Restoring the First-century Church in the Twenty-first Century: Essays on the Stone-Campbell Restoration Movement

IN HONOR OF DON HAYMES

Warren Lewis & Hans Rollmann, editors

Wipf and Stock Publishers
Eugene, Oregon
2005

Restoring the First-century Church in the Twenty-first Century: Essays on the Stone-Campbell Restoration Movement in Honor of Don Haymes is a snap-shot of a major American religious movement just after the turn of the millennium.

When the "Disciples" of Alexander Campbell and the "Christians" of Barton Warren Stone joined forces early in the 19th century, the first indigenous ecumenical movement in the United States came into being. Two hundred years later, this American experiment in biblical primitivism has resulted in three, possibly four, large segments. Best known is the Christian Church (Disciples of Christ), active wherever ecumenical Christians gather. The denomination is typically theologically open, having been reshaped by theological Liberalism and the Social Gospel in the twentieth century, and has been re-organized on the model of other Protestant bodies.

The largest group, the Churches of Christ, easily distinguished by their insistence on *a cappella* music (singing only), is theologically conservative, now tending towards the evangelical, and congregationally autonomous, though with a denominational sense of brotherhood.

The Christian Churches/Churches of Christ (Independent) are a *via media* between the two other bodies: theologically conservative and evangelical, congregationally autonomous, pastorally oriented, and comfortable with instrumental music.

The fourth numerically significant group, the churches of Christ (Anti-Institutional), is a conservative reaction to the *a cappella* churches, much in the way that the Southern *a cappella* churches reacted against the emerging intellectual culture and social location, instrumental music and institutional centrism of the Northern Disciples following the Civil War.

Besides these four, numerous smaller fragments, typically one-article splinter groups, decorate the history of the Restoration Movement: One-Cup brethren, Premillennialists, No-Sunday-School congregations, No-Located-Preacher churches, and others.

This movement to unite Christians on the basis of faith and immersion in Jesus Christ, and to restore New-Testament Christianity, is too little recognized on the American religious landscape, and it has been too little studied by the academic community. This volume is focused primarily on the *a cappella* churches and their interests, but implications for the entire Stone-Campbell Restoration Movement abound. The voices that speak freely within were unimpeded in authoring these essays by standards of orthodoxy imposed from without. All of the contributors are acquainted with Don Haymes, the honoree of the volume, and have been inspired by this friend and colleague, a man with a rigorous and earthy intellect and a heavenly spirit.

David Bundy, series editor
Studies in the History and Culture of World Christianities

*Restoring the First-century Church
in the Twenty-first Century:
Essays on the Stone-Campbell
Restoration Movement*

IN HONOR OF DON HAYMES

TABLE OF CONTENTS

Scripture Studies

Confessional Studies

A Cage of Unclean Birds (Jr 5:27),[1]
or a Word from the Editors[2]

Warren Lewis & Hans Rollmann

This volume is not a *Festschrift* in the ordinary sense of the word; not an exercise in ideological, methodological, or stylistic conformity; not a solemn paean to a beloved old professor by his slightly younger students. This book in honor of Don Haymes at the height of his career is, rather, a mixed choir of the voices of his friends and colleagues shouting, "Thanks, Don!" Some operatic, some rap, some pop, and some as gravelly as Bob Dylan, but all equally meaningful.

This "cage of unclean birds"—50 or so contributors, tweeting and squawking and hooting—defines the very meaning of diversity: Radical to reactionary, conservative to liberal, middle-of-the-road and bourgeois to furious and raving; Black and White, Canadians and Yanks and Europeans, rich and poor, male and female, learned and learning, professors of the academy and those who hold no degree (as Don was for so long); preachers in their pulpits and sitters in the pews, through-the-Word-onlies and mystical charismatics, Stoneite true believers and Campbellite atheists. All kinds of Restorationists (in the Stone-Campbell sense of the word) are here, from party-loyal Stoneites and Campbellites to ex-Restorationists, non-Restorationists, and anti-Restorationists—from liberal Disciples (a.k.a. *Digressives*) to Independent Christian Church folk (a.k.a. *Fiddlers,* or Church of Christ, instrumental) to members of the *a cappella* churches of Christ (a.k.a. *Non-Fiddlers,* Don's own bunch), to charismatic house churches and other renegade groups that have decided to take their congregational autonomy seriously; from those who have "left," those who have "stayed," some who have simply "moved on," others who have "returned," and with an Episcopalian or two, a Lutheran, a Methodist, and who knows what else thrown in for good measure. Others also were willing to write, but time and tide and ill health prevented: A notorious Baptist, Edd Rowell, Don's best buddy at Mercer University Press, deeply regrets his absence from this assembly, as does Tom Death-of-God Altizer, who, when he heard of the volume, pronounced Don Haymes to be "a radically apocalyptic man." Also here are Don's dear wife, Betty; beloved son, Malcolm; dear daughter-in-law, Susan; and delightful grandchild, Rebekah.

In this "Life Award" accolade of the *rara avis* that Don Haymes himself is, we break the rule that only "birds of a feather flock together." Don's truly loyal friends are as diverse in

---

[1] Jr 5:27 (KJV): "As a cage is full of birds, so are their houses full of deceit: therefore they are become great, and waxen rich."

[2] The editors gratefully acknowledge the gracious and able assistance of Freda Elliott Baker and Erika Olbricht, who proof-read the essays, and of Lamar Baker, whose cyber-expertise made this volume technologically possible.

their individual ways as Don himself is individually a man of many parts: radical and renegade and freedom fighter, churchman and pastor and guide to the perplexed; not only a sensitive exegete of scripture but also gifted with that critical endowment of distinguishing spirits; theologian and historian; published author on paper and in cyberspace; professional librarian, memorizer of poetry (which he takes delight in reciting to enchanted listeners), and lover and collector of books and of old automobiles; a friend to all comers, a helper to anyone in trouble, a teacher to everyone who asks, an editor for many writers, a school librarian for all journals, and a hard-headed and ornery cuss who has been gentled by life and his education, and is now set for defense of the truth as he existentially perceives it in all its subjective objectivity.

To embrace literarily as many of Don's friends and interests as we could, we have organized his celebratory volume according to classic seminary departments. As you leaf through the following pages, walk with us down the hallowed halls of Don Haymes Memorial Seminary, visit the several departments, and meet the faculty!

Because Don himself and most of the contributors are Bible-believers, the Biblical Studies Department had to come first: Jack Lewis takes us "beyond the sacred page" into the dirt of archaeological digs to learn about the Sacred Tetragrammaton in antiquity. Lowell Handy explicates the amazing figure of King Josiah (thereby reminding us Campbellites why we have historically had so much trouble with the Old Testament). Doug Geyer gets us as close to the resurrection of Jesus as the Gospels will take us. Carisse Berryhill elevates first-century Christian hospitality to the rank of a sacrament. Roy Bowen Ward, exegete, historian, and social activist, probes biblically, historically, and legally how "traditional" the current notion of "traditional marriage" is not, calling us to a level of tolerance in sexual politics as generous as the *Bill of Rights* and as forgiving as Paul's gospel. Tom Olbricht corrects the homiletic misuse of "another gospel."

The Church History Department, after a look at the watershed between the First-century Church and the Early Church, probes critically the wide variety of Restoration Movement experience: Graydon Snyder, in light of the archaeology of European mortuary architecture of the 3rd and 4th centuries, shows how the European-Christian mind reinterpreted the Jewish-apocalyptic gospel of the resurrection of Jesus and the burial of Christian martyrs as a Hellenistic wake and "eating with the dead." Keith Huey fills in the Scottish and Northern Irish background of Thomas Campbell's thought. Claude Cox observes historically the parting of the ways in Ontario between Baptists and Early Restorationists. C. J. Dull strips the bed sheet off of Gerald L. K. Smith, Disciples preacher and KKK member. Ron Flowers finely etches cameos of the three U.S. Presidents who were Disciples of Christ (Garfield, LBJ, and Reagan), telling us how they held their religion and politics together (or not). Terry Gardner writes an encomium on Foy E. Wallace, Jr., a man whom many loved to hate, but who, Terry says, had another side to him. Hans Rollmann tells us what the Stone-Campbell Movement looked like at long distance in the eyes of German scholars and, more recently, American scholars, who wrote in the major German theological encyclopedias. Richard Goode raises a rattling call to historians and academics to find a way to be faithful to Christian perspectives while engaging in professional, especially historical, scholarship.

The Theology Department comes next: Chris Bryan shows us that preaching the New Testament from pulpit and lectern is not the only way to proclaim the life of Christ, but that we can sing it, pray it, and celebrate it around the Church Year. Leroy Garrett parallels the thought of the great German Reformer with that of the great American Reformer, demonstrating the continuities and discontinuities between Martin Luther and Alexander Campbell. John Mark Hicks opens a window on the problem of evil, North and South, before and after the Civil War.

The Ethics Department, often the case, is next-door to the Theology Department. Richard Hughes, beginning with Jesus and reminding us of a part of the Restoration heritage too little thought about these days, tells the stories of some who conscientiously objected to engaging in charnel violence in the name of politics, thereby reminding us of the gospel call that we are to be peace-mongers. Mike Casey explains in terms of rhetoric and culture where the Restorationist preoccupation with book-religion came from. Mark Tucker reminisces on behalf of many of us White folk on how important Black folk have been to us all along the way. Chris Hutson compares Alexander Campbell's nineteenth-century effort at coming to terms with slavery with Carroll Osburn's twentieth–century wrestling with gender equity for women at church; in so doing, Hutson demonstrates that the possible range of opinion is broader than merely a "right" or "left" either/or. Dianne Bazell and Larry Kant engage in a critique of pop culture to remind us that movies and novels are not the best places to find "evidences" for faith, and to recommend reserve in the apologetic need for "evidences" anyhow. Shaun Casey helps to examine the theoretical oxymoron of a "just war" through an analysis of contemporary Roman Catholic just-war theory and its problematic application to the American war in Iraq. Bill Martin describes the similarities among fundamentalisms in the three Abrahamic religions.

Most seminaries do not have an Education Department, though they need one, for most preachers and professors are woefully lacking in the skills that Kindergarten teachers take for granted: "How to teach so that others may learn." So we have invented the Department of Education: Don Meredith catalogues the ever-growing number of doctoral dissertations written by members of churches of Christ. David Bundy (Don's former colleague in the library at Christian Theological Seminary), now engaged in the most challenging act of theological librarianship in the Early 21st century, building a library to document Christianity around the Pacific Rim, details the promise of this project at Fuller Theological Seminary. Helmut Koester (one of Don's beloved teachers at Harvard Divinity School), foresees effects of the globalization of theological studies now taking place at HDS.

Last (as usual), comes the Department of the Church, where we are allowed to indulge ourselves in confessional statements of what we really do or do not believe: Dwain Evans, the "Moses" of the Exodus/Bayshore Movement, has written a self-revelatory personal memoir. Erma Jean Loveland, in a companion piece to Dwain's memoir, has written a documentary history of the genesis of the Exodus (where Don was a member, off and on). Freda Elliott Baker has compiled an oral history of the early days of the Inner City Faith Corps (a remarkable undertaking co-founded by Don Haymes and some others). Bob Randolph reflects on his upbringing among the churches of Christ in California (nothing like Don's contemporary po'-White upbringing in Kentucky, New Mexico, and Texas). Warren Lewis slams the back door on the Movement, documenting the farewells of those who have written "Why I Left" parting shots. In a companion piece, Melanie Wright brings together a set of nine (counting her own) Canadian "Voices of Concern," a report from the True North that charts the seismic activity running through the Ontario churches of Christ.

Joe E. Lewis, one of the early renegades of the Charismatic Movement in the churches of Christ, ponders spiritual life a generation after the charismatic big bang. Hoy Ledbetter, Gospel Preacher, Elder in the Church, and most frequent publisher of Don's occasional pieces in *Integrity*, reflects gently on his professional ministerial career in three of the main branches of the Restoration Movement. John White, member-in-good-standing of the West Islip Church, tells why he has resolved to blossom where he is potted.

All of the above are people to whom Don Haymes has been in a variety of ways a blessing, a helper, a friend, a servant of the servants of God. We few represent the many who would be delighted to add their voices to this chorus of thanks and praise. Don's wide influence throughout the Stone-Campbell heritage and beyond (for they know him well at AAR/SBL, ATLA, and in many a theological library) is an individual testament to, and parallel of, the path taken in the second half of the 20th century by his own religious community, the churches of Christ, a relatively large communion that has been too little studied and appreciated. Like his religious community, Don came up from bone-breaking poverty and marginalization to intellectual achievement and impact upon Church and Academy.

Don would agree that he has left his tracks on the beach of eternity, then add, "And the tide is coming in." He grumbles against property ownership, and the three-piece suit of respectability makes him itch; but he bears these crosses as part of the mission, for he knows and sings that "earth has no treasures, but perish with using." Therefore, we offer homage to Don Haymes, one who has never allowed poverty and hunger, death and near-death, diseases of the body, operations in hospitals, defections and losses, occupational obstructions and church duties, tired bones and bleary eyes, or other attacks by the Principalities and Powers to hinder him from keeping the faith and finishing his course. And he has been able to do this because God has seen fit to answer Don Haymes's most frequent prayer: "May God have mercy!"

Warren Lewis & Hans Rollmann
Thanksgiving, 2005

List of Contributors

Freda Elliott Baker
Pre-School Teacher, retired
Manhattan Beach, CA 90266
LamarFreda@Adelphia.net

Dianne M. Bazell
Assistant Vice President
for Academic Affairs
Council on Postsecondary Education
1024 Capital Center Drive, Suite 320
Frankfort, KY 40601
859-278-3042
dblk2@qx.net

Carisse Mickey Berryhill
Special Services Librarian
Special Collections, Brown Library
Abilene Christian University
ACU Box 29208
Abilene, TX 79699-9208
325-674-2538
Carisse.Berryhill@acu.edu

Christopher Bryan
C.K. Benedict Professor of
New Testament
The School of Theology
The University of the South
Sewanee, Tennessee

David Bundy
Associate Provost for Library Services
Associate Professor of History
Fuller Theological Seminary
135 North Oakland Avenue
Pasadena, CA 91182

Michael W. Casey
Carl P. Miller Chair of Communication
Pepperdine University
Malibu, CA 90263
310-506-4192
Michael.Casey@Pepperdine.edu

Shaun Casey
Associate Professor of Christian Ethics
Wesley Theological Seminary
Washington, DC

Claude E. Cox
Adjunct Associate Professor of
Old Testament and Hebrew
McMaster Divinity College
Hamilton, Ontario
18 Roslyn Road
Barrie, Ontario, Canada L4M 2X6
c.cox@sympatico.ca

Clifford John Dull
Professor of Greek and Church History
Central Christian College of the Bible
911 E. Urbandale Drive
Moberly, MO 65270
660-263-3900 x130
cjdull@cccb.edu

Joan Ledger De New
Healing Minister,
Church of Healing Energy
www.EnergyChurch.org
Spiritual Dowser
870 Main Street E.
Hamilton, Ontario, Canada L8M 1L9
905-549-7956
JDeNew@cogeco.ca

Russell V. Elliott
Experimental Nuclear Structure
Physicist
Consulting Environmental Engineer,
Industrial Releases in Lakes and
Waterways
183 Heward Avenue
Toronto, Ontario, Canada M4M 2T6
416-463-2900
rve@ympatico.ca

Dwain and Barbara Evans
5426 Fairdale Lane
Houston, TX 77056-6607
713-993-0733
mdevans@Houston.RR.com

Ronald B. Flowers
John F. Weatherly
Emeritus Professor of Religion
Texas Christian University

Terry J. Gardner

Leroy Garrett
1300 Woodlake Dr.
Denton, TX 76210
940-891-0494
Leroy.Ouida@Worldnet.ATT.net

Douglas W. Geyer
811 Chicago Ave #804
Evanston, IL 60202
847-345-4642
dgeyer@AOL.com

Blake Gieg
Journeyman printer, retired
Chaplain, retired
26 Roseland Drive
Carrying Place, Ontario,
Canada K0K 1L0
613-394-6113

Richard C. Goode
Associate Professor of History
Chair, Department of History,
Politics and Philosophy
Lipscomb University
615-279-5748
Richard.Goode@Lipscomb.edu

Lowell Handy
Indexer-Analyst
American Theological Library
Association
250 S. Wacker Drive, Suite 1600
Chicago, IL 60606-5889 USA
888-665-ATLA x4465
lhandy@atla.com

Betty C. Haymes
Teacher
Arlington High School
Indianapolis Public Schools
P.O. Box 88405
Indianapolis, IN 46209
317-508-6469
haymesb@ips.k12.in.us

John Mark Hicks
Professor of Theology
Lipscomb University
3901 Granny White Pike
Nashville, TN 37204
http://johnmarkhicks.faithsite.com

Keith Huey
Chair, Department of Religion and Bible
Rochester College
800 W. Avon Rd.
Rochester Hills, MI 48307
248- 218-2123
khuey@rc.edu

Richard Hughes
Distinguished Professor of Religion
Pepperdine University
24255 Pacific Coast Highway
Malibu, CA 90263
310-506-4526

Christopher R. Hutson
Associate Professor of New Testament
Hood Theological Seminary
1810 Lutheran Synod Drive
Salisbury, NC 28144
www.hoodseminary.edu
704-636-6818
chutson@hoodseeminary.edu

Laurence H. Kant
Associate Professor of Religious Studies
Lexington Theological Seminary
631 South Limestone Street
Lexington, KY 40508
859-278-3042
dblk2@qx.net

Helmut Koester
John H. Morison Research
Professor of Divinity
Winn Research Professor
of Ecclesiastical History
Harvard Divinity School
12 Flintlock Road
Lexington, MA 02420

Hoy Ledbetter
Minister of the Gospel
221 Rivershore Drive
Huntsville, AL 35811
256-859-5799
hoy.ledbetter@worldnet.att.net

Jack P. Lewis
Emeritus Professor of Bible
Harding Graduate School of Religion
1132 South Perkins Rd.
Memphis, TN 38117-5522
(901) 783-1678
jackplewis@juno.com

Joe E. Lewis
Music Man
4899 Drew Rd.
Alpharetta, GA 30004
770-887-4345
joelewis304@bellsouth.net

Warren Lewis
Visiting Research Scholar
Medieval Institute
University of Notre Dame
wwlewis@post.Harvard.edu

Erma Jean Loveland
Librarian and Archivist emeritus
Abilene Christian University
1090 Larned Lane
Abilene, Texas 79602
lovelande@acu.edu

Yvonne MacKay
Administrative Assistant, retired
Grandmom, full-time
75 Summitcrest Drive
Toronto, Ontario, Canada M9P 1H7

William Martin
Chavanne Professor of Religion
and Public Policy
Senior Fellow, James A. Baker III
Institute
for Public Policy
Rice University

Don L. Meredith
Librarian
Harding University
Graduate School of Religion
1000 Cherry Road
Memphis, TN 38117
901-761-1354
hgslib@hugsr.edu

Thomas H. Olbricht
Distinguished Professor emeritus
of Religion
Pepperdine University
14 Beaver Dam Road
South Berwick, Maine 03908
207-384-4469
Tom-Olbricht@comcast.net

David Olson
University Professor Emeritus
Human Development and
Applied Psychology
Ontario Institute for Studies in
Education
University of Toronto
252 Bloor Street W.
Toronto, Ontario, Canada M5S 1V6
416-923-6641 x 2572
dolson@oise.utoronto.ca

Garry Peddle
Teacher, retired
71 Larkfield Drive
Toronto, Ontario, Canada M3B 2H4
416-447-1788
carolyn.garry@sympatico.ca

Robert M. Randolph
Senior Associate Dean for Student Life
Massachusetts Institute of Technology
Cambridge, Massachusetts
Minister, Brookline Church of Christ
94 Main St.
Rockport, MA 01966
617-253-4052
randolph@mit.edu

Hans Rollmann
Professor of Religious Studies
Memorial University of Newfoundland
Adjunct Professor of Church History
Queen's College (St. John's)
Department of Religious Studies
Memorial University of Newfoundland
St. John's, NL A1C 5S7
hrollman@mun.ca

Graydon F. Snyder
Dean, Chicago Theological Seminary
Professor of New Testament, retired
Chicago Theological Seminary
5475 S. Ridgewood Court
Chicago, IL 60615-5314
773-493-2209
graydonsny@aol.com

John Mark Tucker
Dean of Library & Information
Resources
Abilene Christian University
Professor Emeritus of Library Science
Purdue University
Margaret and Herman Brown Library
ACU Box 29208
Abilene, TX 79699-9208
325-674-2387
mark.tucker@acu.edu

Roy Bowen Ward
Professor Emeritus
Department of Comparative Religion
Miami University
Oxford, Ohio 45056
513-529-4300

John D. White
Adjunct-Assistant Professor of History
Dowling College
Oakdale, NY 11769
35 Franklin Street
Islip, NY 11751-1621
631-581-1737
jdw@mail.org
http://johndwhite.net
http://historyweb.info

Audrey Wright
Elementary School teacher, retired
81 Malvern Avenue
Toronto, Ontario, Canada M4E 3E6
416-694-2482

Blenus Wright
The Honourable Mr. Justice,
Ontario Superior Court of Justice
81 Malvern Avenue
Toronto, Ontario, Canada M4E 3E6
416-694-2482

Melanie Wynne Wright
Manager, Program Management
Sapient Inc.
melwwright@hotmail.com

DONAS JACKSON HAYMES III: *BREVIS CURRICULUM VITAE*

BETTY HAYMES[1]

Early in 1940, Donas Jackson Haymes, Jr., a man of practical talent, married Margaret Blair Law, a librarian from Washington, Iowa. Blair Law came from a fine old family in that area; her grandfather had been one of the founders of the town, and his general store had brought the family financial stability and material comfort. Jack's grandfather, by contrast, had been a railroad crew supervisor, forcing hard labor from desperate men for slaves' wages during Depression times—far harder work and less profitable than tending a store. DNA being what it is, Blair stood to inherit from her family, whereas crankcase oil ran in Jack's veins. The automotive vehicle had not yet been invented that he could not repair, neither would it be, until the advent of the computer. Jack had grown up in western Kentucky, and he became an auto shop foreman in Missouri, where he found his bride.

Late in 1940, Jack moved himself and his wife, great with child, to Chicago. In the big city, cars and trucks abounded, most of them in need of fixing at least part of the time, and some of them most of the time. On December 3rd of that year, the importance of making a living for his family became even more urgent for Jack: Donas Jackson Haymes, III—the person honored by the publication of this volume—was born in the Windy City. A year or so later, however, not even war-time Chicago was proving profitable enough for Jack, so he moved Blair and young Don to Iowa City, Iowa.

The marriage of Jack and Blair was not a good marriage; but for the will of far-seeing Providence, it should probably never have taken place. Jack provided adequately, but Blair expected more, and she was more than adequate at complaining. As with many such ill-formed unions, the best part was the child born of it. Don, the little kid one can see in the family album, appears to have been happy. He had plenty of playmates; he had a Scottish Terrier for his best friend; and he had a cowboy suit with twin six-shooters and a hat. What more can a lad with a rich imagination desire?

On the night that Jack left Blair, he gave eleven-year-old Don a choice: "You can stay with your mother, if you want to, or you can come with me. If you want to come with me, then meet me at the corner early in the morning." The choice for Don was not a difficult one: Next morning, with nothing but the clothes on his back, Don met Jack at the appointed corner, and

---

[1] Editors' note: Betty Haymes, the source and principal author of most of this biographical account, wishes you to know, Dear Reader, that she did not write the adulatory paragraphs about herself, and that this writing was accomplished in great part "with too much help from her friends." Much of the detail about Don came from Lamar Baker, Freda Elliott Baker, Robert Arlie Barrett, Dwain Evans, Malcolm Haymes, Leo Kwame Lillard, Lowell Handy, Jack P. Lewis, Warren Lewis, John White, and some unnamed others. Many offered a number of other "Don stories" and matter unprintable here partly because of lack of space.

father and son hit the road for Kentucky. Jack had decided to go back to the place he knew as home, and his boy had chosen to go with him.

Near Walnut Grove, in western Kentucky, on land belonging to the Haymes family, Jack's knack for making-do equipped him to turn the platform of a junked stake-bed truck into the foundation for their dwelling; on it, Jack fashioned a tent-like shelter for himself and Don. Jack bought a cow, and Don's daily chore was to haul water by the bucket up the hill from the creek for the cow. Their conditions were primitive; just to have enough was a struggle; their food habits were inadequate. By the time Don became a teenager, he was unhealthfully underweight and hungry; his teeth, like the teeth of many other children of poverty, were as rotten as they looked; and he was painfully near-sighted, but they could not afford glasses.

A healing light shining on this poor home, as it does on so many poor homes, was the light of Christian religion. At age 11, Don began to attend the Walnut Grove Church of Christ (near Benton, Kentucky), a congregation populated by the Cope family, relatives of Don's Grandmother Haymes, and presided over by Don's Uncle Garfield Cope, who taught Don to love the Bible and fear Hell. Jack *never* attended, but he deeply revered Uncle Garfield.[2] Life at Walnut Grove was simple, but it was possible, until Blair made it impossible.

In 1951, Blair began a legal initiative to gain custody of Don. A mother in pursuit of her rights pleased the court, but without regard for the wishes of the child involved, who was living happily with his father. The local constabulary, friends of the Haymeses and the Copes, privately warned Jack that the court was after him, so Jack took Don and made good their get-away once more. He told everyone that he and the boy were going to Chicago, and then Jack and Don left immediately, headed west, aiming at California.

The money ran out in Albuquerque, New Mexico. But that was far away enough from Blair to be safe, so Jack got a job repairing automobiles, and there he also got a new wife. Beulah Ross by that act also became Don's new mother. Beulah was an extraordinarily good cook, and young Don especially favored her enchiladas, which he ate a pan full at a time. The Ross family owned *Ross Barbeque*, and they were famous for their sauce. The Jack Haymes family stayed in New Mexico for about a year, and then they moved to Lubbock, Texas.

In 1953, teenaged Don was a member of a Bible class and a pretty faithful attender at a church in Lubbock. That congregation invited Brother Willard Collins to preach a protracted series of gospel meetings. As part of the evangelistic effort performed on behalf of the Christians in that local congregation of the Lord's Body, Brother Collins visited the Bible classes attended by all those who were of the age of accountability, and he urged them to obey the gospel.

Don had been attending the evening preaching, so he had seen people going down front during the invitation song. He was aware that, after they said something to the preacher that he could not hear, they went through a door into some secret chamber behind the walls, and then a curtain opened, and after that something happened. Because Don was so near-sighted, however, and still lacking a pair of glasses, he could not see what it was that happened.

That evening following the sermon, when other teenagers in Don's Bible class responded to the gospel invitation, Don did not want to be left behind, so he followed little Tommy Pinkston down the aisle. Like the others, Don and the preacher then engaged in that all-too-

---

[2] See Michael Casey, "Mastered by the Word," in this volume.

brief conversation in which the preacher asks the candidate for baptrism whether he believes that Jesus was/is the Son of God (Don said he did), and then they went through the mysterious door and up the stairs. Next, to Don's amazement, he watched little Tommy Pinkston go down into a pool of water, and he saw the preacher put him under. Now, it was Don's turn; so, having been thus "discipled," Don Haymes, age 13, was baptized into Christ by M. Norvel Young during a Willard Collins Gospel Meeting.

One may presume that since the event, Don has reflected on what happened to him that night, and he can probably explain the terms of the transaction, but if Don Haymes's baptism does not prove the essential truth of Augustine's teaching on the sacraments, then nothing does: Not the age, not the knowledge, not the spiritual status of the recipient, and not the personal holiness or individual state of grace of the officiant, but the act itself of the sacrament—*ex opere operato*—is what effects the good effects of baptism.

Living in Lubbock was bad enough, but a fourteen-year-old living with Jack and Beulah in a small trailer was not an entirely satisfactory arrangement. Teenage Don resented step-maternal supervision, and a young man needs his privacy. Drawing on a coping skill that would save his soul many times throughout the rest of his life, Don escaped into reading. With no brothers or sisters, and being not the kind of kid that made friends easily, Don's companions were books and the ideas and personalities that he met in them. By the time Don got to be 15, however, that trailer was not big enough for them all. Jack took a drastic but inspired step: Now that Don was a Christian, he ought to go to a Christian school. Jack Haymes somehow found money enough to get Don to Abilene Christian High School, and after that, Don took care of himself.

The campus school at Abilene Christian College in Abilene, Texas, was conducted primarily for the benefit of the children of the teachers and staff of the College. Don took no time at all to comprehend two realities about himself that would define his existence for all his years to come: He had already read more than his teachers had read, not to mention his fellow students; and he did not fit in with the nice, polite, obedient kids whose families equated Christian morals with bourgeois behavior. They all operated with certain domesticated assumptions about life and relationships and a cozy mutuality that Don did not share. Living in the tar-paper tent on the back of that stake-bed truck, on the lam to Albuquerque, and in cramped quarters in Lubbock, Don had cloistered himself in the sublime isolation of the hundreds of books he had read, and the thousands more he aimed to read. Don Haymes became sufficient unto himself. Don was unlike all of his schoolmates and all of his teachers, and the parents of those children were unlike Jack Haymes. In among the Christians who seemed mostly to be just like one another, Don was the perpetual outsider, the loner, the renegade, the book-reader.

Don did make a few friends, however. Mike Fanning, who one day would become an English professor and a promising writer, but who would not live long enough to win his Pulitzer), and Pauletta Verrett were two who took the strange boy home to meet their moms and dads. Mike was the first in a long line of intellectually bright male peers, and Pauletta was the first in a long line of sweet women, who would befriend Don Haymes, become his benefactors, and themselves benefit mightily through acquaintance with him. The Fanning and Verrett families accepted Don for what he was, and they adopted him as a friend of their children. Others, by contrast, found Don to be too independent-minded, too self-sufficient, too self-motivated for a young kid; he did not conform to the norms; he did not meet the expectations of the people in charge of the Christian school.

When a kid knows more than most of the people around him, ahead of him, and over him, he's bound to get into trouble. In Don's senior year, the English teacher's course outline promised certain grades in return for certain stated levels of performance. When Don delivered, but the English teacher did not, the inadequate grade kept Don from graduating with his class. The school principal, however, signed Don's diploma and graduated him anyway, grateful to let Don become someone else's problem.

In the autumn of 1959, Don walked across the campus intending to become a student at Abilene Christian College, but he found that his fudged exit from the Christian High School did not guarantee easy entry into the Christian College. So he went, instead, to Harding College in Searcy, Arkansas, there to endure a disastrous semester that, nevertheless, allowed him to earn a few credits that made it possible for him to return to Abilene as a transfer student in the College. In afteryears, Don would usually refer to "Hardly-a-College in Serious, Arkansas."

Don had to work his way through, so he took a job in a dairy while he was at Harding. In Abilene, he went to work for the Abilene Sanitation Department and rode around town on a garbage truck picking up trash. At the College, he worked in the kitchen of the cafeteria, "The Bean." Later, during the summers at Camp Shiloh in Mendham, New Jersey, Don would work as a dishwasher.

Long accustomed to hauling water and dealing with other people's garbage, Don preferred the literary life. The teacher at ACC who made the most sense to Don at the time was Heber Taylor, the Journalism teacher and sponsor of the school newspaper, *The Optimist*. When it came to journalism, Don was a natural. Within two weeks as a Journalism major, he was grading student work done in the Reporting Lab, and he was helping the editor get the paper out. Don landed a job for a while at the *Abilene Reporter-News*, and what might well have become a stellar career in journalism was launched.

Beginning to think of himself as one of the literati, Don affected the non-use of capital letters in his writing, such that the phrase, "i, don haymes," was entirely possible. Perhaps this was a literary affirmation of abject humility, but more likely it was inspired by the direct opposite of that false virtue and by the poet e. e. cummings, who likewise remained aloof from certain literary conventions. The affectation would last for years—it still occasionally crops up—and it has driven Don's friends to the brink more than once. Don said about his journalistic aspirations: "But it now appeared that one could Save The World as a writer, observing the world and writing about it, clearly, for the clear-eyed. i had first to work through that folly."

A few others in Abilene made sense to Don, including his freshman English teacher, Elizabeth Beaty (whose son, Doug, Don would befriend a few years later on Long Island), and the two legendary teachers at the College in those days: James Culp (fabled Chair of the English Department) and LeMoine G. Lewis (Church Historian *extraordinaire*). Don did not immediately become one of "LeMoine's boys," as did so many budding young theologians whom Professor Lewis systematically polished for graduate theological education, mostly at Harvard Divinity School (HDS); in time, however, the association between Don and LeMoine would become everlastingly important for them both. Persistent exhaustion from overwork, little sleep, and too little to eat; perpetual resistance to the social *mores*; and little sense of academic challenge coming at him from most of the teachers at the College—all combined to leave Don uninspired by ordinary post-secondary education; his grades were consistently lackluster. He continued to learn more from reading than he could learn by going to classes.

Don ran afoul of the College administrators on more than one occasion and for a variety of infractions. One memorable time, the academic bureaucrat in view was Garvin Beauchamp, Dean of Students. In those days, Don was (in the words of Robert Arlie Barrett) "imperfectly beautiful." Getting along towards chunky and snaggle-toothed, Don was never attired in anything more refined that jeans and a T-shirt (all he could afford). The way Don looked and acted caused the dean and others grave misgivings, for one of the purposes of a "Christian College" is to turn out the product well scrubbed, all polite, and smelling good. Don's detractors whispered in the dean's ear: "Don is *following* the girls around!" That a red-blooded college man should show interest in co-eds was no novelty, not even at ACC, and Don was no stalker; it's just that he lacked the polish of certain social graces. Authorities in higher education sometimes are given to looking upon the outward man, and that was the problem in this case; the dean haled him in and gave him one of those deanly warnings. Don took a good deal of ribbing, and one of his buddies conferred on him the first of Don's honorary degrees, L.O.M.F.O.W.[3]

The other best thing that happened to Don while he was in the Abilene College called "Christian" was his short-lived editorship of *The Pessimist*, the once-a-year April Fool's edition of the student weekly, *The Optimist*. Don had thought that his wicked humor and intellectual scintillation, on top of the native genius of his natural mastery of journalism, would earn for him the editorship of the official organ, but in this he was also to be disappointed. The job was finessed away from him by a demure young thing and her more prosaic boyfriend. Once more betrayed by polite people, Don turned his back on Christian education and left Abilene without a backward look. He also left without a baccalaureate degree.

Don stayed for a while with Jack and Beulah where they now lived in Arlington, Texas, and in 1961-62, Don worked for a time at the *Fort Worth Star-Telegram* newspaper. But during these same years, a daring young preacher, Dwain Evans, was mustering a group of Southerners and Southwesterners who were only too ready to be led out of their spiritual "bondage in Egypt" into what came to be called "Exodus/Bay Shore," an effort to plant a full-grown, lively, Church-of-Christ congregation on Long Island, up there in the godless Northeast. Don thought the Northeast sounded just about right, so he answered the Abrahamic call to leave home and become great for God. Thus was born a renegade church-of-Christ church—with Don Haymes at its heart and part of its mind—that would serve as a haven for "liberals," a launching pad for theological adventurers, and a consternation to traditional and conservative churcho'Christers for decades to come.[4]

During the Sixties, that all-important decade that sorted out the soul of America, Don was a subtly influential member of the West Islip Church of Christ. Resident prophet and blue-tailed fly on the backside of Mother Church, Don nevertheless functioned for many as a closet theologian. Being far better-read in Scripture Studies and in Theology than most

---

[3] "Leader of Men, Follower of Women"

[4] See Dwain Evans, "A Memoir"; Erma Jean Loveland, "Genesis of an Exodus"; and Freda Elliott Baker, "The Inner-City Faith Corps: An Oral History," all in this volume.

preachers and elders, Don fashioned for himself his own distinctive "existential theology," a kind of gut-wrenching theology of the cross, of unmerited grace, and of Paul's affirmation that "if Christ be not raised, then we are of all men most miserable." Don pursued "Moses" (as Don relentlessly called Dwain Evans) like a guilty conscience, and the remarkable thing is, Dwain wisely listened.

On one embarrassing occasion early after the Exodus arrived, word got around that something called the "the Bayshore Church of Christ" already existed. So "Moses," attended by some "Joshuas and Calebs"—Don Haymes among them—formed up an exploration party and sallied forth. There it was, and when Don tried the front door, it was open. The sign on the building was right, but inside the empty meeting house, the spies immediately spotted the evil piano in the corner and the "Christian flag" behind the pulpit, two idols that marked the church with the stain of Digression; it was a Church of Christ, all right, but an Independent Christian Church, not an *a cappella* singing-only Church of Christ. Don says that he did not laugh out loud, but he did savor the moment more than did the others. In all the preparation and planning for the Exodus, this first-cousin congregation had been overlooked. Luckily for the redeemed of Moses, building the new church building a handful of miles back up Montauk Highway allowed them to change the name; thus Exodus/Bay Shore morphed into the West Islip Church of Christ.

While Don's college chums and other peers were going on to various graduate programs, collecting their respective sheepskins, the inner circle nodded with respect and winked in good humor, repeating the phrase that "Don holds no degrees." Gritting his teeth in the belief that academic paper proves nothing and that reading is enough, Don continuously and without affectation demonstrated his superior learning to his delighted friends not only by schooling them informally in scripture and theology but also in his impromptu poetry recitals. One of the by-products of Don's consuming interest in all kinds of literature was his ability to recite by heart long passages, especially poems, on command. One of his favorites was Oliver Wendell Holmes's witty and wicked elegy on "The Wonderful One-horse Shay." Mr. Justice Holmes had intended his rattling doggerel to be a celebration of the dilapidation of Calvin's theology and the collapse of New England's Puritan oligarchy, but when Don recited it, he and his church-of-Christ-church audiences chortled over the disintegration of another but equally pompous ecclesiastical establishment.

The lack of formal education, however, began to pinch, for people doing the hiring look too much at résumés to see what you've done rather than at the person you are and what you can do. The wannabe journalist worked for a while as an editor at *Dunn and Bradstreet* magazine, and as a reporter/editor for the *Smithtown News*, and when those jobs played out, he spent some months "on the road," hitchhiking across the country, though he always returned.

The West Islip Church remained Don's true north. He loved the beautiful *a cappella* singing (still does) in a congregation whose membership comprised many former members of the *a cappella* choruses of Christian colleges, and others who had always and ever known that God loved to hear them singing. Don was a real presence in his devotion to the weekly Eucharist, and he was perennially engaged with the theological challenges that constantly arose. He nettled the conservatives as much as they could tolerate, and he agitated with Moses and the Elders as much as they would tolerate, sometimes writing pointed notes to Dwain about issues at stake.

One year, when Dwain Evans went to the annual denominational test of orthodoxy, or "Lectureship," at Abilene Christian College, familiarly known by locals as "The Hill," he came under attack by the running dogs of Ira Y. Rice, Jr., heretic hunter of the first water, who had authored *Axe on the Root* (volumes one, two, and three), a full-throttle exposé of "the liberals." Brother Ira had especially singled out Preacher Evans and the West Islip Church. When the battered and bruised Moses came home from that love feast of Christian brotherhood, he found this note that Don had put on his desk: "Home is the sailor, home from the sea, and the *hunted* home from *the Hill*." On a different occasion, rather more nettlingly, another of Don's notes for Dwain popped up unexpectedly on the pulpit when Dwain stood up to preach: "This location is high in entropy."

But Don always knew where home was: The West Islip Church was the one place where he had found adult friends who accepted him, prized him for his mind, and loved this "most unforgettable character" for himself alone. Some of those who loved him best must be called by name: Gary Aday, Robert A. Barrett, Dee Colvett, Hu Gibbons, John White, and Preacher and Moses, Dwain Evans, among others.

Poverty was never far from Don's door. The ordinary jobs did not last long, and the challenging jobs paid little. Don would lodge first with one friend, then with another—he and John White[5] lived in a small motel room on the beach at Babylon, Long Island, for a year, each in his respective state of mental collapse, each supporting the other, John says, "like an inverted V." John remembers that the conversation usually revolved around social injustices with cosmic implications. Don spent some time in the attic of Howard and Margaret Hodgson, and he crashed for a while with Robert Barrett. When Don and his buddies would go out to eat—the Oconee East, a classic New York diner, was a favorite spot, and it was cheaper than the Oconee West—the more affluent (most of them were school teachers) would order tasty-looking items, but Don would order one scrambled egg, which automatically came with toast, and the water and little crackers in packages were free. Friends help friends out, but offering money among equals can be uncomfortable for all.

During the troubled times at the middle of the decade, Don's continuous agitation at West Islip came to fruition in the greatest achievement of Don's young life: Don and some others co-founded an experimental effort in Social Action and the Christian Gospel. Fuelled initially by Don's Christian passions, the "Inner City Faith Corps" (as Don christened it), or "Shiloh" (as it came later to be called), was likewise inspired by two of Don's martyred heroes: JFK and Malcolm X, and by a third, MLK, Jr., to be martyred soon after. What Don and Lamar and Freda planted, Warren watered, and many others tended and weeded, grew eventually both institutionally and in its everlasting effects far beyond the Brooklyn ghetto in East New York, and it shall outlive the genii who devised it.[6]

The evolution of Don's work for social justice in East New York took an emergent leap when Don met Leo Kwame Lillard, a Black activist who vigorously directed a community development organization, East New York Housing Authority, and who now haunts the city fathers of Nashville much in the way he used to terrorize New Yorkers. Don's reading had included the radical social theory of Saul Alinsky, and now, having found a yoke-mate

[5] See John White, "Why I Stay," in this volume.
[6] The story of Don's co-founding of the Faith Corps is told by Freda Elliott Baker, "The Inner City Faith Corps: An Oral History," in this volume.

worthy of him, Don and Leo got things done together. Warren Lewis said that Leo was the first Black person whom he ever heard call a White man—Don Haymes—"Brother" and mean it. Don is, in fact, part Black—the part that counts: the soul. In league with Leo and Walter Thabit, the third member of their poor people's mafia, Don had a way of confronting do-nothing bureaucrats hiding behind their desks until the red tape melted and the files meekly folded into place. Walter Thabit, the third member of this team of Furies and chronicler of the agonies in East New York, mentioned Don in his book.[7]

Kwame Lillard now says of Don's presence in the ghetto, "God knew it would take a pudgy red-haired step-child Church-of-Christ type to clean the Temple of the infidels disgracing the Lord's house." He speaks of Don and himself as a revolutionary "combo" that "spared no *homo sapiens* born of woman, and that got us on everybody's shit list, a place we very much felt honored to occupy."

Don remembers the years from 1968 to 1970 in very much the same way that Kwame does, with the exception that Don was under the scrutiny of the polite racists who still lurked in the Southern churches of Christ. Despite Don's courage and leadership in those days, he was but rarely "asked to speak" at any of the meetings that were held to address the issue; he would, nevertheless, show up and speak up. Don reminisced about his prophetic style:

> By May 1968 i am speaking *ex tempore* somewhere almost every day, but i am rarely, if ever, *invited** to speak in formal gatherings. i speak then with an edge honed in hundreds of community meetings, demonstrations, and confrontations, and it is, assuredly, a "confrontational" manner of speaking. i am then one angry m*f*, and i come by the anger honest. i "address the problem in the terms of the problem" and i do not employ euphemisms.

At that time, Don was the clearest outspoken conscience in the churches of Christ on race and justice. He was opposed not only by avowed and *de facto* racist power structures but also by soft-spoken racists who could not diagnose their own terminal illness with the disease. Among these were Reuel Lemmons, editor of the *Firm Foundation*, the Gospel paper that guarded orthodoxy for the mainline churches of Christ in Texas; and John Allen Chalk, a popular young man in those days among the churches who inherited fame by becoming the speaker on the "Herald of Truth," the national radio program that represented churches of Christ. Lemmons was well to the right of Chalk, and Chalk lived long enough to learn better, but at the time they confronted Don Haymes, they were both standing smack in the middle of the road. Editor Lemmons, who had proudly boasted to Chalk that he had "not an ounce" of racism in him, and did not know of any leader in the Brotherhood who did, turned quietly to Don following a meeting at the Stony Island Church in Chicago, and "staring icily ahead" delivered that classic line: "But would you want your sister to marry one?"[8]

---

[7] Walter Thabit, *How East New York Became a Ghetto* (New York University Press, 2003), a blistering indictment for their ravaging of the neighborhood of East New York by New York City officials, real estate brokers and speculators, and corrupt contractors and managers of low-income housing projects. Towards the close of the book, Thabit described the "hard road to recovery" and talks about the building of affordable housing, job training, recreational opportunities, and health-care planning in which Don Haymes played his part.

[8] See Don Haymes, "Letter of Reuel Lemmons to John Allen Chalk," *Race and the Churches of Christ*: http://www.mun.ca/rels/restmov/texts/race/haymes1.html

Chalk, then the type that tended to put rhetoric above truth, was more oblique in both his church and racial politics. He had heard Don speak at Camp Shiloh in May, 1968, where Don presented much the same speech that he was to deliver at the third annual Unity Forum in Winchester, Kentucky, in July, and that he published in *Mission* in December, said to have been the "first controversial article in *Mission*." Chalk, in an exchange with Walter E. Burch, the publicist for Exodus/Bay Shore, faulted Don for having been too blunt, for not offering "anything constructive," and for "posing problems without offering solutions." Burch defended Don by saying that Don had "exposed racism as a sin," and had "got at the matter (lying dormant in everybody's mind) in a very moving, spontaneous, unorganized, and completely honest way." Burch would soon thereafter engage in a showdown with Reuel Lemmons over similar issues. Dwain Evans likewise defended Don and—Don believes— Evans never again "preached for money" after 1970 because of the trouble Dwain was already in on account of the West Islip Church, the Holy Spirit, the Faith Corps, and "in great part because of the hard time he had spent with me."[9]

Don concluded this remembrance of himself as an angry young man by commenting that his tendency to speak bluntly, colorfully, and in the idiom of the ghetto where he felt so much at home, "remains to this hour...." Don emended this reflection by referring indirectly to the heart attack that would catch up with him some 20 years later, "...although if i were as angry now as i was then, i should not be alive."

Among Don's other good friends at West Islip were a number of single women. One of these, Diana Bush, with that saving practicality and inoffensiveness that turns good women into good mothers, paid to have Don's teeth fixed. The dentist was Dennis Cahill, a Catholic bachelor, whom Diana later married. Don was extremely reticent to accept the charity of his friends, perhaps unwilling to acknowledge that he needed the work done, but finally his better judgment overcame foolish pride. This turning point was the beginning of Don Haymes's new self-image. Eventually, a handsome smile would shine forth atop a trim figure; some time later, an old friend who had not seen Don for years, did not recognize him at first glance: A lean Don Haymes, with dazzling pearly-whites, a neatly trimmed beard, and in a three-piece suit—it seemed an oxymoron!

Among that group of fine young Christian and unmarried women was a certain Ms Betty Carolyn Hollis, a sweet, sane Southern girl from the Protestant part of Louisiana, and Don took notice. Sister Hollis did have beautiful yellow hair; more than that, she had a mind, as well. Their first date began as a dinner party for some of the eligible males given by a household of the eligible females. By the end of the evening, everyone had faded away except Don and Betty. That first date lasted all night long, and all they did was talk—that is to say, Don talked and Betty listened. She was fascinated by his intelligent rap, and she was gratified by his respect: She said that he was the first man she had ever met who talked intelligently about ideas, and, what's more, who talked to her, a woman, in a way that meant he expected her to understand.

They went on other dates, favoring an Indian restaurant in the City that once had been a speakeasy. They listened to the music of B.B. King and Theolonious Monk, among others. Then, they bought rings at a jewelry kiosk in the Village, rings that turned green and then black not long afterward, but that remained perpetually lustrous in other ways. These they

---

[9] See above, note 1.

exchanged, and their vows, and then they called Betty's parents; after that, they announced to friends and to the West Islip Church that they had become husband and wife on March 1, 1968.

Childhood had been a tough patch for Don Haymes, so he was not interested in having children, but Betty was. Malcolm (for Malcolm X) Eldridge (for Eldridge Cleaver) Haymes came into this world on September 18, 1969. Appropriately for a kid with a name as heavy as Malcolm Eldridge Haymes, Malcolm's first home was in the Brooklyn ghetto at 436 Williams Avenue, the original address of the Inner City Faith Corps. Don's booming bass-baritone that made babies cry, terrified young children, and caused *a cappella* singers in the congregation sitting in adjacent pews to search in vain for the melody line, would cause young Malcolm's marrow to quiver more than once. Even so, Malcolm loved his daddy and emulated him: Robert Barrett remembers that the circle of friends took gleeful pleasure in watching young Malcolm loyally imitating his dad's characteristic gait. Because Betty's teaching profession tended to offer more steady work than did Don's calling to change society, Don received the grace that so many men never know: He got to be a stay-at-home dad. During Malcolm's first 11 years, Don, more than Betty, met Malcolm's daily childhood needs both physically and spiritually.

Kwame Lillard observes that since one of his own grandchildren, and Don's and Betty's only child, are both named "Malcolm," that a cosmic and eternal bond of brotherhood prevails among these fathers and sons. Evelyn, Kwame's wife, had been counted among Don's detractors, until he married Betty, when, as Evelyn says, "Don became a person." Evelyn had been irritated that Kwame and Don were "always against everything." She remembers, "Don was never in a good mood the entire time I saw him in East New York." Then, when Malcolm was born, Evelyn had nightmares that Malcolm (contrary to what Kwame devoutly hoped) would become a clone of Don. "We were both disappointed," says Kwame, for Malcolm became his own man. But DNA counts for something, Kwame noted when he and Evelyn saw almost-grown-up Malcolm, age 17, wearing a T-shirt bearing the world-denying message: *I DON'T KNOW—AND YOU DON'T EITHER.*

When Malcolm came to maturity, became a prize-winning director of plays in Chicago, earned an academic degree in Chattanooga, won himself a fine wife (Susan), and became the father of Rebekah Jenise Haymes, that young lady's grandfather would become as silly about her—and as proud of his son—as any other silly, proud grandfather.

In 1970, the Shiloh neighborhood was in trouble again. The Haymes family got burned out of their apartments, and the corner store got bombed. The apartment-house fire at #436 was set on purpose, not aimed at the Haymeses but according to custom: If one's building got burned, then one's name went to the top of the list for subsidized housing. The Haymeses moved temporarily to "the Big House," headquarters of Camp Shiloh, in Mendham, New Jersey. The administration of Don's Inner City Faith Corps had been absorbed by Camp Shiloh, so Don went to work for the new parent organization as a consultant, writer, and in the mail room.

In 1971, the Haymeses moved to Dover, New Jersey, where Betty again took up her career in school teaching that would keep the Haymes family financially afloat for years to come. Like so many other such faithful women, the working wife supported her man of ideals. She was the perfect fulfillment of that prophecy of her in Proverbs 31. Don became a stay-at-home dad with Malcolm and skilled housekeeper, and continued his work for Shiloh in the evenings.

Old Man Jack Haymes lived on until 1972. During Don's days at West Islip, Forrest Wells, one of the Elders of the congregation, had come into the church office one day and remarked to Robert Barrett and some others, "You won't believe this, but as I was driving along, I saw a man who looked as though he could be Don Haymes's father." Robert said that he thought "the undecorative Don was one-of-a-kind, and nobody else would look like him," unless it might be Don's father. Jack had, indeed, started out from Texas, headed for New York, driving a Morris Minor that he intended to give to Don as a gift. In Brinkley, Arkansas, the drive shaft had broken, but Jack did not call AAA. Instead, he took the drive shaft out of the car right there by the side of the road and walked over to a blacksmith shop. "Can I borrow your welder?" he asked. Now the drive shaft of the Morris Minor has tolerances on the order of thousandths of an inch, but Jack eyeballed it, lined it up, welded it together, reinstalled it, and drove on to New York, where he had been spotted by Elder Wells.

DNA, to repeat, counts for something: The crankcase oil that flowed in Jack's veins also flows in Don's. Churchmen of various denominations have secrets in their respective closets of various kinds, and in Don Haymes's two garages, one shed, and a back-porch patio, he has assembled a prize collection of bits and pieces of old cars, carefully harbored, that he is gradually putting together into recycled vintage automobiles. Kwame Lillard testifies that what clinched his respect for Don was when he discovered that Don was a "'50s-type hopeless hod-rodder with all the associated fantasies that no mother, aunt, sister, or girlfriend could comprehend." (Kwame had come to that conclusion, it must be said, before he had met Betty, who has come to love old cars as much as Don does, and thereby has achieved greater understanding of her man.)

In 1972, Jack was driving another car from Texas to New Jersey for Don, but this time he made it only as far as Pennsylvania. Jack had pieced together a 1936 pick-up for Don, and Don and Malcolm (age 2) had gone to Arlington, Texas, that summer where they helped Grandpa Jack finish the reconstruction and then drove the truck back to New Jersey. In September, Jack had loaded up his Valiant station wagon with a few extra parts for Don's truck, intending to arrive in time for Malcolm's third birthday. A two A.M., a call came from the Pennsylvania State Troopers. Jack Haymes—they concluded later from the evidence—had suffered a heart attack, had exited from I-80 in search of help, but was killed when his car failed to take a curve.

Some die and others live. Bruce Hollis, Betty's brother, had survived Vietnam, but just barely. After two tours of duty as a gunner on a helicopter crew, Bruce had earned the nickname "Lucky" because whereas so many of his buddies had been killed, Bruce had lived. Back home in the USA, Bruce battled alcoholism, morphine addiction, and despair that ran deeper than depression. Bruce came to stay with Don and Betty, and Don talked with Bruce and listened to him for the better part of a year. Although the ghosts would never be completely laid, Don saved Bruce's life and redeemed his soul. Bruce married, adopted and successfully raised four children, and lived a contented life until 1997, when cancer took him.

In 1973, the Haymeses moved again, this time to Memphis, where Betty continued teaching, and they worked together to help implement integration of the high schools of Memphis Public Schools. In Memphis, a sort of miracle happened: The Haymes family bought its first house. Over Don's vociferous protest, they signed certain articles of indentured servitude with the banking lords in return for $17,900 so that they might have the monthly privilege and joy of paying high interest on an endless mortgage for "sticks of wood nailed together that Betty wanted." They would buy other houses in years to come, always over the mournful opposition of the principal signatory to the agreement. From pretty teeth to marriage to Betty to the birth of Malcolm to buying a house in Memphis, middle-class normalcy was creeping up on Don Haymes—"May God have mercy!"—and Don was fighting it every step of the way.

Don and Betty both became aggressively involved in implementing racial integration of the Memphis Public Schools. Don worked for the National Conference of Christians and Jews, and he also worked with others to organize "Brotherhood Clubs" in target high schools, aimed at facilitation of interaction between Black and White students. School strikes and a lock-out put Don and Betty on one side of the argument in opposition to an old friend on the other side: Rod Spaulding, who ranked high in the Memphis Public Schools administration, had been a fellow student at ACC, a minister at West Islip, and an administrator of Shiloh.

Push came to shove during a protest over teachers' salaries. Most of the teachers in the public schools were African Americans, and their salaries were so low that Betty's three-person family qualified for food stamps, "had I wanted to apply." Betty got herself placed on the Board of Directors of the teachers' union so she could politick for higher wages. When the teachers struck against the status quo, the school authority threatened firings, if anyone continued the strike. Hungry, dispirited, flagging teachers, unaccustomed to standing up for themselves aggressively and assertively, were inclined to fold. At a rally, St. Don of the Ghetto rose to speak, eloquently addressing all those Black teachers in the *colorful* language that they understood so well. They took heart, stood firm, and Memphis school authorities had the entire Board of Directors of the teachers' union—all but one—jailed overnight. Because Betty was a new appointee of the Board, and her name was not yet on the official documents, she escaped the jailing, remained the only "free" member of the Board, and so became the media spokesperson for the teachers on strike.

By this time, Don should have been accorded the esteem that was increasingly due him as an activist prophet in the churches of Christ, but Jesus had said something about the lack of honor paid to prophets by the people who know them best, and he had been right about that. *Mission* magazine had been founded as the house organ of the Church-of-Christ "liberal" faction, and Don ought to have become its editor, but that was not to be, for Don Haymes "held no degrees."

For ten years, Don had been writing increasingly urgent pieces in Church-related periodicals. For example, his 1966 *The Church of Christ Establishment* was an outrageous graphic spread, from red liberals on the left to blue conservatives on the right, names of famous and infamous Church-of-Christ leaders grouped together under such unlikely sub-heads as "Vatican West," "Vatican East," "Suffragettes," "White Knights," "Still Small Voices," "Court Jesters," "Thorns in the Flesh," "Money-Changers," and "Rich Young Rulers," to list but a few.[10]

---

[10] Don Haymes, "The Church of Christ Establishment" (graphic design by Robert Arlie Barrett): http://www.mun.ca/rels/restmov/texts/dhaymes/cocestab.gif

More sober but nonetheless devastating, Don's "The Silence of the Scholars"[11] was a broadside aimed at the theologically educated among Christian college teachers and other Church-of-Christ intellectuals whose studies had convinced them that the trite biblicisms of the majority of the preachers and Christian college teachers were intellectually bankrupt. The silent scholars met Don's challenge with an even more deafening roar of hushed meekness. No one, not a single one of those bright intellects with their multiple advanced degrees, would stand up and be counted. As prophetically important as were Don's publications in *Mission*, his occasional articles in *Integrity*, edited and published by Hoy Ledbetter,[12] offer equally clear windows into the heart and mind of the author.

Don at last realized that unless he acquired a union card of membership among the university elite, he would be forever barred from working in the closed shop of Academe. Grinding his teeth and biting the bullet, Don went back to school and collected himself a few of those highly touted pieces of academic paper. In 1977, he received an A. A. from Shelby State Community College, and in 1978, a B.A. from Southwestern College (now Rhodes College), both schools in Memphis—all A's except for that B in Astronomy.

In the fall of 1979, he entered Harvard Divinity School. Living in Divinity Hall, and absent Betty's mighty fine Southern cooking, Don commenced a dual regimen of re-forming himself: He registered for as many credit courses as they would allow him to take, and an equal number of audit courses, and he began every day at 4 A.M. running—running and dieting until he had lost 130 lbs. Betty soldiered on, teaching in Memphis; she cherishes the "beautiful letters" she received from Don during the Harvard years. Though Don called often and talked with Malcolm on the phone, Malcolm (now 11) missed his stay-at-home dad, but—Malcolm remembers—he missed Don even more when Don finally came home but got that job he had so badly wanted and started working 14-hour days. The absence of the father hurts less when it is total than it does when his presence seems more possible. Then is when Malcolm started getting into trouble at school for the first time, but Malcolm remained righteously adamant that his behavior was justified, and he has never relented.

Don's admission to America's most excellent Divinity School had been arranged by some of Don's life-long stalwarts, and by one in particular. Although Don had not distinguished himself in LeMoine Lewis's Church History course back in the early '60s, Don had continued through the years to visit with LeMoine in Abilene, to enlarge their relationship, and to collect "LeMoine stories." Don always tells about the time he visited in LeMoine's office at ACU: LeMoine had just come back from helping with Vacation Bible School at church, and was talking about "blowin' up b'loons" for the kids. LeMoine's balance of scholarly teaching at the University and practical Christianity at church became for Don a model of his own Christian vocation. LeMoine Gaunce Lewis was the Trojan Horse in the Church of Christ who brought about the downfall of theological fundamentalism, for he selected each year a couple of the most promising young theologues in his classes, whom he then primed for study at HDS. So successful was he at picking likely candidates for the Divinity School, Ralph Lazaro of HDS once said that, where recommendation of new students was concerned, "LeMoine Lewis had a blank check to Harvard."

---

[11] Don Haymes, "The Silence of the Scholars," in *Mission* 8/3 (September 1974): 70-85.

[12] See Hoy Ledbetter, "Why I Returned: My History in Three Churches," in this volume.

Don said of LeMoine: "I wanted to use my mind the way he used his," and LeMoine saw that Don had made up for lost academic time since those days when Don, exhausted from his work with the Abilene Sanitation Department, would nod off in LeMoine's classroom. "Last of all, as one born out of season," in Don's words and the Apostle Paul's, "he appeared unto me," and so Don eventually became one of "LeMoine's boys." LeMoine wrote the magic letter of recommendation, and Don went to Harvard.

At Harvard Divinity School, Don's interests in Religious Studies led him to focus on the New Testament and on the history of religion in America. He became particularly attached to three giants of Biblical Studies: Krister Stendahl: "I went to Harvard for Stendahl, and he did not disappoint me." George Macrae: "...a great man. His course, 'The Bible and Roman Catholic Theology,' was probably the best course I took." Helmut Koester: "Helmut was kind to me." Don accompanied Koester on one of his New-Testament archeology tours, and he thoroughly absorbed Koester's exegetical method.[13] Don also made solid intellectual connections with Conrad Wright (American Church History), Peter Berger (Sociology), and Frank Moore Cross (Old Testament), all of them equally distinguished scholars in their respective disciplines.

After Don graduated from HDS 1981 with his M. Div. degree, the question nevertheless pressed: How does one make a living with one of these? So he enrolled in the School of Information Science at the University of Tennessee in Knoxville, finished the two-year program in a year and a summer, and received an M.L.S. there in 1982. Of the acquiring of academic paper, there is no end; still, no one would call him "doctor"; but now, with all the degrees, he was said to be overqualified for kinds of jobs he had hitherto been willing to accept as a way at least to pay the light bill. Don decided that enough was enough.

Thanks to an introduction effected by Sam Hill, Don went to work as an acquisitions editor at Mercer University Press (MUP) in Macon, Georgia—a Baptist press that puts out good books anyway—where Don's boss was the most charming Baptist of them all, Edd Rowell. Their hearty collaboration became an enduring friendship. At MUP, Don developed the habit of working 14 hours per day, a habit that he has continued even until now. During Don's years of book-editing, one hardly recognizes him, for he barely got into any trouble at all.

One of the perks of Don's working at the Press was free tuition for Betty at the University, so she earned her Master's degree in English Education, and kept on teaching school in Macon, working in the Georgia heat "below the gnat line." Malcolm graduated from Central High School in Macon with awards in Drama. His strong friendships among the out-group and the earring had kept him from being admitted to the "gifted" classes that he had enjoyed throughout his previous schooling.

In 1986, financial cutbacks at MUP meant that someone had to go. Don volunteered to resign so that a fellow editor whose wife did not have a job would not lose that family's only source of income. Sam Hill to the rescue, again, in 1987 Don became Public Services Librarian at the DuPont Library in the School of Theology at the University of the South. And even when Don left off fellowshipping with the *Babdists* and moved up the ladder to the *Whiskeypalians*, he managed to keep his nose clean, mostly. Leaving the Bible belt for (as Don

---

[13] See Helmut Koester, "Harvard Divinity School and the Future of Theological Education," in this volume.

put it) "the Beretta Belt," Don, Betty, and Malcolm moved well above the gnat line up onto the Cumberland Plateau in Tennessee within "the Domain" at Sewanee.

Men wearing lace and dresses had never especially been Don's cup-o'-tea, but he tolerated the pretensions of Tennessee Anglicanians as well as any good ol' boy from Kentucky or West Texas could hope to do, partly because he found among the eccentric Episcopalians certain intellectuals whose pursuits in the life of the mind mirrored Don's own priorities. Ed Camp (Don's senior librarian), Jack Gessell, and Chris Bryan[14] became Don's abiding good friends. To some extent, the "smells and bells" must have got to him, however; Don for some time had been pleased to wear a cross around his neck, and at Sewanee, he discovered a lot of other people who liked to do that. To this day, from time to time and in the right places, he still wears a pectoral cross--nothing that most Church-of-Christ folk do. But, then, Don's permanent theological stance can best be described as a theology of the cross. Sacramentals are outward manifestations of inward grace.

Even so, continuing their policy of practical Christianity, Don and Betty maintained membership in the Monteagle Church of Christ. Don could put it two ways: Sometimes he said, "The Whiskeypalians make me glad of the Campbellites, and the Campbellites make me glad of the Whiskepalians," and other times he said: "I go to church on Sundays with the church of Christ in order to get over having gone to church on Wednesdays with the Episcopalians, and then on Wednesdays, I go to mass with the Episcopalians in order to get over having gone to church on Sundays with the Church of Christ." To keep the peace, Don took a vow of silence at church services in Monteagle, except for singing while sitting in the pew, and reading scripture when called on. Brother Byers, a member of long standing, told Don that his reading of scripture was the first time that Bro. Byers had understood what was being read publicly from the Bible. To scratch his homiletical itch, Don wrote for an Episcopalian annual liturgics publication.

Betty taught school in Grundy County, the poorest county in Tennessee, so the Haymeses bought a fine old house there. Betty loved it; Don hated it. At last, she had a nice house to fix up and plenty of space for a garden, and Don had a mortgage to pay and endless repairs to make. Not far away, however, was the desolate site of the Highlander Folk School in Monteagle, where Martin Luther King, Jr., Ralph Abernathy, Rosa Parks, Pete Seeger, and the Hortons had prepared the people for "the struggle" in Citizenship School. It was at Highlander that Zilphia Horton had transubstantiated an old union-organizing ditty into the theme song of the Civil Rights Movement, "We Shall Overcome." Local roughians, the KKK, and the Sovereign State of Tennessee had closed Highlander down in 1961, but the ghosts were all still there. Don, now in the lap of White luxury at Sewanee, was no longer living in a ravaged ghetto, but he had nonetheless pitched his tent for a while near a home of his soul.

In 1990, Don and Betty moved to Evanston, Illinois. Betty got a teaching job at Southern School, working with learning-disabled kids; and Don went to work for the American Theological Library Association (ATLA), then under the direction of Al Hurd, later directed by Dennis Norlin. Don became editor of the *Religion One Index*, the one place that anyone smart begins research in contemporary Religious Studies. Daily and massive contact with the serial literature of scholarship about religion placed Don where that once youthful reader of countless

---

[14] See Christopher Bryan, "'Christ our Passover has been sacrificed': *Reflections on the Life of Christ as Represented in the Calendars and Liturgies of the Western Church*," in this volume.

books was meant to be. A bookaholic, a 14-hour-a-day workaholic, Don drove himself in a bibliographizing frenzy.

On top of that, Don had undertaken to establish a scholarship fund in honor of LeMoine Lewis. LeMoine had died in 1987, too young. In 1990 at Don's instigation, Harvard Divinity School established the LeMoine Gaunce Lewis Memorial Scholarship, which it was able to do thanks to the successful fundraising accomplished by Don Haymes and Bill Martin, then Professor of Sociology at Rice University. "I wrote the letters, Bill signed them, Harvard mailed them," Don remembers. Don also contributed the first $1,500.

Shirley Lewis, LeMoine's widow, and Jack Lewis, LeMoine's brother, expressed their thanks to Don for "taking the lead in raising the funds." Jack, emeritus Professor of Biblical Studies at the Harding Graduate School of Religion in Memphis, also says of Don that "they broke the mold after they made him." Jack remembers the time when J. D. Thomas, Professor of Doctrine at Abilene Christian University, assembled a symposium on Bible translations, and someone asked Don (who was not on the program), what he would do if someone said the only Bible they had was *Good News for Modern Man*. Now, no one who knows anything about Bible translations thinks highly of that version, so Don was on the spot. Without hesitation, Don replied: "I would teach them the gospel from out of whatever Bible they had." Jack says, "That was pretty well heresy in the eyes of the person who had asked the question, but Don's answer was just what one ought to do."

Then, in 1993, when the long hours and stress of overwork, the sedentary lifestyle, and the body's memory of former righteousness and rage could not be counteracted by an equally frenetic pace of jogging, Don suffered a massive heart attack that nearly took him from us. Too mean to die young, he recovered and went back to work reading and bibliographizing journals., and attending annual meetings of the ATLA.

Don's annual attendance at the American Academy of Religion/Society of Biblical Literature (AAR/SBL) had begun when he was at MUP and ever on the hunt for publication-worthy manuscripts. The annual meeting now amounts to Don as a family reunion, for he loves to get together with his scholarly and churchly colleagues from over the years. He genuinely enjoys hearing about their current and future research projects. He attends the HDS and the Church-of-Christ functions, and on the Sunday morning, he has been known to lead singing at the gathering of Stone-Campbell scholars. Jack Lewis has even called Don's spontaneous song-leading "a delight." Don would usually lead "O Sacred Head Now Wounded," and then excuse himself by saying that this kind of music was not the kind that predominated at the congregation where he worshiped.

The congregation where the Haymeses worshiped was the Evanston Church of Christ, an almost all-Black congregation. (Chris[15] and Mary Lou Hutson were the only other White couple that regularly attended.) Carrying on in the spirit of LeMoine Lewis's practical Christianity and Don's own passion for racial equity, Don became a leader of the Evanston Church, and for years, he taught Bible classes, led in worship, struggled with divisive church politics, and often preached. Betty, too, taught children's classes, and she was welcomed as a sister among the women and the youth, whom she loved in return. Don spent most of his Saturdays, from mid-morning into the afternoon, reading the Bible with the men, teaching

---

[15] See Chris Hutson, *"Middle Ground? Alexander Campbell on Slavery and Carroll Osburn on Gender,"* in this volume.

them leadership skills, and helping them improve their general literacy. The result was a great spiritual growth for the men and for the whole congregation. "Book religion" may be a fine thing, but the presupposition is that the people read well. Don accommodated and re-learned the power of oral culture.

The *de facto* leaders of the congregation were two strong women, a situation with which Don was comfortable. When, however, he began to encourage all of the women to take public part in the Sunday evening prayers, a reaction set in. Don, therefore, announced that he was "becoming a woman," and to declare his solidarity with the women who were to "keep silent in the churches," Don became prophetically silent. The reaction became sharper, but some women profoundly appreciated the gesture, and about the time that the Haymeses moved away, the controversy seemed to be subsiding. The Haymeses and the Evanston congregation achieved genuine and mutual Christian community, still too rare a thing among Black people and White in Christian America. The West Islip Church and the Evanston Church would be remembered by Don and Betty as their true church homes. Don still champions gender equity at church as powerfully as he has always championed racial justice, and it still gets him into trouble.

The former book editor at MUP had now developed a sideline as acquisitions editor for scholarly books in religion at Scarecrow Press. Combining work at ATLA and Scarecrow, Don's editorial skills guided production of a milestone in Restoration Movement studies on Thomas Campbell's *Declaration and Address*.[16] Authors who have published their own works are the only ones who truly know the inestimable value of the unsung heroes of publication, the editor whose name does not go on the cover of the book.

During these same years, Don—at last—began to work on his own scholarship. In a box in his study somewhere are the first five chapters of a definitive study of the debate in 1837 over Roman Catholicism between Alexander Campbell and Archbishop John Purcell, and of anti-Catholicism in American Protestantism. Collegiality with Hans Rollmann in Newfoundland, moreover, led to Don's greatest scholarly achievement to date, his history of racism in the churches of Christ, an online book at Hans's Restoration Movement website.[17]

In 1999, Don and Betty moved to Indianapolis. Betty took a teaching job at Arlington High School, and Don became Serials and Archives Librarian at Christian Theological Seminary (CTS), working closely with David Bundy, who has since become the librarian at Fuller Theological Seminary, having undertaken the challenge to build a unique library to reflect Christianity of the Pacific Rim. After the move, Don also continued for four years as editor of ATLA's Monograph Series. Malcolm, however, stayed on in Chicago for a while, where his abilities as an actor and director—despite serious health problems—won numerous credits and prizes; thereafter, Malcolm moved to Chattanooga, Tennessee, finished

---

[16] Thomas H. Olbricht and Hans Rollmann, eds., *The Quest for Christian Unity, Peace, and Purity in Thomas Campbell's* Declaration and Address: *Texts and Studies* (ATLA Monograph Series, no. 46; Lanham, Maryland: Scarecrow Press, 2000).

[17] Don Haymes, *Race and the Church of Christ* http://www.mun.ca/rels/restmov/subs/race.html See Hans Rollmann, "'Die Campbelliten': The Stone-Campbell Movement in Major Twentieth-century German Theological Reference Works," in this volume.

his baccalaureate degree, married Susan Foxall, and made Don Haymes a grandfather by begetting Rebekah Jenise Haymes.

Don still works long hours that would kill less sturdy souls, and, indeed, nearly killed Don in 2003. Now, the bionic librarian sports a pacemaker. He especially loves his work with the CTS collection concerning the Stone-Campbell Restoration Movement. In retirement, Don will keep on working: He plans to index the earlier Campbellite serials that have never been indexed, "but that takes money!" quoth he.

Don is a member of the Oldsmobile Club of America, the Vintage Chevrolet Club of America, and Inliners International. Shimmering and shining in the garage are a restored four-door 1952 Chevy deluxe sedan and a 1936 Oldsmobile touring sedan, both of which he owns with Betty. He is currently designing and guiding the restoration of a 1952 Chevrolet deluxe coupe, using a V-6 inline engine with modifications, scheduled to be finished by his 65th birthday in 2005. Kwame is pleased to hear that Don, the grease-monkey, has reemerged.

And as important as the cars are, and his work and his family and his service to so many, a final point of humbling pride remains to be mentioned. Since coming to Indianapolis, Don and Betty have been faithful members of the Fountain Square Church of Christ. When some in that congregation asked Don to become an Elder in the Church, he protested his entire unworthiness, and he meant it. Don acknowledged that no higher calling, and no heavier responsibility, comes to a man on this earth than to be called to be a shepherd and servant of the little flock of Jesus. Neither seeking nor fleeing the office, Don's final response was a willingness to serve, if asked, and that characteristic entreaty, familiar to all his friends and the recipients of his email messages: "May God have mercy!"

YAHWEH: THE GOD OF ISRAEL

JACK P. LEWIS

This collection of archaeological data—inscriptions, mostly—has been gathered from many sources with no previous intention other than to be able to survey the use of theophoric names[1] among the ancient Hebrews, both in the Scriptures and out. Such a collection is, however, relevant to the history of religion in Israel and her neighbors, for the name of God, rather than being "never spoken," as we so often hear, was in quite common, daily usage. Archaeological artifacts do not come up out of the sands and caves with neatly typed interpretive tags attached to them. This material is no different; it is, therefore, susceptible to different interpretations. In the process of assembling and pondering this collection, the possible illumination of the name "Immanuel" (Is 7:14) suggested itself, bringing with it, then, a further possible insight into the "fulfilled" use of that name in the Gospel of Matthew (2:15).

The inscription material of the Middle East offers an abundance of evidence of the worship of various deities mentioned in the Old Testament. Dagon (1 Sm 5:2), in Ebla texts called "Dagon the Canaanite," had first place in the Ebla pantheon,[2] but regard for him is also reflected in Eblite theophoric names. Mari excavations revealed a temple of Dagon there;[3] and at Ugarit, in "The Fight Between Baal and Yam," "The Lament over Baal," "Keret," etc., Baal is the son of Dagon.[4] It has long been illegitimate to represent Dagon as the combined fish-man seen in the imaginary drawing used in the old Bible dictionaries for the Philistine god.

Baal was also worshiped at Ebla as is evidenced in the theophoric element in personal names.[5] Then an abundance of evidence concerning his worship comes from Ugaritic texts; and along with Baal are his consorts Astarte and Anath.[6] Phoenician seals contain the names of Yahziba`al ("May Baal look") and Ba`alnatan ("Baal has given") which are theophoric name-compounds of Baal.[7] In Canaan, place names like Bamoth-baal (Jos 13:17), Baal-meon (Ezk 25:9), Baal-hamon (So 8:11), Baalshalishah (2 Kg 4:42), Baal-peor (Nm 25:3, 5; etc.), Baal-perazim (2 Sm 5:20), Baal-tamar (Jd 20:33), and Baal-zephon (Ex

---

[1] A theophoric name in Hebrew combines within it an element that is the name of a deity, such as *baal* or *'el* or *yah*. In English, "Christopher" is a parallel construction: "the Christ-bearer."

[2] Lorenzo Vigano, "The Ebla Tablets," *Biblical Archaeology* 47 (1984): 11.

[3] André Parrot, "Mari," in *Archaeology and Old Testament Study*, D. Winton Thomas, ed. (Oxford: Clarendon Press, 1967): 137-38.

[4] Walter Beyerlin, ed. *Near Eastern Religious Texts Relating to the Old Testament* (Philadelphia: Westminster, 1978): 203, 216, 224.

[5] Vigano(1984): 11.

[6] Peter C. Craigie, *Ugarit and the Old Testament* (Grand Rapids: Eerdmans, 1983): 61-66.

[7] Ruth Hestrin and Michal Dayagi-Mendels, *Inscribed Seals* (Jerusalem: Israel Museum, 1979): nos. 118, 120.

14:2) are compounds of Baal. Baal-meon occurs on line 9 of the Moabite stone. There are personal names like Jerubbaal (Jd 7:1), Eshbaal, and Meribbaal (1 Ch 8:33, 34; 9:39, 40). A bronze knife of the 13[th] to 14[th] century B.C.E. from Nahal Tavor has the inscription in Proto-Canaanite, "(Belonging) to Si[lli]ba`al so[n of] Pulsiba`al."[8] "Gerbaal" ("client of Baal") and "Azarbaal" ("Baal has helped") occur in other old Phoenician inscriptions on bronze arrowheads from various localities dating from the twelfth to early tenth centuries.[9] "Azarbaal" also occurs on a bronze spatula of the eleventh century.[10] The Ahiram limestone sarcophagus of the thirteenth century B.C.E. from Lebanon, which contains the oldest connected readable text in Phoenician, speaks of Ittobaal which means "Baal is with him" (cf. Ethbaal; 1 Kg 16:31). The Yehimilik inscription dating around 950 B.C.E. has an invocation to Baalshamem.[11] The fragment of a statue of the king of Biblos has the name Abibaal,[12] and that of Elibaal is on a statue of Osorkon I (914-874 B.C.E.); Shipitbaal is his son.[13]

There are numerous inscriptions from the Middle East containing the name of Baal. A Cyprus grave inscription, perhaps of the ninth century B.C.E., speaks of "the hand of Baal."[14] The Kilamuwa (Zenjirli) orthostat[15] speaks of Baal-Semed and Baal-Hammon. The first is a title of Hadad and means "lord of the mace," while the second is the chief god of Carthage.[16] This name is also in an inscription from Malta.[17]

Baal is prominent in the Karatepe gate inscription of the eighth century.[18] The dedicator, Azitiwada, repeatedly gives Baal credit for what he has accomplished. An early eighth century bronze votive inscription has the names of Baalyatan and Abdbaal. The inscription is for Astarte of Hor.[19] A bronze ceremonial bowl is given to "Baal of Lebanon."[20] An ivory box from Ur, probably carried there by a trader or soldier, has a feminine name "Amotbaal."[21]

Six of the theophoric names found on the Samaritan ostraca[22] are Baal names as compared with nine for *Yahweh* names, showing the penetration of the Baal cult into the kingdom of Israel. An inscription on a fragment of plaster from Kuntillet-`Ajrud from the eighth century reads, "Blessed be Ba`al to the day of … "[23] An eighth century Hebrew seal

---

[8] Ruth Hestrin et al., *Inscriptions Reveal*, 2nd. edn., Catalogue no. 100 (Jerusalem: Israel Museum, 1973): 11, no. 3.

[9] John C. L. Gibson, *Text Book of Semitic Inscriptions* (Oxford: Clarendon Press, 1987): 3:6.

[10] *Ibid.*: 3: 9-10.

[11] *Ibid.*: 3: 18.

[12] *Ibid.*: 3 :21.

[13] *Ibid.*:3: 22, 23.

[14] *Ibid.*: 3: 29.

[15] An orthostat is a large stone standing on edge.

[16] *Ibid.*: 3: 35, 39.

[17] *Ibid.*: 3: 74, 75.

[18] *Ibid.*: 3: 47-55.

[19] *Ibid.*: 3: 65.

[20] *Ibid.*: 3: 68.

[21] *Ibid.*: 3:71.

[22] Ostraca are pieces of broken pottery on which someone has written in ink (singlar: ostracon).

[23] Z. Meshel, *Kuntillet `Ajrud: A Religious Centre from the Time of the Judean Monarchy on the Border of Sinai*, Israel Museum Catalogue 175 (Jerusalem: Israel Museum, 1978): n.p.

belonged to a son of Ba`alhanan.[24] Chemosh, the god of the Moabites (cf. Nm 21:29; 1 Kg 11:7, 33; etc.), is met both on the Moabite stone of Mesha and on the fragment from Kerak.[25] Mesha introduces himself as son of Chemosh-gat, a theophoric name that occurs in both inscriptions. An alabaster seal of the seventh century reads "Chemosh" which may be an abbreviated form of a theophoric name.[26]

A seal found in Wooley's excavation at Ur, conjectured to date to the end of the seventh century and to have belonged to a Moabite exile, contains the name "Kemosh-nathan."[27] Another seal of the seventh to eighth century reads "Belonging to Kemosh-m'š," but the meaning of the second portion is uncertain. Avigad proposes that it be interpreted as "Lord."[28]

It is agreed that the Ammonite citadel inscription proclaims the work of Milcom despite the fact that some letters of the name have to be reconstructed.[29] A Moabite seal, apparently from Lebanon, has been found with the inscription which identifies it as the seal of "Kemosh`am (son of) Kemosh'el the scribe."[30]

Milcom is the god of the Ammonites (1 Kg 11:5, 39; 2 Kg 23:13; Zph 1:5). An Ammonite seal reads, "Seal of Mannu-ki-Inurta, blessed by Milcom."[31] A seal impression, dating about 600 B.C.E., was found in 1984 at Tell el-`Umeiri in Jordan which is the first in seals and impressions with a Milcom theophoric name. It reads, "Belonging to Milkom'ur servant of b`lys` ("servant of Ba`alyiss`a")." The name perhaps means "Milcom's Flame."[32] A Baalis, king of the Ammonites, is mentioned in Jr 40:14.

Yahweh Inscriptions

That Israel's God was named Yahweh has never been in dispute. The word is translated "Jehovah" a few times in the KJV [Ex 6:3; Ps 83:18; Is 12:2; 26:4] and often in the ASV, but, following rabbinic tradition, is otherwise "the Lord" in the remainder of the KJV and in other translations. Now, however, use of the name is well attested in non-biblical inscriptions which have been found in Palestine dating from the ninth to the sixth centuries B.C.E., and even later in texts or theophoric names from elsewhere.[33]

The earliest known non-biblical occurrence of the name Yahweh is on the Mesha stone from the ninth century B.C.E., which apart from the Gezer calendar, is the starting place of inscriptions in Palestine. Lines 17 and 18 of the Mesha stone speak of Mesha's taking "the

[24] Nahman Avigad, "Ammonite and Moabite Seals," in *Near Eastern Archaeology in the Twentieth Century: Eassys in Honor of Nelson Glueck,* James A. Sanders, ed. (Garden City, New York: Doubleday & Company, 1970): 297.
[25] Gibson (1987): 1: 76, 83.
[26] Hestrin and Dayagi-Mendels (1979): no. 114.
[27] Avigad (1970): 290.
[28] *Ibid.*: 290-91.
[29] S. H. Horn, "The Amman Citadel Inscription," *Bulletin of American Schools of Oriental Research* 193 (1969): 2-13; Frank M. Cross, "Epigraphic Notes on the Amman Citadel Inscription," *ibid.*: 13-19.
[30] Hestrin and Dayagi-Mendels (1979): 17, no. 2.
[31] Nachman Avigad, "Seals of Exiles," *Israel Exploration Journal* 15 (1965): 222-288.
[32] Larry Herr, "The Servant of Baalis," *Biblical Archaeologist* 48 (1985): 169-72.
[33] An earlier bibliography is found in Frank M. Cross, Jr., *Canaanite Myth and Hebrew Epic* (Cambridge, Massachusetts: Harvard Press, 1973): 60-61; n. 61.

vessels of Yahweh" from the captured town of Nebo and that he "dragged them before Chemosh."[34] The inscription shows that the name of Israel's God was known to the Moabites, Israel's opponents; and, on the other hand, Scripture knows Chemosh as the god of the Moabites (Nm 21:29; Jd 11:24; 1 Kg 11:7, 33; Jr 48:7, 13, 48).

Inscriptions from the ninth to eighth centuries B.C.E. found at Kuntillet-`Ajrud, located fifty miles south of Kadesh Barnea, also know the name Yahweh. A stone vessel has inscribed on it in Hebrew, "(Belonging) to Obadiah, son of Adnah, may he be blessed by Yahweh." An inscription in fragmentary condition on plaster is a blessing that has the words: "Yahweh favored…." An inscription drawn on a pithos[35] reads, "May you be blessed by Yahweh who guards us and his asherah." Another reads, "Amariah said to my lord…may you be blessed by Yahweh and his asherah. Yahweh bless you and keep you and be with you." These occurrences of the word *'asherah* in connection with Yahweh are now provoking much discussion. A female counterpart for the Lord has not previously been attested.[36] However, Joseph Naveh suggests that the third line of the el-Qom inscription be read as "May Uriyahu be blessed by Yahweh, my Guardian, and by his asherah."[37] Epigraphists have debated whether *'asherah* is to be taken as a proper name or as a simple noun.

A later reinterpretation of one of the Kuntilet `Ajrud inscriptions, rather than "Yahweh who guards us and his Asherah," reads, "Yahweh of Samaria and his Asherah." The consonants in the verb "guard" *(shmr)* and those in "Samaria" *(shmrn)* are similar. Another reads, "I bless you by Yahweh of Teman…."[38] Emerton notes a similar structure in another inscription that reads "Yahweh of Teman," and conjectures that they may have been made by travelers from Samaria and from the south which is the meaning of Teman.[39]

---

[34] Gibson (1987): 1:71-83; James B. Pritchard, ed., *Ancient Near Eastern Texts Relating to the Old Testament*, 3rd edn. (Philadelphia: University of Pennsylvania Press, 1969): 320.

[35] A pithos is a large clay jar used for storing oil, water, wine, or grain.

[36] Z. Meshel and C. Myers, "The Name of God in the Wilderness of Zin," *Biblical Archaeology* 39 (1976): 6-10; Meshel, Kuntillet `Ajrud, n.p.; Z. Meshel, "Did Yahweh Have a Consort?" *Biblical Archaeology Review* 5/2 (March/April, 1979): 24-34.

[37] Joseph Naveh, "Inscriptions of the Biblical Period," in *Recent Archaeology in the Land of Israel*, Hershel Shanks, ed. (Washington, D.C.: Biblical Archaeology Society, 1981): 63. The rest of the inscription reads: "(Belonging to) `Uriyahu. Be careful of his inscription! / Blessed be `Uriyahu by Yahweh / and cursed be the hand of whoever (defaces it)! / (Written) by `Oniyahu." The editor of the inscription suggested that the inscription is a graffito of four lines with features comparable to other tomb inscriptions of its period. The deceased is named. The blessing of Yahweh is invoked. A curse is pronounced on anyone defacing the tomb or inscription. The writer of the inscription is named: `Uriyahu means "Yahweh is my light." The name occurs in Jr. 16:20 as well as in other inscriptions for other persons. `Oniyahu means "Yahweh is my strength," and he is likely to have been the writer of the inscription. The name is an addition to the Palestinian name list. See William G. Dever, "Iron Age Epigraphic Material from the Area of Khirbet el-Kom," *Hebrew Union College Annual* 40-41 (1969-1970): 159-162.

[38] J. H. Tigay, *You Shall Have No Other Gods* (Atlanta: Scholars Press, 1986): 26-27.

[39] J. A. Emerton, "New Light on Israelite Religion: The Implications of the Inscriptions from Kuntillet `Ajrud," *Zeitschrift für die altestamentliche Wissenschaft* 94 (1982): 1-20.

A tomb inscription dating in the mid-eighth century from Khirbet el-Qom in the district of Hebron reads, "(Belonging to Uri`ahu). Heed its inscription. Blessed be Uri`ahu by Yahweh. And cursed be the hand of whoever (defaces it)! (Written by) Oniahu."[40]

A seal of the eighth century said to have been found in Jerusalem reading, "(Belonging) to Miqneyaw Servant of Yahweh," is the first with this epithet and is the first occurrence in an inscription.[41] Avigad argues that the owner was a temple functionary, perhaps a musician.[42]

A small ivory pomegranate (only 1.68 inches high and .83 inches wide), thought to have once been the top of a ceremonial scepter carried by temple priests, may be more than 2,500 years old. Pomegranates, one of the native fruits of Canaan (Dt 8:7-10), decorated the capitals of Solomon's temple (2 Ch 3:16; Jr 52:21). Artistic depictions of pomegranates are not unusual in archaeological artifacts. They decorate pottery, metal objects, seals, and coins.

On the shoulder of this small ivory pomegranate is a defective Hebrew inscription conjecturally reconstructed to read, "Holy to the priests, belonging to the H[ouse of Yahwe]h (?). This is granted not to be the only possible reconstruction. From the style of the writing, the inscription, one may conjecture the date to about 765-705 B.C.E., the period from the earliest writing prophets to the time of King Hezekiah.[43] The earliest (and to this point the only) mention of the name of Yahweh found in a Jerusalem inscription was discovered and deciphered by Gabriel Barkay of Tel Aviv University on a silver amulet scroll in a treasure trove found near St. Andrews Church, opposite Mt. Zion in 1981. The letters were scratched into the metal with a sharp instrument and are conjectured to date from the seventh to sixth centuries B.C.E. Both this amulet and a second one also found have the priestly benediction of Nm 6:24-26: "The Lord bless you and keep you; the Lord make his face to shine upon you...."[44]

An Arad ostracon (no. 3), dating in the early sixth century addressed to Eliashib the fortress commander, has the phrases: "May Yahweh inquire as to your welfare," and "In the house of Yahweh he dwells."[45] Y. Aharoni, the excavator, conjectures that the man has found sanctuary in the temple in Jerusalem.[46] On another of these ostraca, Hananyahu says, "I have said a blessing to the Lord for you."[47] One compares 1 Sm 15:13 where Saul says to Samuel, "Blessed be you to the Lord." Yet another has "may the Lord seek your welfare."[48] The editor of the ostraca reconstructs another, inscription 21:2, to read, "I have

[40] Dever (1969-1970): 158-59; Hestrin, *et al.* (1973): no. 141.

[41] Frank M. Cross, "The Seal of Miqneyaw, Servant of Yahweh," *Ancient Seals and the Bible*, L. Gorelick and E. Williams-Forte, eds. (Malibu, California: Undena Publications, 1983): 55-83.

[42] Nachman Avigad, "The Contribution of Hebrew Seals to an Understanding of Israelite Religion and Society," in *Ancient Israelite Religion: Essays in Honor of Frank Moore Cross*, Patrick D. Miller, Jr., *et al.*, eds. (Philadelphia: Fortress Press, 1987): 197-98.

[43] Hershel Shanks, *In the Temple of Solomon and the Tomb of Caiaphas* (Washington, D.C.: Biblical Archaeology Society, 1991): 14-30.

[44] G. Barkay, A. G. Vaughn, M. J. Lundberg, and B. Zuckerman, "The Amulets from Ketef Hinnom: A New Edition and Evaluation," *Bulletin of American Schools of Oriental Research* 334 (May 2004): 41-71.

[45] Hestrin, *et. al.* (1973): 166.

[46] Yohanan. Aharoni, *Arad Inscriptions* (Jerusalem: Israel Exploration Society, 1981): 35-37.

[47] *Ibid.*: no. 16.3.

[48] *Ibid.*: no. 18.2.

blessed you to the Lord."[49] It further reads, "...The Lord will give my master his due."[50] The editor also reconstructs inscription 40:3 as "I have blessed you to the Lord";[51] however, only the final letter *he* of the name is readable.

A tomb-cave near Amasia dating in the early sixth century B.C.E. has the inscription: "Yahweh (is) the God of the whole earth...Jerusalem."[52]

The Lachish Ostraca of the sixth century repeatedly have the phrase, "May Yahweh cause my Lord to hear tidings...."[53] There is also, 'May Yahweh afflict those who report an evil rumor...,"[54] "As Yahweh liveth...,"[55] and "May Yahweh cause thee to see."[56] These ostraca have an abundance of theophoric names: Gemaryahu (cf. Jr 36:10, 11, 12, 25), Hosha`yahu (no. 3:1), Tobyahu (no. 3:19), Shelemyahu (no. 9:7), and Jeremiah (1:4).

A black ink inscription in ancient Hebrew in a cave in the vicinity of Ein Gedi reads "Blessed be" three times. The first, which is line 4, has *brk yh[weh]* which means "blessed be the Lord."[57] The last two letters are restored and the item could be a theophoric name.[58]

Inscriptions from the wall of a tomb at Khirbet Beit Lei, dated to the sixth century by F. M. Cross, are deciphered by him as, "I am Yahweh, thy God: I will accept the cities of Judah and will redeem Jerusalem," as "Absolve [us}, O merciful God! Absolve [us], O Yahweh!" and as "Deliver [us], O Yahweh!"[59]

Though not in Palestine itself, the Elephantine Jews in the late fifth century worshiped a God called "Yaho,"[60] although other deities are also mentioned." Yaho is called "the God of Heaven,"[61] and he has a temple in Elephantine. "The temple of the god Yaho in the fortress of Yeb...."[62] These Jews were seeking aid in rebuilding their destroyed temple. One letter says, "I bless you by Yaho...."[63] The Elephantine Jews made abundant use of Yahweh theophoric names, such as Yedoniah son of Gemariah, Micaiah, Mibtahiah, Nehaeiah, and others. They had written to Deliah and Shelemiah, sons of Sanballat, in Samaria.

Another line of investigation, but also interesting, is the theophoric names that occur in inscriptions and on seals or sealings. If the reconstruction is credible, the Gezer[64] calendar

---

[49] *Ibid.*: 42.

[50] *Ibid.*: 21:4; cf. Rt 2:12; 2 Sm. 3:39; Job 21:31; Pv. 25:22.

[51] Aharoni (1981): 71-72.

[52] Hestrin, *et al.* (1973): no. 79.

[53] Gibson (1987): 1:37, Ostracon 2:1-2.

[54] *Ibid.*: 1, Ostracon II.6.1:32-34.

[55] *Ibid.*: 1:39, 46, Ostracon III:9 and VI:12.

[56] *Ibid.*: 1, Ostracon V:7 and VII.

[57] P. Bar-Adon, "An Early Hebrew Inscription in a Judean Desert Cave," *Israel Exploration Journal* 25 (1975): 226-32.

[58] Naveh (1981): 63.

[59] Frank Moore Cross, Jr., "The Cave Inscriptions from Khirbet Beit Lei," in Sanders, ed. (1970): 299-306.

[60] Pritchard (1969): 491.

[61] *Ibid.*: 492.

[62] *Loc. cit.*

[63] *Ibid.*: 491.

[64] The Gezer calendar, a small limestone tablet (4 1/4 x 3 1/8 inches), discovered at Gezer in 1908, inscribed in Paleo-Hebrew about 925 B.C.E., is thought possibly to be a school boy's exercise. The text

has the name of Abijah in its margin, conjectured to be the name of the scribe. Actually, the theophoric element is reconstructed.[65]

A seal in writing of the ninth to tenth century B.C.E. has a bull image and the name "Shemayahu (Shemiah) son of Ezrayahu (Azariah)."[66] The Shema seal with the lion image from Megiddo has the name of Jeroboam.[67] From the eighth century B.C.E. is the inscription from the Siloam necropolis of the Royal Steward whose theophoric name is defaced but is read by Avigad as "[..]yahu who is over the house."[68] The missing element is usually conjectured to be "Shebna" (cf. Is 22:15; 36:3, 11; 37:2).

Toi of Hamath sent his son Joram to congratulate David over a military victory (2 Sm 8:9). While the Chronicler gives the name as "Hadoram" (1 Ch 18:10), we are puzzled at an Aramean figure of the royal family having a Yahweh compound name. A cuneiform tablet has a name interpreted as Azri-Yau for a ruler of a district of Hamath on the Orontes River of the 8th century B.C.E. Then, after a rebellion against Assyria led by Hamath, Yau-bi'di ruled, probably about 720 B.C.E. How Yahweh names came to be possessed by these figures outside of Israel and Judah is the subject only of uncertain hypotheses.[69]

The Wadi Murabba'at papyrus fragment found in a cave in 1952 is the only known surviving papyrus from pre-exilic times in Palestine and is conjecturally dated eight-seventh centuries. The papyrus is a palimpsest, but in the later writing (*ca.* 650 B.C.E.), the names Hoshea and Shemaiah (son of) Joezer are read on it.[70]

Ostraca from Samaria dating in the seventh century have names that are about one-half compounded with the name of Baal and the others with the name of Yahweh. Such names as Shamaryau ("the Lord keeps"; 1:1-2; 13:2; 14:2; 21:1-2), Jedaiah ("the Lord has known"; 1:8; 42:2; 48:1); Gaddiyau (2:2; etc.) and Ebedyau ("servant of the Lord"; 50:2;) are included.[71]

An eighth-century ostracon from Beersheba has Neryahu and Amaryahu, and a seal impression has Obadyahu and Neryahu.[72]

An ostracon found in an unstratified context on the Ophel hill in 1924, likely dating at the end of the Judean kingdom, has the names Jehizkiah (cf. 2 Kg 18:1; Ezr 2:16; Nh. 7:21), Bukkiah, and Ahijah.[73] An ostracon from Ramat Rahel, dating about 700 B.C.E., has the names Ahiyahu and Hasadyahu.[74] The Metsad Hashvyahu ostracon has the name

---

enumerates the agricultural seasons. For many years, the Gezer calendar was the earliest completely decipherable Hebrew inscription.

[65] Gibson (1987): 1:2.

[66] *Loc. cit.*

[67] Hestrin *et al.* (1973): no. 18.

[68] Nachman Avigad, "The Epitaph of a Royal Steward from Siloam Village," *Israel Exploration Journal* 3 (1953): 137-52.

[69] Stephanie Dalley, "Yahweh in Hamath in the 8th Century B.C.E.: Cuneiform Material and Historical Deductions," *Vetus Testamentum* 40 (1990): 21-32; Ziony Zevit, "Yahweh Worship and Worshippers in the 8th-Century Syria," *Vetus Testamentum* 41 (1991): 363-366.

[70] Gibson (1987): 1:32.

[71] Pritchard (1969): 321; André Lemaire, *Inscriptions Hebraiques* (Paris: Editions du Cerf, 1977): 1:29-38.

[72] Yohanan Aharoni, ed., *Beersheba I* (Tel Aviv: Tel Aviv University, 1973): 72-75.

[73] Gibson (1987): 1:25-26.

[74] Lemaire (1977): 1:157.

Hashabiah (cf. 1 Ch 6:45; Ez 8:19; Nh 3:17).[75] An ostracon of Khirbet el-Meshash has Hananyahu.[76]

A seal, depicting a fighting cock and with the name "(Belonging) to Jaazaniah, servant of the King" (cf. 2 Kg 25:23; Jr 40:8), was found at Tell en-Nashbeh.[77] An ostracon from Horvat `Uza, dating from the seventh-sixth century B.C.E., has the names `Amadyahu, Hosa`yahu, and Hisilyahu.[78]

Of special interest is the abundance of finds made of bullae with theophoric names. A collection of 255 bullae from 168 different seals, the largest ever found, was characterized by the editor as the most significant find since the Dead Sea Scrolls. Dating from the time of Jeremiah,[79] they contain 132 different names. These bullae were formed by impressing a seal into a lump of clay that was attached to a written document by a string. Some have the marks of papyrus fibers on their back; they were baked in a conflagration that consumed the documents to which they were attached but preserved the bullae. Some were presented after purchase to the Israel Museum; others were acquired by a Jerusalem antiquities dealer and collector in October 1975.

About two-thirds of the names of these bullae are names (but not in reference to the biblical persons) mentioned in the Hebrew Bible. Others are previously known from other epigraphic sources. Not one of the bullae belonged to a woman. Most of the names are theophoric, and generally they are compounds of Yahweh. Eighty of them either begin or end with the divine element *yhw*. Of particular interest may be examples where the bulla contains two yahwistic names, such as these: "(Belonging) to Berekhyahu son of Neriyiahu" (No. 9), "Adoniyahu son of Yeqamyahu" (No. 11) or "(Belonging) to Yehoa`az son of Mattan" (No. 74), "(Belonging) to Amaryahu son of Yeho'ab" (No. 31). "(Belonging) to Yeho'ah (son of) 'Eli`az" (Nos. 71-75); and there are others.

Avigad has published three seals or seal impressions which in his opinion have names of special interest. A bulla reads, "(Belonging) to Berachyahu son of Neriyahu the scribe" which may be the scribe of Jr. 36:4. Another reads, "(Belonging) to Jerahmeel son of the king" (cf. Jr 36:26), and a third, "(Belonging) to Serayhu, the scribe" (cf. Jr 51:59). These are conjectured to have belonged to biblical personages.[80]

A discovery of fifty-one bullae, of which forty-one are well preserved, by Y. Shiloh in his excavation of the City of David, yields Hebrew names from the last days before Jerusalem fell to the Babylonians. Fifty different names, including fathers and sons, occur: `Azaryahu and Hosha`yahu occur three times. Three names (as Yehoab) begin with *yhw*. Forty one (or about 50 percent) of the names have the theophoric ending, *yhw*, such as Benayahu, Gadiyahu, `Azaryahu son of Hilkiyahu, etc. A City of David bulla reads,

---

[75] Gibson (1987): 1:28-29.

[76] Lemaire (1977): 1:276.

[77] Gibson (1987): 1:62, no. 14.

[78] I. Beit-Arieh, "The Ostracon of Ahiqam from Horvat `Uza," *Erets-Israel* (1985): 68-9.

[79] Nachman Avigad, *Hebrew Bullae from the Time of Jeremiah* (Jerusalem: Israel Exploration Society, 1986): 20, 116.

[80] Nachman Avigad, "Three Ancient Seals," *Biblical Archaeology* 49 (1986): 51-53; "The Contribution of Hebrew Seals to an Understanding of Israelite Religion and Society," in Miller, ed. (1987): 199.

"(Belonging) to Gemaryahu [so]n of Shafan" who is repeatedly mentioned in the story of the burning of Jeremiah's scrolls (Jr 36:9-12, 25-26). Shaphan is mentioned in 2 Kg 22:3.[81]

In excavations at Arad, sealings were found with names like Eshiyahu (Nos. 105, 106, 107), Shelemyahu and Berakyahu (No. 108).[82] At Tell el-Hesi in 1977, a bulla of the seventh-sixth century was found that has the inscription "Mattanyahu (son of) Ishmael."[83]

We observe with interest a difference in the occurrence of theophoric names in the northern and southern kingdoms, Israel and Judah: While the Samaritan ostraca have numerous theophoric names in which Baal is a part, the Lachish and Arad ostraca, as well as these bullae, have many Yahweh compounds, but they do not have any examples of Baal names. It seems that the cult of Baal was not so popular in Judah as it was in the North.[84] After the reform of Josiah, Yahweh names seem to have increased progressively in Judah.

The use of Yahweh theophoric names continues in the Persian and Greek periods. Aharoni's excavation of the Persian level at Lachish turned up a juglet with seventeen bullae that contain theophoric names, such as Yehokal (cf. Jr 37:3), Yehohay, `Ananyahu, Neriyahu, Shevanyahu [servant/son] of the King, Yirmeyahu son of Sefanyahu. Also found was a weight bearing the inscription, "Belonging to Nedav-yahu."[85] We have already noticed theophoric names in Elephantine. The Murashu documents with names like *yahūnatan the son of mattanyaw* and *yadi`yaw the son of banayaw* attest a like practice among Jews of the Exile in the Nippur region.[86] There are many more examples than those here cited.

Continued use of theophoric names down into the Greek period can be seen in the coin found at Beth-zur in 1931 which has *YHZQYH* ("Hezekiah") in Hebrew from the time of Ptolemy I.[87] Also to be noted are the 128 clay seal impressions from the Wadi ed-Daliyeh, about seventy of which are well-preserved, and two of which have inscriptions. The names are most often Yahwistic, containing a theophoric element. They date about the middle of the fourth century B.C.E One of the Aramaic papyri, now called "Samaria Papyrus I," records the sale of a slave Yehohanan son of Se'ilah by Hananyah to a certain Yehonur in the second year of Arses, the accession year of Darius the King (335 B.C.E). One inscribed seal has the reconstructed reading, "Belonging to Yeshayahu son of Sanballat, governor of Samaria."[88]

---

[81] Yigal Shiloh and David Tarlor, "Bullae from the City of David," *Biblical Archaeology* 49 (1986): 197-209.

[82] Aharoni (1973): 119, 120.

[83] Kevin G. O'Connel, "An Israelite Bulla from Tell el-Hesi," *Israel Exploration Journal* 27 (1977): 197-99; Valerie M. Fargo and Kevin G. O'Connel, "Five Seasons of Excavations at Tell el-Hesi (1970-77)," *Biblical Archeology* 41 (1978): 178.

[84] Jeffrey H. Tigay, "Israelite Religion: The Onomastic and Epigraphical Evidence," in Miller, ed. (1987): 157-94.

[85] Yohanan Aharoni, *Investigations at Lachish. Lachish V* (Tel Aviv: Gateway Publications, 1976): 19-22.

[86] Michael David Coogan, *West Semitic Personal Names in the Murasu Documents* (Missoula, Montana: Scholars Press, 1978): 120-21.

[87] Ovid R. Sellers, "Echoes of the 1931 Campaign" in *The 1957 Excavations at Beth-Zur*, Paul W. Lapp, ed., *Annual of the American Schools of Oriental Research* 38 (Cambridge, Massachusetts.: American Schools of Orental Research, 1968): 2; Nachman Avigad, "A New Class of Yehud Stamps," *Israel Exploration Journal* 7 (1957): 146-53; W. F. Albright, "The Seal Impression from Jericho and the Treasurers of the Second Temple," *Bulletin of American Schools of Oriental Research* 148 (1957): 28-30.

[88] Frank Moore Cross, Jr., "Epigraphic Notes on the Amman Citadel Inscription," *Bulletin of American Schools of Oriental Research* 193 (1969): 13-19; "The Papyri and Their Historical Implications," in

Yahweh Is with Us

The prophet Isaiah speaks of a child named `immanu 'el (Is 7:14). The form is a preposition and its attached object followed by the divine name 'el. It could be a nominal sentence which in Hebrew has no verb and for which one must be supplied in English translation. The same two Hebrew words occur also in Is 8:8, 10. In the Greek transliteration, the two words were joined to make a single name, Emmanouel, and the Vulgate followed this usage. In Is 8:8, 10, however, these same two Hebrew words are translated as declarative clauses: *met' hemōn ho Theos*. The Gospel of Matthew cites the Greek text (Mt 1:29). The Latin Bible renders Is 8:8 as a vocative: *"O Immanuel."* The English Bible follows the Latin, here.

Of particular interest to students of Is 7:14 are the occurrences in the newly published bullae of the name `Immadiyahu (No. 93) which means "the Lord is with me."[89] This sort of name also occurs with a Baal element in the name "Ittobaal" ("Baal is with him"; cf. "Ethbaal"; 1 Kg 16:31) which is found on the Ahiram sarcophagus.[90] Avigad, the publisher of the bullae,[91] calls our attention to a parallel that was also found in the Elephantine papyri in the name `Immanuiah, meaning "Yahweh is with us."[92] Also, Avigad, modifying the vocalization earlier proposed by the excavator of a list of names found at Horvat `Uza in the Negev, reads the name *'mdyhw bn zkr* as "`Immadiyahu son of Zakkur." The name means "The Lord is with me." The declaration of faith—that the deity named is with the person who wears the name—is the same in them all. "The Lord is with us" is met more than once in the O.T. with various pronouns, sometimes with the preposition *'et* (Nm 14:9; Jr 20:11) but more often with *'im* (Jg 6:12; 2 Ch 15:2). "The Lord of hosts is with us" (Ps 46:7, 11), and "God is with us" (2 Ch 13:12).

The only difference between these names and that used in Is 7:14 is that they have the divine element *yahweh* or *'elohim* instead of *'el* in them. Two of them have the first person pronoun instead of the second. The declaration of faith is the same in them all.

The occurrence of these names should lay to rest the contention of those who insist that "Immanuel" can be worn only by a divine child of an incarnation. These names make it likely that any child in Isaiah's day could have been named "God is with us," "God be with us," or "God was with us." Isaiah later speaks of a span of time as a sign to King Hezekiah (Is 37:3). The sign of which Isaiah spoke to Ahaz could have been the time that lapsed between the child's conception, birth, and learning to make choices (cf. Is 8:4). The danger from Peqah and Rezin would pass by that time. Ahaz did not need to hire the Assyrians to fight his battle.

Discoveries in the Wadi ed-Daliyeh," *Annual of American Schools of Oriental Research* 41 (1974): 17-29; "Samaria Papyrus I: An Aramaic Slave Conveyance of 335 B.C.E. Found in the Wadi ed-Daliyeh," *Eretz-Israel* 18 (1985): 7*-17*. A more technical discussion of inscriptions and names is given by J. H. Tigay (1986): 1-114.

[89] Avigad (1986): 71.

[90] Gibson (1987): 3:14.

[91] Avigad, *loc. cit.*

[92] A. E. Cowley, *Aramaic Papyri of the Fifth Century B.C.* (Oxford: Clarendon Press, 1923): 70, 71; no. 22:105.

Though I am concerned in this essay with archaeological finds and not with New Testament interpretation and theology, one can hardly fail to give a passing notice to the Gospel of Matthew.

The Gospel of John suggests that a statement may have import of which the speaker was not conscious at the time of speaking (Jn 11:49-52). The First Epistle of Peter suggests that a prophet was not informed of the final import of his words (1 Pt 1:10-12). If one allows the writer of the Gospel of Matthew to define his understanding of the verb "fulfill" (*pleroō*), one may observe in the infancy narrative that "Out of Egypt have I called my son" (Mt 2:15), a citation of Ho 11:1 in which the prophet was speaking of the Exodus of Israel from Egypt under Moses, is said by Matthew (2:15) to have been fulfilled in Jesus' visit to, and coming out of, Egypt. Also, "Rachel weeping for her children" (Mt 2:18) which in Jr 31:15 speaks of grief over the fate of the Assyrian exiles, Matthew says is fulfilled in the grief over the tragedy of the infants of Bethlehem. If we did not have Matthew's interpretation and understanding of "fulfillment" of prophecy, one might not see either the suggested import in these passages or Matthew's hermeneutical method in his use of the Old Testament. If the writer of Matthew used two passages this way in the infancy narrative, is there any logical reason (despite the long established tradition of interpretation to the contrary) that he could not also have used a third passage, namely Isaiah 7:14, in the same way?

The Good, Bad, Insignificant, Indispensable King Josiah:
A Brief Historical Survey of Josiah Studies
in the Church

Lowell K. Handy

King Josiah of Judah has had a checkered reputation in the history of the church. Never as popular a biblical Old Testament figure as was Moses, David, or Solomon, this king has held a central position in Old Testament studies twice in the two thousand years of the Christian faith. A central figure during the Protestant Reformation, Josiah became the model of the "Reforming" king; again, in the nineteenth century, the notion that the book of Deuteronomy was either newly enforced or newly written during Josiah's reign made Josiah a formidable figure for all succeeding historical reconstructions of ancient Judah and Israel.[1]

Biblical and Foundational Texts

The biblical narratives of Josiah form the basis of all later interpretation of the king; to date, no contemporary extra-biblical references to King Josiah have been discovered. The earliest account of his reign is found in 2 Kings 21:26-23:30; in general, but not universally, scholars agree that 2 Chronicles 33:25-35:27 was based upon the Kings account, with additions and revisions constructed to fill out the Chronicler's theological purposes.[2] The Josiah portrayed in both narratives is a king who, at an early age, turned his back on all forms of apostasy, set about to repair the Temple in Jerusalem, found the scroll of Moses, and proceeded to conform the city of Jerusalem and the territory of Judah (with at least some tampering with Israel) to the norms of the instructions in that scroll. Chronicles expands the passing notice to Josiah's Passover in Kings into a lengthy description of a massive feast in accord with the Mosaic scroll. For doing all these things, he was promised by God, through the prophetess Huldah, that the destruction of Judah, because of its years of infidelity to God preceding his reign, would not be witnessed by Josiah himself and that he would die in peace. He then dies in an ambiguous meeting with Necho, Pharaoh of Egypt; in Kings it is related only that when Necho went to fight the Assyrians, Josiah went to meet him, and "he killed him" (clearly meaning that Necho killed Josiah). By the longer report in Chronicles, Josiah ignores Necho's messengers, who explain that Necho is not

---

[1] Lowell K. Handy, "Josiah after the Chronicler," *Proceedings: Eastern Great Lakes and Midwest Biblical Societies* 14 (1994): 69.

[2] In deference to an old Restoration Movement policy, I do not provide commentary on the biblical passages themselves; see David L. Little, "The Aversion to Biblical Interpretation in the Thought of David Lipscomb and Tolbert Fanning," *Restoration Quarterly* 44 (2002): 162-63.

interested in fighting Judah and that the Egyptian army is doing the will of God/a god; Josiah, nonetheless attacked and was fatally shot with an arrow.[3] In both narratives (2 Kg 22:2; 2 Ch 34:2), Josiah receives "high marks" for being "good."

A short note on Josiah appears in a book of the Protestant Apocrypha, the *Wisdom of Jesus ben Sirach* (=Ecclesiaticus) 49:1-3. The Judean king is remembered liturgically among the righteous, as befits the interests of the author himself. The Passover is ignored in deference to the purification of Judah from the abominations of the religious cult prior to Josiah's reign. For Sirach, Josiah represented the individual who managed to remain good and decent in the midst of a culture that was overwhelmingly evil, an opportunity for Sirach to admonish his own contemporaries not to give in to the cultural wiles of the Hellenistic world. Only three kings of Judah could he classify as righteous: David, Hezekiah, and Josiah (49:4). As Ecclesiasticus was a part of almost all Christian Bibles until the Protestant Reformation, this evaluation of Josiah was part of the scriptural portrait of Josiah for Christianity.

Josiah appears in another book of the Eastern Orthodox canons and the Roman Catholic Apocrypha, the book of *First Esdras* (= Third Ezra). This work begins (1:1-33) with a retelling of the Passover narrative as related in Chronicles, in which Josiah's personal generosity towards the people is expanded. Unlike the Kings or (especially) the Chronicles accounts, Josiah is here pictured as concerned for the care of the Ark of the Covenant, ordering the Levites to bring the ark into the Temple.[4] Other actions taken by Josiah as recorded in the Kings account disappear from this rendition, so that it moves immediately from the Passover to the death story. Here Josiah's attack on Necho is described as that of a foolhardy ruler who disregards Necho's explanation that he is not attacking Judah. The Egyptian ruler emphasizes that he is following the command of the "Lord God." In 1 Esdras, the report in Chronicles, which could be read that the deity whom Necho was obeying was an Egyptian one, has been changed to a clear statement of doing the true God's work. Moreover, Josiah here ignores the direct words of God, that he not attack Necho, spoken to him by none other than Jeremiah. Josiah ignores all divine and human pleas; thus, when the attack is made, he becomes weak and is taken from the field of battle. Josiah's death thereby becomes more of an act of God than of the Egyptian

---

[3] A pair of recent articles furnish examinations of the numerous additions, corrections, and explanations made about the death of Josiah in early Jewish and Christian traditions: Zipora Talshir, "The Three Deaths of Josiah and the State of Biblical Historiography (2 Kings xxiii 29-30, 2 Chronicles xxxv 20-25, 1 Esdras i 23-31)," *Vetus Testamentum* 46 (1996): 213-36, deals primarily with narrative differences in distinct retellings of the same incident; Steve Delamarter, "The Death of Josiah in Scripture and Tradition: Wrestling with the Problems of Evil?" *Vetus Testamentum* 54 (2004): 29-60, sets out the textual variations and their intentional changes in the biblical narrative. The earliest report (2 Kg 23:29-30) is the least descriptive and is quite ambiguous about the intentions both of Necho and of Josiah, but it clearly has Josiah die at the scene of the battle, which in the Hebrew is at the "fortress" rather than according to the usual emendation, "Megiddo."

[4] Christopher T. Begg, "The Ark in Chronicles," in *The Chronicler as Theologian: Essays in Honor of Ralph W. Klein*, M. Patrick Graham, Steven L. McKenzie, and Gary N. Knoppers, eds., *Journal for the Study of the Old Testament* Supplement Series, 371 (London: T. & T. Clark, 2003): 141. Begg highlights the significance of the Chronicler's variation from both the Kings narrative and from Torah legislation.

army, suggesting the expected results of failing to obey the word of God. A popular text of the Early Church, 1 Esdras colored the image of Josiah in the early centuries of Christian reading of the Old Testament.

While rabbinic references to Josiah are common enough, and some Early Christian authors were familiar with them, the church as a whole paid little-to-no attention to these texts.[5] This was not the case with the works of Josephus, however, for his histories were saved, copied, and avidly read for over a thousand years by Christians and not by Jews. Josiah was "of considerable interest to Josephus." Using biblical texts as well as First Esdras, Josephus rewrote the story of the Judean king to demonstrate to the Roman readership of his *Antiquities* that Jews were, like them, obedient to ancient laws and that, moreover the Jewish King Josiah had embodied both the cardinal virtues of the classical world as well as being the very model of the philosopher king.[6] Combining his sources, Josephus explains that the differences in the texts conform to multiple cleansings of the land by Josiah, once when he was very young, just because he was wise enough to know the land needed purification, and again to conform everything to the book of Moses after it was found in the Temple. As for the death of Josiah, Josephus sees destiny at work where Necho slays Josiah, who was defending his righteous land Judah/Israel from Necho's invasion. Finally, Second Baruch 66 reveals an apocalyptic vision of the truly righteous Josiah, alone good in his time, being raised to heaven having forcefully commanded piety on a corrupt nation.

The Early Church

The earliest Christian reference to Josiah appears in Matthew 1:10-11. In this genealogy of Jesus' ancestors, Josiah's name is listed in the second of three groups of 14 stylized ancestors.[7] The direct lineage from David is made clear in this grouping of Judean royal names. It has been noted since Patristic times that the list of kings is incomplete and that the genealogy does not match that of Luke 3:23-38, wherein Josiah does not appear at all.[8] Matthew's list highlights the royal Christ in a way that Luke's does not, no doubt reflecting themes played out in the respective gospels. No other reference to Josiah occurs in the New Testament.

---

[5] Rabbinic additions to the Josianic material of the Old Testament can be briefly summarized: 1) Josiah hid the Ark of the Covenant so the Babylonians could not find it; 2) Josiah's life and death both prove the truth of prophecy; 3) Josiah's Passover was foundational for the Jewish Second Day of Passover; 4) Josiah's hearing of the Torah without reciting it is the scriptural basis for observant Jews to hear their lectionary text (*hallel*) without repeating it aloud; 5) Jeremiah convinced the Israelites (Northern Kingdom) to accept Josiah as their ruler; 6) Josiah was slain not by one arrow but by a fusillade such that his body was a "sieve"; 7) his righteousness was so great that on his merit even his father Amon was to be allowed into heaven, some rabbis even claiming that Josiah was one person who could be said to have never sinned; and 8) the mourning for Josiah became the gauge by which all mourning was to be measured. See Handy (1994): 98-99, for expansion and source citations.

[6] Louis H. Feldman, "Josephus' Portrait of Josiah," *Louvain Studies* 18 (1993): 111 (quote), 113 (cardinal virtues), 129 (philosopher king).

[7] Jack Dean Kingsbury, *Matthew as Story* (Philadelphia: Fortress Press, 1986): 43.

[8] Raymond E. Brown, *The Birth of the Messiah: A Commentary on the Infancy Narratives in Matthew and Luke* (Garden City, New York: Doubleday & Company, 1977): 84-94.

Josiah was not a significant figure among Early Christian writers. Eusebius of Caesarea (260?-340?) collected material from scriptural and classical sources to compile his *Chronicle,* in which Josiah is placed in a time-frame augmented by citations of Herodotus's report of a Scythian invasion of Palestine, which Eusebius takes to have been Josiah's kingdom. In the mingling of biblical and classical sources, Eusebius follows the lead of Josephus, whose work Eusebius used. Being a chronology, Eusebius's work includes numerous observations and corrections of dates and periods of time in both biblical and classical texts, always attempting to correlate them. The Latin translation of Eusebius's *Chronicle* by Jerome (382) became a standard historical work for the next thousand years.[9] In other historical surveys, like Augustine's *City of God* 18.33, Josiah's name appears solely as a date-marker for prophets (*e.g.* for Jeremiah).

Clement of Alexandria (150?-215) in his *Stromata* (1.21) expands on the received biblical and Josephan traditions of Josiah a bit. Clement stresses the violent manner in which Josiah imposed proper cult practice on his kingdom. In accordance with Leviticus 26:30, idol worshipers were killed on the very idols they worshiped. In addition, Clement accepts that the High Priest Hilkiah was the same Hilkiah as Jeremiah's father, and that the "book" he found was, in accord with rabbinic tradition, the Torah (= Pentateuch = first five books of the Old Testament). The death of Josiah, along the lines of 1 Esdras, is seen as the result of Josiah's ignoring the true prophecy of Jeremiah.

The most resilient major Early Christian addition to the traditions regarding Josiah was the decision that the "book" found by Hilkiah and presented to Josiah was not the Torah, as claimed by the Jewish scholars, but was instead the book of Deuteronomy. The origin of this idea eludes us, but by the time of Athanasius (296?-373), John Chrysostom (347?-407), Jerome (342-420) and Theodoret (393?-466?) it was well established; they all cite it as an established fact that they do not need to defend.[10] Given the apologetics concerning sacred scripture in the Early Church, we may reasonably assume that the Christian insistence that the reference to Josiah's "book" was Deuteronomy only and not the entire Torah, contrary to rabbinic tradition, was part of the church's attempt to downplay the importance of the Pentateuch in favor of their own much larger reliance on prophetic materials.[11] In any case, most Christians thereafter insisted that the "Book of the Law" found by Josiah was Deuteronomy or some part thereof.

---

[9] The Greek text that Jerome used to translate the work was one that had already been altered and edited by someone else before Jerome worked with it. Eusebius's *Chronicle* was, however, known in the Western Church solely through Jerome for a millennium. Alden A. Mosshammer, *The* Chronicle *of Eusebius and Greek Chronographic Tradition* (Lewisburg: Bucknell University Press; London: Associated University Presses, 1979): 37-38.

[10] Cited in defense of the early notion of the scroll as Deuteronomy by Eberhard Nestle, "Das Deuteronomium und II Könige xxii," *Zeitschrift für die alttestamentliche Wissenschaft* 22 (1902): 170, 312-13; and James A. Kelso, "Theodoret and the Law Book of Josiah," *Journal of Biblical Literature* 22 (1903): 50.

[11] Handy (1994): 101. Note that Jewish scholars did not accept the possibility that Deuteronomy could be the referent in the Josiah narrative until the Late Middle Ages in Spain, where Christian and Jewish scriptural studies mutually influenced each other. General acceptance in Jewish circles of a Deuteronomic book of Josiah, to the extent that it appears in scholarly circles, is a twentieth-century phenomenon under the influence primarily of the American School of Bible studies.

The Middle Ages

Josiah in the Middle Ages was not a central concern for the Christian community. Nevertheless, three aspects of his tradition carried theological weight throughout the thousand-year period, and all three appear in artistic representations. First was the biblical record of his destruction of idols, portrayed in medieval art as classical Greek and Roman statues being burned in flames. The second was the popular illustration of the King Josiah listening to the priest read the Law to him. In religious circles this scene placed the secular ruler in his proper dependence on the religious hierarchy: the king obeys the priest. Third was the Matthean citation that Josiah had been a direct ancestor of Jesus, the genealogy of Matthew having been more popular throughout the medieval period than Luke's. The "Tree of Jesse" was an early and continuously popular motif throughout the Middle Ages and on into modern Catholic architectural art.[12] In these pictorial representations of Matthew 1:2-16, Josiah appears primarily in one of three manners: 1) as a stylized king, usually in the dress and emblems of the region in which the art is found; 2) a kingly figure upon whom the face and costume of the patron who had commissioned the work of art was imposed, or the face of one of the patron's friends or benefactors; or, 3) as an artistically rendered name, as in the Tree of Jesse in Michelangelo's Sistine Chapel.

As far as written Josianic portrayals in the Middle Ages are concerned, they tended to be restricted to collections that related the biblical narratives along with accruals added in the Patristic Period. So, for example, George Synkellos, in his lengthy ninth-century *Chronography*, relies heavily on Eusebius as well as all the extended canon at his disposal.[13] A classic medieval scholar, he sees the idols removed from the Temple as having been Greek and Roman deities. He accepts Eusebius's use of Herodotus in positing a large Scythian invasion into Judah during Josiah's reign. He relates the Early-Jewish equation of Hilkiah the High Priest with the fathers of the same name of the prophet Jeremiah and of Susanna in Daniel 13.[14] The list of actions taken by Josiah are referred to as signs of his devotion and piety, and are set in opposition to the impurity and pollution of those he was deposing. In accordance with the word of the "book" found in the "house of the Lord," he slew (by burning) diviners and idols alike.

The Reformation

If the good King Josiah had played only a minor role in the Patristic and Medieval Periods, he became the lauded icon of the good king alongside David and Solomon in the Protestant lands of the Reformation.[15] Indeed, a 1572 Luther Bible was graced with a

---

[12] See Arthur Watson, *The Early Iconography of the Tree of Jesse* (London: Oxford University Press, 1934).

[13] See William Adler and Paul Tuffin, eds. and trs., *The Chronography of George Synkellos: A Byzantine Chronicle of Universal History from the Creation* (Oxford: Oxford University Press, 2002): xxix, for date (808-810). The Josianic narrative of the history appears on pp. 312-315.

[14] The Roman Catholic and most Orthodox Bibles include the Apocryphal works of Susanna and the Elders as chapter 13 and Bel and the Dragon as chapter 14; neither appears in the Jewish or Protestant canons, but they are presented separately as Apocrypha in some Protestant Bibles.

[15] For overviews of this phenomenon, see Christopher Bradshaw, "David or Josiah? Old Testament Kings as Exemplars in Edwardian Religious Polemic," in *Protestant History and Identity in Sixteenth-*

woodcut of Frederick the Wise, Elector of Saxony, portrayed as Josiah, listening to Martin Luther, in the role of Hilkiah, reading from the word of God.[16] Moreover, England's Edward VI was raised, complete with school lessons, to *be* good king Josiah with an eye to the destruction of the (literally, as they saw it) idolatrous religion of Roman Catholicism that had grown up in England, now to be "reformed" by the "reformer king" in the Reformation of the church in line with the "Reform of Josiah."[17] The phrase "Josiah's Reform" was the Reformation's way of identifying itself with this biblical "good" ruler, and the phrase has passed into general usage among biblical scholars of all religious backgrounds.[18]

The Reformers saw much in Josiah that they could claim for themselves in their reforming work. Like good King Josiah, they were leaders of a religious movement for the whole nation seeking to divest itself of years of impiety and replace it with a pure faith restored from the distant past. Josiah's foundation for the reformation of Judah had been his hearing the word of God read directly to him without intermediaries; likewise, the Reformers put Bibles directly into the hands of the people for themselves to read.[19] The emphasis changed a bit as depicted in artistic renditions of the reading of the Word. Now, it was not that the king was listening to the priest, but that the king was listening to the Bible, understood that the clergy's job was to convey scripture directly to the king and everyone else. Josiah's Passover could be read as the equivalent of the church's Eucharist; Reformers declared that the Eucharist had been improperly presented ever since the Early Church.

Josiah's example of destroying idols was taken up with a vengeance. Now, "idol" was understood to include all those saints and relics of the Catholic Church, and the destruction was severe and in some places total.[20] And as the tradition had Josiah slaying the corrupt priests of ancient Judah and Israel, so the rounding up of corrupt priests suited the Reforming kings just fine; by definition, a Catholic priest *was* a corrupt priest. In several areas, the Josianic ideal of destroying all those who bowed down to idols along with their idols led to the wholesale slaughter of Catholic laity as well. Josiah's action to rid the land of necromancers, false prophets, and witches was brought to bear on the

---

Century Europe, Volume 2: The Later Reformation, ed. Bruce Gordon, St. Andrews Studies in Reformation History (Aldershot: Scolar, 1996): 77-90; Graeme Murdock, "The Importance of Being Josiah: An Image of Calvinist Identity," *Sixteenth Century Journal* 29 (1998): 1043-59.

[16] Margaret Aston, *The King's Bedpost: Reformation and Iconography in a Tudor Group Portrait* (Cambridge: Cambridge University Press, 1993): 41, ill. no. 30.

[17] *Ibid.*: 26-36; and Diarmaid MacCulloch, *The Boy King: Edward VI and the Protestant Reformation* (New York: Palgrave, 1999): 57-104.

[18] The name given to Josiah's actions has changed from writer to writer; the phrase "Josiah's Reform" passed from Protestant authors to be used across the spectrum of Christian scholars because of the vast amount of Protestant writing dedicated to Josiah. Denis Diderot's *Encylopédie* (1778) s.v. "Josias," uses the standard Protestant *renouvella*, but with regard to the overthrow of Assyrian influence (s.v. "Assyrie") the word is *revolution*.

[19] Aston (1993): 37-40.

[20] MacCulloch (1999): 71-72.

Protestant lands and "Josiah" was hauled in to approve witch-hunts (real ones).[21] Finally, Josiah was set forth as the example of the pious king who properly worships God, the good ruler who watches over his subjects, and even the aggressive king who is not loathe to use force to correct errant persons and to extend the kingdom, as Josiah had extended Judah by annexing Israel. By 1614, *The History of the World*, attributed to Sir Walter Raleigh, but published anonymously, had already proposed that good King Josiah had "reconquered" the northern kingdom for Jerusalem, thereby recreating the United Empire of David and Solomon.[22]

The Reformation's vision of Josiah would remain central to the Protestant biblical understanding until the nineteenth century, although the central importance of the king would wane dramatically in scholarly circles as a result of Benedict de Spinoza's *Tractatus theologico-politicus* (1677) and Richard Simon's *Histoire critique du Vieux Testament* (1678; soon translated into English as *A Critical History of the Old Testament*, 1682). Both works rejected the Mosaic authorship of the Pentateuch; this caused Moses to become the central concern of Protestant scholars for over a century.

Nineteenth-century European Scholarship

Josiah returned to the center of Protestant thought with the coming of the nineteenth century. In reaction to the beginnings of skeptical investigations of sacred writ, several branches of European academic Protestantism took up the pursuit of "questioning everything" about the Bible.[23] One of their central concerns became the dating of the biblical writings and the text-critical reconstruction of a history of ancient Judah and Israel. Though several scholars stressed Josiah's significance through the nineteenth century, three scholars in particular proposed a reconstruction of Josiah's reign that placed the obscure Judean King in the middle of biblical studies and made of him the indispensable peg for dating all other Old Testament texts.

Wilhelm Martin Lebrecht De Wette (1780-1849) was the foundational figure for the rise of Josiah to prominence in nineteenth century biblical circles. He proposed in his dissertation at Jena (1805) that the Deuteronomy found by Josiah was not in fact an old book at all, but a work written in Josiah's own time reflecting what was taking place

---

[21] Stuart Clark, *Thinking with Demons: The Idea of Witchcraft in Early Modern Europe* (Oxford: Oxford University Press, 1997): 567. James VI & I of Scotland and England, who used the Josiah material in his *Daemonologie* (1597), tired of the actual pursuit of witches as soon as those who had personally offended him were rounded up; see Alan Stewart, *The Cradle King: The Life of James VI & I, the First Monarch of a United Great Britain* (New York: St. Martin's Press, 2003): 128.

[22] Walter Raleigh, *The History of the World*. The Works of Sir Walter Raleigh, vol. 4 (Oxford: Oxford University Press, 1829): 785. Raleigh argued that one had to have control of a territory to be able properly to reform its religion. The exact date of the publication and its authorship remain debatable, but on December 22, 1614, King James VI & I of Scotland and England suppressed the work at the insistence of the Archbishop of Canterbury; see Christopher M. Armitage, *Sir Walter Raleigh: An Annotated Bibliography* (Chapel Hill: University of North Carolina Press, 1987): 6.

[23] Thomas Kelly Cheyne, *Foundations of Old Testament Criticism: Biographical, Descriptive, and Critical Studies* (New York: Charles Scribner's Sons, 1893), wrote an interesting survey of the rise of "higher criticism" by one of the seminal figures in its English guise. For a survey of the "higher critical" movement in its intellectual environment, see Emil G. Kraeling, *The Old Testament since the Reformation* (New York: Harper & Brothers, 1955).

under Josiah's leadership.[24] In De Wette's 1817 introduction to the Bible he set out this theory in a few short paragraphs; this work, much more widely read than his dissertation, provoked a rapid response in Germany, but it went essentially unknown in England and America, where an English edition of the work did not appear until 1843.[25] De Wette argued that the unity of worship presented as law in Deuteronomy was never actually a part of Judean cult until Josiah first carried it out. He argued that the treatment of the Ark by Josiah conflicted with Deuteronomy 31:26 and 1 Kings 8:9. He reasoned that the lament appearing in Deuteronomy 32:5-33 suited the period of Josiah and even the Exile, not a much earlier time before the Conquest of Canaan.[26] This placed the composition of the final form of the Pentateuch not only "late" but also as a product of King Josiah's court.

The work of Abraham Kuenen (1828-1891) in 1869-70 and translated into English in 1875 was more widely distributed in the English-speaking world around the time of its composition.[27] Kuenen's extensive study is a reconstruction of the religion of Israel, in which he accepted the notion, already widespread, that the deities inherited by Josiah from his grandfather were really Assyrian (or perhaps Babylonian) imports.[28] For Kuenen, a "Mosaic party" saw in the death of Amon a chance to instill in the nation their own vision of the righteous kingdom by manipulating the child-king Josiah. They adapted principles formulated earlier in the time of Hezekiah and produced the "book" that Hilkiah presented to Josiah. The two-fold strategy of the Mosaic party was publicly to promulgate their own laws in the name of their chosen ancient master, Moses, and then to win the young king Josiah over to their side in order to implement those regulations. The Mosaic party was successful on both counts. The book of Deuteronomy, or, more specifically, Deuteronomy 4:44-26:19 plus chapter 28, was the document redacted by the Mosaic party, although Kuenen assumed that only a portion of this work was actually handed to King Josiah, and Kuenen was careful to suggest that declaration of the book as having been written *by* Moses probably came after its proclamation. The Mosaic reformation of Judean religion, as seen by Kuenen, was vastly superior to, and

---

[24] Arthur J. Droge, "'The Lying Pen of the Scribes': Of Holy Books and Pious Frauds," *Method and Theory in the Study of Religion 15* (2003): 120, and n.2, notes the "daring and radical" statement regarding Deuteronomy's having been written in the time of Josiah; however, Droge does not appear to be aware that other aspects of the dissertation, such as the rejection of Moses as the author of the Pentateuch, were well established in numerous European academies by the time De Wette wrote. The equation of the "book" found by Hilkiah with the Book of Deuteronomy (or some part thereof) was not an odd occasional theory, as Droge seems to suppose, but had been a prevailing position among Christians for over a thousand years; see the discussion in the widely read popular work, George Sales, *An Universal History from the Earliest Account of Time to the Present: Compiled from Original Authors* (Dublin: George Faulkner, 1744): 843, n. E.

[25] Wilhelm Martin Lebrecht De Wette, *A Critical and Historical Introduction to the Canonical Scriptures of the Old Testament*, vol. 2, Theodore Parker, tr. & ed. (Boston: Charles C. Little; James Brown, 1843): 2.150.

[26] *Ibid.*: 150-51.

[27] Abraham Kuenen, *The Religion of Israel to the Fall of the Jewish State*, Alfred Heath May, tr. (London: Williams and Norgate, 1875).

[28] *Ibid.*: 3.3-4. For the following summary, 3.6-43. Sale (1744): 372, had already recorded the Western scholarly tradition that the "foreign" deities in Judah and Israel were Assyrian in origin, imposed by Assyrian kings from the time of Tiglath-pileser III.

advanced beyond, any earlier form of religion in Israel, and it was in line with the prophetic teachings.[29] He then explains how the book of Deuteronomy reflects, or rather, instigated, the "revolution" of Josiah, which is presented as a violent but necessary reform for a better society.[30] Josiah additionally sought to recreate the Kingdom of David by asserting his rule over the former tribal territory in the north. For Kuenen, Josiah's death at the hands of Necho resulted from the brave military act of a king protecting his kingdom from Necho's attempt to add Syria and Palestine to Egypt; yet, Kuenen notes, Josiah's decision to face Necho alone showed a foolishness that reflects an ignorance of dealing with foreign powers.

Julius Wellhausen (1844-1918) combined the earlier studies of the higher critics with an interest in social evolution. European intellectual circles had become fascinated with a social understanding of the history of religion since David Hume overturned the Deist notion that a primal monotheism had developed to polytheism but then returned to monotheism. Social evolution had become a field of research in and of itself with the work of Auguste Comte (1798-1857), whose vision of a world evolving from individualistic polytheism to a speculative communitarian positivism, was set out in an extensive evolution of human religious thought that Comte supposed to conform to all peoples everywhere. Wellhausen combined the century-old study of the literary sources of the Pentateuch with an evolutionist reading of Old Testament passages so as to place texts in an evolutionary line of development. His central work in this pursuit was the monumentally influential *Prolegomena to the History of Ancient Israel* that first appeared in 1878, with a 2nd edition in 1883. By 1885, an English translation was already being widely studied.[31]

In Wellhausen's reconstruction of religion among the ancient Hebrews, Josiah's "reformation" took the central place and produced a "breach of historical continuity."[32] Taking the accepted notion that the Priestly source of the Pentateuch predated the Deuteronomic source, he set out to see whether this fit into a progression of religious history. Assuming, as he did, that the polytheism of the far distant past had moved through a time of having a high god with lower deities, and local worship through sacrifice, Wellhausen posited that the governments of Judah and Israel had put some clamps on religious activity, although religion in Judah and Israel remained nonetheless cultic, ritualistic, and centered on sacrificial traditions. Wellhausen was in complete agreement with Kuenen that Josiah's reform had brought about Deuteronomic social morality as a central ideal, along with the disestablishment of local customs, replaced by control under centralized laws and moral demands. Wellhausen saw this as a great step forward, for he, along with large numbers of the intelligentsia of his time, believed that religions move to moral and communal traditions based on individual ethical behavior. For Wellhausen this moment of change was reflected in the book of Deuteronomy, which he could date to the reign of Josiah. He saw two religious movements deriving from this

---

[29] Kuenen (1875): 3.14.

[30] *Ibid.*: 38; Kuenen was writing in the nineteenth-century Netherlands where the revolutionary spirit was at a peak.

[31] Julius Wellhausen, *Prolegomena to the History of Ancient Israel*, Mr. Menzies, tr. (Cleveland: Meridian Books, 1957).

[32] *Ibid.*: 27-28.

period: One was Josiah's own positive, prophetic, personally moral, liberating tradition, and the other was the conservative, rigid, legal, ritualistic, and controlling Judaism of the Priestly Source, which Wellhausen understood to be a later development. What was significant for the understanding of Josiah was that the date of Deuteronomy was set; indeed, was the only solid date for Old Testament texts. Hence, everything else could be dated approximately from its distance along religious evolutionary lines from this lynch-pin event. The group that had followed Josiah's reforms, Wellhausen proposed, were the ones who had returned from the Babylonian Exile and reconstructed postexilic Judah.

In the course of the 19th-century, Josiah's reform acquired the status of being the foundation for biblical studies. Deuteronomy's equation with the book of Moses handed to Josiah was transformed through scholarly deduction into the key by which all of the Old Testament could now be read. The importance of Josiah's religious kingdom in the academic world was paralleled in the notion of the importance of Josiah's reign in the ancient world. First, as the period that defined true worship for the Old Testament, Josiah's reform became the pivot for Old Testament theologies and religious histories. Second (though more pronounced in the twentieth century), the territory attributed to Josiah's kingdom was increased to conform to the importance of the king newly supposed in 19th-century European scholarship.[33] Josiah became the indispensable figure in Old Testament higher criticism for the next century.

Restoration Movement Responses

The Restoration Movement of early-nineteenth-century America did not concern itself with the Josiah scholarship of Europe. The major reasons for this were two: 1) The founding leaders of the movement, when they dealt with the current debates of the "higher critics," overwhelmingly entered into the debate on the origin of the Pentateuch, firmly standing with the traditional position and arguing for Moses' authorship 2) The English editions of the higher-critical work on Josiah appeared after the active writing period of the Early Restorationists. However, Josiah does manage to appear obliquely in the works of Alexander Campbell and Walter Scott. Alexander Campbell needed to confront Josiah directly only once, and that in his edition of the Doddridge translation of the New Testament, but he never commented on the Judean king.[34] Further, in lists of Old Testament worthies in Campbell's writings, Josiah's name is conspicuously absent. Because Campbell insisted that the way to the true Christianity that he espoused was through the Mosaic covenant and the kingdom of ancient Israel, one may assume that

---

[33] Lowell K. Handy, "The Rise and Fall of the *sogenannt* Josianic Empire," *Proceedings Eastern Great Lakes and Midwest Biblical Societies* 21 (2001) 69-79. The second influence on the expansion of reconstructions of Josiah's kingdom was the parallel rise of Zionism and the "Jewish Question" in the nineteenth century.

[34] Philip Doddridge, *The Family Expositor: Or, a Paraphrase and Version of the New Testament with Critical Notes and a Practical Improvement of Each Section* (London: Thomas Tegg & Son, 1838): 15, "...and Amon begat Josiah, that eminently pious prince, whose heart so early and so tenderly impressed with an apprehension of God's approaching judgments...." Alexander Campbell, *The Living Oracles: The Sacred Writings of the Apostles and Evangelists of Jesus Christ Commonly Styled the New Testament* (Cincinnati: Franklin & Rice, second edition, 1870): 57, made no comment on Josiah at all; though Campbell used "begot" in place of "begat."

this included Josiah.[35] Campbell did make evident his appreciation of Josiah as one of the Old Testament worthies for he listed the king among those men who had demonstrated "woman's true and proper sphere" of giving great men to the world.[36] Walter Scott made use of the Old Testament perhaps more than any other Restoration founder.[37] He expounded extensively on Moses, but he did not deal explicitly with Josiah; however, he twice cited material clearly from the Josiah narratives. When commenting on the Jewish kingdom as the "most prone people to idolatry that ever existed," and in noting that only eight of twenty kings in Judah after David were good men, he was referring to Josiah texts.[38]

The succeeding Restorationists dealt with Josiah in widely differing ways. Isaac Errett devoted a chapter to Josiah showing that the king was forced violently to suppress the evil imposed on Judah by Manasseh, after the abortive and superficial reform of Hezekiah. Since the population was not behind the reforms, preferring instead the lax and sinful life under Manasseh, it was only through Josiah's "pious and patriotic efforts" that the "reformation" could be brought about.[39] Only a small group followed Josiah, but a weakened Assyria and a populace devoted to idolatry and heathen fanaticism made the situation "desperate," so that violence was the only manner in which to deal with the problem. According to Errett, Josiah's mother and grandmother had been responsible for his proper piety and zeal for the Law of God that led him to his attempt at reform; "attempt" because again, the people only superficially conformed, and the movement collapsed after the king's death.[40] Like other scholars of his time, Errett believed that Necho was attacking Assyria when Josiah fatally interfered. Errett's book was written for family devotions, and his Josiah is that of the Bible with a few standard Christian traditional comments.

John McGarvey, on the other hand, produced an academic volume intended to counter the entire nineteenth-century theoretical reconstruction of Josiah's reign. The

---

[35] *Idem, The Christian System, in Reference to the Union of Christians and a Restoration of Primitive Christianity as Plead in the Current Reformation* (2nd ed.; Cincinnati: Bosworth, Chase & Hall, 1839): 140-41.

[36] *Idem,* "Address on the Amelioration of the Social State," in *Popular Lectures and Addresses* (Philadelphia: J. Challen & Son; Cincinnati: J. B. Lippincott; Bethany, Virginia: A. Campbell, 1863): 65. Note also that A. Campbell published a short reprint on "The Worship of Moloch" from D. Kimchi with an editorial preface praising the extinguishment of this religious practice, cited to Second Kings 23:10 as Josiah's action; see *Millennial Harbinger* 2 May 4 (1831): 229-230.

[37] Lowell K. Handy, "Where the Scriptures Speak, We Quarrel: Biblical Approaches in the Disciples Founders," in *Interpreting Disciples: Practical Theology in the Disciples of Christ*, L. Dale Richesin and Larry D. Bouchard, eds. (Fort Worth: Texas Christian University, 1987): 92-93.

[38] Walter Scott, *The Gospel Restored: A Discourse on the True Gospel of Jesus Christ in which the Facts, Principles, Duties, and Privileges of Christianity Are Arranged, Defined, and Discussed, and the Gospel in Its Various Parts Shewn to Be Adapted to the Nature and Necessities of Man in His Present Condition* (Cincinnati: O. H. Donogh, 1836): 181; and *idem, The Messiahship: Or Great Demonstration, Written for the Union of Christians, or Christian Principles as Plead in the Current Reformation* (Cincinnati: Bosworth, Chase & Hall, [1859]): 64.

[39] Isaac Errett, *Evenings with the Bible: Old Testament Studies* (Cincinnati: Standard Publishing, 1887): vol. 2, 277. The following sentence based on p. 282.

[40] *Ibid.*: 281, 287.

villains of his tome are De Wette, Kuenen, and Wellhausen.[41] Alhough McGarvey dealt almost exclusively with the scholars who had followed their lead. He attacked the central theses of the higher critics regarding Josiah and Deuteronomy: McGarvey maintains the authorship of Moses for the entire Pentateuch. McGarvey demonstrates that the late date proposed for the Deuteronomic laws of Moses conflicts with earlier narratives in the Old Testament. The attempt to single out Deuteronomy alone as the book found by Josiah is doomed, according to McGarvey, for at least three reasons: 1) Josiah's reforms conformed to more than just Deuteronomy in the Pentateuch; 2) Josiah is said to have read the covenant to the assembled elders; therefore McGarvey insists that *only* the covenantal sections of the Pentateuch were read which cannot preclude an existing full Pentateuch at the time of Josiah; 3) if parts of Josiah's reforming actions sound like Deuteronomy this does not mean that only Deuteronomy was what Josiah had before him since the Pentateuch *contains* Deuteronomy and McGarvey argues for the entire Pentateuch existing and known prior to Josiah. Other minor discrepancies that McGarvey admitted exist in the narrative were due to divine revelation, which always takes precedence over any written word, even holy scripture (p. 21). McGarvey reasons, moreover, Josiah had known all about the Law; just because Manasseh had abandoned it did not mean that it was not well known. McGarvey argued that the reactions of the people show that they had known the Law all along. So, instead of being a "pious fraud" (p. 17) as the higher critics claimed, Deuteronomy was truly an ancient book (p. 19, 23) and Josiah a pious and devout king who kept the traditional faith. In the end McGarvey concludes that the text stands on its own and needs no imagination to manipulate it (p. 25); he maintains a good Restoratonist (and Reformation) position.

On the other side of the critical debate stood Herbert Willett. Willett early on accepted the basic premises of the higher critics, but produced a portrait of Josiah that remained traditional.[42] He accepted the biblical decision that Josiah was a good king and that the reform was a good and ethical movement, though doomed because people, then as now, preferred "free and easy institutions" and a sinful life. The entire reform was based on Deuteronomy 12-26, a document written only shortly before the reform activities took place themselves. Idolatry and heathenism had been entrenched through the personnel of Manasseh, but Josiah made use of the widely known traditions of Moses to rally the people with a new law code in Moses' name, including a couple of newly emphasized aspects: 1) centralized worship must take place in the Temple in Jerusalem; 2) invading heathenism was prohibited in the land. Willett's later presentation of Josiah was clearly much more influenced by higher-critical studies, including the then current state of Assyriology and biblical archaeology and the twentieth-century inclination to expand Josiah's territory.[43] Willett still saw Josiah's falling in a battle with Necho who

---

[41] John William McGarvey, *The Authorship of the Book of Deuteronomy: With Its Bearings on the Higher Criticism of the Pentateuch* (Cincinnati: Standard Publishing, 1902): vii, xv, identified the "radical," "destructive critics" (pp. 17, 1) as the three commented upon above. The following synthesis is taken from pages 1-27, after which McGarvey dealt in detail with each point made in the preface and opening chapter.

[42] Herbert L. Willett, *The Moral Leaders of Israel: Studies in the Development of Hebrew Religion and Ethics* (Chicago: Disciples Publication Society, 1916): 188-93.

[43] *Idem, The Jew through the Centuries* (Chicago: Willett, Clark & Co., 1932): 105-110, especially 109.

was fighting against Assyria. Willett saw the stories of Josiah as instructive to Christian families who were to take to heart the word of God *and* take proper social action.

The divide between conservative McGarvey and liberal Willett was a major part of the rending that tore the Restoration Movement in two during the first decade of the twentieth century. The traditionalists, true to founding principles of both the Reformation and the Restoration, held the biblical text as central, but they in general turned away form Old Testament studies. The New Testament became the primary focus of research in twentieth-century Restorationist research. The Movement's Old Testament scholars who sided with Willett's approach, became indistinguishable from the general run of higher-criticism in Europe and America, but the Old Testament and Josiah remained a central concern for the Liberal Restorationists in a manner it did not for the heirs of McGarvey.

King Josiah in the Twentieth Century

Josiah was so important a figure by the beginning of the twentieth century that a respectable survey of Josiah scholarship for the past hundred years would require a volume much larger than this Festschrift altogether. The following half dozen works have had both a tremendous influence on the representation of the reforming king and have splintered the higher-critical schools on thought concerning Josiah. By the end of the millennium, it was not clear whether Josiah was a good ruler restoring moral regulations or a tyrant viciously suppressing the people.

In 1923, G. J. Gadd published the text and translation of the "Babylonian Chronicle" that portrayed King Necho of Egypt as an ally and not an enemy of the last Assyrian king, Ashur-uballit II.[44] Immediately, most scholars switched Josiah from being either a defender of his own territory or a loyal vassal of Assyria, to being in revolt against Assyria and therefore intentionally attacking Necho, who consequently slew the minor king. Until the end of the twentieth century, when the term "friendly fire" crept into the discussion, this version of Josiah's demise held sway.

In the same year, Theodor Oestreicher's study of Deuteronomy emphasized the Assyrian nature of the deities (and other items) removed by Josiah during his reform.[45] The notion that Josiah was removing Assyrian images of political power caught the imagination of the scholarly world. Though plenty of critics dismissed his position, it remains a popular understanding of Josiah's "revolt" against the Assyrians to this day. For this thesis the purity of the old religion in Judah was a central concern of Josiah's.

Martin Noth's 1943 volume on the Deuteronomic History set the stage for placing the composition of the biblical history of Judah and Israel during Josiah's reign.[46] Noth himself argued that the whole work Deuteronomy through 2 Kings was one composition written at one time by an Exilic or Post-Exilic author. While he insisted that the work was post-Josianic, he noted that it held Josiah in highest esteem, and that courtiers from

---

[44] C. J. Gadd, *The Fall of Nineveh* (London: British Museum, 1923).

[45] Theodor Oestreicher, *Das deuteronomische Grundgesetz*, Beiträge zur Förderung christlicher Theologie 27, 4 (Gütersloh: Bertelsmann, 1923).

[46] Martin Noth, *Überlieferungsgeschichtliche Studien I: Die sammelnden und bearbeitenden Geschichtswerke im Alten Testament* (Halle: Max Niemeyer, 1943).

Josiah's reform effort had an influence on its composition. In the period following World War II, Noth's work became seminal in almost all higher-critical Josianic studies in the European and American academic world.

Taking the notions of Oestreicher and Noth one step further, in a widely influential article Frank Cross and David Freedman posited that Deuteronomy was, in fact, the very propaganda material produced by Josiah's court for their revolt against Assyrian hegemony.[47] According to this proposal, Josiah becomes the architect of a renewal movement for recapturing the glory of the United Monarchy. This means that Deuteronomy, *and* the political history of the nations of Judah and Israel (Deuteronomy through 2 Kings) as well as the annexation of Israel to Judah, were *all* part of Josiah's plan to fashion an independent state and were to be dated to Josiah's reign.

In 1967, E. W. Nicholson combined several strands of thought about Josiah and Deuteronomy into his theory that the Deuteronomy presented to Josiah was, in fact, a composition older than Josiah.[48] Nicholson maintained that the work derived from the monotheistic circles in the Northern Kingdom of Israel that had also produced Hosea, and that when the Assyrians conquered Samaria, these people fled south to Judah and deposited their proto-Deuteronomy in Hezekiah's Temple.

A movement in the United States in the Sixties to read the Bible through "social scientific" lenses produced a work by Norman Gottwald who presented the pre-settlement Israelites as an egalitarian and basically utopian society.[49] In his second introduction to the Old Testament, Gottwald attempted to show Josiah as a king restoring Judah (and Israel) to this previously idealistic state.[50] Many commentators on Josiah picked up on this interpretation that incorporated a common, popular notion of Deuteronomy as a much more "moral" and "just" law code than other Pentateuchal laws. Shigeyuki Nakanose, also heavily influenced by Gottwald's work, brought this line of thought virtually to a standstill.[51] He needed only to point out that from the standpoint of the people of Judah, and especially Israel, Josiah was a virulently violent and oppressive king who destroyed people and local customs for the sake of his own accumulation of power. Not everyone who followed Gottwald has yet grasped Nakanose's insight.

Finally, a detailed literary study by H. D. Hoffmann of the Josiah narratives over against other Old Testament "reform" narratives, sent biblical scholars off on a whole

---

[47] Frank Moore Cross, Jr., and David Noel Freedman, "Josiah's Revolt against Assyria," *Journal of Near Eastern Studies* 12 (1953): 56-58. Two "schools" of thought developed behind the German notion of a post-exilic date and the American notion of a pre-exilic date for Deuteronomy; many scholars in each circle are seemingly oblivious to the other tradition.

[48] Ernest W. Nicholson, *Deuteronomy and Tradition: Literary and Historical Problems in the Book of Deuteronomy* (Philadelphia: Fortress, 1967).

[49] Norman K. Gottwald, *The Tribes of Yahweh: A Sociology of the Religion of Liberated Israel* (Maryknoll, New York: Orbis Books, 1979).

[50] *Idem, The Hebrew Bible: A Socio-Literary Introduction* (Philadelphia: Fortress, 1985): 300, 371-72, 389-90. The vision of Josiah presented in this introduction is not markedly different from that in the same author's *A Light to the Nations: An Introduction to the Old Testament* (New York: Harper & Brothers, 1959): 328-29, 344.

[51] Shigeyuki Nakanose, *Josiah's Passover: Sociology and the Liberating Bible*, The Bible and Liberation (Maryknoll, New York: Orbis Books, 1993).

new trajectory in Josiah studies.[52] This approach is an effort to determine how much of the reform material is genuine and how much of it is standardized cult-reform prose, as well as determining the purposes of the author or authors.

Not to be forgotten among twentieth-century Josiah scholarship, the Restoration Movement belatedly spotted a kindred spirit in Josiah. At the 1910 Centennial Convention of the Stone-Campbell Movement, similar historical events in the reform movement of Josiah and the Restorationist reform movement were recognized by two speakers: Jesse James Haley envisioned Thomas Campbell's *Declaration and Address* as the "Deuteronomy of our prophetic reformation" in parallel to Josiah's Deuteronomist reform. Isaac Newton McCash compared the recovery of "the unfettered word of God" as the equivalent of Josiah's finding the "Book of the Law."[53]

Later in the century, T. Salisbury recognized a king who sought to restore an ancient and proper religion based on scriptural principles. He also noted that Josiah's attempt at restoration collapsed due to the superficial nature of the populace's enforced reformed religion.[54] On the Disciples side of the higher-critical schism, a number of academic scholars also have devoted much attention to Josiah. Among the most noteworthy are Dale Patrick's work on Deuteronomy and Old Testament laws generally, Richard Lowery's work on the literary and "ideological" construction of biblical reform narratives that continue Hoffmann interests, Marvin Sweeney's expansion of the Cross/Freedman notion of Josiah's reign as a center of Davidic renewal, and Lowell Handy's interest in the portrayal of Josiah in the narrative accounts.[55]

In the twentieth century, Josiah has been viewed academically almost entirely through the spectacles of nineteenth-century higher critics. King Josiah began the century as the founder of the biblical canon (Deuteronomy) and, through increasing divisions in the scholarly world he ended the century as one of three popular options: 1) the great and good King Josiah whose attempt to recreate the Davidic kingdom was indispensable for the

---

[52] Hans-Detleff Hoffmann, *Reform und Reformen: Untersuchungen zu einem Grundthema der deutero-nomistischen Geschichtsschreibung*, Abhandlungen zur Theologie des Alten und Neuen Testaments, 66 (Zürich: Theologischer Verlag, 1980). Although this was the most influential literary study of the reforms, other studies preceded it, e.g.: Ronny Mins Zorn, "The Pre-Josianic Reforms of Judah" (Ph.D. dissertation, Southern Baptist Theological Seminary, 1977).

[53] Jesse James Haley, "Origin of the Restoration Movement," in *Centennial Convention Report*, W. R. Warren, ed. (Cincinnati: Standard Publishing, 1910): 332; Isaac Newton McCash, "The Renaissance of the Apostolic Church," in *idem*: 517. See the text of these speeches online: http://www.mun.ca/rels/restmov/texts/wwarren/ccr/, part of an extensive collection of authentic material relevant to the Restoration Movement. Thanks to Hans Rollmann, owner and manager of this website, as well a co-editor of this volume, for bringing these texts to my attention.

[54] Thayer Salisbury, "Restoration Dangers," *Restoration Quarterly* 26 (1983): 103-104.

[55] Major works dealing with the subject include the following: Dale Patrick, *Old Testament Law* (Atlanta: John Knox, 1985): 97-144; *idem*, "Deuteronomy," in *Chalice Introduction to the Old Testament*, ed. Marti J. Steussy (St. Louis: Chalice, 2003): 63-78; Richard H. Lowery, *The Reforming Kings: Cults and Society in First Temple Judah*, Journal for the Study of the Old Testament Supplement, 120 (Sheffield: JSOT Press, 1991); Marvin A. Sweeney, *King Josiah of Judah: The Lost Messiah of Israel* (Oxford: Oxford University Press, 2001); and Lowell K. Handy, "A Realignment in Heaven: An Investigation into the Theology of the Josianic Reform" (Ph.D. dissertation, University of Chicago, 1987).

production of most of the current Old Testament canon; 2) a pale, almost inconsequential, shadow of the much more important Hezekiah, to whom many now credit the major cult reforms and the composition of Deuteronomy (and even the Deuteronomic History); 3) the evil despot whose bloody suppression of his people's religions puts him on a par with twentieth-century dictators. Towards the end of the twentieth century, little really new material was produced on Josiah: Looking back, one sees that many of these ideas have been floating around in the tradition for centuries.

No consensus among Christian interpreters of Josiah prevailed at the beginning of the third millennium. As Steven Hollway put it: Josiah has become something of a Rorschach Test by which everyone sees themselves in this king.[56] Josiah will no doubt continue to fascinate and frustrate Christian scholars for centuries to come.

---

[56] Steven W. Holloway, personal observation made to the author.

Fear, Anomaly, and Uncertainty in Daily Life: How the Gospel of Mark Provides for Us

Douglas W. Geyer

We journey and move forward to what, at least to the extent that our honesty allows us to admit, is an uncertain future. In spite of long personal histories of robust conviction, or acquisitions of hard-earned perceptions of reality, or a disposition toward theology, or impressive donations to church budgets, or provision of numerous services to others, that time eventually comes when we sit on the shore of Lake Michigan, in the woods looking out over the water, and wonder whether tomorrow will be like today. Will the world hold? Will we be the same? Will what comes next be like what has come before? For us, future conditions are always uncertain. We seek hints and prognostications. We want less risk. We want assurances. We want indemnity.

Under these conditions of future uncertainty, many on the journey prefer travel in circles to travel in straight lines. As we move in our world of an occluded future, we regularly rely on returns to our pasts, circles that take us back through time and space to earlier versions of our selves and our histories. We desire landmarks, places we have seen before, territories where we once lived. Recognition is everything. We seek memories, any memories—tragedy or joy or elation or shame. Whatever the past might contain for us, we seek its places and people for our comfort, whether the past assuages sorrow or stirs up regret.

Here, twin mountains with a dusting of snow once known. There, a shore by a green lagoon once visited. Or we find a poem in an old book, some verse cherished as an adolescent when newly in love, falling over ourselves and stepping on the toes of our beloved. Or we drive by a church attended years ago, over there just on the right, in need of paint and the front door still not working right. It's the place where we first saw people praying on their knees. Or just below us as we jet over, the campus where we began a career and finished writing that first book. The students' names are forgotten, and not much in that once important book seems so glorious anymore. As we circle back through places past, through either matter or mind, we are reminded of what happened, prompted to think about what might now happen. Uncertainty is briefly abated. The future seems a better bet, with fewer anomalies impending.

In contrast to this, travel along a straight line into the future seems peculiar and daunting. The demands frighten us. Each foot we move is a foot away from a start, another yard away from what is familiar, movement away from what was home, from what seemed yesterday to be known. Each step takes us relentlessly further to what is strange and inexplicable. Landmarks do not exist. If a destination ahead looms soon upon a near horizon, it is nonetheless unknown. But the wait also may be long; we may end up in a place not known, never seen before, perhaps unrecognizable even once we get there. If we get there, will we settle down? Will we move out again, along another line, to another unknown? Will fortune enfold us in its graces, or will we be exposed to turmoil, ill will, or intemperate wilderness? No doubt, travel along far-reaching lines causes us to worry. What is familiar can vanish overnight. What is new may challenge us deeply, sometimes to our very marrow, stealing our breath.

From a point of origin, we move out along the line. Given the rigors of long-distance travel, we desire reminders of something previous, something that might let us know that what we have now is similar to what we had before and what we may expect. Travel along this line compels us to want to take control. We don't want to go somewhere that we won't be able to tolerate or endure. This desire stirs a strong impetus to invent conceptual or imaginary returns to the familiar; that is to say, we theorize in familiar language about ourselves and about our world at large. Out on this journey, we cannot actually visit the past and places previously visited–we cannot externally find past indicators to satisfy our need for future certainty, for we are not allowed to circle back; so we devise a theory of ourselves that allows us an illusion of familiarity with new things thus encountered.

Theory does not mean merely thinking or planning for the future ("Watch out for sharp edges" or "A bird in hand is better than two in the bush"). This comforting use of theory comes from developing a pretense over time while traveling along the straight line to the future. We engage in a gentle self-deception that our viewpoint (whatever it may be) is comprehensive, exhaustive, unencumbered, and will protect us from any anomalies of sudden and radical ambiguity. While traveling on the line, we have the knack of trumping up narratives and hypotheses about our situation. We fancy that we can tame wild nature and push back the jungle of the unknown future as it flies into our faces. We are storytellers and theoreticians who attempt to weave our intangible, unforeseeable futures into some palpable tapestry of whatever we can remember as given to us by our past and controllable by us in our present. A certain amount of prudence and appropriate care of oneself inhere in our habit of trying to explain the journey to ourselves. Even so, when we concoct such stories and theories, we do so, as often as not, in the attempt to protect ourselves from our own inescapable vulnerability.[1]

And so also it could be with the idea of the fulfillment of prophecy, which indeed is a robust theory and full of stories about future horizons. Biblical theology thrives on it. Scripture records promises made by God to Abraham and his line (Gn 15:5), to Moses (Ex 3:17), to David (1 Sm 16:12), and to Israel (Is 61:1-3). We find numerous promises made by Jesus to his disciples (Mt 4:30, Lk 21:7-28, Jn 14:25-26). Apostolic writings also contain their full share of predictions and outlines of future benefactions (Rm 8:38-39, Rm 11:25-27, 1 Cor 13:12, 1 Th 4:17, 1 Pt 2:9-10). Throughout the testimony of scripture, new situations with their unseen consequences are anchored in old promises.[2] Gospel writers anchor in Jesus himself as the fulfillment of prophecies. Mark 1:1-4 contains a condensation of this feature, recording a scene that opens with reminders of scriptural prophecies about the messenger of God (Ex 23:20; Is 40:3; Ml 3:1). This messenger will prepare the way of the Lord in the desert. Subsequently, we find John the Baptist has appeared in the desert, predicting that yet another one is coming. That one turns out to be Jesus, the culmination of past promises in a portentous time. In Mark 1:15, we find Jesus articulating the ultimate promise: "The time is fulfilled and the Kingdom of God is right near."

In spite of these noble examples, is belief about fulfillment of prophecy not really just another way we have of comforting ourselves in our vulnerable condition? Uncertainty is the

---

[1] Jerome Miller, *The Way of Suffering: A Geography of Crisis* (Washington: Georgetown University Press, 1988).

[2] Étienne Nodet, *Histoire de Jésus? Nécessité et limites d'une enqûete*, Lire la Bible (Paris: Les Éditions du Cerf, 2003).

normal status for those traveling along the straight line. As response to uncertainty, one might easily view fulfillment of prophecy as something like a made-up past, pointing to a time when God predicted the things we are experiencing now. With such a tidy theory, rescue could be at hand. Some certainty could be confirmed about our track and direction. Since we prefer homeostasis, a.k.a. business as usual, with as few perturbations as possible, we do not want more coming at us that we can negotiate. We take steps to make it so.[3] The unknown future, when perceived through the present fulfillment of prophecy, comes to be framed by events from ancient times. Even though we might not know where traveling along these lines is taking us, according to the theory we can, perhaps, rest assured that its end will be in accordance with something good from our past, or at least something from our past with which we feel familiar. By means of a theory of prophetic fulfillment, we project a link to a stable past, at least a past in God's history if not our own. With a view like this, God's prophecies act in a way quite similar to landmarks and old haunts: They comfort. In so many ways, fulfillment of prophecy functions to allow us to turn a straight line out into the unknown future into the embrace of a familiar circle.

That said, it must be acknowledged that this is only one possible view of how a theory of prophetic fulfillment may work—the use of prophecy, perhaps, in the Gospel of Matthew—and what its use might be. Another, very different view can be found in the Gospel of Mark, a gospel that is of special relevance for those who sense their own experience to be more akin to travel in a line than to moving in a circle.

Mark starts with prophetic fulfillment. The preparation of the way of God at the opening is an announcement of a final act, a long-expected advent, even an epiphany of God through the messenger. "Epiphany" is not too strong a word to describe what Mark delineates.[4] Depicted at the beginning is a reality that is congruent with the kind of biblical theology we readily recognize. Here we find a culmination of promises. Here we are at the cusp of an actual appearance of God. Certainty, security, and hopefulness are expected as a result. These opening scenarios close, moreover, with a transfer from John the Baptist to Jesus. The future looks more promising than ever. Jesus is the herald of the good-news announcement, forecasting the Big Event coming forthwith. Everything vital is right at hand. The Kingdom of God is open. Come, gather at the river! Come, be baptized by the prophet John in preparation for the final days a-coming!

The expectation of a favorable time filled with divine benefaction is not to be underestimated in its potency throughout ancient cultures.[5] The opposite of hoped-for benefaction is fear, about which we also have much testimony. Israelites often feared God, who was jealous like other gods, especially Greek gods who could be noisy and often were intrusive.[6] Furthermore, anybody could fear death at anytime, especially unnatural or violent

---

[3] Thomas Spence Smith, *Strong Interaction* (Chicago: University of Chicago Press, 1992) on feedback loops, homeostasis, and social trends.

[4] H.S. Versnel, "What Did Ancient Man See When He Saw a God? Some Reflections on Greco-Roman Epiphany," in *Effigies Dei: Essays on the History of Religions*, Dirk Van der Plas, ed., Studies in the History of Religions (Supplements to *Unman*), 51 (Leaden: E. J. Brill, 1987): 42-55.

[5] Bobo Gatz, *Weltalter, goldene Zeit und sinnverwandte Vorstellungen*, Spudasmata 16 (Hildesheim: Georg Olms, 1967).

[6] Walter Burkert, *Greek Religion*, John Raffan, trans. (Cambridge, Massachusetts: Harvard University Press, 1985): 189. Albrecht Scriba, *Die Geschichte des Motivkomplexes Theophanie: Seine Elemente, Einbindung in Geschehensabläufe und Verwendungsweisen in altisraelitischer, frühjüdischer und frühchristlicher Literatur*,

death. Sudden death was thought of as without salvation or without good destiny.[7] The opposite of benefactions are strange events and anomalies. They perplex. Hope and desire are not well matched with bizarre responses or with riddles or with turns of events that deeply dissatisfy. That is to say, hope for God's assuring presence is not much of a preparation for an encounter with the pollution of crucifixion.

Here is where Mark is quite useful. In spite of the comfort of its opening of prophetic fulfillment, Mark ends very differently at 16:8, the "short version" of Mark known to Jerome and Eusebius. The wretched fate of crucifixion cuts abruptly through. At the empty tomb, the women flee. They were afraid, so they spoke of the events to nobody. Even given the young man's announcement that they should head for Galilee, there to encounter Jesus again, nothing commends itself as a lush advent or an epiphany of the coming of the Lord. The end of the story seems somewhat empty and full of foreboding. "Go up there to Galilee!" the young man tells three anxious women, and the disciples will see him. So do they go and tell them? Do they all head north to Galilee? They do not—not, at least, according to Mark—"for they were afraid." So much for victorious endings.

Matthew and Luke must have felt the need to amend a commendation this sparse of the activity of God. The two longer Gospels report truly marvelous reappearances of a risen Jesus after the resurrection. In the two later Gospels, Jesus meets the disciples and reconciles with them, showing them how predictions of his resurrection were indisputably accurate.

What happens between the front and back of the Mark Gospel? The crucifixion, of course. In terms of column inches, to be sure, much more than the crucifixion happens in the storytelling; but even so, crucifixion is the event that gathers together all other events in Mark. The crucifixion is the standard by which everything else in Mark must be measured.[8] Whether parables or feedings of thousands, didactic or action events, everything in Mark falls under the shadow of the cross. The predictions of crucifixion in Mark 8:31, 9:31, and 10:33 are part of this, for sure, and we sense the scent of violence and the spasm of death elsewhere, as well. Controversy swirls around Jesus in Mark, with opponents lurking about and seeking ways to cause mortal harm. They maintain homicidal fantasies.

The very odd story about the death of John the Baptist, the longest telling of that story among the four Gospels, is here in Mark 6:14-29, setting a tone of betrayal, capital punishment, and of the confusion and uncertain results of violent death. Herod Antipas, a foolish man aspiring to power, orders John beheaded with no conceivable justice in the whim. Then Antipas fears that John may be alive again, out in the countryside, seeking to disrupt good government by the performance of miraculous deeds (Mk 6:16). The miracles would not have been

---

Forschungen zur Religion und Literatur des Alten und Neuen Testaments, 167 (Göttingen: Vandenhoeck & Ruprecht, 1995).

[7] Sarah Iles Johnson, *Restless Dead: Encounters between the Living and the Dead in Ancient Greece* (Berkeley, CA: University of California Press, 1999). Gerdien Jonker, *The Topography of Remembrance: The Dead, Tradition and Collective Memory in Mesopotamia* (Leiden: E.J. Brill, 1995). A. D. Nock, "Tertullian and the Ahori," in *Essays on Religion and the Ancient World* (Cambridge, Massachusetts: Harvard University Press, 1972): 2:712-719. Nigel Spivey, "Christ and the Art of Agony," in *History Today* 49:8 (August 1999): 49-58.

[8] Johannes Schreiber, *Theologie des Vertrauens: Eine redaktionsgeschichtliche Untersuchung der Markusevangeliums* (Hamburg: Furche-Verlag H. Rennebach, 1967). For a comprehensive discussion, see Alexander Weihs, *Die Deutung des Todes Jesu im Markusevangelium: Eine exegetische Studie zu den Leidens- und Auferstehungsansagen*, Forschung zur Bibel, 99 (Würzburg: Echter Verlag, 2003).

interpreted as the acts not of a benevolent John but of an avenging John, angry due to his unjust and impure death.

The Gerasene demoniac (Mk 5:1-20) is another long story in Mark that brings death to the fore. In it we find a demonized man living among the tombs, violently tearing at himself and anyone else who comes close. The cemetery setting with demonic activity is pivotal—the story reeks of violent death and of matters unsettled, of old blood debts yet to be repaid, and of old hatreds that had become part of the very earth itself.[9] Strangers were caught up out of place, in the wrong cities, now filled with unclean spirits, inhabiting the cemeteries of others. The entity of *Legiôn* is present, best to be taken as representing a Roman legion and its violent quest for victory and, when angered in defeat, revenge. Members of the Roman army were sworn to the Emperor; they represented his desires and power that were predictably forceful and aggressive.[10] Eventually in the Mark story, only the unique purification of sinking into the sea can clear up the problem. The sinking was an act meant to totally eliminate the impurity.[11]

In Mark 11, death invades yet again, this time befalling a hapless fig tree. Jesus enters Jerusalem to cries from Psalm118 and Psalm148: "Blessed is the one who comes in the name of the Lord!" and "Hosanna in the highest!" The Temple, the House of the Lord, shall now—it appears—be under appropriate new management; but no, Jesus leaves right away, and then he comes again the next day (Mk 11:11), and then the next (Mk 11:15). What kind of "Advent" is this? It seems more a turn away from the Grand Arrival, away from the beginning of the Big Event. Furthermore, all the action around the Temple has to be taken, in Mark, as action focusing on eventual threats of the destruction of the Temple (Mk 13).[12] The Temple's destruction, by anybody's reckoning, is to be construed as immense death, a slaying of the hope and home of territorial and liturgical Judaism. Still more to the point, in Mark 11:12-14 Jesus finds that innocent fig tree without fruit; fruit, however, was not to be expected, for "it was not the season for figs." He curses it, and in Mark 11:21, the tree is found withered, dying. This all occurs around scenes of the Temple and the Mount of Olives. One begins to wonder: What means this arrival of a king who goes so unheralded? Why are there brewing themes of Temple destruction? Why are even the seasons for fruit and no-fruit confused, real time no longer pertinent? A curse by Jesus turns the tree into a withered remnant of what was, and we see that even out of season a tree is expected to bear fruit, which unloosens the given sense of seasons and of fruit-bearing times. What kind of turnabout is this? More to the point, what will become of God's past promises if the Temple is now destroyed? How can one evaluate the natural,

---

[9] See example #30, "spirits of the deceased in cemeteries," John Gager, *Curse Tablets and Binding Spells from the Ancient World* (Oxford University Press, 1992).

[10] John Helgeland, "Roman Army Religion," in *Aufstieg und Niedergang der römischen Welt* ii/16.2 (Berlin: de Gruyter, 1978): 1470-1505. Michael P. Speidel and A. Dimitrova-Milceva, "The Cult of the Genii in the Roman Army and a New Military Deity," *Aufstieg und Niedergang der römischen Welt* ii/16.2 (Berlin: de Gruyter, 1978): 1542-55. R.O. Fink, A.S. Hoey, and W.F. Snyder, "The *Feriale Duranum*," *Yale Classical Studies* 7(1944): 1-222.

[11] O. Gruppe, *Griechische Mythologie und Religionsgeschichte*, Handbuch der klassichen Altertums-Wissenschaft in systematischer Darstellung, 5 (München: C. H. Beck'sche Verlagsbuchhandlung, 1906): 889. Gustave Glotz, "Katapontismos," in *Dictionnaire des Antiquités d'après les Textes et les Monuments*, Charles Daremberg and E. Saglio, eds. (Paris: Libraire Hachette, 1877).

[12] Giancarlo Biguzzi, *"Io distruggerò questo tempio": Il tempio e il giudaismo del vangelo di Marco* (Roma: Pontificia Università Urbaniana, 1987).

seasonal give and take of life and death if this commanding figure, Jesus, overrides even nature with a wish and a command? This is surely madness and miasma.

Themes of death and destruction darken much of Mark's narrative, and they all reach their acme in the crucifixion, antiquity's exquisite violent death. But given even this stark thematic emphasis, the remarkable fact is that Mark, in terms of the amount of column inches, is devoted to the wondrous in a degree far greater than parallel percentages in Matthew and Luke.[13]

That said, we can still observe that—with the exception of the healing of the fever of Simon's mother-in-law (Mk 1:30-33) and the healing of Bartimaeus (Mk 10:46-52)—every event of power or wonder in Mark is written up in such a way to connote responses of perturbation, ignorance, or ill will: Stories of wonder, yes, but each wonder seems to raise questions. The paralytic is healed, but a question of forgiveness of sins and an argument over that question is tied to the miracle (2:1-2). Jairus's daughter is revived, but a cloak of secrecy must be thrown over the amazing deed (5:35-43). An abundant, miraculous provision of bread is linked to mysteries of symbolism that the disciples fail to understand; they are therefore chastised by Jesus (8:14-21). The wondrous works of Jesus are disbelieved by his hometown peers (6:16). The transformation of Jesus into a white, heavenly figure, confabulating with Moses and Elijah up on the mountain, provokes only helpless and befuddled responses from the disciples (9:2-13).

Themes of the miraculous in Mark are almost always linked to other issues that appear to be the whole point of the story. The Gospel of Mark is certainly no straightforward report of miracles, vis-à-vis their marvelous beginnings, unbelievable middles, or amazing ends. The Gospel is not a paradoxography, aretalogy, or collection of votive stories.[14] Instead, Mark completely ties the wondrous to various negative and problematic themes. As a result, not even miracles in Mark seem to be able to function as unmitigated fonts of the waters of life. The wondrous is taken captive, held to work for other ends that include themes of secrecy, doubt, revenge, fear, ignorance, or befuddlement. The touch of death in Mark, with its pervasive themes of anomaly and conflict, I argue has altered the many stories of wondrous events, turning the marvelous into a secretly tainted substance.[15] Miracles of life and episodes of violent death are usually polar opposites, but in Mark, they have a common ground in that each induces the need to come to terms with what is really happening. A sense of unfinished business pervades both miracle and violence, both life and death.

Mark does contain passages of Jesus' teaching as well as the narrative scenes of Jesus' acting as a teacher, but the Gospel of Mark contains nothing like Matthew's Sermon on the Mount or Luke's Sermon from the Boat; discourses, like the ones in the Gospel of John, about the meaning of Jesus, Spirit, life, or God are wholly foreign to Mark. Brief statements occur

---

[13] John Fenton, *More about Mark* (London: SPCK, 2001): 55. Eric Eve, *The Jewish Context of Jesus' Miracles*, Journal for the New Testament Supplement Series, 231 (Sheffield Academic Press, 2002). James McClenon, *Wondrous Events: Foundations of Religious Belief* (Philadelphia: University of Pennsylvania Press, 1994) and *Wondrous Healing: Shamanism, Human Evolution, and the Origin of Religion* (Dekalb: Northern Illinois University Press, 2002). Paradoxogaphy was literature of collected marvels and miracle stories; aretalogy was a liturgical literature used to proclaim the qualities of a divinity; votive stories were not unlike stories we tell about fortunate things that once happened to us, for which we give thanks now for their resolution.

[14] Vincenzo Longo, *Aretalogie nel mondo greco, I: Epigrafi e papiri*, Pubblicazioni dell'Istituto di Filologia Classica dell'Università di Genova, 29 (Genova: Istituto di Filologia Classica e Medioevale, 1969).

[15] Elias Bickerman, "*Latens Deus*: La reconnaissance du Christ dans les Évangiles," in *Studies in Jewish and Christian History* (Leiden: E.J. Brill, 1986): 3: 53-69.

throughout the Gospel about unshrunk cloth (2:21), Satan casting out Satan (3:23), shaking off dust from feet (6:11), stumbling blocks cast before "the least of these" (9:42), rulers and tyrants (10:42), and giving to God what is God's and to the Emperor what belongs to him (12:17), but none of these has been developed into even a sermonette. On the other hand, warnings occur three times that point towards impending events in Jerusalem, and these forebodings grow in form and content with each repetition.[16] The remarkable and exceptional chapter, Mark 13, stands out for how it assigns to Jesus his largest portion of teaching: destruction of the Temple and of the cosmos. The literary rule throughout Mark is brief statements, and Mark 13 is the exception that proves the rule.

And then, to make the point one more time, there are the parables. Similitudes and comparisons were intended in ancient oratory to clear up difficulties in understanding,[17] but in Mark 4:10, a contrary perspective on the parables of Jesus is clearly stated: Parables, identified as rhetorical forms and speech acts characteristic of the teaching (*didachê*) of Jesus (4:2) are said not to clarify but to block the mystery of the Kingdom of God from the understanding of certain people. Citing Isaiah 6:9, a rationale is given for the effect: Some can listen, but not hear; some can see, but not perceive. Whether or not the parables themselves cause the problem in understanding, is debatable. The Isaiah passage may mean that some other problem in the audience causes an inability to catch on to the message. In Mark 4:11, the problem is defined as the audience's "being on the outside." Technically, the designation means that the audience is not part of the band of disciples, but this distinction breaks down in Mark because the disciples sometimes exhibit no more understanding than do the outsiders, as in Mark 8:17 ("Do you neither know nor understand? Is your heart hardened?"). To complicate the picture more, parables in Mark are *not always* misunderstood by those on the outside. In Mark 12:12, for example, the chief priests, scribes, and elders in Jerusalem have very clear understandings of the parable about a vineyard (12:1-11), so much so that they hate its message. Their response to the teaching is a stirring up of homicidal intent.

The central event, crucifixion, receives remarkably little explanation through teaching reported in Mark. Theories of redemption or satisfaction are far less evident in this Gospel than in Paul's letters. Well-developed theories of divine sonship, being sent, returning, and granting life—like those in John—are also absent in Mark. No articulated understanding of how the events fulfill prophecy—like that in Luke or a similar approach in Matthew—is to be found in Mark. What teaching there is about the death events that take place in Jerusalem is brief and, to say the least, paradoxical ("Save your soul by destroying it"—8:35) or terse in the worst way ("After I am raised up, I will go before you into Galilee"—14:28) or cryptic ("I am, and you will see the Son of Man seated at the right hand of the power, coming with the clouds of heaven.") This is to say that in Mark neither actions of teaching nor teaching content are brought to much service in order to satisfy the anomalies and strangeness instigated by crucifixion. Given that crucifixion was a literary and rhetorical topic avoided by other writers of antiquity, and that it was the fate of Jesus, crucifixion would seem to have called out for teaching and explanation, but little is given. Even reports about the process to which Jesus was submitted—from trials

[16] Alexander Weihs, *idem*. Alberto de Mingo Kaminouchi, *"But It Is Not So Among You": Echoes of Power in Mark 10.32-45*, Journal for the Study of the New Testament Supplement Series 249 (London: T & T Clark, 2003).

[17] Marsh H. McCall, *Ancient Rhetorical Theories of Simile and Comparison*, Loeb Classical Monographs (Cambridge, Massachusetts: Harvard University Press, 1969).

through the cross-bearing procession to the hill where he was executed—serve to highlight the inexplicable catastrophe that was taking place.[18] To repeat: The touch of death at work in the Gospel of Mark returns, this time extinguishing statements of rationalization and that might have mitigated the abruptly uncanny nature of Jesus' death. Its horror stands, shielded by nothing.

Death, more than life, spurs complexity and concern. We ignore it, fear it, try to bargain with it, or eventually come to grips with it in some way. Under its influence, we quickly become theoreticians. So it is, for example, in Plato's fiction, where Socrates imparts information as now appears in the *Apology* and *Phaedo*. We find there a teacher who explains his rationale, plans, reasons for actions, and beliefs as he prepares himself for death. Much detail is given, especially about the qualities and immortality of the soul. Socrates' fate may have seemed a bitter pill to swallow, but the speeches and dialogues offer an extended explanation. It's great theory, and it was proved useful as the tradition and example of Socrates became seminal especially for later views about death among Stoics and Early Christian writers.[19] Even in a very different setting, the Maccabee brothers were reported as having been motivated by high-minded reasons for their actions, namely their willingness to undergo a noble death on behalf of their God and their people. In contrast to these examples, we do not find in the Gospel of Mark a just teacher whose unjust death is an exemplar of a noble death for others.[20] We do not find, in fact, any very well developed theory about, or explanation for, the death. Instead, we discover that to die is to live, in that "those who destroy their soul will live," or that great and inexplicable powers were at work to necessitate the death of Jesus, warranting his remand over to a capital process.

Life and abundance is the opposite of death and loss. Among us, and our ancestors, one usually finds the belief, expressed with considerable energy and craftsmanship, that abundance of life is correlated to divine congruence and favor. Divine benefaction preserves life, plenty, and safety. History's artifacts reveal the persistence of this belief.[21] Any instance of a correlation of deities with birth, fertility, safety, healing, long life, good life, good crops, good harvest, safe journeys, good death, love, concord, victory in battle, success in business, or blessed afterlife (plus dozens of other desirable community items) is an instance demonstrating this human penchant to link good results with divine favor. Good money has been paid by many, and countless rituals have been endured by even more, for the opportunity to link unknown fate, with its unavoidable prospect of death, to some type of reliable divine benefaction. Skeptics

---

[18] Thomas E. Schmidt, "Mark 15:16-21: The Crucifixion Narrative and the Roman Triumphal Procession," *New Testament Studies* 41 (1995): 1-18.

[19] Klaus Döring, *Exemplum Socratis: Studien zur Sokratesnachwirkung in der kynisch-stoischen Popularphilospohie der frühen Kaiserzeit und im Christentum*, Hermes Einzelschriften 442 (Wiesbaden: Franz Steiner Verlag, 1979).

[20] Jan Willem van Henten, "Das jüdische Selbstverständnis in den ältesten Martyrien," in J.W. Van Henten, ed., *Die Entstehung der jüdischen Martyrologie*, Studia Post-Biblica 38 (Leiden: E.J. Brill, 1989): 127-161. Adela Yarbro Collins, "From Noble Death to Crucified Messiah," *New Testament Studies* 40 (1994): 481-503.

[21] David Castriota, *The Ara Pacis Augustae and the Imagery of Abundance in Later Greek and Early Roman Imperial Art* (Berkeley, CA: University of California Press, 1995). Katherine M. D. Dunbabin, *The Roman Banquet: Images of Conviviality* (Cambridge University Press, 2003). Vincent Tran Tam Tinh, "État des études iconographiques relatives à Isis, Sérapis et Sunnaoi Theoi," in *Aufstieg und Niedergang der römischen Welt* ii/17.3 (Berlin: de Gruyter, 1979): 1,710-38.

have tended to consider this as foolishness. Believers have offered explanations. Students of religion have tried to sort all of it out like a giant puzzle, and consequently they have published rather large and demanding books.

Linkage of divine benefaction with favorable outcomes finds its expression at many levels. Eschatological satisfaction is a primary venue. Isaiah 61:1-4 contains a classic statement of future benefits flowing from divine favor. In the year of the Lord's favor, a righting of injustices, comfort for those who mourn, repair of ruined places, and a cure for oppression and illnesses will come. These themes are re-worked in the Qumran text, *"Q Messianic Apocalypse"* (4Q521), where it is suggested that in the future, when the Lord pays an earthly visit, "pious ones" will be vindicated, the blind will see, captives will be released, the sick healed, and the dead raised. The ideas are articulated again in Luke 4:18 and, somewhat transposed, in Revelation 21:3-4: "He will dwell with them as their God... he will wipe away every tear from their eyes, death will be no more, mourning and crying and pain will be no more." Future fulfillment and blessedness is a common idea throughout ancient and modern cultures. Many gods and goddesses are required to satisfy our unquenchable thirst for safe futures.[22]

Purity issues are another primary venue for the domestication of death. Impurity and miasma were strongly felt ideas in the ancient world that bespoke a powerful conception of success and failure in the human condition. Death, violence, birth, blood, fertility, food, and sickness are all to be found within the dominions of purity that people subjected to rules and rituals. Specific activities and proximity to certain objects were believed to effect states of moral or ritual impurity that needed resolution.[23] Purification rituals were meant to restore life and to diminish vulnerability. When prescribed by a divinity or on behalf of a divinity, they were thought to link divine benefaction to satisfactory resolution of human dilemmas. Realignment towards purification might re-ignite the possibility that divine favor would be extended to the vulnerable human condition.

The practice of divine wisdom, similarly, was in the ancient sources said to arise from a proper and discretely submissive relationship to divine will and knowledge, which would then lead to divine favor. Divine favor was thought gained when divine wisdom was ascertained. Wisdom books such as *Instruction of Ptahhotep, Instruction of Shuruppak, Book of Proverbs, Instruction of Ankhsheshong, Words of Ahiqar*[24] taught one to construe creation itself as blessed, an expression of divine favor, benefaction, and fruitful ordering.

Concepts of salvation were multi-faceted in antiquity, as they are today. Since instincts about who and what is good, what safety and abundance mean, and what one might do to

---

[22] John Ferguson, *Utopias of the Classical World* (Ithaca, New York: Cornell University Press, 1975). Quite to the point, see Tikva Frymer-Kensky, *In the Wake of the Goddess: Women, Culture, and the Biblical Transformation of Pagan Myth* (New York: Free Press, 1992).

[23] Robert Parker, *Miasma: Pollution and Purification in Early Greek Religion* (Oxford: Clarendon Press, 1983). Mary Douglas, *Purity and Danger: An Analysis of the Concept of Pollution and Taboo* (London: Routledge, 1966). Jirí Moskala, "Categorization and Evaluation of Different Kinds of Interpretations of the Laws of Clean and Unclean Animals in Leviticus 11," *Biblical Research* 46 (2001): 5-41. Howard Eilberg-Schwartz, "Creation, Classification, and the Genealogy of Knowledge," in *The Savage in Judaism: An Anthropology of Israelite Religion and Ancient Judaism* (Bloomington, Indiana: Indiana University Press, 1990).

[24] James T. Pritchard, ed., *Ancient Near Eastern Texts Relating to the Old Testament*, 3rd edition (Princeton, NJ: Princeton University Press): 426-28. Ahiqar was a transnational font of wisdom; cf. Dieter Metzler, "Ahiqar in Trier," in *ΘΙΑΣΟΣ ΤΩΝ ΜΟΥΣΩΝ: Studien zu Antike und Christentum für Josef Fink* (Köln: Böhlau, 1984): 97-107.

merit them, have always been strongly held, the supply of testimonies about these matters is more or less limitless. Ideas of wisdom, pollution and purity, and eschatology are rich and varied, and they are often robustly complex and full of divine personages, entities, and powers. Each hopeful belief points to a desire that congruence with divine disposition may result in divine favor and benefaction. The flip side to the desire to be congruent with the divine is, unfortunately, fear. Once the approach to divine favor and abundance is based on any type of negotiation, the chance always remains that negotiations might fail. But failure was not an option! Where can one go to appeal a failure to communicate after one has failed in a negotiation with the divine?

Dismal and violent death remained—and they remain today—stumbling blocks to a sense that salvation is at hand.[25] Overlay concepts such as noble death, vicarious death, or philosophical or virtuous death are attempts to do something with the anomaly of violent and untimely death. Concepts of mandatory purification rituals in response to disgusting deaths are typical. Expectation of eschatological revenge was—and is—common, as well. "Vengeance is mine" as a promise of coming divine intervention is assurance to those under divine favor who have suffered violence that, in the end, the perpetrators and antagonists will be paid back in kind. The shed blood of martyrs, whether in the 1st-century or the 21st-century Middle East, is thought to provoke divine reaction much more effectively than the spilled blood of a victim in a random automobile accident.

So where does the Gospel of Mark enter in? Neither didactic nor miraculous materials in Mark function to cover over the uncanny and horrible fate of Jesus on the cross. They do not sublimate the violence of that death. Just the opposite, they appear to heighten its anomaly and latent fear. No wise miracle-worker who comes to an unfortunate end speaks soothing words in Mark. Instead, we are shocked witnesses to the startling end of a man whose miracles were also startling in their complicated and uncanny results. The story is about a man whose teachings, as recorded in Mark, often raised more questions than they resolved. The wondrous and the didactic in Mark do not satisfy in terms of a reliable theory of how one might identify with this miracle worker or how one might develop a comfortable understanding of Jesus. Instead, the end of Mark follows the general and consistent impulse found throughout Mark toward the inexplicable and unresolved.

Mark gives very little satisfaction either through the fantastic or the conceptual. This is due, I propose, to the overwhelming influence of Jesus' death on the cross, the least satisfying of events imaginable, the end of the story that pervades the whole book. Ascertainment and appreciation of the anomalous turn of events at crucifixion really do establish in Mark a method for retrospective perception of the rest of the book. That is to say, the continuous narrative in Mark is not only focused upon the crucifixion of Jesus but also the crucifixion erupts within the narrative through other stories in domains of content, feeling, and representation. The violent death in Mark is presented without dilution. In so many ways, it never submits to comprehension; it refuses to be fathomed; rather, its primary effect is to confuse and horrify.

---

[25] H.S. Versnel, "Beyond Cursing: The Appeal to Justice in Judicial Prayers," in *Magika Hiera: Ancient Greek Magic and Religion*, C. Faraone and D. Obbink, eds. (New York: Oxford University Press, 1991). Martin Hengel, *Crucifixion in the Ancient World and the Folly of the Cross* (Philadelphia: Fortress Press, 1977). Donald G. Kyle, *Spectacles of Death in Ancient Rome* (London: Routledge, 1998). Thomas Wiedemann, *Emperors and Gladiators* (London: Routledge, 1992). Michael B. Hornum, *Nemesis, the Roman State, and the Games*, Religions in the Greco-Roman World, 114 (Leiden: E.J. Brill, 1993).

Violent death, and especially crucifixion, raised inevitable questions about the certainty of who was good and who was truly able to favor another. A crucified person in antiquity was not thought of as a possible source of goodness or blessing. Nobody turned to the crucified for help. They were cursed.

In the case of Mark, Jesus certainly is not left as a figure who is friendly and full of blessing. He is left as a figure with a ghastly fate, but one who moved past that fate as easily as he walked on water. He is like a phantom who walks the sea at night, as if the undead were coming back to haunt (Mk 6:49).[26] To be sure, he has an identity of sonship, which is to say he is perceived throughout Mark as kin to the divine. Even a Roman professional peacekeeper took note of this (Mk 15:39). Anybody familiar with the idea of the Voice of God from Heaven (Mk 1:11 and 9:7) would have noted this, too, for the Voice was the voice of a father addressing his son. And, towards the end, Jesus claimed eye-popping things about himself at a hearing before the chief priest, the scribes, and other hangers-on (14:62), indicating that he was the Son of Man, that elusive figure of apocalyptic fame.

Do the events reported to us in Mark add up to the coming of the Lord, salvation of the Jubilee Year, expansion of the Way of God, the Big Event, the Final Culmination? If they do, this meaning is quite hidden from plain sight. Are the events in Mark the fulfillment of any prophecy that can be documented? Definitely not. In fact, events in Mark, as the storyteller tells them, veer away from what was stated in Mark 1:1-4. This Gospel starts up front with prophecies of joyous fulfillment, advertising scriptural prophecies at its opening, making clear a commitment to Israel's past with God, the Israel of Scripture, and to the present as an unfolding of that past. These are indications of a belief that God again is active. What could be more wonderful, then, than the final coming of God and the Kingdom of God? But as the pages turn, fulfillment of biblical prophecy in the ways that one might traditionally and scripturally assume proves to be neither Mark's intent nor its meaning—absolutely not its meaning, if fulfillment means satisfaction, happiness, and all things put right. "Fulfillment" means in Mark that promised times are here, but that the times here are not like anything either that was thought to have been promised or that had been known before. In fact, the outcome is so unexpectedly different – there is in Mark no emergence of a just and luxurious Kingdom but instead the occurrence of a crucifixion with but a hidden resurrection – that Mark is to be seen to present a radically different theory of prophecy and fulfillment. This theory of Mark's, I propose, is very useful to those who travel not in circles but onward along the line.

What is Mark's theory? The theory of prophetic fulfillment in Mark is a theory not of fulfillment of a specific schematic or detailed design from the *past*. This Gospel presents no sense that today is like what yesterday was or what yesterday promised. Nobody before believed that the kin of God would be so contemptibly treated; nobody previously expected teaching and actions of a son of God to appear incipient or difficult to comprehend. Kingdoms and their benefactors were expected to be public and renowned, persons of acclaim and of robust ability to make life better. But the figure of Jesus in Mark, as central and as authoritative and as commanding of healing and demons as he is, does not put before his friends and

---

[26] For supernatural figures around water: *umbra mortua, imagines deorum, ludificatione daemonum, simulacrum Mercurii,* see Martin Ninck, *Die Bedeutung des Wassers in Kult und Leben der Alten: Eine symbolgeschichtliche Untersuchung,* Philologus Supplement-Band 14 (Leipzig: Dieterich'sche Verlagsbuchhandlung, 1921): 56.

countrymen a table of satisfaction, with an overflowing cup and endless sustenance. He instead puts before them the worst of options, and he carries on his own affairs from the point of view that all that was previously expected as good is now uncertain. All that one might have expected from a reasonable fulfillment of past prophecy must be recalculated. What comes with Jesus in Mark is not a recognized object from the past or a past promise. What comes is instead something that holds the present as a time of unusual and inexplicable episodes, full of God's activity even while being anomalous. The present, in Mark, maintains the promise that violent death and crucifixion are not final destinations. In Mark, what is fulfilled *now is* the promise of a *future*—today's awful events and defeating experiences, all of them, are not the last stop in transit. The future, and not the past, makes a claim on the present. We cannot recognize it because it has never happened before. But in Mark's theory, recognition means little.

In Mark, even violent and dismal death is but a point on the forward trajectory of Jesus. In Mark, crucifixion is the most intense and worst of human experiences, and yet one that Jesus comes through alive and unscathed by either pollution or violence. He is neither left to be cast away nor is converted into an angry, vengeful character. Mark picks up his narrative to say that Jesus continued his straight-line march from there, from the tomb, alive, and he could be seen again "in Galilee." If one wished to follow him there, one could find him again, up to more who-knows-what. Death is made contingent by Jesus in Mark, being a worst-case scenario that does not stop the traveling forward. The tomb was empty because it had been emptied. What is ahead is unknown, but it is owned by God and it is a straight line fearlessly walked by Jesus. What was ahead for Jesus' followers was a trip to Galilee, to see him, and beyond that, onward on the line. Mark is saying that something like that path straight ahead is also given to us to walk. The One who lays out that path for us, and he who walks it before us, make all the difference.

Though death is made contingent in Mark, life and living are not. Life and living are our fate, our unavoidable default option, the arena where God has willed to be active in His Kingdom. The activities of our daily lives may remain full of anomaly, uncertainty, and fear because we cannot see through them or ascertain clearly where they will lead us. In fact, they may bring terrible conditions or great suffering, even a cross; but, through the theory of future fulfillment emergent in Mark, they may be received as part of a completely enfranchised situation–a human life whose future has already been won by God, and the condition for living that life is that God requires the cross. Life and living, if there be any, are raised up from the tomb by God. The further outcome is that our journey will be travel on the line today, an unpredictable journey "to Galilee, where we will see him, just as he said," and beyond. That is to say, following Jesus in Mark's view makes us "dead men living." We carry on our living while identified with a death, and that death is neither the last stop nor the worst thing that could happen, even though it looks like it.

Mark, even given the lack of abundant teaching or complicated stories of wonder, is a call to belief. The belief recommended is that what we experience, as problematic as it seems, can be accepted in all its newness, uncertainty, unexpectedness, and anomaly; the promise now is that we will survive it. We will survive it because our lives have been invited to become the ongoing history of God's straight line into the future now made intimately personal through Jesus, a life yet to be completed but with us as part of the action.

Our dismaying experiences may be accepted as stemming from the very intentions of God, although those intentions, even if articulated in frightening ways in the past, and now still seeming to be oblique and anomalous, nevertheless appearing new and lively. How is this possible? It is possible, in the witness of Mark, because of the identity and quality of Jesus, who does indeed have an identity of sonship to God and does indeed survive through the most strange and violent of histories. Furthermore, it is possible because, according to Mark, human beings can be called by Jesus, can follow him, and thus can find their lives attached to his own God-given persistence.

For those traveling on the line, this is good news. We know that circling back to our pasts is often a ruse, a method for trying to deflate the abundant uncertainty of our current situations and our inescapable but occluded future. Good news also because the theory that Mark supports is a theory that does not ask us to pretend that we know where we are going or what will happen next. Mark asks us, instead, to cultivate a relationship with the risen Jesus and with those who are following him to Galilee so that they may see him. We, like those who followed, can have confidence that in surviving our opaque futures, we are being launched not away from the future but towards it boldly.

The violent death of Jesus in Mark is the death knell of any quest for certainty, for absolute prognostication, for perspicuous vision. For Mark, that Jesus survived his own death through rising is not a guarantee or a proof of some past promise having come true. Just the opposite. The resurrection of Jesus in Mark is a guarantee and proof that wherever the future takes us, it will be only just the next step towards what our Jesus is up to next. Step after step, we shall be immersed in his death and led by the promise of his resurrected life, and it will be this way forever. With the band of disciples, starting from the Twelve and expanding through so many even today, we have the option to cast our lot with our champion, the Jesus of the Gospel of Mark, who does not comfort us so much as cause the Kingdom to emerge around and upon us. Full speed ahead, for what lies in front of us, although it is unknown, is all on the other side of the tomb.

From Dreaded Guest to Welcoming Host:
Hospitality and Paul in *Acts*

Carisse Mickey Berryhill

When grim Saul bursts on the scene at the death of Stephen, no one could guess that one day, a prisoner himself, he would welcome all who came to ask him about the Way he had once tried to destroy. But indeed this is the case in *Acts*. At the beginning we see him invading home after home, an implacable foe, dragging off believers to imprisonment and death. At the end, we see him a gracious host in chains, freely offering the mercy of God to all. In between, Luke shows us through Paul's travels how his transformation from enemy to guest to host reflects the mission that revolutionized Paul's own life and the life of the church.

For Luke, the story is about explaining how God's grace irresistibly made its way through the world, incorporating everyone who accepted the message into the Israel of faith and promise, and surprising everyone who thought they had understood what God intended to do in the world. Paul is Luke's poster child for this progress of grace because he was the one who had been most sure that he knew what God required, and the most surprised by what had happened next.

The ways are many to think about Luke's book of *Acts*, to understand what kind of community God is building, and what the Kingdom is about that Paul preached, but I want to talk about all this by tracing a set of trajectories through the story of Paul's life: from enemy to guest to host, from the Temple and synagogue to house, from purity to mercy, from exclusiveness to inclusiveness. I get at these by examining the practice of hospitality as Paul experienced it according to Luke.[1] After considering some preliminary items about ancient hospitality, we shall think about Paul's experiences of hospitality according to Luke in *Acts*; then we shall assess the theological implications of these trajectories as Luke narrated them.

Ancient Hospitality

The word translated "hospitality" in the New Testament is *philoxenia*. Its root is *xenos* "stranger," but its derivatives often bear the notion of "guest" or even "host." "Guest room" (*xenia*) and "to show hospitality" (*xenizo*) are members of the same group, a group that demonstrates the sense of tension that attends the appearance of a stranger in a close-knit community. In Stählin's opinion, the practice of hospitality developed culturally out of the fear of the stranger, as a way to remove the threat by befriending the stranger.[2]

---

[1] I intend neither to attempt to harmonize Paul's own epistolary accounts of his experiences with Luke's account nor to derive a general New Testament doctrine of hospitality but to examine aspects of Luke's theology as hospitality events reveal them.

[2] For what follows, see Gustav Stählin, "Ξένος," in *Theological Dictionary of the New Testament*, Gerhard

Another cluster of New Testament words that show up in hospitality settings includes *lambano* ("receive"), *dechomai* ("receive"), and *propempo* ("to send on"). Called a "technical vocabulary" of hospitality by John Mathews,[3] these words denote welcoming someone and then providing them with resources, such as escorts or supplies, when they go on their way. In the New Testament, *propempo* is used "only in connection with traveling Christians."[4]

Ancient Mediterranean hospitality has been defined as "the process for changing an outsider's status from that of stranger to guest."[5] Different from entertaining family and friends, hospitality first tests the stranger and then admits him to a "temporary social location" as guest.[6] Unless accepted as a guest, the stranger possesses "no standing in law or custom," and may be repulsed, ignored, was considered "a sacred duty in the Levant" of such strength that a guest had a right to expect it.[7] Moreover, the host has the obligation to be responsible to protect the guest, providing whatever is needed, even up to defending the guest with one's life.[8] According to John Koenig, the New Testament shares with the Greek and Near Eastern cultures this sense of a sacred bond between guest and host, with the distinct "nuance" that it may be God who plays the role of either guest or host.[9]

Guests have their responsibilities, too. The Greeks classified as "strangers" those who knew how to follow the rules of hospitality, and as "barbarians" those who neither know the rules of hospitality nor even civilized language.[10] The guest must respect the honor of the host by avoiding any display of "insult, hostility, or rivalry."[11] He must not usurp, make demands, or fail to accept what is offered, especially food.[12]

The outcome of the process of hospitality depends, of course, on the success with which the guest and host play out their respective roles. The guest will leave the host "either as a friend or enemy," to spread the host's praises, or to seek satisfaction for aggrieved honor.[13] The guest is under no obligation to repay the host, since mutual reciprocity is not involved. One reciprocates in Mediterranean society, which appreciated travel between its

---

Friedrich, ed.; Geoffrey W. Bromiley, trans. & ed. (Grand Rapids: Eerdmans, 1967): 5: 1-3.

[3] John Bell Mathews, "Hospitality and the New Testament Church" (Ph.D. diss., Princeton Theological Seminary, 1964): 166-174.

[4] Abraham J. Malherbe, *Social Aspects of Early Christianity*, 2nd ed. (Philadelphia: Fortress, 1983): 68.

[5] Bruce J. Malina, *The Social World of Jesus and the Gospels* (New York: Routledge, 1996): 228.

[6] *Idem*: 230. The test is carried out by officials, citizens, or by a community champion. The test may be either an invitation to speak or some kind of verbal combat. A letter of recommendation can sometimes excuse a stranger from the test.

[7] R. H. Stein, "Entertain," in *International Standard Bible Encyclopedia*, Geoffrey W. Bromiley, ed. (Grand Rapids: Eerdmans, 1982): 2: 105.

[8] *Idem*: 2: 106.

[9] John Koenig, *New Testament Hospitality: Partnership with Strangers as Promise and Mission* (Philadelphia: Fortress, 1985): 2; *ibid.*, "Hospitality," in *Anchor Bible Dictionary*, David Noel Freedman, ed. (New York: Doubleday, 1992): 3: 299.

[10] Malina (1996): 230.

[11] *Idem*: 232-233.

[12] *Loc. cit.*

[13] *Loc. cit.*

communities, by making the same services available to other travelers.[14] Inns generally had a bad reputation.[15]

As part of this society, Early Christians were very mobile, spreading the faith into cities on the major trade routes.[16] As Stählin puts it, "The spread of the Gospel took place almost exclusively by word of mouth, and the evangel was carried by wandering messengers who were sustained by the hospitality of the brethren."[17] He continues: "Whenever the hospitality of Christians is mentioned in the New Testament, the reference is primarily to that extended to apostles and missionaries."[18] Furthermore, according to Malherbe, Christian hospitality not only served the needs of the traveling evangelists but also then provided a site for the house churches they established.[19]

Besides the basic motive of Christian love, Stählin enumerates four subsidiary motives for New Testament hospitality: the charismatic motive, where hospitality is viewed as a gift to be exercised; the eschatological motive, where hospitality is rooted in the Christians' recognition that they, too, are sojourners; the metaphysical motive, which understands that one may "entertain angels without knowing it" (Hb 13:1-2),[20] and that one's guest, even one of "the least of them" (Mt 25:35, 40), may represent the Divine Guest; and the missionary motive, which grasps the practical necessity of providing for the needs of traveling evangelists for the sake of the Gospel.[21]

Certainly the ministry of Jesus himself, and of his disciples when he sent them out two by two, depended on, and assumed the values of, hospitality.[22] Luke shows "an obvious interest" in hospitality in both his Gospel and in *Acts*.[23] To his picture of Paul's life as a guest we now turn.[24]

From House to House: The Narrative

Our first glimpse of Saul the Pharisee in Acts 8:3 is appalling. Uninvited, he invades "house after house" to drag believers, both men and women, away for prosecution as blasphemers. Here is the cold cruelty that lurks behind our fear of what strangers may do to us. This man's threat cannot be contained by the courtesies of hospitality because he is a zealot. Towards the end of Luke's narrative, he depicts Saul towards the end of his life, speaking about his earlier motives:

> I thought to myself that I had to do many things hostile to the name of Jesus of Nazareth. And this is just what I did in Jerusalem; not only did I lock up many of the saints in prisons, having received authority from the chief priests, but also when

---

[14] *Loc. cit.*

[15] R. Earle, "Inn; Lodge; Lodging Place," in Bromiley (1982): 2: 826.

[16] Malherbe (1983): 63-65.

[17] Stählin (1967): 22.

[18] *Idem*: 23.

[19] Malherbe (1983): 95-96.

[20] *New American Standard Bible*, reference ed. (Glendale, California: G/L Regal, 1973). All subsequent biblical references are quoted from this version.

[21] Stählin (1967): 5: 21-22.

[22] Stein (1982): 2: 106.

[23] Stählin (1967): 5: 20.

[24] See on p. 86 a chart showing all incidents in the *Book of Acts* when Paul's stayed as a guest or acted as a host.

they were being put to death, I cast my vote against them. And as I punished them often in all the synagogues, I tried to force them to blaspheme; and being furiously enraged at them, I kept pursuing them even to foreign cities. (Ac 26:9-11)

Saul's murderous rage is rooted in his offended purity code. As a Pharisee, he did not have a Sadducee's vested interest in preserving political position in the Temple and the City. As a Pharisee, he did have a passion for the purity and glory of his religion, which the followers of the so-called "Way," with their failed Messiah, threatened to pollute.

But then, following his dazzling encounter with that Messiah on the road to Damascus, Saul becomes the guest in the home of someone he had been on his way to Damascus to persecute, Judas, who lived on Straight Street (Ac 9:11). Blind and broken-hearted, Saul presents no threat to anyone here, and for three days he prays. He is so desperate that he breaks a fundamental rule of being a guest: He refuses to eat or drink (9:9). Then, when Ananias heals and baptizes him, Saul takes food and is strengthened (9:18). He remains "with the disciples who were at Damascus," the same ones he had planned to extradite to Jerusalem for prosecution, getting stronger and stronger as he debates with the local Jews that Jesus is the Son of God. Eventually, when opposition is so intense that his own life is at risk, the disciples, good hosts protecting the life of their guest, help him to escape by letting him down in a basket over the city wall by night (9:19-25).

Returning to Jerusalem, Saul is now a stranger to his former community, and at the same time the disciples of the Messiah think him to be a terror: "They were all afraid of him, not believing that he was a disciple" (9:26). What he needs is a sponsor, a patron, a host who "as an established member of the community" can offer a "personal bond," so the stranger can be "incorporated as a guest or client/protégé.[25] Enter Barnabas. Because he is open to recognizing the grace of God at work in new ways,[26] Barnabas "takes hold" of Saul and brings him to meet the apostles (9:27). As a good host should do, Barnabas introduces Saul and speaks for him, telling his Damascus story. As a result, Saul is accepted into the community. He goes "in and out among them in Jerusalem," moving freely among the houses of the people he had terrorized before (9:28). When another plot on his life comes to light, the disciples escort him for safe conduct to Caesarea and send him off to Tarsus (9:30).

Changing the subject briefly from Paul to Peter, let us note that the conversion by Peter of the Gentile Cornelius and his household is a turning point in *Acts*,[27] for it sets the stage of the entire mission to the Gentiles that occupies Luke's attention throughout the rest of the book. From the compelling visions with which the story of Cornelius begins (10:3-23), to the debriefing by the Jerusalem disciples (11:1-18), it raises the same issues of *kosher* purity (both of food and people), divine direction toward inclusiveness, and table fellowship that are Luke's themes in the Pauline stories. These constant literary themes alert us to focus on Luke's theological intention as seen through the lens of his narrative about Paul.

When the work among Gentiles begins to take hold in Antioch, Barnabas, having been sent from Jerusalem to Antioch to encourage it, travels to Tarsus in search of Saul (11:22-25).

---

[25] Malina (1996): 231.

[26] Robert C. Tannehill, *The Narrative Unity of Luke-Acts: A Literary Interpretation*, vol. 2, *The Acts of the Apostles* (Minneapolis: Fortress, 1990): 123.

[27] David Lertis Matson, *Household Conversion Narratives in Acts: Pattern and Interpretation* (Sheffield: Sheffield Academic Press, 1996), discussed both Cornelius and Luke's other great household conversion story, Zaccheus (Luke 19), as well as Lydia and the jailer.

He recruits him to come help, and they work together for a year, teaching many. Then they are sent by the church in Antioch to Jerusalem with relief funds for the Judean believers (11:30). Barnabas's patronage in Judea and Antioch brings about Saul's transformation from being feared to being accepted.

In Acts 13, Paul and Barnabas are called by the Spirit to begin the work we know as the First Missionary Journey. Luke describes their preaching and controversies in Cyprus and on the mainland of Asia, but no hosts, guests, houses, or meals are mentioned. Only in Iconium do they "remain a long time" (14:3). Only after the stoning in Lystra, when the hero of the piece is again greatly in need, does Luke depict a group of disciples who cluster around Paul and help him (14:20).

When the great circumcision controversy erupts in Antioch, Paul and Barnabas are among those appointed to go to Jerusalem. The church "sent them on their way" (15:3), i.e., provided traveling funds. As they go, they report joyfully to the congregations along the way. When they arrive in Jerusalem, they are "welcomed by the church and the Apostles and the Elders" (15:4), and they make their report. After the council, the Apostles send the results to Antioch by way of Paul, Barnabas, Judas, and Silas, carrying a letter of introduction (15:23ff) and instructions from Jerusalem. Judas and Silas stay there "for some time," and then are "sent off in peace" to Jerusalem (15:33). Paul and Barnabas stay in Antioch. These words of sending and welcoming and sending again indicate the hospitality of the community of faith.

After his team-building disagreement with Barnabas, Paul chooses Silas to go with him on the Second Missionary Journey, collects Timothy in Lystra, and goes from town to town in Asia Minor, taking news of the Council. Forbidden by the Spirit to go into Phrygia, Galatia, or Bithynia, Paul receives a divine invitation to preach in Macedonia; so the team, now including Luke, travels from Troas to Philippi. When they convert Lydia and her household, she urges them to stay in her home, "if you have judged me to be faithful to the Lord" (16:15). Luke remarks, "She prevailed upon us."

This occasion of hospitality is worth special notice for several reasons. Lydia is the first local host mentioned in Paul's mission.[28] Why is it necessary for her to insist that they stay with her? Why is a simple invitation not sufficient? Room or resources are apparently not a problem, for Lydia's house is capacious enough to host the nascent church (16:40).[29] Her gender may be a hindrance, since no male is mentioned in her household.[30] And since she is described in the text as "a worshiper of God" (16:14), she was probably not a Jew, though she may have been a proselyte. Whatever reason these four men have for needing her "peculiar

---

[28] *Idem*: 196.

[29] So much has been concluded about Lydia's wealth as a merchant that it is refreshing, though not completely convincing, to read a detailed examination of primary sources concerning the social class and wealth of workers in the purple industry. Lydia may well have been a freedwoman working with a few other women in her house in "a subsistence occupation." See Ivoni Richter Reimer, "Lydia and Her House," in *Women in the Acts of the Apostles: A Feminist Liberation Perspective* (Minneapolis: Fortress, 1995): 112.

[30] Gender is often brought up as an issue. Derek Thomas, "The Place of Women in the Church at Philippi," *Expository Times* 83 (January 1972): 117, asserted that Paul taught women at Philippi who would not have had access to "systematic teaching" under Judaism. Feminist interpreters, such as Reimer (1995): 111, see Lydia as the "head of a worshiping community."

talent of making it hard for others to refuse what she insists on,"[31] she puts the matter to them in terms of whether they judge her to be faithful. Clearly, some kind of social constraint is opposed here in Luke's narrative to "the implications that conversion carried for relationships between and among Christ's disciples."[32] The subtle reason for their hesitation (which I judge to have been her non-Jewish status) is the very cause of her urging: Will they or will they not behave towards her (a Gentile woman) as one whom they accept in the Lord Jesus.

The problem of the *kosher* household is pressed even further in the following episode, the conversion of the Philippian jailer, for whereas Lydia had been a "God-fearer," the jailer is clearly an unkosher, uncircumcized Gentile. Nonetheless, he takes his erstwhile prisoners into his own house, cares for their wounds, and feeds them. Paul and Silas are eating with Gentiles, again, and Luke characterizes the meal as one in celebration of that household's conversion to faith in God (16:34). Luke's focus, thus, is not on the purity—or lack thereof— of the meal, but on the reversal of enemy to brother, from fear to faith, from potential suicide to celebration.[33] Dumm observed that "the table-fellowship highlighted in *Luke-Acts* not only... manifests a spirit of generosity but also... frequently serves as an occasion for association with companions who would not normally be invited to table."[34]

In Thessalonika at Jason's house, Paul's host is attacked by a mob of Paul's Jewish opponents. "Jason has welcomed them!" (17:7), the Jews charge Jason, that is, he has entertained the strangers as guests, and then before the city officials, the accusers add a charge of sedition, alleging that the missionaries "say that there is another king, Jesus" (17:7). The mention of Jesus as "king" in the indictment indicates that Paul and the community meeting in Jason's house had been heard often enough talking about a "kingdom" so that the opponents hoped they could distort that language in the public mind as seditious. "The dangers of mission," Tannehill observed, "extend to local supporters, particularly those who open their homes to the mission."[35]

Meanwhile, the believers, as earlier in Damascus and Jerusalem, help Paul and Silas elude the authorities by sending them off to Berea. And when the uproar catches up with the missionaries there, the Berean believers send Paul "away to the coast," with an escort: "Those who conducted Paul," Luke says, "brought him as far as Athens" (17:15). Here Paul is active in the synagogue and marketplace, and ultimately at the Areopagus, where he is questioned about his "strange," i.e., foreign, new teaching. Athens is a city full of strangers, Luke says (17:21), Paul among them, and the Athenians are full of curiosity about strange people and foreign ideas. Paul's speech on Mars Hill capitalizes on the Athenian curiosity about novelties: He introduces God as an unknown Stranger whom they need to meet.

Leaving Athens, Paul and his entourage go to Corinth, where he finds Aquila and Priscilla, artisan tentmakers, like himself, and he "stayed with them, and they were working" (18:3) while Paul preaches and debates in the synagogue. When opposition in the synagogue intensifies, he desists from teaching his fellow Jews, exclaiming, "From now on, I shall go to the Gentiles" (18:6). Paul then moves to "the house of Titius Justus, a worshiper of God,

---

[31] F. X. Malinowski, "The Brave Women of Philippi," *Biblical Theology Bulletin* 15 (April 1985): 60.

[32] Richard J. Cassidy, *Society and Politics in the Acts of the Apostles* (Maryknoll, New York: Orbis, 1987): 58.

[33] See Koenig (1985): 116-119, on meals in *Acts* as occasions of joyful repentance.

[34] Demetrius R. Dumm, "Luke 24:44-49 and Hospitality," in *Sin, Salvation and the Spirit*, Daniel Durken, ed. (Collegeville, Minnesota: Liturgical Press, 1979): 232.

[35] Tannehill (1990): 208.

whose house was next to the synagogue" (18:7). Even though the Corinthian church was to include some prominent Jews, such as Crispus, the leader of the synagogue (18:8), Paul's effort to evangelize the Corinthian synagogue ends here. Over the next 18 months in Corinth, Paul directs his ministry mainly to the Gentiles.

Paul's Second Missionary Journey ends with his return—via Ephesus, where he leaves Aquila and Priscilla—to the port at Caesarea, whence he goes up to greet the Jerusalem church, and thence to Antioch, where he had begun his missionary circuit.

Paul's Third Missionary Journey begins in Antioch "after spending some time there" (18:23). Moving through Galatia and Phrygia, this time Paul arrives in Ephesus and, among other preaching work, he takes up the invitation that the Ephesian synagogue had offered on the inbound leg of his previous trip. But after three months of disputation there, opposition in the synagogue causes Paul to shift his place of daily teaching to the Lecture Hall of Tyrannus, where he stays an unusually long amount of time, two years. Malherbe noted that the School of Tyrannus may not have been a "school" but a *schola*, a guild hall where artisans met, lived, and worked under the patronage of a man named Tyrannus.[36] Paul later recalled that he had supported himself and others in Ephesus by manual labor (20:33-35).

The impact of Paul's teaching eventually brings on a riot fomented by Demetrius and the silversmiths. Two of Paul's companions are dragged off, but the disciples prevent Paul from going to their defense. Eventually the riot is dispersed without bloodshed. Paul then "sends for" the disciples–which may suggest that he was in hiding—encourages them, and says farewell (19:23—20:1). Here, for the first time in *Acts*, Paul is depicted as the host of a gathering, though at an undisclosed location.

Next, Paul travels through Macedonia, staying three months in Greece (Luke does not dwell on this part of the journey). Warned of a plot, Paul backtracks through Macedonia instead of sailing to Syria. Paul's entourage precedes him to Troas, but he and Luke stay at Philippi for the Feast of Unleavened Bread, and then they sail to Troas. They stay a week in order to meet with other believers on the First Day of the week to "break bread." On their last night there, Paul preaches well into the night (poor Eutychus!), and they leave at dawn. Again, Paul's companions precede him by ship to Assos, while Paul travels overland to meet them. By then in haste to arrive in Jerusalem before Pentecost, he bypasses a road trip to Ephesus, inviting the Ephesian Elders, instead, to meet him in the port city of Miletus.

The touching scene in Miletus is the second incident of six in *Acts* in which Paul is depicted as the host of a gathering. He invites them, and they "come to him" where he is (20:17-18). Here we hear afresh a key phrase in Luke's language of hospitality. While Paul reviews his mission in general to "testify solemnly of the gospel of the grace of God" (20:24), he mentions specifically his work with the Ephesian church, "teaching…publicly and from house to house" (20:20). The first time we saw him "going from house to house," it was to imprison and kill, but here he reflects on his ministry from house to house for the sake of the gospel he once opposed. This retrospective speech, moreover, functions in Luke's text to signal that the last part of Paul's story is beginning. The meeting has special importance for them, since Paul knows they will never see one another again. After a prayerful and tearful farewell, they escort him to the ship (20:36-38).

---

[36] Malherbe (1983): 90.

When Paul's ship docks at Tyre to offload cargo, Paul and his team find the disciples—maybe it took some looking—and stay there seven days (perhaps so as to be present for the breaking of bread on the First Day). When it is time for Paul's group to leave, the entire church, women and children included, escorts them to the ship, kneeling with Paul in prayer on the beach.

They sail to Ptolemais, greet the believers, and stay with them one day. The following day they go to Caesarea, where they stay for several days with Philip, an evangelist, and his four prophetic daughters. From there, when they leave for Jerusalem, Caesarean disciples escort them to the house of Mnason of Cyprus, who had been one of the earliest disciples, "with whom," Luke says, "we were to lodge" (21:16). At last they come to their destination, Jerusalem, where "the brethren received us gladly" (21:17).

At the advice of James and the Elders, Paul begins a week of purification in the Temple, but he is arrested toward the end of the week when Asian Jews falsely accuse him of defiling the Temple by bringing one of his Greek companions there. After a hearing before, first, the mob in the Temple, then before the Jerusalem Sanhedrin, the tribune who has Paul in custody, tipped off by Paul's nephew to a murder plot, sends him under guard to Caesarea, where he is imprisoned, pending the resolution of his case. During this period, Paul is allowed to "have some liberty," and his friends are not prevented from "taking care of his needs" (24:23). Eventually, after a series of hearings and defenses, he is remanded to Rome.

On the voyage to Rome, the centurion in charge of the prison detail allows Paul to go to his friends during a stopover in Sidon "to be cared for" (27:3). After a difficult voyage to Crete, they are caught in a late-season storm that rages until they despair. Finally, after fourteen nights, as they seem to be approaching land, Paul prevents the sailors from abandoning the passengers and encourages the debilitated crew and passengers to eat something. Near dawn, he takes some bread, says thanks before everyone, and breaks the bread and eats. Everyone else eats, too, even the perfidious sailors. Paul, a prisoner, takes on for the third time the role of a host, a gracious leader protecting the lives of his ship's company, holding them together for the communal effort they must make in order to survive. This he does without a house or a hot meal to offer, merely storm-soaked bread and words of hope. When the morning comes, the ship's crew fails in the landing attempt, and the ship becomes stranded and begins to break up. The guards plan to kill the prisoners to prevent escape, but for Paul's sake, the centurion, "wanting to bring Paul safely through" (27:43), forestalls the massacre and gives permission for the prisoners to swim for shore. The wrecked boat had, as it were, become Paul's house, and its occupants—Roman soldiers, ship's crew, and traveling companions—were under Paul's protection.

When all, as Paul predicted, reach the shore safely, they are welcomed by the Maltese who show "extraordinary kindness" (28:2), kindling a fire and welcoming everyone around it. For three days, the "leading man of the island," Publius, welcomes Paul and his party and entertains them courteously (28:7). When Paul heals Publius's father of dysentery, a ministry of healing begins on Malta that continues through the winter, and the Maltese respond by bestowing "many honors on us," Luke says; and when it is time to go, they provision the ship with "all we needed" (28:10).

After docking at Syracuse and Rhegium, Paul's party comes to Puteoli, where they find believers and are "invited to stay with them for seven days" (28:14)—again, a seven-day stay. Meanwhile, word that Paul has landed in Italy spreads, and believers from Rome come out to meet and encourage him, first at the Market of Appius, about 40 miles from Rome, and then at Three Inns, about 30 miles out. "And thus," Luke remarks, "we came to Rome" (28:14).

In Rome, Paul is allowed to stay in his own place, but under guard in a state of house arrest. Not permitted to move about the city or visit the synagogues, he initiates contact with the Jewish community another way by inviting its leaders to a preliminary meeting to explain his position and to ascertain theirs. Together they plan a second meeting. This time, a large number of Jewish people come to his home and spend the day in discussions "about the Kingdom of God, [Paul] trying to persuade them concerning Jesus, from both the Law of Moses and from the Prophets" (28:23). When his guests reach a stalemate between those who believe his arguments and those who do not, the meeting breaks up. To the unpersuaded, Paul issues Isaiah's warning as they leave not to close their ears, and he announces that he will preach to the Gentiles, who will listen

Paul's fourth and fifth appearances as a host thus take place when he issues an invitation and receives guests to his *xenia*, which may be translated either as "lodging" or as "hospitality" (20:17-28).[37] Whether Paul spread a table before his guests is not stated, but since the second meeting lasted all day, some refreshment was presumably necessary. That the meeting took place at Paul's dwelling, at his invitation, and as an attempt to offer his guests the banquet of salvation, is clear. His disappointment when they leave is palpable, though one does not sense that he is surprised.

Luke concludes *Acts* with our last view of him, living under Roman guard but in his own place for two years, "welcoming all who came to him, preaching the Kingdom of God, and teaching concerning the Lord Jesus Christ with all openness, unhindered" (28:30-31). Restricted as he is, Paul makes seekers welcome. Koenig's opinion is that the word "welcome" is a reference to meals that Paul shared with his visitors: "His proclamation took the form of a table talk that encouraged lively give and take with his guests."[38] Luke's emphasis is on the paradoxical picture of an apostle in chains teaching "unhindered," and of his eagerness to tell any visitor of the Kingdom and its King.

Transitional Observations

In the natural course of things, Paul ate something and slept somewhere everywhere he traveled. Luke surely did not report every incident of hospitality, for his narrative is not a day-by-day account. Where Luke makes a point of describing Paul's housing arrangements, perhaps he does so for a reason.

Two Jewish hosts, including Barnabas, are named as part of Paul's conversion narrative; none is named in the First Missionary Journey; five hosts–four non-Jews–are named in the Second Missionary Journey; two Jewish hosts are named in the Third Missionary Journey,

---

[37] F. J. Foakes-Jackson and Kirsopp Lake, *Acts of the Apostles*, vol. 4: *English Translation and Commentary*, by Kirsopp Lake and Henry J. Cadbury, *The Beginnings of Christianity*, pt. 1 (London: Macmillan, 1920; reprint, Grand Rapids : Baker, 1979): 4: 346, who opted for "hospitality," as does Earle (1982): 2: 827. I. Howard Marshall, *The Acts of the Apostles: An Introduction and Commentary* (Grand Rapids: Eerdmans, 1980): 423, however, commented: "The Jews were his guests, since he could not follow his former pattern of attending the synagogue, but the phrase does not mean that he provided them with a meal or anything of the kind."

[38] Koenig (1985): 54.

and two incidents are recounted in which Paul acted as host; one Gentile host and the Maltese as a group are named in the Roman Journey, and Paul acts as host on four occasions.

In comparison with the amount of attention Luke gave in *Acts* to miracles and speeches, hosts and hospitality receive but brief notice. They do receive notice, now and then, when some detail of the visit is unusual for its novelty, controversy, or emotional intensity. The Second Missionary Journey and the final Roman Journey are more notable than the other passages as far as the details of hospitality go: the Second Missionary Journey for its number of named hosts and their Gentile ethnicity, and the Roman Journey for Paul's role as host.

The shift in the narrative, moreover, of Paul's role seems significant: The frequent guest becomes a frequent host. This shift is partly the natural outcome of the curtailment of Paul's freedom after his arrest, but now the hospitality of Paul, having appeared as host first in the Third Missionary Journey, becomes one of Luke's themes in the Roman Journey. Paul's function as host is so detailed and so full of his apostolic authority that Luke seems to be emphasizing this role for reasons relating to the completion of Paul's mission that has taken him to Rome.

Hospitality and the Progress of Grace: A Theological Trajectory

Marshall listed five strands of theological ideas in *Acts*: 1) the continuation of God's purpose in history; 2) mission and message; 3) progress despite opposition; 4) inclusion of Gentiles in the people of God; and 5) the life and organization of the church.[39] Koenig gave Luke's primary intentions as two: 1) to encourage his readers in that their faith rests securely on God's ancient relationship to Israel, now being fulfilled in them; 2) to equip his readers for more effective participation in God's mission, so to prepare them to face persecution.[40] In particular, Koenig thought that Luke wished to foster partnership with itinerant believers by encouraging resident believers to see their financial support and hospitality as a contribution to the mission.[41]

Luke Timothy Johnson formulated the theological question that occasioned *Acts* in these words: "How did the good news reach the Gentiles, and did the rejection of it by the Jews mean that God had failed in his fidelity to them?"[42] Haenchen, also, argued that Luke's abiding issue was the continuity of the history of salvation:

> The instigators and leaders of the Christian mission, far from falling away from their Jewish faith, in fact held fast to it…. Luke the historian is wrestling, from the first page to the last, with the problem of the *mission to the Gentiles, without the law* [Haenchen's emphasis], both in its theological and political aspects: Is the mission continuous with salvation history, and can the new movement as separate from Judaism be tolerated by Rome?[43]

Dumm connected the Gentile mission to Luke's understanding that the return of Christ would not perhaps be immediate, that an "age of the church" would take place first.

---

[39] Marshall (1980): 23-33.

[40] Koenig (1985): 85.

[41] *Idem*: 86.

[42] Luke Timothy Johnson, *The Acts of the Apostles*, Sacra Pagina 5 (Collegeville, Minnesota: Liturgical Press, 1992): 476.

[43] Ernst Haenchen, *The Acts of the Apostles: A Commentary*, Bernard Nobel, *et al.*, trans., 14th German ed., 1965 (Philadelphia: Westminster, 1971): 100, 102.

New openness to the future leads to a new understanding of the past....[If a] historical future [is] to be considered [because] history has not been completed, it can only mean that the religion of Israel is meant for the whole world. To be a true Israelite now is to "make room," to show hospitality to the Gentile.[44]

To quote Haenchen again, Luke demonstrated by miracles and visions, such as Peter's housetop vision, the outpouring of the Holy Spirit upon Cornelius, Paul's Damascus road confrontation, and Paul's vision of the Macedonian call, that God "unmistakably and irresistibly steered them into the mission to the Gentiles."[45]

What Koenig called the "guest and host stories"[46] of *Acts* play their part in making these ideas tangible. Matson spelled out three ways that household evangelization contributes to *Acts*: It 1) "inaugurates and expands the Gentile mission," especially guided by divine intervention; 2) "legitimates Gentiles as equal members of the new salvific community by stressing their full acceptance at table with the Jews," and 3) "map[s] out a new 'sacred' space for the inclusive people of God," the house rather than the Temple or synagogue.[47] There is a new house of God.

When the converted Saul began preaching in Damascus, the disciples asked, "Is this not he who in Jerusalem destroyed those who called on this name?" (9:21) Theirs is more than a geographical inquiry. It indicates Saul's identification with the Temple authorities whose warrant he had carried to Damascus. According to Elliott, the Temple in Jerusalem functioned as an institution within a "purity system" that "established and controlled the social identity, social classifications, and social boundaries of the Jewish people as the holy people of God."[48] In Luke's narrative, Elliott wrote, "The temple gradually emerges as an institution whose managers, interests, and ideology stand diametrically opposed to the ministry and mission of Jesus and his community."[49] Gowler observed that this clash is particularly visible in hospitality settings, which "graphically illustrate the societal norms of purity and honor that Jesus seeks to transform."[50]

Luke depicts a Paul who, called to take the gospel to the Gentiles, nonetheless remained loyal at the same time to his own Jewishness. His usual pattern of evangelizing in a new community began with a visit to the local synagogue. Tannehill comments that Paul's "pattern of speaking to Jews first and only later turning to the Gentiles testifies to Paul's sense of prophetic obligation to his own people. He is released from this obligation only when he meets strong public resistance within the Jewish community."[51] When Paul defends himself to his Jewish brethren, he presents his faith, Gowler reasoned, as "the logical and legitimate outgrowth of Pharisaism" and himself as a "biographical paradigm for how Jews

[44] Dumm (1979): 233.
[45] Haenchen (1971): 100.
[46] Koenig (1985): 3: 111.
[47] Matson (1996): 187-192.
[48] John H. Elliott, "Temple versus Household in Luke-Acts: A Contrast in Social Institutions," in *The Social World of Luke-Acts: Models for Interpretation*, Jerome H. Neyrey, ed. (Peabody, Massachusetts: Hendrickson, 1991): 221.
[49] *Idem*: 223.
[50] David B. Gowler, "Hospitality and Characterization in Luke 11:37-54: A Socio-Narratological Approach," *Semeia* 64 (1994): 242.
[51] Tannehill (1990): 223.

should believe the gospel."[52] Tannehill mentioned Paul's vow at Cenchrea (18:18) as an act done by a good Jew "without pressure," Paul's own voluntary proof that his position with regard to the mission to the Gentiles "does not arise from contempt for Jews and their way of life."[53] A catalogue of Paul's accommodation of the Jews also includes his insistence that Timothy be circumcized (16:3), and Paul's full participation in the Temple at Jerusalem with the four men under a vow, whose expenses Paul himself paid (21:20-26). This was no mere political compromise with the "thousands" (21:20) of Jewish Christians who were still zealous keepers of the Law, but Paul's whole-hearted participation in the religious culture of his ancestors, in which he took great pride, and which he never repudiated (cf. Philippians 3:4-6; Romans 11), no matter how critical of it he became.

Even so, Paul's final trip to Jerusalem was a blend of urgency (he by-passed Ephesus in order to be in Jerusalem for the festival) and foreboding of danger from his own beloved people, as both he and Agabus prophesied (20:23, 21:11). He moved toward Jerusalem with a "sense of divine necessity" like "a dark cloud."[54] What had been his "spiritual home is now a threatening place, a place of conflict, arrest, and possible death, as it was for Jesus and Stephen."[55]

Paul knew that the dispensations of God's grace were in transition; what had been would no longer be, and the appearance of the Messiah at "just the right time" signaled the beginning of the end of the Law of Moses and of the centrality of the Temple. Elliot commented: "Through its collusion with Rome and its oppression and exploitation of its own people," Elliott comments, the Temple, "this center of Jewish political, economic, and social power... is no longer the place where the hope of the world's salvation and the universal experience of God's mercy could be realized."[56] Instead, Luke presents the household as "the favored setting of the teaching and healing ministry of Jesus and his followers, ... the typical location of the gospel's reception and the church's growth."[57] "It is primarily by means of the house," Matson likewise states, that "the gospel marches steadily from Jerusalem to Rome."[58] Similarly, Koenig remarked, "Luke presents the house church as the creative hub of God's redemptive work."[59]

The household provided resources necessary to the Christian mission, such as security and a sense of belonging,[60] a social identity that was a "decisive alternative" to other forms of social identity and religious allegiance,[61] and a ready-made model for relationships under a *paterfamilias*.[62] Even after a house church became large enough to spin off others, the "household character of a church would be retained as it became a community with a

---

[52] David B. Gowler, *Host, Guest, Enemy and Friend: Portraits of the Pharisees in Luke and Acts.* (New York: Peter Lang, 1991): 295-296.
[53] Tannehill (1990): 227.
[54] *Idem*: 240.
[55] *Loc.cit.*
[56] Elliott (1991): 223.
[57] *Idem*: 225.
[58] Matson (1996): 26.
[59] Koenig (1985): 106.
[60] Malherbe (1983): 69.
[61] John H. Elliott, *A Home for the Homeless: A Sociological Exegesis of 1 Peter, Its Situation and Strategy* (Philadelphia: Fortress, 1981): 194.
[62] Elliott (1991): 229.

broader constituency than it originally had."[63] So we see that in Luke's narratives, both the Temple and the synagogue yield to the household as the arena of God's new activity, or, as Elliott put it, "The Spirit of God and its sanctifying power moves from temple to household, from the chief symbol of Jewish national identity to the principal symbol of a community united with a heavenly Father."[64]

Matson's study of household conversions in *Acts* links the pattern of household evangelization to Jesus' instructions to his disciples in Luke 10:

1) enter homes of economically established (Gentile) households

2) present the word of salvation to the household

3) stay in the house, eating and drinking as an expression of inclusive table fellowship.[65]

Malherbe commented that Paul "came from the same social stratum" as his hosts, people in the artisan/subsistence industry class such as Lydia or Aquila and Priscilla.[66] Paul "lived with his social equals and used their homes as bases for his missionary operation."[67] Their "necessary partnership" was crucial to the mission.[68] Though his local hosts may have been for the most part Paul's social equals, the more important fact is that many of them were Gentiles, and yet Paul stayed with them and ate with them. Meals are, according to Koenig, "a critical arena for the revealing of God's righteousness in Christ and humanity's response to it."[69] So Paul's suppers with the Gentiles, like the meal provided by the Philippian jailer, are events of "joyful repentance."[70] Furthermore, as Pohl pointed out, "shared meals were where the difficulties of social tensions were worked through to portray a common life."[71] The common meal expresses reconciliation between the guests and the host, and between the Heavenly Father who serves as Host at every such meal and those who enjoy his hospitality. "Repentance," Dumm observed, "is to turn away from obduracy that cannot accept the new and different," an obduracy that "cannot entertain God's mysterious ways."[72] At such banquets of novelty, therefore, Paul accepts those whom God has accepted, just as Paul himself had earlier been accepted by people who would have formerly dreaded him as a mortal threat.

Luke expresses this theme of universal grace symbolically in Paul's storm-lashed meal with his fellow passengers just before dawn on their doomed ship. Luke takes pains to say that Paul "took bread, blessed it, and broke it" (27:35). Only two other times does Luke show a host performing this precise sequence: in Luke 9:16, the feeding of the multitude; and at the supper with the self-revealing Lord at Emmaus in Luke 24:30.[73] Tannehill pointed out the similarity between the Greek wording for Paul's promise that salvation of all on board has

---

[63] Malherbe (1983): 69.

[64] Elliott (1991): 230.

[65] Matson (1996): 37.

[66] Malherbe (1983): 77.

[67] *Loc. cit.*

[68] Tannehill (1990): 196.

[69] Koenig (1992): 3:301.

[70] Koenig (1985): 117.

[71] Christine D. Pohl, *Making Room: Recovering Hospitality as a Christian Tradition* (Grand Rapids: Eerdmans, 1999): 31.

[72] Dumm (1979): 236-237.

[73] Tannehill (1990): 334; Bernard P. Robinson, "The Place of the Emmaus Story in Luke-Acts," *New Testament Studies* 30/4 (October 1984): 481-497, also noted the Eucharistic parallels between the story in *Luke* and the story in *Acts*.

been "graciously granted" (*kekaristai*) and his giving of thanks for the bread (*eucharistesen*): Paul's prayer of thanks over bread is thanks for the promise, too, of salvation from a stormy sea.[74] Paul is encouraging all on the ship to take food and to take heart. His meal and prayer are not limited to his Christian party only. Koenig remarked, "Paul's homely act of sanctifying his meal draws the onlookers, who are mostly nonbelievers, into the sphere of God's gracious providence. And so they, too, can begin to hope."[75] According to Esler, Luke uses this story to "reinforce [his] persistent emphasis on the fact that the old barriers between Jew and Gentile have been decisively shattered in the eucharistic fellowship of the Christian community and that an era of salvation for all humanity has now been inaugurated."[76]

When Paul, though a prisoner at the end of *Acts*, enacts the role of gracious host, he obeys the "radical vision of universal salvation."[77] In Paul's meetings in his lodgings with the Roman Jews, and in his subsequent ministry in his house there, he bears witness to the new community, the inclusive Kingdom of God, and to God's work in Jesus (28:23). Jesus came as a stranger, a *xenos*, as he is called in Matthew 25, one who asks to be received as a guest, but also as a "humble Host who not only entertains his guests lavishly...but who Himself serves them at table,"[78] even washing their feet (John 13:2-16), the perfect act of hospitality. This intermingling of guest and host in Jesus compels Christian hospitality, according to Pohl: "Jesus welcomes and needs welcome; Jesus requires that followers depend on and provide hospitality. The practice of Christian hospitality is always located within the larger picture of Jesus' sacrificial welcome to all who come to him."[79]

Ultimately people are asked to receive God by receiving one another. Since God makes room for human freedom, "the presence of God is felt more as an invitation than a command."[80] Neither Paul nor Peter nor any of the Jews imagined that God would ask them to extend the community of promise to those outside the covenant of purity which was so precious to them. But God did. "This is asking for extraordinary openness and generosity," remarked Dumm, "but it is the condition that will permit God to fulfill the promises in a way that far surpasses human expectations."[81] Dumm continued, "The ultimate hospitality is, then, an entertainment of divine mystery in human life."[82] If we receive God as Guest, God becomes in our lives the Host of a community banquet of grace.

Like Barnabas, who was open to recognizing the mystery of the grace of God at work in new ways, we must show openness to God's work outside our expectations. We cannot anticipate what God will do, only that He will surprise us. We only know that grace is calling, as it did when we first heard, "Behold, I stand at the door and knock." When we admitted him, we began to learn what he deserves:

---

[74] Tannehill (1990): 335-336.
[75] Koenig (1985): 54.
[76] Philip Francis Esler, *Community and Gospel in Luke-Acts: The Social and Political Motivations of Lucan Theology* (Cambridge University Press, 1987): 104.
[77] Matson (1983): 197.
[78] Stählin (1967): 25.
[79] Pohl (1999): 17.
[80] Dumm (1979): 231.
[81] *Idem*: 237.
[82] *Idem*: 236.

Christ, He requires still, wheresoe're He comes,
To feed, or lodge, to have the best of rooms:
Give Him the choice; grant Him the nobler part
Of all the house; the best of all's the heart.
—Robert Herrick, "Christ's Part," 1647

When our hearts have granted Lord Jesus residence, then the presence of the Holy Guest/Ghost gives grace to break down walls, even stained-glass ones, and extend God's welcome to those whom God has called. Welcoming the newcomer may mean remodeling the heart or the worship program. It may mean learning to appreciate others' customs or languages or foods or music, no longer content to compartmentalize them as alien. It may mean doing the work of listening hospitably to the suffering or world view or spiritual insight of others. Like Barnabas, we may be called to see the potential in newly converted persons, only to find that God has invited them to reshape our community. Welcoming the stranger means reconfiguring our buildings to remove barriers to access. It means working through our discomforts with illness, age, physical, and mental disabilities.

Having welcomed one another, we must live an authentic community life. We experience the terrible loneliness of the age and seek a Household that provides community and belonging. Like Lydia, we urge one another to get over those social constraints that oppose relationship, not by making social adjustments, but by affirming our common faith. We counsel and support each other in holy living, in the study of the Scriptures, and in worshipful celebration. Then we sit at table with one another, first at church, than at home. We host small group meetings and meals, we have soup night for college students, we invite someone to go for coffee, or to meet for breakfast. We learn to be gracious to one another by eating together.

Then we seek to share our blessing with our shipwreck of a society. We work at reconciliation with those who have hurt us and whom we have hurt, including other religious people in our community; we do the hard work of forgiveness. We volunteer when the city pleads for hosts for community meals to discuss improving race relations in our town. We have meals with other congregations. We work on Habitat houses. We attend interfaith discussions. We serve meals to the hungry, give clothes to the naked, attend to those in prisons of all kinds. We foster and adopt children who need homes. We provide transitional housing and career development for homeless people.

We supply resources for the preaching of the good news. We receive, provision, and send out missionary teams. We contribute funds and medical supplies to short-term mission projects for students. We teach our children to admire missionaries by housing those who are raising funds or reporting on the work. We remember the dangers in many places to missionaries and their hosts, and we pray for them, and advocate for their release when they are kidnapped, imprisoned, and persecuted. We learn to think that the Kingdom is both near and far, but never foreign, and the people in it, never strangers.

In Luke's *Acts*, the New Testament house church becomes a new sort of sacred space, where the reign of God produces the community of grace, the house of God, *Beth-El*, where God dwells. Like that traveler, Jacob, who lay down – he thought alone – on a stone pillow, we learn that this is indeed the house of God when we see, coming and going, holy strangers who reverence our Lord.

The Acts	Location	Length of Stay	Host(s)	Guest(s)	Remarks
					Hospitality Events Involving Paul in *Acts*
8:3	Jerusalem		house churches	Saul	entered to arrest and kill
9:11	Damascus		Judas	Saul	Ananias visited Saul
9:19	Damascus	several days	Disciples	Saul	aided basket escape
9:26	Jerusalem		Barnabas	Saul	introduced Saul to apostles
9:28	Jerusalem		Brethren	Saul	escort Saul to Caesarea
11:25	Antioch	one year	Barnabas	Saul	recruited Saul from Tarsus
14:3	Iconium	long time		Paul & Barnabas	
14:20	Lystra	one day	disciples	Paul & Barnabas	surrounded Paul after stoning
14:28	Antioch	long time	disciples	Paul & Barnabas	sent them on to council
15:4	Jerusalem		church, apostles, elders	Paul & Barnabas	received them
16:15, 40	Philippi	many days	Lydia	Paul, Silas, Luke, and Timothy	prevailed on them
16:32-34	Philippi	one night	jailer	Paul & Silas	
17:7	Thessalonica	three weeks	Jason	Paul & Silas	dragged Jason before authorities
17:10	Thessalonica		brethren	Paul & Silas	sent them to Berea by night
17:14	Berea		brethren	Paul & Silas, Timothy	escorted Paul to Athens
18:3	Corinth	18 months	Aquila & Priscilla	Paul	tentmaking
18:7	Corinth		Titius Justus	Paul, Silas, Timothy	teaching
19:30-31	Ephesus	2 years	disciples	Paul	prevented Paul from assembly
20:1	Ephesus		**Paul**	disciples	farewell
20:6-12	Troas	7 days		Paul & team	broke bread
20:17-38	Miletus	one day	**Paul**	Ephesian elders	farewell speech
21.4	Tyre	7 days	disciples	Paul & team	family escort to ship
21:7	Ptolemais	one day	brethren	Paul & team	
21:8	Caesarea	7 days	Philip	Paul & team	escort to Mnason
21:16	Jerusalem (?)		Mnason	Paul & team	
21:17	Jerusalem	7 days	brethren	Paul & team	received us gladly
24:23	Caesarea	2 years	prison	Paul	friends took care of him
27:3	Sidon		Paul's friends	Paul	friends took care of him
27:35	On ship		**Paul**	all on board	breaks bread
28:2	Malta		Maltese	shipwreck victims	extraordinary kindness
28:7	Malta	3 days	Publius	Paul & team	welcomed
28:10	Malta	3 months	Maltese	Paul & team	supplied ship
28:14	Puteoli	7 days	brethren	Paul & team	invited to stay
28:15	Rome		brethren	Paul & team	came to meet Paul
28:17	Rome		**Paul**	Jewish leaders	preliminary meeting
28:28	Rome		**Paul**	Jewish leaders	day-long meeting
28:30	Rome	2 years	**Paul**	all who came	welcomed

THE TRADITIONS OF "MARRIAGE"

ROY BOWEN WARD

The majority of Americans currently tout "traditional marriage between a man and a woman," often adding that marriage was intended for procreation. Many people, of course, would agree that marriage is (and ought to be) about much more than procreation only. Love comes to mind, including sexual love and other kinds as well: best friendship, mutual affection, companionship in place of loneliness, and comfort in old age. Mutual financial benefits and security also belong in this list.

"Traditional marriage" ceremonies often include in the vows, "until death do us part," yet today fifty-percent of all marriages end in divorce, including those among devout Christians and Jews. Here the "tradition" has changed over time. In 2005, the debate is focused on gay marriages, now legally possible in the Commonwealth of Massachusetts. Those who oppose same-sex unions want to have a monopoly on the word "marriage." The State of Vermont, which acted before Massachusetts, established by secular law "Civil Unions" that accord to same-sex unions such rights as the right to be parents and the right to inherit from a deceased partner.[1] This *may* lead to a new tradition.

My intent in this essay is to reexamine the Hebrew Bible (Old Testament), the New Testament, and writings from the Early Church to see what these texts tell us on the subject of "marriage." Just how traditional is the current concept of "traditional marriage," compared to the biblical and ecclesiastical traditions?

The Traditions of the Hebrew Bible: The Two Creation Stories

The oldest creation story (from the 10th century B.C.E.) is in Genesis 2:4b-3.24. The text tells the story that Yahweh (the name of the Hebrew God), like a potter, formed the earthling, *'adam*, from the earth, *'adamah*—a pun, that is, a play on words that sound alike.[2] Yahweh then breathed into the earthling's nostrils the breath of life, so *'adam* became a living person (*nephesh*, "one who breathes") (Gn 2:7).[3]

Yahweh caused trees to grow from the earth in the Garden of Eden, most importantly the Tree of Life and the Tree of the Knowledge of Good and Evil (Gn 2:9). Yahweh

---

[1] Patricia Nell Warren, "Traditional Marriage: A Secular Affair," *The Gay Lesbian Review* 12/3 (2005): 10. At the time of this writing, Belgium, the Netherlands, and Spain have legalized same-sex marriage; Denmark, Sweden, Norway, France, and Germany recognize civil unions, and Britain and Switzerland are considering similar legislation; Portugal recognizes common-law marriages between same-sex couples. Those who oppose same-sex unions want to have a monopoly on the word "marriage." The Province of Ontario is also moving toward approval of civil unions.

[2] *'adam*—"someone made of earth"—in this particular story did not sound like a proper name, "Adam," to the first Hebrew hearers and readers.

[3] On the relationship of *nephesh* and breathing, see Roy Bowen Ward, "The Use of the Bible in the Abortion Debate," *Saint Louis Public Law Review*, 13/1 (1993): 394-396.

commanded *'adam,* saying: "You are free to eat of any tree in the garden, except only the Tree of the Knowledge of Good and Evil, of which you are not to eat. For on the day you eat of it, you shall be doomed to death" (Gn 2:16,17). The logic of that statement is that *'adam,* before eating of the forbidden fruit, was immortal.

Then Yahweh searched among the beasts and birds for a suitable companion for *'adam,* and finding none, Yahweh took one of the ribs of the *'adam* and built the rib into an *'issah* (woman) (Gn 2:21, 22). *'adam* said, "This, finally, is bone of my bone and flesh of my flesh. This shall be called *'issah* (woman) because this was taken from *'ish* (man)" (Gn 2:23)— another pun, although the Hebrew words, *'ish* and *'issah,* are from different roots. Because the woman came from a source that was immortal, the man, they both were immortal.

The story goes on with an explanation: "Therefore, a man *('ish)* leaves his father and his mother,[4] and cleaves *(dabaq)* to his woman *('issah),* and they become one flesh" (Gn 2:24). The setting is the Garden of Eden where the woman and man were still immortal. He cleaves to his woman and the two become one flesh, a physical union. But nothing is said in this creation story about procreation. At this point in the story, they are still immortal and there was no need to procreate.

Not until they ate of the forbidden fruit of the Tree of the Knowledge of Good and Evil were the woman and man doomed to become mortal and in a patriarchal relationship. After the eating of the forbidden fruit, Yahweh said to the woman, "I will make your pain intense in childbearing. In pain you shall bear children. For your man *('ish)* will be your desire, but he will rule over you" (Gn 3:16). But not yet, for they were still in the Garden of Eden where the Tree of Life was. So Yahweh said, "Now that *'adam* has become like one of us, knowing good and evil, what if he put out his hand and take also from the Tree of Life and eat and live for ever?" (Gn 3:22). So Yahweh sent *'adam* forth from the Garden of Eden to serve the earth *('adamah)* from which he was taken. At the east of the Garden of Eden, Yahweh stationed the cherubim (winged lions, perhaps) and a flaming sword to guard the way to the Tree of Life (Gn 3:23, 24).[5]

Now out of the Garden of Eden, the pair had to work for a living and survive like the rest of the animal creation, and in this condition, procreation became a necessity. Eve gave birth (in pain) to Cain and Abel, and Cain murdered Abel. Outside of Eden, nature is "red in tooth and claw."

The later Hebrew creation story (6th century B.C.E.) is in Genesis 1:1-2:4a. This story is arranged in seven days of creation, and it involves procreation of both animals and

---

[4] Robert B. Lawton, "Genesis 2:24: Trite or Tragic?" *Journal of Biblical Literature,* 105/1 (1986): 97, noted a problem: "...for a patriarchal society like ancient Israel it would have been more appropriate to say that 'a wife leaves her father and mother and cleaves to her husband,' since the wife more obviously leaves her family than the man his." The setting, however, is not yet "a patriarchal society like ancient Israel. When the serpent, the tempter, appears, it speaks to the woman, and the woman speaks for herself and her man (Gn 3:1-6)." This is not patriarchy.

[5] The story in Genesis belongs to that category of creation story, found in various religions, that begins with a paradise, but something goes wrong and the end of the story explains why the real earth is like it is, fraught with decay and death. A similar creation story from a Pacific island tells about the creator god creating a man and a woman. This god offers them a stone. The couple replies that they don't want a stone; they want a banana. The god gives them a banana, but says, "If you had chosen the stone, you would live forever like the stone. Now, you will be like the banana and rot."

human beings. "On day five, God created the living creatures and blessed them and said, 'Be fruitful and multiply'" (Gn 1:22). On day six, God said, "'Let us make *'adam* in our image,' ... and God created *'adam* in his image, in the image of God he created him; male (*zakar*) and female (*neqebah*) he created them. God blessed them, and God said to them, 'Be fruitful and multiply.'" (Gn 1:27, 28).[6]

The Words "Marriage" and "to Marry" in the Hebrew Bible

The ancient Hebrew language did not have a word either for the verb "to marry" or the noun "marriage." These English words were derived from Latin, *maritare*, "to mate." Nevertheless, the widely used English translation, the *King James Version*, uses "to marry" and "marriage" twenty-five times in the Old Testament, translating ten different Hebrew words.

Thus in Deuteronomy 22:22 the *King James* translation is, "If a man be found lying with a woman married to an husband, then they shall both of them die." The Hebrew word *ba'al* usually denotes ownership. The Hebrew word *'ish* means man. Thus this verse could be translated, "If a man be found lying with a *woman* owned by a man, they shall both of them die."

In Numbers 12:1, the *King James* translation is, "And Miriam and Aaron spoke against Moses because of the Ethiopian woman whom he had married." The Hebrew word *laqach* means "to take." Literally the text says, "And Miriam and Aaron spoke against Moses because of the Ethiopian woman whom he had *taken*." In biblical Hebrew, men take and own women; this is patriarchy.

Hebrew Polygamy

Today and in English, the word "marriage" is sacrosanct for the majority of Americans who reserve this word for the union of one man and one woman. Among the ancient Hebrews, however, not only was there no such single word for "marriage" but also the union was typically between one man and more than one woman.

In an early, antediluvian genealogy from Cain to Lamech, the sixth in line, "Lamech took two women; the name of the one was Adah and the name of the other Zillah" (Gn 4:19). Later on, Abraham had two wives,[7] first Sarah (Gn 16:1), and then Keturah (Gn 25:1)[8]. Sarah was barren, but she offered her handmaid, Hagar, to Abraham, and Ishmael was born as the son of Abraham (Gn 16:15, 16). Miraculously—for Abraham and Sarah were quite old—Sarah gave birth to Isaac, the son of Abraham. Subsequently Keturah gave birth to six sons for Abraham (Gn 25:2). Here we have one man and three women who produced eight offspring. Esau, when he was forty, took Judith and Basemath (Gn

---

[6] Victor Paul Furnish noted that "man and woman" are social terms, while "male and female" are biological terms applied to procreation; "The Bible and Homosexuality," *Homosexuality in the Church,* Jeffrey S. Siker, ed. (Louisville, Kentucky: Westminster John Knox Press, 1994): 22.

[7] *'issah* generally means "woman," but in this context, the Hebrew word may be translated "wife," which distinguishes Sarah and Keturah (Abraham's wives) from Hagar, who was Sarah's "handmaid" and Abraham's "concubine."

[8] Victor P. Hamilton, "Marriage (OT and ANE)," in *The Anchor Bible Dictionary*, David Noel Freedman, ed., 4 (1992): 565, mistakenly identified Keturah as a "concubine."

26:34). Later he took Mahalath (Gn 28:9). Still later he took Adah and Oholibamah. One man and five women produced an unknown number of offspring.[9]

One of the very important stories for Israelites begins in Genesis 29, when Jacob goes to visit Laban, a kinsman, and meets Laban's two daughters, Leah and Rachel. Jacob saw Rachel, the younger of Laban's daughters, first, and he loved her. Asking permission of Laban to take her, Jacob offered to work for Rachel's father for seven years (Gn 29:16-18). After this time of indenture, Jacob said to Laban, "Give me my woman that I may go in to her, for my time is completed." On the wedding night, Laban tricked Jacob by substituting Leah, Laban's older daughter, for Rachel; in the darkness of the evening, Jacob went in to Leah, not to Rachel. When morning came, Jacob saw that the woman he had slept with was not Rachel, whom he loved; "Behold, it was Leah!" (Gn 29:19-24). Jacob would eventually take Rachel, but he had to work for Laban another seven years (Gn 29:25-30). As it turned out, Leah bore six of the sons of Jacob, while Rachel bore only two sons. While only Rachel was said to be the one whom Jacob "loved," in the family history, Leah's procreation proved to be more important.

The culmination of the Jacob saga is given in Genesis 35:22b-26. "Now the sons of Jacob were twelve. The sons of Leah: Reuben, Jacob's first born, Simeon, Levi, Judah, Issachar, and Zebulon. The sons of Rachel: Joseph and Benjamin. The sons of Bilhah, Rachel's maid: Dan and Naphtali. The sons of Zilpah, Leah's maid: Gad and Asher." This is what we call "polygyny," one man and two or more women, in this case the four mothers. Jacob received a new name, "Israel." These twelve sons of Leah, Rachel, Bilhah, and Zilpah would become the progenitors of the twelve tribes of Israel.

The tradition of polygyny among Hebrew patriarchs (Isaac and Rebekah being the sole exception were a monogamous pair) continued among the so-called "Judges" of Israel. "Now Gideon had seventy sons, his own offspring, for he had many wives. His concubine who was in Shechem also bore him a son, and he named him Abimelech" (Jg 8:30, 31). Elkanah had two wives, Hannah and Peninnah. Peninnah had children, but Hannah had no children (1 Sm 1:1, 2). Later, after earnest prayer, Hannah conceived and bore a son, Samuel (1 Sm 1:20).

Likewise among the kings of Israel, the tradition was one man with many wives. David's first wife was Michal, the daughter of King Saul (1 Sm 18:27). Michal was later given to Palti, son of Laish (1 Sm 25:44). David took Abigail, a widow, to be his wife, as he also did Ahinoam (1 Sm 25:42-44).[10] In Hebron Ahinoam gave birth to David's first-born, Ammon. Among some of David's other wives, Abigail gave birth to Chileab, Maach gave birth to Absolom, Haggith gave birth to Adonijah, Abitel gave birth to Shephatiah, and Eglah gave birth to Ithream, the sixth son (2 Sm 3:2-5). In Jerusalem, David's new capital, the king "took more concubines and wives; and more sons and daughters were born to David." No names of the women are given, but the names of the eleven sons are given, including that of Solomon (2 Sm 5:13-16; cf. 1 Ch 1-9).

Bathsheba, David's most famous wife, was the one he stole. "And it came to pass in an evening tide that David arose from off his bed, and walked upon the roof of the king's house: and from the roof he saw a woman washing herself; and the woman was very

---

[9] *Loc. cit.*, Hamilton stated incorrectly that Esau had "three wives."

[10] See P. Kyle McCarter, Jr., *I Samuel* in *The Anchor Bible* 8 (New York: Doubleday, 1980): 400.

beautiful to look upon" (2 Sm 11:2 KJV). David found out that the woman was Bathsheba, the wife of Uriah, the Hittite. That Bathsheba was already married did not deter David, for he sent his messengers to bring the beautiful woman to him, and Bathsheba came to David and he lay with her. The purpose of this tryst was not procreation: David had seen her beauty and desired her. Nevertheless, Bathsheba became pregnant, and she told David, "I am with child" (2 Sm 11:5).

David tried to cover up his adultery by recalling Uriah from the battlefield, but Uriah refused to sleep in his house with his wife because continence was the rule for soldiers on duty in a war. Had David been successful it getting Uriah to sleep with Bathsheba, others might have assumed that Uriah was the father of the child that Bathsheba was carrying. David then sent Uriah back to the battlefield, to the front of the battle, where he was killed.

After the death of Uriah, David took the widow Bathsheba to be his wife and she bore him a son (2 Sm 11:26, 27), but the child died (2 Sm 12:18). David consoled Bathsheba and went in to her and lay with her, and she bore a son, and he named him Solomon (2 Sm 12:24). According to scripture, Solomon had 700 wives, including many foreigners, and 300 concubines (1 Ks 11:3). The only woman whose name is given was Naamah the Ammonite who bore Solomon's son, Rehoboam, the successor (1 Ks 14:31).[11]

Rehoboam, king of the southern country of Judah, "took eighteen wives and sixty concubines, and became the father of twenty-eight sons and sixty daughters" (2 Ch 11:21). His first wife was Mahalath who bore three sons. Maacah bore him four sons. Rehoboam loved Maacah, daughter of Absalom, more than all his other wives and concubines (2 Ch 11:18-21).

One other passage, Deuteronomy 21:15-17, refers to multiple wives. "If a man has two wives, the one loved and the other hated, and they have borne him children, both the loved and the hated, and if the first-born son is hers that is hated, then on the day when he assigns his possessions as an inheritance to his sons, he may not treat the son of the loved as the first-born in preference to the son of the hated, who is the first-born, but he shall acknowledge the first-born, the son of the hated, by giving him a double portion of all that he has, for he is the first issue of his strength; the right of the first-born is his." As in the story about Jacob who loved Rachel, it was Leah who bore Reuben, the first-born of Jacob. But that is not the point in the context of discussing polygyny. The point here is that the practice of polygyny continued among the Hebrews at least as late as the seventh century B.C.E.

During the period from the antediluvian Lamech to the division of Israel into two states, one in the north and one in the south (the time of Rehoboam), the tradition of polygyny was "normal" to the people of that time: one man and two or more women was more the rule than the exception, at least for the famous whose stories came to be told. But traditions change and some are eventually phased out.

David and Jonathan

The relationship between David and Jonathan, son of King Saul, is—at the least—touching. It is a love story about two young men, but it is also a tragedy because of King

---

[11] See Tomoo Ishida, "Solomon," *The Anchor Bible Dictionary* 6 (1992): 105.

Saul's growing hatred for David. Saul's fear of David placed Jonathan in a difficult situation, caught between his love for David and his fealty to his father, the king.

Almost all English translations begin the story thus: "The *soul* of Jonathan was knit to the *soul* of David, and Jonathan loved him as his own *soul*" (1 Sm. 18:1, NRSV). The problematic word here is "soul." The first definition usually given today is this: "The animating and vital principle in humans, credited with the faculties of thought, action, and emotion and often conceived as an immaterial entity."[12] This definition of "soul" goes back to the body/soul dualism perpetuated in the philosophy of Plato and first appearing in his dialogue, *The Phaedo*. Plato wrote: "The soul *(psyché)* is most like that which is divine, immortal, intelligible, uniform, indissoluble, and ever self-consistent and invariable, whereas body is most like that which is human, mortal, multiform, unintelligible, dissoluble, and never self-consistent."[13]

By contrast, the Hebrew word for "soul" in the David-and-Jonathan story is *nephesh,* "a living person," the same word used in the older creation story where Yahweh creates *'adam,* the earthling from the earth *('adamah)* and breathes into the earthling the breath of life. Whereas Plato's "soul" has no beginning or end (truly immortal and immaterial), the *nephesh* does not exist without breath, not before birth and not after death. The Hebrew text in question is holistic, not dualistic, and refers to the breathing person (or animal):

> The breathing person of Jonathan was knit to the breathing person of David, and Jonathan loved him as his own breathing person.... Then Jonathan made a covenant *(berith)* with David, because he loved him as his own breathing person. Jonathan stripped himself of the robe that he was wearing, and gave it to David, and his armor, and even his sword and his bow and his belt. (1 Sm 18:2, 4)

The use of the word "covenant" is noteworthy since it usually implies oaths and rituals of mutual commitment, in this case, Jonathan's gifts to David.[14] Hebrew did not have a word for "marriage," as noted above, but David and Jonathan had entered a covenant relationship of mutual commitment and love.

At the end of 1 Samuel, the Philistines are victorious over Saul and his army: "Saul died, and his three sons, and his armor-bearer, and all his men, on the same day together" (1 Sm 31:6). At the beginning of 2 Samuel, David receives the message that Saul and Jonathan were dead. David rent his clothes and mourned and wept and fasted for Saul and Jonathan. He also delivered an elegy that ends with these words: "Jonathan lies slain upon your high places. I am distressed for you, my brother Jonathan; greatly beloved were you to me; your love to me was wonderful, passing the love of women" (2 Sm 25, 26 NRSV). The love of David and Jonathan was a love of "until death do us part."

---

[12] *The New Oxford American Dictionary*, Elizabeth J. Jewell and Frank Abate, eds. (Oxford University Press, 2001): *soul*: "[T]he spiritual or immaterial part of a human being or animal, regarded as immortal." Cf. *The American Heritage Dictionary of the English Language* (Houghton Mifflin Co. 4th edn., Boston, 2000).

[13] Plato, *The Phaedo* 80: A, B.

[14] See also 1 Sm 20:17: "And Jonathan made David swear again by his love for him as he loved his own breathing person."

The Traditions of the New Testament: The Apostle Paul and Marriage

The Apostle Paul himself was not married, and to the unmarried and the widowed, he gave advice to remain as they were (1 Cor 7:8). If they were Roman citizens,[15] they would be subject to the Augustan marriage law, the *Lex Julia de maritandis ordinibus* of 18 B.C.E., and its revision of 9 C.E., the *Lex Papia Poppaea*. According to these laws, men should be married between the ages of 25 and 60, and women, from ages 20 to 50. P.A. Brunt noted that the practice of remaining unmarried and childless was too deeply rooted in Roman society for the Augustan legislation to be successful, but it was not repealed until the time of Constantine, more than 300 years later.[16]

What motivated Emperor Augustus was the increasing number of unmarried and childless citizens. Cassius Dio described the emperor's assembling the Equestrian class in the Forum, and dividing the unmarried from those who were married with children; the unmarried far outnumbered the married. Augustus was concerned for the future: The need for procreation was great, if Rome was indeed to be the Eternal City.[17]

What motivated Paul, however, to remain unmarried and to encourage others to do likewise, was his expectation that Jesus Christ would return (*parousia*) in Paul's own lifetime. In one of his first extant letters, 1 Thessalonians, written about twenty years after the death of Jesus, Paul dealt with the issue of those Christians who had died before the return of Jesus. Paul gives a "word of the Lord" that "we who are alive"—that included Paul—"who are left until the coming of the Lord, shall not precede those who have died. For the Lord himself will descend from heaven.... And the dead in Christ will rise first; then we who are alive, who are left, shall be caught up together with them..." (1Th 4:14-17). Under these circumstances, there was no need to marry and procreate. In another early letter, Galatians 3:27, 28, Paul made this statement:

> For as many of you as were baptized into Christ have put on Christ.
> There is *neither* Jew *nor* Greek;
> there is *neither* slave *nor* free;
> there is *no "male and female."*

Both the Jew/Greek and the slave/free pairings represent two different kinds of people, and Paul says that Christ has removed those differences with "neither/nor." But the last two, "male and female," in Greek, *arsen kai thelu*, appear in the Greek Septuagint in Genesis 1:27. As mentioned above, "male and female" are biological terms, whether in Hebrew or Greek, and are necessary to fulfill the command, "Be fruitful and multiply," that is, to procreate. But Paul wrote also that "in Christ," there is "NO male-and-female." In Christ, procreation is not necessary.

The Romans who chose not to marry, however, did not necessarily abstain from sexual pleasures. For one example, prostitution, which was legal and taxed, was widely available. The Greek word for prostitution was *porneia*, a male prostitute was a *pornos*,

---

[15] In *The Acts of the Apostles* (16:37-39; 22:25-29), Paul is said to have been a Roman citizen, but that may be a later apologetic interpretation.

[16] P. A. Brunt, "The Augustan Marriage Laws," *Italian Manpower: 225 B.C.- A.D. 14* (Oxford: The Clarendon Press, 1971): 560, 565. Cf. Roy Bowen Ward, "Musonius and Paul on Marriage," *New Testament Studies* 36/2 (1990): 281-289.

[17] Cassius Dio, *Roman History* 56:1-10.

and a female one was a *porné*. Paul used these words, but English translations are deceptive, using the vague word "immorality."[18] Paul opposed prostitution, but not on the basis one might think. Female prostitutes were considered to be the handmaidens of the goddess Aphrodite and also of the Nymphs and Pan and Priapus. They were involved in dancing and singing and offering sacrifices and libations.[19] But Paul was, above all, a monotheist. The key passage is in 1 Corinthians 6:13b-20:

> The body (*soma*) is not meant for prostitution (*porneia*), but for the Lord, and the Lord for the body. And God raised the Lord and will also raise us up by his power. Do you not know that your bodies are parts (*melos*) of Christ? Shall I therefore take the members of Christ and make them members of a prostitute (*porné*)? Never! Do you not know that he who unites (*kollao*) himself to a prostitute becomes one body? For it is written, "The two shall be one flesh (*sarks*)" [Gn 2:24b]. But he who is united to the Lord becomes one spirit (*pneuma*). Shun prostitution! Every other sin that a man commits is outside the body, but the one prostituting sins against his own body. Do you not know that your [plural] body is the temple of the Holy Spirit within you [plural] that you have from God? You are not your own. You were bought with a price. So glorify God in your [plural] body.

Paul was not condemning sensuous pleasure; rather, his text was written in opposition to Christians' uniting their bodies with handmaidens of Aphrodite.

In 1 Corinthians 7:1, Paul was replying to a letter from the church in Corinth concerning whether or not it is well for a man to touch a woman. Paul replied that because of the temptation to engage in prostitution, each man should have his own woman and each woman her own man.[20] Paul instructed a man to render due affection (*eunoia*) to his woman, and likewise the woman to her man. The woman has no authority over her own body, but the man does; likewise, the man has no authority over his own body, the woman does. The reciprocity between the woman and the man is noteworthy. Paul went on to say that they should not refuse one another, except for a fixed time, that they might devote themselves to prayer, but then come together again, lest Satan tempt themselves through their lack of self-control (*akrasia*).

We cannot tell from the text whether the man and the woman were married or not, and nothing is said about procreation; in Galatians 3:26, 27, noted above, Paul had written that "in Christ" there is "no male and female," that is, no procreation. Paul's advice seems to be about bodily intimacy between a man and a woman, which might have involved only hugging or kissing, but this intimacy could also have included intercourse. If so, oral contraceptives and oral abortifacients had been available for centuries.[21]

---

[18] Roy Bowen Ward, "Porneia and Paul," *Proceedings: Eastern Great Lakes Biblical Society and Midwestern Society of Biblical Literature* 6 (1986): 219-227.

[19] Alciphron, *Letters*, Book 4.

[20] In Greek, *aner* can mean either a "man" or a "husband," and *gyné* can mean either a "woman" or a "wife."

[21] John M. Riddle, *Contraception and Abortion from the Ancient World to the Renaissance* (Cambridge: Harvard University Press, 1992): 5, "There is little if any evidence for usage of a condom or sheath during antiquity to prevent conception." Oral prophylactics were taken, and they worked.

Paul was far more interested in the coming of Jesus—in Paul's opinion, soon!—than he was in either sexual relations of any kind[22] or having children. In 1 Corinthians 7:25-31, Paul wrote:

> Now concerning the unmarried (*parthenoi*), I have no command of the Lord, but I give my opinion as one who by the Lord's mercy is trustworthy. I think that in view of the *impending distress* it is well for a person to remain as he/she is. Are you bound to a woman? Do not seek to be free. Are you free from a woman? Do not seek women. If you should marry (*gameo*), you do not sin, and if an unmarried girl (*parthenos*) marries, she does not sin. Yet those persons will have worldly problems, and I would spare you that. I mean, brothers and sisters, *the appointed time has grown very short;* from now on let those who have women live as though they have not, and those who mourn as though they were not mourning, and those who rejoice as though they were not rejoicing, and those who buy as though they had no goods, and those who deal with the world as though they had no dealings with it. *For the form of this world is passing away.*

The Gospels and Marriage

All four of the canonical Gospels end with the death and resurrection of Jesus, and three of the Gospels (Mt 24, Mk 13, Lk 21) predict the coming of the resurrected Jesus in the future. In these respects, the Gospels and Paul share the same world view. This eschatological world-view has implications for marriage and the family.

In Luke 14:26 Jesus preached: "If any one comes to me and does not hate (*miseo*) his own father and mother and children and brothers and sisters, yes, and even his own life, he cannot be my disciple." There is no question that *miseo* means any other than "hate."[23] The parallel in Matthew 10:37 has a different tone: "He who loves father or mother more than me is not worthy of me, and he who loves son or daughter more than me is not worthy of me." In Mark 3:31-35, the text says:

> And his mother and his brothers came, and standing outside they sent to him and called him. And a crowd was sitting about him; and they said to him, "Your mother and your brothers are outside, asking for you." And he replied, "Who are my mother and my brothers?" And looking around on those who sat about him, he said, "Here are my mother and my brothers! Whoever does the will of God is my brother, and sister, and mother."

The parallel passages in Matthew 12:46-50 and Luke 8:19-21 are basically the same. Kinship is redefined in terms of a voluntary relationship among those who do the will of God, not in terms of marriage, procreation, and family. Similarly, Luke 11:27-28 reads: "[A] woman in the crowd raised her voice and said to him, 'Blessed is the womb that bore you, and the breasts that you sucked!' But he said, 'Blessed, rather, are those who hear the word of God and keep it!'" And in Luke 23:29, Jesus' saying on the road to

---

[22] The meaning of Paul's advice in 1 Cor 7:9, that "it is better to marry than to burn," is unclear: One cannot tell what "burn" meant in that context: Was Paul trying to regulate the fires of the libido or save souls from Hell or something else?

[23] *The Living New Testament* mistakenly translates *miseo*: "Anyone who wants to be My follower must love Me far more than he does his own father, mother, …"

Golgotha is similar: "For behold, days are coming when they will say, 'Blessed are the barren, and the wombs that never bore, and the breasts that never gave suck.'"

In Mark 12:18-27, the Sadducees, who did not believe in a general resurrection, posed a question based on the levirate marriage law (Dt 25:5-10) that stipulates as follows:

"If brothers dwell together, and one of them dies and has no son, the wife of the dead shall not be married outside the family to a stranger; her husband's brother shall go in to her, and take her as his wife, and perform the duty of a husband's brother to her. And the first son whom she bears shall succeed to the name of his brother who is dead." The Sadducees said, "There were seven brothers; the first took a wife and when he died left no children; and the second took her, and died, leaving no children, and so on through all the brothers. Last of all, the woman also died. In the resurrection whose wife will she be? For the seven had her as wife."

The Sadducees hoped to convince others that there would be no resurrection, but, rather, when we all die, that is the end, period. But Jesus countered them, "For when they rise from the dead, they neither marry nor are given in marriage, but are like angels in heaven" (Mk 12:25). The parallel passage in Luke 20:34-36 expands; Jesus says, "The sons of this age marry and are given in marriage, but those who are accounted worthy to attain to that age and to the resurrection from the dead neither marry nor are given in marriage, for they cannot die any more, because they are equal to angels and are sons of God, being sons of the resurrection." Marriage, according to Jesus, is not eternal.

In the Roman Empire, divorce was easy to come by, whether initiated by the wife or the husband. In marriage, the woman was not under the power of her husband; they were legally independent. The Hebrew Bible allowed divorce. The rabbis of the first century allowed divorce, although for the school of Shammai only for adultery, but for the school of Hillel, for any cause. In the school of Jesus, however, divorce was forbidden (Mk 10:1-12, Lk16:18, Mt 5:31-32; 19:1-12). On the surface, this teaching appears to be pro-marriage with no way out, but Matthew 19:1-12 must be read carefully. Jesus' disciples reacted to the no-divorce teaching in Matthew 19:10: "If such is the case of a man with his wife, it is not expedient to marry." Who would marry if one could not get a divorce?[24] Jesus responded, "Not all men can accept this teaching. Some eunuchs have been so from birth, others have been made eunuchs by men, and others have made themselves eunuchs for the sake of the Kingdom of Heaven." Eunuchs were men who could not procreate[25] and, therefore, could not marry.

Same-Gender Sex in the Gospels and in Paul?

In the canonical Gospels, nothing is said on the subject of same-gender sex.

Under Roman law in the 1st century C.E., same-sex couples could not marry since the purpose of marriage was procreation, but same-sex persons could and did have sex

---

[24] In my university classroom, I often ask my students whether they would enroll in such a class if it were impossible to drop the course. Always they say, "No."

[25] Eunuchs could not procreate, but some could engage in penile/vaginal intercourse. Cf. Martial, *Epigrams*, Vl.67: "Do you ask, Pannychus, why your Caelia consorts with eunuchs only? Caelia wants to be fucked, not to procreate."

with each other; it was not illegal. In light of this practice, the text in Luke 17:30 is curious. Jesus was speaking of the day of the coming appearance of the Son of Man. In verse 34, Jesus went on to say, "In that night there shall be two men on one bed, the one man shall be taken and the other man left."[26] I know of no way to determine what these two men in one bed were doing.

The Apostle Paul, on the other hand, appears to have condemned same-gender sex between two men in 1 Corinthians 6:9, at least in the English translations of that verse. One must look at the context—in this case, 1 Corinthians 5:1 to 6:20. The dominant words in these two chapters are *porneia* (prostitution) or *pornoi* (prostitutes). At the beginning of the passage (1 Cor 5:1), Paul wrote that he had received a report of a case of prostitution (*porneia*) within the church at Corinth, for a man was living with his father's woman. Paul tells the Corinthians that this man must be removed from the congregation. In this letter, as elsewhere in his other epistles, Paul used a common rhetorical device, namely, lists of vices. The first list (1 Cor 5:9-11) names four vices: prostitutes *(pornoi),* greedy ones, robbers, and idolaters; the second list (1 Cor 5:11) repeats the four vices and adds two more: vilifiers and drunkards; the third list (1 Cor 6:9-10) adds four more vices: adulterers, thieves, and two others: *malakoi* and *arsenokoitai.* The meaning of these two Greek words is currently under debate. In all three vice lists, the word *pornoi* is at the top of the list.[27]

English translations available today are problematic in several ways. Although two separate words (*malakoi* and *arsenokoitai*) appear in the text, some translators collapse the two into a single word or a noun with an adjective. *The New American Bible* has "sodomites;" the original *Revised Standard Version* has "homosexuals;" and *The Living New Testament* has "homosexuals." *Today's English Version* has "homosexual perverts," and *The New English Bible* has "homosexual perversion." The *King James Version* reflects that two separate words appear in Greek, and translates "effeminates *and* abusers of themselves with mankind"; *The Jerusalem Bible* (catamites *and* sodomites), and the *New Revised Standard Version* (male prostitutes *and* sodomites).

And there are other problems. *The New American Bible* and the *New Revised Standard* translate *arsenokoitai* as "sodomites," but the words "sodomy" and "sodomites" did not exist before the 11th century C.E. when Peter Damian (ca. 1007-1072) invented the Latin word *sodomia.*[28] Likewise the word "homosexual" did not exist before 6 May, 1868, when Karl Maria Kertbeny wrote a letter to fellow sexologist, Karl Heinrich Ulrichs. A made-up label, "homo-" (Greek) was prefixed to "sexualis" (Latin) to achieve the effect.[29] Paul,

---

[26] *The Living New Testament* speaks of the two men as "in the same room," but the Greek clearly reads "bed" (*klinē*), not "room." Another mistranslation translation, in *God's Word to the Nations,* speaks of "two people," but the Greek clearly says "two men."

[27] The topic of prostitution continues in 1 Cor 6:13-20, and is discussed above.

[28] Mark D. Jordan, *The Invention of Sodomy in Christian Theology* (Chicago: University of Chicago Press, 1997).

[29] Kertbeny, in his 1868 letter, also invented the word "heterosexual." *Hetero-* is Greek and means "other, different, or strange." As Kertbeny used it, "heterosexual" referred to a person who had an "unfettered capacity for degeneracy," one who had a stronger sexual drive, and thus would be apt to assault males or females, members of his own family (incest) or animals. It was not until the 1930s that "heterosexual" shifted to the meaning it has in 2005.

who wrote in 1st-century Greek, could not have known either of these terms. At least in terms of language, the Apostle did not have in mind what is now meant either by "homosexuality" or "sodomy."

Paul did know and use the word *malakos,* an adjective meaning "soft," a word often used to describe something to be touched, such as a soft pillow, and also to describe soft words, gently spoken. These examples are of a positive use, but Paul was writing a list of vices, and those who are guilty of these vices, he exhorted, "will not inherit the kingdom of God" (1 Cor 6: 9a). The negative use of *malakos* often meant faint-hearted, lacking in self-control, weak, or morally weak.[30] Neither a necessary nor an apparent link connected *malakos* with same-gender sexual behavior.[31]

The meaning of the word *arsenokoitai* is problematic partly because it is a compound word. *arseno-* means "male" and *koit-* means "bed." The plural ending *–ai* is the same for both genders, masculine or feminine. *arsenokoitai* could, therefore, mean either "men who bed women" or "men who are bedded" (whether by women or other men). Boswell used as a parallel the English compound "a lady killer," which can mean either "a lady who kills" or "someone who kills ladies."[32] No evidence in Greek literature suggests that *arsenokoitai* had anything to do with prostitution. Paul's vice list begins with *porneia,* the word for "prostitution," so *arsenokoitai* probably referred to something else.

A further difficulty with *arsenokoitai* is that no example is extant of its use before it appeared in Paul's vice list. To establish the meaning of any word, we need to see it in it linguistic context, in its grammatical setting within a sentence. For example, what does the English word "lead" mean? Does it refer to a heavy bluish metal, or does it mean to "go ahead" or "show the way?" Without a sentence, a context, we cannot know. Boswell noted that the word *arsenokoitai* "appeared very infrequently after [Paul],"[33] and where the word did appear in the centuries following Paul, the meanings differed. For example, Eusebius of Caesarea (d. 339) understood *arsenokoitai* to apply to prostitution of men directed towards women rather than to other men.[34] We may never know precisely what *arsenokoitai* meant.

Romans 1:26-27 is a passage in which Paul evidently wrote about same-sex acts, but reading carefully in context, we find that the Apostle left his own opinion unstated. Calvin L. Porter has argued, "Rom[ans] 1:18-32 is a self-contained discourse similar to that used in Hellenistic Judaism in order to establish and strengthen a well-defined boundary and distance between the Jewish community and the Gentiles…. [T]he ideas in

---

[30] H. G. Liddell and R. Scott, comp., H. S. Jones and R. McKenzie, rev., *A Greek—English Lexicon* (Oxford: The Clarendon Press, 1940): 1,076, 1,077.

[31] John Boswell, *Christianity, Social Tolerance and Homosexuality* (Chicago: The University of Chicago Press, 1980): 340, closed his study of the use of *malakos* with these words: "So many people are denigrated as *malakoi* in ancient literature, for so many reasons, that the burden of proof in this case must be on those who wish to *create* a link with gay people. In the absence of such proof, the soundest inference is that *malakos* refers to general moral weakness, with no specific connection to homosexuality."

[32] *Idem*: 342.

[33] *Idem*: 341.

[34] *Idem*: 351

Rom. 1:18-32 are not Paul's. They are ideas which obstruct Paul's Gentile mission."[35] The imaginary speaker, a straw man, rhetorically speaking, warns of the wrath of God against those gentiles who worship idols. The imaginary speaker offers no hope for the gentiles; they "deserve to die" (Rom. 1:32). But this does not sound like Paul. Paul's apostolic mission was addressed to the gentiles,[36] and he had been successful in converting gentiles and in founding Christian churches in Corinth, Ephesus, Galatia, Philippi, and Thessalonica.

This diatribe against the gentiles sounds not like Paul but like the argument of the Hellenistic Jew, Philo of Alexandria, a contemporary of the Apostle Paul.[37] Philo, in his *The Special Laws*, Book 3: 37-38, wrote, "The transformation of the male 'nature' to that of the female 'nature' is practiced by them [gentiles] as an art without blushing. These persons are rightly judged worthy of death." Paul's imaginary critic speaks as follows in Romans 1:26-27:

> God gave them up to disgraceful passions. For their females exchanged the natural (*physiké*) use for that which is contrary to nature (*para physin*). And likewise the males, leaving the natural (*physiké*) use of the females, were burned up in their desire for one another, males working shame with males and receiving punishment among themselves which their deceit demanded.

The language used here is similar to that of Philo. Although he was a Jew, Philo did not read Hebrew, a language that had neither a word for "nature" nor for "unnatural." Philo was dependent on the Greek philosopher, Plato, who had maintained that sexual activity should be engaged in exclusively for the purpose of procreation.[38] For both Plato and Philo, procreation was "according to nature" (*kata physin*), and any other sexual act involving sensual pleasure (*hedoné*) was "contrary to nature" (*para physin*) and deserved "punishment."

But Paul was neither a Platonist nor a follower of Philo. Paul believed that Jesus would return in Paul's own lifetime, and thus marriage and procreation were no longer necessary, as we have noted above. Paul never mentioned *hedoné* in his letters, but he did not debunk sexual mutuality; rather, as we have also noted above, Paul did acknowledge the use of sexual affection, and he affirmed a certain belonging of the man's body to the woman, and of the woman's body to the man; he also thought of appropriate sexuality as a means of avoiding temptation.

Paul used the word *physis* several times in his letters. In 1 Corinthians11:13-15, Paul wrote: "Is it proper for a woman to pray to God with head uncovered? Does not nature (*physis*) itself teach you that for a man to wear long hair is degrading to him, but if a woman has long hair, it is her pride? For her hair is given to her for a covering." In this context, "nature" is a social construct in the Roman world at that time, for "nature" has taught the opposite to other people in other times and places.

---

[35] Calvin L. Porter, "Romans 1:18-32: Its Role in the Developing Argument," *New Testament Studies* 40/2 (1994): 215.

[36] Rm 15:16-20; the Apostle Peter's mission was to the Jews (Gal 2:7).

[37] Roy Bowen Ward, "Why Unnatural? The Tradition behind Romans 1:26-27," *Harvard Theological Review* 90/3 (1997): 263-84.

[38] Plato, *The Law* 636B – 636C, 841B – 841E; see Ward (1997): 264-269.

In Romans 11:17-24, Paul used the olive tree as an example of the destiny of the Jews and gentiles. At the time Paul wrote, his mission to the gentiles was successful, but the mission of Peter and others to the Jews was less so. The roots and trunk of the olive tree, said Paul, represent the Jews. In Romans 11:24, Paul wrote: "For if you have been cut from what is by nature *(kata physin)* a wild olive tree, and grafted, contrary to nature *(para physin)*, into a cultivated olive tree, how much more easily will these natural *(kata physin)* branches be grafted back into their own olive tree."

Paul also used the phrases "according to nature" and "contrary to nature" in other ways, but all of Paul's usage of these phrases is far from what the imaginary speaker in Romans 1:18-32 said. That speaker ends his rhetorical diatribe against the sinners in severe judgment: "Those who behave like this, and worse, who encourage others to behave in the same way, deserve to die." Paul, on the other hand, was for life based on the gospel, "the power of God for salvation to every one who has faith, to the Jew first and also to the Greek" (Rm. 1:16).

The Traditions of the Post-biblical Christians: 2nd to 5th Centuries

The Apostle Paul counted himself to be among those who would be alive when Jesus came again (1 Th 4:17), but time passes. The author of 2 Peter responded to the new situation:

> But do not ignore this one fact, beloved, that with the Lord one day is like a thousand years, and a thousand years are like one day. The Lord is not slow about his promise, as some think of slowness, but is patient with you, not wanting any to perish, but all to come to repentance. But the day of the Lord will come like a thief, and then the heavens will pass away with a loud noise and the elements will be dissolved with fire, and the earth and everything that is done on it will be disclosed. (2 Pt 3:8-10)

The apocalypse will come, the writer affirmed, but he pushed it into an indefinite future. The Gospels and Paul had not encouraged marriage, as noted above, but as time went by, procreation was still needed. Clement of Alexandria *(c.* 150 - *c.* 215 C.E.), for example, wrote: "The purpose [of marriage] is good breeding of children *(euteknia).*" Clement believed—erroneously—that Moses had instructed the philosopher Plato, whom Clement quoted, as follows: "Do not inseminate rocks and stones, since a fruitful nature is not obtainable from their roots,"[39] and then went on to say: "Sow not where you do not desire to reap, nor touch anyone at all besides your own wife, with whom alone it is licit for you to enjoy the pleasures of the flesh for legitimate succession."[40] Here, Clement followed Plato who had believed that mutual orgasms of both wife and husband were necessary to procreate.[41]

---

[39] Plato, *The Laws* 839A.

[40] Clement of Alexandria, *Paedagogus* 11:10.

[41] Plato, *The Timaeus* 91A-91 D. Long before Plato, Greek physicians believed that mutual orgasm was necessary to procreate. This medical tradition continued down to the 18th century. See Thomas Laqueur, *Making Sex: Body and Gender from the Greeks to Freud* (Cambridge: Harvard University Press, 1990).

At about the same time, Tertullian of Carthage went further in his argument. In *An Exhortation to Chastity* (c. 210 C.E.), Tertullian taught three degrees of virginity. The first degree is that of life-long virgins (either male or female), from the time of birth; the second degree is from the time of one's second birth, that is, baptism; the third degree of virginity is that of monogamy; that is, after the death of one's spouse, Tertullian exhorted Christians, "Do not re-wed!" Tertullian was against marriage, and he argued that it is nothing but a kind of *stuprum* (Latin for illicit sexual intercourse in any form, whether forced or voluntary): "For what is it that all men and women do in both marriage and *stuprum*? Fleshly coitus, obviously, and the eager desire for this the Lord made equal to *stuprum*." [42]

Augustine of Hippo not only was influenced by both the teaching of Clement and Tertullian but also he perpetuated the ideas of Plato. Writing ca. 420 C.E., Augustine repeated the Platonic-Christian tradition: "The natural good of marriage is thus sexual intercourse between male and female for the sake of procreation. But a person uses this good of marriage badly if he uses it bestially, so that his purpose is in the pleasure of lust rather than in the desire for offspring." [43] Augustine's teaching was similar to Clement's, but the influence of thinking like Tertullian's had caused Augustine no longer to allow a couple the enjoyment of the "pleasures in the flesh" along with their procreating. "It is one thing to have sexual intercourse only from the desire to bring forth children, which is not sinful," but, Augustine wrote, "it is something else to long for the pleasure of carnal intercourse which entails venial sin, even when the act is done with no one but the spouse." Augustine emphasized his point, saying: "Those who take contraceptive measures, even if they are called spouses, are not; they retain nothing whatever of true marriage, but make the honored name a cover for shamefulness." [44]

Earlier, Augustine had described himself as being "at odds with himself." He went on to say, "I felt that I was still the captive of my sins, and in my misery I kept crying, 'How long shall I go on saying "Tomorrow, tomorrow"'?" All at once, he heard the sing-song chant of a child in the street, repeating the refrain of a game: "Take it and read, take it and read!" Interpreting the voice to be a divine command, Augustine took up his book of Paul's letters lying near him, and opening it, he read the first passage he saw: "Not in reveling and drunkenness, not in lust and wantonness, not in quarrels and rivalries. Rather, arm yourselves with the Lord Jesus Christ; spend no more thought on nature and nature's appetites." (Rm. 13:14) Augustine added, "I had no wish to read more and no need to do so." He went to his mother, Monica, and said, "I no longer desire a wife or place any hope in this world." [45] Augustine thereafter remained celibate till his death. Not all priests were celibate in Augustine's time, but eventually celibacy became the rule for priests, and only laypersons married and procreated.

The traditions of marriage, we can see in the various biblical sources and during the centuries of Early Christianity, were different and varied. The Hebrews read the command to the first man and woman, "Be fruitful and multiply!" and understood that

---

[42] Tertullian, *An Exhortation to Chastity* 9.

[43] Augustine, *On Marriage and Concupiscence* 1:4:5.

[44] *Ibid.*: 1:15:17.

[45] Augustine, *Confessions* 8:10, 12.

they had divine approval to procreate, and the patriarchs knew that multiple wives facilitated keeping the original commandment. In the opposite direction, the apocalyptic eschatology found in Paul and the Gospels made marriage for procreation no longer necessary. Once expectation of the immediate return of the risen Jesus had relaxed, Clement defined marriage as being for procreation, and allowed sexual pleasure for the spouses. Tertullian, a Roman lawyer, held to biblically apocalyptic morality in a legalistic way, keeping the command but without an expectation of the soon-returning Jesus; Tertullian opposed marriage and favored virginity for both men and women. Once the Platonic philosophical dualism of body and soul had seeped thoroughly into the church, Augustine took a vow of celibacy according to his understanding of sexual self-denial as a life-long commitment to Christ. From Genesis until now, one thing is clear: "Traditional marriage" is a concept with a variety of meanings.

Postscript: Gay Marriages?

We no longer live in Bible times or in the Ancient Church. Here, in the United States, and now, in 2005, the question of gay marriages has become a legal and political issue. Do we have a new tradition of marriage emerging?

Had the Founders of the United States been completely logically consistent in their advocacy of the separation of church and state (prohibiting the establishment of religion and interference with the free exercise thereof), marriage would never have been part of the legal code except as recognition of a contractual civil union, to be regulated and enforced as any other contractual obligation. That is, the religious nature of the rite of marriage would have been left to the churches, synagogues, and other religious institutions as a matter of free exercise, and the state would have had an interest only in the civil, contractual matters of property ownership, debt liability, inheritance, reciprocal responsibilities, and the like.

In fact, neither the authors of the Constitution nor members of the early Congress had to consider this question because separation of church and state applied only to national legislation, and the national government's sphere of responsibility as outlined in Article 1 of the Constitution did not include authority to legislate in the realm of domestic relations, an area of law reserved to the States. The doctrine of the separation of church and state at the federal level was not applied to State governments until the mid-to-late 20th century, when the Supreme Court "incorporated" some of the rights from the Bill of Rights into the protections that citizens enjoy from State governments under the 14th Amendment. By this time, however, many religious tenets had been written into State legal codes, establishing aspects of religion, their provenance either largely forgotten or attributed to "the logical arrangement of human affairs" or "the way things have always been."[46]

By 1960, all of the 50 states had sodomy laws, and in most cases these laws cited actions, such as oral sex and anal sex, whether between heterosexuals (married or not) or homosexuals. In 1955, the American Law Institute had promulgated the *Model Penal Code*, which did not provide for "criminal penalties for consensual sexual relations conducted

---

[46] I am indebted to S. A. Kay, professor of Political Science at Miami University, for helping to draft these three paragraphs.

in private."[47] In 1961, the State of Illinois was the first to change its laws to conform to the *Model Penal Code*, and other States soon followed, especially in the 1970s. But in 1986, 24 States (mostly in the South) and the District of Columbia continued to outlaw sodomy.

Michael Hardwick, a gay bartender in Atlanta, brought a civil suit challenging Georgia's sodomy law. The case, *Bowers v. Hardwick 478 U.S. 558 (1986)*, eventually went to the U.S. Supreme Court, and the Court ruled, 5 to 4, that the U.S. Constitution does not guarantee a right to engage in homosexual sodomy; the Court expressed no opinion about the constitutionality of the Georgia statute as applied to acts of heterosexual sodomy. In 1998, the Georgia Supreme Court struck down Georgia's anti-sodomy law.

In 2003, the U.S. Supreme Court ruled, 6 to 3, in the case of *Lawrence v. Texas 539 U.S. 558 (2003)* — overruling *Bowers v. Hardwick* — that the remaining sodomy laws in 13 States were unconstitutional. Justice Anthony Kennedy, a Republican and a Roman Catholic, wrote the majority opinion, concluding with the following words:

> The case...involve[s] two adults who, with full and mutual consent from each other, engaged in sexual practices common to a homosexual lifestyle. The petitioners are entitled to respect for their private lives. The State cannot demean their existence or control their destiny by making their private sexual conduct a crime. Their right to liberty under the Due Process Clause [5th and 14th Amendments] gives them the full right to engage in their conduct without intervention of the government. "It is a promise of the Constitution that there is a realm of personal liberty which the government may not enter."[48] The Texas statute furthers no legitimate state interest that can justify its intrusion into the personal and private life of the individual.[49]

Sanford Levinson, the Garwood Regent Chair in Law, University of Texas at Austin, writing in 1992, referred to *Bowers v. Hardwick*. "Although *Bowers* concerned bedroom conduct, what was ultimately at stake in the case was the integration of gays and lesbians into all aspects of American public life. Thus, had the decision gone the other way, it might have been increasingly difficult to maintain the prohibition of gay and lesbian marriage."[50] But *Bowers v. Hardwick* has now been overruled. The time has come at the national level to open the legal doors to gays and lesbians, following the example of various individual States and other countries. Since gays and lesbians are allowed to enter legally binding contracts and obtain driver's licenses from the States, they should also be able to obtain wedding licenses and enter into marriage contracts, if they so choose. All Americans should have the same rights that all other Americans have, whether they be Whites, Blacks, or Latinos; males or females; heterosexuals or homosexuals.

Equal rights before the law should be no threat to "traditional" marriage as defined by religion. The First Amendment states, "Congress shall make no law respecting an establishment of religion, or prohibiting the free exercise thereof." We have had many

---

[47] Cited in *Lawrence v. Texas 539 U.S. 558 (2003)*.

[48] Citing *Planned Parenthood of Southeastern Pa. v. Casey 505 U.S. 833 (1992)*.

[49] *Lawrence vs. Texas, 2003*.

[50] Sanford Levinson, "Privacy," in *The Oxford Companion to the Supreme Court of the United States*, Kermit L. Hall, ed. (Oxford and New York: Oxford University Press, 1992: 675; 2nd edn., 2005): 782-783.

traditions in the history of Judaism and Christianity, some for the better, some for the worse, depending on one's point of view. Within the political state, however, we should all have equal rights, not special rights.

Justice Kennedy closed his opinion with wise words about the past and hopeful words for the future:

> Had those who drew and ratified the Due Process Clauses of the Fifth Amendment or the Fourteenth Amendment known the components of liberty in its manifold possibilities, they might have been more specific. They did not presume to have this insight. They knew times can blind us to certain truths, and later generations can see that laws once thought necessary and proper in fact serve only to oppress. As the Constitution endures, persons in every generation can invoke its principles in their own search for greater freedom.[51]

The same can be said about the right of gays and lesbians to marry.

---

[51] *Lawrence v. Texas*, 2003.

"Another Gospel," Then and Now

Thomas H. Olbricht

Don Haymes has many interests, so it seems appropriate to honor him with a multitasking essay in which I explore several of these. Don has been throughout his career a champion of Paul's gospel that we are justified not on the basis of any human merit but solely on the basis of faith in Jesus Christ, a gift to us from the grace of God. Don has equally proved himself to be a champion of the poor, of those who have been excluded on account of their race, and of gender equity at church. He is likewise a champion of rigorous historical-critical exegesis of the New Testament. All three of these concerns are at the heart of my chief intent in this essay, namely, to explicate what Paul meant by the "truth of the gospel" in Galatians. I want to do this exegetical and hermeneutical work in conversation with the homiletical tradition in use among Churches of Christ as applied to Paul's pronouncement of "anathema upon those who preach another gospel."

Questions of interpretation arise immediately: Is it appropriate to denounce any teaching or practice at all that a twenty-first-century person may view as "another gospel," even if it has no relationship to what Paul was anathematizing? Should one denounce only those deeds and words that are identical to the ones addressed by Paul? Is a third option, a middle way, open to us, namely to address issues that are parallel or similar to, or at least analogous to, Paul's concerns? In the last case, an exegetical effort must be exerted first to lay bare what Paul had in mind when he contrasted the "truth of the gospel" with the "other" gospel. The "truth of the gospel"—as Paul himself wrote—is that humans are accepted by God because of their faith in Jesus Christ (Gal 2:16), and neither through circumcision or the keeping of the feasts—nor by ethnic identity (Jew or gentile) or social status (slave or free) or gender (male or female) (Gal 3:28).

If we take the strictest possible constructionist approach, then we shall be limited primarily to two issues that no longer trouble most of us: Jewish law-keeping and the insistence that gentiles also keep the Law, and slavery. A parallel issue that does keep plaguing us has to do with relationships among persons of different races. If we take a loose-constructionist approach, then we can extend the meaning of the "false brother" to just about any "brother in error," and read "another gospel" as the preaching of just about any set of ideas, whether liberal or anti-liberal practices, or anything else we happen not to like. If we take the middle path, then we shall focus on issues that are at least similar to the ones that Paul confronted. Examples of these might be either the imposition of a new system of rules-keeping (not the Law of Moses) as a means of making us acceptable to God or the exclusion of any human being on the basis of their social class or color or race or gender.

We who teach and preach in the Churches of Christ do not have an official chain-reference Bible or a Code of Canon Law. If we did, one of our basic rules would be the oft-quoted Gal 1:8: "But even if we or an angel from heaven should proclaim to you a gospel contrary to what we proclaimed to you, let that one be accursed!" Our preachers quote that text so often that we would be wise to expend effort in identifying those false brothers and that false gospel, so as to be circumspect in applying Galatians, chapters 1 and 2, in denouncing apostasy. In our traditional eagerness to denounce certain beliefs and practices, however, we have seldom limited our definition of "false teachers" to either identical with or even similar to the "false brethren" whom Paul denounced in Galatia. This, in part, is because we have been little interested in defining what that "other gospel" was that Paul opposed among the Galatians. We have become accustomed to a loose construction of the passage and a broad application of it to just about anyone perceived as a religious adversary, for we have heard it applied liberally and generally to any teacher and any idea with which the preacher of the occasion seriously disagreed. We have watched missiles launched against various and sundry "apostates" with little regard for whom and what Paul historically had in mind.

This essay, announced as having to do with the "then and now" of this biblical text, requires a two-step procedure: First, a thorough exegesis is demanded to determine what Paul *meant* in his time and place; and then a hermeneutic exercise is required to determine whether what Paul *meant* there and then can and ought to *mean* the same or something similar for us here and now in our own time and place. I must, therefore, set forth the hermeneutical principles upon which I propose that we get from "then" to "now."

I begin with the following hermeneutical presuppositions: I believe that a responsible use of these texts demands that we employ them chiefly to reprove persons who have forsaken Paul's gospel of inclusion by way of the grace of God and faith in Jesus Christ, and that we anathematize anyone who contradicts that gospel by teaching a gospel of exclusion because of law-keeping, racism, classism, or genderism. Whether or not that shall prove to be "strict" or "loose" or some other construction, I do not know, but I sense that we shall have our hands full if we do nothing more than what Paul did. I also believe that application of these texts to any matter at all, and any person at all with whom we happen to disagree, is irresponsible. Our use of these texts should be to combat the same type of opponents that Paul combated so that the "truth of the gospel" may be upheld, namely, that "a person is justified by faith in Christ, not by doing the works of the law" (Gal 2:16). Who, then, were the "false brothers" (Gal 2:4), and what was that "other gospel" that was being taught (Gal 1:6).

Identity of the "False Brothers"
according to Traditional Preaching in Churches of Christ

In 1937, Foy E. Wallace, Jr.,[1] preached a series of sermons in Port Arthur, Texas, titled "The Certified Gospel," revised and published 30 years later as a book.[2] Wallace commenced the series by quoting Gal 1:11 (KJV): "But I certify you, brethren, that the gospel which was preached of me is not after man."[3] Wallace then proceeded to attack those who preached a "human" gospel. His first example was preachers "who pray for

---

[1] See Terry Gardner, "The Influence of Foy E. Wallace, Jr.," in this volume.

[2] I examined these sermons in a 1967 extended edition, Foy E. Wallace, Jr., *The Gospel for Today* (Nashville: Foy E. Wallace Jr., Publications, 1967).

[3] Wallace (1967): 1

God to send down the Holy Ghost saving power upon sinners"[4] Next, in a section titled "The Essential Elements," Wallace listed the first "element" as "The Being of God." Though Wallace said little about the being of God, he contended in considerable detail that evolutionists[5], skeptics, infidels, and atheists[6] have it all wrong. They, therefore, proclaim "another gospel." Certain twentieth-century religious organizations he also included among the "false gospels."

There are several hundred religious organizations in the world now that are called churches. A better designation for them would be fraternities for they bear little resemblance to the church revealed and described in the New Testament.[7]

Wallace presented another list of false proclamations, this one involving another "Gospel Plan of Salvation." "For years every union evangelist has had his patent method of conversion. Billy Sunday shouted 'hit the sawdust trail.' Gipsy Smith pleaded 'sign a decision card.'"[8] Later in the book, Wallace denounced Seventh-Day Adventism, the Jehovah's Witnesses, the Boll Millennial Movement, Premillennialism, Modernism, the Neo-orthodox movement, and the "perversions of the so-called New Versions of the Bible."[9] "False gospels," all.

I do not fault Wallace for attacking his perceived enemies (though his time might have been better spent preaching faith in Christ and the grace of God). I do fault his having made no effort to determine who the real enemies of Paul were in Galatians. It may well be that some of Wallace's enemies would have been Paul's enemies, too, but only after one has determined who the false brothers were in Galatians can one ascertain which modern opponents of the gospel are similar to the ones Paul denounced.

A second example, "Thoughts regarding Another Gospel," comes from a commentary on Galatians by Burton Coffman. In a concluding section on Galatians 1, he wrote:

Some advocate the gospel of salvation by morality, supposing that the only requirement for eternal life is to live respectably before one's contemporaries. Others advocate the gospel of an infallible church, whereas no church was ever infallible, not even any that were founded, or planted, by the apostles themselves, as detailed in the first chapters of Revelation. Still others preach the gospel of salvation by faith only, notwithstanding the fact that such a so-called gospel is anti-scriptural, delusive, deceitful and contrary to everything in the NT. The great fad of our own times is the gospel of humanism....[10]

Like Wallace, Coffman was less interested in "other gospels" from Paul's perspective than he was in those that Coffman himself perceived as "other." In traditional Church-of-Christ preaching, the "other gospel" *du jour* has typically been the hot issue of the day—from instrumental music to institutionalized cooperation among churches, from new translations of the Bible to the charismatic movement. Any brother with whom one

---

[4] *Ibid.*: 2.

[5] *Ibid.*: 7.

[6] *Ibid.*: 9.

[7] *Ibid.*: 28.

[8] *Ibid.*: 30.

[9] *Ibid.*: 235-236.

[10] James Burton Coffman, *Commentary on Galatians, Ephesians, Philippians, Colossians* (Austin: Firm Foundation, 1977).

substantially disagreed has been labeled a "false brother," and whatever heresy one thought he was spouting has been tagged "another gospel."

New Testament Evidence for the Identity of the "False Brothers"
in Jerusalem and the Galatian Opponents
according to Church-of-Christ and Other Commentators on Galatians

I have sampled the views of Church-of-Christ commentators on Galatiansby examining the works of David Lipscomb, B. W. Johnson, J. W. McGarvey, Robert Johnson, Burton Coffman, and George Howard.[11] I have also reviewed the opinions of several other commentators on Galatians.

All the Church-of-Christ commentators took for granted that Paul was the author of Galatians—likewise an uncontested consensus in contemporary scholarship.[12] Commentators in the Restoration Movement typically prefer the "south Galatian view" that the recipients of Paul's letter lived in the Roman province where the cities of Pisidian Antioch, Iconium, Lystra, and Derby were located.[13] All but Howard equated Gal 2:1-10 with the so-called Jerusalem conference of Acts 15. Most of the authors dated the writing to between 55 and 58 A. D., except for Coffman and Howard who dated it to 49-50 A. D.[14]

The south Galatian view runs counter to the current consensus among other scholars, except among conservative British and American scholars.[15] At the turn of the 20th century, the standard British view held by J. B. Lightfoot, James Moffatt, and the American George B. Stevens was the north Galatian view.[16] The south Galatian view was first seriously argued by Sir William Ramsay.[17] Most of those adhering to this view have been either British or persons who had studied in England. An exception is Herman N. Ridderbos of the Netherlands.[18] G. W. Hansen argued a fresh case for the south Galatian view.[19] Bruce

---

[11] David Lipscomb, *A Commentary on the New Testament Epistles, with additional notes by J. W. Shepherd,* 5 vols. (Nashville: Gospel Advocate Company, 1936); B. W. Johnson, *The People's New Testament* (Delight, Arkansas: Gospel Light Publishing Company, n.d.); J. W. McGarvey and Philip Y. Pendleton, *Thessalonians, Corinthians, Galatians and Romans* (Cincinnati: The Standard Publishing Company, 1919); Robert L. Johnson, *The Letter of Paul to the Galatians* (Austin: R. B. Sweet, 1969); Coffman (1977); George Howard, *Paul: Crisis in Galatia: A Study in Early Christian Theology,* 2nd ed. (Cambridge: Cambridge University Press, 1990).

[12] Hans Dieter Betz, "Galatians, The Epistle to the," *The Anchor Bible Dictionary,* David Noel Freedman, ed. (New York: Doubleday, 1992): 2: 872.

[13] Lipscomb (1936): 3: 181-183; B.W. Johnson (n.d.): 163, 164; McGarvey (1919): 245, 246; R. L. Johnson (1969): 7-29, Coffman (1977): 1-6; Howard (1990): ix.

[14] Commentators now propose earlier dates, even those who hold to the "northern" address of the letter. Richard B. Hays, "The Letter to the Galatians," *The New Interpreter's Bible* (Nashville: Abingdon Press, 2000): 193, noted that 50-51 A.D. is the recent date, though he himself offered a range from 50 to 56 A.D., holding an exact date to be difficult to pin down.

[15] Betz (1992): 2: 872-874.

[16] James D. G. Dunn, *The Epistle to the Galatians* (Peabody, Massachusetts: Hendrickson Publishing, 1993): 6, note 4.

[17] William Ramsay, *A Historical Commentary on St. Paul's Epistle to the Galatians* (London: Hodder, 1900).

[18] Herman N. Ridderbos, *The Epistle of Paul to the Churches of Galatia* (Grand Rapids: William B. Eerdmans, 1953): 30-31, "…the evidence…points to South rather than to North Galatia." More

wrote, "...the majority view is that the visit of Gal 2:1-10 is identical with that of Ac 15:2ff."[20]

Though writers in the Restoration Movement have endorsed the south Galatian hypothesis, they have favored a later date. James D. G. Dunn pointed out that "the south Galatian hypothesis, however, usually implies a much earlier date."[21] Our writers have also, with the exception of George Howard, identified Gal 2:1-10 with the Jerusalem conference of Ac 15. Bruce, by contrast, argued that the events of Gal 2:1-10 are to "...be identified with the visit of Ac 11:30," in which Paul and Barnabas traveled to Jerusalem with relief for the famine.[22] The view of Bruce is a minority view. If his hypothesis be accepted, then Galatians is the earliest of Paul's letters.[23] Regardless of what positions scholars occupy, we do not know enough about circumstances in either Jerusalem or Galatia between 46 and 55 C.E. to determine which time frame is more likely, though it is significant that Jewett and Lüdemann agree on 51 C.E.[24]

Who were the "false brothers?" At least we know they were located in Jerusalem. They tried, in Paul's words, to prevent "the truth of the Gospel." Who were the "spies" and what was the "spying" in which they engaged (Gal 2:4)? As to the occasion, Paul tells us that fourteen years after the trip to Jerusalem during which he met with Cephas and James, the Lord's brother (1:18-24), he returned once again with Barnabas and Titus (2:1). The "spying" was their manner of trying to enforce the keeping of the Law of Moses.

According to Ac 15:1, some members of the church in Jerusalem believed that adherents of the new "Way" were not saved unless they had been circumcised. The main concern of church leaders in Jerusalem when Peter returned from preaching to and baptizing the gentile household of Cornelius was that Peter had eaten with uncircumcised persons (Ac 11:3). We might assume that Peter's report of his vision approving table fellowship settled the matter, but such was not the case. In fact, some of those who believed that circumcision was necessary for salvation were likely among the visitors from the Jerusalem church who provoked Peter to cease table fellowship with the uncircumcised.[25]

---

recently Ben Witherington III, *Grace in Galatia: A Commentary on Paul's Letter to the Galatians* (Grand Rapids: Eerdmans, 1998): 8-20, dated the letter in 49 A.D. and therefore the earliest of Paul's letters (10-13).

[19] G. W. Hansen, "The Letter to the Galatians," in *Dictionary of Paul and His Letters: A Compendium of Contemporary Biblical Scholarship*, Gerald F. Hawthorne and Ralph P. Martin, eds. (Downers Grove: InterVarsity Press, 1993): 326.

[20] F. F. Bruce, *The Epistle to the Galatians, A Commentary on the Greek Text* (Grand Rapids: William B. Eerdmans, 1982): 108. See Hans Dieter Betz, *A Commentary on Paul's Letter to the Churches in Galatia* (Philadelphia: Fortress Press, 1979): 3-5.

[21] Dunn (1993): 8.

[22] F. F. Bruce (1982): 108, 109.

[23] See Karl P. Donfried, "Chronology," in Freedman (1992): 2: 1016; cf. Ernst Haenchen, *The Acts of the Apostles* (Philadelphia: Westminster Press, 1971): 65.

[24] Ridderbos (1953): 31. Both Robert Jewett and Gerd Lüdemann date the apostolic conference in 51 C. E., Robert Jewett, "Chronology, New Testament" in *Dictionary of Biblical Interpretation*, ed. John H. Hayes (Nashville: Abingdon Press, 1999): 1:197; Gerd Lüdemann, *Paul, Apostle to the Gentiles: Studies in Chronology*, F. Stanley Jones, trans. (Philadelphia: Fortress Press, 1984).

[25] So argued by Ernest DeWitt Burton, *A Critical and Exegetical Commentary on the Epistle to the Galatians* (Edinburgh: T. & T. Clark, 1921): 78, 79.

We might further assume that those who disapproved of Peter's vision would have been disciplined by the church, but that was not the case, either.

In Acts 15, certain persons in the Judean church, if not of numerical significance then at least with great boldness and conviction asserted, "Unless you are circumcised according to the custom of Moses, you cannot be saved" (Ac 15:1). These persons may or may not be the ones Paul mentioned in Gal 2:12, and described as "certain people [who] came from James." Are we to believe that James himself ordered the cessation of the table fellowship of Jewish and gentile Christians? It is not possible to determine from the texts. Even if those newly arrived from Jerusalem opposed the table fellowship, it is not necessarily the case that James himself charged them to do so. They could well have exceeded their commission. Some have affirmed that Peter's waffling on the matter of uncircumcised Christians may have resulted from reports of increased Jewish nationalism in Jerusalem which, in turn, inflamed the friction between Jews and Jewish Christians.[26] Jewish Christians who were openly eating with the uncircumcised in Antioch may have, as the result, become alarmed over the new developments and isolated themselves at meal times from the uncircumcised. Dunn wrote:

> Why "the false brothers" should raise the issue now, when mission work among the Gentiles had been having considerable success for years, is also unclear; but it may indicate both the increasing success of the mission in Judea and the increasing religio-political tensions in Palestine.[27]

The circumcision party within Early Christianity in Palestine, rather than decreasing over time, apparently increased. In Acts 21, the Jerusalem church leaders told Paul that there were "thousands of believers among the Jews, and they are all zealous for the law" (Ac 21:20).[28] In order to avoid a confrontation between Paul and this significant contingent, James and the Elders recommended that Paul undertake a standard cleansing ceremony in the Temple so as to establish his reputation as a Jew who still observed and guarded the Torah (Ac 21:24). Despite these precautions, Jews from Asia—not Jewish Christians, apparently—became aware of Paul's presence and charged that he taught "against our people, our law, and this place; more than that, he has actually brought Greeks into the Temple and has defiled this holy place" (Ac 21:28).[29] The result was that Paul might have faced certain death had not the Roman tribune come to his rescue.

We conclude therefore that either the visit in 46 A.D., when Paul came bearing gifts, or the visit of 48 A.D., when Paul went up to Jerusalem to settle the Antioch dispute, was adequate to stir up the circumcision party so much that they commissioned certain brothers to spy out the uncircumcised from among Paul's companions. Paul considered their spying despicable. Should Edgar Krentz be correct—and I have reservations about this—these false brothers are significant to our study since they are the same persons who

---

[26] See Josephus, *Wars of the Jews* 2:18, *Antiquities* 18:23. See Robert Jewett, "The Agitators and the Galatian Congregation," *New Testament Studies*, 17 (1970-71): 198-212.

[27] Dunn (1993): 98.

[28] Gerd Lüdemann, *Opposition to Paul in Jewish Christianity* (Minneapolis: Fortress Press, 1989): 55-63.

[29] Lloyd Gaston, *Paul and the Torah* (Vancouver: University of British Columbia Press, 1987): 24-33, made a good case that Paul was not guilty.

went to Galatia and disturbed the churches.[30] Paul argued against these Judaizers that believers are saved by faith in Christ, not by an exterior characteristic such as circumcision.

Proposals have been legion as to who these Judaizers in the Pauline churches were. Ferdinand Christian Baur in his famous book, *Paulus*, set the agenda in 1845 for understanding Paul's opponents.[31] He argued that two parties had opposed each other in the Early Church: Jewish Christianity, which differed from Judaism only in that it affirmed Jesus as Messiah, and Pauline or Hellenistic Christianity. Jewish Christianity, later known as the Ebionites, comprised Paul's Judaizing opponents in all his letters. Baur further argued that it was not only the false brothers who opposed Pauline Christianity but also the Jerusalem Apostles themselves.[32] They reluctantly approved Paul's mission to the gentiles, but they took no interest in restraining those who trailed Paul as far as Galatia, urging the practice of circumcision, feast-keeping, and (perhaps) the dietary laws of kosher, though the latter are not mentioned in Galatians.

Baur was opposed by J. B. Lightfoot in his 1865 commentary on Galatians. Lightfoot argued that Paul's relationship with James, Cephas, and John was one of mutual recognition. The Judaizers therefore were not supported by the Apostles.[33] Later, Johannes Munck argued that Paul and the church leaders in Jerusalem were at one in message but not in method. The leaders in Jerusalem believed that the Jews should be converted first and the gentiles would follow. Paul argued to the contrary that the gentiles should be converted first, whereupon the Jews would come to believe in Jesus as Messiah.[34] The Judaizers were therefore, according to Munck, gentiles rather than Jews. These Judaizing gentiles misunderstood Paul and were impressed with the Jewish religion of the Law of Moses. Walter Schmithals argued in 1956 that the opponents were Jewish or Jewish Christian Gnostics who had no connection with the Jerusalem Apostles.[35] He also argued that only non-Christian Jews in Jerusalem would have an interest in the Law; therefore, in his view the "false brothers" must have been non-Christian Jews who were appointed by the Jewish hierarchy to monitor the activities of the Jewish Christians.[36] The consensus of current scholarship sides with the view of Lightfoot that the "false brothers" were recruited by a right-wing party of Judaizing Jerusalem Christians, and that the Jerusalem Apostles were supportive of Paul's gentile mission.[37]

---

[30] Edgar Krentz, "Galatians," in *Galatians, Philippians, Philemon, I Thessalonians* (Minneapolis: Augsburg Publishing House, 1985): 35.

[31] F. C. Baur, *Paul the Apostle of Jesus Christ, His Life and Work, His Epistles and His Doctrine: A Contribution to a Critical History of Primitive Christianity*, 2 vols., E. Zeller, trans. (London: Williams and Norgate, 2nd ed., 1876).

[32] Horton Harris, *The Tübingen School: A Historical and Theological Investigation of the School of F. C. Baur* (Grand Rapids: Baker Book House, reprint, 1990).

[33] J. B. Lightfoot, *St Paul's Epistle to the Galatians* (London: Macmillan and Co., 1865).

[34] Johannes Munck, *Paul and the Salvation of Mankind*, F. Clark, trans. (Richmond: John Knox Press, 1959).

[35] Walter Schmithals, *Paul & the Gnostics*, J. E. Steely, trans. (Nashville: Abingdon Press, 1969).

[36] *Idem*: 14f.

[37] Luke Timothy Johnson, "Book of Luke-Acts," in Freedman (1992): 2: 415-417. To review current scholarship on this subject, see Mark D. Nanos, ed., *The Galatians Debate: Contemporary Issues in*

In the Church-of-Christ tradition, our commentators have had a reasonably clear vision of Paul's opponents, even though for the most part, our preachers have ignored these insights. David Lipscomb identified the false brothers as "Certain false brethren of the Judaizing party...."[38] He earlier wrote of "their assertion of the necessity of circumcision for Gentile Christians (Gal 5: 2, 11; 6:12) which involved as a necessary consequence the obligation of the whole law."[39] This point is supported from Ac 15:5. Paul did not claim that those mentioned in Galatians required keeping the whole Law of Moses, though he argued later that this was the logical outcome of their position even if they did not teach it: "Again I declare to every man who lets himself be circumcised that he is obligated to obey the whole Law" (Gal 5:3).[40] The general consensus now is that the demands of the opponents were limited to circumcision and the keeping of the feasts, not keeping the whole Torah.[41] Although Lipscomb also wrote of the circumcision party in Galatia, he did not set forth its origin, whether they came from Jerusalem or elsewhere. His assumption seems to be that Judaizers were everywhere among the churches, so some were probably from Jerusalem. Lipscomb alleged that the matter at stake was whether the Judaizers would "succeed in the Galatian churches despite their failure in the case of Titus."[42] They were either the same party or these same persons who had tried to force Titus's circumcision in Jerusalem but had been withstood by Paul.

B. W. Johnson thought that the false brothers were non-Christian Jews. "These false brothers were really Jews who had slipped into the church."[43] Johnson's view that they infiltrated the church runs counter to the statement that they were "brought in," unless they were assisted internally with their infiltration (Gal 2:4). At minimum, even if they were Jewish rather than Jewish Christian, they did the spying under Christian auspices. It seems unlikely to me that Jews who believed in Jesus as the Messiah would have had working relations of this sort with Jews who did not believe in Jesus.

J. W. McGarvey likewise argued that these false brothers were non-Christian Jews. They were: "...certain Jews, who were members of the church and yet not Christians at all, but had entered the church to further Jewish interests, and who were even then present in the council as spies of the Jews to spy out our liberty which we have in Christ, that they might bring the church of Christ back into the bondage of the law."[44] This point of view implies the hardly tenable position that Jewish Christians in Jerusalem were no longer living by the Law, and it seems to run counter to the statement of James that "thousands" of Jewish Christians in Jerusalem were zealous for the Law (Ac 21:20). How Johnson and McGarvey came to their conclusions is unclear in their writing. Few other scholars, either within the Churches of Christ or out, have argued for this position, Walter Schmithals,

---

Rhetorical and Historical Interpretation (Peabody, Massachusetts: Hendrickson Publishers, 2002), beginning with the introduction.

[38] Lipscomb (1936): 3: 203.

[39] *Idem*: 182.

[40] *Idem*: 200f.

[41] See Joseph B. Tyson, "'Works of Law in Galatians," *Journal of Biblical Literature* 92 (1973): 430. See also Gaston (1987): 69-71.

[42] Lipscomb (1936): 3: 284.

[43] B. W. Johnson (n.d.): 168.

[44] J. W. McGarvey (1919): 257-258.

being a later exception.[45] This viewpoint seems anti-Jewish, perhaps fueled by the progressive vision at the turn of the 20th century that Judaism was primitive, whereas Christianity represented a later, more enlightened religion; accordingly, the effort to restrict Christian freedom must have come from the retrograde Jewish religion.[46]

Robert L. Johnson argued that the Judaizers were from Jerusalem, and that Judaizers troubled the gentile mission, but he had doubts that those who influenced the Galatians were necessarily from the outside:

> Though the identity of Paul's opponents cannot be stated with certainty, it is quite clear that their attack centers on two major issues: the question of Paul's apostolic credentials and his gospel.... The chief purpose of [Galatians] was to expose the perverted gospel of the Judaizers and to win the Galatians back to faith in Jesus Christ apart from works of law.[47]

Coffman labeled Paul's opponents in Galatians "Judaizers," but he was more concerned with defending Paul against the Reformationist claim that Paul advocated salvation "by faith alone," than in specifically identifying the Judaizers.[48] He believed that the denunciation of those who proclaimed a false gospel applied especially not only to persistent Judaism but also to "all counterfeits."[49] Coffman had no specific observations as to who the "false brothers" might be. "The Judaizing part in the church were prepared to go to any lengths to enforce law-keeping and circumcision upon all who became Christians, whether Jew or Gentile."[50]

George Howard, a long-time Professor of Religion at the University of Georgia, earlier at David Lipscomb, came to the following conclusion, rather unusual when first proposed, but which has gained some support:

> [R]ather than assuming that the opponents held the opposite position from the one they ascribed to Paul, they held in fact the same position they ascribed to him and considered him as their ally. If this is true it is most likely that the agitators were Jewish Christian Judaizers from Jerusalem who preached circumcision and who said that Paul did the same because he like them was dependent on the Jerusalem apostles for his gospel.[51]

Howard did not comment specifically on the "false brothers" in Jerusalem, but his comments on the "one gospel which he (Paul) received by revelation from Jesus Christ" are on target for our discussion:

> Any action on the part of one to erase the ethnic nature of the other would constitute an automatic eradication of his gospel. This is not to say that observance of the law for the Jewish Christian was necessary for his individual salvation. In other words, Paul would never say that a Jew had to be circumcised to be saved.

[45] Walter Schmidthals, *Paul and James*, D. M. Barton, trans. (Naperville, Illinois: Allenson, 1965): 66-67.
[46] Charles M. Sharpe, "The Idea of Doctrinal Progress," in *Progress: Anniversary Volume of the Campbell Institute on the Completion of Twenty Years of History*, Herbert L. Willett, Orvis F. Jordan and Charles M. Sharpe, eds. (Chicago: The Christian Century Press, 1917): 96-103.
[47] R. L. Johnson (1969): 29.
[48] Coffman (1977): 16-18.
[49] *Idem*: 18.
[50] *Idem*: 35.
[51] Howard (1990): 9.

Such notions were beyond his realm of thought. With Paul all men are saved alike by the grace of God. On the other hand, Paul would say that observance of the law by Jewish Christianity was important for the salvation of the Gentile world and that non-observance of the law by Gentile Christians was important for the salvation of the Jewish world.[52]

Among others, Jerry Sumney, a graduate of David Lipscomb University, now teaching at Lexington Theological Seminary, argues that Paul's Galatian opponents likely were surprised that he perceived them as teaching "another gospel." They thought, rather, that they were essentially preaching the same gospel as Paul.[53] While few recent scholars think that the "teachers"[54] or "missionaries"[55] troubling the Galatian Christians were non-Christian Jews, some—including J. Louis Martyn—argue that they were Jewish Christians from Jerusalem who followed up on Paul's church plantings:

> Data in the letter show that the Teachers have connections with both Diaspora Judaism and with Palestinian, Christian Judaism. Whatever their birthplace and locale of education, the Teachers are messianic Jews, at home among Gentiles, in the sense of being able not only to live among them but also to make effective, apologetic contact with them....From Galatians itself, we can also see that the Teachers are in touch with—indeed, understand themselves to represent—a powerful circle of Christian Jews in the Jerusalem church, a group utterly zealous for the observance of the Law.[56]

I am inclined to think, however, that the situation in the Galatian churches was such that these new developments emerged from social forces in Galatia and not as the result of "Messianic Jews" who traveled from Jerusalem. While the majority of the converts in Galatia were gentiles, some were Jewish. The Jewish Christian had a difficult time explaining to their Jewish relatives and friends why they were participating in table fellowship with gentiles. Their solution for reducing the friction was to encourage the gentile Christians to undergo circumcision and to keep the Jewish feasts.[57] "It is those that want to make a good showing in the flesh that try to compel you to be circumcised—only that they may not be persecuted for the cross of Christ" (Gal 6:12). The Jewish converts therefore developed a line of argument seeking to show the gentile Christians that they, by taking up certain standard Jewish practices, could enhance their status before God. Paul, however, remained adamant that such a requirement would undercut the new relationship that God had graciously opened up through the death of Christ. The "truth of the gospel"

---

[52] *Idem*: 81.

[53] Jerry L. Sumney, "The Opponents of Galatians," unpublished book manuscript; see also Sumney's *Identifying Paul's Opponents: The Question of Method in 2 Corinthians* (Sheffield: JSOT Press, 1990).

[54] The preferred designation according to J. Louis Martyn, *Galatians*, in *The Anchor Bible 33A* (New York: Doubleday, 1997): 117-126.

[55] The preferred designation according to Dunn and Hays (2000): 184-187.

[56] Martyn (1997): 118-119.

[57] Mark Nanos, "The Inter- and Intra-Jewish Political Context of Paul's Letter to the Galatians" in Nanos (2002): 396-407. While I do not fully agree with every detail of Nanos's depiction of the situation in Galatia, I concur that these troubles could have arisen there without the coming of "Messianic Jews" from Jerusalem.

is that one is justified by faith in Christ, not through physical attributes and religious formalities. The latter would, indeed, be another gospel!

The implication of the "other gospel" taught by the "false brothers" at Antioch and in Galatia was to make second-class citizens in the church out of the uncircumcised Christians, both by refusing to share table fellowship with them on earth and by denying them a place in the heavenly banquet to come. According to the "false brothers," a common faith in the saving power of the cross was not enough. The "other gospel" that they wanted the Galatians to embrace was not a different confession of faith, not a different creed, not a different set of doctrinal propositions, but a style of behavior that was rooted in returning to the vain effort of trying to be justified by keeping the Law of Moses, imposing external regulations (circumcision, dietary laws), and keeping religious festivals. This "other gospel" was a serious and far-reaching matter for Paul because it meant that faith in Jesus as Christ was not enough: According to the "false brethren," gentiles must also "become Jews" in order to be Christians, and Paul was opposed to that.

False Brothers and Other Gospels Today

Now that we have some perception of the "false brothers" opposed by Paul in Galatians, what conclusions may we draw as to who "false brothers" are today? What if we were to direct Paul's comments on "false brothers" *then* to persons of the same or similar views *now*?

We have seen that Paul's opponents urged on all believers the Torah-keeping of circumcision, the observance of certain holy or feast days, and (perhaps) keeping kosher. Paul specifically stated his disapproval in regard to keeping special days as a means of making oneself righteous: "You are observing special days, and months, and seasons, and years" (Gal 4:10). Does this mean that we ought not to keep Christmas or Easter, or celebrate Passover or Pentecost? In some quarters of Evangelical Christianity, a strong appreciation for the Old Testament leads many to want to celebrate the Holy Days of Judaism, sometimes in table fellowship with practicing Jews, sometimes with a Christian overlay. Ought Christians who are gospel-free in Christ Jesus decline the invitation of friends and relatives to engage in these kinds of celebrations? What about visiting synagogues or other churches? What about association with people who stand outside the Judeo-Christian faith altogether? What about observing diets, such as vegetarianism or teetotalism, not for reasons of health but as a matter of spirituality?

"The truth of the gospel," according to Paul, was—and is—that salvation is through faith in Jesus Christ. Faith in Jesus Christ is a story that each of us re-tells in our own way, based on the story of the gospel of Jesus' life, crucifixion, burial, and resurrection. When we confess our faith, are buried with Christ in baptism, and then celebrate the Lord's Supper in memorial re-enactment of the breaking of his body and the pouring out of his blood, all of that is our act of faith by which we re-tell the gospel story and make it our own. After that, as far as Paul was concerned, other forms, practices, celebrations, acts of devotion, and styles of spirituality were neutral matters of opinion to be tolerated in the observant by the non-observant, but not to be imposed by the observant on the non-observant. Paul called this spirit of mutual accommodation "liberty and love" (Gal 5:1, 13-15). Be circumcised or do not be circumcised; circumcision or non-circumcision avails nothing, but do not allow someone else to force you to be circumcised on the pretext that God will accept you more readily if you become a Law-keeper (Gal 6:15). Eat and drink what you like; worship on any day that you prefer; celebrate any special days that are meaningful to you; praise God for His grace in company with anyone who will praise God with you, including "going into the Temple" as Paul did (Ac 21:20-26), even if there be "brethren in error" inside that temple. In other words, be spiritual and keep healthy in whatever way works for you, but do not impose your piety and practice on other people, and do not let them impose theirs on you. Be a new creature, build up the Body of Christ, be loving rather than harmful, do not use your liberty as a license for mischief. Augustine summarized Christian morality in this famous phrase: "Love God and do as you please!" Instructed by Paul and the "truth of the gospel," we can improve on Augustine to say: "Love God, love your fellow human being, and do as you please!" (1 Cor 10:23-33, Rm 14:1-15:6)

Some in our time insist that those with whom they fellowship religiously be of a certain kind or behave in certain specified ways. From a Pauline perspective, these requirements are incidental to the justification that results from faith in Jesus and ultimate salvation by the grace of God. For example, in the 1960s and '70s, some insisted that in order to serve in the church, men had to have short hair and be clean-shaven. Others declared that women must dress in plain styles and keep their heads covered. Others required "thee's and thou's" in prayers, intoning certain words in a certain manner with a certain solemn accent. Others said that only the KJV ought to be read. Others insisted on certain spellings for certain words, and certain phrases of in-house vocabulary. All of this, I affirm in parallel with Paul's teaching against "another gospel," amounts to a return to law-keeping when it is imposed by some on others.

Only recently have the churches begun to integrate racially, and some brothers and sisters are still uncomfortable when persons of a different race come through the door: Jews and gentiles! Status with God, I affirm with Paul, is not based on skin color, customs, religion, or ethnicity. In America, these days, polarized into "red States" and "blue States," political allegiance and socio-economic levels are perceived by some as making some people more "faithful to the gospel" than others. Others behave in a superior manner towards those who lack a certain level of sophistication and education. Still others look down their noses at those whom they perceive as unclean and lacking in attention to personal hygiene. And others anathematize those who eat the wrong things, drink the wrong things, and smoke the wrong things. The list is endless.

None of these behaviors on their own are grounds either for salvation or damnation. For Paul, to demand observance of any one of them as a condition for acceptance in Christ would be to deny the "truth of the gospel" that salvation depends solely upon faith in Jesus Christ. Those who make these demands are upholding a form of legalism parallel to that "other gospel" of Law-keeping. By affirming such extraneous traits, foreign to grace, they are turning their backs on the "truth of the gospel" and its love and liberty.

My father-in-law, who infrequently discussed race relations, once declared to me that a certain Brother Calvin, where he went to church, would make an excellent deacon, but he had not been appointed because he was Black. My father-in-law then nominated this fine brother to the Elders, suggesting that he be appointed a deacon, but they took no action. Was their failure to act not a denial of the "truth of the gospel" according to Paul's phrase? Leaders such as these make distinctions that "pervert the gospel of Christ" (Gal 1:7). Preachers who focus on anathematizing propositions rather than accepting persons have misunderstood what Paul meant when he wrote Galatians. Some would say that racial integration of the churches, helping the poor, and participating in similar social concerns is itself "another gospel"—the Social Gospel. Paul, on the other hand, identified the acceptance of all persons, regardless of the presence or absence of exterior marks, such as circumcision, as "the gospel" (Rm 1:16, 15:7). Preaching on the acceptance of all people of faith in Christ Jesus, whatever the color of their skin, their race or ethnicity, their religion or customs, their practices or propositions, or their gender, is not the Social Gospel; it is *the* gospel!

THE ARCHITECTURE OF DEATH AND RESURRECTION

GRAYDON F. SNYDER

The art and architecture of any society reflects more the concerns of the social matrix than it does the philosophical or theological maxims of the given culture. Granted that an interchange between the great culture and the local culture is continuous, the practices regarding death and belief in continued life reflect, nevertheless, primarily the social matrix, with some elements of the great or translocal tradition. Death and resurrection are community concerns.[1] A study of this topic rightly depends more on architecture than literature.

Hellenistic Tradition

Philosophical concepts of immortality and eternity aside, Greeks and Romans in actual practice behaved as though they assumed the continuing presence of the deceased person near the place of burial. Friends and family of the departed could continue a relationship from time to time, especially on the anniversary of death. Even simple graves were constructed in such a way that loved ones—by means of a tube or *mensa* (table) as part of a tomb that accommodated eating with the dead—could share a meal with the deceased. More elaborate burials included a table and/or a *triclinium*—a Roman style dining table with benches around a table—at which a meal could be shared, much as meals had been shared and enjoyed during the deceased's historical existence.

In special instances, the burial site was a monumental edifice erected to honor a hero. In these cases, the entire community could enjoy the presence of the honored leader and share in the meals. These edifices, called *heroa* (singular: *heroon*), were spread throughout the Greco-Roman area, and some are still extant. A prime example, at Trysa in eastern Greece, exhibits remarkably the standard characteristics of a *heroon*.[2] The murals on the walls surrounding the *heroon* depict historic battles, such as the attack on Troy, though, unfortunately, we do not know the relationship of the hero there buried to these battles. Other portrayals depict communion with the dead hero, including women dancing and the meal itself.[3] *Heroa* somewhat like this can be found at locations such as Kalydon, Limyra, Marmara, and Charmyleion.[4]

---

[1] Robert Redfield, *The Little Community: Viewpoints for the Study of a Human Whole* (Chicago: University of Chicago Press, 1955): 34-36, makes the distinction quite clearly and lists the parts *sine qua non* of a social matrix.

[2] Thomas Marksteiner, *Trysa, eine zentrallykische Niederlassung im Wandel der Zeit* (Wien: Phoibos Verlag, 2002): pictures, 181 and 188.

[3] Wolfgang Oberleitner, *Das Heroon von Trysa: Ein lykisches Fürstengrab des 4. Jahrhunderts v. Chr.* (Mainz: P. von Zabern, 1994).

[4] Janos Fedak, *Monumental Tombs of the Hellenistic Age: A Study of Selected Tombs from the Pre-classical to the Early Imperial Era* (Toronto: University of Toronto Press, 1990): 65-101. On the function of the circular tomb, the *tumulus*, see *ibid.*: 22. Howard Colvin, *Architecture and After-Life* (New Haven: Yale

The Jews, by contrast, did not "eat with the dead," neither in the context of the gathered community nor in the tombs of the deceased, and they did not assume the continuing presence of the deceased within the living community. Consequently no Jewish architecture of death and resurrection suggests a cultural sense of afterlife. Neither did the ancient Jews believe, or behave as though they believed, in an infinite heaven to which souls go after death. Normative Israelite cosmology had no place for a heavenly abode, and mainstream Jewish anthropology did not countenance a dualistic division between body and soul. Jews called personal unity the *nephesh*. So the *nephesh* of the Jewish dead did not cease to exist (non-existence was not conceived by the Semitic mind[5]). Rather, the dead, both good and evil, entered *Sheol* – a concept difficult both to discern and define (see Gn 37:35).[6] In any case, though the dead were not available for table fellowship, as in the Greco-Roman world, neither were they absent. Though consultation with the dead was normally forbidden in Israel, one could communicate with the dead by calling them up from *Sheol*. Saul's famous encounter with Samuel recounts the king's forbidden request:

> The woman said to Saul, "I see a divine being coming up out of the ground." He said to her, "What is his appearance?" She said, "An old man is coming up; he is wrapped in a robe." So Saul knew that it was Samuel, and he bowed with his face to the ground, and did obeisance. (1 Sm 28:14)

Continued existence in the faith of Israel depended on participation in the ongoing people of God. Jews did not ascend up to heaven – that was the residence of God (Is 66:1, Ps 115:14-18).[7] Jewish life was horizontal rather than vertical, so any ancient Jewish hope after death consisted of continued remembrance in the community. We know this in several ways: If a man died childless, a brother was obliged to keep his name alive, i.e., so that his name might not be blotted out of Israel (Dt 25:6). Ruth 4:10 best describes the meaning of Levirate marriage: "And Ruth the Moabitess, the widow of Mahlon, I have bought to be my wife, to perpetuate the name of the dead in his inheritance, that the name of the dead may not be cut off from among his brethren...."

If someone broke a law or ordinance, the worst punishment was to be cut off from the people (first mentioned in Gn 17:14 and frequently thereafter, especially in Leviticus). In contrast to being cut off, the reward for a good life was to be found by name in the "book of the living" (Ps 69:28), a metaphor used also in the book of Revelation and by Paul in Philippians 4:3. Given this horizontal understanding of life, the Hebrew word *olam* (*aion* in

---

5 The Jews did not conceive that the creation had taken place *ex nihilo*. The world had been created by ordering chaos (Gn 1:1-2). Because existence resides in the relationship between the *nephesh* and God, life after death would depend on remembrance of one's name (i.e., tangible, relational identity).

6 Sheol would appear to be the abode of the wicked because it is dark (Jb 17:13) and designates the farthest distance from the heavens (Is 7:11). Nevertheless, the Lord has access to the very depths of *Sheol* (Ps 139:8), and people as good and famous as Jacob are there. *Sheol* as the Israelite underworld might best be understood as the collectivity of all graves. See Johannes Pedersen, *Israel: Its Life and Culture* (Copenhagen: Branner og Korch, 1926): 460-462.

7 Enoch (Gn 5:24) and Elijah (2 Kg 2:1-12) might be exceptions.

University Press, 1991), places the circular tomb as early in almost every culture (1-4). A rectangular *heroon* comes later (18).

Greek) has rightly and often been translated "everlasting" rather than "eternal" (e.g., "everlasting covenant" throughout Genesis and "everlasting life" in John 6:47 [NIV]) [8]

For these reasons, an architecture specifically for death or indicative of belief in resurrection never developed in Judaism and played no part in Jewish burials, even up to the time of Jesus when considerable Hellenistic influences had already permeated Jewish culture. There were tombs and monuments in Palestine, to be sure, but not as signs of continued life for the deceased. Jesus spoke of tombs as "whited sepulchers" (Mt 23:27 KJV).[9] Even in later Roman catacombs, Jewish inscriptions, unlike early Christian *loculi* (catacomb graves at which we find inscriptions at individual burials), never mentioned any communion with the dead. Like the Christians, Jews inscribed *en eirene* ("at peace"), but they did not mention *vive* ("long life!") or other drinking salutations.[10]

The New Testament Tradition

The Agape/The Eucharist

The prime Christian event that could have been understood by Hellenistic Christians in parallel to a Hellenistic hero cult occurs with the Lord's Supper. Presumably Jesus was believed to be present at the *agape* meal eaten by his followers (1 Cor 11:17-22), and surely at the sharing of the bread and wine. The Jesus followers were his body. Paul's ritual acclamation makes that clear:[11]

> ...and when he had given thanks, he broke it (the bread) and said, "This act (of breaking bread) is [creates] my body for you. Do this (breaking of bread) as a reenactment [of the Last Supper] with me." In the same way he took the cup also, after supper, saying, "(The act of drinking from) this cup creates the new covenant through my blood. Do this, as often as you drink it, as a reenactment [of the Last Supper] with me. For as often as you eat this bread and drink the cup, you proclaim the Lord's death until he comes. (1 Cor 11:24-26; author's translation.)

The martyred Jesus was present whenever the Jesus people reenacted the Last Supper in his name. Hints of that presence can be seen in the New Testament. Jesus appears to grieving disciples in the Emmaus story as they break bread together (Lk 24:31). The same is true at the breakfast communion described in the Gospel of John (Jn 21:12-13). Beyond these meals with Jesus, no Christian hero meal appears in extant literature or archaeology until the second century. The reflection of Early Christian art makes possible that these Jesus meals might have been eaten around a semicircular table rather than a *triclinium*. In a

---

[8] Walther Eichrodt, "Heilserfahrung und Zeitverständnis im Alten Testament," *Theologische Zeitschrift* 12 (1956): 103-125.

[9] See the extensive list of tombs in Joachim Jeremias, *Heiligengräber in Jesu Umwelt (Mt 23,29; Lk 11:47): Eine Untersuchung zur Volksreligion der Zeit Jesu* (Göttingen:Vandenhoeck and Ruprecht, 1958).

[10] See especially the Vatican Jewish inscriptions 1, 3, 9, 10, 14, 15, 17 and 18 in Harry J. Leon, *The Jews of Ancient Rome* (Philadelphia: Jewish Publication Society of America, 1960). More recent data can be found in the revision by Carolyn Osiek, *The Jews of Ancient Rome* (Peabody, Massachusetts: Hendrickson, 1995).

[11] On the translation of *anamnesis* as "reenactment," see Nils Dahl, "Memory and Commemoration in Early Christianity," in *Jesus in the Memory of the Early Church* (Minneapolis: Augsburg, 1976): 11-29; and Graydon F. Snyder, *First Corinthians: A Faith Community Commentary* (Macon: Mercer University Press, 1992): 157-159.

late-first-century narrative account of the Last Supper, Jesus had risen from the table to wash feet (Jn 13:4, 12) while the assembled disciples are sitting close enough together so that they can dip the morsels and share the food, eating with their right hands (13:26). In the lowest level of mausoleums in the catacomb of S. Sebastiano in Rome, a fresco appears with several such semicircular tables and many people. The furniture of the Johannine meal was both actual and symbolic.[12]

Baptism

In addition to the meal with the resurrected Jesus, "death and resurrection" occurred at yet another key moment in the believer's life. Followers of Jesus themselves considered conversion a form of dying and rising. Baptism signaled a death to an old life and a resurrection into a new life of faith. Baptism marked the shift from the blood family to the faith family. Paul made it clear:

> Do you not know that all of us who have been baptized into Christ Jesus were baptized into his death? Therefore we have been buried with him by baptism into death, so that, just as Christ was raised from the dead by the glory of the Father, so we too might walk in newness of life. For if we have been united with him in a death like his, we will certainly be united with him in a resurrection like his. We know that our old self was crucified with him so that the body of sin might be destroyed, and we might no longer be enslaved to sin. For whoever has died is freed from sin. But if we have died with Christ, we believe that we will also live with him. We know that Christ, being raised from the dead, will never die again; death no longer has dominion over him. The death he died, he died to sin, once for all; but the life he lives, he lives to God. So you also must consider yourselves dead to sin and alive to God in Christ Jesus. (Rm 6:3-11)

As far as we know, Christians did not use baptisteries during the first century; they preferred "living water" (running water). John the Baptist used the Jordan River and the Ethiopian Eunuch was baptized by Phillip in a desert pond (Ac 8:36). The sense of dying to self and rising in the body of Christ by means of immersion in water deeply impacted the art and architecture of the Early Church.

Heaven and Hell

In the Septuagint (Greek translation of the Hebrew Scriptures) and the New Testament, the Greek mythological term *Hades* (the Greek name of the god who presided over the realm of the underworld, and by extension also the name of that realm), translated the Hebrew *Sheol*. In the New Testament, "Hades" continued to be used as a location for the dead, not always a place of punishment (e.g., Acts 2:27, 31). Belief in the resurrection of Jesus thus marked an alteration in Jewish end-time expectation. While Israelites in the Hebrew scriptures thought of punishment as exclusion from the people of God at the end, in the New Testament many references are made to punishment in an afterlife (Lk 16:19-31; Mt 5:29-30, *et al.*). More than the residence of God, "Heaven" now becomes the place of reward for those who are faithful (Mt 5:12, *et al.*) While the dead are present in Hades (1 Pt 3:18-22), the New Testament suggests no continuation of fellowship with them. We should not understand this

---

[12] Dennis E. Smith and Hal E. Taussig, *Many Tables: The Eucharist in the New Testament and Liturgy Today* (Philadelphia: Trinity Press International Press, 1990): 63.

shift in language as the impact of Hellenistic dualism but as the impact of Jewish apocalypticism. Heaven and hell were new ideas among first-century Jews, end-time concepts that came to be associated with more familiar ideas, such as the "Book of Life," in which one's name might or might not be written.[13]

Early Christian Heroon

On his way to a voluntary martyrdom in Rome, Ignatius of Antioch indicated that he wished his body would disappear in the tomb of the lions, but at the same time he wrote of himself as "God's wheat" which, when ground by the teeth of the wild beasts, would become "the pure bread of Christ." That is, just as the death of Christ produced the bread of the hero meal, so would the death of Ignatius produce a similar bread (Ignatius, *Letter to the Romans* 4). Soon thereafter, language befitting the cult of the dead began to appear in Christian writing and inscriptions. As far as literary and archaeological resources are concerned, the first known Christian cult of the dead started with Polycarp (died ca. 156). In the document entitled *Martyrdom of Polycarp,* companions and fellow-disciples explained their reverence for the relics of the dead saint:

> Thus we, at last, took up his bones, more precious than precious stones, and finer than gold, and put them where it was meet. There the Lord will permit us to come together according to our power in gladness and joy, and celebrate the birthday of his martyrdom, both in memory of those who have already contested [an athletic term referring to martyrdom], and for the practice and training of those whose fate it [martyrdom] shall be. (*Martyrdom of Polycarp* XVIII, 2-3).[14]

We do not know the location or structural nature of Polycarp's burial place, but it must have been some type of Christian *heroon* where his martyrdom could be celebrated.[15] Generally speaking, no Christian monuments were visible to the public in the first two centuries.[16]

In Rome and some other locations, Christians were buried in catacomb graves, or *loculi.* Catacomb galleries were too narrow to accommodate a memorial meal in honor of the dead, though there were occasional larger spaces (crypts). Despite the problem of adequate space, Early Christian art leaves no doubt that meals among the living were "eaten with the dead" (e.g., *Capella greca* in the Priscilla catacomb with its fresco depicting the meal and a location for it [ca. 180 C.E.]). Inscriptions on catacomb *loculi* such as *vive* (live!) or *pax* (peace!) derived from Roman eating and drinking salutations. In the latter part of the third century, when the Roman Empire determined to eliminate the Christian menace, we know

---

[13] George Nickelsburg, *Ancient Judaism and Christian Origins: Diversity, Continuity, and Transformation* (Minneapolis: Fortress Press, 2003): 119-146.

[14] *The Apostolic Fathers*, Kirsopp Lake, trans., Loeb Classical Library 25 (Cambridge, Massachusetts; London: William Heinemann, [1917],1970): 337.

[15] Bernhard Kötting, *Der frühchristliche Reliquienkult und die Bestattung im Kirchengebäude* (Köln: Westdeutscher Verlag, 1965): 10.

[16] A unique exception might be the Inscription of Abercius found in Hieropolis. It was written in 216 and was intended for public viewing. See William Tabbernee, *Montanist Inscriptions and Testimonia: Epigraphic Sources Illustrating the History of Montanism* (Macon: Mercer University Press, 1997): 50. Vera Hirschmann, "Untersuchungen zur Grabschrift des Aberkios," *Zeitschrift für Papyrologie und Epigraphik* 29 (2000): 109-116. Graydon F. Snyder, *Ante Pacem: Archaeological Evidence of Church Life before Constantine* (Macon: Mercer University Press, 2003): Plate 48. Deep appreciations to Don Haymes for editing the first edition of *Ante Pacem.*

that many believers were killed for their faith. Some martyrs, like Polycarp before them, were buried in marked graves and honored as Christian heroes. By the end of the third century, we begin to find archaeological remains of these hero burials. Such sites might include a *triclinium*, a *mensa* or table, and openings in the *mensa* to eat with the deceased.

The earliest known Christian *heroon* lies close to the Bonn Münster. It has a *triclinum* and two *mensae*.[17] About the same time (end of the third century), one or more appeared in Salona (Yugoslavia). The best known Christian *heroon* can be found under the floor of present-day S. Sebastiano, south of Rome. The room now consists of a large memorial *triclinium* with hundreds of inscriptions honoring the presence of Peter and Paul at the meals, or prayers and communications with the beloved deceased. Definite connections with the remains of Peter and Paul, however, have not been established. The supposed location of Peter's grave under St. Peter's Church in the Vatican, by contrast, shows no sign of the faithful having eaten together in the apostle's honor. As such, St. Peter's is less of a *heroon* than is the ancient site on the Via Appia that later came to be St. Sebastian's Church.[18] Since the traditional site of Paul's beheading is the Via Appia, it might be that the remains of both apostles rested there, until Peter's "trophies" were moved to what is now Vatican City.

While the Hellenistic *heroon* builtform varied, it appeared in the early Christian world primarily as a circle. The buried body of the deceased was no longer mobile, so a circular space allowed the maximum number of burials close to the critical point. When Christianity became the accepted faith of the Roman Empire, Constantine built circular *heroa* that, later, were elongated to make room for more burials.[19]

These covered cemeteries, or *coemeteria subteglata*, were built close to third-century *martyria*. By so doing, Constantine enhanced the cult of the hero martyrs in a powerful way. In Rome he built S. Lorenzo, Sta. Agnese, and SS. Pietro e Marcellino. These had the circular *heroon* -like apse with an elongated nave. They served as cemeteries, not churches; they were built a few feet from the original *martyrium*; no altars have been found in them, and they were not mentioned in ecclesiastical sources. Over the Peter and Paul *triclinium* on the Via Appia (now S. Sebastiano), Constantine built another complex, covered cemetery that allowed some access to the memorial underneath.

On top of the necropolis near Nero's circus, the location of Peter's martyrdom, Constantine built the original St. Peter's Church, where the much larger St. Peter's Basilica and the Vatican now stand. The *coemeteria subteglata* allowed some access to the Peter monument, and was later amplified by a transept. Constantine's modified St. Peter's became

---

[17] *Ibid.*: 164-166.

[18] G.F. Snyder, "Survey and New Thesis on the Bones of Peter," *Biblical Archaeologist* 32 (1969): 2-24.

[19] Major contributions to the study of early Christian *martyria* can be found in Friedrich Wilhelm Deichmann, "Martyrerbasilika, Martyrion, Memoria und Altargrab," *Mitteilungen des Deutschen Archäologischen Instituts. Römische Abteilung* 77 (1970):144-69; Ejnar Dyggve, *Dødekult, Kejserkult og Basilika* (København: P. Branner Forlag, 1943); Theodor Klausner, "Christlicher Märtyrerkult, heidnischer Heroenkult und spätjüdische Heiligenverehrung," *Arbeitsgemeinschaft für Forschung des Landes Nordrhein-Westfalen* (Köln: Westdeutscher Verlag, 1960): 27-38; *idem*, "Vom Heroon zur Märtyrerbasilika," *Gesammelte Arbeiten* (Münster: Aschendorff, 1974): 275-91; Richard Krautheimer, "Mensa-Coemeterium-Martyrium," in *Studies in Early Christian, Medieval and Renaissance Art* (New York: University Press, 1969): 35-58; J.B. Ward-Perkins, "Memoria, Martyr's Tomb and Martyr's Church," *Journal of Theological Studies* 17 (1966): 20-38.

the standard form for many later churches, especially basilicas, in Western Christianity. Finally Constantine's family, in particular Helena, the Empress Mother, built the Church of the Holy Sepulchre in Jerusalem, another covered cemetery, to commemorate in its apse the location of the tomb of the paradigmatic hero martyr, Jesus.[20] Later (sixth century) martyr-shrines, such as that of St. George in Syria or Seleucia Pieria near Antioch, maintain the *heroon*-like apse (often octagonal) but without the extended nave.[21]

Early Christians understood death as the cessation of historical existence. Within a fairly prescribed proximity to the grave, however, the deceased became a present reality. Family and friends could, and did, eat with those who had died.

That continued presence and communal celebration was understood in terms of the resurrection of Jesus, first noted in the Gospels, and the Last Supper that Jesus had eaten with his disciples before he died. By the third century, Christians were continuing to celebrate the death and resurrection of Jesus by eating the Eucharist and "eating with their dead" hero martyrs whom they honored with Hellenistic *heroa*.[22] They wished to be buried close to the grave of the martyrs, and to eat with the martyrs, even as they had eaten with their own dead.

By the fifth century, the architecture of the Christian *heroon* had become standard church architecture, but the celebration of a separate meal for the dead did not survive the sixth century. The reasons are somewhat complex, since the cult of the martyrs actually expanded during this period. One reason for the loss of "eating with the dead" was conflict between suburban cemetery groups and the more urban churches. Those who frequented the cemeteries (located outside the city) sometimes opposed the authority of the local urban bishops (Hippolytus *Refutation of all Heresies* 9:12). Celebrating with wine, food, dancing, and family fellowship, the cemetery events could sometimes become rowdy, even dangerous. We do know that Augustine asked his mother, Monica, to cease her daily trips to the cemetery (*Confessions* VI, 2). About the fifth century, in any case, the meal with the dead was transferred from covered cemeteries to authorized churches. In the presence of martyrs' remains, the meal was limited to the Eucharist in authorized churches. The meal with the dead disappeared.

Conversionary Death and Resurrection

In the first centuries of the church, the Pauline sense of baptism prevailed. Adults died with Christ and were raised with/in him. It seems reasonable to suggest that the architecture for this type of conversionary dying and rising would reflect in the form of a baptismal pool, that, in turn, was shaped like the circular Hellenistic *heroon* and the covered cemeteries.

---

[20] Ejnar Dyggve, *Gravkirken i Jerusalem: Konstantinske problemer i ny Belysning* (København: P. Branner Forlag, 1941): 6. For the architectural development of the Jesus *martyrion* into a tomb, see the figures on Planche II, IV, and V.

[21] Robert Milburn, *Early Christian Art and Architecture* (Berkeley: University of California Press, 1988): 130.

[22] While no portrayals of the death or the resurrection of Jesus are to be found in Early Christian art (before Constantine), several portrayals of the resurrection of Lazarus are extant. All in sepulcher situations, the scene references the return of the dead to the living community. (*Capella Greca*, Chapels A2 and A6 of the Sacrament Chapels in St. Callixtus). See Robin Jensen, "The Raising of Lazarus," *Bible Review* 11/1 (1995): 20-28, 45.

Our first certain example of a baptistery was constructed from a side room inside a *domus ecclesia* (house church). While under attack in 258, the defenders of Dura-Europos covered the houses next to the city wall. Much to the appreciation of later archaeologists, they covered a synagogue and a house church. Inside the house church was a baptistery, rectangular in form. Other, later baptisteries, however, were round or octagonal.[23] If the House of Fish in Ostia was indeed a third-century house church, then the round pool in front of the *triclinium* may very well have been a baptistery more like the shape of a *heroon*.[24] Other early baptisteries might include the octagonal structure in S. Gregorio of Milan or the octagonal pool in a supposed Christian house in Gabia la Grande in Spain.[25] Post-Constantinian examples, as in Carthage or Ephesus, for example, are round with steps leading into the water. In Rome, Constantine himself built a *heroon*-like baptismal edifice at the primary urban church, St. John Lateran.

The circular *heroon* architectural builtform, as a location for communion with martyrs and deceased loved ones, did not function much beyond the fourth century. It continued as the apse of major churches or basilicas. As for baptismal death and resurrection, by the end of the third century, inscriptions indicate that children were being raised as Christians (with names like "Agape" and "Timotheus"). Consequently, the need had become less for conversionary *heroa* where adults died to sin, were buried in baptism, and were raised to new life in Christ. Nevertheless, buildings that housed baptisteries tended to keep the *heroon* architecture well into the Renaissance.

Summary

Two major religious cultures influenced Early Christianity. Within the primary culture, Judaism, life was understood as corporate existence as the family and nation of Israel, the people of God. That existence would continue until the End Time for both the living and the dead, though the deceased were not available to the living. Consequently, no architecture of death and resurrection would have been functional. In the social form of the other influence, Hellenism, life was also corporate; in contrast to Judaism, however, the deceased were believed to be available to the living, so burials were arranged in such a way that the living could associate with the dead by means of prayers and common meals. In the case of famous people, the tombs (*heroa*) were architectural structures built to accommodate many people.

Early Christians of the Mediterranean area adopted this Hellenistic mode of burial. They said prayers and ate meals with the dead, and they built *heroa* for martyrs and leaders. The sense of apocalyptic death and resurrection reported in the New Testament was celebrated not only in the Eucharist but also in conversionary dying-and-rising baptism. Just as Christian burial and "eating with the dead" was embraced architecturally in the builtform of the *heroa,* so also was eschatological immersion celebrated in baptisteries constructed in shapes reminiscent of Hellenistic *heroa* and the tombs of the saints.

---

[23] J.G. Davies, *The Architectural Setting of Baptism* (London: Barrie and Rockliff, 1902): 3-4.

[24] L. Michael White, *The Social Origin of Christian Architecture II* (Valley Forge: Trinity Press International, 1997): 436-437. Snyder (2003): 206-207.

[25] For examples of circular and octagonal baptisteries, see A. Khatchatrian, *Les baptisteries paléochrétiens* (Paris: École pratique des hautes études, 1962).

Thomas Campbell, "New Light," and the *Declaration and Address*

Keith Huey

Defrocked from his itinerant ministry in Western Pennsylvania, Thomas Campbell established the "Christian Association of Washington" in 1809. From its beginning, the Association was defined by Thomas's *Declaration and Address*, a classic statement of non-creedal Christian polity. Campbell's son, Alexander, would soon overshadow his father, and he would similarly inspire (and enrage) his audiences with a "democratized" gospel of anti-creedal, anti-clerical independence.[1] Predictable in retrospect, the *Declaration of Independence*, penned by another Thomas, then only one generation old and so relevant to the mind of the New Republic, had to resonate in Thomas's own *Declaration*;[2] that observation, however, should not be pressed too far. Let us remember that Thomas was an Irish immigrant, forty-six years old and relatively "fresh off the boat." His primary influences had scarcely been forged in his brief American sojourn.

Lynn McMillon and Leroy Garrett have emphasized the Scottish instincts at work in the Campbell movement,[3] but the most obvious context, the one in Northern Ireland, has been largely neglected. This deficiency has been corrected, in part, by the work of Hiram Lester, who studied Thomas against the background of the Evangelical Society of Ulster. The E.S.U., as Lester demonstrated, was an ecumenical association in which Thomas held brief membership, and its charter bears striking resemblance to the *Declaration and Address*.[4] Building on Lester's work, I now seek to go further, beyond the evangelical context, to the heritage of the Antiburgher Seceder Presbyterians. This was the context in which Thomas had served as minister and Synod member.

At first blush, the Antiburgher Seceders might seem to provide an unlikely setting for anti-creedal ideology. After all, they were formed in radical allegiance to the Westminster

---

[1] Alexander Campbell plays a major role in the discussion of Nathan Hatch, *The Democratization of American Christianity* (New Haven, Connecticut: Yale University Press, 1989). This is also true for Barton W. Stone, whose "Christian" movement merged with the Campbells' "Disciples" in 1832.

[2] Donald H. Yoder, "Christian Unity in Nineteenth-Century America," in *A History of the Ecumenical Movement, 1517-1948*, 2nd ed., R. Rouse and S. C. Neill, eds. (London: SPCK, 1967): 237; Leroy Garrett, *The Stone-Campbell Movement: The Story of the American Restoration Movement*, rev. ed. (Joplin, Missouri: College Press, 1994): 104.

[3] Lynn McMillon, *Restoration Roots* (Dallas: Gospel Teachers, 1983): 1. Leroy Garrett puts it more strongly in his article: "It Began In Scotland," *Restoration Review* 19/2 (February 1976): 230-34.

[4] Hiram Lester, "The Form and Function of the *Declaration and Address*," in *The Quest for Christian Unity, Peace, and Purity in Thomas Campbell's* Declaration and Address, Thomas H. Olbricht and Hans Rollmann, eds., ATLA Monograph Series, No. 46 (Lanham, Maryland: Scarecrow, 2000): 173-92. [This landmark volume, written and edited by Olbricht and Rollmann in association with others, was guided from manuscript through publication by our honoree, Don Haymes.]

Confession. By the time of Thomas's ordination in 1798, however, they, like almost all other Presbyterians, had largely succumbed to the pressures of "New Light." Indeed, very little in the *Declaration and Address* could not have been uttered in the Irish Synod itself. This realization helps us to understand the origins and intentions behind Thomas's landmark document.

Who Were the New Lights?

The New Light label defies precise identification, but it was used in a fairly consistent way among the Presbyterians of the seventeenth and eighteenth centuries. An early example can be found in 1649, where it was used by the Presbytery of Belfast to describe an alternative (and obviously heretical) fountain of religious inspiration. The Presbytery exhorted its readers to avoid the "Sectaries," who "...withdraw from, and villifie the publique Ordinances; speak evil of Church-Government; invent damnable errors, under the specious pretence of a Gospel-way, and new Light...."[5]

In the early 1700s, the term was similarly applied to free-thinkers who eschewed the Westminster Confession, and who favored the inward light of "personal persuasion." A leading instance can be found in 1705, when the Synod of Ulster attempted to address a contagion of trinitarian heterodoxy that had been discovered in Dublin. They voted to require confessional subscription from every ministerial candidate,[6] and thereby they provoked a generation of New Light declarations (and "Old Light" rejoinders).

In Ulster, New Light subversion flowed largely from the Belfast Society, established in 1705 by a Presbyterian minister named John Abernethy. What seemed a new light to others was for Abernethy the "Light of Conscience," and he stood opposed to creeds and confessions of faith. In 1719 he proclaimed:

> Since it is so evident that our Lord Jesus Christ has not only granted all his Disciples the Privilege, but strictly enjoin'd them to enquire into his Will revealed in the Gospel, that from thence they may learn what to believe and what to practice, and without submitting implicitly to human Declarations and Decisions in any Point of Faith or Duty, may by following impartially their own Light, the full Persuasion of their own Minds, obtain his Approbation: Let us use this Privilege and obey this Precept, having always a close and immediate Regard to him; and as being accountable to him only, not to Men: Let us stand fast in the Liberty wherewith he hath made us free: Let us call no Man or Society of Men our Masters; for one is our Master even Christ, and all we are Brethren.[7]

Abernethy, let it be said, was not seeking to justify the boundless, individualistic expansion of doctrinal whimsy. Instead, he appealed to human reason, and, especially with the clinching reference to Mt 23: 8-10, to the unmediated authority of Christ. Hence, New

---

[5] Presbytery of Belfast, *A Necessary Representation of the present evills, and eminent dangers to Religion, Lawes, and Liberties,* in John Milton, *Complete Prose Works* (New Haven: Yale University Press, 1962): 3: 299.

[6] The act of 1705 reiterated a decision reached in 1698, but on the New Light controversies of the early 1700s, see Ian McBride, *Scripture Politics: Ulster Presbyterianism and Irish Radicalism in the Late Eighteenth Century* (Oxford: Clarendon, 1998): 43-52.

[7] John Abernethy, "Religious Obedience founded on Personal Persuasion," in *Scarce and Valuable Tracts and Sermons, Occasionally Published, By the Late and Learned John Abernethy, M. A.* (London: R. Griffiths, 1751): 252-53.

Lights frequently spoke of the exclusive authority of the Scriptures, which, in the words of the Rev. Samuel Haliday, provided "a sufficient test of orthodoxy."[8] According to Ian McBride, they struggled to "peel away the layers of human superstition that had obscured the divine word, and to restore Christianity to its pristine condition."[9]

This was primitivistic, restorationist rhetoric, but the New Lights were not chiefly concerned either with the "ancient order" of the first-century church or with the living of "ancient lives." Their arguments were turned toward latitudinarian purposes, designed to restrain the jurisdictions of dogma and discipline in points that were not "essential."[10] In this respect they were consistent with the spirit of Puritan Dissent, but they naturally raised suspicions. Latitudinarianism seemed to its critics to be a mask for heresy, and New Lights were routinely implicated with heterodox notions concerning original sin, soteriology, and the trinity.

An indicative controversy involved John Simson, Professor of Divinity at the University of Glasgow. He subjected established Presbyterian doctrines to the tests of Scripture and rational inquiry, thus undermining the traditional consensus on a wide range of issues. For instance, he challenged the doctrine of original sin as "inconsistent with the justice and goodness of God;"[11] moreover, he elsewhere asserted that "if Adam was made a federal head, it must be by divine command, which is not found in the Bible."[12] From 1714 to 1717, the General Assembly considered his allegedly Arminian indiscretions, and from 1726 to 1728 they examined his trinitarian viewpoints. In the end, Simson proved to be an elusive quarry who knew "the art of teaching heresy orthodoxly ";[13] so the General Assembly was slow to condemn him. His professorial chair was not revoked until 1728, too little and far too late to mollify the Assembly's conservative elements.

The New Lights and the Secession

Thus disturbed, the Assembly's solidarity was increasingly tenuous, and in 1732 it was finally ruptured by a new dispute. Presbyterian congregations did not possess their own lands or buildings, but occupied the properties of "patrons;" by an act of Parliament, these patrons were permitted to select ministers for the churches they sponsored. This prerogative was offensive to the Presbyterian doctrine of church government, according to which ministers could be chosen only by their prospective congregations. Nonetheless, the Assembly formulated a major concession in which clerical elections were entrusted to a mixed committee of patrons and congregational Elders. To a disaffected coterie of Old Light

---

[8] Cited by A. C. Anderson, *The Story of the Presbyterian Church in Ireland* (Northern Ireland: Bell, Logan, & Carswell, 1965): 166.

[9] McBride (1998): 60.

[10] For example, as in Abernethy (1751): 247-48.

[11] John Simson, *Answers to Mr. Webster's Libel*: 225 (cited in Associate Synod, *Act, Declaration and Testimony, for the Doctrine, Worship, Government, and Discipline of the Church of Scotland* (Glasgow: J. Bryce and A. M'Lean, Jr., 1740); Mitchell Library, Glasgow, A53368 (hereinafter *ADT*): 56.

[12] Simson, *Answers*: 146 (*ADT*: 56).

[13] James Coutts, *A History of the University of Glasgow* (Glasgow: J. Maclehose, 1909): 45.

ministers, this compromise seemed treacherous; consequently they seceded in 1733 to form the confessionally irredentist Associate Synod.[14]

Though Robert Richardson, Alexander Campbell's biographer, highlighted the patronage issue, he rightly identified the Secession as a response to something larger. The Seceders were opposed to the Assembly's reputedly heterodox and "arbitrary" spirit,[15] and their ranks had been formed before the fault lines were revealed by the patronage question. The controversy of 1732 was, as David Stewart described it, "only the occasion, or proximate cause" of the Associate Synod's protest.[16] In their own words, the Seceders justified their withdrawal with a long list of grievances, including the protracted schedule of John Simson's trial. They complained as follows:

> The processes carried on against him were kept several years in dependence before
> the judicatories; and particularly the last process, which concerned his impugning
> the *supreme Deity of the Son of God...* tho' the evidence was so clear, that the
> discipline of the church should have been *summarily* exercised upon him.[17]

In this particular context, a "New Light Seceder" would have presented a startling anomaly, for the Seceders were formed as a protest against New Light encroachments. In their *Act, Declaration and Testimony*, they pointedly denied that salvific knowledge could be revealed by the "light of nature;"[18] moreover, they emphasized the "perpetual obligation" of the Scottish Covenants and the *Westminster Confession*.[19]

Later, in the 1747 breach between Burghers and Antiburghers, the Antiburghers would prove themselves to be the most rigorous branch of the Secession. This debate revolved around the Freemasons' Oath, which was strictly a Scottish concern (the Secession had not yet spread to Ireland). The formula of the oath, which was sworn in certain towns, was designed to sanction the Church of Scotland as the "true religion presently professed within this realm, and authorized by the laws thereof."[20] This, of course, posed a problem for Seceders, who regarded the National Church to be apostate; nonetheless, there were some who managed to rationalize the language. These people, called Burghers, explained that the Secession was the "true" Church of Scotland, and the oath could be construed as a reference to themselves.[21] Antiburghers, repulsed by the oath's clear intention, refused to

---

[14] This is the shortest version of a rather long story. See also Peter Brooke, *Ulster Presbyterianism: The Historical Perspective, 1610-1970*, 2nd ed. (Belfast: Athol, 1994): 85; David Stewart, *The Seceders in Ireland with Annals of Their Congregations* (Belfast: Presbyterian Historical Society, 1950): 47-49; and Associate Presbytery [Adam Gib], *The Present Truth: A Display of the Secession-Testimony; in the Three Periods of the Rise, State, and Maintenance of that Testimony*, vol. 1 (Edinburgh: R. Fleming and A. Neill, 1774); Mitchell Library, Glasgow, A55543: 41-42.

[15] Robert Richardson, *Memoirs of Alexander Campbell* (Philadelphia: J. Lippincott, 1868; reprint, Indianapolis: Religious Book Service, n. d.): 1: 51-53.

[16] Stewart (1950): 42; see also Associate Presbytery (1774): 1: 45-47.

[17] *ADT*: 91. Simson is discussed at great length; see also pp. 53-64, 85-92. By contrast, very little is said concerning the patronage controversy (pp. 92-93).

[18] *Ibid.*: 101.

[19] *Ibid.*: 109-10.

[20] Stewart (1950): 51.

[21] ADT: 11, as indicated on the less-than-subtle title page of the Associate Synod's *Act, Declaration, and Testimony* (see note 11, above).

swear.[22] If a "New Light Seceder" was anomalous, then a "New Light Antiburgher Seceder" was absolutely incomprehensible—for awhile.

Tensions within the Secession

As a matter of formal rhetoric, the Seceders maintained their conservative posture throughout the eighteenth century; in truth, however, they were forced to re-interpret their traditional foundations, even as they reiterated their orthodoxy and denied every hint of innovation. Burghers and Antiburghers were vigilant to check New Light encroachments, but even before their breach in 1747, they faced other troubling questions, especially the question of church/state relations. With respect to this issue they were forced to reconsider the rhetoric of the *Solemn League and Covenant* and of the *Westminster Confession* itself.[23]

The *Solemn League and Covenant* had been published in 1643, in a time when Presbyterians enjoyed a brief period of political hegemony. It pledges the "extirpation" of popery and episcopal prelacy,[24] but for the politically disenfranchised Seceders of 1742, this was an absurd (and politically incorrect) injunction. Consequently they proposed blandly, instead, to pursue the "Preservation of the Reformed Religion."[25] This new language was approved with only one dissenting voice: Thomas Nairn, a minister from Abbotshall, who complained as follows:

> In the Solemn League and Covenant, we swear, not only to endeavour the Preservation of true Reformed Religion, but also to bring the Churches of the three Kingdoms to the nearest Conjunction and Uniformity in Religion, Confession of Faith, Church Government, &c. And to endeavour the Extirpation of Popery and Prelacy, &c. But this last is altogether omitted in this present Oath or Covenant.[26]

In response to Mr. Nairn, the Presbytery explained that the language of "extirpation" was removed for the sake of "present circumstances," and they professed their total fidelity to the Covenant's original intent:

---

[22] Lester G. McAllister, *Thomas Campbell: Man of the Book*. (St. Louis: Bethany, 1954): 29, completely missed the point when he wrote that Burghers endorsed the national church, and that the Antiburghers did not.

[23] The church/state issue was particularly fluid among Presbyterians, as noted by Isaac Kramnick, "Religion and Radicalism: English Political Theory in the Age of Revolution," *Political Theory* 5 (1977): 505. By the time of the American and French Revolutions, wrote Kramnick, the Dissenters offered "the boldest voices attacking the traditional order; they were the secular prophets, the vanguard, of a new social order."

[24] "The Solemn League and Covenant, 1643," in *Documents of the Christian Church*, 2nd ed., Henry Bettenson, ed. (London: Oxford University Press, 1963): 287-88.

[25] This line was officially reiterated in 1743, as seen in Associate Presbytery, *Act of the Associate Presbytery, for Renewing the National Covenant of Scotland, and the Solemn League and Covenant of the three Nations, in a Way and Manner agreeable to our present Situation, and Circumstances, in this Period* (Edinburgh: T. W. and T. Ruddimans, 1744); Glasgow, Mitchell Library A43841: 97.

[26] Cited in Associate Presbytery, *Answers by the Associate Presbytery, to Reasons of Dissent, given in to the said Presbytery...by the Reverend Mr. Thomas Nairn, Minister of the Gospel at Abbotshall* (Edinburgh: T. W. and T. Ruddimans, 1744); Glasgow, Mitchell Library A77845: 27.

As for the Presbytery's not using there the Word [*Extirpation*] it is well enough known that *that* Word has been, of *late* Years, abused to a *sanguinary* Sense, for *propagating* Religion by *offensive Arms*, quite *contrary* to the Mind of our Reformers.[27]

Similarly, the Seceders also subjected the church/state doctrines of the *Westminster Confession* (another product of the 1640s) to an ostensibly faithful revision. Especially problematic was the Confession's twenty-third chapter, where civil magistrates were authorized to take action in churchly affairs:

...to take order, that unity and peace be preserved in the Church, that the truth of God be kept pure and entire; that all blasphemies and heresies be suppressed, all corruptions and abuses in worship and discipline prevented or reformed; and all the ordinances of God duly settled, administered, and observed. For the better effecting whereof, he [the magistrate] hath power to call synods, to be present at them, and to provide, that whatsoever is transacted in them be according to the mind of God.[28]

These lines arguably sanctioned an Erastian arrangement, in which the church was obliged to follow the lead of a Christian magistrate. Presbyterian ecclesiology, however, was forged in opposition to an Erastian system,[29] and the inconsistency proved to be somewhat embarrassing.[30] Hence, in their foundational *Act and Testimony*, the Seceders condemned the Erastian concept, and seized the benign language of Westminster's thirty-first chapter to summarize (and re-interpret) the twenty-third. The civil magistrate is "always free," they averred, "to call synods and assemblies of ministers and elders, for consulting and advising with them, in matters of religion."[31]

The Secession's creative tension was particularly evident in their dealings with Mr. Nairn. In that protracted statement, they offered this striking caveat:

The public good of outward and common order, in all reasonable society, to the glory of God, is the great and *only* end which those invested with magistracy can propose, in a sole respect to that office ... as in prosecuting this end civilly, according to their office, it is only over men's good and evil works that they can have any inspection, so it is only over these which they must needs take cognizance of, for the said public good... without assuming any lordship

---

[27] *Ibid.*, 39; brackets appear in the original. See Stewart (1950): 71, who wrote that the Seceders "resiled somewhat from the stipulations of the Covenants."

[28] *Westminster Confession of Faith*, 23.3.

[29] James Kirk, "'The Politics of the Best Reformed Kirks:' Scottish Achievements and English Aspirations in Church Government after the Reformation," *Scottish Historical Review* 59/1(1980): 30-31.

[30] Alexander Campbell later argued that the Westminster divines "were in fact sworn to act, if not to believe, as Erastians. The form of oath is predicated upon Erastian principles." See A. Campbell, "A Narrative of the Origin and Formation of the Westminster or Presbyterian Confession of Faith. No. II," *Christian Baptist* 2/11 (6 June 1825): 155. For a modern appraisal, see William B. Hunter, preface to John Milton, *Treatise of Civil Power* and *Considerations Touching the Likeliest Means* in *Complete Prose Works* (New Haven: Yale University Press, 1980): 7: 231-32, who described the Confession as "strongly Erastian."

[31] *ADT*: 106. This statement is taken directly from the *Westminster Confession of Faith*, 31.2.

immediately over men's consciences, or making any encroachment upon the special privileges or business of the church.[32]

In McKerrow's opinion, this passage "virtually rejected" the doctrine of Westminster's twenty-third chapter,[33] but the Synod predictably maintained that it had faithfully defined the Confession's true intent. Until the 1790s, its ministers were informed (unofficially) by the qualifications of 1743, and when they professed the "whole doctrine contained in the Confession of Faith," it was an unmistakably provisional declaration. This does not mean that the Seceders constructed their doctrines on a foundation of wishful thinking,[34] but the scrupulous Seceders could not sustain these accommodations forever.

New Oath, New Testimony, and New Lights

The issue was forced in 1796, when the General Associate (Antiburgher) Synod considered the petition of licentiates Thomas M'Crie and William M'Ewan. It seems that these two men were satisfied with the qualifications of 1743; nonetheless, they wished to formalize their exact position.[35] The Synod accordingly canonized the qualifications, and amended the oath of subscription: Licentiates were still required to receive the Confession as it was stated in 1647, but they now understood it, officially, "according to the declaration of the General Associate Synod, 1796."[36] Despite the misgivings of a conservative minority, this amendment was quietly proposed and swiftly passed.

The minority became more vocal, however, when the Synod began to review rough drafts of the *Narrative and Testimony*. This document had been commissioned in 1791 to revise and simplify the Secession's growing collection of declarations and statements, and was ironically destined to provoke great confusion.[37] It expressed viewpoints that generally prevailed in the Synod already,[38] but its inception marked a milestone in the erosion of confessional rigidity. In the latitudinarian style of John Abernethy, the edition of 1804 drew on Mt 23:8-10 to state: "We call no man nor church, Master. One is our Master, even Christ, and his word is our only unerring rule."[39] With reference to the *Westminster Confession* and its catechisms, the Synod further declared:

---

[32] Associate Presbytery (*Answers*, 1744): 71.

[33] John McKerrow, *History of the Secession Church*, rev. ed. (Edinburgh: A. Fullarton, 1854): 379.

[34] Ian Hamilton, *The Erosion of Calvinist Orthodoxy: Seceders and Subscription in Scottish Presbyterianism* (Edinburgh: Rutherford House, 1990): 28-29, n. 40, described a background of substance.

[35] McKerrow (1854): 380.

[36] General Associate Synod, *Acts and Proceedings of the General Associate Synod* (Handwritten manuscript, Scottish Record Office, Edinburgh): 4:40. Robert Gaston Hall, "Archibald Bruce of Whitburn (1746-1816) with Special Reference to His View of Church and State" (Ph.D. dissertation, University of Edinburgh, 1954): 178-80, gave the best summary because he included helpful footnote references. See also McKerrow (1854): 381-82; and Hamilton (1990): 11. Meanwhile, a parallel story was developing in the 1796 meeting of the Burgher Synod. See Stewart (1950): 185-86.

[37] On the intent of the *Narrative and Testimony*, see Stewart (1950): 431, and David Scott, *Annals and Statistics of the Original Secession Church: Till its Disruption and Union with the Free Church of Scotland in 1852* (Edinburgh: Andrew Elliot, n. d.): 80.

[38] As explained by McKerrow (1854): 468, and Hall (1954): 207-9.

[39] General Associate Synod, *Narrative and Testimony, Agreed Upon and Enacted by the General Associate Synod; Together with an Act Respecting Procedure in Covenanting Work....* (Edinburgh: A. Neill, 1804), New College Library, Edinburgh (hereinafter *N&T*): 9.

That as no human composure, however excellent and well expressed, can be supposed to contain a full and comprehensive view of divine truth; so by this adherence, we are not precluded from embracing, upon due deliberation, any further light which may afterward arise from the word of God, about any article of divine truth.[40]

The terminology of an old debate had been resurrected, so the new testators were tagged with the oxymoronic label of "New Light Antiburgher Seceders."

Aside from the scandal of confessional amendment, the New Light Antiburghers now issued some significant statements on the subject of church/state relations. The new *Testimony* generally approved the Presbyterian reformations, but it faulted the Covenanters for "embodying the matter of their religious profession with the laws of the country, and giving it the formal sanction of civil authority."[41] In one of their strongest statements, they declared:

A liberty of worshipping God in the way which they judge agreeable to his will, is a right common to all men. They may and often do err, and offend the most High God, by substituting a false worship in the place of that which he requires: but no power on earth may take that right from them.[42]

These sentiments evoked a storm of controversy, and the conflict between Old Lights and New Lights ultimately hinged on the church/state issue.[43] Ironically, Thomas M'Crie became an articulate defender of the Old Light position, and argued that "irreligion, impiety, profanity, and blasphemy" were not matters of conscience, but were "external interests" that the magistrate could properly proscribe.[44] Similarly, James Hog contended that magistrates must "forbid what God has forbidden in his word,"[45] and he complained that the new definitions were "Latitudinarian and Sectarian."[46] However, the most significant member of the Old Light minority was surely Archibald Bruce, professor of theology in the Antiburgher Divinity Hall. In response to the ratification of the *Narrative and Testimony*, Bruce withdrew in 1806 to lead another secession, called the "Constitutional Associate Presbytery."[47]

---

[40] *Ibid.*: 13. Similarly, on p. 14 the Synod expressed its concerns about "some expressions" in the *ADT*, and sought to replace them with language that might be "less exceptionable."

[41] *Ibid.*: 10.

[42] *Ibid.*: 194-95. This line appears also in an earlier version of *N&T*; see General Associate Synod, *Testimony, Agreed Upon, and Enacted by, the General Associate Synod; Met at Edinburgh, October 16, 1801* (Belfast: J. Blair, 1802), Linenhall Library, Belfast: 82-83.

[43] Richardson (1868): 1: 55-56, wrote that the controversy was "a question…as to the power of civil magistrates in religion, as asserted in the twenty-third chapter of the Westminster Confession."

[44] Thomas M'Crie, *Statement of the Difference between the Profession of the Reformed Church of Scotland as Adopted by the Seceders, and the Profession Contained in the New Testimony and Other Acts* (Edinburgh: C. F. Lyon, 1871); Glasgow, Mitchell Library A275362: 82.

[45] James Hog, *Address to the Associate Congregation of Kelso; in which the Difference between the Former and Present Testimony of the Associate Synod is Briefly Stated; and the Unwary Are Guarded Against Imposition*, in *Professor Bruce's Works*, 2nd. edn., (Edinburgh: George Caw, 1808); New College: 8: 8.

[46] *Ibid.*: 11; similarly, John Thomson, *An Apology for Seceders* (Glasgow: John Thomson, 1798); Glasgow, Mitchell Library A153759: 31-32.

[47] McKerrow (1854): 446-58; Richardson (1868): 1: 56; and Stewart (1950): 382-83. Similar controversies had already ruptured the Burgher Synod in 1799, when the Old Lights departed to form the "Original Burgher Synod." See Stewart (1950): 185-86, 381-82.

The Loyalties of Thomas Campbell

Thomas Campbell was an authentic member of the Antiburgher heritage. As Richardson observed, Thomas seemed to admire the doctrinal rigidity that characterized the Secession churches, and he had even been drawn to the hyper-confessional Covenanters.[48] He used the *Westminster Confession* as a part of his rather intense household instruction, as Alexander would recall in 1830:

> I had to memorize and digest the Assembly's Catechism.... The good effects of memorizing the New Testament were neutralized by the trash which the "Westminster Divines" had obliged me to interlard with it. This gave a coloring and taste to all that I learned from the scriptures.[49]

In 1804, Thomas was still defending the secession of 1733 on account of the General Assembly's "heterodoxy," and he appealed to the Confession as a basis of commonality.[50]

In search of the very best Antiburgher training during the 1790s, Thomas traveled to Scotland for five annual sessions with Archibald Bruce.[51] This might explain why, since at least 1930, Thomas's biographers have repeatedly introduced him as an "Old Light Antiburgher" in the Seceder Presbyterian Church.[52] Membership with the Old Lights, however, was impossible for Thomas, who belonged to the Irish Synod. "In Ireland," explains Stewart, "there was no division on the subject of the Narrative and Testimony. It was approved of willingly, for society here was characterized by the same defections as those which prevailed in Scotland."[53] Brooke also observed that the Old Lights were exclusively Scottish and never established themselves in Ulster.[54] Moreover, even in

---

[48] Richardson (1868): 1: 22.

[49] A. Campbell, "Education – No. 2," *Millennial Harbinger* 1/6(7 June 1830): 251 (This page, incorrectly numbered, should read "252.")

[50] A. Campbell, *Memoirs of Elder Thomas Campbell, Together with a Brief Memoir of Mrs. Jane Campbell* (Cincinnati: H. S. Bosworth, 1861): 210, 213; and McAllister (1954): 54.

[51] The matriculation date is based on Stewart (1950): 437; Richardson (1868): 1: 26 described the five-year schedule of instruction. McAllister (1954): 31, asserted that Thomas began the program in 1787 and finished in 1791, but Stewart's chronology fits more precisely with Thomas's likely ordination in 1797 or 1798. See also David Thompson, "The Irish Background to Thomas Campbell's *Declaration and Address*," *Discipliana* 46/2 (summer 1986): 23, n. 5.

[52] Benjamin Lyon Smith, *Alexander Campbell* (St. Louis: Bethany, 1930): 46. Many others have repeated this identification; for example, see Earl I. West, *The Search for the Ancient Order: A History of the Restoration Movement 1849-1906* (Nashville: Gospel Advocate, 1974): 43, McAllister (1954): 46, Richard M. Tristano, *The Origins of the Restoration Movement: An Intellectual History* (Atlanta: Glenmary Research Center, 1988): 63, and Gary Holloway and Douglas A. Foster, *Renewing God's People: A Concise History of Churches of Christ* (Abilene: ACU Press, 2001): 41.

[53] Stewart (1950): 100.

[54] Brooke (1994): 93. Irish minds had never been duplicated from Scottish originals, and they possessed a long, independent heritage of liberal political viewpoints. See Caroline Robbins, *The Eighteenth-Century Commonwealthman: Studies in the Transmission, Development, and Circumstances of English Liberal Thought from the Restoration of Charles II until the War with the Thirteen Colonies* (Cambridge, Massachusetts: Harvard University Press, 1959): 135-76.

Scotland the Old Light secession was very small, and aside from Bruce, Hog, and M'Crie, only James Aitken joined the Constitutional Associate Presbytery.[55]

Let us note also that Thomas's ideology bore little resemblance to the Old Light sentiments of his esteemed Professor Bruce. For instance, the Irish Synod of 1804 commissioned Bruce (along with three others) to revise the *Formula of Confession and Obligation*, a statement that parents professed when their children were baptized. After some deliberation, the committee resolved that parents "and others joining with us" should not be required to make an "explicit approbation" of the Confession, Catechism, or *Act and Testimony*. Instead, they were exhorted to become "fully acquainted" with such definitions, so they might approve them "in judgment & in truth."[56] If the Synod was relaxed about confessional identity, Thomas was even more so. Shortly after his ordination, he became the only Antiburgher to join the Evangelical Society of Ulster, which the Synod deemed to be "completely Latitudinarian." At the insistence of the 1799 Synod, he humbly withdrew his "official intercourse" with the Society, though he continued privately to fraternize with its members.[57]

The most telling incident, however, involved the adoption of the new *Testimony*. In 1802, the Irish Synod reviewed a draft of the document,[58] and its members, in remarkable contrast to their Scottish counterparts, had very little to say. One reluctant minister, however, expressed his reservations:

> Would it not be highly expedient for this Synod to advert to the 18th & 23d chapters of the New Testimony, seeing that a number of difficulties have occurred from said chapters of a very embarrassing tendency to many ministers & others, whom it must materially affect if it be made a term of communion in its present form?[59]

These were the words of Thomas Campbell, and the chapters he flagged were entitled "Public Religious Covenanting" (chapter 18) and "Church and State, and the Difference Between Them" (chapter 23).[60] His overture was considered too weighty for the context of the present meeting, and was deferred to an "extra-judicial conversation." That meeting, however, ended inconclusively, and the matter was postponed again, till the following year.[61] Accordingly, Thomas delivered a written statement in the meeting of 1803; once more, however, the matter was shelved. The Synod merely ordered that "copies of said paper

---

[55] Scott (1852): 80. McKerrow (1854): 475, was adamant that none of the other ministers followed Bruce's lead, though Hall (1954): 187, noted that Robert Chalmers joined them shortly thereafter.

[56] Associate Synod of Ireland, *Acts and Proceedings, 1788-1808* (Handwritten manuscript, Gamble Library, Belfast): 179-81.

[57] *Ibid.*, 117-20. The story of Thomas's involvement with the Evangelical Society of Ulster has been told by Lester (2000): 181-85, and by Thompson (1986): 24-25.

[58] The draft was issued by the General Associate Synod in 1801, and in 1802, it was published in Belfast. See McKerrow (1854): 438, and Stewart (1950): 381-82.

[59] Associate Synod of Ireland, *Acts and Proceedings* (1788-1808): 151.

[60] Thompson (1986): 25, incorrectly identified the chapters that Thomas opposed because Thompson took his citations from the final (1804) edition of the *Testimony*. The 1802 and 1804 editions are materially different, and an additional chapter was included in the 1804 edition in which the chapter numeration was changed. Thomas did question the chapter on "Public Religious Covenanting," but he also questioned the chapter entitled "Church and State, and the Difference between Them," instead of—according to Thompson—the chapter on "Church Discipline."

[61] Associate Synod of Ireland, *Acts and Proceedings* (1788-1808): 154.

should be transmitted to each Pby [presbytery] to be considered,"[62] and the discussion was postponed each successive year (in the meetings of 1804-1806) until Thomas left for America in 1807.[63] To discover the exact substance of his qualms, someone must recover the statement of 1803; until then we must refer to the *Declaration and Address*.

The *Declaration and Address* could not have passed an Old Light muster. It was one thing to say that "terms of communion" should be drawn exclusively from "the word of God,"[64] but it was something else entirely to divorce the word of God from the interpretations of Presbyterian orthodoxy: "…the Westminster Confession and Catechisms, may, with many other excellent performances, prove eminently useful. But, having served ourselves of these, let our profiting appear to all, by our manifest acquaintance with the Bible."[65]

Most dramatically, Thomas sarcastically challenged the hallowed definitions of Nicea as an affront to the sufficiency of Scripture: "Happy emendation! Blessed expedient! Happy, indeed, for the church, that Athenasius [*sic*] arose in the fourth century, to perfect what the holy apostles and prophets had left in such a rude and unfinished state."[66]

With a telling reference to Mt 23:8-10, Thomas also dismissed the "abstract speculation and argumentative theory" that characterized Calvinistic and Arminian distinctions.[67] He was relatively silent about church/state relations,[68] but against the backdrop of Irish Presbyterianism, the New Light affinities of Thomas Campbell are sufficiently manifest.

Hence, it is doubtful that he opposed the eighteenth and twenty-third chapters because of their doctrinal formulations. Indeed, in his brief synodical statement of 1802, he was chiefly concerned with the "many ministers & others" who would be marginalized by "terms of communion" that they could not accept. His fears were justified by the ultimate defection of Bruce, Hog, M'Crie and Aitken, and his exasperation was still evident in 1809:

> …a partial neglect of the expressly revealed will of God; and …an assumed authority for making the approbation of human opinions, and human inventions, a term of communion…are, and have been, the immediate, obvious, and universally acknowledged causes, of all the corruptions and divisions that ever have taken place in the church of God.[69]

Nothing should be instituted as a "term of communion," he insisted, "that is not as old as the New Testament."[70] Furthermore, as for "inferences and deductions from scripture premises," he would only bind them on a conscience that perceived their logical force.[71]

---

[62] *Ibid.*: 164-65.

[63] *Ibid.*: 182, 203, 226, 257.

[64] T. Campbell, *Declaration and Address of the Christian Association of Washington*, Olbricht and Rollmann (2000) (hereinafter *D&A*): 16: lines 23-30.

[65] *Ibid.*: 42: 33-36.

[66] *Ibid.*: 41: 2-5.

[67] *Ibid.*: 48: 39-46. The passage from Mt 23 is also referenced: 14: 48-15: 1.

[68] Thomas, *D&A*: 7: 49-8: 1, referred to the United States as "a country happily exempted from the baneful influence of a civil establishment of any peculiar form of christianity," but this language is too generic to qualify as a New Light declaration.

[69] *Ibid.*: 18: 8-15.

[70] *Ibid.*: 17: 2-5. Thomas addressed "terms of communion" also in *D&A*: 42: 16, 44: 49.

[71] *Ibid.*: 17: 8-10.

With the ratification of the *Narrative and Testimony*, the New Lights had ironically transgressed their own principles, and had erected their own restrictive standard. With this lesson behind him, Thomas issued a wary caveat in his *Declaration and Address*:

> Let none imagine that the subjoined propositions are at all intended as an overture towards a new creed, or standard, for the church; or, as in any wise designed to be made a term of communion; –nothing can be farther from our intention. They are merely designed for opening up the way....[72]

Indeed, the "subjoined propositions" were anything but creedal, and, judging from the Campbells' own writings, they were seldom invoked.[73]

Conclusion

True statement: The movement of Thomas and Alexander Campbell emerged "from a Scottish background."[74] An unfortunate tendency prevails, however, among primitivistic historians to emphasize the Scottish inspiration of the Glasites, Sandemanians, and Haldanes, and to overlook the evolving Presbyterian heritage that Thomas publicly embraced. The identity of the Seceders has always been accessible: Significant nineteenth-century treatments are available,[75] as well as recent productions of substantial interest.[76] Moreover, the Secession's creedal formulations can be found in published form,[77] and their numerous controversies are volubly chronicled by the disputants themselves.[78] More specifically, the Irish Seceders have been immortalized by David Stewart,[79] and their minute-books lie intact (though rarely disturbed) in a Belfast library. In 1983, Earl West suggested that the Irish Presbyterian context might provide useful insights into the restorationist impulse; such a study, however, still "remains to be done."[80] I hope that this essay demonstrates the fruitful possibilities of that line of research.

By comparing these records with the testimonies of Richardson and the Campbells themselves, it is clear that Thomas, despite the confessional isolation of his Antiburgher

---

[72] *Ibid.*: 15: 47-16: 2.

[73] Doug Foster, "The Understanding and Impact of the *Declaration and Address* among Churches of Christ," Olbricht and Rollmann (2000): 389-90, noted the difficulty in tracing the "reception history" of the *Declaration and Address* among Churches of Christ. In the balance of Thomas Campbell's literary corpus, he reflected in five significant passages on the *D&A* and its original purpose. The earliest retrospection took place in 1832, twenty-three years after the *D&A*'s composition, and the latest, in 1844, thirty-five years after the publication of the defining document: *Religious Reformation* (n. p., [1832]); *Millennial Harbinger* (August 1833): 421-22; (June 1835): 272-73; (March 1839): 142-43; (May 1844): 199.

[74] McMillon (1983): 1; Garrett (1976): 230-34.

[75] David Scott (1852); McKerrow (1854).

[76] For example, Hamilton (1990), Brooke (1994): 87, 92, and McBride (1998).

[77] Chief among these are the *ADT*, the *Testimony* of 1802, and the *N&T*.

[78] See Associate Presbytery (*Present Truth*, 1774), Archibald Bruce, *A Review of the Proceedings of the General Associate Synod...in Reference to the Ministers Who Protested Against the Imposition of a New Testimony* in Bruce (1808): vol. 8, Thomas M'Crie (1871), Hog in Bruce (1808).

[79] Stewart (1950).

[80] Earl West, "Introduction" to McMillon (1983): i. A similar observation was made by Michael Casey, *The Battle Over Hermeneutics in the Stone-Campbell Movement, 1800-1870*, Studies in Religion, 67 (Lewiston, New York: Edwin Mellen, 1998): 9-10.

heritage, had ready access to the New Light principles that would later characterize his *Declaration and Address*. In addition, long before he encountered the Chartiers Presbytery in Pennsylvania, his quest for Christian unity was surely inspired by the divisive wranglings that surrounded the *Narrative and Testimony*. His sentiments in the *Declaration and Address* quite possibly found their earliest expression in the ill-fated statement of 1803.

Finally, if the *Declaration and Address* owes any debt to the spirit of eighteenth-century British New Light ideology, then its reputedly restorationist accent must be reconsidered.[81] The New Lights were not defined by primitivistic restorationism; they were obsessed, instead, with dreams of theological liberty. This priority was so compelling for Thomas that he practically conceded the "latitudinarian" label, and his hermeneutic was ultimately designed to limit the authority of creeds and presbyteries.[82]

> If we take no greater latitude than the divine law allows, either in judging of persons, or doctrines... may we not reasonably hope, that such a latitude will appear to every upright christian, perfectly innocent and unexceptionable? If this be Latitudinarianism, it must be a good thing – and therefore the more we have of it the better; and may be it is, for we are told, "the commandment is exceeding broad."[83]

The *Declaration and Address* was inspired by Thomas's own protracted heresy trial and his eventual deposition.[84] This is significant for several reasons, including his attempt in a number of passages to turn the "latitudinarian" label against his tormentors. Thomas insisted that it properly belonged to those who imposed their "private opinions" upon each other.[85]

Other historians have hailed the *Declaration and Address* as a charter for Christian unity,[86] and this emphasis cannot be denied (the document is saturated with condemnations of division). Even here, however, the unity emphasis is largely derivative, a happy consequence of ecclesiastical liberty. For Thomas, the "bitter root" of division was always the imposition of

---

[81] For striking examples of the Restorationist interpretation, see Tolbert Fanning, "Sketches in the Life of Alexander Campbell, No. 1," *Gospel Advocate* 8 (15 May 1866): 308-9, and Bill J. Humble, *The Story of the Restoration* (Austin: Firm Foundation, 1969): 19. Note also the surveys by Foster (2000): 389-409, and C. J. Dull, "The *Declaration and Address* among Independents" in Olbricht and Rollmann (2000): 411-34.

[82] Thomas Olbricht, "Hermeneutics and the *Declaration and Address*" in Olbricht and Rollmann (2000): 248-49.

[83] *D&A*, 30: 43-31: 2. Thomas completely rejected the latitudinarian label to the degree that it implied a vague and unprincipled application of Scripture. See Christopher Hutson, "Thomas Campbell's Use of Scripture in the *Declaration and Address*" in Olbricht and Rollmann (2000): 219, and Lewis Leroy Snyder, "Forbearance as a Means of Achieving Unity in the *Declaration and Address*" in Olbricht and Rollmann (2000): 306.

[84] The fullest account of this event is in William Herbert Hanna, *Thomas Campbell: Seceder and Christian Union Advocate* (Cincinnati: Standard, 1935): 31-100.

[85] *D&A* 35: 21-23, and see *D&A* 32: 6-7, 33: 37-39, 42: 8-12.

[86] Garrett (1994): 97-117, Holloway and Foster, *Renewing* (2001): 43-44, Harold Kent Straughn, "Unity, Biblical Purity, Spiritual Maturity: Theological Synthesis in the *Declaration and Address*" in Olbricht and Rollmann (2000): 269-92, and Snyder (2000): 303-21. This emphasis has been popularized among Churches of Christ with such presentations as Rubel Shelly, *I Just Want to Be a Christian*, rev. ed. (Nashville: 20th Century Christian, 1984): 65-66.

"private opinions" as "articles of faith or duty," and the alienation of independent minds like his own.[87]

These observations are also important for understanding Alexander Campbell, who, like his father, left the Antiburgher Secession in 1809. Their stories were similar, but not coincidentally so; Thomas was, without question, the most significant influence in his son's ideological development. Moreover, when Alexander began to publish his *Christian Baptist* in 1823, it was scarcely coincidental that his masthead should display a sloganized version of Mt 23:8-10:

> Style no man on earth your father, for he alone is your Father who is in heaven, and all ye are brethren. Assume not the title of Rabbi, for ye have only One Teacher; neither assume the title of leader, for ye have only One Leader.
>
> — the MESSIAH.[88]

This was the ethos of liberty and latitude appropriate for a distinctly American movement, but it had been conceived in the Irish homeland where it had been first illumined by New Light.

---

[87] *D&A* 35: 19-30.

[88] A. Campbell, masthead, *Christian Baptist* 1/1 (4 July 1823): 1. This masthead appears on all subsequent issues of the *Christian Baptist*.

WHY ELDER DONALD MCLAREN'S BAPTIST CHURCH DID NOT HAVE COMMUNION WHEN ELDER WILLIAM TROUT CAME TO VISIT[1]

CLAUDE COX

The first annual meeting of the Canadian Churches of Christ Historical Society took place in the historic Disciples stone meetinghouse at Everton, Ontario. Don Haymes was among those who attended, having made the trip from Indianapolis. He stayed over the Saturday night with our family and worshiped with us the next day. It was good to renew acquaintances with this fascinating individual, a walking encyclopedia of the Stone-Campbell movement. I offer this essay with great pleasure in his honour. The situation I depict was doubtlessly played out many times on the North American frontier as Disciples and Baptists came to terms with each other. In this case, Donald McLaren's refusal of commune with William Trout led Trout to form the Disciples Church at Meaford.

Trout

William Trout's father settled on 800 acres of land in Erin Township in 1821, land given by the Government in compensation for losses suffered at Fort Erie during the War of 1812.[2] The Trouts attended Methodist services, but William found no assurance at the mourner's bench. Then "he incidentally heard of a few families that were not Methodists who met in a private house some distance away." Donald MacLaren was the leading man in the group. "They were Scotch Baptists…. It was not long after this that father was baptized—immersed, in one of those beautiful spring creeks of Erin."[3]

In the late 1830s, Trout had a lease on a flour mill at Norval, Esquesing Township. The family attended meetings in the large family home of Elder John Menzies, who was the usual preacher. A log meetinghouse was built on Menzies' farm, and Trout became "second to the elder in the leadership of the congregation."[4] Indeed, the congregation's records mention the arrival of William Trout as "pastor" in 1838.[5] The Trout family remained with that congregation until 1845. Trout's son told a story about the time when his father challenged Menzies on the propriety of examining baptismal candidates using "old hard catechetical questions." He wrote that Menzies pondered the challenge, then said, "Go on and have it

---

[1] This essay was first presented at the third annual meeting of the Canadian Churches of Christ Historical Society, meeting at Cape Rich, about seven miles north of Meaford, Ontario. Meaford is on the shore of Georgian Bay, Lake Huron, about 100 miles NW of Toronto. See www.ccchs.ca
[2] W.H. Trout, *Trout Family History* (Milwaukee: Meyer-Rotier Printing Co., 1916): 30.
[3] Trout (1916): 48.
[4] *Idem*: 61.
[5] Reuben Butchart, *The Disciples of Christ in Canada since 1830* (Toronto: Toronto Headquarters' Publications, Churches of Christ [Disciples], 1949): 390.

your own way."[6] In 1841 or 1842, Trout and Alexander Anderson were sent by the Esquesing church on a preaching trip to Prince Edward County. About the same time, Trout attended the June Meeting at Bedford, Ohio, a big, annual, evangelistic event among Disciples in the States and soon to become an annual event in Ontario as well.[7]

During these years (1843-46),[8] Trout worked at Collingwood; he built mills at Owen Sound and Sydenham Falls.[9] At Collingwood, the Trouts gathered a small congregation each Sunday, and Trout usually presided.[10] In the spring of 1847, Trout moved to St. Vincent Township, purchasing 50 acres three miles north of Meaford on the shore of Georgian Bay.

McLaren

Donald McLaren was "some 55 years" old when he arrived at Cape Rich in 1838.[11] He had been born, therefore, about 1882. When he had come to Canada and settled in Erin Township is not precisely known. He was an Elder in the Erin Township (Centre) church, which Butchart characterizes as a "Scotch [probably understand *Scottish* by this] Baptist" congregation. This comment is likely dependent upon Alexander Anderson's obituary of Trout, in which he wrote that Trout "was baptized and united with a group of Scotch Baptists in Caledon under the care of Elder Donald McLaren."[12] At the earliest, McLaren would have come to Canada West in the 1820s, i.e., in his late 30s.[13]

McLaren had baptized Trout before 1837, for in 1838 both of them left Erin Township: Trout moved to Esquesing Township, and McLaren went to St. Vincent Township. The direction of the Erin Township Baptist gathering was determined by the preaching efforts of James Black, who lived in the adjoining Eramosa Township, and who, in 1836, began preaching in a schoolhouse in Erin Township.[14] Both McLaren and Trout would have had contact with Black. Much later, in 1863, Trout brought Black to preach at Cape Rich for three nights.[15]

Black's early attempts at Eramosa Township brought a number of people to the point of wanting to be baptized. At that stage, he wrote to a mission board in Scotland, requesting that an ordained Baptist minister come and do the baptizing. Before the missionary arrived, however, Black came to the conclusion that no scriptural warrant prevented any follower of Christ from preaching or administering the ordinances of the

---

[6] Trout (1916): 61-62.

[7] *Idem*: 63.

[8] *Idem*: 43.

[9] *Idem*: 67.

[10] *Idem*: 82.

[11] Frank N. Harding, "The McLarens," *Meaford Express*, May 7, 1942, part of his series, "History of Meaford and St. Vincent."

[12] Trout (1916): 172-173.

[13] "The St. Vincent Book" at the Meaford Public Library says that Duncan McLaren was born in Scotland in 1815, and settled in 1838 at Conc. 6, Lot 31, i.e., across the 7th line from Richard Cox. However, the Census records for St. Vincent in 1871 (District 37, North Grey, Sub-district, St. Vincent Township, Division 3; Reel # C-9955) record Duncan to be 56 years old, born in Ontario. That would put Donald McLaren, Sr., in Ontario in 1820. Perhaps his arrival coincided with that of James Black and several others who came about 1820.

[14] Butchart (1949): 420.

[15] *The Adviser* 2/12 (May 1863): 190. This was a Disciples journal, published in Toronto between 1861 and 1864.

Gospel, i.e., baptism and the Lord's Supper. This change in Black's thinking was a move from a Scottish Baptist understanding to what he would read in Campbell. Did McLaren share that view? Trout did share it, even though his second wife was baptized by Dugald Sinclair, an ordained Baptist, in Scotland.[16] W.H. Trout wrote that at Esquesing Township, his father usually did the baptizing, in the river.[17]

Trout and McLaren Meet in St. Vincent

St. Vincent Township was surveyed in 1833-35, and settlers began to arrive even before the surveying was finished.[18] Among the first of these was Donald McLaren, who settled in the extreme north end of the township, on parts of lots 36 and 37, concession 6 and 7. Harding wrote that McLaren arrived with a wife, two sons, and a daughter, but is not sure whether there were yet other children in the family. The sons' names were Donald; Duncan—born in Scotland in 1815;[19] and Alexander.[20] McLaren gathered together a group of people to meet as a Baptist church. The group apparently included Richard (lot 31, conc. 7) and Joseph Cox. Had they also been baptized by McLaren at Erin? Possibly.

George Jackson, a Disciple for whom Trout worked at Collingwood, preceded the Trouts to St. Vincent in 1846.[21] In fact, when Jackson left, Trout lost interest in being in Collingwood. Jackson had a store in St. Vincent, and Trout built him a small house at the end of it. David Layton, a Disciple, clerked for Jackson. Trout constructed a nice house for Layton, to which he brought his bride, Ellen Stephens, in the winter of 1848-49.[22] Before Trout arrived in St. Vincent Township, a number of Disciples known to Trout already lived there. William Trout's early encounters with Donald McLaren at Cape Rich were described by Trout's son as follows:

> Father was never long in any place without seeking religious affiliation or making some. So considering the prospect of St. Vincent, he thought the likliest [*sic*] way was to renew his old acquaintance with old Elder McLaren, who had baptized him at Erin. The old man, with several sons and daughters, had come north in advance of us, and along with a few neighbors of like mind, met as a Baptist congregation, at McLaren's point or later cape Rich, which was six and one-half miles north of us. We had a boat that we used for a little fishing, and as our principal means of travel. So after we became settled in our new home, and there came a Sunday of nice weather, father and the whole family took the boat, and we rowed up to the point.

---

[16] *Loc. cit.*

[17] *Idem*: 75.

[18] [Bruce Cox,] "After the Redcoats and the Voyageurs," in *St. Vincent. A Beautiful Land. An Illustrated Township History* (Meaford: St. Vincent Heritage Association, 2004): 31. The original title of this essay was "Pioneers in St. Vincent Township, 1830–1850"; I saw it in typescript. The book is excellent. According to its introduction, it had five major contributors—who are named, but unfortunately we are not told who contributed what.

[19] "St. Vincent Book," at the Meaford Public Library. American readers may be interested to know that one of Duncan's sons, Donald, born in 1851, became a Baptist minister in the United States. He died at Walla Walla in 1927. This detail is recorded by Harding in "The McLarens."

[20] Cox, "The Mallory Story," typescript copy: 36. This is an earlier form of the chapter that appeared in *St. Vincent. A Beautiful Land* (2004).

[21] Trout (1916): 43.

[22] *Idem*: 84.

We got there before their meeting time, and were most heartily received, as old friends should have been. *At the meeting father was called upon for the principal speaking. There was no communion service that day.* They said they had no wine. By a pressing invitation we remained to dinner, and through the afternoon, getting home for supper. This Sunday journey was made several times during the summer. *They were always kind, but religiously not approachable. Father finally asked one of the members if they refrained from having communion on his and mother's account, and was told that was the case.* So he abandoned that effort, and endeavoured to start a meeting in our own home.[23] (Italics added.)

The Disciples Church in Meaford began with those meetings in Trout's house, starting in 1848. Our interest is not to follow that story but to inquire about what happened between these old acquaintances, McLaren and Trout that led to a break in their communion.

No Communion: Why?

Theological and personal differences among Christians have often found their flash point at communion. It was during the examination of worthiness in the Presbyterian church that Alexander Campbell put down his communion token—symbol of a passing grade—on the table and left without communing. What was it in this frontier situation in St. Vincent, where the inhabitants were few, and old friends valued, that saw Elder McLaren withhold communion from the Trouts?

Butchart was of the opinion that the Baptist church at Cape Rich practiced closed communion. He put it this way: "[McLaren] founded a strictly Baptist congregation, from which group William Trout had evidently doctrinally emerged, after mixing with the advancing Esquesing church. Trout found the practice of close [sic] communion repugnant to his ideas of Christian fellowship, with its freedom."[24]

In Ufland's brief comments about the Baptists in St. Vincent Township, she wrote that McLaren was "an ordained minister."[25] McLaren had left the Erin Township church while it was making the transition to a Disciples congregation. The church he organized at Cape Rich was not a Disciples church or a "Church of Christ" (the name used at Esquesing) but a Baptist church of the English order, such as he had known in Scotland. Several other immigrant preachers, like Dugald Sinclair, came from that same background. In the case of Sinclair, he retained the central role of an ordained minister, and that means he presided at communion throughout his life at the Poplar Hill (Lobo Township) church.

The late 1830s was a formative period for the Disciples impulse in Canada West. Ideas were in flux; differing understandings of ecclesiology and ministry stood alongside each other. Only the beginnings had been achieved; much needed to be done. When McLaren moved into St. Vincent and gathered a handful of adherents, he organized what he knew best, a Baptist church that practised "closed communion." This meant that members only of that congregation could commune. Trout's presence was awkward for McLaren: The Trout and his family were not communicants of that congregation, and yet McLaren could not honourably refuse to serve communion to a man whom he himself had baptized. McLaren decided that the solution was not to serve the Lord's Supper on days when non-members were present for worship.

---

[23] *Idem*: 89.

[24] Butchart (1949): 417.

[25] Vina Ufland, *History of the Schools of St. Vincent Township and Other Chronicles, 1847-1967* (n.p., n.d.): 237.

One may wonder, however, whether closed communion was the entire issue. In the Old Country, nearly all Scotch Baptists and Scottish Baptists practiced closed communion; communion between the two groups was "rigidly discountenanced."[26] In pioneer Ontario, the situation was more fluid. The Trout family worshiped with Baptists at different times, e.g., at Peterborough, without incident.[27] Baptists of different stripes and Disciples went back and forth—at least some did. McLaren and Trout had been in communion together at Erin Township, but the situation there had changed after McLaren departed.

When Trout had moved to Esquesing Township, he had turned increasingly in the Disciples direction. Young Trout had become a "mover and a shaker" in Disciples circles, a leader in "new ways"; McLaren had stayed where he was. Trout, a successful businessman, was about ten years younger than McLaren, and when the two men met again at St. Vincent, the junior may have posed a threat to the senior's position and theology. McLaren thus made the decision to be cordial but to limit his relationship with Trout.

Perhaps that decision was not made the first time the Trouts showed up at McLaren's for worship. As a Baptist church, the McLaren church would not have celebrated communion every Sunday. Once a month was typical. It took a few visits before the communion question arose seriously in Trout's mind. Surely they would have communion this time! In not having communion, McLaren was protecting his group from Trout's new ideas—Trout was now a "Disciple"—and sending an unspoken message to Trout. So, Trout took the signal and troubled McLaren no further.

Continuing Contacts between the Baptists and Disciples at Cape Rich

In St. Vincent Township, settled in the late 1830s and '40s, Baptists and Disciples had increasing contacts. McLaren's youngest son, Archibald, "a son of the old man, that refused [W. H. Trout's] father communion with him,"[28] married a Disciple, and Trout held meetings in the home of Archibald and his wife when Trout was working at Wilson's mill. W.H. Trout commented that Archibald's marriage indicated that he was "open minded to new settings of the truth." This is a jaundiced comment, but it suggests that McLaren was not open to new ways represented by the Disciples.

Donald McLaren, Jr., was an entrepreneur who had envisaged a town, or at least a village, at Cape Rich. By 1842,[29] he had built a wharf where vessels could dock, take on wood and off-load goods.[30] His brother, Duncan, took over the leadership of the church,

---

[26] George Yuille, *History of the Baptists in Scotland from Pre-Reformation Times* (Glasgow: Baptist Union Publications Committee, 1926): 60. All who were Scottish might be called "Scotch," so the distinction between "Scotch" and "Scottish" is somewhat arbitrary. "Scottish" is used here of Baptists in Scotland who were the product of evangelization by English Baptists, i.e., they were Baptists after the English order, whereby an ordained clergy led the congregation; this was not true of "Scotch" Baptists.

[27] Trout (1916): 167, 168.

[28] *Idem*: 92.

[29] Harding (1942) specifies the date to be 1840. [Bruce Cox,] "The Mallory Story," in *St. Vincent. A Beautiful Land* (2004): 45, puts the date at 1848.

[30] Cox (2004): 43–44, refers to hand-written documents relating to Donald McLaren's dealings with land-dealer Price Mallory. The full version of Cox's paper, "The Mallory Story," appropriately filed under the author's name is on file at the Meaford Public Library. See above, note 18 concerning the failure to ascribe the authors' names in *St. Vincent. A Beautiful Land* (2004).

and by 1868 they were able to build a church building.[31] Not long after this, C.J. Lister, farmer, editor, and preacher, reported in his journal that he had held meetings at Cape Rich and used the Baptist meetinghouse. He wrote:

> At Cape rich [sic] the Baptist Meetinghouse was given us for a few evenings, and was well filled. The clergyman attended twice. Obviously he and the writer did not speak the same things—not perfectly joined together in the same mind and in the same judgment. And while arranging for another evening the deacon sturdily said, "It is settled, sir, that you don't get this house any more." From what had been said about the clergyman, his "friendliness," "agreeableness" and his "preaching so much like the Disciples" and his oft repeated wish to hear them—it is confessed that the brakes were put down rather unexpectedly.— The School House has been occupied a few times since.[32]

Who was this "clergyman?" It may have been "Mr. Ross the Baptist clergyman," who gave lodging to James Black during a series of meetings some weeks later.[33] What were the differences between him and Lister? Had Lister abused the invitation somewhat? Whatever happened, this set-to likely precipitated the construction about this time of a Disciples meetinghouse, a log structure, along the lane of Richard Cox's place (lot 31, conc. 7), which was, by the way, across the road from Duncan McLaren's (lot 31, conc. 6).[34] Then in 1886, the Disciples built a new meetinghouse, much more substantial, on the front corner of the Cox place, just at the road. In the early days, Richard Cox was "the elder": "[He] for many years presided at the Lord's day meetings";[35] later, his son, William, was "the elder" of the congregation. William died in 1915. Note the model of ministry: one elder.

Ufland wrote that the Baptist church waned during the 1870s, sharing the fate of the village. She stated that the building was used on occasion for years and then torn down.[36] Families with the names of McIntosh, Carson, Boyd, and Kennedy had been its mainstay. When the Baptist church at the Cape closed, some of these folk, McLaren's progeny, became connected with the Disciples Church after all. The end came, too, for that small congregation when the whole area was expropriated for a military Tank Range in 1942.[37] By that time, the communion issue of almost a hundred years before had long been forgotten. Baptists and Disciples alike eventually found their places in larger sister congregations in town.

---

[31] Ufland (n. d.): 237.

[32] *The Bible Indicator* 2/8 (Jan. 1870): 126. This journal was published between 1869 and 1872, first in Owen Sound, in 1869, then in Meaford. It was published irregularly and not all issues are extant, but it is a source like no other because of its local interest.

[33] *The Bible Indicator* 2/10 (Mar. 1870): 160.

[34] "St. Vincent Book" (2004).

[35] Joseph Ash, "Reminiscences, No. 14. History of the Rise and Progress of Our Cause in Canada," *Christian Worker* (Beamsville, Ontario: Gospel Herald Foundation, Monograph Series reprint, 1998): 91. Ash wrote twenty-one "Reminiscences," published between 1882 and 1884.

[36] Ufland (n.d.): 238. A photo of the Baptist meetinghouse appears on this same page. P. B. Doran, compiler, *First Baptist Church, Meaford, Ontario, 1884–1984* (n.p., n.d.): 2, wrote that after Meaford became a town, Cape Rich died. The church continued to serve area residents, primarily in the summer, but the building fell into disuse and was torn down during the 1930s or '40s.

[37] See a photo of the last meeting of the Cape Rich church, gathered in front of its frame building, in *St. Vincent. A Beautiful Land* (2004): 388.

A LETTER ON GERALD L. K. SMITH
AND THE KU KLUX KLAN

C. J. DULL

Probably the two most unpleasant names in the history of the Disciples of Christ are Jim Jones and Gerald L.K. Smith. The former is almost universally remembered as the cultic instigator of a mass suicide. The latter now largely endures in popular memory as the founder of a popular passion play and related theme park, although during his active political career, he was known as a "rabble-rouser" and the "dean of American anti-Semites."

One of the more significant but sparsely documented periods of Gerald L. K. Smith's career is the time he spent as a minister in Indianapolis. Smith moved to Indianapolis in January of 1924 and left in September of 1929. From his arrival until October of 1926, he was the minister at Seventh Christian Church, a mostly working-class congregation in the section west of Crown Hill Cemetery known locally as North Indianapolis. The sanctuary of that congregation no longer exists. The addition built by Smith's predecessor, Clay Trusty, is now part of the physical plant of First Baptist Church of North Indianapolis, a predominately African-American congregation. Seventh Christian Church merged with Eighth Christian Church to form Seventh-Eighth United Christian Church. From October of 1926 to September of 1929, Smith was the minister at a congregation near Butler University that was known as Capitol Avenue Christian Church when he took the position. The name was changed during his tenure to University Place Christian Church. In January of 1930, the congregation merged with North Park Christian Church to form University Park Christian Church. Both of these successor congregations are still active congregations of Disciples of Christ.

One issue about Smith's time in Indianapolis is whether he was sympathetic with, or a member of, the second Ku Klux Klan. During Smith's ministry at University Place, the membership included a number of professionals, including F. D. Kershner, who appointed a rabbi as lecturer in Semitic Languages;[1] Dr. Rolla Neil Harger, the pathologist whose testimony was crucial in the conviction of D. C. Stephenson, the head of the Indiana Klan;[2] and a young Jewish dentist, Dr. George F. Goldman, whom Smith baptized.[3] The last two

---

[1] Keith Watkins, *Christian Theological Seminary, Indianapolis* (Zionsville, Indiana: Guild Press of Indiana, 2001): 48. Watkins reported (p. 47) that 7.7% of Disciples in Indianapolis were members of the Klan, and its total membership in Indianapolis approached 40,000.

[2] Dr. Robert Harger, son of Dr. Rolla Neil Harger, author's taped interview, May 7, 1995, about his father's membership at University Place Christian Church. See M. William Lutholtz, *Grand Dragon: D. C. Stephenson and the Ku Klux Klan in Indiana* (West Lafayette, Indiana: Purdue University Press, 1991): 257, 283-4, on Dr. Rolla Harger's testimony in the Stephenson trial.

[3] Russell Blowers, author's taped interview, October 2, 2001, who conducted Dr. Goldman's funeral.

were to break with Smith but not over the Klan.[4] It seems quite clear that Smith's years there were not marked by any outward sympathy with, or involvement in, the Ku Klux Klan. Strangely, during his later, anti-Semitic phase, Smith's enduring reverence for the memory of Huey Long ensured an absence of any sympathy for the Klan.[5]

The situation at Seventh Christian Church had been quite different: The resources of the largely working-class Seventh congregation were considerably less than those of University Place. Smith's predecessor at Seventh, Clay Trusty, who had built two additions to the church, also ran a business, a chain of neighborhood newspapers.[6] The official reason he resigned was that his minister's salary was insufficient for the educating of his five children,[7] although his opposition to the Klan may have been the real reason.[8] He died a little over a year later at age 47. Blacks were beginning to move into that area, also a concern elsewhere in Indianapolis.[9] Other churches in the same area were known to have active Klan chapters.[10]

Most of the literature on Smith's involvement, or not, with the Klan consists of reports of the opinions of various individuals—often years later—that he was or was not a member. At least one significant document from the period also levels the charge, a letter written by W. E. M. Hackleman of Indianapolis[11]. Typed on stationery of The Congress of

---

[4] Dr. Robert Harger (interview, 1995) did not recall the exact nature of the disagreement but was certain it was not concerned with the Klan. Goldman's comments on Smith at Board meetings, as related by Blowers (interview, 2001), are striking: "Board meetings were displays of inordinate behavior on the part of Smith. He demanded his way. He intimidated the Board. At the last meeting Goldman attended, Smith yelled and screamed and got down on the floor and beat the floor."

[5] On Long's denunciation of the Klan, see T. Harry Williams, *Huey Long* (New York: Alfred A. Knopf, 1970): 703.

[6] Joan Cunningham, "*Home-News* (1922—early 1930s)," *The Encyclopedia of Indianapolis*, David J. Bodenhamer and Robert G. Barrows, eds. (Bloomington and Indianapolis: Indiana University Press, 1994): 704.

[7] "They Built Wiser than They Knew: Historical Sketch of Seventh Christian Church, 1883-1933," Prepared and Presented by Mrs. E. E. Shelton at the Fiftieth Anniversary Celebration, June 18, 1933 (Archives of Christian Theological Seminary): 24.

[8] Edwin L. Becker, "1923: Year of Peril for Indianapolis Disciples Pastors," *Encounter* 54 (1993): 381-384. The evidence for Trusty is not so clear-cut as for the two other ministers whom Becker cited. Author's taped interview, May 15, 1997, Mary Holman Weeks: Mary Weeks thought that the Klan controlled Seventh when Smith came, which was one reason her family left for Capitol Avenue Christian Church.

[9] Paul Bogigian, author's taped interview, October 11, 1993, on the appearance of a Black family in North Indianapolis and ensuing Klan harassment. Bogigian's parents had been born in Armenia, thus he was considered a "foreigner," but he seemed not to have had difficulties fitting in at Seventh. A burned cross was inflicted on one Black family that had recently moved into the area, but a family that had lived there for some time was not bothered. See *History of North Park Christian Church and University Place Christian Church and Their Merger into University Park Christian Church and History to June, 1937* (Indianapolis: University Park Christian Church, 1937): 7, in the archives of Christian Theological Seminary.

[10] Bogigian (interview 1993) thought St. Paul M. E. Church, where he had attended, had the most active chapter, with less activity at Seventh Christian, and even less at the Baptist Church.

[11] Guy Israel Hoover papers, Box 22, Folder 22, at Christian Theological Seminary. I wish to thank two deans at Christian Theological Seminary, D. Newell Williams and Clark Williamson, for their assistance in making the CTS archival materials available. Don Haymes has, appropriately, provided

the Disciples of Christ, of which Hackleman was the Executive Secretary-Treasurer, the letter was addressed to G. I. Hoover, who had been chosen State Secretary for Indiana earlier that year.

Exact Text of the Letter

5757 University Ave., 7-22-1926

Dear Brother Hoover:

I take it you are back from the Coast and that you have been inaugurated as State Secretary. While I am away from the state, I want you to know that I am thinking of you and wishing the best things for you in your new work. I wish I were on the Board, now, that you are the Secretary. Somehow, I was a mere figurehead, more or less, of recent years, and while I wanted to do something, the way did not seem to open before me.

Of course, you are more interested in Bethany Assembly than ever. You recall our meetings, both of the Board and our private meeting in the hotel when we paid for the room for an evening[12]–Shelton donating the money.

Shelton has been to see me and he is quite sure that <u>now</u>[13] is the time to change the personnel of the Board. He also wishes to see G.L.Smith made President. Since I am away, and since conditions are as they are, I am very much puzzled as to what I ought to do.

Under conditions, it is hardly fair to a real friend to put him on the Board and expect him to sign notes and tide things over. Then, can the Assembly be tided over? What hope is there?

I would like to see Pritchard and Todd go on the Board. My stock will likely be the balance of power. If I should not come home, I would like for you to vote it—256 shares. It will cost me $25. to come home.

Is Smith the man? He was not the man for State Secretary. I was told he was a Klansman, and also too conservative, and too sensational. I was told those three things eliminated him. Should they eliminate him from consideration for the Presidency of Bethany? I want to do the best thing for Bethany. I have no other desire; but what is best? The Stockholder's meeting is Aug. 4th, Wednesday. Board meeting one week later.

Can you advise me about matters? Will you vote my stock, if I do not get home? What is the outlook?

Yours most truly
Hackleman [handwritten]

---

considerable assistance in these matters. Special thanks are owed to the staff of the Indiana State Library for their assistance.

[12] The "n" in "evening" is inserted by hand. The "hotel" may well refer to a building at the camp; cf. Cauble (1930): n. 14, below.

[13] The underlining is inserted by hand by Hackleman.

P.S. Where are they getting the money to pull off the Fairview Assembly? Railroad fares alone for the talent advertised would be a good-sized amount. Other expenses must be somewhat large under the circumstances.

[the following line is handwritten]
Have done fine work--so my Profs. say!!

Commentary on the Letter

A foolscap copy of the reply is also extant, which, unfortunately, does not illuminate this issue.

Hackleman, who died in an automobile accident the following year, was a beloved figure among Hoosier Disciples.[14] He seems to have been attending a summer session at the University of Chicago.[15] Shelton is in all likelihood E. E. Shelton, a member of Seventh Christian Church and a real estate entrepreneur.[16] He was also a cousin of Dr. Albert Shelton, the missionary killed by bandits in China in 1922.[17]

The nomenclature "G.L. Smith" may seem unusual, but Smith often used his initials. His high school yearbook in Viroqua, Wisconsin, of which he was editor, gives "G.L.K." as his nickname.[18] *The Indianapolis Christian* gives his name as "G. L. K. Smith" in recounting the election of officers, as does the *Indianapolis Star* in its account of a later site consecration.[19] The directory listings in the *Year Books* uniformly say "Gerald L. K. Smith," but in the detail listing by congregation for 1919, this exact form "G. L. Smith" is found.[20] Initials may well have been something of a fashion, since many prominent Disciples ministers of the period went by their initials.[21]

The letter is revealing on a number of levels. While Smith was trumpeting the growth and future program at Seventh, he was pursuing, unsuccessfully, the position of State Secretary. This letter does not prove he was a member of the Klan as much as it shows that

---

[14] C. M. Cauble, *Disciples of Christ in Indiana: Achievements of a Century*, (Indianapolis: Meigs Publishing Company 1930): 216-8. Henry K. Shaw, *Hoosier Disciples* (Bethany Press for the Association of Christian Churches in Indiana, 1966): 191, n. 31. On Bethany Assembly, see Cauble (1930): 219-21, and Shaw (1961): 239-42, 245-6, 290, 291-3, 330-1, 337, 405-6.

[15] W. Barnett Blakemore, *Quest for Intelligence in Ministry* (Chicago: Disciples Divinity House of the University of Chicago, 1970): 155, puts Hackleman in the class of 1926-7.

[16] Shelton (1933): 6, carries an advertisement for the E. E. Shelton Agency, Mrs. Shelton's husband's company, which dealt in cash for real estate, writing insurance, mortgage loans, and the execution of wills and management of estates. A similar ad is found in *The Home-News (South Side)*, March 14, 1924: 4. According to *World Call* 35 (November 1953): 35, Shelton held a life-membership in the Marion County Sunday School Association.

[17] "Seventh Christian Church News," *The Home-News (Visitor)*, January 9, 1925: 6, col. 3.

[18] Yearbook, *The "Pipe of Peace"* (Viroqua Senior High School, Viroqua, Wisconsin, 1915): 17 (original quotes).

[19] *The Indianapolis Christian* 1.1 (April 1926): 1; "Consecrate Ground for Church Building," *Indianapolis Star*, July 25 (1927): 3.

[20] *Year Book of the Disciples of Christ* (1919): 416.

[21] The most prominent was P. H. Welshimer. Others included W. R. Walker and J. H. O. Smith. Gerald L. K. Smith sponsored a revival in 1927 right after the first North American Christian Convention. The evangelist was E. E. Violette; the music evangelist was V. P. Brock.

the leadership of his state denominational machinery accepted it as fact.[22] An FBI file cites a Greenfield, Indiana, informant to the effect that Smith was a Klan lecturer during 1923 or 1924—Wisconsin was his assigned territory, although he spoke in a number of Midwestern States.[23] Some Disciples ministers were known to be Klan lecturers.[24] Edward Jackson, a Disciple and later member at the merged University Park Church, was elected Governor of Indiana with Klan support.[25] George Rutledge, an editor of the *Christian Standard*, was a national officer.[26] The Klan was known to be active in the area Smith came from.[27] Perhaps that distance made it easy to jettison and obscure such ties. Orval Baylor, later "Cincinnati's Klan Preacher," was also in Valparaiso, Indiana, during Smith's student days there.[28]

Getting Smith in Focus

On his being sensational, Smith was remembered in Indianapolis for dedicating a plot of land by cutting down a tree and using the stump for a pulpit.[29] He suggested to Holman Weeks and Mary Ann Hill that they follow him to Shreveport and be married on an airplane.[30] The more dignified P. H. Welshimer was also known for promotions.[31] At Seventh Christian Church, Smith regularly initiated various types of promotions and

---

[22] See both L. Ribuffo, *The Old American Right* (Philadelphia: Temple University Press, 1983): 134, and G. Jeansonne, *Gerald L. K. Smith: Minister of Hate* (New Haven and London: Yale University Press, 1988): 23, on the charge that Smith was a Klan member.

[23] FBI report, September 9, 1943, FBI file 62-43818-339, Indianapolis office file number 100-4754: 1-4; online at http://foia.fbi.gov/gsmith/gsmith8a.pdf : 45ff.

[24] Becker (1993): 371, 372 n. 8. David Siebenaler, "Indiana Disciples of Christ and the Modernist-Fundamentalist Controversy, 1919-1930," *Discipliana* 64/4 (2004): 82.

[25] Becker (1993): 373-4. H. R. Greenapple, *D. C. Stephenson, Irvington 0492: the Demise of the Grand Dragon of the Indiana Ku Klux Klan* (Plainfield, Indiana: SGS Publications, 1989): 164, stated that Edward's brother, James G. Jackson, was listed as Great Titan and (perhaps appropriately!) superintendent of the Home for Feeble Minded at Fort Wayne. Greenapple (157), also listed "Ura Seegar" of West Lebanon as Klokann Chief of Warren County--in all likelihood, despite the different spelling, the Ura Seeger, an Indiana legislator, after whom the chapel at Milligan College (my own undergraduate alma mater) is named. Seeger lived in West Lebanon at the time and was an active Mason, a group the Klan was active in recruiting; "Seeger, Ura" in Justin Walsh, ed., *A Biographical Dictionary of the Indiana General Assembly* (Indianapolis: The Select Committee on the Centennial History of the Indiana General Assembly, 1984): II, 375; on recruiting Masons, see Nancy MacLean, *Behind the Mask of Chivalry* (New York: Oxford University Press, 1994): 7.

[26] James D. Murch, *Adventuring for Christ in Changing Times* (Louisville, Kentucky: Restoration Press, 1973): 59, opposed him in a congregational fight over Klan control. It may be worth noting that F. D. Kershner preached Rutledge's funeral; see "G. P. Rutledge Dies at Middletown, Ohio," *The Christian-Evangelist* 85 (1947): 703.

[27] *The Republican Observer* (Richland Center, Wisconsin), December 2, 1926: 6, col. 5, carries a short piece by "A. Klansman" relating the giving, "in full robe", of a sum of money to a minister in a small community north of town.

[28] O. W. Baylor, "Valparaiso Bible College," *Christian Standard* 52 (1916): 293; on Smith's chronology, see Jeansonne (1988): 17-19, Ribuffo (1983): 130-1.

[29] Shelton (1933): 24

[30] Weeks (interview 1997).

[31] F. Arant, *"P. H.": The Welshimer Story* (Cincinnati: Standard Publishing, 1958): 44, 46-7, 62-3.

"special days," ranging from Mother's Day to honors for fraternal lodges.[32] Henry Halley of the widely used *Handbook* gave a Bible memorization seminar there.[33]

As to Smith's conservatism, Siebenaler, following Alva Taylor, a modernist, suggested that fundamentalists were the basic constituency of the Klan,[34] and he described Smith as a fundamentalist, though he did not connect him directly with the Klan.[35] Hackleman did state in the letter that Smith was "too conservative," but would he have qualified as such? It is worth noting that he is not called a fundamentalist by these two experienced churchmen, Hackleman and Hoover. Deciding whether Smith was a fundamentalist may well contribute to a more accurate assessment as to whether fundamentalism was basic to the constituency of the Klan.[36]

Ribuffo made the point that Smith became more conservative theologically as a result of his far-right political activism.[37] A comparison with his political views may indicate the divergence of the the better-known Smith of the 1940s and '50s from Smith of the 1920s. The words "America First" have become almost synonymous with Smith, who became virtually a paradigmatic isolationist; yet in 1925, Smith had been part of a committee that brought Hamilton Holt, described by one biographer as the "quintessential internationalist," to speak at Roberts Park Methodist Church in Indianapolis on the World Court Movement.[38] In the early 1930s, Smith was a pro-labor and socially liberal, taking positions almost diametrically

---

[32] Smith himself was a member of the Clifton Lodge of the Knights of Pythias; see "K. of P. to Attend Church," *The Home-News (Visitor),* November 7, 1924: 1, col. 1.

[33] "Seventh Christian Church News," *The Home-News (Visitor),* January 2, 1925: 1, col. 5.

[34] Siebenaler (2004): 111.

[35] *Idem*: 113.

[36] This is not a new charge by a representative of what I call the "Old Disciples," who consistently blame fundamentalists for the break between the Disciples and Independents. The *bête noire* has most recently been Burris Butler, the combative editor of the *Christian Standard* from 1944 to 1957. See Henry Webb, *In Search of Christian Unity* (Abilene: ACU Press, 2003): 352-4; Kevin Kragenbrink, "Dividing the Disciples" (unpublished Ph.D. thesis, Auburn University, 1997): 357. The essential stance of the "Old Disciples" is that, had certain events turned out differently, the Disciples/Independents split might not have occurred. Most of all, their reverence for the Commission for Restudy—see Webb (2003): 329-348, especially 335—generally resulted in a negative view of the foundation of the North American Christian Convention, which the Commission judged "tending to divide," even though Dean Walker had served as its president. On this group, see C. J. Dull, "Intellectual Factions and Groupings of the Independent Christian Churches," *Seminary Review* 31 (1985): 95-8, and "The Declaration and Address among Independents," in T. Olbricht and H. Rollmann, eds., *The Quest for Christian Unity, Peace, and Purity in Thomas Campbell's Declaration and Address* (Lanham, Maryland and London: Scarecrow Press, 2000): 417-20.

[37] Ribuffo (1983): 167f., contrasted Smith with Gerald Winrod, whose theological conservatism led to far-right politics; he also mentioned that Smith did not call himself a fundamentalist even during this more conservative period.

[38] "Seventh Christian Church News," *The Home-News (Visitor),* January 16, 1925: 6, col. 4. On Holt, see Justus D. Doeneck, "Holt, Hamilton Bowen," in John Garraty and Mark Carnes, eds., *American National Biography* (Oxford and New York: Oxford University Press, 1999): vol. 11: 98-99. The term "America First" does occur in Disciples missionary literature. Stephen Corey, long-time UCMS executive, condemned it; see his *The Preacher and His Missionary Message* (Nashville: Cokesbury Press, 1930), 146-7; *idem, Missions Matching the Hour* (Nashville: Cokesbury Press, 1931): 40-41.

opposed to his views a decade later—even before his association with Huey Long.[39] Known later for his anti-Semitism, Smith had earlier spoken to Jewish organizations and synagogues.[40] Nothing is more likely to deceive the interpreter of Smith's early career than his later career.

Smith was a protégé of Claude Hill,[41] best known for being minister of First Christian Church in Tulsa. Head of the Peace Committee in 1925,[42] Hill died an active, Cooperative Disciple.[43] Smith was clearly a Cooperative supporter. In a 1926 article, Smith is mentioned as serving on the Board of Recommendations of the 1925 International Convention in Oklahoma City, and being a member of the evangelistic committee of the Indianapolis Church Federation and treasurer of the National Evangelistic Association.[44] Among those making appearances at Seventh Christian Church were a Miss Harris of the UCMS, [45] a Miss Montague, who was a delegate to the International Convention in Colorado Springs,[46] and two elementary-school workers from the College of Missions.[47] The Seventh congregation also supported a UCMS missionary, R. A. MacLeod.[48]

Early in his career, Smith was supported by the Christian Restoration Association during Murch's presidency;[49] that seems to have ended when he left Beloit, Wisconsin, in autumn 1922. He was once a friend of C. G. Kindred, one of the few premillennialists of significance among the Disciples, who performed Smith's wedding ceremony.[50] Yet, when he stole the show at the 1922 Restoration Congress in St. Louis, differences arose between the management of the Congress and a more conservative group led by R.C. Foster, which was planning another congress.[51] Smith certainly was not sectarian in the sense often attributed to the North American Christian Convention.[52] One of the first things he did in Indianapolis

---

[39] Jeansonne (1988): 24-7; Donald Meyer, *The Protestant Search for Political Realism, 1919-1941* (Berkeley and Los Angeles: University of California Press, 1960): 342, pointed out that Alva Taylor praised Smith's work during this period.

[40] Jeansonne (1988): 24, 65, 67. For the transition to his later views, *idem*: 64-79.

[41] Gerald L. K. Smith, *Besieged Patriot: Autobiographical Episodes Exposing Communism, Traitorism, and Zionism from the Life of Gerald L. K. Smith,* Elna M. Smith and Charles F. Robertson, eds. (Eureka Springs, Arkansas, 1978): 144, 283; cf. Ribuffo (1983): 133f.

[42] Webb (2003): 300-1.

[43] "Claude E. Hill Dies," *The Christian-Evangelist* 95 (1957): 281; Hill's last entry in the *Christian Standard* was in 1941.

[44] L. Peres Buroker, "Two and One-Half Years of Fruitful Service," *The Christian-Evangelist* 63 (1926): 857.

[45] "Seventh Christian Church," *The Home-News (Visitor),* April 11, 1924: 1, col. 6.

[46] *Idem,* April 18, 1924: 1, col. 2.

[47] *Ibid.*: 1, col. 3.

[48] "MacLeod's to Arrive in America June 7th," *The Home-News (Visitor),* May 16, 1924: 1, col. 4.

[49] Murch (1973): 82-3.

[50] Smith (1978): 132.

[51] "New Testament Church Congress," *Christian Standard* 58 (1922): 97.

[52] Smith advertised a month-long revival in the first NACC program but did not speak at it. The assertion of Becker and Siebenaler that the NACC was an assembly of fundamentalist Disciples seems at best simplified. Both F.D. and Bruce Kershner spoke there, and the first session was presided over by J.W. Atherton, a Butler administrator with a Ph.D. from the University of Chicago. In the middle of the publicity about its program, the *Christian Standard* printed an article by G. I. Hoover, "Some Definitive Objectives of the Indiana Christian Missionary Association," 62 (1927): 892. Even

was to take part in union evangelistic services with Methodists, Baptists, and Presbyterians.[53] He also urged his young people to attend evangelistic services at United Brethren and Baptist churches.[54] His chorus director, Raymond Harris, preached his first sermon at a Community Church.[55] In regard to Cooperative institutions, often opposed by fundamentalists and many conservatives, Smith certainly did not oppose them. Ribuffo pointed out that Smith remained aloof from the World Christian Fundamentals Association, considered both sides in the Scopes trial to be too rigid, and showed no interest in dispensationalism; indeed, Smith later remembered that he had "toyed with modernism."[56] Calling Smith a "fundamentalist" seems inappropriate for this earlier period.[57]

Perhaps most fascinating about Hackleman's comments is that being a Klansman in and of itself was apparently not sufficient to disqualify Smith for the position of State Secretary; rather, the combination of those three things—sensationalism, conservatism, and Klan membership—did so. Indeed, Hackleman seems to be referring obliquely to Smith as a "true friend." That brings up the issues of whether a direct relationship prevailed between the Klan and fundamentalism, and how opposed to the Klan some of those preachers actually were. What is fascinating is the frequent personal association of those allegedly opposed to the Klan with those allegedly active in it.

For example, aspects of Trusty's career make it difficult to assume in a facile way that his opposition to the Klan was absolute. In all likelihood, his opposition to the Klan may have been somewhat more nuanced and particular, conceivably incremental. When Professor Morro left Butler University—apparently under pressure—to join the College of Missions, Trusty published an indignant and impassioned editorial.[58] Nothing remotely like that followed either Trusty's own departure from the pulpit of Seventh or any hint, as

---

Welshimer, its president, regularly cooperated with the local council of churches in Canton, Ohio ; cf. Murch (1973): 190.

[53] "St. Paul M. E. Church," *The Home-News (Visitor)*, January 18, 1924: 4, col. 1.

[54] "Seventh Christian Church News," *ibid.*, February 20, 1925: 6, col. 5; "Seventh Christian Church News," *ibid.*, April 24, 1925: 4, col. 4.

[55] *Ibid.*: 4, col. 5.

[56] Ribuffo (1983): 133.

[57] Even Smith's participation in the Indiana Christian Institute is not certain. The local publicity— printed in a Trusty paper—does not mention Smith ("Institute at Englewood," *The Home-News [East Side]*, February 2, 1924: 2, col. 3); neither did Baylor mention Smith in his article about the Institute: O. W. Baylor, "Indiana Christian Institute," *Christian Standard* 59 (1924): 647. The big issue at the Institute seems to have been the UCMS, which had both opponents and supporters present who engaged in spirited discussion. If Smith were there, he probably was one of the UCMS proponents. The program for the Institute lists him only as leading a discussion. B. L. Allen, "Indiana Notes and News," *Christian Standard* 59 (1924): 646, commented that Daniel A. Sommer of the *Apostolic Review* attended the Institute and enjoyed it. Daniel Sommer's opposition to missionary societies was well known, which would certainly have made him at home with opponents of the UCMS. Sommer was also a vigorous critic of restrictive racial policies among the Churches of Christ, which makes it unlikely that such policies had been advocated at the gathering in Indiana; otherwise, Sommer would have registered his disapproval. I wish to thank Terry Gardner for this background on Daniel Sommer's views on race.

[58] "Professor Morro's Resignation," *The Home-News (East Side)*, December 14, 1923: 2, cols. 1-4.

in the case of Griggs's resignation from his congregation, of another issue.[59] If Trusty had strong feelings about the ministries of Trinkle and Smith, they did not stop him from publishing regular notes and short articles about the activities at Englewood and Seventh, often on the front page.[60] This included not only such things as revivals and special programs but also such personal details as Trinkle's being involved in a car/train collision,[61] Smith's having the flu,[62] and even such banalities as Smith's going for a ride in a "new sedan."[63] More to the point, Trusty printed a three-column ad just before the Easter *following* his termination for a "100% American Service" at St. Paul M.E. Church.[64] This service was scheduled from 9:00 a.m. to 10:00 a.m. so men could attend it and still make it to the regularly scheduled worship at other churches. Seventh was one of the few in the vicinity that would qualify. Seventh's started at 10:30. It is easy to talk about the complexities of commerce or the compromises involved in making a living, but in this case, opposition to Klan-related activities did not extend to the commercial realm.

Moreover, stereotypical cartoons of blackface characters appeared in Trusty's publications. One, apparently by Paul Kettner, shows a blackface character looking over a fence at a field called "North" eying a watermelon entitled "big wages."[65] One issue of "Mickie, The Printer's Devil," related a conversation between Mickie and a blackface character named "Snowball," who was deserting his wife.[66] A number of Disciples congregations put on blackface minstrel shows; the Downey Avenue Church's was the best known, and the president of the Bible class that staged the show was Trusty's brother, Floyd.[67] After Trusty's death, an ad for Klan songs appeared in his newspapers, as did news of Jewish happenings.[68]

---

[59] Trusty's newspaper chain was doing very well at this time; he had just added two papers; cf. "The Home-News Closes Greatest Year," *ibid.*, December 28, 1923: 1, col. 7.

[60] Trusty certainly lost no opportunity to mention subsequent favorable news about Davison, even after he had left the area; cf. "Rev. F. E. Davison Doing Outstanding Work in Chicago," *ibid.*, September 25, 1925: 1, col. 2.

[61] "Rev. Trinkle and Family Have Narrow Escape," *The Home-News (East Side)* November 2, 1923: 6, col. 3.

[62] "Personal Mention," *The Home-News (Visitor)*, March 28, 1924: 1, col. 2; "Sick List," *ibid.*, October 3, 1924: 1, col. 2.

[63] "Personal Mention," *ibid.*, April 25, 1924: 1, col. 6.

[64] *Ibid.*, April 18, 1924: 3. This congregation probably gets more ink in the paper than any other. The speaker was Vinson Manifold, who in a later issue, *ibid.*, November 6, 1925: 1, is addressed as "Judge" in an ad for an Armistice Day celebration. In "City News in Brief," *The Home-News (East Side)*, August 24, 1923: 1f, col. 3, Trusty does report that an exclusively anti-KKK ticket was elected at the Central Labor Union Delegates Meeting on August 17, 1923.

[65] "Tempting," *ibid.*, July 13, 1923: 1.

[66] *Ibid.*: April 4, 1924: 3.

[67] "Will Appear in the '1924 Minstrel' at the Masonic Temple, April 3," *ibid.*, March 28, 1924: 1, cols. 3-5. "Big 1925 Minstrel Coming Soon," *ibid.*: col. 3; the subheading runs, "Men's Bible Class in Black-Face Speciality."

[68] For example, *ibid.*, March 27, 1925: 4, col. 6. This seems to illustrate the point of Leonard J. Moore, *Citizen Klansmen: the Ku Klux Klan in Indiana, 1921-1928* (Chapel Hill and London: University of North Carolina, 1991): 143-4.

During this period of apparent Klan control at Seventh, both Alva Taylor[69] and C. W. Cauble[70] filled the pulpit there to positive responses. If, in fact, Klan control were that strong[71] —and their views were well known—it is difficult to believe they would have been asked to preach at that church. Unless relations were then what the British might call "terribly civilized" rather than increasingly polarized, at least one of the two previous conditions must not be true. Both Trusty and Taylor served on the Disciples Board of Temperance with Edward Jackson,[72] who was later elected Governor with Klan support. Either their opposition was not so well known as that of Davison or Griggs or they were not so opposed as later sources—including themselves—have portrayed.[73] For many, what had been acceptable before Stephenson's conviction undoubtedly was not so afterwards. An understanding of Taylor's appeal to a congregation sympathetic to the Klan—and perhaps Smith's later passion against miscegenation—may be gleaned from a 1926 article on race. Even as he argued for justice for Blacks, Taylor also made the following comments: "Social intermixing is desired by the better men of neither race. The immoral have done the intermixing."[74]

Since Trusty had been an active member of the National Board of Temperance and Social Welfare of the Disciples of Christ for several years and had been re-elected shortly before his death,[75] one can reasonably conceive that he and others found the Klan's support of prohibition a positive development, or that the Klan found his Temperance efforts admirable.[76] He was

---

[69] "Personal Mention," *The Home-News (Visitor)*, September 9, 1924: 1, col. 5.

[70] "Seventh Christian Church News," *ibid.*, August 21, 1925: 1, col. 2. The article states that Cauble "is always a welcome guest."

[71] Irving Leibowitz, *My Indiana* (Englewood Cliffs, New Jersey: Prentice-Hall, 1964): 213, quoting Trusty, Jr., to the effect that only four or five families at Seventh were not sympathetic to the Klan.

[72] On Trusty, the elder, see Leibowitz (1964): 213; on Taylor, see W. E. M. Hackleman, "The New Governor of the Hoosier State," *The Christian-Evangelist* 62 (1925): 82.

[73] Many, if not all, of the statements about Trusty's opposition derive from his son, Clay Trusty, Jr., later an editor for the Indianapolis News. He was approximately 7 years old during these events, and the information for one version of these events is a letter written in 1983, sixty years after; cf. R. Tucker, *The Dragon and the Cross* (Hamden, Connecticut: Archon, 1991): 210, n. 18. Trusty, Jr., represented his father as an advocate for the inclusion of Catholic youth in the activity center. Leibowitz (1964): 213, the earlier account, mentioned the invitation from the elder Trusty to Bishop Chartrand to be guest lecturer at a YMCA religion class. The younger Trusty married a Roman Catholic and subsequently converted to Catholicism. For his obituary, see Russell B. Pulliam, "Clay Trusty Jr. had been an editor at *The News*," *Indianapolis News*, December 14, 1996: C9.

[74] A. W. Taylor, "Tilt Up the Color Line," *World Call* 8 (February, 1926): 12. According to the title of Taylor's obituary in the same periodical, he was "A Modern Christian Prophet," *World Call* 39 (November 7, 1957). On Smith see Ribuffo (1983): 165, and especially Jeansonne (1988): 125.

[75] "Death Takes Founder and Manager of Home-News Papers," *The Home-News (Visitor)*, October 31, 1924: 1, col. 1. For an example of Prohibition news, see "Twenty Gallons of Liquor Seized," *ibid.*, July 18, 1924: 1, col. 3.

[76] Leibowitz (1964): 213, quoting Trusty, Jr., related a cross-burning: "One night Dad came home and told us we were going to eat dinner early. He packed the whole family in the car, all five kids, and we drove to Clifton and 37th Street, where members of his own congregation burned a cross in his honor." I doubt that this incident was meant to intimidate Trusty, since it took place at a neutral site, not Trusty's home. He had known the incident was coming. One might suggest "in his honor" is meant ironically, but the younger Trusty had been an editor for over four decades, so he could be expected to

also a member of the North Park Masonic Lodge, which was reputed to have an active Klan chapter.[77] After leaving Seventh, Trusty became a member at Central Christian Church, where his funeral was held in October 1924; the situation there was not polarized enough to keep Smith from speaking for a youth banquet at the same church in May 1924.[78] Perhaps the pendulum had swung back somewhat. One of the honorary pallbearers at Trusty's funeral was George Graves, who had been elected Board chairman at Seventh earlier that month.[79] In January of 1925, a newspaper item indicated that internal difficulties were not yet completely resolved:

> Last Sunday was the first anniversary of Rev. Gerald Smith's coming to the Seventh Christian Church. At the morning service he gave a beautiful talk, asking that the people work together with him in the same fine spirit they had in the past year. … He implored that we all start the new year's work right by putting aside any malice, hatred or jealousy which we might feel toward our fellow men.[80]

In regard to the more general equation of fundamentalists and Klan members, a number of difficulties arise. In particular, Murch, head of the Christian Rrestoration Association and *ex officio* president of Cincinnati Bible Seminary during this period, also fought Orval Baylor, "Cincinnati's Klan Preacher," helping to oust him from his pulpit.[81] On the other side, the identification of Charles Gunsolus as a fundamentalist seems bizarre. He had graduated from Butler in 1920, at a time when the dominant influence was Professor W. C. Morro. The last year Morro was at Butler (1923) was also the last year Gunsolus can be found in the Disciples *Year Book*.[82] He went on to write a B.D. thesis (1930) at Butler on the "History and Doctrines of Theosophy," and an M.A. thesis the same year on an "Investigation into Theories of Metempsychosis." He seems never to have held a permanent Disciples pastorate. The two speaking engagements cited by Siebenaler are both to Congregational Churches.[83] The first Disciples periodical to mention him is a Cooperative one, the *Year Book*, and the last is a

---

have added quote marks or some qualifier to make the irony evident. It seems more reasonable to interpret this incident as a genuine attempt to honor the elder Trusty, however questionable the gesture may appear subsequently. Trusty had not been afraid to take his whole family, including small children, to the event.

[77] On Trusty's Masonic burial, see his obituary (note 74, above). On a Klan chapter at the Lodge, see Bogigian (interview 1993), who had joined the Lodge in 1937, and by that time, he said, they merely wanted to forget the Klan years.

[78] "Reverend Smith Guest of Honor," *The Home-News (Visitor)*, May 2, 1924: 1, col. 4.

[79] "Seventh Christian Church," *ibid.*, October 10, 1924: 1, col. 1; see note 74, above, for funeral.

[80] "Seventh Christian Church News," *ibid.*, January 9, 1925: 6, col. 3.

[81] Murch (1973): 59. Baylor also had written for a Cooperative publication, "The Idle Christian," *The Christian-Evangelist* 55 (1918): 633. At the time, he was pastor of First Christian Church in Ottumwa, Iowa (628), now a Disciples congregation.

[82] The spelling in the *Yearbooks* is "Gunsaulus."

[83] Cf. Siebenaler (2004): 124, n. 100; the correct page number for the *Christian Standard* reference is 3,782; *idem*, "Indiana Disciples of Christ and the Modernist-Fundamentalist Controversy, 1919-1930" (unpublished M.A. thesis, Ball State University, 2004): 66.

Cooperative one, *World Call*.[84] We can perhaps get some feel for the theological climate at Butler in this period by noting that a Unitarian minister spoke in chapel.[85]

The identification of fundamentalist with Klansman also runs contrary to Moore's research, which is both transdenominational and surprising.[86] No one would have predicted a significant involvement in the Klan by Quakers, yet there it was. No one would have expected that Churches of Christ (and perhaps some conservative Disciples congregations, who often used the same name, are included in that group) would have been one of the denominations least involved with the Klan, but there that was, too.[87] Above all, as an Agatha Christie character (the Greek doctor in *Murder on the Orient Express*) comments, "The psychology is wrong." Fundamentalist Disciples were often opposed to cooperation with institutions within their own group and very sensitive to attempts to impose control on themselves by institutional forces. To think they would easily and quickly accept cooperation with, much less control by, some outside institution simply does not fit. The greater sectarianism of conservative Disciples and Churches of Christ would, in addition, not seem congruent with not only an outside group but also one that included many who did not practice baptism by immersion—an anti-ecumenical stance that saved them from KKK involvement. Even as Baptists, with their strong tradition of congregational independence, were less likely than Methodists to be Klan members, so it would be logical among Restorationists that those who cared about congregational autonomy theologically would be less likely to go in the direction of actual membership in the Klan. To talk about Klan membership as a means of local control[88] is at best illusory since every state Grand Dragon could overrule a local chapter, and the Imperial Wizard could overrule every Dragon. All state and national Klan officers were appointed from above.[89] When Stephenson was deposed by the Wizard, local support did not reinstate him.

Fundamentalists might seem to have been a fertile recruiting ground for Klan membership since conservative Christian theological intolerance or rigidity would seem a natural correlation to Klan rigidity and intolerance of race and sect.[90] Historically, however, the politicization of fundamentalism during this period was somewhat haphazard and unstable.[91] In the related area of anti-Semitism, fundamentalists saw the dangers of the Nazis earlier and clearer than did most on the left, whose record in this area was much less praiseworthy, including *Christian Century* editors.[92]

---

[84] The first mention of Gunsolus in the *Year Book* is for 1919; the last mention of which I know is "Busy Days on the College Campus," *World Call*, December 1932: 32.

[85] "Dr. Frank Wicks at Butler Chapel," *The Home-News (East Side)*, March 21, 1924: 1, col. 4.

[86] Moore (1991): 70-5.

[87] Cf. H. Leo Boles, "Query Department," *Gospel Advocate* 69 (10 March 1927): 232 for a typical argument against participation in the KKK.

[88] Siebenaler in *Discipliana* (2004): 110.

[89] MacLean (1994): 19-20.

[90] Comparisons of both parallels and differences between Christian and Islamic fundamentalisms are significant in our time. See Bernard Lewis, *The Crisis of Islam* (New York: the Modern Library, 2003): 23-4, and William Martin, "Three Paths to Eden," in this volume.

[91] George Marsden, *Fundamentalism and American Culture* (New York and Oxford: Oxford University Press, 1980): 208.

[92] Joel Carpenter, *Revive Us Again* (New York and Oxford: Oxford University Press, 1997): 93. On Disciple modernists, see C. Williamson and C. Blaisdell, "Disciples and Mainstream Protestant

What in fact deserves a closer look is the interaction between the Klan and Cooperative Christian Churches. It is certainly clear that Cooperative congregations did have Klan chapters within their membership. Becker mentions four Cooperative churches that had KKK difficulties, and three of these remained Cooperative.[93] Klan-supported Governor Jackson was a member at Downey Avenue Christian Church and University Park Christian Church,[94] both of them congregations that were Cooperative and would play significant roles in the Restructured Disciples.

Again, the career of Clay Trusty, Sr., deserves mention. He is remembered in his obituary for having preached at Seventh for sixteen years, with 1,400 additions, and for building one major building. Thus, in those years until his resignation, this congregation was consistently exposed to non-fundamentalist preaching. His ministry seems to have been successful and reasonably popular. Where, then, was the source of the supposed fundamentalism that so suddenly came to dominate the congregation to the degree that only four or five families were exempt? The sources do not suggest a general drift theologically to the right but rather only a specific objection to the Klan. Rather than positing fundamentalism as an intermediate step to the Klan, it seems more logical to infer a direct move, however perverted, to the KKK from the theology that Trusty had long propounded. In fact, all the congregations mentioned by Becker had been served by non-fundamentalist, often socially activist preachers, in the years before the problem with the Klan occurred.[95] Fundamentalism, therefore, came into the picture only after the Klan appeared, if at all. What seems more likely than conservative theology's leading to adoption of the Klan is that some congregations saw in the Klan a means of fulfillment or carrying out of the socially based Christianity that had been preached to them for years. These congregations were accustomed to cooperating not only with their own organizations but also with local ecumenical and other organizations before the KKK appeared. One of the first things Smith did at Seventh Christian Church was set up a Christian Endeavor chapter.[96]

Finally, in some sense Cooperative churches, organizations, and rhetoric may have formed something of a (to use Eusebius's phrase) *praeparatio evangelii* for the coming of the Klan. In the same issue of the *Christian-Evangelist* with Baylor's article—so we can be fairly certain he read it—is a striking editorial. It is unsigned and thus probably by B.A. Abbott,[97]

Theology," in D. Newell Williams, Editor, *A Case Study of Mainstream Protestantism* (Grand Rapids and St. Louis: William B. Eerdmans and Chalice Press, 1991): 132-4.

[93] Becker (1993): 369-86.

[94] Cf. Hackleman (1925): 82, and Becker (1993): 373.

[95] Becker (1993): 369-86.

[96] Smith began at Seventh on January 1, 1924; the February 1 issue of *The Home-News (Visitor)*: 1, col. 3, contains the news about the Christian Endeavor chapter.

[97] B. A. Abbott, *The Disciples: an Interpretation* (St. Louis: Christian Board of Publication, 1924): 238—words on things worth cooperating for may well be pertinent: "There is a very wide range of movements for Christian cooperation. They include local crusades for community betterment; nation-wide campaigns for the uplift of the people; local and world "drives" for the relief of sufferers from accident, drought, oppression or persecution; efforts to Christianize industry; enterprises for better schools and better homes; and endeavors to enforce laws in the community and in the nation at large. The establishment of permanent world-wide peace is the greatest cause of all and probably includes all

since editorials by the editor emeritus, J. H. Garrison, are so marked. The title—"Shall We Have a Nation-wide Life-extension Campaign?"—is pretty mundane; the subtitle—"The Call of the Fiery Cross"—is not. Toward the end, the editorial begins to conclude with this rhetorical flourish, quoting a "great writer": "In olden times when danger threatened, the Scottish clansmen sped the call to arms over hill and moor by the Fiery Cross—two charred sticks dipped in blood...."[98] Slightly later, W. R. Warren made a reference to these same Scottish Highlanders as a "superior race."[99]

"Clansmen?" "The Fiery Cross?" "Superior Race?" It should not surprise us that a second Klan found fertile ground.

---

the rest." Abbot did not mention the Klan but did mention as particularly noble the Women's Christian Temperance Union, the Anti-Saloon League, and Christian Endeavor (240-42).

[98] *The Christian-Evangelist* 55 (1918): 627-8.

[99] W. R. Warren, *The Life and Labors of Archibald McLean* (St. Louis: Bethany Press for the United Christian Missionary Society, 1923): 17.

DISCIPLES IN THE WHITE HOUSE

RONALD B. FLOWERS

The three presidents of the United States who were nurtured in the Disciples of Christ tradition were James Abram Garfield, Lyndon Baines Johnson, and Ronald Wilson Reagan. My focus in this essay is on the thinking of each about church and state.

Disciples valued religious liberty from their inception. In the *Declaration and Address*, Thomas Campbell sang the praises of freedom in Christ. Calling on Christians to put away their denominational names and loyalties, he naturally pointed out that Christ had not only made them free from sin but also enabled people to move away from previous alignments to restore the primitive church, although anything in this passage about civil or political liberty is implicit.

> Resume that precious, that dear bought liberty, wherewith Christ has made his people free; a liberty from subjection to any authority but his own, in matters of religion. Call no man father, no man master upon earth;—for one is your master, even Christ, and all ye are brethren. Stand fast therefore in this precious liberty, and be not entangled again with the yoke of bondage.[1]

Ronald Osborn made explicit the civil implications of Campbell's religious thinking: "To Campbell's Scotch-Irish constituents…'setting Christ on his throne' had meant repudiating all pretensions by any earthly power, civil or ecclesiastical, over the soul of the Christian. Divine sovereignty and Christian liberty were two sides of a coin."[2] Osborn's thesis is that "insistence on freedom has been a dominant strain in the Disciples' self-consciousness."[3]

Campbell wrote more specifically about political religious liberty. He was aware the religious freedom guaranteed by the American Constitution made politically possible his call for a reformation of the churches to begin something new. This gift of possibility was not only the largess of government, although it was that, but also a gift of God.

> The favorable opportunity which Divine Providence has put into your hands, in this happy country, for the accomplishment of so great a good, is a consideration of no small encouragement. A country happily exempted from the baneful influence of a civil establishment of any peculiar form of Christianity—from under the direct influence of the anti-Christian hierarchy—and at the same time,

---

[1] Thomas H. Olbricht and Hans Rollmann, *The Quest for Christian Unity, Peace, and Purity in Thomas Campbell's* Declaration and Address: *Text and Studies* (Lanham, Maryland: The Scarecrow Press, 2000): 16(14)-17(15).

[2] Ronald E. Osborn, *Experiment in Liberty: The Ideal of Freedom in the Experience of the Disciples of Christ* (St. Louis: The Bethany Press, 1978): 23.

[3] Osborn (1978): 14.

from any formal connection with the devoted[4] nations, that have given their strength and power unto the beast; ... Can the Lord expect, or require, anything less, from a people in such unhampered circumstances—from a people so liberally furnished with all means and mercies, than a thorough reformation, in all things civil and religious, according to his word?[5]

Alexander Campbell followed his father in praise of religious liberty. The younger Campbell believed in a strict separation of church and state,[6] so much so that he disapproved of church-sponsored moral societies to try to change society. The church had no business in trying to reform the state.

Alexander Campbell changed his mind on many things as he grew older and as the Disciples matured into a more structured movement. On church and state, however, he seems to have remained fairly consistent. In 1830, he wrote:

This government proposes only to guard the temporal and worldly rights of men. It regards this world as the only appropriate object of its supervision and protection. It permits every man to be of no religion, or of any religion he pleases. It has no partialities for the Jew, the Christian, the Turk or the Indian. Such is its creed. Here the affairs of another world are left to themselves. The government says to all the rival sectarian interests, "FAIR PLAY AND THE RIGHTS OF MEN!" It will not help by its statutes, nor retard by its proscriptions, any religion, any sect of religionists, now on the theatre... Whenever a sect calls for the governmental arm to help her—to hold her up—she proclaims herself overmatched by her competitors, and declares her consciousness that on the ground of *reason* and *evidence* she is unable to stand.[7]

In 1854, Campbell contrasted the American experience with countries in which Catholicism was established:

Religion, in its essence and spirit, can never be compulsory, as in the Papal States and territories; but it can, and of political right and immunity ought to, be left to the free choice and spontaneous action of every human being. And such is its exact position in these United States; and it is as it ought to be, the pre-eminent source and fountain of all our national prosperity, dignity, honor and happiness. And may it ever be the boast and the glory of our common country that every citizen, and even every alien, may freely worship Almighty God according to the last and the best dictate of his reason, his conscience and his affections! We regard this not as an act of mercy, but as an act of justice, not to ourselves only, but to our species—to our common humanity.[8]

These two principal founders of the Disciples movement were committed to separation of church and state and its corollary, religious freedom. To what extent, then,

---

[4] Garrison and DeGroot interpret "devoted" to mean "doomed." Winfred Ernest Garrison and Alfred T. DeGroot, *The Disciples of Christ: A History,* rev. ed. (St. Louis: The Bethany Press, 1958): 60.

[5] Olbricht and Rollmann (2000): 9(7)-10(8).

[6] See Harold Lunger, *The Political Ethics of Alexander Campbell* (St. Louis: Bethany Press, 1954): 38-52.

[7] Alexander Campbell, "An Oration in Honor of the Fourth of July, 1830," *Popular Lectures and Addresses* (Cincinnati: The Standard Publishing Company, 1863): 373 (emphases in original).

[8] Campbell (1863): 298.

were the three Disciples presidents influenced in their thinking about church and state by their original Disciples heritage?

James Abram Garfield, 1831-1881

In a flourish of eulogistic exuberance, *The Evangelist* editorialized: "As long as the story of American history shall be told, James A. Garfield will be named as one of its most illustrious and honored dead."[9] That prediction turned out not to be true. An heir to that magazine got it right when, mentioning the approaching centennial of Garfield's election to the presidency, said: "We find that his image has grown dim to most Americans."[10] One could probably say that aside from scholars of Disciples history, most Disciples do not know that Garfield was a Disciple.

Garfield's is a "rags to riches" story. Born in 1831 on the Western Reserve (northeastern Ohio) to Abram (who died a year and one-half later) and Eliza Ballou Garfield, the boy was raised under the strong hand of his mother, a faithful Disciple. Life was hard, but Eliza saw to it that her son learned to read and became educated. They went to church regularly, and James at 19 was baptized in 1850; he remained a lifelong Disciple. In 1851-1853, he attended the Western Reserve Eclectic Institute, later known as Hiram College, where his intellectual life flourished and he began to preach at Disciples churches.

Garfield decided not to attend Bethany College, although he had great respect for Alexander Campbell. He chose, instead, to attend Williams College in Massachusetts, believing it would broaden his intellectual and geographic horizons. It did, in no small part because of the influence of Williams's president, Mark Hopkins. After Williams, Garfield returned to Hiram to teach and serve as president of the institution.

Along the way, Garfield's interests turned to politics and the law. In 1859, drawing on his Disciples constituency, he was elected to the Ohio Senate. At this point, he radically departed from Alexander Campbell's stated belief that Christians should not enter the political arena because Christians, with a true sense of values, would not want to hold public office but would, instead, devote themselves to more important religious interests.[11] Campbell came to this understanding through personal experience, having served as a delegate to the Virginia Constitutional Convention in 1829-30. Ten years later, Campbell wrote clearly of his disapproval of politics:

> It is about as hard for a Christian man to please unchristian constituents, as it is for anyone to serve God and Mammon. The true politician rises by descending to cater for the lusts and passions of men.[12] ...Ought Christians to take an active part in politics—in the present politics of this country? ...I am decidedly of opinion that they ought not. One of my reasons is, American politics are full of avarice and ambition. They are national and mammoth forms of pride and cupidity; or they are a concentration of selfishness in its most repulsive attributes.... Now can there be any thing in its spirit and character more opposite

---

[9] "The Departed Ruler," *The Evangelist* 16 (September 29, 1881): 610.

[10] Phillip J. Woodworth, "Clouds Over a Pastor-President," *The Disciple* 6 (July 1, 1979): 4.

[11] Lunger (1954): 59.

[12] *The Millennial Harbinger* (1839): 8. Quoted in Lunger (1954): 60; see *idem*: 75-104.

to the spirit and genius of Christianity than the cultivation and display of concentrated selfishness?[13]

Though other Disciples encouraged Garfield not to leave the ministry of education and preaching to enter politics, Garfield was not Campbell; he nevertheless made the career shift hesitantly.

> I will now say to you, my much neglected journal, that I have for some years had it in contemplation to enter the field of statesmanship, either at the legal or educational portal, and if this plan succeeds I shall have gained a step in the direction of my purpose.[14]

The "plan" he referred to was running for the Ohio Senate. When anti-political Disciples confronted him with their objections, he replied: "I believe that I can enter political life and retain my integrity, manhood, and religion. I believe that there is vastly more need of manly men in politics than of preachers."[15]

Garfield was elected to the State Senate from the Republican Party. About the same time, he began reading for the law and, in 1861, passed the Ohio Bar. But the Civil War erupted and Garfield, who hated slavery, volunteered to fight for the Union—another point at which he departed from the New Testament piety of many of his Campbellite brethren. He recruited hundreds into the regiment of which he was given command. He saw considerable combat and rose through the ranks to major general. He parlayed his political experience and war record into election to the U.S. House of Representatives. He resigned his commission and entered Congress in 1863.

Garfield's career in Congress was so successful that he was reelected until 1880, when he was nominated for president. Some said that nothing got through the House without Garfield's support. Meanwhile, his relationship with the Disciples never flagged. Although he rarely preached, he served on the Hiram College Board, was faithful in church attendance wherever he happened to be, and attended the Vermont Street Christian Church in Washington, D.C.[16]—known then as the "Campbellite shanty," which, many years later, became National City Christian Church. In 1866, he was among the founders of the *Christian Standard*, a magazine representing the "progressive" side of the Disciples Movement, with which he clearly wanted to be identified.

In 1880, the Republican national convention found itself deadlocked between six aspirants for the presidency. Garfield was not among them, and he had even nominated another man. On the first ballot, Garfield received no votes. By the 35th ballot, U. S. Grant and J. G. Blaine were the leading contenders, and Garfield got 50 votes. On the 36th ballot, most of Blaine's support disappeared and Garfield got 399 votes—enough to

[13] *The Millennial Harbinger* (1840): 14. Quoted in Royal Humbert, ed. *Compend of Alexander Campbell's Theology* (St. Louis: Bethany Press, 1961): 262.

[14] Harry James Brown and Frederick D. Williams, eds. *The Diary of James A. Garfield* , vol. 1, *1848-1871*, entry for August 22, 1859 (East Lansing: Michigan State University Press, 1967): 340.

[15] Jerry B. Rushford, "Political Disciple: The Relationship between James A. Garfield and the Disciples of Christ" (Ph.D. dissertation, University of California, 1977): 117--an excellent work.

[16] "The Nation's Only Preacher President and His House of Worship," *Christian Standard* 65 (October 18, 1930): 1, 3-5.

make him the party's nominee. He defeated his Democratic opponent, Winfield S. Hancock, by only 9,464 votes, but Garfield won the electoral vote 214-155.[17]

Garfield had relied heavily on his Disciples connections for votes, and the Disciples, in turn, enjoyed the visibility the church attained through the election of a favorite son. Indeed, Disciples numbers rose as a result of Garfield's election.[18] Garfield, however, became annoyed that many Disciples expected political patronage. The president-elect made clear the brethren should not anticipate privilege from his election.

> Our people must not use me as the promoter of the views of our brethren. While I shall cheerfully maintain my old relation to them, I want it understood that it is the broad general views and not the special peculiarities of our faith that I desire to promote.... Let us not flaunt ourselves in the face of the American people as though we had made a special conquest, but by modesty and moderation bear our part worthily and take whatever resulting advantage may come.[19]

On July 2, 1881, two days short of four months after his inauguration, Garfield was shot by a disgruntled—and possibly deranged—patronage seeker (not a Disciple!). Charles J. Guiteau knew that Garfield went to church every Sunday. Guiteau followed Garfield to church one Sunday, took his place in a pew, in order to shoot the president during worship. However, he realized someone else might be killed or wounded, so he decided to wait for another opportunity, which came in a train station a few days later. An assassin with a conscience.[20] Garfield lingered for 80 days and died on September 19. Amidst national and international expressions of grief, the funeral was preached by longtime friend and editor of the *Christian Standard*, Isaac Errett.

Because Garfield's presidential service was so short, one has to look at Garfield's church/state thought while he was in Congress.[21] Most of his remarks on the subject were made in reference to protecting public education from ecclesiastical (Catholic) control, but he made some more general remarks, as well. In a debate that included comments about the structure of government, Garfield noted he had read that Kaiser Bismarck said the principal purpose of the German government was to "maintain and defend the gospel of our Lord Jesus Christ." Garfield's rejoinder was based more on his concept of separation of powers than on explicit reference to the no-establishment and free exercise clauses of the First Amendment:

> Our fathers, though recognizing in common with Germany and the other Christian nations of the earth the supreme importance of religion among men, deliberately turned to the great nation they were to establish and said: "You shall never make

---

[17] Thomas Hudson McKee, *The National Conventions and Platforms of All Political Parties, 1789 to 1905* (Baltimore: Friedenwald Co., 1906, republished by St. Clair Shores, Michigan: Scholarly Press, 1970): 186, 198-99.

[18] Tony A. Conley, Jr., "Garfield and the Disciples," *Christian Standard* 85 (May 7, 1949): 15.

[19] Letter from Garfield to Burke A. Hinsdale, November 17, 1880, quoted in Rushford (1977): 270.

[20] Paul Moore, "'A Hero of the Westernland': President Garfield and the Disciples of Christ." *Christian-Evangelist* 68 (October 2, 1930): 1299.

[21] W. W. Wasson, *James A. Garfield: His Religion and Education* (Nashville: Tennessee Book Company, 1952): 139, says that Garfield's last public statement on religious freedom was in his inauguration address. See also W. W. Wasson, "James A. Garfield and the Issue of Church and State," *The Christian-Evangelist* 88 (March 15, 1950): 246-47.

any law about religion": and to the States they virtually said: "You shall never make any law establishing any form of religion." In other words, here was an interest too precious to be trusted either to the nation or to the States. Our fathers said: "This highest of all human interests we will reserve to the people themselves. We will not delegate our power over it to any organized government, State or national. We will not even allow Legislatures to make any law concerning it."

To my mind it is the sublimest fact in our American system that, in defining the boundaries of delegated powers, they chose to entrust the most precious of all the interests of human beings on this earth absolutely to the voluntary action of the individual people of the Republic, not to be voted upon by their representatives, but to be regulated, protected, and cherished by their own voluntary action, leaving themselves perfectly free to have no religion if they chose or any religion that they pleased.[22]

Garfield developed his notions of the relation of church and state under the prevailing, mid-19th-century Protestant (and Disciples) ethos of anti-Catholicism, wary of Catholic loyalty to a foreign potentate, the pope, and of Catholic designs to get their hands on American tax money to support parochial schools. His first significant contact with a Catholic was when he served on the staff of General William Rosencrans. Rosencrans liked Garfield, regarded him as an intelligent conversation partner, and invited Garfield to his tent night after night for long talks about military matters—and about religion. Garfield gained a new respect for Catholicism and even went to mass with Rosencrans on occasion. He wrote to his mother about this and concluded his letter with the reassurance: "I hope you are not alarmed about my becoming a Catholic. You ought to be glad that I take time to think and talk about religion at all. I have no doubt that the Catholics have been greatly slandered."[23]

Garfield's commitment to separation of church and state caused him to oppose government funding of religious institutions or projects. Once in the House, he voted against an appropriation bill that would have paid off a building debt and completed the building of a charitable group, the Little Sisters of the Poor. Garfield praised their charitable work but explained his opposition as a church/state issue:

Here is an organization composed exclusively of people of one religious denomination. Under its charter the members are wholly and only of one religious sect, and of one society within that religious sect…. [W]e ought never to commit ourselves to the aid of an exclusively sectarian institution. I would say the same were this institution under the control of a Protestant church, even if it were a church to which I myself belonged. The divorce between the church and the state ought to be absolute. It ought to be so absolute that no church property anywhere in any State or in the nation should be exempted from equal taxation;

---

[22] *Congressional Record*, 45th Congress, 3d session, vol. 8, pt. 2, (February 11, 1879): 1209.

[23] Margaret Leech and Harry J. Brown, *The Garfield Orbit* (New York: Harper and Row, 1978): 342, n. 9. For Garfield's conversations with Rosencrans about Catholicism, see Allan Peskin, *Garfield* (Kent, Ohio: Kent State University Press, 1978): 167-70.

for if you exempt the property of any church organization, to that extent you impose a church tax upon the whole community.[24]

When it came to the parochial school question, Garfield was firmly opposed to the Catholic initiative. With the growth of the public school movement from the 1830s, the public accepted that tax-supported schools ought to teach civic virtue and instill in students those values that would make them good citizens. Catholics correctly perceived this "civic virtue" to be thinly disguised, lowest-common-denominator Protestantism. To protect their children from that, they launched an ambitious parochial school program. Because of the expense of the program, the Catholic Church began to agitate for public funding of their schools. Reiterating widespread nativism, Disciples publications addressed the school issue: "The bishops do not condemn that system [public schools] but insist that the Catholic youth of the country shall be educated in Catholic establishments."[25]

> In all our large cities Romists are busily engaged in organizing and sustaining parochial schools, in which Catholicism is the principal thing taught.... There is a marked antagonism between our American institutions and those of Rome. Rome is not in harmony with America.... If Rome succeeds in her purposes our Republic, about which we have boasted so much, will go down. The two governments are opposites, and can not be joined together in harmony.[26] ... Their war on our public schools is familiar to almost everyone. There is scarcely a Roman priest in the land but what would vote to have all our public schools closed. So long as the present school system is carried on, they cannot succeed in their work as they wish. They want this great enemy of Romanism out of the way, hence their opposition.... Give Rome the power and she would close every public school in America; yes, and every private school not Roman, and every Protestant place of worship.... Let the Jesuits have control of this country and the end of our nationality and freedom is near at hand.[27]

Finally: "Protestants shut their eyes to the fact that a crafty, sleepless, unscrupulous religious power is seeking control of city councils, school boards, police and all public institutions."[28]

Garfield was, therefore, consistent with the Disciples when he opposed the Catholics on the school question. In a campaign speech at Warren, Ohio, in 1875, he addressed the issue at length. He stated the issue was not one Americans had generated, but it had been thrust upon the country "by the boldest and most aggressive movement of modern time." It was not started by the laypeople of the Catholic Church, but by the hierarchy:

> [T]he ecclesiastical powers above them...have challenged the American school system, and demanded its overthrow.... The common schools of the United States are a part of the secular machinery of our State governments, believed to be absolutely essential to the safety of our Republican institutions.... [T]he attack is made upon our free schools. It comes from the Bishops and Priests, who are

[24] "Sundry Civil Appropriation Bill," *Congressional Record*, 43rd Congress, 1st Session, Vol. 2, part 6, June 22, 1874: 5,384.
[25] "The Catholic Council at Baltimore," *Christian Standard* 1 (November 10, 1866): 253.
[26] "Papal Education," *The Christian* 18 (February 26, 1880): 4.
[27] "Rome in America," *The Christian* 18 (January 29, 1880): 4.
[28] "Our Catholic Rulers," *The Evangelist* 15 (May 5, 1880): 291.

acting in concert and under orders. [The effort is not truly to get funding for Catholic schools, but] the main assault is directed at the existence of our schools.... [T]he church is the attacking party. In the name of religion they have attacked a cherished institution, a vital principle of our political system [*i.e.* church/state separation].[29]

In 1875, Garfield's good friend, James G. Blaine, Representative from Maine, sponsored a constitutional amendment in the House of Representatives,[30] designed to prevent government money from going to religious schools. Blaine's amendment was motivated not only by preexisting anti-Catholicism[31] but also by his consistent belief that the separation of church and state prohibited government aid to religious institutions, and he wanted to extend this principle to the States. Although Garfield did not participate in the House debate on the proposal, he voted for it,[32] and similar sentiments were part of the Republican platform on which he ran for president in 1880.[33]

When Garfield gave his inaugural address on March 4, 1881, he included two paragraphs on church/state relations, with a surprising twist:

The Constitution guarantees absolute religious freedom. Congress is prohibited from making any law respecting an establishment of religion or prohibiting the free exercise thereof. The Territories of the United States are subject to the direct legislative authority of Congress; and hence the general government is responsible for the violation of the Constitution in any of them. It is therefore a reproach to the government, that, in the most populous of the Territories, the constitutional guarantee is not enjoyed by the people, and the authority of Congress is set at naught. The Mormon Church not only offends the moral sense of mankind by sanctioning polygamy, but prevents the administration of justice through the ordinary instrumentalities of law.

---

[29] Garfield, "Address at Warren, Ohio, August 31, 1875," *Garfield Papers*, Library of Congress.

[30] "Constitutional Amendment," *Congressional Record*, 44th Congress, 1st Session, vol. 4, part 1, December 14, 1875: 205, "No State shall make any law respecting an establishment of religion, or prohibiting the free exercise thereof; and no money raised by taxation in any State for the support of public schools, or derived from any public fund therefore, nor any public lands devoted thereto, shall ever be under the control of any religious sect; nor shall any money so raised or lands so devoted be divided between religious sects or denominations."

[31] Marie Carolyn Klinkhamer, "The Blaine Amendment of 1875: Private Motives for Political Action," *The Catholic Historical Review* 42 (April 1956): 49, reasoned that the Blaine amendment itself did not introduce nativism, for "that unlovely sentiment already existed in many parts of the country," but it did inflame the anti-Catholic, anti-foreign, anti-Negro passions of many.

[32] Neither did Garfield discuss the amendment with Blaine in correspondence. Klinkhamer (1956): 23, n. 23. The vote was 180 for, 7 against, 98 not voting. *Congressional Record*, 44th Congress, 1st Session, vol. 4, part 6, August 4, 1876: 5,191. The amendment was not approved by the Senate.

[33] Item #4 of the platform: "The Constitution wisely forbids Congress to make any law respecting an establishment of religion, but it is idle to hope that the nation can be protected against the influence of secret sectarianism while each state is exposed to its domination. We therefore recommend that the Constitution be so amended as to lay the same prohibition upon the legislature of each state, and to forbid the appropriation of public funds to the support of sectarian schools." McKee (1906, 1970): 188.

In my judgment, it is the duty of Congress, while respecting to the uttermost the conscientious convictions and religious scruples of every citizen, to prohibit within its jurisdiction all criminal practices, especially of that class which destroy the family relations and endanger social order. Nor can any ecclesiastical organization be safely permitted to usurp in the smallest degree the functions and powers of the national government.[34]

Garfield's statement on Mormonism is surprising[35] because he had apparently made no previous public statement on the "Mormon problem," whereas the Republican platform on which he ran, denounced it.[36] In 1862, Congress passed an anti-polygamy law that applied to the territories of the United States, including Utah.[37] In 1879, the Supreme Court ruled the free exercise clause of the First Amendment did not protect a polygamist from prosecution because polygamy was harmful to families and threatened the moral fabric of society.[38] The considerable discussion of the issue in Disciples publications was virtually all against the Mormons. For example, referring to Mormon defiance of the Supreme Court opinion, an editor wrote: "They are seeking to colonize in other Territories, and are evidently aiming to preoccupy the ground with a view to obtain, by a balance of power, political control, so as to bring new States into the Union with polygamy as a fixed institution."[39] Another wrote: "Mormonism and Republicanism are so irrevocably hostile that they can never agree. Again I say to my countrymen, that this evil must be speedily checked, or it involves us in another war."[40] A third wrote:

[Polygamy] should receive no sympathy, complaisance, or quarter on any grounds. The morals of our nation, the reputation of modern civilization, and our political welfare, all demand that it should be crushed out by all the weight of law and, if need be, of the sword that "rulers do not bear in vain."[41]

But like Garfield's encounter with a real Catholic in General Rosencrans, however, Garfield had gained closer exposure to, and greater appreciation for, Mormonism. On two separate trips west, he attended Mormon worship (including preaching by one of the twelve apostles of the Latter-Day Saints), toured the Salt Lake City Tabernacle and Temple, and had two conversations with Brigham Young. Garfield found Brigham (as Garfield called him) to be interesting and engaging.[42]

---

[34] Burke A. Hinsdale, ed., *The Works of James Abram Garfield,*2 vols. (Boston: James R. Osgood and Company, 1882): II, 794.

[35] Peskin (1978): 539, called the statement on Mormonism "a passionate and unexpected denunciation" and "a jarring note."

[36] In condemning polygamy, the platform made a powerful comparison. In an article affirming a number of goals, it said: "[T]hat, slavery having perished in the states, its twin barbarity—polygamy—must die in the territories." McKee (1906, 1970): 188.

[37] 12 *Statutes at Large* 501 (1862).

[38] *Reynolds v. United States* 98 U.S. 145 (1879).

[39] "Mormon Polygamy," *Christian Standard* 14 (February 22, 1879): 60.

[40] "Mormon Polygamy," *Christian Standard* 14 (March 8, 1879): 76, quoting the Cincinnati *Gazette*.

[41] "The Mormons and Polygamy," *The Evangelist* 17 (March 2, 1882): 130.

[42] Brown and Williams (1967): II (1872-1874) 75-76, entry for August 12, 1872; III (1875-1877) 93-94, entries for June 4 and 5, 1875.

On another occasion, Garfield toured the former Mormon Temple in Kirtland, Ohio, and wrote about that visit:

> I never think of that strange people without a mixture of admiration and contempt. Admiration for the boldness of the attempt they made in the world of ideas and actions, and contempt for what appears to be the hollow shams and deceptions by which they carried out their objects. In looking at this deserted temple, I can not repress a feeling of regret at the monument of failure they left. Yet they deserve a grander failure than this.[43]

The new president's inaugural address seems to have been the moment of decision when his human sympathy for the Mormons settled into political antipathy.

James A. Garfield seems to have believed vigorously in the separation of church and state, and its corollary, religious liberty. He spoke of it occasionally in the abstract, but more often his expressions were in reference to the practical problems of whether public funds should be spent on sectarian schools and the perceived social threat of Mormon polygamy. Both of those issues were widely debated during the years leading up to his presidency. His positions on them were consistent with the published opinions of leaders in the Disciples of Christ, a church he loved dearly and of which he was proud to be a part.

After the president died from the gunshot wounds, his body lay in state in the Capitol, where the minister of the Vermont Avenue Christian Church, Frederick D. Power, led memorial services. Garfield was buried in Cleveland, Ohio, where the final oration was preached by his longtime friend, Isaac Errett. In 1884, the new building erected for the Vermont Avenue Church was called the Garfield Memorial Church. In 1930, a new building was built on Thomas Circle and named National City Christian Church. On April 5, 1981, the James A. Garfield Presidential Window was dedicated at National City Church and is still in place today.[44]

Lyndon Baines Johnson, 1908-1973

Lyndon Johnson was born in the family farmhouse in Blanco County, Texas, in the Hill Country, August 28, 1908. His parents were Sam Johnson, Jr., and Rebekah.[45] Sam and Rebekah were poor folks in an area of poor folks. In late 1913, they moved to Johnson City, Texas (founded in 1879 by a nephew of Lyndon's grandfather). Although they moved back to the farm for a while, LBJ always thought of Johnson City as his home town.

Rebekah was a huge influence on her son. He was her first child, and she doted on him. A refined woman with education, she taught him at home and challenged him to learn at school. A bright child, Lyndon learned quickly; at age seven and already in the third grade, he made good grades, except in deportment. Rebekah came from a long line

---

[43] Brown and Williams (1967): II (1872-1874) 215, entry for August 25, 1873.

[44] Hilda E. Koontz, *A History of the National City Christian Church* (Washington, D.C.: Privately printed, 1981): 5-8, 96; J. Edward Mosley, "James A. Garfield and the National City Church," *The Christian-Evangelist* 77 (February 2, 1939): 132-33; "Funeral Sermon of Pres. Garfield," *The Evangelist* 16 (October 6, 1881): 628-29; "Church Honors Two Presidents," *The Disciple* 4 (July 7, 1974): 12; *The James Abram Garfield Presidential Window* (Washington, D.C.: National City Christian Church, 1981).

[45] See LBJ's family tree in Rebekah Baines Johnson, *A Family Album* (New York: McGraw-Hill, 1965): 12-13.

of ministers, Baptists mostly; LBJ's maternal great-grandfather served as president of what is now Baylor University, 1861-1863.[46] Schooled in the Bible and fundamentalist in her interpretation of it, Rebekah was a devoutly religious woman; she taught her son the Bible and the moral values derived from it.[47] He once said to a group of women: "In my childhood, I...had the great blessings of a devout and faithful mother. In our home ... there was always prayer—aloud, proud, and unapologetic."[48] From LBJ's perspective, his mother had fulfilled the commandment in one his favorite passages, "Train up a child in the way he should go; and when he is old, he will not depart from it."[49] From his mother's perspective, however, there was a snag. Johnson City had three churches: Baptist, Methodist, and Christian (Disciples of Christ). When LBJ was twelve years old (or fourteen, depending on which account one reads), he attended a revival meeting at the Christian Church and responded to the gospel invitation. He was baptized along with several other youths. Rebekah did not approve of his decision, but the denominational die was cast. LBJ remained a Disciple the rest of his life.[50] Lyndon seems to have been impressed with the Disciples' ecumenical spirit, for he attended the services of many denominations, both Catholic and Protestant, including the Episcopalians, of which Lady Bird was a member.[51] LBJ honored the religious diversity of the country and believed he could be inspired in various worship settings.[52] Lady Bird called him "my

---

[46] During his presidency, LBJ once told a group of Southern Baptist leaders: "I am not fortunate enough to be a Baptist. I am a member of the Disciples of Christ, but I have always felt very close to your denomination. Everybody else in my household that I grew up in was Baptist. My part of the country was Baptist. My mother was a Baptist. My grandfather and great-grandfather were Baptists. George Washington Baines was an early Baptist preacher who became the second president of Baylor University during the Civil War. He came to Texas in a buckboard to be a circuit-riding preacher. He came the way that most of the Baptists came to the frontier: very early, by the cheapest form of transportation. He was determined to do one thing—and that was save souls." *Public Papers of the Presidents of the United States: Lyndon B. Johnson; Containing the Public Messages, Speeches, and Statements of the President*, book 1, 1968-69 (Washington: United States Government Printing Office, 1970): 441.

[47] Ronnie Dugger, *The Politician: The Life and Times of Lyndon Johnson* (Old Saybrook, Connecticut: Norton, 1982): 59-75; Monroe Billington, "Lyndon B. Johnson: The Religion of a Politician," *Presidential Studies Quarterly* 17 (summer 1987): 519-20.

[48] "Remarks at the 12th Annual Presidential Prayer Breakfast," February 5, 1964 in *Public Papers (1963-64)* 1 (1965): 262.

[49] Pv 22:6 (KJV).

[50] Dugger (1982): 72, 88; Billington (1987): 520.

[51] Once, when the minister of the Episcopal Church in Williamsburg, Virginia, excoriated the President in a sermon for his conduct of the Vietnam War, LBJ said to Lady Bird when they were alone after the service, "Greater love hath no man than that he goes to the Episcopal Church with his wife." Lady Bird Johnson, *A White House Diary* (New York: Holt, Rinehart and Winston, 1970): 589.

[52] The President's brother commented on LBJ's attendance at various churches: "There were a number of cynics who openly accused him of 'courting the church vote' by going from one denomination to another—Episcopalian, Baptist, Methodist, Catholic, Quaker, everything but a Jewish synagogue. They were dead wrong. I am personally convinced that the Presidency, with all its terrible and awesome burdens, made him feel a desperate need for greater spiritual comfort. In going from one church to another, I think he was unconsciously searching for some special kind of solace, a kind of spiritual ease that no President can hope to have." Sam Houston Johnson, *My Brother Lyndon* (New York: Cowles Book Company, 1970): 35.

very ecumenical husband."[53] During his presidency, LBJ attended National City Christian Church more than any other.

Sam Johnson served in the Texas Legislature during LBJ's youth, so the son grew up listening to his father discuss politics and elections with his friends and associates. Sometimes Lyndon went to Austin with his father to witness legislative sessions. He learned from his father not only the interest and excitement of politics but also its potential for good. A liberal Democrat; Sam believed government was for doing good for people. From his mother, LBJ learned a Christian concern for people; from his father, a political concern for people. Church and state might remain separate, but religion and politics went together in the mind of a man who wanted to help people.[54]

When LBJ was elected vice-president in 1960, the Disciples made much of his connection to the church.[55] When President John F. Kennedy was assassinated, and LBJ became president, the Disciples were proud to have one of their own in the White House. They immediately offered him their support, while simultaneously letting the country know that he was a Disciple, an active member of the Johnson City Christian Church.[56] Soon after he took office, LBJ was given a life patron membership in the Disciples of Christ Historical Society.[57] In August 1964, he attended National City Christian Church, and Billy Graham, with whom LBJ was a good friend, preached.[58] When LBJ was elected to the presidency in his own right, National City Church played an important role. On inauguration day, prior to the swearing in, a prayer service was held at the church. Both the minister of the church, George R. Davis, and Billy Graham spoke. The service had been requested by President Johnson.[59] Rev. Davis was also one of four to say a prayer at the inauguration ceremony at the Capitol.[60]

---

[53] Lady Bird Johnson (1970): 745.

[54] Dugger (1982): 84; Billington (1987): 523-26.

[55] For example, A. T. DeGroot, "Lyndon B. Johnson," *The Christian* 99 (January 15, 1961): 29 [a feature entitled "Distinguished Disciples"]; "Vice-Presidential Sermon on Faith," *The Christian* 100 (January 14, 1962): 11; "Disciple Meets Pope," *The Christian* 100 (October 21, 1962): 14.

[56] "Pray for President Johnson!" *Christian Standard* 98 (December 14, 1963): 2; "Disciple Offered Final Public Prayer Heard by President Kennedy," *The Christian* 101 (December 22, 1963): 20; "Disciples Pledge Support to President Lyndon Johnson," *World Call* 46 (January 1964): 4; "'Dr.' Lyndon B. Johnson," *The Christian* 102 (January 12, 1964): 11; "President National City Church Visitor," *The Christian* 102 (February 23, 1964): 20; "Any News is Good News," *The Christian* 102 (February 16, 1964): 8.

[57] "President Patron Member of D.C.H.S.," *The Christian* 102 (May 17, 1964): 20.

[58] "A Great Day at National City Church," *The Christian* 102 (November 8, 1964): 12. George R. Davis was pastor of National City Church. LBJ and Davis were close friends. LBJ had met Davis, whom he regarded as a fellow Texan, at Wichita Falls where Davis had served the Disciples church before he went to National City. They were very much alike: both headstrong and opinionated. It helped that Davis was an ardent supporter of LBJ's Vietnam policy. On the Sunday that Billy Graham preached, as the three were coming out of church, LBJ said to Graham, "Billy, don't you wish you and I could draw a crowd like George?" Davis loved it. (Interview with Lawrence Schreiber, organist at National City Christian Church, 1960-2000, August 4, 2004.)

[59] "President at Private Services in National City Christian Church," *The Christian* 103 (February 7, 1965): 20; "Prayer Service at National City Christian Church," *Discipliana* (March 1965): 6, reported that the service was attended by about 1,300 people, including major government officials, such as the

LBJ attended worship frequently, fifty-five times at National City Church during his presidency. He had his own pew and was able to attend services with a minimum of disruption to the normal service, although the Secret Service inevitably provided security. After services, the president went to the coffee hour and mingled with the congregation and guests.[61] He was named an honorary elder of National City Christian Church and an elder at Johnson City Christian Church.[62]

Why did LBJ go to church both at National City and at other churches so much? His wife suggested three reasons: (1) the responsibilities of the office required more resources than one could generate from within oneself, (2) no one could accuse him of going for political reasons, given he was already "at the top," and (3) he wanted to set a good example for others.[63] LBJ believed politics was largely about doing good for others. He believed doing good was rooted in religious faith. Though the cynical or those who know LBJ's faults, which were many, may think his religion was superficial or window dressing, it appears it was deep. It was the primary motivator in his work for civil rights, expansion of educational opportunities, the Great Society, or even his ultimately failed prosecution of the Vietnam war, in short, his attempts to do good.[64]

On the last Sunday of his presidency, LBJ attended National City Church.[65] Apparently on his own initiative, he wrote a prayer. When Pastor Davis learned of it, he asked and received permission to use the president's prayer in worship.[66]

Cabinet, justices of the Supreme Court, and members of Congress, as well as some governors and mayors of major cities. The service had been planned, however, for only about 100 persons in addition to LBJ's family. The *Washington Post* printed a story that Francis B. Sayre (dean at the National Cathedral) was to have a prayer service on the morning of the inauguration. But he had failed to ask LBJ to attend, apparently assuming that plans at the National Cathedral would take precedent over any other plans. LBJ was furious! He sent telegrams to some 1,000 people, inviting them to the prayer service at National City Christian Church. The Disciples church was packed, but few showed up for Sayre's service at St. John's Episcopal. The President certainly did not attend. (Schreiber interview [2004]).

[60] "Disciple Offers an Inaugural Prayer," *The Christian* 103 (January 31, 1965): 12.

[61] Schreiber interview (2004), related that one Sunday the White House called to see if Dr. Davis were preaching, i.e., to determine whether the President should attend. The receptionist said, "No, it is Youth Sunday. Tell him not to come." But LBJ would not be told what to do! Young people led worship, three of whom gave a sermonette. LBJ loved it! Mingling, as usual, during coffee time following the service, this Sunday LBJ spent a full hour schmoozing with the young people and posing for photo ops with the youthful leaders of the service.

[62] "President Honorary Elder at National City Church," *The Christian* 104 (February 20, 1966): 21. Generals Omar N. Bradley and Maxwell D. Taylor were named honorary elders at the same time; see"Elder Lyndon B. Johnson," *The Christian* 104 (December 8, 1966): 1620.

[63] Lady Bird Johnson (1970): 71.

[64] Billington (1987): 522-26. Billington says: "Concepts of Christian duty, benevolence, morality, and principle were as inseparable from and as deeply rooted in his character as his legendary political skills and his inordinate pursuit of and use of power." (526). See Dugger (1982): 153-63, who hinted at a mystical quality in LBJ's faith. Dugger also suggested that LBJ nearly became Roman Catholic after his daughter, Luci, converted to Catholicism, and as LBJ's despair about Vietnam deepened.

[65] For the final full day in office and a brief summary of LBJ's religious life, see Joseph A. Califano, Jr., *The Triumph & Tragedy of Lyndon Johnson: The White House Years* (New York: Simon and Schuster, 1991): 334-35.

Attendance at National City Church increased during the time President Johnson worshiped there, but when his presidency ended and he went home to Johnson City, attendance fell off and the newspapers quit reporting on services at National City Christian Church.[67] As they had during his presidency, some denominational leaders praised LBJ after he left office.[68]

The last time President Johnson went to National City Christian Church was for his funeral. He died January 22, 1973, at his beloved ranch in the Texas Hill Country. His body was brought to Washington; a State Funeral was held at the church on January 29, George R. Davis presiding.[69] On March 15, 1981, a window was dedicated at National City to President Johnson and is still in place at the church.[70]

Although LBJ believed in separation of church and state, he was strangely silent on the issue, given the opportunities he had to speak about it. When it came to the

---

[66] George Davis, "A Message from the Minister," *The National City Christian* 24 (January 30, 1969): 1, 4. The text of the President's prayer:

We come before Thee with grateful hearts, thankful for the days that have been ours and for the works we have been permitted to do together.

In these hours now, our thoughts are not of ourselves but of our country. Thou has blessed America greatly; may we, in the conduct of her affairs, be always worthy in Thy sight—and in the sight of our fellow man.

Deliver us from the follies of power and pride. Show us the uses of our strengths that will make life better on this earth for all Thy children. In season and out, help us to hold to the purposes Thou has taught us, feeding the hungry, healing the sick, caring for the needy, trusting our young, training them up in the way they should go.

Lift our visions, Father, renew our faith in Thee, and in ourselves. Stir our spirits and disturb our consciences that we may seek not rest from our labors but right for neighbors. Blind our eyes to the colors of men's skins, close our hearts against hate and violence, and fill our souls with a love of justice and compassion.

May we, as a nation, deserve no enemies and be worthy of all our friends, striving without ceasing for a day when mankind shall not war anymore.

Watch over this city and keep it from strife and sorrow.

Guard this Republic and guide us in its service.

These things we ask in Thy name. Amen."

"Text of the President's Prayer Read at Church Services Attended by the First Family," January 19, 1969 in *Public Papers (1968-69)* 2 (1970): 1367-68.

[67] Schreiber (2004) said that George Davis took the decline in attendance hard; he was no longer able to bask in LBJ's reflected glory.

[68] "Dale Fiers Praises President Johnson's Restraint on 'Pueblo,'" *The Christian* 106 (March 3, 1968): 20; "Fiers Thanks Johnson for Service to Nation," *The Christian* 107 (February 9, 1969): 20.

[69] Koontz (1981): 95-96; George R. Davis, "Davis Dots and Dashes," *The National City Christian*, 28 (February 1, 1973): 1, 4; A. Dale Fiers, "The Scene," *World Call* 55 (April 1973): 33; George R. Davis, "L.B.J.: A President's Pastor Remembers a Layman Whose Faith Stayed Strong," *The Disciple* 4 (January 2, 1977): 7-8, is more a reflection on the President's life and faith than a description of his funeral.

[70] *The Lyndon Baines Johnson Presidential Window* (Washington, D.C.: National City Christian Church, 1981); "Church Honors Two Presidents," *The Disciple* 4 (July 7, 1974): 12; "Dedication Service Honors Johnson," *The Disciple* 8 (June 7, 1981): 25.

legislation for which he worked extremely hard and of which he was most proud, he compromised his separationism.

In 1962[71] and 1963,[72] the Supreme Court decided state-required prayer and Bible reading in public schools is unconstitutional, a violation of the no-establishment clause of the First Amendment. The opinions were vehemently opposed both in the public and in Congress. By May of 1964, more than 145 proposed constitutional amendments had been submitted in the United States House of Representatives for the purpose of reversing the public school prayer opinions.[73] Apparently LBJ made no comment on the controversy at all. The chaos associated with President Kennedy's assassination and the uncertainty connected with LBJ's becoming the president on November 22, 1963, may have diverted his attention. Given that the controversy did not die down throughout LBJ's tenure in the White House, however, one would think he would have at least commented on it. So far as I can tell, he did not.

Perhaps the best encapsulation of President Johnson's understanding of church/state relations is a sentence from a commencement address at Catholic University. He informed the audience he had come to speak "about the morality of nations." Then he said: "For while I believe devotedly in the separation of church and state, I do not believe it is pleasing in the sight of God for men to separate morality from their might."[74] In other words, although the American system does not allow government to dictate or impose religion on the people, it is a political duty and a religious duty for rulers and citizens alike to do good for the public welfare. This predominant theme in all LBJ's words and actions he further elaborated in the speech at Catholic University, emphasizing religious freedom: "In the principles that guide us abroad—as in the principles that govern us at home—we of the United States cherish the right of others to choose for themselves what they shall believe and what their own societies and institutions shall be." Then, saying that American policy would consist of "a spirit of compassion and caring," he stated: "For we believe, as Pope John said, "There is an immense task incumbent on all men of good will, namely the task of restoring the relations of the human family in truth, in justice, in love, and in freedom." Like a Disciples preacher extending the gospel invitation, the president offered an invitation on behalf of the American people to the leaders of the world's nations: "[W]e extend to you our invitation—'Come, now, let us reason together.'[75] As peace knocks, our door is unlatched. Our table is set. We are ready, and we believe mankind is ready with us."[76]

He made the same point again when addressing Holocaust survivors, calling attention to the "both/and" nature of church/state separation and the obligation to do good.

---

[71] *Engel v. Vitale* 370 U.S. 421.

[72] *Abington Township School District v. Schempp* 374 U.S. 203.

[73] See Steven K. Green, "Evangelicals and the Becker Amendment: A Lesson in Church-State Moderation," *Journal of Church and State* 33 (summer 1991): 541-67.

[74] "Commencement Address at Catholic University," June 6, 1965 in *Public Papers (1965)* 2 (1966): 640-41.

[75] Is 1:18, one of LBJ's favorite Bible verses.

[76] "Commencement Address at Catholic University," June 6, 1965 in *Public Papers (1965)* 2 (1966): 642-43.

[O]ur Constitution wisely separates church and state, separates religion and government. But this does not mean that men of government should divorce themselves from religion. On the contrary, a first responsibility of national leadership, as I see it, is spiritual leadership, for I deeply believe that America will prevail not because her pocketbooks are big, but because the principles of her people are strong.[77]

At the first prayer breakfast to which he spoke after he became president, LBJ described his belief in the separation of church and state.

We who hold public office are enjoined by our Constitution against enacting laws to tell the people when or where or how to pray.[78]

All our experience and all our knowledge proves that injunction good. For, if government could ordain the people's prayers, government could also ordain its own worship—and that must never be.

The separation of church and state has served our freedom well because men of state have not separated themselves from church and faith and prayer.... I believe ... that our children should be taught to pray; but I know and I believe ... that this teaching is our task in our homes—a task much too sacred to ever be touched by the state.[79]

But the state may and must draw on religious motivations to do good in the world. Speaking to a group of civil rights leaders, rallying support for what later became the Civil Rights Act of 1964, LBJ said:

---

[77] "Remarks in Austin at the Dedication of the Agudas Achim Synagogue," December 30, 1963, *Public Papers (1963-64)* 1 (1970): 102. In the same speech (101), he said: "Out of the evil visited upon us just recently [the assassination of President Kennedy], blessings can come and have come, for Americans have found strength to bear their sorrows in the only place that real strength is to be found—close to God *and the works that He would have us do.*" (emphasis added)

Lady Bird attended the dedication of the synagogue, and she said, "Lyndon was never better" than in this speech, which she also described as "beautiful." The Master of Ceremonies had mentioned that many Jews had been able to escape the Holocaust because of LBJ's work when he was a U.S. Senator. Lady Bird said: "[One] of the most memorable things about the day [was] the way, as we started out of the synagogue, person after person plucked at my sleeve and said, 'I wouldn't be here today if it weren't for him. He helped me get out.' That both frightens you and makes you happy." Lady Bird Johnson (1970): 28.

[78] LBJ made similar comments on two other occasions: "In putting my name to this paper, I cannot proclaim that all Americans will pray on October 20th. Nor would I do so even if I could." "Remarks Upon Signing Proclamation 'National Day of Prayer, 1965,'" October 7, 1965 in *Public Papers* 2 (1965) (1970): 1053. When his despair about the Vietnam War was deepest, Lyndon said: "In this great office of all the people, it is not my right or my privilege to tell citizens how or when or what they should worship. I can—and I do—tell you that in these long nights your President prays.... We cannot know what the morrow will bring. We can know that to meet its challenges and to withstand its assaults, America never stands taller than when her people go to their knees." "Remarks at the Presidential Prayer Breakfast," February 1, 1968 in *Public Papers (1968-69)* 1 (1970): 121-22.

[79] "Remarks at the 12th Annual Presidential Prayer Breakfast," February 5, 1964 in *Public Papers (1963-64)* 1(1970): 261, 262-63.

[M]en of God have taught us that social problems are moral problems on a huge scale.... They have preached that the church should be the first to awake to individual suffering, and the church should be the bravest in opposing all social wrongs. This tradition is deeply imbedded in America's history.[80]

Four years later he still articulated the same theme:

Belief in a divine providence is not ... an escape or a tranquilizer. It is, rather, a compelling challenge to men to attain the ideals of liberty, justice, peace, and compassion.... We can never be so arrogant as to claim God's special blessing for America, but we can express the hope that in His eyes we have at least tried to help make possible a new vitality of the human conscience—not only here in America, our beloved land, but we have tried it and are still trying it throughout all the world.[81]

LBJ believed the country was founded on the principles of the Bible,[82] that it was to be judged by the standard of "our love of freedom for all people," that America's obligation to its own people and to the world "can be met if we only follow the Golden Rule: Do unto others as you would have them do unto you."[83] He believed religious and political leaders had to consider the ancient biblical question, "Who is my neighbor?" because "the roots of public policy must lie in private morality."[84]

At one point, the president became specific about religious morality playing itself out in public policy. Addressing a group of Methodist leaders, he observed that the Methodist church "was founded on social conscience—that was founded on the dream of social justice for all human beings." He then read several items from the *Social Creed of the Methodist Church*, written in 1940:

We stand for equal rights and complete justice for all men in all stations of life...for adequate provision for the protection, the education, the spiritual nurture, and the wholesome recreation of every child...for the abatement of poverty and the right of all men to live.... We believe that it is our Christian duty to do our utmost to provide for all men the opportunity to earn an adequate livelihood.... We believe that society has a right to expect that every person, not physically or mentally incapacitated, shall be constantly engaged, so far as possible, in some vocation productive of common good.... We oppose all forms of social, economic, and moral waste.

He then said:

[I]t would be very hard for me to write a more perfect description of the American ideal—or of the American commitments of the 1960s.... [The President and Legislators] are trying to write [these principles] into the laws of the country today—and in the hearts of all of our people. For our people—of every faith— have come to believe that the works of compassion are the legitimate and are the

---

[80] "Remarks to a Group of Civil Rights Leaders," April 29, 1964 in *Public Papers (1963-64)* 1 (1965): 588.

[81] "Remarks at the Presidential Prayer Breakfast," February 1, 1968 in *Public Papers (1968-69)* 1 (1970): 122.

[82] "Remarks at a Ceremony Marking 1966 as the 'Year of the Bible,'" January 19, 1966 in *Public Papers (1966)* 1 (1967): 34. This is the closest thing I have found to a belief in a "Christian America."

[83] "Remarks in Washington Square, San Francisco," October 11, 1964 in *Public Papers (1963-64)* 2 (1965): 1,297-98.

[84] "Remarks to the Christian Citizenship Seminar of Southern Baptist Leaders," March 26, 1968 in *Public Papers (1968-69)* 1 (1970): 442-43.

necessary concern of the entire Nation and particularly of the National Government, and of the States and of the cities, and of the churches and the schools, and of industry and labor and the private citizen.[85]

The only traditional church/state issue, i.e., involving the no-establishment clause, was the problem of how to fix American education. Even before President Garfield's time, the Catholic Church and other church-related school systems tried to get public money to help support their schools. All the presidents and the majority of the Congress had been consistently opposed to that idea generation after generation. But LBJ believed education to be in crisis; so, consistent with his impulse to do good for the people, he sought ways for the federal government to improve all kinds of education. In spite of his belief in the separation of church and state, LBJ, himself once a teacher, sought ways to get around traditional prohibitions to provide aid to private schools as well as public.

The method he and his advisors settled on was the "child benefit theory." The Supreme Court, in *Cochran v. Louisiana Board of Education*[86] and *Everson v. Board of Education*,[87] had declared constitutional plans to lend textbooks to children in parochial schools and provide transportation on city buses to parochial schools, all paid for with state money. This idea was justified by saying that the children, not the religious schools, were the beneficiaries of the state programs, and certainly the churches that sponsored the schools received no public support. In 1965, when crafting the legislation, agreement was reached that only indirect aid was to be given to parochial schools, such as tax-supported public school teachers teaching after-hours programs in parochial schools, so long as the instruction were not on religious subjects. The principal purpose of spending federal funds in this way was to lift the educational level of poor children, whether in public or private schools.[88]

In 1965, the Elementary and Secondary Education Act (ESEA), containing the child-benefit plan, became law.[89] LBJ signed the bill in the one-room schoolhouse in Johnson City, Texas, where he had gone to elementary school. He was ecstatic that Congress had produced the bill for him to sign. It was the handmaiden of the Civil Rights Act of 1964, which was so important because it attempted to overcome racial discrimination in the country. The president said:

> From our very beginning as a nation, we have felt a fierce commitment to the ideal of education for everyone. It fixed itself into our democratic creed.... By passing this bill, we bridge the gap between helplessness and hope for more than five million educationally deprived children.... As President of the United States,

[85] "Remarks in Baltimore at the Celebration of he Bicentennial of American Methodism," April 22, 1966 in *Public Papers (1966)* 1 (1967): 447. This long piece is a good summary of the legislative accomplishments of the Johnson Administration for social good.

[86] 281 U.S. 370 (1930).

[87] 330 U.S. 1 (1947).

[88] Califano (1991): 71-73; Lyndon Baines Johnson, *The Vantage Point: Perspectives of the Presidency 1963-1969* (New York: Holt, Reinhart and Winston, 1971): 207-12; Hugh Davis Graham, "The Transformation of Federal Education Policy," in Robert A. Divine, ed., *Exploring the Johnson Years* (Austin: University of Texas Press, 1981): 161-63.

[89] *79 Statutes at Large* 27.

I believe deeply no law I have signed or will sign means more to the future of America.[90]

A few days later he told a gathering of members of Congress:

I will never do anything in my entire life, now or in the future, that excites me more, or benefits the Nation I serve more, or makes the land and all its people better and wiser and stronger, or anything that I think means more to freedom and justice in the world, than what we have done with this education bill.[91]

LBJ may never have realized the extent to which the aid-to-parochial-schools feature of his beloved school law was contrary to the separation of church and state that he had so often expressed. One can speculate that some advisor told him the "child benefit theory" was not incompatible with separation of church and state. Justice Hugo Black, author of the majority opinion in *Everson v. Board of Education*, wrote a paragraph of extremely separationist language,[92] concluding with these words: "The First Amendment has erected a wall between church and state. That wall must be kept high and impregnable. We could not approve the slightest breach. New Jersey has not breached it here."[93] But Justice Black decided the state could pay for the transportation of children to parochial schools. He said it was merely a public welfare program, like fire and police protection for churches. So it is entirely possible LBJ and his advisors saw no disconnect between their plan of government aid to religious schools and the separation of church and state.

Many others did see a disconnect, however. Among these were voters at various International Conventions of the Christian Church (Disciples of Christ). In the very years of Johnson's presidency, the Disciples were speaking to church/state issues, among others. Although LBJ apparently never addressed the issue of prayer in public schools, the Disciples International Convention in 1962 endorsed the decision in *Engel v. Vitale* in which the Supreme Court held unconstitutional a state-written prayer required to be said in public schools, a violation of the no-establishment principle. The resolution stated:

---

[90] "Remarks in Johnson City, Texas, Upon Signing the Elementary and Secondary School Education Bill," April 11, 1965 in *Public Papers (1965)* 1 (1970): 413-14. Lady Bird quoted LBJ as saying: "I have been in public life thirty-four years. But of all the things I am glad to be the architect of, it is putting the Catholics and the Protestants and the Jews together in the Education Bill." (Lady Bird Johnson (1970): 295.)

[91] "Remarks to Members of Congress at a Reception Marking the Enactment of the Education Bill," April 13, 1965 in *Public Papers (1965)* 1 (1966): 416.

[92] 330 U.S. 1 at 15-16. "The 'establishment of religion' clause of the First Amendment means at least this: Neither a state nor the Federal Government can set up a church. Neither can pass laws which aid one religion, aid all religions, or prefer one religion over another. Neither can force nor influence a person to go to or to remain away from church against his will or force him to profess a belief or disbelief in any religion. No person can be punished for entertaining or professing religious beliefs of disbeliefs, for church attendance or nonattendance. No tax in any amount, large or small, can be levied to support any religious activities or institutions, whatever they may be called, or whatever form they may adopt to teach or practice religion. Neither a state nor the Federal Government can, openly or secretly, participate in the affairs of any religious organizations or groups and *vice versa*. In the words of Jefferson, the clause against the establishment of religion by law was intended to erect 'a wall of separation between church and state.'"

[93] 330 U.S. 1 at 18.

"We commend the court's defense of the rightful role of the church from encroachment by the state."[94] In *Abington Township School District v. Schempp*, the Court struck down laws requiring reading ten verses of the Bible and a prayer at the beginning of each day in public schools, but it also said the objective teaching of religion (without endorsing or disparaging religion or seeking to elicit faith responses from students) was not only constitutionally permissible but also a good idea. The 1963 Disciples International Convention passed a resolution that did not mention the prayer dimension of the case but did endorse the Court's recommendation of teaching religion in the public schools.[95]

Somewhat more to the point, given the provision of aid to parochial schools in the ESEA, the Disciples disagreed with such aid. As early as 1948 the International Convention had gone on record as opposing government aid to religious schools and subsequently had reaffirmed that position.[96] In 1963 the International Convention approved a long resolution rehearsing the earlier history of government aid to schools and the church's response. The resolution concluded by saying: "Therefore, be it resolved that the International Convention...reaffirms its previous statements on education, especially those supporting the principle of public funds for public education only."[97]

I find it hard to believe LBJ would not have known of these resolutions of the Church in convention assembled, given that Disciples leaders had contact with him from time to time, but I have found no evidence he took note of them. Certainly his Church's resolutions did not prevent the president from negotiating the aid to parochial schools that so much featured in his beloved education law. LBJ took pride in his Disciples

---

[94] The Convention approved Resolution No. 64, "Concerning Approval of the Supreme Court Action Regarding Prayer in Public Schools," *Disciples of Christ Year Book* (1962): 55.

[95] Resolution No. 54, "On Increasing Elective, Objective, Courses in Religion and the Bible in Secondary Schools and Colleges," voted approval by the Convention Assembly, *idem* (1963): 50-51.

[96] In 1947, the Convention had passed a "Resolution Concerning the Separation of Church and State," *idem* (1947): 18-19, in which it explicitly opposed the "child benefit theory" and said that government aid should be limited to public schools.

In 1948, the Convention passed "A Resolution on Separation of Church and State," *idem* (1948): 21, in which it strongly recommended a law "specifically forbidding the appropriation of federal funds to support sectarian schools or any activity thereof."

In 1949, the Convention passed a "Resolution on Federal Support for Public Education," *idem* (1949): 38, in which it said, "This convention favors the enactment of legislation to provide federal assistance to public school education, provided that such assistance is limited to public schools and the law is so worded that expenditure of public funds for private parochial or sectarian schools is prohibited." In Resolution 57, furthermore, it explicitly rejected the transportation at public expense of children to parochial schools.

In 1952, the Convention passed a "Resolution on Public Funds for Schools and Hospitals,"*idem* (1952), urging Congress "to enact legislation providing for federal assistance to public education, limiting such assistance to tax supported and publicly administered schools." In the same year, it replicated earlier language in Resolution 61, *idem* (1952): 77.

In 1954, the Convention passed a "Resolution on the Use of Public Funds for Education," *idem* (1954): 87, stating:"That we affirm our continued adherence to the American principle of the separation of church and state, and to the principle that *public* funds for education should be used for only *public* education, and that we record our unalterable opposition to the use of any public funds for schools conducted under religious or sectarian auspices." (orginal emphasis in Resolution 57).

[97] Resolution 56, "Concerning Federal Aid to Education," *idem*, (1963): 51-53.

heritage, his church membership, and the separation of church and state in principle, but he went his own way in a specific matter that touched upon education of the poor. LBJ nonetheless resolutely maintained the separation of church and state where he was personally concerned: He did not allow his Disciples Church to dictate public policy to their presidential member and honorary elder!

Ronald Wilson Reagan, 1911-2004

Ronald Reagan was born February 6, 1911, in Tampico, Illinois, the second, and last, child of Jack and Nelle Reagan. When Ronald was born, Jack said he looked like a little Dutchman. The nickname "Dutch" was attached to him his entire life. During Dutch's first nine years, Jack's family lived in five different towns, for Jack was infected with wanderlust, and when they did settle down in Dixon, Illinois, in 1920, they lived in five different houses. Not that Jack was an irresponsible nomad, but he was always looking for a better job in retail clothing sales. Jack did the best he could to support his family, "the proverbial traveling salesman...peddling bright promise from dingier briefcases."[98] Jack was also an alcoholic, and sometimes he was absent from his family. Dutch vividly remembered finding his dad passed out in the snow on the front porch. Nelle persuaded her two sons, Dutch and Neil, that their dad's drinking was to be understood as a disease, consequently he was not to be despised as a man.[99]

Young Dutch's life was as grounded through Nelle's influence as it was turbulent thanks to Jack. Nelle, a committed, active Christian, transmitted her enthusiasm for the faith to Ronald. Baptized in the Disciples church in Tampico, Illinois, on Easter, May 27, 1910, she became "a new creature," transformed from her earlier indistinct religious life into vigorous Christian life, teaching Sunday School, activism in the women's missionary and temperance societies, and editorship of the Disciples church newsletter in Dixon. She distributed tracts to jail inmates and, in spite of her family's own modest means, took meals to people who had fallen on hard times. Of lasting influence on Ronald, Nelle had a flair for the dramatic. She wrote little morality plays, or sometimes "elocution readings," that were given at church functions. She invariably starred in these, and as he got older, so did Dutch. Nelle raised her boys with a "hands on" approach to expressing faith in life; in the process, she turned Dutch into an actor.[100]

---

[98] Garry Wills, *Reagan's America* (New York: Penguin Books, 2000): 18, see 9-19; Ronald Reagan, *An American Life* (New York: Simon and Schuster, 1990): 19-43.

[99] Reagan (1990): 32-34; Garry Wills, "Nelle's Boy: Ronald Reagan and the Disciples of Christ," *Christian Century* 103 (November 12, 1986): 1005; Ronald Reagan to Scott Osborne, January 28, 1985, in *Reagan: A Life in Letters*, Kiron K. Skinner, Annelise Anderson, and Martin Anderson, eds. (New York: Free Press, 2003): 674; Lou Cannon, *President Reagan: The Role of a Lifetime* (New York: Public Affairs, 2000): 174-77.

[100] Wills (1986): 1002-6; Wills (2000): 20-32; Stephen Vaughn, "The Moral Inheritance of a President: Reagan and the Dixon Disciples of Christ," in Michael W. Casey and Douglas A. Foster, eds., *The Stone-Campbell Movement: An International Religious Tradition* (Knoxville: University of Tennessee Press, 2002): 248-68; Paul Kengor, *God and Ronald Reagan: A Spiritual Life* (New York: Regan Books, 2004): 1-32. Reagan (1990): 32: "All my heroes weren't college football stars. A wonderful book about a devout itinerant Christian—*That Printer of Udell's*—made such an impact on me I decided to join my mother's church, the Disciples of Christ. Although Jack and Nelle were married by a Catholic priest, Nelle assumed responsibility for the spiritual preparation of my brother and me. She first took us to

Nelle also taught her son about divine providence, her view that everything happened for a purpose. She instilled in him a kind of determinism that resulted in both fatalism and optimism. Even if something bad happened, it must have been for a purpose, but it was also an opportunity to rise above the bad event and make something good out of it.[101]

Jack was Roman Catholic; Nelle was a Disciple; Dutch followed his mother's influence, Neil followed his dad's. The future president learned the lesson of religious tolerance and respect for other people's religion.

> My dad believed passionately in the rights of individuals and the working man, and he was suspicious of established authority.... My parents constantly drummed into me the importance of judging people as *individuals*. There was no more grievous sin at our household than a racial slur or other evidence of religious or racial intolerance. A lot of it, I think, was because my dad had learned what discrimination was like firsthand. He'd grown up in an era when some stores still had signs at their door saying, NO DOGS OR IRISHMEN ALLOWED.[102]

Reagan summarized the influence of his parents: "I learned from my father the value of hard work and ambition, and maybe a little something about telling a story. From my mother, I learned the value of prayer, how to have dreams and believe I could make them come true."[103]

Another person in Dixon had great influence on Ronald Reagan: Ben Cleaver, minister of the Disciples church from 1922 until 1931. Dutch was in love with Cleaver's daughter, Margaret (called "Mugs"). Consequently, Dutch spent an inordinate amount of time in the Cleaver home; Ben Cleaver became his second father. Cleaver was

---

Sunday school, then, when we were older, to the main services, but always said she'd leave it up to us to decide whether we wanted to actually join the church. At twelve, I made my decision and was baptized as a member of the Disciples of Christ."

For the impact of the book, *That Printer of Udell's*, see Kengor (2004): 17-26. For other reminiscences of his parents and an anecdote about Nelle's "helping hand" attitude, see Reagan's "Remarks During a Visit to the Jeanne Jugan Residence on Mother's Day," May 13, 1984 in *Public Papers of the Presidents of the United States: Ronald Reagan*, book 1, 1984 (Washington: United States Government Printing Office, 1986): 690-91.

[101] Reagan (1990): 20-21: "I was raised to believe that God has a plan for everyone and that seemingly random twists of fate are all a part of His plan. My mother—a small woman with auburn hair and a sense of optimism that ran as deep as the cosmos—told me that everything in life happened for a purpose. She said all things were part of God's Plan, even the most disheartening setbacks, and in the end, everything worked out for the best. If something went wrong, she said, you didn't let it get you down: You stepped away from it, stepped over it, and moved on. Later on, she added, something good will happen and you'll find yourself thinking—'If I hadn't had that problem back then, then this better thing that *did* happen wouldn't have happened to me.'" See also Reagan to Elena Kellner, July 20, 1979 in Skinner, *et al.* (2003): 681.

[102] Reagan (1990): 22, 30. Emphasis in original. Jack's family had come from Ireland.

[103] Reagan (1990): 22. Skinner, *et al.* (2003): 2, adding emphasis, quoted Reagan: "My boyhood was spent in the typical midwestern American melting pot. The schoolroom was a mix of races and creeds and so was my circle of friends. In fact, in my own home my father was Catholic and my mother was Protestant. *He left our religious upbringing to my mother.*"

conservative; he believed Christians should help the needy, that welfare should be done by friends, neighbors, and institutions such as the church, not the government. He believed in progress, capitalism, and that America's future was God's special concern; he opposed communism as an enemy of Christianity. Belief in providence and prayer, hesitation to use the power of government to protect civil rights for minorities, view of poverty as an individual problem best left to charity rather than the state, trust in the work ethic, admiration for capitalism, aversion to communism, association of America's mission with God's will, sensitivity to personal problems (alcohol and drugs), uncomfortable with literature and art that questions the family or challenges notions of proper sexual behavior—in many ways, Nelle's and Cleaver's explicit faith "coincided with the words, if not the beliefs, of the latter-day Reagan." [104] Reagan acknowledged the strong influence of the Dixon church when he wrote to Ben Cleaver in 1973:

> One thing I do know—all the hours in the old church in Dixon (which I didn't appreciate at the time) and all of Nelle's faith, have come together in a kind of inheritance without which I'd be lost and helpless.... My faith is unshakable, and because all of you were so much responsible, I thank you for a peace beyond description. [105]

In 1928, Dutch went to Eureka College, a small Disciples school in Illinois, where he maintained his Disciples identity. He majored in economics but, an acknowledged "big man on campus," his primary focus was football and various campus activities, including acting. [106] After graduation in 1932, Dutch got jobs in radio, principally as a sports broadcaster. He rightly hoped radio would be a gateway to a career in acting—in 1937, he moved to Hollywood and began the career that defined the middle part of his life. [107]

Reagan attended Hollywood Beverly Christian (Disciples) Church—as did Nelle when he moved his parents to Hollywood—but church attendance for the professional actor was sporadic, and he acknowledged he did not attend "as regularly as I should. I suppose it's true that a man can be religious without going to church." [108] That supposition seems to have dictated his church attendance for the rest of his life. In 1963, Reagan began attending Bel Air Presbyterian Church, although he and Nancy never joined, because they could never find the time to attend the ten week membership class. They attended from time to time, except for the time they were in Washington. Bel Air

---

[104] Vaughn (2002): 259-60; Kengor (2004): 32-36.

[105] Reagan to Ben and Mrs. Cleaver, in Skinner, *et al*. (2003): 279.

[106] Reagan (1990): 53-54: "Although my grades were higher than average, my principal academic ambition at Eureka was to maintain the C average I needed to remain eligible for football, swimming, track, and the other school activities I participated in—two years in the student senate, three years as basketball cheerleader, three years as president of the Eureka Boosters Club, two years as yearbook features editor, and, during my last year, student body president and captain and coach of the swim team. Despite my preoccupation with extracurricular activities, I'm convinced I got a solid liberal arts education at Eureka, especially in economics. It was a major I chose because I thought, one way or another, I'd end up dealing with dollars, if not at my father's store, in some other business."
See also, Wills (2000): 44-63; Howard E. Short, "A Campus Pathway to the White House," *The Disciple* 8 (January 18, 1981): 10-11, 34.

[107] Kengor (2004): 41-56.

[108] Reagan, "My Faith," *Modern Screen* (June 1950): 37, 88, quoted in Kengor (2004): 49.

Presbyterian was not intensely sectarian, neither fundamentalist nor evangelical,[109] but the theologically and politically conservative Ronald Reagan found it a compatible church home. Although he claimed to be a "member" of the Disciples church as late as 1976, and he always affirmed his Disciple heritage, during both his governorship and his presidency, Reagan's relationship to the Disciples was more nostalgic than actual.[110]

After Reagan became president, he virtually never attended church. The rationale was to protect the members of whatever congregation he attended from inconvenience and, much more importantly, from danger. If this was his attitude before the attempt on his life, March 30, 1981, it intensified afterward. When he was asked why he did not go to church, he said:

> I have gone to church regularly all my life, and I started [to do so] here in Washington. And now, in the position I hold and in the world in which we live, where Embassies do get blown up in Beirut...I pose a threat to several hundred people if I go to church.

> I know the threats that are made against me. We all know the possibility of terrorism. We have seen the barricades that have had to be built around the White House. And therefore, I don't feel—and my minister [Donn Moomaw of Bel Air Presbyterian] knows this and supports me in this position—I don't feel I have a right to go to church, knowing that my being there could cause something of the kind that we have seen in other places, in Beirut, for example. And I miss going to church, but I think the Lord understands.[111]

On the day of Reagan's first inauguration in 1981, National City Christian Church held a worship service, just as it had done for LBJ's inauguration, but President Reagan did not attend, and he did not inform the church that he would not attend.[112]

---

[109] Richard G. Hutcheson, Jr., *God in the White House: How Religion has Changed the Modern Presidency* (New York: Collier Books, 1988): 164-66; Roland Evans and Robert Novak, *The Reagan Revolution* (New York: E. P. Dutton, 1981): 209-10; James Combs, *The Reagan Range: The Nostalgic Myth in American Politics* (Bowling Green, Ohio: Bowling Green State University Popular Press, 1993): 107. Although Reagan quit attending Hollywood Beverly Christian Church in 1963, he continued to send a monthly check to that church, at least as recently as October 2002. (Kengor [2004]: 49.)

[110] Reagan to Dorothy D. Conaghan, "Circa 1976" in Skinner, et al. (2003): 256. Conaghan had inquired about the relation of his religion to his seeking the presidency (unsuccessfully in 1976). He wrote: "By coincidence [I do not know what this means—perhaps Conaghan had identified herself as a Disciple], I am a member of the Christian Church and attended a Christian Church school, Eureka College in Illinois."

[111] "Debate between the President and Former Vice President Walter F. Mondale in Louisville, Kentucky," October 7, 1984 in *Public Papers (1984)*: 2 (1987): 1447. Reagan to Jerry Mueller, May 31, 1984 in Skinner, *et al.* (2003): 461: "I'll admit I was very frustrated when the press carried stories that I never had been a churchgoer and therefore was a hypocrite when I referred to God and his place in our nation's life. We have always been churchgoers and would be now if it were not for the terrorist threats. We could handle the usual kind of kooky threat directed only at me. But the situation has changed as we saw in Beirut. Our intelligence now indicates the possibility of attack which could endanger a great many people." He continued that they do not have religious services in the White House, as Richard Nixon had done, but that they receive communion there sometimes. He concluded: "As I said, we miss going but prayer is very much part of our daily life."

[112] Schreiber interview (2004).

The early Ronald Reagan was a New Deal Democrat, but in the 1950s and early 1960s, he "moved from soft left to hard right," so much so that he was willing to give a speech in 1964 in support of Barry Goldwater's campaign for president.[113] Ben Cleaver's politics and social theory and Nelle Reagan's religion and charitable activism had been combined in Dutch in his youth, and in the 1960s he reformulated their faith in a way that made sense to the emerging Religious Right, although his Disciples categories of conversion did not match their Evangelical "born again" jargon.[114] The emerging political power of the Religious Right contributed to Reagan's election as president because conservative Christians saw him as compatible with their theology and social agenda. Reagan became a symbol of the joining together of traditional secular conservatism and the new Religious Right, "not a matter of one influencing the other," but in the Reagan presidency, "of the two having become a single movement."[115] The Moral Majority, the most obvious expression of the Religious Right, had been formed only in 1978, but Reagan had been theologically and socially conservative before then. If Reagan were "born again," it was not as an Evangelical Christian but as a liberal Democrat rebaptized as a conservative Republican. When the Religious Right began looking for a person to run for president, Reagan was a natural choice because he fashioned his ideological platform long before the Moral Majority or the Religious Roundtable had seen the light of day.

Reagan's conservative theological and social beliefs, some of them church/state issues, had been fundamental to public policy in American politics. Like many of his nineteenth-century Disciples forebears,[116] Reagan identified American national interest with God's will. He believed God had chosen America to be a beacon of hope and righteousness not only to its own people but also to the world. He frequently invoked Puritan John Winthrop's phrase, "We shall be as a city upon a hill, the eyes of all people

---

[113] Evans and Novak (1981): 23-29.

[114] In Reagan's Disciples heritage, "born again" was not part of the vocabulary, but the litmus test of post-Calvinist Evangelicalism is that one confess oneself to have been "born again." Reagan answered potential Evangelical supporters by saying biblically-theologically accurately that he had been born again at his baptism. "'I know what many of those who use that term mean by it, but in my situation in the church I was raised in, the Christian Church, there you were baptized and you, yourself, decided that you were, as the Bible says ... born again. In the context of the Bible, by being baptized, you were [born again],' he said." ("Reagan Claims 'Born Again' Heritage," *The Disciple* 7 (July 20, 1980): 21.)

In a campaign debate between Reagan and his Democratic challenger, Reagan was asked if he considered himself a born-again Christian. As a part of a long, rambling, answer, he said: "I was raised to have a faith and a belief and have been a member of a church since I was a small boy. In our particular church, we did not use that term 'born again,' so I don't know whether I would fit that—that particular term." Then he went on to speak of his mother's influence and to affirm that he prayed. ("Debate Between the President and Former Vice President Walter F. Mondale in Louisville, Kentucky," October 7, 1984 in *Public Papers (1984)* 2 (1987): 1446.)

[115] Hutcheson (1988): 174; see Evans and Novak (1981): 204-25.

[116] David Edwin Harrell, Jr., *Sources of Division in the Disciples of Christ, 1865-1900: A Social History of the Disciples of Christ*, vol. 2 (Tuscaloosa: University of Alabama Press, 2003): 22-24.

are upon us."[117] One of the roles of God-selected America was to expose and defeat godless communism, especially in its most threatening form, that "evil empire" of the Soviet Union. First articulated in the 1950s, this bedrock of Reagan's political faith persisted throughout his presidency.[118] Reagan expressed this tenet in a variety of ways:

> Our nation exists for one purpose only—to assure each one of us the ultimate in individual freedom consistent with law and order. God meant America to be free because God intended each man to have the dignity of freedom.[119]

> We are a nation under God. I've always believed that this blessed land was set apart in a special way, that some divine plan placed this great continent here between the oceans to be found by people from every corner of the Earth who had a special love for freedom and the courage to uproot themselves, leave homeland and friends, to come to a strange land. And coming here they created something new in all the history of mankind—a land where man is not beholden to government, government is beholden to man.... We can make our beloved country the source of all the dreams and opportunities she was placed on this good Earth to provide. We need only to believe in each other and in the God who has so blessed our land.[120]

> We Americans are blessed in so many ways. We're a nation under God, a living and loving God. But Thomas Jefferson warned us, "I tremble for my country when I reflect that God is just." We cannot expect Him to protect us in a crisis if we turn away from Him in our everyday living. But you know, He told us what to do in II Chronicles. Let us reach out to Him. He said, "If my people, which are called by my name, shall humble themselves and pray and seek my face and turn from their wicked ways, then will I hear from Heaven and will forgive their sin and will heal their land."[121]

Reagan's biblical exhortation contains a cautionary note: If Americans fail to fulfill their purpose, they will not be conforming to God's plan for the nation. Reagan's explanation for that includes two classic church/state themes: prayer in public schools and tuition tax credits for parents who send their children to parochial schools. Reagan

---

[117] John Winthrop, "A Model of Christian Charity," in *American Christianity: An Historical Interpretation with Representative Documents*, H. Shelton Smith, Robert T. Handy, and Lefferts A. Loetscher, eds., vol. 1, *1607-1820* (New York: Charles Scribner's Sons, 1960): 102.

[118] Kengor (2004): 89-99.

[119] Reagan to Kenneth Wells, "Circa 1967-68," in Skinner, *et al.* (2003): 257.

[120] "Remarks at a Spirit of America Rally in Atlanta, Georgia," January 26, 1984 in *Public Papers (1984)* 1 (1986): 101-2. A similar statement rings with Dutch's faith learned at Nelle's knee: "I've always believed that we were, each of us, put here for a reason, that there is a plan, somehow a divine plan for all of us. I know now that whatever days are left to me belong to Him. I also believe this blessed land was set apart in a very special way, a country created by men and women who came here not in search of gold, but in search of God. They would be free people, living under the law with faith in their Maker and their future." ("Remarks at the Annual National Prayer Breakfast," February 4, 1982 in *Public Papers (1982)* 1 (1986): 109.)

[121] "Remarks at a Dinner Honoring Senator Jesse Helms of North Carolina," June 16, 1983, *Public Papers (1983)* 1 (1984): 880. The passage, one of President Reagan's favorite verses, is 2 Chronicles 7:14; he quoted it often from memory.

believed the Supreme Court decisions of 1962 and 1963 declaring state-mandated prayer and Bible reading in public schools unconstitutional had been terrible mistakes that hastened the nation down a path of indifference to God:

> No one must be forced or pressured to take part in any religious exercise. But neither should the freest country on Earth ever have permitted God to be expelled from the classroom. When the Supreme Court ruled that school prayer was unconstitutional almost 21 years ago, I believe it ruled wrong.[122]

Just after a statement describing America as a "blessed land," he said:

> Sometimes, it seems we've strayed from that noble beginning, from our conviction that standards of right and wrong do exist and must be lived up to. God, the source of our knowledge, has been expelled from the classroom. He gives us His greatest blessing, life, and yet many would condone the taking of innocent life. We expect Him to protect us in a crisis, but turn away from Him too often in our day-to-day living. I wonder if He isn't waiting for us to wake up.[123]

Reagan believed the country was ready for a spiritual renewal, the people wanted a spiritual renewal, and he was the person to inspire and lead it:

> What I have felt for a long time is that the people in this country were hungry for what you might call a spiritual revival, a return to values, to things they really believed in and held dear. And I always remembered that Teddy Roosevelt said this office was a bully pulpit, and I decided that if it was possible for me to help in that revival, I wanted to do that.[124]

One of the ways President Reagan intended to stimulate national spiritual revival was to restore prayer to America's public schools, and to do that would require an amendment to the Constitution. Reagan believed the Supreme Court had removed prayer completely from the public schools. He told a group of evangelical Christians: "I'm convinced that passage of this amendment would do more than any other action to reassert the faith and values that made America great.... [T]ogether we can show the world that America is still one nation under God."[125] "The Great Communicator," as he was called, took his case directly to the American people, often speaking over the radio:

> I happen to believe that one way to promote, indeed, to preserve these traditional values we share is by permitting our children to begin their days the same ways the Members of the United States Congress do—with prayer. The public expression of our faith in God, through prayer, is fundamental—as a part of our American heritage and a privilege which should not be excluded from our schools.[126]

---

[122] "Remarks at the Annual Convention of Religious Broadcasters," January 31, 1983. *Public Papers of President Reagan (1983)* 1, (1984): 152.

[123] "Remarks at the Annual National Prayer Breakfast," February 4, 1982 in *Public Papers (1982)* 1 (1983): 109.

[124] Bob Slosser, *Reagan Inside Out* (Waco, Texas: Word Books, 1984): 166, quoted in Kengor (2004): 166.

[125] "Remarks at the Annual Convention of the National Association of Evangelicals in Columbus, Ohio," March 6, 1984 in *Public Papers (1984)* 1 (1986): 309-10.

[126] "Remarks at the Annual Convention of Religious Broadcasters," January 31, 1983 in *Public Papers (1983)* 1 (1984): 152.

[I]n recent years, well-meaning Americans in the name of freedom have taken freedom away. For the sake of religious tolerance, they've forbidden religious practice in our public classrooms. The law of this land has effectively removed prayer from our classrooms.

How can we hope to retain our freedom through the generations if we fail to teach our young that our liberty springs from an abiding faith in our Creator?....[C]urrent interpretation of our Constitution holds that the minds of our children cannot be free to pray to God in public schools. No one will ever convince me that a moment of voluntary prayer will harm a child or threaten a school or State. But I think it can strengthen our faith in a Creator who alone has the power to bless America.[127]

At the conclusion of a radio address on education issues, he said: "And, once again, I'll continue working for the restoration of voluntary school prayer, for nothing is as basic as acknowledging the God from whom all knowledge springs."[128]

Because Reagan gave so much attention to the school prayer issue, he was compelled to interpret the First Amendment and comment on what he thought the founding fathers meant by the religion clauses. One of the clearest expressions of this was written in a couple of letters to Norman Lear, the TV producer (famous for producing "All in the Family") and founder of People for the American Way. Lear had written to criticize Reagan on a number of fronts, including his school prayer views. The president replied:

I do believe the First Amendment is being somewhat distorted or misinterpreted by some who would, by government decree, make freedom *of* religion into freedom *from* religion. The First Amendment plainly is to ensure that in this nation there shall be no official state church. The amendment says the government shall not establish religion, but it also just as plainly says the government shall not interfere in the practice of religion.

But isn't the government doing the latter when it decrees that a child cannot ask a blessing before lunch in the school cafeteria—particularly when we remember the child is compelled by law to attend school? ... I believe that Madalyn Murray O'Hair, who brought about the anti-school prayer decision, was imposing her atheism on those of us who believe in God. The goal of our nation must always be the ultimate in individual freedom consistent with an orderly society.

In a second letter referring to school prayer, Reagan indicated his religious ecumenism:

Madalyn Murray O'Hair demanded and got denial of anyone's right to pray in school. I simply ask that they be allowed to pray if they so desire—and that prayer can be to the God of Moses, the man of Galilee, Allah, Buddha, or any others.[129]

On at least twelve occasions during his first term alone, Reagan commented on the meaning of the First Amendment. Usually, he offered a paraphrase, for example the following: "The first amendment of the Constitution was not written to protect the people from religion; that amendment was written to protect religion from government

---

[127] "Remarks at a White House Ceremony in Observance of National Day of Prayer," May 6, 1982 in *Public Papers (1982)* 1 (1983): 574.

[128] "Radio Address to the Nation on Education," May 12, 1984 in *Public Papers (1984)* 1 (1986): 690.

[129] Reagan to Norman Lear, May 22, 1984 and June 25, 1984, in Skinner, *et al.* (2003): 643-44.

tyranny."[130] He believed the founders, in building a wall of separation between church and state, had guaranteed religious freedom for all, never envisioning the government would, as he believed the Supreme Court had done, "construct a wall of hostility between government and the concept of religious belief itself."[131]

Advocating his proposed school-prayer amendment, Reagan summarized the rationale in one sentence: "The public expression through prayer of our faith in God is a fundamental part of our American heritage and a privilege which should not be excluded by law from any American school, public or private." The amending language proposed was: "Nothing in this Constitution shall be construed to prohibit individual or group prayer in public schools or other public institutions. No person shall be required by the United States or by any State to participate in prayer."[132] Under the amendment, no one would be forced to pray, but anyone who wanted to do so voluntarily would be able to. He argued against the many opponents of the proposed amendment who believed it would somehow mandate prayers in schools.

> [W]e were asking nothing of the kind. Quite the contrary, we were asking that the Constitution be restored to neutrality with regard to religion. The government is to neither be an advocate of, nor a controller of, or preventer of the practice of religion. And all the amendment would do is say, if someone wants to pray in schools, they can, under the Constitution. And then we did add some provision that no one could mandate, no one could write or prepare any prayer for them.[133]

---

[130] "Radio Address to the Nation on Prayer in Schools," February 25, 1984 in *Public Papers (1984)* 1 (1986): 261. Then, after quoting the religion clauses in the First Amendment, he went on: "What could be more clear?" He was far less clear when he tried to quote the religion clauses from memory; he botched it grandly. See "Interview with Eleanor Clift, Jack Nelson, and Joel Havermann of the *Los Angeles Times*," June 23, 1986 in *Public Papers (1986)* 1 (1988): 830.

[131] "Remarks at the Annual Convention of the National Association of Evangelicals in Orlando, Florida," March 8, 1983 in *Public Papers (1983)* 1 (1984): 361.

[132] "Message to the Congress Transmitting a Proposed Constitutional Amendment on Prayer in School," May 17, 1982 in *Public Papers (1982)* 1 (1983): 647-48. The President introduced the amendment the following year, also: "Message to the Congress Transmitting the Proposed Constitutional Amendment on Prayer in Schools," March 8, 1983 in *Public Papers (1983)* 1 (1984): 365-66. He never again introduced the amendment, although he urged its passage throughout his tenure.

[133] "The President's News Conference," April 4, 1984 in *Public Papers (1984)*1 (1986): 465. See also "Question-and-Answer Session With Students at Thomas Jefferson High School of Science and Technology in Fairfax Country, Virginia," February 7, 1986 in *Public Papers (1986)* 1 (1988): 180: "I have simply said that I believe that students should have the right and privilege to voluntarily pray within school if they want to. And that's up to them, and no one that doesn't care to or whose religion is different—they can pursue their own courses. But I don't think there should be any place in this nation where anyone is denied the right to appeal to whatever God they worship." For another exposition on the voluntary nature of prayers enabled by the amendment, see "Remarks and a Question-and-Answer Session With Local High School Honor Students," May 23, 1983, *Public Papers of President Reagan (1983)* 1, 1984, 755-56.

On another occasion, he observed, "The prayers, I think, would obviously have to be non-sectarian so that you are not showing favor to one particular religion or another."[134]

Congress never approved President Reagan's amendment, but Reagan never gave up. Late in his administration, he was still promoting voluntary prayer in the public schools and a constitutional amendment to restore it. In a speech summarizing some of the accomplishments of his administration, he said:

> And there's another measure that we've worked for: school prayer. So far, we haven't succeeded in persuading the Congress to enact legislation that would once again permit voluntary prayer in America's schools. But I'm convinced that one day soon, such a measure will be passed.[135]

A second issue with First Amendment implications to which President Reagan gave some attention was government aid for parochial schools. Reagan favored government aid to parochial schools and spoke principally of tuition tax credits as the method to provide that support. His primary argument was fairness. Those people who sent their children to parochial schools obviously had to bear the expense of that, but they also continued to pay taxes for the public schools. As Reagan frequently put it, they were paying for two school systems but using only one. Consequently, he believed, such parents, who were predominantly middle and lower-income families, deserved some relief through a reduction in their federal income tax for the money they spent in private school tuition. Among the many times he mentioned this issue,[136] the following is the clearest and most complete articulation of it.

> Today, 5 million American kids attend private schools because of the emphasis on religious values and educational standards. The overwhelming majority of these schools are church-supported—Catholic, Protestant, and Jewish. And the majority of the students are from families earning less than $25,000. In many parochial schools, the majority of students are from minority neighborhoods. In addition to private tuition, these families also pay their full share of taxes to fund the public schools. I think they're entitled some relief, since they're supporting

---

[134] "Remarks and a Question-and-Answer Session during an Administration Briefing in Chicago, Illinois, for Editors from the Midwestern Region," May 10, 1982 in *Public Papers (1982)* 1 (1986): 591.

[135] "Remarks to the Student Congress on Evangelism," July 28, 1988 in *Public Papers (1988-89)* 2 (1991): 962. Reagan did not pursue the school-prayer issue with equal ardor throughout his administration. Perusal of the indices of all fifteen volumes of the *Public Papers of President Reagan* shows that he spoke on the issue mostly from 1982 through 1984. After that, the number of pronouncements falls off sharply, and what he did say was not nearly so expansive or vigorously stated as in the earlier years. Cannon (2000): 728, argued that Reagan's "constitutional amendment to restore prayer in schools [along with other points on Reagan's "social agenda"] were never more than throwaway lines intended to comfort the Religious Right or some other element of his conservative constituency." Kengor (2004): 176-77 argued to the contrary that Reagan was deeply committed to the school prayer issue and worked hard on it. My own thought is between these extremes. Reagan, it seems to me, was fairly passionate about his views on school prayer, but beginning just before the end of his first term and throughout the second, he ran out of gas on the issue.

[136] Reagan spoke about tuition tax credits fifty-six times while he was President. A review of the indices of the fifteen volumes of *Public Papers of President Reagan* shows that, like his statements on prayer in public schools, the bulk of these statements was made during his first term. In fact, after 1984, he mentioned tuition tax credits only three times, and never after 1986.

two school systems and only using one. Last year, as a matter of tax equity, we introduced legislation to give these families a break. We don't seek to aid the rich, but those lower- and middle-income families who are most strapped by taxes and the recession. In proposing tuition tax credits, we hope to provide greater choice and educational opportunity for our children.[137]

Only once did Reagan even hint that he thought there might be church/state problems with the plan, so he simply denied them, but without articulating why his blurring of the separation of church and state did not violate the principle: "And the bill we proposed does not violate the separation of church and state."[138] Earlier he had used "child benefit" and more accurately "parent benefit" language that could have explained why tuition tax credits did not violate separation: "Now, it's important to understand that we do not propose to aid schools. This bill will provide direct benefit to individuals."[139] And again: "Well, this [tuition tax credit bill] will not allow any government interference in any way in education, because the aid is going directly to the parents of children who are going to the schools. So, this will not lead to any government direction or interference in any way in education...."[140]

The issue here, stated simply, is that religious schools teach denominational religion, i.e., the theology of the sponsoring church. Government aid to those schools would mean some taxpayers' money would be financing the teaching of a religion with which those citizens did not agree, a violation of the no-establishment clause. Also, a frequent argument against government aid to religious institutions, such as parochial schools, is that government requirements and supervision follow government money. Such government intervention in the workings of a religious institution, however, creates "excessive entanglement" between the two,[141] the very thing the First Amendment was designed to prevent.

President Reagan could have used these and similar arguments to assert that, because the aid was in the form of indirect tax credits to individuals, church schools would not receive government money, and this would avoid excessive entanglement, thereby causing no violation of the no-establishment clause of the First Amendment. He did not, however, make that connection. In only one sentence in eight years did the president acknowledge that a church/state problem might inhere in the aid to parochial education bill, and he did not elaborate on that single sentence in any way. The bill

---

[137] "Radio Address on Domestic Issues," January 22, 1983 in *Public Papers (1983)* 1 (1984): 95; See also "Message to the Congress Transmitting Proposed Tuition Tax Credit Legislation," February 16, 1983 in *idem*: 236-37, and "Radio Address to the Nation on Education," March 12, 1983 in *idem*: 390-92.

[138] "Remarks to the New York State Federation of Catholic School Parents," April 5, 1984 in *Public Papers (1984)* 1 (1986): 475.

[139] "Remarks to the National Catholic Education Association in Chicago, Illinois," April 15, 1982 in *Public Papers (1982)* 1 (1983): 466.

[140] "Question-and-Answer Session with Students at St. Peter's Catholic Elementary School in Geneva, Illinois," April 15, 1982 in *Public Papers (1982)* 1 (1983): 470.

[141] At the time, the Supreme Court used a three-part test to determine whether a law or program violated the establishment clause. Called the *"Lemon* test" from its use in *Lemon v. Kurtzman* 403 U.S. 602 (1971), a law was deemed constitutional if it had a secular purpose, a primary effect that neither advanced nor hindered religion, and did not cause excessive entanglement between religion and civil authority. A law had to fail only one of the three to be declared unconstitutional.

favoring federal tuition tax credit for parents sending their children to parochial schools never came to a vote in the Congress.[142]

Did Reagan's church/state views have anything to do with the views of the Disciples during his two terms in office? Hardly anything. Although he had a nostalgic identity with the Disciples, he had severed any meaningful relationship with the denomination long before he became president. No evidence is extant that he looked to the Disciples in any way for any guidance or suggestions as he formulated his church/state beliefs.

Did Disciples acknowledge Reagan's Disciple heritage? Barely. In terms of Disciples publications, aside from occasional mention of Reagan's Disciples background and his ongoing relationship with his alma mater, Eureka College, they gave Reagan scant attention. Compared with the attention that had been paid to Presidents Garfield and Johnson, precious little notice was given to President Reagan in Disciples periodicals. The relationship between Ronald Reagan and the denomination of his youth was one of benign neglect—from both directions; each essentially ignored the other.

Furthermore, at least in terms of the pronouncements or resolutions of the Disciples in convention assembled, they were essentially silent on these issues during Reagan's two-term presidency. In spite of Reagan's first-term full-court press for a constitutional amendment favoring prayer in public schools, the Disciples, apparently content in their agreement with the Court's school-prayer decisions in the 1960s, remained speechless on the issue. Likewise, apparently comfortable with their earlier strong recommendations of public money only for public education, the closest the Disciples came to commenting on education policy was a 1984 reaffirmation of the General Assembly's commitment to public education, a resolution that did not mention private education, much less the president's proposal to subsidize it with public money.[143] In terms of these two church/state issues, he and the Disciples were like two ships passing in the night.

---

[142] The cause of Congressional inaction may have been that members of Congress knew the Supreme Court had earlier declared a New York State tuition tax credit law to be a violation of the establishment clause, in *Committee for Public Education and Religious Liberty v. Nyquist* 413 U.S. 756 (1973). The Court said the plan had a primary effect that advanced religion in that it provided a government incentive for people to send their children to parochial schools. Perhaps they believed a similar federal law would receive the same fate.

[143] Resolution 8347, "Resolution Concerning Public Education," *Year Book* (1984): 262. I thank Dr. Mark Toulouse, professor of American Religious History at Brite Divinity School, Texas Christian University, for sharing with me his compilation of all the resolutions of Disciples General Assemblies from 1968 to the present.

The Influence of Foy E. Wallace, Jr.

Terry J. Gardner

Richard Hughes described Foy E. Wallace, Jr., as he was during the 1930s and 1940s, as "perhaps the most pivotal and influential figure in Churches of Christ."[1] Robert E. Hooper stated that in the 1930s "no other person was as important"[2] as Wallace. Earl West found Foy to be "unusually appealing" and wrote, "I admired him immensely."[3] David Edwin Harrell, Jr., noted that in the 1920s and 1930s, "No individual contributed more to defining the doctrinal direction of churches of Christ"[4] than Foy E. Wallace, Jr. Leroy Garrett wrote that "few men sacrificed more for the cause of Christ than Foy E. Wallace, Jr."[5]

Some, who see Wallace as a person of extraordinary influence, represent that influence as negative. Harrell claimed that Wallace was by "many measures the rankest 'dogmatist' in the movement."[6] Harrell further attributed Wallace's influence to a "McCarthy-like gift for intimidation."[7] The tendency in recent years has been to demonize Wallace, perhaps in part as a reaction to the efforts of others who lionized him. My purpose in this article is to attempt to understand why he was a person of exceptional influence. What were the sources of the influence of Foy E. Wallace, Jr., and how did he use that influence?

The Boy Preacher

Foy E. Wallace, Jr., was immersed into Christ by his father in 1909. On an April Sunday in 1912, fifteen-year-old Foy, Jr., in one of his first sermons, preached with a maturity that amazed and delighted his audience. Arthur Wilkinson filed this report:

> Last Sunday was the day for Foy E. Wallace, Jr., to occupy the pulpit at the Christian church at Sunset. Foy is known as the "boy preacher," which is indeed true. He is only 15 years of age, and is still wearing his knee pants, but his ability as a preacher is indeed wonderful.
>
> The house was crowded to its fullest capacity, and judging from the expression on the faces of the departing crowd, not one was disappointed over their

---

[1] Richard T. Hughes, *Reviving the Ancient Faith: The Story of Churches of Christ in America* (Grand Rapids: Eerdmans, 1996): 183.

[2] Robert E. Hooper, *A Distinct People, A History of the Churches of Christ in the 20th Century* (West Monroe, Louisiana: Howard Publishing Co.): 132.

[3] Earl Irvin West, *Searcher for the Ancient Order: The Golden Odyssey of Earl I. West* (Nashville, Tennessee Gospel Advocate Company, 2004): 88.

[4] David Edwin Harrell, Jr., *The Churches of Christ in the 20th Century: Homer Hailey's Personal Journey of Faith* (Tuscaloosa, Alabama: University of Alabama Press, 2000): 92.

[5] Leroy Garrett, *The Stone-Campbell Movement: The Story of the American Restoration Movement* (Joplin, Missouri: College Press Publishing Company, rev. ed., 1994): 455.

[6] Harrell (2000): 43.

[7] Harrell (2000): 93.

attendance at either the morning or evening discourse, but all were agreeably surprised, and no doubt greatly benefited by the lessons presented.

Brother Foy not only has the startling ability to entertain his audience, but presents the Scriptures in meekness and love, causing all to realize that what he says, though it falls from the lips of a boy, comes from a heart that is sincere, and is intended to point people from the hopelessness of sin to the light of life in a risen Lord.

It makes us rejoice to see such interest and earnest zeal manifested by one so tender in years, and we can almost feel the just pride of the father and mother of so noble a son. And as this thought leaves our mind a sadder one comes to take its place, and we think what a pity it is that there are fathers and mothers whose heads are made to bow low in shame over the disgraceful conduct of their boy. This being true, we think that [in] the giving to the world [of] such a noble character in the young Christian, such as Brother Foy, is made even more commendable, though it be that their parents have only done their duty.

Now, we do not believe in singing the praise of one gospel preacher over that of another, but we do believe that the efforts of our young preachers deserve the commendation and that they should have our encouragement and prayers, therefore we have written the above.[8]

D. F. Draper reported that fifteen-year-old Foy, Jr., preached at Georgetown, Texas, on Sunday night, May 19th, and that he "is one boy with a man's head. Brethren you will make no mistake in calling him out in the regular work. He is a wonder."[9]

A. J. Kirkpatrick wrote of the fifteen-year-old preaching prodigy's gospel meeting that, "There was not standing room, and many left because they could not get in.... He is a preacher of ability for one of his age. The last night his subject was 'The Great Salvation.' He got all out of the subject there was in it. He certainly is a power for good in the gospel. We want him four weeks next year."[10]

The praise elicited from the young Wallace's seniors was remarkable. There was something about him that set him apart from the very start of his preaching career. Other young men preached with power and ability but did not receive the comment reserved for Wallace. In 1917, Jesse P. Sewell, then president of Abilene Christian College, heard the twenty-year-old Wallace preach, and he wrote:

I heard Foy E., Jr., preach in his Goldthwaite meeting. I have heard good preaching all my life; and Foy, while still a boy, is a great preacher. He is a great preacher, not because he is exceptionally "smart," not because he is such a fine speaker, not because he knows so much of history, literature, science, philosophy and the arts, but because he knows and loves the gospel, and in an earnest, simple, self-banishing, humble manner presents them directly to the hearts of the people, with strong confidence, not in his power, but in the power of the gospel.[11]

---

[8] Arthur D. Wilkinson, "Sunday at Sunset," *Firm Foundation* (hereinafter: *FF*) 28/17 (April 23, 1912): 5.

[9] D. F. Draper, "Georgetown Notes," *FF* 28/22 (May 28, 1912): 8.

[10] A. J. Kirkpatrick, "News and Notes," *FF* 28/35 (August 27, 1912): 6.

[11] Jesse P. Sewell, "Among the Churches at Goldthwaite," *FF* 34/34 (July 17, 1917): 8.

The "visible results" of the youthful preacher matched the positive press. In 1920, Wallace baptized at least 233 souls, including 100 in a single gospel meeting in Lometa, Texas. The effect of the Lometa sermons was electrifying. F. W. Dent wrote, "We cannot begin to seat the people, streets and alleys crowded with cars."[12] D. W. Nichols telegraphed the *Firm Foundation* in the midst of this meeting, "Ninety-five additions. Great rejoicing."[13] Wallace reported the final results of the Lometa meeting as "one hundred and forty-nine additions. One hundred baptisms, all grown, not one under sixteen years of age. Men out of duty fifteen years come home."[14] This meeting suggests one source of Wallace's influence, that he was quick to share the credit for extraordinary success with others. Wallace wrote his conclusion to the meeting by stating, "I want to say that its great success is due to the untiring efforts of the membership of that church. They were ready when I got there. We started in high gear and never changed to low. The church at Lometa deserves the credit and God the glory."[15]

Wallace preferred to take his own song leader with him when he held meetings. One of his early song leaders was the well known hymn writer, Tillet S. Teddlie. Teddlie and Wallace traveled together holding gospel meetings for two years from 1921 through 1922. During these two years, the following results are documented:

Year	n. Baptized	n. Restored
1921	281	90
1922	274	81

When Leroy Garrett interviewed the ninety-nine-year-old Teddlie, he asked him to "name the greatest preacher he had sung for in revivals." Teddlie replied immediately, "Foy Wallace." Garrett wrote:

Teddlie told of working with Wallace in towns across Texas, planting the churches that today owe their existence to him. It was tiring work in hard places. Teddlie told of Foy's love for the hymn "Millions in heaven are singing it now," which Teddlie had composed. As people came forward during the invitation, Wallace would cry out to his singer, "Sing it again, Tillet!"[16]

Austin Taylor, another Wallace song leader, reminisced of his days singing for Wallace, "Foy Wallace, Jr., and I have 'blazed the trail' throughout eight different states... In a few places there have been more than one hundred people baptized, while I stood by singing 'O Happy Day.'"[17]

In 1923, Wallace's influence as a preacher would begin to extend east of the Mississippi River as he held his first meeting in Nashville, Tennessee, for the Russell Street congregation. S. H. Hall was the preacher for this very active congregation and the meeting created a sensation. Hall wrote of the meeting:

[12] F. W. Dent, "News and Notes," *FF* 37/38 (September 21, 1920): 4.
[13] D. W. Nichols, "News and Notes," *FF* 37/37 (September 14, 1920): 4.
[14] Foy E. Wallace, Jr., "News and Notes," *FF* 37/38 (September 21, 1920): 4-5.
[15] *Idem,* "News and Notes," *FF* 37/39 (September 28, 1920): 4.
[16] Garrett (1994): 455.
[17] Austin Taylor, "Bring on the Book," *FF* 72/40 (October 4, 1955): 657.

This is the only revival that I have ever been in that it seemed the crowds hindered the work... it was estimated that some six hundred or a thousand were turned away for lack of room. The house was packed at the last three services the last day of the meeting, and at the final night service it was considered that more than two thousand were in the building, and hundreds were turned away.[18]

Among the members of this congregation was J. C. McQuiddy, the owner of the *Gospel Advocate*, and his son, Leon McQuiddy. Wallace recalled that during the Russell Street meeting, the aged E. G. Sewell, "David Lipscomb's colleague and co-laborer, sat in an arm chair a few feet from me."[19] During this meeting, Wallace also became acquainted with F. W. Smith and F. B. Srygley, influential members of the *Gospel Advocate* staff. The impression made by the twenty-seven-year-old Wallace on the aged giants of the Churches of Christ in Nashville was remarkable. Wallace seemed a kindred spirit. From 1923 through 1930, Wallace held several more meetings in middle Tennessee that solidified the impression made in 1923 and added to his influence.

Editor of the Gospel Advocate

In 1930, Leon McQuiddy, who succeeded his father as the general manager of the *Gospel Advocate*, summoned Foy E. Wallace, Jr., by wire to move from Los Angeles to Nashville and become the editor of the *Gospel Advocate*. The August 14, 1930, issue of the *Advocate* was the first edited by Foy E. Wallace, Jr., only thirty-three years old at the time. Even David Lipscomb had been almost thirty-five years old when he began to edit the *Gospel Advocate* in 1866.

In addition to his youth, Wallace had never edited a paper, had written fewer than a dozen articles, and had held only three debates, none of which was significant. G.H.P. Showalter, long-time editor of the *Firm Foundation*, wrote of Wallace's appointment to the editorial chair, "While Brother Wallace is without experience in office work and in the almost infinite detail of the work of an office editor, we believe he will make good…. He is little known before the brotherhood as a writer, but we believe he will make a success of this as he has in gospel meetings."[20]

When Wallace became the editor of the *Gospel Advocate*, David Lipscomb had been dead only thirteen years. The *Advocate* was the most influential paper among Churches of Christ in the era before television and when even radio was still a new medium. In those years, Christians still read, and much of their reading was from the Bible and in the *Gospel Advocate*. In a sense, the mantle of David Lipscomb had fallen onto the shoulders of Foy E. Wallace, Jr. Whatever else Wallace would accomplish in his long career as preacher, he would always be remembered as having once been the editor of the *Gospel Advocate*. R. H. Boll's influence had been boosted in a similar way in 1909, when he became the front-page writer of the *Advocate*. Now here was Foy E. Wallace, Jr., younger than Boll had been, writing not only the front page of the *Advocate* but also serving as the paper's editor-in-

---

[18] S. H. Hall, "The Russell Street Revival," *Gospel Advocate* (hereinafter: *GA*) LXV/47 (November 22, 1923): 1,124.

[19] Carroll B. Ellis, "Foy E. Wallace, Jr. Talks to Young Lipscomb Preachers," *GA* CVIII/13 (March 31, 1966): 197.

[20] G. H. P. Showalter, "A New Regime," *FF* 47/34 (August 26, 1930): 2.

chief. Wallace's considerable natural charisma was thus boosted by the legendary status of his predecessors in the editor's chair he now occupied.

James W. Adams's Review of the Life of Foy E. Wallace, Jr.

At the 1981 Florida College Lectures, James W. Adams delivered a speech[21] on the life of Foy E. Wallace, Jr. Adams made many positive comments about Wallace but also many pointed criticisms. Unlike many of Wallace's other critics, James Adams had been fairly well acquainted with Wallace for part of his life. Adams wrote with certitude about what he called Wallace's "spots of vulnerability."[22] In examining many of these areas of "vulnerability," however, it may be that they are inaccurate or actually added to Wallace's influence.

"Difficult to Forgive"

Adams wrote that Wallace "found it difficult to forgive and forget injuries real or imagined. To be guilty of a personal transgression against him was to him a mortal sin." Most human beings find forgiving others at times challenging. This charge is especially applicable to preachers who in the heat of controversy sometimes say and do things that they later regret. Certainly Wallace made his share of mistakes along this line. Also apparent, however, is that Wallace often apologized for his mistakes both publicly and privately. Wallace both sought and gave forgiveness.

One of Wallace's first major controversies occurred in 1933 with James A. Allen over the Morrow Foundation. Wallace said things he later regretted. In 1936, Wallace wrote a clear-cut apology to Allen:

> I regret beyond words the occasion of the articles that passed between Brother James A. Allen and me several years ago, and I especially regret the severity of my own articles. Brother Allen and I occupy common ground on vital issues and in the truth's defense on these questions. He has stood by his convictions and his courage is praiseworthy. I want all who are interested to know that no issue or feeling exists between us and that my sincere best wishes go with Brother Allen in his militant advocacy of the primitive faith.[23]

Wallace and Burton Coffman had a difficult personal controversy in the 1940s over a matter that seemed of little import by 1966. Wallace wrote of his problem with Coffman, "But for the blunders of the men [whom] you and I know better now than then, the tragic situation in Houston would not have existed."[24]

Burton Coffman responded to Wallace, "I am so thankful for your words to the effect that my letter to Brother Loe 'removed all past feelings, etc.'"[25] Coffman then sent the following telegram to the Wallace testimonial dinner held at Freed-Hardeman in 1966:

---

[21] James W. Adams, "Foy E. Wallace, Jr.: Militant Warrior," in *They Being Dead Yet Speak*, Melvin D. Curry, ed. (Temple Terrace, Florida: Florida College Bookstore, 1981): 171.

[22] *Ibid.*: 183.

[23] Foy E. Wallace, Jr., "A Statement," *FF* 53/46 (November 17, 1936): 7. This same statement also appeared in Allen's paper, *The Apostolic Times* 5/7 (November, 1936): 78.

[24] Personal letter from Foy E. Wallace, Jr., to Sam Loe, 1966 (author's private collection).

[25] Personal letter from Burton Coffman to Foy E. Wallace, Jr., ca. March 5, 1966 (author's private collection).

The Scriptures command honor to whom honor is due; and it is my privilege to join the countless thousands who today honor that valiant soldier of faith, Foy E. Wallace, Jr. It was my happy fortune as a young preacher to sit spell-bound and moved to tears by the magic of his golden voice proclaiming the Word of God. Only eternity can reveal the good that was done by Foy E. Wallace, Jr.

Brother Wallace, I thank God for you and for your ability in the Holy Scriptures and for the love you have inspired among so many. I love you and honor you this day and invite you at your convenience to preach for us some of these days when you are in New York City. Our congregation would be the poorer if they did not have an opportunity to hear you.[26]

On another occasion, Wallace delivered some sermons in Plainview, Texas, that caused some local difficulties for the congregation and its Elders. Wallace paid a personal visit to apologize and followed up the visit with a formal letter of apology in which he wrote in part:

I blame myself for that unhappy incident, which before now should have been rectified—and I now extend unreserved apology to the elders and to the congregation for having been the cause and occasion for the occurrence … It is my whole desire to make this statement a forthright acknowledgment of a mistake made in your midst several years ago, which I should have had the foresight and the wisdom to prevent; and I ask your acceptance of it, and your forgiveness.[27]

Other examples could be cited of Wallace's apologies. The fact that Wallace could and did apologize added to his influence. As Wallace noted in an apology to C. R. Nichol, "When we fight, we fight; and when we apologize, we apologize."[28] Wallace's apologies, like his "fighting," were clear, direct, sincere, and to the point, and they added to his influence.

"Intolerance of Those with a Different Point of View"

A second charge leveled by Adams is that Wallace was "utterly intolerant of a point of view different from his own. Any person who ever engaged in a personal confrontation with him found this out." Both Hugo McCord and E. G. Creacy were pacifists. One of the major issues Wallace discussed in *The Bible Banner* was the Christian's role in civil government. Wallace argued with force and effect that Christians could serve as police officers and combat soldiers. Rather than being intolerant of his friends' views, he remained close to them both for as long as they lived. McCord and Wallace also differed on the Holy Spirit. Again, neither did they fall out over this difference nor did McCord find Wallace "intolerant." In 1966, Hugo McCord wrote of Wallace:

For a third of a century I have gone near and far to be close to Foy E. Wallace, Jr. If ever a man were gifted with five talents in mental strength and quick thinking with a big and a warm heart, it is Foy E. Wallace. At Crawfordsville, Indiana, in the early thirties, it was Foy E. Wallace who took an interest in me as a young preacher, and his interest in me made me feel as if I were on a mountain top. At Chattanooga, he took me and my wife to his family's quarters on Signal Mountain,

---

[26] Coffman telegram (author's private collection).

[27] Personal letter from Foy E. Wallace, Jr., to J. W. Eatman, dated July 15, 1965 (author's private collection).

[28] Foy E. Wallace, Jr., "Personal," *The Bible Banner* VI/2 (September 1943): 6.

and encouraged me to write. Not accidentally my paths have crossed his in many states, and I am always stronger and better because of such contacts. One occasion, after I had driven 450 miles to Washington, North Carolina, to hear him preach, he got up and announced that I would do the preaching, and he sat down. Embarrassing this was to me, and unfair to the audience, but still encouraging to me. He is one of the unforgettable men of God in my life. Always clean morally, when he married, it was to one woman for keeps, and her he has loved more than he loves himself. He loves with a big and warm heart, and grieves just as deeply when men defect from the faith. He loves the truth of the Gospel more than he loves any human being. Many men can look over him physically, but spiritually nobody stands higher.[29]

M. C. Kurfees wrote that preachers "especially" needed to understand their duty to apologize when in the wrong. Kurfees wrote that the apologies which many preachers did make were accompanied by "doubtful 'ifs' or conditions which … would leave one in doubt as to whether there is any real confession of wrong or wish to make matters right."[30] Wallace's apologies were of that rare type that Kurfees characterized as "clear, distinct, and directly to the point, bearing on its very face its own genuine sincerity and noble wish to make everything right." This quality added to Wallace's ability to influence many.

"Intellectually Arrogant"

Adams also charged that Wallace "was intellectually arrogant. Young preachers of intellect and ability, hence with bright promise, he had time for. Those less talented, he merely tolerated." Adam's charge is inaccurate. Wallace did, in fact, spend significant amounts of time with preachers who had no "bright promise" and relatively little talent, but who were conscientiously devoted to doing God's will.

In 1955 David T. Reeves wrote to Wallace and asked that he hold a gospel meeting in La Follette, Tennessee. Reeves wrote Wallace that the church was small and could not offer much in the way of support like one of the big churches in Memphis. Wallace replied, "If I can be of help, I would just as soon be with you as the largest church in Memphis."

Wallace went and held the meeting, spending much time with Reeves. Reeves asked Wallace a number of Bible questions, which Wallace patiently answered. Later, back at his hotel room, Wallace wrote out fourteen pages of notes to help Reeves in his Bible study. Of these notes Reeves wrote that they were a "personal gift," and "I had not requested [the notes], so I have prized this effort." Wallace had the engaging ability to put himself on the same level as anyone, regardless of intellect. This humility made a profound impression and added to Wallace's influence.

Independent Spirit

Wallace was an independent spirit. No one could tell him where to preach, what to preach, or how to preach. He was often encouraged to ease up on his criticism of the excesses

---

[29] Letter from Hugo McCord, March 6, 1966, to the Master of Ceremonies, Appreciation Dinner (author's private collection).

[30] M. C. Kurfees, "A Noble Example for All Christians, and Especially for Preachers," *GA* LXV/27 (July 5, 1923): 651.

of the Christian Colleges, and people pointed out to him that things would go better for him if he would do so. But Wallace always called it like he saw it; he would not bend, stretch, or twist the truth as he saw it to curry favor.

Wallace's independence of spirit meant that he could not be bought. Other preachers longed to be on college lectureships or celebrated in other ways. These emoluments meant nothing to Wallace. Older preachers especially appreciated this aspect of Wallace's personality, and it gave him great influence with the generation that had preceded him.

Certitude of Belief

Wallace deeply believed what he preached. B. C. Goodpasture noted this Wallace quality in 1966, stating, "I like to hear a man preach who preaches what he believes, … he writes what he believes and he believes the Bible."[31] This certainty of conviction sometime led to the charge that Wallace was dogmatic; however, Wallace was constantly reexamining his beliefs, and it may be observed that he did not hesitate to change his views as he matured.

The best known example of Wallace's changing his mind on a significant issue was on the question of a Christian's relation to civil government. Wallace's view changed from the non-combatant view to an understanding that Christians could serve as police officers and combat soldiers. This led some Wallace critics to excoriate him as "unstable—unsafe—unsound"…all for his failure to cling dogmatically to a view that he had come to reject.

Wallace had strong convictions, but his mind could be changed. He was a man that one could reason with, even about vital issues. Furthermore, when the case was made, Wallace would change his view. This was a quality that R. L. Whiteside, Wallace's friend and mentor, strongly encouraged, writing "A Christian should start with the high and holy purpose of learning all the truth he can, eliminating all errors as he finds them, and of practicing every practicable thing he learns."[32] This quality added to Wallace's influence.

Generosity

Wallace's wife, Virgie, noted that her husband "would rather do without and help a friend than anything in the world."[33] Those who were suffering financial hardship would always find a welcome in the Wallace home. Among those who lived with the Wallaces for a year or more were Tillit S. Teddlie and W. E. Brightwell.

Earl Irvin West recalled that Wallace was very generous toward him as a young preacher. When Wallace would come to Indianapolis, West and Wallace would set out for Cincinnati to visit the used bookstores of that city. During these trips, Wallace would insist on paying for the meals, gasoline, the books, and any other miscellaneous expenses. West

---

[31] Speech by B. C. Goodpasture delivered at the Foy E. Wallace, Jr., Appreciation Dinner in Bader Gymnasium at Freed-Hardeman College on 10 March 1966. Transcription of the original tape recording in the collection of the author.

[32] R. L. Whiteside, "Consistency," *The Bible Banner* 10/1 (January, 1948): 14.

[33] 1982 taped interview with Virgie Wallace, conducted by Wilson Wallace. See Noble Patterson and Terry J. Gardner, *Foy E. Wallace, Jr., Soldier of the Cross* (Fort Worth, Texas: Wallace Memorial Fund, 1999): "Appendix," 324, for a transcription of this full interview.

was at this time an unknown young preacher, yet Wallace treated him as an equal while acting as his patron.[34]

In the late 1940s, John Bannister needed a hernia operation, which was both a painful and expensive procedure. Wallace traveled to Oklahoma City and transported Bannister to the Scott & White Clinic in Temple, Texas. Wallace paid for the operation and, after Bannister was released from the hospital, he convalesced in Wallace's home until Wallace took him back to Oklahoma City.[35] Wallace also helped Will M. Thompson and many other preachers pay for their operations.

The Pastoral Side of Foy E. Wallace, Jr.

In 1970, Raymond Miller of Billings, Montana, became deeply troubled regarding the appropriateness of his marriage. Miller had been briefly married as a very young man, and he and his first wife divorced; Ray had then married his second wife, to whom he had been married for more than forty years. After his first marriage had ended and he had remarried, Miller became a Christian. In 1970, the Billings congregation had a preacher who had been trained under Roy Lanier, Sr., and Lanier had held at least one meeting in Billings. It had been recommended to Miller that "he might live with, but not sleep with nor have sex with, his wife of about 40 years."[36] Lanier also recommended that Miller not be used in any "leadership capacity" at Billings, including serving communion.

Miller was a conscientious man, so this matter deeply troubled him. In December of that year, he wrote to Foy E. Wallace, Jr., placing a question mark in the salutation after "Dear brother," and in the final greeting after "in Christ," not wishing to seem presumptuous. Miller posed four questions: 1) Should an evangelist inquire into a person's marital background when that person decides to become a Christian? 2) Did the preacher who baptized Miller err when he did not ask about Miller's marital status? 3) Was it Wallace's practice to ask about a prospective Christian's marital background? 4) Did Paul fail to teach adequately to the Corinthians? – for Paul had written, "such were some of you."[37] Wallace promptly replied as follows:

Dear Brother and Sister Miller

First, you may erase the question mark after "brother" in addressing me, and after "in Christ" in your signature – for I accept you as "brother Miller" — my brother in Christ.

Second, in your letter you fairly answered your questions, as it appears to me, quite correctly. The Lord did not prescribe any such course of action which a preacher referred to would bind, nor did his apostles do so in epistles to the churches in dealing with such past conditions. Restitution for sins is required only

---

[34] Conversation of the author with Earl West in 1996, and West's speech delivered at the Foy E. Wallace, Jr., Appreciation Dinner in Bader Gymnasium at Freed-Hardeman College on 10 March 1966.

[35] E-mail communication from John Bannister, Jr., August 8, 1996.

[36] Personal letter from Jacob Vincent to the author, dated July 20, 2000.

[37] Raymond Miller's original letter is believed not to be extant; however, Miller later wrote out the questions he had asked Wallace (author's private collection).

when and where restitution is possible. This is not possible in the classification of "sins that are past"— Romans 3:25.[38] The incidence in your life in the far past is outside restitution, but is within "the remission of sins" — and a preacher who makes it mandatory now for you to break up your home, separate from your family and to thus scandalize your children and destroy them, is legislating his own opinions & there is no scripture for that course of action — and it is very doubtful that in the same circumstances he would do so himself.

My advice and counsel to you, as it has always been to others in like circumstances, is to stay with your family, live right, be Christians, bring up your children "in the nurture and admonition of the Lord" in the church, and strive to go to heaven, as all of us, as full of mistakes as we are, should strive to do.

In my commentary on the "Sermon On The Mount"[39] there is a section which deals with this portion of the Lord's teaching — I've marked it in the enclosed folder.

It was a pleasure to have you in the meeting at Roanoke, Texas.[40] I would be happy if such a thing should occur again.

Wishing for you and yours all the blessings of divine providence, I am
Your friend and brother in the Lord,

Foy E. Wallace, Jr.[41]

The tenderness and compassion of Wallace's pastoral side was also demonstrated by the comfort he gave to those who lost loved ones in death. Often Wallace would travel many miles to comfort the bereaved. In February of 1919, Wallace traveled from Fort Worth to Mill Creek, Oklahoma, to lend comfort and encouragement to the family of A. Leroy Elkins in the death of their daughter, Mary. Wallace wrote of the occasion, "Circumstances were such that made the occasion a very sad one. Her husband, F. G. Dye, is on the far-away battlefields of France and does not even know that his wife has been sick. Mary was a devout Christian girl and always had a smile and a word of cheer for everybody."[42]

Wallace often traveled great distances to conduct funerals. In March of 1937, Wallace returned to Vernon, Texas, to assist in the funeral of Sister Joe Smith.[43] In April of 1954, Wallace traveled to Cookeville, Tennessee, to assist in the funeral services for Fannie Terry Barnes.[44] Many other examples could be given of Wallace's traveling far distances to assist in the funeral services of his friends and loved ones.

---

[38] "Whom God hath set forth to be a propitiation, through faith in his blood, to declare his righteousness for the remission of sins that are past, through the forbearance of God." Rm 3:25 (KJV).

[39] See Foy E. Wallace, Jr., *The Sermon on the Mount and the Civil State*, (Nashville, Tennessee: Foy E. Wallace, Jr., Publications, 1967): 40-41.

[40] Foy E. Wallace, Jr., had held a gospel meeting in Roanoke, Texas, in September or October of 1970.

[41] Letter to Raymond Miller of Billings, Montana, handwritten by Wallace (thermofax copy in author's private collection).

[42] Foy E. Wallace, Jr., "News and Notes," *FF* 36/7 (February 18, 1919): 4.

[43] L. N. Moody, "News and Notes," *FF* 54/15 (April 13, 1937): 6.

[44] Gilbert E. Shaffer, "At Rest," *GA* XCVI/17 (April 29, 1954): 340.

Solomon wrote, "A word fitly spoken is like apples of gold in pictures of silver." Wallace's words were often comforting. In 1935, when Wallace's close personal friend, A. W. Lee,[45] suffered the loss of his wife, Wallace wrote as follows:

From the church service a slow and solemn procession, guided through city and highway traffic by uniformed patrolmen, followed the flower-sprayed Hearse to the majestic Memorial Park Cemetery, a burial landscape situated on an eminence of the undulating prairie which gives Oklahoma City and vicinage its geographical grace. There interment was made, near Highway 77, in the unobstructed view of the world that passes by. There the body of "Sister Lee" will repose in peace beneath Oklahoma's azure heaven and crystalline firmament, where the west winds blow and wild flowers grow, until the morning of joy when the dead shall arise and splendor immortal shall envelop the skies.

Shall we weep? Yes; it will do us good. Often our only coinage is tears. The bard of Israel said, "They that sow in tears shall reap in joy," and "He that goeth forth weeping shall doubtless come again with rejoicing bringing his sheaves with him." Thank God for tears that yield such harvest of rejoicing! It is so with Brother Lee. His loss, though timely and temporary, brings to him pain nevertheless piquant and grief none the less poignant. But though his sorrow is deep it is also sweet, for there is faith, his comfort, and hope, his solace.

Sister Lee is gone from his home but not from his heart. She shall henceforth be his silent partner—she shall live in his soul![46]

Perhaps the best example of Wallace's moving words came with the untimely death of Harley Emerson Woodward:

The many friends of Sister E. F. Woodward, including many who have never known her personally but to whom she is known as Dorcas by her good works, enter into her sorrow upon the tragic and untimely death of her only son, Harley Emerson Woodward. It came as a shock, and but for Sister Woodward's firm faith and lofty hope she could hardly have passed the ordeal with the calm resignation that characterized her, visible in marked degree to those of us who were present when the last rites were held. We sympathize with Sister Woodward, and rejoice too. Harley was a fine man, faithful to the church, believed God's Word, and his charred Bible was found in the debris of the plane that crashed him to his death. This will ever be his mother's comfort, and his wife's, who is also a Christian. The services at Houston were simple; held in the Heights Church where Harley served as a deacon and in which he was reared. A scripture selection was read by Flavil Colley and talks were made by Oscar Smith and E.C. Coffman.

It is not the length of the life that necessarily counts. It is not the length of the story that makes it worth reading. The greatest stories ever written are the parables of Christ; and the greatest life that was ever lived was the life of the Son of God—just thirty three years. It is *how* we live, not how *long* we live, that

---

[45] A. W. Lee and Foy E. Wallace, Jr., were so close that Wallace named his second son Albert Wilson Wallace in honor of A. W. Lee.

[46] Foy E. Wallace, Jr., "Sister Lee," *FF* 52/4 (January 22, 1935): 2.

counts in the great Reckoning Day, for "it is appointed unto man once to die, and after that the Judgment."[47]

Austin McGary's widow, a fellow member at Houston Heights, called Mrs. Woodward's attention to Wallace's words. Mrs. Woodward was moved by Wallace's words and wrote of the obituary, "It was one of the sweetest that has been written of him, and is very comforting to us. With so many good Christian friends to comfort us we should be able to bear our loss with greater fortitude than we have shown here-to-fore."[48]

Conclusion

When I first began to write about Foy E. Wallace, Jr., some years ago, one Wallace friend asked me if I had known Wallace personally. "No," I replied. "Well," he then responded, "You can't possibly capture the spirit of Foy Wallace." Perhaps he was right. Wallace was a charismatic figure who would cross land and sea to help a friend. He was also a powerful and sometimes cutting public speaker. Wallace himself justified his staunch matter of preaching with these words:

> Preaching that gets the right results has to be drastic. It takes surgery. And whenever the surgeon's knife is needed, a rubbing doctor won't get the job done. I'm not a masseur in my preaching. No sir. I'm not a masseur. I'm a surgeon. And I try to keep the knife sharp enough to cut as deep as it needs to be done.[49]

The direct and powerful influence of the early pioneer preachers has been replaced by the age of politicians in the Church. In their fear of offending anyone, they also fail to motivate or move anyone. In 1984, four years after Wallace's death, his abiding friend, Homer Hailey, wrote:

> Speaking of preaching today – it has been a long time since I have heard a sermon that really stirred my soul. Maybe, as we grow older, we expect too much. But I do expect to be instructed, stirred up, or moved in some way. The gospel is supposed to do something to one: make him glad, make him mad, or [make him] get out of his comfortable chair and do something. But so much of it is blah."[50]

Much of Wallace's influence was due to his convictions and his desire to instruct, stir up, and motivate men and women.

The influence that most men wield is due to something they possess, whether position or wealth or institutional connections or something else. Wallace cared for none of these things. His influence was driven by who he was, and his loss of the editorship of the *Gospel Advocate* did relatively little to diminish his influence. Foy E. Wallace, Jr., as he wrote in the letter to "Brother and Sister Miller," exhorted that we all "strive to go to heaven, as all of us, as full of mistakes as we are, should strive to do."[51] He himself strove in just that way, and it made him a powerfully effective preacher and an influential Christian.

---

[47] Foy E. Wallace, Jr., "Harley Emerson Woodward," *Gospel Guardian* 2/3 (March-April, 1936): 46-47.

[48] Letter dated April 17, 1936 (author's private collection).

[49] Quotation from a sermon delivered in Louisville, Kentucky in 1950. Transcribed by the author from an audio recording.

[50] Personal letter dated May 14, 1984.

[51] See fn. 41.

DIE CAMPBELLITEN: THE STONE-CAMPBELL MOVEMENT IN MAJOR TWENTIETH-CENTURY GERMAN THEOLOGICAL REFERENCE WORKS

HANS ROLLMANN

The church-historical significance of the Stone-Campbell Movement (SCM) stands in no true relation to its obvious neglect shown by many historians outside the movement. Although Michael Casey and Doug Foster have recently published a useful anthology of writings on the SCM that appeared in academic journals, only after World War Two did the movement and the churches it spawned begin to be treated with a modicum of appreciative scholarly seriousness by outsiders.[1]

A test case of how the SCM was viewed by thoughtful outsiders can be gleaned from German scholarly reference literature in church history and theology in a country that in the nineteenth century pioneered historical-critical scholarship in religion.[2] Otherwise exemplary for its historical-critical research, even in areas such as Methodism and Mormonism, the German encyclopedic literature on the Stone-Campbell Movement has until very recently been mixed, at times quite derivative and selective, and often missing crucial theological emphases and a realistic historical estimate of the movement in all of its institutional expressions.

In this essay, which is a small token of my appreciation for Don Haymes's generous help in research and journalism, I discuss the reference literature on the SCM that theologians and educated lay people had available in Germany throughout the twentieth century. The study is limited to major Protestant and Roman Catholic encyclopedias, with the exception of one monograph on the Disciples and the exceedingly scant literature on sects and smaller religious groups.

Protestant Reference Works before World War One

Among the older Protestant theological encyclopedias and reference works, the third edition of the *Realencyklopädie für Protestantische Theologie und Kirche* (RE3), published by J.C. Hinrichs at Leipzig in 24 volumes from 1896-1913, represents the most mature fruit of nineteenth-century German historical-critical scholarship. The work achieved almost canonical status among German Protestants as a theological and church-historical authority and gained a reputation similar to the eleventh edition of the *Encyclopedia*

---

[1] Michael W. Casey & Douglas A. Foster, eds., *The Stone-Campbell Movement: An International Religious Tradition* (Knoxville: University of Tennessee Press, 2002).

[2] See http://www.swbv.unikonstanz.de/depot/media/3400000/3421000/3421308/ 94 0421. html for Albert Raffelt's discussion in connection with the third edition of the *Lexikon für Theologie und Kirche* (Freiburg, Basel, Rome, Vienna: Herder, 1993-2001) in *Informationsmittel für Bibliotheken* 2 (1994) 3/4.

Britannica, with which it shared such a prominent contributor as Adolf von Harnack as well as others. Beginning in 1914, in its English version, *The New Schaff-Herzog Encyclopedia of Religious Knowledge*, by Philip Schaff, it exerted some influence in the English-speaking world, although the article, "Disciples of Christ," was written anew for the American edition. It is safe to assume, however, that during the first half of the twentieth century, most German Protestant theologians, historians, and educated lay people, if they were aware of the Stone-Campbell Movement at all, likely knew it through this reference work.

More radical Protestants would likely have consulted an alternative encyclopedia, *Die Religion in Geschichte und Gegenwart* (*RGG*), published in four editions between 1909 and 2004. Originally a product of the so-called *Religionsgeschichtliche Schule* [History-of-Religions School] that had formed in the 1890s in Göttingen and was characterized by an uncompromising historicism and comparative approach in biblical studies and church history, the *RGG* rejected any dependence in the historical disciplines upon ecclesiastical and theological programs, although not being free itself of tacit agendas. Editors-in-chief of the first edition (*RGG1*; 1909-1913, 5 vols.) were F.M. Schiele; the well-known Old Testament scholar, Hermann Gunkel; and Otto Scheel. Ernst Troeltsch, the systematician of the *Religionsgeschichtliche Schule*, also wrote many articles for the first edition, articles that were later republished in a revised form in his collected works.

Die Campbelliten in RE3

Beginning in the 1850s, Baptists, under the leadership of Johann Gerhard Oncken (1800-1884), represented an indigenous German *believer's church*. As such, they were recognized as "brothers" by Alexander Campbell and the Disciples. But only after World War Two did Disciples, Christian Churches, and Churches of Christ (*Gemeinden Christi*) become for Germans–sociologically and demographically speaking–an institutionally negligible post-war phenomenon. The Disciples and Independent Christian Churches exerted only an educational and benevolent presence in Germany and did not engage in any sustained missionary activity.[3] An institutional SCM presence in Germany, Austria, and Switzerland became a native option as a result of missionaries from America, strengthened by resident American soldiers who were members of *a cappella* Churches of Christ (vocal music only). These efforts grew into a small fellowship of congregationally autonomous churches that today numbers about 46 congregations in German-speaking Europe.[4]

Thus, despite a minor institutional presence of Disciples in the British Commonwealth, historians and theologians in Germany viewed the SCM largely as an American phenomenon, and hardly any encyclopedia articles noted an institutional link between German *Gemeinden Christi* and Churches of Christ in America. Not only was the movement viewed as being American in origin and presence, the *RE3* did not even treat

---

[3] See Dennis R. Lindsey, "Europe, Missions in," *The Encyclopedia of the Stone-Campbell Movement* (Grand Rapids, Michigan: W. B. Eerdmans, 2005): 311-312. On Churches of Christ in Germany, see also Otis Gatewood, *Preaching in the Footsteps of Hitler* (Nashville: Williams, 1960); Mark Martin, "The Churches of Christ Evangelize Germany: The First Years After World War Two," *Discipliana* 65/1 (spring 2005): 23-36.

[4] See http://www.gemeinde-christi.org/adressen/adressen.htm for an up-to-date map.

it as a separate ecclesiastical body. Anyone searching under the heading "Alexander Campbell" was referred to the article *"Baptisten"* (Baptists) by Rudolf Hoffmann.[5] In this article, the SCM was discussed in a sub-section dealing with North American Baptists, titled "Ancillary Parties" (*Nebenparteien*), where the following groups were covered: Anti-Mission Baptists, Free Will Baptists, Seventh-Day Baptists, Six-Principle Baptists, Church of God, Tunkers, Christian Connection, United Brethren in Christ, and *Campbelliten*, the German rendering of the polemical term "Campbellites."

Although last in this list, Hoffmann paid most attention to the *Campbelliten* or Disciples of Christ. His references consist, however, exclusively of literature written by Baptists, although by that time major biographical and historical works from within the movement had appeared in print, among them Rogers's *The Biography of Eld. Barton Warren Stone, Written by Himself, with Additions and Reflections by Elder John Rogers* (1847), Richardson's *Memoirs of Alexander Campbell* (1868), Baxter's *Life of Elder Walter Scott* (1874), and Hayden's *Early History of the Disciples in the Western Reserve, Ohio* (1875), as well as Alexander Campbell's own encyclopedic treatment of the "Disciples of Christ" in *Fessenden's & Co's Encyclopedia of Religious Knowledge* (1838).[6] Hoffmann, who provided membership data (837,929), justified his encyclopedic inclusion of the *Campbelliten* among the Baptists because of their common baptismal practice (*Taufweise*), but he was quite aware that Baptists and Disciples differ on baptismal doctrine (*Tauflehre*) and thus diverge in their soteriology.

After a brief historical sketch, the rest of the section on the *Campbelliten* features their teachings, ostensibly based on the Baptist literature, particularly Armitage's *History of the Baptists* (New York, 1887). According to Hoffmann, *Campbelliten* consider attentive Bible reading their duty, which results in the conviction that Scripture is true and Christ is the Son of God. Faith is largely a rational conviction that results in confession and baptism. Baptism brings with it forgiveness of sins and a change of the old self. This process, Hoffmann tells us, is not to be understood as a transformation but as an initial act of obedience toward God and thus a first step in a life of obedience. *Campbelliten* thus "receive salvation through faith, baptism, and obedience" and reject as unscriptural the penitential struggle of Baptists and their notion that the Spirit is already active prior to baptism. According to Hoffmann, they also disavow the value of religious experience and the Holy Spirit as a person. Scripture-reading and obedience are equated with receiving the Holy Spirit. While, according to Hoffmann, *Campbelliten* reject the Trinity and "the eternal creation of the Son of God from the being of the Father as well as the eternal procession of the Spirit from the Father," they affirm nevertheless the fullness of God's presence in Christ. Because of their unorthodox Christology and soteriology, American Presbyterians, Congregationalists, Baptists, and Methodists do not recognize Campbellites as fellow "evangelical Christians."

While Hoffmann exculpated *Campbelliten* of the charge of being Arians or Unitarians, he considered them to "have strong Pelagian and rationalizing tendencies." The article ends with a brief statement about demography, that the *Campbelliten* are most populous

---

[5] Rudolf Hoffmann, "Baptisten," in *Realencyclopädie für Protestantische Theologie und Kirche (RE3)*, Albert Hauck, ed. (Leipzig: J.C. Hinrich, 3rd edition, 1897): 2: 385-393.

[6] Published in Brattleboro, Vermont, by the Brattleboro Typographic Company, 1838: 462-464.

in states north and south of the Ohio and outnumber all other churches in Kentucky. While the group has several educational and benevolent institutions, unlike nearly all other American Protestants, *Campbelliten* do not, Hoffmann wrote, engage in foreign missions and had never even attempted to proselytize Germans.[7]

Campbelliten in RGG1

The 1909 article, "Campbelliten," in *RGG1* was not written by a well-known theologian or historian but by Albert Hoefs, a Baptist minister from Stettin.[8] Unlike Hoffmann, Hoefs consulted for his article not only Baptist literature, such as Armitage's *History of the Baptists* (1890), but also a nineteenth-century SCM classic, Richardson's *Memoirs of Alexander Campbell*.[9] Hoefs's article provides a brief background of Alexander and Thomas Campbell as Presbyterians, their recognition of paedobaptism as being invalid, and their subsequent baptism and reception into the Baptist fold. This decision was viewed by Hoefs as a consequence of their strict biblicism.

Next, Hoefs observed Alexander Campbell's dissatisfaction with Baptist theology. Hoefs listed the following as being theologically distinctive of the movement: (1) Unlike the Baptist belief in the instrumentality of the Holy Spirit in effecting rebirth even prior to baptism, *Campbelliten* conceive no operation of the Holy Spirit independent of the Word of God. (2) Immersion is a necessary act leading to rebirth, while soteriological certainty for Baptists precedes baptism, the latter then being an act of public confession only. (3) The *Campbelliten's* regenerative notion of baptism as "rebirth" stands in contrast to the Baptist understanding of baptism as a church ordinance.

Hoefs noted the forensic proclivities of the movement, but he observed the divisive effect that debates had for the relations between Disciples and other religious groups. He also draws attention to Campbell's own Bible translation and its theologically sensitive vocabulary ("immersion" for baptism). Subsequent important stages in the movement, according to Hoefs, revolved around the person of Alexander Campbell: the organization of the Disciples in 1827, the founding of Bethany College in 1841, and his death in 1866. Left out of this chronology, however, is the pivotal merger of Campbell's Disciples and Stone's Christians in 1832. The contemporary (ca. 1909) statistics are given as 11,307 congregations and 1,285,123 members.

The SCM is presented in these two major German Protestant reference works in close proximity with the Baptists. There are, of course, historical reasons for this, including the early association of Alexander Campbell and the Disciples with the Baptists. But the discussion is also affected by the choice of literature, notably in the *RE3* article, which is based largely on Baptist treatments of Campbellites. Thus the early internal development and relationship between Christians, the Christian Connexion, and Disciples are not mentioned at all. The polemical nature of the Baptist literature also affects the attempt to differentiate *Campbelliten* from Baptists doctrinally in terms of their differing soteriology and pneumatology. The observation that the *Campbelliten* have "strong Pelagian and rationalizing tendencies" represents a valid observation from the distance, but was

---

[7] Rudolf Hoffmann, "Baptisten," *RE3* (1897): 2:390-91.

[8] *RGG*, Friedrich Michael Schiele, Hermann Gunkel and Otto Scheel, eds. (Tübingen: J.C.B. Mohr [Paul Siebeck], 1913): Index volume, col. 59.

[9] [Albert] Hoefs, "Campbelliten" *RGG* (1909): 1: 1,565.

already a standard topic in the extant Baptist polemical literature on Alexander Campbell and the Disciples.

Protestant and Roman Catholic Reference Works between the Wars

No new edition of the *RE* appeared between the wars, but in 1927, a thoroughly revised second edition of *Die Religion in Geschichte und Gegenwart* (6 vols, 1927-1932) appeared under the general editorship of Hermann Gunkel and Leopold Zscharnack. At that time, "Religion," the key category of the *Religionsgeschichtliche Schule*, had become suspect among Karl Barth and his associates, but little attention was paid in the encyclopedia to Dialectical Theology, one of the most vital directions in post-war German theology. Thus the names of such key thinkers as Karl Barth, Friedrich Gogarten, and Rudolf Bultmann are not found in this reference work at all.

Instead of a new edition of the *RE*, the years between the wars saw the publication of a major Roman Catholic undertaking, the *Lexikon für Theologie und Kirche* (1930-1938, 10 vols.). Edited by Michael Buchberger, and proceeding cautiously in the wake of the anti-Modernist decrees of the papacy, this collaborative reference work had been preceded by two editions of Wetzer & Welte's *Kirchenlexikon* (1st edition 1846-1856, 2nd edition 1882-1901).

Disciples in RGG2

Hoefs, who had written the *Campbelliten* article in the 1909 first edition of the *RGG*, also wrote the article–now titled "Disciples"–for the second one, as well as a small biographical entry on Alexander Campbell.[10] The main source for Alexander Campbell is, appropriately, Richardson's *Memoirs of Alexander Campbell* and contains a brief theological characterization reminiscent of the earlier article, that for Campbell the Holy Spirit "works only through the Word" and that rebirth is accomplished through baptism for the remission of sins.[11]

The article "Disciples" appears to have been revised, and, although Hoefs lists only Armitage's *History of the Baptists* (1890) as his source, the information in Hoefs's article goes well beyond that provided by the Baptist historian. This time, the thought of Thomas and Alexander Campbell is emphasized in their rejection of sectarianism by recourse to a Bible-based apostolic Christianity, and the development of the early Disciples movement is presented in greater detail. Hoefs also stressed the educational, literary, and missionary efforts of Disciples, yet he seems to have been unaware of the bifurcation of the movement into Disciples and Churches of Christ, which found official expression in the 1906 census.

As far as doctrine is concerned, Hoefs presented Disciples as an anti-creedal and biblically based church that was striving for unity and for which a Christ-centered saving and justifying faith was central. Church organization and polity were, according to Hoefs, congregational and democratic, and leadership followed the New Testament model of elders and deacons with preachers and pastors.[12] The article concludes with

---

[10] "Alexander Campbell" and "Disciples of Christ" in *RGG* (Tübingen: J.C.B. Mohr [Paul Siebeck] 1927): 1 : 1,442; 1,948-49.

[11] *Ibid.*: 1,442

[12] *Ibid.*: 1,949.

statistics for 1925 in America and a report of the presence of Disciples in foreign countries and mission territories. Since the missionary efforts listed are confined to those administered by the United Christian Missionary Society in St. Louis, the article's empirical data do not cover the congregationally autonomous Churches of Christ. In fact, Hoefs's understanding of the SCM was limited to the Disciples only.

Disciples in the Roman Catholic LThK1

In 1930, German Roman Catholics were informed briefly about the SCM, not in a separate article but as part of the article *"Baptisten,"* just as had been done in the first edition of the Protestant *RE3*.[13] The article by Konrad Algermissen is hardly original. To judge from Algermissen's *Konfessionskunde*, which was published in the same year as his article in the *LThK1*, his sources were Hoefs's *RGG2* article and Armitage's *History of the Baptists* (1890).[14] Algermissen declared Disciples to be the second-largest division among independent Baptists (after the Regular Baptists). The brief doctrinal profile and discussion of activities are based not on any independent research but rely instead on the existing Protestant encyclopedic treatments, although the American *Catholic Encyclopedia* (1907-1914), while thoroughly judgmental, provided by contrast a treatment of Disciples that was based on J. H. Garrison's works.[15] If the German Roman Catholic author had consulted his American confrere James L. Loughlin, his article would have been much better informed. Algermissen viewed Disciples, like the article in *RE3*, as rejecting all creeds and denying both the Holy Spirit as a person and the eternal creation of the Son, while believing nevertheless in the Divinity of Christ. For Roman Catholic theology, Trinitarian doctrine represents an important category by which to measure the orthodoxy of any religious group. The Disciples obviously fell short in this department. Like *RGG2*, Algermissen also stressed the Disciples' educational and literary activities.

The Stone-Campbell Movement in Post-WWII Reference Works

After the war, we see two revisions and one adaptation of previous encyclopedias that benefit from their greater contact with America and the availability of English literature. In the 1950s, a thorough revision of the *Lexikon für Theologie und Kirche* (1957-1968, 14 vols., including supplements) was carried out under the editorship of Otto Hoefer and the most influential twentieth-century Roman Catholic theologian, Karl Rahner. The second edition breathed the new freedom in biblical and historical scholarship and the heady spirit of Vatican II, whose key documents were published in supplemental volumes.

The *RGG3* (1956-1965, 7 vols.) retains its historical-critical orientation during a period when Bultmann and his students raised new questions for theology, just as Bultmann

---

[13] Konrad Algermissen, "Baptisten," *LThK* (Freiburg: Herder, 2nd edition, 1930): 1: 952-54.

[14] Konrad Algermissen, *Konfessionskunde* (Hannover: Giesel, 1930): 580. Algermissen repeated his 1930 information up to the 7th edition of his book in 1957, when he finally referenced some Disciples literature. This literature did not prevent him, however, from attributing a strict Calvinism to the Churches of Christ as distinct from the Disciples.

[15] See http://www.newadvent.org/cathen/05029b.htm for James F. Loughlin, "Disciples of Christ" in *Catholic Encyclopedia Online*, which reproduces the article in volume 5 of the printed version, originally published by Robert Appleton Company in 1909.

himself was engaged in religio-historical work alongside his systematic interests in demythologization and hermeneutics.

Despite its practical orientation and narrower scope, the *Evangelische Kirchenlexikon* (*EK*) (1956-1961, 4 vols.) features the best article on the Disciples of Christ prior to *RGG4*, as well as a separate entry for Churches of Christ. Edited by Heinz Brunotte and Otto Weber, and published by Vandehoeck & Ruprecht, the dictionary took over some articles from the *Calwer Kirchenlexikon* and the *Nordisk teologisk uppslagsbok*. Serendipitously, Arndt Ruprecht was the author for the article "Disciples of Christ." Scion of the oldest theological German publishing house, Vandenoeck & Ruprecht in Göttingen, and himself a professional theologian, Arndt Ruprecht had been an exchange student after the war at Butler University, a Disciples institution in Indianapolis. Since Ruprecht had encountered Disciples first-hand,[16] his article witnesses to this direct contact and a more appropriate selection of literature.

The SCM in the LThK2

As in the first edition of the *LThK*, Konrad Algermissen wrote the article on the *Baptisten* but revised it somewhat for the second edition, and he seems to have borrowed insights from Ruprecht in *EK2*. Again, the Disciples of Christ are featured as the most important independent Baptist group. Their theological distinctiveness consisted, according to Algermissen, in "a rationalist doctrine" and a theology influenced by Liberalism and the Social Gospel. He also noted an ethos of free faith for the individual, congregational autonomy, a pronounced missionary consciousness, and practical ecumenism.[17]

For the first time in the *LThK*, the non-instrumental Churches of Christ are mentioned, and their separate designation since the 1906 census is noted. Oddly, however, their doctrinal profile totally misses the mark, for Algermissen viewed these churches as a "narrow Calvinistic group" (*eine calvinistisch-enge Gruppe*), a misjudgment also repeated in the seventh edition of his *Konfessionskunde*.[18] The Roman Catholic expert in symbolics and *Konfessionskunde* must have confused the non-instrumental Churches of Christ with the Regular Baptists. Closer to accuracy, he further characterized them as being congregationally autonomous, anti-creedal, and as rejecting any supra-regional synod and ecumenical cooperation. Historically wrong, however, is the statement that in 1957, the Disciples of Christ and Churches of Christ merged and became the United Church of Christ. Presumably the ecumenical discussions between Disciples and the United Church of Christ caused this confused statement. In 1989, Disciples would indeed enter into a partnership of full communion with the United Church of Christ but without any reciprocal relationship on the part of the non-instrumental Churches of Christ.

The Disciples in RGG3

In 1958, yet a new and revised third edition of the *RGG* contained the article "Disciples of Christ" by Otto Eggenberger, ostensibly based on relevant American literature, however still largely of Disciples provenance.[19] At the time, Eggenberger

---

[16] Private conversation of Arndt Ruprecht with the author.

[17] Konrad Algermissen, "Baptisten," *LThK* (1957): 1: 1,230.

[18] *Ibid.*; *Konfessionskunde* (Celle: Giesel, 7th edition, 1957): 772.

[19] O. Eggenberger, "Disciples of Christ," *RGG* (1958): 2: 207-208.

judged Garrison's and DeGroot's *The Disciples of Christ: A History* justly as the best treatment of SCM history; the bibliography includes R.F. West's *Alexander Campbell and Natural Religion* (New Haven, 1948) and the *Biography of Barton W. Stone* (Cincinnati, 1847). Based on literary resources thus improved, it is not surprising that the article exhibits a greater level of understanding than did any previous treatment. Not only are Disciples' origins detailed in precise fashion but also, and for the first time, Barton W. Stone and the "Christians" became a historiographical factor in German writings on the SCM.

Doctrinally, the faith of the Disciples is said to embrace both "unity and restoration" in a Christianity that rejects creeds but is oriented on the Bible. Congregational autonomy and lay-ministry of elders, deacons, and preachers are as characteristic for Disciples as simplicity and lack of formalism in worship. As far as baptism is concerned, Eggenberger missed the mark in stating that in baptismal doctrine Disciples and Baptists are in agreement. (Hoffmann, in *RE3*, had already seen this point more clearly, namely that both groups practice believer's immersion but differ significantly in their baptismal doctrine.) Eggenberger correctly drew attention to the importance and weekly celebration of the Lord's Supper. The public activities and distribution of the churches, based on 1946 figures, cover only the Disciples, highlighting especially their ecumenism and missionary work. No mention is made of the more conservative *a cappella* wing, the Churches of Christ.[20]

Disciples of Christ and Churches of Christ in EK2

Arndt Ruprecht's article on the Disciples is a masterpiece in succinctness and yet covers most significant points. For him, the Disciples were a unity movement influenced by the Great Awaking and the challenge represented by church divisions on the nineteenth-century frontier. He saw the movement as uniquely American and with a twofold origin: Stone's Christians and Campbell's reformed Baptists, who joined forces in 1832. Ruprecht is well acquainted with the synodical struggles of the New Lights about free grace, and with Thomas Campbell's reform program, the *Declaration and Address* (1809), as well as the restorationist agenda of Alexander Campbell and his reasoned approach to evangelization, based on a "rational appropriation of basic salvific facts." Characteristic for the Disciples is the weekly celebration of the Lord's Supper, the non-hierarchical/lay character of church structure, and unitary faith, the latter with full recognition of individual freedom of opinion. Disciples also came to be moved, according to Ruprecht, by a "philanthropically inclined missionary con-sciousness," influenced by theological Liberalism and the Social Gospel. The article concludes with relevant statistics for 1954 and refers the reader to the separate article on the Churches of Christ. In the bibliography, we recognize well-known American and British Disciples authors: W.E. Garrison, A.T. DeGroot, C.C. Morrison, W. Robinson, H.E. Short, and A.C. Waters.[21]

---

[20] *Loc. cit.*

[21] A[rndt] Ruprecht, "Disciples of Christ (*Jünger Christi*), International Convention of," *EK* (Vandenhoeck & Ruprecht, 1956-1961): 1(1956): 940-941.

Hanfried Krüger's brief article on "Churches of Christ" in the same encyclopedia is the first time that they are treated separately in German encyclopedias. The article is based on J. W. Shepherd's treatment of Churches of Christ in the U.S. census of 1926, Frank Mead's *Handbook of Denominations* (1949), and the 1955 *Yearbook of American Churches*. Krüger recognized that the rejection of organized missionary societies and the introduction of instrumental music in worship from 1859 on were formative for Churches of Christ, although formal separation was not publicly acknowledged until 1906. Krüger listed the scriptural reasons for the name of the churches, their thoroughly biblicist ethos, weekly celebration of the Lord's Supper, and their non-cooperative character as far as other denominations were concerned, despite the practice of open communion. Krüger misjudged only the self-understanding of the Churches of Christ when he asserted that they "view themselves as a separate denomination by renewing the strict principles of Alexander Campbell." It takes an insider to understand the true extent of the denial of history and anti-institutional pathos among these churches, which not only reject any official founding figures besides Christ but would find particularly offensive any hint of being a "denomination."[22]

Recent Theological Reference Works

Ecumenical cooperation and a de-confessionalizing of theology have continued into the new millennium, as also the greater cooperation of scholars and the easier accessibility of academic resources in the electronic global village have done. German encyclopedias, which were long a victim of academic parochialism, have now taken on a more international character. Thus *EK3* had an international editorial board, while *RGG4* went so far as to recognize the value of experts from the denominations that are treated in the encyclopedia. One major German church-historical biographical-bibliographical reference work, *Biographisch-bibliographisches Kirchenlexikon* (*BBKL*), has also moved from the printed medium to the Internet, where it can be accessed world wide.

Alexander and Thomas Campbell in BBKL

The articles on Alexander[23] and Thomas[24] Campbell in volume one of the *Biographisch-bibliographisches Kirchenlexikon*, an academic reference work, are competent, short overviews of two SCM founding fathers. Mention is made of the delicate amalgamation of Disciples and Christians in 1832. The article on Thomas Campbell highlights the significance of the 1809 *Declaration and Address*.[25] As secondary literature, *BBKL* lists Alexander Campbell's *Memoirs of Elder Thomas Campbell* (1861) as well as Lester G. McAllister's *Thomas Campbell: Man of the Book* (1954). In treating the doctrine of the Disciples, mention is made of congregational autonomy, lay Christianity, weekly observance of the Lord's Supper, believer's baptism for the remission of sins, and the rejection of creeds in favor of a Bible-oriented Christianity. The bibliography for Alexander Campbell represents the most comprehensive selection in any German

---

[22] H[anfried] Krüger, "Churches of Christ" in *ibid.*, 1: 797.

[23] Friedrich Wilhelm Bautz, "Campbell, Alexander," *BBKL* (Hamm: Traugott Bautz, 1990): 1: 897-898.

[24] *Ibid.*, "Campbell, Thomas," *BBK* (1990): 1: 899-900.

[25] http://www.bautz.de/bbkl/c/campbell_t.shtml

reference work, with a concentration on Disciples literature, particularly the works of Winfred Ernest Garrison, who himself, however, has no article in this international reference work.[26] Surprisingly, Barton W. Stone received no mention in the *BBKL* either. When discussing the churches that formed as a result of the work of Alexander Campbell, only the Disciples are mentioned. The author seems to have been unaware of Churches of Christ or Independent Christian Churches.

The Non-Existence of the SCM in the TRE

From 1976 on, when the first volume appeared of the *Theologische Realenzyklopädie* (*TRE*), completed with volume 36 in 2004, an ambitious effort had been undertaken to develop a Protestant theological encyclopedia of a scope even larger than *RE3*, its turn-of-the-century predecessor. Already the name of this undertaking, *Theologische Realenzyklopädie*, reminds one that this encyclopedia is a modern successor of the earlier initiative. Any doubt as to its literary continuity is removed by the online advertisement, which states that the *TRE* "resumes the work carried out on the threshold of the twentieth century for the *Realencyclopädie für protestantische Theologie und Kirche* (3rd edition, Leipzig 1896-1913)." The self-congratulatory comments, that the *TRE* "with its comprehensive coverage" represents "an indispensable tool and reference work for theologians, scholars in the humanities, and all those interested in religion and theology," holds true for most conventional areas of theological scholarship.[27] The articles are excellent and convey a true impression of the current state of contemporary theological knowledge.

Hence a reader of the *TRE* would rightly expect a thorough and competent treatment of the SCM in its own right, at least the equivalent of the articles on the Jehovah's Witnesses and Christian Science, but this time removed from the suffragan status among the Baptists, where the *TRE's* predecessor had left the movement. The disappointment, therefore, is great, for the SCM is not treated at all! It has totally fallen through the cracks. Under "Disciples of Christ" there is a cross-reference to the article "*Baptisten,*" which indicates that some treatment was intended in the article on the Baptists similar to its fin-de-siècle ancestor. But when one surveys the article on the Baptists in volume four of the *TRE*, written conjointly by John David Hughey and Rudolf Thaut, one finds no mention at all of the SCM or the churches spawned by the movement.[28] Only once, in an article on Latin America, are the Disciples mentioned, where the reader is merely told that the Disciples of Christ had a presence as missionaries but is then referred to the italicized item "Disciples of Christ," which, however, is a phantom entry: It does not exist either as an article in its own right or as treated under the Baptists.[29] Obviously, something went wrong in the planning or execution of the article on the Baptists, but the very fact that the editors intended to discuss religious groups with distinct ecclesiastical identities under a denomination that no longer is institutionally linked with the SCM, represents an unfortunate throwback in conception to nineteenth-century historiography, a failure of awareness, and a lack in historical knowledge, and even this subordinating

---

[26] http://www.bautz.de/bbkl/c/campbell_a.shtml
[27] http://www.degruyter.de/rs/5753_6844_ENU_h.htm
[28] *TRE* (Berlin & New York: Walter de Gruyter, 1979): 5: 190-197.
[29] See *TRE*, 20 (1990): 468; see also the *Index* volume for vols 1-27, *TRE* (1998): 218.

treatment of the SCM as a shoot off the Baptists was never carried out. The total omission of the SCM in the TRE is a serious flaw in the encyclopedia, and one wonders what other worthy subjects might have trickled through the scholarly fingers of the editors.

The Christian Church (Disciples) and Churches of Christ in EK3

In 1985, a truly international encyclopedia appeared at the press of Vandenhoeck & Ruprecht under the title of the older *Evangelisches Kirchenlexikon* (*EK*) as its third edition. In the meantime, this encyclopedia has, with minor revisions, been translated into English and was published in 1999 by Eerdmans under the title *The Encyclopedia of Christianity*. In the German original, readers were presented with a good differentiation between the Christian Church (Disciples of Christ) and Churches of Christ, which are treated in two separate articles.[30] Both articles were written by the American religious historian Edwin S. Gaustad, who had published previously on the SCM. The article on the Christian Church (Disciples of Christ) has a very brief but appropriate bibliography, listing three titles only: Garrison and De Groot's history, the two-volume social history by David Edwin Harrell, and the German translation of Beazley's multi-authored monograph on the Disciples.

Beazley's work deserves special mention since it is the only scholarly monograph on the SCM that ever appeared in Germany. Multi-authored in English, the volume was edited for a German audience and appeared in 1977 under the revealing title *Die Kirche der Jünger Christi (Disciples): Progressiver Amerikanischer Protestantismus in Geschichte und Gegenwart* [The Church of the Disciples of Christ (Disciples): Progressive American Protestantism in the Past and Present], volume 16 in the series "Die Kirchen der Welt." [Churches of the World].[31] In the German volume, Beazley's own contributions, an attempt at theological and ecclesiological contextualization of the SCM and of the Disciples in particular, are somewhat abbreviated. Since Beazley died before the German version appeared, Howard E. Short, former editor of the Christian Board of Publication, saw the translation through its publication process. The volume is more than a history; it represents a compendium of the thought of leading Disciples theologians and strategists of the 1970s. The book has 13 chapters; the German edition opens with a foreword by Günter Wagner, alerting German readers to the exemplary contribution of this American church to Christian unity. After a historically oriented sketch by Beazley of who the Disciples are, chapters follow on theology by Ronald Osborne, worship by William Barnett Blakemore, organization and restructuring by A. Dale Fiers, pastoral and practical topics by Paul A. Stauffer and William Jackson Jarman, social issues by Albert M. Pennybacker, higher education by Harold E. Fey, ecumenism by Paul A. Crow Junior, and on literature of the Disciples by Howard E. Short, followed by a "Statistical Profile" by Howard E. Dentler, with a concluding chapter by Beazley on the future of the Disciples of Christ.

This book is a *summa* of Liberal Disciples thought in the early 1970s, and so pays little attention to Churches of Christ or Independent Christian Churches. Since it is the

---

[30] "Christian Church (Disciples of Christ)," *Evangelisches Kirchenlexikon* (Göttingen: Vandenhoeck & Ruprecht, 1986): 1: 681-683; "Churches of Christ," *ibid.*: 1: 752-753.

[31] Published by Evangelisches Verlagswerk in Stuttgart.

only monographic presentation from the SCM in the series, it reinforces the impression that the productive and progressive heritage of the movement consists solely of Disciples. Beazley characterized Churches of Christ briefly in the introductory historical chapter but then dismissed them as nostalgic conservatives with a rural past. About the post-1906 developments, he wrote:

> Churches of Christ continued to proclaim the brand of Disciples Scholasticism on which they were founded and have grown into a large church, the exact size of which is difficult to determine, since no accurate statistics are kept.[32] They flourish in the rural South and have congregations in many city suburbs. Usually these are made up of rural minded people, now living in the city, who resist efforts to incorporate them into modern metropolitan society.[33]

Churches of Christ and other Protestant conservatives posed a major "problem" for Beazley. While they have "nostalgia for the old-time religion," they are "people caught in the complexities of megalopolitan culture, yet homesick for the simplicity of frontier and small town life." It is this "nostalgia" and conservative mindset that is, according to Beazley, responsible for their placing obstacles in the path of ecumenical cooperation among the churches and by maintaining a "way of looking at things which has prevented the churches from confronting modern secularism positively and effectively."[34] Although Beazley's book appeared in 1977, only Gaustad lists it as a relevant German title, but judges Churches of Christ quite differently than does Beazley.

Gaustad's article on the Disciples is divided into two parts: (1) Conditions and Intentions and (2) Development. He viewed the SCM as an expression of the American frontier with its sense of unlimited possibilities, where the movement sought to realize its "dream of apostolic purity."[35] The original quest of the SCM for unity is understood as a response to the pluralism that religious freedom had fostered in America. A second impulse came from the movement's frontier origins, with its absence of traditional authorities, where only one authority, namely that of the Bible, prevailed and supplied a religious and ethical road map for life in the present and the hereafter. According to Gaustad, the SCM's ideal of apostolic purity is rooted in the progressivist restorationist thinking of the nineteenth century, whereas the Enlightenment does not seem to play any significant role.

Gaustad's treatment of the movement's development though brief is accurate. He observed an irony of history in that a movement whose goal it was to overcome ecclesiastical divisions engendered three new denominations: the Disciples of Christ, Churches of Christ, and Independent Christian Churches. Among these three "denominations," a term eschewed by the groups themselves, Disciples are seen as being by far the most liberal and ecumenically open, whereas Churches of Christ are at the conservative pole and are "still in search of a denominational identity and direction."

---

[32] Beazley wrote prior to Mac Lynn's *Directories*, which start with Mac Lynn, *Churches of Christ in the United States: Inclusive of her Commonwealth and Territories* (Nashville: Gospel Advocate, 1991).

[33] Cited here from the English original, which was translated into German: George G. Beazley, Jr. (edit.), *The Christian Church (Disciples of Christ): An Interpretative Examination in the Cultural Context* (no place: The Bethany Press, 1973): 31.

[34] *Ibid.*: 31-32.

[35] Edwin S. Gaustad, "Christian Church (Disciples of Christ)," *EK* (1986): 1: 681

Independent Christian Churches, which are not treated separately in the encyclopedia, lie theologically in the middle, but for all three, according to Gaustad, the ideal of Christian unity remains alive despite the perennially fissiparous situation.

The separate article on Churches of Christ refers the reader to Gaustad's own 1969 article as well as an article by Samuel S. Hill published in a now-defunct progressive journal issued by members of the Churches of Christ.[36] Gaustad viewed Churches of Christ as being engaged in an unavoidable development from sect to denomination, still resisting the spirit of modernity and the ecumenical opening of the religious life. He directed attention to the Southern and agricultural origins of Churches of Christ and the eventual efforts undertaken at overcoming this regionalism, a development that, according to Gaustad, had succeeded best in California. The Churches of Christ shared the notion of biblical authority and a return to the ecclesial model of the apostolic age, according to Gaustad. Writing in the 1980s, Gaustad judged the conservative wing of the SCM as having the greatest vitality but an unpredictable future as far as worship and religious life were concerned.

The Disciples in LThK3

Approaching the new millennium, a new edition of the authoritative German Roman Catholic encyclopedia, *Lexikon für Theologie und Kirche* (*LThK*), was started in 1993, and was completed in 2001 with volume eleven. The SCM is treated by Thomas F. Stransky, a Paulist priest and original staff member of the Vatican Secretariat for Promoting Christian Unity, who enjoyed a long association with the Tantur Ecumenical Institute for Theological Studies in Jerusalem. Stransky wrote his article with a focus on the Disciples of Christ.[37] In the literature section, the reader is referred to two monographs, both of Disciples provenance: the 1975 history by McAllister and Tucker, and K. Lawrence's *Classic Themes of Disciples Theology* (Fort Worth, 1986), and to a Cincinnati-based journal, *Mid-Stream*. It is surprising that an ecumenist like Stransky seems to have been unaware of Beazley's German volume.

This brief historical profile shows an awareness both of the 1832 merger of Stone and Campbell churches and of the ecumenical and restorationist heritage of the movement. Since the focus is on the Disciples only, their ecumenical initiatives and world-wide spread are emphasized as well as their mergers with other churches in India, Great Britain, Japan, and Zaire. No mention at all is made in the article about the trifurcation of the movement into three separate institutions. While representing a relatively well-informed summary on the Disciples and their ecumenical ethos and initiatives, the article thus totally neglects the conservative (Churches of Christ) and evangelical (Independent Christian Churches) faces of the SCM.

The SCM in RGG4

Most recent reference works show an effort to tone down blatant denominational polemics and strive for greater objectivity in presenting religious groups. The international *EK3* engaged an American historian of religion with a prior publication

---

[36] Samuel S. Hill, "The Churches of Christ and Religion in the South," *Mission* (August 1980).
[37] *LThK* (Freiburg, Basel, Rome, Vienna: Herder, 1995): 3: 259-60.

record in the area, but only in *RGG4* (1998-2005) did the editors commission some of the most prominent international historians in the field, including those from within the traditions discussed in the articles. Thus Richard T. Hughes was asked to write the article "Churches of Christ," and David Edwin Harrell, the articles "Christian Church (Disciples of Christ)" and "Christian Churches/Churches of Christ (Independent)."[38] Harrell also wrote the biographical article on Alexander Campbell,[39] and Mark Noll, the prominent Evangelical historian at Wheaton College, the one on Barton W. Stone.[40]

Harrell's magisterial and insightful social history of the SCM is cited along with the history by McAllister and Tucker as is also Mark Toulouse's *Joined in Discipleship* (1997) as literature for the article on the Disciples. Harrell presented a brief sketch of the history of the SCM in the nineteenth century, with its quest for unity within the context of a simple organization of congregationally autonomous churches. The Disciples are described as having evolved into a mainstream Protestant denomination that pioneered parti-cipation in the world-wide ecumenical movement. The first and definitive division of the movement between the Disciples and the Churches of Christ was marked in the U.S. census of 1906, which listed the conservative Churches of Christ, then numbering ca. 12%, separately. The next formative split between the Disciples and the Independent Christian Churches occurred over fundamentalist/modernist issues. Like other liberal denominations, the Disciples also experienced a sizeable numerical decline since 1980s.

In the article on the Independent Christian Churches, Harrell mentioned the emergence of a separate North American Christian Convention in 1927 as a consequence of a struggle for control within the Disciples, which eventually led to a formal separation with separate facilities for clergy training and the journal, *Christian Standard*, as the periodical voice of the Independent churches. The division became more permanent through increased restructuring and institutionalization of the Disciples, when ca. one-third of their congregations joined the fellowship of Independent Christian Churches, who were now led by prominent Fundamentalists and Neo-Evangelicals. Two titles are referenced as literature on the Independent Christian Churches: Murch's *Christians Only* (1961) and Webb's *In Search of Christian Unity* (1990).

Richard T. Hughes in his article on the non-instrumental Churches of Christ presented to the German readers specifics about the original separation from the Disciples: instrumental music in worship and missionary societies. He also mentioned the regional nature of the northern Disciples and the southern Churches of Christ and the significance that the Civil War played in the division. More recent issues among Churches of Christ, namely Premillennialism and the institutional use of church funds, are mentioned as further causes of dissension. This largest fellowship of churches in the SCM was said to have numbered ca. 1.6 million members in the 1980s. These congregations continued to espouse a restorationist agenda, but the claim to be "the one true church" had now been softened, for these churches were moving closer to the American evangelical mainstream with its pronounced theology of grace. Relevant

---

[38] David Edwin Harrell, "Christian Church (Disciples of Christ)," *RGG* (1999): 2: 255, and "Christian Churches/Churches of Christ (Independent)," *ibid.*: 2: 255-256; Richard T. Hughes, "Churches of Christ," *ibid.*: 2: 377.

[39] David Edwin Harrell, "Campbell, Alexander" *RGG* (1999): 2: 46.

[40] Mark A. Noll, "Stone, Barton Warren," *RGG* (2004): 7: 1,748.

literature about the movement is, according to Hughes, West's encyclopedic *Search for the Ancient Order* (1949-1988), Hooper's *A Distinct People* (1993) and Hughes's own *Reviving the Ancient Faith* (1996).

In Harrell's biographical article on Alexander Campbell, he contextualized the restorationist founder for the German readership and identified as an important early influence the primitivism of the Haldane brothers.[41] Only one factual error mars the otherwise excellent article: Alexander Campbell is said to have arrived in America in 1808; in fact, Campbell arrived in 1809 in New York, after a first attempt to reach the United States resulted in a shipwreck during the previous year. Harrell depicted 1832 as an important date for the movement, when the Reforming Baptists led by Alexander Campbell joined forces with Barton W. Stone's Christians.

Mark Noll's exceedingly brief article on Stone contains more than just one inaccuracy.[42] While Stone was a co-signer of the *Last Will and Testament of the Springfield Presbytery*, he was not—contrary to Noll—its "author," which was most likely Richard M'Nemar, who subsequently defected to the Shakers. The merger of the two movements left the individual congregations on both sides congregationally autonomous; this fact is viewed in a Disciples retrospect by Noll in the following misleading words: Stone "and his followers founded together with A. Campbell the Christian Church (Disciples of Christ)...in 1830." Neither Campbell or Stone nor their followers were "founders" in 1832 [not 1830] of a monolithic church body with the much later designation of "Christian Church (Disciples of Christ)." One hundred years later, the northern Disciples were beginning to approach something like denominational status, which they formally espoused only in 1960s, although the direction they were taking had become entirely clear earlier. At most, the nineteenth-century SCM pioneers were leading figures in an amorphous fellowship of congregationally autonomous churches, the majority of which had become loosely aligned in 1832, but were joined by no formal creedal statement or organizational bonds. Noll listed only Richard T. Hughes's *Reviving the Ancient Faith* (1996), and while it does contain a chapter on Stone, a more appropriate reference would have been D. Newell Williams, *Barton Stone: A Spiritual Biography* (2000).

The SCM as Viewed in Protestant and Roman Catholic Literature on Sects and Ideologies

Besides encyclopedias, two major reference works, Protestant and Roman Catholic, registered denominations, sects, and groups with a distinct religious or quasi-religious world view. While their treatment was not as accessible to the general reader as the available encyclopedias, the two major ones deserve at least a brief treatment and comparison: Kurt Hutten and Konrad Algermissen.

Kurt Hutten's *Seher, Grübler, Enthusiasten: Sekten und religiöse Sonder-gemeinschaften der Gegenwart* [Prophets, Ruminators, and Enthusiasts: Sects and Independent Religious Groups Today] went through multiple editions, of which we will examine the eighth edition of 1962.[43] Hutten was also the founder and long-time director of a Protestant watchdog organization, Evangelische Zentralstelle für Weltanschauungsfragen (EZW),

---

[41] Harrell (1999): 2: 46
[42] Noll (2004): 7: 1,748.
[43] Kurt Hutten, *Seher, Grübler, Enthusiasten: Sekten und religiöse Sondergemeinschaften der Gegenwart* (Stuttgart: Quell-Verlag der Evang. Gesellschaft, 8th edition, 1962).

which monitored religious groups outside of the larger, state churches. The EZW issues a newsletter to the Protestant clergy and other interested subscribers.[44]

Unlike the German encyclopedias that view the SCM as an American church, Hutten dealt with the missionary presence of non-instrumental Churches of Christ in Germany, the *Gemeinden Christi*, beginning in 1958. In his largely theological classification of sects and religious groups, *Gemeinden Christi* are classed with the group whose self-definition is not in line with the Protestant notion of justification by faith only. Hutten saw the *Gemeinden Christi* as a style of "perfectionist community" with an ecclesiological focus who absolutize the true church and its constitution. For Hutten, *Gemeinden Christi* share theological views with the Church of God (Anderson, Indiana) and a circle of German Perfectionists who followed Willy Cordier. Cordier had emigrated in the 1950s to the Falklands and eventually established a utopian community in Argentina.[45]

Whatever one may think about the company in which Hutten placed *Gemeinden Christi*, his treatment of Churches of Christ in Germany at mid-twentieth century was remarkably well informed both in its historical detail and in Hutten's theological estimate. He drew on the extant periodical, tract, and correspondence-course literature in German. The only other literature listed, from which Hutten derived historical background information, is Elmer T. Clark's *The Small Sects in America* (1957). Hutten was aware of the two major roots of the movement, the motivation of its principal founders, the union of the Disciples and Christians in 1832, and the eventual bifurcation of the SCM over instrumental music and missionary societies, and the demographic base of Churches of Christ in the rural South. Hutten's important historiographical omission is his failure to mention the emergence of Independent Christian Churches from the Disciples. Hutten was relatively well informed, however, about the post-war missionary activities of Churches of Christ, their temporary educational base for Germany in Frankfurt, and the consequences of their strict congregational ideal for the many individual congregations scattered across Europe.[46]

In terms of doctrine, he sees correctly the anti-creedal, Biblicist foundations of the *Gemeinden Christi*, their individualist exegesis, and some of the dangers that arise from a subjective hermeneutic. Perfectionism was, according to Hutten, not located so much in the churches' soteriology as in their ecclesiology. He saw the confinement of biblical authority to the books of the New Testament, which are also the foundation for the ecumenical ideal of church union on the basis of Scripture. Hutten then sketched some highlights of SCM restorationism, including baptismal immersion, the weekly observance on the Lord's Day of the Lord's Supper, and a "bibliocratic" constitution of the churches with their not always consistent offices. He concluded this largely descriptive section by pointing out the claim of the *Gemeinden Christi* to be the only

---

[44] On *Gemeinden Christi*, see the EZW's *Materialdienst* 21/1 (1 January 1958): 19; 21/22 (15 November 1958): 262; 36/17 (1 September 1973): 268-270; 36/18 (15 September 1973): 286; 37/17 (1 September 1974): 266-268; 40/5 (1 May 1977): 127, 136-137; 42/6 (1 June 1979): 165; 42/7 (1 July 1979): 188. I am grateful to Marion Löfflmann and Dr. Reinhard Hempelmann for supplying the relevant literature.
[45] The *Gemeinden Christi* are treated in Hutten (1962): 449-455, 475-477.
[46] *Ibid.*, 450-452.

legitimate, biblically authorized churches, and their allegation that all others are biblically unfaithful denominations.[47]

In his theological evaluation of *Gemeinden Christi*, Hutten anticipated much of the self-criticism of Churches of Christ from the 1960s on. After stating the dual motives of SCM ecclesiology, namely obedience to Scripture and Christian unity, he observed as well the empirical reality: a new perfectionist organization. According to Hutten, the main mistake of the churches lay in their misconception of the New Testament as a legal statute. (Hutten's view of Scripture was that it is proclamation and encouragement.) Based on the motto that commanded silence where Scripture is silent, the claim of *Gemeinden Christi* to be the correct church reconstructed from the New Testament was, according to Hutten, mistaken not only because of inconsistent selectivity of their exclusivist scriptural practices but also—and more significantly—because they lacked the presence of the living Spirit.

In terms of hermeneutics, the individualized and leveling Biblicism employed by the churches ran counter to what Hutten considered a more appropriate understanding of scriptural authority: the quest for the center or core of Scripture. In this effort, Hutten articulated a similar criticism of SCM hermeneutics offered from within Churches of Christ by Thomas H. Olbricht, notably in his book *Hearing God's Voice: My Life with Scripture in the Churches of Christ* (Abilene, Texas: Abilene University Press, 1996).[48]

Hutten concluded his treatment of *Gemeinden Christi* by identifying as "the decisive mistake of the *Gemeinde Christi* that it misunderstands biblical authority legalistically and did not evaluate "law" in the Bible in terms of the central message of Christ."[49] The evaluation offered by Hutten thus proceeds along well-known Lutheran lines of distinguishing between material and formal principles of Reformation Christianity and Luther's hermeneutic of a "canon within the canon," judging everything by whether it speaks of Christ or not.

Unlike Hutten, who based his estimate of *Gemeinden Christi* on their own literature, Algermissen's treatment of the SCM in the various editions of his *Konfessionskunde* from 1930 to 1969, relied largely–as in his *LThK* articles–on Protestant secondary literature. Algermissen's understanding thus improved through the years only insofar as this literature became better informed. Algermissen listed as resource literature Ruprecht's well-informed *EKL2* article, Howard E. Short's *Doctrine and Thought of the Disciples of Christ* (1952), and Garrison and DeGroot's *Disciples of Christ* (1948), but there is little indication that he had himself read this literature.[50]

Furthermore, Algermissen treated the SCM as late as 1969 not as denomination or fellowship of its own but as an institutional derivative of the Baptists (*Baptistische Zweiggruppe*), and he linked the SCM as such directly with American Baptist Churches, listing them under "Free Churches and Sects" as "The Baptist Free Churches: Mennonites, Baptists, Neo-Baptists." The only historical difference from the Baptists proper is the Disciples' more emphatic "American character," whatever may be implied

---

[47] *Ibid.*, 452-455.

[48] On this hermeneutic, see Hans Rollmann, "Tom Olbricht as Theologian," *Restoration Quarterly* 43/3&4 (2004): 235-248.

[49] Hutten (1962): 477.

[50] Konrad Algermissen, *Konfessionskunde* (Paderborn: Bonifatius, 8th ed., 1969): 742.

in this judgment. The historiography of the book accounts for the two roots (Campbellites and Stoneites) and the 1832 merger, basically reproducing the content of Algermissen's *LThK* article. Mixed in with more or less accurate historical detail, however, one finds the completely erroneous notions that Churches of Christ in Germany had their "headquarters" (*Zentrale*) in Frankfurt, had been "a unique Baptist community" since 1906, and were "strictly calvinistic"[!]. More on target, Algermissen mentioned the pronounced congregationalism, and the rejection of missionary societies and instrumental music. Viewing the SCM through Baptist-tinted spectacles, Algermissen concluded that the Churches of Christ were the outcome of divisions within the Baptist movement, which can be traced back to the fundamental religious individualism of Baptists, with the only truly unifying element being adult immersion.[51]

Conclusions

The early-twentieth-century German historiography of the SCM as found in the major Protestant and Roman Catholic religious encyclopedias exhibits an undue dependence on secondary Baptist literature at a time when significant biographies and histories had been written and were available. Consequently, *RE3* and *RGG1* do not treat the SCM as an independent movement but as a Baptist sect. This mistake is most obvious in *RE3* in that no separate article is devoted to any SCM group; and even in *RGG1* the name adopted for the SCM, "Campbelliten," is a Germanization of the pejorative term "Campbellites," which originated in the polemical literature of Baptist provenance. While Alexander Campbell was affiliated for a while with a Baptist church after he left the Seceeder Presbyterians, his own separation from the Baptists was made clear early in his career as a reformer, and the normative self-definition of Campbell's Disciples as an independent fellowship of congregationally autonomous churches was part of the restorationist agenda from the very beginning of the movement. The Stone half of the movement never had any formal affiliation with Baptist churches.

The alleged suffragan status of the SCM among the Baptists was reinforced in the minds of the authors of these German essays largely because they used Baptist literature, notably Armitage's *History of the Baptists*. In the case of *RGG1* and *RGG2*, the Baptist perspective was further enhanced in that a German Baptist pastor wrote these articles. The supposed institutional proximity to the Baptists was retained longest in the Roman Catholic encyclopedic literature, notably *LThK1* and *LThK2*, the latter representing the state of Roman Catholic theology after WWII and prior to Vatican II. In both editions, Algermissen dealt with the SCM as part of the article on Baptists. How far and long this Baptist shadow extended is illustrated by the editors of the most recent and comprehensive Protestant theological encyclopedia, the TRE, who intended but then either forgot or decided not to deal with the SCM in the article on the Baptists, as the dead reference links to the Disciples of Christ suggest. The overall picture of the SCM that emerges from the German literature of the first half of the twentieth century is that of a Baptist ecclesiastical offshoot.

As far as the historical development of the SCM is concerned, it took considerable time until even the larger outline of its history was sketched with some accuracy.

---

[51] *Ibid.*, 742-744.

Throughout German historiography, the history of the Disciples outweighs significantly that of Churches of Christ and Independent Christian Churches, a picture reflecting the greater institutionalization and especially the ecumenical involvement of Disciples, reinforced by the translation of Beazley's monograph on the Disciples in the German series *Kirchen der Welt*.

The contribution of Stone to the SCM remained unclear until the post-war literature, and even the merger of the two groups in 1832 cannot be found in the earliest literature. That Stone was neglected until very recently even within the SCM did not help in establishing a balanced view of the relative contributions of the Disciples and Christians to the movement.

Further complexities of the SCM's prehistory, such as the influences from the Christian Connexion, never surface in the German discussion. Also the intellectual and religious roots reaching back to the philosophical Enlightenment and First and Second Great Awakenings remain largely unarticulated.

The difficulty of finding meaningful categories through which to understand and describe the institutional development of congregationally autonomous churches becomes obvious in these German reference works. The authors, accustomed to thinking in terms of denominational hierarchy, inevitably overdraw the institutional cohesion of the SCM. Thus *EK2* states—in unwitting violation of the strict autonomy of all the congregations as well as of their anti-creedal ethos—that the conservative Churches of Christ "view themselves as a separate denomination" by following Alexander Campbell's principles strictly. This assertion is amusing in view of the general lack of awareness of Campbell's actual teachings even among well educated members of Churches of Christ, and the resistance of many members even to acknowledge Campbell's role as an historical founder of the movement.

The challenge of describing accurately the amorphous nature of a movement of individual and independent churches, and the differing degrees to which the three main branches of the movement developed their varying institutional structures, persists in the present, as the most recent *RGG4* article on Stone illustrates. Here, a generally insightful senior American church historian such as Mark Noll can speak quite anachronistically and without the necessary caveat about the unofficial status of an historical founding and the significant figures involved.

Personal acquaintance with the movement, as evidenced in the case of the Disciples article of Arndt Ruprecht in *EK2*, and in the most recent presentation of the SCM in *RGG4*, leads to a more competent presentation of the reasons for the institutional formation of the SCM, notably the trifurcation of the movement into the Disciples of Christ, the Churches of Christ, and the subsequent emergence of the Independent Christian Churches. Only in the most recent reference works, penned by scholars from within the movement, can the German readership become acquainted with the finer distinctions of the divisions in Churches of Christ over premillennialism and the anti-cooperation/anti-institutionalism dispute. Social historians, such as David E. Harrell and Edwin S. Gaustad, have discussed the frontier context, demographics, and the sectional character of the several branches of the SCM.

With the exception of *RGG4*, no encyclopedia links the German *Gemeinden Christi* with their American equivalent, the Churches of Christ, although *Gemeinden Christi* had been detected earlier on the ideological and denominational radar by German experts on sects and ideologies.[52] Remoteness of the SCM in the wider German religious consciousness is further illustrated in that the most comprehensive modern German theological encyclopedia, the *TRE*, could omit any mention of the SCM. Not even the ecumenically active Disciples were any longer visible to its editors.

Awareness of *Gemeinden Christi* on the basis of their literature is generally not registered in the encyclopedias but only in the specialized literature on sects and denominations, notably in Hutten's *Seher, Grübler, Enthusiasten*, where a theological critique of *Gemeinden Christi*, based on the Lutheran hermeneutical principles—rather than on strengths and weaknesses inherent to the SCM itself—is offered. In so doing, Hutten came independently to a similar judgment as that of theological revisionists in Churches of Christ, especially that found in the work of Thomas H. Olbricht.

The theological profile that emerged in the literature during the first half of the twentieth century was largely shaped by the differences between the SCM and the Baptists in the perception of the German commentators. Issues that received special attention are the regenerative nature of baptism, the action of the Holy spirit in salvation, particularly before and during the baptismal process, the relationship of Word and Spirit, and trinitarian issues, in particular the nature of the divinity of Jesus. Most of these topics have their own history in German Protestantism and Roman Catholicism, so the German essayists were sometimes casting in German terms what they thought the issues must be in an American Baptist sect.

Unfamiliarity among the German observers with the actual heritage of Stone's Christians prevented further discussion of the movement's anti-trinitarian thought. Although its SCM theological and Christological heterodoxy is occasionally touched upon, it is not highlighted so much as the earlier Baptist charge of Pelagianism directed against Alexander Campbell and the Disciples. Most of the differences articulated by Armitage and other Baptists, as well as the association of Campbell and the Disciples with Pelagianism, repeat historical charges expressed in the report of the Dover Baptist Association of Eastern Virginia of December 1830, which alleged four principal doctrinal errors: "the denial of the influence of the Holy Spirit in the salvation of man–the substitution of reformation for repentance–the substitution of baptism for conversion, regeneration or the new birth–and the *Pelagian* doctrine of the sufficiency of man's natural powers to effect his own salvation." Campbell, in reply, reduced these charges to two, "the denial of their mystic influences of the Holy Spirit and immersion for the remission of sins." He rejected the alleged association with Pelagian self-salvation by natural human means and reaffirmed "grace and the blood of Jesus" as the biblical base for his soteriology. One cannot deny, however, that in refusing to involve the Holy Spirit in the conversion process before baptism, Campbell and the SCM laid themselves open to charges of Pelagianism. This was reinforced by the importance accorded to reason in religious conversion, spiritual formation, and ethical decision-making, as well as by the activity of the Spirit in human minds and hearts "through the word only."[53]

---

[52] See notes 43, 44, 45, 50, and 51.

[53] For the Dover indictment and Alexander Campbell's response, see http://www. mun.ca/ rels/restmov/texts/ acampbell/tmh/ MH0202.HTM; *The Millennial Harbinger*, 2/2 (7 February 1831): 76-84.

What is missing almost entirely from the German encyclopedias are epistemological and hermeneutical issues as well as the relative contribution of the philosophical Enlightenment in establishing an ideological context for the movement. The two foci of restoration and unity as well as a Bible-oriented restitutionism are discussed but never adequately situated. Also the significance of Alexander Campbell's dispensationalism in his *Sermon on the Law* and its importance for limiting the scope of biblical authority to the New Testament is not discussed. Likewise the pathos with which Stone and his New Light Christians overcame and rejected Calvinism and the thoroughgoing polemic against Calvinism throughout SCM history, though the topic is raised by Arndt Ruprecht in *EK2*, it is never discussed elsewhere.

The SCM through German eyes remains myopic and distant. For the first half of the twentieth century, the movement was poorly referenced, and it was pressed into the straitjacket of another religious group that did have a German presence, the Baptists. The SCM and its first three institutional expressions came into their own only when a closer association with those institutions and the movement's own literature was achieved in the post-World War Two period. Before this, German scholarship on the SCM suffered from continental scholarly isolationism.

The lack of a German SCM presence prior to World War Two may have contributed to this deficiency of historiography, yet even though the SCM has now been on the German scene for over 50 years—admittedly in an easily negligible way—the Roman Catholic encyclopedias and the *TRE* continue to reflect ignorance of the Restoration Movement either in its American or German manifestation. Although Ernst Troeltsch and Max Weber pioneered the methodology and ideal types with which American social historians, notably David Edwin Harrell, came to understand the movement, the SCM remains for German theological scholarship in 2005 an erratic rock jutting from the evangelical ocean. The complexity of this oft-splintered movement has defied categorical oversimplification. Its provisional institutionalization, separatist ethos, eclectic sacramental theology, radical congregationalism, understated and at times dubious trinitarianism, near Marcionite pathos for the exclusive authority of the New Testament, along with semi-Pelagian insistence on human cooperation in salvation and Arminian emphasis on free will, while resisting for much of the 20th century any activity of the Holy Spirit except "through the word only" still defies the often crude and inaccurate categories through which the SCM has often been misunderstood.

The internationalization of scholarship has remediated the situation somewhat in that American experts on the SCM have written the relevant articles in the latest editions of *EK* and *RGG*, but the neglect of the SCM in a major encyclopedia such as the *TRE* is a reminder of how absent the movement and its churches remain from the consciousness of German Protestantism. Neither the institutional presence of *Gemeinden Christi* nor the minor educational and benevolent activities of Disciples and Independent Churches of Christ in Germany have changed this patent lack of awareness.

THE RADICAL IDEA OF CHRISTIAN SCHOLARSHIP: PLEA FOR A SCANDALOUS HISTORIOGRAPHY

RICHARD C. GOODE

> *Our very ability as Christians to lead lives of witness*
> *has been compromised by our inability*
> *to sustain a Christian intellectual witness*
> *worthy of the martyrs.*
> —Stanley Hauerwas[1]

"Is there such a thing as a 'peace church historiography'?" John Howard Yoder once asked. At first glance, a reader might suppose Yoder was inquiring into the body of scholarly literature on groups like Anabaptists, Quakers, or the Church of the Brethren. Upon further investigation, however, we find that he was not interested in histories *about* nonviolent Christians. Instead he was calling for more and better histories *from* nonviolent Christians. Yoder was searching for Christian historians who deliberately re-read the past through the lens of their Radical faith.[2] He acknowledged that such a recommendation might "occasion a horror-struck reaction from professional historians." Nevertheless, because the Gospel is inherently nonviolent, Christian historians should, he pleaded, strive to "rehabilitate" historical writing by taking it "back from the grasp of the military historians and the chroniclers of battles and dynasties."[3]

Unfortunately, Yoder's call remains largely ignored. In fact, most Christian historians seem to operate from the presumption that they can appropriately reconcile (or even integrate) the canons of their faith with those of their chosen profession. In so doing, however, these historians appear to go about their professional work as if Easter had not occurred. At least the gospel of Jesus Christ does not seem radically to have reconstituted all of life for these Christian historians that they feel compelled to tell peculiar stories with shocking meanings.

But could it be otherwise? Must a Christian historian, even to be a professional historian, become a "methodological atheist?" Should Christian historians see the past in ways similar to their unbelieving colleagues? Or does the Christian *kerygma* so reshape

---

[1] Stanley Hauerwas, *With the Grain of the Universe: The Church's Witness and Natural Theology* (Grand Rapids: Brazos Press, 2001): 232.

[2] "Radical" is used here in the sense of the Anabaptists of the 16th-century Radical Reformation. To see how this historic tradition relates to other radical Christian movements, see *Radical Christian Writings: A Reader*, Andrew Bradstock and Christopher Rowland, eds. (Oxford: Blackwell Publishers, 2002).

[3] John Howard Yoder, *The Royal Priesthood: Essays Ecclesiological and Ecumenical*, ed. Michael Cartwright, (Scotdale: Herald Press, 1994): 208. Stanley Hauerwas (2001): 234, echoes Yoder's call.

our vision and thinking that it would be impossible for historians who hold faith to tell a story that their non-believing colleagues could appreciate or approve? Not quibbling with Yoder, might we not rephrase his question to ask: "Should Christian historians generate anything other than a 'peace church historiography,' and what might that historiography look like?"

In this essay, I briefly survey the work of George Marsden, a respected Christian historian who has achieved prestige in the academy, in part, by finding ways to hold his faith and professional commitments in tension. Although Marsden has depicted his synthesis of faith and professional scholarship as an "outrageous idea,"[4] I argue here that Marsden's honest and well-intended attempt to accommodate the Christian faith to the standards of the academy unavoidably detracts from the genius of the Christian message and serves the powers-that-be. Moreover, the history provided by Christian scholars such as Marsden fails to provide the church with the impertinent message it needs to fulfill its task of resisting this world's Principalities. Because the mission of the church is to wage an "irrepressible conflict"[5] against the Powers of this world, the church must have a body of resistance literature to sustain its work.[6] My plea in this essay, therefore, is for Christians to generate a body of history—Yoder's "peace church historiography"— to augment and improve the corpus of resistance literature that will inform and nurture the insubordinate life and work of Christ's peculiar community—the radical idea of a scandalous historiography.

The Example of George Marsden

Over the last quarter-century, perhaps no individual has been more zealous in envisioning a "faith-informed" life of the mind than the historian who teaches at the University of Notre Dame, George Marsden. He has been both critical of, and evangelistic for, the cause of Christian scholarship. In so doing, he has carefully considered his two primary audiences and crafted arguments for each. On one hand, he encourages Christian scholars, as disciples of Christ, to own the vocation of scholarship because the world needs Christians among the front ranks of the world's intelligentsia. On the other hand, Marsden explains to the larger, non-Christian academy why it ought to grant Christian scholars a seat at the table.

---

[4] George Marsden, *The Outrageous Idea of Christian Scholarship* (New York: Oxford University Press, 1997).

[5] David Lipscomb, *Civil Government: Its Origin, Mission, and Destiny, and the Christian's Relation To It* (Nashville: McQuiddy Printing Company, 1913): 29.

[6] As Barbara Harlow has found, "[R]esistance narratives propose historically specific analyses of the ideological and material conditions out of which they are generated." Consequently, resistance literature exists to challenge the ways "the interests of power" exploit power, and "create a distorted historical record." The texts become "immediate interventions into the historical record, attempting to produce and impart new historical facts and analyses…. This requires that the historical record and the present agenda be rewritten." See, Barbara Harlow, *Resistance Literature* (New York: Methuen, 1987): 116. Because resistance literature self-consciously arises out of, and strives to oppose prophetically, the historical context in which it is written, this historiography is by nature "high maintenance." As the context changes, resistance-minded historians must generate new histories, challenging the ways new powers are using knowledge for their purposes. No historical narration is good for all people in all places. Thus, there will be few, if any, "standard" histories.

Elaborating on his message to fellow Christian scholars, Marsden has proposed two interrelated approaches. First, Christians must honor the academy's rules for doing good history. The discipline of history has criteria for remaining professionally engaged, "a basic set of rules on which Christian perspectives should not intrude."[7] Second, although neither forsaking the believer's "God-talk," nor denying Christian beliefs, Christian historians should simply reserve such vocabulary and discussions for their religious subcultures and enclaves where such conversations are appreciated and not inflammatory. Historians, of course, need not be unbelievers, and Christian historians might occasionally consider the actions of God in history and the transcendent moral claims of God on the world. For Marsden, however, these discussions must remain intramural Christian conversations held within the religious subcultures—neither pursued in the pluralistic academy, nor written for popular consumption.[8]

What then becomes of distinctively Christian scholarship? Marsden reassures his Christian colleagues that the criteria for remaining professionally engaged in the academy's conversation is neither particularly burdensome nor threatening to the faith—as if the academy required Christian historians to betray some "set formulae for the Christian perspective."[9] Academic research techniques used by Christian historians, for example, seldom differ from those of any other historian. After all, historical fact is historical fact, available to the Christian and the non-Christian alike. All practitioners are duty-bound to read and interpret the facts with professional "detachment," and to "present a balanced account of what happened."[10] Because the academy demands verifiable factual support or evidence, everyone must be able to replicate the research and confirm the plausibility of the conclusions. Stated differently, one's religious perspective might influence the selection of a research topic, and even the questions that one brings to the research; the methods for culling out the facts and crafting the supporting narrative should, nevertheless, be neither significantly influenced by faith nor different from the methods used by non-believing historians. An atheist must be able to replicate the same research project and arrive at essentially the same conclusions. Thus, Marsden finds an "inverse relationship between how Christian a bit of history is and how good it is as history. If Christian motives are obtrusive, or if a hidden Christian agenda is uncovered, Christian and non-Christian historians alike usually agree that it is bad history." Again, personal tastes might incline an atheist and a Christian to pursue different research projects, yet nothing innate or automatic in one's Christian commitment should necessarily affect research methodology. Consequently, "much of

---

[7] George Marsden, "Common Sense and the Spiritual Vision of History," in *History and Historical Understanding*, eds. C.T. McIntire and Ronald A. Wells (Grand Rapids: Eerdmans, 1984): 56. This essay also appeared as "The Spiritual Vision of History," *Fides et Historia* 14 (fall 1981): 55-66.

[8] Marsden (1984): 65-68, and "Christian Advocacy and the Rules of the Academic Game," in *Religious Advocacy and American History*, Bruce Kuklick and D.G. Hart, eds. (Grand Rapids: Eerdmans, 1997): 10.

[9] George Marsden, "What Difference Might Christian Perspectives Make?" in *History and the Christian Historian*, Ronald A. Wells, ed. (Grand Rapids: Eerdmans, 1998): 13.

[10] George Marsden, "A Christian Perspective for the Teaching of History," in *A Christian View of History?* George Marsden and Frank Roberts, eds. (Grand Rapids: Eerdmans, 1975): 36. See also Marsden (1997): 9.

the history we [Christians] do turns out to be not much different from what is done by our secular colleagues." Marsden concluded, therefore, that perhaps "the best way to be a Christian historian is simply to be a good historian."[11]

Towards this end, Marsden borrowed an illustration, popularized by William James, that envisions the modern academy as a corridor accessible by numerous office doorways. Respective offices represent particular ideological or methodological departments. Although the scholar's individual office might be his/her domain, the corridor is an academic commons available to all who prove themselves academically worthy. No one can bar another from the commons solely on account of the other's ideological viewpoint. Designed to propagate and defend pluralism, in other words, the secular academy must be open to academicians with a religious orientation, with participation in the academy's dialogue dependent only on the degree to which any scholar honors the rules that govern professional research.[12]

Thus one can read the corpus of Marsden's writing on Christian scholarship as a proposed covenant. The academy should not banish Christian scholars on account of their faith, as long as Christian scholars work as good, rule-abiding members of the academy. "The same rules [should] apply to all. No matter what commitments one brings into one's academic work," Marsden proposed. "One would have to argue for one's scholarly interpretations on the same sorts of publicly accessible grounds that are widely accepted in the academy."[13]

Marsden would probably affirm Aileen Kraditor's doctrine that "interest and curiosity," rather than "didactic motives" should determine a "scholar's choice of [research] topic."[14] In the secret recesses of a Christian scholar's soul, Marsden confessed, religious passion undeniably inspires the Christian scholar's curiosity, and thus the selection of a research topic; nevertheless, that interest should not lead to Christian scholarship as a "didactic" or proselytizing enterprise. Likewise, the academy must not "automatically exclude one's views from acceptance in the academy, so long as one argues them on the other, more widely accessible grounds."[15] Again, this means that Christian scholars promise not to bring their "God-talk" into the academy's deliberations, and that the research offered will be civil, cautious, and tentative, driven more by themes of ambiguity and irony than triumphalism.[16] Marsden's proposed

---

[11] Marsden (1984): 56.

[12] Marsden (1997): 7.

[13] *Idem*: 16.

[14] Aileen K. Kraditor, *The Ideas of the Woman Suffrage Movement, 1890-1920* (New York: W.W. Norton, 1981): v.

[15] Marsden (1997): 10.

[16] Ronald Wells, *History Through the Eyes of Faith: Western Civilization and the Kingdom of God* (San Francisco: HarperCollins, 1989): 3, models a version of this chastened style when he argues to a primarily Evangelical audience, "Knowing the 'author of truth' gives us an advantage in knowing truth over our secular neighbors, but it does not insure that we know the truth, which surely exists in the mind of God but comes ambiguously to us. Once in a while we experience moments of clarity, and for these we are grateful. But, since the images remain blurred, we should practice the Christian virtue of humility in what we claim to know and to have 'right' in our historical perspectives."

standard of acceptable scholarship requires, in summary, that Christian historians narrate history in ways that make good sense to all readers—believers or not.

Marsden is hardly alone in his thinking. Douglas Sweeney has discerned, for example, a "Calvin College School of Historiography" that is closely aligned with Marsden.[17] Introducing the essays written by this group, Ronald Wells confessed that the various authors in that collection affirmed "our membership in the academy," which means that these Christian historians "proceed with care and civility," avoiding the use of some "interpretive (i.e., religious) trump card." "For us, a Christian perspective is more about our angle of vision than about the actual subject matter of history. After all, we see what most other *honest* scholars see."[18] Westmont College Provost and former President of the Conference on Faith and History, Shirley Mullen, largely concurred when she wrote, "My point here is simply that integrating one's faith and history must result in history that honors the regulative principles of the discipline.... In short, we must do history in a way that it is seen to be good history."[19] Perhaps the clearest statement of all comes from D.G. Hart and his call for "Christian historical agnosticism." In other words, historiography undertaken by Christian academicians ought to leave God explicitly out of the picture.[20]

Toward a Scandalous Historiography

Although highly respected for his craft, Marsden (and the position he articulates) has not been without detractors. William Speck was one of the first voices to question Marsden's "secularization and professionalization." "Christian historians have defined their central task in essentially the same manner as secular historians, namely, the writing of 'good' history; that is, history with scientific and literary merit, history that is thoroughly researched, readable, and concerned with plausible mundane causes and connections." Although Christian scholars like Marsden tried to cast their "positivist" work in vocational terms (i.e., the cost of doing business in the academy), Speck saw it as an "abandonment of a discernable religious role." In contrast, Speck pleaded for a "prophetic" historiography in which historians "responded to their age of crisis by analyzing and judging events from a dual religious-historical perspective." In other

---

[17] Douglas A. Sweeney, "Taking a Shot at Redemption: A Lutheran Considers the Calvin College School of Historiography," *Books and Culture* 5 (May/June 1999): 43-45. Although Sweeney confesses the imprecise nature of the grouping, he nonetheless finds the leading members of the School to include George Marsden, Frank Roberts, Ronald Wells, James Bratt, Harry Stout, Dale Van Kley, Joel Carpenter, Nathan Hatch, and Mark Noll. Like others, Sweeney questions the distinctively "Christian" nature of the historiography written by this Evangelical group. "Ironically," Sweeney noted, "just as the Calvin school has gained a hearing for Christian scholarship, it has denied the importance of Scripture—or better, the explicit use of Scripture—in fleshing out Christian perspectives." "In an otherwise admirable effort to allay the fears of secular colleagues, it seems the Calvin School has decided to minimize the importance of the only thing that makes Christian scholarship singular at all."

[18] Wells (1998): 4 (emphasis added). Elsewhere, Wells (1989): 3-4, went further in arguing that historians study humans and not God. "Historians with research degrees [conferred by the academy] agree on this. I know of no working historian whose subject is God in history."

[19] Shirley Mullen, "Faith, Learning, and the Teaching of History," in *Teaching as an Act of Faith: Theory and Practice in Church-Related Higher Education*, Arlin C. Migliazzo, ed. (New York: Fordham University Press, 2002): 281-2.

[20] D.G. Hart, "History in Search of Meaning: The Conference on Faith and History," in Wells (1998): 85.

words, Christian historians would study the non-religious world of ideas, culture, and politics, for the express purpose of having their religious perspective bear judgment on the world's faulty assumptions.[21] More recently, after reviewing Marsden's recommendations for faith-informed scholarship, Michael Baxter confessed he was left with the query, "What is so outrageous about that?[22] Likewise, Elizabeth Newman has concluded that Marsden's model of Christian scholarship "ultimately erases Christian identity."[23]

The question that comes to us, therefore, is this: Can a historiography that meets the approval of the academy really serve as resistance literature for the Christian community? Can a diet prescribed and regulated by one of the more entrenched and privileged social institutions, truly nourish a counter-cultural community? Can historians who work for the academy genuinely serve the *ecclesia*; can we simultaneously serve these two masters? I agree with Marsden's critics. What passes for "good" history in the academy is not good enough for the church. Allow me to explain.

Back in 2000, I assigned John Dear's *The Sacrament of Civil Disobedience* in one of my "Religion and American Culture" classes. In the book, Fr. Dear explains his activism this way:

> The Gospel of Jesus reads as a manifesto of nonviolent civil disobedience to systematic violence and societal sin. Everything in Jesus' life is seen as one illegal act of peacemaking after another…. Once we understand the world as a reign of violence into which God is bringing forth God's reign of nonviolence, Jesus' life becomes a testimony of nonviolent civil disobedience as a way to challenge the kingdom of violence and death.[24]

I challenged my students, therefore, to compare their theology of social engagement with Fr. Dear's. "Do you agree with the ends Dear establishes for Christians and the church?" I asked. "How about the means? Explain." Several students questioned the effectiveness of such Christian resistance on the larger culture. In other words, these students could not imagine that anyone following Dear's prescription could be taken seriously. Engaging in nonviolent civil disobedience squanders any real chance to influence society, as both the society and the church will ignore such radicals as embarrassing "renegades and fanatics." Christians, one student wrote, are called to live in harmony with the rest of society. So, "why would one break a perfectly good law to protest a law that is bad when most people find the law acceptable?" Moreover, "more

---

[21] William Speck, "What Should be the Role of Christian Historians," *Fides et Historia* 8 (fall 1975): 76-81.

[22] Michael J. Baxter, "Not Outrageous Enough," *First Things* 113 (May 2001): 14-16.

[23] Elizabeth Newman, "Hotel or Home? Hospitality and Higher Education," in *Conflicting Allegiances: The Church-Based University in a Liberal Democratic Society*, Michael Budde and John Wright, eds. (Grand Rapids, Brazos Press, 2004): 95. Even non-believers have questioned the plausibility of Marsden's approach. Bruce Kuklick, for example, has asked "Why doesn't George Marsden tell us in *Jonathan Edwards* what he really thinks about the Great Awakening? How can he say that he just chooses to play by the rules of the professional game of history but that those rules need not constrain his genuine belief? What kind of professional ethos is this?" (See "Believing History: An Exchange Featuring Bruce Kuklick, Mark Noll, and Richard Bushman," *Books and Culture* 11 (March/April 2005): 6.)

[24] John Dear, S.J., *The Sacrament of Civil Disobedience* (Baltimore: Fortkamp Publishing Company, 1994): 42.

people can be brought to Christ if the church and Christians look more moderate, and are not out there ruffling any feathers."

Clearly, the students were speaking from conventional wisdom. Living as good, obedient citizens and functionaries of the system, they were reasoning, Christians would earn a limited amount of political capital. Pragmatic budgeting of that capital would not allow for incessant protests against popular political positions, which would merely squander their political resources. Peace and justice might be laudable social dreams, students admitted, but Christians are naive to imagine that the world would live by those values. "I believe those who practice such utter nonsense," one student wrote, "are really hippie flower children that are stuck somewhere back in the sixties." Another student noted that resistance will not change "reality." No one "will listen to simple pleas for mercy. They only respond to power." Thus, John Dear and other Christian resisters, according to some of my students, waste their time and energies fighting social problems. "I suppose I feel sorry for Dear," reflected one student, "because he seems like he is throwing himself at something God Himself has said won't change." Perhaps the most honest example of this save-the-personal-reputation reasoning came when a student confessed: "I think about how that criminal record, albeit minuscule, would only hurt my future chances of employment or achievement. I am just as concerned with making the best of my earthly life and providing for my needs and the needs of others that are important to me. A lengthy criminal background would not benefit my career aspirations." [25]

Where does reasoning like this come from? How do disciples of a scandalous Savior come up with such conformist statements? In their own way, these student comments corroborate what Colman McCarthy had found in his own teaching experience. For over a decade, McCarthy gave a standard quiz to thousands of students. First, he asked them to identify Robert E. Lee, Ulysses S. Grant, Napoleon, Julius Caesar, and Dwight Eisenhower. Typically, the students passed this stage with little difficulty. Then, McCarthy asked students to identify Sojourner Truth, A.J. Muste, Adin Ballou, John Woolman, and Dorothy Day. To date, he has never found a student who could identify the second group of five. [26] Students like McCarthy's and my own, cited above, may be unable to appreciate the call of resistance because the only history they know affirms the hegemony of the Principalities and Powers. If our principal historical actors are agents of the powers-that-be, then "common sense" for us will be "the wisdom of this world."

---

[25] These student comments are in my possession. I intend the use of these quotations neither to denigrate my students, nor to ridicule their positions. These students, like most Lipscomb students, are sincere Christians who are willing to engage in serious discussion, but they often articulate mainstream American Christianity and American values, not the radical historiography that I advocate in this essay.

[26] See Colman McCarthy, *The Universe Bends toward Justice: A Reader on Christian Nonviolence in the U.S.* (Philadelphia: New Society Publishers, 1990): ix, and *I'd Rather Teach Peace* (Maryknoll: Orbis Books, 2002). In a similar vein, how many students enrolled in our Christian colleges and universities could identify the First Amendment, and would the percentages surpass those able to identify the First Commandment? To test this issue myself, one evening I asked my daughters, then 11 and 6, whether they could recite the U.S. "Pledge of Allegiance," which they rattled off with no problem. Then I asked them to say the Lord's Prayer. When neither managed to get very far, I realized my failure to catechize them in a distinctive Christian story.

If we expect Christians to act differently from conventional society—to be transformed people—we must tell them different histories. The "good history" we are acquiring from the academy and accepting as true and normative, is unavoidably forming our identities and defining our actions in ways that are consistent with conventional wisdom. People who think conventionally in a conventional society and desire conventional careers and conventional lives, cannot be God's distinct people, for as long as we continue to recycle the same academy-endorsed conventional history that our conventional colleagues teach in their classes, we shall continue to graduate conventional graduates. As Dorothee Soelle reminded us, "[T]hat would mean to go on dancing to the tunes of the bosses of this world."[27] If we expect Christians to live lives of distinction and resistance, we must have histories that recount not the power and grandeur of victorious domination, but Christianity's peculiar genius. We must have histories that take their cue not from the academy's axioms, but from Christianity's apocalyptic vision.[28]

An Apocalyptic Historiography

In popular parlance, the term "apocalyptic" often implies some schematic for successfully deciphering end-time scenarios encoded in the *Book of Revelation*. Martinus DeBoer has recently illustrated, however, that the Pauline epistles may help us better discern the theological meaning of "apocalyptic." In these letters, for example, Paul announced that God is not absent, waiting off-stage for the right moment to reenter history and set matters aright. God is engaged in the "sovereign action of putting an end to this world-age and replacing it" with God's own dominion. Paul's apocalyptic point, therefore, is that God abrogates human reason and eclipses conventionality. Christ is now "the true nature and destiny" of "*this* age."[29] From the moment of the crucifixion, Elizabeth Johnson concurred, the Cross has been apocalyptically "disorienting the prevailing structures of power and reshaping them in its own image of weakness."[30] For Christians, this abolition of "things as they are" encompasses all of today's existence. Nothing falls outside the apocalyptic rubric inaugurated by Christ's crucifixion and resurrection.

In a similar vein, Gordon Zerbe explained that the apocalyptic theme of Paul's letters is far from politically passive, otherworldly, or even socially conservative. Throughout Paul's writing, to the contrary, an apocalyptic perspective provides unique "modes of reaction and resistance to imperial, colonial, and cultural domination across time and place." Zerbe found in these "millennial moorings" the "true scandal for those who would seek to follow Messiah Jesus." In Paul's teaching, the Cross "unmasks the powers

---

[27] Dorothee Soelle, *The Silent Cry: Mysticism and Resistance* (Minneapolis: Fortress Press, 2001): 230.

[28] Richard T. Hughes, *Reviving the Ancient Faith: The Story of Churches of Christ in America* (Grand Rapids: Eerdmans, 1996): 3, 106-34, and *Reclaiming a Heritage* (Abilene: Abilene Christian University Press, 2002): 8-9, demonstrated that an apocalyptic orientation has been a trademark of the Stone-Campbell tradition. My students were unaware of this aspect of their religious tradition.

[29] Martinus C. DeBoer, "Paul, Theologian of God's Apocalypse," *Interpretation* 56 (January 2002): 21-33.

[30] E. Elizabeth Johnson, "Apocalyptic Family Values," *Interpretation* 56 (January 2002): 35.

and their imperial terror," and creates "solidarity with the lowly."[31] This act of creation in death and resurrection then fulfills what Christiaan Beker purports to be the "central question of the apocalypticist: How to overcome the discrepancy between what is and what should be?"[32] Apocalyptic thinking, far from either accommodating to conventional norms or withdrawing into a-political retreat, inspires an irrepressible conflict with the powers-that-be.[33]

As Stanley Hauerwas and Jeff Powell have warned, a contrary acquiescence to "the *non*apocalyptic vision of reality" is the conventional Christian view that "dominates American public life" and "tempts American Christians to accept the inevitability and thus the goodness of things as they are."[34] A radical apocalyptic in our time, therefore, must incite an epistemological crisis. For Christians to appreciate the genius of God's apocalyptic action, "the church must precede the world epistemologically," and refuse, as Phil Kenneson explained, to "engage the world on the world's terms."[35] Or as Hauerwas and Powell have argued, apocalyptics must become the "epistemological prerequisite for [authentically] understanding *how things are*."[36]

Establishing the apocalyptic epistemological privilege—or what John Milbank has called "metanarrative realism"—has been a primary emphasis in his lament over the tendency among Christians both to borrow their history from the Principalities and to subordinate their "reality" to the intellectual canons of the Powers. Christians must invert that relationship. Milbank proclaimed that "theology itself will have to provide its own account of the final causes at work in human history, on the basis of its own particular, and historically specific, faith." Milbank explained: "The Church is *already*, necessarily, by virtue of its institution, a 'reading' of other societies." God's dominion

---

[31] Gordon Zerbe, "The Politics of Paul: His Supposed Social Conservatism and the Impact of Postcolonial Readings." *The Conrad Grebel Review* 21 (winter 2003): 86.

[32] J. Christiaan Beker, *Paul's Apocalyptic Gospel: The Coming Triumph of God* (Philadelphia: Fortress Press, 1982): 30.

[33] What is often mistakenly seen as political passivity among the apocalyptic is better understood as "antipolitical politics." Robert Inchausti praises Dorothy Day, Thomas Merton, Martin Luther King, Jr., E.F. Schumacher, and Wendell Berry as representatives of this countercultural antipolitical political activism. See Robert Inchausti, *Subversive Orthodoxy: Outlaws, Revolutionaries, and Other Christians in Disguise* (Grand Rapids: Brazos Press, 2005): 83-127.

[34] Stanley Hauerwas and Jeff Powell, "Creation as Apocalyptic: Homage to William Stringfellow," in *Radical Christian and Exemplary Lawyer*, Andrew McThenia, Jr., ed. (Grand Rapids: Eerdmans, 1995): 40.

[35] Phil Kenneson, *Beyond Sectarianism: Re-Imagining Church and World* (Harrisburg: Trinity Press International, 1999): 97 and 33.

[36] Hauerwas and Powell (1995): 37. Hauerwas subsequently elaborated on his understanding by noting that the essence of "apocalyptic" is not found in some forthcoming "imminent crisis," but in what "has happened in Christ." Therefore, Christians cannot withdraw from the complexities of the contemporary life, but "must carry on with the small acts of kindness and mercy that are made possible by our conviction that God has redeemed the world. Such a conviction is the background of my oft-made claim that Christians are called to nonviolence not because we think nonviolence is a strategy to rid the world of war, but rather in a world of war, as faithful followers of Christ, we cannot imagine being anything other than nonviolent." Stanley Hauerwas, *Performing the Faith: Bonhoeffer and the Practice of Nonviolence* (Grand Rapids: Brazos Books, 2004): 235-6.

provides the exclusive lens by which disciples discern both what really has been, is, and should be. "The mission of the church is to tell again the Christian mythos, pronounce again the Christian logos, and call again for the Christian praxis in a manner that restores their freshness and originality. It must articulate Christian difference in such a fashion as to make it strange." The apocalyptic orientation equips and enables Christians to think and act from their own distinctive axiomatic principles. All claims to knowledge are based, therefore, on the "interruption of history by Christ and his bride, the Church." It is "a gigantic claim," Milbank admitted, that the church can and should "read, criticize, and say what is going on" in all other societies from the position that the church is *the exemplary* form of human community. Nevertheless, this principle captures the meaning of "apocalyptic" and the church as an *altera civitas*. The gospel is "not just different, but *the* difference from all other cultural systems."[37] To comply with, or operate by the axioms of, the culture's conventionalities in the face of God's *what should be* is to impede the progress of God's dominion.[38]

The point here is that Christianity's epistemological orientation is peculiarly apocalyptic. "Unsurpassed and unsurpassable," Douglas Harink notes, "there is no reality, no historical or mythical figure, no system, framework, idea, or anything else that transcends the reality of Jesus Christ." To profess that "Jesus is Lord," is to confess that the Jesus, who smashed history's natural evolution, is indeed the final, once-for-all Truth, and that, moreover, Christ today continues to efface competing truth claims and knowledges. An apocalyptic world view is a "totalizing" theology, Harink rightly concluded, leaving

---

[37] John Milbank, *Theology and Social Theory: Beyond Secular Reason* (Oxford: Blackwell, 1993): 380-8. As Vernon Eller, *Christian Anarchy: Jesus' Primacy Over the Powers* (Grand Rapids: Eerdmans Publishing Company, 1987): 179, argued that the Christian operates on an utterly different level, and thus meaningful discourse within society's political, economic, and cultural arena is generally futile. Recall Jesus before Pilate, Eller encouraged, to see a classic example of the inverted relationship between "Christ" and "culture." Although Pilate presumed to act as the sane, rational political principal in this encounter, from the perspective of the church, Pilate was actually devoid of real power.

[38] From a lifetime of eloquent writing, Thomas Merton, "A Devout Meditation in Memory of Adolf Eichmann," in *Raids on the Unspeakable* (New York: New Directions, 1964): 45-49, offered a concrete example of this apocalyptic perspective when he questioned the sanity of egotistic nation-states. At Adolf Eichmann's trial, for example, psychiatrists attested to the former Nazi leader's "sanity," which led Merton to ponder the implications. He found the gravity of such a psychiatric evaluation less in what was said about Eichmann than in the judgment it pronounced on the sanity of conventional wisdom. Is something not learned about a world in which the history of mass murder is not accidental but intentional? "It begins to dawn on us," Merton noted, "that it is precisely the *sane* ones who are the most dangerous. It is the sane ones, the well-adapted ones, who can without qualms and without nausea aim the missiles and press the buttons that will initiate the great festival of destruction that they, *the sane ones*, have prepared…. No one suspects the sane, and the sane ones will have perfectly good reasons, logical, well-adjusted reasons, for firing the shot." In view of humanity's history of mass murder, "The worst error," he concluded, "is to imagine that a Christian must try to be 'sane' like everybody else, that we *belong* in our kind of society. That we must be 'realistic' about it." In a world ordered by conventional wisdom, perhaps the "worst insanity is to be totally 'sane.'"

"no reserve of space or time or concept or aspect of creation outside of or beyond or undetermined by the critical, decisive, and final action of God in Jesus Christ."[39]

Consequently, the apocalyptic cannot help but be "an offense to the modern mind," averred Walter Lowe: "By its very nature, it contradicts the assumption of diachronic continuity without which both the procedures of historical research and the promise of future progress are null and void."[40] Consistent apocalyptic interpretation of ordinary reality will turn Christian historians into people unsettling to the academy. Apocalyptics and nonapocalyptics simply cannot agree on "good" history because their epistemologies are antithetical. Accepting God's scandalous incursion into events, and the eclipse of conventionality, apocalyptic thinking shatters one of the academy's foremost axioms—a presumed cause-and-effect timeline intelligible to the natural, unaided mind. What passes as "good" historical narration, therefore, must simply be different, depending on one's apocalyptic or non-apocalyptic perspective.

Moreover—and this point is crucial—the real impact of apocalyptic thought is not merely or even primarily intellectual (i.e., epistemological or apologetic). The tangible and material "apocalyptic sting," as Johann Baptist Metz noted, is found in the "apocalyptic praxis of imitating Christ."[41] Precisely because the cause and sequence of events is under the control of God and not as it might "naturally" appear, Christians are enabled to strive to incarnate the scandalous ethics of Jesus. When God is not part of the historical process, conventional realism makes perfect, or common, sense. But now, as Christians believe, that God's dominion is the central motif of history, apocalyptic realism makes common sense. A synonym for this apocalyptic praxis is Justo Gonzalez's phrase "incarnate marginality," which means touching the "lepers," eating with the "unclean," listening to women, and championing the "unwanted." "We must affirm," Gonzalez dares, "that the proper place for those who follow Jesus Christ is the margin rather than the center; it is the valley rather than the hilltop; it is the cross rather than the throne."[42] In other words, the apocalyptic sting occurs when disciples implement the axioms of God's dominion by incarnating nonviolent *agape* love (self-sacrificial reconciliation and inclusion of alien others) and privileging the disinherited. Because of this world's realism, "the world will think you an idiot for trusting God more than men or idols," William Stringfellow warned.[43] Nevertheless, because Christian apocalyptic realism takes its cue from Christ's self-immolating *kenosis*, his church needs histories that help catechize disciples for their own self-abnegation.

A friend seeking greater clarity about God's apocalyptic presence in this world, asked: "Would 'Christian military narratives,' then, be on 'how to lose a war?' Would 'Christian

---

[39] Douglas Harink, *Paul among the Postliberals* (Grand Rapids: Brazos Press, 2003): 68-9.

[40] Walter Lowe, "Prospects for a Postmodern Christian Theology: Apocalyptic Without Reserve," *Modern Theology* 15 (January 1999): 18.

[41] Johann Baptist Metz, *Faith in History and Society: Toward a Practical Fundamental Theology* (New York: Seabury Press, 1980): 73-4 and 169-79.

[42] Justo L. Gonzalez, *The Changing Shape of Church History* (St. Louis: Chalice Press, 2002): 153. Earlier (114) Gonzalez correctly attributes the loss of "the countercultural and even subversive nature of early Christianity" to the misguided historical narration of historians in the tradition of Eusebius of Caesarea.

[43] William Stringfellow, *Free in Obedience: The Radical Christian Life* (New York: Seabury Press, 1964): 47.

economic narratives,' similarly, be on 'how to become poor?'" The short answer to his questions is "Yes." Emerging out of Christianity's apocalyptic logic, radical Christian scholarship would teach disciples not how to dominate, but how to die. A scandalous historiography would inspire Christians not to take power, but to volunteer for poverty. Admittedly, these are hard concepts to get our minds around. Allow me to illustrate.

A few years ago I asked a U.S. History survey class to consider the possibility that Cold War policy remade the U.S. into something other than Americans intended or even desired. Toward that end, I asked students for their reactions to the following quotation from William Stringfellow:

> The practical ending of the Second World War in the surrender to the Allied Powers of Nazi Germany, and then Japan, was morally inconclusive. As a defeat for, or destruction of, totalitarianism or of the reliance upon war, brutality, deception, fear, or other forms of physical or psychological violence characteristic of totalitarianism, it accomplished little or nothing. Although militarily and territorially, America and the Allies won the war, little more can be claimed. It has lately been evidenced, ruefully, that economically the war was no victory for the United States. It has been increasingly evident since 1945, that morally the demonic spirit incarnate in the Axis powers won the war. The illusion has been that, in the aftermath of the Second World War, America has succeeded British imperialism and French colonialism in the world, but the truth is that America succeeded Nazi Germany. That is to say, the ethos of Nazism, the mentality of Nazism, the social ethic of Nazism survives, prospers, and more and more prevails in the specific American versions—not literally identical to the particulars of Nazism, but nonetheless having the same moral identity as Nazism—which can be symbolized and summarized in three words: *war, racism, genocide*.... What, then, must be said of the Second World War? The very magnitude and versatility of the power of death incarnate in Nazi Germany and the heavy and urgent reliance upon that very same power of death in prosecuting war against Nazism would seem enough to edify human beings that death is the only possible victor in *any* war, that from a human point of view there are no glorious wars—no wars which humanize, no wars of salvation, no just wars.[44]

Although most student reactions were so academically sterile as not to offend, one student was blisteringly clear. "This William Stringfellow needs to be taken out of the United States and shot," he exclaimed. My student was outraged that anyone—especially a so-called "Christian"—would connect the United States and Nazi Germany. However, his frustration with Stringfellow went deeper. "To say that there is no such thing as a just war is pure stupidity at work. The Bible says 'an eye for an eye.' It is the United States' civil duty to protect itself.... God has delivered our enemies into our hands. People who lash out against war are anti-patriotic, and they hurt this great nation and what it stands for!"[45]

Like the other students already cited, this student's reaction illustrates what happens when Christians have a historical narrative that operates out of the epistemology of the

---

[44] William Stringfellow, *An Ethic for Christians and Other Aliens in A Strange Land* (Waco: Word Books, 1973): 125.

[45] This student paper, like the ones cited above, is in my possession.

Principalities and the realism of the Powers. While Stringfellow operated from an apocalyptic reality, the standard U.S. history narrative served as this student's primary "operating system." Without a contrasting historical narrative informed by the apocalyptic certainties of the Christian *kerygma*, Christians fill the void in their search for certainty with the realism of the powers-that-be. Thus, the culture's power of domination, rather than God's dominion and the apocalyptic power of self-sacrifice, comes to define "common sense."

Christians, if they are going to follow the Crucified and glory in the Cross as Paul did, need histories that subvert this-worldly power and defy death. "What a strange prescription is this," Walter Wink confessed, "that offers release from the power of death by the power of dying."[46] Invariably, conventional wisdom will ask some variant of the "will-it-work" question. In other words, conventional realists rhetorically ask whether we need a more pragmatic historiography, one that will help us survive in our Machiavellian world.[47] The short answer this time is "No." Because we have a faith that calls us to die, we need a historiography that can teach us how to get killed. "Folks who are determined enough to hold on to unlimited love usually wind up on a cross, like Jesus," warned Clarence Jordan.

> Their goods get plundered and they get slandered. Persecution is their lot. Surely nobody would be inclined to call this practical. Yet in its final stages, unlimited love seems to be the only thing that can possibly make any sense. Crucifixions have a way of being followed by resurrections. Only one who is foolish enough to lose one's life, finds it. It is the grain of wheat that falls into the ground and dies, that lives. Jesus didn't tell his followers to love their enemies because love would work, or would not work…. Christians are at the complete mercy of their enemies, since by complete surrender to the divine will they no longer have the freedom to cease being what they are. Bound by this higher loyalty, the argument of practicality is irrelevant.[48]

As apocalyptic realists, nevertheless, we have secured our lives with the Easter guarantee that the realities of God's dominion are coming to fruition through history, precisely by means of voluntary suffering and death rather than through domination and control. Although conventional political science ridicules such weakness as suicidal and irresponsible, Wink sensed that a "whole host of people [is] simply waiting for the Christian message to challenge them, for once, to a heroism worthy of their lives."[49]

---

[46] Walter Wink, *The Powers That Be: Theology for a New Millennium* (New York: Doubleday, 1998): 93.

[47] Undoubtedly one of the boldest of such calls comes from Robert Kaplan, *Warrior Politics: Why Leadership Demands a Pagan Ethos* (New York: Random House, 2002): 36, who argued, "Livy shows that the vigor it takes to face our adversaries must ultimately come from pride in our own past and our achievements. Romanticizing our past is something to be cultivated, rather than to be ashamed of."

[48] Clarence Jordan, *Sermon on the Mount* (Valley Forge: Judson Press, 1952): 48-9.

[49] Walter Wink, *Violence and Nonviolence in South Africa: Jesus' Third Way* (Philadelphia: New Society Publishers, 1987): 34 and 69. Wink noted a few pages later, "It takes far more courage to walk into a situation voluntarily, knowing that suffering is inevitable, choosing to draw the poison of that violence with one's own body rather than perpetuating the downward spiral of hate. But that is what we celebrate in every Eucharist as Jesus' way." (72)

I suspect that Wink is correct because I, too, am aware of Christians ready to give their lives to subvert the powers-that-be. Again, however, we need a body of resistance literature that will help us justify—even if only to ourselves—the quest to incarnate marginality.[50] We know that the Christian *kerygma* was originally of, for, and by persecuted individuals. Now we need narrative support to become persecuted individuals again—to cast our lot with the colonized, conquered, or otherwise disinherited. But, I must ask, can professional historiographers of "good" history help relocate us to these hated margins of society? Is there anything that Marsden or most other professional Christian historians are writing that will get us ready to be persecuted?[51] Do they tell the story of history in a way that inspires us to die in the cause of resisting the powers-that-be? Do we not, rather, in the process of pursuing good, conventional history, become sycophants of the status quo?

Lesslie Newbigin has rightly challenged that "the place of the church is not in the seats of the establishment but in the camps and marching columns of the protesters.... [Just] as Jesus was crucified outside the walls of the city, so the place of the Christian must always be outside the citadel of the establishment and on the side of its victim. *Only from this position will things be seen as they truly are.*"[52] If, as Christian scholars, we are pursuing that apocalyptic truth, will we make progress professionally inside the halls of academe with its conferences and university presses, or apocalyptically on the world's trash heaps with society's disinherited?[53]

---

[50] Stanley Hauerwas, "The Politics of Witness: How We Educate Christians in Liberal Societies," in *After Christendom?* (Nashville: Abingdon Press, 1991): 133-52, noted: "If we are to educate as Christians we cannot fail to introduce our children and one another to the gospel in a manner that helps us name those powers that would determine our lives. The only way to do that is by telling a counter story to the commonly accepted story of the United States and/or its correlative presumptions that underwrite the necessity of what we call the nation-state system [and all other Principalities and Powers]. The moral and intellectual courage required for the task is great. Indeed, we cannot pretend to possess such courage on our own but we can only hope to fulfill that mission, as we would anticipate from the story itself, by being part of a community that can help sustain such witness." Essentially the same essay also appears under the title "On Witnessing Our Story: Christian Education in Liberal Societies," in *Schooling Christians: "Holy Experiments" in American Education,* Stanley Hauerwas and John Westerhoff, eds. (Grand Rapids: Eerdmans, 1992): 214-34.

[51] George Marsden, "The Soul of the American University: An Historical Overview," in *The Secularization of the Academy*, George Marsden and Bradley Longfield, eds. (New York: Oxford University Press, 1992): 31, and Marsden (1975): 40-48; George Marsden, "The Soul of the American University: An Historical Overview," in *The Secularization of the Academy*, George Marsden and Bradley Longfield, eds. (New York: Oxford University Press, 1992): 31; and Marsden (1975): 40-48, following the lead of the Cold Warrior and realist, Reinhold Niebuhr, suggested that history written by Christians should be tentative in assessments. Marsden, therefore, substituted irony and tragedy in the place of the apocalyptic.

[52] Lesslie Newbigin, *Foolishness to the Greeks: The Gospel and Western Culture* (Grand Rapids: Eerdmans, 1986): 125 (emphasis added).

[53] Although not coming from a theologically informed perspective, Dipesh Chakrabarty has warned "So long as one operates within the discourse of 'history' produced at the institutional site of the university" the past will continue to serve the oppressive powers-that-be—in particular, nation-states. "Nation states have the capacity to enforce their truth games, and universities, their critical distance notwithstanding, are part of the battery of institutions complicit in this process."

How to Write History in the Apocalyptic Mode

On one level, George Marsden is right: All research topics should be open to Christian historians. Nothing about the Christian faith restricts our choice of studies to some list of "sanctified subjects." Apocalyptic Christian historians, for example, are not limited to writing histories of pacifism. Christian historians, therefore, might teach and write on the U.S. Constitutional Convention, or the rise of Mao Zedong in Chinese history. Nevertheless, as Robert Brinlow counseled: "There is only one calling we should recognize—discipleship—and one vocation—to follow Jesus." Christianity "is a life that refuses to be defined by the categories of this world, but by the categories of the Kingdom of God."[54] Because of our apocalyptic realism, any attempt on the part of Christians to narrate history must be undertaken with the explicit purpose of subverting conventional ideology of domination, whether of the U.S., E.U., Chinese, or any other Principality or Power, that does not bow its knee to the Crucified. The pedagogical purpose in studying the U.S. Constitution or Chinese Communism is to expose and demythologize these as illegitimate powers that desire to seduce individuals to their allegiance.[55] Whatever project the Christian historian chooses, by contrast, the didactic motives of God's dominion must be paramount. A Christian, for example, might produce a military history; nevertheless, from an apocalyptic perspective, while that history might be "accurate," it cannot be "good" unless its author was seeking to subvert the logic that supports the very existence of militarism.

Fleshing out this iconoclastic vocation, Will Campbell envisioned a distinctively Christian education that would celebrate the radical revolution of conscience. A history class headed by this kind of teacher would not "teach to the test" but towards personal transformation:

> [This kind of Christian educator] makes it impossible to "study" war or racism or the New Testament and come away the same person, impossible to study physics or chemistry and not dedicate one's career to opposing their enslavement to the horrors of 20th-century technological inhumanity, impossible to study money and banking and come away lighthearted at what our economics have done to those who originally had property rights to the land which supports us so richly, and to those whom we purchased as chattel and continue to treat as such. [56]

Bluntly stated, Campbell argued that Christian colleges and their faculties ought never to justify their expensive tuition with the "cheap trick of trying to put 'Christ in the classroom.'"

See Dipesh Chakrabarty, "Postcoloniality and the Artifice of History," in *The Post-Colonial Studies Reader*, Bill Ashcroft, Gareth Griffiths, and Helen Tiffin, eds. (London: Routledge, 1995): 383-8.

[54] Robert Brinlow, *Paganism and the Professions* (Chicago: The Ekklesia Project, 2001). See also Robert W. Brimlow, "Who Invited Mammon?: Professional Education in the Christian College and University," in *Conflicting Allegiances*: 156-70.

[55] On the topic of the U.S. Constitution, Michael Parenti's *Democracy for the Few* provides iconoclastic support. See especially the chapter "A Constitution for the Few." Likewise, James Juhnke and Carol Hunter undermine the popular perception of the American Revolution as a "just war." See their chapter, "The Holiest War on Record: War for Independence" in *The Missing Peace: The Search for Nonviolent Alternatives in United States History* (Kitchener: Pandora Press, 2001): 35-52.

[56] Will D. Campbell and James Y. Holloway, *Up to Our Steeples in Politics* (Mahwah, New Jersey: Paulist Press, 1970): 142.

A peculiarly *Christian* approach, in other words, would not try to "graft Christ" either onto a profession already defined by the maxims of the Principalities and Powers or onto an academic product conformed to the intellectual conventionalities of society.

Affirming Campbell's point, Michael Budde lamented: "Too often we think we know what a college or university is—with the usual range of departments, majors, programs, services, and students—and that the object of the exercise is in trying to establish a Christian knock-off of the same." To the extent that Christian scholars perpetuate this mistake, we "remain a prisoner of received notions that oblige would-be innovators to replicate the institutional wherewithal of 'good' colleges and universities as defined by non-Christian norms, structures and ends."[57]

Whatever context we find ourselves in, historians operating out of Christianity's apocalyptic realism should be open to the indictment of political and academic treason, if not outright nonviolent "terrorism."[58] The "we" in Christian historiography should no longer make sense to an academy, a nation, or any institution whose allegiance is to the conventional wisdom of racial partiality, gender discrimination, class inequity, and national triumph. Christian historians should be first in line to expose any national executive's attempt to drum-up the war gods of popular support. Christian historians should work to make imperialistic appeals to history and "our way of life" ring hollow and shameful. Christian historians should be the scholars who expose patriotism as fundamentally the same logic as racism. If we are going to deliver the "apocalyptic sting" by, in part, writing subversive narratives for seditious communities, Christian historians could take a small, necessary first step by engaging in professional nonconformity and disobedience. The world that God so loves needs historians who help sustain the church in its uncompromising, unending, antagonistic resistance to the Principalities and Powers.

---

[57] Michael Budde, "Assessing What Doesn't Exist: Reflections on the Impact of an Ecclesially Based University," in Budde and Wright (2004): 256. Budde and Robert Brimlow, *Christianity Incorporated: How Big Business is Buying the Church* (Grand Rapids: Brazos Press, 2002): 11, decry the tendency of Christian scholars to become "chaplains" of the powers-that-be. "In order for chaplains to understand, serve, and empathize with persons who lead and serve such powerful institutions, chaplains must themselves submit to the formative processes (physical, emotional, affective, and spiritual) of the institutions.... The assumption that such intensive formation leaves the gospel untouched seems entirely insupportable. Instead, in deciding to serve the 'principalities and powers' (Eph 3:10 RSV) on their own turf, the gospel becomes trimmed to conform to the requisites of these principalities and powers."

[58] Stanley Hauerwas, "The Nonviolent Terrorist: In Defense of Christian Fanaticism," in Michael Budde and Walter Brimlow, eds., *The Church as Counterculture* (Albany, New York: SUNY Press, 2000): 103, defining the church's apocalyptic realism, argued that it, "like many terrorist organizations, can be understood as an international conspiracy against all politics based on 'self-preservation.'"

CHRIST OUR PASSOVER HAS BEEN SACRIFICED: REFLECTIONS ON THE LIFE OF CHRIST AS REPRESENTED IN THE CALENDARS AND LITURGIES OF THE WESTERN CHURCH[1]

CHRISTOPHER BRYAN

I am delighted to offer these reflections in honor of my dear friend and colleague, Don Haymes. "A faithful friend," says the Scripture, "is a strong defense," and I have experienced Don as a man truly faithful: faithful to God and faithful to his friends.

The 1979 *Book of Common Prayer* of the Episcopal Church (hereinafter: *BCP*)[2] notes that "all Sundays of the year are feasts of our Lord Jesus Christ,"[3] but we could press the matter further. All Christian worship on any day and at any time commemorates Christ. Hence a mark of all Christian liturgies–Eastern or Western; Roman, Anglican, or Protestant–is or ought to be a continuing acknowledgment of God's grace to us in Christ's life, death, and exaltation. Indeed, because all Christian worship commemorates Christ, some have argueed argued that the church should not call specific occasions "feasts of Christ" at all, lest we seem to deny Christ's universal presence and sovereignty. On the other hand, St. Paul allowed Christians the choice to keep any day as holy: "If someone keeps certain days as holier than others, and someone else considers all days to be equally holy, each must be left free to hold his own opinion. The one who observes special days does so in honor of the Lord." (Rm 14:5)

In my experience, most people need focal points in time as well as place at which to concentrate on what is important to them. Just as we love our spouses, children, and friends all the time, still we celebrate special events—birthdays, anniversaries—to remind us of our love and to intensify it. The New Testament without comment holds a record of the tendency of Christians to focus their worship on a special day, the first day of the week, the day of the Resurrection, "the Lord's day" (Ac 20:7, 1 Cor 16:2, Rv. 1:10[4]

---

[1] One might write this essay in the light of the rites of the Eastern churches and come to similar conclusions. I, however, am most familiar with the Western liturgical tradition, and primarily its Anglican forms.

[2] *The Book of Common Prayer and Administration of the Sacraments and Other Rites and Ceremonies of the Episcopal Church Together with The Psalter or Psalms of David According to the Use of the Episcopal Church* (New York: The Church Hymnal Corporation, 1979).

[3] *BCP* 16.

[4] While the intention of *hē kuriakē hemera* "the Lord's Day" (Rev 1: 10) to signify Sunday is not absolutely certain, it remains the most likely interpretation: see Wilfred J. Harrington, O.P., "Revelation," *Sacra Pagina* 16 (Collegeville, Minnesota, 1993): 50; M. Eugene Boring, *Revelation*

compare *Didache* 14.1), but many Jewish Christians continued to worship God on the Sabbath (the seventh day) and according to the liturgical calendar of the Jerusalem Temple. St. Paul himself took part in Temple worship when he was in Jerusalem, and the first-generation Church of Jerusalem worshiped in the Temple for as long as it stood (until 70 A.D., when the Romans destroyed it). The point is this: The principle of keeping special days is both permitted and established in the Early Church. Hence the overwhelming majority of Christians in all denominations over the centuries have appointed throughout the year particular commemorations of the events of Christ's life. In the words of Richard Hooker:

> The sanctification of dayes and times is a token of that thankfullnes and a part of that publique honor which we owe to God for admirable benefites,...but the daies which are chosen out to serve as publique memorials of such his mercies ought to be clothed with those outward robes of holines whereby theire difference from other dayes maie be made sensible... This is the daie which the Lord hath made saith the prophet David, *Let us rejoice and be glad in it.*[5]

The Jewish festival of *Shabuot* (the Feast of Weeks or Pentecost) was early associated by Christians with the gift of the Spirit (see Ac 2:1-42). Similarly, Christians came in time to associate the Jewish *Pesach* (Passover)[6] with the celebration of the Resurrection—an association manifest not only in the re-interpreted Exodus traditions that dominate every strand of Easter liturgy[7] but also by the connection of the name of the festival (in almost every language except English)[8] with the Aramaic word for the Passover, *Pascha*: for example, Italian *Pasqua* (Easter) = *Pasqua degli Ebrei* (Passover).

Subsequently, various other events of Christ's life were commemorated on other days, such as the Ascension on the fortieth day after Easter (following the chronological hint in Acts 1:3), the birth of Christ on December 25, the Annunciation to Mary nine months earlier on March 25, the Birth of John the Baptist (six months earlier) on June 24,

---

(Louisville: John Press, 1989): 82; Thomas J. Talley, *The Origins of the Liturgical Year* (New York: Pueblo Publishing, 1986): 13-18.

[5] Richard Hooker, *Of the Laws of Ecclesiastical Polity* 5.70.1, 2, in W. Speed Hill, ed., *The Folger Library Edition of the Works of Richard Hooker,* vol. 2 (Cambridge, Massachusetts/London, England: The Belknap Press of Harvard University Press, 1977): 363.

[6] The original meaning of *pesach* is uncertain. In the Hebrew Bible it is used to speak of the Angel of Death passing over the houses of the Hebrews, which had been marked with the blood of the sacrificed lambs (Ex 12:1-28); so it is translated "Passover."

[7] A connection between Easter and Passover had probably been made as early as the time when the New Testament books were being composed. See Ellen Bradshaw Aitken, *The Morphology of the Passion Narrative* (D. Phil. Thesis, Harvard University, September 1997), but see my reservations in note 69.

[8] The English word "Easter" needs no apology. Its associations with Eostra, Goddess of Dawn (whose symbol was the fleet and mysterious hare, now ludicrously degenerated into the Easter bunny), are not inappropriate for the festival of Christ's resurrection. "At night Christ was born, a light in darkness; noonday turned to night when Christ suffered and died on the Cross. But in the dawn of Easter morning, Christ rose in victory from the grave... The early morning belongs to the Church of the risen Christ." Dietrich Bonhoeffer, *Life Together,* John W. Doberstein, trans. (New York: Harper and Row, 1954): 40.

and the Presentation of Christ in the Temple on February 2 (the appropriate number of days after the birth of the boy).

The calendar of the *BCP*[9] is broadly typical of the pattern that has become characteristic of churches in Europe, the British Isles, and America.[10] This calendar names among "Principal Feasts" the following that celebrate specific events of our Lord's incarnation, passion, and exaltation: Christmas Day, The Epiphany, Easter Day, and Ascension Day.[11] In addition, the following are also referred to as "feasts of our Lord": The Holy Name, The Presentation, The Annunciation, The Visitation, Saint John the Baptist, The Transfiguration, and Holy Cross Day.[12] To these one might add the First Sunday after Epiphany, which in all three years of the *Lectionary* cycle recalls our Lord's baptism; the First Sunday in Lent, which in all three years is a memorial of his temptation in the wilderness; and the Last Sunday after Epiphany, which, also in all three years, provides a second memorial of the transfiguration. Taken together with the major days of Holy Week (Palm Sunday, Maundy Thursday, Good Friday, and Holy Saturday) commemoration of these special days amounts virtually to a "Life of Christ" acted out in the church throughout the year.

Such an acted-out "life" is different from the romantic "Lives of Jesus" in nineteenth-century Liberal-Protestant biblical criticism, and from the reductionist modern quests for the so-called "historical Jesus"[13] undertaken by scholars such as John Dominic Crossan, John P. Meier, and N. T. Wright.[14] The "life" of Jesus throughout the Church's year is also different from the "Lives" of Jesus, basically Greco-Roman biographies in form, that are presented by the canonical Gospels.[15] The Church's "life of Christ" celebrated in worship is, nonetheless, parallel in at least two ways to the "Lives of Christ" presented in the four Gospels.

First, the liturgical "life" as enactment and presentation is, at least in its public aspect, a reflection on the *public* acts and career of its subject, as is the case in a Greco-Roman biographical "life"), rather than a study of inner life and motivations in the

---

[9] *BCP* 19-30.

[10] See *The Alternative Service Book 1980* (Cambridge, England: Cambridge University Press / Colchester: William Clowes / London: S.P.C.K., 1980): 15-25; *Lutheran Book of Worship* (Minneapolis: Augsburg / Philadelphia: Lutheran Church in America, 1978): 9-12; *The Revised Common Lectionary* (Nashville: Abingdon, 1992): 21-24; *The Roman Missal, Revised by Decree of the Second Vatican Council and Published by Authority of Pope Paul VI* (1973): 72-81.

[11] *BCP* 15.

[12] *BCP* 16.

[13] By "historical Jesus," I mean the "Jesus" whom we can, at least in principle, recover and examine by using the tools of modern historical research, as does John P. Meier, *A Marginal Jew: Rethinking the Historical Jesus*, vol. 1: *The Roots of the Problem and the Person* (New York: Doubleday, 1991): 21–40.

[14] John Dominic Crossan, *The Historical Jesus: The Life of a Mediterranean Jewish Peasant* (New York: HarperSanFrancisco, 1991); John P. Meier (1991); N. T. Wright, *Christian Origins and the Question of God*, vol. 2: *Jesus and the Victory of God* (London: S.P.C.K. /Minneapolis: Fortress Press, 1996).

[15] On the canonical gospels as examples of the Greco-Roman genre *bios/vita* (i.e., a "life"), see Richard Burridge, *What Are the Gospels?: A Comparison with Graeco-Roman Biography.* SNTS Monograph Series 70 (Cambridge, England: Cambridge University Press, 1992); also Christopher Bryan, *Preface to Mark: Notes on the Gospel in Its Literary and Cultural Settings* (New York: Oxford University Press, 1993): 3-64, and literature there cited.

manner of modern biography.[16] Second and, again, much like a Greco-Roman "life," a liturgical life of Jesus focuses a great deal on the events, manner, and significance of the *death* of its subject. In the ancient view, how and why a hero died told a great deal about who that hero really was. Nearly half of these commemorations focus on our Lord's passion, and all but two of them (Good Friday and Holy Saturday) are celebrated within the context of the Eucharist: "This do in memory of me"—as the *BCP* emphasizes, "the principal act of Christian worship on the Lord's Day and other major Feasts."[17] And as St. Paul pointed out, the Eucharist is by its nature a proclamation of Christ's death (1 Cor 11:26). So it is that under this discipline of the cross, even Christmas—which we all love to sentimentalize—plunges us towards Calvary. "The holly bears a berry," we sing, "as red as any blood"—and we all know whose blood we mean. If we do not remember, the "Great Thanksgiving" that follows in the liturgy will surely remind us.

The liturgical "Life of Christ" of which we are speaking is, then, a construct arising in unceasing dialogue and proclamation from almost two millennia of faith and joy. Three questions about this proclamation of Christ's "life" in our worship require consideration: Our commemorations of Christ's "life" normally take place in the context of the eucharistic Lord's Supper: Why do we do it that way? What is the calendar and pattern of the "life of Christ" as presented by the Church through these commemorations? What is the theological *significance* of the Church's focusing so much of its devotion on the specific events of Christ's life and death rather than on "timeless truths" (so to speak), as is the case in the early alternative to a Gospel, the *Gospel of Thomas*?

Commemorations of Christ and the Eucharistic Celebration

Christian insistence on celebrating the festivals of Christ in the context of the Eucharist is important not only because the Eucharist points us to Christ's death but also because of the words that Jesus himself spoke about the celebration of his death. According to Sts. Luke and Paul, Jesus added to his words of interpretation at the Last Supper as a "rubric" (that is, a direction for worship): "Do this in remembrance of me (*eis tēn emēn anamnēsin*" Lk 22:19, 1 Cor 11:24). Although this rubric has been omitted from the Markan version of the tradition, that omission is not hard to explain. As Paul Benoit observed, "*On ne récite pas une rubrique, on l'exécute*"—"One does not repeat a rubric, one obeys it."[18] The Early Church ate and drank in memory of Christ because he had asked his disciples to do so.

What would the first Christians have understood by such a "remembrance?" Current discussion of ways in which biblical words for "remembrance" are to be understood is

---

[16] See Bryan (1993): 42-47, 63. This distinction between modern "biography" and the Greco-Roman *bios/vita* as it developed before and after the first century of our era is one reason that I prefer to avoid the word "biography" altogether in speaking of the older genre. The Greek word *biographia*) is, as far as I know, nowhere evidenced in the extant literature before the fifth century A.D.

[17] *BCP* 13.

[18] Pierre Benoit, "Le récit de la Cène dans Lc. XXII, 15-20: Étude de critique textuelle et littéraire," *Revue Biblique* 48 (1939): 386.

lively and complicated, and can hardly be summarized here.[19] I believe that "in remembrance of me" ("for my remembrance") derived from Jewish tradition and comprised at least two ideas: that *God* should remember, and that *God's people* should remember.[20] Of these, the former—that God should remember—is the more difficult for us, now, to grasp.[21] Difficult or not, it is plainly present in biblical texts. After Noah's Flood, for example, God declared: "I set my bow in the cloud, and it shall be for a token of the covenant between me and the earth…. *and I will remember my covenant*, which is between me and you and every living creature of all flesh…. " (Gn 9:13-15) Here, as elsewhere, when God "remembers" something or someone, God acts—or, in this case, refrains from acting—in judgment and grace (compare Gn 19:29, 30:22-24; Ex 2:24-3:8, 6:5-8). According to the Targum, Abraham prayed that God should remember Isaac's offering of himself on behalf of Israel, and that God would *act* by delivering Israel: "And now, when his sons are in the hour of affliction, remember the binding of their father, Isaac, and listen to the voice of their supplication and hear them and deliver them from

---

[19] Joachim Jeremias, *The Eucharistic Words of Jesus* (Oxford: Basil Blackwell, 1949, 1955): 59-65, is foundational. See also Louis-Marie Chauvet, *Symbol and Sacrament: A Sacramental Reinterpretation of Christian Existence;* Patrick Madigan, S.J., and Madeleine Beaumont, trans. (Collegeville, Minnesota: The Liturgical Press, 1987, 1995): 229-65, 275-89; Paul F. Bradshaw, *The Search for the Origins of Christian Worship: Sources and Methods for the Study of Early Liturgy* (New York: Oxford University Press, 1992): 15-17; David N. Power, O.M.I., *The Eucharistic Mystery: Revitalizing the Tradition* (New York: Crossroad, 1992): 42-51; Fritz Chenderlin, "'*Do this as my Memorial': The Semantic and Conceptual Background and Value of Anamnesis in 1 Corinthians 11:24-25,"* Analectica Biblica 99 (Rome: Biblical Institute Press, 1982); Brevard S. Childs, *Memory and Tradition in Israel.* Studies in Biblical Theology, No. 37 (London: SCM Press, 1962): 74-80; Max Thurian, *The Eucharistic Memorial,* Ecumenical Studies in Worship, Nos. 7 and 8 (London: Lutterworth Press, 1960/61). In view of the likely connections between Christian "remembrance" and the riches of the Jewish tradition, I am not persuaded by suggestions of direct influence on Christian liturgy from pagan ceremonies of *anamnēsis,* i. e., memorials in honor of the departed; see discussion of this in Hans Conzelmann, *1 Corinthians* (Philadelphia: Fortress Press, 1969, 1975): 198-200; C. K. Barrett, *The First Epistle to the Corinthians* (London: A. & C. Black, 1969): 266-68; Jeremias (1955): 159-161; and *Paul Beyond the Judaism/Hellenism Divide,* Troels Engberg-Pederson, ed. (Louisville: Westminster John Knox Press, 2001).

[20] I thus adopt a more nuanced position than that of Jeremias, who insisted on "that God may remember me" as the *only* sense of *eis tēn emēn anamnēsin.* See Jeremias (1955): 159-65, but contrast Childs (1962) throughout, and Chenderlin (1982): §27. Those who find it difficult to conceive of words or expressions being bivocal could do worse than look at G. B. Caird, *The Language and Imagery of the Bible* (London: Gerald Duckworth, 1980): 27-30; see also Christopher Bryan, *Preface to Romans* (New York: Oxford University Press, 2000): 71-72, 109-10. At least the better educated in Luke's and Paul's audiences would likely have looked for significant words to mean more than one thing, for their education had taught them to expect language and Scripture to be full of multiple levels of meaning.

[21] To speak of God's "remembering" is an anthropomorphism that embarrasses us: Did God forget? But everything we say about God must suffer from the limits of human speech. See Hans Kosmala, " 'Das tut zu meinem Gedächtnis' " *Novum Testamentum* 4 (1960): 81; Norman Hook, *The Eucharist in the New Testament* (London: Epworth Press, 1964): 129.

all tribulation."[22] Abraham's prayer that God should remember is also an assertion that God is faithful: God will not fail to do what God has promised.[23]

When the Eucharist was celebrated in "remembrance" of Jesus, first-century Christians, still close to their Jewish roots, were most likely expecting that God would "remember" the Messiah, the new Isaac, and in remembering, He would act graciously. When celebrating the Eucharist according to the *Didache*,[24] the church was to pray as follows:

Remember (*mnēsthēti*), Lord, your church,

in order that you may deliver it from all evil

and perfect it in your love

and gather it together from the four winds

into your kingdom which you have prepared for it,

for yours is the power and the glory for ever.[25]

They give thanks for their deliverance, looking to God to complete His gracious work for them and the whole creation when the Kingdom is finally manifested in glory.

Different Eucharistic rites accomplish "remembrance" in different ways. In the *BCP*, Eucharistic Prayers I and II of Rite I and Eucharistic Prayer A of Rite II[26] focus attention almost exclusively on God's action in the birth, life, death, and resurrection of Jesus the Messiah—sometimes, in specific prefaces, limiting themselves even to particular aspects of that story. By contrast, Eucharistic Prayers B, C, and D of Rite II[27] draw attention to entire salvation history, offering a christologically oriented recollection of the whole biblical story as the setting for God's mighty act in the Messiah.

Moreover, our Eucharistic remembering of God's grace carries with it an ethical imperative: Grace looks for grace. "For I have set you an example, that you also should do as I have done to you" (Jn 3:15; compare Rm 15:7). Not for nothing did the Fourth Evangelist introduce the story of the feet-washing as the climax and defining moment of his narrative of the Last Supper. By that imperative, the Christian memorial is always subversive of the ways of the world, for it sends us forth to live in the world by the spirit of Jesus, "to do the work you have given us to do, to love and serve you *as faithful witnesses of Christ our Lord.*"[28] Not only do we pray that God will remember His Messiah

---

[22] *Targum Neofiti* Gen. 22:14; text and translation in Alejandro Díez Macho, *Neophyti I: Targum Palestinense ms. de la Biblioteca Vaticana* Vol. 1 *Génesis*, Martin McNamara and Michael Maher, English trans. (Madrid: Consejo Superior de Investigaciones Científicas, 1968): 129, 552.

[23] Jeremias (1955): 159-65; Childs (1962): 31-44, 74; Thurian (1960-61): 1:27-39.

[24] The date of the *Didache* is not entirely certain, but in the opinion of the majority of scholars, internal and external evidence alike favor a date towards the end of the first century, a time when "apostolic men" who had known Paul and other Early Christians were still alive: See Kurt Niederwimmer, *The Didache*, Linda M. Maloney, trans. (Minneapolis: Fortress, 1998): 52-53.

[25] *Didache* 10:5; text in T. Klauser, *Doctrina Duodecim Apostolorum. Barnabae Epistula* (Bonn: Hanstein, 1940); text and translation in Kirsopp Lake, ed. and trans., *The Apostolic Fathers* vol. 1 (London: William Heinemann/Cambridge, Massachusetts: Harvard University Press, 1912): 308-32.

[26] *BCP* 333–36, 340–43, 361-63; Eucharistic Prayer II in *The Roman Missal* (1973): 527–30; Great Thanksgiving §32 in the *Lutheran Book of Worship* (1978): 69-70, 89-90.

[27] *BCP* 367-75; Eucharistic Prayer IV in *The Roman Missal* (1973): 535–39; Great Thanksgiving §31 in the *Lutheran Book of Worship* (1978): 69-70, 89-90.

[28] *BCP* 366.

but also that we ourselves may remember and proclaim Jesus' death for us "until he come" (1 Cor 11:26) The Eucharist, therefore, sends us out to become in our turn and in our place living memorials of Jesus and pledges of his final advent in glory.

The Life of Christ as Presented by the Church

To note that the Church Calendar presents what amounts to a "life" of Christ is not to suggest that the events commemorated are experienced throughout the church year in chronological order as events in Christ's life, or even that in different years they are necessarily experienced in the same order. General usage in the churches of the West presents the life of Christ not in a biographical order but in terms of two cycles of feasts and holy days, one dependent on the fixed festival of Christmas (December 25), the other dependent on the moveable Sunday of Easter (the Sunday following the first full moon occurring on or after March 21).[29] Similar to the rhetoric and style of Greco-Roman "lives," the church is concerned not with niceties of chronology but with emphasizing the significance of the actions and words of the subject of this "life," Jesus Christ. In the following, therefore, I list the usual commemorations *broadly* in order as events in the chronology of Christ's life, but this orderly, post-Enlightenment approach can work only in part. Where the date of the commemoration is fixed, I have indicated it; where the moveable commemoration is part of the fluid Easter cycle, it is marked (*) with an asterisk.

The life of Christ as presented by the church's calendars begins, in the manner of many ancient "lives," before the birth of its subject,[30] with *The Annunciation of Our Lord Jesus Christ to the Blessed Virgin Mary* (March 25),[31] a commemoration first attested in the seventh century but which had surely been established earlier.[32] "In the mystery of the Word made flesh," says the appointed preface of the Epiphany, "You have caused a new light to shine in our hearts...,"[33] and the Festival of the Annunciation makes clear to us that the life of Christ is from its beginning God's own act. God's act (not Mary's "purity") is the point at issue in the Gospel reading appointed in all the churches (Lk 1:26–38).

The force of Mary's words to the angel is that by all human reckoning what she is being promised is impossible. Luke's intention is that we shall see in Mary's conceiving that God alone is the source of human fruitfulness, and that God alone is the source of *this* fruitfulness, which will lead to the redemption of Israel.

The angel indicates this by comparing the promise to Mary with the experience of her cousin, Elizabeth, "who was called barren" but who will also bear a child, "for with

---

[29] *BCP* 15.

[30] Bryan (1993): 50-51.

[31] Earlier Anglican Prayer Books (e.g. *BCP* 1662) referred to the commemoration simply as "The Annunciation of the Blessed Virgin," a title whose emphasis was reflected in everyday speech by the name "Lady Day," originally "Our Lady Day," and formerly used not only of March 25 but also of August 15 (Assumption), September 8 (Nativity of the Blessed Virgin), and December 8 (Conception of the Virgin). The change of emphasis to Christ himself represented by *BCP* 1979 is clear; compare the new Roman calendar's "The Annunciation of the Lord."

[32] St. Sophronius (*c.* 560-638), Patriarch of Jerusalem from 634, wrote a homily on the Annunciation (J. P. Migne, *Patrologia Graeca*, vol. 87): 3,217; see further Louis Duchesne, *Christian Worship: Its Origin and Evolution* (London: S.P.C.K., 1903): 272; Hatchett (1980): 56-57.

[33] *BCP* 378.

God nothing shall be impossible" (Lk 1:36–37). The rabbis observed that "wherever [in Scripture] it is written, 'she was barren,' it means that she would bear."[34] Such were the births granted to Sarah (Gn 16:1), Rebecca (Gn 25:21), Rachel (Gn 30:1), the (un-named)[35] mother of Samson (Jg 13:2), and Hannah (1 Sm 1:2), *and always they are for Israel's deliverance*. Luke wanted his hearers to have this tradition in mind throughout his entire birth narrative, and nowhere is this made clearer than in Mary's words when she visits Cousin Elizabeth.

In the passage immediately following the appointed Gospel, in the *Magnificat*, perhaps the best known of all Christian hymns, again and again Mary echoes the phrasing and sentiments of another barren woman, Hannah, who also had sung praise to God for the promise of a child who was to be great in Israel (Lk 1:46–55 cf. 1 Sm 2:1–10). The *Magnificat* is therefore very appropriately used, as the *BCP* permits,[36] in place of a Psalm at the Eucharist on this day.[37] The exaltation of the woman of low estate, as is made clear in the *Magnificat*, is a sign of that reversal of human values that marks God's presence and kingdom. Throughout the gospel tradition, not the powerful, not the wealthy, not the hierarchical leaders, but the outcast, the poor, and the women recognize Jesus. Moreover, God's creation of something from nothing in the fruitfulness of the barren woman becomes in Luke's account of the virginal conception a prefiguration of the resurrection: a point to be stressed by the preacher when, as often happens, the festival of the Annunciation falls in close proximity to Easter.[38]

While the faith and obedience of Mary are not the central concern of this commemoration, Mary's faith and obedience do have their place, for when Mary responds in the affirmative, "Let it happen to me!" she was speaking for all her people, Israel. "It is for her obedience at that moment, the climactic obedience of Israel, that we not only invoke Mary but revere her."[39]

Neither Jerome's Latin in the Vulgate: *Fiat mihi secundum verbum tuum!* nor the English of the Authorized Version: "Be it unto me according to thy word" quite gets the force of Luke's Greek, which unambiguously expresses neither mere resignation nor mere acceptance, but graceful eagerness. Mary is saying: *"Please* let this happen to me!

---

[34] *Pesikta de Rav Kahana,* S. Buber, ed. (Lyck: Mekize Nirdamim, 1868): 20 (141b); *Pesikta Rabbati* 32, M. Friedmann, ed. (Vienna: Moritz Güdemann, 1880): 148a.

[35] Omission of the name of Samson's mother is the more remarkable because the mother is presented as a character more interesting and stronger than her husband, for she receives the initial angelic annunciation (Jg13:3–5), shows both common sense and humor at the climax of the story (13:21–23), and names the child (13:24). On the theme of the barren woman in Scripture in general, see Mary Callaway, *Sing, O Barren One: A Study in Comparative Midrash,* SBL Dissertation Series, 91 (Atlanta, Georgia: Scholars Press, 1986).

[36] *BCP* 922.

[37] I find it regrettable that the first part of the story of Hannah was not appointed in the *Lectionary* to be the Old Testament reading (i.e. 1 Sm. 1:1–20) since Luke evidently had that passage from the Septuagint in mind when he wrote the birth narrative. See note 46 on the Visitation. As an alternative, Dn 7:13–14, which is in mind at Lk 1:32–33, would have been appropriate.

[38] Several have noted the connection between Luke's narrative and early formularies about the resurrection, such as Rm 1:3–4. See Callaway (1986): 103, and literature there cited.

[39] Robert Jenson, *Systematic Theology* 2 (Oxford and New York: Oxford University Press, 1999): 203–204.

Grant me this favor, that it shall be to me according to your word!" Later on, her son will say: "Thy will be done!" Our Lord himself had no better model in prayer than the words of his mother. On his knees in Gethsemane, preparing for the cross, he was praying his version of the prayer that his mother had prayed when she was a teenager: "Behold the handmaid of the Lord: let it be to me according to thy word" (Lk 1:38). Mary's own joyful faith and obedience would bring her to the foot of her son's cross and to the prophesied sword that would pierce her own heart (cf. Lk 2:35), yet her prayer and that of Jesus are the way through pain to true human joy. For such faith and obedience as theirs we pray in the appointed Collect, which in its Anglican form asks that we, like Mary, may "by his cross and passion be brought to the glory of his resurrection"[40] — the liturgy again reminding us of the connection between the mystery of Christ's conception and the mystery of his passion and exaltation.

In the next moment of celebration, *The Visitation of the Blessed Virgin Mary*[41] to her cousin Elizabeth (May 31), we are still in the time before the birth of the Messiah. Luke continued writing about Mary's faith: "Blessed," says Elizabeth in the Gospel passage, "is she who *believed* there would be a fulfillment of what was spoken to her from the Lord." Then the church proclaims the prophetic reading appointed from Hebrew Scripture: "Sing aloud, O daughter of Zion...! The King of Israel, the LORD is in your midst... the LORD your God in your midst" (Zph. 3:14, 15, 18a). Rabbi Berekiah said that Rabbi Isaac had said: "The latter deliverer will act as the former."[42] As Moses had been protected and nurtured by women, by Miriam and by Pharaoh's daughter, so women, our Lady and her cousin Elizabeth, are the first to proclaim their faith in the Coming One while he is still in the womb. In just the same way, women will be the last, standing by his cross, to be faithful to him at the end; and women, again, will be the first to proclaim him risen.[43]

The *Nativity of Saint John the Baptist* (June 24) comes in the chronological scheme of things after the Annunciation to Mary (Lk 1:36). Mark quoted the prophecy of Isaiah, and then began his story: "John came..." (Mk 1:2, 4). Eastern Christianity ranks St. John second only to the Blessed Virgin among the saints. Certainly the New Testament's understanding of the witness of the Baptist roots the coming of the Messiah in the hopes and aspirations of ancient Israel. Zachariah and Elizabeth represent, as the Gospel reading from Luke makes clear, the very finest in Israel's faith, the ones most fit to beget and bear the forerunner. Yet, as in the Gospel narrative itself,[44] so in the liturgy, when we

---

[40] *BCP* 188, 240.

[41] This festival was officially established by decree of Pope Urban VI on April 6, 1389.

[42] *Qoheleth Rabbah*, 1.9, A. Cohen, trans., in H. Freedman and Maurice Simon, eds., *Midrash Rabbah*, vol. 8 *Ecclesiasticus* (London: Soncino Press, 3rd ed., 1983): 33; compare *Shirim Rabbah* 2.9, Maurice Simon, trans., in H. Freedman and M. Simon, eds., *Midrash Rabbah*, vol. 9 *Song of Songs* (London: Soncino Press, 3rd ed., 1983): 120.

[43] Again, I think, the second part of the story of Hannah (1 Sm 1:19b–2:11) would have been appropriately appointed in the *Lectionary* to be read for the Old Testament lesson at the Visitation, since that passage seems to have been in Luke's mind when he wrote the narrative that forms the gospel.

[44] "What precedes [the Baptist] takes its shape from what follows [Jesus]. This means that the Baptist has no significance in himself. There can be no 'doctrine' of or about the Baptist; instead, the statements concerning the Baptist are christological," Willi Marxsen, *Mark the Evangelist: Studies*

speak of the Baptist, it is not finally the Baptist who is our concern but the Coming One whom he proclaimed, as St. Augustine pointed out in a sermon on this day:

John's mother was old and barren while Christ's mother was young and a virgin…. John marks the boundary between the Old and the New Covenants…. He represents the Old, yet also brings in the New. His parents were aged, as befitted his former role, yet while still in the womb of his mother he was hailed as prophet, as befitted his second… . Zachariah became silent and lost his power of speech until John, the Lord's forerunner, was born and restored his speech. Is not Zachariah's silence a hidden prophecy? …Zechariah's speech was restored because a voice was born. When John announced our Lord's advent, he was asked, "Who are you?" He answered, "I am the voice of one crying in the wilderness." John was a voice; but, in the beginning, the Lord was the Word. John was a voice for a time; Christ, who was the Word in the beginning, is the Word for eternity.[45]

Nine months exactly after the celebration of the Annunciation, the Church's "life" moves to the *Nativity of Our Lord* or *Christmas Day* (December 25). In the Julian calendar, December 25 was the day of the winter solstice. As established by the Emperor Aurelian in 274 a festival day of "the birth of the unconquered sun" (*dies natalis solis invicti*), the imagery involved quite suited Christian understanding of the coming of "Sun of Righteousness" (Ml 4:2, cf. Lk 1:78-79). Since the biblical evidence for the date of Christ's nativity is ambiguous,[46] the Christian and pagan rites may have influenced one another to some degree.[47]

---

on the Redaction History of the Gospel (Nashville: Abingdon Press, 1969): 33. Marxsen wrote specifically of Mark, but his observations could stand for the entire gospel tradition surrounding the Baptist, and would apply particularly well to the Lukan birth narratives, a part of which is used as the gospel reading for the Nativity of the Baptist. It is evident that Luke's account of the Baptist's birth is in its entirety designed to stand in relationship to, and in some sense as a foil for, his account of the Birth of Christ.

[45] Augustine, *Sermon* 293; in Brother Kenneth C.G.A., ed., *From the Fathers to the Churches* (London: Collins Liturgical Publications, 1983): 700-701.

[46] Folllowing Lk 2:8, some have suggested that the actual time of Jesus' birth must have been between March and November, when the shepherds would have been out in the fields. As early as Clement of Alexandria (*ca.* 200), one theory was that Jesus was born on April 20-21; another, on May 20 (Clement, *Stromata* 1.21). The exact date of Jesus' birth must have been a matter of little concern to the first-generation Christians, or else they would have made sure we knew it. See Raymond Brown, *The Birth of the Messiah* (Garden City, New York: Doubleday, 1979): 401. See below, notes 47, 56.

[47] The "history of religions" hypothesis, that the Christian festival was a deliberate attempt to Christianize the associations of the pagan rite, is still probably the most widely held view of the origin of the Christmas festival: e.g. John Gunstone, *Christmas and Epiphany* (London: Faith Press, 1967): 11–14, 15–21; Hatchett (1980): 39, 86. Thomas Talley's revival of the "computation hypothesis," first propounded by Duchesne, challenges the notion of pagan borrowings without totally rejecting the possibility of influence from the coincidence of the *Sol novus*; nonetheless, Talley regarded as "most satisfactory" the view that "the date for the birth of Christ was fixed from the assumed starting point of His Passion." See Duchesne, *Christian Worship* (1903): 261–65; Talley (1986): 87–103. For an excellent summary and evaluation of the discussion to date, see J. Neil Alexander, *Waiting for the Coming: The Liturgical Meaning of Advent, Christmas, Epiphany*

The Christmas festival is marked in the first place by the four weeks of Advent that have led up to it—through which four-week period we are urged not merely to recall Christ's first coming "in great humility" but expectantly to look forward to his final coming "in his glorious majesty to judge both the living and the dead."[48] The Proper for Christmas itself offers a choice of Gospel passages: we may either (1) commemorate Christ's coming as experienced by the shepherds (suitable for the midnight Eucharist) (Lk 2:1–14 and 15–20)[49] or else (2) we may use the prologue to John's Gospel (especially suitable for Christmas morning) to commemorate the cosmic significance of the Incarnation, speaking of the Word-made-flesh in terms owing something to both Hebrew and Greek wisdom—a link further emphasized by the selection of Hebrews 1:1–10 as the Epistle to go with this Gospel.[50] This commemoration in its *BCP* form also offers a choice of three Collects, the first encouraging us to continue Advent's double focus on the Second Coming of Christ "to be our Judge" alongside our present acceptance of him as "our Redeemer"; the second speaking of the "true Light" which has illumined "this holy night" (thus being particularly suitable for the midnight Eucharist) and praying that "as we have known the mystery of that light upon earth, so we may also perfectly enjoy him in heaven"; and the third focusing on the birth of Christ from the womb of the Virgin Mary: "You have given your only-begotten Son to take our nature upon him and be born of a pure virgin."[51] Other ceremonies associated with the commemoration, such as processions to, and prayers before, a crib (a model of the manger scene at Bethlehem) have no formal place in the various books because they are of 13th-century vintage, thanks to St. Francis of Assisi. They seem nonetheless suitable, however, provided either that they do not overwhelm the liturgy itself or distract from the central mystery of the Incarnation.

The festival of *The Holy Name of Our Lord Jesus Christ* (January 1) speaks of Jesus' person and work. Names are of great significance in antiquity. Earlier calendars referred

---

(Washington, D.C.: The Pastoral Press, 1993): 46–51. I express my gratitude to my friend and colleague, Neil Alexander (now Bishop of Atlanta), for a number of helpful comments about this paper, including his drawing my attention to his own intriguing suggestion that *if* pagans and Christians influenced each other over the date of Christmas, the influence might as easily have passed from the Christians to the pagans as the other way round. What if Aurelian's new feast at Rome in 274 were actually an imperial *response* to the increasing size and influence of the Christian movement? Using elements of pagan people's *superstitio* in the process of guiding them to true *religio* has often been a tool of Christian missionaries, but why might pagans not have used a similar ploy on the Christians? The Romans, from whose point of view Christianity was the *superstitio*, and the worship of the Roman gods was *religio*, might just as easily have attempted to co-opt Christian faith in Christmas to enhance the Roman festival of the "new Sun." See Alexander (1993): 51; and on Roman understanding of *religio* and *superstitio*, see Mary Beard, John North, and Simon Price, *Religions of Rome: A History* (Cambridge University Press, 1998): 215-27.

[48] *BCP* 211, *Collect for the First Sunday of Advent*; cf. *BCP* 159.

[49] *The Lectionary*, Christmas Day I and II, in *BCP* 889, 990-1, 911.

[50] *Idem*, Christmas Day III, in *BCP* 890, 901, 911.

[51] *BCP* 212–13, cf. 160-61. The Roman Rite entails three masses: midnight, dawn, and during the day, a threefoldness held to symbolize the thrice born Christ: eternally in the Father's bosom, in time from the womb of the Blessed Virgin, and mystically in the hearts and souls of the faithful.

to this commemoration as the Feast of the Circumcision,[52] but the newer title certainly better reflects Luke's concern in the Gospel (Lk 2:15–21). Luke was stressing Jesus' being named in clear parallel to the naming of the Baptist earlier in his narrative (Lk 1:57–80), while his deliberate reference to the angel's message insists that we recall the gifts there associated with Jesus' name (Lk 1:32–33).[53] How, then, are these gifts to be understood? The Gospel passage affirms the spontaneous joy of the shepherds, and even more the thoughtfulness of Mary who, Luke wrote, "treasured these things and pondered them in her heart" or, more precisely translated, "tried to hit upon their true meaning" (Lk 2:19).[54] Mary's faith was a faith seeking understanding (*fides quaerens intellectum*, as St. Anselm liked to say), and in this she became a further model for the Christian disciple. Even so, the experience of this questioning faith and spontaneous joy arrest us with yet another reversal of human expectation: Joy raining on shepherds was an angelic expenditure on a class of people reckoned in that society among the lowest and least valued of the working class;[55] Mary and Joseph, likewise, were among the poor and powerless, people spiraling down into homelessness as the result of an imperial decree, hence finding themselves with a lack of resources sufficient to support the new mother in her childbearing (Lk 2:1–7).

After Christmas we come to *The Epiphany* (January 6). The Greek word *epiphaneia* means "manifestation."[56] The day was early associated with the Lord's nativity, with the

---

[52] For example in the 1662 *Book of Common Prayer* of the Church of England. In *The Alternative Service Book 1980* of the Church of England (Cambridge University Press/Colchester: William Clowes/London: S.P.C.K., 1980): 752, an attempt was made—perhaps not wisely—to preserve both names, referring to "The Naming of Jesus, or the Circumcision of Christ."

[53] When preaching on this passage from Luke, one does so quite inappropriately if one imports the explanation of the name "Jesus" implied in Mt 1:21. If the "two-source" hypothesis of the Gospels is correct, Luke did not know of this explanation. Alternatively, if Luke *did* know of Matthew's explanation, then Luke's approach suggests that he thought little of Matthew's idea. See Austin Farrer, "On Dispensing with Q," in D. E. Nineham, ed., *Studies in the Gospels: Essays in Memory of R. H. Lightfoot* (Oxford: Blackwell, 1955): 55-58; and Mark Goodacre, ed., *Mark without Q*, available online: http://www.bham.ac.uk/theology/q/farrer.htm

[54] Joseph A. Fitzmyer, S.J., *The Gospel according to Luke (I-IX)*, in *Anchor Bible* 28 (New York: Doubleday, 1981): 413, citing W. C. van Unnik, "Die rechte Bedeutung des Wortes treffen, Lukas II 19" in *Sparsa collecta: The Collected Essays of W. C. van Unnik* Novum Testamentum Supplementum 29 (Leiden: Brill, 1973): 72–91.

[55] Cf. *Midrash Kiddushin* 4:14.

[56] Many have asserted that the eastern provinces of the Roman Empire had observed January 6 as the day of the winter solstice (following the ancient calendar of Amenhemhet I of Thebes), a day celebrated in Egypt as the day of the rising god, Osiris, marked by light, water, and wine; and that, therefore, Christians appropriated an older pagan festival for their own purposes—another "history of religions" view still widely held: See Gunstone, *Christmas and Epiphany* (1967): 14–15; Hatchett (1980): 39, 48. This, however, like the "history of religions" view of Christmas (see note 53) has been challenged by revival of the "computation hypothesis"—and on weightier grounds. Talley (1986): 103-29, argued that no calendar of Amenhemhet I existed, and that clear evidence of a pre-Christian pagan festival on January 6 is likewise lacking. Roland Bainton, "The Origins of the Epiphany," *Early and Medieval Christianity: Collected Papers in Church History.* Series One (Boston: Beacon Press, 1962): 22-38, showed that Orthodox Christians late in the second century already believed that January 6, 2 B.C., had been the date of Christ's birth.

coming of the pagan Magi (thus emphasizing the incarnation as a manifestation of God's grace for the gentile nations), with Jesus' baptism, and with his turning the water into wine at the wedding in Cana of Galilee,[57] which was, according to the Fourth Evangelist, the beginning of the signs whereby he "manifested forth (*ephanerōsen*) his glory" (Jn 2:11).

The *BCP* Proper for the celebration on January 6 focuses on the coming of the Magi, and clearly requires us to consider Jesus' manifestation to the nations, a theme taken up elsewhere in the liturgy, i.e., in the Collect ("by the leading of a star you manifested your only Son to the peoples of the earth"), as well as in the Readings. In case, however, we become too obsessed with this outgoing vision, the Preface (which is used throughout the season, including the Presentation, as well as at the Annunciation and the Transfiguration) reminds us that what has happened through this manifestation is that God has caused "a new light to shine in *our* hearts."[58] If we do not have that, we have nothing—and certainly nothing with which we need trouble anyone else.

The First Sunday after the Epiphany reflects on one of the other themes that most ancient churches associated with the Epiphany, namely *The Baptism of Christ*.[59] Like Jesus' circumcision, his baptism was, as Matthew's narrative in particular reminds us, the sign of his willingness to be identified with us in all things. In the gospels, the baptism of Jesus is also closely associated with his temptation, or testing, in the wilderness. The church, however, pauses for a while in its presentation so that we may contemplate various aspects of the manifestation of God in our world during the Sundays in the season of Epiphany. Not until the *First Sunday in Lent** do we come fully to consider Jesus' Temptation, being encouraged to associate ourselves with his faithfulness to God's will in our own practice of the Lenten fast. "Displease yourself," Austin said of this fast, "and have fellowship with Christ. For he pleased not himself, and his prayers were heard. And for what did he pray? He prayed for, and obtained, our salvation."[60]

---

[57] The lessons provided in the Armenian Lectionary (representing the liturgy of Jerusalem in the first half of the fifth century; hereinafter *AL*) are all concerned with the Nativity (*AL*, # 1–9). Readings during the octave are connected with the Visit of the Magi, St. Stephen's martyrdom, the Massacre of the Innocents, and the Circumcision on the eighth day. Those readings not connected with the Nativity appear to be connected with the places where they were read. The Armenians apparently did not associate this season with the Lord's baptism, although an early association in the churches of Egypt did associate that event with January 6 (e.g. Clement of Alexandria, *Stromateis* 1.145, 146). The *Armenian Lectionary* speaks of December 25, incidentally, as the commemoration of James and David, noting, however, that "in other cities they celebrate Christ's nativity" (*AL* 71). For text and introduction to the *AL*, see A. Renoux, *Le Codex Arménien Jérusalem*, 2 vols. (Turnholt, Belgiums: Brepols, 1969, 1971); and John Wilkinson, trans., *Egeria's Travels* (London: S.P.C.K., 1971): 253–77.
[58] *BCP* 346, 378.
[59] Compare the Church of England *ASB 1980*, Epiphany 1 (463-66). The other ancient association of Epiphany—namely, with the Wedding at Cana—is maintained in the *Book of Common Prayer 1979* by the Proper for the Second Sunday after Epiphany in Year C (912); cf. *ASB 1980*, Epiphany 3, Year 1 (473-74).
[60] Farrer (1952): 22.

The *Presentation of our Lord Jesus Christ in the Temple* on February 2 (in earlier calendars referred to as "The Purification of Saint Mary the Virgin") takes us out of the chronology to an earlier point in the story. The passage from Ml 3:1-4 that is normally used as the reading from the Old Testament appropriately picks up the force of Luke's narrative: that the Coming One is entering into his own, as is testified prophetically by the aged Simeon and by Anna, and by a note of warning in the Gospel.[61] Egeria, the pilgrim who wrote an account of her experiences of the Holy Land some time between 381 and 384, felt that this festival was "observed with special magnificence, ... things are done with the same solemnity as at the feast of Easter."[62] The One who came as Savior must by that very fact come also as Judge, and therefore is set "for the fall and rising of many" (Lk 2:34).[63] If God is love, then by that very truth much that passes for human greatness must painfully be set aside.

Between the Temptation and the Entry into Jerusalem, only one event from Jesus' ministry is singled out for attention in the "life" presented by the Calendar, namely *The Transfiguration of Our Lord Jesus Christ* (August 6), a festival celebrated in the East as early as the fourth century, but a special day that appeared much later in the West.[64] *Transfiguration* centers on a narrative that is a watershed in the Gospel tradition itself, pointing both backward to the nature of Jesus' ministry as the disciples thus far had seen it, and forward to his passion, death, and the glory that was to follow.

Preaching on this appointed Gospel (Lk 9:28-36) is an occasion to make the important point that in Luke, as in all the synoptics, the account of the Transfiguration follows immediately on Jesus' statement that his messiahship involves suffering and death for him and, therefore, also for those who choose to identify with him (Lk 9:18-27). A temporal link, "after eight days" (Luke's adaptation of Mark's "after six days") connects Jesus' words about suffering and death with the mountain-climbing to the Transfiguration. Temporal links are unusual in the synoptic tradition (outside of the Passion narrative), so we may infer that the before and after were thus connected in the thinking of the gospel-writers. When Jesus, then, is seen by his disciples in transfigured glory—for "his raiment was dazzling white" (Lk 9:29)—they have seen a theophany not only of a glorious Messiah but of the Messiah who is to be crucified. Jesus, here, reminds us of Moses receiving the tablets of the Law at Sinai, and in case we did not catch the reminiscence, the *Lectionary* specifically directs our attention to it in the Old Testament reading, as does also the appointed passage from the Psalter (Ex. 34:29-35, Ps. 99:5-9).

---

[61] If Luke's narrative is to be set in the context that Luke had in mind, then Leviticus 12:6–8 ought also to be read. In view of the Old Testament reminiscences that dominate this part of Luke's account, a case could be made for reading both the passages from Leviticus and Malachi, and dispensing with the New Testament reading.

[62] Egeria (1971): #26. Pierre Maraval, *Egéria Journal de voyage: introduction, texte critique, traduction, notes, index et cartes*. Sources chrétiennes 296. (Paris: Les Editions du Cerf, 1982); E. Francheschini and R. Weber, *Itinerarium Egeriae* in *Corpus Christianorum, Series Latina* 175 (Turnholt, Belgium: Brepols, 1965): 37–90. Egeria referred simply to the feast as "the Fortieth Day after Epiphany," and it was evidently celebrated not on February 2 but on February 14; see also *AL*, no. 13.

[63] Egeria (1971): #26, specifically identified this as the content of the Gospel passage interpreted by the presbyters and the bishop; *AL*, No. 13 confirms the Gospel reading as Luke 2:22–40; cf. *BCP* 922).

[64] Hatchett, *Commentary*, , 70.

With Jesus "in glory" on the mountain appear two of Israel's heroes, Moses and Elijah, and they are speaking with Jesus "of his *exodus* (RSV: "departure") which he is to accomplish at Jerusalem" (Lk 9:31). This reference to the Exodus is Luke's own detail, and it points forward once more not only to Jesus' death but also to the significance of that death: our deliverance. In what follows, we catch a re-echo of the heavenly Voice that had spoken at Jesus' baptism (Lk 3:22) and echoed in further witness to Jesus' Sonship to God and his being chosen to die (Lk 9:35). The Transfiguration in the synoptic Gospels makes clear that Jesus does not first suffer only then to receive glory: For those with eyes to see, the Chosen One who accepts suffering for the world is *already* in glory. As the Fourth Gospel puts it on the eve of Christ's passion, "*Now* is the Son of Man glorified" (Jn 13:31).

Martin Kähler's dictum: "A Gospel is a passion narrative with an extended introduction," has perhaps been taken more seriously either than he intended or it deserves.[65] Like an ancient "life,"[66] the Church's liturgical "Life of Christ" emphasizes the aspect of Jesus' life that the Gospel writers considered to be the most significant, namely Jesus' death. The focus of all the holy days in the Calendar of which we have still to speak is on Jesus' passion, death, and resurrection. No fewer than five major days in Holy Week are devoted to this, as is also *Holy Cross Day* (September 14).[67]

The view that the passion narrative is the oldest part of the gospel tradition, substantially pre-dating Mark, although questioned recently,[68] remains—in my opinion—likely to be correct. While I remain largely unconvinced by attempts to document forms of the Christian Paschal Vigil to the New Testament period,[69] I do not doubt that in dealing with Easter generally, we are dealing with some of the oldest

---

[65] Martin Kähler, *Der sogenannte historische Jesus und der geschichtliche biblische Christus* (Leipzig: A. Deichert [Georg Böhme], 1896): 80. Kähler himself, on the same page, observed that he offered his description "etwas herausfordernd"—"somewhat provocatively." Indeed.

[66] Burridge (1992): 164-67; Bryan (1993): 41-42.

[67] *Holy Cross Day* originally commemorated the dedication of the Church of the Holy Sepulcher erected in Jerusalem over the sites of the crucifixion and the burial, as identified by the Empress Helena, a British princess and mother of Constantine the Great. This festival functions in the *1979 Prayer Book* as it does in other churches and other Anglican provinces (see the Church of England's *ASB 1980*, 832-34) largely as a commemoration of Christ's death, the center of attention not only in the Readings and Preface "of Holy Week" (*BCP* 192) but also in the Collect's memorial of "our Savior Jesus Christ [who] was lifted high upon the cross that he might draw the whole world to himself." (*BCP* 244).

[68] See Bryan (1993): 112-124, 132-135, and literature there cited.

[69] See Massey Shepherd, *The Paschal Liturgy and the Apocalypse* (London: Lutterworth Press, 1960): 77-84, who suggested a direct link between the Paschal Liturgy and the Book of Revelation; Michael Goulder, *Luke: A New Paradigm*, Journal for the Study of the New Testament: Supplement Series 20 (Sheffield: Sheffield Academic Press, 1989): 1: 151-2, who suggested a link between Luke's chronology of Jesus' death and an (alleged) day-long Christian Passover in memorial of the Passion; and Augustine Stock, O.S.B., *The Method and Message of Mark* (Wilmington, Delaware: Michael Glazier, 1989): 12-19, who connected Mark to a Christian Passover. All these theories are testimony to the respective authors' lively imaginations, but they are supported by little or nothing that could actually be described as evidence. See Bradshaw (1992): 35-6, for a critique of Shepherd and Goulder.

material in the Christian tradition.[70] Thus, the major commemorations of Holy Week—marked in the Roman Rite and in the *BCP* not only by Propers for the Eucharist but also by Proper Liturgies[71]—contain many details that are evidently quite old. Egeria, describing Holy Week in late-fourth-century Jerusalem, tells us that on Palm Sunday, they read Matthew's account of Our Lord's entry into Jerusalem (Mt 21:1–11), then went in procession with the people waving palm branches, "with psalms and antiphons, all the time repeating, 'Blessed is he that comes in the name of the Lord!'"[72] She wrote of celebrations of the Eucharist on the afternoon of Maundy Thursday,[73] the reading of John's account of the trial before Pilate early on Good Friday,[74] and devotions before the wood of the cross later the same day.[75] Other elements in the Proper Liturgies, though not documented quite so early as these, are nonetheless old. Among these are forms of the *Exultet* by Bishop Ennodius of Ticinium in the sixth century;[76] the practice of singing the ninth-century hymn, "All glory, laud, and honor," during the Palm Sunday procession, with the first stanza sung as a refrain after each succeeding stanza, and the singing of the entire Passion narrative as the Gospel in the Palm Sunday mass, both featured in the Sarum use.[77] Reading Philippians 2:5-11 for the Epistle at the Palm Sunday mass was appointed in the earliest Roman lectionary.[78]

In many respects, the magnificent liturgies for Holy Week are the jewel in the crown of Christian worship, as represented particularly in the Roman Catholic and Anglican traditions. Used with sympathy and sensitivity, they furnish for those taking part in them an unforgettable *anamnēsis* and proclamation of Christ's passion and triumph.

To repeat Benoit's dictum, "One does not recite a rubric, one obeys it." In the same vein, we might say that the Proper Liturgies of Holy Week can hardly be described, they can only be experienced. Through them, we may enter into Jerusalem with the disciples

---

[70] Hatchett (1980): 240; Duchesne (1903): 239–40, 247–57. Our earliest description of a Christian Paschal ceremony (including baptism) *may* be that in the *Apostolic Tradition*, attributed to Hippolytus, that possibly had its origin in Rome about 215 AD. This work has survived, however, only in a few fragments of the original Greek and in a number of ancient translations that differ considerably among themselves. We cannot take for granted that they provide us with information about the Roman church in the early third century: see A. F. Walls, "The Latin Version of Hippolytus' Apostolic Tradition" in F. L. Cross, ed., *Studia Patristica 3/1* (Berlin: Akademie-Verlag, 1961): 155-62; Marcel Metzger, "Nouvelles perspectives pour la prétendue *Tradition Apostolique*," *Ecclesia Orans* 5 (1988): 241-59; Bradshaw (1992): 89-92. For the reconstructions, see Paul Bradshaw, Charles Whitaker, and Geoffrey Cuming, *Essays on Hippolytus* (Bramcoate, Notts.: Grove Books, 1978); Gregory Dix, *The Treatise on the Apostolic Tradition of St. Hippolytus of Rome, 2nd* ed. (London: S.P.C.K., 1968); Bernard Botte, *Hippolyte de Rome: La Tradition apostolique d'après les anciennes Versions*. Sources Chrétiennes 11 (Paris: Les Éditions du Cerf, 2nd ed., 1968).

[71] *BCP* 270–95.

[72] *The Book of Common Prayer and Administration of the Sacraments and Other Rites and Ceremonies of the Episcopal Church Together with The Psalter or Psalms of David According to the Use of the Episcopal Church* (New York: The Church Hymnal Corporation, 1979): 16.

[73] Egeria (1971): #35.2.

[74] *Idem*: #36.4; *AL*, No. 42 confirms this as John 18:28–19:16; see Wilkinson (1971): 136; cf. *BCP* 277.

[75] Egeria (1971): #36.5-37:7; cf. *BCP* 281–2.

[76] Ennodius, *Opusculum*, 9, 10; see Hatchett (1980): 245; Duchesne (1903): 253 n.3.

[77] Hatchett (1980): 224; cf. *BCP* 271, 272.

[78] Hatchett (1980): 227; cf. *BCP* 272.

and the crowd on Palm Sunday.* Four days later, on Maundy (or Holy) Thursday,* we recline with the disciples at the Last Supper, sharing the table, having our feet washed by the Lord, even washing others' feet with him. At last, the altars are stripped and, all signs of festivity swept away, we are led out to watch with him in Gethsemane—and, no doubt, to know that we, too, faithless disciples that we are, will fall asleep while he prays, will betray him with a kiss, and later deny him.

On Good Friday* Jesus' arrest, trial, and death on the cross will be the center of our attention. We listen to John's account of his passion, we venerate the cross, and in communion from the reserved sacrament,[79] we feed on what Christ has given us, but we do not celebrate the Eucharist. Communion in silence from elements consecrated the previous evening powerfully represents to us our utter dependence on Christ's gift, and our utter inability to do anything about it. "Have you seen how Christ has united his Bride to himself?" St. John Chrysostom asked his catechumens: "Have you seen with what kind of food Christ feeds us all? By that food we are formed and fed. As a woman feeds her child with her own blood and milk, so Christ himself continually feeds those whom he has begotten with his own blood."[80]

Throughout Holy Saturday,* Christ's body lies in his borrowed tomb, and we will not (and may not)[81] celebrate the Eucharist on this day. The Church, in so restricting itself for this one day in the year, allows itself to contemplate what life might be like if God in Christ had not triumphed. "What is happening? Today there is a great silence over the earth, a great silence, and stillness, a great silence because the king sleeps.... But arise, let us go hence. The enemy brought you out of the Land of Paradise; I will reinstate you, no longer in Paradise, but on the throne of heaven."[82] Holy Saturday is a day of waiting, as the Collect and the Readings make plain.

At last, the Easter Vigil begins in the darkness and silence that are broken by the new fire, the lighting of the paschal candle, and the glorious proclamation of the *Exultet*.[83] The deacon calls heaven, earth, and the church to bear witness to God's victory in the resurrection of Christ. Then we pause again, listening as passages from Scripture rehearse for us the long tale of our flight from God and God's search for us, until at last we are ready to affirm the history of our flight as our own history of being found, thereafter to renew our baptismal vows, for we, too, are among those who have "put on the Lord Jesus."

What would God's victory in Christ be to us, if it were victory for Christ only? Baptism reminds us that Christ's victory is *for us*, and was shown to be ours in our

---

[79] *BCP* 282.

[80] St. John Chrysostom, *Instruction to Catechumens* 3:19, in Brother Kenneth (1983): 297.

[81] *BCP* 283.

[82] "From an ancient Homily for Holy Saturday," in Brother Kenneth (1983): 297, 298.

[83] I yield to no one in my admiration for the Holy Week Proper Liturgies of the *BCP*; nonetheless, in connection with the *Exultet*, a criticism is in order. I cannot imagine what possessed those who drafted the Prayer Book version to omit the great passage that used to begin in the Latin liturgy with the words *O felix culpa quae talem ac tantum meruit habere redemptorem!* ("O happy fault, that merited such and so great a redeemer!") "A happy fault"—that daring image, sanctioned by antiquity and thoroughly in accord with the best insights of the Reformation. Let us hope that any future revision will restore this passage!

baptism wherein, as Paul pointed out in the passage appointed for the Epistle, "We were buried with him by baptism into death, so that as Christ was raised from the dead by the glory of the Father, we too might walk in newness of life" (Rm 6:4). "Baptism," St. Augustine said in an Easter sermon, "is the sacrament of the new life, beginning in the present age with the forgiveness of past sins, but only to be completed in the resurrection of the dead."[84]

So we are prepared to burst into that triumphant cry and response whereby we witness to Jesus Christ, the first fruits of the promised resurrection:

Alleluia. Christ is risen.

The Lord is risen indeed. Alleluia.

Then the Eucharist begins.

Easter lasts for fifty days, as opposed to only forty days of Lent. The period of fifty days between Easter and Pentecost is defined by the Scriptures themselves (Lv. 23:16; Ac 2:1); nonetheless, as C. S. Lewis's Screwtape was well aware, the God of Christians is a hedonist at heart, and so it is appropriate on other grounds that there will always be more feasting than fasting in the church. "From Easter till Pentecost," wrote Egeria, "not a single person fasts, even if they are apotactites [i.e. monks or nuns]."[85] One mark of this continued celebration is the use of the Proper of the saint:[86] During the Great Fifty Days, "since the triumphs of the saints are a continuation and manifestation of the Paschal victory of Christ, the celebration of saints' days is particularly appropriate."[87]

Easter moves through Ascension Day* to culminate in Pentecost,* marking the triumph of Jesus' exaltation to the right hand of God and the giving of the gift of the Spirit to the Church.

The Incarnation speaks of the union of God with our flesh; the Ascension speaks of the triumph of our flesh resulting from that union. We must say more than that death of human flesh has been conquered in the Resurrection. At least since the latter years of the fourth century, Christianity has affirmed the celebration of the exaltation of our very humanity in divine glory: *theosis* is the teaching more prevalent in the Eastern churches than in the West that "in Christ, God became human, so that in Christ humans might become divine." The seventeenth-century divine, Peter Heylyn, put it thus: "Not altering thereby the nature which before it had, but adding a perfection of that glory which before it had not, and making it, though a natural body still, yet a body glorified."[88] Jesus' glorified humanity is the pledge of our own some-day-to-be-glorified humanity. He has gone before us, as the appointed Preface points out, "to prepare a place for us; that where he is, there we might also be, and reign with him in glory."[89] Despite present

---

[84] Augustine, *Sermon 8 in the Octave of Easter*; in Brother Kenneth (1983): 309.

[85] Egeria (1971): #41.

[86] *Lesser Feasts and Fasts, together with The Fixed Holy Days,* 3rd ed. (New York: The Church Hymnal Corporation, 1980): 20.

[87] *Idem* (1980): 56

[88] Peter Heylyn, *Theologia Veterum* (1654): 270; cited in Paul Elmer More and Frank Leslie Cross, eds., *Anglicanism: The Thought and Practice of the Church of England, Illustrated from the Religious Literature of the Seventeenth Century* (London: S.P.C.K., 1957): 273.

[89] BCP 379, Preface of the Ascension.

appearances, we humans are star children, created by God for an eternal and infinite destiny.

Two earthly corollaries must, however, attend this heavenly truth: First, as one of the Collects appointed for the day teaches, despite Christ's ascension into Heaven, "according to his promise, he abides with his Church on earth," nonetheless, "even to the end of the ages."[90] We are not left comfortless while remaining on earth. Second, as baptized Christians, we do not have to wait until the end for glory, for even in the midst of present griefs, we may, if we choose, "in heart and mind thither ascend, and with him continually dwell."[91] So the whole matter of the Ascension was remarkably summarized by Austin : "…[H]ere Christ ascends in fire; the fire is kindled in the Christian heart, and we ascend. He says to us all, 'Lift up your hearts;' and we reply, 'We lift them up unto the Lord.'"[92]

Ten days later, Ascension is followed by Pentecost* and commemoration of the first fruits of future glory already received in the church on earth, that is, the outpouring of the Holy Spirit. It is appropriate that in contemporary usage, on Pentecost rather than (as in previous Western usage) on Ascension Day, the Paschal Candle is finally extinguished. What is celebrated above all at Pentecost is that moment at which the church through the gift of the Spirit is enabled to become *itself* God's Paschal Candle, shining out in Christ's light to the nations. As Austin Farrer observed with his usual penetration, Pentecost is not the festival of the Holy Spirit, it is the festival of the Holy Spirit's descent upon us:

> [A]s the Holy Ghost grows in us, it is… we who grow. The Holy Ghost does not grow up and leave us behind, we grow up into the Holy Ghost… [who] becomes the spring and substance of our mind and heart… the never failing fountain of which Jesus spoke to the Samaritaness. We break up the stony rubbish of our life again and again, to find and release the well of living water.[93]

St. Cyril of Jerusalem had made the same point in his own way:

> One spring watered all Paradise, and the same rain comes down on all the world, yet it becomes white in the lily, red in the rose, purple in the violet… shaping itself to each that receives. Just so the Holy Spirit, being one, and of one nature indivisible, yet apportions grace to each person individually… . One in nature, the Spirit yet brings forth many excellent things by God's will and in Christ's name.[94]

Celebrating the Life of Christ

Why celebrate the *events* of Christ's life in the liturgy of the church?[95]

---

[90] *BCP 226*, Collect for Ascension Day.

[91] *BCP 226*, second Collect for Ascension Day.

[92] Farrer (1955): 34.

[93] *Idem*: 36.

[94] St. Cyril of Jerusalem, *Catechetical Lectures* 16.12, in Henry Bettensen, *The Later Christian Fathers: A Selection from the Writings of the Fathers from St. Cyril of Jerusalem to St. Leo the Great* (London: S.P.C.K., 1970): 38.

[95] See Bryan (1993):166-70.

The Old Testament asks us, "Who is on the Lord's side?" (Ex 32.6)—and insists on doing so in the context of Israel's story, frequently an unpleasant story with a significance by no means always evident to us, just as it was manifestly not always evident to those who lived it. The New Testament asks a second question, Christ's question: "Who do you say that I am?" (Mk 8.29)— also in the context of a story that was not always pleasant, the story of Jesus' life, death, and exaltation.

Narrative, better than argument and proposition, binds us directly to the grief and ambiguity that must be involved when we offer *any* human answer to the questions asked of us by God. Only the narrative of history—talking about the lives of particular persons in particular times and places—can enable us to identify both with the disciples in their confusion and uncertainty, and with Jesus in his frustration at their lack of understanding; or with Peter in the agony of his betrayal, and with Jesus in the loneliness of being betrayed. Only a story can involve us in the promises made at the Last Supper and the treachery already planned. Only a story can face us with the irony either of those who called Jesus "King of the Jews" in mockery, and so spoke the truth though they did not know it, or of the pagan soldier who crucified him but was then first to confess him crucified. Only a story can allow us to hear the angelic witness to the resurrection and yet identify with the awestruck silence and fear of the women who had heard it.

All such stories are a burden to us. They remind us as we encounter the ambiguity and confusion of our own lives. We, too, seldom find clear answers to our questions, and even when we do, we seldom have the courage to act upon those answers. Yet the church binds us precisely to a story such as this, year after year, Sunday after Sunday, day after day, the story of that "life" told through the liturgy of the festivals in the Calendar of Christ. The story of that life then obliges us to understand that any hope we have, however broken we may be in our ambivalent individuality, comes to us for the present when we respond to God's call, rather than resisting it.

Some have ever objected to this aspect of the Christian religion, from Gnostics and Docetists in the early years of the church who wanted a Christianity without Jewish history and a Christ who had not been crucified, to 21st-century teachers who proclaim a Cosmic Christ whose incarnation in Jesus of Nazareth, as Angela West put it, "becomes an awkward little detail in a much more significant universal."[96] Against this evaporation of the concrete and particular, the churches' insistence on commemorating year by year the specific events of Christ's life abides—like the creeds and the canonical Gospels—a bedrock of faith in the One who was real, personal, tangible, and historical. These commemorations, and the liturgy that enshrines them, work on us like a good poem in which the universal and eternal are to be found either in and through the individual and the local or not at all. The foundation of the Gospel tradition, and the liturgy focused upon the events of Christ's life found within it, "always starts from something personal in order to declare things and values that are of universal significance."[97] Why this centrality of the individual, the temporal, and the local? Because God will deal with us through nothing save reality, and in the realm of history

---

[96] Angela West, "Matthew Fox: Blessing for Whom?" *Sewanee Theological Review* 38/4 (1995): 336.

[97] Anna Maria Chiavacci Leonardi, ed., *Dante Alighieri: Commedia: Inferno* (Milan: Arnoldo Mondadori, 1991): 1: 238–39, thus describes Dante's poetry: "*Sempre, Dante parte da un fatto personale per dichiarare fatti e valori di portata universale.*"

in which we live, the individual and the local are the moment-by-moment reality that we know. On account of all our weakness and transience in time and place, none of us has anything to sustain us other than that God is source of each one of us, and our end is the promise of resurrection.

So the liturgy takes us through the drama of Christ's life. To take part in just *some* of these commemorations—to visit a church, for example, only for the liturgy on Easter Sunday without having experienced the rest of Holy Week—is like entering a theater and watching only the last act of a great play. One does not say that the experience will be meaningless or that we cannot profit from it; by missing the first parts, however, we have certainly failed to share the total event, and therefore we cannot fully appreciate the climax and completion.

The church's liturgy presents us with the drama of Christ's life and, indeed, with the drama of salvation history in its entirety. Like all drama, this acted-out life requires that we participate in it if we are to be moved by it, and the more we participate, the more we shall be moved. To what end? Drama can change us, as Aristotle knew: In the case of tragedy, the action on stage works through the arousal of our pity and fear to effect a *catharsis* of these emotions.[98] By taking part in the liturgical life of Christ, we begin to feel our self-love turning to love of others, and our fear of death and crosses turning to hope for resurrection.

We have compared the liturgy several times to rhetoric, in particular the rhetoric of the ancient *bios*. The rhetoricians of antiquity were aware, however, that rhetoric must have a moral effect or else it is meaningless, and they knew that both the speaker and the audience share responsibility for that effect. We commemorate Christ through the liturgical "life" in order to drench ourselves in Christ's person, his deeds, and his life. We seek so to be drenched that we may live hopefully in the world, and so living, by grace, bring to the world some measure of grace in His name.

---

[98] Aristotle, *Poetics* 6.1449b.

REFORMATION AND RESTORATION:
A COMPARATIVE STUDY OF
MARTIN LUTHER AND ALEXANDER CAMPBELL

LEROY GARRETT

The Principle of Available Light

> *No man can be justified today by living in accordance with*
> *the knowledge he had yesterday.*
> — Alexander Campbell

My interest in this comparative study was kindled by the frequent—and sometimes quite unusual—references in Alexander Campbell's writings to Martin Luther. I wondered what influence Luther had had on Campbell, particularly in reference to the motifs that appear to distinguish them: reformation and restoration. If reformation is especially associated with Luther, and restoration with Campbell, then the comparisons—and the distinctions—might prove interesting.

Campbell, however, also talked about reformation, even describing his own efforts as "the new Reformation," and he talked about reformation as much as, if not more than, he did about restoration. Sometimes he used the terms synonymously. Similarly for Luther, the restoration motif is present in his writing, if by that term one means an appeal to primitive Christianity in reforming the church.

My thesis in this essay is that while Campbell virtually equated "the Protestant Reformation" with Martin Luther, and saw it and him as the providential work of God, and as a turning-point in human history for both the church and the world, Campbell—like generations of Anabaptists before him—was persuaded that Luther and the German Reformation had not gone far enough. Not that Campbell blamed Luther for leaving the task unfinished, for Campbell understood Luther to have responded faithfully to the opportunities afforded him and to have followed the light that he had been granted. Both Luther and Campbell believed the idea behind the motto: *Ecclesia semper reformanda*, "the church must always be reforming herself." Luther did not, contrary to the claim, coin this phrase, just as Campbell did not express some of the Restorationist mottos often ascribed to him, and some of those that he did express he had borrowed from others. Luther, in Campbell's view, had been raised up by God to usher in the renewal of the church, and he had made considerable headway. Campbell heard his call three hundred years later to take up where Luther had left off. Both reformation and restoration of the church, he believed, are ongoing.

Campbell set forth the "principle of available light" in an imaginary conversation he penned between Luther and a monk named Erastian. Campbell made his literary Luther hold anyone responsible to follow only the light that one may have:

Erastian: Friend Luther, what think ye has become of your pious father?

Luther: He has gone to heaven, sir, I doubt not.

Erastian: And your mother, too?

Luther: Yes, and my mother too; and my grandfather and grandmother also, for Saxony can boast of no Catholics more devout than they.

Erastian: Then in the name of both Saint Paul and Saint Peter, why have you caused all this fuss in Germany and throughout the world? Do you expect anything better than to go to heaven when you die?

Luther: Nothing better than to enjoy heaven.

Erastian: If then, your pious ancestors, who lived and died in the bosom of the Holy, Catholic, and Apostolic Church, have gone to heaven, as you believe, how dare you separate from that church? Are you sure that, separated from that church, you can arrive at heaven? Besides, you say that you can promise yourself no more than heaven where you now stand; why not, then, have the good company of your virtuous ancestors, and walk with them in the good old way, rather than be enrolled with heretics, and hazard so much for nothing gained!

Luther: "For nothing gained!?" Why, sir, I have gained everything in renouncing the Pope—peace of mind and the joyful hope of heaven.

Erastian: Remember, you have conceded that your ancestors gained heaven in the Church of Rome; and why could not you?

Luther: Because they were pious members of that church, which I could not possibly be.

Erastian: Why not?

Luther: Because I have been favored with more knowledge than they were.[1]

As the extended conversation continues, Campbell has Luther say of his ancestors: "They lived in conformity to all they knew, and died in the church; I live in conformity to what I know, and have left that church."[2] Luther goes on to say, "Certainly as the brain grows, the heart should grow."[3] And finally Campbell has Luther tell Erastian that one must obey the light that God has given him.

One can see that Campbell put himself into that conversation. What Campbell called "piety" we today would call "spirituality." Piety is the basis of one's acceptance before God, Campbell understood, and it means to respond faithfully to such knowledge or light as God has given. Luther's ancestors had been saved in the Roman Church because they had been pious—faithful to the knowledge they had of the gospel. Luther had received more knowledge, so he believed that he had been required to leave that church. As Campbell's Luther asks the monk: "...for have we not both agreed that the ratio of piety is the ratio of conformity to the revealed will of God...?" And finally, "Indeed, no man can be justified today by living in accordance with the knowledge that he had yesterday."[4]

Campbell saw himself as one who, due to the contingencies of history, had been given more light than Luther had been given. Just as Luther had enjoyed more light than

---

[1] Alexander Campbell, "Dialogue between Martin Luther & The Monk Erastian," *Millennial Harbinger* (December 1837): 539ff.

[2] *Ibid.*: 540.

[3] *Ibid.*: 541.

[4] *Ibid.*: 540

his parents had done, and had to go beyond where they were, so Campbell, having more light than Luther had, was required by the will of God to go beyond where Luther had gone. In another context, Campbell put it a different way: The light that would dispel darkness is sometimes hindered by the traditions that have long held the light in bondage. Referring to Luther's effort to remove the darkness that the Roman Church had brought upon the world, Campbell insisted, "The darkness has been only partially dissipated." He went on to explain:

> The Bible was brought out of prison, and Luther bid it march. He made it speak in German, and thus obtained for it a respectful hearing. It was soon loaded with immense burthens of traditions, drawn from the cloister and the cells where it had so long been incarcerated. It soon became unable to travel with its usual speed—and then stopped the Reformation.[5]

Campbell saw his effort as one of getting the Reformation back on track, but from a perspective different from Luther's. Campbell referred to "the present generation"— meaning his people and his movement—as having begun "a new order of things" that was bringing both political and religious freedom. He identified this as "the hopes of the expectants of the restoration of the ancient order of things."[6]

From our perspective in the 21st century, we can see even more clearly what Campbell saw about Luther and "more light"; we can also see that since Campbell, yet more light has broken forth; and we expect, believe, and hope that even more light is yet to shine. Campbell had the advantage over Luther of 17th-century developments in toleration of religious differences, and 18th-century developments in the use of rationality to dispel superstition and ignorance. We now, similarly, have the advantage over both Luther and Campbell in 19th- and 20th-century developments in the sciences, and in the application of the sciences to Religious Studies. Campbell's interest in phrenology, for example, has been superseded by psychology, and his overly optimistic attitudes concerning the Anglo-Saxon race must now be tempered by awareness of our multicultural world—although Campbell's prophecy about the English language as the global tongue has come to pass (for a while).

The Bible As Centerpiece

> *One thing, and one thing alone is necessary to life, the word of God.*
> —Martin Luther

> *The Bible and the Bible alone is our rule of faith.*
> —Alexander Campbell

As the particulars of Luther's and Campbell's efforts gradually become relativized by history, their permanent contributions become clearer by contrast. The restoration of the ancient order of things became the centerpiece of Campbell's plea, and this desire to connect with Early Christianity, I affirm, is what gave continuity from Luther's reformation to Campbell's restoration, and permanence to their common appeal. Campbell spent several years spelling out in his journals what he meant by a restoration

---

[5] Alexander Campbell, "Prefatory Remarks," *Millennial Harbinger* (4 January 1830): 4.
[6] *Loc. cit.*

of the ancient order of things. His word "order" did not mean a "pattern" to be duplicated; and it is more descriptive than prescriptive. For Campbell, "order" was centered in "ordinances" rather than in a code of biblical law, and ordinances were what God had instituted for his church, through which God bestows grace, and which Campbell believed needed to be re-formed and restored. And for Campbell, as for Luther, the sure and certain way to the recovery of the ancient order was through the scriptures.

In one instance, Campbell expanded the meaning of "ordinances" by referring to them as means of spiritual enjoyment, including the reading of the scriptures: "What, then, under the present administration of the kingdom of heaven, are the ordinances which contain the grace of God?" Campbell asked. "They are, preaching the gospel— immersion in the name of Jesus, into the name of the Father, and of the Son, and of the Holy Spirit—the reading and teaching the Holy Oracles—the Lord's day—the Lord's supper—fasting—prayer—confession of sins—and praise."[7]

Like Luther in 1522, early in his Reformation, so Campbell in 1827, early in his Restoration, published his own translation of the New Testament. Luther's New Testament was the first translation into German that reached the masses, and Campbell's was the first American translation. Luther and Campbell were, before all else, men of the Book.

Where else in all history does one find such a moving appeal to scripture as when Luther stood before his accusers assembled for the Diet at Worms in 1521? When asked if he would repudiate the views expressed in the books lying before him that he had authored, Luther replied that he could not unless he were convinced from the Bible that they were erroneous. Questioned further, he insisted that his conscience was captive to the word of God, and that unless he were convicted by scripture and plain reason, he would not recant. He no longer accepted the authority of popes and councils, for they contradicted one another, he charged. He closed with a ringing prayer: "God help me. Amen!" Another version of his closing words has him saying, "Here I stand. I can do no other."

Luther could "do no other" because he was captive to the word of God, and his captivity to scripture was evident throughout his reforming efforts. He spoke in absolute terms when it came to the Bible: "One thing, and one thing alone, is necessary to life, justification, and Christian liberty; and that is the most holy word of God, the gospel of Christ."[8] From the time he issued his famous ninety-five theses, challenging indulgences in particular, it was the Bible that was his ultimate source of authority. While early on he had no intention of breaking with the pope or the Catholic Church, he at last took the position that no ecclesiastical institution is authoritative. Pope and church may err; only the scriptures are authoritative.

In one of his pamphlets, *The Babylonian Captivity of the Church*, Luther questioned the church for withholding the Communion cup from the laity, arguing his case from the Bible. Likewise, he challenged the doctrine of transubstantiation, appealing to scripture. Equally significant, he denied that the mass is a sacrifice to God and therefore a good work by which God's favor is earned. The Bible teaches, he argued, that salvation comes

---

[7] Alexander Campbell, "Extra," *Millennial Harbinger* (1834): 423, 424.

[8] Martin Luther, *The Freedom of a Christian* (1520), John Dillenberger, ed. & trans., *Martin Luther: Selections from his Writings* (Garden City: Anchor Books, Doubleday, 1961): 54.

only through God's incomprehensible grace, and that the mass is a gift of God to be received with faith and thanksgiving. Likewise, Luther rooted two of his most famous Reformation doctrines–the priesthood of all believers and justification by faith apart from works–in scripture alone.

Luther, hiding out in the Wartburg castle for a year after the Diet at Worms, translated the New Testament. He would translate the Old Testament later. Nothing underscores Luther as "a man of the Book" as much as his passion to translate the Bible into the language of the German people – "real German" and "not Latin or Greek couched in German," as he put it. Working alone and painstakingly (Melancthon looked over the New Testament translation with a critical eye before it was published, but Luther had done the work), Luther said he sometimes spent a fortnight to find the right expression for a single word!

Translating the Old Testament Luther found more daunting than he did translating the New. Self-taught in Hebrew at first, he had studied Hebrew with rabbis during his trip to Rome in 1510. In a letter to his friend, Wenceslaus Link at Nürnberg in June 1528, Luther lamented over his struggle to translate the Old Testament:

> We are sweating over the work of putting the Prophets into German. God, how much of it there is, and how hard it is to make these Hebrew writers talk German! They resist us, and do not want to leave their Hebrew and imitate our German barbarisms. It is like making a nightingale leave her own sweet song and imitate the monotonous voice of a cuckoo, which she detests.[9]

One of Luther's guidelines, "A revelation should reveal," led him to disparage some portions of scripture, even though he took equal pains to translate them to match the parts that he preferred. He concluded that the Book of Revelation does not help anyone to understand anything, and he found James "a right strawy epistle." Luther's guiding principle of canon was a Christological criterion: *solus Christus* (Christ only) and *sola fide et gratia* (faith only and grace only). Scripture that does not advance Christ (*was Christum treibet*), Luther was willing to leave out of the canon. Another of his rules was that no sectarian–however well versed in the languages–can translate scripture correctly. And he realized that–however unbiased one may be—no absolutely correct translation of the Bible is possible, including his own.[10]

Luther's sense of the limits of translation caused him to revise his translation with each new printing, year after year, even to the day of his death in 1546. Luther was ahead of his time in realizing that every translation is an interpretation of the Bible and, therefore, is an ongoing task. Of his own efforts he said: "This version won't last forever, either. In time the world will need something new again, and throw it away."[11] Luther thought that his translation would not outlast him, but it took root in Germany, furthered

---

[9] Martin Luther, *WA, DB* 9I, x–xii; Martin Luther, *Word and Sacrament I: Luther's Works* vol. 35, Jaroslav J. Pelikan, Hilton C. Oswald, and Helmut T. Lehmann, eds. (Philadelphia: Fortress Press, 1960, 1999).

[10] On Luther's Christological interpretation of biblical books and his "canon within the canon," see his "Prefaces" to the New Testament. Some of the key texts are assembled in Dillenberger (1961): 18-19, 35-37; see also Bernhard Lohse, *Martin Luther's Theology: Its Historical and Systematic Development* (Minneapolis: Fortress Press, 1999): 189-191.

[11] Cited by Edith Simon, *Luther Alive* (New York: Doubleday, 1968): 292.

the Reformation, and inspired Tyndale's English translation (1525-35), and thereby fed directly into the translations that we read in English today.

However much Luther extolled the Bible, particularly in reference to doctrinal issues, one is left to marvel that its ethical teaching appears to have had so little impact upon some of his attitudes and actions. Here, again, we must understand Luther as a creature of his times, the 16th century, one whose behavior was shaped—as was Campbell's in his century and as is ours in our century—by the conventional habits and legal structures of society and according to the light that he had then (and that Campbell had and that we now have). Whereas, for example, Luther at first strongly condemned the medieval church for burning heretics, well aware that he himself might meet such a fate, he reversed his position later on when he had an ecclesiastical establishment of his own to protect, and he had to deal with heretics. One of the ironies of history is that Martin Luther gave consent, however reluctantly, to the burnings, beheadings, and drownings of heretics, particularly the rebellious Anabaptists. Social, political, and legal toleration of differences in religion was unknown in Luther's century, and it would come about only under the liberalizing aegis of the Enlightenment in the 17th and 18th centuries, partly in reaction to the blood-guilt of the Protestants that had matched that of the Catholics during the Wars of Religion.

Campbell in the 19th century was, and we in the 21st century are, beyond the physical punishment of heretics in religion. We may only devoutly hope that our current crusade against Islam; our relaxation of humane policy against torture; our lurch to the social, political, and religious Right; and our temptation to re-unify religion and politics, will not take us back to Luther's era and the Wars of Religion. Nevertheless, old habits die hard: Leaders of Churches of Christ have burned other Christians' books as heretical, dissidents in religion have been treated harshly and fired from their jobs, and women are still told to "keep silent in the churches."

Luther's language was often caustic and hateful, particularly toward the pope, whom he described in terms of apocalyptic evil. As one of his biographers put it, "Luther lost all self-control and abused the papacy in the filthiest terms."[12] Luther prided himself on the roughness of his working-class German language. He is infamous for his classist advice against the rebellious peasants: "Club them like lemmings!" And he was viciously anti-Semitic, even to the degree of recommending that Jews be deported to Palestine and approving of the destruction of synagogues. Martin Marty, unlike some Luther scholars through the centuries, made no excuse for Luther's offensive and repulsive anti-Semitism.[13] Roland Bainton expressed the wish that Luther might have died before he wrote such things about the Jews.[14] The translators of the 55 volumes of *Luther's Works* considered not translating Luther's anti-Jewish diatribes, but they decided that they owed it to history to present a full and honest Luther.

Campbell and his associates struggled with analogous problems. The great ecclesiastical challenge in mid-19th-century America was to hold the North and South elements of the Stone-Campbell restorationist reformation together when half the

---

[12] Walter Nigg, *The Heretics* (New York: Alfred A. Knopf, 1962): 297.

[13] Martin Marty, *Martin Luther* (New York: Penguin, 2004): xi.

[14] Roland H. Bainton, *Here I Stand* (Nashville: Abingdon, 1950): 379.

brethren either believed in or practiced slavery, and the other half was ready to kill to abolish it. Campbell tried to walk down the middle, but in so doing, he let his biblicism triumph over his morality: He correctly upheld that the Bible teaches slavery, while he himself was no longer in favor of it. Half immersed in his culture, Campbell did not have the same amount of light on human rights that we now enjoy.[15] But even in our own time, our Christian colleges were among the last to achieve racial integration, and 20th-century racism and segregation remain a feature of the Southern churches even into the 21st century, as Don Haymes is documenting in his excellent on-line studies, "Race and the Churches of Christ."[16] Don would say: "May God have mercy!" And I say, *O Lord, let new light shine upon us all!*

Campbell translated only the New Testament, but in the matter of biblical interpretation, Campbell went beyond Luther. Luther as a student of the Bible in the 16th century had benefited spectacularly from the literary work of the Humanists; Campbell as a student of the Bible in the 19th century enjoyed three more centuries of light, including the illumination of the 18th-century Enlightenment. Especially in the science of hermeneutics (interpretation), Campbell was able to articulate a more adequate approach to understanding the historical text of the scriptures. We, now, benefit from the new light that is ever breaking forth from scripture and shining upon our minds by way of such windows as *The Restoration Quarterly*, that fine journal wherein some of our best minds publish their best exegetical work.

One of Campbell's rules of hermeneutics was his emphasis on the *facts* of scripture. The "facts," Campbell insisted, are what matters most. For his definition of "facts," Campbell drew on Francis Bacon.[17] Revelatory facts in scripture are what God has said or done, and facts demand consensus; theories about the facts, on the other hand—that is to say, theology—are matters of opinion, and in matters of opinion there must be liberty. Campbell was—or would have been—comfortable with the motto that his people eventually borrowed from the ecumenically minded, both Protestants and Catholics: "In essentials [facts] unity; in opinions [theology] liberty; in all things, charity."[18] To put it another way, facts are what the Bible actually says, whereas opinions (theories) are what one thinks it means by what it says.[19]

---

[15] See Chris Hutson, "Middle Ground? Alexander Campbell on Slavery and Carroll Osburne on Slavery," in this volume.

[16] http://www.mun.ca/rels/restmov/subs/race.html

[17] On the hermeneutical issues, see Michael W. Casey, *The Battle over Hermeneutics in the Stone-Campbell Movement, 1800-1870* (Lewiston, New York: Edwin Mellen Press, 1998).

[18] Hans Rollmann, "In Essentials Unity: The Pre-history of a Restoration Movement Slogan," *Restoration Quarterly* 39/3 (1997): 129-39: http://www.restorationquarterly.org/ Volume 039/ rq03903rollmann.htm.

[19] For this reason, when a simple Christian gathered with other Christians around the open Bible becomes dumbfounded by a passage of scripture difficult to understand, and that Christian affirms of the knotty text that "it means what it says," far from uttering an unlearned tautology, he or she is affirming in all epistemological humility the heart of Campbellite faith in the facts of scripture: It *meant* to the writer what it says, whether we now can tell what it *means* to us or not. This reverence for the historical meaning of text, "what it meant," leads spiritual descendents of Campbell to forego subjective overindulgence in expressions of "what it means to me" in preference for reaffirmation of "what it meant to the author who wrote it," whether we understand it 2,000 years later or not.

The gospel, Campbell reasoned, is made up of facts: the mighty acts of God *done* through Jesus Christ, and this is the gospel that is, Campbell held, the basis of Christian unity. The gospel is at the center, which is Christ; all other matters are marginal, even when a matter is important. Christ the center of everything for the Christian—this was also Luther's position, and it became the hallmark of Campbell's plea for unity in diversity. "So long as they hold to Christ as head"—I paraphrase to encapsulate Campbell's plea—"we don't care how many opinions they have, so long as they do not bind them upon others."[20] The Bible was the foundation of Campbell's restoration of the ancient order, but the facts of the gospel recorded in the Bible were the centerpiece of Campbell's plea. None of the lesser details—even those that seemed more important than others—held for Campbell the centrality of God's "facts": the death, burial, and resurrection of Jesus, the Son of God, the Messiah, the Savior.

Another of Campbell's rules of interpretation, unique in its time, anticipated the Biblical scholarship of our time: *We must come within understanding distance of the text.*[21] This curious exhortation was Campbell's way of saying that we are to interpret with the heart as well as with the head, and Campbell went so far as to say this: "All beyond that *distance* cannot understand God; all within it can easily understand Him in all matters of piety and morality. God, Himself, is the center of that circle, and humility is its circumference."[22] To put it another way, to understand we must *want* to understand. Campbell's was a "common sense" approach to scripture, influenced as he was by the Scottish philosophers who popularized that term, particularly Dugald Stuart, whom Campbell called the greatest of the metaphysicians. Early in his career as a restorer of the Bible to the heart of religion, Campbell put it this way: "I took the naked text and followed common sense; I read it, subject to the ordinary rules of interpretation, and it became to me a new book."[23]

Whereas both Luther and Campbell clearly esteemed the Bible as authoritative in their plea for reformation and restoration, substantive differences nevertheless prevailed between them in their grasp of its teaching.

Campbell was aware that Luther, for example, had expressed his preference for baptism as immersion. Luther believed immersion to be baptism as taught in the New Testament:

> Baptism is *baptismos* in Greek, and *mersio* in Latin, and means to plunge something completely into the water, so that the water covers it. Although in many places it is no longer customary to thrust and dip infants into the font, but only with the hand to pour the baptismal water upon them out of the font, nevertheless the former is what should be done. It would be proper, according to the meaning of the word "baptism," that the infant, or whoever is to be baptized, should be put in and sunk completely into the water and then drawn out again. For even in the German tongue, the word *Taufe* [baptism] comes undoubtedly from the word *tief* [deep] and means that what is baptized is sunk deeply into the

---

[20] This sentiment expressed in *Millennial Harbinger* (December 1840): 558, 559.

[21] Alexander Campbell, *Christian System* (Cincinnati: Standard, reprint, n. d.): 4f.

[22] *Loc. cit.*

[23] Alexander Campbell, "Reply to Brother Semple," *Millennial Harbinger* (March 1830): 135-139.

water. This usage is also demanded by the significance of baptism itself. For baptism, as we shall hear, signifies that the old man and the sinful birth of flesh and blood are to be wholly drowned by the grace of God. We should therefore do justice to its meaning and make baptism a true and complete sign of the thing it signifies.[24]

And yet, Luther was never immersed as an adult after having had water poured on his head for baptism in infancy. Luther did not believe in anabaptism (re-baptism) because, thinking with Augustine, he believed that sacraments are unrepeatable, and that each sacrament conveys its own indelible "character" on the soul of the recipient. Even imperfect sacraments are still sacraments and, as such, efficacious; baptism, therefore, need not be repeated. We understand this point: Who of us, baptized at 10 years old, understood then as much or as well as we do now at 70 about baptism (not to mention God's grace and the gospel)? Does this mean that we need to be re-baptized every ten years or so? No, there is "one baptism," whether it was perfect or not, and it does not need to be repeated.

Luther as a Catholic, and Campbell as a Presbyterian had both been christened in the same traditional non-biblical way. Although Luther also preferred believer's (adult) baptism (immersion), he never made either the form of baptism or the baptism of infants an issue, not even with his own children. Here Campbell parted from Luther, helped along—once again—by greater available light and where he stood in history: After Campbell had left the Presbyterians, he became a Baptist, for a while, before he became a Restorationist. When he left the Baptists, he took with him what they had taught him. Then, after a thorough study of the scriptures, Campbell decided against pouring water on his infant daughter and calling it baptism.[25]

We must therefore conclude that Campbell the restorer was closer to the Bible on the practice of baptism than was Luther the reformer. Luther was more "theological" in his rationalization of traditional Catholic baptism; Campbell was focused more on the "facts" and "ordinances" of the Bible—things that God had done and that we are to do. According to the ancient order evident in scripture, baptism had been central to the faith and practice of the first-century Christians, for baptism was the way that a believer entered into Christ and the forgiveness of sins that God through grace had made available in the gospel of the death, burial, and resurrection of Jesus. Because Campbell was endeavoring to restore the New-Testament order of things to the church of his day, he was captured by the scriptures and "could do no other." All the biblical facts made clear to Campbell that the ordinance of baptism in the New Testament was immersion in water of people who had expressed belief in Christ.

---

[24] *Luther's Works* (1960, 1999): 35: 18-21. While various forms of ritual washing have been practiced by many religions in all periods, the earliest Christian ablution was by immersion. In the Latin Church it prevailed until the twelfth century, and in some places until the sixteenth century (*The Catholic Encyclopedia*, II, 261–262). In Luther's world, the oldest baptismal order of the Münster bishopric (*ca.* 1400–1414) prescribes triple immersion. The 1521 order of the Schwerin diocese allows a choice between immersion and washing [*abwaschen*]. Luther's 1528 order of baptism prescribed dipping the child into the font (*PE* 6, 201). Bucer and Zwingli both favored pouring (*CL* 1, 185, n. 12).

[25] Robert Richardson, *Memoirs of Alexander Campbell* (Philadelphia: J. B. Lippincott, 1868): 1: 390-405.

Unlike Luther, Campbell did not *"prefer* baptism by immersion"; rather, Campbell, the Greek scholar, was compelled by the language of the New Testament to respond in faith through total immersion, for that is the action of the Greek word when it is properly translated (as Luther himself had agreed). In Campbell's translation of the New Testament, he translated the Greek word literally; thus, "John the Immerser." Immersion in the New Testament was an ordinance ordained by God to be the fact of faith by which sins were to be washed away. Campbell therefore reasoned that being immersed was the response of faith to the act of God, and that pouring water on babies had not been ordained by God. Campbell rejected baby baptism along with his rejections of popes and councils. In an encyclopedic article about the movement he had helped to launch, Campbell wrote in 1838 the following about "Disciples of Christ":

> They regard all the sects and parties of the Christian world as having, in greater or less degrees, departed from the simplicity of faith and manners of the first Christians, and as forming what the apostle Paul calls "the apostasy." This defection they attribute to the great varieties of speculation and metaphysical dogmatism of the countless creeds, formularies, liturgies, and books of discipline adopted and inculcated as bonds of union and platforms of communion in all the parties which have sprung from the Lutheran reformation. The effects of these synodical covenants, conventional articles of belief, and rules of ecclesiastical polity, has been the introduction of a new nomenclature, a human vocabulary of religious words, phrases, and technicalities, which has displaced the style of the living oracles, and affixed to the sacred diction ideas wholly unknown to the apostles of Christ.[26]

Equally significant is that Campbell's plea for a restoration of the ancient order was also a plea for "uniting the Christians in all the sects," a motif not present in Luther's Reformation. Luther initially saw Christians as already united in the Catholic Church, a church badly in need of reformation, but a church that (except for some noisy heretics) was still essentially a single cultural phenomenon in the earl 16th century. Luther eventually came to believe that the Church of Rome was apostate and beyond reformation, and he lived long enough to see the final end of church unity conceived of as Euro-Catholicism—a cultural phenomenon that his own German Reformation helped to destroy.

Three centuries later, Campbell saw all around him the fallout of Luther's Reformation. In Campbell's view, nothing but a restoration of primitive, first-century, biblical Christianity could mend the once seamless garment of Christ, now torn and shredded by dozens and dozens of sects and denominations, on the way to becoming hundreds and thousands. No mere "reformation" of an existing ecclesiastical institution would do; only a radical "restoration" of the primitive gospel might succeed. This difference between reformation and restoration sent these two men in different directions in their use of the Bible.

---

[26] Alexander Campbell, "Disciples of Christ," *Fessenden's & Co.'s Encyclopedia of Religious Knowledge* (Brattleboro', Vermont: Brattleboro Typographic Company, 1838): 462-64: http://www.mun.ca/rels/restmov/texts/acampbell/DOC-ERK.HTM.

Catholicity: The Rule for Unity

> *Martin Luther was always a good Catholic.*
> —Hans Küng, Professor of Ecumenical Theology
> University of Tübingen, Germany

> *I am very catholic.*
> —Alexander Campbell

Despite his vitriolic attacks on Rome, Martin Luther never denied that the Church of Rome was the Catholic Church. Even though Rome had become, in Luther's opinion, worse than Sodom and Gomorrah, the Babylonian Harlot still had the gospel, the ministry, the scriptures, and the sacraments. Many years into the Reformation, Luther intended to be and to remain a Catholic. He never entertained the notion of a new church, a "Protestant" church, and certainly not a "Lutheran" church. New churches were the inventions of the Anabaptists and other sectarians whom Luther cordially detested. The Old Church could be reformed, Luther believed; she could even experience an evangelical awakening, and yet remain the historic Church.

Luther would have always agreed with Ignatius of Antioch, the first Christian writer who used "catholic" (universal) to describe the church: "Wherever Jesus Christ is, there is the catholic church."[27] Luther and other German fellow reformers in the 16th century, and Campbell three centuries later, believed alike that the *catholic* faith in Jesus Christ is "that which has been believed always, everywhere, and by all," according to scripture. And yet, as Luther's break with Rome gradually developed, he came to use "Christian" to describe the church more and "Catholic" less. When, at last, an ecclesiastical movement loyal to Luther had grown up, Luther could not abide to hear people of catholic faith being called "Lutherans," though at last he reluctantly consented. Today, sixty-four million Lutherans worldwide bear his name. Campbell had better luck in dissuading his co-religionists from allowing themselves to be called "Campbellites"—it is a nickname that never stuck, at least not with the Campbellites themselves! Nowadays, however, people do freely speak of the "Stone-Campbell Restoration Movement," a frank recognition that "these Christians" are different from "other Christians."

Hans Küng, the most notorious Roman Catholic theologian of the second half of the 20th century, himself a German professor accustomed to ecumenical dialogue with Protestants, described Luther as "the Catholic Luther," insisting that he "should by no means have been condemned sweepingly as un-Catholic." Küng further argued that Luther's excommunication in 1520 should be repealed: "It is one of those acts of reparation that should follow the pope's confession of guilt today." Küng claimed that the basic tenets of Luther's call for reform–including justification by faith only–were consistent with Late-Medieval Catholic piety.

Luther's "Christ alone," "grace alone," and "justification by faith alone" were all consistent, as well, with the theology of Augustine of Hippo, a 5th-century Western Catholic point of view that had been maintained by the Order of the Hermits of St. Augustine, the monastic community of which Luther had been a member. None of this

---

[27] Ignatius of Antioch, *Letter to the Church at Smyrna* 8.

was heretical in Catholic theology, Küng insisted, so the Reformer should be seen as faithfully Catholic to the very end. In fact, Rome's refusal to effect obviously needed reforms, in Küng's opinion, caused the Reformation and the dissolution of Christian unity more than did Luther's obstinacy. If the pope in Rome had only listened to the monk in Wittenberg, a church split might never have taken place, at least not along Roman Catholic/German Protestant lines. (The Anabaptists—I must say—would not have been placated had the Pope Leo and Friar Martin kissed and made up!) Even in the face of the Protestant exodus, Küng argued in his 1957 doctoral thesis, rapprochement could still have been effected over the doctrine of justification.[28]

On Reformation Day, October 3l, 1999, Roman Catholic officials and leaders of most of the Lutheran churches convened to sign a *Joint Declaration on the Doctrine of Justification by Faith*, thereby bringing the two communions closer together than they had been for soon-to-be 500 years. Hans Küng is proving to be a true prophet.[29]

Campbell, the catholic (small "c")

Alexander Campbell's claim, "I am very catholic," would likely surprise many of his followers today. In lectures and in debates he insisted that his restoration plea was eminently *catholic* – not Greek Catholic or Roman Catholic but just catholic. His people wore a catholic name: "Disciples" or "Christians," one that all believers could wear. They practiced a catholic baptism: immersion in the name of the Father, Son, and Holy Spirit, a baptism that all Christians can accept. They served a catholic Communion Table: "We neither invite nor debar; it is the Lord's table."[30] They had a catholic rule of faith and practice: the teaching of the Apostles.[31] Campbell challenged his critics, daring them to try to make his "Disciples" into a sect, proclaiming them and himself to be "catholic."[32]

---

[28] Hans Küng, *The Catholic Church* (New York: Random House, 2003): 120-121.

[29] Marty (2004): 194.

[30] Carey E. Morgan, "The Place of the Lord's Supper in the Movement," *Centennial Convention Report*, W.R. Warren, ed. (Cincinnati, Ohio: Standard Publishing Co., 1910): 466.

[31] Campbell's insistence on "Bible only" was more Protestant than either Catholic or catholic, the equivalent of Luther's *sola scriptura*. The Church of Rome has never premised her teaching solely on scripture. The Ancient Church of at least the first two centuries did not have either a doctrine or practice of "Bible only." The Bible that Campbell read was the Bible that Luther had read, a Protestant Bible, and neither the catholic nor the Catholic Bible, including the Apocrypha, that had been read nearly universally by the Great Church before Luther.

[32] Alexander Campbell, "The Bible Cause," in *The Millennial Harbinger* (January 1847): 5-7: "We have something called a catholic faith and a catholic Bible. Let us, then, have a catholic spirit, and co-operate with those who are doing all they can."

During Campbell's widely read debate[33] with Roman Catholic Bishop Purcell in Cincinnati in 1836/37, the reformer made some of the same charges against the Roman Church that Luther had made; nevertheless, Campbell saw his own position as more truly catholic than the bishop's sectarian commitment to Rome. Like Luther, Campbell charged that "Roman Catholic" is a contradiction in terms (and Hans Küng would later call it an oxymoron): A church that is particularly Roman cannot be truly catholic; a church that is universally catholic cannot be particularly Roman. Unlike Luther, who at times called both the Church of Rome and the pope "the Antichrist" and wax as hostile towards Rome as Rome was hostile towards him, Campbell, safe in the 19th century and in America from the predations of Church and Empire, could be gracious towards his debate opponent in Cincinnati; he and the bishop in fact became friends. Purcell afterwards opined that Campbell might well take a place in history alongside Luther and Calvin!

In 1839, Alexander Campbell, now three decades into his restoration movement, made a mid-course correction having to do with the principle of catholicity in reference to his plea for the unity of all Christians. He wrote in his journal that year that while unity had always been his "darling theme," he had lately come to see clearly "the ground on which all true Christians could form one visible and harmonious union."[34]

In an ecumenical gathering in Lexington, Kentucky, in 1841, Campbell restated his "catholic rule of union," formulated first in 1839, proposing it this time as a resolution and asking the audience to vote on it: "When convened according to appointment, the rule of union shall be, that, whatever in faith, piety, and morality is catholic, or universally admitted by all parties shall be adopted as the basis of union; and whatever is not by all parties admitted as of divine authority, shall be rejected as schismatical and human." The audience rose to its feet and gave its approval by an overwhelming standing vote.[35]

Thereafter, Campbell tended to make his plea for unity more in terms of "the catholic rule" than of the "restoration of the ancient order." He came to see that general agreement on what constituted "the ancient order" was not possible because the New Testament is susceptible to a divergent variety of interpretations, not unlike the variety

---

[33] *Debate on the Roman Catholic Religion: Held in the Sycamore-Street Meeting House, Cincinnati, from the 13th to the 21st of January, 1837. Between Alexander Campbell, of Bethany, Va., and the Rt. Rev. John B. Purcell, Bp. of Cincinnati. Taken down by Reporters, and Revised by the Parties* (Cincinnati, Ohio: J. A. James, 1837; reprint, Nashville: McQuiddy, 1914): 11:

> In the first place, the very term *Roman* Catholic indicates that she is a sect, and not the ancient, universal and apostolic church, the mother and mistress of all churches. If she be the only universal or Catholic church, why prefix the epithet Roman? A Roman Catholic church is a contradiction, The word Catholic means universal—the word Roman means something local and particular. What sense or meaning is there in a particular universal church? It is awkward on another account. If she pretends to be considered the only true and universal church of Christ among all nations and in all times, why call herself Roman ? To say the Roman Catholic church of America, is just as absurd as to say the Philadelphia church of Cincinnati,—the London church of Pittsburgh,—the church of France of the United States. The very terms that she chooses indicates that she cannot be the universal church.

[34] Alexander Campbell, "Union of Christians No. 1," *Millennial Harbinger* (May 1839): 212.
[35] *Idem*: "Union Christian Meeting," *ibid.*(1841): 258f.

that prevailed among Christians of the first century; consequently, Campbell now saw that general agreement in every detail could not be required because it is not possible and had never been historically the case. I summarize Campbell's shift by reformulating the famous motto, as follows: *In things catholic, unity; in things not catholic, liberty; in all things, charity.*

Here we find a distinct difference between Luther and Campbell on catholicity. Whereas both were catholic, Luther's catholicity was more historical, and Campbell's more biblically theological. To Luther's 16th-century mind, the Roman Church was still the catholic church, however apostate she might be and in need of reform under the word of God. The Church of Rome had been the Body of Christ historically present in Rome throughout the centuries since the days of Peter and Paul and Clement.

Campbell, in 19th-century America, saw catholicity less in terms of history than in terms of biblical principles, which Campbell called "facts" (as discussed above), distinguishing them from theories about facts. He referred to the seven "facts" of Ephesians 4, the seven *ones* there listed as the basis of unity: one Body, one Spirit, one Hope, one Lord, one Faith, one Baptism, and the one God and Father of all. This was Campbell's "catholic rule of union," based in the "fact" or principle of Jesus Christ himself, who is the ground of unity. When encouraging Christians to unite in spite of their differences, I paraphrase Campbell's plea: "So long as we hold to the Head, which is Christ."

The difference between Luther and Campbell here was Luther's passion to reform the existing church but Campbell's passion for the unity of Christians. While both reformers were catholic in principle, Luther thought more in terms of changing an ecclesiastical institution, whereas Campbell thought more in terms of uniting the Christians in all the sects, the very sects that had grown out of Rome's apostasy and Luther's reformation.

Reformation and Restoration: What Did They Mean?

> *I do not accept the authority of popes or councils.*
> —Martin Luther

> *We advocate the great and good cause of Reformation,*
> *or restoration of the ancient order of things.*
> —Alexander Campbell

Edith Simon, Luther scholar, summarized "the root of it all" in six propositions that she conceived Luther to have had in mind in his effort to reform the Church:

1. Man is saved by faith alone.
2. Faith is by divine grace only, merit an unearned boon.
3. Every baptized Christian has access to God without intermediaries.
4. The papacy was not instituted by Jesus, as claimed, but was a relatively recent fiction. From Luther's 16th-century perspective, the muscular development of the papacy had gathered steam with the 11th-century Gregorian Reform.
5. When ecclesiastical authority refuses to rectify flagrant ecclesiastical anomalies and abuses, secular authorities have not only the right but also the duty to act.

6. First and last and always, the Bible comprises the sole, definitive record of God's purpose and commandments, in which everyone should be thoroughly instructed, whereas the man-made code of canon law was an obstructive, cancerous excrescence that would spell death unless it were cut away.

Euro-Christian civilization was torn apart in the quarrel over these propositions, Simon concluded; Luther thereby defined a new way to periodize history: The thousand-year-long "Middle Ages" came to be seen as standing between antiquity and modernity.[36]

Another Luther scholar, Heiko A. Oberman, saw the issue in terms of "the Reformation breakthrough" (Simon's proposition #1, listed above): That sinners are saved by faith only, based on Paul's dictum that "the just shall live by faith," was "the central Reformation discovery." Salvation by faith only, said Oberman, was not merely new, it was unheard of, and it rent the very fabric of Christian ethics. Reward and merit–so long undisputed as the basic motivation for all human action–were robbed of their efficacy. Salvation through good works–long maintained as an indisputable doctrine–was stripped of its basis in scripture.[37]

Reformation scholar William Stevenson, however, weighing Luther's work in more personal terms, said that Luther's reformation changed the world through the freedom it brought to every believer by proclaiming the "priesthood of all believers." This Protestant dogma (implicit in Simon's proposition #3, above), was revolutionary in that it asserted the right of every believer, apart from any ecclesiastical intermediary, to go straight to God in prayer for pardon and for the strength to live. This individualization of Christian experience, essentially a restatement of Late-Medieval mysticism, marks a turning point in intellectual history away from collective consciousness and towards the personalization and psychologization of just about everything, religion included.

Since the political power play of the Gregorian Reform of the 11th century, Stevenson pointed out, the Church of Rome had exerted centralizing control over local and regional churches throughout Euro-Christendom. If a prince or king offended the pope, the whole political domain might be placed under interdict (the priests were forbidden to celebrate the sacraments in that place), and this impasse could last for years: No child might be baptized, no public services were allowed, no celebration of the eucharist was permitted, no lawful marriages were performed, no approved consolation to the dying was offered. Luther challenged this kind of "ecclesiastical tyranny," as Stevenson described it, and the new reforms brought freedom, not the least of which was that believers could commit themselves entirely to God's mercy, trusting in Heaven's promise of redeeming grace, with or without the blessing of an intermediary priest.

Beyond emancipation from papal tyranny, however, Stevenson argued that freedom of the mind and spirit was even more important. In this, Luther shared the values of Renaissance humanism and the freedom to think and to act for oneself. For over two hundred years, the scent of freedom had been on the wind. Dissident Franciscans in the 13th century had seen that the established church and the pope could become the "Whore of Babylon" and "the Antichrist" in opposition to the restoration of the gospel in St.

---

[36] Edith Simon (1968): 5-6.
[37] Heiko A. Oberman, *Luther: Man between God and the Devil* (New Haven: Yale, 1982): 154.

Francis. Renaissance Humanists in the 14th and 15th centuries raised the cry *"Ad fontes!"* (back to the original sources of the Greek and Hebrew languages of scripture and the ancient manuscripts), while applying their historical-critical methods to debunk the fake historical claims to the Church of Rome. Luther's 16th-century reformation was a northern-European religious expression of this pan-European liberation movement of the spirit. To apply Campbell's dictum, "New light had become available." Stevenson summarized to describe Luther's reformation as "the most vital and far-reaching event in all Christian history since the Gospel had been preached by Christ Himself and by His apostles."[38]

Hans Küng summed up Luther's reform in these words: "[Luther] called on the church to return to the gospel of Jesus Christ." In the place of traditions, canon laws, and scholastic authorities, Luther gave them "scripture alone." In the place of thousands of saints and mediators, Luther gave them "Christ alone." In the place of all pious achievements and devout works to attain salvation, Luther gave them "faith only."[39]

Emphasis on the religious principles alone, however, is inadequate to explain either the success of Luther's reformation or the effectiveness of telling everyone to read their own Bible. Luther's reformation could not have succeeded, and everyone could not have had their own Bible, without the new technology of a recent invention: the printing press—part of the Humanist Renaissance, mentioned above. Luther hailed Gutenberg's revolution as "God's finest work." In the first ten years of the Reformation, 1517-1526, Luther published 300 books and pamphlets, and in the next decade, 232 more; by the time of Luther's death in 1546, his bibliography numbered 715—an average of twenty-five publications per year! Alexander Campbell, himself no slouch when it came to publishing, admired Brother Luther's remarkable literary output.[40]

Alexander Campbell agreed with all of Luther's reformation principles. He joined in the applause that generations before and since have given the German Reformer. Hailing Luther as "the reformer of popery," one who gave "the Man of Sin" a mortal blow from which he has not and will not recover, Campbell especially applauded Luther for the place he gave to the Bible. Luther, translator of the Bible into the ordinary language of everyday Germans, told his fellow countrymen—Campbell loved this!—"I would not advise anyone to place his child where the Holy Scriptures are not regarded as the rule of life."[41] Campbell was also impressed by the way Luther upbraided the German universities: "I fear keenly that the Universities will be found to be great gates leading down to hell, unless they take diligent care to explain the Holy Scriptures, and to engrave them upon the hearts of our youth."[42]

---

[38] William Stevenson, *The Story of the Reformation* (Richmond: John Knox, 1963): 177.

[39] Küng (2003): 122.

[40] Alexander Campbell, "Martin Luther's Activity," *Millennial Harbinger* (September 1844): 425. Just as Luther's Reformation could not have succeeded (as similar efforts before had failed) without the new technology, so also Campbell's reformation was greatly abetted by the expansion of the "print culture" in Frontier America of the 19th century. See Michael Casey, "Mastered by the Word: Print Culture, Modernization, and 'the Priesthood of All Readers' in the Churches of Christ," in this volume.

[41] Alexander Campbell, "Weighty Words of Luther," *Millennial Harbinger* (March 1842): 143.

[42] *Loc. cit.*

Campbell liked to quote D'Aubigne's celebrated work on the Reformation.[43] The renowned French historian, viewing the priesthood of all believers as central to the Reformation, quoted Luther as having said: "We all have one baptism, one faith, and it is this that constitutes the spiritual man.... We are all alike consecrated priests in baptism." Campbell approved of Luther's saying according to D'Aubigne: "The unction, the tonsure, ordination, consecration by the bishop or by the pope, may make a hypocrite, but never a spiritual man." Campbell also found quotable, according to D'Aubigne, Luther's move towards spiritual egalitarianism. Luther made no distinction between laity and priests, and princes and bishops, except in their functions: "They all belong to the same estate, but all have not the same work to perform."[44]

Campbell could have said these things himself, and he did in fact make the same claims in his debate with Bishop Purcell. Campbell, however, out-Luthered Luther, for he lived—to make the point one last time—three centuries later, and he enjoyed, therefore, a greater availability of light. One may say that Campbell picked up where Luther had left off. For example, in the debate with Purcell, Campbell affirmed a position that Luther, even in old age, would not have agreed to affirm: "The Roman Catholic Institution, called the 'Holy, Apostolic, Catholic Church,' is not now, nor was she ever, catholic, apostolic, or holy; but a *sect* in the fair import of that word."[45] In another proposition, Campbell asserted that the Roman Church was not only apostate but also "unsusceptible of reformation."[46] This difference between Luther, whose mission was to reform the existing church, and Campbell, whose mission was to restore primitive, first-century Christianity, well defines the seismic divide between the two reformers. Campbell may have been catholic, but he was also baptist, and as such, he was closer to the Anabaptist *Schwärmer* whom Luther had loved to hate.[47] As the Anabaptists themselves often said, so Campbell would have agreed: The Reformation was good as far as it went, but it did not go far enough. Restoration goes all the way.

For Campbell, nonetheless, the terms "reformation" and "restoration" could be used synonymously. By 1837, Campbell was using "reformation" as much or more than "restoration." In that year, he published "a synopsis of the grand items of the reformation for which we have contended and still contend." The following list of the first five items, "For the healing of divisions," reveals an area in which Campbell's primitivist plea for reform-as-restoration differed significantly from Luther's reformation-of-the-existing-institution:

1. *The restoration of a pure speech, or the calling of Bible things by Bible names.*

Under this heading, Campbell charged that religious controversies are often about words of foreign importation, which have supplanted the diction of the Holy Spirit. Calling Bible things by Bible names, he argued, would serve as a cure for Protestant partyism.

2. *The Bible must be proposed as a book of facts, not of doctrines nor opinions.*

[43] *Idem*: "D'Aubigne's History of the Reformation," *Millennial Harbinger* (August 1846): 455-456.
[44] *Idem*: "Luther on Apostolic Succession," *ibid.* (March 1845): 142.
[45] Campbell/Purcell Debate (1837): vii.
[46] *Ibid.*: 315.
[47] Richard Hughes, "A Comparison of the Restitution Motifs of the Campbells [1809-1830] and the Anabaptists [1524-1560]," *The Mennonite Quarterly Review* 45/4 (October 1971): 312-330.

Campbell explained that a "fact" is what God has said or done, whereas "doctrines" and "opinions" are theories about the facts (as discussed above). Believers can unite upon the facts–what the Bible actually says–while allowing freedom in matters of opinion.

3. The Bible alone, instead of any human creed, as the only rational and solid foundation of Christian union and communion.

Campbell contended that "every reformation of a human creed has produced a new party in religion." He drew the equation: "So many creeds, so many parties."

4. The reading and expounding of the sacred scriptures in public assemblies instead of text preaching, sermonizing, and philosophizing.

Campbell avowed that "text preaching"[48] was a modern invention, and that some charged that it had begun with Luther and Protestantism. It had, Campbell complained, filled the pulpit with "a race of pigmies in the Bible as diminutive as ever lived."

5. The right of private opinion in all matters not revealed in contradistinction from the common faith, without forfeiture of Christian character and Christian privilege.[49]

Campbell claimed that holding to "unity in the faith" while allowing freedom of opinion is the only way that the church can enjoy the "unity of the Spirit in the bond of peace."

However much Luther esteemed the Bible, he remained a "magisterial" reformer—a top-down professor and teacher, a *doctor ecclesiae*, and a Late-Medieval mind who conceived that the secular power had a role to play in reforming ecclesiastical institutions. By contrast, Campbell lived on the 19th-century American Frontier, in a nation that had disestablished all forms of state-supported religion, and more than 400 years after the invention of the printing press: Everyperson's Bible was now a part of the democratic legacy. Campbell's movement differed from Luther's in proportion to these time-wrought changes. Luther looked backward towards the historic church in need of reform; Campbell looked millennially forward, issuing his restorationist plea for the unity of Christians in all sects in view of a new dawn rising, and calling for unity in essentials and liberty in opinions. Moreover, Campbell saw Luther and other reformers as having stripped away theological opinions and dogmas of the Roman Church only to impose different ones in Protestantism, thus eventually fomenting a multiplicity of new sects.

---

[48] "Text-preaching," Campbell defined, "…authorizes a man to make as many sermons as there are verses in a chapter; and oftentimes these sermons on these texts are as detached from the scope on which they stand, as if the whole New Testament was a book of proverbs." This "text-taking" and "sermon-making" we today would call "interpreting words out of context." Campbell's 22nd reply of the *Campbell-Owen Debate*; see http://www.mun.ca/rels/restmov/texts/acampbell/cod/COD44.HTM. Text-preaching is as old, at least, as Origen of Alexandria, and goes back in principle to Philo of Alexandria and his hermeneutic of interpreting the "spiritual" meaning of the text apart from its historical, literal, factual meaning.

[49] Alexander Campbell, "Synopsis of Reformation and Objects," *Millennial Harbinger* (December 1837): 530-533.

Campbell's movement, too, it must regrettably be acknowledged, eventually divided into numerous sects that, likewise, gladly would impose their opinions as facts. Alexander Campbell, however, died an optimist who was blessed with not having to live long enough to see his followers growling at one another over the scraps of his legacy. Campbell went on record to affirm that the Restoration would never divide, as Protestantism had done, if it would remain true to his unity principles. Either he was mistaken, then, or his heirs did not remain true to the principles of Restorationism.

Robert Richardson, Campbell's close associate and biographer, and the first historian of the Restoration Movement, named still another distinction between Restorationist "Protestantism," which Richardson traced back to Luther. The *furor doctrinalis*, as Richardson called it, was the congenital disease of Protestants that sets a love for doctrine above devotion to Christ. Faith is personal, Richardson insisted, and not doctrinal. It centers in a person, not in tenets. The reformers' undue zeal for special doctrines had led partisans to love each other not for Christ's sake but for opinion's sake. This was especially true during the period of Lutheran Orthodoxy, when *fides quae* (faith in the doctrines to which we give mental assent) took priority over *fides qua* (the faith by which we trust in Christ). This was paralleled during a similar period of 20th-century Restorationist scholasticism when bickering splinter groups led by pugnacious preachers turned Campbell's biblical "facts" into the pesky details of this or that "pattern" of detailed religious practice supposed to be evident in the New Testament. The Protestant sects demanded confessions based on various sets of doctrinal tenets, Richardson charged, but the Restoration required only a simple confession that Jesus is Messiah, the Son of God.[50] Had Richardson lived into the twentieth century, he would have seen that old Protestant habit kick in again among the Restorationists.

Richardson's emphasis on the *personal* nature of faith conforms to another principle that Campbell had listed in his *Synopsis* under the heading of "Personal and Family Reformation." Campbell charged that the church was filled with ignorant, carnal, and immoral members, and that "a radical and thorough reformation in family religion and family education" was imperative. "As personal intelligence, purity, and happiness is the end of all public and private, theoretic or practical reformation, the present standard of personal knowledge, faith, piety, and morality must be greatly elevated."[51]

Two Great Reformers and a Friend on the Front Porch of Heaven

I imagine that Brother Luther and Brother Campbell are now well acquainted and have spent any number of everlasting afternoons sitting in their cloud-cushioned rocking chairs on the front porch of Heaven, viewing the scene below, discussing the relative merits of their respective endeavors, and confessing their faults one to another. They have a lot to talk about, pleased as they are that "reformation" and "restoration" turned out, at least in principle, to be sisters, though not identical twins. In Heaven, where we are immortally transparent to one another, they speak freely to one another, for hiding one's feelings Over Yonder is no longer either necessary or possible.

---

[50] Robert Richardson, "Reformation No. VIII," *Millennial Harbinger* (May 1848): 253-254.

[51] Alexander Campbell, "Personal and Family Reformation," *Millennial Harbinger* (December 1837): 537.

Rocking and chatting, Brother Luther has just expressed his regret about the Anabaptists: "Crazy as lemmings, they were, those *Schwärmer*, and yet they were my brothers in Christ! Oh, I wish I had treated them more kindly! And I wish, too, that I had been more true to my own Bible study about the nature of baptism as immersion."

Speaking a word of forgiveness on behalf of baptists of all kinds, in all places and times, Brother Campbell replies: "Now, Martin, we see what we can see, but only by the candle-power of our available light."

Brother Luther persists in repentance: "So true! But oh, Brother Alec, the Devil did everything he could to blow out my flickering light! Think how much damage my unChristian attitude did to the Jews in centuries to come! *Ach*, that was devil's work! It will take the Jews an eternity in Heaven to forgive me!"

Brother Campbell persists in forgiveness for them both: "And I must say the same about African slaves, for I spoke out much too weakly on their behalf. But, Martin, there's plenty of time to forgive and be forgiven, for an eternity in Heaven is exactly what we've got."

About that time, Pope Leo X comes strolling along, and Luther greets him: "*Ach, guten ewigen Morgen,* Your Holiness! Have you met my friend, Alec?"

"Oh, yes," Brother Campbell answers for the pope. "We've met. Good day to you, Brother Leo! Come on up and sit a spell!"

"*Dominus vobiscum!*" the pope extends his usual, cordial greeting, pulls up a rocking chair, and joins the conversation. "I suppose you're talking about forgiveness, again" says the pope, getting right to the point, reading their hearts in the light of the Father's face. "As I am always telling to Martino, I should have listened to him more carefully with a pastor's tender heart. You know, Alessandro, no matter how sinful a Christian becomes, faith in Jesu Christo is what counts, and you can't say that we Catholics didn't have faith in *nostro domino Christo!*"

Brothers Luther and Campbell nod in agreement. "But the people who followed me," laments Martin, still worrying about penance, "now say that they are *of Luther* rather than *of Christ!*"

"And the people who followed me," laments Alexander likewise, "say that they are 'of Christ' and not 'of Campbell,' but still they have torn the seamless garment of the Lord into shreds and tatters!"

Leo nods soberly and comments: "There are many kinds of apostasy, my dear, separated brothers."

That starts the three old friends off on a favorite topic: "The church must always be reforming herself," says Martin.

"So long as that reformation is ever a restorative return to the deepest well for the purest water," says Alexander.

"Amen," agrees Leo, remembering the Gregorian Reform and the restoration of the gospel brought about by St. Francis before him, and pondering the similar movements that followed him. "I firmly believed Christ's promise that he would *be with us always, even unto the end of the world.* What I see now is that all these reformations and restorations were inspired by the Holy Spirit's moving humans to do the good works of salvation. We Catholics have a longer memory than do you Protestants—we remember that miracles have never ceased, that the Holy Spirit has never stopped working through the church, and that Christ has never failed to keep his promise that *the gates of Hades shall not prevail* against the faith."

"And not through the church only," Campbell agrees. "Truth is where you find it—perhaps among the thinkers of the Enlightenment, perhaps among the natural scientists; and progress is made by inventors and explorers and by any frontiersman walking behind his plough."

"It finally comes down," Luther taps the arm of his rocking chair with finality, "to each individual conscience! We are *all* priests."

"And to freedom from all man-made institutions to accept the grace of God in Christ Jesus," Campbell adds.

"And freedom, as well, for each individual to become his own little pope!" Leo chuckles. "Let's take a look at your Missouri Synod, Martino; and Alessandro, how about some of those uncooperative, anti Elderships of yours! I only wish I had been as infallible as they all think they are!"

The three spirits laugh jovially together, and Brother Campbell sighs: "Each of us believed—and we still do: *In essentials, unity; in opinions, liberty; in all things, love.* And yet, look down there! What do you see? Disunity over essential facts! Liberty being used to push opinions as essentials! Not nearly enough love in anything!"

Leo replies: "What was your best line, Martino? *Ecclesia semper reformanda!* The emphasis must fall on *semper*, I think, for the church must *always* be reforming herself. The job is never finished, Alessandro. Every generation must discover its truths, both new and old, for itself."

"Available light," muses Campbell.

"I was a reformer in my time," agrees Luther, "and you were a reformer in your time, Alec."

"*Signior* Campbell was a *Lutherano*, and *Signior* Luther, without knowing it, had been a... uh... what does one say?"

"Some people say *Campbellite*," Campbell fills in, "but I always preferred *Disciple of Christ*—just a *Christian*, Brother Leo, and a *Christian only*."

"So did I!" Luther nods his agreement.

"But neither of you, alas, a Roman!" Leo holds up his hands, empty.

"That's right!" Brothers Luther and Campbell heartily agree in unison.

"Ah, well," Leo concedes, "You can't always get what you want. But come, dear brothers, all of this is ancient history. Now that we have learned our lessons, we must apply our spirits to the human future, if there is to be one. We must ask ourselves: What good in the world is the church? Cast your eyes upon our dear old sorrowing earth: Wars! Religious wars and political wars! Wars of greed and pride! Harm and hurt everywhere, more often committed by people of good intentions than by ordinary criminals! What can we do?"

"Let us be spirits of sweet reasonableness!" Brother Campbell immediately replies.

"And let us prompt kings and rulers to act in accord with the spirit of Christ!" Brother Luther concurs.

"And let us be truly catholic, as we do so!" Brother Leo admonishes. "See that man over there, standing out in the garden? That's Brother Muhammad. Have you met him? I once thought he was the Antichrist! Let us go and talk things over with him, and see if there be anything the four of us together might do to bring peace down below." Leo stands up from his rocking chair.

Luther stands up, too, and makes one of his German jokes: "Might as well consort with a Saracen antichrist as with a papal one!"

"Does he speak English?" Campbell asks.

"No," Brother Leo replies, "but he's on speaking terms with Gabriel, and he can interpret for us, if we need him to."

Theodicy in Early Stone-Campbell Perspectives

John Mark Hicks

"Every theological system," B.U. Watkins wrote in 1867, "has, by implication, a corresponding theory of theodicy."[1] Deism, Optimism,[2] Universalism, and Calvinism each have their distinctive theodicies. Since the "reformation of the nineteenth century has obtained sounder theological sentiments than any of our contemporaries," according to Watkins, "the world has a right to expect of us a corresponding sound and lucid theodicy."[3] Watkins embedded his critique in fourteen articles published in 1867,[4] and although they contain principles that, in part, form his own theodicy, he offered no distinctive alternative to the four theodicy systems. The question, then, is whether the "sounder" theology of the Stone-Campbell "reformation of the nineteenth century" actually did produce a correspondingly "sound and lucid theodicy."[5]

Watkins believed that the shift from deductive, metaphysical idealism to inductive Baconianism touted by Campbell's approach provided hope for a sound theodicy. "The only foundation for a popular Theodicy—one that can be understood by the masses—is God's providential and verbal revelations."[6] The biblical narrative must have precedence over speculative theories. According to Alexander Campbell, philosophy is impotent "in all matters and things pertaining to a spiritual system." Scripture provides "no explanations" or "speculations" but only a "narrative."[7] Theology, in Campbell's view, is a system of "facts" rather than of theories.

---

[1] B. U. Watkins, "Essays on Theodicy—No. 1.," *Christian Standard* 2 (February 2, 1867): 38.

[2] Optimism, the least familiar term in this list of four, is (according to Watkins, "Essays on Theodicy—No. 3," *Christian Standard* 2 [February 16, 1867]: 54), the theological view that "the universe is the very best that could be made," so that "moral evil" is "an essential element of the universe." God created the best of all possible worlds, and though he did not create sin, he does overrule it "for some good purpose." Philosophically and historically, optimism is associated with Leibniz's *The Theodicy: Essays on the Goodness of God* (1710).

[3] Watkins, No. 1 (1867): 38.

[4] The fourteen articles ran from February 2 to May 11, 1867.

[5] No scholarly treatment of this question in the history of the Stone-Campbell Movement has been written; correspondingly, no entry for "Evil" or "Theodicy" appears in the recently published *Encyclopedia of the Stone-Campbell Movement*, Douglas A. Foster, Paul M. Blowers, Anthony L. Dunnavant, and D. Newell Williams, eds. (Grand Rapids: Eerdmans, 2004).

[6] Watkins, No. 1(1867): 38.

[7] Alexander Campbell and Robert Owen, *The Evidences of Christianity: A Debate between Robert Owen, of New Lanark, Scot. and Alexander Campbell, President of Bethany College, Va. containing an Examination of the "Social System" and all the Systems of Skepticism of Ancient and Modern Times, Held in the City of Cincinnati, Ohio, in April, 1829* (Nashville: McQuiddy Printing Co., 1946; reprint of 1829 edition): 90.

Antebellum Arminianism: Alexander Campbell

Reared in the context of Scottish Presbyterianism, Campbell's basic theological structure is Protestant and Reformed. Within this Reformed frame, however, his Arminian soteriology is an emphasis on human freedom. The emphasis on freedom shapes his understanding of providence and ultimately his theodic postulates.

High View of Providence

In 1833, Campbell published substantial extracts from William Sherlock's *A Discourse Concerning the Divine Providence.*[8] First published in 1694,[9] it had been reprinted for the Methodist Episcopal Church in 1823.[10] Dean of St. Paul's Church in London in the late seventeenth century, Sherlock represented a moderate Anglican Arminianism with a rather traditional theology of meticulous providence. Sherlock attempted to steer a middle course between Deism and Calvinism. Campbell endorsed Sherlock's views:[11]

> Your commendations of Sherlock I think are well deserved. They are not exaggerated. He is a writer of good sense, and has chosen a very interesting subject. As far as I have perused his work, it appears to be well adapted to refute the scepticism of some professors on the doctrine of special providence. It would be well if our philosophists, who disbelieve the superintending care of the Almighty Father, would give Sherlock a candid hearing.[12]

Campbell's traditional understanding is clear when he speaks of "special providence": "They who admit a general providence, and, at the same time deny a special providence, are feeble and perverted reasoners and thinkers."[13] In the face of deists and rationalistic speculators, Campbell advises us to "place our hand upon our lips and be still."[14]

Campbell's pedagogical example is the story of Joseph, which is filled with "apparent contingencies."[15] While Campbell spoke of "chance," he used it only accomodatively, that is, "Whatever occurs, the cause or instrument of which we do not perceive, is said to happen, or to come by chance." But "in the strict sense of the word chance, as respects God, there is no such thing."[16] "Blind fortune" and "good luck" are the "creatures of Pagan imagination" and are "wholly incompatible with Christian

---

[8] Alexander Campbell,"Sherlock on Providence," *Millennial Harbinger* 4/5 (May 1833): 205-12, 4/6 (June 1833): 247-51, 4/7(July 1833): 296-300, 4/8 (August 1833): 389-95, 4/9 (September 1833): 435-9.

[9] William Sherlock, *A Discourse Concerning the Divine Providence*, 2nd edition (London: William Rogers, 1694).

[10] William Sherlock, *A Discourse Concerning the Divine Providence* (Cincinnati: M. Ruter, 1823; reprint of 2nd edition, 1694).

[11] Likewise, Robert Richardson, Campbell's son-in-law, endorsed Sherlock and followed the extracts with his own complementary series on providence, "The Providence of God," *Millennial Harbinger* 7/5 (May 1836): 219-224, 7/6, (June 1836): 246-51, 7/7 (July 1836): 305-7, 7/8 (August 1836): 360-364, 7/9 (September 1836): 385-89; 7/10 (October 1836): 441-48.

[12] Alexander Campbell, "Reply to J. A. Waterman," *Millennial Harbinger* 4 (June 1833): 243.

[13] Alexander Campbell, "Providence, General and Special," *Millennial Harbinger* (New Series) 5 (November 1855): 602.

[14] *Ibid.*: 603.

[15] *Ibid.*: 604.

[16] Alexander Campbell, "Chance," *Millennial Harbinger* (New Series) 1 (November 1851): 617.

sentiment and style."[17] Our histories, like Joseph's, are filled with "links of chain of designs" which terminate "in the eternal destiny of the world."[18] Indeed, "in this life many of our so-called misfortunes are the choicest blessings, and all things do work together for good to them who love God and keep his commandments."[19] Providence is benevolent, Campbell believed, even in misfortunes; he was careful to note, however, that none of this undermines human moral freedom. Special providence does not conflict with the "freedom of thought, of speech, or of action, in any issue involving or controlling the moral character or the eternal destiny of any man."[20]

Campbell's understanding of special providence includes the death of infants and good men. In 1847, Campbell wrote on the mystery of providence in response to the death of several young ministers. He opined that God has a role for the "disembodied spirits of men" after death—they are his ministers, like angels.[21] Indeed, he surmised that "the Lord may need the services of infants and adults, and that for this purpose he often selects the purest and the best of our race and calls them hence to minister in his hosts of light, in other fields of labor, according to the wants of his vast dominions."[22] God's special providence includes the time of death, at least for some.

Campbell was explicit about the role of angels in special providence. While God's ministry is not carried out "exclusively" by angels, Campbell nevertheless affirmed, "I do believe that much has been done, and still is done by them."[23] Campbell's Lockean epistemology meant that angels could influence human beings only through the five senses. Hence angels take on empirical form in order to influence events and persuade human thinking. He supposed that angels, whether good or bad, influence human beings to good or evil. They do this in a variety of ways:

> ...assuming a form of some sort—the form of a man—of any creature—of a thought—of a word, and by presenting it to the outward senses; or by an acquaintance with our associations of ideas, our modes of reasoning, our passions, our appetites, our propensities—and by approaching us through these avenues, they lead us backwards or forwards, to the right or to the left, as their designs may require....It is more than possible—it is probable.[24]

Campbell extended this influence not only to angels but also to natural evils:

> I limit not human agency, nor angelic agency, nor divine agency in the government of the world; in providence, general or special; nor in the power of circumstances to arrest the attention and to fix the mind upon the arguments and motives which give to the gospel its potency over the mind of man. Men, good

---

[17] *Ibid.*: 617-8.

[18] *Ibid.*: 619.

[19] *Ibid.*: 620-1.

[20] Alexander Campbell (1855): 608.

[21] Alexander Campbell, "Mysteries of Providence," *Millennial Harbinger* 18 (1847): 707. In his "Address on Demonology," *Popular Lectures and Addresses* (Philadelphia, Pennsylvania: James Challen and Son, 1866): 379-402, Campbell defended the thesis that demons (both good and bad) are the spirits of the dead. See http://www.mun.ca/rels/restmov/texts/ acampbell/pla/PLA17.HTM.

[22] Alexander Campbell (1847): 708.

[23] Alexander Campbell,"Waterman" (1833): 244.

[24] *Ibid.*: 245.

and bad, evil spirits, angels, dreams, pestilences, earthquakes, sudden deaths, personal and family afflictions, may become occasions of conversions to God.[25]

Through these direct and indirect means, God manages the world, including its evil, toward its destiny, and he uses his means to awaken humanity to his redemptive presence. Robert Richardson, Campbell's son-in-law, expressed a similar understanding of both special and meticulous providence in his lengthy 1836 series on providence.[26]

Theodicy

Consistent with a traditional Arminian understanding of special providence, Campbell emphasized human freedom as his primary theodicy. While hesitant to engage in speculative discussion, human freedom is the origin of human evil. The following extended quotations highlight this significance for him:

> It may, then, in the spirit of true devotion, and genuine humility be affirmed that God could not, with a reference to all final results, give birth to a more perfect system of things than the present. In other words, God could not make an infallible fallible creature. Now before your difficulty becomes too heavy for the strength of an ordinary mind, it must be proved that God could have given birth to a system in which moral evil could find no place, and in which there would be no need of a governor, and that he did not…. [I]f God had given birth to a system which in its very nature excluded the possibility of evil, it would have also excluded the possibility of his being a governor.[27]

> Some talk of his preventing moral evil by an exertion of Almighty power; of his having 'greater power to prevent it than the immediate cause;' of his being stronger than Satan. But all such notions, if they have any foundation at all, are built upon the most palpable inattention to rational nature. And here I would affirm that it is impossible to conceive of a rational creation of an infallible nature. But in affirming this I am brought to the shore of an immense ocean where weak heads are sure to be drowned. Let us try whether we can swim a short distance in sight of land…. None of them could have been capable of moral good. For it is essential to moral good that the agent act freely according to the last dictate, or the best dictate of his understanding…. Please consider that if a rational being was created incapable of disobeying, he must, on that very account, be incapable of obeying. He then acts like a mill wheel, in the motions of which there is no choice; no virtue, no vice, no moral good, no moral evil…. There are some things impossible to Omnipotence….It is impossible to create a being that shall be capable of obeying, and at the same time incapable of disobeying.[28]

Campbell's theodicy is a version of the "free-will defense," yet Campbell was uncomfortable with this sort of metaphysical reasoning. He pursued it only as a negative apologetic.

---

[25] Alexander Campbell, "Editor's Reply," *Millennial Harbinger* 4 (July 1833): 333-6.

[26] See especially Robert Richardson, "The Providence of God—No. 7.," *Millennial Harbinger* 7/10 (October 1836): 441-8, on the divine government of evil.

[27] Alexander Campbell, "Replication.—No. 1.," *The Christian Baptist* 4/1 (August 7, 1826): 14.

[28] Alexander Campbell, "To Mr. D.—A Skeptic.—Replication.—No. III," *Christian Baptist* 4/4 (November 6, 1826): 23-24.

To launch out into the development of views purely metaphysical, in order to correct metaphysical errors, is at best only calculated to create a distrust in those visionary problems on which some build as firmly as if on the Rock of Ages. I never wish to establish any one point in this way; but I desire to throw a caveat in the way of those who are willing to risk eternity itself upon a visionary problem.[29]

Consequently, Campbell rarely spoke of theodicy. Apparently, it was not a focus in his setting since providence overruled evil in the progress of the world. Theodicy was not even raised as a polemical argument pro or con in his 1829 debate with the skeptic, Owen.

This "free-will defense," however, is combined with an Augustinian understanding of natural evil. Thomas Campbell, for example, had affirmed that natural evils are the "just and proper results and consequences of" moral evil. They "are ordained by God as punishments, preventives, or correctives."[30] Alexander Campbell concurred: "Before the rebellion in Eden," Alexander wrote, "all was good." There was "no gloom, no pain, no sorrow any where. But the instant man rebelled…[n]ature was immediately diseased in all her members."[31] The original sin "is the root of all this bitterness and grief. This brought death into the world, and all our woe."[32] Consequently, "all the sins of all the word, and all the evils attendant on them, are developments of the sin of Adam (or of Eve,) and must be all taken into view with all the train of natural evils consequent upon them, before we can think aright of what sin is."[33] Humanity inherits a "fallen, consequently sinful nature" from Adam; human nature was "corrupted by the fall of Adam."[34] Moral evil, then, according to Campbell, is the result of human freedom. Natural evil is the consequence of that evil, as sin corrupted the cosmos. This is a fairly traditional, classic Arminian theodicy.[35]

Postbellum Rationalism: Thinking about Evil

Despite the traditional character of Campbell's theology of providence, the primary antagonist in Stone-Campbell theodicy was Calvinism. While Campbell primarily opposed Deism, most thinkers in the Stone-Campbell Movement were responding to Calvinism. Eight of Watkins's fourteen "Essays on Theodicy" focused on Calvinism. Both Wilkes and Christopher, the two authors considered below, also had Calvinism in their

[29] *Loc. cit.*

[30] Thomas Campbell, "To Mr. D.—A Skeptic.—Replication—No. V.," *Christian Baptist* 4/6 (January 1, 1827): 39.

[31] Alexander Campbell, "History of Sin, Including the Outlines of Ancient History—No. I.," *Millennial Harbinger* 1 (March 1830): 108.

[32] *Loc. cit.*

[33] *Ibid.*: 110.

[34] Alexander Campbell, *The Christian System* (Nashville: Gospel Advocate, 1970; reprint of 1839 edition): 15.

[35] Robert Richardson added an Ireanean "soul-making" dimension to his theodic thinking, even to the extent of affirming, to some degree, what is traditionally known as the "Happy Fall." See Richardson's "Sin—A Dialogue," *Millennial Harbinger* (New Series) 3 (September 1839): 406, and (October 1839): 443, 445-6.

crosshairs. The two most extended attempts at theodicy in the late nineteenth century were written by two significant leaders from the ultimately Disciples North. One concerns moral evil and the other natural evil.

Moral Evil

Lanceford B. Wilkes (1824-1901) authored a 200-page volume entitled *Moral Evil: Its Nature and Origin.*[36] J. H. Garrison, editor of the Christian-Evangelist, introduced the book with considerable praise. As a former writer for *Lard's Quarterly*; co-editor of the *Apostolic Times* with J. W. McGarvey; onetime President of Columbia College in Columbia, Missouri; and co-editor of the *Pacific Church News* in California, Wilkes's views are representative of late-nineteenth-century Disciples.[37] McGarvey commended Wilkes's "national reputation" as well as his talent as a "logician" whose "preaching was characterized by close and severe argumentation."[38]

While building on biblical axioms, Wilkes approached the task with methodical, rational inquisition as he proposed and answered questions that built a cumulative and deductive understanding of the origin of moral evil. He began by stating the classic problem of evil. If God is omnipotent, why does he not rid the world of evil, and if he is willing, why is evil still here?[39] Wilkes did not get hung upon either horn of the dilemma. He limited the definition of omnipotence to those things "of a purely physical character" that God cannot do, but "preventing or removing sin" is not "the exertion of physical power. Hence God's omnipotence has nothing to do with the question of the original or continued existence of sin."[40]

But could not have God made humanity without the capacity to sin? Wilkes retorted: "God could not have made man different from what he did make him. If he had made him so he could not have sinned, he would not have been man."[41] Humanity is no longer human if humans have no capacity for moral evil. Further, if the capacity for moral evil be lacking, then capacity for moral good would also be absent. Thus, the capacity to choose good or evil is part of humanity *qua* humanity. As "free moral" agents, our nature "excludes, ex necessitate rei, the idea of moral necessity."[42]

God, however, neither intended nor "designed [moral evil's] existence."[43] God does not design what he forbids. Indeed, Wilkes argued, God did not even permit sin since "it ought not to be said that one permits what he could not prevent."[44] That God did not

---

[36] Lanceford B. Wilkes, *Moral Evil: Its Nature and Origin* (St. Louis: Christian Publishing Co., 1892). Unless he was a plagiarist, Wilkes is the author of the essay "Moral Evil," *Lard's Quarterly* 5.2 (April 1868): 132-143, signed "L." That article is fundamentally focused on rebutting a Calvinist understanding of "moral evil."

[37] These biographical data are taken from Mary K. Dains, *Partners with God: Biographical Sketches of Our Ministers, 1832-1982* (Columbia, Missouri: First Christian Church, n.d.).

[38] J. W. McGarvey, *The Autobiography of J. W. McGarvey* (Lexington, Kentucky: The College of the Bible, 1960): 76.

[39] Wilkes (1892): 23.

[40] *Ibid.*: 24.

[41] *Ibid.*: 25.

[42] *Ibid.*: 27.

[43] *Ibid.*: 28.

[44] *Ibid.*: 31.

prevent sin is "proof, entirely satisfactory, that he could not do so" since a loving God would certainly prevent whatever evil he could. [45] God did not permit sin because he cannot prevent it. The sanctity of human choice is absolute by God's own design. Every human act is their "own act" and is without any divine "resisting, restraining, or controlling force."[46] Such a force is not a "moral possibility."[47]

The origin of moral evil, then, lies within the creature, not the Creator. Ultimately, it originated in the will of angels. We have no knowledge of how the desire for evil arose within them, but "our ignorance is no premise for the conclusion that it did not."[48] The sin of Adam and Eve originated within their own wills, as well, though they were tempted by the angelic evil one.[49] God created the world with moral meaning, which entails that humanity could create evil out of their moral capacity.

Wilkes's moral theodicy is rooted in the nature of moral agency. God created moral capacity that entails the capacity for good or evil. Moral capacity is concreated, but human evil acts are the sole responsibility of the human actor. God cannot create moral life without moral capacity, and he cannot prevent the exercise of that moral power for evil without subverting his own creative work. Where it concerns moral evil, however, we cannot doubt that "God has done, is now doing and will ever do all he can to put an end to moral evil."[50] In other words, God is doing the best he can with the world he made.

Natural Evil

Hiram Christopher, a St. Louis physician, authored one of two nineteenth-century redemptive-historical systematic theologies in the Stone-Campbell Movement, entitled *The Remedial System*.[51] His understanding of the "irruption of sin" (or moral evil) in the cosmos is essentially the same as Wilkes's. Due to the nature of rational finite beings (both human and angelic), they are "necessarily and unavoidably peccable."[52] It "was impossible for God to create a universe in which the disaster of sin was not possible" because God cannot accomplish "self-contradictory things."[53] The nature of finite rationality is inherently peccable. Consequently, it is improper to say that God "permits" sin since it is not within his power to prevent it. "God has done all in his power to prevent it" consistent with finite rationality, and having "exerted all the psychical powers of his being to prevent it, which alone was capable of effecting any good results, and if these failed, the failure cannot be attributed to him or the powers exercised; but to the perverse will of the creature."[54] Christopher's theodicy agrees with Wilkes's.

---

[45] *Loc. cit.*

[46] *Ibid.*: 44.

[47] *Ibid.*: 53.

[48] *Ibid.*: 86.

[49] *Ibid.*: 87.

[50] *Ibid.*: 181.

[51] Hiram Christopher, *The Remedial System; or, Man and His Redeemer* (Lexington, Kentucky: Transylvanian Printing and Publishing Co., 1876); the other redemptive-historical systematic theology is by Robert Milligan, *The Scheme of Redemption* (Cincinnati, Ohio: Carroll, 1868).

[52] Christopher (1876): 36.

[53] *Ibid.*: 35.

[54] *Ibid.*: 37.

In 1900, Christopher published a meticulously argued theory of providence and miracle, entitled *The Relations of God to the World by 1. Immanency. 2. Intervention. 3. Incarnation.*[55] In the first part of the book, Christopher explored the idea of divine providence in the relation of force and matter, but in the second and third parts, he addressed the miraculous work of God through historic interventions in redemptive history and climactically in the *kenosis* of the Logos.

According to Christopher, God, by the creative act, correlated force and matter, establishing a divine government over the cosmos. As the history of this government unfolded, divine "interventions were necessary as emergencies arose in the progress of the race." It was "necessary in order to assure the race of the reality of a divine government."[56] All "intervention" is "essentially and necessarily miraculous."[57] Whatever is not a matter of intervention (miracle), is natural and embedded in the nature of creation itself. Providence, then, relates to what is natural, but miracle is interventionist.

To explain God's relationship to his natural creation, Christopher employed the scientific distinction between force and matter. Matter is inert and is, therefore, "wholly passive under the influence of force."[58] Force is immanent within matter when it moves it. This force is ultimately God's own creative power, but God placed it in matter as a reality, embedded his own power in creation itself as part of his orderly creation. The "force is God," but it is immanent within matter.[59] It operates in an immanent way according to the laws of nature. Consequently, what is natural is orderly and is only interrupted by miraculous interventions. Providence, then, is simply another name for the ongoing function of natural laws by the energy immanent within matter—ultimately traceable to God, but now embedded in the natural order with regularity and predictability. God is distinct from that order; therefore, Christopher is not a panentheist, but the natural has such independent status that his understanding entails a functional Deism.

Christopher developed his argument by noting that this "force" became "vital force" in living organisms. The life force is God's own power, but now it is part of the natural order.[60] The climactic event in creation was the investment of "psychic personality" in human beings.[61] The "psychic" force is the moral and religious ground of humanity.[62] Humans, of course, exist as free moral agents. Though the "psychic" force is rooted in God's creative act, it now exists in human beings as their own capacity to live out God's law in community with others.[63]

---

[55] Hiram Christopher, *The Relations of God to the World by 1. Immanency. 2. Intervention. 3. Incarnation* (Nashville, Tennessee: Gospel Advocate Publishing Co., 1900).

[56] *Ibid.*: 91.

[57] *Ibid.*: 119.

[58] *Ibid.*: 17.

[59] *Ibid.*: 7.

[60] *Ibid.*: 40.

[61] *Ibid.*: 48.

[62] *Ibid.*: 55.

[63] *Ibid.*: 54.

God, then, has embedded force in matter in such a way that it sustains, moves, preserves, and regulates nature, and he has embedded psychic force in humanity in such a way that grants them freedom and religiosity. Just as God is not blameworthy for the moral evil of free human actions, so God is not blameworthy for the natural acts of force in matter as part of the natural order. Nature will sustain its order, whether humans get in the way or not. This is not evil; it is simply the nature of the cosmos. Consequently, there is no natural evil; tragic events within the cosmos are merely natural, not moral. We call them "evil" only in an accommodative sense because they describe the effects of natural events upon the human condition, but the events themselves have no moral meaning.[64]

When moral evil was introduced by Adam and Eve, nature was not changed. Indeed, nature had spent ages developing into a place specifically prepared for humanity. Christopher did not see any contradiction between Darwinian geology and the biblical account of Moses in Genesis 1.[65] What changed with the introduction of moral evil was the loss of the Tree of Life. The Adamic sin entailed no further consequence, even to the point that our present "moral nature" at birth is no more depraved than Adam's was at his creation.[66] The loss of the Tree of Life meant that humanity was left unprotected from the natural forces in the universe such that humanity became subject to nature's orderly processes.[67]

Accordingly, evil is a property that is potential only for moral actions and agents. God does not intervene to deliver his people from nature except in redemptive-historical events such as the Flood, the Exodus, etc., but guides them through miraculous revelation and delivers them from evil by his redemptive power. His ultimate redemptive-historical intervention is the *kenosis* and incarnation of the Logos, but his providence is the force he embedded in the cosmos, which he does not interrupt or against which he does not intervene except for redemptive-historical purposes (i.e., miracles of redemption and revelation).

Postbellum Conclusion

The combination of Wilkes and Christopher constitutes a rationally driven theodicy. God is not the actor in moral evil, and there is nothing he can do to prevent it other than to have refused to create moral capacity in the first place. God cannot prevent moral evil. "Natural evil," not really evil, is but the result of the natural order operating in a material universe absent of the Tree of Life.

This emerging view generated discussions about the nature of general and special providence within the Stone-Campbell Movement. Some denied any kind of special providence at all other than miracles,[68] while others (such as Isaac Errett) limited special

---

[64] This understanding of moral and natural evil is evident in Thomas B. Warren, *Have Atheists Proved There Is No God?* (Jonesboro, Arkansas: National Christian Press, 1972).

[65] Christopher (1876): 61-75.

[66] *Ibid.*: 104.

[67] *Ibid.*: 97.

[68] George T. Smith, "Is There a Special Providence?" *Christian Standard* 15 (February 28, 1880): 65. Everything is regulated by law so that even suffering lacks mystery because there are laws that govern suffering. Prayer is not a matter of special providence because "there are as many

providence only to spiritual ends in relation to the soul and the gospel.[69] Others clung to belief in a kind of special providence, which earlier Reformers (such as Campbell and Richardson) had articulated.[70] The legacy of a more rational theodicy in the Stone-Campbell Movement, however, was the development of a modified Deism according to which God had intervened in the past with miracles, but now works only through the mediation of the created order and its natural laws and through scripture.

The soteriological counterpart to this theodicy, evidenced in the rise of a "through the word only"—that is, through scripture only—approach to spiritual influence, is the exclusion of the Holy Spirit from any direct work on the human heart. Indeed, those who adopted a "word only" pneumatology were inclined to a modified Deism much like Christopher. James A. Harding, whose perspectives are similar to those of David Lipscomb's (described below), battled those who equated Spirit and word, and he correlated a "word only" theology of the Spirit with their deficient understanding of providence. In the context of opposing a deistic understanding of prayer, Harding asked: "Does the Holy Spirit do anything now except what the Word does? Do we get any help, of any kind or in any way, from God except what we get by studying the Bible?... Does God answer our prayers by saying, 'Study the Bible...'?"[71] Harding conducted a discussion with L. S. White of Dallas, Texas, on this very point. White advocated a practical Deism, while Harding, sharing the same milieu as David Lipscomb, defended a version of special providence.[72]

Postbellum Two-Kingdom Theology: David Lipscomb

One might expect a rather different conception of providence in the war-torn South after the 1860s. Theodicy looks different to people who have lost a war than it does to the victors. Even though this perspective is a generalization that could die the death of several qualifications, it is a useful generalization, for late-nineteenth-century Southern theodicy differs remarkably from its Northern counterparts. While Wilkes and Christopher were pursuing a rational and scientific understanding of moral and natural evil, David Lipscomb, who lived in Nashville, Tennessee, articulated a dynamic understanding of moral and natural evil under God's meticulous sovereignty. Lipscomb

---

conditions of successful prayer as for raising corn" according to the "laws of the Spirit." Another example is S. H. Brown, "Sickness and Death Governed by Law, not Providence," *Christian Standard* 49 (May 31, 1913): 890.

[69] Isaac Errett, "Prayer and Providence," *Christian Standard* 15 (January 17, 1880): 20; (January 24, 1880): 28.

[70] In one discussion, for example, Joseph Lowe denied any kind of special providence other than what is consistent with embedded laws, while R. P. Anderson defended more traditional notions of special providence. See Lowe's articles and Anderson's responses in *Christian Standard* 31 (September 21, 1895): 902, (October 12, 1895): 975, and (November 16, 1895): 1094. For other traditional perspectives, see Joseph H. Fox, *Special and General Providence* (St. Louis: John Burns, 1880) and J. S. Lamar, "What Most Interests Me Now," *Christian-Evangelist* 38 (March 28, 1901): 393-4.

[71] James A. Harding, "Questions and Answers," *The Way* 4/16 (17 July 1902): 123.

[72] James A. Harding and L. S. White, *The Harding-White Discussion* (Cincinnati, Ohio: F. L. Rowe, 1910): see http://www.mun.ca/rels/restmov/texts/jharding/hw.htm.

believed that God's role in the world was sadly underestimated and that "no question" needed more study "than the principles of God's dealing with men."[73] Lipscomb located the problem of evil in the context of a cosmic spiritual war.[74]

Two Kingdoms

Lipscomb's fundamental understanding of God is that of "ruler" or "governor." While love is a function of that government, it is not his core conception of God. "First and highest to him and the world," according to Lipscomb, "is the recognition that he is Ruler."[75] God's "fundamental relationship to the universe" and "the first highest truth" is that God is the "ruler of the world."[76] This is the ground of providence and ultimately of theodicy.

Lipscomb's theodicy is Augustinian. Prior to sin, humanity "knew no toil, no weariness, no care, no anxiety, no pain, no sickness, no sorrow. The Spirit of God brooded over it all and impregnated every breath of air with his own life-giving, life-perpetuating and health-inspiring elixir."[77] When humanity rebelled, the cosmos fell. Humanity transferred its allegiance to the Evil One. "By this treason the evil one became the ruler"[78] of the cosmos. Humanity "chose the devil to be his god and the god of his kingdom instead of the Lord God."[79] God left his dwelling place upon the earth and "with grief withdrew to heaven."[80]

[God] cannot dwell in a defiled and sin-polluted temple. He has since dwelt on this earth only in sanctified altars and temples separated from the world and consecrated to his service. He will again make this earth his dwelling place, but it will be only when sin has been purged out and it has been consecrated anew as the new heaven and earth in which dwelleth righteousness.[81]

The earth, once "the paradise of God," now "became a dried and parched wilderness. Toil, pain, sickness, anxiety, care, sorrow, mortality, and death became the heritage of humanity."[82]

Hence the cosmos was divided into two kingdoms. The kingdom of God withdrew to heaven, but the earth was left to the vicissitudes of sin and Satan. The "earth was cursed for man's sin."[83] Humanity was enslaved to sin and Satan. The "act of Adam, the ruler, supplanted the reign of God's Spirit in the world with the rule or inspiration of the

[73] David Lipscomb, "God Uses the Evil as Well as the Good," *Gospel Advocate* 22 (September 30, 1880): 634.

[74] Lipscomb's most thorough articulation of this spiritual conflict is *Civil Government: Its Origin, Mission and Destiny, and the Christian's Relation to It* (Nashville: McQuiddy Publishing Co., 1913): see http://www.mun.ca/rels/restmov/texts/dlipscomb/civgov.html.

[75] Lipscomb, "God—Who and What is He?" in *Salvation from Sin*, by J. W. Shepherd, ed. (Nashville, Tennessee: McQuiddy Printing Company, 1913): 32.

[76] *Ibid.*: (1913), "Difficulties in Religion": 340.

[77] *Idem*, "The Ruin and Redemption of the World": 110.

[78] *Ibid.*: 111.

[79] *Idem*, "The Blood of Christ": 159.

[80] *Idem*, "Ruin": 111.

[81] *Idem*, "God": 36.

[82] *Idem*, "Ruin": 111.

[83] *Ibid.*: 113.

spirit of the evil one, [and] caused man to be born into this kingdom of the evil one."[84] Satan reigns over humanity and its kingdoms, but God seeks to restore his original reign. "The mission of Christ is to root up all the briers, thistles, and thorns that grow in the material, moral, and spiritual world, and so restore this home of man to its primitive and pristine relations to God, its Maker and rightful Ruler."[85]

"The chief end" of the divine rule, according to Lipscomb, "is to reestablish the authority of God *on earth as the rightful ruler of the world*, to so bring the world back into harmonious relations with the universe that the will of God shall be done on earth as it is in heaven."[86] Thus the whole cosmos is engaged in a spiritual conflict. God is sovereign, and God shall win; however, God invests humanity with the freedom to choose and respond to his work in the world. "He must serve God or the evil one; he can make a choice." But humanity's "liberty is not very wide," though it is "broad enough to show his character." [87] Humans are not autonomous, but they are free. They are free to develop their chosen characters, but they may do so only under God's sovereignty. Consequently, though human beings are free to choose their character, "God has the right to rule and direct all persons and all things for his own ends and purposes." God "is able to direct and control them so as to bring about his desires and purposes."[88] Human freedom, then, does not obstruct God's purposes or undermine his sovereignty. On the contrary, human freedom ultimately serves God's purposes, whether they choose either evil or good.

The central question of human history is this: "Who shall rule in the world—God or the devil?"[89] Human history will unveil the victorious kingdom of God. God will win over evil. Humanity, however, must choose which ruler it will serve. Everyone has and makes this choice, but God is so sovereign over those choices that he uses them for his own purposes.

Humanity lives in this present fallen world as a moment of trial or probation. "The idea is plainly set forth in the sacred Scriptures," Lipscomb wrote. "This is a life of preparation, of probation, of trial or choice, in which we make our choice, undergo our schooling, develop the character that will decide our destiny and work out our fate in the world to come."[90] Humanity lives under the dominion of Satan but under this dominion still has a choice. Through this choice, God develops character, trains disciples, and prepares people for the coming reign of God. God "tries all spirits, tempts them so they can fully prove each his character, and by the rule of the eternal fitness of things each will find his own congenial home."[91] God is at work in the fallen world to prepare for his full reign. "God's aim in creating" humanity "is to prove and test men and see who is worthy to stand in his everlasting kingdom."[92]

---

[84] *Idem*, "Rewards and Punishments": 379.

[85] *Idem*, "Ruin": 115.

[86] *Idem*, "Difficulties": 341 (italics his).

[87] *Idem*, "God": 47.

[88] *Loc. cit.*

[89] *Idem*, "Rewards": 375.

[90] *Ibid.*: 403-4.

[91] *Ibid.*: "Foreknow, Did God, That He Would Punish Certain Men," in *Questions and Answers by Lipscomb and Sewell*, M. C. Kurfees, ed. (Nashville: McQuiddy, 1921): 256.

[92] *Idem*, : 257.

Lipscomb complained that humanity swings like a pendulum between two extremes: One excessive conclusion is the theological affirmation of total depravity according to which humans are not able to "understand or know or desire to do the will of God or to do any good thing."[93] The other excess is that humans are supposed to be "in need of no guidance, no rule of right from without. He needs not God to guide and direct."[94] Between total depravity (Calvinism) and total autonomy (deistic rationalism), Lipscomb postulated a human freedom that is circumscribed by God's sovereignty. God gives human beings enough freedom to choose under whose dominion they will live, but whichever way they choose, they nevertheless live subject to God's providential government.

God's Reign Over Evil

God actively blesses the world through his loving care. "All his provisions are for good to his creatures; none for evil to any." But "evil comes" when they violate the laws and pervert the provisions which he has made to bestow good."[95] When either these provisions are perverted or the laws violated, his creatures "pervert their own characters" and the "laws ordained for good bring evil to them."[96] A legal order embedded in the universe terminates in either good or ill, for either blessing or punishment, according to God's intended purpose.

God's power is not, however, merely immanent within the embedded order; rather, God is actively permitting and directing events in the world for both blessing and punishment. For example, as Lipscomb contemplated the Civil War, he discerned a divine purpose in the conflict similar to the purpose expressed by Lincoln in his Second Inaugural Address: "Since the end of the war," Lipscomb wrote, "we have never had a doubt but that it was the purpose of the great Father of the universe to destroy slavery. For purposes known to himself he tolerates and ordains such relationships."[97] God raised up a people to overcome the sinfulness the South should have relinquished on its own. If the South "from Christian principles" had willingly "freed the slaves," then "they would have been blessed." Instead, "for a time, at least, a desolating and destroying scourge was visited upon them."[98] God accomplished "his end by the hand of violence." That the Northern army was God's battle-axe, Lipscomb wrote, "we have no doubt."[99]

> Yet, the North should not think of itself as a righteous avenger. "We believe that every man that God used as a battle-axe he used because he was a sinful man and needed punishment."[100] The North, Lipscomb prophesied, would also experience its divine judgment. "It is folly and deception for a people to think that because they are used to punish other nations and are successful in war,

---

[93] Lipscomb (1913), "Difficulties": 335.
[94] *Loc. cit.*
[95] *Idem*, "God": 33.
[96] *Loc. cit.*
[97] Lipscomb, "God Uses the Evil as Well as the Good," *Gospel Advocate* 22 (September 30, 1880): 634.
[98] *Loc. cit.*
[99] *Loc. cit.*
[100] *Ibid.*: (1913), "God Uses the Evil": 634.

therefore they are better or more favored of God than the nations they conquer. The wicked are the sword of the Lord."[101]

Lipscomb also commented on the Franco-Prussian War of 1870: While "rationalistic philosophy" believes that "God has nothing to do" with human wars and conflicts, Lipscomb countered by attributing the European war to "God's overruling the wickedness of these nations."[102] God functions through "direct imposition," just as he did between Judah and Babylon. "We believe the same laws that governed in the punishment of Judea, the destruction of Babylon, Chaldea, and all the nations of antiquity are now in full force and vigor with reference to the church of Christ and the nations of earth."[103] In particular, France "has been the nursing mother of infidelity, scoffing atheism and fashionable licentiousness," and though "France has long been an avenging rod in the hand of God to punish surrounding nations," now "God is punishing wickedness with the wicked."[104] "Prussia," according to Lipscomb, "is the rod in the hand of God to punish her own seducer," and "when the days of her power are accomplished, then some other power in turn must visit even a more fearful destruction of her people."[105] This is how God deals with nations, and "so will it continue until all the institutions of earth will be destroyed save the kingdom of God through which God proposes to rule the world in peace and righteousness."[106]

God's reign over evil extends to human freedom though without violating it. Genuine freedom means real choice, but God's providence means that those choices are used and overruled toward divine ends. God's goal is to conform us to his image, and he uses all his resources for that goal. "We are thus gradually trained through successive stages, and molded in character into the likeness of God, and so fitted to stand beside his Son, to bear his likeness, and, with him, share all the blessings and glories of the Father's throne."[107] He intends "to train him into fitness to dwell with God and the spirits around his throne forever."[108] When we respond in humility to this training, God gives "life and hope again to the heart that is bruised and crushed with a sense of its own guilt and helplessness. This heart is sustained and guided now by the Spirit of God."[109] God's purpose is to dwell with his people. He abides now to prepare them for the future dwelling with God in the new heaven and new earth.

Not everyone, however, responds with humility. Many respond with arrogance and defiance. When the heart is corrupt and perverted, "God permits" it "to believe a lie that he may work out his own ruin and accomplish his destruction."[110] God uses human freedom to serve his own purposes. "When they make themselves wicked, he appoints them to do evil

---

[101] *Idem*, "God": 47.
[102] *Ibid.*: "The Visitations of Providence: The War of Prussia and France," *Gospel Advocate* 12 (October 27, 1870): 1,001.
[103] *Ibid.*: 1,002.
[104] *Ibid.*: 1,002-3.
[105] *Ibid.*: 1,003.
[106] *Loc. cit.*.
[107] *Idem*, "God" (1913): 42.
[108] *Ibid.*: 50.
[109] *Ibid.*: 42.
[110] *Ibid.*: 33-34.

work and then to destruction for the evil done. I have no doubt Jesus selected Judas because he knew his character and that he was fitted to do the work of treason. God did not make him bad; he chose him to do a wicked work because he found in him the character fitted to do it."[111] Thus, "God never sends an evil spirit or a delusion upon a good man, or upon those willing to obey him; but he sends these upon the wicked and disobedient that they may go down to ruin. All spirits are subject to God, the evil as well as the good. He sends the evil spirits to afflict the wicked and lead them to deeper ruin."[112]

Evil, therefore, is not autonomous. It serves divine purposes. God reigns over it so that he uses it to carry out his ends and achieve his goals. Evil will not hinder the kingdom of God. God permits evil because he values authentic human decisions; he permits everyone to choose whom they will serve. At the same time, he nonetheless circumscribes that freedom so that it serves his purposes and ends. That ultimate end is the reign of God over the new heaven and new earth. This present probationary period is a time of training and discipline when the character of the people of God is to be educated and shaped in preparation for their role in that coming kingdom.

Conclusions

Several factors shaped the history of theodicy in the beginnings of the Stone-Campbell Movement. First, the movement was born in the context of Baconian induction. The earliest "Reformers" rebelled against metaphysical and theological speculation. Instead of pursuing rigorous logical deduction as a theological method, they embraced the historical induction of "facts" within the biblical narrative. Consequently, the narrative took precedence over theological metaphysics. Theodicy in the Stone-Campbell Movement was initially shaped by biblical induction rather than theological deduction.

Second, the Movement participated in the new nation's cultural optimism. Most thoughtful 19th-century Americans assumed progress and anticipated a millennial utopia; indeed, Campbell believed the American frontier was the cutting edge of that millennial dawn. Consequently, theodicy was not a particularly significant topic because, in the optimistic perception of the age, the evils of human experience were being progressively overcome. Providence, in the first half of the nineteenth century, was perceived fundamentally as divine benevolence. In the early 1820s and 1830s, for example, most were optimistic that even slavery would end through governmental compromise and action. In fact, Barton W. Stone's disappointment with governmental intervention on this point helped move him towards a premillennial eschatology.[113] Stone's move from postmillennialism to premillennialism certainly affected his theodicy, but on this, Stone wrote too little for us to be certain of his theodic moorings.

Third, the earliest frontier "Reformers" were influenced by classical Arminianism, a post-Calvinist theology of providence tempered by the affirmation of human freedom. Campbell and Richardson, for example, held a high view of providence that was both special and meticulous; the idea of "chance" they viewed as more pagan than Christian.

[111] *Idem*, "Foreknowledge and Predestination, God's" (1921): 254.
[112] *Idem*, "'Evil Spirit,' How 'From God'?": 219.
[113] D. Newell Williams, "From Trusting Congress to Renouncing Human Governments: The Millennial Odyssey of Barton W. Stone," *Discipliana* 61 (fall 2001): 67-81.

While these three points characterized theodicy of the antebellum Movement, postbellum Restorationist theology shifted significantly. In the face of the horror and evil of the Civil War, the problem of evil became existentially compelling. The North— particularly in circles whose perspectives would characterize the Disciples of Christ in the 20th century—turned toward a more rational and metaphysical understanding of the problem. In the South—particularly in circles whose perspectives would characterize the Churches of Christ early in the 20th century—the biblical story was radicalized through the perception of cosmic conflict. The earlier, more rationalist tradition, a classic Arminian theology of providence, continued in both sections of the country, but these other alternatives also emerged within the Movement.

The Northern emphasis tended towards a rational theodicy focused on the origin of moral evil through human freedom; Northern Disciples explained natural evil in the light of natural law. The Northern emphasis tended toward a modified Deism and a denial of special providence. The Southern emphasis saw evil in more radical terms. Without denying the origin of moral evil in human freedom, the Southerners emphasized the role of God and Satan in the human drama. Human history is a cosmic conflict concerning who will reign over the world. This high view of providence was accompanied by a coequal radicalization of evil.

The Northern victory in the War enriched a cultural context in which one could explain evil in terms of human choices, and developing scientific theories pointed to the regularity and order of natural law, requiring no theory of angelic or human fall to explain harmful natural events. When humans make ignorant choices, harmful natural consequences result; when humans make morally bad choices, evil moral consequences result. The Northern victory enabled a continued optimism in the North that explained evil through rationalistic means well into the early 20th century.

The Southern defeat and the attending experience of suffering radicalized evil. The Northern victory gave evidence of the reign of Satan in the world. In the eyes of David Lipscomb, God nonetheless controls both Satan's reign and the South's defeat; he had used the North to punish the South for the evil of slavery. Lipscomb had lost the earlier frontier-American, cultural optimism; he saw no end to the reign of Satan except through the progress of the kingdom of God, identified as the church, and God's ultimate creation of a new heaven and new earth.

At the end of the 19th century, then, three broad theodic views were operative in the Stone-Campbell Movement. Some continued the optimistic, high view of providence that Campbell and Richardson articulated consistent with classic Arminianism, including the strong sense of special or meticulous providence. Others embraced a modified Deism and defended God's righteousness through a form of theological rationalism and scientific naturalism. Some, such as conservatives in Texas, did not embrace the Darwinianism of Christopher but nonetheless absolutized the natural order after the New Testament period in Newtonian fashion, so that post-biblical divine interventions were denied (e.g., L. S. White). The net effect of both is a practical Deism. A third group, however, reframed the problem of evil in the context of a cosmic conflict between God and Satan, affirming that God is absolutely sovereign over Satanic and human evil. The Southern view—primarily located in the Deep South—retained a high view of providence, but saw providence in a fallen world as disciplinary, pedagogical, and preparatory for better things to come.

Despite their differences, all three strands assumed two fundamental theodic positions. First, they affirmed a form of the "free will defense." Human freedom is the origin of human evil. Humanity qua humanity has moral capacity for good or evil. Second, they affirmed an Augustinian understanding of natural evil. Natural evil is the result of Adam's sin, even if it be entailed only in the removal from the Tree of Life. Sin introduced human death into the cosmos along with all its attendant curses (disease, pain, grief, et al.) In these two points, the theodicy of the Stone-Campbell Movement was not fundamentally dissimilar from other Arminian nineteenth-century theodicies.

While Campbell had promised a narratival reading of scripture rather than metaphysical speculations, he did not produce a narrative theodicy. Instead, he restated Arminian principles that had congealed in late-seventeenth-century Latitudinarian England. Given his cultural circumstances and lack of engagement with theodicy, perhaps Campbell simply went into "default mode" on this topic. Wilkes and Christopher significantly abandoned the narrative reading of scripture for philosophical and scientific models of theodicy. Their theodicies are substantially extra-Biblical and reflect new methodological approaches to theology emerging in the northern regions of the Stone-Campbell Movement. Ultimately, this tendency betrayed the primal impulse of the Movement by moving away from narrative to metaphysics.

Lipscomb's theodicy, however, is a narrative reading of scripture. In *Civil Government*, he followed the redemptive-historical flow of Creation, Fall, Israel, Church, and Eschatological Kingdom. He affirmed the text: God is an actor in the tragic events of history (the Flood, destruction of Canaanites, the Exile, etc.). God ordains and orders these events for his own purposes—not only for redemption but also for punishment. And God still acts in history in similar ways for similar purposes. In *Civil Government*, Lipscomb's reading of history is at times naïve and uncritical, but his theodicy in narrative form is powerful. Lipscomb was faithful to the Movement's original vision of scripture: inductive Bible study, not deductive theology.

Given contemporary theology's orientation to narrative and the reality of evil in the modern world (e.g., the Jewish Holocaust), the restoration of first-century Christianity in the twenty-first century is ripe for the development of a narrative theodicy by a God-conscious mind that seriously reads scripture in all of its diversity.[114] Theodicy is too often encumbered by metaphysical assumptions, too driven by hermeneutical harmonization, and too distant from the affirmations and particularities of the text. A Stone-Campbell theodicy, consistent with the originating principles of the Movement, will be heavy on the text (speaking where the Bible speaks) and light on metaphysics (being silent where the Bible is silent). However, the promise that Watkins made on behalf of the nineteenth-century Reformation—"a sound and lucid theodicy"—remains as yet unfulfilled.

---

[114] E. Frank Tupper, *A Scandalous Providence: The Jesus Story of the Compassionate God* (Macon, Georgia: Mercer University Press, 1995), is one such attempt in the Baptist tradition, though it fails to account for God as actor in the tragic events of human life. In fact, Tupper's theodicy is fundamentally a narrative presentation consistent with that of Christopher and Wilkes.

THE REAL HEROES

RICHARD T. HUGHES

In the aftermath of September 11, 2001, the American people honored some genuine heroes—fire fighters, police officers, civilians on American Airlines flight #93, and a variety of rescue workers who risked their lives—and in many instances gave their lives—for other human beings. The tribute we paid these heroes was not misplaced.

Soon, however, the mission of rescue gave way to the mission of war. The ease with which the nation made that transition is staggering. The ease with which many Christians embraced the cause of violence and retribution is even more staggering and offers a context in which we should consider another impressive set of heroes—heroes who consistently pursued non-violent solutions to human conflicts.

Jesus

Jesus heads that list of heroes, for it was Jesus who said to Pilate, "My kingdom is not of this world. If it were, then my servants would fight."[1] And it was Jesus who rebuked a companion who struck the servant of the high priest with his sword and cut off his ear. Jesus told the man, "Put your sword back in its place, for all who draw the sword will die by the sword."[2]

But Jesus also demonstrated that non-violence at its highest and best goes far beyond mere passivity. "Love your enemies," Jesus said. "Do good to those who hate you, bless those who curse you, pray for those who mistreat you…. Do to others as you would have them do to you."[3]

According to Scripture, Jesus embraced this radical sort of non-violent outreach as a way of life and a way of death. This is the meaning of the cross that stands at the center of the Christian faith, for the path of non-violent suffering is finally the path of love, and love is the power of redemption.

Jesus' non-violent death is all the more impressive since he died for human beings who were and are completely undeserving of such a gift. As Paul wrote in Romans:

At just the right time, when we were still powerless, Christ died for the ungodly. Very rarely will anyone die for a righteous man, though for a good man someone might possibly dare to die. But God demonstrates his own love for us in this: While we were still sinners, Christ died for us.[4]

This is the reason we celebrate the heroes of 9/11 as we do, for in a very real sense, their actions emulated the work of Jesus whether they were Christians or not. For they

---

[1] Jn 18:36
[2] Mt 26:51-52.
[3] Lk 6:27-28, 31.
[4] Rm 6:6-8.

risked themselves and gave their lives for men and women they had never seen and did not know. In this sense, they, too, were redeemers.

But when we move from non-violent redemption to violent destruction, from the work of rescue to the work of war, even if we think of that war as a war of redemption, then we have turned a radical corner and have placed our feet on a path that Jesus refused to tread.

This is why the "Battle Hymn of the Republic" makes very little sense when it proclaims that God "hath loosed the fateful lightning of His terrible swift sword," or "I have read a fiery Gospel writ in burnished rows of steel." This sort of rhetoric stands in stark contrast with the admonition of Jesus: "Put your sword back in its place, for all who draw the sword shall die by the sword."

Some Other Heroes

If Jesus heads the list of heroes who embraced a non-violent way of living and a non-violent way of dying, who are some of the other heroes who also stand in this tradition? There have been many, to be sure, but several come to mind immediately.

Unanimously, the leaders of Churches of Christ and Disciples of Christ in their early years spoke against violence and the practice of war. In his famous "Address on War," delivered in 1848, Alexander Campbell asked satirically:

> But if anyone desires to place in contrast the gospel of Christ and the genius of war, let him suppose the chaplain of an army addressing the soldiers on the eve of a great battle, on performing faithfully their duty, from such passages as the following: "Love your enemies; bless them that curse you; do good to them that hate you, and pray for them that despitefully use you and persecute you, that you may be the children of your Father in Heaven, who makes his sun to rise upon the evil and the good, and sends his rain upon the just and the unjust."
>
> Again, in our civil relations: "Recompense to no man evil for evil." "As much as lieth in you, live peaceably with all men." "Dearly beloved, avenge not yourselves; but rather give place to wrath." "If thine enemy hunger, feed him; if he thirst, give him drink." "Be not overcome of evil; but overcome evil with good." Would anyone suppose that he had selected a text suitable to the occasion?[5]

Likewise, Barton W. Stone, who professed his allegiance to the Kingdom of God and refused allegiance to the kingdoms of this world, even the United States of America, made non-violence central to his witness. He chastised America when he wrote in 1844, "A nation professing Christianity, yet teaching, learning and practicing the arts of war cannot be of the kingdom of Christ." On the other hand, he suggested, "If genuine Christianity were to overspread the earth, wars would cease, and the world would be found together in the bonds of peace."[6]

David Lipscomb, the great third-generation leader of Churches of Christ, also carried the banner of non-violence, and during the Civil War, refused to designate northern soldiers or northern citizens as enemies. He recalled in 1881: "In the beginning of the late strife that so fearfully desolated our country, much was said about 'our enemies.' I

---

[5] *Congressional Record*, November 22, 1937.
[6] Barton W. Stone, "Lecture on Matt. V. VI. And VII. Chapters," *Christian Messenger* 14 (July 1844): 65.

protested constantly that I had not a single enemy, and was not an enemy to a single man North of the Ohio River." Nonetheless, he lamented, "Thousands and hundreds of thousands who knew not each other... were made enemies to each other and thrown into fierce and bloody strife, were imbued with the spirit of destruction one toward the other, through the instrumentality of human governments."[7]

All these were heroes. But there have been others, from other Christian movements, in other periods of Christian history. One thinks, for example, of the sixteenth-century Anabaptists, the forbears of today's Mennonites, Amish, and Hutterites. The irony of the Anabaptist tradition lies in the persecution of those people in that age, for in part the authorities killed these people because they, like Jesus, also refused to take human life. Indeed, to identify oneself as an Anabaptist in the sixteenth century was tantamount to signing one's own sentence of execution.

Derk Willems, a Dutch Anabaptist, had been imprisoned for his beliefs and was awaiting execution in 1569, when but Derk managed to escape from the palace that confined him. It was winter and the moat that surrounded the palace was frozen solid. A small man, Derk scampered across the moat to freedom. Then he heard the palace guard in hot pursuit.

Unfortunately, the guard was heavier than Derk and broke through the ice to his certain death. Clearly, Derk was now free, though tragedy had befallen his pursuer. But Derk refused to take advantage of this opportunity, which he might have interpreted as providential. Instead, he turned around, walked back to the middle of the moat, and pulled the man to safety. The man was completely stunned by this incredible turn of events and wished to release Derk. But the sheriff, also in close pursuit, demanded that the palace guard seize Derk once again. Several days later, the authorities burned Derk Willems at the stake, just as Derk had known would happen.[8]

Derk Willems was neither a loser nor a fool. A man who might have resisted and saved himself, Derk chose instead to follow the way of the cross. What did he accomplish through his commitment to non-violent behavior?

The Merits of Non-Violent Resistance

The merits of non-violent resistance are many, and we can observe at least some of those merits in the life and work of another in my list of heroes, Martin Luther King, Jr. First. King understood that if Blacks responded to white racism with violence, the White community could easily dismiss those Blacks with the taunt, "Well, that's what we expected from those kinds of people!" But if Blacks responded with non-violence, they would maintain their integrity and reveal their oppressors before the world as the racists they were. Indeed, this is the very first thing we accomplish when we embrace non-violent behavior as a way of life.

This strategy paid rich dividends for Martin Luther King and Southern Blacks when, in Birmingham, Alabama, in 1963, Sheriff Eugene "Bull" Conner and his police attacked non-violent marchers, most of whom were children, with police dogs and high-powered

---

[7] David Lipscomb, "Babylon," *Gospel Advocate* 23 (2 June 1881): 340.

[8] Thieleman J. van Braght, ed., *Martyr's Mirror*, 1660 (reprint, Scottdale: Herald Press, 1950): 741.

fire hoses. That night, coverage of this unprovoked brutality against non-violent protesters aired on television stations everywhere. That night, the world saw who was right and who was wrong, and King was on the road to victory, based solely on the moral superiority that he had demonstrated over the racists of the South.

Derk Willems has been less fortunate than King, for no television cameras filmed either his rescue of the palace guard who fell through the ice or Derk's destruction at the hands of wicked men. But we can read the report of his death in the great Anabaptist document, the *Martyr's Mirror*, and even today, we know who stood tall on the moral high ground, and who wallowed in the gutter of violent behavior against a man of peace. This suggests that non-violence is itself a powerful method of resistance, and no one understood that better than did Martin Luther King.

Second, non-violent resistance breaks the vicious and seemingly endless cycle of retribution that is inevitable when men and women succumb to the ethic of "an eye for an eye and a tooth for a tooth." We should know this by now, simply by observing the endless cycle of revenge that has characterized the Israeli/Palestinian conflict for so many years. In like manner, King understood that if Blacks opposed white racism with violence, they would only trigger more violence against themselves, which in turn would provoke an endless cycle of violence and mutual revenge.

Third, at its highest and best, non-violence replaces revenge with deeds of human kindness. We have seen this already in the life and work of Derk Willems, and we can see this truth again in the life and work of Martin Luther King, Jr.

In 1967, only a year before he was assassinated, King marshaled his philosophy of non-violence as the basis for his opposition to America's war in Vietnam. "We are called to speak for the weak, for the voiceless, for victims of our nation and for those it calls enemy," he proclaimed, "for no document from human hands can make these humans any less our brothers."

And when critics turned on King for taking this stand, he reminded them that he had taken this position not simply as an activist but more so as a Christian. "Have they forgotten that my ministry is in obedience to the one who loved his enemies so fully that he died for them? What then can I say to the 'Vietcong' or to Castro or to Mao as a faithful minister of this one? Can I threaten them with death or must I not share with them my life?"[9]

Fourth, non-violent resistance is incredibly efficient. While we often think of non-violent people as altogether passive, as people who are willing to roll over and play dead before their enemies, non-violence often requires energetic levels of active, thoughtful, and strategic planning.

Several years ago, only weeks before the United States embarked on the war we call "Desert Storm," I was on a plane, returning from Chicago to Los Angeles. In the seat pocket in front of me was a newspaper, and I found on the back page of that paper a full-page statement offering constructive and strategic ways to resolve the conflict between Iraq and Kuwait, short of going to war. As I read through that statement, I was amazed at the depth of insight that informed it. Why was I not surprised when I finally reached

---

[9] Martin Luther King, Jr., "A Time to Break Silence," 1967, in *I Have a Dream: Writings and Speeches that Changed the World*, James M. Washington, ed. (San Francisco: HarperSanFrancisco, 1986): 140.

the end of the statement? On the bottom line, I learned that Mennonites—descendants of the Anabaptists, spiritual heirs of Derk Willems, Christians devoted to the ethic of non-violence—had crafted the statement.

If Americans were to seek to solve with non-violent measures the crisis we face today, the first, simple question we might ask is this: "Why do they hate us?" In 1967, Martin Luther King reasoned that one must ask why an enemy hates someone who intends no harm:

> Here is the true meaning and value of compassion and non-violence when it helps us to see the enemy's point of view, to hear his questions, to know his assessment of ourselves. For from his view we may indeed see the basic weaknesses of our own condition, and if we are mature, we may learn and grow and profit from the wisdom of the brothers who are called the opposition."[10]

By seeing ourselves as our enemies see us, we shall learn something about ourselves.

My fifth point is the most obvious point of all, but in many ways the most important: Non-violence rejects killing in the interest of peace. It is easy enough to glorify violence and war, but we often fail to realize the incredible levels of destruction and devastation that war inevitably brings.

Mark Twain understood that point amazingly well. In 1904, he dictated a document to his family that he insisted should not be published until after his death, which occurred in 1910. Twain called that document *The War Prayer*.

In *The War Prayer*, Twain described a Sunday morning worship service on the eve of war. The volunteers had taken their places in the church along with their families, and they were listening to the pastor who prayed that God would grant these young soldiers victory. "Help them to crush the foe," the pastor prayed. "Grant to them and to their flag and country imperishable honor and glory."

Then Twain described an aged stranger who moved slowly and silently down the aisle. He announced himself as a messenger from Almighty God who had been commissioned to put into words the full meaning of the prayer the pastor had prayed. A prayer for victory, he said, was a prayer "for many unmentioned results which follow victory—*must* follow it, cannot help but follow it."

Then the old man said, "Upon the listening spirit of God the Father fell also the unspoken part of the prayer. He commandeth me to put it into words. Listen!

> "O Lord, our Father, our young patriots, idols of our hearts, go forth to battle— be Thou near them! With them—in spirit—we also go forth from the sweet peace of our beloved firesides to smite the foe. O Lord, our God, help us to tear their soldiers to bloody shreds with our shells; help us to cover their smiling fields with the pale forms of their patriot dead; help us to drown the thunder of the guns with shrieks of their wounded, writhing in pain; help us to lay waste their humble homes with hurricanes of fire; help us to wring the hearts of their unoffending widows with unavailing grief; help us to turn them out roofless with their little children to wander unfriended the wastes of their desolated land in rags and hunger and thirst, sports of the sun flames of summer and the icy

---

[10] *Ibid.*: 143.

winds of winter, broken in spirit, worn with travail, imploring Thee for the refuge of the grave and denied it—for our sakes who adore Thee, Lord, blast their hopes, blight their lives, protract their bitter pilgrimage, make heavy their steps, water their way with tears, stain the white snow with the blood of their wounded feet! We ask it, in the spirit of love, of Him Who is the Source of Love, and Who is the ever-faithful refuge and friend of all that are sore beset and seek His aid with humble and contrite hearts. Amen." After a pause. "Ye have prayed it; if ye still desire it, speak! The messenger of the Most High waits."

Twain finished by saying: "It was believed afterward that the man was a lunatic, because there was no sense in what he said."[11]

Conclusions

One may dismiss this sort of rhetoric easily enough on the grounds that it reflects an earlier age before the time of smart bombs. The best estimate that I have seen, however, suggests that our "smart bombs" are not so smart as they are said to be. By the end of November 2001, "at least 3,006 Afghan civilians had died in U.S. bombing attacks"[12]—roughly the same number as died in the Twin Towers of the World Trade Center. And by the summer of 2004, conservative estimates suggested that American and Coalition firepower had taken the lives of more than 10,000 noncombatant civilians in Iraq.

We rightly mourn the dead who died in those buildings on our shores, but who in America mourns the civilian dead of Afghanistan, victims of American bombs, unleashed in the attempt to rid the world of "evildoers"" Who in America mourns the civilian dead in Iraq? The logic of war regards those deaths as "collateral damage."

But there is One who has mourned and will continue to mourn the deaths of them all, and His name is Jesus, the Christ. He is the one who has taught us to walk in the way of the cross and the way of non-violent resistance. He is the Ultimate Hero.

---

[11] Mark Twain, *The War Prayer* (New York: The Mark Twain Company, 1923, 1951; reprint, Harper and Row, 1970).

[12] Marc W. Herold, "Who Will Count the Dead? U.S. Media Fail to Report Civilian Casualties in Afghanistan": http://www.media-alliance.org/mediafile/20-5/.

MASTERED BY THE WORD:
PRINT CULTURE, MODERNIZATION, AND "THE PRIESTHOOD OF ALL READERS"[1] IN THE CHURCHES OF CHRIST

MICHAEL CASEY

> *"Be baptized every one of you in the name of Jesus Christ*
> *for the remission of your sins, and you shall receive*
> *a New Testament."*
> —Walter Scott satirizing those who thought
> the Holy Spirit was a retired author

> *"Now the Word of God is in the Book—the written word—*
> *and the direct possession of the Holy Spirit*
> *is unnecessary and superfluous."*
> —Foy E. Wallace, Jr.

At age 11 at the Walnut Grove Church of Christ near Benton, Kentucky, Don Haymes first attended a Church of Christ. There his great uncle, Garfield Cope, presided over the worship, and soon young Don was sitting in a class with other young men as his uncle taught them. Here Don encountered the classic clash between the "facts" of science and the "facts" of the Bible, for Uncle Garfield insisted that it is "hot" at the center of the earth because that is where hell is to be found. Don reflected years later:

> I had never heard of the three-story universe, as Uncle Garfield explained it now. I did not know that young men must live in terror of hell, in order to be sanctified. Nor had I met anyone who cared so much for the Bible, who attended so lovingly to its language, who tried to live his life so completely in accordance with its precepts, as Uncle Garfield Cope. I came to know that Uncle Garfield was among the very few men of whom my father spoke with absolute reverence and respect.[2]

Like so many conservative and fundamentalist groups, the Churches of Christ pride themselves as being a "people of The Book." However, unlike most other such groups, that common moniker plays itself out in some unusual ways in the Churches of Christ, a peculiarity explored in this essay.

---

[1] The phrase "priesthood of readers" is taken from David Paul Nord; see Leonard I. Sweet, "Communication and Change in American Religious History: A Historiographical Probe," in *Communication and Change in American Religious History*, Sweet, ed. (Grand Rapids: Eerdmans, 1993): 5.

[2] Don Haymes, "Walnut Grove: A Remembrance," *Integrity* 9 (October 1977): 76.

W. T. Moore (1832-1926) is credited with the line that the Restoration Movement churches "do not have bishops, they have editors."[3] Early leaders of the Churches of Christ discovered the power of print. Periodicals multiplied while a deluge of books and debates were published. The "editor-bishop" became a powerbroker in the tradition, ensuring some consensus in doctrine across the initially far-flung congregations. The earliest preachers emphasized *reading* Scripture, and many were leaders in public education, helping to increase the literacy and rationality of all Americans. The rise and proliferation of religious journals, books, and pamphlets was a part of the flood of printed Christian material called "the institutionalization of print culture."[4] This new "communication environment" produced the "modernization of knowledge." Nineteenth-century America had a print culture with high literacy rates.[5]

Catholic scholar Walter Ong explained the profound impact of the print medium on communication. In ancient oral culture, speech literally could not save itself. Once words were uttered, they were lost—they went out of existence. Words could exist only as sounds that were fleeting, and they existed only in specific contexts in which the speaker and audience were both present. Then came one of the first communication technologies in the world, the alphabet. When oral words were "captured" by writing, they could exist as symbols fixed in clay or stone or on paper and be removed from the context of a living speaker and audience. Writing and printing suggests that words are not fleeting but— according to Ong—are "fixed and neatly segmental too." Words are removed from time and, in fact, become "locked" in time—they are permanently "frozen" on paper. In a print culture, the focus is on the literal meanings of words. Since the words appear in a linear style, one pays more attention to the details, style, and arguments of writers. Therefore, a person who reviewed and reread a written document, as opposed to one who listens to a conversation, more easily notices the omissions and inconsistencies of an author.[6]

Moreover, with the transition from handwritten, copied books to moveable print and mass-produced books, printed text took on an authority of uniformity. Medievals had been accustomed to their holy books disagreeing with one another because copyists had copied incorrectly, and because other copyists had taken it upon themselves to "help" the author by "improving" the text. By the time of 19th-century religious controversy, people assumed that all copies of the printed Bible ought to say the same thing.

Among the Churches of Christ, the traditional conception of "restoration" fits print culture. The 19th-century restoration of the New Testament church was seen by 20th-century members of the Restoration Movement as a permanent structure or pattern that was "frozen" or "locked" in time, just as printed words appear to be. The lost patterns could be restored by an inductive search of the appropriate verses of Scripture where the puzzle pieces of the pattern were presumed to lie. The Movement's preaching was linear,

---

[3] W. T. Moore, *Comprehensive History of the Disciples of Christ* (New York: Fleming H. Revell Co., 1909): 12.

[4] Sweet (1993): 27-28.

[5] *Idem*: 4-49.

[6] Walter Ong, *Orality and Literacy: The Technologizing of the Word* (New York: Methuen, 1982). Much of the following section exploring Ong's ideas are adapted from my book, *Saddlebags, City Streets and Cyberspace: A History of Preaching in the Churches of Christ* (Abilene: Abilene Christian University Press, 1995).

rational, and argumentative, fitting the print culture, as Larmar Reinsch, Professor of Communication at Georgetown University, perceptively wrote:

> [A] Church of Christ sermon or lesson always included a number of Bible texts. The speaker was careful to cite "chapter and verse" so that the listener could follow along in his or her own Bible. The intricate analysis, both of the "silences" of the texts and of the "necessary inferences" to be drawn from them, frequently required visual aids in the form of elaborate charts or graphs. Sometimes the speaker used a chalkboard to diagram a sentence taken from the Bible. Very often the Bible was treated as a set of word equations to be analyzed with theological algebra. Each significant word was assumed to have a single, simple, literal meaning which was either immediately apparent or could be discovered by manipulating the equations. Always the listener was assumed to be interested in a detailed grammatical analysis of what isolated passages of Scripture did or did not say.[7]

Preachers also might explore in their sermons the intricate meanings and nuances of various Greek words found in New Testament passages. The "plan of salvation" or the correct and limited number (5) of "acts of worship" would be laid out; various linear constructions from Scripture of the "patterns" of behavior or worship or organization that needed to be restored would be explained in terms of yet another "pattern" of formalistic logic: To be "binding," a Scriptural principle requires a "direct command," an "apostolically approved example," or a "necessary inference." Evangelistic sermons or Bible studies emphasized these intricate logical structures of knowledge, and potential converts usually had to master this method before they would be immersed. Sunday school lessons consisted of fill-in-the-blank reviews of appropriate blocks of Scripture. Occasionally, the preacher's audience wrote out the sermon outline while listening to the preaching as a way to master the knowledge being presented. Preachers would sometimes print collections of their sermons either identical or nearly identical to speeches in other, similar books of sermons. These books served as résumés to show Elders and congregations that the preacher was "sound" and that he had mastered the necessary biblical knowledge and logical lore.[8] People in the Churches of Christ wanted permanent, immutable, uniform knowledge, and print culture provided the means for obtaining it.

Alexander Campbell was the leader in forming the print culture of the Restoration tradition.[9] Campbell certainly fits Leonard Sweet's description: "From here on, one could live in the backwoods but still be part of the cultural mainstream; isolation was not mutually exclusive with association."[10] Campbell, while based in isolated Bethany, Virginia, was able to engage national and even international audiences through his books, printed debates, and the two religious journals that he himself published, *The*

---

[7] Lamar Reinsch, Jr., "How Churches Are Challenged by the New Technologies," Paper presented at the Conference on Religious Communication in the Restoration Tradition, Abilene Christian University, July 1985.

[8] I acknowledge Professor Mark Love, Abilene Christian University, as the source of this astute insight into the use of books of sermons.

[9] For an assessment of Campbell as *litterateur*, see Gary Holloway, "Alexander Campbell as a Publisher," *Restoration Quarterly* 37 (1995): 28-35.

[10] Sweet (1993): 28.

Christian Baptist and the *Millennial Harbinger*. He became an international celebrity, entertaining a steady stream of interested visitors who came to Bethany; and when he traveled to preach or debate, large crowds flocked to him. The communication technologies of book production and the United States Post Office enabled Campbell to spread his Restorationist agenda. In addition, Campbell, following the same path as the American Tract Society, had his agents who peddled subscriptions for his publications. Exactly who these agents were is not entirely clear, but Campbell followed the same marketing strategies as other 19th-century publishers.[11]

But the effect of the technological word, i.e. print, did not end there. Ong argued that writing and print influence the content of messages and alter human consciousness in the process.[12] As we have already noticed, the rational message of the Churches of Christ fits the linear bias found in Western writing. With Campbell and other early leaders of the Restoration Movement, the ideology that fit the print culture of Early America was what Mark Noll called "theistic Enlightenment science," an ideology that 19th-century American Evangelicals mastered.[13] Scholars call this ideology "Baconianism," derived from Scottish Common Sense philosophy.[14] Baconianism, simply put, was the idea that the Bible could be studied scientifically through an inductive method of observing the relevant "facts" of Scripture. Campbell and others after him used the language of the "facts" of Scripture to say that Christians are to believe the reports of Scripture much as one is to accept the events and numbers that result from experiments in natural science. In fact, Campbell believed that persons needed to study the Bible and analyze Christianity in the same objective manner as a scientist studies the world of nature. Campbell wrote: "The inductive style of inquiring and reasoning is to be carried out in reading and teaching Bible facts and documents, as in the analysis and synthesis of physical nature."[15] What many have not recognized is that whereas Baconianism fits print culture, i.e., the technological effects of writing and print, perfectly, it does not necessarily result in an accurate account of how ancient literature was written, what it meant to the people who wrote and read it, and how its meaning, embedded in long-forgotten culture, can best be recovered by readers thousands of years later.

Churches of Christ have always prided themselves as a people of "The Book," and quite often, preachers have claimed to be "one-Book people." Restorationist Christians view the Bible as central to their identity. They desire to "speak where the Bible speaks, and be silent where the Bible is silent." They claim to "call Bible things by Bible names." We observe, here, that speech itself is to be determined by the very words of the printed

---

[11] This dimension of Campbell's publishing efforts has not been explored and begs for investigation. For the wider context, a model to use in exploring Campbell's marketing through agents was presented by David Paul Nord, "Systematic Benevolence and the Marketplace in Early Nineteenth-Century America," in Sweet (1993): 239-269. For an example of Campbell and his agents, see "Monthly Receipts for the Millennial Harbinger," *Millennial Harbinger* (June 1830): 288.

[12] Ong (1982): 78-116.

[13] Mark A. Noll, "The Evangelical Enlightenment and the Task of Theological Education," in Sweet (1993): 270-300.

[14] Michael W. Casey, *The Battle over Hermeneutics in the Stone-Campbell Movement, 1800-1870* (Lewiston, New York; Queenston, Canada; Lampeter, United Kingdom: The Edwin Mellen Press, 1998).

[15] Alexander Campbell, "Schools and Colleges—No. 2," *Millennial Harbinger* (March 1850): 172.

Scriptures, and that what one has found in print has been taken to heart in a way that alters the content of what one teaches and preaches.

Leonard Allen and Danny Swick identified other effects of Baconianism in the philosophy that Robert Richardson, Alexander Campbell's biographer, pejoratively called "dirt philosophy" because of its total "dependence upon material things."[16] If humans can only know empirical or material reality, that ultimately denies to humanity the ability to know anything spiritual. Robert Richardson recognized that Baconianism, among other effects, squeezes the life out of the doctrine of the Holy Spirit.[17]

Among the Churches of Christ, the orthodox position that arose to dominate thinking about the Holy Spirit was that "the Spirit works through the word only," which means that the influence of the Holy Spirit could be felt or experienced not directly but only through the mediation of the scriptural word in teaching and preaching. The extreme statement of this point of view was that the Holy Spirit is nothing more than the word or words, or the moral and psychological influence of the words, found in the Bible. The Holy Spirit was reduced to, and equated with, the written New Testament! Most of the early leaders of the Restoration Movement, however, opposed this view. Walter Scott, a prominent evangelist famous for his preaching of the "five steps of salvation" (namely "believe, repent, confess, be baptized, and receive the Holy Spirit"),[18] made this clear:

> When Bro. John S_____ was preaching, shortly after the public restoration of the immersion of remission, he was asked what he meant by the Holy Spirit, for he urged the people to be baptized that they might receive the Holy Spirit, he answered that he meant the word of God—for he did not believe that the Spirit was any thing distinct from the word. Then replied Bro. M_____, you should say, and people will understand you, "Be baptized every one of you in the name of Jesus Christ for the remission of your sins, and you shall receive a New Testament."[19]

Even Alexander Campbell, who at times seemed to equate the Holy Spirit and the word, did not take the extreme view that the Holy Spirit is simply the New Testament. In the *Christian System*, Campbell stated:

> The Spirit is said to do, and time have done, all that God does and all that God has done. It has ascribed to it all divine perfections and works; and in the New Testament it is designated as the immediate author and agent of the new creation, and of the holiness of all Christians. It is therefore called *the Holy Spirit*. In the sublime and ineffable relation of the deity, or godhead, it stands next to the incarnate Word…. To us Christians there *is*, then, but one God, even the Father; and one Lord Jesus Christ, even the Saviour; and one Spirit, even the Advocate, the Sanctifier, and the Comforter of Christ's body—the church.[20]

---

[16] C. Leonard Allen and Danny G. Swick, *Participating in God's Life: Two Crossroads for Churches of Christ* (Orange, California: New Leaf Books, 2001): 43.

[17] *Idem*: 3-56, 74-76.

[18] Later in Restoration Movement developments, this five-step *ordo salutis* was changed to "hear, believe, repent, confess, and be baptized." The Holy Spirit, as either an experiential reality or in its hardcopy print edition, fell out of the five-point picture.

[19] Walter Scott, *The Evangelist* (2 September 1833): 210.

[20] Alexander Campbell, *The Christian System* (Nashville: Gospel Advocate, 1974): 11-12.

Despite the opposition of most of the early leaders to the theory of "through the word only" and its extreme formulation that "word as Spirit," one of the most influential preachers and debaters of the Churches of Christ in the twentieth century, Foy E. Wallace, Jr., a Texan, championed it:

Apart from the inspiration of the apostles and prophets, it is impossible for spirit to communicate with spirit except through words. God and Christ never personally occupied anyone; and for the same reason, the Holy Spirit does not personally occupy anyone."[21]

Wallace went on to say, "Now the Word of God is in the Book—*the written word*—and the direct possession of the Holy Spirit is unnecessary and superfluous."[22] Thus he made evident the writing bias of print culture.

Allen and Swick further pointed out that Christian life and worship have also been affected by the "dirt philosophy." Christian development "becomes simply a matter of reading, learning and memorizing Scripture."[23] This idea goes back to the influence of the development of printing. Elizabeth Eisenstein noted that the cry of the Protestant Reformation, *sola scriptura* (Scripture alone) meant, "Bible-reading might take precedence over all other experiences to a degree and with an intensity that was unprecedented in earlier times."[24] While this had not been the intention of Martin Luther, whereas "through the word only" was the stated intention of Foy Wallace, the new print culture made possible "an introverted spiritual life developed among solitary readers who received silent guidance from repeatedly re-reading the same book on their own."[25] Eisenstein argued that the development of print recast the Scripture tradition of Christianity and set the stage for Enlightenment thought.[26]

Allen and Swick also reasoned that a "works righteousness mentality" emerged from the "dirt philosophy": "If God cannot work personally in our lives but only through the Bible and the five senses, Christians…must by their own power seek to meet the rigorous demands of the Gospel."[27] Worship is focused on the preaching event where "it becomes basically the place where the words (not so much the story) are recited, clarified and reinforced."[28]

While Allen and Swick correctly diagnosed the general problem with Baconianism, they failed to observe that the print-culture bias inherent in the Churches of Christ had caused the problem that they deplored. Silent reading of text isolates the reader from other hearers of the text—each individual reading in silence reads alone. This individualization is intensified through the printing and mass production of books, for whereas in ancient and medieval times, only the elite read alone and in silence, now

---

[21] Foy E. Wallace, Jr., *The Mission and Medium of the Holy Spirit* (Nashville, Tennessee: Wallace Publications, 1967): 7.

[22] *Idem*: 8.

[23] Allen and Swick (2001): 77.

[24] Elizabeth L. Eisenstein, *The Printing Press as an Agent of Change: Communications and Cultural Transformations in Early-modern Europe* (Cambridge: Cambridge University Press, 1979): 366.

[25] *Loc. cit.*

[26] *Idem*: 303-450.

[27] Allen and Swick (2001): 77-78.

[28] *Loc. cit.*

everyone has his or her own Bible and reads silently and alone. This reinforces the idea that each Christian in the isolation of his or her private Christian experience is left to their own devices in confronting the text, issues and implications of the text, and the application of text in the solution of personal problems. The communal practice of public worship, where a relatively small amount of biblical text may be read aloud, is not enough to overcome the focus of the individual reading Scripture silently and privately. One no longer *"hears* the word of the Lord" but, rather, "reads and digests it inwardly." The result is to make Bible-reading more of a private, individual event than a communal, congregational experience. The communal nature of humanity found in primary orality and which is partially recaptured in the secondary electronic culture, is missing from the print bias that has defined the Churches of Christ.[29]

The effect of print culture extends even further. The traditional worship of the Churches of Christ can be characterized by its emphasis on simplicity to the point that it is almost minimalist in appreciation of aesthetics. A sense of anything sacred is lacking in most worship assemblies (except for the Lord's Supper). The room where the congregation gathers is usually plain and unadored with religious imagery or visual symbols; it is not called a "sanctuary"—said to be an unbliblcal word—but it is readily called an "auditorium"—no more biblical a word than is "sanctuary" but very much more appropriate to the main event that takes place there: preaching. The "auditorium" is more a venue for Bible reading and study and classroom-style discourse than for worship or attendance upon the *mysterium tremendum*.

Christians from other traditions are often surprised at the absence of a cross, stained glass, and iconography. One might understand this post-Calvinist resistence to visual images as a soft form of iconoclasm, but Bibles, children's Bible-story books, and other literature are repleat with icons. As long as they are in books, images are OK. Ong reasoned that writing "distances the word from the plenum of existence."[30] Spoken words are part of a non-verbal context with its attendant personal relationships and relationship with objects. In Churches of Christ, however, the context of written words is merely other words. The nonverbal is stripped away and substituted in writing. Even the icons are Baconian, written words: "This Do In Remembrance of Me" is the sacred phrase that adorns the communion table, carved into the wood. A sign board announces songbook numbers of the hymns to be sung. And (still in many rural churches) another sign board announces the results of another of the "five acts of worship" in Churches of Christ, the collection: The amount of last week's collection and the running total of the building fund are posted for all to read.

The effect of print culture, moreover, is apparent in the traditional worship of the Churches of Christ. As with writing, so with worship, much of the nonverbal is stripped

---

[29] Secondary orality is Ong's idea for the electronic media. He points out that they release words frozen in print back into an oral form. Unlike primary orality though, speech is preserved and can be played back. Secondary orality helps bring back the communal nature of orality, yet it does not recover the strong need for memory found in primary orality because it preserves speech. Ong also explores other effects, such as the demise of reading, that go beyond the scope of this essay.

[30] Walter Ong, "Writing Is a Technology that Restructures Thought," in *The Written Word: Literacy in Transition*, Gerd Baumann, ed. (Oxford: Clarendon Press, 1986): 39.

away. Typically, the preacher's pulpit occupies center stage, although the communion table usually stands in front of it, so that—in a sense—the Lord's Supper and the sermon take turns as the focus of the congregation, the former for about ten minutes, the later for from thirty minutes to an hour. The functional purpose of the pulpit serves the rational delivery of a sermon usually devoted to the characteristic logic of Baconian Bible study. The communion table is a table, not an altar, with its printed phrase, worked in the wood for all to see, as mentioned above. The Lord's Supper is understood to be neither a reenactment of Christ's death nor a miracle of Real Presence, but a commemoration dependent on the psychological state of the believing individual, dependent for its efficacy to convey grace "through the word" on a rationalized act of human faith, *ex opere operantis*. This is made clear in the near-universal liturgy (at last, a touch of oralcy, for this traditional prayer for the "fruit of the vine" cannot be found written in a prayer book):

> In like manner, our Heavenly Father, we thank thee for this fruit of the vine which so fitly represents the blood of our Lord and Savior, Jesus Christ. May each one here examine himself, and partake in such a manner that is pleasing in Thy sight. In Jesus' name, amen.[31]

Baconianism and the bias for print has encouraged a cognitive and forensic focus that often is expressed in the Churches of Christ in a legalistic way. God has been understood to be so transcendent (wholly other) that the divine presence, whether as Father, Son, or Holy Spirit, has been removed from this earth, and only a book, the Christian Bible, has been left behind. Believers are expected to apply their human logic, and a failure of logic is more often determined to be a defect of will than a failure either of the learner to understand or of the preacher/teacher to communicate. No doctrine of Original Sin is part of the creed to undermine the 19th-century optimism in Baconian, rationalistic logic at work in the essentially unfallen human mind. Reading the plain words of Scripture is said to be all one needs to figure out logically what one needs to do to save oneself.[32] No doctrine of personal grace, whether prevenient, justifying, or sanctifying, is part of the creed to afford divine assistance in this all-human system of salvation by words and works. "Grace" is understood, as Pelagius understood it, to have been God's great gift in giving us the Law, the Prophets, the Messiah, and—now above all—the canonical Scriptures.

The study of the Scriptures, as devised by 19th-century Baconian frontiersmen, is analogous to the work of a strict constructionist of the Constitution. Each person has to figure out God's will from the words of Scripture, which is variously said to be our "blue print" of salvation and our "road map" from earth to Heaven. Campbell and those who followed him argued that by studying the Bible scientifically and objectively, any rational person could figure out God's will *easily*—it is "easy," Campbell reasoned, because a merciful, self-revelating God would not have made it hard for humans to find Himself in His own book. The task is to sort out which commands, which approved apostolic examples, and which necessary inferences in Scripture are "binding," as opposed to those that are considered to be "not binding," being logically deemed to have been

---

[31] I observe that both the rational sermon and the form of Communion are rapidly changing into almost unrecognizable forms in the new, postmodern suburban congregations under the influence of Evangelicalism and secondary orality of the emerging electronic media.

[32] Shaun Casey, "From Illusions of Innocence to the Wisdom of Serpents," *Leaven* 1/3 (1990): 21.

merely "local customs" of the first century. Baptism by immersion, singing *a cappella* only (no instruments of music), and celebration of the Lord's Supper each week and on Sunday only, and the silence of women in church, were customs of the first-century church, but they are said to be "binding" because they are backed by the logic of command, example, and inference; as such, they are received as permanent sacramental features in Churches of Christ. Foot-washing (a potential sacrament of Christian humility), holy-kissing (a potential sacrament of Christian friendship), and the wearing of veils by those silent women (a potential sacrament of Christian modesty), by contrast, are said to have been merely "local customs" of the Early Church and are, therefore, "not binding"—this, despite their likewise being backed in Scripture by similar command, example, and inference. One must look beyond the demands of logic to deetermine why some "local customs" are "binding," and other "local customs" are "not binding."

Latter-day casuistry aside, this approach was believed by 19th-century readers of the Bible-in-print, their *McGuffey's Reader* of religion, to lead to clear and certain practices and laws for Christians to follow and obey. J.S. Lamar, one of Campbell's students at Bethany College, said that when the Bible was studied scientifically, it spoke "to us in a voice as certain and unmistakable as the language of nature heard in the experiments and observations of science."[33] Campbell argued that only by a "full induction," that is, by looking at all the relevant verses or biblical "facts" on an issue, could one understand the correct teaching of the Bible on a topic.[34] Moses Lard, another of Campbell's students at Bethany College, was confident that the will of God in the Bible could be understood. He said, "The Bible, then, being assumed true, we hold that the mind has…the highest possible assurance that its knowledge is correct." The mind through the "necessary laws of thought" could study and "by these the meaning of Holy Writ may be determined, not doubtfully, but with absolute certainty."[35] With this utter lack of epistemological humility, and with no sense that pervasive sin as assuredly corrupts human logic as it does the human heart, will, and body, Lard presumptuously but confidently proclaimed: "[I]f a man knowingly holds one false doctrine, or one which with reasonable effort he might know to be false…it is simply certain that he cannot be saved if he remains in this condition."[36]

Whenever persons outside the Churches of Christ did not reach the same conclusions that the followers of Campbell did when they studied Scripture, then those conclusions were viewed as unscientific and therefore erroneous and therefore damning. The persons reaching those mistaken conclusions were viewed as either irrational because they used subjective, emotional methods, or unintelligent because they lacked either the ability or motivation to study all the biblical evidence, or possessed of a willful stubborness in their refusal to see the plain and obvious meaning of Scripture.

---

[33] James Sanford Lamar, *The Organon of Scripture: Or the Inductive Method of Biblical Interpretation* (Philadelphia: J.B. Lippincott, 1859): 176.
[34] Alexander Campbell, *Christian Baptism with its Antecedents and Consequents* (Nashville: Gospel Advocate Co., 1951): 184-5.
[35] Moses Lard, "The Reformation for Which We are Pleading—What Is it? *Lard's Quarterly* 1 (September 1863): 14, 16.
[36] Moses Lard, "Have We Not Become a Sect?" *Lard's Quarterly* 1 (March 1864): 246.

Devotion to the technological, written word has necessarily exacerbated the cognitive, forensic, logical, legal, and argumentative nature of Church of Christ debaters. Ong argued that written words divorced from their nonverbal context have a "verbal precision" enforced by other words:

> In a text, the entire immediate context of every word is only other words, and words alone must help other words convey whatever meaning is called for. Hence texts force words to bear more weight, to develop more and more precisely "defined"—that is "bordered" or contrastive—meanings. Eventually words used in texts come to be defined in dictionaries, which present the meaning of words in terms of other words.[37]

This squarely fits the Baconian bias prevalent in Churches of Christ. Lard stated: "For as, of yet, our Heavenly Father has no medium through which he holds intelligible intercourse with us, except words." So Lard argued, "How important, then, that the mind should be profoundly skilled in the use of terms, and in the best and surest methods of ascertaining their exact import." For Lard, "theoretic discussions" or debates about religion were the best way to acquire this skill because "they cultivate and develop especially the logical faculty." He added:

> They lead us to study intimately the structure and meaning of propositions, the nature of premises, the relation between them and conclusions—in a word everything constituting the validity of arguments or in any way vitiating them. They serve, furthermore, to make us acquainted with the laws of evidence, the force and relevancy of testimony, the nature of proof, together with the various and proper methods of refutation and disproof.[38]

For the next hundred years, public debate—a favorite spectator sport in the Churches of Christ—would be wrangling arenas in which champions of rhetoric would engage outsiders and insiders alike over the parsing of Greek verbs, the meaning of text, the interpretation of scriptural passages, the logical exercise of the mind, and the proper wording of formal debate propositions. They even would construct convoluted analogies and highly theological propositions as they sought to slay all comers through cantankerous argument and clever "logical" structures that baffle most outsiders (and many insiders): The reason that one must sing only (and not play) church music is the same reason that Noah built the Ark of gopher wood (and not some other wood): because God said so.

The Churches of Christ were learning their lessons well, as Lard had boasted: "In no denomination in Christendom…can an equal number of discriminating critics, accomplished logicians, and skillful debatants be found." Lard inadvertently acknowledged the embarrassing truth of the situation, that the "intellectual powers" of debaters in the Restoration Movement were so well developed that they were accused of "having only *a religion of the head.*"[39]

The legalism and print bias of the Churches of Christ focuses on the propositions ("facts") found in the Bible, similar to the difference between oral words and words frozen in writing, mentioned above. For example, Ong showed that the word *nevertheless*

---

[37] Ong (1986): 40.

[38] Lard (1963): 18.

[39] *Loc. cit.*

appears as a single word in print; however, to a person with a completely oral background, the entire word cannot be entirely simultaneously present. By the time *the-less* is uttered, the *never* is gone. "To the extent that it makes all of a word appear present at once," Ong stated, "writing falsifies." He added:

> Recalling sounded words is like recalling a bar of music, a melody, a sequence in time. A word is an event, a happening, not a thing, as letters make it appear to be. So is thought: "This is a paper" is an occurrence, an event in time. We grasp truth articulately only in events.[40]

Truth in oral cultures was narratively based and grasped in poetry and ritual. By contrast, the idea of propositional objective truth that is at the core of the technology of writing and print requires that we must assent to laws or truths found in propositions embedded in individual verses of Scripture. These segments of truth are then reassembled like pieces of a jigsaw puzzle according to an imposed Baconian logic, the whole construct a thoroughly modern invention made possible through freezing words in writing. This view of propositional truth spread across modern human culture with the proliferation of print technology.

The focus of propositional doctrine comes to fall on belief of the facts of the Bible (as opposed, say, to faith in God), just as one believes the facts found in a biology or history text. An experiential gulf is fixed between the person and the ideas presented. To this impersonal truth, one may respond in a variety of ways: One can mentally assent to the facts, but those facts remain disconnected from one's behavior. One can believe that something is true but still not care about that truth. One can subscribe to the facts as imposed, and then supply them with one's own personal meaning, whether that meaning arises from the alleged facts or not. While this is not always the case, the results can be devastating and leave people morally and spiritually bankrupt, even though they make every effort to believe in the facts of Scripture.

The triumph of print culture in religion brought about a further result from the emphasis on the precise meaning of words in print, and on the cognitive assent to intellectual meaning, namely the "priesthood of all readers" in the Restoration Movement. With the printed book ascendant, and in particular with the Bible as the preeminent authority in religion, Campbell and most other Americans believed that each individual reader had a religious right and freedom (equal to democratic rights in the political culture) to interpret Scripture for himself or herself. Borrowing a word from Jefferson, Campbell argued for "the inalienable right of all laymen to examine the sacred writings for themselves."[41] Campbell took this to heart for his own study when he claimed, "I have endeavored *to read* the Scriptures as though no one else had *read* them before me."[42]

Many observers have noted that this individualistic hermeneutic led not to uniformity of meaning but rather to the babble of legion interpretations in the many competing

---

[40] Ong (1986): 25.

[41] As cited by Nathan O. Hatch, "The Christian Movement and the Demand for a Theology of the People," in Michael W. Casey and Douglas A. Foster, *The Stone-Campbell Movement: An International Religious Tradition* (Knoxville: The University of Tennessee Press, 2002): 128.

[42] As cited by Richard T. Hughes and C. Leonard Allen, *Illusions of Innocence: Protestant Primitivism in America, 1639-1875* (Chicago: University of Chicago Press. 1988): 143.

denominations on the American scene. Within the Restoration Movement, a similar babble of division emerged over the correct application of Baconian logic and the ever-elusive pattern of the New Testament Church. Originally a unity movement to unite all Christians, the Stone-Campell effort resulted in the spawning of several new schisms, or "splits" as they are called, within Restorationism, some of them numerically sizeable, some of them not.

A member of the Church of Christ in Texas reasoned that the New Testament pattern meant that males only may be allowed to sing during corporate worship, since singing is commanded in Scripture as one way to "teach and admonish," but women are commanded to "keep silence" and are not allowed to teach or usurp authority over men when they are "in church." No one agreed with this rural Texan, so he ended up worshipping with his family out in the country, himself presumably the only one doing the singing (unless he had sons). Eventually, even his family disagreed with him and went back to their local congregation, leaving him alone to sing by himself. When the man came to die, he believed that the true primitive church would disappear with him from the planet![43]

The focus on reading, nevertheless, has also had a positive side, for many from the Churches of Christ have become accomplished scholars, educators, lawyers, and doctors by reason of their critical faculties that were sharpened by the pulpit and in Bible class. The ability to read, discuss, analyze, and think has opened up wider venues for many than the rural world offered at Walnut Grove. Even now in postmodern America, the Churches of Christ are alive and well and not likely to disappear anytime soon. Don Haymes reflected on one of the last times he saw his then 90-year-old Uncle Garfield:

He was frail, but he moved and spoke with the same dignity and power I remembered. He searched through the house until he found a small New Testament to give to my son. In it he wrote:

Book of all Books
Gift of all Gifts

Gar. A. Cope

My son is a fortunate young man. If one may not own a Bible inscribed by the Author, the autograph of one who cared for it so much must be the next-best thing.[44]

Modern print culture with its individualistic propensity is being altered by the emergence of postmodern electronic culture; postmodern culture is replacing modernization and the "priesthood of all readers"; people and churches are searching for greater community and closer connection to others. Now, as fewer and fewer are "mastered by the word," will Churches of Christ discover the Word who is beyond and above the words?

---

[43] Author's interview with J. Ervin Waters, September 13, 1990.
[44] Haymes (1977): 76.

SIX BLACK WOMEN WHO INFLUENCED MY LIFE:
A JOURNEY IN SPIRITUAL AND INTELLECTUAL FORMATION

JOHN MARK TUCKER

The opportunity to honor Don Haymes has led me to address one of his abiding passions, reconciliation among races. I approached this topic by tracing the roots of my own race consciousness. As my journey proceeded, I encountered six African-American women who made enduring contributions to my intellectual and spiritual development.

Something that the apostle Paul wrote also compelled me: "For whatever was written in former days was written for our instruction, so that by steadfastness and by the encouragement of the scriptures we might have hope." (Rm 15:4, NRSV) Paul offered a rationale for examining the lives of people depicted in the biblical accounts, those who lived their lives sometimes learning—and sometimes not learning—the ways of God. Their experiences inform those of us who choose to live in hope, a compelling rationale for an autobiographical account.

The six Black women I want especially to tell you about have been a rich blessing to me, for having led, nurtured, taught, challenged, served, and befriended this White male. Through something they had in common by way of their race and gender, they advanced radically my education and race consciousness. I grew up in the South, living in three States of the former Confederacy, a White child in the churches of Christ, part of that indigenous American Frontier effort in the early-19th century to unite Christianity by restoring the first-century church through following what we believed to be New Testament patterns in faith and practice. Our churches had as much trouble as any other group in dealing with Black and White issues. Though living, worshipping, and studying in segregated settings, I came routinely in contact with African Americans. Their lives were separate from mine but not necessarily distant.

My dad, Paul M. Tucker, was a minister; our home was filled with religious conversations, ideas, and books. Where we lived depended on where he preached. In 1945, when I was born, he was serving the Church of Christ at 315 Rankin Street, which later moved to 29 Fourth Street (now Covington Road) in Natchez, Mississippi. During our Natchez years, Dad sought desperately to reach out to the Black community with the simple Restoration plea. He brought the world-renowned Black evangelist, Marshall Keeble, and a small contingent of Keeble's students from Nashville Christian Institute (NCI). Keeble had sent my dad a portrait of himself and four young preachers in training (one of whom was Fred Gray, later a Civil Rights attorney for Rosa Parks and Martin Luther King, Jr.). Dad intended to advertise the meeting, in part, through publicity in the *Natchez Democrat*. In that time and place, however, it was unthinkable that a photograph of a Black person would be printed in the city newspaper. I have often wondered what motivated Dad to attempt this particular innovation. An honest conviction that this was the best way to publicize? A simple desire to succeed where others had failed? A stubborn determination? Naiveté? Dad's failed attempt to publicize the Keeble meeting in the Natchez city paper survives in our family folklore, and our photographs include one of "Keeble and his boys." Not coincidentally, the building constructed on Fourth Street in Natchez during my dad's ministry now houses the Black church of Christ, likely established through Keeble's meeting.

A second phase of the Keeble story occurred the night before his meeting in Natchez. Members of my dad's congregation had erected a tent; an unusually heavy rainstorm arose and the tent collapsed into thick mud. Brother Keeble responded calmly, saying that he and his boys would take care of the tent, as he gently quipped: "I could have told you a bunch of White folks don't know how to put up a tent!"[1]

In 1948 our family moved to Tuscaloosa, Alabama. Dad preached at the Central Church of Christ at 6th Street and 26th Avenue, later relocated to Hargrove Road. In 1952, we moved to Nashville, Tennessee, where he preached at Jackson Park, Wingate, and Crieve Hall, respectively. These were White middle-class churches, although small businessmen and blue-collar workers, some with union membership, were a large part of the group at Wingate. We lived in segregated, middle-class suburbs during the years my brother and I were coming of age.

Three Black Women in My Early Years

My earliest memories, traceable to about age four, include images of Annie May and Robert Tyson, janitors for the church building in Tuscaloosa. Annie May spent much time baby-sitting my brother, Tim, and me. I recall a meal that she prepared for us in our home. We asked her to join us at the kitchen table. Instead, she served us and stood across the room, back to the door, her lunch on the kitchen counter, not explaining why she would not sit with us. I also recall being in the Tyson home, a shotgun shack, the first building to the left, and north of the bridge over the Black Warrior River leading from Tuscaloosa into Northport. Annie May demonstrated an inquisitive and welcoming spirit.

The second Black woman whom I remember was Dorothy Way. Attractive, personable, and immensely fun to be around, she was married to the Black preacher in the Black Church of Christ in Tuscaloosa. On Thursday evenings, my dad preached at Dorothy's church. She and her husband had a small fenced back yard—I remember playing there one afternoon with Dorothy's six children. Like Annie May, Dorothy did some baby-sitting. My earliest memory of learning how to spell words like *dog, cat, boy, hat, sun,* and other simple words dates from the time that Dorothy wrote them on the blackboard in our bedroom. She identified letters and words, helped me to pronounce them, taught me to write them on the board, and made an effort to help me connect the words and the objects they named. My brother, four years older than I, needed none of this instruction, so he does not have this early literacy recollection. Dorothy, like Annie May, provided both of us with a variety of lasting memories.

---

[1] J. E. Choate discussed the same events in *Roll Jordan Roll: A Biography of Marshall Keeble* (Nashville: Gospel Advocate, 1974): 119.

I am not quite sure when the thought entered my mind that Blacks were different from me and that, due to that difference, other people expected me to treat them with less respect than I treated Whites. I do recall, however, that, in my preschool years, I found racial distinctions to be somewhat puzzling. I also remember not having ever heard a racial epithet at home. I heard only words of respect toward people, regardless of color, class, level of education, or other distinctive. But after we moved to Tennessee, I began to adopt the derogatory language and racist impulses of my public school classmates. At the time, these changes were subtle enough that I did not recognize them for what they were. Much later I would come to regard them as attitudes and terminology elaborated by White power structures to maintain the *status quo*, a system of racial apartheid, designed to serve a wide variety of social, cultural, political, and economic purposes.

The third Black woman from this time was Deeandrew Bell. We called her "Dee." She came to our house usually twice a month to assist the family with laundry, sometimes cleaning, occasionally cooking. My mom, Edith, needed the help. A full-time employee at Lipscomb College, she was for several of those years a student at George Peabody College for Teachers. As a preacher's wife, she also provided hospitality for church functions, traveled for meetings and related church activities, and taught an adult Sunday Bible-study class, something she has done continuously since 1965. She also reared two independent-minded sons without undue embarrassment to our family.

I admire and appreciate Dee to this day. Irrepressibly cheerful, she expressed her concern for us in the form of a gentle inquiry and a prayer for a favorable outcome, but her faith went far beyond the warm, responsive person we witnessed. She sang as she worked, always a hymn; she peppered her conversation with deep concern for those around her, immediate friends and family and the friends and family of others she served. Her faithfulness in every circumstance both to the task at hand and to the people in her circle modeled Christian devotion.

Over the years, I felt a growing sense that any of Dee's pay increases could not possibly compensate for what she meant to us. I occasionally wondered how she managed to work all day for others, and then have the energy to cook and clean for her own family. If I ever asked her about such things, I do not recall her reply. I knew she did not have much money because I had seen her home on 2nd Avenue South. That she had minimal resources was further underscored for me when I heard that she had brain surgery at General Hospital, the Nashville city hospital for those who could not afford Vanderbilt, Baptist, Parthenon Pavilion, or St. Thomas.

In our talking with Dee, political topics rarely emerged, though on a couple of occasions they did. Among several college students to take room and board at the Tucker house in the 1960s was Felton Spraggins, a ministerial student from Gadsden, Alabama. Unusually bright and personable, Felton had been granted a full scholarship to study Engineering at Auburn University but, following his freshman year, he transferred from Auburn to Lipscomb, a Christian college; after graduation, Felton served as pulpit minister for several congregations in Georgia. He also read voraciously, challenging me to read in and beyond my usual fields of interest. In 1964 Felton read a book by Martin Luther King, Jr., *Strength to Love* (1963), and he asked Dee if she had ever read it. Dee asked who wrote it. Felton replied that it was King. Dee responded, "He's the one who's always getting us in trouble," thus ending that conversation.

I wish I could say that I had engaged Dee in conversation about politics or theology or some topic beyond the daily issues of life, but I never did. My brother, Tim, did, however, and in 1970, he asked, "Do you think that new Civil Rights laws and improved attitudes toward Blacks came about as a result of the demonstrations?" Dee answered, "Yes," and that conversation ended as the earlier one had, quickly and without further elaboration.

Tim and I have some residual ambivalence about our relationship with Dee. Our family had employed her in a position that was typical in that time and place for people of low estate, and yet those were also times of emerging new consciousness regarding race and human rights, of which Dee's presence made us freshly aware. Dee meant much to us on a personal level; I am sure that I expressed gratitude for her service and devotion but, now, I long for an opportunity to say those things again. I trust that she is resting in the arms of Jesus and forgiving me for not having said more completely how I felt when I had the opportunity. I love you, Dee—deeply, deeply.

Decades later, I realize that these three Black women of my childhood would, today, be stereotyped in more radical minds in an unfavorable light as among those who accommodated and compromised. They were not outspoken, not radical, and seemingly not impatient for change; they never marched or protested. Their personal gifts and Christian graces facilitated their acceptance of what life had given them with balance and good humor. I am not foolish enough to imagine that they were the "happy negroes" of our racist notions, but every person is, in part, a creature of his or her own times, so Annie May, Dorothy, and Dee could hardly have been other than what they were. To me they were wonderful, also wise, compassionate, resourceful and, upon further reflection, vastly underestimated and underappreciated.

A Critical Incident

A seed of racial innovation had been planted in 1964 that would sprout, grow, and bear fruit in the coming years. I do not recall in great detail the circumstance that took me off campus, at age nineteen, to speak at NCI. But I was there in that hot summer to meet Marshall Keeble in his office, to attend an elementary-school class, to visit with NCI students, and to make a talk in chapel. Following my innocuous and hopefully harmless remarks, Keeble spoke extemporaneously. He commented not on the contents of my sermon but on my apparent personal attributes, which he credited to my father's influence.

He followed this introduction with a message of his own. Among his students, he was leader, teacher, mentor, spokesman, prophet, and friend. He was fretting over the presidential election of that year: Republican Barry Goldwater was challenging President Lyndon Johnson. The Civil Rights Act of 1964 was under consideration; if passed, it would become the most sweeping legislation of its kind in a century. Keeble spoke of freedom, recounting years of slavery, struggles for the right to vote, the right to educational and economic opportunity, the unfettered right to an integrated society. He longed for a prophet to lead his people to freedom; he likened Johnson to Moses. Tears welled up as he beseeched the God of us all not to "put Mr. Goldwater on us." If necessary, he said, he and his people could "take" Mr. Goldwater. They had, after all, taken slavery. But they would pray and hope for a better outcome, one that would place Blacks securely on the road to freedom. I felt as if I had been allowed to pull back a curtain and to peer into the heart of another universe, a culture that I had known existed but had never seen. I pondered these things in my heart; the images they produced became seared forever into my brain.

The 1960s

I came of age in the 1960s, a tumultuous yet promising time for our country. Our family was probably more politically aware than most in our environs, though we were never activists or party regulars. Politics engaged our reading interests and conversation but not our time-intensive service, which was reserved for church, family, and education. Our political awareness was owed to the intellectual and avocational obsessions of Tim. He loved American geography, history, and politics, and long before he graduated from the elementary grades, he began lecturing our parents and me on matters of public policy. He did this without being prompted, often supplying us with more information than we might have requested or could absorb. Relatives and friends began to seek Tim out for political information.

During this revolutionary decade, I came alive politically, placing too much hope in the processes and the people involved. I was angry about the war in Vietnam and the divisive spirit it had incited in the country. I was both fascinated and repelled by the counter culture. I was disturbed by the violence and destructive rioting in the nation's cities. I was concerned about the plight of the poor—mostly Blacks—in urban ghettoes. While on a church-related trip to New York in 1966, I endangered my life and that of a student from Middle Tennessee State University, Jean Thweatt (later Jean Cobb), by driving us several miles out of the way so I could see first hand the poverty and decay of the Bedford-Stuyvesant section of Brooklyn.[2]

With formal education temporarily behind me, I had the leisure and opportunity to pursue my interests. I had developed a thirst to know why big cities would flare into race riots, to know the hopes and concerns of Black Americans. The following books became the formative canon of my education about African America: Anthony Lewis, *Portrait of a Decade: The Second American Revolution* (1964); William Bradford Huie, *Three Lives for Mississippi* (1965); Claude Brown, *Manchild in the Promised Land* (1965); and John Howard Griffin *Black Like Me* (1960).[3]

---

[2] Little did I know at the time that only a few blocks away Don Haymes and his Inner City Faith Corps were in even greater danger. That "long hot summer" of 1966 was a time of awakening for many of us, and Brooklyn drew us like a magnet to reality. See Freda Elliott Baker, "The Inner City Faith Corps: An Oral History," in this volume.

[3] Anthony Lewis, reporter for *The New York Times*, reviewed key events in the Civil Rights movement from 1954 to 1964. William Bradford Huie investigated the murders of Andrew Goodman, James Chaney, and Mickey Schwerner, civil rights activists slain in Philadelphia, Mississippi, during Freedom Summer, 1964, and one of whose murderers was brought to justice only as I was writing this essay over 40 years later. Claude Brown offered a searing, candid autobiographical account of life in crime-ridden Harlem in the 1940s and 1950s. He subsequently earned a college degree and graduated from Harvard Law School. John Howard Griffin, a White journalist, sought the aid of a physician who chemically darkened the pigment of his skin with

Once in Jackson, Tennessee I heard a speech by the head of the local N.A.A.C.P.. He assured us that Blacks and Whites had never really been separate as evidenced by the light brown hue of his skin. He added that the critical issue in America was not about race but about the chasm between rich and poor—that poor Whites were oppressed as much as poor Blacks and that hope for a better life lay in partnerships among the poor regardless of race.

Jessie Carney Smith

In 1971 I returned to Peabody to pursue an Ed.S. in Library Science. I was ripe for new perspectives on African Americana, so I enrolled in "Bibliography of the Negro," a course taught by Jessie Carney Smith.[4] This course had a radical impact on my intellectual, professional, and spiritual life, providing the missing links in my undergraduate liberal arts education.

Smith's academic career is that of a pioneer. She earned a B.A. from North Carolina A & T, an M.A. in Child Development from Michigan State, and an M.A.L.S. from Peabody; in 1964 she graduated from the University of Illinois as the first Black to obtain a Ph.D. in Library Science. She was appointed library director at Fisk University in 1965, succeeding her mentor and friend, the author-librarian, Arna Bontemps. Smith obtained hundreds of thousands of dollars in federal grants to train teachers and librarians in the rich, but historically neglected, print culture of African Americana. In 1977, she published *Black Academic Libraries and Research Collections: An Historical Survey*, an instant standard for professional librarians. Smith soon emerged as one of the nation's leading academic librarians, and in 1985 was so honored by the Association of College & Research Libraries. In 1997, she was named the William & Camille Cosby Professor in the Humanities, honoring years of leadership, grant-proposal writing, teaching, mentoring, and scholarship. She has written or edited twenty books specializing in biographical, historical, and statistical reference sources.

Smith immersed her students in African-American culture. My classmates and I read John Hope Franklin's *From Slavery to Freedom: A History of Negro Americans* (4th ed., 1971, now in the 8th edition) and Alain Locke's *The New Negro* (1925, reprinted several times), which provided our foundation for Black history and literature. Smith led us, literally, into Fisk University's rich treasure trove of African-American archives and rare books. Under Smith's sure and wise tutelage, we discovered vitally important reference sources: *A Bibliography of the Negro in Africa and America* (1928) by Monroe Nathan Work; *Negro Anthology* (1934), an oversized collection of nearly 900 pages by Nancy Cunard; *The Negro*

---

serious long-term health effects. He then toured a number of Southern states in order to experience being treated as Black rather than White. Though not especially well received by Black reviewers, Griffin's book was immensely popular, selling eleven million copies in fourteen languages and being made into a movie. For more recent insights, I recommend Bernestine Singley, ed., *When Race Becomes Real: Black and White Writers Confront their Personal Histories* (Chicago: Lawrence Hill Books, 2002).

[4] Smith later revised this course into "Bibliography of Cultural Minorities." The impact of this and similar courses on instruction in graduate schools of Library and Information Science is a topic that merits further research.

Almanac (1st edition, 1967, now in the 9th edition, under a new title); and *The Negro in the United States: A Selected Bibliography* (1970) by Dorothy Burnett Porter. Thus began my fascination for topics in Black culture, an abiding interest that continues to flourish.

In 1972 I enrolled in a course by another remarkable African American, Akbar Muhammad, then director of the Afro-American Studies Program at Vanderbilt University. A brilliant, engaging teacher, Akbar had earned his doctorate at the University of Edinburgh. In his course, "Black History and Historians," he introduced us to foundational works such as those by George Washington Williams, Benjamin Brawley, and Carter G. Woodson.[5] He also brought Berkeley professor Winthrop Jordan to lecture to our class. Jordan had published *White over Black: American Attitudes toward the Negro, 1550-1812* (1969), winner of the National Book Award.

One memorable dialogue from this class involved the role of Christianity in the Civil Rights movement. Some students argued—in Marxist terminology—that Christianity served as an opiate and, with its focus on the afterlife, encouraged believers not to think about injustice in the present age. These students claimed that Christianity had stifled political protest and related activity. Others, including me, argued that Christianity had been essential to the movement's success. I could not conceive of a successful rights effort apart from Martin Luther King, Jr., and the Southern Black churches.

Professor Muhammad missed numerous class sessions due to health problems, reportedly ulcers. As the semester proceeded we learned—so we hypothesized—why his ulcers defied medical control. Years earlier he had been disowned by his father, Elijah Muhammad, leader of the Black Muslim movement in the United States. Akbar had rejected his father's particular version of Islamic faith, choosing, instead, another path. His alienation from the Black Muslim rendition of Islam began when Akbar studied Islamic law at Al-Azhar University in Cairo, where his father had sent him and where he was able to compare traditional Islam with that of the Nation of Islam. The gulf between Akbar and his father had widened still further in the course of Akbar's doctoral studies. Hans Rollmann, co-editor of this volume in honor of Don Haymes, also studied under Akbar Muhammad (1972 to 1974), enrolling in courses on Classical and Medieval Islam, and enlarging his own understanding. Likewise, my own appreciation of Professor Muhammad's journey of faith, and the revision of the ideas he had inherited, subsequently deepened. The mantle of Elijah Muhammad's leadership has since passed to Akbar's older brother, Wallace Muhammad.

My reading about African-American subjects, stimulated strongly by Smith's course, has continued with a focus on Civil Rights. I especially enjoyed *Parting the Waters: America in the King Years, 1954-63* (1988) and *Pillar of Fire: America in the King Years, 1963-65* (1998) by Taylor Branch, and *Freedom Summer* (1988) by Doug McAdam. I also read the classics by W.E.B. Du Bois, including *The Suppression of the African Slave Trade to America, 1638-1870*

---

[5] Representative titles include Williams's *History of the Negro Race in America, 1619-1880* (New York: G.P. Putnam's Sons, 1883); Brawley's *A Short History of the American Negro*, 4th rev. ed. (New York; Macmillan, 1939); and Woodson's *The Education of the Negro Prior to 1861*, 2nd ed. (New York: G.P. Putnam's Sons, 1919). August Meier and Elliott Rudwick provide scholarly context for these sources in *Black History and the Historical Profession, 1915-1980* (Urbana: University of Illinois Press, 1986).

(1896), *The Souls of Black Folk* (1903), and *Black Reconstruction in America, 1860-1880* (1935). I delved into the major biographies of Du Bois and Booker T. Washington, which together provide an excellent short course on African-American intellectual and political history during the first fifty years of the 20th century.[6] I have felt challenged by James Baldwin, in *The Fire Next Time* (1963), *Go Tell It on the Mountain* (1953), and *No Name in the Street* (1972). And I have been entertained and inspired by the poetry of James Weldon Johnson and Langston Hughes and, during the 1970s, through public lectures by Arna Bontemps, John Hope Franklin, Imamu Amiri Baraka (LeRoi Jones), and Dick Gregory.

Eventually I began writing about African Americans. My first publications about Blacks appeared in the general studies and biographical chapters of *American Library History: A Comprehensive Guide to the Literature* (1989), which I co-edited with Donald G. Davis, Jr. Later I wrote an essay on the Tuskegee University sociologist, Monroe Nathan Work.[7]

The highly satisfying opportunity to collaborate with Jessie Smith came in the academic year 1993-94 when I chaired the American Library Association's (ALA) Library History Round Table and planned the program session and research forum that we sponsored as part of the ALA summer conference in 1994. Thirty years after the Mississippi Freedom Summer seemed an excellent moment to recall the contributions of Civil Rights workers to literacy and libraries and the historical development of African-American librarianship. We set the theme for the Program Session as "Libraries, Books, and Civil Rights"; the Research Forum topic was "Black Librarianship in America."

Smith's participation ensured the success of these programs. Having her as a speaker helped us to draw well attended, racially integrated sessions. She presented a paper based on her book, *Notable Black American Women* (1992), and she recruited Casper Leroy Jordan as a moderator. Papers from the summer conference formed the core of the essays collected for *Untold Stories: Civil Rights, Libraries, and Black Librarianship* and published by the University of Illinois Graduate School of Library and Information Science in 1998. This collection features the autobiographical account of Edward G. Holley, coincidentally a member of the churches of Christ, on his experiences with racial integration of faculty and staff at the University of Houston. Subsequently, I contributed to some of Smith's reference works, including *Notable Black American Women Book II* (1996), *Notable Black American Men* (1998), and *Handbook of African American Business* (forthcoming). My debt to Jessie Smith is immeasurable, for she cultivated thoroughly my reading interests and intellectual and spiritual growth in a way that brought to substantial harvest seeds that had long been planted in the soil of my mind and desire.

[6] Louis T. Harlan, *Booker T. Washington: The Making of a Black Leader, 1856-1901* (New York: Oxford, 1972) and *Booker T. Washington: The Wizard of Tuskegee, 1901-1915* (New York: Oxford, 1983); and David Levering Lewis, *W.E.B. Du Bois: Biography of a Race, 1868-1919* (New York: Henry Holt, 1993) and *W.E.B. Du Bois: The Fight for Equality and the American Century, 1919-1963* (New York: Henry Holt, 2000).

[7] "'You Can't Argue with Facts': Monroe Nathan Work as Information Officer, Editor, and Bibliographer," *Libraries & Culture* 26 (1991): 151-68; reprinted in *Reading & Libraries*, D. G. Davis, Jr., ed. (Austin: University of Texas, Graduate School of Library and Information Science, 1991): 151-68.

Those first, few lectures in the summer of 1971 wrought something in me more powerful and abiding than either she or I could have thought possible at the time.

Evelyn Curry

In 1977, I entered the doctoral program in Library and Information Science at the University of Illinois. The University then, as now, boasted the third-largest academic library in the United States (and the largest in a public university). The Library School, the second in the nation to offer doctoral work, traces its origins to 1893, and remains unique as having the most comprehensive publishing program of any school of librarianship. The faculty brought to the classroom a fine mixture of scholarly depth, international experience, and practical wisdom. The doctoral curriculum, freshly redesigned for the fall term of 1977, focused on research in the context of seminars intended for mutual support and critique.

Six of us began the program at this point: a school librarian from Montana, technical service specialists from Brazil and Iran, and three (including Evelyn Curry and me) who had worked in academic libraries in the Midwest. Like most doctoral students, we needed a few weeks to conclude that we could work at this level and then learn how to encourage and support each other through the process. Many doctoral programs pursue a Darwinian approach, one that emphasizes survival of the intellectually fit individual while undervaluing teamwork and mutual support. The professional culture of librarianship is more mutually supportive than most, and Illinois seemed well attuned to ways that doctoral students can help each other. When the doctoral committee interviewed me, for example, I was able to meet three students—all working on dissertations—who offered great, informative insight. Like me, Evelyn benefited from this supportive environment long before mentoring emerged as an important value in higher education.

Evelyn had grown up in Marshall, Texas, in a large, loving family. She was the sibling who had launched the farthest geographically in establishing a career. Having completed a B.A. at Prairie View A & M, a school known for high-quality programs in the helping professions such as Teaching, and in technical fields such as Engineering, she had earned her M.A. at the University of Wisconsin. Evelyn then served as reference librarian at the University of Northern Iowa before entering the Illinois doctoral program. After graduate school, she taught briefly at the University of Oklahoma and then moved to Texas Women's University where she is teaching at the time of this writing. Over the years, she focused her research and teaching on information retrieval, technical services, and international and multicultural librarianship. She has a strong affinity for Africa, having held Fulbright lectureships in Kenya and Zimbabwe.

While graduate students together, we sometimes lunched, talking over professors and courses *ad infinitum* and also, eventually, other topics. We discovered mutual interests in music and literature and, finally, in our Christian faith. We learned—through prayer and persistence and seeking sound advice—the challenges that must be met to complete a Ph.D. and feel good about the process. Our personal contact over the intervening years has, alas, been slight due to diverging career paths. Still, when I would fly to Abilene, Evelyn and I would get together for brief visits during stopovers in the Dallas-Fort Worth Airport.

One way that Evelyn shows her love for others is to remember birthdays. By the end of October, I have come to expect having in hand my card from Evelyn reminding me that I am a year older. One year she sent a book, an early edition of Henry T. Blackaby's *Experiencing God*. Initially, I did not give this book the attention it deserved; several years later, I bought a subsequent edition and worked through it. The lessons it teaches require close attention to study and prayer, but they became sources of strength and guidance. Evelyn was prescient in understanding what I needed spiritually.

After Barbara and I moved to Abilene so that I could work at Abilene Christian University, I was able to bring Evelyn to the University in 2004 as part of a team of scholars in Library and Information Science to assist our library faculty with research projects. Her enthusiasm and experience enriched her interactions with several participants. She was a blessing to us all through her expression of deep joy in following our Lord, and living a life of love, trust, and responsibility.

Emily R. Mobley

I met Emily Mobley in 1986, when she came to Purdue University as Associate Director of the University Libraries, where I was then Senior Reference Librarian in the Humanities, Social Science & Education Library. She arrived with excellent credentials, having earned an A.M. in Education and an A.M. in Library Science from the University of Michigan. She was also "ABD" from Michigan, having been awarded a CIC (Committee on Institutional Cooperation) Doctoral Fellowship. She had served in the library system at Wayne State University and as library director at General Motors Engineering & Management Institute. Active professionally, she wrote a book on special libraries and served as president of the Special Libraries Association. She had also served in consulting capacities to the Library of Michigan, the Library of Congress, and the Smithsonian Institution.

Emily Mobley is "life writ large." She is large in personality, intellect, political skill, and physique. Few seem more at ease when it comes to "working a room" at a cocktail party. In smaller groups, she does not merely enter a room; she takes it over. She had been with us about three years when our director died of cancer. As chair of the Libraries Faculty Affairs Committee, I joined a small entourage that met with the University administration to recommend Emily as interim director. Those were tense times for us, and they gave Emily the opportunity to display both confidence and sensitivity. Later that year, Emily was appointed Purdue's first Dean of Libraries, a position she held for the next fifteen years. In 1997, she was named the Esther Ellis Norton Distinguished Professor of Library Science.

Emily is a skilled administrator. She has taken the Purdue Libraries far beyond a traditional, decentralized outlook and structure. She launched a strategic planning process that gave the library much clearer direction and that pioneered strategic planning at Purdue. She thus modeled for all of us how to establish priorities in order to address our most critical needs. She earned high marks from administrators and faculty for careful stewardship of library resources and effective communication about services and collections. She attracted new support for computers, technological infrastructure, online databases, and remodeling projects. She established the Digital Learning Collaboratory, a unique library-computing center partnership to assist faculty and students in preparing course-related assignments. By any measure, she placed the Library solidly on the University's agenda in fresh and visible ways.

Library faculty who had served at other universities or who had been at Purdue long enough to compare her with previous administrators routinely recognized the uniqueness and power of her contributions. She appointed the Libraries' first development officer, planning librarian, and training coordinator, and she restructured the Library to expand both middle management and cross-functional input. She raised enough money to ensure that library staff would be paid at the same level as other university staff.

She also had her detractors. Some complained that she did not speak when she passed us in the hall (she would have had to know all 225 library employees). After public discussions, people would sometimes express anger or dismay. After one meeting, a Library faculty member asked if we were going to withdraw our status as a U.S. Government Publications Depository (a designation that had been awarded by U.S. Congressional action in 1907). After another meeting, someone complained that Emily did not support information literacy. Consternation and gossip were not uncommon, but their cause was virtually always a reaction to Emily's attempts to stimulate more innovative and flexible approaches, to help us think through difficult problems, and to become more capable for challenges that lay ahead.

Emily is a natural teacher and mentor. When I was appointed Humanities, Social Science & Education Librarian, I knew I could count on her for sound advice about the large issues. Her mentoring abilities had been finely honed as a career counselor for the Special Libraries Association. She was a master at résumé evaluation and sound career advice.

Like others, I was sometimes frustrated and perplexed, but I felt that my relationship with Emily was rooted in deep mutual respect. Even though she grew up in Detroit, she had been born to Southerners in Valdosta, Georgia, and her speech patterns and word choice—laced with regional color and hyperbole—made sense to this Southerner. Early in our relationship she "came out" to me as a member of the churches of Christ, but she had chosen not to participate in church life since she regarded negatively her early church experience. Although we devoted little time to non-professional topics, our common cultural and theological heritage laid the cornerstone for a fruitful relationship. Now, in semi-retirement, Emily Mobley has taken on a new role as Mrs. Bill Royston.

Emily acknowledged and honored my personal interests and spiritual values in three particularly memorable ways. At a gathering of library faculty and donors, she asked me to lead the invocation. I found myself praying for Purdue University in a way that I had not previously, an important lesson that prompted me to fresh perspectives. On another occasion, she brought the Nobel Prize-winning author, Toni Morrison, to Purdue for a lecture, and in conjunction with this event, Emily and I designed a brochure featuring my brief history of the Purdue Libraries. She also asked me to chair the search committee when Purdue's Black Cultural Center appointed a new librarian. New challenges sometimes unearth hidden talents.

Six Magnificent Women

Jessie Smith, Evelyn Curry, and Emily Mobley are three vital forces whose faith and works shall remain to influence those who come after them. Smith and Mobley, nearing retirement age, continue to serve the institutions with which they have been most closely connected, Fisk and Purdue, respectively. Their achievements are lasting; their work as mentors and scholars continues to encourage and inspire younger generations. Curry's cross-cultural contributions and her international influence reach far beyond her small-town Texas origins and her current teaching position.

Annie May Tyson, Dorothy Way, and Deeandrew Bell are among those who "died in faith, without having received the promises, but from a distance they saw and greeted them.... God has prepared a city for them." (Hb 11:13, 16b NRSV) Their part in my education and my maturing race consciousness is a gift from God that I gratefully acknowledge. The Maker has created a richly diverse world, and I am blessed to have been lovingly and thoughtfully nourished by the best that our world has to offer.[8]

---

[8] I gratefully acknowledge the wise, incisive counsel of Carisse M. Berryhill, Special Services Librarian, Abilene Christian University, and teacher and writer, who read and edited this essay. Her encouraging words and evaluative observations have vastly improved the writing. [Berryhill is the author of "From Dreaded Guest to Welcoming Host: Hospitality and Paul in *Acts*," in this volume.]

MIDDLE GROUND?
ALEXANDER CAMPBELL ON SLAVERY
AND CARROLL OSBURN ON GENDER

CHRISTOPHER R. HUTSON[1]

"I have two daughters," he said. He was a leader in a congregation in Tennessee where I conducted a workshop on women's roles in the church in 1995. Afterward, he thanked me because the topic mattered to him. "My daughters are both strong in their faith, and I'm so proud of them. Both are married to good men who love them and go to church with them. But neither of their husbands has the strong faith that my daughters have. As a father, it hurts me to see my daughters stunting their own spiritual growth waiting for their husbands to be the spiritual leaders of their families." He had an earnest commitment to the Bible. He grew up in a church that taught women to submit to men at home and in church, and it had always seemed right and biblical to him. After all, everyone he cared about said the same, but his experience as a father was raising new questions. He wanted to look again at the scriptures to see whether he had missed something all those years, something important to his daughters' spiritual development.

The question for this man was not whether to follow the Bible, but how. The experiences of his life had always confirmed his reading, but now they caused him to question whether he had read clearly. Sensitivity to his daughters caused him to look through their eyes, and he began to see things in scripture he had never seen through his own eyes.

This essay is an exercise in looking through other eyes. I believe it makes a difference whether you look at the Bible through the eyes of the dominant group or those of the dominated. I wish to test some current arguments about women in the church by lining them up against arguments on slavery in the nineteenth century.[2] As test cases, I take

[1] I dedicate this essay to Don Haymes with whom I have shared fruitful conversations on race and gender, and who showed me that how one lives is the most forceful argument. I received comments on earlier drafts from students in my "Women in the New Testament" course, and from Thomas H. Olbricht. I thank the editors of this volume and my colleagues in the faculty colloquy at Hood Theological Seminary who helped sharpen my argument. Where these failed to persuade me, I must take responsibility for any weaknesses that remain.
[2] Many have noticed similarities between current arguments about gender and antebellum arguments about slavery. Willard M. Swartley, *Slavery, Sabbath, War, and Women: Case Issues in Biblical Interpretation* (Scottdale, Pennsylvania: Herald Press, 1983), presented classic interpretations on each side of these debates, along with helpful comments on interpretive methods. See also Philip S. Foner, ed., *Frederick Douglass on Women's Rights* (Westport: Greenwood, 1976; repr., New York: DeCapo, 1992); Floyd E. Rose, *An Idea Whose Time Has Come* (Columbus, Georgia: Brentwood Christian Press, 2002).

Alexander Campbell on slavery and Carroll Osburn on women. Each of these positions himself on the moderate left side of the debate. Both argue for an end to oppression, and both are deeply committed to the Bible as a guide. I wish to address those who are similarly positioned, who see a need for change but who fear a slide into secularism. Like Campbell and Osburn, I am committed to the Bible as foundational for Christian faith and practice. But I believe that a clearer reading of the Bible pushes us to the left on these questions, that what holds us back is not our faithfulness to Jesus but adherence to our own cultural values which have skewed the ways we read the Bible.

In the 1845 *Millennial Harbinger*, Alexander Campbell tried to expound a moderate position on slavery that would be acceptable to both Northern and Southern Christians.[3] These articles constituted neither his first nor his last statement on slavery, but they did amount to what Garrison called his "magnum opus on the subject."[4] Over the years, Campbell seemed to offer comfort sometimes to opponents of slavery and other times to its defenders, but always he aimed for a middle position.[5]

More recently, ACU Press has issued a revised edition of Carroll Osburn's *Women in the Church*.[6] In many ways, Osburn is to the current debate over gender what Campbell was to the antebellum debate over slavery, and it is striking to observe similarities in the ways they approached their respective tasks. Time and distance allow us to view Campbell with some objectivity, and perhaps the comparison will suggest insights that

---

[3] Campbell's views are found in the following places in the *Millennial Harbinger* (hereafter, *MH*) for 1845: "Preface": 1-3; "Elder Thomas Campbell's Views of Slavery" [by Thomas Campbell, with additional comments from Alexander Campbell]: 3-8; "Our Position to American Slavery," 48-53; "Our Position to American Slavery—No. II": 67-71; "Our Position to American Slavery—No. III": 108-112; "Free Masonry, Odd Fellowship, Abolitionism, &c., &c.—No. I": 134-135; "Associations, Communities, Phalanxes": 135-136; "Our Position to American Slavery—No. IV": 145-149; "Our Position to American Slavery—No. V": 193-196; "Reply to 'A Disciple' on the Subject of Slavery" [by Thomas Campbell]: 196-200; "Our Position to American Slavery—No. V [sic]," 232-236; "Our Position to American Slavery—No. VI [sic]": 236-240; "Our Position to American Slavery—No. VIII": 257-264; "Weekly Herald and Philanthropist": 266-271; "The Question Settled": 271-272; "American Slavery": 306-398; "Abolition, Masonic, and Odd Fellow Intolerance": 313-318; "American Slavery": 355-358; "American Slavery": 418-419; "Abolitionism": 505-507.

[4] Winfred E. Garrison, *Religion Follows the Frontier: A History of the Disciples of Christ* (New York: Harper & Bros., 1931): 179. Campbell would have agreed with Garrison's assessment. He read from *MH* (1845) when he lectured on slavery in Scotland in 1847, since he did not think he could state his views any more clearly. In 1849, he declined to reiterate his arguments, saying, "I have fully and at all hazards expressed my views" (reply to "Letter from Brother Smith," *MH* [1849]: 414).

[5] On Campbell's views on slavery over the years, see Harold L. Lunger, *The Political Ethics of Alexander Campbell* (St. Louis: Bethany Press, 1954): 193-232; David Edwin Harrell, Jr., *Quest for a Christian America: The Disciples of Christ and American Society to 1866* (Nashville: Disciples of Christ Historical Society, 1966): 91-138: Jess O. Hale, Jr., "Ecclesiastical Politics on a Moral Powder Keg: Alexander Campbell and Slavery in the *Millennial Harbinger*, 1830-1860," *Restoration Quarterly* 39/2 (1997): 65-81. On slavery in the broader Restoration movement, see Robert O. Fife, *Teeth on Edge* (Grand Rapids: Baker, 1971); Paul M. Blowers and Robert O. Fife, "Slavery, The Movement and," *Encyclopedia of the Stone-Campbell Movement* (Grand Rapids: Eerdmans, 2004): 685-688, and related articles.

[6] Carroll Osburn, *Women in the Church: Reclaiming the Ideal* (Abilene, Texas: Abilene Christian University Press, 2001); originally published in 1994 with the subtitle *Refocusing the Discussion*.

twenty-first-century Christians might draw from the nineteenth-century debates so that by God's grace we may learn from our forebears and avoid their pitfalls.

Response to Threat of Division

Campbell's 1845 essays were a response to the crisis threatening American Christianity in the 1830s and 1840s, as fissures appeared in various denominations.[7] The Presbyterians split along theological lines in 1837 with slavery as a background issue. Slavery was the central issue when the Methodist Episcopal Church split dramatically in 1844. In theory, their episcopal polity and connectionalism should have held them together, but after years of controversy, the slavery issue put asunder what God had joined. By 1845, the controversy was coming to a head among Baptists, and Campbell was following the debate closely.[8] In response to these schisms, he took up his pen, determined to hold the "Christian movement" together:

> The necessity of a timous [*sic*] consideration of our position and of our duties and obligations in relation to a crisis rapidly approaching in this controversy on this subject, may be argued, were it at all questionable, from recent developments in other religious associations.— The Methodists, Baptists, and some other denominations are threatened with new schisms and new centres of association on this ill-fated institution. Mason's and Dixon's political metes and boundaries, the established bourne of the Slave States and the Free, are about to be the extreme latitude of Methodistic charities between Northern and Southern professors. One denomination of Presbyterians has already declared non-fellowship with any and every master of a slave in the whole nation. The Baptist Board, regulating missions, has recently passed resolutions on this subject indicative of schism; and unless retracted, or nullified by other measures, must eventuate in the disruption of the denomination.

> Apprehending that we are all men of like passions, and that in our communities there are persons of different opinions and theories on this subject, it becomes us to recur to first and fundamental principles, to anticipate any unfavorable issue of views and feelings, and to fix our minds upon the profession of allegiance to the Lord, and the ground of union, communion, and co-operation which we have assumed before the universe in our ecclesiastical relations and duties.[9]

The threat to the movement was real, as congregations were concentrated in Border States, where opinion was most divided. Even though Campbell's moderation prevailed

---

[7] On the battle over slavery in American Christianity, see Martin E. Marty, *Pilgrims in Their Own Land: 500 Years of Religion in America* (Boston: Little, Brown & Co., 1984): 227-246; Mark A. Noll, *A History of Christianity in the United States and Canada* (Grand Rapids: Eerdmans, 1992): 314-317.
[8] *MH* (1845): 52, 67-71, 109-112, 146-149, 194, 233, 271-272, 306-308.
[9] *MH* (1845): 233-234. Cf. similar sentiments at 51, 194-196, 262-263, 271-272, 313, and 357.

on the surface, and the movement did not formally split over slavery,[10] individuals held strong convictions and later bore arms on both sides.[11]

So also now, debates about biblical perspectives on gender have proven highly divisive in many denominations. For example, the much ballyhooed revision of the "Baptist Faith and Message" in 2000 restricting the office of pastor to men,[12] was symptomatic of a deep rift between moderate and ultra-conservative wings of the Southern Baptist Convention. That rift now appears irreparable. Similarly, the synod of the Christian Reformed Church in North America adopted diametrically opposed statements on the ordination of women in two consecutive years, 1994 and 1995. According to Belleville, the impact on that denomination has been devastating.[13] In 2004, the Vatican issued its "Letter to the Bishops of the Catholic Church on the Collaboration of Men and Women in the Church and in the World," which garnered much reaction in major news outlets.[14]

In this climate, Osburn's concern is the potential for controversy over women's roles to tear apart the Churches of Christ:

> I fear that the way we are now addressing the matter can only lead to extremism, chaos, and hardening of attitudes. If we are to investigate the matter afresh, we must find a more productive approach....What is greatly needed is clear understanding of each view, biblically and culturally, and a keen awareness of the influences at work in each view.[15]

Osburn models respect for opponents while debating an important topic of religion. Honest debaters must consider the weaknesses of their own positions, and Osburn wants to help both sides see where their arguments need work.[16] He seeks common ground and

---

[10] On the debate within the American Christian Missionary Society, which did not force the issue, see W.E. Garrison and A. T. DeGroot, *The Disciples of Christ: A History* (St. Louis: Christian Board of Education, 1948): 332, 335-336.

[11] Garrison & DeGroot, *Disciples* (1948): 332-335. John H. Hull, "Underground Railroad Activity among Western Pennsylvania Disciples," *Discipliana* 57/1 (1997): 4-12, includes Campbell's own sisters among the staunchest anti-slavery activists. On the pro-slavery extreme, see Barry C. Poyner, *Bound to Slavery: James Shannon and the Restoration Movement* (Fort Worth: Star Bible Publications, 1999).

[12] See the "Baptist Faith and Message," revised, 2000, available on the official website of the Southern Baptist Convention: http://www.sbc.net/bfm/default.asp/. The controversial text is in Article VI.

[13] Linda L. Belleville, *Women Leaders and the Church: Three Crucial Questions* (Grand Rapids: Baker, 2000): 19-20.

[14] Online at: http://www.vis.pcn.net/doc/040731x_en.htm. For a reading of the document as mediating between extremes, see M. Cathleen Kaveny, "What is the Vatican Saying about Women? Conservative Catholics Might Be Surprised," *Washington Post* (August 5, 2004): B03. For a critique of it as still failing to grasp women's perspectives, see Sidney Callahan, "Ratzinger, Feminist? Not Quite," *Commonweal* 131/15 (September 10, 2004): 9-10.

[15] Osburn, *Women* (2001): 2, 85.

[16] Unfortunately, Osburn concentrated so much on the strengths and weaknesses of others' positions that he sometimes failed to make clear his own reading of key passages. He is clearest on 1 Cor 14:34-35, but he never quite ties all the pieces together on 1 Cor 11:2-16 or 1 Tm 2:8-15.

helps both sides hear one another. But I wish to ask whether Osburn's or Campbell's way of framing the debate truly bears witness to the cross of Christ.

Four-fold Schema

A rhetorical commonplace defines positions to one's left and right as "extreme," and argues that one's own position is "moderate." But for those interested in maintaining dialogue, a four-part schema allows for a broad middle ground where moderates on both sides of a question can come together. This is the rhetorical strategy adopted by both Campbell and Osburn.

Osburn defines four positions on the roles of women. From left to right, these are: Radical Feminism, Evangelical Feminism, Hierarchal Complementarianism, and Patriarchalism. Campbell was less explicit in naming his categories, but four positions emerge in his arguments as well. Ranging from left to right, I call these Abolitionism, Anti-slavery, Benevolent Slavery, and Abusive/Exploitative Slavery.[17] Both Osburn and Campbell eschew extremes. Both adopt positions on the moderate left and seek dialogue with the moderate right.[18]

The Extreme Left

On the extreme left, Campbell decried Abolitionists, by whom he meant those who took an absolute position that slavery is immoral and aimed to end it immediately. First, Campbell argued that the Abolitionists were moving too fast. By forcing the issue, they were provoking a pro-slavery backlash and, ironically, delaying the demise of slavery in America. "Action at the North produces reaction at the South, and these are always equal to each other. Is there any instance on record in proof that slavery has fallen by foreign interference!"[19] Campbell disapproved of Northerners who meddled in affairs they didn't understand.[20]

Moderates in the gender debates often resist "moving too fast," but it is a weak argument, and in hindsight Campbell must be criticized. If we wait for people to come around on the basis of reason alone, they never will. We must actively create conditions and opportunities for people to experience the unfamiliar thing and get over their fears

---

[17] Harrell (1996): 137, identifies four positions as operative among Disciples of the period: abolitionists, antislavery moderates, proslavery moderates, and proslavery radicals.

[18] By contrast, Wayne Grudem, *Why Human Sexuality is at the Center of Many Current Controversies* (Libertyville, Illinois: CBMW, 2000), offered five positions on women, placing his own complementarian position predictably in the center, but he drew only laughable caricatures of even the moderate positions on either side of his own.

[19] *MH* (1845): 195.

[20] In "Tracts for the People–No. XXXIII: A Tract for the People of Kentucky," *MH* (1849): 242-243, Campbell wrote that he first publicly asserted this position in a debate with some Quaker Abolitionists in Philadelphia in 1831. However, the idea appeared already in a letter from "T." of Essex, Virginia, in *MH* (1830): 188-190, and Campbell reiterated it in his "Response to 'T.,'" *MH* (1830): 191. "T." may have been Thomas M. Henley, *MH* (1833): 565; (1841): 334. Campbell's "Tract for the People of Kentucky" was itself criticized by one Kentuckian as the unwanted meddling of a Virginia outsider, "Letter from Brother Smith," *MH* (1849): 413. On reaction to Campbell's "Tract," see Lunger, *Political Ethics*: 218-219.

of it. If gender justice is biblical, there should be no question of delaying action but only of pastoral sensitivity in helping weak sisters and brothers embrace the insight.[21]

Second, Campbell viewed abolitionism as an extra-ecclesiastical phenomenon. Frequently invoking 1 Cor 5:12 against "judging outsiders," he preferred to debate slavery within the church.[22] In his view, reform would come not by political activism but by converting individuals to Christianity, thereby making them subject to the Bible.

> The Church cannot constitutionally undertake to reform the State. It may seek to convert the citizens; but can never assume, by any political expedients, to reform the State. As American citizens, we may be Free Masons, Odd Fellows, Pro-Slavery men, or Abolitionists; but as Christians, we cannot be any one of these.[23]

In a similar vein, Campbell objected that Abolitionists were willing to subordinate the Bible to human reason and experience, disregarding Bible statements that ran contradictory to their philosophical presuppositions.

> Our premises are not the Declaration of American Independence, the bills of political rights or wrongs, natural religion, natural conscience, natural liberty; but the Christian Oracles. I launch my feeble bark upon no such shoreless ocean, I steer by no such misty metaphysics, I have no such sandy anchorage in my horizon....I am no believer in the infallibility of the dictates of natural religion, natural reason, natural conscience, natural liberty, natural law. I stand or fall by supernatural religion or revelation.[24]

Campbell suffered under no illusions that the American political system was founded on Christian principles. But he presented a useful distinction that Osburn does not make. If we ask what is truly "radical" about Osburn's Radical Feminism, it is neither the feminists' absolute position against oppression nor their impatience, but that some of them reject the Bible and rely on a secular ideology.[25] I return to this, below, but for now suffice it to say that when Osburn lumps together secular and Christian feminists in his Radical Feminists, he confuses things. If the topic is "Women in the Church," it would be better to follow Campbell's lead, allowing secular theorists to go their own way and engaging those who speak in a Christian context.

The Extreme Right

On the extreme right, Campbell disapproved of abuse,[26] though he showed no real awareness of the conditions that slaves endured. The one specific abuse mentioned most frequently was disruption of marriages, but even that was raised more by his

---

[21] Christopher R. Hutson, "Martha's Choice: A Pastorally Sensitive Reading of Lk 10:38-42," *Restoration Quarterly* 45/3 (2003): 139-150. For a scathing attack on "gradualism" in relieving oppression, see Martin Luther King, Jr., *Why We Can't Wait* (New York : Harper & Row, 1963): 137-141.

[22] *MH* (1845): 108, 145, 193, 237, 238.

[23] *MH* (1845): 108. Campbell equivocated in likening the amorphous Abolitionist movement to a fraternity (cf. *MH* [1845]: 108, 134-136, 313-318) or political party (*MH* [1845]: 195, 234, 356, 505).

[24] *MH* (1845): 236; cf. 53, 194, 271.

[25] Osburn (2001): 24-41.

[26] *MH* (1845): 260, 261, 262, 356.

correspondents than by himself.[27] Campbell rejected man-stealing, although he viewed it as a moot question, since the African slave trade had been discontinued by 1845, and he took the position that all born in slavery were legitimate slaves regardless of how their parents or grandparents became slaves.[28]

Campbell was tone deaf to arguments against slavery as inherently exploitative. His portrayal of slavery seems to have been derived from a limited experience of the smiling faces of house slaves among his prosperous friends. He seems oblivious to the deplorable conditions of the majority of slaves in the South. He assumed that "cruel masters are few compared with the humane."[29] And when he spoke against slavery, it was only in vague and general terms, as when he replied to Abraham Smith's complaint about his meddling in the affairs of Kentucky: "[S]lavery, as now legalized and generally carried out, is not in harmony with what the Lawgiver, and Judge, and Rewarder of all men, has expressed by his Apostles and Prophets to the church and to the world."[30] Here he seems to acknowledge the cruelties, and yet the wording is not specific. Campbell opposed slavery more on economic than humanitarian grounds.

If Campbell was not completely callous to the suffering of American slaves, he certainly failed to emphasize it, which points up his concern not to alienate moderates on the right. His rhetoric was consistent with what Peter Kolchin describes as "one end of a pro-slavery spectrum" in antebellum political rhetoric.[31] He appealed to "the slave owner's self-image as a loving, paternalistic master who provided for his people."[32]

Campbell's failure to acknowledge the human suffering exacerbated by slavery antagonized Abolitionists, as was apparent when they hounded him through Scotland in 1847.[33] Responding to pressure, he delivered a public lecture on slavery in Edinburgh on August 13, 1847, which was printed in the Edinburgh *Journal* and reprinted as a tract. Here is an excerpt:

> For myself, I greatly prefer the condition and the prospects of the free to the slave States, especially as respects the white portion of the population. Much as I

---

[27] *MH* (1837): 272; *MH* (1845): 270; cf. 267 (quotation of Dr. Bailey), 507 (letter from M. Winans).

[28] *MH* (1845): 419. For Campbell's disapproval of man-stealing, see also "To Mr. William Jones, of London: Letter II," *MH* (1835): 17 (cf. Thomas Campbell, *MH* [1845]: 6). Campbell and the Abolitionists talked past one another on this point. He used "man-stealing" to refer only to the capture and sale of free persons into slavery, whereas Abolitionists used it as a broad pejorative for the whole system of slavery.

[29] *MH* (1849): 251.

[30] *MH* (1849): 414.

[31] Peter Kolchin, *American Slavery, 1619-1877* (New York: Hill & Wang, 1993): 196. Cf. below, n. 43.

[32] *Idem*: 194.

[33] Campbell's version of events is recorded in "Letters from Europe—XIV" [from Glasgow Prison, September 10]; *MH* (1847): 625-632; "Letters from Europe—XV" [from Belfast, September 17]; *MH* (1847): 633-641; "Letters from Europe—XVI" [Glasgow Prison, September 11]; *MH* (1847): 641-648; "Letters from Europe—XVII" [n.d.]; *MH* (1847): 683-685; "Letters from Europe—XVIII [n.d.]; *MH* (1847): 686-695; "My Imprisonment in Glasgow," *MH* (1848): 45-53. Accounts of the events sympathetic to Campbell are in W. Faulds, "Letter to the Editor," *Renfrewshire Reformer* (September 18, 1847); Robert Richardson, *Memoirs of Alexander Campbell* (1897; reprint, Indianapolis: Religious Book Service, n.d.): 2: 551-566; Thomas Chalmers, *Alexander Campbell's Tour of Scotland* (Louisville: Guide Printing, 1892; reprint, Nashville: Gospel Advocate, n.d.).

may sympathise with a black man, I love the white man more. As a political economist, and as a philanthropist, I have many reasons for preferring the prospects and condition of the free to the slave States; but especially as a Christian, I sympathise more with the owners of slaves, their heirs, and successors, than with the slaves which they possess and bequeath.[34]

Especially as a Christian? The editor of the Glasgow *Christian News* responded, "What are we to think of such Christianity as this?"[35] And the editor of the *Renfrewshire Advertiser* retorted, "This appears to us a very remarkable method of proving himself the friend of the slave.... Out upon the religion which could tolerate such 'sympathies'."[36] Anti-slavery newspapers in Scotland had a field day at Campbell's expense.[37]

Here is a significant distinction between Campbell and Osburn. Osburn shows more concern for the oppression of women than did Campbell for the plight of slaves. In fact, it is precisely this concern, says Osburn, that prompted him to study the question in the first place.[38] He listens patiently even to the strident "Bitch Manifesto," because, "I am convinced that the hurt, frustration, and anger lying behind such an acrimonious plea are not imagined, but very real."[39] Patriarchalist Christians must be challenged for insensitivity to the liberating voices in scripture and to the plight of women who suffer under religiously legitimated oppression.

So much for the extreme right and extreme left. Campbell, like Osburn, attended mainly to negotiating understanding between the moderate left and the moderate right. He assumed Christians could find common ground by taking the Bible alone as their guide, so he staked out a position based on careful reading of what the Bible says and does not say about slavery. Biblical teaching, he argued, should be the sole basis for

---

[34] "Lecture on Slavery Delivered by Alexander Campbell, President of Bethany College, Virginia, U.S., within the Waterloo Room, Edinburgh, on Friday, August 13, 1847" (Edinburgh: R.M. Walker, 1847): 12; which drew from *MH* (1845): 234.

[35] Editorial, "Mr. Alexander Campbell's Pro-Slavery Principles Reviewed," *Christian News* No. 57 (Thursday, Sept. 2, 1847): 2, cols. 2-3.

[36] "Manstealing in America, and the Rev. Alexander Campbell," *Renfrewshire Advertiser* 1195 (Saturday, September 4, 1847): 2, col. 4.

[37] In addition to those cited in the two previous notes, lively accounts critical of Campbell appeared in the newspapers of Scotland, including, "American Slavery Defended," item from Edinburgh *Weekly Express*, in Glasgow *Christian News* 55 (Thursday, Aug. 19, 1847): 1, col. 6; "Alexander Campbell and American Slavery," *Christian News* 55 (August 19, 1847): 1, col. 6; "Alexander Campbell and American Slavery," *Christian News* 55 (August 19, 1847): 4, col. 1; "Mr. Alexander Campbell & Slavery," [letter to the editor, signed, "A Wellwisher to Humanity"], *Christian News* 56 (August 26, 1847): 4, col. 2; "Beware of the Manstealer," *Renfrewshire Advertiser* 1194 (Saturday, August 28, 1847): 2, cols. 1-2; "Mr. Campbell's Attack on the Emancipation Society," *Christian News* 57 (September 2, 1847): 3, col. 1; "Advocacy of Slavery," item from the *Ayr Advertiser*, in *Renfrewshire Advertiser* 1195 (Saturday, September 4, 1847): 1, col. 3; item under "Local Intelligence," *Renfrewshire Advertiser* 1196 (Saturday, September 11, 1847): 2, col. 4; item from the Edinburgh *Evening Post*, under "Scotland," *Renfrewshire Advertiser* 1197 (September 18, 1847): 4, col. 4.

[38] See "Preface to the First Edition," in Osburn (2001): vii-x.

[39] Osburn (2001): 21. Osburn summarized feminist perspectives on societal oppression of women (21-23) and acknowledges the abusive tendencies of patriarchalism (47-48).

Christian fellowship. So also, the burden of Osburn's book is a painstaking review of the exegetical strengths and weaknesses of scholars from the moderate right and left who purport to explain what the Bible says about gender.

The Moderate Right

On the moderate right, Campbell fellowshipped Christian masters who treated their slaves well according to biblical principles. He took pains to point out that the Bible does not condemn slavery *per se* but only abuse. He argued that faithful people of God in both Testaments were slave owners (e.g., Abraham, Philemon). He argued that the New Testament directs the behavior of masters toward slaves and slaves toward masters, and therefore a New Testament Christian could legitimately own slaves.

The idea of a truly benevolent slave owner may be an oxymoron to twenty-first century ears, but Robert Fife recounts the story of Numeris Humber, who went to the extraordinary lengths of migrating to Kansas for the purpose of freeing his slaves and purchasing land for them. But Kansas law did not permit free Negroes to own land, so Humber retained them as his property only so they could have a means of livelihood on his land.[40] Fife further documents that Stone-Campbell churches in Southern states typically received blacks—both free and slave—as members in good standing, although segregation persisted in congregational worship and polity.[41] We may consider the possibility, therefore, that at least a few benevolent slave owners actually existed, in spite of the inherent oppression of the institution. If Campbell's arguments seemed ham-handed to Abolitionists, he nevertheless made it clear that he fellowshipped benevolent Christian slave owners, even as he tried to persuade them to free their slaves.

For his part, Osburn reaches out to moderates on the right, whom he calls Hierarchal Complementarians. This position is "essentially a hierarchal reaction against evangelical feminism."[42] It is hierarchal in that it "still maintains a very strong view of male leadership and female submission."[43] It is complementarian in arguing that male and female each has a god-given role to play, and these roles are complementary. Complementarians have repudiated extreme forms of chauvinism and abuse and accepted women's leadership at the highest levels in secular affairs. They have even made room for the ministries of women in the church under a glass ceiling. But they maintain steadfastly that God has given final authority in the church and in the family to the male alone, settling with easy confidence into the traditional readings of 1 Cor 11:3; 14:34-35; 1 Tm 2:11-13; and Eph 5:21-24.

Like Campbell, Osburn maintains dialogue with the moderate right. The majority of Christians in the world still live under patriarchal structures, and progressives need to entertain the possibility that some of them do so with genuine goodwill; men not oppressing women, nor women with a sense of being oppressed. Osburn sees examples

---

[40] Fife (1971): 48.

[41] Fife (1971): 51-73. After the war, congregations became much more segregated as color prejudice came to the fore.

Osburn (2001): 67, noticed that the conversation was among evangelicals, with little or no engagement of mainstream feminist scholarship.

[43] *Loc. cit.*

of such goodwill among the Complementarians, but what he most admires about them is that they stand firmly under the authority of the Bible. As such, they are his brothers.

The Moderate Left

Campbell took his stand on the moderate left, a position he defined as anti-slavery. He opposed slavery not because it was inherently immoral or unbiblical but because he thought it was an impractical economic system.[44] While citizens should work to end slavery, such an end could come only gradually, not by extreme fiat.[45] As a biblical warrant for emancipating slaves, Campbell cited 1 Cor 7:21 (interpreting the ambiguous phrase "use it rather" as legitimating a slave's bid for freedom); Col 4:1 ("just and equal"); and the Golden Rule.[46] Campbell himself acquired two or three slaves, for whom he provided instruction in reading and religion and whom he freed as soon as they were old enough to care for themselves.[47] He did not, however, insist that all Christian slave owners follow suit, only that they treat their slaves justly.

Osburn adopts a similar stance on gender, arguing that the weight of biblical texts is on the side of egalitarianism while arguing that Evangelical Feminists and Hierarchal Complementarians should fellowship one another as Christians, all dedicated to following the Bible. He insists only that Complementarians repudiate abusive treatment of, and oppressive attitudes toward, women.

First, Osburn builds a case for female leadership. He starts in chapter 5 with Gn 1-3, arguing that the pristine ideal for men and women was equality and that male domination is a result of the Fall. Chapter 6 surveys Jesus' view of woman, emphasizing his egalitarian approach to questions on marriage and divorce and his understanding of power as service. In chapter 7, Osburn is wary of those who use Gal 3:28 as the rallying cry for women's liberation, although he thinks traditionalists are wrong to limit the text to matters of salvation. The text is important, but it is neither the starting point nor the final word on the matter. In chapter 8, Osburn discusses examples of women leaders in the early Christianity, including especially Phoebe (Rm 16:1-2), women deacons (1 Tm 3:11), and Priscilla.[48]

Next, working carefully through the battleground passages, Osburn demonstrates the weaknesses of Complementarian interpretations. In chapter 9 on Eph 5:21-24, Osburn argues that the command is for voluntary submission, not subjugation, and that the mutual submission in verse 21 entails all Christians, not only wives. Chapter 10 on 1 Cor

---

[44] *MH* (1849): 244-248; cf. the letter from "T." of Essex, Virginia in *MH* (1830): 189. On Campbell's position, see T. Brian Pendleton, "Alexander Campbell and Slavery: Gradualism and Anti-Slavery Rhetoric in the *Millennial Harbinger*," *Restoration Quarterly* 42/3 (2000): 149-154.

[45] For similar arguments by preachers of the time, see Swartley (1983): 31-37. Roland Bainton, "Alexander Campbell and the Social Order" in *The Sage of Bethany: A Sage in Broadcloth*, Perry E. Gresham, compiler (Joplin: College Press,1988): 125-127, argued that Campbell's position was consistent with that of moderate Northern theologians of the time, including "the Yale circle and such men as Nathaniel W. Taylor, Leonard Bacon, and Moses Stuart."

[46] *MH* (1849): 248.

[47] Richardson (1897): 1: 502.

[48] See Christopher R. Hutson, "Laborers in the Lord: Romans 16 and the Women in Pauline Churches," *Leaven* 4/2 (1996): 29-31, 40, online: http://gal328.org/articles/Hutson-Laborers.html

11:2-16 argues that a hierarchalist reading of verse 3 misses the point about relationships between men and women. Likewise in chapter 11, "let women be silent" (1 Cor 14:34-35) applies to a specific, local situation in Corinth and cannot be a general rule for all, since Paul allows women to pray and prophesy in the assembly in Corinth (1 Cor 11:5). Finally, in chapter 12 on 1 Tm 2:9-15, Osburn shows that the injunction, "I permit not a woman to teach or usurp authority over a man," applies to a specific, local situation in Ephesus, and should not be understood as a general rule. Further, "teach or usurp authority" is better translated, "teach in a domineering manner."[49] According to Osburn, the issus in 1 Tm and 1 Cor are much more about the *manner* in which women speak than about *whether* they ought to speak.

While I would approach some details differently and push some issues harder (the implications of Gal 3:27-28, for example), my purpose here is not to set forth all the exegetical details. For now it is enough to see that Osburn, who began as a committed hierarchalist, concluded as follows:

[T]here is no biblical mandate for hierarchalism in either the church or society. Hierarchalism is a legacy from remote antiquity, originating in the post-Fall era of Gn 3. It was not designed by God, but was the result of human frailty. Jesus did not overthrow hierarchalism, as some feminists suggest. Instead, he worked within the hierarchal society of his time. He gave women greater respect, freedom, recognition, involvement, and responsibilities. This view of Jesus continued in the earliest churches for a limited time before patristic churches reverted to the patriarchalism that has become a dominant part of our Christian heritage for centuries.[50]

Yet, in spite of these conclusions, Osburn is reluctant to turn his back on Complementarians, as long as they repudiate the abusive and domineering attitudes of the Patriarchalists. The analogy between Campbell and Osburn is instructive. We might crosscheck our arguments about gender by asking how they sound when applied to the issue of slavery. Hale sums up the situation this way:

The Disciples could make slavery a matter of opinion and divide over having an organ for worship services. One might wonder if that skillful exercise of political skills was worth it. There is an element of the tragic in this heritage—is there not?[51]

Campbell was stuck in a biblical scholasticism that gave equal weight to every text in scripture without regard to the theological center. As Christian theology, it failed utterly, and this should give pause to moderates in the gender debates. Osburn is a more sophisticated exegete than was Campbell, and yet, like Campbell, he is uncomfortable standing with progressives who, he suspects, may be influenced by ideological viewpoints from outside scripture.[52] He admires the Hierarchalists' devotion to biblical authority. In the end, he leaves Hierarchalism as a matter of opinion.

---

[49] See Christopher R. Hutson, "A Study Guide to 1 Tm 2:8-15," online: http://www.gal328.org/articles/Hutson-1Tim2Study.html.
[50] Osburn (2001): 260.
[51] Hale (1997): 81.
[52] Osburn (2001): 56.

I agree with both Campbell and Osburn that biblical exegesis is essential, but it is not sufficient. The Bible contains more than one viewpoint on slavery and on women. Biblical exegesis can expose these, but how do we choose among them? Biblical interpreters must engage in serious theological reflection in order to weigh and consider how to apply ancient biblical texts to modern questions. I would like to offer some suggestions for consideration.

Rethinking Categories: Biblical Egalitarianism

Osburn's categories become a procrustean bed, since not all interpreters fit snugly into one of his four boxes. This is especially true of those who do not fit easily into either Radical Feminist or Evangelical Feminist categories. While Osburn recognizes that "feminists are not all alike,"[53] Phyllis Trible is the only Christian feminist he notices who seeks "to maintain the relevance of the Bible."[54] But Trible is not alone, and much fruitful discussion is emerging among feminist scholars who read the text closely on its own terms and express the liberative voices in scripture.

Osburn expresses some discomfort at calling his position Evangelical Feminism, because the term feminist "carries so much baggage."[55] He is suspicious that it is tainted with secular ideology. For my part, I am less concerned about the term "feminist" than with "Evangelical," because the latter implies a commitment to biblical inerrancy. Now here is an ideology imposed upon scripture from the outside with disastrous consequences.[56] Those who suppose that every word in scripture is phrased exactly as God intended it have difficulty discounting any text, no matter what oppression it may foster. Inerrantists will always wonder anxiously whether God really meant, "Let women keep silent in the assembly." But once we admit that inerrancy is a human invention imposed upon scripture from a modernist ideology, we can let Paul be a human being who is trying to bear witness to Christ in a difficult, real world context. Paul himself can say that he has no word of the Lord on a matter and is giving his opinion (1 Cor 7:25). We need to abandon the notion of inerrancy and learn to read the biblical writers as human beings, faithful but fallible. This does not mean giving up on the Bible. It means we must work all the harder both to understand the words of those ancient witnesses and to develop a strong theological framework that can make those ancient texts live again in our time.

If the terms "Feminist" and "Evangelical" are both problematic, perhaps we should rename the category, even taking Osburn's own suggestion, and call it "Biblical Egalitarianism."[57] This would allow us to broaden the conversation beyond Evangelicals and take into account all those who find in the Bible strong voices for liberation.

---

[53] *Idem*: 23.

[54] *Idem*: 31. See also Phyllis Trible, "If the Bible's So Patriarchal, How Come I Love It?" *Bible Review* 8/5 (October 1992): 44-47, 55.

[55] Osburn (2001): 67.

[56] *Idem*: 255, quoting J. D. G. Dunn to the effect that biblical inerrancy is "exegetically improbable, hermeneutically defective, theologically dangerous, and educationally disastrous," but he himself does not commit to this view.

[57] *Idem*: 67.

Broadening the Conversation

If we include all Christian feminists in the conversation, not merely Evangelicals, we must still recognize that these display a variety of approaches to the Bible.[58] Pushing the left edge of the envelope would be those feminists who view the biblical texts as hopelessly androcentric and apply postmodern analytical methods to deconstruct the patriarchal biases of biblical writers. Foremost among these is Elisabeth Schüssler Fiorenza.[59] But this approach tends to ground theology in hypothetical reconstructions of early Christian history, which must be freed from the encrustations of androcentric biblical writers and subsequent interpreters.[60] While there is value in seeing biblical writers as human beings with culturally conditioned blind spots, such deconstructive work leaves little foundation for theological reflection. Feminist theologians must offer a constructive theology that embraces the liberating voices within scripture itself. Still, I note that Schüssler Fiorenza hears that liberating voice. Even as she rejects the Bible as theological archetype, she retains it as prototype. That is, she rejects it as a blueprint to be followed rigidly, but she embraces it as a "model for Christian life and community," as the thing that gives direction to Christian life.[61] Schüssler Fiorenza cannot be dismissed as a secularist. She approaches the issues as a Christian theologian and takes the Bible into account.

Furthermore, Christian feminists cannot be dismissed for subordinating the Bible to human reason and experience. For Schüssler Fiorenza, "a feminist critical interpretation of the Bible cannot take as its point of departure the normative authority of the biblical archetype, but must begin with women's experience in their struggle for liberation."[62] Although Campbell would have recoiled at this, Schüssler Fiorenza is merely being an honest interpreter.[63] The naïve conceit of Modernism was that interpreters could be "objective" and "neutral." In fact, human beings are always influenced by their own experiences of life to be more sensitive to some things and less to others, a point that

---

[58] *Idem*: 28-32, aware that variety exists, does not discuss the spectrum of opinion. Elisabeth Schüssler Fiorenza, *But SHE Said* (Boston: Beacon, 1992): 20-50, surveyed ten approaches to biblical authority among Christian feminists, though with some overlap; she summarized a number of strategies used by moderate and conservative feminists (144-150). See also Alice Ogden Bellis, *Helpmates, Harlots, Heroes: Women's Stories in the Hebrew Bible* (Louisville: Westminster/John Knox Press, 1994).

[59] Schüssler Fiorenza (1992): 79-101, and see Elisabeth Schüssler Fiorenza, *Bread Not Stone: The Challenge of Feminist Biblical Interpretation* (Boston: Beacon, 1984).

[60] For example, Mary Rose D'Angelo, "Women in Luke-Acts: A Redactional View," *Journal of Biblical Literature* 109/3 (1990): 441-461.

[61] Schüssler Fiorenza (1984): 14; she defined "archetype" on p. 12. Sarah Heaner Lancaster, *Women and the Authority of Scripture: A Narrative Approach* (Harrisburg, Pennsylvania: Trinity Press International, 2002): 23, illustrated the point this way: The Wright brothers' flying machine was not "an archetype to which subsequent flying machines had to correspond," but rather "a prototype that was later improved and developed in a variety of ways." This obviously flies in the face of a "patternist" hermeneutics, but it still values the Bible as impetus for Christian theology.

[62] Schüssler Fiorenza, "Bread Not Stone" (1984): 13.

[63] Daniel Patte, *The Ethics of Biblical Interpretation: A Reevaluation* (Louisville: Westminster/John Knox Press, 1995).

Osburn acknowledges.[64] The call to see biblical texts afresh through women's eyes is akin to the call of Abolitionists to see through the eyes of the slaves.

These examples illustrate that moderates have something in common with Christians on their left. One man's radical is another woman's prophet. If we can learn from the left wing, then surely we can learn also from those feminist Christians who, like Trible, place a premium on diligent reading of scripture.[65]

Asking the Right Questions

Historically, the Churches of Christ have focused on the meaning and performance of worship rituals (Lord's Supper, baptism, music) as the essential elements of first-century Christianity that needed to be restored, and they have scarcely attended to central theological or ethical dimensions of early Christianity.[66] So it is not surprising that the debate about "women's roles" in the Churches of Christ has tended to focus on which rituals women may perform in the congregational assembly. But Osburn shifts the focus significantly from ritual to ethics:

> To ask what *roles* women can have in the church and its worship is, I think, to ask the wrong question. It is true that the role of women in the church and its public worship are important topics. But... I am more concerned with widespread problems of abuse and inequity in our society and, more than I care to admit, in our churches. I am particularly bothered by any view of women that demeans, depreciates, and exploits women as merely tools for man's enjoyment and service. The question is not "What *roles* can women have in church?" but *"How shall we view women?"* [67]

This is a great improvement, and yet I would reframe the question as, "Women, what do *you* think?" because biblical ethics is relational, regarding the other person as "you." We may think of Jacob's words to Esau: "To see your face is like seeing the face of God" (Gn 33:10). If I regard a human face as reflecting the "image of God" (Gn 1:26-27),

---

[64] Osburn (2001): 102-103, 106.

[65] Space does not allow for exegetical studies of key passages here, but see the growing body of studies online at http://www.gal328.org. See also Phyllis Bird, "What Makes a Feminist Reading Feminist? A Qualified Answer," in *Escaping Eden: New Perspectives on the Bible*, H.C. Washington, S.L. Graham, & P. Thimmes, eds. (New York: New York University Press, 1999): 124-131; Turid Karlsen Seim, *The Double Message: Patterns of Gender in Luke & Acts* (Edinburgh: T&T Clark, 1994); Luise Schottroff, *Lydia's Impatient Sisters: A Feminist Social History of Early Christianity* (Louisville: Westminster/John Knox Press, 1995); Emily Cheney, *She Can Read: Feminist Reading Strategies for Biblical Narrative* (Valley Forge, Pennsylvania: Trinity Press International, 1996); Bonnie Thurston, *Women in the New Testament: Questions and Commentary* (New York: Crossroad, 1998); Amy-Jill Levine, ed., *A Feminist Companion to Paul* (Sheffield: Sheffield Academic Press and Cleveland: Pilgrim Press, 2004); *idem*, *A Feminist Companion to the Deutero-Pauline Epistles* (Sheffield: Sheffield Academic Press, and Cleveland: Pilgrim Press, 2003).

[66] For other types of restoration movements, see C. Leonard Allen & Richard T. Hughes, *Discovering Our Roots: The Ancestry of Churches of Christ* (Abilene: Abilene Christian University Press, 1988).

[67] Osburn (2001): 2 (emphasis Osburn's); cf. the preface Osburn (the first edition, 1994): vii.

then I should relate to that person as if relating to God.[68] Likewise, in Mt 25:31-46, Jesus offers a criterion for separating the sheep from the goats at the Judgment. Each individual is assessed in terms of how she/he responded to "the least of these," understood as a response to Jesus himself (Mt 25:40, 45). Taking a cue from Matthew's Jesus, we might assess each position in terms of its effects on "the least of these."[69] Taking a cue from Jacob, we should not ask *about* the least of these, but we should turn to the least of these and ask, "Does this interpretation of scripture bear witness to *you* about God?" We need to talk less *about* women and talk more *to* women who are hurting or asking questions or simply leaving.

Applying the "Least of These" Test

In case anyone doubted it, the testimonies of slaves demonstrate that slavery in the American South failed the "least of these" test.[70] Yet it would be fair to say that most owners perceived themselves as "good" masters, and we have granted that a few may indeed have been benevolent. Certainly Campbell viewed them so. Let us ask the slaves how they feel about life with a "good" master.

Tom Robinson was ten when he was sold away from his mother in North Carolina. His chief memory of her was kneeling to pray. "She'd pray that the time would come when everybody could worship the Lord under their own vine and fig tree—all of them free." In Texas, Tom's master, Dave Robinson, "treated me almost like I was one of his own children...He was good to me." After the war, Tom kept the name Robinson and named his own son Dave, reflecting fond memories of his former master. Still, nothing compared with freedom. "Was I happy? Law, Miss! You can take anything—no matter how good you treat it—it always wants to be free. You can treat it good and feed it good and give it everything it seems to want—but if you open the cage—it's happy."[71]

---

[68] I acknowledge the thinking of Tamara Cohn Eskenazi, "Introduction—Facing the Text as Other: Some Implications of Levinas's Work for Biblical Studies," in T.C. Eskenazi, G.A. Phillips, & D. Jobling, eds., *Levinas and Biblical Studies*, Semeia Studies 43 (Atlanta: SBL, 2003): 10. Eskenazi quoted Emmanuel Levinas, *Totality and Infinity* (Pittsburgh: Duqesne University Press, 1961, 1969): 215: "The Other who dominates in his transcendence is thus the stranger, the widow, and the orphan, to whom I am obliged."

[69] David Lipscomb applied Jesus' admonition about "the least of these" in a similar way when he intervened in an exchange between S. E. Harris, and E. A. Elam that appeared under the title "The Negro in the Worship," *Gospel Advocate* 49 (July 4, 1907): 424-425; (August 1, 1907): 488-489; (August 15, 1907): 521. The text, with introduction and comment by Don Haymes, appears at http://www.mun.ca/rels/restmov/texts/ race/ negro.html.

[70] Ira Berlin, Marc F., and Steven F. Miller, eds., *Remembering Slavery: African Americans Talk about Their Personal Experiences of Slavery and Emancipation* (New York: New Press, 1998); M. Shawn Copeland, "Wading through Many Sorrows," in *A Troubling in My Soul: Womanist Perspectives on Evil and Suffering,* Emilie M. Townes, ed. (New York: Orbis, 1993): 109-129.

[71] G. P. Rawick, ed., *The American Slave: A Composite Autobiography* (Westport, Connecticut: Greenwood, 1972-79), ser. 2, vol. 10 (Arkansas, part 6): 64-69, quoted in Berlin, *et al.* (1998): 275-277.

So also nineteen-year-old Frederick Douglass spoke of servitude under a "good" master. In 1835, Douglass was transferred from the brutal Mr. Covey to Mr. Freeland, "a well-bred southern gentleman."[72] Of his state of mind in 1836, Douglass wrote:

> I was not through the first month of my second year with the kind and gentlemanly Mr. Freeland before I was earnestly considering and devising plans for gaining that freedom which, when I was but a mere child, I had ascertained to be the natural and inborn right of every member of the human family. The desire for this freedom had been benumbed while I was under the brutalizing dominion of Covey, and it had been postponed and rendered inoperative by my truly pleasant Sunday-school engagements with my friends during the year at Mr. Freeland's. It had, however, never entirely subsided. I hated slavery *always*, and my desire for freedom needed only a favorable breeze to fan it to a blaze at any moment. The thought of being only a creature of the *present* and the *past* trouble me, and I longed to have a *future*—a future with hope in it.[73]

Now even if we accept the testimony of the slaves themselves that these masters were good to them, how can we look Robinson or Douglass in the face and turn away? Do slave owners pass the "least of these" test simply by being nice? Did Freeland relate to Douglass the way he would relate to Jesus?

What, then, about Campbell's moderately progressive position? Campbell took his stand on biblical precedent for slavery, while he argued for its demise. This seemed to be a sober position that was biblically defensible without fomenting chaos. And yet what was the impact of that reasoned sobriety on "the least of these"? Douglass decried the hypocrisy of Protestant Christians who exhorted every believer to "search the scriptures" but who broke up his own attempts to teach fellow slaves to read the Bible on the grounds that they might be influenced by its revolutionary ideas.[74] He understood the logic of their position, but he could not discern in it any "good news." Howard Thurman's grandmother expressed a similar view when she explained why she never read any of Paul's letters:

> During the days of slavery, the master's minister would occasionally hold services for the slaves. Old man McGhee was so mean that he would not let a Negro minister preach to his slaves. Always the white minister used as his text: 'Slaves, be obedient to them that are your master...as unto Christ.' Then he would go on to show how it was God's will that we were slaves and how, if we were good and happy slaves, God would bless us. I promised my Maker that if I ever learned to read and if freedom ever came, I would not read that part of the Bible.[75]

White preachers read the Bible to slaves, but they did not proclaim the gospel to them. Campbell failed to come to terms with the fundamental problem that he valued

---

[72] Frederick Douglass, *Life and Times of Frederick Douglass* (revised edition 1892; reprint, New York: Crowell-Collier, 1962): 149.

[73] *Idem*: 155-156.

[74] *Idem*: 152.

[75] Quoted in C. Michelle Venable-Ridley, "Paul and the African American Community," in *Embracing the Spirit: Womanist Perspectives on Hope, Salvation & Transformation*, Emilie M. Townes, ed. (Maryknoll: Orbis, 1997): 213.

Africans less than Caucasians.[76] The problem with moderation is that it merely moves the line of discrimination over a little without challenging the fundamental categories. A kinder, gentler racism is no solution to the problem of racism. We cannot simply move from slavery to Jim Crow to school segregation to racial profiling, and congratulate ourselves for Christian enlightenment. On this point, Martin Luther King, Jr. is instructive:

> I have almost reached the regrettable conclusion that the Negro's great stumblingblock in his stride toward freedom is not the White Citizens' Counciler or the Ku Klux Klanner, but the white moderate, who is more devoted to "order" than to justice; who prefers a negative peace which is the absence of tension to a positive peace which is the presence of justice; who constantly says: "I agree with you in the goal you seek, but I cannot agree with your methods of direct action"; who paternalistically believes he can set the timetable for another man's freedom; who lives by a mythical concept of time and who constantly advises the Negro to wait for a "more convenient season."[77]

When we turn to women today, what do we hear? Billie Silvey presents voices of thoughtful women in Churches of Christ.[78] Most of these have accepted a moderate position that moves the line of "permission" over a little without erasing it. Women should be "allowed" to do everything except _____. Congregations draw the line in different places and fill in the blank any number of ways.[79] And yet, in reading their stories, one cannot help but notice how each revels in whatever limited opportunities she's had to develop her spiritual gifts. How much has their spiritual growth been stunted by well-meaning spiritual horticulturists who believe that plants of certain species should grow only so high and no higher? How many women among us are like pot-bound plants, fertilized and watered every Sunday but never allowed to grow? We should not be surprised when some send roots through the hole in the bottom of the pot or threaten to burst it altogether.

Osburn asks, "How shall we view women?" and his answer is firmly biblical. After detailed discussions of key passages, he concludes, "A clear understanding of and appreciation for the authority of scripture does not necessitate a hierarchal stance. In fact,

---

[76] See note 34, above, excerpt from Campbell's 1847 "Lecture on Slavery." Harrell (1966): 100-111, documents Campbell's slide to the right after 1845, as his biblicism forced him to rationalize and justify slavery, and even to repudiate the declaration that "all men are created equal."

[77] King (1963): 87.

[78] Billie Silvey, ed., *Trusting Women: The Way of Women in Churches of Christ* (Orange, California: New Leaf, 2002). For stronger voices of frustration, see the "forum" online at http://www.gal328.org/.

[79] Ironically, most of the so-called "progressives" among Churches of Christ, who draw supposedly "liberal" lines of discrimination, are still well to the right of historical precedent within the Restoration Movement. On women preachers in the early 19th century, see C. Leonard Allen, *Distant Voices: Discovering a Forgotten Past for a Changing Church* (Abilene: Abilene Christian University Press, 1993): 22-31. By 1888, the line had moved to the right, when Silena Moore Holman published four articles in the *Gospel Advocate* offering biblical arguments for women teacher—discussed in Allen (1993): 126-135. See the text in Hans Rollmann, ed., *The RM Homepage*: http://www.mun.ca/ rels/restmov/people/sholman.html.

a high view of scripture might just lead one to be an egalitarian."[80] Amen! But then Osburn makes the same move that Campbell made on slavery:

> [E]galitarianism is certainly preferable as far as the ideals of the kingdom are concerned. My studies have led me to conclude, however, that there is no biblical mandate for egalitarianism either, although it was the pristine ideal in the pre-Fall era of Gn 1-2. It is recovered in the thinking of Jesus and is behind much of the practice of the earliest churches, but was later lost again in the strongly patriarchal world of the eastern Mediterranean.

> However, is egalitarianism so necessary that all forms of hierarchalism must be obliterated? Feminists certainly want one to think so! However, neither Jesus nor the earliest churches took this radical view. Just as they did not overthrow slavery, but worked with that system and the evil sometimes present, so they did not overthrow hierarchalism, but worked within the system and the evil sometimes there.[81]

How does this brand of moderation affect the "least of these?" If we truly regard the faces of Christian women, we may discover profound expressions of the gospel as a world-changing force from women who have been dismissed as "radical."[82] If we close our eyes to them, we may fail to see some of the most eloquent portrayals of the pain and frustration felt by some sisters for whom Christ died, not to mention their theological insights.

We can all agree on the importance of scripture and the need to find common ground with Complementarians. But citing a scriptural example is not the same as proclaiming the gospel. A kinder, gentler sexism is no solution to the problem of sexism.

Placing the Cross at the Center as Interpretive Guide to Scripture

The moderate positions adopted by Campbell and Osburn are based on biblical precedent, but they can be arrived at only by reading the Bible on the flat, giving equal weight to every sentence without regard for the theological center. The question "Is a thing Biblical?" is insufficient, for all biblical statements do not proclaim the gospel equally. The question should be, "Does the thing bear witness to the God who is revealed in the cross and resurrection of Jesus?" In Gal 6:14-16, Paul establishes the cross as the criterion by which he evaluates every question:

> But far be it from me to boast, except in the cross of our Lord Jesus Christ, through whom the world is crucified to me and I to the world, *15]* for neither circumcision is anything, nor uncircumcision, but new creation. *16]* And those

---

[80] Osburn (2001): 255.

[81] *Idem*: 262.

[82] For women's expressions of pain, see Ursula King, ed., *Feminist Theology from the Third World: A Reader* (Maryknoll: Orbis, 1994): 103-179; Susan Brooks Thistlethwaite, "Every Two Minutes: Battered Women and Feminist Interpretation," in Letty M. Russell, ed., *Feminist Interpretation of the Bible* (Philadelphia: Westminster, 1985): 96-107; J. Cheryl Exum, *Fragmented Women: Feminist (Sub)Versions of Biblical Narratives* (Valley Forge, Pennsylvania: Trinity Press International, 1993). For a more moderate approach, Phyllis Trible, *Texts of Terror: Literary-Feminist Readings of Biblical Narratives* (Philadelphia: Fortress, 1984).

who conduct themselves by this canon, peace be upon them and mercy also upon God's Israel.

The cross of Christ proclaims the "new creation." It proclaims a renunciation of "the world" (Gal 6:14), a declaration of the end of "this present evil age" (Gal 1:4). The cross is Paul's "canon," his yardstick for evaluating right and wrong. Or, to switch metaphors, it is the new interpretive lens through which he has learned to read the Hebrew scriptures.[83] Looking at Torah through Jesus-colored glasses, Paul sees the gospel already proclaimed to Abraham, "through you all the nations will be blessed" (Gal 3:8, quoting Gn 12:3).

The problem is not with scripture. For Paul, "Torah is holy, and the commandment is holy and just and good" (Rm 7:12). The problem is that Sin (personified) "works death through what is good" (Rm 7:13). That is, Sin influences even the way we read and apply Torah. This happens whenever we interpret scripture in self-serving ways or ways that support (or fail to confront) violence, coercion, abuse, discrimination, exploitation, or benign neglect. The cross challenges us to read scripture self-critically, to reorient our thinking to the "new creation."[84]

Sally Purvis offered an example of constructive feminist theology grounded in reflection on the cross. Like many feminists, Purvis resists theological models that support authoritarian or coercive structures; she seeks out those that support relationships and respect individuals. She critiques traditional notions of "power as control" that tend toward abuse, and she offers an alternative model of "power as life" that better reflects the life-giving power of God. On 1 Cor 1:18-25, she comments: "God's power as shown forth in 'Christ crucified' is the reversal of power as violent control. It is the power to bring life, even in the face of the worst, most destructive power that can be brought to bear."[85] Reflecting on 1 Cor 13, she wrote:

> If we learn to trust the cross as a resource, as a symbol of the power of God that is not controlling but is trustworthy, then we are constantly called back from the temptation to think that because God does not control, God is impotent. The cross as a symbol claims that goodness and power are *not* opposites. It is only when we continue to [think] that power must be controlling to be powerful that we have to posit a contradiction between power and goodness. Understanding power as love, as life, changes the terms of the conversation.[86]

---

[83] C. R. Hutson, "The Cross as Canon: Gal 6:16," *Leaven* 12/1 (2004): 49-53.

[84] Eschatology is important in feminist thinking. Letty M. Russell, *Household of Freedom: Authority in Feminist Theology* (Philadelphia: Westminster, 1987), framed the center as an "appeal to the future" (recognizing eschatological dimensions of biblical theology) and as a call for freedom from oppression (recognizing biblical critiques of ideologies of domination). Cf. E. Elizabeth Johnson, "Apocalyptic Family Values," *Interpretation* 56/1 (January, 2002): 34-44; Venable-Ridley (1997): 222-227; Ada María Isasi-Díaz, "The Task of Hispanic Women's Liberation Theology—Mujeristas: Who We Are and What We Are About," in Ursula King, ed., *Feminist Theology from the Third World: A Reader* (Maryknoll: Orbis, 1994): 100-101.

[85] Sally B. Purvis, *The Power of the Cross: Foundations for a Christian Feminist Ethic of Community* (Nashville: Abingdon, 1993): 50.

[86] *Idem*: 90.

It may be that a feminist perspective on the cross can help us see the center again more clearly. Purvis would be a good conversation partner for Osburn, who sees in both Jesus and Paul a redefinition of power in terms of service.[87]

Prospects for the Future

Much can be said for careful Bible reading, listening to one's opponents, and maintaining fellowship despite disagreement. Campbell and Osburn both reflect such concerns. Yet as moderates, both in effect tolerate discrimination and congratulate themselves for their broadmindedness. We need to erase altogether any line that favors one group over another. We need to live as people baptized into Christ, people clothed with Christ, people for whom there is no ethnic or class or gender discrimination (Gal 3:27-28). If the slavery issue in America is any indication, then those who defend gender discrimination will someday appear as awkward and misguided as Campbell now does in his "biblical" defense of slavery. Campbell knew the Bible, but the Abolitionists knew Jesus. If we would know Jesus, our first concern must be how we relate to the "least of these." Let us not be conformed to this age, but be transformed by a renewal of the mind. And may God have mercy!

---

[87] Osburn (2001): 129-130.

First-century Christians in the Twenty-first Century: Does Evidence Matter?

Dianne M. Bazell and Laurence H. Kant

Since the turn of the new millennium, we have seen an immense resurgence of interest in the world of the Early Christians. Even as many biblical scholars have pared Gospel pericopes into fewer and fewer passages they are willing to attribute to Jesus, and some have even abandoned altogether the search for the historical Jesus as a naive and futile enterprise, the public appetite and demand for evidence of "the way it was" in Jesus' time appears to be increasing.

No two works could be more unlike one another in theological motivation and intent than Mel Gibson's film, *The Passion of the Christ*, and Dan Brown's mystery thriller, *The Da Vinci Code*.[1] Yet popular audiences have turned them both into resounding commercial successes and generated spin-off industries for their interpretation and further appreciation. Indeed, both Protestant and Catholic congregations have used showings (or critiques) of *The Passion* as a vehicle for religious education, while *The Da Vinci Code* has become a staple of book clubs and inspired guided tours across Italy and France tracing the adventures of its protagonists.

Both works present themselves as accurate, evidence-based renditions of Christian history, and it is this popular demand for evidence, as well as its use and abuse in these two blockbusters, that we find most intriguing. No "faith in things unseen" for the modern orthodox—or for earnest heretics, either! Both Gibson and Brown appeal to source documents and reference ancient languages in their efforts to confirm or refute, respectively, specific institutional accounts of Christian history. And while many critics have praised the aesthetic experience each work offers, they also find the ways in which each work uses evidence as disingenuously selective, distorting at best and, at worst, blatantly manipulating to arrive at false conclusions.

The Passion of the Christ

Many found the cinematography of the film and its set visually compelling. The acting (especially Monica Bellucci's performance in the role of Mary, Jesus' mother) received critical acclaim. The use of Aramaic with English subtitles in a popular film about Jesus is groundbreaking. The portrayal of brutality, for which the film received some criticism, forces us to reckon with the savage environment characteristic of many parts of the ancient world—and the modern one, as well. And the entire visual texture of the film, right down

---

[1] Dan Brown, *The Da Vinci Code: A Novel* (New York: Doubleday, 2003).

to the depiction of Jesus' wounds, reminds one of Late-Medieval and Early-Renaissance paintings and sculptures, cracked with age and begging restoration.

This leads us to the problem of *The Passion's* claims to "historicity." In interviews given in a range of popular print and broadcast media, Gibson characterized the Gospels as eyewitness accounts, "reliable sources. These are guys who were around." He dismissed over two centuries of historical-critical analysis of the New Testament by minimizing differences among Gospel accounts. "The Gospels don't contradict one another. They mesh….Because if they didn't, you wouldn't have so many people hooked into this."[2]

Gibson's claims notwithstanding, even eyewitness accounts cannot be naively "meshed." (At the scene of the auto accident, was the van white or blue? Did it leave the parking lot at 8:00 p.m. or at 10:30 p.m.?) One cannot simply toss all accounts into the hopper, average them out, assume that information offered by one fits into others that fail to mention some specific detail, and then arrive at a harmony without oneself doing some selection.[3] To take these canonical sources seriously, one must do what New Testament scholars do, and have been doing now for generations: One must note significant differences among the four canonical Gospel accounts and ponder why this one says "this" but the others say "that."

Gibson selectively appropriated these renderings, depicting the healing of the soldier's ear (Lk 22:51), the dream of Pilate's wife (Mt 27:19), the blood libel (Mt 27:25), and Pilate's question regarding truth (Jn 18:38). Gibson adopted the synoptic Gospels' chronological sequence of the Passover *seder* preceding the crucifixion in preference to John's different ordering of the events.

Moreover, whereas New Testament scholars seek external amplification from contemporary or near-contemporary sources (for example, regarding the character of Pontius Pilate, discussed below), Gibson included many additional details drawing either on artistic license or on the spiritual visions of a nineteenth-century mystic, Sister Anne Catherine Emmerich, whose *The Dolorous Passion of Our Lord Jesus Christ* inspired Gibson during a difficult life passage and whose work is now enjoying a revival due to the film it helped shape.[4] Scenes of Jesus' childhood relationship with his mother, his building a comically out-of-proportion table for her at home, stamping on the snake in the garden, the devil appearing in human form, Peter's addressing Mary as "mother," identification of the adulterous woman with Mary Magdalene—none of these details can be found in the Gospels. Neither in the Gospels are found Jesus' being dropped on a rope from a bridge after his arrest and coming face-to-face with Judas, demonic children appearing in physical form to harass Judas, Caiaphas's attending the scourging and following Jesus to the cross, Pilate's wife bringing linens to Mary and Mary Magdalene, and the latter wiping Jesus' blood from the floor after the scourging, the dislocation of Jesus' shoulder

---

[2] Peter J. Boyer, "The Jesus War: Mel Gibson's Obsession," *The New Yorker*, 9/15/03: 64-65.

[3] The first to attempt a Gospel harmony was the second-century Assyrian Christian, Tatian, in his *Diatesseron*.

[4] Ann Catherine Emmerich, *The Dolorous Passion of Our Lord Jesus Christ*, Klemens Maria Brentano, ed. (El Sobrante, California: North Bay Books, 2003). Originally published in 1833 as *Das bittere Leiden unsers Herrn Jesu Christi*. See Tim Challies, "The Passion of the Christ according to Emmerich," for a useful compilation of references in the film to Emmerich's writing: http://challies.com/archives/000197.php. Gibson also used the writings of Mary of Agreda.

to fit him to the cross, a black crow flying among the crosses, a heavenly teardrop, the soldier showered with blood when Jesus' side is pierced—all these and other additions come from Emmerich's visions and Gibson's other non-biblical sources.

Gibson further reshaped and limited the Gospel accounts by rendering a film that is a narrative of the Passion alone. The Gospels devote comparatively little space to the death process. In doing so, Gibson drew more on the medieval genres of the classic *Passion Play* and the Stations of the Cross than on the Gospels, and, in fact, the scenes of Jesus' multiple fallings on the way to the cross, his encounter with his mother on the road to Golgotha, and the character of Veronica who wiped his face with her veil, all come from the Stations and Emmerich's visions.

Other historical errors include the use of Latin in the film. Residents of ancient Palestine (Jews and non-Jews alike) spoke Greek as a second language, and inscriptions suggest that Greek rivaled Aramaic as the language of the region at that time. Thus Pontius Pilate and Jesus would probably have conversed in Greek (certainly not in Latin, as they do in the film). Neither did Pilate likely address the crowd in Aramaic, as the film would have it, but in Greek. Jews would probably have used Hebrew, especially in their traditional prayers and references to scripture.

The film devotes its attention to Jesus' torture, and here, too, its rendering draws from medieval veneration of the instruments of the Passion rather than ancient practice. In the Gospels, the Romans used reeds to whip Jesus,[5] not the metal instruments depicted in the film.[6] In the Graeco-Roman world, victims of crucifixion were not clothed, but naked, and Romans focused less on the preliminary torture and more on their victim's public humiliation, as the Gospel accounts suggest, for crucifixion was a Roman punishment for sedition and a message to anyone who might contemplate it. Victims carried a horizontal crossbeam only, not an entire cross, and nails (only occasionally used) were not driven into the palms of hands but into the wrists (and sometimes the ankles) to keep the victim from falling.[7]

Gibson's *The Passion* achieved notoriety partly because of its depiction of Jews and Judaism and the traditions it evokes. In general, the film treats the Temple high priest,

---

[5] Mk 15:15.

[6] Andrea Berlin and Jodi Magness, "Two Archaeologists Comment on the Passion of the Christ" http://www.archaeological.org/pdfs/papers/Comments on The Passion.pdf discuss the methods of torture then in use. Thanks to Ross Scaife of the Department of Classics of the University of Kentucky for alerting us to this fine article.

[7] On crucifixion, see the following: Martin Hengel, *Crucifixion in the Ancient World and the Folly of the Message of the Cross*, John Bowden, trans. (Philadelphia: Fortress, 1977); and A. Berlin and J. Magness, *op cit.*: 3. For analysis of the burial of a crucifixion victim in Jerusalem, see the following: Vassilios Tzaferis, "Jewish Tombs at and near Giv'at ha-Mitvar," *Israel Exploration Journal* 20 (1970): 18-32; J. Zias and E. Sekeles, "The Crucified Man from Giv'at ha-Matar: A Reappraisal," *Israel Exploration Journal* 35 (1985): 22-27; William D. Edwards, Wesley J. Gabel, and Floyd E. Hosmer, "On the Physical Death of Jesus Christ," *Journal of the American Medical Association* 255 (1986): 1455-63; and Joe Zias, "Crucifixion in Antiquity: The Evidence": http://www.centuryone.org/ crucifixion2.html.

Caiaphas, more harshly than he appears in any of the Gospels.[8] At Jesus' trial, in the film, Caiaphas supports the accusations against Jesus by appeal to Jesus' Sabbath violation, but the Gospels do not note this; the question of Sabbath observance did not occupy the priests, but rather the Pharisees, who, along with the Sadducees and other competing Jewish groups, are absent from the film, although they figure importantly in the Gospels. Rather, the film has Caiaphas and the priests stand as proxies for "the Jews" collectively, and the androgynous devil is depicted as circulating among them, as if Jews were somehow collectively inspired by the Prince of Darkness. Then Caiaphas is present at Jesus' scourging and thereafter follows him to the cross—none of this to be read in any of the Gospels.

At the same time, the film portrays Pontius Pilate more sympathetically than he appears in the Gospels, and certainly more sympathetically than he does in ancient sources. The film's Pilate is a weak and vacillating fellow who'd like to do the right thing but just can't bring himself up to it. In Mark and Matthew,[9] Pilate is very much in control of the situation, perhaps manipulating it to his advantage. In John, however, Jesus tells Pilate that he is not so much to blame as those who are demanding his execution (Jn 19:11), and he is fulfilling a divine plan. Further, the *Passion's* portrayal of Pilate's wife as giving Mary and Mary Magdalene linens during Jesus' scourging (scenes taken from Emmerich's visions) serves to render Pilate more sympathetic. Near-contemporary sources outside the Gospels, i.e. Josephus and Philo, however, depict Pilate as a cruel, brutal, and very confident and decisive Roman procurator.[10]

Most troubling of all is how Jews and Judaism are portrayed in the film. Women are dressed in apparel that resembles nuns' habits. The priests wear robes and hoods unlike the simple tunics they probably donned. Physically, Jesus and his disciples do not resemble olive-skinned, sunburned, shorthaired Middle Easterners. In their height, weight, and dental condition, the Jews in the film seem more like well-fed American Bible Study participants than Galilean peasants and tradesmen.[11] Historically, Simon of Cyrene (from Libya) might well have been black-skinned. In the film, he wears a head covering (*kippah/yarmulke*), which Jews did not wear until the High Middle Ages.

The above is not mere historicist nit-picking, for Jesus, as a Jew, does not wear a head covering in the film, and the effect of this difference in portrayal is a clear theological statement: Jesus, together with his disciples (the first "Christian converts"), view Judaism as a religion of the past, and the "real" Jews are Caiaphas, the priests, and the angry mob that clamors for Jesus' crucifixion. Granted, Simon of Cyrene, a Jew, is depicted as being kind to Jesus; yet it is intriguing that, as he aids Jesus in carrying the cross down the Via Dolorosa, our eyes rest on a man resembling a northern European Jew assisting a man resembling a medieval Christian—the first Jewish-Christian interfaith dialogue, as it were.

---

[8] Helen K. Bond, *Caiaphas: Friend of Rome and Judge of Jesus?* (Louisville: Westminster John Knox Press, 2004). See also Margaret M. Mitchell, "The Passion of the Christ" in *Sightings* (March 11) (University of Chicago: Martin Marty Center, 2004).

[9] Mk 15:1-15; Mt 27:1-2, 11-14.

[10] Helen K. Bond, *Pontius Pilate in History and Interpretation*, Society for New Testament Studies Monograph Series, 100 (Cambridge: Cambridge University Press, 1998).

[11] For a possible visual representation of Jesus, see the attempt of the CNN program, "The Mystery of Jesus," narrated by Liam Neeson; for the related photos by David Gibson, "What Did Jesus Really Look Like?" *The New York Times* (February 2, 2004): see www.nytimes.com/2004/02/21/arts/21JESU.html?th.

Gone is the Jesus who lived until his death as a Torah-observant Jew ("Do not think that I have come to abolish the law or the prophets....[N]ot one letter, not one stroke of a letter, will pass from the law until all is accomplished," according to the Gospel of Matthew 5:17-18), who kept kosher and usually observed the Sabbath, who worshipped in the Temple sanctuary and went up to the feasts in Jerusalem, and who accepted many of the principles and ideas of Pharisaic Judaism (while disputing some of their implementation).[12] Even worse, there are no Jewish prayers (even at the Passover meal), no references to the Hebrew Bible (except a predictive use of Isaiah 53 at the film's opening), no indication of Temple rituals and sacrifices, no mention of Jewish dietary practices, no identifiable clothing such as fringes or tassels (*tzitzit*) that observant Jewish males (probably including Jesus) typically wore, no substantive references to Jewish culture and ethics, and no reference to Jewish nationalism and opposition to Roman rule (to illuminate the tensions between Jews and Romans and provide some sense of why Jesus offended the Temple priests and the Roman rulers alike).

Absent are Jesus' defense of the poor, the homeless, and the marginalized. Missing is his critique of the plutocrats—the reigning priests and politicians, and his calling the Temple hierarchy to task for its religious and economic dominance. His agreement with the Pharisees on religious questions is not mentioned, with their emphasis on piety outside the Temple and the cultivation of a holy life distinct from the Temple (though Jesus thought the Pharisees went too far in some ways and not far enough in others). In the film, we do not see Jesus in the company of tax collectors, prostitutes, and adulterers, or the poor Jewish Galilean peasants who were among his first followers. When Jesus preached in parables to his followers to feed the hungry and thirsty, clothe the naked, nurse the sick, visit the imprisoned, and welcome the stranger, he said, "Just as you did it to one of the least of these who are my brothers and sisters, you did it to me" (Mt 25:40). These are core Jewish values, presumably as threatening to institutionalized authority then as now. But a Jesus this Jewish does not appear in the film.

Gone also is Jesus, the rabble-rousing, trouble-making Jew, not unlike his spiritual descendents who organized exploited workers into unions and helped disenfranchised Black Americans gain and exercise their right to vote. The prophetic call to change oppressive social, economic, and religious structures is a concern that Jesus and many of his Jewish contemporaries shared (including Jesus' disciples, one of whom was a Zealot). It is a call that many Jews and Christians still share, but one that is not shared by the film.

---

[12] The bibliography on Jesus' place within Judaism is massive. See Albert Schweitzer, *The Quest of the Historical Jesus: A Critical Study of Its Progress from Reimarus to Wrede* (New York: Macmillan, 1968; originally published in 1910 as *Von Reimarus zu Wrede*); Geza Vermes, *Jesus the Jew: A Historian's Review of the Gospels* (London: William Collins, 1973); *ibid., Jesus and the World of Judaism* (London: SCM, 1983); E. P. Sanders, *Jesus and Judaism* (Philadelphia: Fortress, 1985); Geza Vermes, *The Religion of Jesus the Jew* (Minneapolis: Fortress, 1993); Brad H. Young, *Jesus the Jewish Theologian* (Peabody, Massachusetts: Hendrickson, 1995); Brad H. Young, *The Parables: Jewish Tradition and Christian Interpretation* (Peabody, Massachusetts: Hendrickson, 1998); Peter J. Tomson, *'If this be from Heaven': Jesus and the New Testament Authors in their Relation to Judaism* (The Biblical Seminar, 76; Sheffield, England: Sheffield Academic Press, 2001); Geza Vermes, *Jesus in his Jewish Context* (Minneapolis: Fortress, 2003); David Instone-Brewer, *Traditions of the Rabbis from the Era of the New Testament* (vol. 1): *Prayer and Agriculture* (Grand Rapids, Michigan: Eerdmans, 2004).

Biblical religion is not a private matter, but a community responsibility in which we share in one another's failures and successes, mistakes and good deeds.

Gibson's film, however, articulates none of this. We are left with no real explanation of why Jesus was so disliked. Perhaps a more realistic and Jewish portrayal of Jesus would have offended today's contemporary institutionalized authority. *The Passion* distorts and selectively uses the Gospels (focusing on the last portion of the Gospels and excluding the rest of their scope), ignores other contemporary evidence, and adds medieval and later material, thereby obliterating the Jewishness of Jesus and Jewish foundations of Christianity.

The Da Vinci Code

Turning to *The Da Vinci Code*, we encounter a very different figure of Jesus—one who married, fathered a child, and left a biological bloodline of descendants unacknowledged by the church that took his name. Brown's book is an easy-to-read page-turner of a suspense novel, with no chapter exceeding ten pages in length. Its immense appeal to readers from young adult and beyond, and of widely varied levels of educational attainment, has led to its translation into more than forty languages. A film version of the book, directed by Ron Howard and starring Tom Hanks, is scheduled for release in 2006.

Like Gibson, Brown presents his story as fact based on historical sources, which he announces explicitly on the page preceding his prologue: "All descriptions of artwork, architecture, documents, and secret rituals in this novel are accurate"—actually a stronger claim than Gibson makes, for Brown more directly (and quite positively) assesses his own use of source material. The sources for the life of Jesus on which Brown draws include several non-canonical gospels.

The plot, in brief, is as follows: The curator of the Louvre, Jacques Saunière, has been murdered. His naked body, positioned in a contorted manner and surrounded by strange symbols and codes, some written in his own blood and others in invisible ink, lies in the Grand Gallery adjacent to the room where Leonardo Da Vinci's painting, *The Last Supper*, hangs. A Harvard symbologist, Robert Langdon, is summoned to investigate, along with Sophie Neveu, a police cryptographer and granddaughter of Saunière. They discover that Saunière, from whom Neveu had been estranged for years, was the head of a centuries-old, secret society, the Priory of Sion, which has kept the secret of the whereabouts of the *true* Holy Grail. Following clues they find while traveling in France and England, and with the aid of a wealthy independent scholar, Sir Leigh Teabing, they learn that the Holy Grail is not the chalice from Jesus' Last Supper, but the very person of Mary Magdalene, who not only held a primary role among the apostles but also married Jesus, bore him a daughter, and transmitted his royal bloodline which continues to this day. The Holy Grail, guarded by the Priory of Sion, consists of the Magdalene's remains which rest in a secret tomb along with documents attesting to her life and the "complete genealogy of the early descendants of Christ" (256). Also seeking the whereabouts of this burial site and all clues pointing to it are members of Opus Dei, a conservative Catholic order that seeks to suppress the truth about Jesus' earthly nature, his sexuality, the apostolic role that Mary played, and, indeed, the role of women in the Early Church. The Priory of Sion's leadership has included Sir Isaac Newton and Leonardo Da Vinci, and it is in Leonardo's depiction of the beloved figure to Jesus' right in *The Last Supper* that the truth about Jesus and Mary is proclaimed, for the clean-shaven figure is not "the beloved disciple," but Mary Magdalene.[13]

Brown's argument is that the earliest documents of Christian history, which included sources that never made it into the canon, such as those discovered at Nag Hammadi, portray Jesus in more human terms, and women more powerfully, than subsequent church authorities could tolerate. Only in the fourth century, Brown posits (through Sir Leigh) did the Emperor Constantine, overseeing the Council of Nicaea, fix the Gospels of Mark, Matthew, Luke, and John as canonical.

Bart Ehrman and others have admirably reviewed some of Brown's key misuses of source material and missteps of inference. Included among these are the following: a misdating of the discoveries of the Dead Sea Scrolls and mischaracterizing them as "among the earliest Christian records" when they are in fact Jewish texts that make no reference to Jesus; misattribution to the Nag Hammadi documents of an account of the Grail story and an emphasis on Jesus' human nature; a glossing over the nearly three-centuries-long process by which multiple Christian communities came to determine a shared collection of authoritative texts; mischaracterization of the date at which multiple Christian communities came to accept the Gospels of Mark, Matthew, Luke, and John as authoritative—the date was much earlier than Brown suggested; misrepresentation of these four Gospels as sources that emphasize Jesus' divine nature and minimize his humanness; a false claim that Constantine "commissioned and financed a new Bible" which was voted on at the Council of Nicaea, and which omitted Gospels that emphasize Jesus' human traits and embellished Gospels that make him godlike; exaggeration of the number (eighty) of Gospel accounts of Jesus' life, and mischaracterization of these sources as "recordings" of Jesus' life by thousands of his followers; and attribution of the hypothetical "Q" source as Jesus' own writing.[14]

Brown's aim was to address two distinct concerns: a) the place of the "feminine" in conceptualizations of divinity, and b) women's standing in the Early Church. His argument is that a) non-canonical sources emphasize the human aspects of Jesus' nature and the feminine aspects of divinity (while, conversely, canonical sources unduly divinize Jesus and remove him from contact with women), and b) ecclesiastical decisions redacted the importance of women in the Early Church, removing it from official canonical records, while non-canonical texts show that women were more positively viewed and that they took a more central leadership role.

Ehrman and others more than adequately show that both canonical and non-canonical sources either belie these claims or reveal strong ambiguity. In addition, neither do views of the feminine divine reflect a social reality in which women are necessarily prominent, nor can one infer positive theological renderings of the feminine from prominent roles of women in a community.[15] Jesus' human nature is patent in the

---

[13] Brown (2003): 244, Sir Leigh proclaims, "*The Last Supper* practically shouts that Jesus and Magdalene were a pair."

[14] Brown (2003): 231-34, 256; Bart D. Ehrman, *Truth and Fiction in the Da Vinci Code: A Historian Reveals What We Really Know about Jesus, Mary Magdalene, and Constantine* (Oxford: Oxford University Press, 2004): xiv-xv *et passim*.

[15] The worship of the Syrian goddess, Atargatis (*Dea Syria*), involved male priests (eunuchs, *galli*) exclusively, not women. On this cult, see also Monika Hörig, "Dea Syria—Atargatis," in *Aufstieg*

canonical Gospels, especially in the Synoptics, where he fraternizes, preaches, eats, drinks, and emotes; the docetist view that Jesus only appeared to be human and suffer was condemned as heretical.[16] Jesus as depicted in the gnostic *Gospel of Thomas* (114) speaks of the need for every woman to "make herself male" in order to enter the kingdom of heaven,[17] while it was Paul for whom gender differences were eliminated "in Christ."[18] In all four canonical Gospels, Mary Magdalene and her female companions are the first to learn of Jesus' resurrection,[19] whereas the Magdalene's private revelations and post-resurrection visions of Jesus are disputed by Andrew and Peter in the *Gospel of Mary* precisely because the Magdalene was a woman.[20]

While no sources either canonical or non-canonical identify Jesus as being married, the central passages on which Brown rests his case for the marriage of Jesus and Mary are found in the *Gospel of Philip*. The first is where Mary Magdalene is described as Jesus' companion and partner, to distinguish her from his mother Mary and his sister; the other depicts a rivalry between Mary and the other disciples and (gaps in the manuscript notwithstanding) implies that Jesus kissed Mary and loved her more than he did the other disciples.[21] Setting aside the singularity of this source, the ambiguity of the status of "companion" and "partner," and possible implications (other than sexual or marital) implied by kissing, a more basic, and feminist, question remains: Why is it necessary for Mary to be Jesus' wife and bear him children for her to be either important or even his favored, or favorite, disciple? Why would her possible roles as financial supporter, organizer, strategist, theological interpreter, private recipient of revelations, and family confidante to his mother and sister alone not render her operationally critical to the nascent movement of Jesus-followers?

Gibson and Brown Together

Despite the stark contrasts between Mel Gibson's and Dan Brown's theologies and interpretations of Christian history, they share some remarkably similar historiographic

---

und Niedergang der römischen Welt (Berlin: Walter de Gruyter, 1983), ser. 2, vol. 17, fasc. 4: 1536-81; and Robert Turcan, *The Cults of the Roman Empire*, Antonia Nevill, trans. (Oxford: Blackwell, 1996): 133-43. The prominent place of Priscilla and Maximilla in the Christian Montanist movement did not prevent Tertullian, himself a Montanist, from disparaging women—"each an Eve," "the devil's gateway," and destroyers of "God's image," and hence the cause of Jesus' need to die. See Ehrman (2004): 173-74.

[16] Pheme Perkins, "Docetism," in *Encyclopedia of Early Christianity*, E. Ferguson, ed. (New York: Garland Publishing, 1998): 341-42.

[17] "Simon Peter said to them, 'Mary should leave us, for females are not worthy of life.' Jesus said, 'See, I am going to attract her to make her male so that she too might become a living spirit that resembles you males. For every female (element) that makes itself male will enter the kingdom of heaven.'" Bentley Layton, trans., *The Gnostic Scriptures* (New York: Doubleday, 1987): 399.

[18] Gal 3:28, and Jesus appears to diminish gender roles in the kingdom of heaven when he says that humans will not need to marry because they will be like angels (Mk 12:25, Mt 22:30, Lk 20:35-36).

[19] Mt 28:1-10; Lk 24:1-10; Mk 16:9; Jn 20:11-18.

[20] *The Gospel of Mary*, in *The Nag Hammadi Library*, 3rd ed., James M. Robinson, gen. ed. (New York: HarperSanFrancisco, 1988): 526-27. See also Karen L. King, *The Gospel of Mary of Magdala: Jesus and the First Woman Apostle* (Santa Rosa, California: Polebridge Press, 2003).

[21] Layton (1988): 339: *Gospel of Mary* 59.6-10; 63.32-64.5.

leanings. Both Gibson and Brown claim that the Gospels (though they differ about which ones are more credible) are "eye-witness accounts" and "recordings" of Jesus' followers. Ironically, however, both *The Passion* and *The Da Vinci Code* focus to an extraordinary degree on Jesus' physicality as a foundation for their respective claims about Jesus: Gibson's film lingers on Jesus' bodily abuse, omits most of the Gospel accounts of Jesus' teaching, and only briefly touches on the resurrection; Brown conceives of Jesus' continuing presence in the world through biological progeny, identifies the Grail with the body (now relics) of Mary Magdalene, and frames her elevated status in Christian history in terms of child-bearing wife, yet little of this is to be found in the "eye-witness accounts" and "recordings" so prized by both the film-maker and the novelist.

Further, both Gibson and Brown envision (in different terms) a cosmic battle of good and evil. For Gibson, the battle is between God and Satan (graphically depicted as flitting among the Jews—and perhaps also envisioned among those who sought to suppress Gibson's film). For Brown, the battle is among human protagonists who try to cover up the true nature of the divine, including the struggle between the two groups, the Priory of Sion and Opus Dei. Each raconteur displays a world view not unlike that reflected in a medieval mystery play, where events on earth reflect drama at the cosmic level.

Both Brown and Gibson are conspiracy theorists—Brown charging the Constantinian Church with conspiring to suppress Jesus' true nature and the Magdalene's leading role in the spread of Christianity, Gibson finding conspiracy in the opposition to his film.

The Ossuary of James

To set the use (and misuse) of evidence in a different light, let us turn from documentary to material sources. Over the last ten to fifteen years, a large number of finds, apparently verifying biblical texts, have come to light. Seemingly out of nowhere, a veritable treasure trove of these objects has spawned a scholarly publishing industry that has further drawn the lay public into its intellectual vortex. These intriguing artifacts include an ivory pomegranate inscribed in paleo-Hebrew with a reference to the Temple of Yahweh; the Mattanyahu decanter, believed to be an offering from the Temple of Solomon; the Shishak bowl that bears an inscription of the king of Egypt who invaded Israel in the tenth century B.C.E.; the Jehoash tablet, which lists a series of repairs made by King Jehoash (Joash) in the ninth century B.C.E.; the King Manasseh seal; the Moussaieff ostraca, inscribed potsherds from the seventh century B.C.E. that mention King Josiah, and one of which was thought to constitute one of the only physical remnants of Solomon's Temple; the Baruch ben Neriyah bulla, apparently a seal belonging to the scribe of the prophet himself, Jeremiah; and the ossuary of James, a bone box that bears an inscription in Aramaic referring to a deceased man named James, son of Joseph and brother of Jesus.[22] And John the Baptist's Cave has already been on

---

[22] See the various articles in the Society of Biblical Literature (SBL) *Forum* (March 11, 2005) for full discussion of the evidence, especially the following, which also have extensive bibliography: Christopher A. Rollston and Andrew G. Vaughn, "The Antiquities Market, Sensationalized Textual Data, and Modern Forgeries: Introduction to the Problem and Synopsis of the 2004 Israeli Indictment":http://www.sbl-site.org/Article.aspx?ArticleID-373; and Yuval Goren, "The Jerusalem Syndrome in Biblical Archaeology": http://www.sbl-site.org/Article.aspx?ArticleID-374.

television.[23] These finds made headlines in news outlets and especially in the journal that popularizes biblical archaeological scholarship, *Biblical Archaeology Review* (*BAR*), which announced several of the finds.[24] The ossuary of James proved of such great interest that almost immediately the editor of *BAR* and a New Testament scholar collaborated to produce a best-selling book.[25]

From the outset, however, some scholars doubted the authenticity of these objects: The scripts are not quite right; multiple chisels seem to have carved inscriptions; the contents of the inscriptions seemed too good to be true; the inscriptions involved appear to be out of sync with other, comparable inscriptions; and the objects have all been purchased without regard to provenance, that is, in alleged ignorance as to how they were acquired, where and by whom, and under what circumstances in some murky antiquities market. None of the finds had a connection to an archaeological context in which scholars might verify dates and context with greater precision and certainty. The collector of the ossuary of James, Oded Golan, claimed to have found the inscription some twenty-five years before his announcement of its existence: Such a gap between discovery and disclosure invites suspicion. After travel from Tel Aviv to Toronto for display at the Royal Ontario Museum in 2002, the ossuary developed a significant crack, casting further doubt on the professionalism of the entire enterprise. Then, under the aegis of the Israel Antiquities Authority, a team of epigraphers and geo-archaeologists studied the ossuary and declared it a forgery with a decipherably modern patina. Finally, in December 2004, Israeli authorities indicted several individuals and accused them of fabricating these and other objects.

We still await the full investigation and trial of these persons, but the final determination of the authenticity or inauthenticity should not preclude our asking some basic questions. In the case of the ossuary of James, why did a number of scholars assume veracity in the face of so many doubts? Jodi Magness has convincingly demonstrated that James was much more likely buried in a trench grave (where the poor and marginalized nearly always found themselves) than in an ossuary in a wealthy tomb.[26] No extant texts indicate that James was ever taken up after his burial and interred by Jewish-Christian followers of Jesus.[27] Nor do we have evidence for reburials of those previously interred in the trench graves of the less well-to-do. The reference to "brother of Jesus" is odd and very uncommon in funerary inscriptions in the Mediterranean world, where parental lineage (especially that of the father) almost always holds sway. Ancient inscriptions generally follow set patterns and rarely deviate from them. While these observations seem rather straightforward now, the emotions during the period immediately following the discovery may have caused many to forget such obvious and mundane matters.

Why should we care about these objects in the first place? What difference do they make? What do they prove? Perhaps some doubt the existence of the first Temple or the

---

[23] http://www.msnbc.msn.com/id/5724143

[24] For discussion of the role of the *BAR*, see Edward M. Cook, "The Forgery Indictments and *BAR*: Learning from Hindsight": http://www.sbl-site.org/Article.aspx?ArticleID-371.

[25] Hershel Shanks and Ben Witherington III, *The Brother of Jesus: The Dramatic Story & Meaning of the First Archaeological Link to Jesus & His Family* (New York: HarperSanFrancisco, 2003).

[26] "Ossuaries and the Burials of Jesus and James," *Journal of Biblical Literature* 124 (2005): 121-54.

[27] If the community had reburied James, it would be surprising for Josephus, Eusebius, or other commentators not to have mentioned it.

existence of certain biblical kings and other figures; yet, virtually no one questions the historicity of the central figure of the Gospels, Jesus (Joshua or Yeshu, son of Joseph). Many debate his historical mission, his purpose, his theology, his religious beliefs, and his political attitudes, but almost all scholars now accept the fact of his existence. Why then do we need the ossuary of James, and why do we need it to refer to the New Testament James and Jesus?[28] On the one hand, proof of their historical existence, and perhaps their importance to some people in the ancient world, would add one more brick to the wall of our understanding of antiquity; on the other hand, persons of faith—like doubting Thomas—very often crave tangible evidence for what they want to believe.

Does Evidence Matter?

If "evidence matters," why does it matter? Why do people of faith need such evidence to believe in things of ultimate concern? Well before the time of the Enlightenment, both Jews and Christians sought to show that divine commandments were rational—for example, Maimonides's explanation of the healthfulness of kashrut (Jewish diet and purity regulations), and Anselm's ontological "proof" of God's existence by reason alone, apart from scriptural authority. But we can say that the Enlightenment accentuated the need for the "reasonableness" of things believed and heightened the demands for evidence as a condition of faith. It is no small irony that Enlightenment thinking, which set the stage for the modern biblical scholarship that Gibson so disregards, also fomented the worldwide public appetite for a visually compelling account, purportedly based on eye-witness accounts, focused on the physical agony of Jesus during his last few hours.

For many moderns, indeed, nothing is truly real until it is made tangible, and yet the more we are delighted by computer-generated realities on monitors and silver screens, the more slippery our hold on external reality becomes. Actual objects allow us to touch, to see, and to feel—to use our senses. While this desire has existed for centuries, the triumph of radical empiricism, or to quote a colleague, "empiricism run amok,"[29] has made the imagination and the abstract world of the mind less relevant or helpful or meaningful. Physicists may accept the existence of tiny particles (electrons, quarks, etc.) that no one has ever seen, and mathematicians may live in a symbolic world of numbers (with some numbers that are literally "imaginary"), but the ordinary public—movie goers and novel readers—adheres to more tangible standards before we are willing to believe. Despite the talk of "faith"—"the evidence of things not seen"—many of us depend almost exclusively on the support of corporeality, without which we are lost and become unhinged. Evidence and its proper use have both practical and ethical dimensions not to be minimized. No one would doubt the superiority of DNA over eye-witness accounts (of, say, whole communities who watched the application of red-hot tongs to the flesh of heretics or the dunking of alleged witches and confessed Anabaptists in the town pond) as an evidentiary basis for determining criminal responsibility, and reports regularly surface nowadays of prisoners released from death row because some group of law students compelled the authorities finally to get the evidence right.

---

[28] Even proving the antiquity of the ossuary and its full inscription would not establish the precise identity of the named individuals, James and Jesus. Many people in ancient Israel were named James (Jacob) and Jesus (Joshua or Yeshu).

Tampering with evidence can ruin individual lives and oppress peoples by erasing their histories. Minorities and subaltern populations struggle to counter the dominant histories of those with more powerful pens and word-processors.

Conquerors know this, and so do movie makers. The conscious destruction of evidence in an effort to annihilate a people is nowhere more vividly expressed than by the character of Amon Goeth, the Nazi commandant of Plaszow, in Steven Spielberg's film, Schindler's List. Surveying the city of Krakow before a raid to decimate its Jewish ghetto, he says, "Today is history.... For six centuries there has been a Jewish Krakow. By this evening those six centuries will be a rumor. They never happened." A respect for evidence is a pre-condition for our respect for truth.

At the same time, could our modern demand for hard evidence and certainty be infringing upon, and even eroding, our commitment to truth? Can evidence matter too much? Can it matter so much that, in its absence, modern faith requires its fabrication to persist? Who are the most despairing? Are they the biblical critics who have found the "quest for the historical Jesus" to be so elusive as to border on Zeno's paradox, either because their methodological standards are too demanding or the available sources are too unyielding? Or are the modern faithful in greater dismay because their devotion to their version of the divine requires suppression of sources that point to unwanted conclusions, the misreading of sources to arrive at foreordained results, and even the forging of evidence to fill in the gaps?[30] The ironic parallel of Gibson and the Enlightenment persists: The Enlightenment commitment to the idea of truth has paved a path to the Postmodern disregard and contempt for it.

Evidence matters, but to require it as a condition of faith—to the point where one would forge it—is nothing less than idolatry. Making evident fact alone the criterion of faith constricts the hermeneutical space, as it were, between what we can actually prove at the moment and a larger scope of living. Understanding the limits of our understanding requires intellectual humility, a willingness to "watch and wait," in the words of the *Gospel of Mark*, until we may gain further understanding. A willingness to act provisionally "as if" a divine reality were so, even before we can prove it to be so, requires not *blind* faith, but epistemological reserve—humility before an enormous task— that is the foundation of our capacity for further rigorous inquiry. Those with this kind of faith need neither to disavow, misattribute, abuse, or forge their sources nor to rely on a theological foundation that is liable to crack with the next archaeological find.

"Blessed are those who have not seen and yet have come to believe." (Jn 20:29) Don Haymes is one of these.

---

[29] Jerry L. Sumney in an oral communication.

[30] Forgeries exist everywhere in the world; for example, recently in Japan where Shinichi Fujimora, an amateur archaeologist nicknamed "God's hand," apparently faked numerous prehistoric finds. A few years ago, a find, "Hitler's Diaries," duped some of Germany's best historians, at least for a while. The "Piltdown Man," a famous archaeological fake of a prehistoric human skeleton, has become synonymous with the game of hoaxes that forgers seem to enjoy perpetrating on a gullible public, both professionals and ordinary people alike.

Observations on
Contemporary Catholic Just War Thinking

Shaun Casey

One of the most interesting recent developments in the Churches of Christ is the rediscovery of our historic pacifism. Thanks to the work of Lee Camp, Michael Casey, and Richard Hughes, we now have a much better understanding of, and appreciation for, our pacifist legacy. This new awareness comes ironically at a time when the denomination as a whole is sliding deeper into the throes of the Bush Administration's neo-pagan doctrine of preventive war masquerading as Christian truth.[1]

What these scholars have recovered, however, Don Haymes never lost. For the twenty-six years I have known Don and benefited from his friendship, wisdom, humor, and counsel, he like no other has consistently maintained a learned pacifism.[2] As a near-pacifist, I dedicate this essay on "just war" to him, knowing full well that he will not be buying what I am selling.

In this essay I unapologetically commend a version of the just war ethic to my brothers and sisters in the Churches of Christ as an alternative to the Bush doctrine of preventive war.[3] As many aspiring Evangelicals within our movement, and beyond, seek closer ties to some conservative Roman Catholics in order to pursue a conservative political agenda that includes, among other things, defeating Democratic candidates, the issue of war and peace presents something of a stumbling block, for efforts in this direction find themselves in contradiction to the opposition of John Paul II and Benedict

---

[1] For a moral analysis of the current, second Iraq war and the Bush doctrine, see my essay, "Iraq, the Just War Ethic, and Preemptive War," in *War and Border Crossings: Ethics When Cultures Clash*, Peter French and Jason Short, eds. (Lanham, Maryland: Rowman and Littlefield, 2005).

[2] As I was preparing to traverse the once well-worn path from Abilene Christian University to Harvard Divinity School in the fall of 1979, LeMoine Lewis, of blessed memory, told me to be on the lookout for Don Haymes who also had been accepted into Harvard. LeMoine proceeded to pay Don the ultimate compliment, scholar to scholar: "I always learn something important from Don's writing."

[3] By "unapologetic" I mean to signal that I am engaging in a type of argument many Campbellites find difficult. Perhaps the best statement of my "method" is from Hans Frei's description of Karl Barth: "He took the classical themes of communal Christian language molded by the Bible, tradition and constant usage in worship, practice, instruction, and controversy, and he restated or redescribed them, rather than evolving arguments on their behalf." See Hans Frei, "Eberhard Busch's Biography of Karl Barth," in *Types of Christian Theology*, George Hunsinger and William C. Placher, eds. (New Haven and London: Yale University Press, 1992): 158. For exemplars, see William C. Placher, *Unapologetic Theology* (Louisville: Westminster John Knox Press, 1989); Ronald F. Thiemann, *Revelation and Theology* (Notre Dame: University of Notre Dame Press, 1985); and most daringly, Eugene F. Rogers, Jr., *Sexuality and the Christian Body* (Oxford: Blackwell Publishers, 1999).

XVI to the current Iraq war. In other words, I believe we are learning the wrong lessons from the wrong Roman Catholics. In these pages, I describe one trajectory of Catholic social teachings on war, and towards the end I briefly argue that the moral wisdom of this tradition leads to a condemnation of the current Iraq war as immoral.

One could tell the story of the current state of just war thinking many ways. I offer a portrait of just war thinking in the legacy of Catholic thought that descends from John Courtney Murray (1904-1967), who was primarily responsible for the resurrection of the tradition among Catholics in the middle of the 20th century. I discuss Murray's contribution vis-à-vis the teaching of the Roman Church, especially Vatican II (1962-65) and after, and focus the entire concern in terms of J. Bryan Hehir's critical extension of Murray's thought. At the end, I summarize Hehir's analysis of the Persian Gulf War from his just war perspective, and then, using the contemporary Catholic theory of just war as my analytical model, I assess the Iraq War to determine whether I think it be just.[4]

Catholic Just War Theory according to Vatican II

Recent Roman Catholic teaching on war and peace should be seen in the theological context of the Second Vatican Council, specifically as expressed in the text of *Gaudium et Spes*, the final document of the Council.[5] The achievement of *Gaudium et Spes* is the articulation of a theological conception of the social ministry of the Church using the combined resources of eschatology, Christology, and ecclesiology; the document places social ministry on an ecclesiological basis previously lacking in Catholic thought. The Church thereby gained a theological rationale for its *ad hoc* entrance into public affairs, which includes serving a catalytic role for public discourse.[6] According to *Gaudium et Spes*, the reason the Church enters into public or social ministry is to protect and promote the transcendent dignity of the human person. The "Introduction" states as follows:

> At all times the Church carries the responsibility of reading the signs of the time and of interpreting them in the light of the Gospel, if it is to carry out its task. In language intelligible to every generation, she should be able to answer the ever recurring questions which men ask about the meaning of this present life and of the life to come, and how one is related to the other. We must be aware of and understand the aspirations, the yearnings, and the often dramatic features of the world in which we live.[7]

This ecclesiological shift helped underwrite an explosion of social ministry by the Church during the four decades after Vatican II. The pastoral letters of the U.S. Conference of Catholic Bishops written in the Eighties should be seen as examples of the local Church

---

[4] The other significant contemporary trajectory of the just war ethic is represented by the work of Paul Ramsey and his student James Turner Johnson.

[5] Two standard commentaries on *Gaudium et Spes* are *The Church Today: Commentaries on the Pastoral Constitution on the Church in the Modern World*, Group 2000, ed. (Westminster: Newman Press, 1967) and *Pastoral Constitution on the Church in the Modern World*, Herbert Vorgrimler, ed., *Commentary on the Documents of Vatican II*, 5 (New York: Herder and Herder, 1969).

[6] J. Bryan Hehir, "Church-State and Church-World," *Proceedings of the Catholic Theological Society of America* 41 (1986): 56-58. Also see his "Catholicism and Democracy," in *Christianity and Democracy in Global Context*, John Witte, Jr., ed. (Boulder: Westview Press, 1993): 19-23.

[7] *Pastoral Constitution* (1969): 4.

working according to the parameter of the vision for social ministry set out in *Gaudium et Spes*.[8] The context for assessing the morality of war is now the whole Church. Contemporary ecclesiology in the Churches of Christ, I add parenthetically, lacks any such theological justification for the Church's role in the world in general, and it lacks as well any biblical, theological, or ethical analysis of the morality of war specifically.

As the paragraph quoted above demonstrates, a direct relationship connects this life and the life to come. The notion of finding total emancipation through human effort is rejected.[9] Chapter III, "Man's Activity in the Universe," is nonetheless an affirmation that the efforts of humanity to improve the circumstances of the world correspond to the plan of God.[10] The Council argued later in this chapter that the knowledge of a coming world does not diminish the need of concern for this world; on the contrary, knowledge of the world's need is an incentive for action:

> Far from diminishing our concern to develop this earth, the expectancy of a new earth should spur us on, for it is here that the body of a new human family grows, foreshadowing in some way the age which is to come. That is why, although we must be careful to distinguish earthy [sic] progress clearly from the increase in the kingdom of God, such progress is of vital concern to the kingdom of God, insofar as it can contribute to the better ordering of human society.[11]

This eschatological theme continues in the beginning of Chapter IV, "Role of the Church in the Modern World," with the affirmation that the Church has a saving and eschatological purpose that can be fully attained only in the next life. Since, however, the Church is present here and now, it believes it can contribute much to the humanizing of the world and its history through each of its members and its community as a whole.[12]

The Council recognized the presence of sin in human history and its corrosive effects, and yet the bishops confessed an eschatological vision of the world to come which fuels the activity of the Church in the world with a belief that the Church can have a meliorating effect. *Gaudium et Spes* is thus a chart according to which Catholics are to steer a course between a purely realized eschatology in which all the promises of the kingdom of God are seen as attainable here and now, and a purely futurist eschatology that might cause human effort in the world to be rejected as worthless. [13]

---

[8] Hehir made this case very soon after the publication of *The Challenge of Peace* in "From the Pastoral Constitution of Vatican II to *The Challenge of Peace*," in Philip Murnion, ed., *Catholics and Nuclear War: A Commentary on The Challenge of Peace: The U.S. Catholic Bishops' Pastoral Letter on War and Peace* (New York: Crossroad, 1983): 71-87. See also Hehir (1986): 67-70.

[9] *Pastoral Constitution* (1969): 10.

[10] *Ibid*.: 34.

[11] *Ibid*.: 39.

[12] *Ibid*.: 40.

[13] Charles Curran argued that *Gaudium et Spes*, while integrating the old natural law optimism of *Pacem in Terris* into a more theological approach, still comes out on the optimistic side. Curran pointed to a more realized eschatology in the theoretical sections of the document while noting the futurist eschatology in the sections of the document here cited. See the essays in *Commentary on the Documents of Vatican II*, vol. V, that give some of the details of some aspects of the composition of the different sections of the document. Taken as a whole, *Gaudium et Spes* seems to me to preserve

The Teaching of the American Catholic Bishops on Just War

The Challenge of Peace, the pastoral letter of the United States Conference of Catholic Bishops, is perhaps the most widely read moral document that was written in the United States during the 1980s. Bryan Hehir is known best for his having been its primary author. Hehir has also written widely on the application of Murray's model to other issues, including the history of Roman Catholic teaching on war and peace, and on the role of the Church in the world (discussed below).

The American bishops in *The Challenge of Peace* followed the eschatological orientation of Vatican II's *Gaudium et Spes* in the section, "Kingdom and History."[14] Here the bishops affirmed that while the kingdom of God is never fully realized in history, the Church lives in the tension between the "already" and the "not yet," that is, we live in the grace of the kingdom but not yet in the completed kingdom. "Christ's grace is at work in the world; his command of love and his call to reconciliation are not purely future ideas but call us to obedience today."[15]

The bishops noted further that this is the eschatological context in which Catholic social teaching has been addressed to the problem of war. This understanding of history, at once hopeful and confident but also sober and realistic, anchors hope in the belief in God as creator and sustainer, and the belief that the kingdom will come in spite of human sin. Recognition of sin, however, prevents the realization of the peace of the kingdom as permanent or total.[16]

The eschatology of *Gaudium et Spes* had begun a movement away from a more traditional natural-law position with its explicit theological and biblical tone, a tone quite different from the social teachings of the popes from Leo XIII to Pius XII,[17] a new tone that "becomes a staple of Catholic social teaching under John Paul II."[18] While clear traces of natural-law arguments remain in the post-Vatican II discussion of war and peace, these arguments are often in the background. This development is important because it narrows the gap between Catholic and Protestant styles of public theology. The Churches of Christ, by contrast, no longer possess any consensus on eschatology, whether realized or future; hence, appeals to any form of proleptic politics based on a mutually shared eschatology opens the door for colonization by conservative political ideologies such as President Bush's declaration that the United States is ridding the world of evil in the war on terror.

The final point regarding the theology of *Gaudium et Spes* is the prominence given to the problem of war. In the final chapter, "Fostering Peace and Establishment of a

---

an eschatological balance. See Curran's *The Living Tradition of Catholic Moral Theology* (Notre Dame: University of Notre Dame Press, 1992): 59, and *Directions in Catholic Social Ethics* (Notre Dame: University of Notre Dame Press, 1985): 43-69.

[14] *The Challenge of Peace*: 56-65.

[15] *Ibid.*: 58. See also Charles Curran, "Roman Catholic Teaching on War and Peace," *The Journal of Religious Ethics* 12 (1984): 69-71, on the role of eschatology in Catholic teaching on war and peace.

[16] *The Challenge of Peace*: 57, 61.

[17] J. Bryan Hehir, "The Social Role of the Church: Leo XII, Vatican II, and John Paul II," in Oliver Williams and John Houck, eds., *Catholic Social Thought and the New World Order* (Notre Dame: University of Notre Dame Press, 1993): 38.

[18] *Loc. cit.*

Community of Nations," the Council put the question of war at the center of its theological purview. The now famous call for "a completely fresh reappraisal of war,"[19] on the one hand, picks up Murray's earlier call for reviving the just war tradition, and on the other hand, this impetus supports much of the Catholic theological and moral analysis of war in the decades following the Council. This call for a reappraisal of war comes within a theological vision of how the Church relates to the world.

Catholic Just War Theory in the Thought of John Courtney Murray

Murray's approach to just war thinking is a "holist model" because of his willingness to incorporate theological, historical, and philosophical insights into his view.[20] At a superficial level it might appear to make sense to call this model "the Catholic model." The holist approach, however, while centered in Catholic social teachings, includes both the full scope of the tradition back to Augustine and the work of ethicists outside of the Catholic Church. Enough influences impinge on this trajectory that are from non-Catholic sources to render that designation too facile, and other Catholic visions of a just war ethic are available as well as this one.

The importance of history in the just war tradition resides primarily in Catholic social teachings and to a lesser extent in the Catholic social tradition.[21] Murray's landmark work was essentially a recovery of the just war ethic for the post-World War II Church. The holist model is a continuation of this legacy in Hehir's moral cartography of Catholic social teachings on war and peace. In his historical work, he dealt with the social tradition in its transition out of the High Middle Ages, but he concentrated mostly on twentieth-century papal and conciliar texts as well as the work of the U.S. Catholic bishops. In addition he chronicled the policy evolution of the nuclear age as part of the context for much of the social thought he examined.

According to the holist position, the historical development of doctrine does occur in Catholicism but neither simply nor quickly.[22] For example, as Hehir described Murray's

---

[19] "Pastoral Constitution": 80. See Hehir's analysis, "From the Pastoral Constitution of Vatican II to *The Challenge of Peace*," in Philip Murnion, ed., *Catholics and Nuclear War: A Commentary on* The Challenge of Peace: *The U.S. Catholic Bishops' Pastoral Letter on War and Peace* (New York: Crossroad, 1983): 71-86. See also Dominique Dubarle, O.P., "Schema XII and War," in Group 2000, ed., *The Church Today: Commentaries on the Pastoral Constitution in the Modern World* (Westminster: Newman Press, 1967): 229-282.

[20] John Courtney Murray, *We Hold These Truths* (New York: Sheed and Ward, 1960), remains his classic work.

[21] Here I am following the distinction between Catholic social tradition and Catholic social teaching as set out by Hehir, "Catholic Social Teaching," in *The HarperCollins Encyclopedia of Catholicism*, Richard McBrien, ed. (New York: HarperCollins, 1995): 280. The social tradition refers to biblical teaching, patristic writers, Augustine, Thomas, and the Spanish Scholastics, Suarez and Vittoria. Catholic social teaching refers to papal, conciliar, and synodal teaching on the political, social, economic, and international order. For another description of Catholic social teaching see Francis Fiorenza, "Church, Social Mission of," in Judith Dwyer, ed., *The New Dictionary of Catholic Social Thought* (Collegeville: The Liturgical Press, 1994): 151-171.

[22] J. Bryan Hehir, "Catholicism and Democracy: Conflict, Change, and Collaboration," in *Christianity and Democracy in Past Contributions and Future Challenges*, John Witte, Jr., ed. (Boulder: Westview Press, 1993): 18. See also J. Bryan Hehir, "The Right and Competence of the Church in

scholarship, thinking in tandem with papal teaching had led to profound changes in doctrine regarding the status of democracy:

> Murray's work, an individual achievement of scholarship, extended over 25 years; it often was done in tension with ecclesiastical teaching authority, and it found acceptance only after the event of the Council provided a new context for theological work in the Church. Murray once described the theologian's role as standing on the growing edge of the tradition. It was exactly where Murray placed himself, between the experience of American democracy and the pre-conciliar teaching on church and state. Murray mediated that dialogue and helped to revise the teaching of Catholicism on democracy.

> Murray worked with the categories of the tradition like a master craftsman. He took each of the major terms of the teaching and either redefined them (e.g., the state) or placed them in a new context (the idea of religious liberty). The end product of his effort was to provide an historical and theological explanation of Catholic tradition, which allowed Vatican II to affirm a relationship with the political order substantially different from the nineteenth-century teaching on democracy, the state, and human rights. Murray stressed, before and during the Vatican II debate on religious liberty, how the church could restructure its relationship with a democratic state without simply contradicting the teaching of the past. He wove a complex argument which stressed continuity of key themes, while calling for change in the conclusions of earlier teaching.[23]

Here we see how the historical development of doctrine takes place and how a scholar acts within that process. The stages of development of Catholic teaching on Church and state will continue.[24] Catholic social teaching is a living tradition in which each succeeding generation of the Church must engage with its ethos.[25]

Catholic social teaching on war and peace has functioned in a manner similar to Murray's work on church and state. Two important contributions have been to display the continuing relevance of the just war ethic in the face of a changing international system, and to help make moral and intellectual space for pacifism as a legitimate view for personal conscience in the Church, if not for policy. Hehir saw Murray's work as the single most important event in the renaissance of the just war tradition in Catholic social teaching. Murray summarized Pius XII's statements and compared them to the broader historical tradition. At the same time, Murray was also pushing the tradition as he

---

the American Case," in *One Hundred Years of Catholic Social Thought*, John Coleman, ed. (Maryknoll: Orbis, 1991): 63-65, for an elaboration of what changed in the Catholic view of democracy at Vatican II.

[23] J. Bryan Hehir (1993): 19-20; see also "The Perennial Need for Philosophical Discourse," *Theological Studies* 40 (1979): 710-713.

[24] J. Bryan Hehir, "Church and State," in McBrien, ed. (1995): 316. These five stages are: the Church and the Roman Empire; the Church in the medieval Christian period (*Respublica Christiana*); the Church confronting the post-Reformation nation-state; the Church and nineteenth-century liberalism; and the twentieth-century Catholic teaching before and after Vatican II.

[25] See Charles E. Curran, *The Living Tradition of Catholic Moral Theology* (Notre Dame: University of Notre Dame Press, 1992): 59.

grappled with the new realities of the Cold War and the nuclear age. In a manner similar to his work on the Church/state question, Murray was nudging the tradition to comprehend new realities. Without Murray as a catalyst, it is difficult to predict where Catholic thought on war and peace might have headed.[26]

Catholic Just War Theory according to J. Bryan Hehir

The bulk of Hehir's historical interest resides in the social teachings of the twentieth century. From the standpoint of content, at least six developments within the teaching on war and peace are noteworthy: the overall re-emergence of the just war ethic since Murray, the emergence of pacifism, the endorsement of selective conscientious objection, the application of the ethic to specific cases during and after the Cold War, the development of an ecumenical dialogue among scholars, and the engagement with policy specialists in international relations.

The re-emergence of the just war ethic after Murray came first with John XXIII and *Pacem in Terris*. In the years since John XXIII took up the papal ministry, Catholic teaching on war "has been in a state of movement, with the principal development being the legitimation of a pacifist perspective as a means of evaluating warfare."[27] *Pacem in Terris* is notable for three reasons: First, the strong critique of the arms race and its balance of terror is seen as evidence of the structural defects of the international political and legal system. Second, *Pacem in Terris*, unlike any other papal document, provides no explicit endorsement of the right of self-defense for people and states. Third, the most explicit moral judgment asserted in the section on war seems to call into question the very rationale of just war thinking: "Therefore, in this age of ours, which prides itself on its atomic power, it is irrational to think that war is a proper way to obtain justice for violated rights."[28]

Hehir went on to show that John XXIII did not provide an endorsement of a pacifist position here, as some commentators had argued, but that the tenor and the text of *Pacem in Terris* does signal a change in the Catholic evaluation of war. A specific endorsement of pacifism was to come, however, in *Gaudium et Spes*.

Endorsement of a pacifist position is to be seen within the endorsement of a non-violent philosophy and support for conscientious objection.[29] At the same time, the right to self-defense as articulated in the just war tradition continues to be endorsed in Catholic teaching in sources from Pius XII to *Gaudium et Spes*, as well as in much of the thinking of John Paul II. In a world of states devoid of an effective international political and legal authority, the right to legitimate defense remains an option for sovereign states.[30] Hehir rightly raised the question of whether the range of teaching between pacifism and just war thinking can be coherent.

---

[26] J. Bryan Hehir, "Murray on Foreign Policy and International Relations: A Concentrated Contribution," (Paper prepared for the Woodstock Center-Notre Dame Joint Project on John Courtney Murray, S.J., April 3-5, 1992).

[27] J. Bryan Hehir, "The Just-War Ethic and Catholic Theology," in *War or Peace? The Search for New Answers*, Thomas A. Shannon, ed. (Maryknoll: Orbis, 1980): 19.

[28] *Ibid.*: 20. *Pacem in Terris* as cited in *Gaudium et Spes*: footnote to fn. 80.

[29] *Ibid.*: 21-22.

[30] *Ibid.*: 22.

The development of the social teachings on war and peace come up to date in the statements of John Paul II.[31] Five basic thrusts in the pope's conception of international order are aimed at providing a moral structure for the decentralized international system: First, he demanded a concept of order in which the need of states and peoples unable to demand attention will be taken seriously. Second, he called for a devolution of superpower control in world affairs. Third, he desired that the devolution of the big powers would make space for others to surface, particularly the developing countries and a united Europe. Fourth, while concerned about the nuclear threat and the political life of nations, his most urgent demand was a revision of the rules and practices of international economic relations as they affect developing countries. Fifth, he affirmed that the test for international relations, as for domestic affairs, is individual human rights.[32]

The question of the implicit statecraft of the just war tradition is an area of increasing importance as the shape of the post-Cold War international system continues to evolve. The holist position calls for a concentration on the political-ethical demands of the tradition, since the focus on questions of means has receded as the Cold War threat subsided.[33] This emphasis on the shape of the international arena as a legitimate question of justice goes back in Catholic thought at least to Pius XII in modern times, and it is emphasized in *Gaudium et Spes*. In "Establishment of an International Community" (section 2, chapter 5), a series of norms is listed, intended to guide international bodies to promote the cause of peace and justice. One may reasonably expect that a significant part of future thinking within the holist orbit will focus on questions of the shape of international politics in light of normative concerns. Hehir summarized this methodological shift:

> The fear of proliferation [of nuclear systems particularly, but also of ballistic missiles and chemical weapons] fixes superpower attention on the systemic questions, but the agenda will inevitably go beyond safety in the system [from a superpower perspective] to justice in the system [from developing nations] and finally to the kind of moral order that can accommodate the needs of a world which is both nuclear and interdependent. Neither the moralists nor the strategists have spent enough time thinking about this question. Its appearance is a welcome sign for ethics and politics.[34]

This renewed examination of the political character of the just war ethic reveals that the content of the politics of the ethic includes several components: the need to examine

---

[31] J. Bryan Hehir (1991): 60-62; "War and Peace: Reflections on Recent Teaching," *New Catholic World* 226 (1982): 60-63; "Catholic Teaching on War and Peace: The Decade 1979-1989," in Charles Curran, ed., *Moral Theology: Challenges for the Future: Essays in Honor of Richard A. McCormick* (New York: Paulist Press, 1990): 359-364; "John Paul, Geopolitician," *The Boston Sunday Globe* (August 8, 1993): 69; "The Social Role of the Church: Leo XIII, Vatican II, and John Paul II," in Williams and Houck, eds. (1993); "John Paul II: Continuity and Change in Social Teaching," in Charles Curran and Richard McCormick, eds., *Readings in Moral Theology No. 5: Official Catholic Social Teaching* (New York: Paulist Press, 1986): 253-255.

[32] Hehir in Williams and Houck, eds. (1993): 40.

[33] J. Bryan Hehir, "Just War Theory in a Post-Cold War World," *The Journal of Religious Ethics* 20 (1992): 237-259.

[34] J. Bryan Hehir, "There's No Deterring the Catholic Bishops," *Ethics and International Affairs* 3 (1989): 295- 296.

war and strategy in relation to political judgment; concern for political authority and legitimacy; a test of last resort, requiring that political means be used to resist injustice before military means; emphasis on right intention as embodied in *jus ad bellum* criteria of the ethic.[35]

According to the holist model, one must address how the post-Cold War structure and substance of world politics can and should be fashioned. To be concerned with arms control, the decreasing chance of nuclear war, and non-proliferation means that a political ethic, rather than a strategic ethic, should be at the heart of the just war ethic.[36]

While advancing this argument for a renewed political ethic shaped by the just war ethic, Catholic social teaching is typically focused on the shape of international order. While most theorists of international relations posit an anarchical world system, Catholic teachers argue that the lack of any adequate political authority in world politics is an unfortunate and morally significant structural defect that frustrates the normal expectation for the international community.[37]

With the sweeping changes in the international arena, the normative questions of Catholic social thought may now be put realistically to the theorists of international relations. We may be seeing a convergence between the normative concerns of Catholic thought and the empirical concerns both of analysts and actors in world politics.[38]

The Challenge of Peace also reflects this concern for the need to establish just international venues as a means to make peace a reality. In the section, "World Order in Catholic Teaching," the pastoral letter is a recapitulation of Catholic teaching that the establishment of international order is the way to bring about a political order that, in turn, will bring about peace. "This positive conception of peace sees it as the fruit of order; order, in turn, is shaped by the values of justice, truth, freedom and love."[39]

The holist position is a demonstration of the use of philosophical concepts to express and clarify the moral force of the ethic in a manner that preserves the theological and historical integrity of the tradition. Around the time of the Vietnam War, two ethicists conceptualized the just war ethic in philosophical terms that were incorporated into the holist model. Drawing on the work of two Protestant ethicists, Ralph Potter and James Childress, Hehir argued that the tradition can be seen as a presumption/exception style of reasoning.[40] The presumption of the moral argument is against the use of force, and the burden of proof resides with those who argue the necessity of resorting to war.

---

[35] J. Bryan Hehir, "Just War Theory in a Post-Cold War World," *The Journal of Religious Ethics* 20 (1992): 252-253.

[36] *Ibid.*: 253.

[37] J. Bryan Hehir, "Christians and New World Disorders": 231-233.

[38] *Ibid.*: 233.

[39] *The Challenge of Peace*: 235. Perhaps the strongest critic of Hehir on international order is George Weigel, *Tranquilitas Ordinis* (Oxford: Oxford University Press, 1989). Weigel represents what might be called the right-wing heirs of Murray's legacy. Weigel argues, incorrectly, if my analysis is accurate, that Hehir represents a break with Murray and Catholic theology and the search for sound international political community.

[40] J. Bryan Hehir, "The Just-War Ethic Revisited," in Linda Miller and Michael Joseph Smith, eds., *Ideas and Ideals: Essays on Politics in Honor of Stanley Hoffmann* (Boulder: Westview Press, 1993): 144-161; J. Bryan Hehir, "The Just-War Ethic and Catholic Theology: Dynamics of Change and

In response to a prime question, whether or not lethal force may be employed, the just war tradition shares with pacifism an original presumption against violence. Whereas pacifism perceives this as an absolute prohibition of all force, the just war ethic sets out rules-governed exceptions, to use Potter's language; or, in Childress's view, it views the prohibition of force as a *prima facie* duty that may be overridden. Thus the just war presumption is not the pacifist's absolute opposition to all use of lethal force, but a presumption that yields to morally justified exceptions.

Three tests frame these justifiable exceptions: First, why may force be used? Second, when may force be used? And third, how is force to be used in a morally acceptable fashion?

These questions then yield the more specific technical criteria that have been traditionally seen in the *jus ad bellum* and *jus in bello* categories of the just war tradition. The first question, why may force be used, generates the just-cause criterion. The three historic justifications for just cause are first, to defend innocents from unjust attack; second, to restore rights wrongfully denied; third, to reestablish an order necessary for decent human existence. The "when" question generates a second set of tests designed to show that not every just cause provides a justification to go to war. Even with just cause, other considerations—such as right intention, proper authority, last resort, reasonable chance of success, and proportionality of ends—must be met. Once both the "why" and "when" tests are met, the moral debate shifts to the "how" question over the means of war. Here the criteria of discrimination, or non-combatant immunity, and of proportionality of means, come to the fore.

Hehir's Analysis of the Persian Gulf War according to Just War Theory

The Persian Gulf War (under the first President Bush) presented Hehir a straightforward case for the application of the just war ethic. His analysis is a nuanced application of the holist version of the just war tradition, and a complex moral analysis of the entire war effort.[41] Not intending to set forth here a full ethical evaluation of that war,[42] I present his judgments on the *jus ad bellum* criteria first and then the *jus in bello* criteria.

Continuity," in *War or Peace? The Search for New Answers*, Thomas A. Shannon, ed. (Maryknoll: Orbis, 1980): 18-19. Ralph B. Potter, Jr., "The Moral Logic of War," *McCormick Quarterly* 23 (1970): 203-233. James Childress, "Just-War Criteria," in *Moral Responsibility in Conflicts: Essays on Nonviolence, War, and Conscience* (Baton Rouge: Louisiana State University Press, 1982): 63-94. Both Potter and Childress are now more easily found in *War in the Twentieth Century*, Richard B. Miller, ed. (Louisville: Westminster/John Knox Press, 1992).

[41] J. Bryan Hehir in Miller and Smith, eds. (1993); *idem*, "Short-Term, Long-Term: Proper Means in the Gulf," *Commonweal* 117 (1990): 536-537; *idem*, "Baghdad as Target?: An Order to Be Refused," *Commonweal* 117 (1990): 602-603; *idem*, "The Moral Calculus of War," *Commonweal* 118 (1991): 125-126.

[42] A full evaluation would require consideration of the modest but robust literature on the morality of that military action: David E. Decosse, ed., *But Was It Just? Reflections on the Morality of the Persian Gulf War* (New York: Doubleday, 1992); Kenneth Vaux, *Ethics and the Gulf War* (Boulder: Westview Press, 1992); Alan Geyer and Dolores G. Green, *Lines in the Sand: Justice and the Gulf War* (Louisville: Westminster/John Knox Press, 1992); David Smock, *Religious Perspectives on War: Christian, Muslim, and Jewish Attitudes toward Force after the Gulf War* (Washington: United States Institute of Peace Press, 1992); Brien Hallet, ed., *Engulfed in War: Just War and the Persian Gulf War* (Honolulu: Spark M. Matsunaga Institute for Peace, 1991); Andrew Dean Walsh, "Political Realism and Just-War

Hehir noted that adequate reasons to affirm a just cause for war had to be put forward, and he indicted the inadequate reasons that had been alleged for war but that did not meet the standards for just cause.[43] The strongest case for just cause was the need to repel Iraq's invasion across an internationally recognized border. A complementary just cause was the response of preventing an invasion of Saudi Arabia in the face of the massive deployment of Iraqi troops near the Saudi border. To the contrary, Hehir noted that the expansion of the causes cited by the Bush Administration undermined the moral quality of the case for war. Specifically he argued that the "serious issues" of oil and nuclear proliferation were not just causes for war. An expansion of just cause to include these and similar arguments would be dangerous for world politics.[44]

The next *jus ad bellum* criterion is that for force to be justified, the action must be undertaken by a legitimate authority. Hehir cited approvingly the multilateral action in assembling the initial defensive force in Saudi Arabia. He did not grapple with the closeness of the Senate vote, and he did not speculate on what effect a negative Senate vote might have had on the concept of right authority. President George H. W. Bush's remark, that he did not need Congressional approval and would have proceeded without it, was not addressed.[45]

Hehir argued that the criterion of proportionality was the most controversial of the *jus ad bellum* criteria. His assessment of proportionality is complex. Because just cause reasons existed, and a chance of success seemed reasonable, judgments about proportionality were the major restraints on the decision to go to war. The costs of this success were unknown before the fighting started. The moral consideration of cost had to take into account casualties on both sides, some idea of the consequences in the short and long views, including political, material, and ecological considerations. Hehir also argued that the acknowledged losses had to be weighed in terms of a hierarchy of values. Any such comparison before hostilities is clearly a rough guess at best, but advocates of the just war ethic presume, nonetheless, that such assessments can morally be made.[46]

Hehir's analysis through the first two of the three phases of the moral discussion parallels the process of the war. In the initial period, September and October 1990, the

---

Rhetoric: The Case of the Persian Gulf War," (Ph.D. dissertation, Drew University, 1994), supervised by Robin Lovin.

[43] Hehir in Miller and Smith, eds. (1993): 154.

[44] *Loc. cit.,* Hehir noted that this is not to say they could not ever constitute just causes but that in this case they do not suffice.

[45] The whole question of the Constitution and the power to declare war stands in need of reassessment from the perspective of the just war tradition. While many people assume that the Constitutional process for declaring war worked flawlessly in the case of the Gulf War, such was not the case. Since World War II, the Executive branch has increasingly usurped war-declaring power from the Legislative branch. What constitutes right authority in our Constitutional framework is hardly a settled question. For analysis of the Constitutional issues, see Louis Fisher, *Presidential War Power* (Lawrence: University Press of Kansas, 1995), and Michael Glennon, "War and the Constitution," *Foreign Affairs* 70 (1991): 84-101.

[46] Hehir in Miller and Smith, eds. (1993): 157.

discussion focused on the criterion of just cause. Hehir saw just cause for a defensive deployment of coalition troops in Saudi Arabia but not for an offensive move.[47]

The second phase of the debate, from November 1990 to January 1991, shifted from questions of "why" go to war to questions of "when." Hehir elaborated that he opposed offensive action by the coalition forces against Iraq because it would be a disproportionate strategy.[48] He saw three different arguments pointing to enormous human and political costs.

First, he foresaw a ground war in which some forecasters were already predicting tens of thousands of American and Arab casualties. The accompanying air war would also produce unacceptable civilian deaths. Second, the scope of the war threatened to extend beyond Iraq and Kuwait, and kindle a war across the Middle East. Third, because of this uncertainty, the war undertaken to vindicate state boundaries in the Middle East could end up erasing most of the borders that currently defined the region. This outcome would not be proportionate.[49] In retrospect, these judgments were not accurate. We do not know the number of Iraqi civilian or military deaths, so it is impossible to assess fully the first concern. The second fear did not materialize, and thus neither did the third. All of this goes to show the provisional nature of much just war reasoning.

Hehir argued for a stringent observation of last resort.[50] In February 1991, he wrote that if he had been asked on January 17, 1991, he would have maintained that force not be used because of the likelihood of disproportionate outcomes and, therefore, the consequent need to honor the last-resort criterion stringently.[51] Here it is important to recall Ralph Potter's observation regarding last resort: "Every peaceable means of obtaining redress must have been tried and exhausted. Only a strict necessity can legitimate resort to force. Thus a 'preventative war' cannot be justified."[52]

After the war began, Hehir offered an explanation of his view that, despite his reservations about proportionality and last resort, he would not call the entire war unjust "purely and simply."[53] He cited two kinds of reasons for this position:

First, the weight of the moral case: Proportionality is by definition a consequentialist argument, always open to further debate; I had and have my ongoing doubts about the moral worth of war as the means to address Iraq, but I know that such a judgment, especially made *a priori*, as I did, is open to differing conclusions. Similarly, the judgment about last resort is by definition open to prudential calculations about what is possible, what is wise, and when have all efforts been exhausted.[54]

Hehir concluded that it was right to press the "when" criteria, but that the moral weight of the case does not compel a judgment that the war was unjust. This conclusion

[47] Hehir, "Short –Term…" (1990): 536.
[48] Hehir, "Baghdad…" (1990): 603.
[49] *Loc. cit.*
[50] Hehir, "Moral Calculus…" (1991): 125.
[51] *Loc. cit.*
[52] Ralph Potter, "The Moral Logic of War," published most recently in Richard Miller, ed., *War in the Twentieth Century* (Louisville: Westminster John Knox Press, 1992): 206.
[53] Hehir, "Moral Calculus…" (1991): 126.
[54] *Loc. cit.*

is reinforced, according to Hehir, when the consequences of such a judgment are assessed. These implications would include encouraging the persons involved in the war effort to cease and desist and oppose the policy of going to war. Hehir concluded in February 1991 that the war was just but unwise.[55]

The discussion of the *jus in bello* criteria shows an evolution in Hehir's thinking. Writing in 1993, he offered a modification of his earlier view of the justice of the war. While he was not willing to declare the whole war unjust on proportionality grounds, he was less likely to endorse "another enterprise with similar prospects" because the standards of justification in moving from the "why" and the "when" needed to be raised higher in light of the results in Iraq.[56]

Hehir reasoned that the principle of discrimination had been observed while proportionality of means was violated at times, hence resulting in civilian deaths and—in a "harder judgment"—disproportionate combatant deaths.[57] Hehir set out three tests for assessing the application of the *jus in bello* criteria of discrimination and proportionality: First, the targets chosen; then, the rules of engagement; and last, the results. The first two touch on intentionality and means; the third presumes right intention but requires an examination of the gap between intentions and consequences in warfare. In terms of the targets and rules of engagement, Hehir concluded, the principle of discrimination was observed by coalition forces in Iraq.

Hehir argued that the repeated bombing of sites in and near Baghdad violated proportionality limits and "verged on a policy of simply seeking to traumatize the leadership and, possibly, the population of Iraq."[58] Moreover, Hehir indicted the bombing of infrastructure that reduced much of Iraq to pre-industrial status.

Hehir acknowledged that the combatant aspect of proportionality of means was more difficult to assess in Iraq. First, no official statistics were released. Second, the traditional concern to reduce non-combatant casualties may have led to ignoring the costs of combatant casualties. Some estimates of up to 100,000 Iraqi combatant deaths may force reconsideration of the traditional criterion. He concluded that the rules of engagement used in bombing the retreating Iraqis in the last days of the war violated proportionality standards. Adding up all the moral analyses, Hehir came to this conclusion:

> These themes, combined with the enormous suffering that resulted from the suppression of the Kurds by Saddam Hussein, illustrate the inherently unpredictable character of modern warfare. The accuracy of "smart weapons" made it possible to avoid targeting civilians, but they also enhanced the allied capabilities to strike the infrastructure of water, sewage and electrical systems which an industrial society needs for the survival of its civilian population.

---

[55] *Loc. cit.*

[56] Hehir in Miller and Smith, eds. (1993): 158, was unwilling on purely consequentialist grounds to rule the war unjust; after the war, however, he seemed more inclined to raise the bar of *jus ad bellum* criteria.

[57] *Loc. cit.*

[58] *Loc. cit.*

...This mix of unintended consequences, human choices and vast technological power place great stress on the old categories. They also make judgments about clear verdicts of "just war" seem fragile.

Among the lessons of the Persian Gulf war for moralists are the need for a tighter set of proportionality tests, and attention to all those methods and means of policy which will make the presumption against war a difficult standard to overcome. The Gulf war shows that modern warfare fought under just-cause legitimation is still, at best, marginally moral. The emphasis must be placed on finding ways to meet just-cause concerns and preserve international peace and justice.[59]

In summary, Hehir's trajectory of the just war ethic is grounded theologically, is historically aware, is politically sophisticated in the face of the profound changes in the international system, and appropriates philosophical analysis (such as Potter and Childress do) in a theologically responsible manner. But the proof of the power in Hehir's holist approach is its faithfulness in fulfilling Murray's vision of the Church's teaching on war in assessing specific cases: It condemns war as evil, it seeks to limit the evil of war, and it seeks to humanize the conduct of war to the extent possible.

Three Concluding Observations

In conclusion let me offer three observations. First, as I have argued at length elsewhere, the current Iraq war fails to pass muster with this conception of the just war ethic.[60] From just cause to the other *jus ad bellum* criteria such as legitimate authority, right intention, last resort, and proportionality of ends, the current war fails to pass moral muster.

Second, while the Churches of Christ do not seem to possess the requisite theological gifts to develop a doctrine of the role of the Church in the world that is analogous to the eschatological view that fuels *Gaudium et Spes*, it is conceivable that these theological resources might be developed.

Third, it may take eating the bitter fruit of the current war before the people who populate our congregations and the men (and women) who lead them awaken from their slumber and see a different vision.

---

[59] *Ibid.*: 159.
[60] See footnote 1.

THREE PATHS TO EDEN:
CHRISTIAN, ISLAMIC, AND JEWISH FUNDAMENTALISMS

WILLIAM MARTIN

Most of the contributors to this volume have been touched—some of us walloped—by the socio-religious phenomenon known as fundamentalism, although we may not have called it that. As a student in "Denominational Doctrines" at Abilene Christian University, I was taught that fundamentalists believe in premillennialism, which was not part of the New Testament Church that our spiritual ancestors had perfectly restored in the 19th century after well more than a millennium of darkness; fundamentalists, therefore, were quite different from ourselves. Sociologically speaking, however, we were indeed fundamentalists, though we might be *left behind* when Jesus returns to rapture the saints from this *Late Great Planet Earth*. These decades later, I remain a Christian—of sorts—though my faith is a cyclical performer and seldom wanders far into orthodox territory, but my fascination with various forms of fundamentalism still abides with me as fast falls the eventide, faster than I had anticipated.

Because I have had personal acquaintance with fundamentalist religion, I use "fundamentalism" not in a pejorative sense but to refer to movements grounded in the fundamentals of a religious tradition, fundamentals that its proponents seek to reassert—or restore—in the face of perceived threat or loss. "Fundamentalism" is not a perfect term, and many to whom it is applied do not much like it, given the negative response it often generates, but it can be useful and is worth retaining. Typically, fundamentalism has a reactive, oppositional quality that distinguishes it from orthodoxy, which is more concerned with remaining faithful to a tradition than with fending off or conquering an opposing force. Fundamentalists are fighters, facing a serious threat.

Threats to fundamentalism tend to flow from the common and widespread processes of modernization and secularization. These processes are not so inextricably related to one another as many have thought. The USA, for example, is at or near the top on almost any measure of modernization, yet it remains one of the most religiously vital countries in the world. Islamic revival often finds its most fervent advocates not in rural villages but among well-educated professionals and engineers in major urban centers. Fundamentalists have, moreover, proved quite skilled at using the tools of modernity—radio, television, computers, the Internet—to spread and support their message. Still, modernity or, more specifically, "modern consciousness," does pose a distinct threat to any traditional order, religion included. As business, medicine, education, politics, law, the military operate more and more "without benefit of clergy," without reference to what God wants us to do, religion becomes compartmentalized and loses its power and influence in other institutional spheres. Fundamentalism, then, is a reassertion of religious authority, an attempt to revitalize a sacred tradition and administer it as an antidote to a society that has strayed from its cultural moorings. Fundamentalism rejects the separation between the sacred and the secular that has evolved with modernization; it is an attempt to bring religion back to center stage as an important—indeed, the overriding—factor in public policy decisions.

Fundamentalism can take numerous forms. Within days preceding my writing of this essay, I have read a book about Mormon fundamentalism, discussed a type of Catholic fundamentalism with a relative, and thought actively about a form of Indian nativism referred to as Hindu fundamentalism. In this essay, however, I want to concentrate on three forms of fundamentalism with particular relevance to contemporary world affairs: Protestant Christian, Islamic, and Jewish. These three differ from each other, and fundamentalist factions within each tradition differ among themselves, but they tend to share a number of characteristics.

Common Characteristics of Fundamentalisms

Fundamentalism typically involves an attempt to reclaim the values and practices of a Golden Age, an earlier, allegedly finer and more pristine era with a good and just moral order: for example, the New Testament Church, early America as a Christian Nation, a City Set on a Hill; the era of the Prophet Muhammad and his Rightly Guided Companions; the Lithuanian *Shetl*, where true Judaism was authentically practiced; the description of the pristine time includes an account of how this idealized and romanticized social order went astray. Reminiscent of the story of the Garden of Eden, found in both the Bible (Genesis 2-3) and the Qur'an (Sura ii and vii, v. 19-25), fundamentalism identifies symbols of evil, delineates moral breakdown, and condemns the corruption of values.

A second key characteristic is an authoritarian interpretation of God that allows the fundamentalist easily to sort humanity into two groups: those who believe and those who do not, the saved and the unsaved, the true followers of God and the disciples of the Great Satan. There are no shades of gray between light and dark. Opposing thought is to be condemned and stifled.

Closely related to this authoritarian view of God is an emphasis on the authority of scripture and related sacred traditions with a corresponding rejection of critical history, empirical science, and the claims of human reason. This often manifests itself in a preference for schools that emphasize subjects and approaches supportive of the fundamentalist tradition's worldview.

Fundamentalists often give greater attention to superstructural issues than to foundational matters. For example, they may show more concern about drinking alcohol, sexuality, pornography, profanity, modes of dress, segregation of the sexes, observance of a sacred day (the Muslim Friday, the Jewish Sabbath, or the Christian Sunday), performance of ritual (baptism, prayers, ceremonial reading), keeping fasts, eating or not eating certain foods, resisting innovation (for example, the Southern half of my 19th-century fundamentalist background, the Stone-Campbell Restoration Movement, resisted the encroachment of instrumental music in worship, a prohibition that endures to this day in about one-half of the congregations associated with this movement), and abstaining from dancing and such like. Fundamentalists tend to "major in minors" like these rather than focusing on "the weightier matters" such as justice, economic fairness, fair treatment of religious and ethnic minorities, preservation of the environment, or war and peace.

Fundamentalisms are typically patriarchal. Women are consistently regarded as properly subordinate to men.

Fundamentalists usually show a preference for theocracy, or at least greater unity between church and state. This is strongest among Muslims, muted among American Christians by the firmly entrenched tradition of church/state separation but under increased challenge (for example, the growing favor for government support of "faith-based" charities and provision of vouchers for use in private schools), and quite alien to some forms of Jewish orthodoxy, while intrinsic to others.

Fundamentalists make a claim of absolute knowledge. All that is truly necessary is part of the tradition; anything that contradicts the tradition is wrong. They lay claim also to absolute values that contrast with the cultural and ethical relativism that is part of the definition of modernity.

The major forms of contemporary fundamentalism all claim that human history as we know it will end by supernatural intervention, typically featuring the appearance of a messiah and initiation of a new Golden Age.

Protestant Fundamentalism

Fundamentalism has swept through Christianity in America in two great waves, the first of which was at approximately the three-quarter-point of the 19th century, following on the heels of the Second Great Awakening. Evangelical Christianity was then the dominant form of religion in America, characterized by confidence in the reliability of scripture, an emphasis on personal piety, and heavy involvement in an impressive variety of reformist voluntary associations. Following the Civil War, Protestant orthodoxy was hit with a series of major challenges. Darwin's theory of evolution challenged the Biblical account of creation; if Darwin was right, then the Bible was in error and God was not needed to explain the origin of species. German Biblical Criticism challenged the inspiration of scripture; if this "higher criticism" was right, then the Bible, like other ancient books, had been assembled from various sources, some with competing agendas, was not of supernatural origin, and its history and its science were not to be regarded as authoritative. At about the same time that Protestants were becoming cognitively dismayed, immigration by Jews, Catholics, Eastern Europeans, and Mediterranean Europeans challenged and weakened the traditional hegemony in America of Northern-European Protestants. Industrialization and the attendant urbanization brought about an increase in secularization and, with the growth of poverty and associated ills, undermined optimistic views of progress and human nature that had characterized evangelical preaching, particularly before the war. Some churches, especially those whose clergy had been influenced by the new Biblical studies and had lost some confidence in the reality of heaven and hell, began to proclaim a Social Gospel that placed more emphasis on this-worldly outcomes than on questions of eternal life. Ironically, because evangelicals associated the Social Gospel with decline in conservative views of scripture, they largely retreated from their earlier involvement in service-oriented efforts. In response, then, to these late-19th-century and early-20th-century developments, Protestant Christian Fundamentalism arose and took on the characteristics by which we still recognize it.

Before the rise of Biblical Criticism, American Christians had no strong, well-delineated doctrine of Biblical inspiration. As Christians had done for centuries, they simply assumed that the Bible, as the word of God, was true and reliable. Now, they needed to formulate a defense against the new attacks and articulate a position on inspiration. The crucial work was done at Princeton Theological Seminary. The heart of the "Princeton Theology" is that God could not and would not convey truth through an errant document; therefore, any doubting of scripture is heresy, a sign of unChristian attitude. This remains the position held by most Protestant fundamentalists today. Those who deviate from this position and suggest that some of the moral and cultural prescriptions found in the Bible need to be revised to reflect a new situation after the passing of two or three millennia, or who give the wrong answer to test questions specifically designed to smoke them out, can be thrown out of a church, fired from a seminary, removed from power in a denomination, taken off a Christian radio or television station, ostracized from circles of friends, and marked as persons whose views should no longer be considered.

Closely related to firm belief in biblical inspiration, and utterly dependent on it, was increased interest in biblical prophecy, and particularly in the doctrine of premillennialism—the notion that Christ would return to reign on earth for a thousand years before the final wrap-up of history. In its current form, this doctrine teaches that ordinary human history will occur in accord with a detailed plan laid out by God in the scriptures but overlooked by Christian theologians for 1800 years. (Many Protestant premillennialists are unaware of their 19th-century forebears among the Darbyite Dispensationalists.) When Christ comes again, he will "rapture" faithful Christians up into the heavens where they will escape "the tribulation," seven truly terrible years on earth; he will exercise command over his triumphant forces during the "Battle of Armageddon" and will then set up his millennial kingdom on earth and reign from his capital, Jerusalem. Because this will happen "soon," human efforts to change social conditions and preserve the environment are pointless. The key task is to bear witness to as many souls as possible before the Lord returns. This doctrine (or some version of it) is widespread within the Christian Right and has enormous consequences for American foreign policy.

Between 1910-1915, a widely distributed set of twelve small volumes entitled *The Fundamentals: A Testimony of the Truth*, written by some of the most respected men in the movement, established "fundamentalist" as the most common term to identify the conservative wing of American Protestantism. In 1919, the term gained further currency by the founding of the World Christian Fundamentals Association (WCFA) at a Philadelphia meeting attended by 6,500 delegates and led by the luminaries, most of whom lived in major northern cities. Fundamentalists of this period were fond of drawing up lists of "Fundamentals of the Faith," from which no deviation could be tolerated. They tried to purge their denominations of "Modernists," whom they considered to be unfaithful. Not surprisingly, this confrontational approach met with considerable resistance. The worst conflicts came among the Presbyterian and Northern Baptist churches, which eventually opted for a more flexible form of Christianity and squeezed the fundamentalists out. Not all the action was in the North. In the South, anti-evolutionists made concerted efforts to prohibit the teaching of evolution in public schools, culminating in the Scopes Trial in 1925. Though Scopes was convicted, fundamentalism was held up to ridicule throughout the world.

In 1920, fundamentalism had seemed to be on a roll. It was energetic and growing. It counted Billy Sunday and William Jennings Bryan, two of the most famous men in America, among its leaders, and it celebrated a great victory with the passage of Prohibition in 1919. By the end of the decade, however, fundamentalists were in retreat, seemingly defeated and perhaps even headed for extinction. Instead, they consolidated, built on their strengths, and transformed themselves in anticipation of new opportunities. They formed numerous fundamentalist alliances, similar to the World Christian Fundamentals Association. They built large independent congregations, the forerunners of today's megachurches. They established Bible Colleges and Institutes to train people for various ministries, without exposing them to the corrupting influences of the liberal arts. They made extensive use of print and electronic media, laying firm foundations for today's religious broadcasting and the enormous popularity of religious publications.

In the early 1940s, an influential group of more moderate leaders decided it was time to come out of the wilderness and re-engage the world on less confrontational terms, to emphasize evangelism more than the protection of sound doctrine. That wing eventually became what we now call Evangelicalism, with Billy Graham as the best-known representative and most influential leader. The more conservative segment was led by Carl McIntire, who had broken away from Princeton and who continued to be a fundamentalist firebrand until his death in 2002 at the age of 95.

Fast-forwarding a few decades to the 1960s and after, we encounter a morphed fundamentalism, the Christian Right, also a reactive movement. Most of its founders and members share a background of non-involvement with the secular world: As a matter of theological conviction, they once believed their primary task was to win souls, not elections. Millions did not even vote. That has changed, they claim with considerable justification, because perceived threats have forced them into the political arena. During the 40 years since the Consciousness Revolution of the '60s (another Great Awakening in America), a series of catalyzing events and developments—Supreme Court decisions prohibiting school-sponsored prayer and Bible reading, the widespread introduction of sex education into the schools, feminism, abortion, gay rights, AIDS, soaring divorce rates, sex and violence in the media, etc.—either generated direct response or fomented situations that continue to call for Christian moral action.

Beyond these concerns, fundamentalist Christians have also been deliberately, carefully, and aggressively recruited into politics by such conservative operatives of the New Right as Richard Viguerie, Paul Weyrich, and Howard Phillips, associated with such organizations as the Heritage Foundation and the Free Congress Foundation, a process that I describe in detail elsewhere.[1] It is easily possible to under- or over-estimate the real impact of the Christian Right, but the following assertions seem reasonably safe:

---

[1] William C. Martin, *With God on Our Side: The Rise of the Religious Right in America* (New York: Broadway Books, 1996; revised edition, 2005), the companion book to the 1996 PBS television series by the same title, also available

Thousands of fundamentalist and evangelical pastors and millions of their flocks who were not much involved in politics until about 1980 have become convinced their Christian duty compels them to get involved. They represent millions of rather easily mobilized votes, and they are likely to cast their votes on the same side of a number of identifiable issues. Moreover, many who were recruited into politics by the Christian Right no longer see themselves as needing to wear that theological label. They are simply Republicans, the Party of traditional values, now possessing a great deal more sophistication and knowledge of how our political system works.

Christian fundamentalists dominate Republican Party organizations in at least 18 States, and they have substantial influence in at least 26 other State Republican organizations, for a total of 44 States—all the States but six in the Northeast and the District of Columbia. In about half of the 26 States, more moderate Republicans are offering strong resistance. In the Republican-majority Congress in place in January 2005, the top echelon of Republican leaders in both the House and the Senate received approval ratings of 87-100 percent on the 2004 Christian Coalition Scorecard, indicating their vote on issues of key interest to Christian conservatives; the highest score received by their Democratic counterparts was 16 percent.

The Christian Right controls the Party platform. Though political platforms tend to be more symbolic than substantive, they are an important symbol. Because they are "official," they have a way of causing people to think they ought to be taken seriously. Christian conservatives have thus been phenomenally successful at getting their agenda on the record, and they are working to get their beliefs incorporated into public policy.

Their agenda is the same list of aversions to modernity and secularity mentioned above: opposition to abortion, gay rights, pornography, violence and sex in the media; secular humanism in the schools, the teaching of evolution, and any form of sex education that is not abstinence-based. They support student vouchers for private religious schools; they favor a greater presence in public venues for religious symbols such as crosses and the Ten Commandments, and for rituals such as prayer in the schools and other public settings, and including "...under God" in the Pledge of Allegiance. Since many of these issues fall under the jurisdiction of the courts, they press for the nomination and confirmation of conservative judges—from the Supreme Court on down.

On foreign policy issues, they push hard for sanctions against nations that persecute Christians or that restrict evangelistic work among native populations. They oppose giving aid to countries or to organizations such as the United Nations or the World Health Organization if any of the money can be used to pay for abortions. In large measure because of opposition from the Religious Right, the United States has cancelled or severely reduced contributions to the U.N. Population Fund, jeopardizing a program that provides contraceptives to nearly 1.4 million women in 150 countries. Pressure from Christian conservatives has also led to legislation stipulating that all federal monies for sex education in U.S. schools ($167 million in 2004) go to abstinence-only programs that are forbidden to provide information about contraceptive options. In a similar spirit, Congress currently requires that one-third of all funds allocated to the global HIV/AIDS pandemic ($2.9 billion in 2004) be spent on abstinence-only programs, rather than for such proven disease-reduction measures as instruction about safe sex and distribution of condoms.

Surprising to some, fundamentalist Christians also tend to be critical of multinational or broad-scope organizations such as the European Union, the Trilateral Commission, the Council on Foreign Relations, The International Court of Justice, and the World Council of Churches. In part, this stems from standard-issue isolationism and a fear of compromising American safety and economic interests and sacrificing national sovereignty to an international, liberal world order. But it also relates to the premillennialist doctrine that before Jesus returns, a great consolidation of power will take place under the headship of The Antichrist in the area that covers the old Roman Empire. Any significant transnational organization—especially the E.U.—is an easy target for suspicion.

This same doctrine of premillennialism is responsible for the Christian Right's unwavering and uncritical support of Israel, making Christian fundamentalists the greatest friends that Israel has in America, apart from Jews. This doctrine also teaches that Jesus will not return until Jews are in possession of the whole Land of Promise, both Judea and Samaria, including those parts now called "the West Bank;" and until the Temple has been rebuilt in Jerusalem, on Temple Mount, where the Dome of the Rock and the Al-Aqsa Mosque now stand, the third holiest site in Islam after Mecca and Medina. By this standard, then, dismantling the settlements in Palestinian areas cannot be condoned, whereas a takeover of all Jerusalem by Israelis is permissible. If the settlements go, and the Temple is not rebuilt, Jesus will not come, and the millennium will continue to be postponed.

Although the fundamentalist Christian Right is not a juggernaut that can level all opposition, it is clearly a formidable movement with a powerful set of resources. Enmeshed in webs of churches and clergy, reinforced by the intense personal networks common in congregations, and exposed repeatedly to a clear theological and political message in sermons, religious publications, mass mailings, email, television, and talk radio, its members tend to have a missionary zeal seldom matched by those on the left and almost never by the more moderate middle. Even more important, they are determined not to give up the fight, especially since they seem to be winning more and more rounds.

Islamic Fundamentalisms

The worldwide resurgence of Islam, which includes a fundamentalist response but is not limited to it, is also a reaction to crisis. The crisis for Islam has been painfully acute. The rapid expansion of Islam during its formative period, much of it by conquest, seemed to be self-evident confirmation of its truth. Within a hundred years after Muhammad's death in 632 C.E., Islam spread from Arabia westward to Spain and eastward to India, consequently becoming the enlivening spirit of rich and flourishing civilizations that reached into Asia, swallowed up the Christian Byzantine East, and are still effectively working their way southward through Africa. The spread of Islam, a religion that teaches the common brotherhood of all men and simple allegiance to the Almighty, is one of the more remarkable movements in human history. Its success was seen as proof that it was of God.

Beginning in the 17th century and progressing steadily until after World War I, the great Ottoman Empire—that is to say, Islamic civilization centered in Turkey—began to be overrun and dismantled by European forces, primarily the French, the British, and the

Russians. These European nations, once scorned by Muslims as backward and inferior—and they were right about that at the time—had become the beneficiaries of Modernity, Enlightenment, and the Industrial Revolution, and now possessed superior weaponry, superior strategy, superior science, superior technology, superior organization. If Islam ("complete submission to the will of Allah") is invincible, how could such a new thing in history have come about? The collapse of international Islam into squabbling national and ethnic enclaves precipitated a crisis in the religion itself, a challenge to the legitimacy of Islam. If Muslim power had been a sign of divine favor, its decline could only mean that favor had been lost. Divine revelation warned that departure from the straight path of Islam meant the loss of God's guidance and protection, and now it had happened. The decline of Islam demanded a response, and several were forthcoming.

On the radical left, some leaders met the onslaught of modernity by opting for a secularist approach. They discarded much that stood in the way of accommodating the West, and they rejected Shari'a (the legal tradition based on the Qur'an, the holy book), the Sunnah (sayings of the Prophet), and the Hadith (traditions about the Prophet) as the basis for law and society. The most successful example of this approach was in Turkey, where Mustafa Kemal Ataturk and the Young Turks called for, among other unthinkable changes, the separation of the religious and political realms and the complete emancipation of women.

Others, sometimes called Islamic Modernists or Reformists, tried to bridge the gap between Islamic concepts and modernity, and to adapt the new technologies and political and administrative ideas to the structures of Middle Eastern societies. They stressed the need for independence from foreign control, but they did not repudiate the Western ethos and Western ways. They also urged a revival of *ijtihad*, the use of reason and common sense, rather than upholding a traditional ethos that was no longer working.

A third and increasingly prominent response was, and continues to be, fundamentalist Islam—also known as Islamic Activism, Political Islam, or simply Islamist—an insistence on an overwhelming rejection of non-Muslim, secular society, and on exact fulfillment of the Shari'a, with strong emphasis on the comprehensive and universal nature of the message of God as presented in the Qur'an.

In this view, religious leaders are justified in trying to get, seize, and infiltrate power. The American model of church/state separation is viewed as false and inferior. Some Muslim fundamentalists are willing to use violence, armed *jihad*, in their efforts to make Muslim countries more Muslim and eliminate secularists as well as Christians and Jews, and to strike out at non-Muslim powers in their own lands. If this cannot be managed by force, by the strong form of *jihad*, then *hijrah* (separation) is mandatory.

The fundamentalist response grows most when Muslim societies experience modernization intensely. The first leaders to encounter the West typically experiment with secularism and reform. As the masses begin to get caught up, fundamentalist leaders perceive the threat and attempt to preserve traditional ways. One way to do this is to keep the sacred canopy over culture and society securely in place. This reaffirmation of the past is understandably attractive to sincere Muslims, for it depicts Islam as a divinely inspired, comprehensive, self-sufficient ideology that offers a way to fend off the secularizing influences and practices that threaten the tradition.

Though Islamic fundamentalism came to full flower in the 20th century, it is important to note that by the 18th century, before the confrontation with the European powers became critical, Muslim societies were showing serious signs of strain, as large empires always do, and some reformers had begun to call for a socio-moral reconstruction of society on the foundations of Islam. The most important early voice of reform was the Wahhabi movement, established on the Arabian peninsula by Muhammad Ibn 'Abd al-Wahhab in the mid-1700s. Wahhab challenged the compromises and moral laxity he believed the Muslim states had made. He and his followers did not like compromise and sought to purify and perfect the faith of individual believers and to call on rulers to assist them in this effort. They also emphasized the universalistic character of Islam, the global community of the faithful—the ummah. Wahhab was supported by Muhammad al-Sa'ud, a local ruler (1745-65).

The Wahhabi state is based on the close cooperation of a learned teacher (shaykh) and an able commander (emir), a combination of religious and political leadership advantageous to both. The original Wahhabis helped the Saudis gain control of most of the Arabian peninsula and solidified "Wahhabism" as a major reform movement in modern Muslim history. Osama bin Laden is a current example of Wahhabism. The Saudi monarchy needs cooperation and approval of the ulama (the religious authorities) to enhance its legitimacy; the ulama need royal support to maintain their privileges and wield some influence over policy-making. Although considerable tension exists, the royal family winks at the excesses of the Wahhabis in return for their support, and the Wahhabis tolerate the royal family's excesses in return for monetary and political support. Wahhabism today continues to call for the Islamization of society and the creation of a political order that gives appropriate recognition to Islam. It continues to operate within the modern world but was not initiated as a result of conflict with the modernized Western powers. It is the most enduring experiment within the broader mission of Islam, and it has provided a standard against which other movements and states have been measured. Wahhabism's export has been made possible by the sale of Saudi petroleum products. Apart from oil, and financed by it, Wahhabism is Saudi Arabia's chief export.

The first major movement in the 20th century was the Muslim Brotherhood, founded in Egypt in 1928 by Hasan al-Banna, who organized groups dedicated to improving the moral life of students and helping people to live more strictly in accord with Islamic law and to resist what he regarded as a new crusade to destroy Islam by means of social corruption and unbelief. Though the Muslim Brotherhood was not an official political party, it became a significant political force, primarily through organizing or participating in mass demonstrations. After a member of the Brotherhood assassinated the Egyptian prime minister in 1948, al-Banna was murdered and the Brotherhood was officially suppressed, but it did not disappear. When members of the group tried to kill President Nasser, who took control of Egypt in 1952, many of them were executed or put into prison, where a substantial number became even more radicalized. Muslim Brotherhoods developed in Syria and the Sudan, and similar groups arose in other countries. Though without formal ties, they shared many common interests and tactics. The Brotherhood remains active today, but has become somewhat mellowed as it has gained ground in professional associations of doctors, lawyers, pharmacists, engineers, and university professors.

A second key figure, with ties to the Muslim Brotherhood, was another Egyptian, Sayyid Qutb (1906-1966). Qutb visited the United States in 1948 and was thoroughly repulsed by what he saw. In his voluminous writings, the most important of which is *Milestones*, he provided an intellectual and theoretical foundation for the rejection by Muslims of both Nasser's attempts to develop a distinctive Arab Socialism and other Western-based ideologies. Qutb told Muslims that they must combat—violently if necessary—*jahiliyya* (unbelief; also, the state of society before Islam) wherever they find it, especially in regimes that claim to be Muslim but whose implementation of Islamic precepts are seen as imperfect. Because of his harsh criticism of Nasser's regime, Qutb was arrested in 1954 and spent ten years in prison before being brought to trial and hanged in 1966. He was, however, allowed to write while in prison and he is often regarded as the true father of modern Islamic fundamentalism.

The only person whose thought and writing have rivaled Qutb's in popularity and influence was Maulana Abul Ala Maududi, the founder in 1941 of Jamaat-I-Islami, a militant Pakistani movement that also helped spawn the Taliban. Southeast Asia also gave rise to the Tablighi Jamaat, which is more concerned with personal piety than with political activism, and is extremely conservative on matters such as the role of women, proper dress and appearance, and strict observance of devotional practices, and which spreads its message by means of itinerant evangelists working in teams.

The cultural challenge of the North Atlantic civilization presents Muslim fundamentalism with several targets. One is imperialism—the historical fact that the Islamic world began to crumble under the impact of Early Modern European civilization deeply disturbs fundamentalists of Islam. Now in its 14th century, Islam in many countries is quite "medieval" (to use a fine word in a pejorative way); many Muslims know this, and resent being looked down on by sophisticated Europeans and Americans. Modern and secular values are also seen as threatening to a godly life. Muslim fundamentalists condemn, for example, Western materialism, sexual and other forms of immorality as seen in movies and on television and in the addictive use of alcohol and drugs. Capitalism and communism, both of them North Atlantic models of social and economic organization, are seen as dangers contrary to the revealed truth of God and destructive to Muslim culture. Moderate Muslims have new models of Islamic economics, including Arab Socialism, but these have not been notably successful.

Patriarchal subordination of women is common, reaching extremes in those Islamic societies where women may not appear in public without a male escort, may not drive, may not receive an education beyond learning how to be a wife and mother, may not engage in a range of occupations, and certainly may not vote. This varies from Muslim country to Muslim country; in Egypt, for example, the liberation of women is far more advanced than in most other Muslim countries, but even in Egypt, fundamentalist elements are agitating to return to the purity of patriarchal control. Even where women have been granted certain rights, a fundamentalist takeover can quickly rescind them, as occurred in Afghanistan under the Taliban.

The State of Israel looms large in the consciousness of Muslims. The partitioning of Palestine and the founding of the State of Israel in 1947-48 was a severe blow to Arab pride and Palestinian nationalism when a half-million Jews re-entered the Land after a 2,000-year absence, occupied the Holy City (Palestinian Muslims think of Jerusalem as their "Mother"), appropriated their houses and orchards, and forced an entire generation of Palestinians to grow up inside the barbed-wire confines of Arab concentration camps. The combined efforts of five Arab states and indigenous Palestinians were unavailing against this new Conquest of Canaan, a wound that bled for 20 years, only to be deepened in 1967 by the Six-Day War, when the Israelis, in a lightning show of military power and strategy, seized everything west of the Jordan, including Jerusalem, and south to and including the Sinai Peninsula. At this lowest point of decline in Arab fortunes, jokes and cartoons poking fun at Arab impotence were humiliating to Arabs. In this state of war, fundamentalist Jews carried the encroachment farther by settling on Palestinian land, which continued to feed Arab outrage. To the Muslim mind, the suggestion that a tiny nation, officially secular but overwhelmingly Jewish and backed by European and American power, can dominate nations that believe themselves to be in complete submission to God, is intolerable. Muslims are convinced that were it not for American-made *Apache* helicopters and F-16 fighter planes and billions of dollars from American Jews and the U.S. government, this history would have been different.

American foreign policy offers other causes for offense: sanctions and then war against Iraq, failure to offer sufficient support to Muslims in Chechnya and Kashmir, support of corrupt regimes in various countries, and the presence of American troops in Saudi Arabia, the home of Mecca and Medina, Islam's two most hallowed sites.

For those involved—and it is important to insist that they are not the majority of Muslims—this is a true Culture War, whose aim is not only to defeat or drive out the infidel, but also to rediscover or recreate a satisfactory personal and communal identity. It is a search for authority, for roots, for a new birth. This is the perfect soil for fundamentalism.

Islamic fundamentalism differs from region to region and group to group, based mainly on intensity of commitment. Some are so consumed that they cannot tolerate the failings of their own governments, so they declare war on their rulers. The most famous example of this, of course, is the 1979 revolution in Iran, where Shi'a forces inspired by such as Ayatollah Ruhollah Khomeini ousted the modernist (but dictatorial) regime of the Shah and established the most successful fundamentalist regime to date. In Algeria, a strong showing by the Islamic Salvation Front in 1991 elections led to a crackdown by the military, which led in turn to the rise of the Armed Islamic Group, a powerful organization that launched a brutal guerilla war against government forces, journalists and intellectuals, and, eventually, ordinary Algerians who did not follow the Shari'a. Though they have failed to achieve their goal of reforming their societies, fundamentalists in Egypt engineered the assassinations of Anwar Sadat in 1981 and radical Islamists continue to bedevil the monarchy in Saudi Arabia. Because they enjoy the certainty of knowing God's will, they feel justified in using any means, and they readily adopt violent methods, including terrorism. If they reach power, they attempt to implement a program based on Shari'a. This inevitably arouses resistance and makes it necessary to exercise coercive control.

The fundamentalist response became so widespread during the last quarter of the 20th century, particularly after the success of the Iranian Revolution and again after the *mujahedin* drove the Russians out of Afghanistan, enabling the Taliban to seize power, that an Islamic leader who fails now to appeal to religion to bolster his regime will squander important political capital. Appeal to religion makes strategic sense when one considers the widespread revival of Islamic practice, as reflected in dress, observance of prayers and other obligations, involvement in youth organizations, and energetic missionizing.

Fundamentalism has strong appeal as masses of people try to preserve their traditional way of life, and those whom fundamentalist leaders such as Osama bin Laden recruit are not only the oppressed. They are often people who have a good education, who come from good backgrounds, and who are socially conscious and eventually radicalized by their desire for reformation and restoration of pristine Islam. Islamic governments vary from the arguably democratic regimes in Turkey and multi-cultural Indonesia to the oppressive, divine-right monarchy of Saudi Arabia, but all of them clearly feel the pressure of the fundamentalist impulse, a threat that those in power correctly perceive as ominous.

Jewish Fundamentalisms

Within Judaism, one finds forms of fundamentalism that are similar in a number of respects to those found in Christianity and Islam, but most quite conservative forms of Judaism do not fit the criteria for fundamentalism that I am using. Just as the Amish, a doctrinally and socially conservative Christian sect whose members are quite resistant to modernization do not fit the criteria, so other acutely conservative groups that feel threatened by secularity and modernity do not necessarily become fundamentalists.

Israel was founded in 1948 as a social-democratic state, but since the Six-Day War of 1967, and the Yom Kippur War of 1973, that liberal ethos has lost much of its central importance. Surrounded by the threat of Muslim nations that would gladly see the State of Israel destroyed, Israeli consciousness has been challenged by an ultra-nationalist, eschatologically based ideology aptly characterized as Jewish fundamentalism. The implications of this shift to the religious right (analogous to a similar shift in American religious life and politics) entails profound implications for Israel itself, the Middle East, American policy, and much of the rest of the world.

Zionist Jews in the late-19th, early-20th century were inspired and led by Theodor Herzl to begin the return to Palestine to establish Jewish nationhood, contending that anti-Semitism resulted from the abnormal condition of Diaspora Jews. If they had their own land, according to the Zionist argument, Jews could be a nation like any other nation, without needing to be religious. When these international immigrants, many of whom were secular, came to Palestine, they overwhelmed the smaller number of Orthodox Jews who had already filtered back to settle there.

Ultra-Orthodox Jews, known as *haredi* or *haredim* (those who "tremble" at God's word), both then and now oppose secular Zionists. The Haredim are critical of Zionists because the latter believe that they can redeem the nation by their own actions, instead of waiting on God, and also because they believe one can be a complete Jew while being secular, with no need to keep the Law of Moses scrupulously in its rabbinic interpretations.

The Haredim fall into two major divisions, the Hasidim (Hasidic Jews) and the Misnagdim. They contend between themselves as to who represents Judaism most authentically, but they share a resistance to changes in Judaism, to pluralism, and to the modernizing effects of contemporary gentile culture. Their participation in politics has focused mainly, though not exclusively, on protecting and providing for the religious needs of traditional Orthodox Jews.

A third component of Judaism can be characterized as religious, messianic Zionists. These Jews are nearest in spirit and practice to Christian and Islamic fundamentalists. The best known and most influential of these in recent years have been the Gush Emunim (Bloc of the Faithful). They are less visible as a distinct group in the early 21st century, but the influence of their outlook and policies remains strong. The Gush Emunim believe that the coming of Messiah can be hastened through Jewish settlement on land they believe God has allotted to Jews. Gush leaders established the first settlement (Kiryat Arba) in Hebron shortly after the Six-Day War in 1967. Since then, more than 150 settlements, backed by the Gush, the Likud Party, and the financial and military strength of the Israeli government, have been established in the West Bank and Gaza Strip, to the outrage of Palestinian Arabs who regard the West Bank and Gaza as belonging to them. In Israel/Palestine, two armed bands of fundamentalists—Jews and Muslims—confront one another in a struggle to the death over a tiny strip of Holy Land that each claims for itself.

The Gush seek to occupy the West Bank, to which they refer in biblical terms as "Judea and Samaria," with the ultimate goal of permanently incorporating this territory into the State of Israel, thereby hastening the fulfillment of Jewish destiny. This includes establishing Jewish sovereignty over the entire biblically described Land of Israel, substituting authentically Jewish forms of governance for Western-style liberal democracy, rebuilding the Temple in Jerusalem, and implementing the divinely ordained messianic Redemption. Direct political and military action, including acts regarded by the recipients and much of the rest of the world as terrorism, can be used to accomplish this cosmically ordained imperative. By abandoning territory, Israel is weakened, and the imperatives God placed on Jewish people to inherit the land are contradicted and redemption is delayed. The Covenant must be fulfilled in one particular chosen place, the Land of Israel, and the holiness of the Land outweighs any other consideration. Any peace through compromise, as in Camp David or Oslo or Wye River accords or the Bush administration's "Road Map," is ipso facto invalid. Abandoning the settlements and giving up Judea and Samaria would be a mortal sin. Palestinian Arabs correctly realize, of course, that this agenda leaves no room for an autonomous Palestinian state.

As noted, the Gush Emunim as a distinct organization have lost prominence, but its fundamental outlook and policies have filtered into the mainstream of Israeli life and leadership and have been supported even by those who do not share its religious convictions. (This is similar to the situation in America, where the Christian Coalition is a shell of its former self as a distinct organization, in part because its ideals and goals have become a central part of the agenda of the Republican Party.)

Implications of Fundamentalisms in the 21st Century of the Common Era

I have described forms of fundamentalism as they appear in the three main Abrahamic religions. Although numerous variations could be counted within the broad outlines, these are sufficiently similar to allow us to identify several common implications:

Each form of fundamentalism has considerable potential for causing problems for human society. We are keenly aware of the disruption and harm Islamic fundamentalists have caused in America and elsewhere, and they clearly have potential for a great deal more. If the deeply held convictions of Christian and Jewish fundamentalists carry the day with respect to Israel, hope for a peaceful solution to the Israel/Palestine conflict remains dim, and until some resolution to that complex problem is reached, much of the world will remain in great peril.

James Davison Hunter, through his book, *Culture Wars*, planted that suggestive term in our consciousness. He contended that the prospects for resolving the differences between fundamentalists and either secular people or liberal religionists are not especially bright because these parties "do not operate on the same plane of moral discourse." They do not merely disagree over goals and tactics; they represent, instead, "allegiances to different formulations and sources of moral authority." This makes constructive debate quite difficult.[2] One ideal in public debate is to engage in constructive moral reasoning. Given the nature of the divide, this is not feasible, because neither side can ever persuade the other. Each side attempts to discredit the other, replacing dialogue with stereotyping, name-calling, denunciation, efforts to capture important symbols for themselves, and bigotry. Both sides are such outsiders to the other's cultural world that they do not understand why the other is so insulted by their criticism. Only the naïve imagine that everything will work out in the end, and even hostile coexistence seems possible only so long as neither side gains decisive advantage over the other.

Samuel Huntington has made a similar argument, contending that the West and Islam are locked in a life-or-death struggle, a "clash of civilizations."[3] Neither Huntington nor Hunter is terribly encouraging, and Huntington's view is starker than Hunter's. Hunter at least explicitly recognized that not everyone has enlisted in the Culture Wars, that these polar positions are not the whole picture. Alan Wolfe made this point more strongly by showing that most Americans are by no means absolutist about a wide range of beliefs and values.[4] In a more recent work,[5] Wolfe described the effect of dominant, pluralistic American values in shaping religious belief and practice, yet with a strong disinclination among most people, even devoutly religious people, to pass judgment on the religious and moral beliefs of others.

Just as Christian fundamentalism is subject to the moderating influences of American society and culture, so also are Jews and Muslims, both in the USA and elsewhere, learning to appreciate the benefits of pluralism. Jihad is preached in some mosques, but not in others, and not all Muslims go to mosque. Many Muslims are in America precisely because they left Iran or other places where fundamentalist religion had made life

---

[2] James Davison Hunter, *Culture Wars: The Struggle to Define America* (New York: Basic Books, 1991): 181.

[3] Samuel P. Huntington, *The Clash of Civilizations and the Remaking of World Order* (New York: Touchstone, 1996).

[4] Alan Wolfe, *One Nation, After All: What Middle-Class Americans Really Think about God, Country, Family, Racism, Welfare, Immigration, Homosexuality, Work, the Right, the Left, and Each* Other (New York: Viking Penguin, 1998).

[5] Alan Wolfe, *The Transformation of American Religion: How We Actually Live Our Faith* (New York: Free Press, 2003).

intolerable. In some of those countries, the tide of Muslim fundamentalism is being strongly resisted, even rolled back. I agree with Huntington's thesis to the extent that significant segments of Islamic society in some countries do see themselves in a struggle to the death with secular, modern society, but many report that these fundamentalists are far from a majority. Even a tiny minority, however, can make life miserable for the rest of us, if that is their intention. America is less free since 9/11, not because an invading army has overrun us but because we have surrendered many of our personal liberties in the interests of "Homeland Security."

Overall, fundamentalisms have difficulty with modernity and pluralism. Let me point to just three aspects that I find particularly notable.

First, fundamentalists tend to assume, at least in the realm of religion, that all that needs to be known is already known. Young boys in Pakistani *madrassas* (Wahhabi schools built and funded by Saudi petrodollars) rock back and forth as they chant memorized portions of the Qur'an. If we could look inside yeshivas in Israel, we would also see Israeli students rocking back and forth as they memorize Torah and study traditional interpretations of it handed down from the rabbis of the past. In America, we can watch fundamentalist Christian children in private schools that use the Accelerated Christian Education curriculum, raising their small American flags (instead of their hands) to ask a question, and being told, "All the answers are in the text."

All these limited and limiting approaches share the view that to challenge received knowledge, or even to seek to add to it, is to risk offending God. I believe that view is mistaken. I not only believe it but, as a university student and professor for fifty years, I have bet my life on it.

Secondly, fundamentalisms assume that women are not equal to men. In so doing, they deprive themselves of the full talents, intelligence, energies, and participation of approximately half of their population. This mistaken assumption will inevitably undermine the vitality of any human culture, especially if it must coexist with cultures where women are encouraged to develop their talents and energies.

And thirdly, Christian, Muslim, and Jewish fundamentalisms invite civil war when they assert that politics must be subservient to religion. Jesus did his followers a great favor by saying, "Render unto Caesar the things that are Caesar's, and unto God the things that are God's," thereby acknowledging a distinction between religious and civil (or secular) society. James Madison and Thomas Jefferson, drawing both on Jesus and the lessons of history's millennia of religious wars, said (I'm paraphrasing): "Let's not let the state use religion to reinforce and extend its authority, and let's not let religion use the state to impose its doctrines or rules on others." This separation of church and state was a novel notion in their time, perhaps the only truly novel notion in the U.S. Constitution, and it has worked wonderfully to maintain our peace. We must not surrender it. We ought to commend it to others.

Worldly power in religious hands—Islamic, Roman Catholic, Protestant, Jewish, whatever—has hardened into more than one tragic episode. Men and women convinced of the correctness of their convictions and the purity of their ideals need to be aware of a crucial truth: certainty corrupts; absolute certainty corrupts powerfully. We do well, even when speaking knowledgeably and authoritatively of fundamentalism, to remember the words of Oliver Cromwell, a man well acquainted with the tension between noble ideals and the will to power: "I beseech you, in the bowels of Christ, think it possible that you may be mistaken."

In the title of this essay, I refer to the Garden whose name summons an image of ideal earthly existence. In the story of Eden, honored alike by Jews, Christians, and Muslims, Adam and Eve were tempted by the illusion that they could be perfect, like God, completely in charge. When they swallowed that poisoned fruit of pride, they became like us: fallen, imperfect, often mistaken—human. And they were cast out of Eden. Permanently. The cherubim and the sword that turned in every direction set the limits of their humanity. God told them (I'm paraphrasing, again): "You found out about good and evil. Now you must live in a world in which they are always mixed up together. The proportions will differ, but you will never get rid of evil. You will never return to Eden."

Eventually, according to the story, God said (still paraphrasing): "I know it is difficult being human. I'll make a covenant with you. I'll tell you how to live, how to be the best humans you are capable of being. I know you will disappoint me, but I'll do it anyway. This is what I require of you: Let justice roll down like waters, and righteousness like an ever-flowing stream....Do justice, love kindness, walk humbly....Love your neighbor as yourself. If you do that, then someday,... well, We'll see, but that will be up to Me. In the meantime, you can never return to Eden. You must not try. My sword will cut you down. And besides, you wouldn't like it. It's crawling with snakes."

Theological Doctoral Studies
by Members of the Churches of Christ, 1904-2004

Don L. Meredith

Many scholars and their reports have been helpful to me over the past 30 years in compiling the bibliography that follows, and I am grateful for their efforts. In no way do I imagine that the list is complete. I would appreciate notification of anyone who has been omitted from this work ever in progress.

As early as 1958, Alex Humphrey, Jr., published a list of 29 doctoral dissertations by members of the Churches of Christ compiled from responses to a questionnaire published in three periodicals.[1] In 1974, Don Haymes discussed theological scholarship in the Churches of Christ in the 1950s and 1960s, particularly as reflected in articles published in the *Restoration Quarterly*.[2] A number of the scholars he mentioned had completed doctorates at that time, and others finished theirs subsequently. Eight years later, Everett Ferguson in his discussion of higher education within the Churches of Christ from 1957 to 1982 did a brief analysis of doctoral work done during this period based on a list that I shared with him.[3] In Atlanta, 2003, at a special session of the Society of Biblical Literature celebrating scholarship in the Churches of Christ during the previous 50 years, James Thompson presented a brief history of theological doctoral work done by members of the Churches of Christ, its reception, and influence on subsequent study.[4]

Dwayne Van Rheenen compiled an extensive list of masters and doctoral theses produced on religious communication in the American Restoration tradition.[5] Many of these were doctoral dissertations produced by members of the Churches of Christ. The volumes of *Preachers of Today* include a section on training for each preacher and were helpful in surfacing graduate training in the 1950s and 1960s.[6]

Other techniques—word of mouth, taking note of announcements of new faculty members at schools associated with the Churches of Christ, noting credentials for authors

---

[1] Alex Humphrey, Jr., "A List of Some Doctors of Philosophy and Doctors of Theology Dissertations by Members of Churches of Christ," *Restoration Quarterly* 2 (1958): 71-2.

[2] Don Haymes, "The Silence of the Scholars," *Mission* 8 (Sept. 1974): 70-85.

[3] Everett Ferguson, "Higher Education in Religious Studies among Members of Churches of Christ, 1957-1982," *Restoration Quarterly* 25 (1982): 206.

[4] James Thompson, "Reflections on the Last Fifty Years," *Restoration Quarterly* 46 (2004): 131-8.

[5] Dwayne D. Van Rheenen, "Bibliography of Research on Religious Communication in the American Restoration Tradition (through 1982): A Preliminary Report," paper presented to the Religious Speech Association, Louisville, Ky., Nov. 1982, 1-28.

[6] Batsell Barrett Baxter and M. Norvel Young, eds., *Preachers of Today: A Book of Brief Biographical Sketches and Pictures of Living Gospel Preachers,* 4 vols. (Nashville: The Christian Press and Gospel Advocate Company, 1952-70).

of books and periodical articles received in the Harding Graduate School library, and follow-up on graduates of the Harding Graduate School of Religion—have also contributed to the bibliography.

My principle of selectivity was to include those who were members of the Churches of Christ (*a cappella* singing) at the time they wrote the dissertation. Some of these scholars are no longer associated with this fellowship. I have also included only those dissertations completed at conventional, accredited institutions. I have not included Doctor of Ministry projects or dissertations. Unless otherwise indicated, the dissertations were submitted for the Ph.D. degree. Many of these doctorates were not completed for degrees in Theology, but the dissertation centered on a topic in Religious Studies; therefore, many doctorates in Education, Speech, History, Psychology, Counseling, and Literature are included because they deal with Theology-related themes, Christian Education, morality or religious life in some way, such as the speech or rhetoric of a preacher or theologian, religious aspects in literature, and the historical treatment of a religious subject.

Of these 462 dissertations written at 114 institutions, 163 were completed at state-supported institutions and 23 at 15 non-U.S. institutions. Hall Calhoun's dissertation at Harvard in 1904 is the earliest. The most dissertations were completed at the following schools: Baylor (22), Harvard (21), and Vanderbilt (21). Ten or more were completed at Southwestern Baptist Theological Seminary (15), New Orleans Baptist Theological Seminary (14), University of Iowa (14), University of Southern California (13), Emory (12), Southern Baptist Theological Seminary (12), Louisiana State University (11), University of Chicago (11), Yale (11), George Peabody (10), and Princeton (10). Only 55 were written before 1960, but the numbers spiked to 108 in the 1970s and 114 in the 1980s.

The dissertations cover a wide range of subjects. As would be expected within the fellowship of the Churches of Christ, the largest number is in biblical studies: 85 in the New Testament, 47 in the Old Testament, and 2 in general biblical studies. There are 88 that I have classified in the area of church history, 28 of these more specifically in the history of the Restoration Movement. It is sometimes hard to categorize a dissertation. Some of those I classified as church history treat early church history and in some cases may technically be New Testament dissertations. I included 11 as studies in Judaism and 7 in ancient Near Eastern studies that might in some cases be regarded as Old Testament dissertations. Some of the 54 speech/communication dissertations treat the preaching of the Restoration Movement or an individual preacher in the movement, and a number of the 64 education dissertations treat schools and/or individuals connected with the Churches of Christ. Other areas represented are ethics/philosophy (26), theology (20), missions (20), counseling/ psychology (19), ministry (11), religion & literature (8), and hymnology (2).

Others may wish to make observations on this list based on the choice of schools in particular periods, the writer's previous education, a professor or school's reputation, the people that influenced the choice of the school, the theological perspective of the institutions, the author's gender or geographical factors. I hope this list will at least be a working document for the study of theological scholarship in the Churches of Christ.

Bibliography: Theological Doctoral Studies by Members of the
Churches of Christ, 1904-2004[7]

Abernathy, Elton. "An Analysis of Trends in American Homiletical Theory since 1860." State University of Iowa, 1941.

Alexander, Thomas C. "Paul's Final Exhortation to the Elders from Ephesus:The Rhetoric, Acts 20:17-38." Emory University, 1990.

Allen, C. Leonard. "The Restauration of Zion: Roger Williams and the Quest for the Primitive Church." University of Iowa, 1984.

Allen, Holly Catterton. "A Qualitative Study Exploring the Similarities and Differences of the Spirituality of Children in Intergenerational and Non-Intergenerational Christian Contexts." Talbot School of Theology, Biola University, 2002.

Altman, Ted Max. "The Contributions of George Benson to Christian Education." Ed.D., North Texas State University, 1971

Aquino, Frederick A. "Communities of Informed Judgment: The Significance of John Henry Newman's Notion of the Illative Sense for Issues in Theological Prolegomena." Southern Methodist University, 2000.

Armour, Michael Carl. "Calvin's Hermeneutic and the History of Christian Exegesis." University of California, Los Angeles, 1992.

Ash, Anthony Lee. "Attitudes toward the Higher Criticism of the Old Testament among the Disciples of Christ: 1850-1905." University of Southern California, 1966.

Ash, James Lee, Jr. "The Social Construction of Historical Reality: An Intellectual Biography of William Warren Sweet." University of Chicago, 1976.

Ashlock, Rodney O. "As the Lord Commands: Narrative Endings and Closure Strategy in Exodus, Leviticus and Numbers." Baylor University, 2002.

Atkinson, Kenneth. "Toward a Redating of the Psalms of Solomon: Implications for Understanding the Sitz im Leben of an Unknown Jewish Sect." Temple University, 1999.

Bailey, Fred Arthur. "The Status of Women in the Disciples of Christ Movement, 1865-1900." University of Tennessee, 1979.

Bailey, Jon Nelson. "Repentance in Luke-Acts." University of Notre Dame, 1993.

Bailey, Randall C. "Images of the Prophets: An Analysis of the Metaphors and Epithets Used in the Old Testament to Describe Prophets and Prophetic Activity." Drew University, 1987.

Baird, Harry Russell. "An Analytical History of the Church of Christ Missions in Brazil." D. Miss., Fuller Theological Seminary, 1979.

Baird, Jim. "Human Rationality as Evidence for Theism." Oxford University, England, 1991.

Baker, Harold Stanford. "A Rhetorical Study of the Preaching of John McMillan from 1820 to 1830." Louisiana State University, 1967.

---

[7] Editors' note: We have reproduced the titles of the dissertations exactly and without the usual literary indicator of error, [*sic*], even when spelling, punctuation, and other norms of style are incorrect.

Balch, David Lee. "'Let Wives Be Submissive....' The Origin, Form and Apologetic Function of the Household Duty Code (Haustafel) in I Peter." Yale University, 1974.

Bales, James David. "A History of Pragmatism in American Educational Philosophy." University of California, 1946.

Banister, Mickey Dean. "Changes in Religious Emphasis among Selected Colleges and Universities Associated with the Churches of Christ." Ed.D., Oklahoma State University, 1985.

Banowsky, William S. "A Historical Study of the Speech-Making at the Abilene Christian College Lectureship, 1918-1961." University of Southern California, 1963.

Barton, Fred J. "Modes of Delivery in American Homiletic Theory in the Eighteenth and Nineteenth Centuries." University of Iowa, 1949.

Barton, John. "Causation in Modern Africa and the Postmodern West: A Study of Cultural Similarities with Special Reference to the Worldviews of the Basoga of Uganda and the Proposals of the Vatican Observatory/CTNS Project." Makerere University, Kampala, Uganda, 2002.

Barton, John Marion. "Preaching on Herald of Truth Radio, 1952-1969." The Pennsylvania State University, 1975.

Barton, William Bryan, Jr. "A Defense of the Direct Realist's Interpretation of Intentional Consciousness and its Metaphysical and Religious Implications." Harvard University, 1955.

Bates, Jack Ward. "John Quincy Adams and the Antislavery Movement." University of Southern California, 1952.

Batey, Richard Alexander. "The Church, the Bride of Christ." Vanderbilt University, 1961.

Baxter, Batsell Barrett. "An Analysis of the Basic Elements of Persuasion in the Yale Lectures on Preaching." University of Southern California, 1944.

Baxter, John Douglas. "Divorce Adjustment among Church of Christ Members: A Survey of Selected Factors Including Perceptions of the Church as a Support System." Ed.D., George Peabody College, 1984.

Bennett, Weldon Bailey. "The Concept of the Ministry in the Thought of Representative Men of the Disciples of Christ (1804-1906)." University of Southern California, 1971.

Berryhill, Carisse Mickey. "Sense, Expression and Purpose: Alexander Campbell's Natural Philosophy of Rhetoric." Florida State University, 1982.

Bever, Ronald Doyle. "An Analysis of Speaking in the American Restoration Movement, 1829-1849." Northwestern University, 1968.

Beyer, Jimmie Lee. "The Educational Concept of Parent-Child Development Based on Major Jewish and Christian Philosophies to the Second Century." Ed.D., New Orleans Baptist Theological Seminary, 1971.

Black, Mark Cothran. "The Rejected and Slain Messiah Who Is Coming with His Angels: The Messianic Exegesis of Zechariah 9-14 in the Passion Narratives." Emory University, 1990.

Black, Robert Allen. "The Conversion Stories in the Acts of the Apostles: A Study of Their Forms and Functions." Emory University, 1985.

Blackburn, Barry L. "A Critique of the *Theios Aner* Concept as an Interpretative Background of the Miracle Traditions Used by Mark." University of Aberdeen, Scotland, 1986.

Bland, Dave Lawrence. "A Rhetorical Perspective on the Sentence Sayings of the Book of Proverbs." University of Washington, 1994.

Bledsoe, W. Craig. "The Fundamentalist Foundations of the Moral Majority." Vanderbilt University, 1985.

Bowen, Bill D. "Knowledge, the Existence of God and Faith: John Locke's Influence on Alexander Campbell's Theology." Michigan State University, 1978.

Bowie, Dennis Harold. "A Study of Certain Factors Affecting Non-Enrollment in Selected Church-of-Christ-Related Private Schools." Ed. D., Memphis State University, 1968.

Bowling, Jerry. "An Examination of Spirituality Based on Howard Gardner's Theory of Multiple Intelligences." Southern Baptist Theological Seminary, 1998.

Bowman, Craig Douglas. "An Analysis of the Chronicler's Use of Sources: Methodological Concerns and Criterion." Princeton Theological Seminary, 1997.

Boyd, H. Glenn. "A Model Program for Primary Health Care Delivery in Ghana, West Africa, for the African Christian Hospitals Foundation (Churches of Christ)." D. Miss., Trinity Evangelical Divinity School, 1988.

Brecheen, Freddy Carl. "A Leadership Study of the Elder in the Churches of Christ." D.R.E., Southwestern Baptist Theological Seminary, 1965.

Briley, Terry Ray. "Josephus, the Historian and the Man: An Analysis of Josephus as an Historian of the Jewish War against the Romans." Hebrew Union-Jewish Institute of Religion, 1990.

Brock, Gary L. "Musical Pews: The Circulation of the Saints in Springfield, Missouri." St. Louis University, 1982.

Brown, Douglas Eugene, Jr. "The Evolution of Augustine's Theological Method." Southern Baptist Theological Seminary, 1981.

Brumfield, Joe Stephen. "The Effect of a Christian Home Course on Awareness of Attitudes and Relationship Expectations." Ed.D., Oklahoma State University, 1995.

Bryant, David James. "Theological Imagination and Symbolic Heritage: An Examination of the Role of Imagination in Constructive Theology." Princeton Theological Seminary, 1986.

Bryant, Rees Odell. "The Role of Baptism in Pauline Theology of Conversion." D. Miss., Fuller Theological Seminary, 1990.

Burke, Gary Tapp. "Celsus and Late Second Century Christianity." University of Iowa, 1981.

Burks, David Basil. "The Development of Model Faculty Recruitment and Retention Programs for Selected Senior Colleges Supported by Churches of Christ." Florida State University, 1974.

Butts, John R. "Rhetorical Study of the Preaching and Speaking of Batsell Barrett Baxter." Michigan State University, 1970.

Cage, Gary Thomas. "Essentialism and Reference." University of Tennessee, 1978.

Cail, James Thomas. "A Christian Doctrine of Man in Light of the Psychology of B. F. Skinner." Baylor University, 1976.

Caillouet, Larry Martin. "Comparative Media Effectiveness in an Evangelistic Campaign: A Survey of Communication in the Campaign for Christ." University of Illinois at Urbana-Champaign, 1978.

Calhoun, Hall Laurie. "The Remains of the Old Latin Translation of Leviticus." Harvard University, 1904.

Camp, Lee Compton. "The 'Primitivist-Pacifism' of Alexander Campbell, Adin Ballou, and Leo Tolstoy: An Atypical Type." University of Notre Dame, 1999.

Camp, Phillip Glenn. "According to the Word of the Lord: The Degree of Correspondence between Prophecies and Fulfillments in the Deuteronomistic History." Union Theological Seminary & Presbyterian School of Christian Education, 2004.

Campbell, Norris Clyde. "A Study of the Need for Counselor Preparation in the Department of Bible and Religious Education in Abilene Christian College." Ed.D., University of Colorado, 1959.

Campbell, Thomas Lee. "The Contributions of David Lipscomb and the *Gospel Advocate* to Religious Education in the Churches of Christ." D.R.E., Southern Baptist Theological Seminary, 1968.

Cannon, Russell Carroll. "A Source Book in Training Christian Education Leaders: Prepared for Use in Harding College, a College of the Churches of Christ, Searcy, Ark." Ed.D., New York University, 1953.

Carmack, William Ross. "Invention in the Lyman Beecher Lectures on Preaching: The Lecturers' Advice on Gathering and Selecting Sermon Material." University of Illinois at Urbana-Champaign, 1958.

Carpenter, Robert Terrance. "Religious Competition and the Spread of Alternative Spirituality in Contemporary Brazil." University of California, Santa Barbara, 2001.

Carruth, Theodore Raymond. "The Jesus-as-Prophet Motif in Luke-Acts." Baylor University, 1973.

Carver, Francis Grace. "From Sanctuary to Saloon: Carry A. Nation and the Religious Ethos of the Midwestern United States, 1850-1910." Princeton Theological Seminary, 1997.

Casey, Michael Wilson. "The Development of Necessary Inference in the Hermeneutics of the Disciples of Christ/Churches of Christ." University of Pittsburgh, 1986.

Casner, Paul. "Blessed Assurance? Reason and Certainty of Knowledge of God in Karl Barth and Hans Küng." Marquette University, 1997.

Castleberry, Ottis L. "A Study of the Nature and Sources of the Effectiveness of the Preaching of Benjamin Franklin in the Restoration Movement, 1840-1878." The Pennsylvania State University, 1957.

Chancey, Dudley. "Economic Distress and Psychological Outcomes: Using Objective and Subjective Measures of Economic Distress as Predictors of Depressive Mood and Self-Satisfaction Moderated by Religiosity." University of Tennessee, 1997.

Cheatham, Carl Wade. "Social Christianity: A Study of English Nonconformist Social Attitudes, 1880-1914." Vanderbilt University, 1982.

Chesnutt, Randall D. "Conversion in Joseph and Aseneth: Its Nature, Function, and Relation to Contemporaneous Paradigms of Conversion and Initiation." Duke University, 1986.

Childers, Jeff W. "Studies in the Syriac Versions of St. John Chrysostom's Homilies on the New Testament." Oxford University, England, 1996.

Chouinard, Larry E. "A Literary Study of Christology in Matthew." Fuller Theological Seminary, 1988.

Christlieb, Terry Joe. "Theism and Evil: Consistency, Evidence and Completeness." Syracuse University, 1988.

Clark, Paul A. "An Emerging Church Sponsored College." Ed.D., University of Kentucky, 1959.

Clark, Wayne Royce. "The Relation of Present Experience to Eschatological and Christological Uniqueness in Schleiermacher, Tillich, and Pannenberg." University of Iowa, 1973.

Clevenger, Eugene W. "The Human Element in the Writing of the New Testament as Related in the Pauline Epistles." Th.D., Southwestern Baptist Theological Seminary, 1968.

Cloud, Rodney Eugene. "The Pre-Literary Prophets and the Rule of Kings." Hebrew Union, 1971.

Cochrane, Murray Ross. "Teaching Them to Observe All Things: A Practical Rationale for Teaching Scripture in Evangelical Colleges." Boston College, 1994.

Coker, Dannie Carroll. "The Influence of United States Financial and Administrative Support upon Two Mexican Theological Institutions as Perceived by Former Students of Those Institutions." University of Florida, 1976.

Collins, Johnnie Andrew. "Pacifism in the Churches of Christ, 1866-1945." Middle Tennessee State University, 1984.

Collins, William. "A Study of the History of Ideas: The Concept of God in Twentieth Century Anglo-American Process Philosophy." University of St. Andrews, Scotland, 1983.

Cooper, David Lipscomb. "The Use of en and eis in the New Testament and the Contemporaneous Non-Literary Papyri." Th.D., Southern Baptist Theological Seminary, 1930.

Cope, Glenn Melvin. "An Analysis of the Heresiological Method of Theodoret of Cyrus in the *Haereticarum Fabularum Compendium.*" Catholic University of America, 1990.

Cosgrove, Owen. "The Administration of Don Heath Morris at Abilene Christian College." Ed.D., North Texas State University, 1976.

Cox, Claude Edward. "The Textual Character of the Armenian Version of Deuteronomy." University of Toronto, 1979.

Cox, Monte B. "'Euthanasia of Mission' or 'Partnership'? An Evaluative Study of the Policy of Disengagement of Church of Christ Missionaries in Rural Kenya." Trinity Evangelical Divinity School, 1999.

Craig, Mack Wayne. "The Role of the Academic Dean in Selected Church-Related Colleges." George Peabody College, 1958.

Crain, Matthew Kent. "Transfer of Training and Self-Directed Learning in Adult Sunday School Classes in Six Churches of Christ." Ed.D., Southwestern Baptist Theological Seminary, 1987.

Crenshaw, Scot. "An Examination of the Relationship between Biblical Authority and Self-Disclosure in Preaching." Southwestern Baptist Theological Seminary, 1997.

Crump, Warren Wayne. "The Structure and Soteriology of Romans in Light of the Function of 5:1-11 in the Argument of the Epistle." Princeton Theological Seminary, 1979.

Cukrowski, Kenneth Larry. "Pagan Polemic and Lukan Apologetic: The Function of Acts 20:17-38." Yale University, 1994.

Cunningham, Thomas S. "A Study of Some Family Influences and Other Social Factors Affecting Participation in Religious Activities among a Group of College Students Professing a Common Faith." Ed.D., Oklahoma State University, 1966.

Curry, Melvin Dotson, Jr., "Jehovah's Witnesses: The Effects of Millennarianism on the Maintenance of a Religious Sect." Florida State University, 1970.

Daniel, Jerry Leroy. "Apologetics in Josephus." Rutgers University, 1981.

Danner, Dan Gordon. "The Theology of the Geneva Bible of 1560: A Study in English Protestantism." University of Iowa, 1969.

Darnell, David Rancier. "Rebellion, Rest, and the Word of God (An Exegetical Study of Hebrews 3:1-4:13)." Duke University, 1973.

Davis, Oliver Jennings, Jr. "Physical Education in Christian Colleges: With Reference to Colleges Operated by Members of the Churches of Christ." Columbia University, 1955.

Davis, William Hatcher. "The Philosophy of C. S. Peirce." Rice University, 1965.

Dean, Camille K. "Evangelicals and Restorationists: The Careers of Robert and James Haldane in Cultural and Political Context." Texas Christian University, 1999.

Deason, Gary Bruce. "The Philosophy of a Lord Chancellor: Religion, Science and Social Stability in the Work of Francis Bacon." Princeton Theological Seminary, 1977.

Denman, Stan C. "Theatre and Hegemony in the Churches of Christ: A Case Study Using Abilene Christian University Theatre." University of Pittsburgh, 1998.

Dodd, Carley Henry. "Predictive Correlates of Innovativeness in the Diffusion of a Non-Technological Innovation in an African Setting." University of Oklahoma, 1974.

Douglas, Robert Christy. "Power: Its Locus and Function in Defining Social Commentary in the Church of Christ, Illustrated by a Case Study of Black Civil Rights." University of Southern California, 1980.

Dudrey, Russell Paul. "The Social and Legal Setting of I Corinthians 7:17-35: De Facto Slave Marriages in the Church at Corinth." University of Minnesota, 1998.

Duke, Johnny Ivy. "The Interaction of Parents and Church in the Christian Education of Children." Ed.D., Southern Baptist Theological Seminary, 1986.

Duncan, Harold Downey, Jr. "Christian Religious Conservatism and Help-Seeking Behavior." North Texas State University, 1981.

Duncan, Robert Lee. "Protestant Themes and Theses in the Drama of John Bale." Indiana University, 1964.

Durham, Kenneth Ray, Jr. "An Experimental Study of the Effects of Religiosity, Social Attitudes and Self-Esteem on the Reception of Homiletical Fear Appeals." Louisiana State University, 1974.

Durham, Ronald Oatis. "Process Thought and Theodicy: A Critique." Rice University, 1974.

Eckstein, Stephen Daniel. "The History of the Churches of Christ in Texas, 1824-1950." Texas Technological College, 1959.

Edwards, Bruce Lee, Jr. "A Rhetoric of Reading: A Study of C. S. Lewis's Approach to the Written Text." University of Texas, 1981.

Edwards, Earl D. "A Plan for Initiating a Major in Missiology at Freed-Hardeman College, Henderson, Tennessee." D. Miss., Trinity Evangelical Divinity School, 1985.

Ellis, Carroll Brooks. "The Controversial Speaking of Alexander Campbell." Louisiana State University, 1949.

Elrod, Mark Alan. "The Churches of Christ and the 'War Question': The Influence of Church Journals." Vanderbilt University, 1995.

Enzor, Edwin Harold. "The Preaching of James M'Gready: Frontier Revivalist." Louisiana State University, 1964.

Ethridge, Franklin Maurice. "Sect-Denomination Evolution: A Dialectical Model of Organizational Change." University of Texas, 1973.

Evans, Warren Donald. "Educational Expenditures within Liberal Arts Colleges and Colleges Maintained by Members of the Church of Christ." Ed.D., The Pennsylvania State University, 1963.

Fair, Ian Arthur. "The Theology of Wolfhart Pannenberg as a Reaction to Dialectical Theology." University of Natal, South Africa, 1975.

Faulkner, Paul B. "An Analysis of a Process of Integrity Therapy in a Local Church." D.R.E., Southwestern Baptist Theological Seminary, 1968.

Fay, Greg. "Paul the Empowered Prisoner: Eph. 3:1-13 in the Epistolary and Rhetorical Structure of Ephesians." Marquette University, 1994.

Ferguson, William Everett. "Ordination in the Ancient Church: An Examination of the Theological and Constitutional Motifs in the Light of Biblical and Gentile Sources." Harvard University, 1959.

Filbeck, James Orval. "The Christian Evidence Movement as Related to American Schools." University of Texas, 1944.

Finley, Lewis F. (Tony). "A History of Harding Academy, 1924-1984."Ed.D., University of Arkansas, 1985.

Fitzgerald, John T. "Cracks in an Earthen Vessel: An Examination of the Catalogues of Hardships in the Corinthian Correspondence." Yale University, 1984.

Flatt, Billy Way. "An Evaluation of the Degree Programs of the Harding Graduate School of Religion as Perceived by its Graduates, 1964-1973." Ed.D., Memphis State University, 1973.

Flatt, Dowell Edward. "The Relationships of the Father, Son and Disciples as Reflected in Jesus' Prayers and Related Teachings in the Fourth Gospel." Th.D., New Orleans Baptist Theological Seminary, 1975.

Fleer, David. "Martin Luther King, Jr.'s Reformation of Sources: A Close Rhetorical Reading of His Compositional Strategies and Arrangement." University of Washington, 1995.

Fletcher, William Harold. "Amos Sutton Hayden." University of Oklahoma, 1988.

Floyd, Harvey Leroy. "Nigel's *Speculum Stultorum*: A Study in Literary Influences." Vanderbilt University, 1969.

Forshey, Harold Odes. "The Hebrew Root *NHL* and its Semitic Cognates." Th.D., Harvard University, 1973.

Fortner, John. "Adjudicating Entities and Levels of Legal Authority in Lawsuit Records of the Old Babylonian Era." Hebrew Union, 1996.

Foster, Douglas Allen. "The Struggle for Unity during the Period of Division of the Restoration Movement: 1875-1900." Vanderbilt University, 1987.

Fredenburg, Brandon L. "With Horns of Irony: The Implications of Irony in the Account of Ahab's Reign (1 Kings 16:29—22:40)." Iliff School of Theology & University of Denver, 2003.

Freeman, William Webb. "Was Paul a Sacramentarian?" Th.D., Southern Baptist Theological Seminary, 1927.

Fryer, William Neal. "Faculty Counseling at Abilene Christian College." Ed.D., Columbia University, 1964.

Fuentes, D. Cortes. "Eyes to See and Ears to Hear: Echoes of Moses in Matthew's Portrayal of Jesus." Northwestern University, 1999.

Gallagher, Neil. "The Concept of Blame." Brown University, 1981.

Gardner, Donald Earl. "College Decisions of Members of the Churches of Christ in California." Ed.D., University of California, Los Angeles, 1967.

Garner, Donald Paul. "George S. Benson: Conservative, Anti-Communist, Pro-Americanism Speaker." Wayne State University, 1963.

Garrett, Leroy. "The New Jerusalem: A Study in Jewish and Christian Apocalyptic." Harvard University, 1956.

Geer, Thomas Carter, Jr. "An Investigation of a Select Group of So-Called Western Cursives in Acts." Boston University, 1985.

Gieger, Loren Glen. "Figures of Speech in the Epistle of James: A Rhetorical and Exegetical Analysis." Southwestern Baptist Theological Seminary, 1981.

Gifford, Carey Jerome. "Space and Time as Religious Symbols in Ante-Bellum America." Claremont Graduate School, 1980.

Gilbert, Kevin James. "The Rule of Express Terms and the Limits of Fellowship in the Stone-Campbell Movement: T. W. Brents, a Test Case." Southern Baptist Theological Seminary, 2004.

Gilmore, Donald Ralph. "The Concept of a Person and Survival of Death: A Strawsonian Approach." University of Tennessee, 1981.

Glover, Robert Alan. "Factors Relating to the Referral Practices of Dallas Christian Clergy Members to Marriage Family Counselors." Texas Woman's University, 1984.

Goldman, George II. "The Contribution of Joel 2-3 to the Restoration of Israel Theme in Acts." Trinity Evangelical Divinity School, 2002.

Goldstein, Robert Morris. "On Christian Rhetoric: The Significance of Soren Kierkegaard's Dialectic of Ethical and Ethical-Religious Communication for Theological and Philosophical Pedagogy." Princeton Theological Seminary, 1982.

Goode, Richard. "The Only and Principal End: Propagating the Gospel in Early Puritan New England." Vanderbilt University, 1995.

Goree, Balfour William, Jr. "The Cultural Bases of Montanism." Baylor University, 1980.

Gragg, Douglas L. "The Parable of the Workers in the Vineyard and Its Use in the Gospel of Matthew." Emory University, 1990.

Graham, Matt Patrick. "The Utilization of 1 and 2 Chronicles in the Reconstruction of Israelite History in the 19th Century." Emory University, 1983.

Granberg, Stanley Earl. "A Critical Examination of African Leadership and Leadership Effectiveness among the Churches of Christ in Meru, Kenya." Open University, United Kingdom, 1999.

Grasham, William Wesley. "The Priestly Synagogue: A Reexamination of the Cult of Qumran." University of Aberdeen, Scotland, 1985.

Gray, Edward A. "A Holistic Analysis of Stress with Implications for Stress Management as a Function of Pastoral Counseling." Ed.D., New Orleans Baptist Theological Seminary, 1981.

Green, William McAllen. "Fifth Century Paganism as Implied in Augustine's City of God." University of California, 1931.

Greene, Kenneth Wayne. "An Analysis of the Teaching of Religion in the State Universities of Texas." North Texas State University, 1974.

Gurganus, George Pope. "An Audience Analysis of Three Missionary-Supported and Three Indigenous Christian Congregations in Tokyo, Japan." The Pennsylvania State University, 1963.

Hacker, William Joe. "A Study of the Learning Theories of E. L. Thorndike and Evidence of Their Similarities as Reflected in Southern Baptist Adult Curriculum Materials, 1964-1965." D.R.E., Southwestern Baptist Theological Seminary, 1967.

Hailey, Mel. "The Political and Social Attitudes of Church of Christ Ministers." Texas Technological University, 1988.

Hamilton, Clinton David. "Theory of the Roman Catholic Church in the Support and Control of Education, with Special Reference to the United States." Florida State University, 1965.

Hamilton, Mark Wade. "The Body Royal: The Social Poetics of Kingship in Ancient Israel." Harvard University, 2000.

Hardeman, Thomas Patterson. "The Philosophy of Lucius Annaeus Seneca." University of Illinois at Urbana-Champaign, 1956.

Hardin, Daniel Col. "An Analysis of the Relationship of Institutional Goal Specificity and Faculty Morale in Liberal Arts Colleges." Ed.D., Oklahoma State University, 1970.

Hardin, Joyce Faye. "A Study of the Relationship of Moral Development to School Setting, Comparing Students in a Church Related School with Students in a Public School." Ed.D., Oklahoma State University, 1978.

Harrell, David Edwin. "A Social History of the Disciples of Christ to 1866." Vanderbilt University, 1962.

Harrell, Patrick Edwin. "A History of Marriage and Divorce in the Ante-Nicene Church." Th.D., Boston Univiversity, 1965.

Harrison, Calvin Wesley. "Andreas Ehrenpreis and the Hutterian Brethren of the Seventeenth Century: The Period of the Reformation and Crystallization of Faith and Practice." University of Oregon, 1991.

Harrison, John Pal. "Did Jesus Teach Obedience to the Law?" University of Edinburgh, Scotland, 1992.

Harvill, Jerry G. "Aristotle's Concept of Ethos as Ground for a Modern Ethics of Communication." University of Kentucky, 1990.

Haynie, Paul David. "A Peculiar People: A History of the Churches of Christ in Washington and Madison Counties, Arkansas." University of Arkansas, 1988.

Hazelip, Herbert Harold. "Stephen Marshall: Preacher to the Long Parliament." University of Iowa, 1967.

Henegar, Richard James. "Discipling Churches of Christ: An Assessment of Pre, Peak, and Post Involvement of Former Members Using the Myers-Briggs Type Indicator." United States International University, 1992.

Hester, Samuel Edward. "Advancing Christianity to its Primitive Excellency: The Quest of Thomas Grantham, Early English General Baptist (1634-1692)." Th.D., New Orleans Baptist Theological Seminary, 1977.

Hicks, Dixie Crawford. "Marcus Garvey and Pan-Africanism." Memphis State University, 1992.

Hicks, John Mark. "The Theology of Grace in the Thought of Jacobus Arminius and Philip Van Limborch: A Study in the Development of Seventeenth-Century Dutch Arminianism." Westminster Theological Seminary, 1985.

Hicks, L. Edward. "A Case Study of Conservative Political Education: Dr. George S. Benson and the National Education Program." Memphis State University, 1990.

Highfield, Ronald Curtis. "The Doctrine of Sin in Ecumenical Perspective: A Comparison of Karl Barth and Karl Rahner." Rice University, 1988.

Hines, Roger Herman, Jr. "Caught between Two Worlds: Tertullian's Use of Time and History." Baylor University, 1998.

Holladay, Carl Roark. "*Theios Aner* Hellenistic-Judaism: A Critique of the Use of This Category in New Testament Christology." Cambridge University, England, 1974.

Holland, Harold Edward. "Religious Periodicals in the Development of Nashville, Tennessee, as a Regional Publishing Center, 1830-1880." Columbia University, 1976.

Holloway, Gary Nelson. "The Form and Function of Church of Christ Preacher Anecdotes." Emory University, 1987.

Hooper, Robert Eugene. "The Political and Educational Ideas of David Lipscomb." George Peabody College, 1965.

Hoover, Arlie Jack. "The Gospel of Patriotism: The Nationalism of the German Protestant Clergy (1806-1815)." University of Texas, 1965.

Houston, Michael Victory. "The Identification of Torah as Wisdom: A Traditio-Critical Analysis of Dt. 4:1-8 and 30:11-20." University of Iowa, 1987.

Howard, George Eulan. "The LXX Book of Amos." Hebrew Union, 1964.

Howard, James Edwin. "A Critical Evaluation of the Thesis that the Roots of Jewish Apocalyptic Are in Israelite Wisdom Rather than Prophecy." Baylor University, 1971.

Huey, Keith B. "Alexander Campbell's Church-State Separation as a Defining and Limiting Factor in his Anti-Catholic Activity." Marquette University, 2000.

Huffard, Everett W. "Thematic Dissonance in the Muslim-Christian Encounter: A Contextualized Theology of Honor." Fuller Theological Seminary, 1985.

Hughes, Richard Thomas. "Henry Burton: A Study in Religion and Politics in Seventeenth-Century England." University of Iowa, 1972.

Humble, Bill Joe. "The Missionary Society Controversy in the Restoration Movement (1823-1875)." State University of Iowa, 1958.

Hutson, Christopher H. "My True Child: The Rhetoric of Youth in the Pastoral Epistles." Yale University, 1997.

Isom, Allan Lloyd. "A Study of the Financial Condition of Church of Christ Preachers." Ed.D., New Orleans Baptist Theological Seminary, 1972.

Jackson, Donald Edward. "Feedback in Preaching Communication." University of Southern Mississippi, 1988.

Jackson, James L. "Music Practices among Churches of Christ in the United States, 1970." D. Mus. Ed., University of Oklahoma, 1970.

Jewell, Jason. "Authority's Advocate: Samuel Parker, Religion, and Politics in Restoration England." Florida State University, 2004.

Johnson, Robert Lee. "A Critical Comparison of the Teachings of New Testament Christianity and Early Stoicism." New York University, 1957.

Jolivet, Ira Joseph, Jr. "The Structure and Argumentative Strategy of Romans." Baylor University, 1994.

Jones, Gary L. "Effects of Religiosity on the Initial Decisions of the Counseling Process." University of Oklahoma, 1989.

Jones, Jerry Lee. "A Survey of the Audience Expectation Factors with an Analysis of Preaching in the Churches of Christ in the South in 1972." Th.D., New Orleans Baptist Theological Seminary, 1974.

Jones, Joseph Ferdinand. "The Educational Contributions of Jesse Parker Sewell." Ed.D., Oklahoma State University, 1961.

Jones, Mike. "The Hermeneutical Controversy in the Churches of Christ and Implications for Preaching within that Tradition." Southern Baptist Theological Seminary, 1995.

Jones, Warren Saunders. "G. C. Brewer: Lecturer, Debater, and Preacher." Wayne State University, 1959.

Jones, William Edward. "A Study of the Covenant Concept in Ancient Israel and Its Influence on the Formation and Maintenance of the Israelite Community." Southwestern Baptist Theological Seminary, 1966.

Kearley, Floyd Furman. "The Early Jewish and Christian Interpretations of the Throne and Reign of David." Hebrew Union, 1970.

Keckley, Paul H., Jr. "A Qualitative Analytic Study of the Image of Organized Religion in Prime Time Television Drama." Ohio State University, 1974.

Kelcy, Raymond Coy. "A Grammatical and Syntactical Analysis of I Thessalonians." Th.D., Southwestern Baptist Theological Seminary, 1963.

Kendrick, William Gerald. "Prayer in Colossians and Ephesians: Its Theology and Meaning." Baylor University, 1976.

Kinder, Donald Michael. "The Role of the Christian Woman as Seen by Clement of Alexandria." University of Iowa, 1987.

King, Daniel Hayden. "Ideological Confluence in the Wisdom of Solomon." Vanderbilt University, 1982.

Kirk, Willis Edward. "A Study of Faculty and Student Attitudes toward Cheating at Selected Church-Affiliated and Secular Colleges." Ed.D., Oklahoma State University, 1970.

Kirkpatrick, Foy Leo. "An Educational Program for the Church of Christ." Southwestern Baptist Theological Seminary, 1960.

Kline, Leslie Lee. "The Sayings of Jesus in the Pseudoclementine Homilies." Harvard University, 1971.

Kooi, William E., Jr. "Transvaluation of Metaphysics in Christian Tradition: Toward a Narrative-Liturgical Theology." Baylor University, 1999.

Kraftchick, Steven John. "Ethos and Pathos in Galatians Five and Six: A Rhetorical Analysis." Emory University 1985.

Kyker, Rex Paxton. "William Winans: Minister and Politician of the Old South." University of Florida, 1957.

Lambert, Bill. "Using an Adaptive-Mastery System to Teach Inductive Exegesis in the Greek and English New Testament: A Course in How to Study the Greek and English New Testament." Ed.D., University of Arkansas, 1991.

Langford, David Ross. "Celebrative Versus Reformative Religion: The Impact of Religious Models on Family Dynamics and Family Satisfaction." Texas Technological University, 1992.

Langford, Thomas A. "The Ethical and Religious Thought of Walter Pater." Texas Christian University, 1968.

Larsen, Dale Russell. "A History of York College." Ed. D., University of Nebraska, 1966.

Lavender, Earl Dale. "The Development of Pelagius's Thought within a Late Fourth Century Ascetic Movement in Rome." St. Louis University, 1991.

Lawrence, John M. "Hepatoscopy and Extispicy in Graeco-Roman and Early Christian Texts." Miami University, Oxford, Ohio, 1979.

Ledlow, William Franklin. "The History of Protestant Education in Texas." University of Texas, 1926.

Lewis, Jack Pearl. "An Introduction to the Testament of the Twelve Patriarchs." Harvard University, 1953.

Lewis, Jack Pearl. "A Study of the Interpretation of Noah and the Flood in Jewish and Christian Literature." Hebrew Union, 1962.

Lewis, LeMoine Gaunce. "The Commentary: Jewish and Pagan Backgrounds of Origen's Commentaries with Emphasis on the Commentary on Genesis." Harvard University, 1958.

Lewis, Warren. "Peter John Olivi, O.F.M. (1248-1298), Prophet of the Year 2000: Ecclesiology and Eschatology in the *Lectura super Apocalipsim* (1297)." Dr. Theol., Tübingen, Germany, 1975.

Lightfoot, Neil R. "A Critical Examination of the Revised Standard Version of the New Testament."Duke University, 1958.

Lipe, David Lee. "Religious Versus Secular Ethics: A Religious Response to Some Contemporary Secular Views of Ethics." University of Tennessee, 1986.

Lisi, Luigi F. "La Poesia Biblica dell'Inferno: Immagini e Richiami Scritturali nella Lingua della Prima Cantica." University of California, 1974.

Long, Ellis Eugene. "Communication and Social Change: The Verbal and Nonverbal Protest of Selected Clerical Activists Opposed to the Vietnam War, 1965-1970." Florida State, 1971.

Long, Jesse Ceymour, Jr. "Sedentary Adaptations at the End of the Third Millennium B.C.: Khirbet Iskander and the Excavated Settlement Sites of Early Bronze IV Palestine-Transjordan." Drew University, 1988.

Long, Larry R. "Walden and the Bible: A Study in Influence and Composition." Ohio State University, 1976.

Long, Loretta M. "A Fellow Soldier in the Cause of Reformation: The Life of Selina Campbell." Georgetown University, 1998.

Looper, Travis Dayton. "The Poetry of Lord Byron: A Compendium of Biblical Usage." Baylor University, 1976.

Love, Bill R. "A Rhetorical Study of Selected Speeches by Reinhold Niebuhr (1930-1960)." Louisiana State University, 1979.

Lynn, Joe Mac. "A Curriculum for the School of Biblical Studies of Columbia Christian College." S.T.D., San Francisco Theological Seminary, 1972.

McAllister, Ted Vernon. "Revolt against Modernity: Leo Strauss, Eric Voegelin and the Search for a Post-Liberal Order." Vanderbilt University, 1994.

McCall, Brent Eugene. "Changing the Transformational Leadership Paradigm Perspective, Power by Perception Not by Position: Transperceptional Leadership and Organizational Effectiveness in Churches of Christ." University of New Mexico, 1999.

McCampbell, Duane. "A Critical Analysis of the Ethical Theories of A. C. Ewing." University of Arkansas, 1977.

McCann, Forrest Mason. "The Development of the Hymn in Old and Middle English Literature." Texas Technological University, 1980.

McCasland, Selby Vernon. "The Genesis of the New Testament Narratives of the Resurrection of Jesus." University of Chicago, 1926.

McCauley, Morris L. "The Preaching of the Reverend Rowland Hill (1744-1844), Surrey Chapel, London." Louisiana State University, 1974.

McCord, Carl Hugo. "The Significance of Yir'ath Yahweh Book of Proverbs." Th.D., New Orleans Baptist Theological Seminary, 1960.

McDonald, Michael David. "The Prophetic Oracles concerning Egypt in the Old Testament." Baylor University. 1978.

McFarland, Sam Grady. "Dogmatism and the Reduction of Cognitive Inconsistency Involving Important Beliefs by Logical and Illogical Repercussion Effects." Vanderbilt University, 1971.

McGaughey, Don Hugh. "The Hermeneutic Method of the Epistle to the Hebrews." Th.D., Boston University, 1963.

McGill, James Reuel. "An Experimental Study of the Effect of King James Version Archaisms upon Reading and Listening Comprehension and Retention." George Peabody College, 1970.

McKee, Timothy Gene. "A Formative Evaluation of a Church of Christ Missiological Rural Training Program in El Petén, Guatemala." Ed.D., Pepperdine University, 1981.

McKelvey, Cecil Carl, Jr. "An Investigation of Selected Active Adult Church Members Who Were Church Dropouts during Adolescence." D.R.E., Southern Baptist Theological Seminary, 1968.

McKenzie, Steven Linn. "The Chronicler's Use of the Deuteronomistic History." Th.D., Harvard University, 1983.

McLean, Mark Thurston. "An Analysis of Congregational Leadership Factors and Growth of Middle-Sized Churches of Christ in the Western United States." Ed.D., Southern Baptist Theological Seminary, 2003.

McMillan, G. Earle. "Wisdom-Logos Christology and Gnostic Speculation." University of St. Andrews, Scotland, 1969.

McMillion, Phillip Eugene. "Judges 6-8 and the Study of Premonarchical Israel." Vanderbilt, University, 1985.

McMillon, Lynn Allan. "The Quest for the Apostolic Church: A Study of Scottish Origins of American Restorationism." Baylor Univeristy, 1972.

McNicol, Allan James. "The Relationship of the Image of the Highest Angel to the High-Priest Concept in Hebrews." Vanderbilt, University 1974.

McRay, John Robert. "The Use of I Corinthians in the Early Church." University of Chicago, 1967.

Malherbe, Abraham Johannes. "The Supplicatio pro Christianis of Athenagoras and Middle Platonism." Th.D., Harvard University, 1963.

Manor, Dale Wallace. "An Archaeological Commentary on the Josianic Reform." University of Arizona, 1995.

Marrs, Rick Roy. "The SYRY-HM'LWT(Psalms 120-134): A Philological and Stylistic Analysis." Johns Hopkins University, 1983.

Martin, Dale R. "Slave of Christ, Slave of All: Paul's Metaphor of Slavery and 1 Corinthians 9." Yale University, 1988.

Martin, William Curtis. "Christians in Conflict." Harvard University 1969.

Mathews, Edward Frank. "A Comparative Analysis of the Attitudes of the Graduates of Caribbean Christian College and Leadership Training by Extension in Puerto Rico." D.Miss., Fuller Theological Seminary, 1980.

Matlock, R. Barry. "Unveiling the Apocalyptic Paul: Paul's Interpreters and the Rhetoric of Criticism." University of Sheffield, England, 1993.

Mattox, Fount W. "The Teaching of Religion in the Public Schools." George Peabody College, 1948.

Merritt, John Hilton. "A Study of Change in Circumcision Rituals among the Abaluyia of Bungoma and Kakamega Districts of Western Kenya since 1910 A.D." University of Nairobi, 1976.

Meyers, Robin Rex. "Preaching as Self-Persuasion: A New Metaphor for the Rhetoric of Faith." University of Oklahoma, 1991.

Miles, Johnny Edward. "When is a Wise Man a Fool? A Semiotic Analysis of Proverbs 1-9 as Satire." Baylor University, 2001.

Miller, David L. "The Status of Homiletics in Speech Communication Journals." Southern Illinois University, 1988.

Miller, Kenneth L. "The Relationship of Stages of Development in Children's Moral and Religious Thinking." Ed.D., Arizona State University, 1976.

Miller, William Allen. "The Cost of Vandalism and Its Prevention in Church of Christ Schools in the Southeast United States." George Peabody College, 1984.

Mitchell, Carl Gene. "A Comparison of the Values of High and Low Creative Seventh-Grade Students in Selected Junior High Schools in the Los Angeles District." University of Southern California, 1967.

Mitchell, Lynn Evans. "Two Ages and Two Communities: Implications of an Eschatological Duality for the Development of a Social Ethic." Rice University, 1979.

Money, Royce Lynn. "Church-State Relations in the Churches of Christ since 1945: A Study in Religion and Politics." Baylor University, 1975.

Moore, Lewis L. "Divorce: A Study of Coping Behaviors and the Interrelatedness with Religiosity, Loneliness, and Well-Being." University of Nebraska, 1980.

Moore, Marlin K. "An Empirical Investigation of the Relationship between Religiosity and Death Concern." Memphis State University, 1991.

Moore, Michael S. "The Balaam Traditions: Their Character and Development." Drew University, 1988.

Moreland, Milton Carl. "Jerusalem Imagined: Rethinking Earliest Christian Claims to the Hebrew Epic." Claremont Graduate University, 1999.

Morgan, Dennis Dale. "Needs Assessment in Churches: A Christian Community's Need for Professional Counseling Services." Rosemead School of Psychology, 1982.

Morgan, John Henry. "Communitarian Communism as a Religious Experience Exemplified in the Development of Shaker Theology." Hartford Seminary Foundation, 1972.

Morrison, Matthew Clifton. "Daniel Sommer's Seventy Years of Religious Controversy." Indiana University, 1972.

Moss, Carl Michael. "Origen's Commentary on John, Book XIII: A Translation with Annotations." Southern Baptist Theological Seminary, 1982.

Muncy, Raymond Lee. "Sex and Marriage in Nineteenth Century Utopian Communities." University of Mississippi, 1971.

Muse, Clyde. "The Educational Philosophy of Martin Luther King, Jr." University of Oklahoma, 1978.

Myer, Charles Franklin, Jr. "The Use of Aromatics in Ancient Mesopotamia." University of Pennsylvania, 1975.

Myers, Edward P. "A Study of Baptism in the First Three Centuries." Drew University, 1985.

Myers, Kippy Lee. "Philosophical Issues concerning the Bible and Animal Telos." University of Tennessee, 2000.

Neller, Kenneth V. "The Gospel of Thomas and the Earliest Texts of the Synoptic Gospels." University of St. Andrews, Scotland, 1983.

Niccum, Larry Curt. "The Book of Acts in Ethiopic (with Critical Text and Apparatus) and its Relation to the Greek Textual Tradition." University of Notre Dame, 2000.

Nichols, Jim. "A History of Harding College, 1924 to 1984." Ed.D., University of Arkansas, 1985.

North, Ira Lutts. "A Rhetorical Criticism of the Speaking of James Abram Garfield, 1876-1880." Louisiana State University, 1953.

North, Ross Stafford. "Joseph Priestley on Language, Oratory, and Criticism." University of Florida, 1957.

Northam, Gary J. "A Survey and Analysis of Family Life Ministries in the Churches of Christ."University of Nebraska, 1983.

Norton, Howard. "Sermões anti-Judaicos Pregados nos Autos-de-Fe em Lisboa de 1706 até 1750." Universidade de São Paulo, 1981.

Olbricht, Thomas Henry. "A Rhetorical Analysis of Representative Homilies of Basil the Great." State University of Iowa, 1959.

Osburn, Carroll Duane. "The Text of the Pauline Epistles in Epiphanius of Salamis." University of St. Andrews, Scotland, 1974.

Oster, Richard E., Jr. "A Historical Commentary on the Missionary Success Stories in Acts 19:11-40." Princeton Theological Seminary, 1974.

Owen, Dan Randall. "A Criterion-Referenced Instrument for Use as a Curriculum Evaluation Tool in Biblical Studies Departments in Universities Associated with Churches of Christ." Southern Illinois University, 1996

Pack, Frank. "The Methodology of Origen as a Textual Critic in Arriving at the Text of the New Testament." University of Southern California, 1948.

Pack, Rolland William. "Case Studies and Moral Conclusions: The Philosophical Use of Case Studies in Biomedical Ethics." Georgetown University, 1988.

Palmer, Roy Virgil. "The Problem of Talent Migration and the Role of the Small Private College in Foreign-Student Education." University of Michigan, 1968.

Parker, Floyd Oscar, Jr. "A Study of the Akedah in Paul's Letter to the Galatians." Drew University, 1994.

Patterson, George William. "Human Nature, Organization Theory, and Interpersonal Relations: An Investigation of Consistency among Leaders in Churches of Christ." Ed.D., New Orleans Baptist Theological Seminary, 1969.

Patty, Stacy Lee. "Corporations as Moral Persons with Responsibility for the Environment: A Judeo-Christian Challenge." Baylor University, 1994.

Pemberton, Glenn D. "Rhetoric of the Father: A Rhetorical Analysis of the Father/Son Lectures in Proverbs 1-9." Iliff School of Theology & University of Denver, 1999.

Perdue, Leo Garrett. "Wisdom and Cult: A Critical Analysis of the Views of Cult in the Wisdom Literatures of Israel and the Ancient Near East." Vanderbilt University, 1975.

Perry, Lowell Gordon. "The Description and Analysis of a Process of Religious Persuasion." Northwestern University, 1956.

Peterson, Jeffrey Earl. "The Image of the Man from Heaven: Christological Exegesis in 1 Corinthians 15:45-49." Yale University, 1997.

Petrillo, Dennis Dale. "An Identification and Examination of the Educational Philosophy of Adult Education among the Graduates of the Bear Valley School of Biblical Studies." University of Nebraska, 1989.

Petty, Daniel Wade. "Anabaptism and the Edwardian Reformation." Texas Christian University, 1988.

Phillips, Myer. "A Historical Study of the Attitude of the Churches of Christ toward Other Denominations." Baylor University, 1983.

Pitard, Wayne Thomas. "Ancient Damascus: A Historical Study of the Syrian City-State from Earliest Times until its Fall to the Assyrians in 732 B.C.E." Harvard University, 1982.

Plunket, Rodney Lamar. "'Between Elim and Sinai': A Theological Interpretation of Exodus Sixteen Shaped by its Canonical Context." University of Durham, England, 1996.

Pollard, Jesse Paul. "The Problem of the Faith of Christ." Baylor University, 1982.

Pope, Jesse Curtis. "The Restoration Ideal in American Religious Thought." Florida State University, 1990.

Potts, Michael. "Individuality, Metaphor, and God." University of Georgia, 1992.

Poyner, Barry Cole. "Role Duality as Represented in the Anti-Abolitionist Speeches of James Shannon." Louisiana State University, 1990.

Priest, James. "Judicial and Governmental Ethics in Hebrew Scripture and Rabbinic Literature—A Comparative Study." St. Mary's University, 1977.

Proctor, William Henry, Jr. "Herald of Truth: A Study of Religious Television Program Format Changes from 1954-1979." University of Mississippi, 1980.

Pryor, Neale Thomas. "The Concept of Da'ath 'Elohim in the Book of Hosea. Th.D., New Orleans Baptist Theologial Seminary, 1969.

Pulley, Kathy Jean. "Study of Secularization in Selected British Secondary County Schools' Religious Education Curricula, 1944-1985." Boston University, 1989.

Rambo, Lewis. "The Strenuous Life: William James's Normative Vision of the Human." University of Chicago, 1975.

Randolph, Paul Gene. "The Role of Protestantism in the Founding of Public Primary Instruction in France, 1814-1833." University of Michigan, 1972

Randolph, Robert Eugene. "The Development of the Synoptic Tradition." Emory University, 1968.

Ray, Vernon Oliver. "A Rhetorical Analysis of the Political Preaching of the Reverend Jerry Falwell: The Moral Majority Sermons." Louisiana State University, 1985.

Rayburn, Gary Keith. "Paul Tillich's Philosophy of Communication." University of Oklahoma, 1969.

Reese, Jack Roger. "Routes of Conversion: A Sociopsychological Study of the Varieties of Individual Religious Change." University of Iowa, 1988.

Resner, Andre, Jr. "Preacher and Cross: Person and Message in Theology and Rhetoric." Princeton Theological Seminary, 1998.

Reynolds, James Glen. "Justification by Faith in Reinhold Niebuhr's Thought." Th.D., Graduate Theological Union, 1974.

Rhoads, Forrest Neil. "A Study of the Sources of Marshall Keeble's Effectiveness as a Preacher." Southern Illinois University, 1970.

Riall, Robert Archie. "Athanasius, Bishop of Alexandria: The Politics of Spirituality." University of Cincinnati, 1987.

Richardson, Robert Randolph. "Speaking Where the Bible Speaks: The Rhetoric of the American Restoration Movement." Wayne State University, 1994.

Rideout, Holbert Leon. "Criteria for the Development of Curriculum Materials for Churches of Christ." D.R.E., Southwestern Baptist Theological Seminary, 1962.

Roberts, J. W. "Use of Conditional Sentences in the Greek New Testament as Compared with Homeric, Classical, and Hellenistic Uses." University of Texas, 1955.

Roberts, Jimmy Jack McBee. "The Early Akkadian Pantheon: A Study of the Semitic Deities Attested in Mesopotamia before Ur III." Harvard University, 1969.

Robinson, Edward Jerome. "'Like Rats in a Trap': Samuel Robert Cassius and the 'Race Problem' in Churches of Christ." Mississippi State University, 2003.

Robinson, Thomas Lonzo. "Theological Oracles and the Sanctuaries of Claros and Didyma." Harvard University, 1981.

Rockey, Edward H. "John Haynes Holmes's Published Opinions on Human Freedom." New York University, 1966.

Rodriguez, Daniel Arthur. "No Longer Foreigners and Aliens: Toward a Missiological Christology for Mexican-Americans in Southern California." Fuller Theological Seminary, 2000.

Rogers, Glenn F. "The Missiological Implications of God's Desire for a Relationship with All Peoples." Fuller Theological Seminary, 2002.

Rollmann, Hans-Josef. "The Historical Methodology of William Wrede." McMaster University, 1980.

Roper, Coy Dee. "Factors Contributing to the Origin and Success of the Pre-Christian Jewish Missionary Movement." University of Michigan, 1988.

Rotenberry, Paul Wilson. "A Translation and Study of the Qumran Hodayot." Vanderbilt University, 1968.

Royse, Nyal Dailey. "A Study of the Environment of Harding College as Perceived by its Students and Faculty and as Anticipated by Entering Students." Ed.D., Memphis State University, 1969.

Ruffner, Kail D. "Demographics Associated with Non-Participation in Church-Based Adult Education:A Factor Analytic Study." Ed.D., Indiana University, 1982.

Rushford, Jerry Bryant. "Political Disciple: The Relationship between James A. Garfield and the Disciples of Christ." University of California, Santa Barbara, 1977.

Salisbury, Thayer Allyn. "Textbooks for African Bible Colleges: Investigating the Narrative Option." D.Miss., Concordia Theological Seminary, 2000.

Samuel, James H. "Luke's Presentation of Jesus' Journey to Jerusalem: A Study in Redaction Criticism," Th.D., Southwestern Baptist Theological Seminary, 1968.

Sanders, Joel Pilant. "The Concept of God in the Philosophical Writings of James Bissett Pratt." University Southern California, 1947.

Sanders, Joseph Enloe. "Major Theological Beliefs of the Churches of Christ and Their Implications for Christian Education." Boston University, 1957.

Savage, James Charles. "Josephus: Jewish Historian and Translator of Sacred Scripture." Hebrew Union, 1993.

Savage, James Charles. "Psychotherapy and Exegesis: A Study of Parallel Processes." The Union Institute, 1998.

Scarboro, Charles Allen. "A Sectarian Religious Organization in Heterogeneous Society: The Churches of Christ and the Plain Folk of the Transmontane Mid-South." Emory University, 1976.

Schubert, Joe David. "The Impact of Selected Colleges on Students' Values." Ed.D., University of Southern California, 1967.

Schulz, Dorris M. "A Study of Third Culture Experience in Relation to the Psycho-Social Adjustment of Returned Church of Christ Missionary Families." University of Nebraska, 1985.

Schulz, Thomas N. "A Study to Determine the Basic Needs of MK's upon Re-Entry to the United States and to Define and Describe a Re-Entry Program Designed to Meet the Needs." University of Nebraska, 1985.

Scott, Jack Alan. "A Critical Edition of John Witherspoon's 'Lectures on Moral Philosophy.'" Claremont Graduate School, 1970.

Scott, John Atwood. "The Pattern of the Tabernacle." University of Pennsylvania, 1965.

Sears, Lloyd Cline. "Shakespeare and the Problem of Evil." University of Chicago, 1936.

Seesengood, Robert Paul. "Running with Endurance: Nascent Christian Use of Athletic Metaphors." Drew University, 2004.

Selby, Gary Steven. "Apocalyptic and Rhetoric in the Epistles of the New Testament." University of Maryland, 1996.

Sensing, Timothy R. "Pedagogies of Preaching." University of North Carolina at Greensboro, 1998.

Shackelford, Robert Donald. "The Concept of Knowledge in the Book of Job." Th.D., New Orleans Baptist Theological Seminary, 1976.

Shank, Harold. "The Sin Theology of the Cain and Abel Story: An Analysis of Narrative Themes within the Context of Genesis 1-11." Marquette University, 1988.

Shaver, Thomas Austin. "A Critical Analysis of William C. Bagley's Concept of Essentialism and Evidence of its Similarity in Church of Christ Youth Curriculum Materials, 1963-1966." D.R.E., Southwestern Baptist Theological Seminary, 1967.

Shaw, John Paul, Sr. "Proof for the Existence of God at Two Extremes." University of Nebraska, 1980.

Shelly, Thomas Rubel. "Theodicy in Plato's Timaeus." Vanderbilt University, 1981.

Shipp, Glover Harvey. "Research As a Tool for Urban Evangelism in Developing Countries." D.Miss., Fuller Theological Seminary, 1986.

Shipp, R. Mark. "Of Dead Kings and Dirges: Myth and Meaning in Isaiah 14:4B-21." Princeton Theological Seminary, 1998.

Shults, Fount Lee. "Shalem and Thamim in Biblical Hebrew: An Analysis of the Semantic Field of Wholeness." University of Texas, 1974.

Sikes, Walter W. "The Gospel of Life: An Inquiry into the Significance of the Idea of Life in the Fourth Gospel and the Johannine Epistles." Union Theological Seminary, New York, 1939.

Sime, Donald R. "The Effect of Interpersonal Encounter in Small Groups on Attitudes Relevant to Faith in God." University of Chicago, 1962.

Sinclair, Cameron. "A Linguistic Analysis of Neo-Assyrian Syntax." Dropsie College, 1971.

Skaggs, W. Jack. "Work Values of Faculty Members in Selected Small Liberal Arts Colleges: A Comparative Study." Ed.D., Oklahoma State University, 1987.

Slate, Carl Philip. "Communication Theory and Evangelization: Contributions to the Communication of Religious Innovations in the Euroamerican Culture Area." D.Miss., Fuller Theological Seminary, 1976.

Smith, Dennis Edwin. "Social Obligation in the Context of Communal Meals: A Study of the Christian Meal in 1 Corinthians in Comparison with Graeco-Roman Communal Meals." Th.D., Harvard University, 1980.

Smith, Derwood Cooper. "Jewish and Greek Traditions in Ephesians 2:11-22." Yale University, 1970.

Smith, Jay. "A Study of the Alleged 'Two Messiah' Expectation of the Dead Sea Scrolls against the Background of Developing Eschatology." Vanderbilt University, 1969.

Smith, Thomas Vernor. "Philosophic Bases of the American Doctrine of Equality." University of Chicago, 1922.

Smythe, James Erwin. "The Religious and Moral Philosophy of Sir Walter Scott." University of Illinois at Urbana-Champaign, 1955.

Sneed, Mark Ronnie. "The Social Location of Qoheleth's Thought: Anomie and Alienation in Ptolemaic Jerusalem." Drew University, 1990.

South, James Thomas. "Corrective Discipline in the Pauline Communities." University of Virginia, 1989.

Southern, Paul. "The New Testament Use of the Preposition kata with Special Reference to Its Distributive Aspects." Th.D., Southern Baptist Theological Seminary, 1948.

Spain, Carl. "A Study of the Evangelistic Ministry in Churches of Christ." Th.D., Southwestern Baptist Theological Seminary, 1963.

Speck, Henry Eli, Jr. "The Educational Contributions of a Religious Reformer—Alexander Campbell." University of Texas, 1951.

Srygley, William Leake. "A Study of Some Factors Basic to the Religious, Moral, and Social Education of Adolescents." Ed.D., New Orleans Baptist Theological Seminary, 1972.

Steed, Tom. "Alexander Campbell's View of Reality and the Church: A Phenomenological, Rhetorical,and Metaphorical Analysis." Southern Illinois University, 2000.

Stephens, Robert William, Jr. "Predictors of College Choice for First-Time College Students at American Colleges and Universities Associated with the Church of Christ." Ed.D., West Virginia University, 1995.

Stephenson, Charles Bell. "The Christology of the Pastoral Epistles." Th.D., New Orleans Baptist Theological Seminary, 1978.

Sterling, Gregory E. "Historiography and Self-Definition: Josephos, Luke-Acts, and Apologetic Historiography." Graduate Theological Union, 1989.

Stewart, John David. "Paul Ricoeur's Phenomenology of Evil." Rice University, 1965.

Stockstill, Daniel Brady. "Intelligence and Faith in Adolescents: A Study of the Relationship between Multiple Intelligences and Faith Formation during Adolescence." The Union Institute, 1999.

Storm, Melvin R. "Excommunication in the Theology and the Life of the Primitive Christian Communities." Baylor University, 1987.

Stowers, Stanley Kent. "A Critical Reassessment of Paul and the Diatribe: The Dialogical Element in Paul's Letter to the Romans." Yale University, 1979.

Such, William A. "'To Bdelugma tes Heremoseos' in Mark 13:14: Its Historical Reference and Its Impact in Mark 13 and in the Context of Mark's Gospel." University of St. Andrews, Scotland, 1998.

Sumney, Jerry L. "Paul's Opponents: A Method for Determining Their Identity and a Proposal for the Identity of the Opponents of 2 Corinthians." Southern Methodist University, 1987.

Sutherland, Arthur Marvin. "Christology and Discipleship in the Sermons of Karl Barth, 1913-1916." Princeton Theological Seminary, 2000.

Tabor, James Daniel. "Things Unutterable: Paul's Ascent to Paradise." University of Chicago, 1981.

Tate, Francis Vincent. "Kangemi: The Impact of Rapid Culture Change on Community and Family. A Study of Change and Stability in a Newly Developing Urban Community." University of Nairobi, 1973.

Taylor, Donald Ross. "Andre Gide's Application of Biblical Parable to Express a Moral Philosophy." University of Southern Mississippi, 1987.

Teague, William Jack. "Characteristics of Donors and Non-Donors to Higher Education among Members of Churches of Christ in the United States." Ed.D., University of California, Los Angeles, 1965.

Terry, Ralph Bruce. "An Analysis of Certain Features of Discourse in the New Testament Book of I Corinthians." University of Texas, Arlington, 1993.

Thomas, James David. "The Greek Text of Tobit." University of Chicago, 1957.

Thomas, Theodore Norton. "Women of the Confessing Church, 1934-1945: Theologians and Pastors' Wives." University of Maryland, 1992.

Thompson, James Weldon. "'That Which Abides': Some Metaphysical Assumptions in the Epistle to the Hebrews." Vanderbilt University, 1974.

Thompson, Robert Edward. "An Analysis of Fund-Raising Methods and Techniques Used by Church of Christ-Related Four-Year Colleges in the United States of America." Ed.D., George Peabody College, 1983.

Tippens, Darryl Lee. "John Milton and St. Paul: A Comparative Study." Louisiana State University, 1973.

Tollerson, James. "The Role of the Samaritans in the Ministry of Jesus." Th.D., New Orleans Baptist Theological Seminary, 1979.

Trimble, John Clifton. "The Rhetorical Theory and Practice of John W. McGarvey." Northwestern University, 1966.

Trotter, James Marion. "Reading Hosea in Achaemenid Yehud." Emory University, 1998.

Tyler, Ronald L. "The Pauline Doctrine of Jesus Christ as Last Adam." Baylor University, 1973.

Tyson, John Nelson, Jr. "Paradigms of Religious Expression: An Analysis of Religious Broadcasting." University of Texas, 1990.

Ulrey, Evan A. "The Preaching of Barton Warren Stone." Louisiana State University, 1955.

Vancil, Jack Wayland. "The Symbolism of the Shepherd in Biblical, Intertestamental and New Testament Material." Dropsie University, 1975.

Vanderpool, Harold Young. "The Andover Conservatives: Apologetics, Biblical Criticism, and Theological Change at the Andover Theological Seminary, 1808-1880." Harvard University, 1971.

Vanderpool, Kenneth Gene. "The Attitude of Selected Nineteenth-Century Disciples of Christ Leaders Regarding Physical Activity." Ed.D., Temple University, 1972.

Van Rheenen, Dwayne D. "The Process of Persuasion: A Field Experiment on Changes over Time within, between, and across Speeches." University of Missouri, 1975.

Varner, Jeanine Baker. "Henry James and Gustave Flaubert: The Creative Relationship." University of Tennessee, 1981.

Verkler, Billy D. "An Application of Cognitive Dissonance Theory to Reference Group Behavior: A Study of Racial Attitudes of Church Members in Searcy, Arkansas." University of Mississippi, 1971.

Walker, David Ellis. "The Rhetoric of the Restoration Movement: The Period of Inception: 1800-1832." University of Florida, 1969.

Wallace, David Paul. "Texts in Tandem: The Coalescent Usage of Psalm 2 and Psalm 110 in Early Christianity." Baylor University, 1995.

Walters, James Christopher. "Ethnic Issues in Paul's Letter to the Romans: An Analysis in Light of the Changing Self-Definition of Early Christianity in Rome." Boston University, 1991.

Ward, Roy Bowen. "The Communal Concern of the Epistle of James." Th.D., Harvard University, 1966.

Warden, Duane. "Alienation and Community in 1 Peter." Duke University, 1986.

Warren, David Harold. "The Text of the Apostle in the Second Century: A Contribution to the History of its Reception." Th.D., Harvard University, 2001.

Warren, Lindsey Davis. "Invention in the Lyman Beecher Lectures on Preaching, 1958-1988." University of Oklahoma, 1991.

Warren, Thomas Bratton. "God and Evil: Does Judeo-Christian Theism Involve a Logical Contradiction?" Vanderbilt University, 1969.

Wasson, Woodrow W. "James A. Garfield and Religion: A Study in the Religious Thought and Activity of an American Statesman." University of Chicago, 1947.

Waters, Kenneth Eugene. "Toward the Successful Christian Publication: A Descriptive Analysis of Four Independent Evangelical Christian Periodicals." University of Southern California, 1982.

Watson, Paul Layton. "Mot, the God of Death, at Ugarit and in the Old Testament." Yale University, 1970.

Weed, Michael Robbins. "Conscience in Protestant Ethics: An Examination of Protestant Views of the Nature and Function of Conscience, Focusing on the Thought of Select Contemporary Theologians." Emory University, 1978.

West, Earl Irvin. "Religion and Politics in the Jacksonian Era." Indiana University, 1968.

West, Earle Huddleston. "The Life and Educational Contributions of Barnas Sears." George Peabody College, 1961.

West, W. B., Jr. "An Ante-Nicene Exegesis of Romans and Galatians." Th.D., University of Southern California, 1942.

Wheeler, Frank. "Textual Criticism and the Synoptic Problem: A Textual Commentary on the Minor Agreements of Matthew and Luke against Mark." Baylor University, 1985.

White, Lloyd Michael. "Domus Ecclesiae—Domus Dei: Adaptation and Development in the Setting for Early Christian Assembly." Yale, 1982.

Whitfield, Thomas Clark Rye. "Administration of Colleges Operated by Members of the Churches of Christ." George Peabody College, 1953.

Wiebe, Ben. "Messianic Ethics: Jesus' Kingdom-of-God Proclamation and the Appropriate Response." McMaster University, 1988.

Wilburn, Ralph Glenn. "Schleiermacher's Conception of Grace in the Light of Historical Development of the Doctrine of Grace." University of Chicago, 1945.

Williams, Joel Stephen. "Ethical Issues in Compulsory Medical Treatment: A Study of Jehovah's Witnesses and Blood Transfusion." Baylor University, 1987.

Williams, Michael A. "The Nature and Origin of the Gnostic Concept of Stability." Harvard University, 1978.

Willis, John Thomas. "The Structure, Setting, and Interrelationships of the Pericopes in the Book of Micah." Vanderbilt University, 1966.

Willis, Timothy M. "Elders in Pre-Exilic Israelite Society." Harvard University, 1990.

Willis, Wendell Lee. "Paul's Instructions to the Corinthian Church on the Eating of Idol Meat." Southern Methodist University, 1981.

Wilson, John Francis. "The Christian Message: Its Place in Ordering the Life of the Pauline Communities." University of Iowa, 1967.

Wilson, Vernon Woodrow. "The Archaeological and Biblical Evidences Bearing upon the Question of the Date and Pharaoh of the Exodus." Th.D., Southwestern Baptist Theological Seminary, 1955.

Winrow, Dewayne. "A Social Ethical Analysis of the Restoration Motif of Churches of Christ." University of Southern California, 2000.

Wolfgang, James Stephen. "Science and Religion Issues in the American Restoration Movement." University of Kentucky, 1997.

Womack, Morris Maloney. "A Study of the Life and Preaching of John Chrysostom." Wayne State University, 1967.

Woodroof, James Timothy. "Religiosity and Reference Groups: Towards a Model of Adolescent Sexuality." University of Nebraska, 1984.

Woods, Clyde Morris. "A Translation of Tosefta Yevamoth with Commentary." Hebrew Union, 1964.

Woods, Robert M. "Imagination, Religion, and Morality in the Shorter Imaginative Fiction of George MacDonald." Florida State University, 1990.

Woodson, William Edgar. "An Analytical History of Churches of Christ in Tennessee (1906-1950)." Th.D., New Orleans Baptist Theological Seminary, 1975.

Worley, David Ripley, Jr. "God's Faithfulness to Promise: The Hortatory Use of Commissive Language in Hebrews." Yale University, 1981.

Yates, Jere Eugene. "Erikson's Study of the Identity Crisis in Adolescence and its Implications for Religious Education." Boston University, 1968.

Yeakley, Flavil Ray. "Persuasion in Religious Conversion." University of Illinois at Urbana—Champaign, 1975.

York, John Oran. "The Rhetorical Function of Bi-Polar Reversal in Luke." Emory University, 1989.

Young, David M. "Whoever Has Ears to Hear: The Discourses of Jesus in Mark as Primary Rhetoric of the Greco-Roman Period." Vanderbilt University, 1994.

Young, Matt Norvel. "History of the Organization and Development of Church of Christ Colleges." George Peabody College, 1944.

Zenor, Charles Wesley. "A History of Biblical Interpretation in the Church of Christ: 1901-1976." Th.D., Illiff School of Theology, 1976.

Zink, James Keith. "The Use of the Old Testament in the Apocrypha." Duke University, 1963.

The Future of Theology
at Fuller Theological Seminary:
Looking around the Pacific Rim

David Bundy

To comment on the future of anything is an undertaking fraught with hazards! Perhaps for that reason, American Christianity and its offspring have been more comfortable with "Primitivism" than with "Prophecy." In this essay, I am compelled by continuity with the past of Fuller Theological Seminary, and by its geographic location, to argue a case for the future. Historically and actively a school with strong ties to the rest of the world, Fuller was founded on the edge of the Pacific Rim. From our home on the westward edge of the North American continent, we look out upon the great circle of the Peaceful Ocean. In full awareness of the immense challenge and in joy of the promise, Fuller Theological Seminary has embraced the Pacific Rim as its primary realm of educational and intellectual activity.

This essay is a thoroughly personal reflection upon a community, and its future, that I joined in August 2002. My job as the Associate Provost for Library Services and Associate Professor of History at the Fuller Theological Seminary is to build a library that will support Fuller's mission. That mission, focused on the Pacific Rim, requires an understanding of the history of Christianity and other religions of the Pacific, missionary responses appropriate to the several cultures and their human needs in the Pacific hemisphere, and ministry and pastoral care of missionary and indigenous churches in their almost uncountable diversity. Essential to the future of Fuller's mission is interaction with the "theologies of the Pacific" as these churches make responsible responses to the grace and love of God for all humankind.

In this essay, I speak in no official capacity for the faculty, administration, or Board of Fuller Theological Seminary. I have discussed these matters with numerous colleagues, and their many suggestions have influenced what I present here; however, this essay is not a statement of institutional policy but, rather, my own individual "prophecy" of "The Future of Theology at Fuller." I begin by looking at the history and context of Fuller Theological Seminary and the development of theology on the Pacific Rim, and then I foresee some of the challenges that Fuller will need to address if it is to play the constructive role in the future of theology on the Pacific Rim that all of us here at Fuller desire.

A Way of Looking at Fuller Theological Seminary

George Marsden, in his magisterial analysis of Fuller Theological Seminary prepared for the fiftieth anniversary of the institution, reasoned that Fuller was to be understood as a continuation of a classical Princetonian Presbyterian tradition. Certainly there was evidence for Marsden's perspective. He is a superb historian with an encyclopedic knowledge of American Fundamentalism; he could see a result of Fuller as "reforming Fundamentalism."[1] A lot of people hoped he was correct, neglecting to acknowledge that most of that supportive Princetonian myth had gone into the formation of—and would be more sympathetic with—the Westminster Theological Seminary of J. Gresham Machen. Marsden was taken to task by Donald Dayton, also with an encyclopedic knowledge of American evangelical religion, who argued that Fuller should more accurately be understood as developing within the context of the American Holiness and Pentecostal movements.[2] Likewise, there was evidence for Dayton's perspective, but fewer people hoped he was correct!

Both of these scholars missed a crucial factor in their analyses: the geographic context of Fuller in California and on the Pacific Rim. From its beginnings in Los Angeles, Protestant Christianity has defied the national models. The theological, social, racial, and cultural boundaries that defined religious life in the East and South have functioned with less severity and clarity on the West Coast. Californians have been less attached to the sectarian emphases of either the right or the left as defined at any particular moment in American history. The tendency in the Far West has been to make common (and often temporary) cause in support of social, educative, and mission projects. This fluidity of identity has extended to a consciousness of the Pacific Rim, and it has developed in parallel with significant portions of the polyglot cultures of our oceanic neighborhood.

These trends were early in evidence among Protestants in California. The first Protestant evangelist and church leader in Southern California, William Money (he pronounced it *Mo-nay*), ordained himself bishop and sought to establish a primitivist New Testament version of Christianity, with no direct reference to similar trends in the Stone-Campbell tradition of the American South and Mid-West.[3] He was followed, with considerably less success, by a series of Methodist, Presbyterian, and Baptist missionaries who had minimal success and established no permanent presence.

The second successful Protestant effort was funded by the Presbyterian Mission Board and founded by William Boardman (from 1859 to 1862). Boardman, however, rather than working under the banner of the Presbyterians, organized (May1859) the "First Protestant Society of the City of Los Angeles." Boardman's Society languished after February1862, when he resigned, having learned that most of his parishioners enthusiastically favored the South in the American Civil War. Boardman, already an internationally known advocate of the Holiness movement, eventually moved to London, and he fulfilled his days as a progenitor of international healing movements and as an influential Holiness evangelist in

---

[1] George M. Marsden, *Reforming Fundamentalism: Fuller Seminary and the New Evangelicalism* (Grand Rapids: Eerdmans, 1987); the second edition (Grand Rapids: Eerdmans, 1995) contains a response to the criticisms of Donald Dayton, cited below.

[2] Donald W. Dayton, "The Search for the Historical Evangelicalism: George Marsden's History of Fuller Seminary as a Case Study," *Christian Scholars Review* 23 (1993): 12-33. This produced a significant debate in subsequent issues of *Christian Scholars Review* as well as a response in the second edition of George Marsden, *Reforming Fundamentalism: Fuller Seminary and the New Evangelicalism* (Grand Rapids: Eerdmans, 1995).

[3] William P. Money, *Reform of the New Testament Church/Reforma de la Iglesia del Nuevo Testamento* (Los Angeles: n.p., 1854).

Europe. Boardman's revivalist activities provoked the establishment of the Holiness Movement Church in Sweden, for example.[4]

Later evangelical activity on the eve of the rise of the Fundamentalist/Modernist controversy was ecumenical. While some quickly assumed the religious values of the dominant Eastern mainline churches, Baptists, Presbyterians, Methodists, Holiness advocates, and Quakers—men and women, rich and poor—shared the platforms as they evangelized among immigrants to Southern California, with special attention to Catholics and non-Northern European immigrants. Their interest in converting non-Europeans contributed to the early development of trans-Pacific revivalism. The racial and class differences of Post-Civil-War churches that led to segregated congregations in the East were more nuanced here. California has been comfortable with its multicultural reality for a long time.

Henry Fuller, after whom Fuller Theological Seminary is named, was supportive of those evangelistic and missionary efforts. He traveled around the world visiting Holiness and Pentecostal and other "free-church" missionaries. Fuller's book describing this tour was published by the Pentecostal Press, located in Pasadena, owned by Phineas Bresee, an urban mission activist and a primary founder of the Church of the Nazarene.[5] The supporters of the ministry of Henry's son, Charles E. Fuller, came from all segments of the religious communities.

The point of this essay is not to engage in an extended analysis of historiographical debates about the origins of Fuller Theological Seminary; nevertheless, essential to understanding Fuller is to grasp that the Seminary's geographical context, on the beach of the Pacific Rim, has made a difference for its past and present, and shall make a difference for its future. We're talking California religion, here; and religion in California, like California itself, has always been, well…different!

What Happens at Fuller Theological Seminary

Theology at Fuller Theological Seminary has generally been promulgated within a version of the Calvinistic Reformed traditions of Christian theological reflection, but not in ways that most Reformed traditions would recognize as Reformed and Calvinist. As is clear from the works of theologians from Carl F. H. Henry and E. J. Carnell to James McClendon and Miroslav Volf, and then to Nancey Murphy, Colin Brown, and Veli-Mati Karkainen, the reality is more complicated.[6] One could perhaps make a more successful argument for a

---

[4] On Boardman, see Mary Boardman, *Life and Labours of the Rev. W.E. Boardman*, forward by Mark Pearse (London: Bemrose & Sons, 1886; New York, D. Appleton and Co., 1887); for an initial appraisal of his role in Los Angeles, see, Michael E. Engh, *Frontier Faiths: Church, Temple, and Synagogue in Los Angeles, 1846-1888* (Albuquerque: University of New Mexico Press, 1992). When Boardman came to Los Angeles, he was already internationally famous as the author of a best-selling Holiness classic: William E. Boardman, *The Higher Christian Life* (Boston: H. Hoyt, 1859; New York: D. Appleton, 1859; Chicago: Wm. Tomlinson, 1859; Edinburgh: A. Strahan, 1860, with many editions/printings, including, London: Dalby, Isbister & Co., 1875; London: Morgan and Chase, 1875; London: James Nisbet, 1875). This book appeared in complete, serialized, or extracted translations in numerous Asian and European languages.
[5] Henry Fuller, *A Californian Circles the Globe* (Pasadena: Pentecostal Press, 1904).
[6] For example, see Carl F.H. Henry, *The Relation between Conduct and Belief* (London: Victoria Institute, 1946) [in the context of Fuller, Henry generally narrowed his theological analysis]; E.J. Carnell, *The*

general, evangelical Pietism.[7] Certainly that understanding would be in continuity with the "Old Fashioned Revival Hour," the famous radio program of Charles E. Fuller.[8] From the days of Henry and Carnell, indeed, voices have been raised at Fuller in discussion with both the left and the right as typically defined in European-American Protestant theology.[9]

Fuller Theological Seminary has always been a difficult place to peg. Its faculty has produced many a Fundamentalist/Evangelical text, but it has also proudly produced what are arguably two of the most important theological works for the English-speaking world of theology, regardless of ideological slant: the English translations of Kittel's *Theologishe Wörterbuch des Neuen Testaments*, and many of the works of Karl Barth in translation by the English scholar, Geoffrey Bromily. These multi-volume works might have been translated at Harvard or Princeton or Chicago, but they were not. They were translated, magnificently, at Fuller—uncensored beacons both of German critical biblical scholarship and of its major Neo-orthodox critic. In addition, critical Evangelical biblical commentaries and analyses of biblical texts have been produced at Fuller by an array of scholars, including Goldingay, Allen, Geulich, Hubbard, Scholer, Hagner, and others.[10]

Kingdom of Love and the Pride of Life (Grand Rapids: Eerdmans, 1960); James McClendon, *Systematic Theology* (Nashville: Abingdon, 1986-1994); Miroslav Volf, *Exclusion and Embrace: A Theological Exploration of Identity, Otherness, and Reconciliation* (Nashville: Abingdon, 1996); Nancey Murphy, *Anglo-American Post-Modernity: Philosophical Perspectives on Science, Religion and Ethics* (Boulder: Westview Press, 1997); Colin Brown, *History and Faith: A Personal Exploration* (Grand Rapids: Eerdmans, 1987); Veli-Mati Karkainen, *Christology: A Global Introduction* (Grand Rapids: Eerdmans, 2003).

[7] Central to Pietism is a determined primitivist impulse that is Biblicist, albeit operating from a philosophical base different from Fundamentalism. On how this has worked in American religion, see Richard T. Hughes, ed. *The American Quest for the Primitive Church* (Urbana: University of Illinois Press, 1988); *idem, The Primitive Church in the Modern World* (Urbana: University of Illinois Press, 1995); Grant Wacker, *Heaven Below: Early Pentecostals and American Culture* (Cambridge, Massachusetts: Harvard University Press, 2001). For a general survey of the role of Pietism in global Christianity, see D. Bundy, "European Pietist Roots of Pentecostalism," *The New International Dictionary of Pentecostal and Charismatic Movements* Stanley M. Burgess and Eduard M. Van der Maas, eds. (Grand Rapids: Zondervan, 2002): 610-613.

[8] Charles E. Fuller was aware of his multi-ethnic audience and addressed the issue frequently. See, for example, his "Old Fashioned Revival Hour" sermon, "Is the Church the Storehouse? Mal. 3:7-11," preached 15 November 1954, re-released 23 November 2003 (Orange, California: Christian Heritage Ministry, 2003).

[9] See especially the inaugural address of Edward J. Carnell, "The Glory of a Theological Seminary," in Russell Spittler, *Fuller Voices: Then and Now"* (Pasadena: Fuller Theological Seminary, 2004): 21-30. This collection of documents central to Fuller's history is a good introduction to the values of the institution.

[10] See for example: John Goldingay, *An Ignatian Approach to Reading the Old Testament* (Cambridge: Grove Books, 2002); Leslie C. Allen, *Ezekiel 20-48*, Word Biblical Commentary 29 (Waco: Word, 1990); Robert Geulich, *Mark 1-8:26* Word Biblical Commentary 34A (Waco: Word, 1989); David A. Hubbard served as an editor for the Word Biblical Commentary Series; David Scholer, *Women in Ministry* (Chicago: Covenant Press, 1987); and Donald Hagner, *Mt 1-13* Word Biblical Commentary, 33A(Waco: Word, 1993); *idem, Matthew 14*, Word Biblical Commentary 33B (Waco: Word, 1995).

Some Fuller faculty members, such as Mel Robeck, have had a major impact on the ecumenical movements of the mainline churches as well as on the newer churches.[11] Fuller early on posed questions about the relationship of theology and psychology.[12] Now, Fuller is taking an independent tack in the burgeoning "theology and the arts" regatta. The approaches of Rob Johnston, Bill Dyrness, Fred Davison, Marguerite Schuster, Clay Schmidt, and Roberta King are quite different from the approaches of either more mainline seminaries (e.g., United Theological Seminary, St. Paul or Christian Theological Seminary, Indianapolis) or of the church music programs of either the Southern Baptist seminaries or Yale.[13] As is usual for Fuller, the faculty and students of the Brehm Center for Theology and the Arts are aware of, and in discussion with, the other approaches, but also as is usual for Fuller, the Southern California context makes a big difference.

The "Church Growth" tradition of teaching and practice in the School of Intercultural Studies has been accused of being "overly American" and interested only in numbers. This accusation can perhaps be sustained, and naïve enthusiasm for the theory has waned at Fuller. As is usual for Fuller (the refrain repeats itself), the reality at Fuller is rather more complicated. Church Growth, as understood by William Taylor, E. Stanley Jones, J. Wascom Pickett, and Picketts's protégé, Donald McGavran, was arguably the first recognition by Protestant mission theorists that non-European Christians in America have a lot to teach European and North American Christians, especially mainline Christians, about mission, evangelism, ethics, and the growth of the church.[14] One can argue about whether these pioneers were actually insightful, but pioneers they were. At a time when Henry P. Van Dusen and John MacKay were observing that something was different about the reality of churches in Latin America and the Caribbean,[15] McGavran and his disciples

---

[11] See for example, C. M. Robeck, "A Pentecostal Looks at the World Council of Churches, *Ecumenical Review* 47(1995): 60-69; *idem*, "When Being a "Martyr" Is Not Enough: Catholics and Pentecostals," *Pneuma* 21(1999): 3-10; *idem*, "Do 'Good Fences Make Good Neighbors?' Evangelization, Proselytism and Common Witness," *Asian Journal of Pentecostal Studies* 2 (1999): 87-103.

[12] See Marsden (1987, 1995) and H. Newton Malony and Hendrika Vande Kamp, *Psychology and the Cross: The Early History of Fuller Seminary's School of Psychology* (Pasadena: Fuller Seminary Press, 1995).

[13] The Fuller Theological Seminary approach is less prescriptive than either UTS (St. Paul) or CTS, determinedly multi-denominational, and fosters close relationships with the churches and the entertainment industries. See, for example, Clay Schmidt, *Too Deep for Words: A Theology of Liturgical Expression* (Louisville: Westminster/John Knox, 2002), and William Dyrness, *Visual Faith: Art, Theology and Worship in Dialogue* (Grand Rapids: Baker Academic, 2001).

[14] William Taylor, *Our South American Cousins* (New York: Nelson and Phillips; London: Hodder and Stoughton, 1878); *idem, Pauline Methods of Missionary Work* (Philadelphia: National Publishing Association for the Promotion of Holiness, 1879); Jarrell Waskom Pickett, *Christian Mass Movements in India: A Study with Recommendations* (Lucknow: Lucknow Publishing House, 1933; New York, Cincinnati, *et al.*: Abingdon Press, 1933); Jarrell Waskom Pickett, Donald McGavran and G. H. Singh, *Christian Missions in Mid India: A Study of Nine Areas with Special Reference to Mass Movements* (Jubbulpore, India: The Mission Press, 1938); Eli Stanley Jones, *The Christ of the Indian Road* (New York, Cincinnati: Abingdon, 1925); *idem, The Message of Sat Tal Ashram* (Calcutta, Association Press, 1932); *idem, Mahatma Gandhi: an Interpretation* (New York Abingdon-Cokesbury Press, 1948).

[15] Henry P. Van Dusen, "My Caribbean Holiday," *Christian Century* 72/33 (17 August 1955): 947, and John MacKay, *Ecumenics: The Science of the Church Universal* (Englewood Cliffs, New Jersey: Prentice-Hall, 1964): 110-111 *et passim*. This Presbyterian former missionary and then president of

were entering into discussion with these groups in an effort to describe them and learn from their experience. This was complemented, at the insistence of McGavran, in congruity with the traditions of Taylor and Pickett, by the incorporation of the anthropological methods of the Australian Methodist scholar, Alan Tippett, and then Charles Kraft.[16] The social sciences and the experiences of Christians outside North America became crucial factors for understanding the mission and theology of the churches. In continuity with this tradition, both the "signs and wonders" experimentation of the 1980s, and the current concerns for dialogue with Islam, "children at risk," and "AIDS," as well as numerous similar projects, are to be understood. These are all at the heart of Christian concern outside of North America and Europe: the quest for transformative spiritual power, healing, and amelioration of the situation of the suffering church and bruised humanity.[17]

All of this has taken place in an institution that now brings together students and faculty from all over the world. About 4,300 students are studying at Fuller in 2005, from more than 120 countries, on campuses scattered from Pasadena to Seoul, Seattle, Palo Alto, Sacramento, Phoenix, and Colorado Springs. Sustained conversations and classroom instruction go on in languages as diverse as Korean, Spanish, Chinese, Japanese, Thai, Russian, French, Portuguese, and Dutch, as well as English. Over 29,000 alumni/ae, around the world serve in diverse posts of leadership in congregations, denominations, and humanitarian agencies, mostly, but not exclusively, on the Pacific Rim. For decades, visitors to the main campus in Pasadena have remarked on the astonishing diversity of the student population at Fuller. This has been less remarked upon by the Fuller community itself. For us, it is merely the reality in which everyone lives. What else would one expect in Southern California and on the Pacific Rim?

As a new participant in the Fuller community, and a traveler of the world, I have discovered that Christian theologians and practitioners everywhere have an opinion, for better or worse, about Fuller. Some are quite hostile to Fuller's roles in the churches. However, most everywhere one meets graduates and people who regret that they had time for only a course or two at Fuller. Unsolicited, they often refer to the particular combination of "heart and mind" that is Fuller. To go back to Marsden and Dayton,

---

Princeton Theological Seminary introduced Pentecostal theologians, including David DuPlessis, to the larger ecumenical world. DuPlessis's archives are at Fuller Theological Seminary.

[16] Alan R. Tippett, *The Deep Sea Canoe: The Story of Third World Missionaries in the South Pacific* (Pasadena: William Carey Library, 1977), and many other titles; Charles Kraft, *Christianity in Culture: A Study in Dynamic Biblical Christianity in Cross-Cultural Perspective* (Maryknoll: Orbis Press, 1979), and many other titles. Kraft's discussion of "spiritual warfare" is to be understood as an effort to engage issues confronting the "global church" in language that relates to their experiences, for example, *idem, Confronting Powerless Christianity: Evangelicals and the Missing Dimension* (Grand Rapids: Chosen Books, 2002), and many other titles.

[17] Marsden's analysis of Fuller makes the "signs and wonders" controversy an aberration in the Seminary's history. Dayton's analysis is perhaps more helpful at this point, but both, to my mind, understand "Church Growth" theory through the voices of its critics rather than in the context of Southern California and the history of the discussion of the principles. This misunderstanding of "Church Growth" theory and its role at Fuller was caused by McGavran's refusal to acknowledge his debt to other thinkers, and his claim of originality about ideas that had been worked out initially in the 1870s, significantly, on the Pacific Rim. McGavran and his heirs have not provided a coherent, historically contextualized articulation or defense of the theory.

graduates in my experience have never described their experience in terms of *either* Reformed theology *or* Pentecostalism. Most would generally describe themselves as "evangelical," (often ill at ease about the ambiguities and term itself!), but they are more eager to talk about the intercultural theological and social experiences involving friendships, prayer meetings, celebrations with friends, and an awed appreciation of the faculty who taught them to think critically as warm-hearted, committed Christians.

Issues of Context and Culture

Theological reflection is going to evolve dramatically for all serious Christian thinkers during the twenty-first century. If for no other reason, minds will change because about two-thirds of Christians are presently underserved in theological education and have developed churches outside of the shadow of the academy or the European-North American norms for theological reflection. I do not mean to imply that the traditional theological encyclopedia of the Catholic and Reformation churches has had and will have no influence. I mean to say that the monopoly of that approach never prevailed in these churches, and that other sources for theological education and reflection are becoming even more viable as the demographic shifts of Christendom during the past century have now placed intellectual and social power in the hands of Christian thinkers outside of Western Europe and North America. In terms of statistical millions, Christendom has moved south and east, and a parallel ideological movement by Christian thinkers is away from European-American cultural analysis of theological issues towards a variety of other, but equally Christian, understandings of the world and of Christian theology.

Theological differentiation, with roots in cultural realities, has been a constant from the earliest days of Christianity. Volumes have been written on the differences between Petrine and Pauline Christians, between Hebrew and Hellenistic Christianity, between Southern and Northern-European expressions of Christendom. However, all Christian traditions have been, and still are, hesitant to warrant perspectives significantly different from their own. When a group is judged to be significantly different, as for example Marcionites, Manichaeans, East Syrians, Mormons, and Moonies, all of the more established branches of the tradition gather to condemn them. When groups like the Mennonites, Methodists, Quakers, and Pentecostals achieve recognizable success, they cease, generally, to be described as heretics and are categorized variously as "separated communions." This recurring phenomenon leads one to suggest that the categories of "heresy and orthodoxy" are not useful tools for discussing the evolution of theological reflection. We need better ways to acknowledge diverse perspectives as being recognizably Christian by other Christians. Decisions regarding fellowship and funding will be made, and those decisions need to be informed by an analysis of the basic features of cultural identity.

What Is Happening on the Pacific Rim

Life around the Pacific Rim has long been turbulent. The arrival of diverse versions of Christianity in league with the European-American gold-seekers, opium traders, gunboat diplomats, together with European diseases and weaponry, has led to complex relationships among churches and the peoples of the Pacific Rim. Despite this historical legacy, Christians enter the twenty-first Christian century with a position of tentative strength around the Pacific Rim. Tentative, that is, because in no place on the Pacific Rim (except illusorily in

Australia and New Zealand) do non-Catholic Christians wield political power based on church/state links.

This worldly strength of Christians comes, moveover, from neither the traditional Protestant Christianities of Western Europe nor their North-American transplants.[18] These perhaps better-known groups are present, but they are a minority among Christians everywhere around the Pacific Rim. Numerical power within Pacific-Rim Christendom lies, instead, with the children and grandchildren of American Revivalism, filtered through local lenses such as Native American experience in Chile and Mexico, Mayan experience in Central America, and Chinese, Korean, and Japanese experiences both on their native soil and in diaspora. The major churches, for example of Vietnam, are the Catholic Church and the Evangelical Church of Vietnam, the latter a product of decades of work by Christian and Missionary Alliance missionaries. An analysis of Barrett's *World Christian Encyclopedia*,[19] for all of its methodological and actuarial problems, indicates that the future of Christianity in these areas is firmly in the hands of assorted Pentecostal, Holiness, and otherwise Evangelical Christians, not always directly connected to Europe or North America. A virtual flood of literature, both micro and macro studies, is now issuing from Australia and New Zealand in exploration of Australian and New Zealand religious experience.

In Latin America, the clergy and theologians of these newer, "Third Force" traditions have generally been excluded from the theological schools both of the Roman Catholics and of the Protestants who originated in Europe and North America. In instances where ideology was not the controlling reason, economics became a dominating factor. The major exception has been the Methodist University in São Paolo. Otherwise, the thinkers of these indigenous traditions have been left to study in seminaries sponsored by North American Holiness or Pentecostal churches; limited to the short-term Bible Schools that are effective at teaching practicing pastors, but not in developing scholars; or, if they have the requisite academic experience to gain admission, they have matriculated in the schools of Anthropology and Sociology at Latin American universities. This has produced a generation of theologians who understand their religious experience not in terms of the traditional categories of theology but in light of the disciplines of the social sciences.

A significant number of theologically educated Christian theologians, church leaders, and social activists around the Pacific Rim gained their higher education through contact with Fuller Theological Seminary, and through Fuller with the historical traditions of the churches. Certainly other universities and seminaries in Europe and North America have made and are making their contributions.[20] The contribution of Fuller Theological Seminary, however, has been massive. Part of the reason for Fuller's success in communicating with

---

[18] The Presbyterians in South Korea might be an exception to this generalization, but the form of Presbyterianism in Korea is heavily influenced by Keswick spirituality and the American Holiness movements.

[19] David B. Barrett and George Kurian, *World Christian Encyclopedia: A Comparative Study of Churches and Religions in the Modern World* (New York: Oxford University Press, 2001).

[20] My first contacts with Chilean Pentecostals took place at the Catholic University of Louvain, where they were refuges from Pinochet's Chile. They told me that study at Fuller Theological Seminary had been a longstanding dream, but that dream had been crushed by the link between Pinochet and the USA.

Pacific-Rim Christians has been that the social sciences are taken as seriously in the understanding of religious experience at Fuller as they are by the people we serve.

The Christian experiences of these newer traditions are focused on the Bible. The cultural discontinuity that has kept them from attachment to historic Protestantism has, likewise, kept them apart from traditional and organized American Fundamentalism. These Christians are to be understood as *biblicists* who read their Christian canon much the way early Christians did, and as *primitivists* whose ideals for Christian norms are based directly on biblical models. They are concerned with social and moral issues in the larger society; they tend to become politically engaged; they are heavily influenced by Pentecostal experience, even when they are not actually a part of the Pentecostal tradition. As a Chilean Catholic theologian expressed it to me, "In Chile, we all are a bit Pentecostal!"

Many efforts have been made to explain the growth of non-traditional Christianities in Latin America. Despite the work J.A. Kessler, J. Miguez Bonino, and Juan Sepulveda, the approaches to the newer churches have not been exactly hospitable.[21] The more tolerant interpreters understand these traditions negatively as avoidance responses to social realities; others continue to produce books on "sects," describing—rarely accurately—the perspectives of these churches. Others attempt to explain them as extensions of American political and social power. Most seem to forget one of the verities of religious belief: People do not believes something because they think it is stupid or in an effort to "turn back the clock." Instead, people believe what they believe because that particular belief system helps them understand themselves in their context, and because they sense that their beliefs, theories, and faith supply tools for dealing with the future. Indeed, Sepúlveda has argued that the phenomenal success of Pentecostalism among Native Americans of Chile is because Pentecostalism allows indigenous leaders to develop and facilitates their ability to struggle and balance between the past and the present and modernity.

All around the Pacific Rim, the publication of Christian theology is in full swing. For a long time, much of non-Catholic, non-English Christian book publishing in our region was generally limited to translations of European or North American theology. Indigenous writers were often limited to contributions submitted to periodical publications or to ephemeral publications such as tracts and pamphlets. Their work almost never made it into discussions in the academies in their own countries,[22] much less the academies of North America or Europe. Now, however, there is an extensive, scholarly publishing project around the Pacific Rim. This undertaking is not yet a major

---

[21] J.B.A. Kessler, *A Study of the Older Protestant Missions and Churches in Peru and Chile, with Special Reference to the Problems of Division, Nationalism and Native Ministry* (Goes: Oosterbaan & Le Cointre, 1967); Georg F. Vicedom and José Míguez Bonino, *Christ and the Younger Churches: Theological Contributions from Asia, Africa and Latin America* (London: S.P.C.K., 1972); José Míguez Bonino, *Rostros del Protestantismo Latinoamericano* (Buenos Aires: Nueva Creación; Grand Rapids: W.B. Eerdmans, 1995), translated *as Faces of Latin American Protestantism*, Carnahan Lectures 1993 (Grand Rapids: W.B. Eerdmans, 1997); Juan Sepúlveda, *The Andean Highlands: An Encounter with Two Forms of Christianity* (Geneva: World Council of Churches Publications, 1997).

[22] Exceptions to this generalization included the work of Gunpei Yamamuro and J. Nakada in Japan, who had an impact on both the academy and popular culture. John Sung, Andrew Gih, and Watchman Nee became major theological forces in China and throughout Asia. Nee has had global impact through his writings, published both by his followers and by Pentecostal presses.

economic force, but it is prolific, often innovative, and tends to defy the traditional categories of European and North American theologies. What is slowly, sometimes fitfully, evolving among Christians on the Pacific Rim, is an independence and diversity of Christian theological reflection, with attention to their own sources. These efforts rarely arise without both promise and problems! Two examples must suffice.

The first example, with connections to Fuller Theological Seminary, is an analysis of David (formerly Paul) Yonggi Cho, pastor of Yoido Full Gospel Church, the largest Christian congregation in the world. Pastor Cho is a prolific writer and influential theologian, many of whose works have been translated into most Asian and European languages. The volume about Cho was co-edited by Fuller graduate, Wonsak Ma.[23] This first effort to understand and evaluate the life and ministry of Cho is a scholarly analysis with contributions by twelve scholars. Not a hagiographical piece, the authors have endeavored to defend Cho's Pentecostal orthodoxy and Nicene "trinitarian" theology. What the authors miss, for they do not sufficiently cite Cho's Korean works, is the Korean context of Cho's work. They never deal, for example, with the question of the Koreanness of his success. Was he successful in Korea only because he was "trinitarian" and an "orthodox" Pentecostal?

Nowhere, to name one specific issue, do these essayists address the "honoring of the ancestors" controversy, during which the Assemblies of God, USA, excommunicated Cho for advocating what the Americans perceived as Asian ancestor worship. Later, the Assemblies realized that their opposition had only increased Cho's popularity in the Pentecostal world. Apparently embarrassed that they no longer had a relationship with the largest congregation in the world and the worldwide network of churches allied with Cho, the Assemblies hierarchy quietly reversed its decision and orchestrated the election of Cho to the presidency of the World Pentecostal Conference. American Christians are comforted by hearing what they already know; however, it is precisely at the points of difference with the "orthodox Pentecostal" and "Nicene trinitarian" that exploration becomes worthwhile and learning becomes possible. What do we have to learn from Pastor Cho about being a Christian on the Pacific Rim?

A second example is the work of Elizabeth C. Salazar Sanzana. This important thesis was presented as part of her degree program, *Bachiller en teología*, at the Comunidad Teología Evangélica de Chile.[24] Although technically unpublished, this work has circulated widely in polycopied form. It is an important, insightful, major study of the development of Chilean Pentecostal ecclesiology and missiology. Although deeply grounded in the sources and history of the Iglesia Evangélica Pentecostal, its focus is theological. She demonstrates how the church adapted to its context and used its history and particularity effectively in both urban and rural evangelism. Ironically missing is a dialogue with the North American and European roots and sources of her church.

Sometimes, Pacific-Rim publications of theology and religious history are composed by non-native English speakers in English or are translated into English. The most important

---

[23] Wonsak Ma, William W. Menzies, and Hyeon-sung Bae, eds., *David Yonggi Cho. A Close Look at His Theology and Ministry*, Asian Journal of Pentecostal Studies Series 1 (Baguio, Philippines: APTS Press; Goonpo, Korea: Hansei University Press, 2004).

[24] Elizabeth C. Salazar Sanzana, "Aspectos ideológicos en las controversias teológicas de la Iglesia Evangélica Pentecostal" (Santiago, 1989).

material, however, is typically in an Asian language or Spanish. A major challenge for scholars at Fuller Theological Seminary, and other groups of Christian scholars, will be acquisition of the linguistic tools necessary to participate in the expanding theological dialogue around the Pacific Rim, not to mention the rest of the world! Fuller has begun to tackle the problem. One can do a complete M. Div. in Spanish and all Fuller degrees in Korean. Some course work and symposia involve other languages, but the multi-lingual and intercultural nature of theology in the twenty-first century will require more, much more sophistication in language than has hitherto been the norm.

Fuller Theological Seminary and the Challenges for Christian Theology in the 21ˢᵗCentury

During my pre-Fuller career, a Korean colleague of mine who was theologically opposed to Fuller nonetheless responded favorably to my questions about Fuller's extension campus in Seoul, Korea. "The importance of Fuller in Korea," he told me, "is that it provides the only neutral theological venue in Korea where all perspectives can sit side by side to discuss Christian traditions." Providing space for Christian theological diversity is one of the hallmarks of Fuller Theological Seminary in the U.S.A. as well. Fuller is characterized by cultural and theological diversity made possible by its context in Southern California on the Pacific Rim. Academically, Fuller is committed to intense, careful scholarship, understood as a Christian undertaking in the context of an equally intense but tolerant, evangelical Pietist spirituality. The location and perspective situate Fuller Theological Seminary in the right place at the right time to address the challenges for Christian theology during the 21ˢᵗ century; these are formidable and it will require effort, persistence and courage to address them.

Among the challenges confronting Christian theology, especially at Fuller, are the following:

1. To develop Christian understandings of God and of the goal of humanity that do not depend only on European traditions.
2. To speak in irenic ways with followers of other religious traditions, and together with them to seek the common good, while competing with them for the minds and hearts of adherents.
3. To speak to and with the larger cultural structures in evangelism and culture formation.
4. To develop an understanding of suffering and evil as they are experienced by and in the church.
5. To develop an understanding of the world, its resources, its limitations, and its preservation.
6. To find forms of ecclesiology and ministry that allow fulfillment of individual and community aspirations, and Christian contribution to society.
7. To develop a nuanced and independent analysis of the political challenges of particular and globalizing economies and socio-political structures.
8. To undertake theological reflection with both particular and global specificity.
9. To provide space for evolving theologies in the theological curricula.
10. To bring the European-based philosophies and theologies into peer evolving theologies.
11. To provide theological education to the underserved populations of Christians (perhaps as many as two-thirds of Christians worldwide).

12. To invite evolving theologies into the international theological academies, without destroying either the values of the academy or of the developing theologies.

13. To invite adherents of the evolving theologies to take their place in the circles. (The current ecumenical structures, both of the left and right, make little room for experimentation and independent reflection.)

14. To warrant the biblical faithfulness of theologies built in non-European, non-North American frameworks.

15. To build a massive, comprehensive library of documentation that will support all of the above.

At the beginning of the twenty-first century, these issues, and others, are being addressed by the faculty and students at Fuller Theological Seminary, usually in partnership with Christians from around the world. To do this work on the Pacific Rim means that the work takes place in the context of cultural and religious diversity. Engaging with the people of the Pacific Rim, and warranting the voices of these traditions in the search for what it means to be Christian in the 21st century, is the future of theology at Fuller Theological Seminary.

We are familiar with the phrase "knowledge explosion." A theology explosion is now taking place all around the Pacific's "Ring of Fire." The theological challenges, broadly understood, now facing communities of Christians around the Pacific Rim are daunting. Fuller Theological Seminary is destined, I believe, to continue in the future to do what it has done in the past, but at an ever more rapid rate, on an ever more massive scale, and with even more openness to engagement of the newer traditions.

Well placed to do its work, contextually shaped by its particular experience on the Pacific Rim, Fuller benefits from the culture of Los Angeles, California, one of the world's great cultural crossroads. Theological diversity is as natural to our region as is cultural diversity, and our cultural and theological diversity are served by Fuller's geographically, linguistically, and religiously diverse academic programs, abetted not least by Fuller's special blend of Pietist "heart and mind". Fuller's ecumenical and convening mission is sustained by a commitment to theological reflection beyond the categories of any one ecclesial tradition. Its globe-encircling network of graduates, former students, faculty, and friends provides an international grid of cultural latitudes and theological longitudes within which to chart future conversations.

The extent to which these resources are wisely used will determine whether Fuller Theological Seminary shall be but a footnote in the history of American theological education or a formative influence in the development of unprecedented theological education and reflection around the Pacific Rim and beyond.

Harvard Divinity School
and the Future of Theological Education

Helmut Koester

The Situation Today

What I say in this essay may sound strange, outlandish, and perhaps revolutionary for most of the readers of this Festschrift in honor of my dear friend, Don Haymes, but Harvard Divinity School is the institution where Don studied the New Testament and received his well-earned Master's degree. Now that I have been retired from HDS for six years, though I am still an active member of the faculty as a Research Professor, I wish to tell Don what is happening at his and my beloved Harvard school and reflect on the future of theological education, and say why I am convinced that present developments are right and necessary.

On a personal note, I was baptized and confirmed as a Lutheran Christian, eventually entering the ministry of the Lutheran church, in which I am still active in the ordained ministry. In order to receive my doctoral degree in Theology fifty years ago at the University of Marburg in Germany, I still had to submit certificates of my baptism and confirmation. Even to teach at the University of Heidelberg in Germany required that I be a practicing Protestant Christian—and not something horrible like a Roman Catholic!

I encountered a somewhat different world of theological studies when I came to the Divinity School at Harvard University, where I have taught for more than forty years. When I arrived in Cambridge, HDS was an "interdenominational" school—implication: Students and faculty of all Christian denominations were welcome. In the years before my arrival, Unitarian-Universalist and Congregationalist students had been the largest two groups, but that was changing. More and more students from other denominations arrived, even some Roman Catholics—and something worse than that! Students from the Churches of Christ, Don's denomination, had already been going there for some years, and more were coming, most of them with degrees from what was then still called Abilene Christian College. Rumor had it that the Anabaptists were about to take over the Divinity School!

I came to understand that Harvard was for Church of Christ students and others devout in their belief in the Scriptures a kind of safe place, a reputable school of advanced theological learning where they could earn a degree and no one would try to steal their faith. Thus Harvard Divinity School, both in terms of the composition of its faculty and of its student body, became indeed interdenominational, but in the safety we provided, we remained neutral and objective, unwilling to challenge anyone's faith commitments.

By the end of the 20th century, a remarkable shift could be observed that had been inaugurated slowly during the preceding decades. Roman Catholic students had become a very strong constituency within the student body. The number of African-American students had likewise increased. Mainline Protestant denominations had meanwhile become less strongly represented. Students enrolled in the new, non-ministerial degree program, "Master of Theological Studies," began to outnumber those in the more traditional program, "Master of Divinity" (formerly the "Bachelor of Divinity") that had been designed especially for the training of ministers. Another new reality: Over 50% of the students were women, and the numbers of students from other religions were increasing. This development had begun 45 years earlier with the establishment of the Center for the Study of World-Religions, grew slowly but increased visibly towards the end of the century. Along with these students from non-Christian religions, more and more Christian students were applying for doctoral programs in the study of other religions; and Jewish students in increasing numbers were also enrolling, not only in doctoral programs in Hebrew Bible but also in other world religions as well as New Testament and Christian Origins. The new emphasis in the reshaped Master's programs facilitated these changes by requiring from all students a substantially broad-range study of the many aspects of religion.

Major changes also took place in the composition of the faculty. Traditionally—and this was still the case when I arrived at Harvard—almost all members of the faculty had been ordained Protestant Christian ministers. The establishment of the Stilman Chair in Roman Catholic Studies in 1958 raised the question whether a Roman Catholic could possibly be accepted as a faculty member of the Harvard Divinity School. The compromise reached was that a Roman Catholic philosopher, a layperson, not an ordained priest, was accepted. No harm done! When this first incumbent retired after a few years, the Catholic question arose again, and the result (after several failed attempts) was the appointment of a New Testament scholar who was a Jesuit priest, George MacRae, of beloved memory. Now it was not the Anabaptists but the Catholics who were taking over! At the same time, pressure was growing that drove HDS to an even worse fate: the appointment of more women to the faculty! This move, as well as other considerations, resulted in the formation of a new faculty: Ordained Protestant male clergy and even Roman Catholic clergy (of whom, even yet, are all males) became a smaller percentage. HDS was not what it used to be!

The new wave extended even as far as the leadership of the school. Whereas Unitarians or Congregationalists had always occupied the office of the dean, now an American Baptist minister, Samuel Miller, was appointed dean in 1959, breaking a tradition over 300 years old. Thereafter, the deanship passed safely back into the hands of a Lutheran, then a Presbyterian; but then, danger struck and a Roman Catholic became acting dean; after him, all breathed more easily when another Lutheran took over; but then, another Roman Catholic rose up! And now, a scholar of the study of Islamic religion, who is a Protestant Christian but not an ordained minister, holds the position of leadership. Thus our complex faculty and its leadership is radically different from what it was when I arrived at Harvard almost half-a-century ago.

The contrast is evident between, on the one hand, the new HDS and, on the other hand, the situation in European theological faculties and faculties of most denominational seminaries in the United States and Canada. In other schools, the curriculum is structured primarily to prepare people for the ministry in a particular Christian denomination through courses in Bible, history of the Christian church, and especially through study of the denomination's own past, particular theology, and courses in pastoral theology. Protestant and Catholic theological education of most future clergy still takes place in clearly separated institutions. Only token courses, if any, are offered in the study of other religions of the world. To offer a single example: The Lutheran and the Roman-Catholic faculties at the University of Munich in Germany share *one* professor who teaches all the courses in non-Christian religions, while at Harvard, almost a third of the courses offered are concerned with topics in the study of religions other than Christianity.

The multi-denominational and even multi-religious scene of the United States is certainly reflected in the striking differences of the curricula of theological studies at HDS, but that alone does not explain the differences. Germany, for example, includes a 3.5 million Muslim population, more than two million of whom are from Turkey. The percentage of Muslims living in France, for another example, is larger than the percentage of Muslims in the United States. Schools of religion in those two countries, however, do not offer courses in Islam. Even Eastern-Orthodox Christians in Central and Western Europe have to fight hard to maintain a foothold in universities. We should not be surprised, however, for denominations even in the United States are suspicious of candidates for the ministry who were educated in non-denominational theological schools like Harvard or Yale or Chicago. If you are a Lutheran candidate for the ministry, you usually have to spend an additional year at a Lutheran theological seminary before you can qualify for ordination. Some other denominations have similar rules, and the Roman Catholic Church will not accept any candidate for the priesthood who has received his ("her" does not apply in this case) ministerial degree at a non-Catholic theological faculty. Of course, no one dares to ask what is happening to the very large and increasing number of Catholic women who have received their degrees qualifying for the ministry at such institutions as Harvard or Yale, or even at the Catholic Union of Chicago, even though the Roman Catholic Church in the United States (and elsewhere in the world) has a severe shortage of priests! In any case, even in the U.S.A., most theological discourse in the education of ministers and priests is still confined to the parochial languages and biases of the confessionally oriented schools of the several denominations.

The International Language of Music

Gisela and I were at Tanglewood in the early days of August. The old estate in the Berkshire Mountains of Massachusetts is now the summer home of the Boston Symphony Orchestra. On the first evening in Ozawa Hall, the Orchestra of the Age of Enlightenment, a small British ensemble playing without a conductor, made beautiful music, mostly of Johann Sebastian Bach, on original instruments of the 18th century. My wife and I, though we are from Germany, had never heard our beloved Bach's *Brandenburg Concertos* played so beautifully and with so much clarity and originality as here in the United States by this British group! To be sure, here we were still within the confines of the Western European/American tradition of music and music- making, which, as ever, continues largely to dominate the concert scene of the United States. The musicians, the selections, and the venue—the entire scene was international but not yet stepping out beyond the confines of the Western tradition.

The second evening, in the Music Shed with the full Boston Symphony Orchestra, we listened to Robert Schumann's *Second Symphony* and to Johannes Brahms's *Second Piano Concerto*. I refrain to describe the joy, wonder, and exaltation that we experienced while listening to this wonderful performance on a lovely summer evening. I only wish that you, dear reader of this *Festschrift*, had been there! The music was, once again, German, but who were the musicians? The conductor was a German of Hungarian extraction; the concertmaster, a woman from Serbia; the Assistant Concert Master, a Chinese woman; the soloist came from Israel. I could go on to give a long account of international origins of the rest of the orchestra. They had all come together as a performing unit of incredible harmony and beauty beyond description.

The third evening went beyond the first two in its international quality. The first half of the program was *Music from the Silk Road*, the ancient trade route that stretched from China through Mongolia, Afghanistan, Persia, and Turkey to southeastern Europe. At Tanglewood, ensembles were playing orchestral arrangements of tunes from Mongolia, India, Armenia, Turkey, and Roma (Gypsy). In the second part of the program, the Boston Symphony Orchestra performed the *Concerto for Cello, Orchestra, and Video* by the Chinese composer, Tan Dun. This combination of folk music from a Chinese province, including exquisite singing usually heard at weddings, was answered by the indescribably beautiful sound of the solo cello played by Yo-Yo Ma, accompanied also by stunning tunes and local instruments recorded in China, such as someone blowing on a leaf and someone else sounding out stones. Throughout the performance, videos of the native players and singers were being shown on a large screen.

What happened at Tanglewood is a message to us theologians and scholars of the study of religion. These musical presentations of the Boston Symphony Orchestra spoke a truly international language, crossing oceans and cultures. Especially the music from the Silk Road and the concerto by the Chinese composer—Tan Dun, the composer, himself was conducting—daringly mixed Western and Eastern traditions of music, blending them into a new communication that did not offend but greatly enriched our own classical musical sensitivities. This music shows a way to step out of one's traditional and parochial boundaries and listen to others speaking in their own languages in such a way that minds and hearts meet on a new plain of human experience.

The "Babylonian Captivity" of Christian Theology

Listening to these concerts, I became much aware of the self-imposed walls behind which Western Christian theology and church ideology have been hiding. The strict separation of Roman Catholic and Protestant theological faculties in German universities is a strangely antiquated situation, and German public schools, in which religious instruction is mandatory, give separate instruction to Roman Catholic and Protestant children, but the schools are then helpless when it comes to the question of religious instruction for children of Muslim parents!

And if that is a problem in such European countries as Germany, we Christians in the United States have even less excuse. The following is an extreme case, to be sure, but a Roman Catholic bishop recently declared that the first communion of a little girl using a rice wafer would be illegal and ineffective according to Canon Law. The little girl had a gluten allergy, and Eucharistic bread made of wheat flour would have been unhealthful for her. Less extreme was the case in a university in the so-called "Bible Belt" of the South: When a professor assigned readings from the Qur'an, many students and parents objected strenuously, alleging that "separation of church and state" prohibits the reading of sacred texts in a tax-funded school.

Luther entitled one of his important Reformation tractates "The Babylonian Captivity of the Church." I want to suggest that all Western Christian denominations today are once more imprisoned by an analogous Babylonian captivity, in a way reinforced by sister denominations in developing countries. European and American churches have exported their parochialism as well as their faith, and new churches in the so-called "third world" are both as true to that faith and as naïve as the historic churches once were. Each denomination is guarding its turf and drawing very close boundary lines, some closer than others, but the differences among them have little, if any, relationship to the substance of Christian faith. In fact, several Christian denominations are divided within themselves over questions that—in my opinion—clearly lie outside of the fundamental tenets of Christianity: acceptance and ordination of women and of gay people; abortion rights; war and peace; and even such trivial questions as the use of grape juice instead of real wine in the Eucharist services. We are all doing ecclesiastical gymnastics in a non-Olympic sport: outdated models of church and Christian identity. And then, Christian theology either follows this course of parochial calisthenics or else it stretches beyond these limits only to be ignored or even condemned. Many theological schools limit theological education to their own traditions only; they are not even trying to become ecumenical, not to mention inter-religious, in their dialogue and theological reflection. As a consequence, most Christian denominations, and even groups within these churches, are busily working at throwing up retaining walls around their own turf, not realizing that their walls serve as bulwarks that keep us in as well as keeping others out. We make ourselves prisoners within a new "Babylonian captivity," captives of our own righteousness and our own pride, arrogance, superiority, and parochialism.

The New Testament and Self-Righteousness

In Luke's Gospel, Jesus told a story about a Pharisee and a Publican at prayer: The scummy Publican went home forgiven, whereas the elevated Pharisee, who had done all the right things, was not justified.

Then there is the story about the Samaritan who tended the traveler who fell among robbers, whereas the pious priest and the religious Levite, eager to perform their churchly duties, left the man in the ditch to die of his wounds.

Not to forget Jesus' statement that he had come not to be served but to serve, and to give his life for others.

The teaching of Jesus and of the New Testament requires that Christian behavior towards others be the love of all human beings without limits. Jesus commanded that we love even our enemies. Jesus also said that one should not judge others. That command seems to be entirely forgotten in Christian circles.

Nothing in Jesus' teaching justifies the self-righteous condemnation of others. Jesus' principles of reaching out in love beyond the boundaries of faith, ethnicity, and culture were proclaimed in a world where everyone hated everybody else: The ruling elite despised the common people, the Pharisees judged the impure working-class people from the countryside, the Jews hated the Roman occupation, the pure-bloods hated the half-breeds, the religiously elect sneered at the denominational outsiders as untouchables and dogs (Jesus himself, in conversation with the Syro-Phoenician woman, had to get over that bit of prejudice), the rich and wealthy neglected the poor and cheated their employees out of their wages.

The Apostle Paul and others brought Jesus' message of God's universal welcome out of the cultural confines of the Palestinian Aramaic, Jesus' language, into the Greek-speaking world of the vast Roman Empire. Paul, who spoke the language of the world at large, translated Jesus' message into a new language, foreign even to Jesus himself, a language that everyone in that world was able to understand. Paul had been a devout and law-abiding Pharisee, one who was proud to be a Jew and—as a law-abiding Jew—he judged and despised gentile sinners, all slaves, and most women. If there were reasons for self-righteousness, Paul had plenty. Why did he give up his record of perfect religious and moral accomplishments? Not in order to become an even more pious and righteous person, a truly moral Christian—in fact, Paul did not even know what it meant to be a "Christian." Rather, his call to preach to the gentiles told him that God's righteousness was God's will to establish justice for all kinds of people, all peoples, all nations, Jews and gentiles alike. Whereas human righteousness only divides, separates, and engenders pride and judgmental attitudes towards others, God's righteousness makes us all one. For Paul, therefore, that human beings might or might not be moral and righteous was completely irrelevant.

And yet, the way we in America look at others is widely dominated by a judgmental attitude, born of a hypocritical self-righteousness. If we define ourselves as heterosexuals, we quote our Bibles and judge homosexuals as sinners. If we are against abortion rights, we denounce as "baby-killers" those who advocate a woman's right of choice; at the same time, many of those same "pro-life" people quote their Bibles, again, and call for the re-institution of the death penalty.

All this selective Bible-quoting is of the essence of religious hypocrisy, for the same people who abhor homosexuality and uphold the death penalty on the premise of Biblical authority, wink at Jesus' prohibition of divorce and the condemnation in both Testaments of usury. I, too, can quote the Bible: "For *all* have sinned and fall short," both the homosexual and the heterosexual, and "**none** is righteous, *no not one*," neither the Bible-quoter nor the one who knows no Bible. "No matter who you are, if you pass judgment, you have no excuse. *In judging others, you condemn yourself.*" And that includes me, too! Do we think of ourselves as members of a righteous Christian nation, but then judge other nations of different religious adherence to be not merely enemies but even as part of an "axis of evil" and empire of Satan? They call us "the great Satan" and commit 9/11 against us; we call ourselves "Christians" and retaliate by raining fire on their cities, killing their women, children, and old people. Is either axis more Satanic than the other or of greater evil?

Self-righteous people (Christians and Muslims alike) quote their Bibles and their Qur'ans against one another and against all other religions, and yet all that counts is that human beings love and respect each other. "In Christ," Paul wrote, "there is therefore no longer Jew or gentile, free or slave, male and female." And we can add today: There is no longer Christian or Muslim, heterosexual or homosexual. We are all one in Christ, and one before the righteousness of God. How can that ideal become human reality? By converting everyone to my Christian church, the Evangelical Lutheran Church? No, for

Jesus also said, "If they are not against me, they are for me." Jesus' commandment to love others as he has loved us, knows no limitation on just who "the others" are. No merit lies in loving only those who agree with us and share the same religious and moral values. Carrying each other's burdens does not mean to carry only the burdens of members of our own denomination or our own religion or our own nation. The love of Jesus extends absolutely to everyone. God is not a "respecter of persons" because he intends for us to respect all persons, no matter their religious, social, or national identity and moral convictions. God's justice extends to all people.

But does not the Bible set certain moral standards? Does not Paul, for example, condemn homosexuality in Romans 1? By no means! What Paul says here is that *all* human beings are condemned, notwithstanding their sexual orientation, because they have *all* failed to worship God, but have worshiped instead their own idols, be they pagan gods, or money, or their own righteousness, or their own nation's pride and superiority. We are all sinners, but we are acceptable before God and only because God's gracious will is to include us sinners in the merciful rule of justice that he wants to create on this earth. Paul therefore worked towards God's goal for the creation of a new community that would work, in the words of Jesus, like light in the darkness, salt on the meat, and leaven in the dough. The creation of the community of the new age does not require that we all become "righteous" persons; it requires only that we learn to respect and love each other; and embrace whatever is good, honest, and beneficial; and do not hurt others but, rather, do good to them.

Of course, the universal love of Jesus does not imply that "anything goes." Anything that does harm to others is out. Stealing, murder, breaking a marriage, rape, pederasty, putting one's business competitor at a disadvantage, terrorizing others, treating others disrespectfully on account of their racial or sexual identity, favoring the rich and depriving the poor of their legal rights and living wage and welfare—all these things do harm to others and are therefore immoral. By this rule of God's righteousness, then, if two homosexuals want to live together in mutually faithful commitment, or if a woman wants for good reasons to interrupt her pregnancy, neither is anyone hurt nor is anyone else forced either to abort her fetus or to become homosexual. Who am I to judge others? People are different. How do I know better than anyone else when human life begins—at conception, at birth, in a former life? After God's creation becomes "a breathing soul," then we are commanded to do no harm. How sure can I be of my own normal religious behavior and conventional ideas? By what right would I judge others who worship differently or pray in a different way to God known by another name?

In 1 Corinthians 9:20–22, Paul stated his great principle of Christian compromise: He made himself to be like a Jew for the Jews, to be like a gentile for the gentiles; although he himself was no longer under the Law, he became someone under the Law for the sake of those who were under the Law, but for those outside of the Law, he became as one who also was outside of the Law. Paul understood himself to be under the "law of Christ" to become anything and everything to anyone in order to win them to Christ. Did that make Paul a chameleon? Certainly not! It made him free and useful to God's will of righteousness and love.

Paul made clear that any emphasis on our own self-righteousness, morality, and religious standing, and especially our prejudices and emotional dislikes, more often than not, benefit no one. What does it matter that I abide by certain religious and moral standards, keep certain customs and traditions? All that matters is that I respect the great range of human differences smartly enough to be able to love and benefit others.

If we religious people and proud theologians were better at practicing Paul's ethic of unconditional love, we might do better at learning each other's languages and opening the windows and doors to a better understanding of our fellow human beings. We might make some headway with international and inter-religious dialogue.

It seems to me, therefore, that Harvard Divinity School is on the right path when it revises its degree programs beyond the limits of a Christian ecumenical school, truly to become a school that welcomes people from all the world's religions who are wanting to study the religions of all the world. I trust that Don Haymes, to whom we dedicate this Festschrift, will appreciate the developments taking place at his old *alma mater*.

Two Final Stories

My first final story concerns the reelection of the president of the Lutheran Church Missouri Synod. His reelection was in doubt and challenged by many members of the synod meeting. Why? Three years earlier, he had permitted a district president of his church to participate in an ecumenical prayer service held in Yankee Stadium in New York after the terrorist attack on the twin towers of the World Trade Center on 9/11/01. At that time, he had to undergo a disciplinary hearing before a committee of his church because he had violated the biblical command "Do not associate with the unbelievers." Another objection to his reelection was the suspicion that he might seek closer relationships with the Evangelical Lutheran Church of America, which allows the ordination of women. Both Jesus and Paul would be disappointed to see the candidate treated this way.

My second final story comes from a study tour taken in 2001 by the Harvard Seminar on New Testament and Archaeology. (Don Haymes was a member of this seminar many years ago during his time at Harvard Divinity School). We were staying in a small village hotel in Turkey. As it happened to be a Sunday, we decided to celebrate the Eucharist together. We agreed that a student member of the seminar, an ordained Jesuit priest from Slovakia, would lead the service and bless the bread and wine. While we were sitting in a circle in the yard of the hotel, just at the moment of the Eucharistic prayer with the words of institution of the Lord's Supper, the call to prayer began to sound from the minaret of the nearby mosque. The celebrant interrupted the recitation of the Eucharistic prayer, and all of us listened in silence to the Muslim prayer, continuing with our service only after the prayer to Allah had come to an end. Then we passed our bread and wine from one to another, including to the one member of the seminar who was a Muslim. He did not eat the bread or drink the wine as they were passed, but he did receive them devoutly and hand them to the person sitting next to him. Jesus and Paul would like that.

A Memoir

Dwain Evans

I was born on a black-land cotton farm four miles north of Palmer, Texas, on April 4, 1933. I arrived with a clubfoot on my right, but by the grace of God, something could be done. I was carried to Dallas where successive plaster casts, each exerting a little more pressure, succeeded in straightening the foot. I was left with a usable but rocker-shaped foot. The left foot was not much better. The doctors described them both as "flexible feet," so flexible that I could slip a laced-up shoe on and off. My playmates had a different description: "flat-foot floogie with a floy, floy."

My uncle, D.A. Epps, owned the farm where I was born. Grandfather and Grandmother Madison Epps had previously owned it. My uncle purchased it when the estate was settled. We always called it the "Home Place." Only Grandmother Epps was still alive when I was born, and she died shortly thereafter; both of my grandfathers had been born in 1850, before the Civil War began.

We lived there as tenant farmers. My mother had been born in that house, and so was my younger sister, Faye. I was born in the middle of the Depression, the fourth child of my mother, coming after Ralph, 18; Marcreta, 16, and Dell, 14. My mother was forty, and my father was fifty. Faye's arrival, about a year later, was equally unplanned.

The Home Place was a cut above most farms, for though we were on a black dirt road, a gasoline powered Delco unit would, when we could get it to run, generate electricity. We mostly used kerosene lamps. The house was big and comfortable and painted white. The orchards of pear, peach, apricot, and plum were extensive. I remember helping Mother spread peaches and apricots on the sheet-iron roof of a shed to dry. Mother would then make fried pies that were delicious indeed. The land was good for cotton, when the rains came on time. Even without a tractor, my father was able to produce good crops with our team, Nat and Biggun, a horse and a mule, respectively. My father was a hard-worker, but he was a poor manager. Mother said that in the fall, he would always hold out for a higher cotton price, and when prices plummeted and he was forced to sell, he could scarcely repay the bank for the loan he had taken to put in the crop. During these hard times for nearly everybody, my father worked for the Works Projects Administration (mostly road work) in addition to his farming. Hard times, dirt farming, and always owing the bank helped to shape my political thinking later on.

I do not remember any time that my father ever went to church, but without fail, every Sunday morning, my mother saw to it that we five children got loaded up in the Model A Ford Phaeton and headed to the Trumbull Church of Christ where my uncle, Rufus Epps, was the Bible class teacher, song leader, and from time to time the preacher. Ironclad determination on Mother's part saw to it that, come rain or shine, we were going to church. The Model A was an ideal mud car. It had 18" wheels and a high wheelbase, but the black mud would bog up on the wheels until they would not turn. When that happened, someone had to get out and dig the mud out from the wheels so we could then go on. Fortunately I was young enough to escape the mud-digging.

Ralph courted and married Eva Sue Farrar, and he graduated from Trinity University with a degree in Economics. He was able to accomplish this achievement thanks to a loan from my uncle, D.A. Epps. I was four, and Faye was three. When Faye and I were disappointed in not being invited to one of the wedding showers for Sue, Ralph loaded Faye and me up in the Model A and drove down the road to an overhanging tree. He reached up in the tree and mysteriously retrieved two pieces of candy. From then on, that was the "candy tree."

From this point on, things went downhill. Circumstances required a move from the Home Place when I was four. We moved a few miles away to the Jack Risinger place, but this time, our house was an unpainted "hand house," that is, a house where field hands normally lived, and that was usually Blacks who worked for the farmer at less than basic wages. Life on the Risinger farm was not all bad: I remember my father reading stories from the Old Testament to Faye and me by the light of a kerosene lamp. The stories were always from the Old Testament and never from the New. I learned to count to 100 while we sat on the front porch in the evening.

Life for us at the Risinger farm had gotten harder. One day, my mother went to Ferris, the closest town, stood on a street corner and prayed, "Lord, don't let my children starve." My mother was a firm believer in prayer. Then she went to the residence of Mrs. Smith who lived alone in a two-story home, who greeted her by saying: "Mazie, I have just been thinking about you. Would you be willing to help me with my housework?" We moved into the second story of Mrs. Smith's home.

I can only imagine the negotiations it must have taken to get my father to move with us. My father worked as farm labor from sunup to sundown six days each week for $1.00 per day. As poor as we were at Risinger farm, we managed through it all to keep our Jersey cow. I never had to milk her, but my task every morning before school was to take her to a different vacant lot with plenty of grass and stake her out. I found this to be a very humiliating task. I was always afraid that someone like Joe Green (one of my more sophisticated class mates) might see me with that cow on somebody's vacant lot.

Our next move was to a rented house on Railroad Avenue in Ferris where the rent was $10.00 per month. I remember my first Christmas in that house. Although it had no indoor plumbing, it did have electricity, and Santa brought me an electric train (courtesy of my sister and brothers who were by then working in Dallas and Ferris.) I celebrated my good fortune with my friend, Royce Flippen, but I was deeply chagrined when he told me that all Santa had brought him was an apple and an orange.

I started first grade in Ferris, and there I first fell in love—with my teacher, Miss Fleetwood, and also Janie Ruth Jeffers, who had long curly hair. I never worked up enough courage to speak to Janie Ruth during our entire first-grade year.

Dell had attended high school at Ferris and was a halfback on the football team. He was offered a small athletic scholarship to go to college, not enough to make it possible, so he went to work at a service station in Ferris. Ralph and Sue meanwhile were teachers at Barry, Texas, where he coached the basketball team. Ralph then received his Master's degree from North Texas State Teachers College in Denton (now the University of North Texas), and he later completed course work for the Ph. D. After teaching at Marshall, Texas, he went to work for North American Aviation. Marcreta had finished business school in Dallas, and was attending Pearl and Bryan Streets Church of Christ where she met, fell in love with, and married Jack Carrington. Jack, too, went to work for North American. Marcreta and Jack had two sons, Bryce Lee and Jack Hulen.

Then came World War II. Dell was called up. I was frightened when he left to catch the train to Ennis and then Dallas to take his physical, but late that evening, we were as delighted to see him returning as we had been frightened to see him leave. He had failed the physical because one leg was shorter than the other: That leg had not kept him from playing football, but it did keep him out of the army. One of the young men called up with Dell died in the conflict. Dell met Martha Jo Mann in Dallas and they married. Dell, too, went to work for North American Aviation. Martha Jo and Dell had had two children, Nick and Karen.

I was deathly afraid of the dark. I was convinced that myriad demons were ready to pounce on me at any moment. We had an outdoor toilet located about 75 feet from our back door. Only an extreme urge could persuade me to make the trip out after dark, on the return trip, I set all kinds of records for speed between the little house and the big house. Our outhouse, like many others, was state-of-the-art equipped with last year's Sears & Roebuck *Catalogue*.

We took an annual trip in to Dallas on the Interurban (a glorified electric street car). Our unmarried aunt, Ollie Epps, met us, and she would outfit Faye and me for the coming school year. Towards the end of the Depression, Aunt Ollie had one of the better-paying jobs with the U. S. Postal Service. Getting outfitted included a visit to the Health Spot Shoe Store where my ungainly feet would be shod with a pair of high-tops. I could not wear a low-quarter shoe because of my rocker-shaped feet. I was grateful for the ugly shoes, yet they embarrassed me because no one else in my class wore shoes like that.

We attended church every time the doors were open. The minister was Lynn Browning, and he was one of my heroes. Even though my father never attended, neither did he ever allow Faye and me to beg off. He had grown up a Methodist, but somewhere along the way he fell out with preachers and churches. My mother had a stainless steel faith. She believed in the power of prayer and spent a lot of time at it every day. Although her life was hard beyond my ability now to remember it, she seemed always to be singing one of the old gospel hymns. Her favorite was "Sun of My Soul," and I heard her singing it when she was dying in the hospital. Each evening she would gather Faye and me, and we would read a chapter in the Bible, taking turns, a verse at a time.

When my father, as Ralph, Dell, and Brother-in-law Jack had done, got a job with North American Aviation in Grand Prairie, life took a turn for the better. North American built the AT6 Trainer and, later, the P51 Mustang. The new job meant a move to Dallas where we rented a house at 1016 Griffith in Oak Cliff. Except for Mrs. Smith's, it was our first house with indoor plumbing. What a delight!

Church in Dallas was as important as church in Ferris had been. We placed membership with the Page and Cumberland Streets Church of Christ. Faye and I had a Bible teacher named Mrs. Luck, who took a dispensational view of biblical history, dividing it into three ages: Patriarchal, Mosaic, and Christian. We studied the Bible once a week at Mrs. Luck's house.

Faye and I went to public school at John F. Peeler Elementary School, where I entered the fourth grade, skipping grade 3. This was not because I had superior intellectual skills but because the state had decreed that school would now last for 12 grades. I was one of the last to go to school for only 11 years. What I remember most about Peeler was always being chosen last for the athletic games we played. My classmates discovered my poor athletic skills the first week. I had been taught by my mother never to fight—that "turn the other cheek" business. My classmates also discovered my pacifist philosophy, and my life became a daily torture. Finally, an all-determining fight became impossible to avoid. My opponent had a reputation for being really tough. The time and place was set for our encounter after school one day. The usual hangers-on gathered to watch. After our first few rounds, I discovered something that surprised me: I was stronger than he was. Before long, he had all he wanted, and that ended further demands that I fight.

My first job was mowing lawns in our neighborhood. I was making my own money for the first time, and I was elated. But then I was troubled to discover that my mother also worked outside our home. One morning as I was walking to school, I had another little skirmish, and my shirt got torn. I returned home to change shirts and was surprised to encounter my mother leaving the house with a sample case. She was on her way to sell *Hurlbut's Story of the Bible* door to door. Her book selling career had gone on for several years, and I had never known it. She had kept the knowledge of her part-time work from Faye and me.

My friend Monte introduced me to smoking. At first we puffed on grapevine that grew in abundance in nearby woods; then we graduated to Monte's father's pipes—Monte's father was away in the Army. I had been told that if I would suck on a lemon, no one could tell that I had been smoking. Each time I returned to the house, I would go by the refrigerator, suck on a lemon, and feel safe. One night, my mother came in and sat on the edge of my bed. I had come home from Monte's, made my usual trip by the refrigerator, and had gone to bed with no worries. "Dwain, how long have you been smoking?" she asked with deep disappointment in her voice. She did not ask *whether* I smoked or if I had *thought* about it; the case was already closed, the facts were in, and she required to know only how long it had been going on. After she left my bedroom, I thought I would have preferred to be beaten with a cat-o'-nine-tails rather than face her disappointment. That ended my youthful smoking experiments.

After the fourth grade, we moved to Grand Prairie. Our new church was the 4th and Church Streets Church of Christ where Logan Buchanan was the minister. I was eleven, and for good reasons, I had a strong consciousness of personal sinfulness. I wanted to be baptized at the earliest possible time. With trembling and fear, I went forward when the Invitation Song was sung, and Logan plunged me beneath the water. I came up with a great sense of relief.

In Grand Prairie, I fell in love again, this time with Betty Ruth Burns. I never spoke to her, either, but I admired her from a distance. One of my classmates was in the skunk-trapping business with his father. People could always tell when my friend had been in the classroom, more easily that Betty Ruth could ever have detected my affection for her.

My Uncle Marshall, who lived in Santa Ana, Texas, was wealthy by our standards. He took pity on my mother and made her a gift of $5,000.00. With that she bought a house in the Oak Cliff section of Dallas, and we moved to 1227 South Brighton in time for the 6th grade at Winnetka Elementary School; after that, I attended W. E. Greiner Junior High. During this time, I carried a paper route for the *Dallas Times-Herald* and later got a job as a soda jerk in a drug store on Hampton Road.

The church continued to play the dominant role in our lives—really, church was my entire social life. Preachers like Jim Pillow, George Chaires, Claude Chaires, B. C. Ballard and Ed Rheinfelt were strong influences in my life. Wilken "Big Chief" Bacon trained all of us in a chorus that went to a Sunday-afternoon singing almost every weekend. And about this time, I found the courage to invite a girl on my first date. Claudia Chaires was a lovely person, but we had to go on the streetcar, and I was miserable. I never had another date on the streetcar. What was soon to become an obsession with automobiles had already set in. Dell had a 1939 Chevrolet; Ralph, a 1940 Ford; and Jack, a 1941 Chevrolet. I waxed and polished them whenever I had the chance, longing for the day.

The problem with my feet became severe, causing me a lot of pain. The orthopedist, Dr. Felix Butte, told my mother that I had to have surgery on both feet. We had no health insurance, no money to pay for surgery. Dr. Butte directed Mother to take me to the Texas Crippled Children Society, and they agreed to pay for the operation. Dr. Butte fused certain bones and gave me more comfortable feet. I spent that entire summer at St. Paul's Hospital, first with casts on both legs from my crotch down and then with walking casts on both feet. I started school that fall wearing walking casts.

The war was coming to an end, the defense plants were laying off workers, my father lost his good-paying job, and our life was about to come apart. "Pop"—as we called my father—found a job as a night watchman. He was having occasional episodes that the family called "fits" that involved talking under his breath and times of explosive anger. Within the family, we understood that we just had to go through these times with Pop. My two older brothers had experienced worse "fits" with Pop than I had seen, but I did not know it at the time. One evening, Marcreta and Jack had brought three-year-old Bryce and two-year-old Jack for a visit with Grandma and Grandpa. Jack, their father, was sitting in a straight chair with his back to the front door listening to a ball game. My father came home unexpectedly. He was not due until the next morning, but we were all glad that Pop was home. I went out to greet him and walk with him into the house. As soon as we entered, he set his lunch box down, and without any warning, he took out his pistol and shot Jack five times in the back, killing him instantly.

Unable to grasp what was happening, I had the presence of mind to run next door, call the ambulance, call the police, and call my brother, Ralph. Ralph and Sue were now living in Corsicana where, after serving five years in the Army Air Force, he was coordinator of the Veterans Schools. I delivered my unbelievably awful news to him, all the while my own heart was crying out: "God where are you? How could you let this happen to us? Have all of our years of believing in you come to this?"

The next few days were nightmarish. My family was smeared all over the front pages of both daily papers. Jack's funeral was held at the Fourth and Church Streets congregation in Grand Prairie. Jack's favorite song was sung, "When Peace Like a River." But I had no peace in my heart!

Ralph took charge. He and Sue paid for the best criminal attorney in Dallas, Maury Hughes, to represent our father, who was in the county jail facing a charge of murder. Psychiatrists examined him and came to the conclusion that he was suffering from paranoid schizophrenia. He went before a judge, was declared insane, and was remanded to the State Hospital at Terrell, to be confined in the unit for the criminally insane. In the Texas we live in today, as sick a man as Pop was, he might very well have received a death sentence.

I went to see Pop both in the county jail, at Terrell, and later when they transferred him to Rusk. All the institutions reeked of pine-tar disinfectant. We did not talk about the killing. We talked only of our love and affection for each other.

Going back to school was a trial, but for once my classmates were merciful. I pondered the text in Romans 8: "All things work together for good for those who love the Lord." I couldn't see how anything good could come out of this. Years later, I can: I now have a gift that enables me to help others through unbelievable trauma. I have the rock-solid confidence that whatever happens, the Lord will never leave us. Then, I thought He had left us; now, I realize how wrong I was.

Marcreta's situation in widowhood was desperate. She sold her home in Grand Prairie, and she and her two sons moved in with us. She found work at the executive offices of Wyatt's Grocery. With Bryce and Jack in our house, I suddenly had two younger brothers—a real bonus. And then there was the 1941 Chevrolet that I had not-so-secretly coveted. I worked out an arrangement with Marcreta to use the car if I kept it serviced and waxed. I put a lot of wax on that car. At age 14, my love of cars had become an obsession. I went before the county judge and succeeded in getting him to grant me a hardship driver's license. After school, I delivered groceries for A&G food store, driving A&G's Chevrolet panel truck. I also stocked the shelves, swept the store, and filled telephone orders. I loved it, and soon I knew all of Oak Cliff as well as I knew my bedroom. Now I could pay for my own clothes and entertainment.

At Greiner Junior High, my favorite teacher was Mrs. Powledge. One day, she gave us a pop quiz for which I was totally unprepared. Making good grades was terribly important to me, so I stole information from the person sitting next to me. But after I turned in my paper, I was so crestfallen at what I had done, I could not leave the classroom. I went to Mrs. Powledge, confessed, and asked her to give me a zero. I felt much better after that.

Having wheels was a wonderfully liberating experience. My social life was still limited to the church circle, but that now included the guys I knew at 4th and Church in Grand Prairie. We would meet to shoot pool, though—remarkably—never to drink. Going out with girls now began in earnest, but within this church circle. After ninth grade at Greiner, I went on to Sunset High School. In general, high school was a good experience for me, though I always moved on the periphery. My self-image registered somewhere below zero, and I was extremely shy. I dated only the girls at church, never a girl from high school, though there were many—like Janie Ruth and Betty Ruth in grade school—whom I worshipped from afar.

I was destined to go to college—Ralph saw to that. The only question was how the family could afford it. Once more, Texas Crippled Children's Society came to the rescue. They gave me a scholarship that covered tuition at North Texas State. All was going well: The college had accepted me, I had a scholarship, and I had arranged for a part time job. My life was a constant round of activities—school during the day, work at A&G in the afternoon, and social activities in the evening. But one evening, I came home when no one was there, and the house was dark. I sat down on the front porch and reflected on my life. I could see my life before me in Technicolor, and it was not a pretty sight. I was a regular church-goer, and I ran with guys who were Christians, but none of us was living up to our calling. I was suddenly filled with remorse. In tears, I asked for the Lord's forgiveness. I felt that I had to make a dramatic change in the direction of my life. I resolved then and there that somehow, some way, I would go to Abilene Christian College, where I would have a better opportunity to find a real "band of brothers."

I had no idea how we could afford for me to go to the school with a much higher tuition, and in a town where I had no job, but I had two things going for me: I could get temporary room and board in the house of my brother, Dell, and his wife, Jo, who lived in Abilene. And then, D. A. Epps, the same Uncle Arthur who had helped Ralph, agreed to lend me tuition money each semester at a nominal rate of interest.

When I got to Abilene in the summertime, the best job I could find paid 35 cents per hour as a soda jerk—I'd been making 75 cents per hour at A&G! Later, I got a job with Lydick Hooks Roofing at 75 cents per hour. The man who hired me took me out to the Mrs. Baird's Bakery then under construction, showed me a ladder leaning against a 20-foot wall, and told me to climb it and report to the foreman. At the top of the ladder, I discovered that I had to walk along a two-foot ledge to report for work. Always afraid of heights, I wanted to crawl, but I knew I would not keep the job if I did. Screwing up my courage, I walked over and met my foreman, a guy called "Preacher" because he was one of most foul-mouthed people I had ever met. Preacher made it easy for me to keep my language clean! When school started, I had to give up the roofing job because it required 40 hours per week. Drawing on my vast grocery store experience, I landed a job at the A&P. By this time, I had—for the grand sum of $75.00—acquired my own first automobile, a 1936 Chevrolet club coupe. The body was not much, but the motor ran good.

From the moment I set foot on campus, I sensed that everything was different from what I had been used to. The clothes one wore, one's family status, where one was from—none of that mattered. I had found my "band of brothers": Students at ACC for the most part wanted to honor their Christian convictions above all else. In 1950, the college was not yet what it would become in another decade. All the men were housed in U.S. Army surplus barracks. The teachers were underpaid, but no one minded that much. People of great heart and great faith made the college truly Christian. My first roommate, Ken Ford, was elected president of our freshman class. My lifelong case of terminal shyness had been healed. The camaraderie of equals at Abilene Christian was one of my life's greatest blessings. A little late, perhaps, but my four years at what is now Abilene Christian University was my "coming of age." I set no academic track records; rather, I learned that relationships are the most important thing to me. My relationship with my Lord, my fellow students, and my teachers became very important to me.

One good way to evaluate my college experience is to say that I had *fun*. Jasper Howard and I had a contest to see who could date a different girl every night for the greater number of nights. When news of our competition got out, we became socially unacceptable for a while.

In the spring of my freshman year, I met Barbara Bass at church at the 14th and Vine Streets congregation. I called her up, identified myself, asked her out to the Catclaw Picnic. Clearly, I had remembered our introduction better than she did; even so, she accepted, and that was the end and the beginning: We were married in our senior year.

The underlying question facing every undergraduate is this: "What am I going to do with my life?" For me, the answer had to do with service of one of two kinds: I could either become a medical doctor and minister to the physical needs of people, or I could become a minister of the gospel and minister to people's spiritual needs. I was more confident of my ability to become a doctor than to become a minister, although I felt a strong calling in the latter direction. I was not the only one who doubted my future prospects as a pulpit man: Dr. Carl Brecheen, after hearing one of my early attempts at preaching, told a friend of mine that he wanted to come to me and say, "Dwain, there are a lot of things you can do in life, but preaching is not one of them."

During our sophomore year, Dwight Eisenhower and Adlai Stevenson were running for the presidency. During a campus debate, Jon Jones and Max Leach represented Eisenhower, the Republican, and Jack Scott and I spoke out for Stevenson, the Democrat. We lost the debate, and Stevenson lost the election. Then, Rudy Wyatt, who was preaching for a small church in Truby, Texas, invited me to fill the pulpit one Sunday. I worked up a sermon on I Corinthians 13, went over it and over it in the barracks dormitory, and invited Barbara and another couple to go with me on this preaching expedition. I got up to deliver the sermon, quoted every scripture I could think of and some I was not so sure of, and sat down after the elapse of a total time of five minutes. Public speaking was not my long suit, so I became a pre-med major. Barbara and I talked about my becoming a medical missionary. We would move to some exotic place where our services would be welcome. Doctors don't have to talk that much.

Few students at Abilene Christian were less suited for the preaching ministry than I was, but I had a burning desire. Mid-semester of my junior year, I changed from pre-med to being a Bible major, and that shook my relationship with Barbara. She had said "yes" and put on our engagement ring while I was a pre-med major, but our relationship now became so strained that I broke the engagement. We were both miserable because we were genuinely in love with each other. As it worked out, I barely squeezed in enough Bible courses in summer school to call it a major. Barbara—with courage and grace—resigned herself to becoming the wife of a preacher. Giving Barbara's mother very short notice, we were married on September 5, 1953, at the beginning of our senior year at Abilene Christian.

Barbara completed her degree requirements at mid-semester, and taught school in Abilene the spring semester. I was taking a heavy academic load, preaching at Shields, Texas, on Sundays, speaking on a radio program in Coleman, and serving as the night manager of the Hotel Wooten drugstore. I still lacked an English course and a French course to have enough credits to be able to graduate with my class; Barbara graduated with honors. I began looking for a church that would employ me as their minister.

Dr. Overton Faubus arranged a try-out sermon for me with the church in Coolidge, Texas. In proof that miracles do still happen, they hired me. Preaching for me was an exhilarating burden of responsibility, a fearful challenge. I had just turned 21, I realized at the core that I was ill equipped to communicate a word from the Lord to His church. "I had taken the minimum number of Bible courses because I had been so slow in choosing Bible as my major. I had not even been able to squeeze in the course on the "Preparation and Delivery of Sermons." I knew I needed more training, but I could see no way to get it.

Despite my misgivings, the church at Coolidge seemed to do well under my preaching, and I began to receive invitations to speak to other churches in the area. The salary was a modest $65 per week, but I loved the work. I loved every thing about it—the pastoral work: visiting the sick at home and in the hospitals, offering a word from the Lord and a prayer for healing. I especially loved preaching.

Then, Barbara gave me some good news: We were pregnant. Lisa was born on December 23, 1954—an absolute delight! In the spring semester, the local school needed a teacher, so Barbara went to work. We engaged a baby-sitter for Lisa, and with her came a graduate course in Southern culture. Lisa's Black nanny would not enter our house through the front door. Our suggestion that she do so, in fact, horrified her. I, too, was horrified but for the opposite reason. She would not sit down at the table and eat with us. When I insisted, she became anxious and uncomfortable. I gave up on the effort.

This was 1954, the year that the U.S. Supreme Court in *Brown v. The Board of Education* reversed a hundred years and more of school segregation, striking down the old hypocrisy of "separate but equal." As the schools had been, so the churches still were: separate and unequal. I decided that the time had come as well for a word from the Lord to the church on the subject of segregation. In an article on *James*, chapter 2, for the church bulletin that I published weekly, I inserted the words, "black man" instead of "poor man," and "white man" instead of "rich man." After the stir began to subside, only one person had quit the church, a big raw-boned farmer named Gus Bolen from the little community of Delia. I loved Gus and I think he loved me, so I went to see him. When I got to his farm, Gus saw me coming, and by the time I walked up to him, he was red in the face. Gus doubled up his fist, shook it in my face, and said, "Preacher, don't you never mention *Nigger* again!" "Gus," I replied, "I think you know me well enough to know that if I think it is in the Bible, I am going to mention it." Within a few weeks, Gus was back in his pew as if nothing had happened.

Barbara, Lisa, and I attended the Lectureship at ACC that year—the annual week of preaching and teaching by the best. Among the speakers was J. Harold Thomas from Bangor, Maine—Harold had dedicated his career to the Northeast where Churches of Christ were few and far between. His exhortation to become involved in church-planting and strengthening in the Northeast had a strong appeal to Barbara and me because we had already talked about New England. About the same time, we heard that the Skillman Avenue Church in Dallas was looking for someone to serve the small church in Augusta, Maine. Barbara and I talked it over, we contacted the Elders at Skillman Avenue, and—to my surprise—they asked us to go.

Lisa, now eight months old, and I had never been east of the Mississippi River. Barbara had been a counselor in the first year at Camp Shiloh at Mendham, New Jersey. But in August of 1955, we three took our tiny exodus from Coolidge, Texas, bound for Augusta, Maine. Across the upper South, along the Blue Ridge Parkway, through the Shenandoah Valley of Virginia, by way of Washington, D.C., and then northward through the big cities I had heard about but never seen, and through the States whose names I knew from books on American History, a preacher-boy from Texas had a revelation of a bigger world. We rented an apartment directly across from the modest church building that housed the Augusta Church of Christ. The tiny band of Christians there graciously received us.

At the ripe old age of 22, I was now responsible to the Lord and the Skillman Avenue Elders for my work in a mission field. I had no idea how to proceed. I must acknowledge that my message at that time was a narrow and legalistic one, but that was about to change. I got a copy of *Letters to Young Churches*, a modern-speech version of the New Testament by

J. B. Phillips. His translation of the book of *Romans* was the most exciting thing I had ever read. "This is too good to be true," I thought. "He must have missed it somewhere! Surely this is not an accurate translation!" But the more I studied, the more I came to the conclusion that Phillips had it dead on. This message in *Romans* caused a radical change in my preaching. I had been excited about the Lord, the gospel, salvation before, but this new light from *Romans* filled me with much greater excitement and made me more eager than ever before to share the Good News with everyone I met.

Back in that frame house on Railroad Avenue in Ferris, Texas, we used to gather around a little Silvertone Radio to listen to Gabriel Heatter broadcast the news during World War II. He would begin by saying: "Ladies and Gentlemen, I have good news tonight." Now, I too had good news, a good-news message that the Savior had come, abandoning his glory, to walk on earth in human flesh, disguised in a seamless robe and wearing sandals. He had learned what it was like to be like us; he had experienced life the way we experience it; he had been tempted in all the ways that we are tempted but without sinning; and finally he had—because of his great love for us—surrendered his life on the cross so that I—and Barbara and Lisa and the church folk in Augusta and you, Dear Reader, and everyone—might be saved, so that we all might be saved. What a message! What a Savior! It was "grace upon grace!" It was salvation that rested not on our good works but on the sacrificial death of Jesus. And to think that this poor, fumbling, inexperienced, under-prepared, rocker-footed preacher had the privilege of proclaiming this good news. It boggled my mind!

The three years in Augusta were a huge blessing to Barbara, Lisa, and me. Relationships developed there have lasted our lifetime. And there was more good news: Barbara was pregnant with our second daughter, Stephanie. Moreover, "on the ground" at a small mission church, I came experientially to a revelatory conclusion: A more effective church-planting might be accomplished when a few dedicated Christian families would band together to move into a new community to proclaim Christ. We decided to go back to Abilene where I could finish my degree, and where we would gather ten families who would move with us as the nucleus of a new church in a new city. We moved in with Barbara's parents in Abilene, and Stephanie was born on June 5, 1958—yet another great blessing to us! I completed my course work and finally received my B. A. Meanwhile, I was looking for a church.

James Willeford recommended me to the Lamar Street Church in Sweetwater, and our ministry there was blessed, but we found no other family interested in moving with us to some distant city. The next church we served was the Parkway Drive Church in Lubbock, where we found others willing to take the challenge of our ultimate plan.

Robert Qualls, with his wife Annette, joined us as associate minister in 1960, a year when the Civil Rights pot was coming to a boil. Another minister and I studied the segregation issue with Virgil Trout, preacher for the Sunset Church of Christ in Lubbock. I came across a sermon by Will Campbell, a Baptist minister in Nashville, Tennessee, that began with a quotation of David Lipscomb, who had called it a sin to have both a Black church and a White church in the same community. I prepared and announced a Sunday evening sermon, "Is Segregation Scriptural?" planning to use the citation from Lipscomb. One of the Elders, who had been especially generous to Barbara and me, told me that if I preached that sermon, that he would refuse to attend. I told him I felt that I had no choice but to preach it. In the sermon, I stated that one day soon, Black Christians would ask to be members of this congregation, and I said that we must be prepared to accept them into full fellowship. Today, Parkway Drive is one of the most integrated churches in Lubbock.

At Parkway Drive, we found 12 couples, including one of our Elders, who were interested in our new idea of church-planting. We developed a list of 22, which we narrowed to a list of 7, cities of over 100,000 that did not have a Church of Christ in them, all of them in the Northeast, and began to gather information focusing especially on their commercial life and the job market: the Lowell-Lawrence-Haverhill area in Massachusetts; Waterbury, Connecticut; Middletown, Connecticut; Albany, New York; and Bay Shore, New York. Four of us traveled to these cities to gather information. After fasting and prayer, our groups of families selected Bay Shore on the South Shore of Long Island. The project was named "Exodus/Bay Shore."[1] During the 1950s, Long Island had experienced a huge population boom and the existing churches had not kept up with this prodigious growth. The group felt that it was a "field white unto harvest."

About this time, Walter Burch, who worked with Abilene Christian University, came through Lubbock and stopped for a visit. He became excited about our plans and encouraged us to raise the goal to 30 families. Walter had excellent planning skills and a thorough knowledge of promotion. He volunteered his services and, over the years, made a huge contribution to the success of the project. He proposed that we ask the Richland Hills church (near Fort Worth) to be our sponsoring church, and the Elders there—full of vision and courage—readily agreed. Walter enlisted the help of Larry Cardwell, a commercial artist, and they prepared graphics and charts that were as large as they were professional: We had to build a trailer to pull them behind the car. The theme of our presentation was, "Advancing a Bold Idea in Evangelism." Our new goal of 30 families was soon raised to 60.

Our message was centered on a quotation from Dietrich Bonhoeffer: "When Christ calls a man, he bids him come and die." There are many ways to die but we felt that one way was to leave one's job, sell one's home, say good-bye to one's culture, and move across the nation to be a part in planting a new church.

Barbara, the girls, and I bade farewell to the Parkway Drive church and moved to Fort Worth to become members at Richland Hills. We spent about a year visiting churches across the South and Southwest, presenting our plan. Rodney Spaulding and his wife, Pat, recent graduates of ACU, with their daughters, were persuaded to join the team. Rodney and I took separate paths in the effort to recruit members and funds, and we agreed that when we met in Bay Shore, he would be the Minister of Personal Evangelism. Ralph Spencer, a Lubbock architect, and Don Osborne, a Lubbock realtor, agreed to serve as our site location team. They found the four-acre site on Montauk Highway, a principal east/west artery not in Bay Shore but in West Islip, that was to become the ultimate address of the Exodus. The first funds we raised paid off that site. Ralph designed the building: According to plan, it was to be built in two phases, first a chapel and educational plant to be followed by a large auditorium that could seat 2,000.

Rodney and I found the response to our presentations greater than our wildest dreams. The times were ripe for such an idea. President John F. Kennedy in his inaugural address had challenged the nation when he said: "Ask not what your country can do for you but

---

[1] See Erma Jean Loveland, "The Genesis of an Exodus," in this volume.

what you can do for your country." Young people everywhere we went were ready to do something new. They were volunteering for the Peace Corps, taking only subsistence salaries. The same spirit of adventure was penetrating the hearts of church members who were asking this same hard question about the church and their spiritual lives. More than 1,500 families signed commitment cards either to take part or to support in Exodus in some way. We did not take a hard-sell approach. We would make our presentation in some town or city, leave the congregation that evening for our next destination in another city, another state, and then we would find that people who had pledged themselves followed up on their own. The target date for the move was set: August, 1963. We held three retreats—at Glen Rose, Bedford, and Athens, Texas—so interested families could obtain more information. Some of our best speakers at these retreats included A.R. Holton, E.W. McMillan, and Virgil Trout.

As more and more people became committed, the enormity of the undertaking began to settle in. Like the sometime dubious Israelites who left Egypt in their exodus to a land of promise, this wobbly Moses must confess that his faith trembled over the prospect of having asked all these people to sell their homes, quit their jobs, pull up their roots, and move from one section of the country to what to most of us was a "far country," Long Island, New York.

It helped a lot when my brother Ralph and sister-in-law Sue organized an employment conference at the Baker Hotel in Dallas in January, 1963. We collected résumés from all who were getting ready for the move, and Ralph, Sue, and I traveled to Long Island to talk to potential employers. Our list of willing workers included mostly professional people, and their range of talents included "butchers, bakers and candlestick makers." We three explained to Human Resources professionals on Long Island that we represented a group of people who would be arriving in August, motivated by a faith commitment, and we asked them to send employment counselors to our conference at their companies' expense. Grumman sent four, Republic one, and four school superintendents came, as did a professional employment counselor. In one day at the Baker, 150 people were interviewed. The church at Commack, Long Island, had a team of ministers who gave us invaluable assistance in this effort to find employment.

All of us sensed that a power greater than any of us was at work at that conference. I know of no one who was hired on the spot, but the ground was laid for future hiring. As time drew near for our departure, we made another trip to Long Island and we rented some modest (indeed!) vacation cabins, Wolffe's Cabins, that would provide temporary shelter as our people arrived. A Jewish rabbi in Bay Shore offered the Exodus his premises as our temporary place of worship. Like believers in Jesus in the New Testament, we were made at home first among our brother and sister Israelites. When the day arrived, 86 families made the move.

On February 15, 1963, *Time Magazine* ran an article complete with picture on their religion page, titled "The Campbellites Are Coming." Unfortunately they used phrases we had not used, for example, that we had chosen the South Shore of Long Island because of a "novel blend of wholesomeness and godlessness." Other articles were appearing in the Fort Worth *Star-Telegram*, Long Island's *Newsday* and other papers.

That year of travel in recruitment and preparation had taken a toll on Barbara and our two daughters. Just before the departure, Barbara and I took a trip to New Orleans for some desperately needed time alone. Then we loaded our furniture, packed our car, and headed to New York. As we drove through New York City and out Southern State Parkway, Barbara became disillusioned. The suburban sandbar of Long Island's South Shore is nothing like the rural hills and dales we had enjoyed in Maine. With Barbara's rare kind of courage, she soldiered on.

On the first Sunday of August 1963, we met in the Jewish Center with 136 in attendance. I preached on the text that records the words of Elisha, "Fear not, for those who are with us are more than those who are with them." (2 Kg 6:16). By this time, we had begun to believe it. The Lord was working very powerfully in the lives of all of us, and the consciousness of Heavenly assistance was beginning to dawn on us. As cramped as we all were, we had arranged for the youth group from the Richland Hills church to come to Long Island and help us in a campaign. We could see no way that we could house them and feed them, so we called Fort Worth to cancel the trip. The bus full of teenagers and adult leaders had already left. We had to move quickly.

From the start, we had a full-time staff: Rodney Spaulding, Minister of Personal Evangelism; Richard Salmon, Minister of Education; Ruth Stillinger, Secretary and Office Administrator; and Alfred Holeman who was shortly made an Elder of the church. We found three store-front buildings on Main Street in Bay Shore and converted these into classroom space, a worship center, and offices. These buildings had stamped tin ceilings, so with the many in our group who had sung in *a cappella* choruses at Lipscomb, Harding, and ACU, the singing during our worship was truly marvelous.

We welcomed the Richland Hills group in our three store-fronts. Rod Spaulding did a masterful job orienting and preparing them to go door to door with a simple message: "We represent a new church in this community and we are eager to arrange Bible studies in your home, if you so desire." The response was overwhelming, and we suddenly had a crisis. Scores of classes had been arranged, but we had no one prepared to teach them. Rod began a crash-course training our recently arrived members; before long, we had over 70 classes in session each week. In the first 18 months, over 150 were baptized.

Meanwhile, James Hance, who was acting as general contractor in the construction of the church building, was soon—with Forrest Wells and Alfred Holeman—to become an Elder of the church: The church's organization was quickly taking shape. Housing and jobs, likewise, were found in a very short period of time. The only person I remember going more than two or three weeks in finding a job was Lamar Baker, an electrical engineer, so when Lamar got his job, everyone rejoiced. Grumman and the school districts were the principal employers. Jim Kite arrived from Houston and went to work at Grumman, where he was told: "Mr. Kite, we have never had an opening for a man with your qualifications until today." Incidents like this convinced us that an Invisible Hand was opening doors.

A few weeks before, I had received a call from one Don Haymes. He was a young single man whose 1953 Morris Minor had broken down on Sagtikos Parkway only a few miles short of his goal. He, too, was joining the Exodus. Little did I know at the time how deeply he would influence my life. He had been asked to leave reputable institutions such as Harding College and Abilene Christian College, not for any moral reason but for his failure to fit in. He had made it across the country with a borrowed credit card and had spent the last of his money on car repairs in Joplin, Missouri. And what a picture he presented! Broke, disheveled, his eyeglasses taped together, with few academic credentials to offer. No razor had touched his face, but behind this deceptive exterior, the mind was razor sharp. The new church took him in. They fed him, they clothed him, they loved him. He soon gained a reputation as our *"Torchbook* Theologian." I think Don had read every issue of Harper's paperback books on theology; that series had been Don's inexpensive route to a theological education, a route that he had traveled in style. Don Haymes became the permanent "thorn in my flesh," always challenging, always forcing me to think deeper, to study more, to read more broadly. He was no "messenger of Satan," but he clearly saw it his duty to "harass me, too keep me from being too elated." I was deeply blessed when the Lord sent him our way.

The formal opening for our new building took place on September 13, 1964. By then, the church had grown to 236 members. My prayer from the beginning had been that this church would have a world vision. I had become aware of the Park Street Church, a Congregational church on Boston Common, which both its pastor, Harold John Ockenga, and the Harvard students that attended there, referred to as the "hell-fire-and-brimstone corner." That one church was supporting more than 100 missionaries around the world, and they did it through an annual "Missions Conference." Several of us decided to attend that conference. We heard men and women with professional degrees, living on subsistence salaries, speak of the powerful way that Jesus Christ was working in the lives of people who previously had never heard of him. I found it hard to argue against the doctrinal incorrectness of people who had taken the core message of scripture far more seriously than I had done. We came away from this conference with the firm resolve to schedule a missions conference at West Islip.

Our Missions Conference was human folly and divine wisdom. The West Islip Church had been in existence for less than two years. All of its members were already giving liberally, even sacrificially. What more could be asked of them? Yet the Elders agreed, we set a goal to raise $30,000 in addition to our regular contribution (a mountain of money in 1964). We planned to employ a Minister of Missions and inaugurate a program to be called—inspired by JFK, of course—the Faith Corps. Faith Corps would recruit college students to spend two years of their lives at subsistence salaries as apprentice missionaries. They would spend three months in training at West Islip before going out to mission fields around the world.

Speakers at our Mission Conference included Stanley Shipp from Switzerland, Ira Rice from Singapore, Gordon Hogan from Malaysia, Judd Whitefield from Malaysia, George Gurganus from Japan. We fasted and prayed through Saturday and Saturday night; someone was at the building every hour of the night in prayer. The conference started on Sunday and concluded on Wednesday night. Our financial goal had been exceeded, and Carl Phagan became our bright and innovative Minister of Missions. He traveled from college to college, making this simple appeal: "Devote two years of your life in dedication to the Lord. Be responsible for raising your own subsistence support. We will provide the training." In the first year, perhaps a dozen people answered that call; within a short time, more than 100 had gone on mission, many of them to the Inner City Faith Corps.[2]

I keenly felt the need for more education. I made plans to pursue a M. Div. Degree at Biblical Seminary in New York City, but before I could begin this program, a more pressing

[2] See Freda Elliott Baker, "The Inner City Faith Corps: An Oral History," in this volume.

need arose. The stress of earning a living in a new culture combined with the additional demands of our intense church life was more than some of our families could handle. A pressing need for skilled family therapy had arisen. In 1966, I enrolled at Iona College, a Catholic school in New Rochelle, New York, in the Master's program in Pastoral Counseling for priests, nuns, rabbis and Protestant clergy. I completed the course in 1970.

The churches of Christ, with which the West Islip Church was historically and emotionally involved, were changing. Our 19th-century Restoration Movement had changed from being a sect to being a denomination in its form as the Disciples of Christ. In the brotherhood of the churches of Christ, we tried to maintain a more primitive form of congregational autonomy. If the West Islip Church of Christ were truly autonomous, and non-sectarian, then why not drop the name "Church of Christ" and simply be "the church in West Islip." We had to acknowledge, however, that we would soon sectarianize even that bid for complete independence.

In the mid-1960s, social awareness was growing in the mind of the church. Our own Inner City Faith Corps was a part of that movement. Freedom Marches were going on in the South, but we could not easily participate in those. Members of the West Islip Church did take the lead among Long Island churches in getting the Town of Islip to pass the first Open Housing Ordinance.

I had the privilege of being the first non-Roman Catholic to speak at the Catholic Church in Bay Shore. I met with Eugene Smith, then Secretary of National Council of Churches of Christ, and as a result I, along with Robert Raines, was invited to address a meeting of the World Council of Churches held in the Poconos of Pennsylvania. In my speech, I focused on church renewal, but religious talk has to become political discourse when there is little concern for the poor in high places.

Our concept of church-planting, the Exodus, had caught the attention of many across the nation, and I was invited to speak in nearly every State. A group of us young Turks met at lectureships and seminars to lay plans for renewal among the churches of Christ. In 1965, we gathered together in Nashville 75 prominent preachers in the White and Black Churches of Christ. Ira North hosted the gathering, and we discussed the church's mission, race relations, and the work of the Holy Spirit.

I was invited to deliver one of the main lectures the following February at the Abilene Christian University Lectureship. I felt the Lord had given me the opportunity to say some things that were on my heart. I worked very hard on my lecture, "Exodus with the Bible." Don Haymes assisted me greatly. Among other things, I made the case for the Holy Spirit's energy influencing our lives separate and apart from the word of Scripture. I think Barton Stone and Robert Richardson would have called out "Amen!," but Tolbert Fanning would have sat silent. Others still living who agreed with Tolbert Fanning did not, however, remain silent.

When my time to speak came, I was on fire with the word, and I poured out my heart. According to schedule, I was to give the same lecture two nights in a row. After the first night at the University Church, which had been well received (I thought), three members of the University's administration called me in and asked me not to repeat my lecture in Sewell Auditorium.

I asked them to help me correct whatever was wrong with the lecture, and I offered to stand up that night and correct it in public.

They told me that they agreed with my premise, that the Holy Spirit works more than through the Bible only, but that the churches were not yet ready to hear it.

"In that case," I replied, "I have no choice but to give the same lecture again that I gave last night."

One of them said, "Dwain, it is a shame for you to throw away your career over a little thing like this."

I replied that it was no little thing to me.

After two hours of this kind of talk, one of them said, "It will do less damage for us to let him speak than for us to cancel it as this late hour."

Despite this concession, I walked out feeling that I could not possibly speak that night. I spent the next two hours in prayer at my wife's parents' home, where I was staying. I had never been much sensations of spiritual experience, but about 6:00 p.m., a warm feeling of peace and joy swept over me—joy that I had the privilege to preach, and peace that whatever the cost might be, speaking the truth of the gospel is worth it. I told my father-in-law what had happened, and he replied, "I am going with you." Years later at his funeral, I said: "If I had ever been in a street fight, I would have wanted Jay Bass standing beside me."

I gave this lecture in 1966. At the time, I had meetings and speaking appointments scheduled through 1975: They were all cancelled except for two. Gary Freeman and I had been columnists for the *Christian Chronicle*; we both lost our columns. Future appointments at ACU were cancelled, Lipscomb called and cancelled, Oklahoma Christian scrubbed me. Only Pepperdine among the Christian colleges allowed me to come and speak. Barbara and I received bags of hate mail. One said that they had evidence that I was a graduate of the "Oral Roberts School of Healing." Another said that they had heard that I had been involved in raising a dead cat to life. And on it went. Perhaps it was a balancing of my spiritual karma: As much was said to discredit me after my fall that was untrue as has been previously said to flatter me that was also untrue!

Meanwhile I continued with my graduate program at Iona in Pastoral Counseling, and I was beginning to do a lot of personal and family counseling within the West Islip Church. In my final year at Iona, I was assigned a counseling intern position at a Catholic girls school in Nyack, New York—a challenging task.

The group of young Turks continued to meet, though less frequently. We were eager to find a forum where the Black and White churches could come together. We decided on Atlanta as the next meeting place, and we asked Jimmy Allen to host for the White churches, and Eugene Lawton from Newark and Roosevelt Wells from Manhattan to host for the Black churches. Black and White preachers and Elders responded marvelously, and almost everyone in attendance signed the manifesto on race that we drafted and that was published in a full-page ad in the *Christian Chronicle*.

Following the uproar over my Abilene lecture, members at West Islip began to receive letters of alarm from back home, questioning their loved ones about what they had committed themselves to. Our membership began to drop off, and people went to other churches on Long Island. We could no longer support our staff. All of us went off the payroll. After a time, the Elders suggested that I go back on the payroll, so I did. Before my lecture at ACU, Sunday attendance at West Islip had been running over 400; afterwards, we dropped to less than half that number.

In 1970, Barbara greeted me with the news that she was no longer going to teach school. She was making considerably more money than I was, and we clearly could not meet our obligations without her salary. And she had more news. She told me that our marriage was stressed to the limit. This sledgehammer blow greatly focused my attention. Barbara's thunderbolt struck far more deeply than did the ACU debacle. I loved her dearly; I had felt that everything was going well in our marriage. I, the degreed expert in family therapy, had missed the signs that my own marriage was a textbook case of the preacher who is so busy saving the world that he loses his own family. The proverb Jesus quoted kept ringing in my ears, "Physician, heal yourself!"

I asked immediately, and Barbara agreed—thank the Lord!—to go with me to see Dr. Thomas Fogarty, an outstanding family therapist with whom I had studied at Iona. I guess I was secretly thinking, "Fogarty will straighten Barbara out soon enough." Was I in for a surprise! He asked me the question that set my brain to ringing, and I can still hear the echo nearly fifty years later: "What makes you think that God is not going to get his work done in the world without you?" He also asked me, "Why did you ask Barbara to marry you when you knew that she was concerned about living up to the role of a minister's wife?" Mercifully, I do not remember my lame response, but I do remember the clarity: If I wanted to save my marriage, I had to give up the ministry that I loved so dearly.

Breaking the news to the church at West Islip was hard, but finding a job was harder. My academic preparation was strictly in the area of ministry, but Barbara did not want to be married to a preacher. James Walter Nichols set up an interview with the president of an advertising company in Manhattan. I walked into his office and he said, "OK, Mr. Evans, sell yourself!" Whatever else I said during that conversation, I told him that I could sell anything that I believed in. At the end of the interview, he said, "You won't do in our business. We have to sell things everyday that we don't believe in."

The time for repentance had come, and it was not going to be easy. My obsession had been my calling, but I had neglected my dear wife and our two precious daughters. I went to work for Glendale Associates, a real-estate syndication firm on the North Shore owned by Glen Paden and Dale Harper, members of the Commack Church. They bought properties in the path of development of the major growth cities, involved investors in the deals, and managed the real estate until it could be sold at substantial profit to the investors. At first, they had me traveling three or four days a week, first to Atlanta and later to Houston. I found working in the "real world" of business, as opposed to the "ideal world" of a churchly cloister, exhilarating. I took part in the purchase of a $24 million-dollar package of properties in Houston, and Glendale management said I had to move to Houston. But I had planned to spend the rest of my life on Long Island as a member of the West Islip Church.

Dreams are dashed and plans change. I commuted from Long Island to Houston for nearly a year; we moved to Houston in the summer of 1971. I cried out to the Lord, "Where is my ministry?" He showed me. My new call was to a humble service: I was to be a servant to my wife and children. I did household chores, visited the sick, visited people in prison, taught Bible classes, and helped to raise my four grandsons. I accepted the call to be an Elder at the Bering Drive Church where I served four terms of five years each.

Exodus/Bayshore—the West Islip Church—did fine without me. The church-planting movement spawned other exoduses: Rochester, Burlington, Stamford, Dover, Toronto.

Some fared better than others, but the movement—and the Holy Spirit—changed lives. I am proud of what we did. The Exodus Movement is an example of faith and commitment among people in the twentieth century who, like people in the first century, were willing to march off the map for the Lord.

My brilliant idea for church-planting turned out not to be an effective way to do mission work. At Bay Shore/West Islip, there were too many of us. We imported our own culture instead of embracing the culture of Long Island. The words of Gertrude Kriss, a dear lady who was baptized as a result of one of our classes, ring in judgment against us: "Not only do you become a Christian in this church but also you become a Texan." To be sure, we could intellectualize about the challenges of cross-cultural communication, but when that many from the same culture cluster together in a new culture and a foreign land, the ghetto effect takes over. At the end of the century, I conducted a survey of those who had gone with the Exodus to Long Island. Among the fifty responses, not one regretted having taken part. From what people said, I concluded that the greatest thing that came out of our experiences were the changes that took place in our own lives. Would I do it again? No. Am I glad I did it in 1963? I offer a resounding yes!

On September 5th, 2005, Barbara and I celebrated our 52nd wedding anniversary. Whatever price I paid by leaving my beloved ministry, Barbara was well worth it.

THE GENESIS OF AN EXODUS:
THE DOCUMENTARY BASIS FOR A HISTORY OF
THE EXODUS/BAYSHORE MOVEMENT

ERMA JEAN LOVELAND

On Leaving Home for God

"Follow me!" And he rose and followed him. (Mk 2:14) Throughout the Bible, the Lord's people have heard Heaven's call to follow God and go the way He bade them go. Abram and Isaac, Jacob and Joseph, Moses and the disciples of Jesus—all heard the call to go out and away from the familiar paths of the old life to be faithful to God in the new.

Eighteenth-century followers of God and leaders of their people—Pilgrims, Puritans, and Quakers—likewise heard Heaven's call and followed His path across a trackless ocean to a land of opportunity in the New World.

Nineteenth-century land-seekers moved their families into the American wilderness away from the coastlines and cities. They followed not only the frontier and their need for a place to grow but also a quest for religious freedom to worship God their own way. From Baptists on foot and Methodists on horseback to Mormons with handcarts—including some 150 diverse communitarian groups—the early pioneers carried their faith, government, and life style with them wherever they went.[1]

Heaven's call to go out from one's home into a land that God would show the wanderer could still be heard in the twentieth century. A young man and his bride, Dwain and Barbara Evans, gathered a group of trained and educated people to leave the South and Southwest to go with them to what seemed to most of the company to be a "foreign land"—Long Island, New York. Their goal was to teach the people of Long Island about Jesus and his call to men and women to follow him. Called "Exodus/Bay Shore," this soul-stirring experiment has been compared with the faith and mission of the first century and the way Early Christians were sent forth from Jerusalem. In this essay, I explore the genesis of this exodus during its beginnings, 1961 to 1964, from the time of the going out until the time of the settling in, when the Exodus/Bay Shore Group appointed Elders, built a building, and began to carry out their projects.

In 1961, Exodus/Bay Shore wanted to make disciples of all nations. The plan was to leave family, friends, jobs, and houses behind and move with a group of Christians to a great metropolitan area. God opened many hearts for this Exodus. Hundreds of emigrants traveled thousands of miles on their exodus route to a meaningful lifestyle of obedience

---

[1] Jerry Rushford, *Christians on the Oregon Trail: Churches of Christ and Christian Churches in Early Oregon 1842-1882* (Glendale, Arizona: Covenant Publishing, 2001), wrote about the early 19th-century exoduses of the Stone-Campbell Restorationist Christians or Disciples.

and faith in their Lord and Savior. These modern-day Christians willingly gave the honor and glory of their days to God.

Dwain and Barbara Evans

When Barbara Jo Bass said "yes" to Dwain Evans's[2] marriage proposal, she thought she was agreeing to be the wife of a medical doctor. Dwain was a pre-med student at Abilene Christian College (ACC—later University, ACU). His first career choice seemed to be a desire to save physical lives through medical treatment. But then his thinking changed, and he caught the glimmer of hope in saving lives for eternity. Before they were married, Dwain told Barbara, "I want to preach; I want to go where the church is weak."[3] Dwain's personal talents were great; and in answer to his power of persuasion when laying out his call of discipleship to her, Barbara said, as Ruth told Naomi, "Where you go I will go.... Your God is my God." (Ruth 1:16)

Dwain Evans, born in Palmer, Texas, April 4, 1933, was baptized at 12 years of age in 1945 by Logan Buchanan. Evans graduated from Sunset High School in Dallas in 1950 and matriculated in Abilene Christian College. From the pre-med course he changed to become a "Bible major" during his junior year. Barbara and Dwain were married on September 5, 1953, and the next year he began preaching in Coolidge, Texas. Soon, the Elders of the Skillman Avenue Church of Christ in Dallas sent the young couple to minister in Augusta, Maine. Dwain confessed to the 1963 ACC Bible Lectureship crowd that their mindset had been to get their "internship in preaching" finished in a small congregation and then come back to a large Southern congregation with a cushy lifestyle.[4]

Barbara Jo Bass, daughter of J. W. and Josephine Bass, was born May 17, 1932. The Basses were owners of Bass Soap Company on Rose Street in Abilene. After Dwain and Barbara married in 1953, they continued their studies at ACC and graduated in 1954. According to the *1954 Prickly Pear*, the ACC yearbook, Barbara was a member of Girls' Training Class, Mission Study, and the Shiloh Club, a group of students who were interested in furthering Christianity in the Northeast. Her involvement with these groups was preparatory and prophetic of her future direction. Her career choice was to become a primary-school teacher.

The Genesis

Dwain and Barbara lived and learned for three years in Augusta as their understanding of the Word grew. They knew they needed more guidance and research before they ministered in a mission area again.[5]

Returning to Texas, Evans preached at the Lamar Street Church of Christ in Sweetwater, and then at the Parkway Drive Church in Lubbock. He read widely, talked with others, and screened the new ideas through his bright mind and his will to follow

---

[2] See Dwain Evans, "A Memoir," in this volume.

[3] Mrs. Dwain (Barbara) Evans, *Moving for the Lord: Exodus/Bay Shore*. No Date. Center for Restoration Studies vertical file – "Exodus/Bay Shore."

[4] Dwain Evans, "Advancing a Bold Idea in Evangelism," in *The Christian and Morality: Abilene Christian College Annual Bible Lectures* (Abilene, Texas: Abilene Christian College Students Exchange, 1963): 235.

[5] *Loc. cit.*

Christ wherever He might lead him. Dietrich Bonhoeffer's *Cost of Discipleship*, particularly Chapter 4, "Discipleship and the Cross," became a leading conduit in Evans' pathway of discovery.[6] Bonhoeffer had written: "When Christ calls a man, he bids him come and die...because only the man who is dead to his own will can follow Christ."[7] Jesus told the rich young man, "Go sell what you have, and give to the poor, and you will have treasures in heaven, and come, follow me!" (Mark 10:21) Evans grew to understand why we humans need to set our focus on the Lord: When our vision wanders to worldly, materialistic possessions, we become no longer willing to live the sacrificial life.

May 11, 1961, Dr. Walter and Mary Rogers invited three couples into their home in Lubbock, Texas, for conversation about "How can we better approach mission work in the large metropolis area?"[8] The couples were Alfred and Clellie Holeman, Floyd and Pat Stumbo, Dwain and Barbara Evans. The seed of genesis had been planted. The couples believed that a major handicap of loneliness could be removed were an exodus of several families to settle near each other in a large, populated area.[9] Three of the four families at the Rogerses' home that evening said they were prepared to move. They set a target date two years hence—August, 1963—the time to go out.

Because they had experienced the discouragements of a single couple moving into a mission field alone, the Evanses knew the project had to be carefully planned, prepared, and soundly backed financially. Faithful, mature adult Christians would need to commit to staying the rest of their lives wherever they decided to move.[10]

"Our ultimate goal was to bring Jesus Christ into the life of every person on Long Island," Evans stated. "This is the dream that God will make possible!"[11]

By the end of the first week of planning for the Exodus, Walter Burch was asked to be the editor of the Exodus Master Plan and Director of Publicity. Burch prepared a detailed, ingenious plan for everything from the census takers' dialogue to the size of envelopes that would be needed for the mail-outs.

A committee searched for the ripest field of harvest. Twenty-six ministers in the greater New England States were asked, by questionnaire, to recommend seven prime locations that needed a mission group to immigrate there. Walter Rogers, Alfred Holeman, Robert Qualls, and Dwain Evans visited each one of the seven cities, using another paper survey tool to make their selection.[12]

---

[6] Don Haymes, introduction to Evans's article, "Lipscomb is quoted," *Christian Chronicle* (August 6, 1966), wrote that the *Cost of Discipleship* shaped Dwain Evans, his message, and then his mission. Howard Hodgson, a fellow traveler in the Exodus movement, stated that Evans referred to Bonhoeffer in his sermons frequently. (Howard Hodgson, former member of Exodus/Bay Shore Movement. Interview by author, 10 September 2004, tape recorded. Center for Restoration Studies.)

[7] Dietrich Bonhoeffer, *The Cost of Discipleship* (New York: Macmillan Co., 1959): 79.

[8] "Exodus/Bay Shore Chronicled: How Exodus/Bay Shore Developed from Idea into Action." No date. Center for Restoration Studies, 1.

[9] Dwain Evans (1963): 238.

[10] *Loc. cit.*

[11] Don Haymes, "Press Release about Exodus/Bay Shore." No date. Abileene Christian University, Center for Restoration Studies.

[12] "Exodus/Bay Shore Chronicled," *op. cit.*

On the south shore of Long Island, about 60 miles east of Manhattan, Bay Shore was chosen. In the 1960s, the population growth was "exploding" because of the new job openings in the defense/aerospace industries. Long Island, Suffolk County, was agriculturally fertile, held records for production in New York State of potatoes, cabbage, and broccoli, and "Long Island duck" was a famous delicacy on the menu of any number of fine-dining restaurants. The villages were growing into a megapolis such that travelers could drive their cars on the Island parkways from one village to another without leaving inhabited areas.[13] Other vehicles, such as pickups, vans, station wagons, trailers, and school buses, were required to use I-495, Long Island Expressway, rather than the parkways.

Nearby congregations of the Churches of Christ were Manhattan, East Side, Queens, Malverne, Bethpage, Huntington Station, Commack, Patchogue, and Riverhead as listed in the October 17, 1963 *Exodus Milestone*. An Independent Christian Church (Church of Christ), named the "Bay Shore Church of Christ," a congregation that used instrumental music in worship, was overlooked in the survey but would be discovered—with due embarrassment—right there in the very town where the exodus pilgrims had landed.

A mission statement published in a letter of agreement was co-signed by the Elders of the North Richland Hills congregation: R. C. Blevins, T. Berlin Cummings, Wilson Hunt, and Don McHam, and the Committee for the Exodus/Bay Shore Group:

> ...to establish a self-supporting congregation and New Testament Church in the city of Bay Shore, Long Island, New York on or about August 1, 1963. The congregation was to be made up of families desiring to move to the Bay Shore area to fulfill the purpose of the project. It will be the purpose of those concerned to have at least 60 couples of unquestioned Christian character [to] make up the nucleus of this congregation.

According to the plan, the Group would before November 1, 1961, develop promotional materials such as a filing system, mailing list, visual presentations to sell the attractiveness of Bay Shore, and statistical data about the ten Northeastern States. Toler Brannon recalled that they worked with the Jule Miller audio-visual materials: "That was the best we had and it taught those who were ready to listen."[14]

Under Walter Burch's editorship, Larry Cardwell was the artist for the first Exodus/Bay Shore brochure. At Lubbock Christian College Lectureship, February 1962, the official announcement was made that the Exodus was moving to Bay Shore, New York. Next, the news releases were sent to commercial periodicals inviting others to "Come, follow us to Bay Shore." Following the first meeting on May 11, 1961, the Group met May 23, July 3, July 20, and August 3 in Lubbock.[15] Howard Hodgson stated that each family made a verbal commitment: "If we said we would do it, then we would. You put your actions where your mouth is."[16] By August 28, 1961, Doyle and Jean Love, of Brownfield; Dail and Maxine Griffin of Lubbock; Jim and Delores Hicks of Lubbock; an engaged couple, Robert

---

[13] Howard Hodgson (2004).

[14] Toler Brannon, former member of Exodus/Bay Shore Movement. Interview by author, 1 October 2004, by tape recording. Center for Restoration Studies.

[15] Walter E. Burch, *Outline of Master Plan of Action for the Northeastern Missionary Group*, privately printed, circ. 1963. Center for Restoration Studies vertical file, "Exodus/Bay Shore."

[16] Hodgson (2004).

Qualls of Lubbock and Annette Davis of Tyler, had joined the Rogers, Holeman, and Evans families of Lubbock.[17]

The Plan

In Walter Burch's detailed "Outline of Master Plan of Action for the Northeastern Missionary Group," he pointed out procedures, needs, plans, and questions that needed to be addressed. From the beginning, the Group knew that in order to magnify their influence, they should plan to move to the Northeast permanently; each family, except for the Ministers and possibly the Elders, would need to be self-supporting and able to finance their own moving expenses; they would need to buy or build homes as soon as possible.[18]

Some of the questions that needed answering before the Group could move to a new home over a thousand miles away, were these: Does a congregation have to be weak at the beginning or can it be strong? Can the Group be scripturally organized with Elders and Deacons from the start? Can the Group move into its own church building within one year? Can every member be totally dedicated from the beginning? How soon can the congregation become self-supporting? Can a group moved from out of one culture into another abound with faith, zeal, love, and grow to 1,000 members or more?

Part of the plan included cultivation of programs that had been generated during the Group's meetings: One of these was a standard of religious orthodoxy: Anyone straying from a form of religion like that of Churches of Christ would be excluded from the Group's fellowship and social activities. Other plans were less exclusive: A program of benevolence will be encouraged and initiated on Long Island as soon as possible. A mission program will be begun within the first year. Newcomers in Christ will be actively shepherded in their faith, zeal, and love. Every member, new ones included, will be trained to be personal teachers for Christ, so that each can teach Bible classes to friends and neighbors. A defined curriculum will be selected or written, and teaching assignments made. The projects will be carefully orchestrated, goal oriented, and written down. Each member will have a project assignment. Publicity will be planned to announce regular worship services. As early as possible, the Elders and Deacons will make selections and assignments to share the work of the church by way of a committee system.[19]

The Elders of the North Richland Hills congregation (Fort Worth) decided to advance the planning and promotion costs up to $2,500 over a 16-month period, agreeing to manage all financial contributions made into the Exodus/Bay Shore accounts. On June 1, Dwain Evans was placed on full-time salary at North Richland Hills, thereby making the sponsorship of the Exodus/Bay Shore Group an official part of that congregation's work. Rodney Spaulding, Director of Personal Evangelism, was added to the payroll on July 1.

---

[17] The Group grew to include the following: Dale and Sheila Burnett, Oklahoma; Floyd and Pat Stumbo, Lubbock Children's Home superintendent; Aubrey and Gail Cox, Lubbock; Joy and Evelyn Tanner, Lubbock, interior decorators; E. F. and Hazel Williams, Elder of Vandalia congregation in Lubbock; Early and Mary Lou Williams, Lubbock, life insurance underwriters; Gerald and LaWanda Neel, U.S. Armed Forces, Lawton, Oklahoma; Kenneth and Virginia Davidson, Richardson, Texas, instrument engineer; C. L. and Bernice Green, Richardson, Elder; Paul and Mary J. Zanowiak, Sweetwater Elder.

[18] Burch (1963).

[19] *Ibid.*: 3.

Other men employed as ministers were Richard Salmon, Educational Director; Carl Phagan, science teacher, the Minister of Missions; Alfred Holeman, Counselor of New Members and Minister of Teaching.[20]

Among the four paid Ministers from Texas, Richard Salmon was the only one who had been born outside of Texas. The veteran preacher in this group, Dwain Evans, had preached less than 10 years before moving to Exodus/Bay Shore. They were all college graduates, three of them from ACC. Burch's "Master Plan" included short biographies of Dwain Evans and the other three Ministers, the following:

Rodney Allen Spaulding, born in Wichita Falls, Texas, July 27, 1938; baptized at age 13, by C. Dale Brooks, April 1, 1951, had grown up in Bend, Oregon; he had graduated from high school in Hamlin, Texas. Spaulding married Patricia Ann Phagan (sister of Carl Phagan, mentioned above), June 2, 1961. Educated at Abilene Christian College, he had served churches including Artesia, New Mexico, and Loving, Texas. Spaulding traveled for six weeks to raise funds for the salary of Alfred Holeman, who became a full-time Elder. Spaulding was one of the ministers for Exodus/Bay Shore, 1962 – 1963. He wrote a series of "Modern Conversions" for *Exodus Milestone*, ending each essay: "Lord, Lead Me to Some Soul Today."

Richard Farley Salmon, born in Trenton, New Jersey, February 8, 1935; baptized, age 13, November 15, 1948, by Clinton Rutherford. He began preaching in Mendham, New Jersey in 1953. Other churches he served were Bonita, Texas; Lawndale, Houston; Southwest, Houston; and Procter Street, Port Arthur, Texas. His wife was Carolyn Cooper. The Salmons moved to Bay Shore in 1963.

William Alfred Holeman, born in Childress, Texas, March 19, 1911; baptized, age 40, March 20, 1951, by M. Norvel Young. Holeman was thus the oldest of the ministers who served the Exodus/Bay Shore congregation. He had married Clellie Barton on October 7, 1933. His undergraduate work was in Government at Texas Tech. He had served the Parkway Drive congregation, Lubbock, as an Elder. He became a preacher at West Islip, New York, in 1964.[21]

Employment

Exodus workers found the job market to be excellent; most of the jobs were in defense/aerospace and teaching. Housing was a critical need because the expanding defense/aerospace industry had attracted workers in many sectors who had absorbed available housing. Wherever the Group turned, however, they believed that God was meeting their needs—jobs with good salaries as well as financial support from congregations "back home"; land for houses and existing houses, loans; additional families moving to Long Island; national news coverage; community acceptance and prospects for conversion to the new church on Long Island. They recognized God's hand working in the Exodus; they credited the Holy Spirit with providing the strength and power for each day. By 1963, 85 families, including single people (most of whom were school teachers), had

---

[20] *Loc. cit.*

[21] "Introduction to the Elders of the Church on Montauk Highway," privately printed, 1964. Abilene Christian College, Center for Restoration Studies vertical file – Exodus/Bay Shore.

made the journey to Exodus/Bay Shore. As they excitedly talked about the Exodus, they found other families who wanted to go, too; the numbers multiplied.

Three times a week, Bay Shore Christians drove to Commack, L.I., for church services. The ever-larger group needed a place for its own church services near to their homes in the Bay Shore area. Leaders of the Jewish synagogue, impressed that a Christian group would style themselves an "exodus," offered the ministers a place to worship in their educational building until the Christians could locate a place to lease. On Sunday, August 4, 1963, 136 persons gathered in the Jewish educational building. Some remembered that First-Century Christians had often met in synagogues—this relationship with the Jews seemed more than coincidental. This Jewish/Christian relationship—like the ones mentioned in the *Book of Acts*—was, however, short lived, when the Jews found out that the Christians were missionary minded. The Christian congregation soon moved into three glass-fronted commercial buildings at 144 E. Main Street, Bay Shore, New York.[22]

The Exodus Adventures of the Hodgsons and the Brannons

After hearing Dwain Evans's Bay-Shore plea at the Highland Church of Christ in Abilene, Howard and Margaret Kamftra Hodgson visited Long Island during the 1962 Christmas holidays. The E. J. Sumerlins, members of the Huntington Station, L.I., congregation, were traveling during the holidays and offered their home for Bay Shore visitors, like the Hodgsons, who needed a place to stay. Howard and Margaret used the time to look for teaching jobs. Howard recalled his interviews: "As teachers, we had our choice of four to six jobs, and they were good-paying teaching jobs. We returned to Abilene very ready to go and get busy." In those days, Long Island was commonly called the "Gold Coast of Public Education."

As soon as Margaret graduated in May 1963, they departed for Long Island. Howard remembered arriving there with exactly $6 in his pocket. Within the week, they both had signed contracts. Howard's contract was for a new school in the South Haven Consolidated District, 80 miles east of Manhattan on the South Shore. This school district had offered an above-base-pay salary to get the teachers to teach in the South Haven system, with two and three grades per room system; thus Howard started out at the highest level for teachers' salaries on Long Island.

Because of the housing shortage in the expanding economy, the Hodgsons lived with the Ken Russells until they could find an apartment. In this seller's market, landlords were charging high rents. Howard and Margaret found an upstairs two-room apartment, with an unfinished attic, in North Babylon; the kitchen was a hot plate—no stove. When visitors or other new arrivals needed a place to stay, the Hodgsons put them in the attic, unless the guests were elderly, in which case the Hodgsons took the attic and let the newcomers sleep in the "master" bedroom. Cooperation was phenomenal, and good spirits were high among the Exodus/Bay Shore people—everyone was helping everyone to settle in.

Howard particularly mentioned Don Haymes who slept in the attic and ate bread and peanut butter while he was trying to find newspaper work. Haymes wrote for the *Smithtown News* and did the Exodus/Bay Shore press releases for the *Christian Chronicle.* Those releases were the "top stories" of the *Christian Chronicle* in 1962 and 1963.

---

[22] Howard Hodgson (2004); email message to author from Freda Elliott Baker.

After attending one of Exodus/Bay Shore meetings at North Richland Hills, Toler and Ella Ruth Yowell Brannon, decided to go to Long Island too. Long Island's need for schoolteachers beckoned to them.

Suffolk County, L. I., school administrators asked for a Texas Employment Conference to interview prospective teachers. Clyde Austin, Director of the ACC Placement Office, and Bill Adrian, Assistant Director, coordinated the meeting at the Baker Hotel in Dallas. Some of Long Island's top employers were interviewing job applicants: Republic Aviation Company, Grumman Aircraft, Long Island Lighting Company, and eight school districts. Candidates from Abilene Christian, Harding, and David Lipscomb Colleges flocked to the interviews at the Dallas Employment Conference.[23]

After Toler Brannon's flying trip to New York City for an interview with the Huntington Station school officials, he accepted a position as a junior high Science teacher, and Ella Ruth Brannon became a Music and Art teacher there. In August 1963, the Brannons moved into Carolyn and Richard Salmon's basement. As soon as the Salmons moved into their new house, the Brannons moved out of the basement and into the Salmons' old house.

Toler reminisced about the educational philosophies of New York schools that varied from those followed in Texas public schools. Tracking of New York students in the elementary grades determined which educational route a student would be allowed to pursue. All sports received equal attention and time, but none came close to the fervor of Texas high school football. The unionized New York public school teacher organizations were strong. They negotiated with the school board about concerns such as class size and salaries. The Bay Shore teachers soon found out that they were making twice the salary they had made in the U.S. Southwest.[24]

Retreats

As the planning progressed, the Elders of the North Richland Hills church invited Elders from other Texas congregations to a retreat in Athens, Texas. The visiting Elders were asked to brainstorm some of the special problems with the sponsoring Elders. Ronald Bailey of Lubbock was moderator of the meeting. One outcome was that Ralph Spencer, architect, and Don Osborne, a Lubbock realtor, were sent to Long Island where they selected and made arrangements to purchase a four-acre tract on the South Shore of Long Island for the new church building site.

Before the exodus took place, three weekend retreats were held in Texas in Athens, Glen Rose, and at Bedford Ranch at Ft. Worth. The intensified focus of these meetings was for dedication to the project, planning, faith, and prayer to sustain the Group during the time of planning. The new congregation enjoyed another retreat, "Drawing Closer," over the weekend of May 16 and 17, 1964, at Camp Shiloh in Bernardsville, New Jersey.

Census

For five weeks in the summer of 1963, young people from Forth Worth and Midland, Texas, and Memphis, Tennessee, contacted 10,000 homes on Long Island. The purpose of

---

[23] "Seabrook Learns about the Great Evangelistic Move," *Suburban Daily News*, November 23, 1964.
[24] Toler Brannon (2004).

the face-to-face census was to share the message of Christ and to visit with the Long Island public.[25] The workers knew exactly what was expected of them; written dialogue showed them what to say, how to say it, why to say it, who they were, and where they came from. Census takers were to leave printed material in the contact's hand for later review. The outcomes were impressive: 303 home Bible classes were arranged, and 463 Bible correspondence courses were started.

The census takers found that 350,000 Long Islanders lived within the immediate range of the Exodus/Bay Shore building. Among these, 100,000 had no church affiliation; and of that group, most had moved within the past 15 years and had not made any church ties after they were settled again.[26]

1963-1964 Plans

The Planning Conference for the Committees met on Saturday, September 14, 1963, at the Commack Church of Christ building, 25 Old Indian Head Road, and the following committees were appointed: Acting Chairman of Business Meeting for October and November: Carl Phagan; Legal Secretary: Jim Compton; Building Committee: Forrest Wells (chairman), Dan Davis, Dan Mallow, and John Tanner; Corporation Trustees: Nick Buttacavoli, Clayton Crabtree, Ather Ellis, Emmett Gentry, Jim Hicks, and Cleo West.[27] The new church was getting down to business.

Each newly-formed committee planned and outlined their strategies for their first year on Long Island:

The Evangelism Committee planned to start a radio program, advertise on billboards and in newspapers, preach wherever opportunity availed, celebrate the opening of the new building, and make a contribution of $25 a week toward the New York World's Fair Evangelism Project.

The Congregational Welfare Committee planned to make physical changes in the configurations of the three glass-front stores at 144 East Main Street in Bay Shore better to accommodate the worshiping congregation, and to improve facilities for the staff and the nursery.

The Educational Committee planned to get a class for women on Thursday mornings, and classes for young people on Sundays, started by October 1. They planned to complete the full Bible-class curriculum before Christmas. They planned to offer transportation to children to come to Bible classes and church. A double class period might be needed by October 6.

The Benevolence Committee planned to operate a clothing and food storeroom for needy families. A blood bank was to be set up. Hospital and jail visitations were to be arranged. The church members' private homes were to be opened for missionaries departing and returning through the Port of New York.

The Building and Grounds Committee planned to finish the remodeling projects at the 144 East Main storefronts.

[25] Rod Spaulding, "Census Orientation," privately printed, 1966. Abilene Christian University, Center for Restoration Studies, vertical file: "Exodus Bay Shore."
[26] *Exodus Milestone*, newsletter of the Exodus/Bay Shore Movement, December 5, 1963.
[27] *Ibid.*

The Finance Committee gathered and analyzed the various committee budgets.

The Personal Evangelism Committee planned to start the home Bible class program on October 7.

The Worship Planning Committee wanted to have spontaneous singing before worship services. They made plans to start an *a cappella* chorus in October. They began planning a weekend retreat at Camp Shiloh in the spring.

The Building Committee began planning a groundbreaking ceremony at the new building site, 600 Montauk Highway, West Islip. Underbrush and trees had been removed. James Hance and Dwain Evans were working with subcontractors.

The Education Committee had organized the faculty of the Sunday Bible School.[28] This group of people had "committed their life and their resources to the Lord," and they were ready to work. On September 12, 1963, 207 attended classes, 224 were at worship, and the contribution was $1,106.

That same month, Walter Burch spoke on "Advancing the Church through Effective Public Relations" in a communication workshop for the Exodus/Bay Shore congregation. Burch handed out pages of effective techniques to help in setting up the new work of the congregation. His topics were: "Public Relations and the Work of Church," "Creation of News," "Advertising," and the "Church Bulletin." On leave of absence from his position as Director of Development at Abilene Christian College, Burch preached for the Commack church and also served as the coordinator for the New York World's Fair Program of Evangelism, while simultaneously working on his M.A. at Columbia University.

In October 1963, Evans was strongly urging the other committees to do their work, offering the Building Committee as a good example in their construction of the church building.

It is not enough to conduct fifty cottage classes per week – it is not enough to complete a $200,000 church plant – it is not enough to enroll 1,000 in our Bible Correspondence Course – all this is not enough so long as one soul on Long Island… or in the entire creation has not heard the thrilling message of Christ. Let us be bold as we move forward with Him![29]

The committees responded to the invitation: Plans were made for a July Census Campaign with Rod Spaulding in charge; August Vacation Bible School would be under the direction of Richard Salmon; the young people of the congregation would go on a campaign for Christ in Portland, Maine, with Dwain Evans as leader.[30]

The Building

The plan was for the new building to be finished and in use for church service within a year. The congregation would be self-supporting; the church members would themselves be making the bond and interest payments on the building. The architectural plans were

---

[28] Nursery: Doris Newhouse, Gene Ann Masters, Lily Gentry, Betty Crabtree, Shirley Campbell. Beginners: Ruth McClain, Carolyn Fawcett, Vera Lee Compton, Ginger Coffman. Primary: Nadine West, Carleta Roberts, Betty Grant, Liz Kimberlin, June Daniels. Junior: Jack Thomas, Howie Hodgson. Junior High Class: John Tanner, Jim Kite, Dennis Conaway. Senior High: Rod Spaulding. Adult: Dan Mallow, Carl Phagan.
[29] *Exodus Milestone*, October, 1963.
[30] *Idem*, January 9, 1964, lead article: "Commit Your Summer to Christ."

drawn by Fred Van Gaasbeck of Wiedersum Associates, a local architectural firm, and approved by the North Richland Hills congregation in Texas. The men of Exodus/Bay Shore helped with the building of the structure. Both Brannon and Hodgson spoke of the many hours of labor they put on the new building.

James Hance, Superintendent of the Construction; Forrest Wells, Chairman of the Building Committee; Fred Van Gaasbeck, architect; and Dwain Evans, the Moses of this Exodus, handled the shovel at the ground-breaking ceremonies of the classrooms and chapel on September 8, 1963. These men actively oversaw the construction and subcontracted what they themselves could not do on the building to non-union subcontractors.[31]

The total financing of $228,000 (except for furniture expenses and $30,000 for the concrete floor which had to be poured soon because of the approach of freezing weather) had been secured by September. *Exodus Milestone* kept the readers up-to-date on the building progress: It took a while for the Highway Department to decide where to place the curb line. Another $30,000 was raised for the building permit. The building was to be constructed in three units; the first phase was the chapel and classrooms. The other two phases were planned for later, one of them to be a large auditorium when the congregation grew large enough to require a meeting space that size.

Construction continued: Interior duct work, carpentry work, electrical work, painting, and window framing. The electrical union tried to pull all of the trade unions off the job because of the preference for sub-contracting non-union workers. A compromise settlement was reached; the work continued. The steel framework and outside brick work were completed. A concrete roof was poured, and cedar shingles were applied to the roof of the chapel. Within ten months of the groundbreaking, the building was finished. The official opening of the new building took place on September13, 1964.

The Eldership

In March, the Leadership Selection Committee[32] had been named to choose a slate of Elders—only seven months from the time that the congregation had started to meet for worship and fellowship. After six months of research, prayer, and interviews, the Committee nominated James Hance, Alfred Holeman, and Forrest Wells to become Elders of Exodus/Bay Shore congregation. The general business meeting of the congregation approved the recommendations. Short biographies of the proposed Elders were given to the membership:

James Hance, 46, baptized in 1934, had married Vi in 1946, and they had seven children. James was a building contractor. He served on the Building Committee and Foster Home Committee.[33]

Alfred Holeman, 53, was a former Elder at the Parkway Drive church in Lubbock. He had married Clellie in 1933, and they had two married children. His previous occupation

[31] *Idem,* September 26, 1963.

[32] *Idem*, September 12, 1963. Members of the committee were Jim Kite, Carl Phagan, Darrell Ramsey, D. L. Reneau, Ken Russell, and Jack Thomas.

[33] "Introduction to the Elders of the Church on Montauk Highway," privately printed, 1964. Center for Restoration Studies vertical files – Exodus/Bay Shore.

was irrigated farming. He served as Minister for New Members, on the Personal Evangelism and Missions Committee, and taught in the Adult Bible Study Department.[34]

Forrest Wells, 43, had served 11 years as a deacon at the Macgregor Park congregation in Houston. Baptized in 1943, he had married Kay in 1944, and they had three children. He had a B.S. degree in Civil Engineering from Kansas University, and he worked at Grumman Aircraft Engineering Corporation. Forrest was Chair of the Building Committee, a member of the Local Evangelism Committee, and taught in the Adult Department.[35]

The Second Wave

The Second Exodus/Bay Shore Employment Conference was held April 24-25, 1964 in Abilene. Again, Dr. Clyde Austin and Bill Adrian coordinated the candidates from Abilene Christian, David Lipscomb, and Harding Colleges. Interviewers from Long Island met with 73 teachers, and 11 women signed contracts.[36] Dr. E. L. Moreland, Superintendent of Bay Shore Schools, commented: "It is a very refreshing experience to find people moving in on us who [want] to contribute to the welfare of our community. I reiterate, I wish you had moved up a thousand families instead of 60."[37] Hodgson supported Dr. Moreland's statement: "People recognized that we were solid people; we would not do mischief in the community. We received good press in the newspaper; we were wholesome, steady, and well intentioned."[38]

Bud Stumbaugh, Walter Burch, and James Walter Nichols traveled to the Queens congregation in New York to help develop the plans for the Churches of Christ New York World's Fair Exhibit. Arnold Watson of Memphis, Tennessee, and Loyd Rutledge of San Antonio planned and coordinated the exhibit staff, of which the Exodus/Bay Shore membership was a part. Toler Brannon found his work at the Fair exhilarating. Texans are used to grandiose numbers and events, but these transported Texans were daily given opportunities and challenges in the Big Apple greater than they had ever known before. The New York World's Fair would bring them 100 million people to tell about Jesus.

The World's Fair team held well-attended preaching services in the Protestant Orthodox Pavilion. The Pavilion seated 2,100, so because of a great crowd of 2,600 two services were conducted by George Bailey.[39] On June 18, 1964, Dr. Batsell Barrett Baxter spoke to 1,500 people on a rainy day. His topic was "Can the Ecumenical Movement Succeed?"[40]

The Abilene Christian College A Cappella Chorus, directed by Vernon Moody, performed during the Church-of-Christ services at the Fair. The chorus members stayed as

---

[34] *Exodus Milestone*, January 9, 1964.

[35] *Ibid.*

[36] *Idem*, June 11, 1964. The new teachers headed to Long Island were Betty Hollis, Sylvia Aday, Sharon Phillips, Pat Caraway, Weldon Calloway, Charlot Root, Carole Humphreys, Rayma Bailey, Karen Moore, Kathryn Finch, and Sharon Nichols.

[37] *Idem*, November 7, 1963.

[38] Hodgson (2004).

[39] *Exodus Milestone*, April 30, 1964.

[40] *Idem*, July 30, 1964.

guests in the homes of Exodus/Bay Shore members for ten days. Several of the Bay Shore people were ACC a cappella exes.[41]

First-Year Report

The Men's Business Meeting Reports were published in the church bulletin, *Exodus Milestone*, on a regular basis. The yearly report showed the rapid growth of the Exodus/Bay Shore congregation.

The Building Committee: The $228,000 building had been completed and occupied. Roscoe Grant was negotiating to buy more land to add to their lots on Montauk Highway. Church pews had been ordered. Air conditioning was not yet available, so families were bringing oscillating electric fans to recycle the air during church services.

The Evangelism Committee: A gospel meeting, "America's Moral Crisis," preaching by Gary Freeman, was held December 1–4, 1963. The purpose of the meeting was to acquaint outsiders with the Bay Shore Group, their services, and message. Bay Shore men helped to fill area congregations' pulpits.

Leadership Selection: Elders were installed on March 15, 1964.

The Personal Evangelism Committee: Dan Mallow, Committee chair, worked with home Bible classes and correspondence courses. Religious literature was mailed to doctors' offices, hospitals, and other places where people had to wait.

The 1964 Summer Census: Census takers were being recruited from Midland, Abilene, Fort Worth, and Boles Home, Texas. Mallow announced the plans of Rex Tilley of Lamesa, Texas, to bring another Exodus to Long Island in two years.

The Benevolent Committee: A new committee had been formed during the year to provide care for orphaned children. More blood donations were needed. A storeroom for food and clothing for needy families was operational. Hospital and jail visits were being scheduled and completed. Bay Shore homes were being opened to missionaries departing or returning through the Port of New York

The Education Committee: A Bible study curriculum for all ages had been completed. Along a bus route, 18 passengers were being picked up and brought to Bible School. Plans were being made for 800 Vacation Bible School students.

The Financial Committee: A special contribution was taken up to help pay for the Churches of Christ exhibit at the New York World's Fair. The building loan having paid for and furnished the new building, additional funds were needed for the next land payment. Bonds could be purchased from the First National Bank of Abilene.

The Missions Committee: Carl Phagan announced plans for this year's Mission Conference. The speakers were to be Stanley Shipp, Switzerland; Ira Rice, Singapore; Lucian Palmer, Nigeria; S. F. Timmerman, Belgium; Wesley Jones, Canada; Howard Norton, Brazil; Phil Elkins, Memphis; George Gurganus, Japan; Carmella Casella, Australia; and Conrad Steyn, South Africa. The purpose of the Mission Conference was to send at least three missionaries into the field by the end of 1964.

---

[41] Among former ACC A Cappella Chorus singers at Bay Shore were Virginia Brock, Shirley Campbell, Dennis Conaway, Liz Kimberlin, Dick Masters, Doris Newhouse, Richard Salmon, Ruth Scott, Pat and Rod Spaulding, and Mary Lois Thomas.

The Advertising Committee: "Herald of Truth," a radio program, was being broadcast on Long Island. Publicity had been placed in *The Christian Worker, The Christian Leader, The North Atlantic Christian, The Gospel Advocate, The Firm Foundation, The Fort Worth Christian Journal,* and *The California Christian*. Identical releases were sent to area newspapers and church bulletins. Lectureship Exhibits were displayed at Lubbock Christian College and Abilene Christian College. A series of dinner meetings was held to generate interest and build support for the Exodus movement.

An offset printing press was in operation to supply the many printing needs of the congregation: prospective members' folders, response cards, reply envelopes, checks, and pledge cards, among other literature. Toler Brannon's knowledge gained as a pressman at Texas Christian University contributed to the printing of these materials as well as weekly publication of 900 copies of *Exodus Milestone*. In May 1964, *The Window*, a Bay Shore publication, was added to the print production.

Reflections

Exodus/Bay Shore was a noteworthy experiment that attracted the interest of the Churches of Christ brotherhood everywhere. Visiting ministers came to tour and talk whenever they were in the area. Among others, some mentioned in *Exodus Milestone* were John White, Elder at the Broadway Church of Christ, Lubbock, Texas; Elza Huffard, President of Northeastern Institute of Christian Education, Villanova, Pennsylvania; Gary Freeman, Cleveland, Ohio; Andy T. Ritchie, Jr.; Eddie Grindley from Camp Hunt; Batsell Barrett Baxter, Nashville; Athens Clay Pullias, Nashville; R. C. Hunt and Rex Tilley from Lamesa, Texas; Carroll Anderson, missionary to Norway; and Phil Elkins.

The 1960s were turbulent years for the American nation. Young people were becoming adults without benefit of life-survival experiences like war or economic depression to temper their passions like those that their parents had endured. In the search for new life styles and meaning in life, youthful America brought forth new cultural variations in many forms, from long hair on men, psychedelic art forms, an explosion of new kinds of Rock music, and a mounting struggle to achieve racial equality. All of these influences—and more—touched the Exodus/Bay Shore congregation, now called the West Islip Church of Christ. Only one African American, Wondrous Burns, had been a part of the initial exodus, although other Black members were gladly received soon after the Southerners arrived on Long Island. The *a cappella* Churches of Christ were largely a Southern denomination, so most of the Exodus people had come from the South and Southwest. Long Island, where they landed, and New York City (an hour away) were a different situation in terms of ethnicity during the "long hot summers" of 1964, 1965, and 1966. Blacks were in revolt on the Exodus's doorstep. The West Islip Church responded to this challenge, as it had done to so many others, in its own special way, by establishing the Inner City Faith Corps, led by Don Haymes, Lamar Baker, and friends.[42]

Part of the challenge of the Consciousness Revolution then going on in the nation was the theological challenge of the Charismatic Movement—a new awareness of the work of the Holy Spirit. Because the Bay Shore Christians had seen the Lord's Hand at work in so many ways, from calling them to Long Island, to the building of the Montauk Highway

---

[42] See Freda Elliott Baker, "The Inner City Faith Corps: An Oral History," in this volume.

church house, they were convinced of—and Dwain emphasized—the work of the Holy Spirit. The older generation tended not to talk about Exodus successes in terms of the Holy Spirit, but the younger people did, and they coupled their new devotion to the Holy Spirit with a greater sense of Christian ecumenicity, and a new vision of the church's role in social justice issues and race relations.

Toler Brannon said that he and Ella Ruth, in their late-20s and early-30s, were considered to be at the mean average in age among the new church membership.[43] People older than they were tended to be of the older generation of fundamental, orthodox Church-of-Christ believers; people younger than they were tended to be in the more revolutionary set. At West Islip, the two groups were thrown together in a single congregation. This mix caused tensions to run high on occasion as they, both individually and congregationally, discovered and resolved the differences in their faith while accommodating the challenges of an unfamiliar mission setting.

Because of Dwain Evans's leadership in the Bay Shore movement, he was called time and again to tell hungering churches the exciting stories of how people were responding to the Lord's message. Often on the road, he was frequently away from West Islip where the oil and the water of the two generations kept mixing and separating. Brannon felt that the urging of the Mission Conference to send members into foreign countries in less than a year's time since the congregation's own genesis, siphoned off leadership and talent that was still needed at home.

Howard and Margaret Hodgson worked with the exodus congregation for six years before moving on to Vermont. Others also had already moved on to spread the gospel of Christ. The rushed, crowded, urban life style of Long Island was more than they wanted to cope with any longer.[44] The only way off of Long Island is either by bridge or tunnel, unless one takes a boat. Every parkway and expressway always seemed jam-packed full of cars waiting for the car in front to move. The local joke was that I-495 is the longest parking lot in the world.

When asked whether the Brannons and the Hodgsons would make the Exodus to Bay Shore again, each family and individually answer emphatically: "Yes!" Brannon added, "If I had my youthful energy, I would go again today." Hodgson remembered it this way: "It was hard, it was uplifting, it built character. It was extremely rewarding. You learned to work with people in very sensitive areas. The Bay Shore Movement did not exploit the Group mentally, physically or financially. There was a lot of encouragement but no cohesion." Howard and Margaret stayed a total of 34 years on Long Island and in New England States; Toler and Ella Ruth stayed for 9 years.

Alfred Holeman, Bay Shore Elder, summed up the first year of the Exodus/Bay Shore's mission with these words: "Everything we have belongs to God, and it is our duty and our joy to serve Him now and forever more."

---

43 Brannon (2004).
44 Hodgson (2004).

THE INNER-CITY FAITH CORPS:
AN ORAL HISTORY

FREDA ELLIOTT BAKER[1]

The Inner-City Faith Corps of the West Islip Church of Christ[2] was an outgrowth of the recently launched "foreign" Faith Corps. A bold plan in missions, the Faith Corps was the innovative idea of Carl Phagan, West Islip's young minister of missions, and it was carefully patterned after President John F. Kennedy's Peace Corps, organized in 1963 by Sargent Shriver. Faith Corps volunteers had undergone training to live in a foreign environment at subsistence level and were required to raise their own financial support. The first wave of recruits had been sent to Canada and Brazil, and the Church was preparing to host its second mission conference. Then, the Faith Corps concept was hijacked—in the view of some—by Don Haymes and Lamar Baker and taken to a Black and Puerto Rican ghetto in Brooklyn.

Reinventing the Faith Corps

These two Texas transplants with the 1963 Exodus/Bay Shore movement had decided to adapt the foreign Faith Corps to New York's inner city after their experiences with a Black house church in Freeport, Long Island. Don, a multi-talented operative for a weekly Smithtown newspaper, and Lamar, a skilled electrical engineer with Brookhaven National Laboratory, had branched out from suburban West Islip to work with the small congregation closer to New York City. While canvassing a neighborhood, Lamar had met Walter and Pauline Maxwell and their friends, Harold and Daisy Ruff, and started studying the Bible with them in the Maxwell home. He brought in Don to help with the teaching, and he asked me (a transplant from Oklahoma) to work with the children. At that time, the Beatles' movie, *Help!* was playing in a downtown area of Freeport called "Little Harlem," and it caught Lamar's attention. He talked to Don about trying to capitalize on the lyrics of the film's title song to reach people with the gospel, and they decided to hold a public street rally in Freeport.

---

[1] An oral history must be the result of a group effort at mutual memory. My sources include my own recollections and Lamar's, as well as our collection of documents and memorabilia, and telephone, email, and snailmail conversations with other Faith Corps members, church members at West Islip, and other friends. Special thanks go to Carolyn Gauntlett who helped me track down people and information.

[2] See Dwain Evans, "A Memoir," and Erma Jean Loveland, "The Genesis of an Exodus," both in this volume.

Street Preaching in Freeport and Brownsville

Don and Lamar persuaded Dwain Evans, West Islip's minister of preaching, to be their speaker for the rally by telling him, "If you are not interested in doing it, we can get someone else." When the idea was presented to the Elders of the house church in Freeport, the latter were frightened by the notion of street preaching, as they had never done it before. Nevertheless, they mustered courage to go along bravely with the plan. Don composed a brochure and got a friend, Carolyn Hale, to illustrate it. On the night of the rally, Christians from both Freeport and West Islip congregated in the parking lot directly across the street from the movie theater. Finding no crowd there, we moved to another location nearby. For the occasion, Lamar had rigged a homemade lighting and public address system, powered by his car battery. John White, a rally supporter from West Islip, recalls that while Lamar was setting up his equipment, a big, smoky fire broke out not far away, and the sirens and excitement of the fire attracted many of the people away from our meeting. Not disheartened by the diminishing crowd, Dwain delivered a rousing street sermon, while the rest of us talked to the people—some until 1:30 in the morning.

A few weeks later, we held an afternoon street rally in Brownsville, Brooklyn, one of New York City's most impoverished areas. Lamar again recruited a team of people to pray for the rally and support it with their presence. This time, they surreptitiously snagged Don's long-time friend, Warren Lewis, then living in Toronto, to be the street preacher. Warren's experiences had ranged from preaching to Mexican field workers in West Texas and in villages in northern Mexico to a two-year neighborhood ministry with the House of the Carpenter[3] in inner-city Boston. Lamar bought a round trip plane ticket and told Warren to come to New York "on faith." From J.F.K. airport they drove straight to the selected site in Brownsville.

Lamar set up the public address system on the back of his 1954 Ford station wagon while supporters arrived and the locals gathered to see what was going on. Addressing the crowd, Lamar introduced the speaker and handed Warren the microphone, the first time that Warren was told he was to preach that day. Rising dramatically to the occasion, Warren preached for 35 minutes, in English and Spanish. Without hesitation, he began by pointing across the street to an empty, burned-out skeleton-of-a-building, and telling the crowd: "I once felt like that—before I asked Jesus Christ to come into my heart." Photos by John White captured the moment as Warren preached and we talked to the people on the street. When he finished, he asked people to raise their hands if they wanted us to pray for them. Hands went up across the street and down the block. D.T. Niles, speaking to the World Council of Churches, had said: "God is previous to him who witnesses in the life of the person whom he is seeking to win for the gospel, and also previous in whatever area of life he is seeking to make the gospel effective."[4] In Brownsville, as in Freeport, we had sensed the presence of God going before us, and the idea for the Inner-City Faith Corps was born.

---

[3] The House of the Carpenter had been founded in 1963 by Bill Martin, sponsored by the Brookline Church of Christ, and supervised by the Harvard Divinity School Field Work Program. William Martin is the author of "Three Paths to Eden," in this volume.

[4] Alan Walker, *A Ringing Call to Mission* (New York: Abingdon Press, 1966): 17.

Getting the Church Leaders On Board

Using blown-up photos, Don and Lamar challenged the Church's Elders and Missions Committee to extend the foreign Faith Corps ministry to an American city right in our own backyard. Don remarked: "Brooklyn is as 'foreign' to West Islip as any place the Faith Corps has gone—and surely more foreign than Barrie, Ontario!" Their prospectus presented specific ideas for personnel, coordination, training, salary, group structure, and activities. Warren and his wife, Lynne, were recommended to spearhead the project, and Lamar, whose "general qualifications and commitment to this work need no introduction to the West Islip church," to oversee the work on a year-round basis.

Don and Lamar were particularly concerned about one senior and very influential member of the committee who was usually the first one to raise objections. As it turned out, though, someone else spoke up first, asking derisively, "Who in the world would want to go into the inner city?" Lamar calmly replied, "A Christian would." This upset in the group dynamics left the senior member free to support the plan, and the proposal as a whole was accepted. Don used John's photos to design a recruitment brochure, and they called Warren to make plans for a presentation at the upcoming mission conference in late October. Things were happening, not the least of which was the engagement of Lamar and me.

Lamar and I Have Our Own Conference

It took only one week and four "conferences"—as Lamar called our tête-à-têtes on marriage—for us to get engaged. Lamar told me that he had taken notice of me the first day he saw me in August 1963, when I walked into the Church's storefront office in downtown Bay Shore to get help finding a job. Although he was interested in getting married, Lamar had become so involved in personal evangelism that he did not have time for traditional dating. Now, on the last night of the mission conference, when people would be formally committing to the Faith Corps, he realized he had a problem: Given his feelings for me, how would he deal with working together even more closely than we had done for the past two years?

Remembering the Bible story of Isaac and Rebekah, and how Isaac's servant found a wife for Isaac, Lamar followed the servant's example and prayed about his own dilemma. Since he knew that a few young women in the congregation were considering the challenge of the inner city, Lamar bargained with the Lord, "If Freda is the only one to commit to our project tonight, I will talk to her about my feelings." To his amazement, that was exactly the way it happened. With his courage bolstered up, Lamar approached me as I chatted with Lynne Lewis and invited me to dinner.

I thought this was just an occasion to continue our discussion of the Faith Corps, so in the church hallway I asked Don if he, too, were in on the dinner. "Oh, I'm sure I am!" Don replied in his usual, self-confident tone. Lamar drove John, his alcoholic friend, home and when he arrived at my place, Don and I were sitting at the dining table discussing the inner-city project. Lamar asked me if I were ready to go and then turned to Don and said, "We'll see you later, Don." As the full implication of his words sank in, my mouth and Don's both fell open. On the way out to the car, Lamar said, "I bet Don is curious."

Waiting for our food to be served at the Pioneer Diner in Babylon, Lamar touched on various topics but quickly got around to the Holy Spirit. His food went cold while he read aloud Genesis 24 in its entirety and told me about his prayer. He spoke of his longstanding attraction and high regard for me, emphasizing that someone like me was what he wanted in a wife. Moving right along, he suggested it might be a good idea for us to get married. Taking the pressure off, though, he said he would check back with me in a week to see how I was feeling about the idea.

Having been completely taken aback by this sudden onslaught, my feelings were in turmoil all that week; I could neither eat nor sleep. Aside from not being ready to get married, my feelings for Lamar, though respectful, were strictly platonic. On Wednesday night after Bible class at church, Lamar invited me to go out for coffee. In the diner, I related all the ill effects I had been experiencing since we last had talked, saying that I thought we should just call off the whole thing. Lamar's comeback was quick: "The very fact that you are upset might be significant," he said. "Why not pray about it and see what happens?"

At the Friday night T.G.I.F. party, which Lamar was too busy to attend though it was at his house, I impulsively confided to Don, "I had no idea Lamar was even interested in me; he never acted like it." Don, in his big booming voice, bellowed, "*OH YES*, he's interested!" Finally, I submitted to prayer, and after two more "conferences" with Lamar over the weekend, I had been "royally picked up emotionally." Knowing my feelings for him had changed and would continue to grow, I accepted his proposal on October 31. We were married at West Islip on December 5, 1965, before a standing-room only crowd from both West Islip and Freeport. On our honeymoon trip, we traveled to Oklahoma and Texas to meet one another's family and friends, to promote the Inner-City Faith Corps, and to raise support.

Promoting the Inner-City Faith Corps

When Lamar's subsistence-level support from his Austin friend, Joe Carroll, began on March 1, he resigned from Brookhaven and gave his full attention to the promotion of the inner-city project. He had already started sending out letters, reading everything from Bonhoeffer to Baldwin, researching potential locations, and studying urban ministries and social projects. After Lamar had read *The Cross and the Switchblade*, by David Wilkerson, he and I visited Teen Challenge, a dynamic street ministry that was effectively reaching young drug addicts and gang members. At their Brooklyn headquarters, we met and talked with staff members and asked to go along that evening to their rally in a nearby theater. Teen Challenge people asked us whether we had received the baptism in the Holy Spirit, evidenced by speaking in tongues, for they firmly believed the Spirit's power was behind their success with the street kids. We admitted that we did not speak in tongues but affirmed our belief that we had been given the gift of the Holy Spirit upon our baptism. Although the staff member seemed rather puzzled by such a tepid concept, we were allowed to tag along. The night was an inspiration.

Don and Lamar organized a trip to Manhattan's densely populated Lower East Side where a group of us from West Islip, including Dwain Evans, witnessed a powerful Teen Challenge street-preaching effort out of the back of a pick-up truck. Lamar and I later participated in a door-knocking event there, inviting people to a rally, but our involvement with "that Holiness preacher, David Wilkerson" cost us. Friction with Lamar's former church in Texas over both his and Dwain's association with Pentecostals brought a scathing letter of inquiry. Forrest Wells, one of the Church's Elders, replied that he "didn't like the wording of their questions."

In February, Dwain and Don attended the annual Lectureship at Abilene Christian College (now Abilene Christian University), in Texas, and Dwain's allegedly radical views on the Holy Spirit stirred up quite a controversy. In his May 9, 1966, *Exodus Milestones*, Dwain admonished the West Islip Church to "honestly admit that we have given the Holy Spirit no place in our lives."

Controversy followed Don like a devoted dog. Because of his involvement in the inner-city project, some in the West Islip Church were now questioning his theology and even his personality. They did not speak of this to Don personally, however, as Jesus had taught his disciples to do, but instead were making their influence felt indirectly through the Eldership and the Missions Committee. Their beef was not with Don alone; they had suspicions about the whole idea of inner-city work and many of its implications: Social Gospel, Holy Spirit, and Negroes, to mention three. Carl Phagan, acting as liaison, advised Don about the problem and set up a meeting for April 18, 1966, at which time Don would directly address the church's leaders.

Don's Self-defense

On that night, Don rode to the meeting in the back seat of Dennis Conaway's big, blue Oldsmobile, and seated next to him was James Hance, one of the church's Elders and the best possible good ol' boy. Just before they got out of the car, James leaned over, gripped Don's left thigh with his right hand, a hand that usually held a hammer and drove nails, and he said, "I hear you don't believe in the Virgin Birth." Undoubtedly with much eyebrow action and looking over his taped-up glasses, Don replied: "I don't know anything about that kind of biology, but I believe that Jesus Christ is Son of God by the power of the Holy Spirit. It's a spiritual birth, James." James just looked at Don for what, Don said, "seemed like an eternity, and then, just before my leg broke, he let it go and said, 'I guess that'll do.'"

Lamar said that Don had composed a two-page defense, and that the sweat was pouring as Don first quoted Paul Tillich and 2 Corinthians 5:14-18 and then declared his personal stance. He began by clarifying his purpose: "Going into the inner city is not my choice; I would rather be a writer and researcher, but I feel compelled by the love of Christ and by my own sense of salvation to offer myself as a witness in the streets." Otherwise, Don figured that he would be like the man in one of Adlai Stevenson's stories, who stood up in a revival meeting and cried out, "Here am I, O Lord! Use me—in an advisory capacity!"

His message would be simply the New Testament's message—that "man was separated from God because of his sinful nature, but God through Jesus Christ paid the cost of reconciliation and took the necessary steps to free man from the prison of his sin and heal man of the disease of his sin. In taking advantage of this gift of salvation, man becomes an entirely new being, a new creation." Regarding traditionally correct doctrines, Don pointed out that "salvation and a belief in dogmas are not necessarily one and the same. Doctrine pales into minute insignificance beside the *kerygma*,[5] the real point, of the New Testament."

---

[5] Kerygma is the proclamation of the death, burial, and resurrection of Jesus, and his elevation in the power of God, as opposed to didache, the teaching of particular doctrines and practices of first-century Christians.

Regarding what he would do as a Faith Corps worker in the City, Don said that he did not yet know. "I fear that only God knows, and thus we will be forced, finally, to submit to Him for guidance. It will be a great comedown for us, but we may at last taste the humility of discipleship." One thing Don was sure of: "Like anyone else who goes in, I will make mistakes." He thanked the leaders and said, "I must leave the decision to you, and I pray that the Spirit will guide you in the decision best for all of us." The inquisition was over, but the outcome was still unclear. In the end, "the powers that pee" (to use Don's phrase) allowed him to become a part of the Faith Corps.

The Recruitment Flight

Warren and Lynne, who by then was eight months pregnant, had made plans for her to stay with her parents, Morris and Amber Yadon, in Shawnee Mission, Kansas, until after the baby was born. Meanwhile, Warren would be away with Lamar on a recruiting trip. On the day Lynne left Toronto, she and Warren arrived at the airport after the plane was already taxiing out onto the runway. The airline people tried to stop her, but Lynne, an irresistible force if ever there was one, charged down the stairs of the loading area, lumbered out onto the tarmac, suitcase in hand, and stood nose to nose with the plane. Having no other choice, the pilot stopped the plane, let down the gangplank, and took her on board.

Warren connected with Lamar on Long Island. In New Jersey, they picked up Jim Fowler, a friend of Warren's who had agreed to fly them around the country in a Cessna they would borrow in Dallas. Recruitment efforts were concentrated on congregations within the Churches of Christ and their affiliated colleges. Appointments with churches could be arranged by telephone as they went, but the colleges tended to be more standoffish, and recruiting efforts had to be carried out primarily by word of mouth. Instead of being granted opportunities to speak in chapel or classrooms, they were relegated to sitting in the college hangouts where they waited for students with enough sense of adventure to think of an inner-city ministry as alluring. At David Lipscomb College in Nashville, draft deferment tests were being given, so the recruiters scrawled on their signs in large letters: *Ministerial Deferment*.

Lamar said that realization set in: They had overestimated the number of mature young people ready to interrupt their life plans for a year and move into the slums of Brooklyn. Meanwhile, exciting things were happening with Lynne. By the time the Cessna landed in Los Angeles on May 21, Lynne was about to deliver. Warren, on the phone with his brother-in-law, Mike McGuire, heard a moment-by-moment report of the birth of Phoebe Yadon Lewis—the youngest Faith Corps member to be added during the famous recruitment flight. That afternoon, Lamar and Warren walked past the sandbags and the machine gun mounted in the main gate of Pepperdine University. The riots were on in Watts, and Pepperdine was not much involved with its neighbor community. Did anyone want to migrate from one war zone to another?

Raw Recruits in Training

We were a motley assemblage that found our way to rustic Wolffe's Cabins in Great River, Long Island, former temporary home to Exodus families three summers before. Our original recruits included the following: Lamar and Freda Baker, Dale Crain, Ken Gossett,

Don Haymes, Maxine Hill, Don ("Pete") Johnson, Warren and Lynne Lewis, Raymond Scott, Joan Shockley, Daisy Mae Smith, David West, Kenneth Wilson, and Ron Wright.

Training, led by Warren, began June 20, 1966. His lectures on scripture and theology involved many reading assignments, which always came with the instruction: "Readings are to be read BEFORE the lectures!" Most of us had never attempted critical analysis of a text, and we wondered how it might come in handy in Brooklyn.

Warren had us do a self-disclosure exercise through art to depict the concept of grace. Don's was memorable: Using a black crayon only, he drew a tiny picture of a town across the bottom of the page, and above it, and aimed at it, and occupying at least one-third of the whole piece of paper, was a huge black bomb falling on the little city below: "Grace!" he said, and offered no further explanation.

To test our group dynamics, we shared kitchen duties and took turns leading informal worship on the lawn. To help offset culture shock, James Petty, a psychologist, profiled the urban poor and their social conditions. A Public Health official spoke to us of ways to maintain good health and sanitation. I, for one, was glad to hear that we could not contract a venereal disease from a toilet seat.

The training period functioned as a weeding-out process, so we lost several recruits during our month at Wolffe's Cabins. For some, the training was too academic. For others, the ghetto was what they had managed to escape, and they could not bring themselves to go back into it. As they fell away, we became quite dispirited. When the last Black couple left, Don pleaded with them not to go, crying out, "Don't cut off my arm!"

Having Blacks as part of our group had made us Whites more acceptable on the street, and it had even saved our skin on one occasion. Just as Warren had started preaching, a group of young Blacks approached him in a threatening manner. A disagreement broke out, and the situation seemed to be escalating. One of our Black brothers stepped between Warren and the leader of the hostile group, rolled up his shirtsleeve, and, comparing his skin color with that of the Black leader, he challenged, "What do you see?" The leader was both surprised and mystified. Our brother persisted: "Look! Look!" Finally, the Black leader got the message and stood down, "'s cool, man, 's cool!" Conflict avoided.

Though we lost some recruits, others joined us: Robert Barrett, Bob Harris, Norman Porter, Carolyn Cunningham, and later, Vickie St. John. We spent a refreshing weekend on a farm Upstate belonging to Bob Harris's uncle. Warren fashioned this retreat in the monastic style, with plenty of time to go off in the woods for solitude and thought—"Do I really want to do this?" During meal preparations, we had to rely on gestures and body language for communication, but we also spent time in verbal sharing of our experiences and just chatting and enjoying one another's company—a perfect culmination of our month-long training period.

We Move to Brooklyn

When the time came to find a place to live in Brooklyn, we all piled into Lloyd Cameron's Volkswagen bus and headed to East New York, the general area that Lamar and Don had selected. After cruising around, looking for rental signs, we parked on Williams Avenue. What an absurd sight we must have seemed to the people of Williams Avenue as a group of ten Whites got out and started walking around and goose-necking that neighborhood of four-story, walkup tenement buildings that housed Blacks, Puerto

Ricans, and the few reclusive old people who were the remnants of the Russian and Jewish populations that had previously dominated this piece of New York real estate. The names on several of the stores were still Russian, and a Russian Orthodox church stood nearby, but no Russians seemed to be left in the neighborhood to worship there. If there had been, most of them would be too old and feeble to stand up during the lengthy Orthodox liturgy.

Black men out of work were sitting on the stoops, drinking from bottles in brown paper bags, and watching us. Women were carrying their wash to the Laundromat at the corner of Williams and Livonia. The street and sidewalks glittered as if studded with diamonds: So many liquor and pop bottles had been smashed and ground to powder by passing vehicles and foot traffic that the glass fragments gave a gem-like sparkle to the pavement. Lamar said, "Just attempting a ministry in this neighborhood is exciting because it all seems so impossible!" Later, we found further evidence inscribed on the local Laundromat walls that lent credence to Lamar's prediction:

> *Black is beautiful.*
> *Brown is cool.*
> *Yellow is mellow.*
> *White is shit.*

We walked up and down Williams Avenue and then ventured around the corner. On Hinsdale we met a White man named Ed Rosen who said that he and his father had some apartments on Williams. We trooped back around to Williams Avenue with him, nudging one another when we noticed that we had parked right in front of his building. He showed us four vacant apartments, which we took on the spot; so he gave us the special rate of $50.00 each. We contracted through Nesor Realty, with occupancy to begin July 15, 1966. Lamar, acting as agent on behalf of the Islip Church of Christ, signed the lease agreement, and Carolyn witnessed it. Individual leases for each apartment were also drawn up. Two were signed by Lamar, one by Donald P. (Pete) Johnson, and one by Norman D. Porter.

Preparing the Apartments

The apartments were unbelievably filthy. Over a period of three weekends before we moved in, about fifty good folks from West Islip braved the heat to help us get the apartments ready, donating labor, supplies, used furniture, and meals. As the work began, eager children from the neighborhood pitched in to help. Together, we ripped up and carried out the old, worn-out linoleum, sending dust clouds billowing. Then we scooped up shovels full of the dirt of generations of families, sending cockroaches in their myriads scurrying. Adults all up and down that block, where more than 1,000 people lived, looked on with curiosity and amusement, gave the occasional word of advice, and once in a while the loan of a strong back. Some children picked up and carried a mattress inside. They looked like a big soft rectangular caterpillar with lots of legs.

Not all the activity was about roaches, new linoleum, and fresh paint. Forrest Wells, a full-time Elder of the West Islip Church, met Jim Ash, Jr., when Jim paid us a visit in Brooklyn. Jim, a Texas friend of some in our group, was traveling about the country explaining the charismatic gifts of the Holy Spirit to anyone who would listen. While Forrest was laying new flooring, Jim told him about "his Jesus" and arranged a meeting with Forrest in his office. Of Jim's testimony, Forrest said, "I could have never taken him seriously a year ago." Jim laid hands on Forrest and prayed for him to receive the baptism of the Holy Spirit and assured him that, even if he did not feel anything right away, sooner or later the Spirit would become evident in his life.[6]

A few days later, Jim and Warren met in one of the chapels of the Church of St. John the Divine. After talking about the Holy Spirit for a while, Warren said that he did not believe everything he understood about the Holy Spirit, but that if the charismatic gifts of the Spirit were still available, he certainly wanted to receive whatever the Spirit wanted to give. With radiant light streaming down upon them through the stained-glass windows, Jim prayed for Warren. Just as they said amen, the church organist let loose a mighty roar on the organ, startling the two of them and causing them to laugh and wonder whether window-rattling trumpets and the boom of diapason might be almost as good as tongues of fire. Not every member of the Faith Corps had a private audience with Jim, and not all became charismatics; but some did. Lamar and I had been "charismatics" of a sort all along in that we were fully aware of the leading of the Spirit in our lives, but our charismas were different from glossolalia.

Vickie, who joined us in September, had heard much talk while in training at Wolffe's Cabins about people at West Islip, and even in Brooklyn, being baptized with the Holy Spirit and receiving the gifts of the Spirit. Her interest was piqued, and she read books such as *The Cross and the Switchblade* and every scripture in the Bible about the Holy Spirit. She participated in discussions about the Holy Spirit around our communal dinner table, and she finally concluded that the gifts of the Spirit must still be available today. Vickie began praying for the Lord to baptize her with the Holy Spirit, but she did not receive an experiential filling of the Spirit until she was prayed for with the laying-on-of-hands two years after leaving Brooklyn. Then, she started experiencing an overwhelming desire to praise God. She would wake up during the night, praise God, and then fell asleep again. She received the gift of tongues as well as several artistic gifts that she has subsequently used to glorify God.

Mike Ciota and Mike Delaney, two Roman Catholic priest-seminarians who were doing a summer internship in the inner city, were quite a different kind of influence on us. Getting to know these delightful young men well, and on an informal basis, was a rare blessing. Whenever "the two Mikes" would appear in the door of our common apartment, they would salute us with great good humor and priestly blessings: "The Church of Christ salutes the Church of Christ!" We held many a lengthy theological debate, of course, liberally sprinkled with light banter, and each side learned gladly from the other. Our side, for example, held out firmly for the literal existence of the Biblical Hell, but Mike and Mike, being Vatican II *aggiornamento* Catholics, following the liberalization of Catholicism that followed Vatican II, were not so sure. Finally, Ciota found the middle ground: "All right," he agreed, "There's a real Hell, but in the end, there won't be anybody in it."

The Riots

Shortly after we moved in, hell of a different sort flared up all around us. The summer of 1966 was one of the two "long hot summers" of the mid-'60s. "Bronx is burning," the

---

[6] Forrest Wells, in *The Acts of the Holy Spirit in the Churches of Christ Today* (Los Angeles: Full Gospel Business Men's Association, 1971): 23-24, also mentioned by Warren Lewis, "Why I Left," in this volume.

word spread around the City, and the race riots and ghetto violence came home to us there in Brooklyn, too.

The day after we had moved in, an ordination service was held for us out at West Islip, and the Elders blessed and set apart our group with prayer and laying-on-of-hands. Don offered to remain in Brooklyn ostensibly to "stay with all that stuff, lest it be stolen." Personally, he was thinking: "There could be certain ones who might only want to *lay hands* on me to do serious damage."

The morning after the ordination service, Bob and Warren went out exploring and came upon a fight over on the next block. When they tried to break it up, cheering onlookers shoved them out of the crowd shouting, "Get back to your own neighborhood!" People already knew who we were and where they thought we belonged.

In Don's first field report[7] (August 1, 1966), he described our initiation in East New York: "Less than 24 hours after moving in, simmering racial tensions in the East New York-Brownsville area boiled over into a week of violence that plunged the Faith Corps into the thick of the action."

A prolonged feud between two families living a block from Faith Corps headquarters flared up over a woman and came to a climax that Monday evening with a shooting and two tenement buildings being set ablaze by teenagers with Molotov cocktails. Bob had observed that the rival groups started forming in the afternoon by repeatedly circling the block, picking up more people each time around, ever shouting louder and louder. By six o'clock, the two groups—the Blacks and the Ricos—came to blows, chasing each other with sticks, pipes, chains, or whatever they could get their hands on.

Meeting in our fourth-floor communal apartment, we agreed that the riot was our first great challenge, a defining moment for our relationship to the community. We agreed that the men (with the exception of Lamar, who had fragile bones) would dress in white shirts—to stand out against the darkness—and go out into the streets that night. Pete wished he had the protective coloring of a clerical collar to wear, but there was no time to get one; we had to act fast. Norman carried a large crucifix in his hip pocket and flashed it in the faces of raging Puerto Ricans, thinking it might calm them down. The rest of us stayed behind and prayed. Carolyn said, "I was looking out on the street from an upper window with the lights off and praying that no one would set our building on fire, for people were madder than I had ever seen." Each time we heard a fire siren, we rushed to the rooftop to search for the location of the fire.

Out in the street, three gangs were rampaging in great numbers: the Blacks, the Puerto Ricans, and the gang in the blue suits. More than one thousand of "New York's finest" were in full battle gear in our twelve-square-block area.[8] The police strategy was to keep the two other gangs apart, herding the Puerto Ricans up one street, and the African-Americans in the opposite direction down another. When they happened to pass each other at parallel intersections, all hell threatened to break loose.

---

[7] Don periodically sent field reports to the West Islip Church of Christ concerning our activities in East New York. His first report focused on our efforts to quiet the rioting and work toward peace.

[8] Paul L. Montgomery, "1,000 Policemen Move in to Stem Brooklyn Unrest," *The New York Times* (23 July 1966): 1, col. 8 (section unknown).

A crowd would gather in front of some empty building, and people would position their cars with the headlights all trained on the same spot. They would set their car radios to the same favorite music station and turn them up to full blast. Then, after someone torched the building, everyone would dance in the light of the burning building and the cars' headlights. The cops would try to break up the party, shouting through a bullhorn, "Please return to your homes!" One Black woman shouted back, "We *are* home, baby!"

According to Pete, some of the fire fighters were hampered in their work not only by the difficulty in getting their trucks in but also by vandalism. Mischievous kids used forks, knives, or whatever they had to poke holes in the fire hoses. After a while, the firemen quit going up inside the tenement buildings because people were flagrantly knocking big holes in the upper floors and then covering them with rugs as fall-traps for the fire fighters.

Faith Corps members were walking the streets, looking for ways to help. Buildings were being evacuated, and some people were going to a temporary shelter; others were being taken to Kings County Hospital. Pete and Robert used Lamar's station wagon to transport people. Pete said that Robert knew the way to the hospital, so he drove, and Pete rode in the back of the makeshift ambulance with their "patients." The first person they transported was a Black man who had encountered a group of Puerto Ricans waiting for him; he caught a split bag of lye in the face. At the hospital, Robert and Pete saw real ambulances bringing in the injured from the riot. Most of the hurt people they saw had "the telltale vertical gash on the head that comes from being hit with a billy club."

Bob said that he paired up with one of "the two Mikes," and they got caught between two groups fighting with clubs and chains. Bob said, "We prayed hard, thinking surely we would be injured or killed, but they just pushed us back against the building, out of their way. Clearly, they had no beef with us." Against the building proved to be a good place to be; when the police arrived, bricks, pop bottles, and chunks of cement came raining down from the rooftops. One of the cops was hit in the head by a falling cement block and taken away by ambulance.

Don found himself in a tight spot, and according to Leo Lillard, "Don almost got himself killed." As he was watching the parade of angry people, men in front of him were methodically jostling him and moving him ever closer to an alley. Leo helped him get out of there and later said, "They were planning to kill Don if they could have gotten him into that alley." Later still, Leo—now called "Kwame"—said that he remembered Don as a kind of "Braveheart" wandering around in the ghetto. "The passion that Don and I put into this piece of Hell is all but invisible to the untrained eye who has not the benefit of history."

Warren got out of his close call with a different kind of assistance. At the climax of the riot on the third night, when the Puerto Ricans greatly outnumbered the black gang, Warren, who spoke Spanish and had spent most of the evening with the Hispanics, said that he decided to cross over the lines to see what things were like from the Black side. As he approached, their leader menacingly challenged him: "Wha chu wan', Grayboy?" Using quick wit, Warren retorted: "I'm here to pick you up and take you to the hospital when some cop splits open your head with a night stick." The leader grinned at this and nodded: "You can stay." Then, ignoring Warren, he turned to his troops and made the following speech:

This our turf, our neighborhood. We be here 'fore these Ricos ever show up. We Americans! We fought for this country in three wars. Those Ricos come over here from they island, they got no business here. They be dirty, they gots too many kids, and they won' keep they hands off our women. They can jus' go on back to they island where they come from, and take they cucarachas wif 'em!

Just then, the Puerto Rican gang crossed the opposite intersection a block away, and when they saw the Black gang, they gave a great shout and charged. The Black leader quickly grabbed a brick and flung it through a nearby plate-glass window. He picked up a three-foot-long shiver of glass, wrapped a rag around one end, and brandished it like a sword. "This time, we not gonna run. We gonna stand and fight!" And an answering shout arose from Black throats. All-out gang warfare was erupting—with Warren right in the middle.

Enraged Hispanics ran toward him from one direction, and Blacks advanced from the other, each armed with everything from pieces of glass to guns. All around him, objects were raining from the rooftops; pop bottles were exploding at his feet, and he could feel the glass shrapnel splattering and hitting his pants legs. A steel garbage can landed on the roof of a parked car next to him and dented in its roof and stuck there. Warren was so scared that he could not move, and he did not know what to do.

Just then, he sensed a Heavenly presence. The Virgin Mary seemed to appear to him, and he saw her, not with physical eyes, but with spiritual eyes. She spoke to him and said: "Do not be afraid! You will not be hurt." Then—as in the Colgate toothpaste commercials running on TV at the time—a "gardol" shield seemed to surround him, and none of the bricks and bottles and boards could hit him, anymore. He said, "I could see and hear everything around me, but I was no longer afraid. I knew I would be all right."

The wave of onrushing Hispanics crashed against a solid wall of "Blue." Standing with their arms interlocked, the police had thrown a human cordon across the street. The few Puerto Ricans that had somehow managed to crawl between the legs of the police officers got up and looked wildly around for the Blacks, who—having sized up their chances for success—had wisely vanished into the night.

Two cops were holding one short Puerto Rican by the arms while a third cop repeatedly hit him in the crotch and wherever else he could land a blow, and finally, he cracked open his forehead so that the blood spurted out all over the cop wielding the night stick. Warren, standing nearby, said the cop's face went ghastly white when he saw blood spouting like a Texas oil gusher. A fellow Puerto Rican also saw what was happening, and he picked up a 2x4 from the gutter, raised it above his head, and advanced on one of the cops. Warren stepped over to the man and wrapped his arms tightly around him, but the man pulled roughly away, still holding his 2x4, ready to strike.

Speaking his best Tex-Mex to the Puerto Rican, Warren commanded: "Don't do that!" The man shot back in Spanish, "Why not?" Warren replied: "Because Jesus doesn't want you to." When the name *Jesús*—a common Hispanic name—seemed to have little effect, Warren regrouped and came back with greater cultural sensitivity and better aimed theology: "All right, then, Mary doesn't want you to!" *Jesús y María*—the two names spoken together rang a bell. The man looked carefully at Warren in his white dress shirt and asked, once again in Spanish: "Are you a priest?" Pulling himself up to his full priestly height and dignity, Warren looked the man straight in the eyes and lied: "Sí." Slowly, gradually, the man lowered his 2x4, dropped it back into the gutter, and stole away quietly into the night. Warren said later: "That's when I knew why I had been there and why I had been protected: I probably saved the life of a cop, and the Rico from a murder trial."

The next day, while ominous crowds continually tried to gather, Don worked together with a Black cop and a Puerto Rican cop to mediate grievances and establish an emergency truce. Faith Corps workers walked the streets, passing out handbills that explained the negotiated truce. That night, a quite surprising turn of events took place when the Blacks and Puerto Ricans joined together for a "peace riot." Claiming that they could get along and live together in the same neighborhood, they marched arm in arm for something over an hour. Out of the peace talks emerged ideas for possible future Faith Corps projects to help solve some of the area's problems.

Our Day-to-Day Life

With neighborhood tensions calming, we got down to internal Faith Corps business. We had four apartments to pay for and ten people to support, but only four of us had been able to raise our full support ($125.00 per person per month), and two of these were temporary. Taking the bull more by the tail than by the horns, Warren appointed one of our less-qualified members to be the treasurer and empowered him with the Faith Corps checkbook and a key to the cash drawer in Lamar's desk. Though some of us expressed grave concern about having our treasurer be the very chap about whom we had been warned during the recruiting trip, Warren held out hope that it would be a character-building experience for him. Later, when Lamar's electric typewriter disappeared, and then the cash he had contributed for communal use went missing, the honesty of our treasurer was called into question. Though we did not make him leave, Lamar confiscated both his key and his fiscal position and told him, "We love you, but you may not be our treasurer any longer."

We wanted to make a difference in the neighborhood, and Pete recalls that we held brainstorming sessions to come up with what our approach to the people would be. There were places of worship all around us that people could attend if they wanted to, ranging from the traditional Roman Catholic and Russian Orthodox churches to the inauspicious storefront assemblies. With the idea of reflecting our faith as an experiential reality, Don came up with the catchphrase, "Demonstration Precedes Proclamation." Our game plan would be to demonstrate Christ to the people around us rather than talking about religion. In fact, we would not even mention God unless the other person brought up the subject first; we would just let our actions speak by the way we interacted with people.

Right away, Pete had an opportunity to try out this approach when a gentleman came up to him on the street and asked him for a cigarette. Pete, who smoked, gave the guy a cigarette but then slipped up and mentioned God. Immediately, the man heatedly said, "Hey, man, don't talk to me about God! Don't you know that *God* spelled backwards is *dog*—the lowest creature in the world?" Pete had to think fast about how he might apply the concept that we were learning. Inspiration struck, and he sincerely replied to the man, "I am so glad you feel that way about God. It's true that a dog is man's best friend; he will faithfully stick by you through thick and thin, to the very end, just like God. This proves that you actually think more of God than I do." Pete told us that he was completely taken by surprise, then, to see tears falling from the man's eyes.

Due to the turf war ongoing at the local subway station four blocks away, we agreed to use a voluntary buddy system when out and about, in order to watch one another's back.

Don got upset with Carolyn even months later when she borrowed someone's car (without benefit of a current driver's license) and went out alone late at night. Of that little excursion she said, "It was a cold New York winter, and I could not get the car started. Two uniformed policemen stopped and helped me get it going. They were very polite and informed me, 'This is a bad neighborhood.' I replied, 'Yes, I suspected as much; I live around the corner!'"

Don had first got his hackles up when Carolyn let the cops into our apartment— "Something you just don't do in the ghetto," Don instructed her. Carolyn explained, "I was alone in the communal apartment when two New York City detectives came to the door, and, being raised with the belief that 'policemen are our friends,' of course I let them in." Lamar's engineering hobbies had aroused suspicions from the law. They said they had heard we had some kind of electronic devices on the premises. "After I showed them Lamar's radio transmitter set-up," Carolyn concluded her defense, "they were satisfied and left." We all felt a little safer after Lamar's electrical skills were used to install an intercom system in each of our four apartments so that we could keep in touch with one another.

Undaunted by cockroaches, voluntary poverty, and a new baby, Lynne arrived from Kansas City the weekend following the riots and took charge of the communal kitchen, organizing a rotation plan for kitchen duties with everyone expected to do their fair share. Her plan worked well for everyone except Norman and Pete, who not only shirked their kitchen duties but also slept in as long as they pleased, ignoring morning Bible study and Robert's Spanish lessons. They could not understand the social good of eating together with the group, which meant they might or might not show up at mealtimes. To top it all off, those two could not stand each other and made no pretense about it. During a group meeting in the communal dining room, they came to blows, going at one another right across the big table.

In stark contrast, Bob was gung-ho and ready for anything; he even seemed to enjoy our new austere lifestyle of little money and few possessions. Himself a regular guy from the suburbs, Bob was not so sure about most of our group, but he was totally reliable. One morning, when Bob was on his way out of the building, he heard a hissing noise in the Lewis apartment. So he and Robert broke into their apartment and found that the heating pipes had burst and steam was shooting out. "We managed to turn it off while Warren, Lynne, and Phoebe slept through the whole thing."

Warren maintains that the greatest challenge for Baby Phoebe was the sudden and unannounced daily advent of Uncle Don as he came bashing through their apartment door, bellowing, *"Sister Pheebull!"* causing the poor child to wail and tremble in shock. She became accustomed to Uncle Don's bass-baritone arrivals, though, and those early experiences in her first home at 436 Williams Avenue may have influenced her future career as an opera singer, now known by her married name, Phoebe Fennell.

Our group difficulties aside, we had some pleasant times together. In search of an evening breeze, we soon discovered the rooftop and would go up there to sing and pray, or sometimes to just be alone. When the phone rang two floors below, Pete would make a mad dash down the stairs to get the call, prompting an alcoholic woman who lived on the fourth floor to complain for days about our "making so much noise on the roof." Carolyn said, "I think the opportunity to complain to us was probably the highlight of her week, but, of course, we were always polite."

We shopped locally enough to know the plight of our neighbors who had no car to drive outside the area for supermarket sales. The only local grocer took full advantage of this leverage, charging outrageous prices for his poor quality meats and limp produce. We tried to start a food co-op, but it was a dismal failure. Someone in the neighborhood was always having a crisis of some sort. A family across the street had all their food stolen, so we cooked dinner for them that night. While waiting for her nursing license, Vickie took a Red Cross training course and taught a much-needed home nursing class in our building.

I decided to start cleaning the littered street and gutters, and the children joined right in to help. Most of the adults hanging around on the sidewalks just looked on with amusement, but one man offered to do it next time, and two others agreed that we should all clean the street more often. Don and I teamed up to scrub the halls and stairs of all four floors of our building each week. Rag mops, bleach, and buckets of water would be arrayed against grime, urine, and God-only-knows what else in those filthy tenement stairwells. He and I also held a weekly Cockroach Roundup in the communal kitchen. Since roaches lived in the walls of those contiguous old tenements, we could only fight a losing battle in the effort to control them. Don sprayed thoroughly, waited until the roaches died, and then we swept up their dead bodies by the dust pan full.

For the first two months, Carolyn shared our two-bedroom apartment with the communal kitchen. Carolyn remembers that she was usually the first one up, and when she turned on the light in the kitchen, the floor would be covered with cockroaches. She said, "The light caused them to scatter, but I literally could not put my foot down on the floor without crunching a few. The first time Freda got up before me, I was startled awake by a piercing scream."

Lynne took on the challenge to keep the Biblical-sized plague of roaches out of our staple kitchen supplies. She appealed to the women from West Islip, and their gracious donations of Tupperware and storage jars gave us some semblance of sanitation. Our tenement neighbors had long since given up on the roaches. Vickie said: "I watched those nasty things crawl up and down my neighbor's door casing as I chatted with her in the hall, and I was always on the lookout for them sharing my shower." Later on, she was mortified when, in the home of one of her patients, a big roach crawled out of her nursing bag. In a desire to turn all our experiences into gifts from God, we tried praying: "Thank you, Lord, for the roaches." But it's hard to pray a prayer that you really don't believe.

We were about as successful with the rats and mice as we were with the cockroaches. Both Vickie and I had discovered mice jumping up and down in kitchen trashcans trying to escape. I had stoically taken a broom handle to mine. Warren says that he got two cats to do battle with the rodents, also in vain. He said, "We opened the cellar door, shoved the cats inside to do their work, and slammed the door. Soon, we heard hissing and scrambling and yowling, so we cheered our cats on. When the noise subsided, we opened the door. All we ever found of those cats were bits of bloody fur." Warren claims that this is not an "urban legend," but I'm not so sure.

The Children of Williams Avenue

The children had welcomed us from the first day we set foot in their neighborhood, and they paved the way for our acceptance there. Probably one of the most important things we did in East New York was just hang out with them, and they soaked up the attention like dry sponges. In a presentation at West Islip's Third Annual Mission Conference,[9] I said:

> *We feel a deep sense of responsibility to the children, and they take first place in our lives.*
> *We encourage them in their homework, discuss their conduct cards, and monitor their*
> *school attendance, to the extent of delivering them back to school when they play hooky.*

No recreational facilities for the children existed in the neighborhood; even the school across the street locked its playground after school hours and during the summer. Don worked with several agencies to negotiate a locally sponsored play street on our block. During the hottest part of the summer, we arranged for a fire hydrant to be opened so the children could frolic in its spray and cool off.

I noticed that the Black girls were sensitive about skin color—one's degree of blackness or lightness was a frequent topic of conversation, and they could use blackness as a way to dish out the insult, "You black!" I took this as an opportunity to reinforce the new phrase we were all hearing, "Black is beautiful!" Carolyn said that right after moving in, she overheard Peaches, a cute little six-year-old girl, making fun of a dark-skinned alcoholic woman, and Carolyn gave her a sound dressing down. Carolyn had nearly had her blonde hair pulled out by the roots when this same brazen child had tried to see if the hair were a wig. Peaches could be beguiling, though, and Lamar was her next victim. While hanging out with Lamar and me, she was playing with Lamar's hand and doing her usual fidgeting. Suddenly, she gave a quick, sharp jerk to one of his fingers and inadvertently broke one of the bones in his hand.

Vickie said that two sisters who lived in the apartment next door to her seemed to prefer her place to their own. Lounging for hours on her bed while visiting, they infested her mattress with bedbugs, and she worked for days to disinfect before her mother came for a visit. The mixture of strong chemicals caused her to cough for months.

The kids loved for us to go out and play jacks, hopscotch, or jump rope with them on the sidewalk. Turnabout, they had great fun helping us with our work. I usually had an entourage of girls when I went to the Laundromat. While the clothes were drying, "my girls" and I could either talk and play right there or walk over to a small playground a few blocks away. A few of us spent so much time at the Laundromat we got to know the woman who worked there. After the Lewises left, she told us that she really missed Lynne.

We prepared a clubroom in one of the apartments and started "Link Clubs" for both boys and girls. Meetings were twice a week to plan activities and parties. Kids came out of the woodwork like cockroaches to join the clubs; more than one hundred of them became club members. Norman, himself a big kid, found his niche in heading up the Boys' Club, although at times, he would get peevish about something and try to push it off on Pete, who felt no divine calling whatever that suited him for running the clubs. The kids really liked Norman, and he always came round and continued working with the clubs. Using cardboard, he made membership cards for each club member with chain links drawn on

---

[9] "Opportunities for Ministry in the Inner City" was presented at West Islip on October 30, 1966. While composing my report in East New York, Don Haymes gave me a "literary lesson." Pointing out the subtle difference between the words "leery" and "wary," he quipped, "Old men leer." Don's encouragement over the years to write is part of the reason I could accept Warren's request to contribute an essay about the Inner-City Faith Corps to this volume in Don's honor.

them. Some of his boys made drums out of cans of many sizes, called themselves "The Impossibles," and performed for us.

Carolyn headed up the Girls' Club, and she and I organized classes in cooking, sewing, and art. The girls loved to bake cookies for the club meetings, and sometimes they prepared whole meals in the communal kitchen and then cleaned up afterwards. One of my supporters from Oklahoma financed a set of Arch®Book Bible stories, and when some of the kids expressed an interest in reading them with me, we added a Sunday School to our program.

Robert started a Spanish class for Black children who wanted to understand their Puerto Rican neighbors better. Some of the older kids came to us asking if we would do something for them, too. We got a club going with about fifteen teenagers. We arranged for the use of the school gym on Saturdays, and a basketball team was formed. Carolyn recalls that we got a lesson in local customs and mores when a young boy came into the boys' clubroom with a large leather bracelet and an even larger grin on his face. All the boys were teasing him, for the bracelet (ordinarily used in archery) was understood to convey the idea of "mighty hunter." Translation: He had lost his virginity, and all of the people, children and adults alike, were treating it as a matter for congratulations. Rumor had it that his initiator was in her early twenties—which would have made it a crime in the suburbs, but not on Williams Avenue.

On Saturdays, we took the children on field trips to museums, the Bronx Zoo, United Nations headquarters, Central Park, the Staten Island Ferry, and Prospect Park. One day we took a group of kids to Manhattan by subway. When one of the girls got upset about something and attempted to go home alone, Norman had to hang onto her arm for the rest of the trip to keep her with us. Noticing at one point that we were standing in front of the classic Waldorf Astoria Hotel, we decided to add this to the kids' cultural repertoire and took them inside. They had great fun gawking around and riding up and down the elevator, while well-to-do hotel guests enjoyed High Tea in the elegantly understated lobby.

Norman, together with some people from West Islip, organized a trip to a drive-in theater in New Jersey, and 135 neighborhood children got to see "The Greatest Story Ever Told." In his September 10, 1966, field report, Don wrote of West Islip's teenagers helping to "supervise the mayhem" in the two buses, and of the enthusiastic children's clamor to "go again soon." On another occasion, Norman and Julius, a young boy in the Link Club, had been to Manhattan to see a movie. Returning on the subway, Norman gave his seat to a woman and asked Julius to give his seat to another woman. A Black man across the aisle (who appeared to be drunk) thought that the big White man was shoving the little Black kid around, so he caused a disturbance. Several people nearby tried to get him to settle down. Norman let him rant for a while and get it out of his system, and then he quietly told the man that he and Julius had been to a movie together. Julius looked up at Norman and said, "What's with him anyway? Doesn't he know I am a member of the Link Club?"

Mixing West Islip's kids with ours broke some important ice, and we began taking carloads out to Long Island to stay with host families for the weekend. This became such a popular activity, we had to set a minimum age limit of six years, for even the very youngest wanted to jump right into the cars and go along on the adventure. Once we got them out of their natural environment, we learned a lot about our inner-city children. Some of the older, street-smart boys were frightened by the darkness and quiet way out there in the Long Island suburbs, fifty miles from all the streetlights and nighttime noise of East New York. One was heard to say: "Man, I wouldn't walk these dark streets alone!" Urban anxieties, however, never kept them from wanting to go back whenever we organized a weekend away.

We started transporting our kids to the Eastside Church of Christ in Manhattan where we joined busloads of others for a week at Camp Shiloh in Mendham, New Jersey. There, open spaces, rural beauty, and a big grand old house provided the city children a totally different environment, and they relished it. One exception was a girl from our building whose father was in prison and (according to Robert) had been raped in the schoolyard. She commented bitterly: "The trees are ugly." Camp Shiloh's natural beauty seemed not to reach her.

Living in community, combined with having some of the kids with us much of the time, added up to a real problem in finding time for personal solitude. Carolyn tells of the aggressive and abrupt young Black woman who had once found her quietly reading a book, and in great surprise, heavily tinged with disapproval at finding someone in a room alone, had emphatically stated: "I could not stay in a room by myself!" Carolyn said it was as if she were doing something wrong, if not unheard of, and this encounter gave her a real understanding of one of the effects of overcrowding—the young woman did not know how to be alone any better than the kids knew how to be in the dark and the quiet. That same young woman had also been adamant that Carolyn should carry a knife, like the one she always had in her shoe.

Two of Our Neighbors

Annie Johnson, an alcoholic woman who lived across Williams Avenue from us, staggered up to Robert on the street and, slurring her words so much he could hardly understand, told him she had a crippled son named Tony who needed a home tutor. Robert met Tony and described him as "a bright little seven year old." Because he needed a colostomy, Tony's foul body odor kept him out of school. Robert befriended Annie and Tony and took them to the Bronx Zoo on two occasions. He talked with Annie about her drinking and her "men friends" that continually came to her apartment. He also talked with her about Jesus and studied the Bible with her.

Annie and Tony came to our Sunday afternoon coffee hour, and she was all cleaned up and sober. Tony proudly demonstrated the Bible school songs that Robert had taught him. I visited Annie after she had undergone a minor operation and was trying to learn to use crutches. She asked me to wash her hair. I had never worked with her hair type, but it was high time that I did! I washed it, combed it, greased it, straightened it, and then set it for her. We had great fun together, and she basked in the personal attention. We surprised her with a birthday party, and she said, "Y'all are just like my family, and I love every one of you."

When Annie fell ill for two weeks, we visited her each day, taking food and seeing to her needs. Robert followed through with his promise to arrange a home tutor for Tony. George Kriss, a new member at West Islip, arranged for Tony to get a colostomy at a Shriner Hospital. We helped out by writing business letters for Annie and providing transportation and expenses.

Marie Fischer, a wiry little White woman with no teeth and thinning gray hair that she pulled up loosely in a bun, would cautiously venture from her second-floor apartment to wait for the mail. From the way she searched about uncertainly for the wall and handrail, I could tell that she was nearly blind. Thinking she must be lonely, I visited her and was shocked and appalled by the condition of her little apartment. The roaches in her adjoining kitchen never bothered to hide, and they crawled all over the slices of white bread that Mrs. Fischer had laid out to become crusty so that she could "gum them." When I mentioned the roaches on her bread, she dismissed the subject with a wave of the hand and inquired, "Do I have any Pepsi Cola in the refrigerator?"

Mrs. Fischer and her husband, whom she referred to as "Mr. Fischer," had come to New York from Paris. After his death, she had left all their friends in Manhattan and moved to East New York in order to save on rent. She was delighted when I offered to give her place a thorough cleaning. When I started helping her regularly, I threw something away that she missed the very next day; thereafter, I was more careful in my house cleaning.

Mrs. Fischer was especially cheerful one day when she opened the door for me and said with great excitement: "I just discovered I am only eighty-four; I thought I was eighty-six!" Then, with the agility of a chorus line dancer, she kicked one leg high in the air. I shopped for Mrs. Fischer's groceries and other items; so she asked me to get her a new apron at Fortunoff's Department Store. When she saw the colorful kitchen garment that I had carefully selected, she laughed and said, "This is not an apron!" Turns out, an "apron" in Parisian English is a dress.

Mrs. Fischer joined us occasionally for a Sunday meal, and she took delight in the group atmosphere. While I was in her apartment one day, she handed me a studio portrait of her late husband and said earnestly, "Please keep this; I have no one else to pass it on to." When her health began to deteriorate, she confided her great fear of being put under the ground. She made me promise to see that she would be cremated—a promise that I was unable to keep. A year after we met her, she began suffering from frequent falls that resulted in serious injuries. Vickie's diary reflects that after one of Mrs. Fischer's falls, I spent eighteen hours at Kings County Hospital with her. Subsequently, during her lengthy recovery following cataract surgery in the autumn of 1967, I visited her and shared the news that I was expecting a baby. Together with José, the building super, I painted her apartment as a homecoming surprise.

When hospital officials refused to let her go home, Vickie used her resources to arrange for Mrs. Fischer's placement at the Oxford Nursing Home, not a happy place but the best we could find. Mrs. Fischer expressed her fear of going to a nursing home, saying, "If I go there I won't live long." I kept after the staff about her lack of care, but to no avail. The last time I saw Mrs. Fisher, she was lying curled up in a ball, and her shallow, barking cough sounded like pneumonia. The winter wind was whistling through the open window, and there was a strong fecal odor in the room. In reply to my anxious inquiry about the cough and the frigid room, the nurse merely said, "Oh, the open window is good for her." Not long after that, Don got the call that Mrs. Fischer had died—"of hardening of the arteries"—and that someone needed to come to the morgue and identify the body. I offered to go, but Don suggested that I let him take care of it. When I reminded Don of my promise for cremation, he pragmatically replied, "She won't know."

Time to Regroup

A couple of months after moving in, the group began to decline in numbers, and before December, just five of us remained: Don, Carolyn, Vickie, Lamar and I. We had to give up one apartment and find ways to bring in enough income to support ourselves as well as our ministry. Warren's start-up job with us was finished, and it was time for him and Lynne and Phoebe to return to Toronto so he could resume his graduate work at the Pontifical Institute of Medieval Studies. On September 21, they headed back to Ontario, and around the same time, Bob returned to Nyack Missionary College. Lamar took a part-time job repairing television sets in Woodside, Queens. Vickie and Pete got jobs at Fortunoff's. With great curiosity, one of Pete's fellow employees said to him one day: "Everyone else that works here is either Black or Jewish. What are you?"

At the end of October, Robert decided to leave the group and go back to Long Island. We missed him and his big pots of homemade soup. In November, Vickie's State nursing license came through, and she got a job with the Visiting Nurses Association of Brooklyn. Pete quit Fortunoff's and worked for a while as a youth director with New York's Anti-Poverty Program. He said that the supervising priest would have fainted had he known Pete was not a practicing Catholic. He and Norman both left Brooklyn sometime in November. Pete went out to Long Island, and Norman went to Toronto to stay with Warren and Lynne. We later heard that Norman had brought with him a Brooklyn-sized load of cockroaches in his suitcase, and then, when he fell asleep in the upstairs bathtub with the water running, the landlord's downstairs apartment was flooded. Bath time and the roaches got the Lewises evicted.

I remained on site full time to respond to needs in the neighborhood. One day, I rushed a woman in labor to Brooklyn Women's Hospital, bumping along in my little Volkswagen Bug. I continued interacting with the children and our adult neighbors. Vickie and I joined a home Bible study with four women nearby, and Lamar and I studied with a new Christian who said she knew nothing at all about the Bible. For encouragement, I made friends with Mary Murray in the nearby projects, and Mary came to Williams Avenue and gave sewing lessons to our girls. We appreciated supportive friends from West Islip who came for Sunday dinner. Among them were John and Donna White, Forrest and Kay Wells, Dorothy Buice, Marjorie and Lewis Wood, and Ruth and Don Stillinger.

On Sunday evenings, Lamar and I visited Black churches both in Brooklyn and in Harlem, where Roosevelt Wells preached for the Washington Heights Church of Christ. In Brooklyn, we were closely questioned as to our orthodoxy: Had we been baptized by immersion, in a Church of Christ, and by a Church-of-Christ preacher? Fortunately, both of us could say yes to all questions. At Washington Heights, we were readily accepted, and we thoroughly enjoyed the singsong style of sermon delivery, accompanied by the women's soft murmurs of agreement and the men's enthusiastic shouts of "Amen! Preach on, Brother!"

Don, and later Carolyn, started working for the New York Housing Authority in a program called "Operation Rescue," which arranged for housing repairs in slum dwellings and sent the bill to the slumlords. Carolyn said of that job: "It was some of the best work I did with the Faith Corps because it fulfilled a real need." A concerned doctor called about a child he was treating for pneumonia that was living in a building with no heat. Carolyn was instrumental in getting the boiler fixed right away, and the doctor expressed his gratitude. Carolyn got up her nerve and asked him if he were an intern, for he was the first doctor who had made a request on behalf of any poor person in the several months she had been on the job. He acknowledged her statement of fact as "a terrible indictment of the medical profession."

Vickie's job with the Visiting Nurses Association involved making home visits all over Brooklyn. She said that from the beginning, she felt a God-given sense of protection and an assurance that she had been called to be there for that time in her life. While walking to and from the subway, making her nursing rounds, returning late at night from visits to Long Island, and even while staying in her apartment with a broken lock (until Lamar repaired it), Vickie felt safe. On the job, she wore a professional Navy blue uniform with matching cap, carried a black equipment bag, and strode with confidence: No one bothered her. Vickie said the only occasion of abuse she suffered was when she exited a building after seeing a patient, and a man sitting on the stoop spat a wad of phlegm on the back of her leg. She ignored him, walked calmly on, and wiped it off later.

Vickie's work thrust her into situations that were heartbreaking and unsettling. When she had felt stressed before the group started breaking up, she and Pete would walk the neighborhood, talk things over, and she could get it out of her system. Sometimes they would go to a movie or just act silly together. Now, she could not forget the little child with tuberculosis who needed injections, the infant who died of suffocation in her teenage mother's bed, and the depressing sight of so many bright, promising children who would live their lives in poverty, never breaking away from the welfare system. Sometimes she despaired of making a difference in even one life.

One small incident worked for Vickie against the desperation she encountered, and it warmed her heart. While she usually left her car on Long Island with Roscoe Grant, one night she kept it in Brooklyn. The next morning she discovered it had been vandalized. She wondered how the marauders had possibly escaped the watchful eye of her neighbor, Louise, who sat out on the fire escape a lot and had become the self-appointed guard of our cars. Vickie drove to the V.N.A. garage (where, by then, she was allotted a company car to use for her rounds). When she returned to the garage at the end of the day, everything in her car was completely cleaned, fixed, and put in order. The V.N.A. mechanics had taken turns throughout the day working on Vickie's car, and they would take no money in payment from her.

In November, we had several discussions about separating the Brooklyn version of the Faith Corps from the West Islip Church. We had produced no "visible results" (i.e. no baptisms) after four months in the inner city, so were apparently an embarrassment to some of the Church members because other Churches of Christ criticized West Islip for supporting the "Social Gospel." Don continued to be a hot topic at West Islip; in fact, Don had already had a long and infamous history of relationships with Churches of Christ, and his infamy would live on even after the Faith Corps. Lamar said that he saw Don's role at West Islip as that of a prophet. He was not afraid to attack the status quo; in fact, he felt called to do just that when he was convinced that church leaders were misleading the "little ones." He could communicate well with "Moses" Dwain, and would get on his case when necessary. One issue that Don took up with Dwain was the common tendency of churches—some of the West Islip leaders included—to direct evangelistic efforts towards people whose economic status would allow them to support financially a congregation's building fund and ministers.

In Don's field report of January 20, 1967, he portrayed the church's mission in areas like East New York as being "destroyed by practices and attitudes rooted in tradition." Don reported that a young man in a civic committee meeting, speaking of the churches in general, had said: "They don't really care what happens to the people here; they don't really want to do anything." Don continued: "In this place, it is not the Christian's place to conduct ceremonies. He must instead become the servant of his neighbors."

We decided to continue as a Brooklyn extension of the West Islip Church, at least for the time being. Writing about our restructured group, Don said:

> In many ways other than numbers we are not the same group that stumbled into East New York in July. We have grown up together, and we have learned much—only to discover that we have much more to learn. It is a time for taking stock, for evaluating old mistakes, for seeking future opportunities. It is a time of renewing commitment to thankless tasks, remembering the words of St. Paul: 'Forgetting what is behind me, and reaching out for that which lies ahead, I press towards the goal to win the prize which is God's call to the life above, in Christ Jesus.'

Was It Worth It?

Was the Faith Corps a success in East New York? Don had said it well in his second field report: "It is not easy to measure success; progress can be vague and intangible and cannot be compared to the calculating self-satisfaction of statistics." Having no predecessors, we learned as we went along, using smiles, the joyful cry of a child, or a dinner of barbequed ribs and cornbread sent up by a neighbor as signs of progress. Almost twenty years later, we would have the privilege of seeing some of our "Link Club" kids all grown up.

Carolyn stayed out her commitment year and then went to Toronto for a while. She later returned to New York (but not to Williams Avenue) and worked again with Operation Rescue for a time. Vickie stayed on until January 1968, and then moved to Toronto to work at the Hospital for Sick Kids. It was there she met her future husband, John Coutlee.

By the time I became pregnant in October 1967, I was accustomed to seeing so much more color in my world than had previously been the case that when I contemplated my unborn child, a little Black or brown face automatically came to mind. And then, in December, I suffered a miscarriage. I decided that having a baby amidst the rats and roaches was not such a good idea. In January 1968, Lamar and I also moved out. We went back to Long Island and resumed involvement at West Islip. I experienced "reverse culture shock" and had trouble readjusting to White, suburban life, after the intensity of Williams Avenue. I missed the children that I had grown to love and felt guilty for having picked up and left them. Occasionally, I would bring some of them out to Long Island for weekends and summer visits. They were among the first friends of our daughter, Allison, and we kept up with them over the years.

After all of us except Don had moved out of East New York, Rod Spaulding, who by then had left West Islip and was working for Camp Shiloh, asked Don to come over and speak to his young recruits. Don reportedly "scared the poop" out of them with old Faith

Corps stories. Rod started bringing Shiloh workers to Williams Avenue for a follow-up program with the campers. They moved into the newly vacated apartments, and the Inner-City Faith Corps was resurrected as Shiloh, a neighborhood ministry at 436 Williams Avenue. In Toronto, Vickie heard of this and noted in her diary that she now understood why the Lord kept some of us there until January 1968 — to "hold the apartments."

Shiloh reestablished programs for the children and started taking the basketball team on competitive trips outside New York. On June 29, 1975, Shiloh suffered the martyr's death of the onsite director, Phil Roseberry, when he was shot and killed after escorting a female worker home after dark. Shiloh faced the dilemma of whether they should stay on or leave. In a community meeting, a mother of two children helped by Shiloh's after-school tutoring program, answered the question point-blank: "Please don't go! You are the only good White people my children have ever met."

Shiloh's witness of the Gospel continued until 1984 through the efforts of the East New York Christian Fellowship, housed at 405 Williams Avenue, just to the north of where 436 had stood. Our old tenement building had been the last one standing before the whole block became a vacant lot of weeds and trash. The ENYCF paid tribute to the original Faith Corps workers who had paved their way with these words on their day-camp fund-raising brochure:

The East New York Christian Fellowship (ENYCF) stands in a noble tradition of Christians committed to serve Christ in the city. They owe a debt of gratitude to the adventuresome souls who made their way from the West Islip Church of Christ on Long Island to Williams Avenue in June [July] of 1966.

Whether under the banner of the Faith Corps, Shiloh, or ENYCF, we served the Lord in East New York by serving "the least of these" for nearly 20 years. Probably the best measure of success is not the way the people of East New York were changed and blessed by us, but by how each of us who dwelt there for a time were changed and blessed by them.

Editors' Note:
Camp Shiloh had been in operation since 1951. Among the services it performed for the Williams Avenue neighborhood and others like it were the summertime fresh-air camps in the New Jersey countryside with a Christian focus. When the "Big House" burned at Shiloh's headquarters in New Jersey, Camp Shiloh was moved to Upstate New York in the 1970s. New Camp Shiloh was sustained in part by the East New York Christian Fellowship and people from the Eastside and Stamford Churches of Christ.

Shiloh expanded to as many as ten different inner-city sites around New York and New Jersey, and at one time, as many as 150 people were living in community in groups from Williams Avenue to the East Village to Red Bank — an extent of operation that had been Lamar's and Don's original goal for the Inner-City Faith Corps. After Rod Spaulding moved away from West Islip, Bryan Hale and Preston Pierce became two of the main leaders, and with them, Phil Roseberry, until his death in 1975. Don Haymes had remained a stalwart and a leader, but he became less interested in the Faith Corps when mainline church folk took it over. He married Betty Hollis, the only woman alive patient enough to form an alliance with the Christian Sol Alinsky. By then, Don was in league with Kwame Leo Lillard, Brooklyn's unstoppable community organizer. Don and Betty (and their 16-

month-old son, Malcolm) moved away in January 1971. Among the most effective later leaders of Shiloh were Doug Shafer, John Reynolds, and David Hall. Great things were done in those years, especially in the matter of urban housing for low-income people. The neighborhood called individual members of the Shiloh community "Shilohs," and it became a badge of honor and neighborhood protection to announce oneself as "a Shiloh."

Former Shilohs carried the Faith-Corps/Shiloh spirit elsewhere, and new inner-city efforts were begun in Nashville, Chicago, Dallas, Austin, Los Angeles, Flint, Montgomery (and maybe some places we do not know) by Shilohs whose names we do not know. We have made a mere beginning at telling the Faith Corps/Shiloh/ENYCF story, and the story of absolutely every one of these heroes and saints deserves to be told.

GROWING UP CAMPBELLITE, 1940-2004:
WHAT WE SAID AND WHAT WE DID

ROBERT M. RANDOLPH

In the fall of 1941, an announcement appeared in a "gospel paper" serving Churches of Christ that described the progress of the new congregation in North Hollywood, California. J. Emmett Wainwright was the minister of this group then meeting in the Women's Club. The congregation was reported to be growing, and three new babies had been born. I was the third of those three babies, and my advent in the world had first been made known in a gospel paper.

Eventually the congregation became the Burbank Church of Christ, which still exists today, meeting in a building that looks little changed from the way it appeared when it first opened in the late 1940s. It was one of a series of congregations planted by Churches of Christ across the San Fernando Valley during the 1930s and 1940s. While attrition and history have shaped the Church of Christ in this corner of Christendom, sister groups still meet in Glendale, Van Nuys, and Canoga Park. Don Haymes, according to his biography in this volume, grew up poor in Kentucky and Texas and in the Church of Christ; I grew up during the same years in the California middle class and in the Church of Christ, and thereby hangs a tale.

Wainwright was a powerful evangelist who had influenced and planted churches along the southwest corridor from Texas to California. During and after World War Two he had particular influence on young men who became interested in ministry. Serving in the armed services had given them a view of the needs of the wider world, and Emmett Wainwright had an idea of how they could serve. A number of ministers who are still serving Churches of Christ today count him their spiritual father.

Babies born in 1940 and shortly thereafter were often referred to as the "first generation of Californians" since almost everyone else had come from somewhere else. My cohort always felt as though we had been born into a new world. The War had changed everything, but not only wartime conditions swelled the numbers of the congregation meeting in North Hollywood. The Great Depression and the Dust Bowl had sent waves of migrants from the South and Southwest to California in search of jobs, and this influx continued during and after the War. Many others came who were involved in the entertainment industry. Robert Holton, in an early Hollywood attempt to tell the Gospel story, played a blue-eyed Jesus. Holton, who paved the way for Mel Gibson's recent cinematic effort, was a member of the Church of Christ in Burbank and the son of a well-known minister.

The community of members of the Churches of Christ in California was not large. Many had come from the educational institutions founded by the church, including especially Abilene Christian College, but California church members took pride in George Pepperdine College in downtown Los Angeles, founded in the success of Western Auto Stores and the generosity of George Pepperdine. Pepperdine was never named a "Christian" college, but we all knew it was one, more or less. Some of the church folk from farther East in Texas and Tennessee thought thought it was mostly "less," but we local supporters knew better. My mother was a graduate of Pepperdine. They used to say that my father saw her picture in the college yearbook and vowed he was going to marry that girl. We have color movies of their wedding, and those leaving the church building were to become leaders in the next generation of the Church of Christ.

These congregations were made up largely of young couples putting down roots in suburban California. Several, after staying a few years, returned to where they had come from. Later, however, when our time came for post-secondary education, we children of parents who had stayed in California reconnected in college with people our own age that we had known as kids before their families returned to Texas or Tennessee. Membership in the Churches of Christ was like being a member of an extended family.

The moral life was defined differently in California from the way it was defined in other regions of the Campbellite world. Proximity to the ocean required rules different from the maxims applied in landlocked congregations. To spend time on Saturday at the beach scantily attired was acceptable for the young people in California churches. Only years later did I realize that "mixed bathing" referred to swimming together and not to some esoteric sin I dreamed about that involved soap and intimacy. Later, in New England, I heard with pleasure the story of the young minister who in Boston taught the church to go on picnics rather than going to the beach, only then to be called a liberal because he endorsed playing games—horseshoes, in this case—on the Lord's Day. In California we both swam together and played games on the Sabbath. And sometimes, we *danced* after church! We were just too close to Hollywood, I guess.

Leadership in the church during the early years came primarily from preaching ministers. Batsell Barrett Baxter preached for us, as did Frank Pack, while each completed doctoral studies at universities in the area. The congregation grew, and each promotion and each new home or car was celebrated. After church, the men of the congregation would pour out the front door to gather around a new Ford, kick its tires, and comment on style. The end of the war brought many new Fords and Chevrolets, and down the street from the church in a shop window was the sign of things to come: We all gathered to watch the eerie blue glow of the television set on display in the store-front window each evening.

The essence of the gospel we all believed was simple and tended to get simpler with repetition. You put on Christ in no way other than baptism by immersion, and woe to you should you fall and hit your head on the steps into the baptistery and expire before the preacher got you under the water. You took Communion each Sunday and sang without instruments of music. The latter expectation had an unexpected side benefit. We paid attention to music, learned to hold our own in four-part harmony, and grew up valuing music. A good song leader was worth more than rubies, as was a strong soprano, not to mention a moving alto. With so much concern paid to how music was to be produced, when we stepped outside our *a cappella* environment and heard music being done well with instrumentation, some of us felt compelled to follow the piper. One of the first records I purchased in college was a new recording of Händel's *Messiah*, accompanied, of course, by a full orchestra—not the ideal that some of my Christian college teachers had in mind, but I could not resist.

Even so, when *a cappella* singing was done well, we all rejoiced. A high point for many Californian church members was reached in the early 1960s when Pat Boone, at that time a song leader at the Inglewood Church of Christ (near Pepperdine), recorded an LP with the *A Cappella Chorus* from Abilene Christian College. Nearly 50 years later, I can hear those recordings clearly in my head. Today we never sing certain hymns without remembering those with whom we first sang them.

Our world was Protestant, although we would have said that we were not. We feared the Catholics, knowing that they used to burn heretics at the stake, wanted to take over the country as they had already done in Italy, and planned to accomplish that goal through the election of JFK. We heard from returned missionaries what happened to our religious operatives in Catholic countries. We knew first-hand that Catholicism was the religion of repetition, mumbo-jumbo, and repression. It was also the religion of foreigners. Mexicans, French, and Italians were Catholics. We were convinced that church and state ought to have nothing at all to do with each other. No one needed to tell us where to pray—in school or out—and we worried lest the government get involved. After all that was how things had gone from bad to worse in Italy and Mexico.

Education was touted as our key to the future. College was a goal, but fears persisted as to what higher education might do to one's faith. Tales abounded of guileless young people who had gone to UCLA and ceased to believe. One day they were in church and on the road to heaven, and the next day they were in the university, unbelieving, wrapped in sexuality, full of alcohol, and on the broad way to hell. Even Pepperdine was sometimes suspect because the Vermont Avenue Church had ceased to have revivals and was said to read *The Littlest Angel* on the Sunday before Christmas. But Pepperdine also gave us occasional victories. When they beat Loyola in football, it was as good as USC beating Notre Dame (not that anything like that ever happened). And the only remaining question was whether or not the star players were members of the Church of Christ. Thoroughgoing sectarians, this was a question we pondered deeply.

On one occasion, due to a family emergency, we were traveling on Sunday morning while others went to church, and I noticed with alarm that those going into other churches looked just like us, and some of the young women were especially pretty. At that time in my life, I still thought that most of the good people in the world had to be members of the Church of Christ; I just didn't know where they went to church. "Naïve" hardly covers it, but I suspect that I was no more naïve than many raised in other migrant cultures. Our parents had been aliens in a foreign land, and their children were being raised in a spiritual ghetto. I would finally figure out that the alleged golden age our families thought they remembered in the South/Southwest before the Depression was no more real than the golden age of the first-century church that we were trying so hard to re-create.

Growing up Campbellite gave me a clear focus and a sharp-edged yardstick by which to interpret the world. We were among the "not many wise" mentioned in the New Testament, and we were outsiders. We looked to a City whose builder was God, not to the glamour and glitz of the nearby metropolises. The Apostle Paul had written to "you all," so we knew he was one of us. When, then, we accomplished something, it may have been a surprise to everyone else, but not to us. We cultivated the underdog role and took quiet pride in our accomplishments. We wanted to have "our own" version of everything, especially "our own colleges" where the children's faith would be safe. And this approach meant that we worked harder than others who might have social standing, the finances, or better preparation to accomplish their goals. Riding the post-war wave of success that warmed the Sun Belt for everyone who lived there, our sense of cultural alienation lessened, our self-understanding evolved into an at-homeness in our environment, and we changed. We were still the people of God, but we might not be the only ones in Heaven.

Growing up Campbellite meant that we loved books, but the only book that mattered was the Bible, though we valued the New Testament more than we did the Hebrew Scriptures. We were challenged to read it through and through, and to commit portions to memory. We were equally committed to reasoned understanding, however, and that led us inevitably to other books that would help us understand our Bibles better. But there's the rub: You cannot put reason at the top of your mental hierarchy and then limit how far it may roam. Enmeshed initially in a religion of *Bible-olatry*, our faith in a book eventually would become as unsatisfactory as the idolatries it was designed to counter.

At the heart of the simple religion of a cultural outsider lies a strong sense of community that protects and serves the individual. In the 1940s, the Randolph family had little of this world's goods: Three children in a one-bedroom house, Mom and Dad slept on a fold-out couch in the living room; it was Spartan, but it was also a place from which to do the work of God. We were God's people and God had given us hands with which to do, and minds with which to think. We read books, and we viewed the wider world as a place to explore. We were safe and we were cared for. I grew up with basic trust in my family, my church, and the cosmos.

One Saturday the whole church came out to build a new garage on our lot where our car could be parked and tools stored. When the work was finished, we all joined in games to be played and races to be run. As the oldest son, part of the races and games was conversation about my future and what was expected of me. Would I be a preacher? If not, then what? Since I was a boy-child, I was expected to become a leader in the church when I became a man, probably a preacher. Gender was a closed issue in our community: Many of the most able people in the church—we all knew, but no one said—were women who taught school and influenced every waking thought of the husbands who had come to California in the hope they could once again provide for their families. Leadership in the church had to be male—the Apostle Paul had seen to that—so who became the Preacher or the Deacon or the Elder was the result more of one's plumbing and social circumstances than the recognition of gifts given by God. Any male who was the "husband of one wife," i.e. not divorced, and "father of believing children" (not child) usually qualified one to become an Elder in the church. Women of the church often provided the actual leading, but always from the second pew and behind the scenes.

If growing up Campbellite meant that the gender of leadership was never on the table for discussion, it also meant that race was not allowed in the room. My grandfather, E. W. McMillan, went to Japan after World War II to carry the gospel to those who, a few short years before, had sought to destroy us. He came and went through the airport in Burbank. He met with Douglas MacArthur and reported back that MacArthur was lonely for home. During the same period, he also took the lead in creating educational opportunities for Negroes. He became the founding president of both Ibaraki Christian College in Japan and

Southwestern Christian College in Texas. Later, when MacArthur returned home a battered hero, he would fade away betrayed by those whose orders he had carried out. And Negroes would become Blacks and then African Americans, but the impetus for college study that we felt for our White sons and daughters would become less clear for our brothers and sisters in Christ of African descent. Could it be that we were more interested in keeping African-Americans out of "our own colleges" than we were in helping them participate in the American dream? But, then, we had mostly kept them out of "our own churches," as well, scarcely more interested in helping them be faithful to a heavenly vision.

Pepperdine College had integrated in 1944, to the consternation of members of the Churches of Christ in the South. Eventually all of "our own colleges" would follow suit, but not for another 20 years and more, and only when forced. A lack of tolerance and understanding in our California situation of Japanese-Americans were other ugly indicators that our religion ran no deeper than our culture. The federal and States governments had collaborated in the incarceration of Japanese-Californians in internment camps, and this damaged the cause of our churches among the many Japanese who lived near the Pepperdine campus and elsewhere in California. Our churches hardly lifted either a finger to help or—as far as I know—a voice in protest. And when Black members of the Church of Christ from other parts of the country came to visit in California, they did not worship with the White congregations. Even Blacks with close ties to families in our congregation visited only the Black churches of our sect. During the Watts riots in 1965, sand bag bunkers were built at the entrances to the Pepperdine campus, and tanks were in the street. If you don't already have good relations with your neighbors, you may have something to worry about during times of trouble.

According to our family mythology, a well-loved domestic, a Black lady, had cared for the family in Tennessee, and the congregation that helped Grandfather go to Japan had supported her financially in her pursuit of higher education. When Grandfather returned to Southwestern Christian College, he made her Dean of Women and spoke proudly of her mother who owned her own home and gathered her family around her in her old age, each one owning a small plot of land. Though they were this close to us, and members of this Black family would often drop by our house for advice when they traveled to California in search of work, they did not, however, worship with us at the church. Blacks and Whites, then, did not go to church together, just as, today, they mostly still do not do.

When "our own colleges" did finally integrate, I went to Southwestern to share the moment with the Dean. She cried. Her tears were not tears of joy in the realization of opportunity made real, but rather they were tears of fear for the institution to which she had given her life. As late as the 1960s, the White president of the school was found to be living in the Big House, served by students at the school earning part of their tuition by trimming the grass and working in other domestic capacities. After that president was replaced by an African American, the institution did survive, barely, not as a witness to the triumph of inclusion but, rather, in testimony to the sectarianism common in our churches fifty years ago and still today. Some church leaders have kept Southwestern going as a "separate but equal" [!] opportunity in Christian Education with the desired but unstated result of keeping "them" away from "our" other colleges. Leadership differing only in hue has slowly replaced the paternalism that founded the school.

Abilene Christian College (now University) was for me the educational institution of choice and of heritage. My family had contributed to the essence of the school, and when I registered there, I had a feeling that I was almost home. When I shared this feeling with my father, he responded that he understood, but that my sense of comfort was not his experience: "When I come to Abilene, it is as if a dark cloud comes over my head. It doesn't lift until I leave." At first, I thought he was talking about Dust Bowl times and his experience growing up in the region; later, I came understand that he meant much more.

For me, Abilene was a launch pad. I found support and encouragement. Professors challenged me in ways I had not been previously challenged, but their challenges were, nevertheless, all within the framework of expectations that I would grow up and attain leadership within the Church of Christ. Our trust in reason, however, was not abated: Minds were to be used as one uses the muscles God has given us; ideas were to be debated, and no formal limits were placed on my imagination. No one suggested that education is something to be gotten and forgotten; education was to be used to the glory of God, wherever knowledge might lead.

Within that healthy intellectual environment, where education was allowed freely to work its magic, if our self-understanding that we were the chosen people of God were challenged, then that was the way education worked, and it was not to be feared. Orthodoxies were supposed to be challenged. Restoration of New-Testament Christianity was to be an on-going movement of the mind. Views on race and gender were to be challenged, as well, because the very essence of our religious movement was to move us ever forward in our attempts to become more faithful as the people of God. Change was understood to be the nature of God's world, and movements that did not change would necessarily wither away. Static doctrine *versus* a changing world; God known only—or mostly—through an infallible book *versus* an appeal to rational intellect; values, morals, and social norms fashioned in the segregated South by under-educated preachers for congregations that had been mostly "po' Whites" *versus* post-War, educated, upwardly mobile middle-class people in an increasingly tolerant, multi-cultural America of the Civil Rights era. Something had to give.

Part of the saving grace for the generation of my young adulthood was the sense of humor that we maintained in the midst of this tightly woven system with its contradictions and possibilities. We managed smiles and occasional laughter in the presence of the Holy, from the countless baptisms gone awry to the ludicrous preacher who tied a handkerchief on his head to imitate the Pope. Religion is serious business, but so is laughter; and each lightens the other. "First Things First Forever" had been a purple-and-white/school-colors banner that hung on the wall of Sewell Auditorium at Abilene Christian in a recycling of the school's motto for its second 50 years, but the standard disappeared in a hijinks of derring-do, only to resurface in Paris during the late-'60s when youthful Marxist demonstrators waved it with enthusiasm from the barricades; now that West Texas Christian banner reportedly adorns the wall of a bistro on the Left Bank. In the midst of generational change, young and old alike might best be served by not taking themselves (or one another) too seriously—a principle too often honored more in the breach than in observance.

Then I was young, and now I am old. For the past 26 years, I have worked as a dean at M.I.T., and I have been part of the Brookline Church of Christ for 38 years often as minister. Brookline is not like most Churches of Christ. It serves as a home-away-from-home for

Campbellite students attending the several institutions of higher learning in the Boston area; the year-round resident congregation is relatively small. Among the honors that have come to the Brookline Church, one must list its instrumentality (in cooperation with Harvard Divinity School) in founding "The House of the Carpenter," a bellwether effort among Churches of Christ especially focused on improving race relations. The brainchild of William C. Martin,[1] then a doctoral student at the Divinity School and now emeritus Professor of Sociology at Rice University, The House of the Carpenter (1963–1973) served for many Churches of Christ as a model effort in the Social Gospel.

More recently the church has worked to become a congregation that recognizes the giftedness of all of its members. The congregation is led by a Steering Committee made up often more of women than of men. Think of it as Burbank with the women moved forward from the second pew. Small in numbers, Brookline has always exerted a large influence on the Churches of Christ because people go from here believing that they can serve. And they do.[2]

What I describe in this essay is not universal throughout the Churches of Christ, but I suspect that my story will ring true for most who were earnest Church-o'-Christers. The appellation "Campbellite"—a reference to Alexander Campbell, the 19th-century American religious leader who was the dominant founder of our movement to "restore primitive New Testament Christianity"—did not become acceptable until well into the late 20th century, and it is not acceptable to many now. We all have our blind spots.

I view my religious heritage with a great deal of gratitude. My Campbellite upbringing afforded me a place to stand, a sense of identity as a self-conscious Christian, and a love for the Bible, even when we collectively twisted its meaning to our own devices. To be truly Christian, I believe, is to be part of a community in Christ. I have been blessed with a community of faith and observance that is far larger than I would have experienced otherwise, and that community shaped me in profound ways and lasting ways. For all our limitations, the nearness to God that I have enjoyed through membership in a flawed church has led me to understand the grace of God who accepts me with my own flaws. Thank-you, God, for a fallible church!

Don Haymes is a product of this tradition, as well. His roots, his story, and his outcomes are different from mine, but the forces that shaped us are similar. Don and I—although he would be too modest to put it this way—have been made virtuous by our experience, for we are both strong in the faith despite our doubts, and energetic in doing good works in spite of the weakness of the flesh. I make this boast for both of us not on account of our accomplishments, our education, or our socio-economic status, but by the work of Christ on our behalf. Christ lifts the cloud with which lived experience and studied theology befog us. And if in the presence of the Holy we laugh, as well, that, too, is a gift of grace. We have much to find humorous in ourselves and in our Church, and no one knows that better than Don Haymes; and as he himself so often says: "Thanks be to God."

---

[1] See William Martin, "Three Paths to Eden," in this volume.
[2] To see the whole story of what some members call "gender equity," see http://www.gal328.org/articles/Brookline.html.

"WHY I LEFT":
A LITERARY GENRE OF RELIGIOUS DISSIDENCE

WARREN LEWIS

"Why I Left" Statements, both Ancient and Up-to-Date

When I googled the phrase "Why I Left," the web presented me with 42,600 hits. One can read why someone left Bill Gates and Microsoft, the Democratic Party, the Republican Party, and the U.S.A. ("where males are hated") to return to Australia ("where males are not hated"). Why-I-Left religious statements abound on the web. The first listed is by someone who had left the Christian ministry to become an atheist; the next one, by someone who had left atheism to become a Christian. Someone as early as 1700 had left the Quakers. Other Why-I-Left statements tell about exoduses from all kinds of religion: from the synagogue, from Creationism, from the Jesuit Order, from the Missouri Synod; from Catholicism and Protestantism, from the Moonies and the Mormons, from the Baptists and the Methodists, from Islam and Zionism, from Eckankar and Premillennialism. One person told why he had left the Contemporary Christian Music Movement when—presumably—aesthetics reasserted itself and theological sanity returned. "For as long as there has been Christianity, people have been leaving it."[1] All kinds of disaffected religionists are energetically moving the deck chairs around on the *Titanic* of religion, while the rest of us stand together and sing "Nearer, My God, to Thee."

Don Haymes and I remember the Why-I-Left tracts that we fished out of the racks at the back of church houses when we were kids. So impressive to me were those passionate declarations of religious freedom written by Restorationists in the 1940s and '50s that I imagined Why-I-Left essays to be peculiar to our movement. Preachers, editors of Gospel papers, and tractarians seemed to be saying that great waves of people were flowing from "the sects and denominations" to be "added to" (not "join") "the one true church." By the time I got to Abilene Christian College, people were bragging that we were 2.5 million strong, the fastest growing religious group in America, and that we in our non-denomination, "neither Catholic, Protestant, nor Jew," were the only ones who "speak where the Bible speaks, and are silent where the Bible is silent." We alone called "Bible things by Bible names" and stood for the "restoration of pure New-Testament Christianity." Googling on the subject, however, has made me realize that my perception of the uniqueness of the Why-I-Left genre was about as much a self-absorbed fantasy as were the early reports of our numerical ascendancy. And what was missing in those racks were any tracks explaining why someone had left the churches of Christ to go elsewhere. My googling has disabused me likewise of the fancy that it has been a one-way street. From the earliest days of the Restoration Movement, people have been writing Why-I-

---

[1] Paul Murray (Canberra, Australia), editor, www.exchristian.org, lists links to other "deconversion" sites; see http://www.users.globalnet.co.uk/~slocks/decon.html.

Left statements not only about leaving the denominations to come to us but also about leaving the Church-of-Christ denomination to move on elsewhere.

The urge to tell one's fellow humans why one has quit one religion for another (or for no religion) has been widespread both in time and place, and is still very much with us. And people who write about Why-I-Left do not tend to be quitters and soreheads. The Why-I-Left genre has an honorable history, both literarily and theologically. For example, John Henry Newman's *Apologia Pro Vita Sua* is a Why-I-Left statement about a 19th-century English cleric's journey from his Evangelical upbringing to broad-church Anglicanism and then on home to Rome. The first sentence of Thomas Jefferson's Why-I-Left *Declaration* of deistic faith in freedom and liberal democracy fairly defines the genre itself: "When in the Course of human events, it becomes necessary for one people to dissolve the political bands which have connected them with another,… a decent respect to the opinions of mankind requires that they should declare the causes which impel them to the separation." The earliest Why-I-Left essay in Christendom was penned by a man named Saul, a former Pharisee who had been more or less successful keeper of the Law of Moses, "…circumcised on the eighth day, a member of the people of Israel, of the Tribe of Benjamin, a Hebrew of Hebrews; as to the Law, a Pharisee; as to zeal, a persecutor of the Church; as to righteousness under the Torah, blameless…." That gentleman, having become a convert to "The Way" followed by disciples of Christ, wrote that he counted all his former piety and culture religion as so much "slop" when compared to the "surpassing value of knowing Christ Jesus, my Lord." (Phl 3:4-8) Jesus himself expressed a touch of Why-I-Left when he said, "You have heard that it was said of old,…but I say to you…."

Why-I-Left statements are inevitably polemic, for the writer is both anti something and pro something else; the urgency is to explain why old paths are being forsaken for new progress being made along "the road less traveled by." You and I would be both unfair and mistaken to conclude that people who write Why-I-Left statements are necessarily ornery or narrow-minded: Jesus, called the Christ; Paul, called an Apostle; Jefferson, elected President; and John Newman, created Cardinal—a crucified messiah, a renegade Pharisee, a colonial revolutionary, and a man in a red hat—no shoddy company in which to find oneself—all of them Why-I-Left dissidents.

When I googled again, I discovered a better browsing strategy (the terms "Why-I-Left" with "church*-of-Christ") and reduced the number of hits to a mere 2,050. I also ransacked Restoration Movement libraries with the help especially of Don Haymes (Christian Theological Seminary) and Carisse Berryhill (Abilene Christian University) to find the print material. Without telling Don what I aimed to do with my study, I invited his further input, asking advice from someone who shall never "leave." In good Socratic fashion, he had a few Socratic questions that helped to shape my methodological approach:

> What is the literary form of these texts, and how does the form function? Why do we see fewer of these statements now than we used to see? Are there actually fewer of them, or do we not know where to look? If they have diminished, why? Why do people reject one Christian denomination and take up another? Is there any evidence that these testimonies persuade others to "leave" that which the author has "left" and take up with that which the author has taken up? Do these texts witness to conversion or diversion? How have these authors been changed by the process? Surely there are things to be learned from these historical texts.

"Why I Left" and the 19th-century Restoration Movement

The Stone-Campbell Restoration Movement by its very nature stands in the tradition of those who left. The Campbells, father and son, left the Presbyterians, first, and then they left the Baptists; Alexander kept the printers busy issuing the volumes of *The Christian Baptist* and *The Millennial Messenger*, two Why-I-Left journals against religious division and in favor of uniting all Christendom on the basis of a restoration of pure and pristine New-Testament faith and practice.

The most telling Why-I-Left manifesto of the Restoration Movement had already been issued in 1804, before the Campbells showed up, co-signed by Barton Warren Stone, David Purviance, Robert Marshall, John Thompson, John Dunlavy, and Richard M'Nemar. *The Last Will and Testament of the Springfield Presbytery*[2] is quite possibly the most daring, most radical religious statement by anyone, anywhere, in the 19th century, and the report of this opening shot of the Ecumenical Movement has continued to ricochet throughout Christendom for over two centuries. Taking aim at all organized religion other than the local congregation, these dissident denominationalists expressed a desire that their own religious hierarchy should come to its end, and they called upon the entire Christian world to co-commit ecclesiastical suicide: "We will, that this body die, be dissolved, and sink into union with the Body of Christ at large; for there is but one body, and one Spirit, even as we are called in one hope of our calling."

The Springfield brethren went on to list other principles upon which they conceived that their "sister bodies" might also "taste the sweets of Gospel liberty:" No more hierarchies lording it over the churches, radical congregational self-government, free access for all to Bible study as "the only sure guide to heaven," that "preachers…would pray more and dispute less," and that all would sense the coming of the Millennium "and confidently expect that redemption draweth nigh."[3] Alas, since that first moment of original genius, almost no one has agreed to take the founding Restorationists' route of radical ecclesiastical *Gelassenheit*[4] and achieve terminal hierarchical *nihilitas*.[5] Popes, cardinals, archbishops, bishops, superintendents, presiders, preachers, ministers, elders, deacons, administrators, doctors, and rabbis—not to mention editors of Gospel papers and Christian college presidents—have too much ego involved, and even more income at stake, to hearken to the sages of Cane Ridge.

At this early turn, however, I first noted travelers along the two-way street of Why-I-Left diverging before me—some towards, others away from the Movement. Although Stone and Purviance stayed with the "Christians" Movement, M'Nemar and Dunlavy left to join the Shakers, and Thompson and Marshall went back to a modified Presbyterianism. Thus, even before the effort was ten years old, and before it united with Campbell's "Disciples" to become the Stone-Campbell Movement, a new genre of Restorationist literature had been invented: "Why I Left the Restoration Movement." In 1811, two of the founders, Thompson and Marshall, confessed that they were "heartily ashamed to look back at the career we have run." Partly they were in reaction to Stone's theological heresies (Millennialism, low Christology) and Monomer's "eccentric genius" and "alarming ideas" about the Atonement; partly they lamented the mischief caused by the disorganized state of the Movement, a condition that was to become perpetual.

[2] http://www.mun.ca/rels/restmov/texts/marshthom/marshal1.html
[3] *Last Will and Testament of the Springfield Presbytery*:
http://www.mun.ca/rels/restmov/texts/rmcnemar/ocg/OCG.HTM#Will
[4] *Gelassenheit*: German mystical term meaning (in today's parlance): "Let go and let God."
[5] *nihilitas*: medieval Latin mystical term for "nothingness, or nearly so."

The consequences of thus breaking and dissolving all church order were what might have been foreseen. A number of weak and unsettled men, unskilled and unsound in doctrines, crowded into the ministry; impelled, some by their own pride, some by the importunity of mistaken friends, and others, no doubt by an honest zeal for the promotion of religion. Some of them appeared to labor with honesty, and were not without success; but others, most probably, did much more harm than good.... The way being also paved for every error,... we at length became so divided in doctrines, that considerable alarm arose on that subject.[6]

Another who became noteworthy by leaving was Peter H. Burnett, a pioneer lawyer who later became Governor of California, and had become a Campbell-style Disciple in 1840. In 1844, a Baptist preacher lent him a copy of the Campbell v. Purcell debate.[7] In this most famous of 19th-century religious debates, both the great Protestant leader of "the 19th-century reformation" (as some Restorationists liked to call the Movement), and the great hierarch and future Cardinal of Roman Catholicism in America, had risen to the occasion in 1837 and represented their respective positions magisterially. Disciple Burnett, who had begun reading the printed proceedings "with utmost confidence in the capacity of Mr. Campbell as an able debater," concluded, however, that "much could be said in support of the Catholic theory," that many of Campbell's positions seemed "so extreme and ill-founded, that I could not sanction them," and that, in the end, "Mr. Campbell had been overthrown."[8] Burnett started a reading program on Catholicism, converted himself from Restorationism to Catholicism, and wrote a Why-I-Left book to explain the power of deep and ancient religious feelings that are stronger than bright and brittle reason in matters of faith.[9]

Like the Campbellite Disciple who left, so also did a Stoneite Christian. Charles Chilton Moore (1837-1906), a second-generation, birthright *Christian-only*, and the grandson of Barton Warren Stone, became famous in Kentucky for his opposition to drunkenness, and infamous for his opposition to "the whole Bible...a bundle of errors, except a few moral precepts that are found in all religions."[10] Preacher Moore espied the connection between the taverns that fostered excess in the consumption of beverage alcohol and the corn-growing church members who became wealthy by selling their produce to the distillers. A conspiracy of the churches and

---

[6] John Thompson and Robert Marshall, *A Brief Historical Account of Sundry Things in the Doctrines and State of the Christian, or as it is commonly called, New Light Church: Containing Their Testimony against Several Doctrines Held in That Church, and Its Disorganized State; Together with Some Reasons Why Those Two Brethren Purpose to Seek for a More Pure and Orderly Connexion* (Cincinnati, Ohio: J. Carpenter, 1811; reprint, Levi Purviance, *The Biography of Elder David Purviance.* Dayton, Ohio: B. F. & G. W. Ells, 1848; reprint 1940): 255-274: http://www.mun.ca/rels/restmov/texts/marshthom/marshall1.html

[7] Alexander Campbell and John B. Purcell, *A Debate on the Roman Catholic Religion* (Cincinnati: J. A. James, 1837).

[8] Peter H. Burnett, *The Path which Led a Protestant Lawyer to the Catholic Church* ((New York: D. Appleton/ Benziger Brothers, 1859; St. Louis: Herder, 1921, third, abridged edition): xii.

[9] *Ibid.*: xi: "I attended High Mass as a mere spectator, on Christmas, at midnight. I had never witnessed anything like it before, and the profound solemnity of the services—the intense, yet calm fervor of the worshippers—the great and marked differences between the two [i.e. the Catholic and Protestant] forms of worship—and the instantaneous reflection, that this was the Church claiming to be the only true Church, did make the deepest impression upon my mind for the moment. In all my religious experience, I had never felt an impulse so profound, so touching."

[10] Charles C. Moore, *Behind the Bars* (Lexington, Kentucky: Blue Grass Printing Co., 1899): 256.

the taverns landed Moore in jail: "Insults and threats to kill me, made by Christian people, became common."[11] Later, others had Moore incarcerated in a federal prison on the trumped-up charge that he used his periodical, the Blue Grass Blade, to disseminate pornography. Sentenced to serve two years, Moore was pardoned by President McKinley after five months. One can still hear and read the entirely false accusation that C. C. Moore promulgated "free love."

Something else that Moore decided no longer to promulgate was religion. While a preacher at a Christian church in Versailles, Kentucky, Moore concluded that the Old Testament was full of myth and error, and he resolved no longer to preach from it. Not long thereafter, he likewise concluded that he would be compelled to abandon the New Testament for similar reasons, including that the New Testament, like the Old, justified human slavery.[12] Jailed for three months in Lexington, Kentucky, on a charge of blasphemy against the Holy Spirit, Moore opined that "the church will imprison a man for his religious opinions to-day, if it had the power, just as it once did when it had unrestricted power."[13]

And the words for which I was fined and put in jail in Paris, Kentucky, by the "Christian" church were as follows: "If I had a contract to bore for hell-fire, I would pick the place where the earth's crust is thinnest, and rig my derrick right in front of that Christian church in Paris.[14]

20th-century Phases of the Why-I-Left Genre: Classic Patternism

The two-way street of Why-I-Left ran right through the 20th century as church members wrote their statements in both directions. The classic form was that short tract aimed at "the sects and denominations" and against belief in false doctrine and untrue churches. A few of those tracts found their way into collections that appeared as bound books,[15] and some have appeared as articles in Gospel papers such as *Truth Magazine*, *Guardian of Truth*, and *Preceptor* (conservative journals), as well as the *Firm Foundation* and the *Gospel Advocate* (the standards of mainline[16] Church-of-Christ orthodoxy in Texas and Tennessee, respectively). A few printed tracts and two bound books have reincarnated as digital manifestations on the global computer screen.[17]

---

[11] *Ibid.*: 214-215.

[12] *Ibid.*: 104; Moore, *The Rational View* (Louisville, Kentucky: Courier-Journal Job Printing Co., 1890): 14.

[13] Moore (1899): 218-219.

[14] *Ibid.*: 301.

[15] Guy V. Caskey and Thomas Lee Campbell, eds., *Why I Left* The nine speeches of the Vickery Boulevard, Fort Worth, Texas, Lectureship, October 25 to 29 and November 1 to 4, 1948. (Fort Worth, Texas: Caskey-Campbell Publishing Company, 1949); Wayne Price, ed., *Why I Left* (22nd Annual Central Oklahoma Lectureship, McCloud, Oklahoma Church of Christ, 1996): 13 speeches.

[16] By "mainline" I mean the now numerically largest segment of the *a cappella* congregations, generally associated with the "Christian colleges" and their Lectureships, as distinguished from the non-class or one-cup or premillennial or anti-cooperation or other splinter groups of "the Brotherhood" that had been whittled away by the mid-20th century.

[17] Many classic Why-I-Left statements appear online at websites supported by traditional churches of Christ with a doctrinaire bent. The following, among others, are exemplary:

Bangor, Northern Ireland: http://www.churchofchristbangor.com/

Bible.ca: http://www.bible.ca/cath-why-I-left.htm

The Bible Speaks: http://www.thebiblespeaks.com/

Bible Study Guide: http://www.biblestudyguide.org/churches-religions/index.htm

Deckerville (Michigan) Church of Christ: http://www.greatlakes.net/~churchcr/

The majority of pre-1960s statements are strictly doctrinal; they include only hints at individual discomfort or lamentation over interpersonal upset in the church left behind. The authors sometimes even stated that no personal element was involved in their reasons for leaving. Acknowledgement of anything so human would seem to have undermined the ideological purity of their propositional motivation. From the Church-of-Christ perspective, the other churches were just plain wrong, so leaving them had nothing to do with whether people there were friendly or not.[18]

David Riggs, for example, in an oft-reproduced statement about why he left the Church of Rome, articulated the non-personal point clearly and simply: "I did not leave the Catholic Church because of some evil that I had done or that was done to me. I left the Catholic Church because I came to believe that it was contrary to the Bible."[19] Keith Clayton, a generation later, said the same about leaving the Episcopal Church.[20] Without impugning the integrity of the authors, one may nonetheless question whether doctrinal disagreement occurs this intensely in a personal vacuum. One has to wonder whether personal matters did not, even in those stiffer times, enter at least partly into people's decisions to leave their churches.

Another function of this literary form, though less frequently stated in so many words, has been to confirm the reader in the certainty of one's own religious convictions: "If Brother So-and-so learned the truth and left the (____) Church, then I know I'm right to be where I am; they're wrong and we're right." As a teenager, I had collected an entire briefcase full of these tracts and similar publications, a *vade mecum* for the high-school denomination-slayer. With the flick of a wrist, I could produce a Why-I-Left tract against the Baptists or Mormons or any other biblically wobbly group, and demonstrate to my complete satisfaction wherein those sectarians were wrong and the churches of Christ were right. Also a dominant style of traditional

---

Garden City (Michigan) Church of Christ: http://www.garden-city-coc.org/

Gospel Defender: http://www.gospeldefender.com/whyileft-articles.html

Highway 9 Church of Christ (Piedmont, Alabama) "an autonomous congregation of the Lord's church": http://4dw.net/hwy9/index.html

Northside Church of Christ (Tucson, Arizona): http://iwhome.com/spiritualquest/

Oakridge (Tennessee) Church of Christ: http://oakridgechurch.com/riggs/whyileft.htm

Sandia Church of Christ (Albuquerque, New Mexico): http://sandiachurchofchrist.com/

For a vigorous attack on all "denominations," see http://www.members.shaw.ca/completeunity/

Some statements can be found online at the Center for Restoration Studies, Abilene Christian University, Abilene, Texas (hereinafter: ACU/CRS): http://www.bible.acu.edu/crs/

[18] The occasional Why-I-Left essayist has broken this stylistic mold, with an informative and enjoyable result. Mrs. Edward Fleming (1971), had migrated from New England Congregationalism to the Baptist Church and had married an ex-Catholic, but came to find herself among some "happy people who were **ALL** bubbling over with something....What I found here was warmth, sincerity, affection, a sincere desire to study God's will, and a determination to apply these teachings to their own lives." After four months, she became a member of a church of Christ in Woburn, Massachusetts.

[19] David Riggs, "Why I Left the Catholic Church"(1962): found at several websites, including the following: http://iwhome.com/spiritualquest/tracts/leftcath.htm

[20] Keith E. Clayton, "Why I Left the Episcopal Church," *Truth Magazine* 43 (2 Dec 1999): 718 and at various websites. Joe Malone said essentially the same thing about why he left the Catholic Church in 1928: http://www.bible.ca/cath-why-I-left.htm

preaching, this mental contact sport was referred to in folksy parlance as "skinning the sects."[21] Mrs. N. N. Whitworth (of blessed memory), a nice Methodist lady, but an intolerable censor of free speech, pronounced a moratorium on religious debate in her Speech class at Amarillo High School, and compelled me to leave my briefcase at home.

A few choice examples must stand for the entire genre: Dan Goddard explained why he left the Conservative Christian Church (the piano-playing sister denomination of the *a-cappella* [singing-only] churches of Christ) by charging them with, in addition to the use of instrumental music in worship, "Error # VII":

> [They believe that] they are CHRISTIANS, BUT NOT THE ONLY CHRISTIANS… [and that] there are many roads to heaven. You're on one and I am on another. We may differ doctrinally, but we both believe in Jesus Christ as the Son of God. I am a Christian and you are a Christian. [When I was a member of the Conservative Christian Church,] I believed that denominational church members were my brothers in Christ.[22]

Goddard's denial that members of other churches are Christians is telling because he thereby negated another time-honored motto of the Restoration Movement: "We are not the only Christians, but we are Christians only." This hardening of the Restorationist perspective had congealed in the Southern churches of Christ following the War of Northern Aggression and in reaction to the ever-more-liberal *Digressives* (as we termed the Christian Churches [Disciples of Christ]), such that *a cappella* churches of Christ came to believe that "we are not only Christians only, but we are the only Christians."

A further function of the classic form has been to give an ex-member of some "denomination" an opportunity publicly to denounce the false doctrines of his or her former religious identity while approving a comparable list of propositional truths that characterize canonical teaching of the churches of Christ. The lists of errors vary, of course, with the targeted denomination: Catholic errors are different from Baptist errors, but to the extent that all kinds of errors differ from the perceived patterns of truths in the 27-book biblical canon, they are all equally damnable. Roman Catholic errors most often mentioned in Why-I-Left tracts include the following: Catholics are not open to being corrected by the Bible, but the Bible is the only infallible test of religious truth (not tradition, not the Church, not the Pope); Catholics believe that Peter was the first pope, and that the pope (not Christ) is the head of the Church; almost all teaching about Mary is non-biblical (perpetual virginity, immaculate conception, bodily assumption, queenship of Heaven); non-believing infants are sprinkled and it is called baptism; priests are called "father" yet marriage is forbidden to them; priesthood is limited to a few;

---

[21] Martha Armstrong, "The Heart Has Its Reasons," in Robert R. Meyers, ed., *Voices of Concern: Critical Studies in Church of Christism* (St. Louis: [Carl Ketcherside's] *Mission Messenger*, 1966): 230.

[22] Dan Goddard, "Why I Left the Conservative Christian Church" in "Sermons" (n/d): http://www.garden-city-coc.org/sermons/church43.htm. See Floyd A. Decker, "Why I Left the Christian Church" in Caskey and Campbell (1949) and online; Robin Haley, "The Christian Church" in Price (1996); Terry Gunnells, "Why I Left the Christian Church," *Carolina Christian* 33 (1 Nov 1991): 9; Larry Harrington, "Why I Left the Instrumental Church of Christ," *Carolina Christian*, 29 (1 Oct 1987): 12; Terry Sanders, "Why I Left the Christian Church" online at Riggs websites; William S. Willis, *Why I Was Rebaptized*, bound together with *Why I Left the Christian Church* (Austin: Firm Foundation, between 1920 and 1940 [?]) (ACU/CRS). Clarence C. Morgan at http://www.bible.acu.edu/crs/doc/chch.htm, *Why I Left the Christian Church*, Austin, Texas: Firm Foundation Publishing House [1932?] or, "A Sermon Delivered at the Church of Christ, Weatherford, Texas, Lord's Day Afternoon, November 27, 1932" (ACU/CRS).

bishops must not be married; transubstantiation of the bread and fruit of the vine; eating of meat is sometimes forbidden.[23]

The classic Why-I-Left statement entails not only the "95 Theses" in disapproval of error but also an affirmation of the "marks of the one true church." This mini-systematic theology tends to be theologically minimalist (rarely does one find statements addressing the perennial questions of historic theology, e.g. the nature of God and Christology). The items touched on have a certain ideological and methodological sameness, for the Why-I-Left genre tends to be consistent.

The standard Church-of-Christ list of the articles of faith comprises a few concerns notable for their biblical qualities. Campbell's doctrine of sacramental immersion of believers, *e.g.*, is perpetuated in them all. Whether non-immersion of a believer would result in non-salvation, a conclusion drawn by Why-I-Left tractarians, is a result reached strictly by logic and is not based on the biblical text or any pattern within it, because the first-century Christians did not have to face that soteriological question. According to Why-I-Left logic, however, a church that does not baptize the right people (adults; believers) for the right reason (unto the remission of sins) in the right way (immersion) is a church whose members are still in their sins, not "in Christ"; therefore, they are neither Christians nor saved. Baptists baptize the right people and in the right way, but not for the right reasons. Catholics baptize for the right reasons, but neither the right people nor in the right way.[24]

Most of the rest of the Why-I-Left tenets are even more impressionistic and biblically dubious. They are doctrines premised largely on hermeneutics (principles of interpretation) that arise not from the canonical literature itself but from a contrived logic, a hermeneutical casuistry that depends upon a kind of formal and exclusionary rationalism of "command, example, and necessary inference," as though the Bible were a code of canon law or a book of cases. A "pattern" of first-century belief and practice is thus defined to be biblical, and then it is knotted into place with a reinforcing string of proof-texts that seem to assert biblical authority for the perceived pattern: Anyone who does not maintain this pattern is said to be "going beyond the doctrine of Christ" (2 Jn 9), is either "adding to" or "taking away" (Rv 22:18) from biblical

---

[23] Aaron Erhardt, "Why I Left Catholicism," *Truth Magazine* 48 (19 August 2004):18-19, concluded with a remarkable turnabout for one whose own tradition once called itself a "reformation": "The fact that Catholicism has changed and reformed itself proves that it is not of God." See also John A. Cupp, *Why I Left the Roman Catholic Church to Become a Member of the Church of Christ*. Jacksonville, Florida: private publication [195?]; Greg Litmer, "Why I Left the Roman Catholic Church," *Preceptor* 38 (1 Nov 1989): 352.; Samuel Mormino, *Why I Left the Catholic Church* (pamphlet, n.d.) (ACU/CRS); Gary Henson, "The Catholic Church," in Price (1996); Joseph Suchorski, *Why I Left the Roman Catholic Church* (tract, n.d.) (ACU/CRS); Aniceto Mario Sparagna, *Why I Left the Roman Church, and Other Sermons by Aniceto Mario Sparagna*. West Collingswood, New Jersey: Collingswood Church of Christ, n.d.; Dick Weber, "Why I Left the Roman Catholic Church and Why I Will Never Go Back," *Christian Worker* 83 (Dec. 12, 1997): 5: http://www.catholicism.org/pages/stauffer.htm, But see "Joe Stauffer: Church of Christ Convert," n.d. The tables turned when Stauffer left the Church of Christ to become a Roman Catholic in 1989.

[24] The Church-of-Christ doctrine and practice of baptism is becoming more common in 21st-century Christendom as free-church independent groups outside the mainstream of historic Christendom invoke biblical patterns. Even so, my adult daughter, Phoebe, was sacramentally immersed in a kiddie wading pool in the narthex of Holy Trinity Episcopal Church in Uptown Manhattan. All we had to do was ask. Cf. "The Baptism," *Book of Common Prayer* (1979): 307—"Each candidate is presented by name to the Celebrant...who then immerses, or pours water upon, the candidate...."

teaching, and is therefore violating "all scripture, inspired by God" (2 Tm 3:16).[25] Never mind that these sticky bits of proof-texting neither in context nor as stand-alone statements either suggest or support in any way the particular pattern being alleged. Never mind that this kind of book-logic did not mean to the first-century writers and readers anything like the use to which this inferential logic upon logic puts them in isolation from their historical context of meaning.[26]

The search for patterns, let it be said, is not bad method: Naturalists study nature by observing its patterns; literary critics and linguists study literature and language by observing literary and linguistic patterns. The method goes awry, however, when preconceived notions cause one to "find" patterns that are not there: *eisegesis* ("reading into the text") according to the reader's subjective response, rather than *exegesis* ("reading out from the text") according to the author's intention by means of historical-critical hermeneutics that arise from the objective texts themselves.

Among the commonplaces mentioned—some of which, indeed, may have some basis in the texts—none is so clearly patterned as is believer's immersion. These include, for example, emphasis on the name of the church. As no "Catholic church," Lutheran church," "Baptist church," or "Methodist church," and the rest, is named in the Christian Bible, these names are deemed by Why-I-Left tractarians as reprehensible. "Church of Christ," our tract writers argue, is the proper name for Christ's church, partly because in our culture (until recently) a wife traditionally took her husband's name, so since the church is the "Bride of Christ," she must wear his name. The single verse, Romans 16:16, was absolutized into a denominational moniker that appeared on signboards and was engraved on cornerstones: "Church of Christ Meets Here." This "pattern," alleged on the evidence of a single proof-text, can be held firmly only by ignoring evidence for other "names" (if, in fact, they were "names") of the first-century followership of Jesus: e.g., "The Way," "Disciples," "Church of God," "Church of the First-Born Ones," "the Elect Lady," and some other possibles.

The list of other Why-I-Left doctrines is a long one: mandatory weekly observance of the Lord's Supper each Sunday—whereas Paul specifically stated that "one day is as good as another" for worship (Rm 14:5-6); the Sunday collection as one of the mandatory *Five Items of Worship* (preaching/teaching, praying, singing, the Lord's Supper, and the collection)—another one-scripture pattern (1 Cor 16:1-4, a one-time event of charitable fund raising) that has been canonized into a practical dogma to justify the management of "the church treasury" and "the Lord's money," two outstandingly non-biblical concepts—except that Jesus did condemn the notion of "the Lord's money" [Mk 7:8-13]); congregational autonomy and two-tier (Elders and Deacons) church polity only—despite the variety of church polity evident in scripture, including missionary churches under the control of the missionary who planted them, authority of the evangelist, house churches under the presidency of the householder (in some cases—Lydia and Phoebe, for example—these leaders were women); the city-wide church in Jerusalem under the guidance of a synod of Elders and James, its

---

[25] On "patternist" or "Baconian" logic, see Michael Casey, "Mastered by the Word," in this volume, and see *idem*, "The Theory of Logic and Inference in the Declaration and Address" in *The Quest for Christian Unity, Peace, and Purity in Thomas Campbell's Declaration and Address: Text and Studies*, Thomas H. Olbricht and Hans Rollmann, eds. (Lanham, Maryland: Scarecrow Press, 2000): 223-242.

[26] See Roy Bowen Ward, "'The Restoration Principle': A Critical Analysis," *Restoration Quarterly* 8/4: http://www.restorationquarterly.org/Volume_008/rq00804ward.htm

presiding Elder; and the emerging role of "the bishop" in the Pastoral Epistles); and doctrinal non-use of the Old Tetament (except as history and prophecy)—when, in fact, the Hebrew scriptures were the only "Bible" that first-century Christians had.

The one other doctrine (along with believer's baptism and weekly Lord's Supper) that one inevitably finds in Why-I-Left tracts is the affirmation of *a cappella* music in worship (singing only). Instrumental music in worship is the controverted point over which more grief has been poured out than baptismal water in the 200-year life of the Restoration Movement, for this is the Mason-Dixon Line between "the fiddlers and the non-fiddlers."[27] A piano in the church house is also the easiest disqualifier to spot, for almost all churches in Christendom (except some Orthodox churches, some Quakers, and the Primitive Baptists) make it easy to identify "the one true church" that is known best by what it does not do. The patternist logic upon logic expended to prove that God approves of singing-only at church betrays the hermeneutical impossibility of this approach to text and, at the same time, demonstrates the *real* function of this style of theologizing, namely, to make credible a religious conviction that was originally established for reasons other than the ones being alleged, in this case, the cultural, aesthetic, and traditional preferences of the Southern churches over-against the Northern, Liberal, Digressive Disciples whose armies had won the War.

The Why-I-Left argument against instrumental music runs as follows: Christians are (1) *commanded* in scripture to "sing"; and (2) the history of the apostolic church demonstrates an *exemplary pattern* of singing, no mention of playing. Although the biblical canon does not specifically prohibit instrumental music in Christian worship, the command to "sing" is interpreted according to the strict-constructionist legal principle of logical exclusion: "sing" does not include "play"; so (3), therefore, any church that "plays" is, according to *necessary inference*, in violation of that string of proof-texts (mentioned above), adduced to absolutize the "authority of scripture."[28]

One may observe, however, that if this patternist hyper-logic had been more consistently applied—and post-Civil War animosity had contributed less to dogmatic formation—the churches of Christ might as easily have come to an opposite conclusion. When one asks the historical-exegetical, Restorationist question purely: "Did any first-century Christians in their worship of God sing to the accompaniment of musical instruments?" one may come to a conclusion different from the conclusions to which other questions, typically asked, lead: "Do you like it?" "Do you think we ought to do it?" "Is church music better with it or without it?" "Is either *a cappella* singing or instrumental music anything at all to be 'restored,' or are they both nothing more than 'customs of the times'—like holy-kissing, foot-washing, women's veils, and women's silence in the assembly? When the classic Church-of-Christ three-step logic of command, example, and inference is followed, then the answer to the simple question: "Did the first-century church ever worship with instrumental music?" is a simple and biblical yes.

---

[27] *"fiddler v. non-fiddler"*—a bit of Ohio wit to define the distinction, reported to me by Roy Bowen Ward.

[28] On one occasion in Canada, an elderly Elder scolded me for having called upon a preacher from the piano-playing Independent Christian Church to word the closing prayer at Sunday-afternoon singing. The old gentleman reasoned that if we call upon the brother-in-error to pray, then we somehow condone his error. In passionate condemnation of playing instrumental music in worship, the venerable Elder tapped the table with his forefinger and proclaimed: "They're wrong, they know it, but they just won't change!"

1. *Command*: Christians are commanded to "sing …Psalms" and to teach one another by singing the Psalms (Col 3:16, Eph 5:19).[29]

2. *Example*: The first Church of Christ, the Church in Jerusalem, worshiped daily both in house churches and in the Temple (Ac 2:46). All the apostles, living in Jerusalem until they were scattered; James, the Lord's brother and the presiding Elder of the Jerusalem city-church; the apostle Paul and his missionary cohort when they visited Jerusalem (Ac 21:20-26); together with the whole community of Jewish-Christians, living in Jerusalem from the first Christian Day of Pentecost until just before the destruction of the Temple in the year 70, did likewise. That is to say, the first full generation of the life of the church, or half the lifetime of the entire first-century church, Christians continued worshiping in the Temple where instrumental music accompanied their worship—hearty music associated with praise and joy.[30]

3. *Inference*: Because Psalm 150 exhorts worshipers to play all manner of musical instruments, and Early Christians taught one another by singing the Psalms in the Temple, including Psalm 150, to the accompaniment of those very instruments, one may infer a biblical pattern of the teaching, use, and approval of instruments of music in worship among Christians in Jerusalem. This inference is further inferentially supported in that no Early Christian author objected to the music of the Temple, although some words of Jesus, the epistles of Paul, and the book of *Hebrews* abound with criticism of various other aspects of Temple worship.

I offer the foregoing not to argue the case one way or the other on this notoriously moot issue, for cultural and aesthetic passions have invariably determined the issue. For A. Campbell, unaccompanied singing was a matter of aesthetic preference, conditioned by his upbringing as a Scottish Presbyterian, a disposition derived from J. Calvin's dislike for Romanist liturgy. What for Campbell had been not even of doctrinal significance, however, took on the dogmatic weight of embittered politics in the unReconstructed South. My intention here is to demonstrate an enculturated lack of integrity in the awareness and use of scripture as manifest in the repetitiousness of the denominationally homogenous Why-I-Left literature.[31]

---

[29] Note the impeccable Church-of-Christ logic of the Texas farmer (reported by Michael Casey, "Mastered by the Word," in this volume): If women are to "keep silent" and are not to teach, then neither should they sing, for we teach publicly through our singing. Ancient rabbis and medieval monks agreed with the farmer and forbade the women to sing because "the voice of the woman leads to licentiousness" (see Eric Werner, *The Sacred Bridge I* (New York: Columbia University Press, 1959): 323-333.

[30] See *Sukkah* 51a (Babylonian Talmud), *Mishna Arakhim* 2:3-6. Werner (1959): 316-318, stated that the rabbis later banned instrumental music in the synagogue as a sign of mourning, following the destruction of the Temple. Eschatologically joyful Christians did not share this attitude towards the ethnic Jewish cultic center. The Christian temple was said to be in Heaven, where instruments of music were reported by John, the Seer of Patmos, to be in everlasting use.

[31] Lest one think that instrumental music, seemingly a minute point, be deemed no longer important in the Church of Christ, see http://www.christianaffirmation.org/ and the new (2005) "creed" there promulgated (under the euphemism of an "affirmation") by leading members of the mainstream churches (some of them contributors to this volume). In a political effort to hold together their fractious denomination, these theological reductionists sensed an ecclesiastical need so great that they were willing to violate one of the principal mottos of the Restoration Movement, "No creed but Christ." In so doing, they ignored any number of weightier matters to focus on three tenets only of Church-of-Christ dogma: baptism, the Lord's Supper, and *a cappella* singing.

Had our Why-I-Left tractarians been attempting truly to restore first-century practice in the light of the Christian canon, rather than perpetuating late-19th and early-20th century traditions, a strikingly different list of *non*-observed biblical patterns offer themselves as far better represented than is *non*-instrumental music. One may mention foot-washing—the sacrament of service and humility—"a custom of the times" that (like another "custom of the times," ritual washing [immersion]), took on heavy-duty religious significance among first-century Christians under the direct command of the Risen Christ in the Fourth Gospel and numerous apostolically approved examples. Necessary inference argues more strongly for the sacramental character of foot-washing than does the scant evidence require mandatory Lord's Day observance of the Lord's Supper. Also, holy-kissing—the sacrament of welcome and acceptance; various styles of table fellowship, communitarian sharing, love feasts, and hospitality;[32] fellowship with the Jewish synagogue—a regular observance for both Jesus and Paul, the sacrament of unity among God's Abrahamic peoples; the laying-on of hands—the sacrament of ordination; the laying-on of hands and anointing with oil—the sacrament of healing; charismatic worship—the sacrament of mystical contact with the Holy Spirit; no divorce—the sacrament of fidelity; no lending at interest—the sacrament of liberality; no legal litigation—the sacrament of no self-defense; and non-violence—the sacrament of God's peace under the cross; and others. Our theologically reductionist tractarians tended to ignore this richness of biblical lore; as a result, the *non*-restored first-century church is far less interesting, and far less biblical, than it might have been.

20th-century Phases of the Why-I-Left Genre: The Tables Turn

Neither the form nor the functions of classic Why-I-Left statements have changed much since the 1940s, except that in the electronic era, this type of proselytizing and sectarian pastoral psychology is infinitely more widespread than the tract rack ever was. Latter-day statements, moreover, no matter who writes them—from the most liberal to the most conservative leaver—tend to be more personal, more passionate, though no less doctrinal. In response to Don Haymes's question, we can say that we see not fewer but more such statements: Why-I-Left is alive and well and online.

As to the missionary effect of the Why-I-Left genre, no evidence leads me to think that these testimonies ever did persuade people in great numbers to leave those forms of religion that the leavers had left, but the perpetual popularity of the genre indicates that audiences still exist in many churches that enjoy being told that they are doctrinally correct. At the turn of the millennium, the scant statistical evidence supports the stronger anecdotal evidence that far more people are leaving the churches of Christ to go elsewhere than are moving towards them. According to Mac Lynn, counter of the uncountable, although the Church of Christ is still the largest of the numerous splinters of the Restoration Movement, its membership is now in decline.[33]

[32] See Carisse Berryhill, "From Dreaded Guest to Welcoming Host: Hospitality and Paul in *Acts*," in this volume.

[33] See Mac Lynn, *Churches of Christ in the United States 2003* (Nashville, Tennessee: 21st Century Christian, 2003), and *Churches of Christ around the World* (Nashville, Tennessee: 21st Century Christian, 1988). See also Ted Parks, "A Conversation with Mac Lynn," *The Christian Chronicle* (June 3, 2002): http://www.christianity.com/CC/article/0,,PTID25485|CHID127205|CIID1391832,00.html. Lynn stated his sense that "the church has plateaued and perhaps in the last couple of years started downward"; "conservative"

Nowadays, classic Why-I-Left statements tend to be written more by members of conservative and traditional congregations than by members of the mainline Church of Christ. The conservatives and the Antis are right: The mainline denomination has become better educated, more liberal, more institutional; less sectarian and more ecumenical, and that means softer on such shibboleths as instrumental music and immersionist exclusivism. The mainline Church-of-Christ denomination now tends to view other denominations at least as cousins in Christ, if not brothers and sisters. The digressive effects of "our own" universities, large and expensive buildings, educated preachers and other professional clergy, institutionalized efforts at missions and benevolence are taking the Church-of-Christ church down the same highway to Digression that the Disciples traveled one hundred years ago. Socio-economic at-homeness in this world, and a set of social and political values in common with NeoCon Republicanism, have made Why-I-Left statements of denomination-bashing and sect-skinning politically incorrect. The former overweening sectarian claim to being the only ones headed for Heaven is gradually being humbled into the soft Calvinism of "the Wheaties" (Don Haymes's term of opprobrium for the pious graduates of Wheaton Theological Seminary and their Evangelical ilk). "Such worms as we," Don pokes fun to say, "don't know nuthin' 'bout bein' no one-true-church."[34]

The tables began to turn for the churches of Christ following World War Two. Since the 1960s, four emergent groups have made energetic use of the Why-I-Left genre to declare their reasons for leaving the Church of Christ: (1) The "liberals" (so-called by their more conservative critics), from educated elitists to broken-hearted dissidents, from advocates of church kitchens to proponents of whatever the current hot topic may be;[35] (2) charismatics; (3) arch-conservative anti-institutionalists; and (4) the International Church of Christ (ICOC). Other, smaller fractions of the Restoration Movement—the Premillennialists, the One-Cup brethren, the No-Sunday-School congregations,[36] the anti-Located Preacher effort, and some others, all had their single points to make, but mostly have lost energy as movements within the Movement.

---

churches of Christ are not growing; members who move to new locations no longer start new congregations; "fervor for bringing new people in" is lacking; "younger people are leaving, and saying: 'If I'm not getting what I need here, I'll just go somewhere else, so what if it's another group.'" In a private email, Lynn added: "People have been leaving Churches of Christ throughout the body's history, so the idea of exiting is not new…. In the latter part of the 20th century, we may often identify an additional reason [for leaving]: to find spiritual fulfillment." Lynn reported that whereas the number of Church-of-Christ congregations doubled between 1945 and 1965, those numbers are now declining.

[34] Ex-Church of Christ Support Group: http://ex-churchofchrist.com/PurposeCoC.htm: "Many Churches of Christ see themselves as part of the greater evangelical movement in the United States,…[example: Max Lucado]… almost indistinguishable from other evangelical churches from various denominations."

[35] In 2005, a gender-equal public role for women at church is the hot topic. Ann Evankovich, "Why I Left the Church of Christ and Why I Returned": The GAL328.org website, Gender Justice and Churches of Christ: http://www.gal328.org/articles/Evankovich-Why.html is an online clearinghouse of advocacy for the public role of women in the Church. At this same website, see http://gal328.org/articles/Haymes-Theses.html: Don Haymes, "9.5 Theses on the Ministry of Women…" See Chris Hutson, "Middle Ground?" in this volume. A sense of gender justice has not yet, however, been extended to other genders: Issues regarding the public participation and ministry of acknowledged Gay and Lesbian Christians has hardly been raised in the Church-of-Christ church, although the Disciples (and other denominations) have been agonizing over the issue for years. See Roy Bowen Ward, "The Traditions of 'Marriage'" in this volume.

[36] J. W. Hayhurst, "Why I Left the Anti-class Position" in Caskey and Campbell (1949).

The Liberals

The Why-I-Left highway has ever been a two-lane road, one lane leading towards the Church of Christ, the other leading away. The off-ramp sign for exiting liberal dissidents (not a unified splinter group and unlikely to become one) was first marked in the 20th century by *Voices of Concern*[37] who took aim at the chilly piety, legalistic moralizing, exclusivism, and scripture patternism of the traditional churches of Christ. In a way that makes the turning of the tables in the Why-I-Left genre obvious, Ralph V. Graham, who became a minister in the Disciples of Christ, entitled his essay with the canonical phrase upended: "Why I Left the 'Churches of Christ.'"[38]

Contrary to the classic style of essay aimed at other denominations, these newer *Voices* all spoke of acutely personal concerns and in autobiographical terms. Beginning in the 1960s, we witnessed the psychologizing of America, and this change in the *Zeitgeist* allowed for the change from the classic personal reserve. Why *did* these people leave the churches of Christ? Certainly, they found that they no longer agreed with important aspects of the doctrine, but more tellingly their reports are wet with the tears of bitterness, and the blood of frustrations, antagonisms, pain, and spiritual starvation that they have experienced as Church members. No study of the "leaving" phenomenon known to me comes even close to grasping the *real* reasons why people have left and continue to leave.[39]

This change in literary style from classic reserve to the post-psychological invites a correspondingly psychological analysis of the two-sided situation. Those who leave, I suggest, are recognizable psychological types suffering from Ecclesiastical Bi-Polar Syndrome with a touch of Theological Oppositional/Defiant Disorder (EBPS/TODD types), whereas those who

---

[37] Meyers (1966). Seventeen arch critics formed the first rupture of a seismic shift in the Church of Christ that caused a tsunami of opposition and still sends out aftershocks half-a-century later. John Waddey, "Voices of Concern Were Voices of Change," *Christianity Then and Now* http://www. christianity-then-and-now.com/html/hb study 023.html, called the Meyers volume "Apostasy!... apostates...whose words eat like gangrene.... Instead of being a great tragedy that they left us, we are much better off that they did.... Today's agents of change are the lineal descendants of those past apostates."

[38] Meyers (1966): 129.

[39] Dana Larry Gill, "A Study of Church Dropouts in the Merkel Church of Christ, Merkel, Texas" (Memphis, Tennessee: D. Min. thesis, Harding Graduate School of Religion, 1983), in the body of his study barely grazed people's real reasons for leaving, although in his "Conclusion" at least touched the nerve: "Many of these dropouts were tired of hearing constant tirades against their upbringing as well as their loved ones who remain in denominational circles." Gill's solution to the problem, however, was as superficial as his analysis. He recommended that one "speak the truth in a loving manner for the up building of the church," such that "the divisiveness of denominations could best be defeated by positive and loving instruction in the ways of New Testament Christianity." (p. 97) In other words, if we are nice when we tell those "divisive denominationalists" that they are going to Hell for not being members of the one true church, then it will go down more smoothly. Gill's rhetoric indicates his failure to acknowledge that the rampant divisiveness of the group he called "New Testament Christianity" is just as divisive, if not more so, than those terrible "denominationalists." Gill further recommended employment of that tried and true Roman Catholic strategy, that church members marry only other church members, and he called this teaching the church's "duty." (p. 103) One must further question Gill's interview methodology: How could his interviewees have possibly answered his protocol of questions entirely honestly? "All of the Merkel interviews were conducted by the preacher." (p. 104)

cause them to leave are text-book cases of Asperger's Syndrome: High-Functioning Sound-Doctrinal Autists. (ASHFSD types).[40]

EBPS/TODD types, the more sensitive souls, are caught between bi-polar options: On the one hand, their manic expression of inflated self-esteem causes them to resist being told how to feel and what to do by a Preacher or an Elder. On the other hand, this type can be depressive; burdened by grace-neediness, excessive worthlessness, or guilt; fatigued by pew-sitting, hypersomniac during sermons, and lethargic during evangelistic campaigns. They feel trapped in a context of family/community dysfunction; when they experience difficulty in handling frustration, irritability, depression, fear, and hostility, they resort to blaming the leadership; turning their aggression inwards, they become non-compliant, and they underachieve at church. They have an overwhelming need for autonomy that can manifest as inappropriate behavior when threatened by ecclesiastical authorities. These members have a comprehension deficit that keeps them from caring about cognitive fine points or understanding why a system of sound doctrine may be more important than human compassion.

ASHFSD types, the less sensitive souls, being mostly males and therefore the Preachers and Elders, are compulsive systematizers, more interested in patterns than in people. Their brain is trying to build and understand a system that is finite, reliable, rules-based, and predictably regular and regulatory. They tend to occupy a higher social rank (pulpit huggers, not pew-sitters); they are leaders who see members as functioning parts of the system more than as uncontrollable human individuals. High-functioning, intelligent, attentive to detail, and 10-to-1 males over females, they suffer from Empathy Disorder, having difficulty imagining the world through someone else's eyes or responding appropriately to someone else's feelings. When required to function in the social world that they would prefer to control, they may react by trying to impose predictability on the unpredictable, and sameness on the diverse. They are aware that people often seem shocked by their unempathic and sometimes offensive views, but their response is to blame the hearer (the other), not the speaker (oneself): "What I say is what I believe," they assert. "How someone else perceives what I say has nothing to do with me. If they're hurt or offended, that's not my problem. I just say what is true."[41] Ecclesiastical dogmatic dubious translation: "If I tell you that you're going to Hell, it's only because I love you!"

Applying Baron-Cohen's language without need of ecclesiastical translation, many notable theological autists who want to keep the women silent and out of church leadership, believe in "meritocratic misogyny":

> They believe…women have not achieved equally high positions…because they are less able. Their [the ASHFSD types'] views are often held very strongly, and are black or white. They are typically convinced by the rightness of their beliefs, and given the chance will spend hours relentlessly trying to convince the other person to change their view. They do not understand how one's beliefs can be a matter of subjectivity or just one point of view. Rather, they believe that their own beliefs are a true reflection of the world and, as such, that they are correct.[42]

[40] I draw the structure of my analysis from Simon Baron-Cohen, *The Essential Difference: The Truth about the Male and Female Brain* (New York: Basic Books, 2003): 61, 62, 67, 95, 121, 126, 137-139, 141, merely turning his psychological terminology towards church-related behaviors.

[41] *Ibid.*: 142.

[42] *Ibid.*: 147.

When EBPS/TODD types and ASHFSD types confront one another across a pulpit, the rough humor or insensitivity of the latter may tell the former to "keep silent in the churches" and reduce them to tears over the everlasting destiny of some family member who died unimmersed and in sin, and in ignorance of "the way that is right and cannot be wrong" ASHFSD types imagine that their perfect theological systems—e.g., the *Five-Step Plan of Salvation* [hear, believe, repent, confess, be immersed] or the *Five Items of Worship* [mentioned earlier]—ought to engender cognitive satisfaction enough to overcome mere emotion. When, then, an EBPS/TODD type has had more than enough, the choice is between one of these "uncontrollable" EBPS/TODD type's leading a church split, or—more likely—a saddened EPBS/TODD type's quietly slipping away. In either case, another Why-I-Left statement thereby becomes appropriate.[43]

Further in this personal vein, many latter-day leavers begin their essays by rehearsing their Church-of-Christ pedigrees—so many generations on this or that side of the family, baptized by this or that famous gospel preacher—so as to say to the reader: "I started out firm in my faith in, and experience of, the Church of Christ, so I know what I'm talking about."[44] Roy Key, who became a minister for the Disciples of Christ, wrote "A Letter to Daddy and Mother,"[45] expressive of the rending of families and the tearing of loyalties that he and his people felt when he turned his back on what once had been religiously precious to his family and reinforced by filial affection.[46]

Other *Voices* offered other equally intensely personal reasons for leaving. Martha Armstrong, her pen dipped in the inkpot of pain, wrote: "With Foy Wallace[47] in the pulpit, I simply could not stand it any longer. I had to leave. I must, for conscience's sake, leave the Church of Christ.... I left in order to be a free woman in Christ."[48] Logan Fox, an educator (especially in Japan) and a psychologist, took a psychological approach, decrying the Church's "almost paranoid certainty" in its affirmation of being the "one and only true church."[49] J.P. Sanders, himself a blind person, a social activist, and servant of the blind, who left the churches

---

[43] One may wonder whether some ASHFSD-type Preachers and Elders might not be content to see the EPBS/TODD types go. Like Benedict XVI, who foresees a loss of membership during his reign over the Catholic Church, ASHFSD-types prefer a leaner, meaner, more obedient church. See the comment of John Waddey in fn 37, above. As one ASHFSD type sourly commented of the "Voices of Canadian Concern," in this volume, "They're whiny."

[44] Robert Meyers, editor of the volume, confessed to being a "pure-blood" Church-of-Christer: He had read and internalized "all the literature"; he could "vanquish any of my childhood playmates with barrages of proof texts;" he had notebooks full of debaters' points against "sectarians," including answers to "thirty-six arguments made by Baptists who believed in the impossibility of apostasy." He had attended Freed-Hardeman College, "a Church of Christ Bible school in Tennessee," because preachers from Abilene Christian College preached about "love" too much and were not doctrinally "sound"— "Above all else, I wanted to be sound." But then, in the Armed Forces during World War II, Meyers got to know Adventists and Presbyterians "whose devotion to Christ put mine to shame.... Suddenly, my beautifully structured world began to crumble." (248-250).

[45] *Idem*: 115.

[46] *Idem*: 119-121, 245.

[47] Foy Wallace, an infamous denomination skinner, but see Terry Gardner, "The Influence of Foy E. Wallace, Jr.," in this volume.

[48] Meyers (1966): 227, 230.

[49] *Idem*: 14.

of Christ to become ordained in the Disciples of Christ, wrote about mercy and compassion, the triumph of "life-giving spirit over the dead letter," and opposition to "literalism" in scripture study as a way to establish ecclesiastical and spiritual norms. He specifically invalidated the Restoration Plea:

> Restorationism is the effort to catch an historical process at one moment of its evolution and to fossilize it at that point for eternal duplication. Literal interpretation, at the most, can hope to resurrect only the corpse from the past; the experimental, fluid, and dynamic life is too elusive for such capture…. Why should the church of the twentieth century want to be like the one of the first?[50]

For the *Concerned Voices,* motivating factors tended to the intellectual and professional: Norman Parks, a Social Scientist, wrote about the Church of Christ sociologically: "Viewed sociologically, the Church of Christ is far advanced on the sect-denomination continuum,…a lower middle class phenomenon 'on the make' at its socio-economic level…. Viewed either sociologically or scripturally, the Church of Christ is not the church of Christ."[51] Thomas P. Hardeman, an ex-preacher turned philosopher and project director of social services, told the story of his exodus out of the Church's ministry and into the service of fellow humans, *finally* "doing the Lord's work."[52] Because a good philosopher must pay attention to formal logic, Hardeman dismantled the non-biblical logic of doctrine that supports patternism, defined as a type of religious scholasticism that establishes doctrine through appeal to (a) direct commands in scripture, (b) apostolic examples, and (c) necessary inferences deemed to be binding on Christians.[53] Carl Etter, an educator (especially in Japan) and scholar, who became a Congregationalist, enumerated 20 specific reasons for his leaving, including the defective "educational program of the Church of Christ…unwilling to trust the youth of the church with the facts of life and religion."[54]

For still others, spiritual hunger and thirst led them away in search of assuagement: Cecil L. Franklin, having a greater "reverence for truth" than for settled opinion, desiring to be a Christian without having to be a fundamentalist, and sensing himself an heir of "almost two thousand years of Christian history, in many countries, among peoples of many tongues and races," concluded that "to cut ourselves off from any of this heritage is to impoverish ourselves."[55] He was ordained a priest in the Episcopal Church. Ralph Milton Stolz received an experiential outpouring of the Holy Spirit on Saturday morning, October 19, 1963, and like thousands of other members of the churches of Christ caught up in the highly ecumenical Charismatic Movement of the 1960s and '70s, he left the Church to find fellowship with Christians of any stripe who worship "in the Spirit" as well as "in the mind also." Still a Restorationist, Stolz wrote: "The one dominant identifying characteristic of the early church was not its name, or its organization, or even its ritual of worship. It was its supernatural witness."[56] Laurie Hibbett, who became an Episcopalian, wrote her essay sitting in the "perfect stillness" of a Neo-Gothic church, "facing the cross." She remembered the drab architecture of

[50] *Idem*: 39.
[51] *Idem*: 71, 73, 84.
[52] *Idem*: 95.
[53] *Idem*: 97.
[54] *Idem*: 105.
[55] *Idem*: 184.
[56] *Idem*: 202, 213.

the buildings of the churches of Christ, the absence of the cross, "no time for meditation," the starring role of the preacher at "dead center stage, the sole performer."[57] Margaret O'Dowd, wife of a famous preacher, after all those years of hearing the same ol' sermons and the same ol' sermon illustrations, and sitting at the bedside of dying church members fearful of going into eternity because their church attendance had not been as regular as it might have been, found that she had "lost her fervor." "The tradition of our infallibility" and "our empty legalisms" had become as "sounding brass or a tinkling cymbal, words with no life, a form with no spirit.... Every time I read my New Testament...there arose perfect pictures of the Pharisees in almost everything my brethren did."[58] Sister Margaret, trading legalism and fearfulness for grace and assurance, decided to stay home from church.

These diverse essays represent not only individualized unhappiness with "Church-of-Christism" (the book's subtitle) but also a common perspective in airing a long, long list of dirty ecclesiastical laundry: Almost all of the *Concerned Voices* uttered a collective dismay over the self-righteousness of "the-one-and-only" sectarian exclusivism of the churches of Christ, and the Church's commensurate lack of "not-the-only-Christians" Restorationist ecumenism.[59] They also questioned ritual immersion in water as the exclusive sign of one's acceptability to God;[60] verbal inerrancy of the Bible, and the use of "patternism"[61] or "literalism"—a myopic and superficial reading of scripture[62] that leads to "majoring in minors," the over-insistence on some first-century religious behaviors such as *a cappella* singing[63] and keeping women silent at church,[64] but failure to find meaning in other religious behaviors evident in the biblical canon, such as foot-washing, the holy kiss, healing, laying-on of hands, among others;[65] putting one's faith in the Bible rather than in the Savior and the Spirit to whom the Bible points;[66] an inadequate doctrine of grace,[67] and a superficial grasp of many other Christian doctrines and practices;[68] legalism—using the biblical canon as a code of rules and regulations, a "plan of salvation" and "works righteousness" by which to control human behavior and morality in the attempt to avoid the displeasure of God;[69] the doctrine peculiar to traditional churches of Christ

---

[57] *Idem*: 50-51.

[58] *Idem*: 148-149.

[59] *Idem*: 14, 23, 43-44, 51f, 104, 106-107, 122-125, 132, 180f, 198f, 222-225, 232, 240, 248-250, 256f. Margaret O'Dowd focused on the words of Christ in Luke 9:49-50, which one almost never hears in a Church of Christ sermon: In response to the report of the disciples that someone who was "not one of us" was using Jesus' name to cast out devils, Jesus replied, "Do not stop him, for whoever is not against you is on your side." (152.)

[60] Meyers (1966): 17-18.

[61] *Idem*: 77f, 197f, 238-239, 243.

[62] *Idem*: 105.

[63] *Idem*: Ralph Graham: "There is positively and absolutely no Scriptural warrant whatever for opposing instrumental music in the worship or in forbidding any other artistic talent's use for the glory of God....The Bible does not teach that human initiative and spontaneity motivated by adoration of God are to be penalized or outlawed as unscriptural." (133, and see 194-196, 221, 241)

[64] *Idem*: 62-64, 133, 135.

[65] *Idem*: 18-19, 38, 57, 74, 138, 219f.

[66] *Idem*: 132, 203-213.

[67] *Idem*: 54f, 118.

[68] *Idem*: 104.

[69] *Idem*: 40-43, 75f, 109, 134, 153.

that the Holy Spirit works "through the Word only" (i.e. through the Bible);[70] a refusal to see the Restoration Movement as a man-made historical event no better and no worse than other church-historical moments;[71] fear of advanced learning;[72] inflexibility and authoritarianism of the leadership;[73] heresy hunting that strangles the liberty of individual consciousness and stifles free speech;[74] social and intellectual irrelevance; placing dogma—as did the Pharisees—above justice and compassion;[75] and the Restoration Movement's inevitable failure of essential purpose both in principle and practice: "The ideal church can never be restored because it never existed."[76]

Since these dissident *Voices* shouted their concerns in 1966, other voices have continued to indict the churches of Christ in similar ways. Many of the same "Unbiblical Doctrines" listed above have been up-dated on the web by a new generation of ex-Church-of-Christ members.[77]

Perhaps the most heart-rending statement of Why-I-Left is the story of Wendle Scott, a *gringo* teacher and minister to Tex-Mex *braceros* in "the Valley" of South Texas. Against the warning of administrators at Abilene Christian College, Wendle had married Maria Cano, a Mexican. By 1966, supported in part by the Highland Church of Christ in Abilene, Wendle was training church leaders at a small school in McAllen, and Maria had birthed their five children. When, however, Wendle took part in a march in favor of fair wages for *braceros*, he ran afoul of the Highland Church Eldership. Speaking for the Elders, Dr. R. W. Varner required that Scott take no further part in such "communist-led" demonstrations. Wendle remembered the conversation, quoting from his notes: "Dr. Varner never asked, he demanded, and very emphatically at that. After the

---

[70] *Idem*: 54f, 203-213.

[71] *Idem*: 19-20, 28f, 53, 56, 140, 261.

[72] William Floyd, a Speech teacher, lamented the poor preparation of preachers by asking, "Why do our 'brightest' leave?" His own answer: "…education as propaganda! The bright young men, sooner or later, begin to wonder what there is to a faith that needs such cloistered protection." (Meyers (1966): 157, and see 22, 79, 106, 108, 185-186, 190, 216-220, 232.)

[73] *Idem*: 76, 80-84, 133, 157-162, 262; William Floyd described the non-democratic governance of churches of Christ as "preacher worship" (170-174); Charles Warren called it the "divine right of the Elders" (196f); Martha Armstrong drew out a detailed comparison between the pre-Vatican II authoritarianism of "Romanism" and the abiding attitude of traditional "Church of Christism" (233).

[74] *Idem*: 104, 133-134, 172-173, 192, 243-244.

[75] *Idem*: William Floyd: As with many of the 19th-century followers of Campbell on the slavery question, so "the Church of Christ…placed itself on the sidelines of the greatest moral struggle of our times. Without exception, every one of our southern Christian colleges…waited until it was safe before they [racially] integrated. And when they finally integrated (mildly), they blew trumpets and waved flags and sent articles to newspapers announcing their courage and humanitarianism! All this, to their everlasting shame, after they had worked for years to stave off integration as long as possible." (164f. and see 44-47, 60, 74, 134-135, 158-159, 165-170, 186-187.)

[76] *Idem*: 135: Ralph Graham: "The actual church as described in the New Testament did not have a uniform organization, worship, practice, or faith, in all its congregations. The actual church was plagued by heresies, divisions, immoralities, ignorance, indifference, apostasy, and weakness. It has never ceased to be thus plagued. Since it neither disappeared nor ceased being, it is not an object of restoration."(see 31, 40, 57, 104, 137-139.)

[77] http://ex-churchofchrist.com/unbiblicalCoC.htm

march was over and I met with the Highland elders, they also demanded. In that meeting I was demeaned and insulted, mostly by their spokesman, Dr. Varner."[78]

This confrontation with Elders obsessed with their own authority and demanding that church members "obey the Elders," points to the Achilles' heel of Church-of-Christ polity. Ornery Elders, considered to be qualified for office principally in terms of the number of their baptized children, become addicted to uncontested authority and behave as though they were infallible. Dusty Owens faulted the Church of Christ for its Catholic-like self-congratulation at being "the one true church" and investing the Eldership with papal infallibility.[79]

At the opposite end of the liberal-to-conservative spectrum, Wayne Goforth, spokesman on behalf of anti-institutionalism among churches of Christ, charged the Church of Christ with the same flaw that destroyed Wendle Scott's ministry and Maria's life.

> We were informed that once a "game plan" had been drawn up by the sponsoring church for the Arizona work, we were to never "circumvent their plan." Which, they told me, meant that once they had reached a decision about what the church in Arizona was to do, we were not to change anything ("even if found harmful") until the elders at the sponsoring church approved of it first.[80]

Church-of-Christ congregations and lectureships, colleges and universities, theologians and editors seem paralyzed in their inability either to reform this abuse of power or to restore the ideal expressed by Jesus that spiritual authority belongs to one who is the greater servant, not to those who "lord it over" the little flock of Jesus (Mk10:41-45 and parallels).

Canadian voices of concern[81] tend to speak with the softer "eh?" of the Canadian accent, but they are likewise tinged with leaver's "liberalism," and they make many of the same points that dissident Yanks have made. Some of the Canadians left the Church in Ontario in search of,

[78] Read the full account in the collection of letters, news reports, and other documents and texts compiled and commented upon by Don Haymes in his brilliant online book, *Race and the Church of Christ*, to be found within the equally brilliant online collection of documents, about the Stone-Campbell Restortion Movement, managed by Hans Rollmann, co-editor of this volume: http://www.mun.ca/rels/restmov/texts/race/haymes41.html. Don concludes his commentary with these words: "Scott thereafter became a Church-of-Christ agnostic, doing literary battle with all forms of organized religion.... His wife, Maria, ill in body and wounded in spirit, caught in an unbearable dissonance with her husband and her Church and her people, ended her life by suicide. The tragedy of Wendle Scott is the tragedy of the Churches of Christ. While it is true that no white minister of the Churches of Christ marched from Selma to Montgomery, it is also true that Wendle Scott marched from Rio Grande City to San Juan. For that he should be celebrated as a hero. The tragedy is that he marched alone, and alone he is still marching. May God have mercy."
[79] Dusty Owens, "Why I Left the Church of Christ." *The Examiner* 8/6 (Nov. 1993). (Chattanooga, Tennessee, Truth and Freedom Ministry, 2000): See http://www. theexaminer.org/volume8/ number6/leftcoc.htm, also listed creeping denominationalism, everlasting quarrelsomeness and divisiveness, meddlesome moralizing, and preoccupation with church buildings, among others. Owens would solve "the woman problem" by solving the "church building problem." "Arguments today over whether women can speak out in the assembly dissipate when the group meets in a private house. *There* women readily participate and no one objects."
[80] Anthony Goforth, "Why I Left," *Guardian of Truth* 30 (15 May 1986): 296 or "Why I Left the 'Institutional Position' (Why I Left the Institutional Church of Christ)" and found on several anti-institutional websites, *e.g.*, http://www.friendlyval.com/Ed/why i left.htm and http://www.thebiblespeaks.com/Articles/FalseTeachings/Denominationalism/Institution.htm
[81] See Melanie Wright and others, "Voices of Canadian Concern," a book-within-the-book, in this volume.

as they say, "something more." With equal personal passion and with the same finality, however, these Canadians have left and they are not coming back: Several of them employ the metaphor of a spiritual "journey" along a road that goes forever on. This representative group of nine leavers runs the sociological gamut from "ordinary member" to religious professional, from a working-class housewife to a university professor, and includes even a high-ranking member of the Ontario Provincial judiciary. Others who were invited to write—EBPS/TODD types, perhaps—declined, saying, "It's all still too painful." The struggling Church of Christ in Ontario has been no more successful than is the much larger sister denomination south of the border at keeping and challenging a significant number of those who could give it the leadership it lacks.[82]

The Charismatics

The liberal defection from "Church-of-Christism" marked by a book in 1966 was matched by the charismatic defection marked by another literary landmark of collective testimony in 1971.[83] The very title of *The Acts of the Holy Spirit in the Churches of Christ Today* carries poignant ironies in its blatant assault on one of the main dogmas of the "through-the-word-only" Church of Christ that teaches the impossibility of a new *Book of Acts* because "miracles have ceased." Charismatic gifts and their results—so traditional Church-of-Christ preachers nearly unanimously preached throughout 20th century—were 1st-century phenomena not to be "restored" in later centuries because they belonged exclusively to the "apostolic era." Any such miracle would be falsely so-called, and would be, instead, either a magical trick, a psychological effect, or a "lying wonder of the devil," for whereas the devil is powerfully at large, "like a roaring lion, seeking whom he may devour," the influence of the Holy Spirit is said to be bottled up in a book.[84] In the 1960s and after, however, when the pan-denominational Charismatic Movement swept through all of American Christendom, it did not by-pass the churches of Christ. With roots in many traditions, from 2nd-century Montanism (as LeMoine Lewis used to say, "the first Restoration Movement") to American Revivalism, African-American religion, and the Azusa Street Meeting from which denominational Pentecostalism arose, this "Third Force in Christendom" also had one of its remote springs in the Cane Ridge Meeting of Restorationist fame. Whether they wanted to be or not, the churches of Christ were swept by the irresistible Spirit into the broad tradition of the Great Church.

---

[82] Like the Canadians, perhaps the most numerous acts of "leaving" are committed these days without fanfare and simply in search of "something more." Evidence on the internet for low-key leaving is abundant: David P. Crews, http://www.newrational.com/joy/; Edward Fudge Ministries, http://www.edwardfudge.com/ and GracEmail Ministry, http://www.edwardfudge.com/; Cecil Hook, http://www.freedomsring.org/; Ex Church of Christ Support Group, http://www.ex-churchofchrist.com/.

[83] *The Acts of the Holy Spirit in the Churches of Christ Today* (Los Angeles: Full Gospel Business Men's Fellowship International, 1971), a set of essays by Preachers and Elders, mostly, but also by one famous song-leader, Pat Boone (p. 13). I find it curious that no women contributed to the volume, since charismatic religion—unlike one-book religion--is no respecter of gender.

[84] Jim Miller, *Is the Church of Christ Really* THE *Church of Christ? (Confession of an Ex-Campbellite)*. Brenham, Texas: J-M Publications (post 1963), "Tract no. 73-1," 6 pp. (ACU/CRS): http://www.bible.acu.edu/crs/ItemDetail.asp?Bookmark=1974, is, among other things, a defense of the continuation of the charismatic work of the Holy Spirit after the so-called "Apostolic Age."

Joe E. Lewis's self-published statement[85] is simultaneously a book-length account of the discovery of his charismatic spirituality, a narrative of the resulting subtle persecution he endured at the hands of Church-of-Christ folk, and his Why-I-Left farewell. A spirit of intentional kindness flavors the book with Lewis's pious desire not to offend Church-of-Christ sensitivities. Although Lewis had been singing in a Presbyterian choir for decades by the time he wrote, he included the Why-I-Left *de rigueur* recitation of his Church-of-Christ pedigree and an addendum of "Church of Christ Ministers & Evangelists that Touched My Life." The plot thickens, however, with his detailed narrative of firings from two Christian colleges on account of his charismatic experiences. After the initial "baby rattle" stage of charismatic excitement, wrote Lewis, living the charismatic Christian life had matured into awareness and experience of a divine and loving Presence, manifest through the struggles of his family's life as a "Spirit of Healing," "Spirit of Inspiration," "Spirit of Visions of Prophecies," and a Heavenly "Partner" who helped Joe, Mary Ruth, and their children make it through.[86]

James Ash, Sr., a leader in a Church of Christ in Dallas in the late-1960s, has now, in advancing years, become an advanced and consistent charismatic theologian, more muscular than ever in his charismatic leadership. At the time of this writing, he is publishing a newsletter serialization of his experiences, "A Breakthrough Worth Writing About," communicating ecumenically across all lines with other Spirit-led people, and advocating what he calls "the coming Laymen's movement, which will originate from the pew, not the pulpit," and which, he says, has been prophesied to him: "Those in the pew who will hear His voice and respond to his call will be trained, equipped, prepared, ordained and anointed by God Himself *to do every work Jesus did during His visible ministry and yes, even greater works than He did.*"(emphasis belongs to Ash.)[87]

One characteristic effect of the Charismatic Movement is rampant ecumenism. The sense is that, no matter how wobbly a person's doctrinal logic may be, one cannot deny the Christian identity of anyone who, with hands uplifted and "filled with the Holy Spirit," is praising the name of Jesus in a rapture of prayer to the Father. This ecumenical readiness, combined with the exhilaration of spiritual rebirth and freedom, when met by traditional Church-of-Christ dogmatism and resistance, has predetermined that most actively charismatic Church-of-Christ members would inevitably leave to find their ecclesiastical home where they are welcome.[88]

---

[85] Joe E. Lewis, *Leaving the Faith of My Fathers: A Spiritual Journey* (Atlanta: Joe E. Lewis, 2001): 188-193. This book is not available in bookstores. Order from the author, $15.00: joelewis304@bellsouth.net

[86] See Joe E. Lewis, "A Charismatic Christian: One Generation Later," in this volume.

[87] Jim Ash, Sr., *Now Concerning Spiritual Things* (Part Six, April 20, 2005): 4. email: jimashsr@juno.com. A Spirit-led "laymen's movement," one must observe, has been underway in Third-World Christendom for a generation, and for longer than that in various radical Spiritual movements.

[88] *The Acts* (1971): 10. Ben Franklin, a California preacher, wrote that he tried to remain in the Church of Christ, "but found it difficult to serve the Lord as we wished, since it was almost impossible to lead others to Him and then have them exposed to teaching from the pulpit and classroom that was adverse to a complete Gospel." Two others contributors to *Acts of the Holy Spirit* (1971), William Epperson (p. 36) and Dwyatt Gantt (p. 29), had been part of the Church-of-Christ exodus to Toronto (see Melanie Wright and others, "Voices of Canadian Concern," in this volume, for essays by former members of this now defunct congregation). One of the main pressures on the Yanks in Toronto was that all but one of them, having become actively charismatic, became *persona non grata* among their Church-of-Christ families and

Only a few Church-of-Christ congregations are now obviously charismatic, though many more have been subtly influenced. Wherever women now participate in public worship and the music seems spontaneous and "house church" replaces "Wednesday-night prayer meeting," one may detect shy hints in traditional churches of Christ of "the daughter of the Voice" echoing a previous rush of wings of the Heavenly Dove.[89]

The Anti-Institutionalists

It all started in the 1950s with a quarrel over whether it be scriptural to have a kitchen in the church house, that early warning of the Social Gospel. Even before the liberals and charismatics began to leave by ones and twos in the 1960s, the anti-cooperationist split had been gaining momentum with its opposition to any church-related activity (*e.g.*, orphan homes, the *Herald of Truth* national radio program) that was carried on at an organizational level beyond the local congregation and its Eldership. By the end of the millennium, the anti-institutional churches of Christ (as they had come to be known) had withdrawn fellowship from the mainline churches, carrying away an estimated one-quarter of the congregations and one-third of the membership of the *a cappella* Church of Christ. Yet one more time, the Restorationist tradition, enacting its hermeneutics of a silent Bible, had redefined itself negatively by clarifying what it does not do: "We don't baptize babies, we don't use instrumental music, we don't have Sunday School, we don't drink from many communion cups, we don't have a pastor system, we don't support Christian colleges" and now—in a reaffirmation of opposition to Digression like that of the Disciples—"We don't function through any institutional structure larger than the local congregation or managerial frame more complex than the local Eldership."

This next-to-latest denominational dissolution of the Restoration Movement now accurately denominates the mainline churches as "the institutional Church of Christ," an increasingly interconnected denominational network that involves the widespread activity of individuals and congregations in and through organized bodies other than individual congregations under the oversight of local Elders. These biblically unpatterned institutions include not only orphan homes and media evangelism but "sponsoring churches" that funnel "the Lord's money" into variously organized missionary and charitable efforts, professional and higher education, social-gospel adventures such as the House of the Carpenter and Shiloh,[90] and expenditure of church funds for purposes other than evangelism, worship, and care of the saints.[91] Further indictments by the Antis of the Institutionalists include their

---

associates in the Lower Forty-eight. Epperson became an Episcopalian and now teaches at Oral Roberts University in Tulsa.

[89] Also in *The Acts* (1971), Forrest Wells, "a full-time Elder" at the Exodus/Bayshore-West Islip Church of Christ, reported his experience of the "baptism in the Holy Spirit." Freda Elliott Baker, "The Inner-City Faith Corps," in this volume, refers to Elder Wells's charismatic conversion; see also Dwain Evans, "A Memoir," and Erma Jean Loveland, "The Genesis of an Exodus," both in this volume.

[90] See Freda Elliott Baker, "The Inner City Faith Corps," in this volume.

[91] Dan Huddleston, "Why I Left Institutionalism," *Preceptor* 41 (1 June 1992): 160 or *Guardian of Truth* 36/14 (16 July 1992): 6-7: "We could see that it was not a matter of opinion, but a matter of faith. There is no [biblical] authority for general benevolence. There is no authority for the church to establish, to fund from the treasury, and to pool funds from several churches to run institutions such as hospitals, orphan homes, old folks' homes, unwed mother's [sic] homes, etc. There is no authority for the sponsoring church with its pooling of funds from other churches and its centralization of power. There is no authority for one church to make decisions for another church, nor for them to hold the deed to the property of another church.

forsaking of the old paths of Restorationism, permissiveness towards instrumental music, undermining belief in and practice of immersion by admitting unimmersed "members" and practicing "open membership," being corrupted by the Charismatic Movement to believe in the direct and miraculous work of the Holy Spirit, free grace, and—above all—tolerating a changed view of the Bible. The over-arching issue for the anti-institutional Church of Christ is the nature and use of scripture: "The problem is that of authority."[92] Whereas the liberals and charismatics criticized the mainline denomination for being too conservative, the Antis criticize the Church of Christ (Institutional) for being too liberal.

Wayne Goforth, speaking for most Antis, has probably declared with finality the anti-institutionalist split from the mainline Church. A cladistic shove along the seismic rift of biblical authority appears to have made this ecclesiological subduction deep, wide, and irreparable:

> This will most likely be the last generation of conservative-institutionals, those we have a chance of reaching, because we have a common understanding of [biblical] authority. The new line up do not understand the nature and need of authority, and thus we have no common ground with them.[93]

The International Churches of Christ (ICOC)

Kip McKean, the acknowledged leader of the ICOC proclaimed: "The mainline Church of Christ is dead."[94] His cultic followership of Why-I-Left dissidents shouted an enthusiastic amen, and the late-20th century "Boston Movement," a.k.a. "the Crossroads Movement," a.k.a. the "discipling movement," a.k.a. the International Churches of Christ" was born.[95] Not long after--Why-I-Left being ever a two-way thoroughfare—ICOC dissidents were writing their own passionate farewells to the Church-of-Christ cult movement. What had begun in the 1980s as an earnest effort to reform and enliven the mainline churches of Christ,[96] came to the same end as

---

There is no authority for church kitchens, church gymnasiums, church funded camps, church funded ball teams, or for any church sponsored or church funded recreation or entertainment."-

[92] *Ibid.*: 6. Terence Sheridan, "Why I Left Institutionalism," *Focus Magazine's Web Companion* (post 1994): *http://www.focusmagazine.org/Articles/Institutionalism.htm* connected the main issue of biblical authority with materialism and secularism in the Church: "I can only view the megachurch phenomenon as being the logical end of institutional practices. When a church decides to melt into the social fabric of the surrounding society by focusing on social issues (civic charity, recreation, politics, secular education, etc.), it becomes no more than a civic club paying lip service to Jesus. Institutionalism is a spiritual distraction which opens the door for spiritual decay...." Brian Yeager, "Why I Left Institutionalism," *Preceptor* 50 (September 1, 2001): 262: http://www. wordsoftruth.net/ whyileftliberalism.htm, or *Watchman Magazine* IV/8 (August 2001): http://www.watchmanmag.com/ 0408/040823.htm or likewise "filed...most of [the] issues under biblical authority," working within the framework of what he called the "New Testament Law." Accordingly, he concluded that "the Lord's money" (a term that he uses without defining it) may be spent by a congregation on no charitable action that does not benefit Christians, that is to say, whereas individual Christians may expend charity towards anyone in the world, the church itself is to care only for its own.

[93] Goforth (1986): last paragraph.

[94] Kip McKean, *The Movement of God* (ICOC.org: 1994).

[95] http://www.reveal.org/ ; http://www.tolc.org/ .

[96] See Kip McKean, *First Principles* (Woburn, Massachusetts.: DPI, 1993) and numerous other writings and recorded addresses: http://www.newcovpub.com/icc/quotes.htm, http://www.freendeed.org/, and www. RightCyberUp.org.

all the other fragments of this religion founded in leaving: a steady state of shock and dismay over mutual rejection.

The basic doctrinal insight of the ICOC—relatively accurate, as most basic doctrinal insights of most Anti splits have tended to be—is that too many members of the Church of Christ had not been properly "discipled" (thoroughly instructed and committed to following Jesus) before they were baptized (The Church's practice of "adult baptism" had slipped to "believer's baptism," and that can take place at quite an early age). According to Church-of-Christ logic, then, anyone insufficiently "discipled" before baptism needed to be baptized again (that is to say, properly baptized for the first time), just like any other denominationalist who had not been scripturally "discipled" and then immersed. The ICOC had landed a blow on the chin on the practice of the mainline Church of Christ's most precious doctrine, believer's immersion.

For about a decade, the ICOC enjoyed phenomenal growth in numbers and expansion to many cities and countries: The ICOC was what the church of the first century had been, not an established part of the suburban social order but a missionary movement. These evangelistic results came, however, at a high price. As acknowledged in ICOC publications and as alleged in Why-I-Left statements of ex-ICOC members, the ICOC became a well-oiled machine under the heavy-handed hierarchical controls of McKean and his curia. "Recruitment quotas" were imposed on church leaders, pushing them to the usual cult excesses of "heavenly deception"(ruses, pretensions, and seductions made moral in the service of "the Cause") to gain converts, raise funds, and all the rest so familiar to students of the late-20th-century cult phenomenon of "new religions."[97] The ICOC was the Church of Christ on steroids—what the Restoration Movement might have looked like had it been invented by Sun Myung Moon or L. Ron Hubbard instead of by Alexander Campbell and B. W. Stone.

The massive amounts of criticism on the internet of the ICOC, Why-I-Left statements by the dozens, and reliable gossip suggest that the days of the ICOC may be numbered. Rumors abound: Some say that ICOC leaders are "going down front to confess that they have said and done things unbecoming to a Christian"; others say that Kip McKean is alive and well in Portland, Oregon, and gathering his churches once more under his wings. The ICOC as a dissident movement within the Restoration Movement, however, seems to be having a shorter half-life than most Anti splinter groups have done. Stay tuned for late-breaking news!

For all its post-Yuppie qualities as "Power Restoration," the ICOC was, in fact, a New-Age version of old-fashioned Anti-ism. The ICOC founders had realized with equal clarity what the anti-institutionalism group had seen: The Church-of-Christ church had eased into bourgeois denominationhood. The ICOC's focus on a single but telling proof-text—Mt 28:19, "the Great Commission," that requires people to be "discipled" before they are baptized—hit a nerve. Despite waves of Exoduses, numerous reformations in various directions by assorted anti movements, invasive Pietism and Evangelicalism, applied charismatics, Christian College

---

[97] Susan McGunnigle Condon, Why I left the Boston Movement (International Church of Christ): The Emperor's New Clothes, Fort Worth, Texas: Star Bible Publications, 1991; Marion D. Owens, Time to Go: A New Look at the Boston Movement. Fort Worth: Star Publications, 1995; and "Why I Left the Boston Movement," *Gospel Advocate* 137 (Dec. 1, 1995): 27, and other statements on websites: http://www.reveal.org/; http://www.tolc.org/; and http://rightcyberup.org/index.html: *RightCyberUp: Recovery from the International Churches of Christ (ICC)*.

education, and psychologization of the gospel by doctored and degreed pastoral counselors, and a soft sell by radio and TV "personalities," the hearts of benumbed Church-o'-Christchurchers at the turn of the century and the millennium cried out for "something more."[98]

The Last to Leave

When I was a preacher in rural churches of Christ in Texas, my duties as the last to leave included turning off the lights and locking the door. So many have left, and others might as well have left for many reasons—is it time, now, to turn off the lights and lock the door?

Our Why-I-Left essayists have taught us important lessons that point towards this very course of action. After two centuries of jangling fissiparity, if we have any sense of history at all, we ought to realize by now that the Stone-Campbell approach both to Christian unity and to restoration of the "ancient order" has brought us no closer today to a unified Christendom than we were two centuries ago, for we ourselves have spawned a dozen and more new "one true churches," each ready to anathematize the others. Now, our entrenched doctrinal scholasticism, biblical casuistry, and denominational mechanisms keep us from "restoring" anything new or better. Our movement has not worked, does not work, shall never work. Any argument to the contrary puts one in mind of that pop definition of insanity: doing the same thing over and over again but expecting a different result, this time.

Let us realize that we never could have restored "the first-century church" because it was many churches, not a church. Which of those churches ought we to have restored? The Jewish-Christian one that still kept the Law and worshiped in the Temple? The Corinthian charismatic church? One of the incipient Gnostic churches of Syria or Alexandria? The church in Rome? Any of some other types about which we know little or nothing? The historic culture of which these first-century churches were a religious expression, is gone, forever gone; therefore, the religion that made sense in that culture is no longer possible.

And if the first-century church *per se* is unrestorable, what of specific doctrines and practices? Did everyone believe about Jesus in the same way? The Gospels (canonical and non-canonical alike) make clear that they did not. Were all immersed "in the name of the Father and of the Son and of the Holy Ghost?" We do not know that they were. Did all worship alike? How could they? The Jerusalem church worshiped daily in the Temple as well as in house churches, whereas the gentile Christians developed Sunday rituals. Did James and Paul believe alike about justification and the Law? Clearly not. About the only thing that all first-century Christians had in common was an indefinite loyalty to the name of Jesus, whom they understood in a variety of ways. That kind of unity Christendom has ever had, and still does, without need or benefit of restorationism.

Restorationists have built a Jurassic Park of religion, trying to get a dinosaur of specific religion back into our world through the genetic engineering of Bible study, but the dinosaurs of first-century Christendom cannot survive in the twenty-first century. The literary echo of that lost religion, as fine a thing as the Christian canon may be, cannot be a basis either for "unity" or "restoration," for if church history has demonstrated anything at all, it has made plain that agreement premised on our reading and understanding alike the fragments of scripture is not

---

[98] See http://www.exchristian.org/. In our New Age of religious exotica, people leave the Church of Christ for a greater range of destinations than they did 50 years ago, including Wicca, paganism, feminism, and anywhere else that seems to offer fresh air and freedom.

humanly possible. All the vain philosophy of human logic in the world—commands, examples, and inferences—cannot compel agreement in the interpretation of literary texts. Turning the Why-I-Left searchlight on ourselves turns me into some kind of "Campbellite atheist." The motion has gone out of the Movement; our daring but overly optimistic 200-year-long experiment in reductionism has ended in collapse; our enterprise, wrong from the start, fails of essential purpose because of a definitional tautology: "Restorationism" itself is not biblical, so it cannot, therefore, restore "the first-century church" in this or any century.[99] To speak of "the restoration of the New Testament church" is to speak where the Bible is silent, and to call a non-biblical thing by a non-biblical name. We ought to practice what we preach in this matter, and resort to "biblical silence."

What, then, ought we to do? Recognizing that we already have more churches in the world than anybody needs, I propose that we take the honorable step and follow the lead of our Cane Ridge forebears: Let us commit ecclesiasticide! Let us "will that this body"—these Stone-Campbellite, 19th- and 20th-century, sectarian bodies—"die, be dissolved, and sink into union with the Body of Christ at large."

If you, Dear Reader, prefer a different course, you may choose another option. You may choose to "go to the church of your choice," and you may choose to go to one of a number of different "churches of Christ." Whether hard-line, mainline, over-the-line, or out-of-line, you may suit your church to your taste, for congregational autonomy insures variety.[100] In the arch and subtle wit of Patricia Summerlin Martin, "I believe that one can be a member of the Church of Christ and be saved"—though I acknowledge it to be hard, very hard.

The easy way to go for Church-of-Christ culture Christians is to affirm our Southern comfort in religion, sing the "good ol' gospel songs," take pride in a preference for *a cappella* music, and attend one's Christian college reunions loyally. Our Christian rabbis of one-book religion will continue to parse *baptizo* and *psallo* to our sole satisfaction, and we can rely on knowledge of the Bible to stand us in good stead on the Day of Judgment. Those who find this kind of religion exhilarating are welcome to it, but I myself have no taste for being a member of a post-Protestant, Pietist denomination of Evangelical Wheaties that has sold its soul to the Republican Party for a NeoCon mess of bourgeois *potage*.

I, for one, must have either "the one true church" or none at all, for I was poisoned in my cradle with a lust for radically pristine first-century Christianity. By the time I was 17, and a red-handed thief of books from the tract racks at the back of Catholic churches (they charged for theirs; we gave ours away for free), I had realized that it was "either us or them." Longing for historic continuity and the mystical unity of the Seamless Garment, I nevertheless learned at

---

[99] Roy Bowen Ward, "'The Restoration Principle': A Critical Analysis," *Restoration Quarterly* 8/4 http://www.restorationquarterly.org/Volume_008/rq00804ward.htm#N_4: "Nowhere does the NT provide explicit scriptural basis for the Restoration Principle—that is, there is no text within the NT which states explicitly that later generations should go "Back to the Bible," nor are there examples of this principle at work within the NT material (since the NT *qua* NT did not yet exist)."

[100] The radical friends of Don Haymes may find a renegade congregation of desperados now in just about every metropolitan area where Restorationist churches are numerous. See the mini-list of liberal churches:: http://ex-churchofchrist.com/biblioCoc.htm, a sign, perhaps, of incipient denominationalism: Bering Drive, Houston, TX; Cahaba Valley, Birmingham, AL; Macedonia, Florence, AL; Troy, Troy, MI; Oak Hills, San Antonio, TX, to which one would surely add, among others, the West Islip Church on Long Island , the Belmont Church in Nashville, and several congregations in California.

Harvard Divinity School that relativism and sectarianism are the permanent status quo in religion. Hanging out with Episcopalians and Catholics, moreover, soon disabused me of any romantic notion that history and tradition are any better than Bible or reason at shoring up Christendom. Both book-learning and experience, therefore, have made an Anti out of me: I am in moral agreement with the basic premises of most of the Antis of whatever stripe in their criticism of all mainline churches. As Don Haymes loves to say, "The Antis are always right, but for the wrong reasons."

The Restorationist plea is not only non-biblical, it is anti-biblical, and the concept itself is a gross, historic insult to the power and majesty of the Almighty and a contradiction of the promise of the resurrected Lord Jesus: "And lo, I am with you always, even until the End of Days." (Mt 28:29) The audacity and originally sinful self-importance of those 19th-century frontiersmen with their "one book" and their American optimism was sheer egoistic braggadocio. That they by dint of human reason and action could restore the Church that God Himself had somehow failed to sustain throughout the centuries—the very idea! We are a snarling breed of pups, nipping at one another's tails and ears, growling over the "one book" as though it were the torn blanket from our basket, but we come by our habits naturally. The post-Protestant spiritual DNA of the Northern Irish sectarian who whelped us flows in our veins. The Restoration Movement has ever been an ecclesiastical Belfast.

I stand with our Why-I-Left essayists to say—making the right point, this time, for the right reason—we have accepted the wrong authority. In our post-Protestant bibliolatry and rationalism, we have focused on book religion. Like the scribes, Pharisees, and doctors of the Law, we in our dependence on learned professors must also come under the judgment of Jesus, as reported in the Fourth Gospel: "You study the scriptures because in them you think you have eternal life, but these same scriptures testify to me, and yet you refuse to come to me for life!" (Jn 5:39) One cannot nit-pick one's way to Heaven. Nothing that has to be edited, translated, exegeted, interpreted, and numbered can possibly be required of anyone for salvation, for that places human authorities—rabbis and scholars—as squarely between the believer and God as popish priest craft ever did. The lame effort, then, of cobbling together some "Affirmation" or other to make some equally lame "Plan of Salvation" make sense to the people in the pews, is but further proof of the frailty of human religiosity. James and the Jewish Christians in Jerusalem tried to impose their biblicist legalism on gentile Christians, but to no avail. Every creed or affirmation written since James by Christians for Christians has done more to divide the church and put the Spirit to flight than it has done to unify and vivify the people of God.

As I recently said to Don Haymes, "It's all right to read the Bible, and it's all right to think about what we are doing." We must, of course, have our learned elite, up in their Hebrew and Greek, pouring over sacred texts; however, to confuse Bible-reading with spirituality, and to mistake a rationalized defense of sound doctrine for salvation, is to miss the Fisherman's Boat entirely. As our dear hymn sings, "Beyond the sacred page, we seek thee, Lord."[101] so must we seek not a dead letter in codified bodies of knowledge, but, rather, the Living Voice of the Life-giving Spirit who keeps speaking forever, saying to all the churches, faithful and unfaithful alike: "Come!"

---

[101] Mary Ann Lathbury, "Break Thou the Bread of Life," *Great Songs of the Church Number Two* (Louisville, Kentucky: Great Songs Press, 1937): no. 354.

One may begin in many ways to live a Spirit-led life, but eventually one adjustment to be made is to change one's notion of authority in religion from a book (the so-called canon of the so-called *New Testament*) to the very Source of that book, the Life-giving Spirit. Let us "call Bible things by Bible names!"—the 27-book Christian canon is not "the new testament:" The "new testament," according to Jesus himself, is not a book but a covenant between God and humanity effected in the blood of the Cross (Lk 22:20). Let us, therefore, "be silent where scripture is silent," and not refer to a book as "the New Testament." Paul never even saw a Gospel, and the Jewish Christians in Jerusalem did not think much of Paul's epistles, if they ever read one. Certainly, the first Christians read one another's mail (Col 4:16), though some people felt that reading other people's mail was dangerous (2 Pt 3:16), and some biblical writers tried to set the others straight (Lk 1:1-4). One old first-century saint, Papias, said he preferred "the living word" to written texts.

The *New Testament* (the book) began to be put together in the 2nd century and reached its full status as the 27-book canon that we know today only in the mid-4th century under the political maneuvering of Bishop Athanasius of Alexandria and the Emperor Constantine. The same folk who brought us one empire, one emperor, one bishop, one creed, one set of canon (church) laws, and one liturgy, also brought us one canonical Bible. Take one, take all, and you'll have restored yourself not a 1st-century church but an early 4th-century one.

Shall we, then, stop reading our Bibles? By no means! The Bible is the best reflection we have of Jesus & Co. But let us read *all* of the Early Christian scriptures, not just the ones approved by the Emperor and his Bishop. Let us read not only the four approved Gospels but also the *Gospel of Thomas* (as old or older than The Four, and just as inspired), and let us read the equally ancient fragments of the Jewish-Christian Gospels. Let us read Clement's letter to the Corinthians—Clement was as apostolic a man as was the author of *Luke-Acts*, and probably more apostolic than whoever wrote *2 Peter*. Let us read the *Didaché* (the *Teaching of the Twelve Apostles*) to see what church life was like at the end of the first century. All of these—and more—are "first-century" in their inspiration and content, and they have all been read from time to time as scripture somewhere in the Great Church. Let that oft-misapplied proof-text (2 Tm 3:16) speak with full, fresh meaning: "*All scripture* is inspired of God and is profitable...," so why not read it *all*?

Expanding the canon will expand your heart and mind, but reading more books is not the same as opening yourself to the leading of the Spirit. To do that, we Church-of-Christ folk need to repent of our blasphemy of the Holy Spirit. Our notion that "the Holy Spirit works through the word (the Bible) only," is our worst heresy, and too close for comfort to what Jesus pronounced "the unpardonable sin"(Mt 12:31-32). We are sick in soul and body because we have carped that body-healing, soul-saving, life-giving miracles are "lying works of the devil" rather than the work of the Holy Spirit. Here is a sin requiring great repentance.

The living, speaking, guiding, filling, empowering, wonder-working, inspiring Spirit who fell upon the first-century folk is ready to fall upon us, too, as that Spirit has fallen on the saints in every century. By breathing the same spiritual atmosphere that first-century Christians breathed, we shall be like them in the way that truly matters, not by way of imitation and attempted restoration, but by communion with and through God-with-us. The resulting "form of religion" may or may not be the same as it was in the first century--that's up to the Spirit!— but the "power thereof" will be the same power that Jesus sent to them and still sends to us.

Wherein does authority in the church lie? Wherein did Jesus *say* it lies?

Jesus said: I tell you solemnly, whatever you bind on earth shall be bound in Heaven; whatever you loose on earth shall be loosed in heaven. I tell you solemnly once again, if two of you on earth agree to ask anything at all, it will be granted to you by my Father in Heaven. For where two or three gather in my name, I shall be there with them." (Mt 18:18-20)

Did Jesus say that authority lies in a book or canon? No. In a creed or affirmation? No. In pope and council? No. In a Lectureship or Eldership? No. In "the Movement" or "the Brotherhood?" No. Jesus *said* that he would grant the power of the Father, the authority to bind and loose both in Heaven and on earth, directly to us, the church. All we have to do is agree and ask. The crucified and risen Christ, who has now become a life-giving Spirit, comes to us and abides with his worshipful body of believers. Jesus can ever be found among any little two- or three-member congregation living under the cross and in the all-creating power of the Holy Spirit.

The resurrected Lord Jesus is the head of all spiritual hierarchy, in Heaven, on earth, and under the earth (Col 2:9-10). When the Holy Spirit bears witness to our spirits that we are the children of God, we have everything we need (Gal 4:6). The presence of that Spirit permeates all churches, all religions, and the entire universe, for "everyone moved by the Spirit of God is a child of God" (Rm 8:14-17), and ever so many more than just we few are being moved by that Spirit. All of our puny little "one true churches" here on earth are merely gatherings of "brethren in error," but that's OK, so long as we have "the mind of Christ," Jesus' "Abba" for our Heavenly Father, and the One Spirit in and among us. When Jesus in the Spirit is with us, even though *we be brethren in error* (*Brethren in Error*—now *there's* an honest name for a church!), we are the one true church. As fragile and broken, spotted and spoiled as each of us and all of us may be, we are—all sects, all churches, and all religions in all cultures—"the one true church" under the guidance of the One Spirit.

Let us, therefore, the Whole Church of all the first-born ones who are led by that Spirit, join with prophets and apostles, seers and saints from all times and places and peoples, and unite with myriad choirs of angels met in festal celebration (Hb 12:22-23). Turn, please, to that fine old hymn by Brother G.M. Hopkins, and let us stand together and sing praises to our Creator: "Glory be to God for dappled things!"

What Has Happened to the Churches of Christ in Ontario?

Melanie W. Wright

If I were a Church-of-Christ insider, I might answer the question of this essay differently, but as a friendly outsider looking in, I may achieve at least minimal objectivity. Even though I was born into a Church-of-Christ family, and despite my occasional, earnest efforts to be helpful in my inherited setting, I have been—and continue to be—on the outside of the Churches of Christ in Ontario.

My earliest introduction to a real and true relationship with God came via my paternal grandmother. She and my grandfather lived in a modest house in small-town Ontario. From an early age, I would enjoy spending weeks with them. To reach the spare bedroom in the small upstairs of their house, I had to walk through their bedroom, and I vividly recall that each night, my grandfather would see me through their room and into my own because my grandmother would be on her knees, draped over the bed, deep in prayer. She was also the one who asked the blessing at meal times, and she took the initiative to enroll me in the Vacation Bible School at the Presbyterian Church in Tweed the summer I was 5 or 6 years old, the only VBS experience of my life. My grandmother's strong love for God and her commitment to her family and her community left an indelible impression on me as a young girl, but Grandma was not a member of the Church of Christ; she had been an Officer in the Salvation Army.

The eight statements in this section of our book honouring Don Haymes are from former Church-of-Christ members in Ontario. The writers range from people with a secondary-school education to a university professor, teachers and housewives, retired people and religious professionals, and at least one fairly high-ranking civil servant. They touch on issues of rules and legalism and fellowship, doctrinal differences, the public participation of women, exclusivity and baptism, gentleness and spirituality. These and other matters of concern are at the heart of the slow decline of the Churches of Christ in Ontario.

When I was born in 1964, Church of Christ congregations in Ontario numbered approximately 46. One must say "approximately" because no central organization keeps records of the number of congregations and members that exist in the "churches of Christ." Forty years later, approximately 70 congregations are in existence; however, I would not interpret this increase in the number of congregations in Ontario—most of them in rural settings or small cities and towns—with a collateral increase in effectiveness as harbingers of God's word and His love for his children. In no way have the few, small congregations of Greater Toronto kept up with the population explosion that has taken place during these four decades.

My personal impression as a friendly but outside observer is that most of these churches are struggling with declining membership. This is especially the case in Toronto. Now with more than three million inhabitants (not including its vast suburbs), Toronto has trebled in population since 1964, and is said to be the most culturally diverse city in North America, a thriving megalopolis where the broad spectrum of the former British Commonwealth—and beyond—now reside. This on-going, monumental change is overwhelming the backward-looking Churches of Christ. Only four congregations (two fewer than in 1964) with a combined membership of approximately 500 now struggle to exist in Toronto proper. One congregation has gone years without a regular pulpit minister.

I believe that the waning of these immobilized churches is due primarily to their being locked in a time-warp that is firmly set somewhere around 1952, and confined to an ethnically and sociologically enclosed, culturally homogenous group of doctrinally bound folk who have not found a way of updating their religious pursuit in terms of the changing, multi-ethnic, multi-cultural world around them. Toronto is a ready-made market for the Churches of Christ, and two of Toronto's congregations are now greatly populated with persons of Caribbean origin, but no outreach, as yet, is being made to the dozens—perhaps hundreds—of other groups within this large metropolis. Certainly no one in the Church of Christ in Ontario understands what a church might be in which many diverse ethnic and social groups would be welcome. How can the Church of Christ think they are fulfilling the "go, preach, baptize, teach" mission if they remain strangers in their own communities? What is the merit in starting churches halfway around the globe if one is not ministering to the people in one's own neighbourhood? The Churches of Christ in Toronto could, in fact, "go into the whole world" merely by going next door, for the whole world has moved to Toronto. But the culturally alienated Church people are quite bamboozled by the immense cultural mosaic that Toronto has become.

Thus far, one congregation has had an active and somewhat successful mission to the Spanish-speaking community in the east end of the city, but the Hispanic congregation is clearly the poor, second cousin to the parent, white C of C. The Anglo-Christians hardly allow the Spanish-speaking members any say in running their own congregation. White people from the British Isles and white Southerners from the racially divided U.S. tended the roots of the Churches of Christ in Ontario during their spawning years. Our roots are showing.

Most Church members, in my experience, suffer from a dismal lack of forward thinking, unwillingness to plan and prepare to keep pace with the growing needs of our vibrant younger people, and no idea of how to cope with the plethora of stimuli beckoning to everyone's diminishing personal time.

Most households have had to become two-income families out of necessity, so women are now well represented in the workplace in responsible positions. Churches of Christ, however, offer nothing more for the spiritual sustenance, growth, and participation of their female members than they did decades ago. Women in church are still supposed to sit down and keep quiet. That kind of religious non-engagement offers very little to bright, well-educated, articulate women holding jobs of high responsibility in the professional realm. Influenced by my strong, outspoken Christian grandmother, I cannot understand why this "silence of the women" policy continues to be so staunchly promulgated. The official line at church was that women are to "ask their husbands at home." But what if you are a single woman and have no husband at home? What if you are an emancipated young woman who no longer lives at home with Daddy? Why do the men at church want to keep the women either dependent or like children? Why would any adult, intelligent, independent woman—single or married—want to live and worship under such a regime? Already on the periphery of the Church of Christ, I naturally gravitated away from a group that made little or no sense to me as a woman.

Baptism, I believe, is one of the components of a closer relationship with God, a conviction that I learned partially from the extreme emphasis placed on baptism by the Church of Christ. The exclusivist use of baptism made by the Church, however, makes of it "the only way to Heaven" and therefore the only way to achieve acceptance within their ranks. This rigid doctrine also makes very difficult one's effort to "let one's light so shine" in the community, for it colours one's view of those whom one is trying to reach, fostering an "us/them" mentality—"we" are saved and "they" are not.

The rest of the Christian world wholly identifies with the clear and concise symbol of the cross. Why are the Ontario Churches of Christ so reticent to display this all-encompassing moniker on their buildings and in their sanctuaries? They will ornamentally wear a gold cross around their neck or on their lapel to make a subtle statement of their Christian identity, but Heaven forbid that we let the neighbours see a cross on the building! Did not St. Paul write: "In the cross of Christ I glory!"

Similarly, while other followers of Christ joyfully remind one another and tell the world of the significance of Christmas and Easter, the Church of Christ falls silent during these special seasons of the Christian year. How many people from across the backyard fence of the church house might be inclined to learn more about Christ and the Church if they were to enjoy a Christmas Eve, Christmas Day, or Easter Morning service and a hospitable meal? I myself find these celebrations spiritually uplifting.

And then there is Great Lakes Christian College (GLCC) in Beamsville, nestled in the famous wine region of Ontario's Niagara Peninsula. GLCC was established more than 50 years ago by a group of well-intentioned Church of Christ men to provide a facility for private high-school education with heavy Church of Christ influence. GLCC is a "college" (i.e., high school) in the Canadian sense of the word, not a post-secondary "Christian College" familiar to Church of Christ members in the Lower 48. GLCC students now wear uniforms to school, but when I attended for grades 11 and 12, the male students were allowed to wear jeans whereas female students were specifically forbidden. A two-tiered standard was definitely in place, but GLCC, then and now, was turned in upon itself in far more ways than merely its sexist dress code.

The school is no more successful than the congregations themselves, and just as isolated, alienated, and irrelevant to the life around it. One might assume that the presence of a Church of Christ school in southern Ontario for half-a-century would have had a positive impact on the churches that the school strives to serve, but this has hardly been the case. Reviewing the list of my fellow graduates from the Class of '82, I can report that many are very active within their respective churches, but few of these are Churches of Christ!

A decision, to recruit students from Hong Kong and charge the foreign students a higher tuition than Canadian students were paying, was made as financial concerns became paramount in the 1970s. Aside from one notable example of two brothers from

Hong Kong who were Christians actively involved in both school and church, GLCC could not realize its plans for the Chinese students: They were not Christians when they arrived, they did not become Christians while at GLCC, their English skills were so poor that they were barely able to comprehend basic classroom studies and get passing grades, much less begin to understand the Bible teachings offered as part of the curriculum. GLCC failed to foster inter-cultural communication between the Chinese and Canadian students enough even to get the two groups to eat together. The Chinese cooked their own meals in the dormitory kitchen, suffusing the dorm with mouth-watering aromas and the happy chatter of their own language, leaving the Canadian students befuddled about the visitors from Hong Kong.

GLCC continues to suffer financially due to the predominantly rural and non-professional population of the Churches of Christ. Farmers, small-business owners, and labourers do not have the means necessary to send their teenagers to a private school where costs are in line with other private school institutions. GLCC has, therefore, had to accommodate its constituency with lower than standard fees, and this has had a cascading effect on the school's financial position and, consequently, on teacher salaries. GLCC teacher salaries do not compete with salaries at other private or public; therefore, most willing teachers with a recognized teaching certification cannot afford to work at GLCC, and even if they make the sacrifice for a while, they do not stay for long. The devolving financial situation has a detrimental effect on building a qualified long-term faculty of seasoned teachers; students have become less and less inspired either to learn or reach high in their personal goals and achievements, so the student population has declined; with fewer students, the College has less money to hire more teachers and retain the ones already on staff.

This vicious cycle now spins out into yet another cycle of decline for the school and the churches: When low-income parents do make the financial sacrifice to send their children to the Christian high school, expendable funds are then lacking when those GLCC graduates want to attend university. This leaves a student with the decision either to become encumbered with years of debt in order to further higher learning or to settle for entering the workforce at a lower level of performance and pay. GLCC remains a school that cannot build itself up because most of its alumni/ae can ill afford to support their *alma mater*, and this means that the pattern of inadequately educated, low-income non-professionals among the membership of the C of C in Ontario continues.

While U.S. Churches of Christ, especially the ones in the South that had a significant impact on the C of C in Ontario in the 1940s and '50s, have entered into this new century with changes in outlook, programs, worship, and even the negative stance on the highly emotional issue of instrumental music, the time-warp is still firmly in place in Ontario. The C of C in Ontario as it is cannot hope to have a meaningful impact in the future. Its present mission to survive must be turned into a passion to thrive, but this will not happen unless something approaching the miraculous causes the scales to fall from Christian eyes. Fields of ripe harvest lie all around us in Ontario, right outside our very doors. These willing souls—many of them rootless in Toronto's cultural matrix—could be won to the joy of Heaven by a gentle, friendly, generous-hearted welcome of love and grace by bringers of a non-threatening, undoctrinized evangel of the Good News about Jesus Christ. But this kind of Heavenly embrace is incompatible with the exclusivity that has plagued the Churches of Christ in Ontario for far too long.

WHY I STAYED WITH THE CHURCH OF CHRIST— FOR AS LONG AS I DID

YVONNE MACKAY

When I was first asked if I would be willing to write an essay on "Why I Left the Church of Christ," I facetiously replied that I would and should probably title it "Why I Stayed with the Church of Christ"—for as long as I did. The more I thought about it, the more I decided to approach the topic from that direction. A short and simple answer would be this: "Because I waited until close family members and friends were ready to move on."

My early years were spent in the United Church of Canada, a union of some Methodists, Presbyterians, and Congregationalists around 1925. My particular congregation had been Methodist. Bible study was important, and it was still OK to say "Amen" and "Praise the Lord" right out loud! My father was a deacon. I sang in the senior choir for 12 years and became president of the Young People's Union, a closely-knit, active group of 35-40 people in their late teens and early twenties.

All was well with the world until my father died in 1954, leaving my mother and me all alone, but I was engaged to be married by the fall of 1955. God had been a loving presence in my life as far back as I could remember, and I knew in my heart that if I ever married, my husband-to-be would have to be a Christian. Within a short time, and still trying to recover from the loss of my father (I was only 22), I found myself in a new church environment surrounded by Bible-believing folk who seemed to take an interest in me. This was comforting. The historical background of their denomination was completely new to me, and I realized that their distinctions made this church different from what I had been used to, but didn't we all believe in the same God and His risen Son, Jesus?

I was soon shocked and insulted to find out, however, that my fiancé's church considered me to be a non-believer, non-Christian! I was apparently on the road to Hell and did not even know it. If this be true, I asked, then where was my father, the one I had sat at the kitchen table with, the one who had talked to me about the necessity of believing and trusting in God? The first time I voiced this question, the answer I got was a sort of whispered, "Sorry."

My young mind was confronted with a dilemma of monumental proportions. On the one hand, I was in love and looking forward to my new life together with Bill. On the other hand, I felt as though these people were ripping out by the roots everything I held dear, and they wanted me to do the discarding. This and other issues all caused such conflict that the wedding came within a hair's breadth of being cancelled at the last minute, but cooler heads prevailed and we were wedded on schedule.

How could this comparatively small number of people, I asked myself uncompre-hendingly, actually believe with all their hearts that theirs was the one and only "true church," and that they were the only ones going to Heaven? Rules, patterns, and traditions that had been established in the New Testament, they said, must be followed to the letter of the law. Where was the New Covenant in all of this? I asked. But I soon learned that persistent questions and firm dissent were neither encouraged nor appreciated. Every objection was shot down with the appropriate "book, chapter and verse" citation, whether it said what they said it said or not. "Where is LOVE in all of this?" I gasped.

In deference to the choices I had made, I felt that I owed it to myself and to others to explore these beliefs that were new to me and to find some answers. From the very beginning, my spirit sensed inconsistencies and contradictions. I decided that in spite of many pressures, I would delve into the scriptures and other sources to find answers for myself. I prayed for patience, wisdom, and guidance so that I would be honest with myself and not just try to reinforce what I already believed. Perhaps, I reasoned, then, I would be at peace, even if circumstances were not ideal. I was also very concerned for the spiritual well being of the children Bill and I were planning to have.

The next few decades brought times of optimism and growth, discouragement and challenge for me, and my faith, forever weaving its way through my life as a wife and mother. Over the years, I met many kind and loving people who inspired me to keep going. Many times I wondered whether the struggles were really worth it all. I appreciated opportunities to hear some outstanding speakers who seemed to have risen above the stifling confines of legalism in the Church of Christ. Unfortunately, their numbers were few. Most of my inspiration and encouragement came from "outside" sources.

Change, for good or bad, is inevitable, and change did come to the little church to which my husband had introduced me. This change brought a newness of possibility: Some greeted the opportunity with open arms; others, with open suspicion and hostility. For a time, we seemed to be enjoying renewed vitality and hope for the future of our faith community, but these hopes and dreams were to be dashed. Some held on rigidly to old beliefs and unhelpful traditions, finding it frightening and impossible to think of change. Others found new freedoms in Christ, especially the power and presence of the Holy Spirit that had long been denied. Unfortunately, some had more zeal than knowledge, and this proved damaging to many. The confusion and disunity opened a door to "petty tyrants" on power trips with their personal agendas.

The tempests passed, as tempests do, but the little church itself had been shipwrecked. A small group of us began to meet for worship in an atmosphere of peace, harmony, and freedom, with mutual acceptance and respect for each other. This close-knit, loving fellowship met every Sunday for over 20 years, snubbed and ignored by the mainline Church of Christ. By the late 1990s, time and circumstances brought change once again, and this time it meant, for me personally, that I must break my ties with the Church of Christ. It had to be done. There was no alternative. Their concepts of God and of the church were just too small. God cannot be contained within a church that confines itself to narrow, sectarian, party lines.

With this in mind, I accepted the invitation of a long-time zealous Christian friend to visit her church. The good results of that visit tell me that the Lord was surely in the move. Bill and I are now being blessed beyond measure. We are uplifted by worship that brings glory to God in an atmosphere of celebration and praise. The positive preaching and teaching nourish us to an extent that we have never before experienced. We are wonderfully surrounded by a large number of people who love the Lord and each other, and who encourage each other to spread the love of God within the church, into the community, and throughout the nation and the world.

Was the pain of separation worth it? In my view, absolutely! Wounds have healed, and the scars are barely visible. I believe that doubts and fears, criticisms and even insults have strengthened, not diminished, my faith because they caused me to delve more deeply into the things of God. For that I am grateful. "'Tis grace that brought me safe thus far, and grace will lead me home." PRAISE GOD!

THE VOYAGE OF A LIFETIME

AUDREY WRIGHT

My leaving the Church of Christ was not a single event; it has been a voyage. My voyage began when I was a child, and my mother, seeking more than she had experienced in the "denominations," found the Church of Christ in Toronto in 1942 and was baptized. Three memories of my pre-teen years that have stayed with me seem pertinent now:

1. I recall my mother's exclaiming from time to time that so-and-so was a fine person: "It's hard to believe that he won't be in Heaven." Little did my mother know that these seeds of doubt she was sowing would germinate for me in adulthood.

2. A visiting evangelist gave my mother cause to question the validity of her own baptism because she had been immersed while wearing a bathing cap. Fortunately, some wise and comforting person assured her that her baptism was intact, even if her hair had remained dry. As a twelve-year-old, I began to wonder whether a bathing cap would make a difference in an act of faith.

3. I doubt that my Father knew of the bathing cap dilemma. He attended services on Sunday evening with Mother and me and was baptized in 1944. Some years later he agreed to serve as an Elder, so his name was put forth for congregational approval. A dispute arose because he had only one child, me, and did not scripture say that a bishop must be the father of "believing children" in the plural?

As a teenager in the '50s, my Christian voyage brought me together with a large, supportive group of peers who made the entrance into adulthood painless and secure. Then I arrived at Abilene Christian College, thrilled and grateful to be there. My first choice of a major field seemed to lack substance, so I switched to English—we were all astonished in those days by the brilliant James Culp. Then I added Bible as a second major, and I minored in French. Ah, those were my "salad days!"

When I was introduced to *We Be Brethren* by J.D. Thomas, a book in which the concept of "pattern authority" in scripture: (a) command, (b) example, and (c) necessary inference is prominent, doubts began to nag at me about the standard mottos: "the one true church," "restoration of the first-century church," "we speak where the Bible speaks and are silent where the Bible is silent." Where did the Bible itself "speak" about all this tricky logic of patterns?

Then I met Lemoine! Dr. Lemoine G. Lewis taught Church History like no other. (His untimely death continues to sadden me.) By the time his lectures had taken us to the fourth century, I engaged him in his office after a particularly confusing lecture: He kept referring to "the church this" and "the church that." I was determined to know whether this "church" of which he spoke were the Church of Christ as I knew it! My visit to his office was a classic case of The Age of Innocence meets The Wisdom of Solomon: With his smiling eyes and gentle manner, Lemoine spoke words to me that, while I do not now remember them exactly, caused me to leave his office satisfied. By the end of the semester, I would know that "the church" had emerged victorious, and I would have my answer.

The voyage continues: In 1967, the Toronto Churches of Christ presented an exhibit at the Canadian National Exhibition (the world's largest annual exhibition): We offered viewings of the Jule Miller filmstrips to interested folk. Marjorie Cook, a nurse by profession and a member of the United Church of Canada, requested the series, so I spent five evenings showing them in her home. At their conclusion, she saw the need for baptism, which I was happy to arrange. Subsequently, she returned to the worship and fellowship of the United Church. I had assumed, of course, that she would change churches and become a member of one of "our" congregations. The experience gave me pause: Was I seeking to bring people to Christ, or was I seeking to draw Christians from other churches into the Church of Christ?

Late in 1968, I was part of a group who left the merger of two old, established Churches of Christ in Toronto. Those of us who left did not want to have to worry about a roast in the oven that would be overdone if the season of prayer lasted too long. Women, including myself, wanted to participate in the season of prayer. Naively, we thought we left on good terms: "They" were happy to see us go, and "we" were happy to be leaving— but such was not the case. "They" were hurt and "we" were shunned. The healing took some time.

As a new congregation of worshippers, we found a love for each other that I had scarcely believed possible. Further, my father, who had been an Elder at a traditional congregation across town, together with my mother became numbered among us. Little had I known all those years that he and she both had been waiting for "*something more.*" He quietly resigned from the eldership, they joined us, and I was thrilled.

For the next thirty years, I was part of a committed fellowship of believers who worshipped under the official name "Church of Christ," but we did not concern ourselves with whether anyone else approved of what kind of church we were. We welcomed as brethren all who claimed Jesus as Lord. We celebrated the Lord's Supper every Lord's Day. Musical instruments were welcome. Christ was the head of the body, and submission to Him was the priority in our worship and our daily living.

By 2001, on account of deaths in our church family and geographical moves of several of our members, our group disbanded. I am now happily part of a large church fellowship that (a) does not have Communion every Sunday, (b) does not believe baptism precedes salvation, (c) sings *a cappella* infrequently, and (d) allows women to participate publicly in worship and in business decisions. What's more, this church is welcoming, loving and peaceable, enjoys great Biblical preaching, and lifts the name of Jesus throughout the world. I am blessed to have found it.

I extol my early voyage and cherish the memories because I was born to a seeking mother and a wise father. I remember committed Sunday school teachers, great church picnics, abundant church suppers, delightful Christmas concerts, Omagh Bible School (now Camp Omagh) where I was baptized by Charles G. McPhee, June Meetings, the young people's group at the Strathmore congregation, teaching Sunday School, Ralph Perry who performed our wedding, three years at ACC (now ACU), one year of teaching at Great Lakes Christian College, a lifetime of *a cappella* singing that honed my voice and instilled in me a love for choral music, Church of Christ friends scattered across North America, and a good deal more.

Memories such as these are treasures that nothing can take from me, but looking forward towards the rest of my voyage, I see more clearly, now, in the words of Ephesians 2: 8-9, that "by grace I have been saved through faith...not of works that no one should glory." And in the words of Marcel Proust, I also see that "the real voyage of discovery consists not in seeking new landscapes but in having new eyes."

"*MAKING THE MOST OF ONE'S CHANCES*"

DAVID OLSON

Why did we leave the Church of Christ? Fran and I discovered that we had choices!

I myself left because leaving gave me freedom from what I had come to see as a set of arbitrary constraints as to what I should think, believe, and do. At first I was reluctant to challenge these constraints, fearing, as I had been taught, "This way lies danger!" To voice doubts was to border on blasphemy. To the contrary, I discovered that doubt is the route to a new freedom to believe and think freely, not necessarily to believe whatever I want to believe, but to believe that for which there are good reasons to believe. My mind was opened, freed from at least some inherited beliefs and taboos.

The leaving process took some time. Among the more flambuoyant evangelists that visited Western Christian College (formerly in Dauphin, Manitoba, now in Regina, Saskatchewan) was one who proclaimed that, such was his faith in the Bible, even if it had said that Jonah had swallowed the whale, he would have believed it. I began to suspect that this attitude was more a matter of gullibility than of faith. Did the church require one to deny science and logic and to believe in all sorts of nonsense? The song from *Porgy and Bess* still titillates: "The things that you're li'bel to read in the Bible, it ain't necessarily so." To quell my doubts about the contradictions between science and faith, I was encouraged to read a book called *Christian Evidences*, but I found the book superficial and misleading. I mentioned this to my teacher, the legendary Miss Torkelson, who responded that she didn't think much of it either, an opinion that earned my enduring respect for her.

At first, I thought that what was needed was to bring the church into a more enlightened 20th-century frame of mind: Surely, faith did not require suspension of one's commitment to scientific knowledge, did it? All that was required to escape the excessive literalism and fundamentalism of many preachers and church leaders was to learn to read the Bible more metaphorically. All the talk of gods and demons, heaven and hell, was simply an archaic way of talking about life, its meaning, about doing good and avoiding harm, and allowing one to live life "more abundantly." I soon discovered, however, that such a turn towards enlightened liberalism had already been made years and years before. The Church of Christ—along with the Catholic Church and other fundamentalist groups— called it "Modernism."

I came to see that the Church of Christ continues to exist primarily by distancing itself from most advances in human understanding. Church leaders remain wedded to an extreme conservatism that resists rethinking such traditional issues as to whether there be a literal hell, and whether the first-century expectation of a soon Second Coming—their mistake, obviously—were the product of an over-wrought imagination. One person's imagination is as good as another's, I suppose, but I tend to be sympathetic to Robert Frost's relativist vision of the end of time: "Some say the world will end with fire, some with ice; fire is fine, but ice is nice."

I read—indeed, I earnestly pondered—a book by John Robinson called *Honest to God* in which he argues that human rationality—modern science, for example—is not at odds with God's hopes for mankind. I found extremely appealing Tillich's suggestion that God is not "out there" but "in here," not an external power but our "ground of being." I still thought that the Church of Christ could be saved, and enter the modern age, if only it would learn these lessons. And the second step in saving the Church would come close on the heels of the first: If one could recognize that the Bible comprises the tribal legends of a Semitic tribe, written and collected to unite the Jews and justify their land-grabbing behavior to themselves, then it would no longer be necessary to believe as literal truth the magic and superstition expressed there. After the time of biblical miracles, times had changed—I had been taught—and now miracles had ceased." Part of that stuck with me!

My realization that things have not changed, but that there were no more miracles 3,000 or 2,000 years ago than there are today, exploded like bombshell in my brain. What has changed is how we think about nature and history. Most of us, these days, believe that events have natural causes. People speak sweetly of the "miracle of birth," but, in fact, there are no "real" miracles, no "biblical" miracles. Only slick salespeople who prey on the credulous offer miracle cures. But if neither miracles nor angels nor voices from the heavens come to us now, why think that they ever did? When we read that "the sun stood still," we must read that either as a statement of the writer's faith (he believed that the sun stood still) or as the writer's use of metaphor or literary hyperbole (the event was as if the sun stood still). As a writer, I know that writing, rightly or wrongly, is the expression of the beliefs and opinions of the author. That was no less true of biblical writers than it is of writers in our own time: I write what I believe to be true, and so did they; the reader must weigh reason and reality against my statement of faith and perception and similar statements by biblical authors. If I were to write that I had seen the sun stand still, most readers would know to take my statement with a grain of salt—and possibly with an entire salt shaker.

Authors who claim to write what was dictated to them by "inspiration" from an invisible superior power are probably somewhat deluded. To me, this is no less true of biblical writers than of Joseph Smith or Muhammad. Charismatic speakers get their energy and some of their eloquence from the feedback of an enthusiastic audience, but even so, great orators such as Martin Luther King, Jr., express only what they themselves have come to believe. As with miracles then and now, reflection on the talk about an "inspired Bible" then, as opposed to an inspired address by Dr. King, when he was alive, caused me to see the whole structure of church teaching as a great web of fantasy. Nothing written in the Bible, I now realize, is anything more than could have been written by ordinary people such as you and me (and Robert Frost and Martin Luther King). The Bible is a piece of truly great literature, like many other great statements of religious belief throughout human history.[1]

I was astonished to discover that "the faithful" had no interest in benefiting from what I thought of as my remarkable discovery! I recalled that I knew every counterargument to

---

[1] See David R. Olson, *The World on Paper: The Conceptual and Cognitive Implications of Writing and Reading* (Cambridge University Press, 1994), for a more full statement of ways of reading the book of Scripture and the book of Nature.

my new views because I had learned them in Bible class in the Christian College High School I had attended. If one turned away from "the tried and true," it was like "a dog returning to his vomit." If one doubted, one was a Thomas, a backslider, or even a Judas. If one had a new idea, one was a liberal, a modernist, a secular humanist, or an agnostic. At first, my revisionist views were treated by some with patience, seen as a sign of personal failure that time and maturity might correct. People are not easily shaken from entrenched beliefs, so many old friends could not understand how or why I could exchange Christian faith for what seemed to them to be nothing. Was it a product of my own efforts to understand? Was it a product of finding a new home in a more academic environment? Would I have been willing to die at the stake for my new beliefs? Not likely, and I am grateful that I do not have to make that choice! I left the Church of Christ and all such fundamentalisms because *I thought about the matter and changed my mind.* Had I gone the other way—I am horrified now to imagine—I might have been linked to the Evangelical Right! Even I can find reason to pray: "There but for the grace of God go I."

Leaving the Church produced some anguish, at first, mostly because I was using some of the Church's categories to describe myself: I had passed "beyond the pale," I had "become worldly," I had "lost my faith." I felt an unbridgeable gap between myself and some of my dear friends who were more religious than I. Once upon a time, I, too, had regarded "backsliders" negatively, so I knew that my old friends now regarded me in that way. My feelings, however, turned out to be unjustified: Dear Miss Torkelson, my beloved teacher, still regarded me positively—as a person, not a backslider. Some others of my old friends whose religion forbade them to allow skin colour, sexual orientation, ethnicity, or church membership to distance them from their true friends, extended that grace to me. This has been a great comfort to me. Now I know that religious differences need pose no obstacle to serious friendships.

Thirty years later, I realize that for many of the devout, all this talk about doctrine, the correctness of beliefs, literal interpretation of the Bible, and the like, has nothing at all to do with faith: "I know whom I have believed" they say, and all the rest is merely speculation. These are probably the true Christians, and although I am not one of them, I have enormous respect for people for whom their faith is "the ground of their being."

My belief structure now has become completely naturalized: There are no gods, demons, witches; there is no hell fire; there is no vengeful god waiting to get his licks in; there is no rapture and no Second Coming; there are no miracles; there was no special creation; spirit has become synonymous with gusto; wine does not mean the blood of Christ; blood does not take away sin (let there be never an excuse for vengeance killing!); there is no supreme being who craves praise and demands obedience. Like Freud, I find many religious beliefs hopelessly infantile—"Safe in the arms of Jesus"—as if we wished to be babes in arms again.

Giving up religious beliefs does not mean that I no longer feel brotherly love, compassion, respect for others and their views, or that I do not discriminate right from wrong, good from bad, true from false. Gratitude and modesty have changed somewhat for me. I am indeed thankful in a sense when things go my way, but I no longer think of them as a gift from God: "The rain falls on the just the unjust." I no longer pray for favours, although I do have hopes and goals, and I duly appreciate anyone's achievement. I don't believe in Lady Luck, healing hype, the power of prisms, or other magical mysteries. I now set more store on justice than I did before; I count on friends, community, and a civil society to order human life aright. I believe in self-defense, but I hate imperial wars, even when they are declared on "evil empires."

I am modest in the sense that I realize that my beliefs are my own, not special inspiration from divine influence. I am naturally grateful for a good idea, and I acknowledge that good things happen when we least expect them: The universe is abundant! I believe that freedom of thought and belief goes hand-in-hand with the right to express what we have good reasons to believe to be true and important. I no longer believe that I or anyone can be God's spokesperson, can proclaim the words of God by quoting Scripture, in the way that ancient prophets thought they could do, and modern evangelists everywhere claim to do. People need to recognize that when they say something, it is they themselves that are speaking, even when they are passing on some bit of elder wisdom. No one has the right to pretend to speak for God.

I love music and I devote some of my time to careful listening. I acknowledge to a certain amount of innocent hypocrisy, for Brahms's *German Requiem*—an eminently religious composition —draws deep feelings from me. I hope my devoutly religious friends get as much soul-satisfaction from attending church as I do from listening to Brahms! I proselytize for Brahms; they are entitled to do so for the church. I have discovered life outside of the church.

To my friends, both old and new, I say that I would be happy to share my new perspective with them and with you. Please communicate with me at my e-mail address: dolson@oise.utoronto.ca "Life outside of the church"—this sentiment is brilliantly summarized in a brief poem by Frank Kuppner whose title I borrowed for these reflections. I have requested Poet Kuppner's permission to reprint his poem.

> *Making the most of one's chances*
> *Another evening, and in a moment of sheer inadvertence—*
> *that is doubtless what it was; what else could it have been?—*
> *Saint Peter, closing up the gates of Paradise*
> *for the night, no doubt more from habit than anything else,*
> *finds, to his astonishment, that he has locked himself out.*
>
> *A spasm of panic at first. He shouts for help.*
> *(Whose attention, one wonders, is he trying to attract?)*
> *He shouts again. No answer. He opens his mouth to shout*
> *again -- but this time, for some reason, he does not do so.*
> *Instead he takes a look round. What is this place?*
>
> *He takes another look round. What is this place?*
> *It is so long since he had a good look round outside here.*
> *He takes a few steps forward and back, looking round.*
> *He stands motionless for a moment, thinking —*
> *then shakes his head, laughs, and disappears down the road.*

Frank Kuppner

Two Christians' Journey Together

Garry Peddle

I was born in 1935 to a mother who was Roman Catholic and a father who was a member of a church of Christ. Baptized as an infant, I attended Catholic elementary school. My parents divorced when I was 12, and I went to live with my paternal grandparents. My grandfather was a church-of-Christ Sunday School director who preached frequently at local country churches. Immersed in a new theology that made sense to my uncritical mind, I was rebaptized at Omagh Bible Camp when I was 13.

At 19, I fell in love with Carolyn. From solid church-of-Christ stock, her grandfather had been a preacher, and her mother—in her late 70s—went as a missionary to New Guinea. Carolyn and I attended Harding College for our undergraduate education, and returned to Toronto, to marriage, and to graduate work.

In those days, we accepted most of the theology of the church of Christ, except that I had a problem with Scientific Creationism. As a scientist, I was disturbed by the seeming failure of the conservative Christian churches to learn anything from the Roman Church's encounter with Galileo. Later, I gave talks on the subject, took part in a debate, and wrote an article for *Mission* magazine entitled "Galileo Revisited."[2] These experiences led me to examine what I saw as the assumptions underlying conservative Christian theology, namely that the Bible is inerrant and should be taken literally; that the "New Testament Church" can be recreated from a study of the Bible; that any action in addition to actions directly authorized in the New Testament, is wrong.

Questions about Baptism

Early in my analysis of these assumptions, I decided that I could not understand the Early Church without a better grounding in first-century Jewish and Hellenistic culture. Consider what happens when we look at baptism in the context of first-century history: We know that Judaism in the first century was a successful evangelical religion; Jesus himself spoke of the fervor of the scribes and Pharisees in seeking converts. When a man was converted to Judaism he, and all the males in his household, would be circumcised; then, because all the members of the household—children included—would be ritually unclean, they would undergo a ritual washing, literally a baptism.

We know that most of the early converts to the Church came from amongst Jews, proselytes to Judaism, and God-fearers or gentiles attracted to Judaism. *Colossians* states that circumcision had been done away with, and that Christians enter a covenant relation with God through baptism. The question of faith in Jesus asked of adults determined whether they were eligible for baptism. If the normal Jewish practice of including children

---

[2] Garry J. D. Peddle, "Galileo Revisited," *Mission* 7/12 (June 1974): 13-14.

in such conversions were to be continued, nothing needed to be said; were the children, however, to have been henceforth excluded from the covenant relationship—or, at least, excused from being baptized—that would have represented a major change. We would expect a clear teaching that children were no longer to be included in covenantal baptism, but the New Testament contains no such teaching; therefore, we may reasonably conclude that the usual procedure was continued.

This conclusion is strengthened by observing that about a quarter of the baptisms in the New Testament were of whole households. Although no children are mentioned, they would have been included on the basis of their parents' faith. By the second century, we have indirect evidence of the baptism of children, and by the third century, the evidence for the baptism of children is abundant. Polycarp (69-155), a disciple of John, as he was dying a martyr's death, proclaimed that he had "been in the service of the Lord" for 86 years. This suggests that he had been baptized at a very early age. Irenaeus (120-202), a disciple of Polycarp, wrote fifty years later that "Christ came to save all people through himself, I say all who are born again to God, nursing babes, small children, children, young people, and older people...." Many other Early Christian writers refer to infant baptism as an Apostolic tradition. In retrospect, I cannot believe that I ever accepted a teaching that excludes from God's covenant with us the overwhelming majority of all the devout Christians who have ever lived merely because they were baptized as infants.

Efforts to Improve Worship

As Carolyn's and my certainty in doctrinal issues decreased, our desire for a greater emphasis on worship increased. Over the years, we tried a number of times to increase the devotional quality of worship during Sunday morning services. Once, we suggested playing taped *a cappella* hymns for five minutes before the start of the service to help prepare the congregation for worship. Objections were raised concerning the use of "instrumental music" (a tape deck is an instrument) and "choirs," so the idea was dropped. Another time, we suggested that an additional worship hymn be sung during the service. The preacher responded that he was unwilling to give up any of his sermon time for another hymn.

No effort was made on Sundays to coordinate the hymns with the sermon. One Thanksgiving, the minister (a different one) asked Carolyn to plan a service centered on Thanksgiving. When she called the song leader to be certain that he knew all the hymns, and the song leader's wife found that Carolyn had been involved in planning the service, she said that they would be away on Sunday, and they remained away from then on. This of course raised the question of what role, if any, women may have in the services of the church.

Questions about Women at Church

How can one "restore" the "New Testament Church" when the New Testament itself is ambiguous in what it reports about the Early Church? Some texts suggest that women took an active role in the services, and other texts are commands for the women to be silent. History reveals that the lot of women in first-century Palestine was dismal. A father could sell his daughter into a form of slavery or pass her on as a wife into the control of another man. She could be divorced by her husband, but she had no right to divorce him. Sayings of rabbis contemporary with the New Testament make clear this domination of women:

Jose ben Johanan: "Talk not much with woman kind; such talk, even with one's wife, could lead to Gehenna."

Rabbi Elitzer: "If a man gives his daughter knowledge of the Law, it is as though he has taught her lechery."

Little wonder, then, that the morning prayer of the Jewish male ran thus: "I thank Thee, God of my fathers, that I was not born a gentile, a slave, or a woman."

First-century Hellenistic society also regarded women as inferior to men. When Josephus wrote, "The woman is in all things inferior to the man," he was echoing the misogynistic opinions of the Greek philosopher, Aristotle.

In such a society, Jesus' treatment of women was nothing short of revolutionary—a message of liberation. He conversed with women in public, including ritually unclean women; he allowed women to touch him; he made clear to Mary and Martha, Lazarus's sisters, that study of the Law is better for women than is "women's work"; he used a woman as the messenger to spread the Good News to the Samaritans; and a woman, Mary Magdalene, was the first apostle whom Christ sent to tell the good news of his resurrection.

Some first-century Christian women threw off their sexist shackles and became actively involved in the work of the church. Paul, for instance, had a number of women co-workers, one of whom he named in *Romans*, Junia—"outstanding among the apostles." In a sermon on Romans 16:7, John Chrysostom (347-407) exclaimed: "Oh! how great is the devotion of this woman, that she should be even counted worthy of the appellation of apostle!" Paul referred to his "Sister Phoebe, deacon of the church at Cenchreae," as one who presided over her own house-church (Rm 16:1-2).

But something went wrong. When we turn to the writings of other Church Fathers, we find their message to be amazingly more in agreement with the rabbis than with Christ. Consider the following sayings:

Jerome (340-420): "Woman is the gate of the devil, the path of wickedness, the sting of the serpent, in a word a perilous object."

Epiphanius (310-403): "Women are unstable, prone to error, and mean-spirited."

It was as if Christ had never lived.

As the Ancient Church in the Roman Empire built up its hierarchy and consolidated power in the hands of the bishops, women were not viewed as likely candidates for a job in the church. In 245, Archbishop Dionysius of Alexandria echoed Jewish tradition when he wrote: "Menstruating women ought not to come to the Holy Table, or touch the Holy of Holies, nor to churches...."

In segments of the church outside the mainstream, women were involved as leaders and in efforts to resist the centralized power of the bishops. In the second century, Maximilla and Priscilla, two prophetesses associated with Montanus, called for a return to the fundamentals of first-century Christianity. They believed in the priesthood of all believers—women as well as men. Tertullian (160-225), the most famous convert to Montanism, as this first of all restorationist movements may be called, has been described as the first Protestant writer. Tertullian wrote that the church is not a conclave of bishops, but the people of the Holy Spirit. A synod of bishops declared Montanism heretical, and so it has been ever since, and other synods consistently reinforced the exclusion of women from public activity in the church: Council of Laodicea (352): "One ought not to establish in the church the women called overseers"; Fourth Synod of Carthage (398): "A woman may not baptize"; Council of Chalcedon (451): "No woman under 40 years of age is to be ordained a deacon." The logical culmination of such actions occurred in the 13th century when Aegidius of Rome decided that the text of Romans 16:7 was obviously incorrect, and so he changed it: Junia, a woman apostle, became "Junias," a man.

We Leave the Church of Christ

For many reasons, we had not wanted to leave the church of Christ. The most important was that Carolyn's mother would have been hurt by our leaving. Another was the influence of a 1950s sermon by Carl Ketcherside in which he spoke to many like us who were dismayed by the narrowness: We wanted to "make a larger circle of love to include those who would exclude us." Many of our brothers and sisters in the churches of Christ had been dear to us for most of our lives; we did not wish to abandon them. Finally, we hoped to make a difference in the Church, if only a small difference.

Finally, however, we left. Carolyn's mother died. Our congregation's tolerant leadership passed away and was replaced by a more conservative leadership. Our beliefs were disturbing to some of the members. We needed to find a church home where we would feel closer to God. We still believed in God and Jesus and the Holy Spirit. We still believed that God communicates with us through the Judeo-Christian tradition. But we also believed that God's message to us had been, in part, distorted. In good Restorationist fashion, we believed that a clearer message could be restored, and that the circle of God's love is big enough to embrace a wide spectrum of believers.

After two years of searching, we finally found a group where the services are intelligently and affectively planned, where the people sing more, more scripture is read, more prayer is offered, women participate alongside the men, and preaching is not the main event. The services, now, are longer, but they seem shorter. When we leave worship, we know we have been lifted up. Thanks be to God!

GROWING UP IN THE CHURCH OF CHRIST:
ONE CANADIAN WOMAN'S SPIRITUAL JOURNEY (1938-2004)

JOAN LEDGER DE NEW

Along my spiritual path, I have taken a number of hairpin turns that appeared treacherous to some of my friends, but these gripping moments, in my view, have led me continuously towards spiritual wholeness. While my spiritual path, which began in the Church of Christ, has appeared unorthodox and definitely questionable to many family members and friends over the years, I have experienced it as a continuous journey towards increasing wholeness and joy. I trust that my experience may be helpful to members of the Restoration Movement.

My Parents

My dad, Ted Ledger, was raised Anglican but thought of God as "The Great Mechanic" who had set up the world and left it to run on its own. One could thank God for good things, but it was pointless to ask him for favors. Mum, Edith Stevens, came from a Church of Christ background in St. Catharines. When Mum and Dad married, they mutually agreed that the difference in their church backgrounds would never become a source of conflict, and that they would attend the Church of Christ. Dad, not having been baptized "the right way," was never considered a member. After they graduated from McMaster University (then a Baptist college in Toronto) they settled in Toronto and began regular attendance at the Fern Avenue Church of Christ.

Mum was a devoted Sunday School teacher for as long as I can remember. On Saturday nights, she was usually busy preparing handouts for her Sunday students. Dad, the handyman, often ran the projector for Sunday School, drove us to church, along with others, including a family in the neighbourhood that did not own a car. Some members knew that Dad was not a member of the Church of Christ; because he attended weekly services faithfully for years and years, others probably never realized it. The two, or possibly three times that Mum was ill on a Sunday, Dad took me to church anyway. Because of Dad's "non-member" membership, and because Mum was a woman, our family did not take part in the congregation's decision-making processes. We were permanently part of the fringe.

The Fern Avenue Church of Christ

I remember the people of Fern Avenue more than anything else. When I myself became a Sunday School teacher and initiated a Junior Congregation during sermon time, dear Mrs. Hargrave, a retired teacher and widow, gave me some money so that I could buy supplies and books for a lending library for my students.

Margaret and Kay Whitelaw were my Sunday School teachers. A.L.Whitelaw, a bookkeeper, was an Elder in the congregation and a devoted Sunday School teacher of the boys' class, many of which always sat in the pew in front of me during worship services. Every boy in that row, including A.L.'s son, Warren, eventually became ministers of the church. When Great Lakes Christian College opened in Beamsville, A.L. served not only as treasurer of the Board but also as a loyal promoter of Christian education. He approached me about attending GLCC and, later, Abilene Christian College. Because I expected to be a high-school teacher in Ontario, however, my parents encouraged me to take my education within the public school system and to attend a Canadian university so that my professional credentials would be accepted. When A.L.'s wife died, the other close readers of their Bibles at Fern decided that he no longer qualified as an Elder. The Bible says that a bishop must be "the husband of one wife," and A. L. no longer had a wife. He took the ruling in good grace, continued to participate in services, and was frequently called upon to lead in prayer.

Leora Haw (later, Armstrong) was the other church member whom I most respected. She was the mother in the family that we usually drove to church and Sunday School. She lived with her husband, their two children, her own mother, and often her handicapped sister-in-law. Leora's husband dropped dead suddenly one Sunday morning of a heart attack. She had to find work and provide support for her whole household of people. Leora met all her difficulties with a positive attitude, always acknowledging with deep appreciation the help that was offered her. When I was to be married, Leora hosted a lovely bridal shower for me and invited the women of the church. She presented me with a colorful scrapbook that she had made from magazine cut-outs illustrating the highlights of life along with good wishes and thoughtful quotes. Leora was a woman of great faith that had been tempered in the fire of significant adversity.

Dr. Eleanor Robinson, a physician in our congregation, was the only other university-trained person, beside my parents, at Fern. Others, such as Mr. Peckham and Mr. Kennedy, had their own businesses. A number of our younger single women either worked as secretaries or were employed by various companies; most of the other women were wives, and several were widowed. But all of them remained silent at church, for that is the way it was. The women were instructed and expected to leave church leadership to the men.

The many ministers that served Fern Avenue through the years differed considerably. Some specialized in anti-Catholic sermons; emphasis was placed on the Church of Christ doing things "the right way" in contrast to biblically unjustifiable Roman Catholic practices. Most had only limited higher education, though some had attended Bible College. During times "between preachers," Mr. Kimberly, an Elder who had come from England, usually preached for us. He was a gentle, insightful, scholarly man whose preaching was much appreciated in the Ledger household; the same may be said about the scholarly and inclusive spirit, Walter Burr Smith. Mum and I became involved in Willie Bryson's efforts to reach out to neighbourhood children through a Thursday night crafts class. Newman Leonard and his wife were open, loving people; Newman had baptized me when I was 14. It was always a treat to have the members of A.L. Whitelaw's boys' class return on special occasions or as interim preachers—Warren Whitelaw, Murray Hammond, Joe Cannon, and Keith Thompson. We also appreciated the interim services of Geoff Ellis, whose primary involvement was teaching at Great Lakes Christian College.

In 1959, I graduated from McMaster and went on a summer Canadian Youth Hostels bicycle tour to Europe. As was the custom for returned travelers at Fern Avenue, I offered to make a slide presentation to the congregation. Unfortunately, my third slide jammed in the machine, and despite Dad's best efforts to dislodge it, nothing worked. Rather than disappoint people, I began describing in words each of the slides that I would have shown them. I noted in conclusion that I had seen and learned a lot in a short time and commented that this may have been because I expected it. Then, I applied this insight to Fern Avenue's community outreach, suggesting that God might show us opportunities to serve many people if we really expected His guidance. A few weeks later, I heard that the minister had condemned the Elders for allowing a woman to preach in church! It had never occurred to me that I was violating any biblical precepts.

Singing was an important part of church life at Fern Avenue. Born with what is called "perfect pitch," at times I was uncomfortable because I was automatically aware when we were singing off-tune or contrary to the music written in the hymnbook. I began to sing alto and was often the only alto in the congregation. The singing was best at the annual "June Meeting" of the Ontario Churches of Christ, which was usually held in the Niagara region. Hearing all those good voices singing together is one of my strongest memories. The Meeting speakers were excellent, too, and I loved hearing about mission work.

Church of Christ people took pride in being the only church (known to us) that sang only and did not play instruments in worship. But being "the only one" was not exclusive to singing. Throughout elementary school, high school, and university, I was, to my knowledge, the only Church of Christ person in the student body. Church-related experiences with neighbourhood friends were, of necessity, with people of "other denominations," all of which were considered to be wrong because the "only true church" was the Church of Christ, as one could easily tell by its name. Nevertheless, I attended Sunday school a few times with an Anglican friend, and I later joined a local Presbyterian girls' group with my friends. I enjoyed being chosen to read the scripture at the annual services acknowledging the youth groups. I went to camp two summers with this national, ecumenically supported girls' program, and was elected Chief Camper the second summer. (The Chief Camper's main job was to raise and lower the flag each day.)

An important experience at Fern Avenue was reading church papers. One of my own letters, about wanting to be a teacher and work in the north with aboriginal children, was published in *Junior Life*. The teen magazine, *Straight*, included a weekly Bible Quiz section, which I almost always completed. When I was 16, I won a contest because I sent in the correct answers over several months. I received a scholarship to attend a week at a non-denominational evangelical camp where, again, I was the only Church of Christ person present. Reading the church papers compensated somewhat for the small group of young people at Fern during those years: We had only five young people within a five-year age range, and we lived many miles apart.

When I began university in September 1956 in Hamilton, Ontario, Fern Avenue members presented me with a beautiful leather handbag as I set off on a new chapter of my life. I was glad that a Church of Christ congregation in Hamilton was within easy access by bus from the university.

Faith Crisis (1957-60)

Although Mum and Dad were graduates in Math and Sciences, I earned a university scholarship in Modern Languages and enrolled in first year Arts. Whereas I had done an excellent job academically, I discovered rather painfully that I was not experienced in dealing with emotions. After I broke up with my first boyfriend, I suffered a crisis of faith. I had enjoyed the security of a supportive personal family and church family, but now I found myself facing questions that they had not prepared me for. Enrolled in Honours English and History, I was realizing to my consternation that things are not black and white but varying shades of grey. Where was the truth? How could one tell? Is God really there? Is the Bible just a collection of stories that people made up in order to feel better? My self-confidence based on knowing what was right and wrong, began to waiver. Concentrating on my studies became difficult; essay writing became extremely stressful; my grades slipped. My prayer became: "God, if you are really there, help!" Doubt was something that one was not supposed to have, either at home or at the Fern Avenue Church of Christ.

Help came from new directions. I was invited to attend a young people's group at a downtown Hamilton Baptist church on Sunday evenings after service. The minister was excellent. I remember his Christmas sermon: He spoke about how we cannot see the Star unless the sky around is dark. I certainly felt like I was in the dark, and this word gave me hope; yet, by the fall of my third year, I was feeling quite desperate. Meantime, I had begun to re-read the Gospels. I could see how Jesus had put his trust in God and had risked his life on it. I decided to see what Jesus had to say about God, and then, in my own way, to test its validity. I understood that I was to do whatever I could to help others. One day, all I could manage was to hold the door open for other residence students to enter the cafeteria. It doesn't sound like much, but it was about all I felt capable of doing at the time.

At the University morning chapel service one day, I became deeply aware of my crisis. An older seminary student stopped to talk to me for the first time that day as I was leaving the chapel. Within a few minutes, my confusions were spilling out. He assured me that God would help me.

A short time later, as I was soaking in the residence bathtub around 1:30 a.m., I sadly realized that I had no clue what to do to find out for sure whether God were real. However, in the same moment, I received the message that I had a purpose and that a certain seminary student was connected to it. Though I didn't hear any "voices" or see any "visions," I knew that something very special had happened. The whole world was different: Colours were bright, edges looked sharp, and I was keen to find out more about that seminary student. I realize now that this experience could be described as a baptism of the Holy Spirit. At least I was in a bathtub when it happened!

At first, it appeared that God had given me a life partner, but our ages and experiences had placed us too far apart. He had escaped from a Communist country, and through his struggle he had done what I had not done—he had found a faith that was his own. I continued to benefit from him as a pastor, for he was the student minister at my Baptist church. Meeting someone whose faith had been severely tested and had carried him through great difficulty gave me hope.

I enrolled in the Women's Leadership Training School at the McMaster Divinity College. They were talking about God; that year was amazing! Every day, every class, things began making sense. My life had seemed like a jigsaw puzzle that had been swept off the table but was now getting put together again in greater detail and with the missing pieces filled in.

Serving with the Disciples

At the suggestion of a fellow student, I contacted Oliver McCully, General Secretary of the Churches of Christ (Disciples), the "liberal" branch of the Restoration Movement. Offered the position of Associate Secretary to the All-Canada Committee of the Toronto-based organization, I traveled from coast to coast, visiting various congregations, informing them about Christian Education resources, and offering leadership-training opportunities to teachers and youth leaders. No one had held my position for the previous 30 years, so part of the job was discovering what was needed, as well as doing it. After two years of service with the Disciples, I had learned much, and I had shared what I could. I had discovered the vastness of the country we call Canada and the infinite variety of its people. Most important, I had learned that a Power greater than I supported me in my work.

To my surprise, within my first two weeks with the Disciples, the "girl from Fern Avenue" became one of four Canadian Youth Delegates to the Third Assembly of the World Council of Churches in India, November-December, 1961. Thanks to my study of languages, I could bring French, German, and Spanish to the aid of my English in communicating with almost everyone there. Worship services were conducted in a variety of languages and traditions. The singing was inspirational. The Church Universal was real. I met outstanding leaders of the world church and heard them speak of their passion for unity and our common witness as Christians. After my return, I reported extensively to church groups across Canada about my experiences at the World Council. Later, I became chairperson of the Committee on Young People's Work of the Canadian Council of Churches, the group that had sponsored my trip.

With Paul in Montreal (1962-64)

In June 1962, I married Paul De New, who had recently been ordained a minister in the United Church of Canada (UCC). Shortly thereafter, I transferred my church membership to the UCC. I did not so much "leave" the Church of Christ or any of the other churches with which I had been associated; rather, I took them with me as I moved on to what was next. While Paul began a two-year Master of Social Work program at McGill University in Montreal, I was employed by the Student Christian Movement, working on campus with students, helping them plan meetings and conferences and offering support in personal faith struggles.

During that time, the Fourth World Conference on Faith and Order was held at McGill, half-a-block up the street from where we lived. Once again chosen to be a Canadian Youth Delegate, I also co-chaired the reception and transportation committee, as well as helping to organize a public celebration of the conference. The enthusiasm generated by working together on the conference led to the planning of an ecumenical Christian Pavilion at Expo 67 in Montreal.

As Busy As We Could Be (1964-79)

Our family settled down to the business of living in Hamilton. Paul became a social worker at family service agencies. We had three sons, and we adopted a daughter. Though motherhood is a full-time job, I enjoyed my involvement in a new parent-run co-op preschool that met in a local United Church complex. For adult conversation, I also started selling Tupperware.

Paul entered McMaster University Medical School in 1971. I worked for a year as part-time Christian Education director in a downtown United Church, followed by two years at a Baptist inner-city mission church. I took some M. Div. courses at the McMaster Divinity College, taught piano lessons, became a driving instructor, worked for a while at a Tim Horton's doughnut shop, and sold more Tupperware.

I then volunteered with the Canadian Bible Society (CBS), serving as secretary of the local branch for several years, and as a speaker in numerous churches about the work of the CBS, producing a one-hour program on the work of the CBS, and as district president for two years, and as local president for two years. In Hamilton, we sponsored a one-day workshop on "The Church, the Bible, and the Disabled." I enjoyed active participation with the CBS for a total of some 24 years. At Fern Avenue in my youth, I had learned the importance of the Bible, and I had believed in the importance of Christian unity. My years with the CBS were a way of passing on what I had learned at Fern Avenue.

While promoting CBS events in Hamilton, I made sure that the local Church of Christ congregations were notified, even though they had not traditionally participated in CBS efforts. Blake Gieg, then part-time minister at Ivon Avenue Church of Christ, invited me to speak to the young people who were serving in a work camp that was sponsored by the congregation. Our family began to attend the Ivon Avenue services, and we would have continued there had a problem not arisen about acceptance of my husband's baptism as an adult by sprinkling. He did not wish to devalue his previous Christian faith and experience by being re-baptized, and the other Ivon Avenue co-minister could not accept him without baptism by immersion. Sadly, we moved on. Meanwhile, I was delighted that Blake Gieg became active on the Board of the local CBS. Thereafter, he was hired by the National Office to assist the General Secretary with his duties.[3]

Serving with the United Church of Canada (the 1980s)

In the early 1980s, I became involved in the regional UCC Conference Communication Committee, representing it on the National Communication Education Committee, where I served on the planning committee for a national consultation on communication skills. I also edited the eight-page bi-monthly Conference News insert in the national *United Church Observer* monthly for three and a half years. Giving up this enjoyable work was necessary when my husband and I moved to a different Conference area. Once again, what I had learned at Fern Avenue still guided my Christian service: I believed it important to report the news of warmth and caring in local congregations.

Paul having completed his residency in Psychiatry during this time, I worked as his medical secretary/medical office manager. Further, I assisted with the production of two audio-visual resources dealing with violence on television and war toys, the first of which was produced by Canadians Concerned About Violence in Entertainment (C-CAVE), an organization I started in 1983. These audio-visuals, used widely across Canada in churches, showed people how to correct and prevent the harmful effects of violence in entertainment. I spoke in many places, did radio and TV interviews, and was a panelist in Vancouver at the annual meeting of the Canadian Association of Broadcasters when they adopted the voluntary code on violence to which we had contributed. I also addressed the Broadcast Educators' Association of Canada, and a national consultation of provincial Film Review Boards on entertainment violence issues. I had not planned to become a voice against

---

[3] See R. Blake Gieg, "My Spiritual Journey," in this volume.

violence in the media, but sometimes the mission field chooses the missionary. Bible study at Fern Avenue had taught me that what happens in society matters to God. I saw the need for someone to speak up, so I did.

For two years, I was president of the local Council of Women (a group of concerned women that had been formed in 1893, before women were allowed to vote, hold office, or belong to a political party), after which I became the media convener and quarterly newsletter editor for the National Council of Women. Then, without campaigning, I was elected national president of the NCWC and began coast-to-coast travel once again, helping Councils assess their leadership needs and identify available resources.

Among many leadership challenges, including helping the Council to reclaim its effectiveness on a limited budget, I was forced to choose between organizational service and service to a single human being. A young secretary—later diagnosed with multiple personality disorder—embezzled half our operating funds. Both the law and the Council viewed the secretary as our adversary, and I was advised that I would have to cease communication with her if I intended to continue as president for a third year (to which I had been called by acclamation). I chose to resign, instead, so that I could stay in contact with the woman. How could I be the leader of the Council and not take care of its most needy member? When I learned that she had attempted suicide, I saw her as a member fallen from the flock. In a flock of Canada geese, when a member is either injured or becomes ill and falls out of the flight pattern, two geese drop back to wait with the fallen one, either for recovery or death, and thereafter they join another flock. I am happy to report that our "fallen one" successfully completed therapy, teaches in a business college, survived a divorce, is raising three lively children, and has married a university teacher. She also volunteers weekly in her church's soup kitchen. Once again, the faith I had learned at Fern Avenue clarified the situation for me: Had not the good shepherd of Jesus' parable left the 99 sheep in the fold to go in search of the one that was lost? I regretted not being able to follow through with the possibilities for rejuvenating the NCWC and leading it through its 100th anniversary in 1993, but I firmly believe I made the choice that the Good Shepherd would have made.

Dowsing through to the New Millennium

At home in Hamilton again, I developed a case of fibromyalgia, an autoimmune disease that disrupts sleep through painful muscle spasms, and leaves one physically agitated and unable to concentrate in ordinary ways. For an active person accustomed to organizing and getting things done, this debilitation was very frustrating. During a two-year-long, successful treatment by a healer who used massage, shiatsu, and reiki, I discovered that I, too, had "healing hands" that would get warm when I placed them on others for healing.

In late summer of 1994, my massage healer explained the use of a small pendulum (a weight on a string) to guide in making choices for the most appropriate vitamin and mineral supplements to recover health. This technique, called "dowsing," indicated almost the exact doses that I was already taking. Amazed and curious, I wondered what else dowsing might indicate in addition to health guidelines. I gradually realized with great excitement that the answer to my question is "anything one needs to know for highest good."

One of my first dowsing surprises had to do with my eyesight. Shortsighted since a bout with the red measles during the sixth grade, I wondered whether I might become more far-sighted as the years advanced. I inquired of my body by swinging the pendulum ("yes" if it swings one way, "no" if it swings another) whether I would ever be able to take off my glasses: "Yes." Soon? "Yes." Tomorrow? "No." When? "One week." I do not claim a miracle of the pendulum, but I do affirm that the pendulum told truly. I took off my glasses little by little, and three years later, still acting on pendulum advice, when I went to get my eyes tested at the Motor Vehicles licensing office, I was given a non-restricted license—after 46 years of carrying a restricted license—to drive without glasses. Moreover, I have been free of fibromyalgia since 1994, again thanks to dowsing: It helped me understand the emotional causes and stress that had led to the disease, and the relaxation and release that has healed me.

Fascinated by dowsing, I noticed a book in a special display at the public library about dowsing which contained the address of the American Society of Dowsers. I got in touch, started reading books (chosen on pendulum advice), communicated with other dowsers, and attended my first dowsing convention in Vermont in 1997. I tried dowsing for everything I could think of. I began to realize that Einstein was right: Everything is some form of energy. Although dowsing terminology is quite different from religious language, I could see that both describe the same phenomena: dowsing helps us connect with the Source of all energy.

In 1998, I organized the Hamilton and Area Healing Network (HAHN), and we have held meetings nearly every month since then. We have a lending library, a speakers' series on various aspects of healing, a monthly newsletter, a membership of over 80, and an average meeting attendance of about 40. HAHN is an active member of the Canadian Society of Dowers (CSD).

From 2002 to 2004, I served as president of the CSD at a time when my organizational abilities and experience helped the young society develop into a more structured organization able to respond to increasing membership. Some of my articles are posted on the CSD website: www.canadiandowsers.org. While HAHN and the CSD are not church communities, they appear to be my "next flock." Here, I am welcome—as I was not within the Church of Christ—to use my natural and grace-given and ever-developing leadership skills and organizational experience. I am currently a CSD director, policy advisor, and convener for our 2005 annual convention in Toronto. I consider this work to be my current Christian vocation.

For me, dowsing is a way of doing prayer. In 1959, I had chosen Matthew 7:7 for the university yearbook quotation: "Ask and you will receive, seek and you will find." What an appropriate choice for someone who eventually became a dowser! Through dowsing, I can request information, guidance, and intercession. I consider my pendulum to be a sacred tool, receiving "yes" and "no" answers from the Source of all energy. My pendulum also swings in answer to my requests for healing—it's like watching one's prayers go by.

I have been almost a daily dowser for ten years. Much of my dowsing work is distance healing for people who may not even know me personally. Occasional feedback convinces me that remarkable changes have taken place in their lives. I do not profess to be 100% accurate. The answers I receive are what I consider to be "likely." I check with others on important matters, and often ask various related questions to see whether the answers are consistent. I do not feel bound to follow the dowsed guidance I receive, but I give it very careful consideration, and I usually follow it, curious to see what surprises and insights will be revealed en route.

Some people discredit dowsing as a form of divination against which there are warnings in the Bible. A physical form of prayer, dowsing to me means seeking the will of God, which I take to be the calling of all Christians. Some people consider dowsing to be satanic. To them I reply that Satan must be very disappointed, for I give the credit to God for all the great good that has come through my dowsing.

I dowse for healing, for myself and for others. I do "soul's purpose dowsing," helping people to understand themselves and the gifts that they can develop, and how they can encourage family members and others to develop their own gifts and grow in their connectedness with the Source. Now I am applying dowsing to organizational wellness, blending my experience with dowsing for personal wellness together with my training and experience in facilitating organizational transformation. I led an exploratory workshop in June 2004, on this theme at the American Society of Dowsers' convention. Among other results, we have drafted a code of ethics for dowsing in this new area of organizational wellness. My entire professional life has been in the service of organizations that do good; why would I not want to apply the goodness of dowsing to serve those organizations further?

In September 2003, I was ordained a Healing Minister by the Church of Healing Energy, a legally incorporated body in North America that provides public recognition for spiritual healers from a variety of faith backgrounds and a self-regulatory discipline through its code of ethics. My "healing modality" is dowsing. At www.energychurch.org, you can read the code of ethics and learn more at. My background in the Church of Christ makes me uncomfortable with the title of "Reverend" that goes with this religious leadership recognition, but "Healing Minister" feels just fine! We can all be channels of healing in this world as we connect with the energy of God's creative love, and share it joyfully with others.

Reflections on My Journey

I have come a long way since my girlhood in the Fern Avenue Church of Christ. What I learned and came to believe at Fern gave direction to my unique spiritual journey. In order to use the gifts that God had given me, I had to connect with churches that were more ecumenical than was Fern Avenue and that welcomed me as both a woman and a leader. I left Fern Avenue with regret, but without anger; the Fern Avenue congregation is gone, now, but its goodness lives on with me. At the Fern Avenue Church of Christ, I gained a strong sense of the importance of ordinary people giving leadership, of the biblical imperative for unity "that the world may know" the truth of the Good News of God's love, of the importance of the biblical record of God's interaction with people over the ages, of the witness of real people who faced life's challenges with faith, and of the value of tangible signs of support within the church community.

As an adult, I have sought to be a responsible daughter of the loving Father of a worldwide family of loving, joyful, healed, and happy brothers and sisters. In me, my family inheritance has caused me to become an open channel of our Father's healing energies. Our elder brother, Jesus, also a healer, taught us to love one another as his Abba loved us. Jesus remains for me the Way, the Truth, and the Life. By receiving and passing on the gift of healing, I have come to know that God's Spirit is accessible to us abundantly when we seek to be filled and transformed by it. The Good News is that God, the Source of all goodness, is everlastingly with us. Thanks be to God!

MY SPIRITUAL JOURNEY

R. BLAKE GIEG

When does the Spiritual life begin for an individual? Does it happen at birth? Does it happen at christening or some other church-related event? Does it happen at baptism when one confesses Jesus as God's Son and the Messiah, and is immersed for the remission of sins? Or does it happen when an aunt presents a Bible to a 12-year-old? What about a mother's gentle guidance of her child, kneeling beside the bed in the evening and praying: "Now I lay me down to sleep...." What about that mother's commitment to see her children growing up with regular attendance at Sunday school? Could it be during catechism classes held in a Lutheran church school building, taught by a Catholic priest, to prepare some boys and girls for Confirmation in the United Church of Canada?

How does one determine the actual moment at which one's Spiritual journey with God began? Perhaps the important point is that it does begin.

Let me think back to a tiny village in Saskatchewan with a population of 200. The community was served by four denominations: Roman Catholic, Lutheran, the United Church of Canada, and the Holiness Movement. The Catholic priest did not live in town; Lutheran services were in German; the United Church had its own full-time minister; the Holiness group was overseen by their local elders, and known for their rousing evangelistic meetings. Taken to church by my mother, I sampled them all as a young boy, experiences not soon forgotten.

Regular attendance at Sunday school and worship at the United Church was the norm for me and my three-years-younger brother. In our early teens, we were given opportunity to be the caretakers of the church building. That meant doing some dusting and sweeping, straightening the hymnbooks, and lighting the fire in the big furnace in the basement so the sanctuary would be warm when the parishioners arrived for services. It was an old-fashioned furnace with "octopus" arms conducting heat up to huge round grates in the floor. Inevitably, when children tried to contribute the pennies they brought to mark birthdays, they would miss the box that was passed around, and pennies would drop and roll into the big round grate and down beside the furnace. To my brother and me, it was "pennies from Heaven."

Confirmation classes were a summertime event. One Confirmation Sunday, the classes were seated together, our names read out, and we received certificates that marked the successful completion of our studies. We were now full members of the United Church of Canada.

Life took a dramatic turn in my later teens when my family moved to the small village of Thornbury, Ontario. My parents were no longer either farmers or merchants, and I was one of three children (out of a total of 10) still at home, and a high school student with new friends to make and new teachers to meet. The most difficult transition for me was the move from the prairies of western Canada, where the sky never ends, to the trees and forests of Ontario, where I could barely see the sky.

Becoming part of the United Church in our new town was quite easy. My cousins were well established in this town that had been my mother's birthplace and the homes of six generations of our family that had come over from Ireland. Aunts and uncles and cousins—I don't know how many times removed—were just everywhere. They made me feel welcome at the young people's activities on Friday nights at the United Church. The minister's son, who was my age, lived up to the disreputable reputation of many a P.K., but "we won't go there."

I left high school early for reasons that I now do not quite remember. I spent a season on a commercial fishing vessel off the northern shore of Georgian Bay at Point au Baril. That one season in a Spiritual wilderness had more effect on my life journey than I realized at the time. My wages for April through November still have not arrived.

One hungry season of commercial fishing was enough for a lifetime. My uncle informed me that the local newspaper was looking for an apprentice, so on January 1, 1950, I began my work with the Thornbury *Review-Herald*. I worked at least a sixty-hour week for the princely sum of $10.00 per week, but it was an unlimited opportunity to learn from a great employer.

Health reasons prompted me to move to Toronto where I found employment with a printing firm. Now I was exposed to the Jehovah's Witnesses, another learning curve in my Spiritual journey. After about 18 months, I began working for the Thompson Newspapers, traveling on the Ontario Northland railway, continuing my career in the newspaper business, a job that ended less than a year later when I returned home and went to work for the *Meaford Express*. Happy to be back in Meaford, and away from winter in the north, I continued my career in printing for nine years. I rose from being a low-level employee to manager, gaining leadership skills that have been validated over and over throughout my Spiritual journey.

In the fall of '53, my buddy and I were double dating, and the girl he was dating would later turn out to be my lifetime partner. During these dating days, I was first exposed to the Churches of Christ (Disciples)—or so the signboard said on the front of the church building. Older citizens of Meaford and my co-workers always referred to the congregation as "the Disciple church." I attended my first "gospel meeting" under the preaching of Roy Cogdill. Hot summertime with the windows wide open, I'm certain that people on Main Street two blocks away could hear the message!

Regular church attendance and Bible Study on Wednesdays became the norm as dating began to turn into a more serious relationship. One Wednesday afternoon in the spring of 1955, I spoke with Philip Petch, one of the Elders, and told him that I wanted to be baptized. In typical Church of Christ fashion, there was no delay. That evening, after Bible Study, Philip heard my public confession of faith and immersed me.

Our wedding took place that summer. Blake and Marion, boy and girl, became husband and wife, C. G. McPhee officiating. Emma Jay (nee Godfrey), the bride's grandmother, a descendant of the Trout family—pioneers who had established the Church of Christ in the region—was the great influence on us both at this time. Carl Manor, owner/publisher of the newspaper where I worked, printed our wedding picture on the front page, shot photos of all the guests as they arrived for the reception, and—later—the editor wrote an article on us just after our first-born arrived. Mr. and Mrs. Gieg were off to a good start.

During our early years, Bible study, sermons, and a lot of gospel-meeting preachers gave further direction to what was now our spiritual journey together. We began to see a new dimension of the Church of Christ. June Meeting, a traditional time of fellowship among Ontario churches of Christ that dated back to the mid-1800s, and visits to other congregations both local and beyond, and attendance at their gospel meetings, brought about many new relationships that have continued to this day.

On a hectic Thursday morning, while working at the newspaper in Meaford, we were rushing to put the paper to bed for the week. The local minister, Walter Dale, dropped by to inquire about my absence from Bible Study the night before. When I tried in vain to convince him that nothing on earth was more important than finishing the newspaper set-up on a Wednesday evening, he replied: "I'm going to Great Lakes Christian College in August. Why don't you leave your work and bring your family for the new two-year Bible Program beginning in the fall?"

My first response was "no way," but then I found myself talking to Marion about the conversation. We wondered where we could get the money to go back to school, and I was hesitant to approach my employer, but Carl proved himself once more my friend and mentor. "There's an open door," he told me, making my decision easy, and I could always come back to my position with the paper, if it didn't work out. Carl, a Spiritual giant and community leader, helped me take my next major step in our Spiritual journey.

The next two years in the Bible Program was a busy time for our family: I was also Dean of Boys and in charge of the Tuck Shop, in return for which GLCC provided our housing accommodation. Marion was taking care of two preschool girls, and she served as seamstress for the community. We had sold our home in Meaford, and that netted us $100.00/month income during this time. We spent the summer between school terms in our nation's capital. I held down a full-time job with a printing firm, but our reason for being in Ottawa was to help build up the local church, which had been pioneered by Roy and Nelle Merritt.

My teachers at GLCC, among others, were Geoff Ellis (Church History), Walter Dale (Old Testament), Donald Perry (New Testament), Keith Thompson (Speech), and Ila Ellis (English). Between my two jobs and a heavy class load, writing papers, attending local gospel meetings, and attention to Marion and the girls, I was unacquainted with free time.

When I had completed the Bible Program, we returned to Meaford, and I walked gratefully through that "open door" back to the newspaper, but another major turning point was just around the corner in our journey. At the Canadian Weekly Newspaper Association in Ottawa that fall, Nelle Merritt told me she was editing a small community newsletter in the southeast corner of Ottawa, but the owners wanted someone to take over the newsletter and develop it as a local newspaper. Back home in Meaford, Carl, as ever, encouraged me: "Go for it!"

The publishing and printing business in Ottawa involved our family from 1961 to 1967—until the bankruptcy of our business partner forced the sale of my shares in the company. Then, when a call to ministry came, my first response—as it too often has been— was "no way." But God's reply—as it always is—was "yes way." I became the assistant minister in the Riverview Park Church of Christ, where Dean and Ruth Clutter were leaders of the congregation.

My first responsibility was to raise my own support. We needed a monthly income, and in addition to that, the Ottawa congregation had committed to an Ivan Stewart "Campaign for Christ," and not only to one campaign but to two of them. I went to Port Elizabeth, South Africa, to be part of the campaign there as preparation for the campaign in Ottawa. Raising funds for foreign missions was easier than raising funds to support oneself at home. I got what I needed for the month-long campaign in Africa, but upon my return, it took travel through most of Ontario and much of the southern U.S.A. to piece together a livable income for my family. I was frustrated that the Churches of Christ lacked sufficient organization so that those willing to take on ministry in small congregations had to go about the country seeking help to secure financial support.

Having spent most of my time trying to make our ministry in Ottawa possible, we moved from there to Hamilton, Ontario, in the fall of 1968, in answer to a call from the Ivon Avenue congregation. After that, the call came in 1971 from Barrie, Ontario. In conversation with Wesley Jones at the Michigan Christian College Lectureship, he told me that he was leaving for mission work in Indonesia, and he wanted me to replace him in Barrie. My ego being greater than my common sense, it did not occur to me to say "no way," this time, but after we arrived in Barrie, we found out that the congregation was divided. One faction had called me to be the minister even while another person was already fulltime with the work there. After four frustrating years, I resigned my ministry in Barrie and returned to Ottawa to become a sales representative for a greeting-card company.

In 1979, the Hamilton church called again, and we took on the leadership of their program in personal evangelism. The congregation had agreed to bring an AIM team (Adventures In Missions) from the Sunset School of Preaching in Lubbock, Texas. Marion and I graduated from the six-months Coordinator's Course and returned from Lubbock to Hamilton with a team of ten young people intending to infiltrate our community by way of the AIM program. Struggles and disappointments were many, including the never-resolved problem of how to find individual support for the AIM team, but the benefits far outweighed their opposite. During the AIM time, the Hamilton congregation moved its meeting place to suburban Stoney Creek, and this placed even greater financial burdens on the church. Once more, I thought, lack of central organization within the Churches of Christ made fundraising harder than it needs to be.

Marion and I began to contemplate future retirement, and we realized that time was not on our side. Our salary as ministers of the gospel had always been low, and benefit packages were undreamed of. So we began to draw on other resources.

While we continued as members of the Stoney Creek congregation, and I acted in a part-time administrative position, I took advantage of a two-year course in chaplaincy at the Hamilton hospitals. Marion continued working at McMaster University in the Psychiatry Research Department. I felt especially honored when the congregation chose me to be one of the Elders of the church.

During the chaplaincy course, I was asked to take a position with the Board of a local chapter of the Canadian Bible Society (C.B.S.) The contact person was Joan De New,[4] and acquaintance with her put me in touch with a group of people and a whole new ministry about which I had known absolutely nothing. I met the CEO of the national office of the

---

[4] See Joan De New, "Growing Up in the Church of Christ," in this volume.

C.B.S., who soon proposed that I become his personal assistant. I accepted on condition that I might complete the chaplaincy course. Ten years later, at the mandatory retirement age of 65, I had concluded a decade of work with the C.B.S. that had proved to be a fulfilling ministry and also came with a livable salary and, at last, retirement benefits.

During my time with C.B.S., I traveled widely and came in contact with heads of different religious organizations and denominations, both local and worldwide. My appreciation grew immensely for fellow travelers on their own Spiritual journeys. Our vacations became a summertime idyll at a Free Methodist retreat and campsite in Prince Edward County, an island in Lake Ontario. These times were one more opportunity for Spiritual growth and fellowship outside the Churches of Christ.

We retired in the little community called "Carrying Place," at that spot where the island of Prince Edward County joins the mainland of eastern Ontario, a narrow corridor of land across which First Nation Canadians and Early Europeans who did not want to boat around the island had carried their canoes in portage from one part of the Lake to the other. Marion and I were tired of carrying our boat in a portage that had lasted too long. We wanted to become involved with a church in the community where we lived. We thought about becoming members of a small Church of Christ that met nearby—but that is all they did: "meet."

So we tried out the other churches and finally became associated with the United Church in Carrying Place. I soon found my place with the AOTS Men's Club, dedicated with a great Spiritual emphasis to "serving" in the sense of Luke 22:27. Marion became fully involved with the United Church Women. Ironically unlike my Men's Club, Marion's Church Women's program proved to be sadly lacking in the Spiritual dimension. Whereas I seem to have returned to my childhood roots in the UCC, Marion continues to struggle with the drastic change involved in moving away from her family and personal history with the Church of Christ.

Friends and members of the Churches of Christ refer to us as two who "left the church." They ask us why. I reply that their statement is impossible. We *are* the church because of our commitment to the one who is Lord of the church. We both answered that call a long time ago, and we plan to abide in relationship with the One who called us until He comes to get us.

In this essay, I spell "Spiritual" with a capital "S," but I have not specifically mentioned the Holy Spirit. I personally thank a great evangelist, Karl Ketcherside, who through his publication from St. Louis, *Mission Messenger*, opened my mind and eyes to the power and presence of God in every moment of my life through the Holy Spirit's taking up residence in me when He was invited to do so. He remains with us today, still guiding us along the Spiritual journey to which I refer in the title of this essay. "Spiritual" means many things, including surprises, wonderment, and awe. I thank the many mentors and encouragers along my Spiritual journey, for God and I know that they are the ones who put me on the road that leads to the Eternal Presence. To Him be the glory and praise! Amen.

Finding a Scientific Voice

Russell Elliott

Common sense is the collection of prejudices acquired by age 18.
– Albert Einstein

This essay is a description of my efforts, as of 23 November 2004, to emerge from the "primal soup" of family and community values that were based on a literal interpretation of the Bible in my individual evolutionary effort ultimately to embrace a scientific description of the world, and then make sense of it all. When I first started writing this essay, I thought it would be simply a case of telling the story about a person who grew up in a Church-of-Christ family and attended a secular university to study science, only to discover that he could not find the teachings of science to be compatible with Church-of-Christ doctrine, and was thus driven by logic to leave the Church. If that was all there was to it, it probably would not be worth writing about. It turns out to be bigger than that.

Born and raised in a Church family, our congregation was composed mostly of relatives or relatives of relatives. I felt loved and accepted by the Church community and could not imagine wanting to be part of any other church. As a teenager, I remained an outsider at school and where I worked because the church community met my social needs. This church-family structure was also the model for most of the Church of Christ congregations I later attended. I am surprised, now in retrospect, to realize that the fellowship aspect of the Church turned out to be much more important than doctrinal issues when Church of Christ doctrine came into conflict with my emerging understanding of scientific ideas. I wish I had grasped the social aspect of my religion back when I was attempting to resolve my dilemma between science and faith in the Scriptures.

We were expected to study the Scriptures regularly, usually in the context of twice-weekly Bible-study classes that were designed to make sure we understood exactly how God expected us to conduct a righteous life. The system, as taught, seemed to be perfect, although I was aware that in addition to doctrinal conflicts with other denominations, some scientific ideas did not agree with our understanding of specific biblical ideas and alleged facts; however, I was too busy attending to my own salvation to give these concerns much thought.

My complacency was disrupted when I enrolled in Engineering Physics at the University of Saskatchewan. The disruption did not arise from the side of the Saskatoon Church of Christ or its failure to accept me personally. Indeed, I felt the same love and fellowship there that I had known in my home congregation. The difficulty arose as I began gradually to face scientific concepts, for example, as the antiquity of the Earth (much older than the "six thousand" or so biblical years), and scientific paradigms such as Neo-Darwinian evolution. I was—still am—unable to reconcile these with the biblical worldview or with Church-of-Christ teachings.

In university, some of my classmates were religiously neutral and took everything in their stride. Most of the religious ones seemed able to compartmentalize their thinking so they could hold contradictory points of view. Whereas they could move back and forth between religion and science depending on the topic of conversation, I found that I could not do this. For example, one of my classmates, a Roman Catholic and active in the Catholic student organization on campus, could entertain opposing points of view at will and close one of them off when he wanted to affirm the other. I suspect his ability to compartmentalize was due to the clearly established doctrine of the Roman Church that seemed to have been in place for centuries: He believed science with the scientists, and religion with the Church. Religiously, he lived comfortably within an authoritarian but benign religious dictatorship in which one did not need individually to think through the validity of one's religious beliefs.

I, on the other hand, lived in a religious system in which the Bible was to be interpreted literally, and responsibility for interpretation of Scripture rested ultimately on the individual reader. Ours was more a system of religious anarchy, yet with the constraint that one was expected to maintain "correct" views in order to be accepted by the local church group. Under this requirement, I felt it my duty to examine carefully any ideas that appeared to contradict the standard Church-of-Christ interpretation of the Bible. The Church of Christ had taught me not to segregate my cognitive processes and to put my ideas into separate boxes.

I discussed my dilemma with the minister and with some of the congregation members who were university students. Those conversations usually ended in a long exhortation to keep keeping the faith. I no longer remember the details, but I do remember that I was not convinced. I also remember my own recurring exhortation to myself: Why would God have given me reasoning ability if He did not expect me to use it?

The reality of my life at the time was that I was too busy with university studies, helping to raise a family, and going to church to think about the larger religious questions very much. So I continued putting off ultimately resolving these issues, pretended that I believed the party line (which I did do to some extent), and carried on like a regular Church member. Thereby, I avoided internal conflict and conflict with my church family. The stakes were high: I had a wife and a large loving extended family, all of whom were members of the Church, and most of my friends were in the Church, too. I kept my head down with the expectation that I would resolve the issues when I had time. Meanwhile, I presided at the Lord's Table, taught Bible class, and served on the congregation's board of directors.

This half-in, half-out state continued for many years, and I never resolved the issues. My decision, later, to leave the Church was triggered when I caught myself lying to a family member in order to appear acceptable. This event made clear to me that I was tired of pretending to believe Church-of-Christ doctrine and that I was ready to leave, but catching myself in a lie was not the real reason I left. My divided mind, I now realize, had kept me from developing a strong, loving connection with the congregation I was attending, so no compelling reason obliged me to stay. My leaving, however, proved seriously unsettling to members of my family.

After I left the Church, I spent intermittent periods as an agnostic, with occasional forays into atheism. A period of intense self-exploration was precipitated during which I attended workshops, self-help lectures, retreats, fasts, encounter groups, and other personal-growth initiatives. I read a great deal of esoteric literature—Gurdjieff, Castaneda, Jung; I sampled other religious systems—Sufism, Hinduism, Tibetan Buddhism. Later, I took another look at Christianity when I attended The Unity Church of Truth in Toronto for about ten years. Also, I studied Tibetan Buddhism in parallel with Unity. I attended several long meditation retreats, and I found these retreats to be wonderful, enlivening experiences.

Early in this period of self-exploration, I had a very frightening experience with channeling (or "familiar spirits" in biblical terminology) which convinced me that Spiritualism is much more than a parlour game and should be avoided. This experience, more than any other, awakened me to an aspect of spiritual reality that I would normally have ridiculed. Ultimately, my fright turned out to be beneficial because it opened a door to positive realms of spiritual experience that I had previously not known to exist.

I seem to be blessed (or cursed) with an "insistent underlying faith" or belief that the Universe is intelligent, i.e., that it is not a mindless machine. I equate "an intelligent Universe" with the existence of a supreme being. I think it is generally agreed that intelligence of the universe, or not, cannot be proven, one way or the other; therefore, either choice must be an act of faith. To defend my choice, I often use the methods of experimental science to examine my personal spiritual experiences. Many times, however, I really do not know what to make of it all, and I am left to rely on my insistent underlying faith. One of the gifts of the scientific paradigm is that it has made the position of not knowing respectable; therefore, I feel no embarrassment in having to say, "I do not know," and then going ahead and believing by "faith alone."

I cannot deny that atheism is reasonable. The physical evidence for the absence of God is almost overwhelming. For example, the carefully measured homogeneity of the cosmic microwave background radiation throughout the universe and the red shift in the spectra of chemical elements in far-away galaxies, strongly support the contention that the universe started as a small primordial fireball that expanded to form the present cosmos over a period of about 13.5 billion years. Personally, I find it very difficult to conceive of a role for a personal "God" in these processes of this primordial fireball, especially before it expanded beyond quantum mechanical dimensions. Some theoretical physicists who work on these cosmological questions suggest that their models preclude the existence of God at all.

Alternatively, other practitioners of theoretical physics maintain a spiritual outlook and derive their faith, at least in part, from their work. Since 1989, for example, four of the winners of the $US1.2 million Templeton Prize for Progress toward Research or Discoveries about Spiritual Realities have been theoretical physicists, three of whom work in cosmology, and one in quantum mechanics.

After all of the arguments have been made, I find myself able to state with measured conviction that I believe that an intelligent but unknowable "Presence" exists in the universe. This Unknowable Presence, it seems to me, is a better explanation for the spiritual states and visions to which I myself have been subject, and certainly I prefer that explanation to aberrant brain chemistry, although my scientific mind cannot completely dismiss the latter. Atheism as a cognitive choice strikes me as a closing of the door to exploration of the spiritual world, and in that sense, atheism is like being a traditional member of the Church of Christ, for it, too, closes the door to explorations beyond the literal interpretation of the Bible. My spiritual life (or brain chemistry) is far too active to accommodate the restrictions of either atheism or Church-of-Christism.

After I had completed writing this essay, I visited friends in Saskatchewan who are members of the Church of Christ. I was among them long enough to observe the presence of the same sense of love and friendship, fellowship and family that I had felt in most of the congregations I had been associated with before I left the Church. When I attended church, where I knew the people and was known, I felt accepted and was treated like a brother.

Reflecting on that experience, I remembered my old expectations of love and fellowship that flowed with good feelings from the good people in the congregations. Not all groups based on fellowship can be counted on to have such good people, however. So now I wonder whether my good feelings of fellowship might have been a tribal, kinship response that I experienced. Feelings, like everything else, are susceptible of scientific explanation. Members of the churchly tribe, myself included, had unconsciously acted in the way that members of a kinship group are programmed to act. This Darwinian explanation of love and friendship—nurture, protection, identity—at church works equally well to explain the relationship between a mother and baby or the behaviour exhibited among members of any family or tribe. Over long periods of time, harmony within a group would tend to maximize the survival rate of offspring and thereby perpetuate the production of loving, friendly tribal people. Thus, the loving, harmonious behaviour that we experience within the Church is undoubtedly an aspect of the evolutionary genetic heritage of the human race. What better proof for the existence of a loving, caring God do we need than the evidence of this Darwinian effect in the human species? "In the image and likeness of God created He them."

My Spiritual Journey

Blenus Wright

Seventy years ago I was born in the small farming community of Tweed, Ontario, Canada. Tweed is about halfway between Toronto, Ontario's capital, and Ottawa, the capital of Canada.

My father, Elias, had been born to farming parents near Tweed. He spent his working life as a plumber and tinsmith, including the installation and servicing of gas pumps for Texaco stations in the area.

My mother, Mary, was eighteen when she left her home in Glace Bay, Nova Scotia, to attend the Salvation Army College in Toronto. Her first posting was to Tweed, where she met my father who attended the Salvation Army. They fell in love and were married.

But the Salvation Army had rules: One rule specified that if an Officer bought a car, it had to be black. Another required that an Officer be allowed to marry only another Officer, and if an Officer were to marry someone who was not an Officer, that person could not continue as an Officer. "Love conquers all"—even the rules of religious groups. My mother loved my father, and for love's sake, she sacrificed her promising career as an Officer, though she continued as a member of the Salvation Army. I came along soon after, their only child.

My early contact with God and religion thus was nurtured through the Salvation Army. I remember the band playing at every service, and often I would fall asleep on either my father's or my mother's lap listening to the music.

One thing I know for sure: If anyone shall enjoy passage through the Gates of Heaven, it shall be members of the Salvation Army. They are good people whose religion concerns both the soul and the physical well being of humanity. Good people often rise above the rules of their religion to become even better people, and rules that once seemed so important pass away with time. If members of the Salvation Army are excluded from Heaven because they drove black cars only and did not follow other right rules, then there is little hope for the rest of us who drive any colour of car we please and likewise fail to live up to our own, but different, rules.

In 1952, when I was 18, I left Tweed in search of employment. I worked for a couple of years in the dairy business and then for Zurich Insurance, underwriting farm insurance. Realizing that my future without further education did not look promising, I decided to return to school. In 1959, I entered Abilene Christian College (now University). In 1963, I graduated with a B.Sc. in Business Administration and an M.A. in Religious Studies. A wonderful lady who had been my Business Law teacher had inspired me to pursue a career in Law.

I returned to Toronto, entered Osgoode Hall Law School, and was called to the Bar in 1968. I spent the next 23 years in various capacities with the Ontario Attorney General's Office. In 1991, I was appointed a Superior Court Judge. Having reached the age of 70 with the required number of years as a judge, I am now semi-retired. I shall—Lord willing—continue to work as a judge on a part-time basis until I am 75.

When I first moved to Toronto in 1952, I knew one person, a former Salvation Army Officer who had been stationed in Tweed. She knew a family who were members of the Church of Christ. I began attending that family's congregation, and in time, because of the fellowship among congregations, I began attending the Strathmore Boulevard Church, near Coxwell and Danforth, which had a large group of active young people. There I was baptized by immersion and also met my future wife, Audrey. We were married in 1958, and Audrey also attended Abilene Christian College.

I had become a member of the Church of Christ primarily because of the vibrant young people's group at Strathmore. I felt welcomed and comfortable. The congregation was full of "salt of the earth" people. They were a significant part of my life, and I was greatly influenced for good in my spiritual journey.

How many people are members of a particular religious group because either they like the members of the group or else their family is a part of the group? If one feels comfortable within a particular religious group, the rules of the group take a back seat or are largely ignored or tolerated because a person enjoys the company.

In my experience, most members of the Church of Christ have been wonderful, committed Christians. In time, however, I began to wonder to what they were committed. Were they committed to the Body of Christ as set forth in scripture or to a body of Christians with a specific set of rules? The Body of Christ as portrayed by the Church of Christ is a body limited and defined by a narrow set of exclusive rules. No rule covers the colour of car that one must drive, but numerous other rules cover any number of other minute matters in life. The prime issue and main focus in nearly every sermon was the requirement to be immersed. One could not participate in a leading role in worship unless one became a member of the Church of Christ, and to become a member one had to be baptized in a lot of water.

According to one of the rules of the Church of Christ, baptism is essential to salvation; however, many scripture passages more simply instruct: "Believe on the Lord Jesus Christ and you shall be saved." John 3:16, probably the most quoted scripture verse, says, "For God so loved the world that he gave his only begotten son that whosoever believes in Him shall not perish but have everlasting life." Can a person "believe" unto salvation without necessarily being baptized?

Please do not get me wrong! I believe that baptism is important, but is baptism the only and exclusive driver's license if one wants to travel to Heaven? Must one, even to be permitted to sit in the back seat of the black car to Heaven, have a baptismal driver's license acquired no other way than through immersion and "for the right reasons?" My Master's thesis at ACU is entitled: "The Relation of Faith to Obedience in Becoming a Christian." I wrote:

> The moment a person really believes, he or she will want to be baptized. One who has faith in the gospel must have a faith that desires to obey the gospel. A part of this gospel is baptism, and baptism is nothing more than faith in the gospel. As the gospel is the death, burial, and resurrection of Christ, so baptism into Christ is the death, burial, and resurrection of a person as the summit of faith. When the

element of faith expressed in an individual's explicit decision for, and commitment to Christ is stressed, baptism is seen as the crowning moment and goal of faith.

I recently re-read my thesis. I no longer entirely agree with all of the statements I wrote over 35 years ago. That is not an uncommon occurrence for any of us. Our opinions, like time and religious rules, change; and time and religious rules change us, and our opinions—one may hope—for the better. "We are closer to the Lord now than when we first believed."

As a judge, I interpret rules as part of my profession. As I interpret the Church of Christ rules on salvation, one must believe, repent, confess Christ, and be baptized by immersion for the remission of sins—or else one is hell-bound. I can no longer accept that edict. In my life in the Law and as an Officer of the Court, I have learned that laws and rules usually have more than one interpretation. At times, I myself have given a wrong interpretation, only to have it corrected by the Court of Appeal.

Christians, however, are charged not to judge one another. The ultimate Court of Appeal will be a loving Heavenly Father who will judge his children on the deeds of their entire lives. I believe that the Heavenly Court of Appeal will overturn the Church of Christ rule of "no salvation without immersion."

Following the logic of the Law and the usual practice of interpreting rules, we must consider all the cases: What about those who believe in Jesus Christ as their Saviour and live lives according to the principles of Jesus but are never baptized with any amount of water? What about those who are sprinkled or the water is poured or are half-immersed but are never fully immersed? What about those who are immersed but not "for the remission of sin?" What about those who believe that they have been saved before baptism, or who believe that sacramental power is strictly a spiritual matter that has nothing at all to do with physical water or a symbolic physical action?

Although baptism seemed to be the chief and most articulated rule in the Church of Christ, other rules also pertained and needed to be adhered to: no instrumental music in worship; the Lord's Supper each Lord's Day; no women participating publicly in worship. Other rules were also in force, but these three were among the main rules used as a test of fellowship with other Christians. Of course, in the minds of some in the Church of Christ, one was not a Christian unless one adhered completely to all of the rules.

Perhaps the Church-of-Christ rule that has wasted more time and talents and still causes more disunity is the rule that worshipful music must be singing only—*a cappella*—without instruments of music, which are anathema. The debate continues because some firmly believe that the rules must be followed or else hellish consequences shall follow.

As with any of the creative arts, what would life be without music? Each of us has music preferences. One of mine is to sit silently in a great cathedral and listen to wonderful organ music. I can worship either with or without instruments of worship. I believe that God is more interested in our attitude of worship than He is in our methodology.

I have great difficulty comprehending that a loving God would deny someone entrance to Heaven because their worship included instruments of music. It is a sad commentary on Christianity that fellowship among Christians is based in some instances on whether instruments of music are used in worship. I can accept *a cappella* singing as a preference but not as a test of fellowship, and certainly not as a rule that must be followed to gain entrance to eternal life.

In John Grisham's novel *The Last Juror*, Grisham tells the story of the owner of a newspaper in Mississippi who in 1974 decided to visit all eighty-eight churches in Ford County, and describe each visit in his newspaper. This included his visit to the Clanton Church of Christ:

> The Clanton Church of Christ had no musical instruments. The ban was based on scripture, it was later explained to me…. There was also no emotion whatsoever in the service…. A powerful sect was the Church of Christ. They clung to the odd notion that they, and only they, were destined for heaven. Every other church was preaching "sectarian doctrine."

The newspaper owner wrote this summary comment about Protestantism in general:

> The denominations were varied and baffling—how could Protestants, all of whom claimed to follow the same basic tenets, get themselves so divided? They agreed basically that (1) Jesus was the only son of God; (2) he was born of a virgin; (3) lived a perfect life; (4) was persecuted by the Jews, arrested and crucified by the Romans; (5) that he arose on the third day and later ascended into heaven; (6) and some believed—though there were many variations—that one must follow Jesus in baptism and faith to make it to heaven.

The Church of Christ in 1974 that Grisham has described is close enough to the church in which I believed while growing up in Ontario. I bought into the whole nine yards—all the rules of the Church of Christ, and I have no regrets. But times change, and as I continue my spiritual journey, so must I.

For me, a defining time came when I spearheaded *The Churches of Christ Salute You* exhibit at the Canadian National Exhibition in Toronto in 1967. Thousands of dollars were spent on the exhibit that was fashioned after the Churches of Christ exhibit at the 1964 New York World's Fair. For two and one-half weeks, dedicated staff portrayed a message to the public; but what was our message? On reflection, I now realize that we spent most of our time attempting to convince other Christians that they were following the wrong rules. Father, forgive us, for we did not know what we were doing!

In 1968, two congregations of Churches of Christ in Toronto, the Maplewood Avenue and the Fern Avenue churches, merged into what was called the West Toronto Church of Christ. Both of them had enjoyed a lengthy history; the Maplewood congregation reached back to the British Isles and to a time before the Campbells, father and son, had come to America. Even so—and I am not surprised—the merger failed. Changes were required of both sides in the merger, a gulf between the generations was perceptible, and members clashed over different interpretations of the rules. The greatest problem in all religious groups is maintaining unity. All religious groups have produced their splinters, and Churches of Christ are about as full of splinters as a church can be. New groups then form due to a different interpretation of the rules.

Eventually, some of us in Toronto classed by others as "more liberal" began meeting in house churches and in rented facilities for Sunday worship. Our worship was more spontaneous, with more individual participation and sharing, and with women participating publicly. Time brought change again: Some people died, others moved away, and our group became too small to continue; therefore, we disbanded. Audrey and I then began the search for a new church home. We attended other congregations of the Church of Christ, but, sadly, found nothing to meet our needs at this time in our lives.

For the past two years, we have been worshipping at Calvary Church at Danforth and Pape. Calvary has a loose connection with the Associated Gospel Churches, a 76-year history of community outreach, and a considerable foreign missions program. A dedicated team of twelve spiritual elders along with a senior pastor and an associate pastor lead Calvary Church. This loving and caring congregation has warmly welcomed us. While membership gives the privilege of voting on major issues, Calvary does not require a person to be a full member to participate in their multitude of church activities; indeed, participation is encouraged whether one is a full member or not.

Instruments of music are part of worship with a blend of old and new songs and hymns, and occasionally we sing *a cappella*. Worship teams take considerable time planning meaningful and uplifting worship services. Baptism by immersion is encouraged. We have experienced a number of very moving baptismal services. Communion is celebrated monthly and on special occasions. Each celebration of the Lord's Supper has been a meaningful experience. The elders serve communion with dignity, and the congregation is encouraged to "wait on one another," taking time to meditate on the solemnity of the occasion. The sermons have been extraordinary, Bible based, encouraging and inspiring. In the kind of world in which we live today, people need to have their batteries recharged on Sunday if they are to face the long haul of a new work- week. I have yet to hear a message at Calvary that failed to feed my soul and encourage me.

Calvary is not a perfect church. There are no perfect churches because all churches are made up of imperfect people. But, for me, Calvary Church is what I need at this time in my spiritual journey. I hope that my contribution will continue to build up the universal Body of Christ of which Calvary Church is a small part.

Inscribed on the front of the Strathmore Church of Christ building is this verse of scripture, John 8:31: "If ye abide in my words, then are ye truly my disciples." What follows in verse 32 reads, "and ye shall know the truth and the truth shall make you free." The mainline Churches of Christ believe that in following their rules they have embraced the whole truth. I agree that some of their rules may indeed assist some people to salvation, helping to free them from sin. Unfortunately, however, according to the Apostle Paul, a religion of rules brings bondage rather than spiritual freedom. If a person thinks that one cannot be acceptable to God if one drives a car that is not black, the ultimate result will be a stunting of spiritual growth, and if one insists that the rules of the Churches of Christ are the only truth that can set one free and guarantee eternal life, a likewise stunted spiritual growth will be the outcome.

Time and rules change, and so must I. Paul said in Galatians 5:1: "For freedom did Christ set us free; stand fast therefore, and be not entangled again in a yoke of bondage." Paul was freed from the Law of Moses, and I can no longer submit to a yoke of bondage under the Church-of-Christ rules that say that Jesus suffered and died on a cruel cross so that only those persons who belong to certain congregations, are baptized in a certain way and for certain reasons, who worship in a certain way, who have communion a certain way and only on certain days, and who treat women as certainly disallowed from participation in public worship, will be the only certain residents of Heaven. Those rules do not make common sense, and in the Common Law tradition, our rulings must at least make common sense!

Time changes even the Churches of Christ. I understand that some congregations now have worship teams, use instruments of music, and allow women to participate publicly. Praise the Lord! "The truth shall make you free."

What is the end of this matter? When I stand before my Judge, He will not ask me to what congregation I belonged. I am responsible for my own spiritual journey, and I alone must come before my God to account for my life. I believe in God, and in his Son, Jesus Christ who died for my sins and rose again, and in His Spirit who lives in me and around me every day. I have been baptized by immersion which I believe is an important and amazing spiritual experience, but I do not plan to go to Heaven on the basis of a set of rules that I have kept, whether Church of Christ rules or our house-church rules or Calvary rules. Jesus himself gave the rule that leads to eternal life in what he called the two greatest commandments:

> Thou shalt love the Lord thy God with all thy heart, and with all thy soul, and with all thy mind. This is the greatest and the first commandment. And the second like unto it is thus, thou shalt love thy neighbour as thyself. (Mt 22:37-38)

I confess both to you, Brother or Sister in the Journey, and to our only High Judge of Appeal, that I am a long way from fulfilling these two great commandments, but I also believe that a good judge tempers justice with mercy. Therefore, "Forgetting those things which are behind, and stretching forward to the things which are before, I press on toward the goal, unto the prize of the high calling of God in Christ Jesus." (Phl 3:13-14) I shall appeal my case to our loving and forgiving Father in Heaven through Jesus Christ, my Lord.

A Charismatic Christian:
One Generation Later

Joe E. Lewis

A Budding Maverick

Even as a young boy in the 1940s, in the Putnam City Church of Christ in suburban Oklahoma City, I was beginning to question traditions, rituals, and "our" spirit of moral, ethical, and spiritual elitism. Being a "maverick" became my badge of pride, and I trusted no one's conclusions about any facet of "eternal truth" unless I could discern it through my own searching. Having mellowed of late, I now give others credit for honest thinking that can benefit my outlook on life and spirituality; even so, what I learn still has to ring true in my heart of hearts.

By the time I was a freshman majoring in Biblical Languages at Harding University, I had already arrived at a few conclusions considered heretical by my peers: instrumental music in worship is not sinful; elders do not hold an "office" but do a pastoral work; Jesus would not have known what to do with collective church treasuries—except, perhaps, to empty them as he did the money-changers' coffers in the Temple; multi-million-dollar church buildings and "plants" do not proclaim the image of the Lord's Body; perfunctory reenactment of the Lord's last supper is too often a meaningless, choreographed exercise in efficiency; trite, by-rote public prayers do not rise higher than the ceiling.

I changed my major to Vocal/Choral Music, desiring to serve the Lord by making a difference in the spirit and content of corporate worship. After graduate work in Voice at the University of Kansas, I joined the faculty of York College, a Christian college in York, Nebraska. The atmosphere there and in the local church was flexible and open, the school being far enough north to be rather immune to the wrangling over issues of the "Brotherhood" going on to the South and Southeast.

In that relatively fertile soil, I was able to develop deeply moving, spiritual worship services that fed hungry hearts, my own as well as others', both at the college congregation and throughout the region. Over the years, the "new worship" prompted hundreds of college students to "go forward," confessing out of a sense of guilt: "I don't feel close to God." My heart responded to theirs: "Yes, I understand; in spite of all the changes, I still don't feel close to God, either; I have only intensified the hunger and thirst in my heart."

Manna for the Hunger Pains

Break Thou the bread of life, dear Lord, to me
As Thou didst break the loaves beside the sea;
Beyond the sacred page I seek Thee, Lord;
My spirit pants for Thee, O living Word!

In the late fall of 1966, at age thirty-two and in my ninth year as choral director and chair of the Music Department, the dramatically changed lives of a fellow professor and two former students burst on Mary Ruth (my wife) and me like a vision: Our friends had become charismatics. Their experiences and the implications threw me back into intense Bible study, both in English and Greek. What is a "charisma?" What was the "gift" of the Holy Spirit?

I concluded that the contents of my old sermon outline on the work of the Holy Spirit were nowhere to be found in scripture. Mary Ruth and I prayed for each other—with the laying on of hands—to be *filled* with the Spirit of Jesus Christ. This prayer was not accompanied with raised voices or "holy-roller" antics; that would have scared the living daylights out of me! The answer to our prayer came as a calm and reassuring presence of Jesus himself in the room. I now realize that he had been there with us all along, but we had been unable to sense his presence.

My position at York College was terminated one week later. The charismatic professor had just been fired, but the administration, not taking me seriously, issued an ultimatum that I cease speaking about my convictions regarding the Holy Spirit or cease teaching at York College immediately. I resigned the same day, speaking to both faculty and students in separate convocations.

Throughout the college and the church in York an atmosphere of irrational fear arose. We had begun having Saturday-night meetings in our home—a house church for prayer, study, and Communion, usually attended by as many as ten people. Almost immediately, rumors began to circulate that we were using a crystal ball and hosting nude sleeping parties. When I traveled to attend non-Church-of-Christ meetings, "fifth-column tactics" (their words) were used by two church Elders to determine the nature of events and my participation. My honesty was questioned; my wife's accustomed visits with other women in the congregation aroused suspicion and panic—a slice of seamy history from old Salem. It was as if the congregation were fighting off the demonic hordes, all because a few of its members had dared to search for themselves and find answers that were not in the current version of the church's unwritten creed.

I recently received a letter from a former York Elder whose attitude differed drastically from those who had surreptitiously spied on me. Among other kind remarks, he wrote: "Joe, I hope that none of my words or actions back in York caused you unnecessary pain. And I sincerely wish that you had stayed with us, to help us become more like Jesus." I, too, wish I could have stayed, but—old wineskins, you know—evidently I was years ahead of my time. That seems to be the plight of those who think for themselves.

We stayed in York for two more years; I made our living by teaching vocal music at the local high school (with a 73% salary increase). Then an invitation came to teach at Southeastern Christian College in Winchester, Kentucky, a school founded by those ostracized a quarter-century earlier from the mainstream Church of Christ for holding "diabolical" Premillennial views. The people at SCC initially welcomed a "fellow outlaw" with open arms, but alas, their determination to be tolerant of differences in others soon waned. After two years, the Board fired the president, dean of students, me and several other faculty members, all over our faith in, and experience of, the work of the Holy Spirit. Their unwitting, sectarian agenda was expressed eloquently by one Board member: "I don't care if what [the president] says about the Holy Spirit *is* true; it's not what we've always taught!"

At that point, I decided to leave my career in "Christian Education" to open a music store in suburban Atlanta. We attended the Brook Valley Church, a prototype of the Community Church, composed of former Church-of-Christ members and former Baptists, assorted charismatics, and some who were too liberal in other ways to be tolerated at a mainstream church. After two years there, we were again ostracized. When the Elders named as Deacons every man in the congregation but me, I knew how to read the "handwriting on the wall." It was time again to move on.

Our search for a new church home ended at a nearby Presbyterian church. The warmth of the membership and the professional-sounding choir met our family's needs. Mary Ruth and I began singing in the choir, and four of our six children became active in children's and youth choirs as well as bell choirs. After most of our children had left home and we had moved to a rural area north of Atlanta, Mary Ruth stopped attending regularly, but I continued until glaucoma and the driving distance eventually curtailed my ability to travel to choir rehearsals and worship services.

At the Presbyterian church, I became known as their "resident Campbellite," for I was allowed to speak up in scripture-study classes (both high school and adult, which I taught) about baptism as I believed it to be described by Early Church writers. The Presbyterian mode of "baptism" and Calvinist election and predestination were points of doctrinal disagreement, but their "baptizing" of infants was more a ceremony of mutual promises by parents and congregation to join in nurturing the child in the love of God. With appropriate mental reservation, I participated in these dedication ceremonies wholeheartedly; it couldn't hurt the babies, and it might do the parents some good. No other point of doctrinal difference became an issue during my 30 years of joyful worship among them.

Presbyterians, as I experienced them, are a staid and stuffy lot, intent on doing things "decently and in order," refusing even to sing "Amen" at the end of a hymn for fear of appearing Pentecostal. In a way, I had exchanged one worn-out liturgy for another, but I found a quiet contentment in their regular recitations of the Lord's Prayer and the Apostles' Creed. Time spent in the choir loft, lifting my voice with theirs in the choir's highly effective ministry of music, was spiritually fulfilling. I miss that, now, tremendously.

Our house church, begun in York and continued in Kentucky, ceased when we moved to Atlanta. Times of study and prayer in homes of the ex-Church-of-Christ Brook Valley members were frequent and intense, but irregular. The Elders there were zealous in promoting such gatherings as well as times of spontaneous fellowship and love feasts on Sunday evenings, in which women participated in leading the worship and testified to the Lord's working in their lives. One eccentric Gay man also participated, better preparing me to receive the news from my own two daughters who were lesbian. The Holy Spirit's leading and gifts during these informal fellowships—lifting arms in praise, prophesying, admonishing, exhorting, and bearing one another's burdens publicly—were honored by the whole church, and this made our eventual exclusion an enigma that I have yet to understand. I accept the outcome as part of my learning, leading me further down the path set for me.

Was it all worth it? *Absolutely!* My charismatic Christian life has brought me to the sense of intimacy with God I had longed for. I shudder to think of what might have happened, had it not been for the change of heart that the Spirit created in me. Our new prayer life has stayed with Mary Ruth and me as our source of being connected with God continuously. The travails at York and Kentucky I now recognize as periods of lesson-learning, for which I am the better. I was not victimized; I believe I generated my own social reality in those two human contexts. I am responsible for my own life. Now I retain the absolute assurance of my kinship with God, his incarnate manifestation as the precious person of Jesus, and the promised Comforter within and around me. I am safe in my universe.

Who Is the Holy Spirit?

Of late, I have become reluctant to think of God in the masculine gender only. To think of God as "Father," as Jesus did, is certainly comfortable, for as humans, acquainted with the comfort and care of loving parents, we find it comforting to think of our Source as the Divine Parent with all that connotes of caring and nurture. I still use parental terminology when thinking about God, but what I have come to understand gives me infinitely more comfort: God is All That Is, "everything to everyone," the One of which we are the Many. We all (animal, vegetable, and mineral) are related to each other and our creative Source, not only in terms of religion but in terms of our very nature, being part of what God is, for in God we "live and move and have our being." God in scripture says, "I AM," and I, too, say, "I am." For me, then, to claim the same "name," being part of what God is, evokes in me the most intimate, umbilical, molecular feeling of kinship and genetic inheritance possible.

Further, to call the Holy Spirit "it" is an unfortunate limitation of human language, but neither do I want to fall into a sexism of language and call the Spirit *him* all the time. Here, again, scripture helps us: In Hebrew, *ruach Yahweh* (Spirit of the Lord) is feminine; in Christian scriptures, the "Comforter" (*parakletos*) is masculine; and in biblical Greek, "Spirit" (*pneuma*) is neuter. The Holy Spirit, therefore, may be thought of as super-personal – She, He, It – whichever best suits the context of meaning. The Holy Spirit is the trans-personal creative energy that brooded over the primeval waters, like a mother hen broods over her chicks. The Holy Spirit in creation, in Jesus, and in us is that same She, He, and It in all, making us spiritually one, not in some weakly moral and influential sense, but in the essence and power and presence of everything that God is.

An enlarged understanding of the Holy Spirit, then, helps us understand Jesus better. In some ancient, fragmentary Gospels, Jesus called the Spirit "my Mother, the Holy Spirit," and he was himself utterly a Spirit-filled person. He was conceived by the Holy Spirit when *She* prepared and helped Mary receive the creative word. Jesus was baptized in the Holy Spirit when *It* fell upon him like a bird descending out of Heaven. Jesus was driven by the Power of God when *It* led him into the Wilderness to be tempted. Jesus prayed and rejoiced in the Holy Spirit when *She* came to delight his soul. During his own final hours, Jesus was comforted by the Paraclete when the Comforter sent angels to minister to him. Jesus was the consummate spiritual man, come from All That Is God to show us our true nature and teach us how to relate both to our Father-Mother God in Heaven, and to everyone around us on earth, who, like us, "created in the image and likeness of God," are our brothers and sisters. God – Father, Son, and Holy Spirit –"They" are actually "One," and we, "Their" children, are likewise one.

The Holy Spirit is the *Breath of God* (*ruach Yahweh*), breathing the breath of spiritual life into the nostrils of the Church, starting with Acts 2—and before that with the Apostles (Jn

20:21-23)—and after that in every age and in every place, inspiring martyrs, saints, and other heroes; empowering them to work many kinds of miracles; and enabling them and us with every ability and every strength that we are willing to receive, so that we may be the very Body of the New Adam, Christ, alive in the world today and forever. As reminder and revealer of Jesus' teachings, the Holy Spirit is the source of ever-new revelation, equipping the church day-by-day to meet the challenges and obstacles that the Principalities and Powers throw against us. When the church has failed, as we so often have done, it was only because we were unwilling to receive the cloudbursts of blessings that the Spirit was oh-so-willing to pour down upon us through the open windows of Heaven.

The Acts of the Holy Spirit in the Lewis Family

Water of Life

Mary Ruth was ready to ask for the baptism of the Holy Spirit the instant she heard the testimonies of those whose lives we had observed, but she was patient with my need to analyze and search. (Intuition was not yet one of my strong points.) As I began my intense study, reading first the Gospel of John, words of Jesus jumped off the page and into my hungering, thirsting heart. Closing my eyes, I envisioned a deep, artesian well of pure water, flowing ceaselessly from within, quenching the thirst of all life it touched, and all the thirsts of life. For the first time in my life, I said aloud, with feeling, "Praise *God!*" Jesus' words were literally fulfilled in me: "He who believes in me, as the scripture has said, 'Out of his heart shall flow rivers of living water.' Now this he said about the Spirit, which those who believe in him were to receive" (Jn 7:38-39).

The Dove

Just as the Heavenly Dove pointed to Jesus at his baptism, so did the Spirit of God point to Jesus at our Spirit-filling, enabling us to sense his presence in the room. We were not afraid, for now we knew of his infinite care for us. That sense has remained with us through the good and bad times, encouraging us, sheltering us, and sustaining us.

Spirit of Sonship (and Daughtership)

A few days after we prayed for each other, I was alone in our bedroom, praying. Letting my Bible fall open "randomly" (I believe the Spirit was guiding my fingers) to Romans 8, I read a few verses and then prayed with tears, thankful for my new heart. I became aware that I was saying "*Abba*, Daddy!" and it distracted me enough that I resumed reading: "When we cry '*Abba*! ['Daddy!'], Father!' it is the Spirit [Her]self bearing witness with our spirit that we are children [sons and daughters] of God." The sense of assurance gained that night has remained these almost-forty years, and I have never had the slightest doubt of my inheritance. To this day I cannot sing the hymn "Blessed Assurance" without tears. Later, while participating in a "Unity in Diversity" series of worship services at a Christian Church, one of my former students, who had heard this story, led the assembly in prayer, saying at one point, "…because you *are* our Daddy." This was, after all, the way that Jesus taught us to pray: "Our Daddy, who art in Heaven…."

Considering our individual relationships with our fathers and mothers, it may be that some would be more comfortable in praying to "*Mama in Heaven*," and that's fine. Having overcome my ingrained distrust of anything having to do with Roman Catholicism, I find it comforting at times to communicate with Mary, the mother of Jesus, as another source of nurturing care and understanding. But Catholics are not the only ones who know about the Eternal Feminine in godhead: Count Zinzendorf, re-founder of the Moravians, called the Holy Spirit "Mommy." And African-American members of the churches of Christ in Texas likewise knew that the Holy Spirit is female.

Spirit of Unity

Being a worship leader in the above-mentioned weeklong series, experiencing unity in diversity, occurred four months after my being filled with the Spirit. One of the first things I noticed after we prayed for each other was that suddenly I felt a kinship to other believers I had previously avoided—including even the Independent Christian Church, which used instruments in worship but was otherwise a near-clone of the Church of Christ. Why I had not earlier reached out to them is still a mystery to me, since I had long before concluded that using instruments was not a sin. I also discovered that I no longer felt superior to non-immersed believers. I could talk with them freely without fearing I would contract some spiritual disease!

These new attitudes were not the result of analyzing, reasoning, or struggling to re-educate my conscience; the feelings of acceptance and openness and oneness in the Spirit were just there. A new heart had arrived with the Spirit of God when I invited him into my life. For the first time, I comprehended that it is the *Spirit* who creates unity, not we who struggle to fashion it through lowest-common-denominator doctrine or formal ecumenical movement; our job is merely to "keep" what we are given. As Alexander Campbell knew, unity comes first, and *then* agreement. Differing opinions do not constitute disunity; being divisive with those opinions is the culprit. My sense of relief and freedom was enormous when I recognized that the true source of unity is the Spirit Himself, and that our duty, in the face of others' differences, is but to *preserve our Spirit-given unity with an agreement to remain peaceful* – "…maintain the unity of the Spirit, in the bond of peace." (Eph 4:3)

Spirit of Unknown Languages

When the Spirit manifested its presence in our lives through a gift of language, we sensed no feeling of a rising "ecstasy" or overpowering urge to begin speaking unintelligibly. We simply made the decision to open our mouths and speak without intentionally forming familiar words. My "acceptance" of tongues came when I was out in a friend's back yard, at night, alone in the woods behind the garage (Talk about your closet charismatic!). With my heart pumping overtime, I took a deep breath, blew it out, shut my eyes, raised my face and arms in the vulnerable-before-the-Lord "funnel of reception," as I conceived it, and began praising God with sincere feeling. I did not understand the words, but I knew I was being understood by my Lord. Later, my analytical mind got into gear as I tried to recall some of the words, thinking they sounded like a mixture of Middle Eastern and Slavic dialects, none of which I had studied. This "reserved charismatic's" experience of tongues contrasts starkly with that of a Church of Christ minister in Abilene, Texas, who, at the laying-on-of-hands and the prayers for specific gifts from those ministering to him, fell to the floor as if struck by lightning, writhing in the throes of what resembled an epileptic fit. Paul wrote of "different measures" of the Spirit.

I have to smile as I remember Mary Ruth's first gift of new language. We were side by side in bed, I on my back and she on her side, facing away from me. I thought we were both near sleep, but all of a sudden she turned on her back, flung her arms out—one of them across my face—and began speaking in a strange language. My nose was mashed flat, I could hardly breathe, but I was reluctant to move until she finished. We both laughed from relief and joy, and after I drifted into sleep, I was awakened by her shaking the bed with paroxysms of silent laughter. I thought, *Laughter is a gift, too!*

Now, a generation later, Mary Ruth no longer uses the gift of tongues. I still use my private prayer language, especially in times of crisis. We never expressed this gift in a group setting, and only once did any visitor to our house church exercise the gift, after which I immediately interpreted, again not intentionally forming thoughts to utter but opening my mouth and speaking "spontaneously" in English. I remember thinking, when the other started speaking, *Uh-oh, what if no one has the gift of interpretation? Lord, give me the words. I trust them to you.*

Spirit of Love in the Lewis Family

"God is Love"—a truth learned through pain in our household of six children. Many times Mary Ruth and I were at our wits' end, at the point of total despair. What kept us going was the assurance that God was in charge, aware and caring. From sources both scriptural and extra-scriptural (especially C. S. Lewis), we learned the true meaning of agapé-love that we had not theretofore understood. This is how we—and our children— survived.

Our firstborn came home drunk once, threatening to kill me. We woke up our therapist, asking for help. He advised locking him up and calling the police. We thought, *No! We've talked to the wrong person!* We prayed; when finished, we both knew we needed an angel. About half-an-hour later, our dearest friend, a longtime Church-of-Christ minister, showed up and, after assessing the situation, physically restrained our son, took him home with him, sobered him up, gave him a place to sleep, and took him to his job the next morning. Our *angel!*

This son had often been assured of our unfailing love for him, our willingness to be what he needed, no matter what. He felt that our beliefs and standards had ruined his life, but after he submitted to Army discipline to straighten himself out, I received a letter saying, "Now that I'm a little older, I can see what kind of man you are, and I'm proud to call you my Pop." Love is the greatest gift of all—the determination to act in another's best interests, no matter what their response may be and the cost to oneself. This son is now a spiritual person, but he has chosen not to be affiliated with any church; neither has he become charismatic.

When our second child, a daughter, cut off a relationship with a young man, he began leaving notes on her car at work threatening violence. He made the decision to commit suicide by speeding his car through the front of our home, taking as many of us as he could with him. On the way to our house, he wrecked his car and was hospitalized. Our attorney literally yelled at us: "Have him arrested for terroristic threats!" In a moment of bi-polar spirituality, I listened to a conversation in my head: *No! Let there be mercy...forgiveness!* "No! He's crazy! He'll harm us!" *Love...mercy...forgiveness!* Then it dawned on me (the Spirit's prompting, I believe!) that this lad had the same uncommon last name as some of my regular customers in the music store, so I called them. Yes, they were his parents, and he had been under a psychiatrist's care. After I informed them of what was going on, they took the situation in hand, and he was spared a probable prison term that would have had tragic consequences in his struggle to find healing.

Although she was active in the youth choir and bell choir at the Presbyterian church, this daughter continued to commute to as many of the Brook Valley Church's periods of spontaneous fellowship as possible. She is now attending a Church of God, worshiping in their custom. I know her to be gifted, but she does not consider herself to be charismatic.

At age seventeen, our fifth child was sent to prison for eighteen months for burglary to support a crack-cocaine habit. On his eighteenth birthday, he received from me a poem that I felt moved by the Holy Spirit to write after I had prayed, asking, "What does he need to hear from me?" The words reached his heart, and he responded in a treasured letter, saying, "I love you and respect you for what you stand for." Here is my Spirit-inspired poem:

My son –

Today you are a man,
Not so much because you are eighteen,
But because you've grown so much.
My wish for you today is that you
Profit from your experiences
And love yourself,
For you are loved, lovable, and lovely,
And worthy of love.
I long to tell you face to face,
But I cannot.
As you read this, believe it.
I love you.
Dad

Our boy is now the most fervently church-active of our children and is currently associated with one of the Vineyard churches. To my knowledge, he does not, however, claim to be charismatic.

Our fourth child is deeply spiritual, and is gifted with musical talent. She writes beautiful songs, many of which have been recorded. Her voice is now missed greatly in the Presbyterian Chancel Choir. The choir members, pastor, and many of the congregation know of her lesbian nature, and they accept her lovingly, recognizing the gift of God in her. Currently she is struggling courageously with bi-polar disorder, having recently undergone several ECT shock treatments. She is now smiling and laughing again and talking of the future.

Our third child, a daughter, had the least traumatic teen years of the six, but she, too, experienced pain in her maturing. She is the other lesbian daughter, who started out in life as a very shy child but has grown into a powerful, assertive, professional woman.

The sixth child, another daughter, went through an identity crisis that prompted her to leave school one day and meander aimlessly northward to Cincinnati, where she realized she was out of money and improperly clothed for the cold weather. A parents' prayer for angels to watch over her and her car was answered; one day after she left, she pulled into our yard, the car on its last legs, with oil streaking down its sides—but she was home safe.

Her name is the Greek-Hebrew equivalent of the prayer, "Lord, peace." That little prayer, too, was answered.

I sometimes think that when the Spirit is most active, the Other Side rages more furiously. Many people view being charismatic as a life full of roses; new charismatics are often deceived into thinking they must make excessive claims to lend credibility to their experience. With no self-righteous smiles or claims of charismatic immunity from assault, I am here to tell you that Mary Ruth and I most certainly have had our times of terrible hurt, but the gift of love helped us see that our children were hurting worse than we were. Growing up seems to be excruciating for most teenagers, and perhaps more so for kids in a family that turns out to be a battleground of Spiritual Warfare. We knew that deep down they loved us but were so confused and in such pain that they were unable to bring that love to their own consciousness. In time, however, "love conquers all." Our six are now exemplary human beings, successful in their respective fields, and giving loving attention and care to us, their elderly parents. Praise be to the God of Love!

Comforter and Prayer Partner

Prayer is the most basic attitude of Spirit-led life and worship. "Pray without ceasing" for me has meant being connected moment by moment with God, aware always of his oneness with my heart. Prayer at times takes the form of words uttered and thoughts sent out, but for the most part, it is reaching to—yea, embracing—my Abba with wordless yearnings that are immediate and personal. Being thus "present with God" continually, aware of his loving embrace, is prayer in the most sublime sense.

The young boy I once was wondered: *If God is real and is here, why don't our words sound like we believe it?* Then, as the experience came of praying so fervently that I was not even aware of the sounds coming forth from my mouth, I remembered the promises I had read but had not really understood. The Spirit of God was helping me with groanings and sighs too deep for words (Rm 8:26). The *Paraclete* is our "comforter" because He is the one who comes to aid us, to stand by our side like a defense attorney, to understand and interpret our inarticulate thoughts and needs, and to express them in us and for us before the Court of Heaven.

The very process of attempting to articulate the needs, feelings, and praise that come from the belly is self-limited. To be free of limiting constraints at such private, visceral prayer is to be at one's most vulnerable. Praying from the body sets the spirit free to soar and express itself completely, without inhibition, and this lays the whole person open to more healing, new faith, and deeper devotion. In this state of total prayer, everything that we are—heart, mind, body, lips, grunts and groans, unintelligible words, half-conscious desires, unformed emotions—flows outward from us, and the Holy Spirit turns it into praise, love, thanksgiving, longings, meaningful problems, and honest needs being offered in worshipful sacrifice to our caring God.

In private prayer, especially during times of great pain, such as the crises with our children, I know the Comforter is near. Compelled to go to a private place, I prostrate myself and communicate with the Lord without concentrating on the words. At those times, Spirit-given language expresses the pain for me and lends language to the deepest yearnings of my heart. With the Comforter at my side, I turn my palms up, ready to receive comfort and assurance, reaching for an *Abba*-Mama embrace, knowing anew that my wife and my children and I are offspring of the Living God, born of the abundant universe. We are loved, and we are safe.

Spirit of Visions and Prophecies

A former student of mine at York College, now living in Texas, once had a vision of a man's face. He was wearing a unique hat and walking the streets of London. She was convinced she was supposed to find this man and help him "clear the cobwebs from his head" so that he could fulfill whatever destiny was awaiting him.

She and her husband actually flew to London and chose, by the Spirit's leading, to wander the theater district in the old town, ending up in an internet store. While there, she began to feel "antsy and claustrophobic" and went outside. *The man she had seen walked by!* She recognized his face from the vision, and there was the same hat. She called loudly back to her husband while hurrying towards the man, for he was about to cross the street. Rushing up to him, she explained that she had seen a vision of him and wanted to pray with him to have the "cobwebs removed from his head," for she believed God had something special in mind for him. He agreed, saying, "My wife is going to be very interested in this; she prays all the time." As they talked, after praying, it was evident he felt renewed and invigorated, surprised by the love of a God who would send someone such a far distance to pray with him. My former student and her husband were at peace, able to say, like Paul: "I was not disobedient to the heavenly vision."

The only vision I ever had led to the only prophetic utterance I was given to deliver. After we had been in Kentucky a few months, two men from our house church and I were praying together about the sectarian attitudes we had observed in some of the Board members of the college. We considered what action, if any, we should take. I let my Bible fall open and put my finger on a passage that I have since summarized in memory: "Go in and speak to the Princes of Judah." Since then, though I have searched, I cannot find those exact words in my Bible, but something tells me that Jeremiah 34 may be close: "Yahweh says this: 'You have disobeyed me by not granting, each of you, freedom to his brother and to his neighbor....As for the Princes of Judah,...I will put them into the power of their enemies.... It is Yahweh who speaks: '...I am going to make an uninhabited desert of the towns of Judah.'"

My house church brethren and I borrowed a piece of Gideon's fleece, asking for a confirmation while we meditated. Several minutes of silence followed, during which I had a vision of a king sitting on his throne, his scepter standing free on a tiny golden tripod built into its tip. We all raised our eyes simultaneously, and I related the vision. "What does it mean?" they asked. I replied, "The Lord's Word stands on its own. Therefore I am to deliver a concise message about these concerns without adding unnecessary comments, leaving my own pride out of this." These words had not formed in my mind during the vision. I just opened my mouth and they were there.

A few days later, the fall Board meeting convened on campus. I attended as the guest of the president who was later fired. I urged those present to listen closely for God's guidance in the operation of the school, since it could not continue to grow and prosper unless they did so. I learned later that one Board member immediately took my words seriously, thereafter reminding his peers of "the warning." When the school was forced to close a few years later (brotherhood apathy and lack of funds), that Board member spoke to a posthumous assembly of those same men, declaring, "*Now* can you sit there and tell me that God does not speak today? – that he did not send us a warning?" The irony is that another of the Board members was charismatic, and a third, the most vocal in the firing of several of the faculty, later became charismatic and so lost his place of leadership in the premillennial Churches of Christ. Every building on the main campus, except for the Andrew Carnegie-built library, has been demolished. The campus is now a city park – all because a bequest came one day late. The Lord God knows his timing.

Spirit of Inspiration

As a musician and poet, I know naturally that divine inspiration is a factor in the creative process. The Greeks talked about the Muses; my fellow music-makers and I speak of "something in the air," and I have often sensed or intuited an idea swirling in my mind, a feeling of having temporarily tapped into a realm other than my normal consciousness. When I complete a poem or a piece of music, I look at it, listen to it, and wonder: How did I do that! To duplicate the work would be impossible; the moment of inspiration has passed. In the Hebrew scriptures, this kind of divine aesthetics was ascribed to Bezalel and Oholiab and "all the skilled craftsmen whom Yahweh had endowed with the skill and perception to carry out all that was required for the building of the Tabernacle,... all whose hearts prompted them to offer to do the work,... And they did their work exactly as Yahweh had directed." (Ex 36:1-2) David, too, was poetically inspired to compose his Psalms.

The gifted artist's job, then, is to be attuned to the slightest impulse that could, if heeded, become something of beauty to enrich the lives of other human beings. Just as ancient writers of scripture, singers of songs, and builders of beauty revealed their unique personalities in their work, so must all artists and writers necessarily use their own tools and words, their own imagination and worldview, but they must also remember the eyes, ears, and hearts of those with whom they would communicate.

Many of my aesthetic impulses come from inspirations of the Spirit and inspirations coming from all of God's Nature. The noble tree speaks to me mightily, as do the innate qualities of animals. I learn from them all, reading God's "other Book," listening for the revelations of God's Spirit, sensing God's Presence, absorbing the knowledge and wisdom to be gained through this spiritual communion.

One of my biggest struggles has been over an inherited hearing loss which, together with church-college politics, forced me to leave my cherished work as a choral conductor. I understand and sense a kindred spirit in Ludwig van Beethoven, the great composer who lost his hearing. *But that does not keep us from being creative, does it, my friend!* My joy was ever in performing—in weaving the tapestry of choral sound, but now the inspiration has been re-directed: Now I compose the music that has been in my head for decades, and the recently-acquired ability to articulate and write my thoughts (such as in this essay) is an unadulterated joy in my eighth decade of life—another gift from God the Holy Spirit.

Spirit of Healing

Numerous instances of God's healing abound among acquaintances that are or have been in the Church of Christ. The following stories have been related to me by trusted friends.

An elderly woman called her Church-of-Christ minister late one night, saying that her husband was in the hospital, not expected to survive until morning. The doctors could not relieve his suffering or symptom–lungs filling with fluid. The ministers prayed with the woman, asking for the removal of the fluid and complete healing. The next morning the doctors were dumbfounded, finding that their patient's lungs were clear, declaring him to be in good health and ready to go home.

A friend's mother developed terminal heart disease. A charismatic Elder spontaneously showed up and prayed, with the laying on of hands, for the healing of the woman's heart and a "gift of understanding of her healing." Again, dumbfounded doctors. The woman showed no signs of heart disease, and she lived another twenty-five years. The "gift of understanding" led her to found a Ladies Aid Society of women from many and diverse Christian groups who are still ministering to the sick as well as to the doctors and nurses at the hospital where she had once been a patient. This blessed woman's husband, an Elder in the Church, did not find her healing all that convincing. Later on, when the Lord showed this Central Texas rancher in a dream where to find a cow of his that was in labor to deliver a calf, but was in trouble, and he found her right where the dream said he would, he became a firm believer in "modern-day miracles."

A former student of mine was told by his doctor that he had a malignant spot in one lung requiring immediate surgery to remove part of the lung. He took a bold "stand of faith against cancer and surgery," and the subsequent PET scan showed no spot. His cigarette habit of three packs a day was broken instantly after he prayed for deliverance from nicotine addiction. Later he tested himself by lighting up and became violently ill. As he puts it, "The walk with the Spirit is a walk of faith."

A Church-of-Christ minister, sitting as Board chair of a Christian school, listened as one of the Board members requested prayers for his mother who had just been diagnosed as having an advanced stage of cancer with about two weeks to live. The Board put aside their business and prayed. Later in the week, the doctors could find no sign of the cancer.

For almost three decades, I have been an insulin-dependent diabetic, also taking Lesix and concentrated potassium for swollen feet and Lipitor for high cholesterol. Then, five months ago, I began losing weight, but with none of the typical diet struggles. After losing thirty-five pounds (twenty-five more to go), I am no longer on insulin, and have thrown away my Lipitor, Lesix, and potassium supplement. My blood pressure is normal and my last Hemoglobin A1C test for blood sugar was an ideal 6.0, after averaging over 9.0 for more than twenty years. All I had to do was *ask!* God is faithful, but we must choose to walk in faith, trusting his Holy Spirit for healing.

Restorationism Revisited

Over these forty years since my struggles within the Church of Christ, I have become disillusioned with organized religion—"churchianity." Specifically, I no longer regard the Restoration Movement's philosophy as a valid criterion for its partial imitation of first-century Christianity. Yes, total immersion into Christ ought to be taught and practiced, and the Lord's Supper is a vital source of nourishment for all Christians. But as far as success at "restoring primitive first-century Christianity" goes, the non-creed published in 2005 for the Church-of-Christ non-denomination gets only one out of three points mentioned (baptism, Lord's supper, *a cappella* music) anywhere close to my understanding of the Early Church, and the so-called "Affirmation" does not affirm nearly enough.[1]

The Lord's Supper, for example, as practiced formalistically during the canonical Sunday morning hour with a pinch of cracker and a sip of grape juice bears about as much resemblance to the Passover and love-feast that Jesus celebrated with his friends, and that Early Christians celebrated with one another, as bedewing the head of an innocent and unknowing baby resembles immersion into Christ.

This "Affirmation" treads with velvet-soled shoes, avoiding delicate areas of diverse opinion, in effect saying, *Let's get back to what we we've been; let's hold our Brotherhood together, and maintain our denominational distinctiveness.* The twenty-four co-signers are concerned about the Church-of-Christ denomination's getting too far off the path of Restorationism's 19th-century understanding and traditions (echoes of *"It's not what we've always taught!"*). They neglect to affirm what the churches most need to hear in our time. Where is a mention of the power of the Holy Spirit and the everlasting presence of Jesus Christ guiding his church forever? Where do they tackle hard problems and affirm Spirit-inspired new truth, such as the full equity of women alongside men in the worship and service of God? Where do they apply the love of God to human hurt, and affirm Christ's welcome to gays and lesbians?

Which first-century church do twenty-first-century Christians think they are restoring when they spend millions of dollars on elaborate assembly halls, classroom buildings, and peripherals? Why not meet in the Temple, as the Jerusalem Christians did, worshiping alongside their non-Christian Jewish brethren? That might mean for us today to meet with the First Baptists, the Second Presbyterians, the Third United Methodists, or—perish the thought!—the Fourth Assembly of God. Or why not just meet in our homes, as the gentile Christians did? Church buildings are brick idols.

Which first-century "office" is being restored when a congregation hires a highly paid "Preacher" to become the congregational manager and flunky, and to tell the members what they believe? If we want to be like garden-variety Protestants, then this "Pastor system" is just the ticket. Big Preachers are idols of flesh.

Which part of first-century Christianity is restored in the fundamentalist personification and deification of a book? Many of the letters and reports written by first-, second-, and third-generation disciples were lost, edited, and corrected; some were written by someone other than the named authors; and some first-century writings were purged from "the scriptures" in later centuries. The "New Testament" as we have it today was a political compromise, a collection of first- and second-century writings that are far from representative of the whole Early Church. No verse of scripture indicates that God ever intended for this collection—or any other paper idol—to be an absolute, inerrant, infallible guide for faith and practice. The source of absolute guidance for Christians is the living, abiding, indwelling Spirit who points to Jesus—not some book, no matter how fine it may be.

Moreover, the traditional Church-of-Christ insistence on "command, example, and necessary inference" is nothing but a *vain philosophy* of human reasoning that evokes the same legalism of the scribes and Pharisees whom Jesus so heartily debunked. Like rabbis, popes, bishops, synods, and councils in years past, and now, when debaters and preachers

---

[1] "A Christian Affirmation 2005," *Christian Chronicle*, May 2005, signed April 18, 2005, by twenty-four leading thinkers of the Church of Christ.: www.christianaffirmation.org/.

lord it over the pew-sitters, and Elders assert their "authority," they impose commands that neither Christ nor his first followers ever commanded.

But why should I complain about the Church of Christ! We don't go to church there, anymore. Not since 1971 have Mary Ruth and I been formally associated with any Church of Christ, charismatic or otherwise, except for two years at the Brook Valley Church. When I was doing research for my own book,[2] however, I found that many Community Churches and several non-mainstream Churches of Christ are blessed with a charismatic atmosphere in their celebratory assemblies. Their thrust into the world is not directed at winning people to "correct doctrine" or "the one true church" or the "first-century church restored in the 21st century," but to carrying out a Holy Spirit-guided mission to win people to the person of Jesus Christ, and to seek and to save people who truly sense that they are lost, by bringing to them the healing, comforting love of God.

Some of the Churches of Christ that have gone "beyond the sacred page," even those who were not vocal about being charismatic, have been disfellowshipped by traditional churches in their area. No doubt following a clear pattern of behavior detailed in scripture, the anathemas were published in full-page newspaper ads.

On the other hand, I also found that several alternative and breakaway groups have eventually drowned in their own new set of church politics. As with any reformation/ restoration attempt, human nature prevails, resulting in a waning of the original freshness and vigor, replaced by yet another guarding of the new *status quo*, ending the life-flow.

Several large congregations have enjoyed mass charismatic revivals, and the Spirit seems still to be among them. These congregations were not "breakaways"; rather, the sign out front simply changed from "Church of Christ Meets Here" to some new non-denominational designation, such as "Fellowship of Believers," "House of Blessing," and "Oak Hills Church."

The Charismata in Mature Perspective

1 Corinthians 13 is, though concise, surely the most richly abundant statement regarding the charismata and their use. Love is the best and ultimate gift, to be sought especially because it is the regulative principle for all the other charismata. Hope will be fulfilled and will pass. Faith will come to fruition and cease to be needed. Other gifts will serve their purposes and fade away—many of us grow out of tongues, prophecies are fulfilled and recede into history. But rather than saying that I have "cooled down," I want to say that I have gone forward. The "baby rattle" stage is behind, now, and what was once a sparkle of fireworks is now a warming glow. Paul's great chapter, so often read at weddings because it is about "love," may be little understood on wedding day; it comes to be better understood by the old couple in the rocking chairs who have learned that passion turns to compassion, and desire becomes fulfillment. A charismatic Christian, one generation later, learns something similar about the charismas of the Holy Spirit.

---

[2] Joe E. Lewis, *Leaving the Faith of My Fathers: A Spiritual Journey* (self-published, 2001): 237 pp. Available from the author: joelewis304@bellsouth.net or can be found in the libraries at the Harding Graduate School of Religion (Memphis), Oral Roberts University (Tulsa), Christian Theological Seminary (Indianapolis), University of Notre Dame (South Bend, Indiana), or Shallowford Presbyterian Church (Atlanta).

With poetic, Spirit-inspired utterance, Paul gently exhorted the Corinthians to move on toward "the perfect"—the maturing of the whole self, growing up to the "stature of the fullness of Christ." The writer of Ephesians in a similar but different passage commented on the same reality. In both passages, we are taught that charismatic experience is the divine energy that causes each of us, bodily members in our local congregations, to grow up to eschatological fullness in the universal body of Christ that is expanding throughout the entire cosmos. The allure and ecstasy of tongue-speaking mellows into an abiding spirit of prayer. Prophecy is either fulfilled or ignored, but its moment of importance is surpassed by whatever new situation requires a "word from the Lord." As Paul seemed to say, prophecies are as imperfect and transitory as they are hot and inspired. Knowledge—both in religion and in science—is superseded by subsequent knowledge. But love—never wrong, always right—endures, matures, and perdures forever, for "*God* is Love."

To pitch a tent at any one spiritual gift and try to stay there or insist that it be a *sine qua non* for true spirituality would be contrary to the nature and purpose of the charismata. I now consider my own initial enthusiasm for the vocal gifts to have been somewhat of a spiritual or emotional "primal scream" that I had been denied earlier. That gift effected a liberation of my inner self and my vocal chords in the free expression of deep emotions that had been locked up by my Church-of-Christ upbringing. I do not base my faith on these feelings; rather, I affirm the *fact* of the Spirit's working, out of which issues my *faith*, followed by the freely flowing, heartfelt feelings that express my spiritual life: *fact, faith, feeling*—in that order and not the other way around.

I am uncomfortable with the word "charismatic," although it *is* the term in wide use to describe those who have been filled with the Spirit. I am uneasy with it because it seems to focus undue attention on the *gifts* rather than on the *Giver*. Exercise of the charismata is for revealing the grace of God, for pointing to Jesus, for building up his Body and ministering to it, and for giving glory to God—our *Abba Father, Jesus* our brother, and our Spiritual Mother, Friend, Counselor, and ever-present Power.

Both Christian and non-Christian spiritual fireworks of all kinds—tongues included—have been documented by phenomenologists of religion. What is it, then, that makes spiritual gifts truly charismatic, that is, "gifts of grace" and not merely psychological play? Paul's rule of thumb was that a "spiritual gift" is a "charisma" when its effect is to "build up the Body." Jesus, in John's Gospel, said, "When the Spirit of Truth comes, he will guide you into all the truth...." By pointing us to Jesus ("I am the Truth...."), by reminding us of what we already know about Jesus, and by revealing to us new words from the risen Lord, who is now himself a "life-giving spirit," the Holy Spirit guides us faithfully to build ourselves and others up toward maturity in him who is the head of the Body, in which we are all various parts and members.

That Body is one and whole and entire in the smallest house-church gathering, and no less so in the all-embracing Great Church of all who confess themselves to be followers of the Crucified. Within this mystical, universal Body of Christ one can sense when the Holy Spirit is preparing to announce the latest "word from the Lord." By giving close attention to the Spirit's leading, we are prompted to act in our own unique circumstances in ways consistent with what Jesus, the all-transcending model of the Spirit-filled person, "began both to say and do." When you find us "visiting Jesus" in prison, feeding the hungry, healing the sick, aiding the homeless, caring for the weak and elderly, resisting the Principalities and Powers, and bringing reassurance to the hurting and dismayed, then you will know that the Spirit still works miracles, and that Christians are "one," even as Jesus and his Abba are "One." *These are the charismata more to be desired*—the gifts of loving ministry to others.

The Path Goes Ever On

The hymn, "Spirit of God, Descend upon My Heart," was often sung by the York College Chorus during my struggle to find a new path for growth. These poetic lines further kindled the desires of my heart and the hearts of many of the chorus members, who have since followed a similar path to Jesus. The spirit and intent of my searching is expressed so well in the last stanza:

> *Teach me to love Thee as Thine angels love,*
> *One holy passion filling all my frame;*
> *The baptism of the heav'n-descended Dove,*
> *My heart an altar and Thy love the flame.*

As I write, almost four decades have passed since Mary Ruth and I prayed for each other to be filled with the Spirit. We remain committed to listening for the Spirit's voice, knowing that he is not merely a "retired author." Although some concepts of the use of the charismata have mellowed and changed in our experience, we are attuned to the Spirit's promptings as we follow *The Path* toward maturity. Jesus is *The Path*, for he said, "I am the Way...." In relating our generation-long journey to you, I have felt no need to convince you of the psychological, emotional, or scriptural validity of our Spiritual encounters; neither do I wish to suggest that you need to experience the Spirit in the same way we did. "The wind blows where it will, and you hear the sound of it, but you do not know whence it comes or whither it goes; so it is with every one who is born of the Spirit" (Jn 3:8). You are being led along *The Path* in your way, and we are on *The Path* in our way. Following Jesus, we shall meet up with one another on down the road. *Blessings be upon you!*

WHY I RETURNED:
MY HISTORY IN THREE CHURCHES

HOY LEDBETTER

My present church affiliation is, as Samuel Johnson said of a certain man's second marriage, "a triumph of hope over experience," for in some ways, though only in some ways, I am back where I started a half-century ago. My journey has not been like that of the parabolic unclean spirit who wandered through waterless regions looking for a resting place but found none. The climate between my departure and return has been, for the most part, agreeable.

Some people, seeking guidance for their own spiritual odyssey, have wanted to talk with me about my journey. Others have urged me to write about it, imagining, perhaps vainly, that such an enterprise could be edifying to somebody. And so, with some hesitation, I write—but I write from my own, necessarily limited experience.

Intensity

Recently I asked a friend who had switched several years back from the Church of Christ to the Christian Church (Disciples of Christ) what he now missed about the Church of Christ. He capsuled his answer: "The intensity." Good word, used in a good sense, and it may qualify both the good and the bad.

When I emerged from Freed-Hardeman College in 1951, I shared the common conviction that "the whole world is in the power of the evil one." We did not equivocate. People outside the church—*our church*—were lost. We had the remedy for their condition, and we seized every opportunity to apply it. In a flurry of evangelistic activity following World War II, we multiplied "personal work programs" at home and sent missionaries all over the world, people ready to give a quick and unqualified answer to the question, "What must I do to be saved?"

Bible study was considered vital, and the ability to cite passages from memory word for word from the King James Version was widespread. Churches routinely had food banks and other programs for helping the needy. Local leaders were diligent to restore backsliders and to keep watch over all the members, urging and rebuking, as needed, to groom them for heaven. We called it a matter of eternal life and death, and we acted upon our conviction.

On Sundays, we seldom ate in restaurants, yet we seldom ate alone. We either had company or were company in someone else's home, and we often spent a good part of Sunday afternoon around the dinner table or in a living room or out on the porch in spontaneous discussion of the Bible. Perhaps it is a case of distant pastures appearing greener, but I sometimes find myself longing for that old way of life. Of course, dangers lurk behind intensity. We had not quite fulfilled W.E.H. Lecky's prediction:

If men *believe with an intense and realising faith* that their own view of a disputed question is true beyond all possibility of mistake, if they further believe that those who adopt other views will be doomed by the Almighty to an eternity of misery which, with the same moral disposition but with a different belief, they would have escaped, *these men will, sooner or later, persecute to the full extent of their power.*[1]

But we had already moved in that direction: We had the truth, we pressed others to accept that truth, and we took strong disciplinary action against any insiders who wavered. Unfortunately, that sense of having the truth, tended to strengthen our grip on extreme opinions. Illustrations follow.

Negatives

When as a baby Preacher I moved from a delightful rural church in Missouri to the Detroit area in 1952, I landed in a congregation that was strikingly restrictive. For one thing, we could not use quarterlies in our Bible classes, but we were permitted to retype and mimeograph published lessons a week at a time and hand them out. None of those who had made that decision ever imagined that God might be as concerned about plagiarism as he was about using literature "not authorized" in the Bible.

When I first arrived on that scene, I was surprised to learn that a strong body of opinion prevailed against going to movies. My sins found me out one Sunday when a devout brother mistakenly mistook my topcoat for his and discovered two ticket stubs in the pocket, left there after my fiancée and I had taken in a show in Detroit. Some of those same anti-cinema brethren would, however, sit for hours every week with their eyes glued to a new Muntz TV, watching old movies. In relatively little time, the cinema issue died of exposure to technological progress.

The plumbing proved fatal to a similar issue in another congregation. An influential element in the church believed that we ought not to eat in the church building. Consequently, their meetinghouse was outfitted neither with a cook stove nor anything else that could be taken for a kitchen. But, alas, we did have rest rooms, and I suggested that using them was probably not much less offensive to the Divine Presence than eating dinner together. That silenced the objection.

These and other such incidents notwithstanding, we prided ourselves in not being as literalistic as some other churches, like those wherein the Lord's Supper had to be served in a cup, just one cup, according to the well-known text, and moreover the cup had to be authentic—it had to have a handle on it. So the cup handle became a test of fellowship in those churches. We had not honed our exegesis quite that sharp, even if we did come close. (I've never been able to find the proof-text for the handle on the communion cup. If you find it, please write and let me know.)

But our work prospered, and we had to consider enlarging the building. In that connection, our heralded role as "a peculiar people" peaked out one day when one of the Elders said to me, "Brother Ledbetter, I'd like to have an office in the church building, but *the denominations have them!*"

In an atmosphere like that, I should not have been surprised when I accepted into the fellowship a woman from a conservative Christian Church "back home," and some of our

---

[1] Cited by T. Lewis, "Persecution," in Hasting's *Dictionary of the Apostolic Church.*

members were puzzled that I did not rebaptize her. According to their usual custom, they made their objection widely known. With some difficulty, I convinced them that the baptism I administered would not differ from the one she had already experienced. My people were not being unreasonable; they just did not want someone to be lost because of invalid baptism. But one of the harder questions that folk like them have to answer is this: "Who baptized Alexander Campbell? And if it were not a Gospel Preacher for a Church of Christ, how do we know that it took?"

During that pastorate, a troubled member of the congregation and I became good friends and we spent a good bit of time together. Some in the church wondered out loud and half seriously whether I would make a Christian out of him or he would make a drunkard out of me. I won. But after I moved away, he went through a spiritual depression and stopped eating the Lord's Supper, although he attended every Sunday. The Elders opted for edict over encouragement and announced to the congregation that if any member were not eating the Lord's Supper, and then were not to begin to do so within a specified time, he would be disfellowshipped.

When that impressive announcement had no discernible effect on my friend, they announced they were withdrawing fellowship from him. Then one of the Elders, usually a mild and sensible individual, visited the man's wife to discuss her role in that severe assault on sin. Although the Bible disallowed eating with an excommunicated person, he was not quite sure how that would work out in a marriage, where the wife had some duties that resisted setting aside. With some hesitation, the Elder ruled that she might go ahead and eat with her husband, but she should always look sour when she did. Her lack of enthusiasm for his counsel was indicated by her dismissive exclamation, "And then I'm supposed to go in there and go to bed with him!"

In some cases, such rulings by the Elders were not so easily dismissed. According to an Elder in the Flint, Michigan, area, "The members have to do what the Elders say, even if it is wrong. In that case, the Elders will have to answer for it, and not the members." If he had in mind a supporting text for that claim, he did not mention it.

Sometimes when even humble men were made Elders, they became virtual tyrants. The excessive authority generally attributed to the office of the Eldership did not sit well on some. In one congregation, I had an Elder who was often very difficult to work with and who constantly asserted his authority. I actually thought he did not like me, but when I moved on, and he resigned, he would often visit me, and we enjoyed warm friendship. He was a completely different person when he escaped the dictatorial role he thought he had to assume.

On another occasion, I urged the congregation to appoint a man who seemed to be eminently qualified, but once he was in office, power corrupted him, and he became impossible. The congregation often complained about him, and I concluded I had done him a great disservice by urging his selection.

Power joined to insensitivity can be especially ugly. One of my preaching friends in Louisiana was using his vacation time to paint the church building when the Elders called him away from that work and fired him without any warning. Then they kept him sitting with them for an hour while they swapped jokes!

One time a man came to me from a neighboring congregation and asked to place membership. We had heard that he had stirred up some trouble in the other church, but he assured us he had made all necessary apologies and was in good standing. Our investigation indicated that the church had hired a Preacher who was determined to nail all divorced people to their sins, and this brother had gotten in his way. Being a caring conservative, the brother of whom I speak had reached the conviction (not an unusual one at the time) that God's marriage law applies only to Christians, so that, therefore, one gets to start over—so to speak—when one is baptized. But when this brother expressed this opinion in Bible class, he incurred the wrath of the Preacher and Elders. They threatened to excommunicate him as a troublemaker. In the interest of peace, he consented to keep quiet from then on. All seemed to be well, but then one of the Elders examined him further and learned that he had not actually abandoned his belief; he had only agreed to refrain from expressing it in class. The Elder insisted he had to change his belief. He could not, so they cast him out. We took him in. Then they withdrew from us. Ironically, not long afterwards, the Elders fired that Preacher and hired another who believed exactly what they had been so vigorously opposing!

Meanwhile, on the other side of the city, the Preacher and one of the Elders of a suburban church had met with a young couple and, after some study, had persuaded them to be baptized. So they picked them and their two small children up one night and headed for the building to baptize them. On the way, the man said something that would dash the hopes of all involved: "I don't suppose it really matters, but perhaps I should tell you that we have both been married before."

It did matter—far more than he had any reason to imagine. The two churchmen immediately ruled that he and his wife would have to separate and go back to their former mates in order to be right with God. They, of course, declined. Whether they ever went to church again, I do not know, but they never went to *that* church again. We can only wonder what happened to the joy and devotion they felt that night—or how the Heavenly Host felt about being deprived of a night of rejoicing.

At times, things seem so right that we fail to notice how they violate our convictions. For instance, one year the keynote speaker at our annual VBS workshop became ill and therefore was unable to preach his sermon. In view of the prevailing notions about women in the church, I found his replacement interesting. His wife brought his sermon and read it in the church pulpit before a few hundred people. To the naked eye, it seemed that a woman was preaching, and nobody seemed to be bothered by it. Even one of the local conservative Preachers said to me, "You know, if someone should claim that a woman may preach, it would be pretty hard to argue against it." Later events discouraged that idea.

Sometimes, in their eagerness to protest another's errors, people will override other convictions that they hold. I recall teaching an auditorium class of about 80 people in which a mature lady often argued with my interpretation of passages in Romans. She did not seem to realize that she was doing what she thought Paul forbade: a woman speaking up in church and teaching a man. "In church," we may say, because when the class ended and we brought in the children, she continued to sit in the same seat surrounded by the same people, where, according to her convictions, she could not say a word. Just bringing in the children and calling it a "service" required that the women now remain silent—even when that was not their natural inclination.

These experiences, and others like them, together with the insights that resulted naturally from years of study, aroused within me a growing realization that we needed to take a look at how far we had drifted from our Restoration Movement roots. I realized that we had devised a scheme of interpretation that allowed—even demanded—making tests of fellowship out of ecclesiastical trivia and Biblical minutiae: We were the Pharisees, counting every tenth mint leaf and cumin seed, all over again. We had aided and abetted dictatorial Elderships that had a destructive stranglehold on many, if not most, of the churches. The Preachers who worked under these Elders were already aware of this situation, but they were not daring enough to initiate corrections. I realized further the double-mindedness in our view of women and what they should not be allowed to do in the church; I saw that our teaching and practice did not really square with all the evidence in the Bible. The Restoration Movement, I concluded, a body of devoted people who were supposedly dedicated to "uniting the Christians in all the sects," had become, instead, an embarrassing example of persistent disunion.

Congregational splits were exceedingly common, born of doctrinal disputes and power struggles. More new churches resulted from fighting than from evangelism. Proneness to these conflicts was an ugly blot on a marvelous Movement. Inevitably I came to the conclusion that we were avoiding a better way, one that, as it turned out, made it possible for me to enjoy a broader fellowship, especially with the three main branches of the Stone-Campbell Movement.

A Telling Exchange

What our approach had ultimately done was highlighted when two men of my acquaintance, both sensible and seasoned members of the Church of Christ, were working together in a General Motors plant in Flint. They were discussing their respective churches and the doctrines and practices there that they considered necessary but concerning which some members—rumor had it—were inclined to wobble. One of them, with daring honesty, ventured to say that he did not believe it would necessarily be wrong for the church to use instrumental music in worship, or occasionally to eat the Lord's Supper on Wednesday evening. His friend, suddenly fraught with fright at the implications of that statement, replied, "If I believed that, I would quit going to church."

So it had come to that. The second friend, firm on no instrumental music and the Lord's Supper on Sundays only, had to choose between sound doctrine and no doctrine at all. Practices based entirely upon inferences and deductions had turned out to be so important that if one abandoned them, then nothing else was worth keeping. The lordship of Jesus stood or fell with inferred conclusions. No wonder, then, that in most Churches of Christ at the time, mere stumbling blocks had become tests of fellowship. And those Preachers who were "soft" on the issues, and who were both too weak to dig and too ashamed to beg, were in for some lean times.

I understood the psychology of the alarmist brother, and, in fact, had in the past given aid and comfort to it. For years, he had heard trusted ministers point to a cappella music and having the Lord's Supper *every* Sunday and *only* on Sunday as essential marks of the one true church—a member of which he proudly claimed to be. Those two characteristics were emphasized so frequently and firmly that they naturally became more and more important to the people in the pew, finally reaching equivalent significance with the fundamental confession "Jesus is Lord."

Why I Left

While I had no desire to practice the things that man feared, I had become convinced that we should not split churches over such issues, since the Bible does not identify them as tests of fellowship. So I thought it "meet, right, and my bounden duty" to offer a corrective influence.

A number of my fellow ministers agreed that we needed to address the persistent problem of division, which is so often and emphatically condemned in the Bible. One of our efforts was the monthly publication of *Integrity*, a little journal that we intended as a forum in which to give brethren of good will the opportunity to discuss their differences in an atmosphere of respect and friendly acceptance. Although it was warmly welcomed throughout the country, it was too friendly and accepting for many tastes and therefore was vigorously opposed.

We were ostracized, even excommunicated, by congregations we did not know. Letters of denunciation, some of which were not too careful with the truth, were widely circulated. The pressure became so irresistible that sympathetic colleagues and moderate churches were afraid to associate with us. In this way, my once warm relationship with the Church of Christ *as I had known it* came to an end.

This is not to say that I did not have the support of many brethren and churches; I did, and many more than I imagined, as I learned when the encouraging letters came pouring in from all across the country.

When I moved to Atlanta in 1982 to begin work with the Brookvalley Church, one of our so-called "free" churches, a broader field for my ecumenical efforts was thrust upon me. I was asked to chair the Task Force on Christian Unity for the Christian Council of Metropolitan Atlanta, which I did as long as I lived there. That position put me at the same table with all sorts of unity seekers, including representatives of the National and World Councils of Churches.

I have been asked whether that position did not compromise some of my conservative convictions. Not in the least. I could state my position on an issue and listen respectfully to contrary viewpoints. Merely talking neighborly with people in no way implies endorsement of heresy. By that time, I had embraced the propositions of Thomas Campbell's *Declaration and Address*, and I often found opportunities to refer to them in ecumenical dialog. They are useful starting points for discussion with anyone at all interested in Christian unity.

Working on the Task Force put me in repeated contact with some outstanding people from the Christian Church (Disciples of Christ) with whom I developed a warm friendship. Those friends, along with others to whom they introduced me, constituted a fine "welcoming committee" when I decided to become affiliated with the Disciples in 1986. One reason I made that move was my impression that the Disciples were more loyal to our roots than were the Churches of Christ. If you study the history of the Ecumenical Movement, you will always find a Disciple moving and shaking at every turning point of the broader effort to reunite Christendom.

My first Disciples church was First Christian in Albany, Georgia, a fairly conservative church that, as far as I can recall, never had an argument with anything I said or did (except they were kind enough to object when I resigned after ten years to move farther north). I still remember how pleased I was to be able to preach my convictions without having anybody get upset over it.

By serving on various committees, boards, and commissions, I came to know the Georgia Region of the Disciples church very well. I chaired the Commission on Christian Unity for some years, and then the Commission on Evangelism. My wife served on the Commission on Ministry. I also became acquainted with various leaders on the national, or General Church, level.

The Disciples congregations are independent of creedal control, so the theological outlook varies considerably from church to church. In general, the Disciples have no "lick them or join them" mentality, except in situations that affect one's own congregation. The liberal and conservative elements do sometimes clash. For instance, once an effort was made to get the General Assembly to affirm acceptance of Acts 4:12: "And there is salvation in no one else; for there is no other name under heaven that has been given among men by which we must be saved." Although there may have been some unseen reasons why the assembly rejected it, the conservatives were appalled, and for some time there were rumbles throughout the church. We Georgians, for the most part, took Peter at his word.

A similar tension arose over the question of the ordination of homosexuals. It still remains a question of hot debate at the national level, but not in the congregations I have known. On such questions, the debate may be intense in whatever forums are available for public discussion; however, a corresponding reluctance to divide the church prevails that keeps congregations from splitting.

The Disciples take great pride in their diversity. The questions that have plagued the Churches of Christ for generations—how many cups to use during the Lord's Supper, whether or not to have Bible classes on Sunday, whether or not to cooperate in benevolent work, and the dozens of others—would never dawn on the Disciples. In many ways they are staunch Campbellites and advocates of Christian unity, but they sense some tension over traditions. For example, the usual practice is for Elders to preside at the Lord's Supper, and for the Deacons to pass the emblems to the congregation (and in some Disciples churches, the Elders and Deacons do little else!) When, however, a member of my congregation, himself an Elder, advocated allowing all mature members to share equally in those duties—a practice he thought quite Campbellian in spirit—he met with overwhelming resistance.

Disciples services are often weighted with responsive readings, sometimes very long ones. I never did get addicted to them; in fact, I tried to keep them at a minimum because I felt their value was greatly overrated. I am an old man, and yet I have never heard anyone boast of being inspired by a responsive reading.

The Disciples, like many others, are struggling to recover the lost art of evangelism, and some valiant efforts have been made. During my ten years among the Disciples, we had an Evangelism Commission, and each year we held an Evangelism Workshop to which people came from all over the State. Attendance varied from church to church, probably suggesting lack of initiative in some churches.

A matter of concern to me has been the quality of ministerial candidates being turned out by the seminaries. Some of them may not be able to tell the congregations what they need to hear. One person seeking ordination in the Georgia Region was asked, "How would you answer the question, 'What must I do to be saved?'" Her answer: "It depends on what you mean by 'saved.'" She said more, but it became clear that she either did not know how to answer the question or did not wish to commit herself to any specific teaching. Those old "What must/shall/will" sermons were either unknown or unacceptable to her.

The Independents

My relationship with the Independent Christian Churches (also known as Churches of Christ, with the difference that they typically use instrumental music) has always been pleasant. The Independents befriended my reformist associates and me while I was still in Michigan. They invited me to preach and teach in their churches, to speak at both the Michigan Christian Convention and the North American Christian Convention, and to participate in various activities.

About twenty students from Atlanta Christian College (an Independent school) attended Brookvalley Church when I was in Atlanta, and one of them was our youth minister for a while. The area churches embraced us warmly, as their outlook disposed them to do.

When I retired at the end of 2000, my wife and I started attending the West Rome (Georgia) Christian Church. We already had good friends in the congregation, including the minister. We went to all the church meetings and remained in our house group even after I started preaching out of town on Sunday mornings. When we moved to Huntsville, Alabama, in 2003, they gave us a rousing going-away party.

The several Independent churches that I have known well have been uniformly free of the party spirit. Occasional tensions and temperaments flared, and some small "worship war" battles were engaged, even some disagreements over issues like the role of women, but in the broad picture they are loving, tolerant, and evangelistic. Somehow, the Independent Christian Churches have escaped the disruptive concept of "patternism" in the New Testament that has caused so much trouble in the *a cappella* Churches of Christ.

We members of the Stone-Campbell Restoration Movement are familiar with a number of mottos that have been employed through the years to summarize our doctrinal concerns. One of these (ascribed to Campbell, but to be found before his time and in other fellowships beyond the Restorationist fold) is this: "In matters of faith, unity; in matters of opinion, liberty; in all things, charity."[2] More than one has said that you could write the history of our fractured Movement this way: The Disciples majored in opinions and unity; the Churches of Christ majored in faith but disunity; the Independents majored in charity. I've thought for some time that it would be good to get it all together again.

Huntsville

Now, in Huntsville, at an *a cappella* Church of Christ with hundreds of members, the atmosphere is different from any other I have previously experienced. We express both our faith and opinions; we're working on liberty in unity; we rejoice in charity, the greatest gift of the Spirit. At Huntsville, we're trying to get it all together again.

---

[2] In its 17th-century Lutheran version, it ran thus: "In essentials, unity; in non-essentials, liberty; in all things, charity." The Moravians and the Quakers also had their versions. In the 20th century, Pope John XXIII resurrected it as a Catholic motto. See Hans Rollmann, "'In Essentials Unity': The Pre-History of a Restoration Movement Slogan," *Restoration Quarterly* 39/3 (1997): 129-39, or http://restorationquarterly.org/ Volume 039/ rq03903 rollmann.htm.

I have been asked more than once what sort of Church of Christ I would be willing to be a member of. My "ideal congregation" would, of course, necessarily be less than perfect, for no congregation is perfect, and all brethren are brethren in error. But some qualities I would consider very important, to wit:

I would want the church to assume responsibility for Paul's message and ministry of reconciliation, and I think that requires a bi-directional concern. That is to say, the church should strive to seek and save the lost (recovering "God's folly" as best we can, the neglected burden of evangelism), and it should also press for the reconciliation of all believers with each other. My preferred congregation should be open-minded enough to accept different viewpoints, and it would restrict exclusion to that which the Bible clearly enjoins.

Inferences and deductions from Scripture should be kept in their place, as valuable means of discerning the truth, but not as tests of fellowship.

I would like to see flexible, Spirit-filled and spirited worship. Singing suits me fine, and *a cappella* music can be contemporary, traditional, or blended, but it must be done well. The very best available leader should always be used. The worship should extol the majesty of God as well as praise him for his goodness.

I want a congregation that not only allows the Preacher to say what he believes, rather than what he thinks he ought to say, but also insists on it. The sermons and lessons should be biblical and intelligently presented so as to bear conviction to reasonable people. Knowledge and understanding of the Bible should always be one of our chief concerns.

The church should be friendly, inclusive, multicultural (as far as possible), and open to the use of a variety of spiritual gifts, always practicing what it sings about: a "love that will not let me go." We should be taking deliberate steps towards gender equality in all affairs of the congregation.

The congregation should be involved in as many outreach ministries as possible, giving the congregants hands-on opportunities for service and face-to-face encounters with people in all kinds of need. We should also be dedicated to foreign mission work, preferably projects in which it can have more than trivial ownership.

I think I have found my ideal church in Huntsville. The worship is always inspiring. The *a cappella* music is outstanding, a blend of traditional and contemporary, but mostly contemporary. Even very conservative visitors usually find something good to say about it. The congregation has no inclination to make inferences and deductions tests of fellowship. We are still working on some issues, but with true honesty and devotion. The preaching minister is articulate; his lessons are timely. The educational program is excellent. The church abounds in good works, both locally and abroad. The members there are exceptionally friendly; they make all newcomers feel wanted. Praising the Lord in that kind of atmosphere comes easy, so we do it—a lot!

And our congregation is not without twin sisters. Similar churches are springing up all over the country—free churches, churches of no known denomination, Spirit-led churches, churches that major in faith and unity and liberty and—in all things—charity. Yes, I "left," but now I have returned. I rejoice in hope that many wanderers may find what I have found: It's easy to go back home when there's a good home to go to.

WHY I STAY

JOHN D. WHITE

Looking around

Yesterday I stood in the choir loft (formerly the slave balcony) of a chapel in Wading River, Long Island, New York. For their second morning service, a dozen of us had been invited to sing *a cappella* versions of the same Sacred Harp hymns heard there in the 1840s when this church was called the Congregational Church. Now it is called the United Church of Christ, and when I am asked whether the United Church of Christ be the same denomination I belong to, I give the standard answer: "No, I belong to the Disunited Church of Christ." The Uniteds descend from the Puritan and Pilgrim heritage rather than the Scottish Dissenter Presbyterian background from which we "disuniteds" descend.

Most of the congregational hymns, the liturgy, every part of the Christ-centered sermon, prayers, scripture readings, and even announcement style yesterday were interchangeable with those of the West Islip Church of Christ where I have been a member since 1963. While visiting Presbyterian, Methodist, and Lutheran services in recent years, I have felt quite comfortable, despite my having grown up believing their sincerity could not shield them from an inevitable eternity in hell. Now, if my wife and I were to move to another community that lacked a Campbell-Stone/Restoration-based congregation, we could joyfully unite with such a fellowship.

As we drove away, reflecting on the inspirational worship we had enjoyed, Donna thought aloud about our reducing the Lord's Supper *meal* to a thumb-pinch of matzo bread and a thimbleful of pasteurized, nonalcoholic grape juice. Why, she wondered, is that any different from other Protestants and Catholics using a token amount of water for baptism?

A few weeks ago, I was honored to read Scripture in a Catholic service, led mostly by lay people, in which cherished friends renewed their wedding vows. The priest, one of three with whom I enjoy friendly relations, took only a minor part as the couple distributed sacramental wine and consecrated bread to those assembled, including known Protestants. Feeling equal part of admiration and affection for, and exasperation with much of the Roman church, however, I would be far less likely to affiliate with it. Yet, hard as it might prove, I must always remain open to the leading of the Holy Spirit to move into another branch of God's church.

Some years ago a former faculty member of Harding College, Robert Meyers, published *Voices of Concern*.[1] Many of the contributors set forth why they had separated themselves from the Churches of Christ. When I read the stories, I could see that they had some very good reasons for leaving. After some thought and with no regrets to date, however, I have decided to stay. Except for becoming more ecumenical than most of my brothers and sisters, I

---

[1] See Warren Lewis, "Why I Left," in this volume, for a discussion of Robert Meyers's *Voices of Concern*.

have changed little in relation to my traditional church background. I am aware that the Movement is changing, and I become less comfortable each year with what it is becoming, but I have no plans to announce a break.

For now, I want to keep a foot in the legacy of the Churches of Christ while planting the other firmly among the ecumenical riches of the rest of the recognizably Christian community—Orthodox, Catholic, and mainstream Protestants. Now that most Fundamentalists, Evangelicals, and Pentecostals have added the Republican political agenda as part of their gospel message, I am less relaxed with them than when I grew up among them. It may seem odd, but I feel a closer tie—even an obligation for contact—with observant Jewish friends than with the Baptists and Pentecostals that I once thought to be "closer to the truth" than mainstream Protestants. I am distressed to see the apolitical Church of Christ of my youth joining Baptists and Pentecostals in an effort to merge with and take over civil government.

The sects—Mormons, Seventh-Day Adventists, Jehovah's Witnesses—pose a fellowship challenge that remains insurmountable because they reject the validity of my Christian connection. I now understand the exasperation once felt by other denominations in town towards us when they tried to recruit our people for inter-faith efforts. Certainty among many Church of Christ folk that we alone loved the truth, and all others did not, made of us a sect that rejected others in past years just as sectarians now reject us. This precludes neighborliness—much less unity—with other groups of followers of Jesus. What an irony that early-20th century exclusivism rejected the very foundation of the Restoration "unity plea." Donna and I believe that by embracing the whole Christian family in other denominations, we have become truer to the goals of 19th century founders.

Looking back

After growing up in the Churches of Christ[2] and maintaining several layers of connection to them, how can I now enjoy ecumenical worship with non-Restorationist Christians? I'm sorry to say that my growing-up years included almost no experiences of shared worship with other Christian groups. How strange that the unity movement spurred by Alexander Campbell and Barton W. Stone could have become so exclusivist by the time I was born in 1936.

In the 1930s-1950s, the Churches of Christ engaged in "purification by excision" practices that included witch-hunts against premillennialists, "one-cuppers," and "no-class" churches, and that culminated beginning in the late-1940s in an uncivil war that is still raging over "institutionalism." The term referred originally to financial support for orphans' homes when supervised by an independent board or even when sponsored by *a group of churches*

---

[2] Once upon a time, it was almost a dogma that "churches of Christ" had to be spelled with the lower case "c" on the word "churches" to prove that we were a movement, not a denomination. Tricks of spelling, however, do not disprove the thoroughly denominational status of that recognizable body of churches that may be denominated "Churches of Christ." The real name in-house of the denomination is "the brotherhood"—who's in, who's out, whose preacher gets invited to speak at the Christian College lectureships, etc. A more formal institution with elected denominational officers, headquarters, official print organs, and certified educational institutions would be more denominational only by a matter of degree. Informal structures may well be stronger than formal ones.

cooperatively. Support for nationwide "Herald of Truth" radio broadcasts came to be equated with support of an institutionalist heresy, and by the turn of the century, with extra-congregational organizations all around, the "anti-cooperation" brethren have voted with their feet: Approximately one-fourth of the congregations and one-third of the membership of the so-called "mainline" Churches of Christ have withdrawn their fellowship from what they now call the "institutional churches."

Christian colleges, i.e. post-secondary institutions affiliated with Churches of Christ, largely escaped criticism as *institutions* in this debate, perhaps because an earlier split with the Sommer/Ketcherside disciples made college support from the church budget orthodox. In a skeptical mode, however, one must ask whether one institution is not as bad as another, if extra-congregational means of organizing Christian effort be sinful. Christian college and Christian university lectureships function as denominational conventions to watch-dog and harden the dividing lines of dogma. Many congregations, led by some of my father's Freed-Hardeman classmates, launched their own assaults against the mainstream churches of our fellowship. A blizzard of combative debates, books, and periodicals rained down upon the villains, whether to straighten them out or merely to let everyone know who they were.

Despite my father's friendship with these classmates, and his subscribing to their journals for a few years, he lost interest in the controversy. I remember struggling to determine the right side on "the issues" and wondering how illiterate first-century Christians would have sorted the kernels of truth from the chaff of error. Along with Dad, I refocused on the gospel of and about Christ instead of the hair-splitting and put-downs of the opponents. The church—its organization, name, and current theology—not only is not itself the "Good News" but also in too many cases becomes bad news that drives seekers away.

All these latter-day quarrels were but the playing out of a style of religious argumentation that had taken place long before my time, between the Civil War and the turn of 20th century, when mostly Yankee Disciples of Christ, called "digressives" by mostly Southern Churches of Christ, had to be anathematized for their infernal instruments of music and their diabolically federalist "missionary society." By 1906, a great gulf had been dug to prevent contact with the Liberals, and by then, many of the Disciples truly had become "Liberal" in terms of the theological trends of the day, whereas Churches of Christ had remained solidly conservative. A similar great gulf came to be fixed for most members of Churches of Christ between ourselves and the Independent Christian Churches (also known as Churches of Christ in some areas), who play instrumental music in worship (like the Disciples) but are theologically conservative (unlike the Disciples) and have remained independent by refusing to take part in the Disciples restructure of themselves into formal denominational status. What began as microscopic differences came to be Grand Canyons separating us, the *truth-lovers*, from all those others, the *digressives*, who rejected the truth.

Looking within

The Apostle Paul in some of his writings aimed at Jewish-Christian brethren presented his credentials as a mainstream Pharisee and devout Jew. Similarly, I state here my identification with what I consider the middle-middle of the Churches of Christ.

My third- and fourth-grade years were spent in the Demonstration School at Freed-Hardeman College, where my dad was taking courses to prepare for full-time ministry in Idaho and Arizona. Our main recreation consisted of singing, fellowship meals, and board games with church members. Besides attending two services on Sundays, and one on Wednesday nights, we tried to attend a few evenings of "gospel meetings" (revivals) at Churches of Christ within an hour's drive. My parents encouraged me to attend the newly established Central Christian [junior] College in Bartlesville, Oklahoma, where a family friend, L. R. Wilson, was president.

After graduating from Harding College, in Searcy, Arkansas, in 1958, I taught in a nearby public high school for a year, after which I returned to work as the audiovisual director of the College for two years. I also spoke at Wednesday night services at the College Church, taught a well-attended Sunday morning Bible class, and during five summers worked at church-connected Camp Shiloh in New Jersey, and was asked to serve as director of a similar camp in upstate New York, Camp Hunt. During my Harding years, I also preached in various small towns during summers in Arizona and Alaska, including a clumsy sermon in Spanish to Mexican workers on a cotton plantation. My college preaching buddies and I frequently traveled on Sundays to preach, teach adult Bible classes, and lead singing.

In 1969, I received an M.A. in History from Abilene Christian College, where years before I had worked as assistant director of the audiovisual center and graduate assistant instructor in U. S. History. The Hillcrest Church of Christ asked me to substitute at times for teacher Ray McGlothlin's popular college-age Sunday evening Bible class. In time, they asked me to teach a regular Sunday morning class that met in a large room behind the pulpit. The class quickly grew as church dropouts, including Don Haymes, began attending and bringing their friends. One of the Elders eventually told me that they had decided to stop the class because "the Elders did not have time to supervise it." Since none of the classes—even controversial ones—that I had taught in six states had ever been either attended or supervised by Elders, and although no one had complained about my teaching at Hillcrest, I interpreted this message to be that these Elders did not want the likes of my class, including Don Haymes, filing past the pulpit and walking to the front of the building in full view of everybody.

After two years' part-time work on the M. A. in Abilene, friends from Camp Shiloh living on Long Island arranged a job interview at North Babylon, and I began teaching high-school social studies there in 1963. Without intending to do so, I drifted into membership with the newly arriving Exodus Bay Shore church, which settled that same year a few miles away in West Islip, New York. For the church I co-taught a college-level night course in Ephesians with one of the ministers, Carl Phagan, and co-conducted an alternative Bible class in a house next door to the church. This so-called "Carriage House" rump church attracted several that would neither attend classes taught in the church building nor participate in the main worship service. Despite objections by some members of the congregation, an Elder or two visited the class occasionally and gave it their blessing. Some of these renegades (Don Haymes included) and I during the 1960s published and distributed at no cost to the readers *An Uncertain Sound,* a short-lived religious rag that carried articles that were both humorous and serious. We were trying to call the Churches of Christ back to their historic roots and away from petty preoccupations that had risen to excessive importance.

In that decade, the West Islip Church attracted the hostility of a self-appointed scold named Ira Y. Rice, Jr., who whipped us roundly and soundly in his three-volume work of ecclesiastical pulp fiction, *Axe on the Root.* In the years following, the West Islip Church was often shunned by more conservative churches both nearby and far away, for we were striving to follow a congregationally autonomous course led by Scripture and the Holy Spirit without regard to meandering, channel-shifting, Southern-based Church of Christ orthodoxy. Occasional visits to churches in the South and Southwest made me wonder whether they had not strayed more than had our little body of Christ's followers on Long Island.

Churches for which my father preached during the 1960s in western Tennessee, northern Mississippi, southern Kentucky, northern Idaho, and several towns in Arizona were small and typical of mainline Churches of Christ in that era: They met in white, wood-framed buildings built and maintained by the members, most of whom were farmers or blue-collar workers. If there were a prestigious location in the community, the Church of Christ building was certain to be located elsewhere. Members accepted their status as a minority religion because "narrow is the way" trod by the righteous. Their limited success in attracting converts reinforced their sound theology. The "wrong side of the tracks" was the right place to be.

In 1953, when I attended for the first time a sophisticated urban church with opaque tinted glass windows and an office for the minister right there in the church house, I found myself worshiping on the better side of the tracks. The 6th & Dewey church in Bartlesville, Oklahoma, stood just across a shady street from the Price Tower, an awesome Frank Lloyd Wright structure. The church leaders were either executives at Phillips Petroleum or held comparable places in the city's establishment. Over the next generation, other Churches of Christ surpassed 6th & Dewey, moving into lavish multi-structural complexes rivaling those of the Methodists and Southern Baptists. Shrill fire-and-brimstone sermons became kinder, gentler with doses of sociology and psychology; "give 'em hell" gave way to contemporary marketing techniques and the Social Gospel as various "programs" replaced revivals. For better and sometimes for worse, the Churches of Christ came to focus on upwardly mobile middle-class niceness, beginning to resemble neighboring denominations. And the political climate at church began to change, as well, as nouveaux-riches Republicans replaced otherworldly Democrats, and a tendency towards pacifism and political non-involvement gave way to Americanism and a tendency towards the Religious Right.

Looking right here

Absent compelling reasons to repudiate one's background, I believe one who denies the effects of formative years will suffer from that suppression of one's history. Rural people can celebrate the riches of their childhood after moving to a great city or its suburb; they can bring an enriching difference to their adopted community. Farm communities gain from the arrival of former urbanites that share their experience in their new rural environment. Neither should feel threatened by the other. I, therefore, affirm my Church-of-Christ upbringing—warts and all—for the following reasons:

Growing up in the Churches of Christ meant for me an intense sense of community in my home congregation as well as on the road. The signboard on the highway announcing the presence of a Church of Christ in the town up ahead was a beacon of welcome. I knew that wherever I roamed, the sign out front, "Church of Christ Meets Here," was a guarantee of safety and hospitality. After a quick survey of the building (no piano, communion trays with individual thimble-sized cups instead of a single chalice, no flags and usually no crosses, a cornerstone with either the text of Romans 16:16 chiseled on it or the deliciously quaint message: "Church of Christ, established 33 A.D.," told me that I was home. Submitting to a subtle check of my own doctrinal soundness was no inquisition: Who was the preacher in my home congregation? Who usually held the gospel meetings? Had I attended Christian College? Then we all settled in to celebrate our similarities in Bible class and public worship.

No, the churches of Christ were not a "denomination," but we were a "brotherhood." This meant that attendance at a Christian college guaranteed a certain Bible-true, morally upright point of view. It meant that after two songs and a prayer, a Bible-based sermon would follow, and somewhere along the line, matzos would be broken and nibbled and Welch's grape juice would be sipped in memory of the Last Supper, following the orally transmitted but inevitable liturgical words: "In like manner, our Heavenly Father, we thank thee for this fruit of the vine, which so fitly represents...." Annual lectureships at the colleges served the same purpose as synods and councils to sort out the latest issues. Missionaries to other lands spread this familiarity of our small but tight nationwide community, so that one could sing hymns by Tillet S. Teddlie and Austin Taylor even overseas, albeit in foreign tongues.

Just as "all history is local history," so also all church membership is local church membership. In the Church of Christ, I have *my* favorite hymns and songs, *my* favorite preachers, and—more importantly—*my* preferred missionaries and works of Christian service. One cannot support all worthy charities, so one must choose a finite few to support. Growing up in the Church of Christ meant hearing reports from actual returned missionaries and watching slide shows of foreign congregations of real people, often in gritty situations, that we back home were helping to support. We understood that the very definition of Christ's church was that it had been called and sent by the Man Himself to "go into the world and preach the gospel"—the Great Commission—and lo! He would be with us always. I still believe that, and I still support *my* missionaries.

I support the PrediSan program in Catacamas, Honduras. I've known Doris Clark, who directs the program, over several decades and also their stateside liaison, Charlie Walton, through an old Camp Shiloh connection. These godly people and their staffs work long days all year not only to preach a grace-filled gospel but also to minister to those with medical and substance-abuse problems. I know *my* missionaries.

I also support the Ezell Clinic in Montellano, Suchetepéquez, Guatemala. They conduct several kinds of major surgery at the main clinic, and they travel out on bad roads in pickups to conduct one-day clinics. I have been blessed to work at three weeklong clinics there. One of those times, I acted as translator for an American doctor who gave thorough exams to 40 children in a single day—a few miles from a smoking volcano. Most of these volunteers pay their own way to do the Lord's work for Mayan Indians in the highlands. The clinic and staff minister to the spiritual needs of the area via a church that meets just across the highway on a river bluff and at other congregations in villages that are miles away. Not all the workers come from the Church of Christ, but the variety of believers there are united in their desire to serve, and share God's love with, the needy.

In the same sense that I have *my* missionaries, I also have *my* saints. I mention one only, a Church of Christ saint: Each year I make a small contribution to the Harvard Divinity School in memory of LeMoine Gaunce Lewis, one of the most influential teachers in the three Christian colleges I attended. Forty years after sitting in his Church History classes, his spirit, teaching style, sense of humor, and high-mindedness shape my own college teaching of Western Civilization and Latin American history. From a humble, small-town background, Dr. Lewis had attended one of our colleges, and then went on to Harvard and brought back vast learning to share with students from many backgrounds. He was a bridge for me. I achieved safe passage from my limited, provincial outlook and my parochial theology to a grander understanding of God's interaction with all His people, and to an understanding of the Great Church, from the first century through the Middle Ages to the Reformation, and even the Restoration Movement, into what was then the 20th century. I would love to hear what LeMoine would say about our 21st-century situation! I also send modest contributions to *my* three Christian colleges (now "universities") in the hope that these institutions will continue—whether they intend to or not—to help students like me pass over that bridge from their backgrounds to their futures.

Membership in a Church of Christ meant for me a sense of personal responsibility to read my Bible, pray, and attend the public worship services of the church. Each person was to pray along in silence with the man standing in the front. Each was to read the Bible daily, whether at home or when traveling, and everyone was expected to have a Bible in hand and turn to the sermon text, no matter how familiar (Mk 16:15-16, Ac 2:38, Rm 6:3-4 came up more than others). My first trip through the entire Bible, from Genesis—including Leviticus and Numbers—through to Jude and Revelation, was completed by age ten. I've probably been through the New Testament over 100 times. I continue the habit to this day, and I read the New Testament aloud in Spanish two or three times a year.

Above all, everyone was expected to sing when at church. Where neither piano nor organ is available either as crutch to support timid voices or as instrumental competition to those who would rather hear one another sing than be drowned out by the accompanist, one learns to sing heartily, listen to others, and love singing. "If I do not sing, there will be no music," is a thought that naturally occurs to each member of a Church of Christ. No professional musician, I am certain that I am a much better singer than I would have been, had I been raised in a church where they played instrumental music. Now, I am an avid singer of the "Sacred Harp," not the music of my youth and childhood, thanks in part to my upbringing in the *a cappella* churches of Christ.

Being tutored mentally in the Church of Christ meant for me a healthy skepticism about requirements or pronouncements imposed by religious authorities other than my Bible and my own conscience. An unresolved tension accompanied this stubbornly rationalist streak because, whereas doubt was expected about the unscriptural beliefs of "the denominations," exceptions to this ecclesiastical agnosticism that followed no consistent hermeneutic allowed me to sing hymns by non-members Fanny J. Crosby and Charles Wesley, read the definitions of *baptizo* and *psallo* in Thayer's Greek *Lexicon*, and consult B. W. Johnson's *Commentary on the New Testament*, even though it had been published by the Christian Church instead of by one of "our" publishing houses. This inconsistent tolerance for authorities and poets from outside our fold taught me a tacit ecumenism: When tensions arose over the interpretation of some Scripture passage, or we young people challenged the orthodoxies of the preacher, a Sunday School teacher, our parents, some Restoration pioneer, a tract writer, or an editor of the *Gospel Advocate* or the *Firm Foundation*, we learned to deal with disagreement by not dealing with it. When no one could untie some particularly knotty Bible verse of Scripture, we would commend our faithfulness by ignoring our ignorance: "Well, it means about what it says." I learned to overlook that no two people ever agree 100% with one another.

The Church of Christ taught me a kind of rugged individualism of higher performance in religion and in everything I do—after all, in those days, "we were right, and everyone else was wrong." That has mellowed for me into a sense of the importance of each individual's private commitment to God. Religion is not, for me, a spiritual social club, an ideological collective of the like-minded, a right place to be and be seen with the right crowd. At its worst, perhaps, the moral and intellectual *perfectionism* required by being the only ones in religion who were right, tended to crowd out hope for God's grace to cover one's failings— what if, for example, my mind wandered a bit during Communion to the pretty girl in the second pew where the teenagers all sat, perched like birds on a wire? Jimmy Carter is not the only one who has broken the counsel of perfection lusting again and again, and at church at that, but lucky for the President emeritus, he is a Baptist, and they believe in grace. I am a churcho'Christ, and we believe in works.

All that picking the Scriptures apart, one verse at a time, taught me a rigorous attention to detail. Even if sometimes we carried our "close reading of the text" to extremes and with neglect for great principles and broad outlooks, at our best, we took Scripture seriously and probed deeply to mine its riches. To reverse the usual saying, "God is in the details." The i-dotting, t-crossing habits I learned at church are part of the reason people still hire me to proofread their documents, and I would be much less of a historian had I grown up inattentive to detail.

Everyone is proud of his or her circle of friends, I suppose, but the warm association with the vast network of members of this fellowship comprises the most treasured part of my heritage in the Church of Christ. From my earliest childhood, the folks who showed up for church three times each week (Sunday morning, Sunday evening, and Wednesday evening) became closer than blood kin. My dearest friends remain the people who once were my Sunday School companions, Christian college roommates, fellow counselors at Christian camps (Wyldewood, Shiloh, Hunt), faculty colleagues, members in churches in nine states that I have attended through the years, and brother and sister members of the West Islip Church of Christ with whom I have been in loving and caring association for four decades.

If I were to "leave," in the sense of making a formal break and possibly affiliating with another denomination, I could maintain some of these associations, but most would probably fade. My high school reunions included instant re-connection with some friends from 50 years ago, but seeing others sparked only a faint recognition that nostalgia could not fan into friendship. A reunion of Central Christian College alumni at the original Bartlesville campus two years ago, on the other hand, was much warmer than the high school reunions. At the same time, however, I was saddened to encounter a few who had retreated deeper into a narrower sectarian view of "the truth" held in common in earlier years. Many were still active in the Church of Christ, but a surprising number had moved on to different denominations while holding onto this Church of Christ *college* connection with special fondness. The two Camp Shiloh reunions have revealed a similar composition of former members and active members but no nostalgia about returning to allegedly golden years of 1935-1960. I would hate to weaken this tie to currently active members, although many of these good people will be distressed to learn of my ecumenical leanings.

Looking towards other strugglers on this path

Many remain active supporters of their congregations while longing for something better. At Harding, a few brave faculty members probed directions away from the mainstream and kept their jobs. Erle T. Moore—behind the scenes—challenged the conservative political and religious assumptions prevalent on campus, discussing with small groups of students a thought-provoking range of ideas from outside our religious box. Andy T. Ritchie, Jr., led well-attended evening devotionals and door-knocking campaigns in the Northeast as a pacifist rejecting participation of any kind in civil government. Professors Moore and Ritchie made alternatives available in an otherwise ideological and religiously homogenous environment. I was enriched by their lives and teachings, and I was—am— blessed because they chose not to "leave." The spirit of my mentors continued to inspire me in the Bible classes I taught at college churches in Searcy, Arkansas, and Abilene, Texas, and at the West Islip Church, where I have ever attempted to reach out to the malcontents and thoughtful probers. I might easily have walked on both feet out of the Church of Christ and into the larger Christian world, but I hope that, by my staying, I can pass along the Moore/Ritchie blessings to the generation that follows.

In the issue of the *Christian Chronicle* that arrived today, a letter appears from a Bob Meyers of Wichita, Kansas—possibly the Bob Meyers who edited *Voices of Concern*, mentioned above—in which he argues convincingly against cultural adaptation and in favor of reconsidering the underlying spiritual significance of first-century Christian practices of the "holy kiss" (now abandoned in favor of shaking hands), the subdued role of women in worship, and the significance then and now of personal modesty or its lack as manifest in braided hair, gold, pearls, and expensive clothing. From the late-1950s through publication in the mid-1960s of his infamous book, Meyers forced thousands in the Churches of Christ to think thoroughly about Scripture and our interpretation of it. Although Professor Meyers left Harding for a Quaker university in Wichita, I am delighted to see that in his later years he is still afflicting the comfortable. Some "leave," and others "stay," and each has his gift from the Lord.

Two decades ago, I was aware only of the West Islip, New York, and Brookline, Massachusetts, congregations that were serving as beacons to those looking for an escape from ill-thought-out practices that had hardened into tradition and finally to dogma. Today, many more such congregations exist—proving yet once more the viability of congregational autonomy in a "brotherhood" of congregations as opposed to a "denomination." For better or maybe for worse, no congregation can be kicked out of the Churches of Christ for failing an orthodoxy test. Congregations do withdraw fellowship from unruly individual members who disturb the peace of the Body of Christ at that place, but even members who have been shunned are free to migrate to another congregation that will receive them. An official, worldwide denomination from which either an individual member or a whole congregation might be excommunicated, does not exist. Unholy gossip and malicious judgment are the worst that anyone can do. From the orneriest anti and sectarian Church of Christ in existence, across the progressive spectrum, to West Islip or Stamford, Connecticut, or Cahaba Valley (Birmingham, Alabama), there's a congregation somewhere that will welcome all sinners. Conservative congregations, 1935-vintage, may fume and sputter in their favorite gospel paper, but finger-wagging is the worst they can do. We are—*God be praised!*— congregationally autonomous. No matter who disagrees with what I believe, I can stay if I want to. And as long as our congregation holds together in mutual love and respect, no bureaucrats in some over-arching denominational structure can kick us out.

We at West Islip have been blessed to offer inspiration for better times elsewhere, especially through our affirmation of the full participation of women in public worship and church administration. Through these decades, many have lingered in our congregation long enough to discover a new spirit of Christian liberty, only then to pass onward and carry elsewhere what they enjoyed discovering among us. We joke about serving as lightning rods: "Congregation X wants to move in that direction, but, of course, not so far or so fast as Brookline or West Islip."

We remain truly a priesthood of all believers. We who remain at the West Islip Church—many of us from very traditional Christian college backgrounds—still identify ourselves congregationally as a non-instrumental-music church that emphasizes believer's baptism by immersion and a weekly Lord's Supper, whereas most of our former paid ministers later left the Church of Christ. Professional necessity and preference took them to Presbyterian or Lutheran or Anglican churches, or to none at all. But, then, it's easier to be a pew-sitter than it is to be the man (or woman!) in the pulpit. This is, perhaps, an argument for yet one more Church of Christ oddity—mutual ministry. Do churches really need a paid ministry, after all?

Looking up and down the pew

I would like to see survey data showing who left and who stayed, why they left and why they stayed. What were the experiences of those who left? Better, worse, about the same? Did the leavers feel occasional nostalgia for that totally predictable sermon on baptism and wish to hear again that identical prayer uttered each time by ol' Brother So-and-So?

What are the real reasons that people leave the Church of Christ? In search of a spiritually-stimulating liturgy, less confrontational sermons, escape from guilt-based theology or perfectionism, release from a sectarian focus on our supposedly non-denominational group, a more open probing of Scripture, greater emphasis on grace? In their new church home, did they find it difficult to adopt a different vocabulary or organization style? What goes through their mind when the infant being baptized lets out a squeal? Does that organ always seem too loud?

As we used to tell our campers who reported being mistreated, "It's better to be persecuted than ignored." We used the campfire to illustrate that a glowing coal when removed from the other coals soon goes out. I still believe in the value of fellowship. I have always doubted the staying power of solitary devotion detached from a congregation. Even the tradition of devout hermits—in most cases—has been about hermits who were sustained in their hermitages by devoted followers. In the deserts of Egypt, as many as 10,000 hermits lived and prayed and fasted alone in their tiny cells, each a few yards from the next, but they gathered on Sundays to celebrate the Lord's Supper. The history of monasticism is more a history of monastic communities than of solitary hermits.

Why, then, do I stay? Everybody's gotta be somewhere! Old Brother Bradford of the Swenson Church of Christ in West Texas used to say: "The Church of Christ may not be the best church they are, but it's better'n most, and that's where I'm at." Brother Bradford was pleased to be where he was at, and so am I. There cannot be a perfect church, can there? All churches are populated by people; all people are sinners, a.k.a. "brethren in error;" all churches, ergo, are imperfect. I'm sticking with the West Islip Church of Christ, even though it may not be the best church in Christendom, and certainly it is not a perfect church, but I'm staying with it because—in addition to all the reasons cited above—I like it, and for me, it's better than the rest. I already know the lingo, the expectations, and how to sidestep minor confrontations. To go to a different church would mean that I would have to start over. No thanks!

Within the brotherhood of Churches of Christ, the increasing diversity—indeed, *unpredictability*—surprises frequent travelers. As never before, "we" truly are, and increasingly so, a "brotherhood" or a "movement," not a structured "denomination." No two congregations, it seems, are alike. I judge that to be a good thing.

I expect never again to have to sit through another one of those Bible-slapping diatribes against neighboring churches that were so typical of revival evangelists in my youth. On the other hand, if I have to suffer one more PowerPoint sermon full of misspellings and spacing errors, I may reconsider atheism. Similarly, I dislike simple-minded, repetitive "praise songs" projected on a big screen, but I tolerate bad taste in music; the very variety of worship styles now abounding points to a positive future.

Seriously, what could change my mind about staying? Aside from sloppy PowerPoint presentations, other, more serious infractions against the Good News of Jesus do give me pause. If the Churches of Christ generally were to become more and more attached to a *right*-side-of-the tracks posture, more remote from the needy, more tied to Republican platforms than to Christ's teachings and deeds of merciful concern for the poor and sinful, I might be too embarrassed—and too angry—to stay with a congregation associated with a brotherhood like that. But, in spite of Neo-Con tendencies here and everywhere, I am hopeful on many fronts.

Looking at the women next to me in the pew

Before Abigail Adams became First Lady, she wrote to husband John, who was helping to set up a country, and said: "Remember the ladies!" One trend that makes me hopeful is the current moving through our churches to make a better place both in the church and the world for women. I want girls growing up in the churches to expect to be song-leaders, preachers, deacons, and elders, as well as continuing—if they want to—to teach in elementary Sunday Schools and prepare and serve the common meals ("dinner on the grounds," as we called them Down South). I hope men will be willing to share formerly female roles as well.

At the West Islip Church, we have consciously and conscientiously worked for more than 30 years towards achieving gender equity among our membership. When the Holy Spirit moved in a new way among us, He/She/It moved powerfully among our women. When we "invented" the office of "church administrators," we did so because no one in the Restoration Movement had ever heard of that office before, so no one had said that a woman could not officially exercise the charisma of "administration." Now, as far as I know, our beloved co-minister Katie is the only woman in the Churches of Christ who serves as full-time pulpit preacher, adult Bible-class teacher, and counselor—Katie is truly a pastor to us. Katie and her husband, Lance, both preach and teach; they thus serve as a new role model for young women and men in Church-of-Christ higher-education institutions now in training for future ministry. Our summer interns and visitors from Christian colleges have been inspired by Katie's life and work. And, as I am finishing this essay on Saturday afternoon, I can report that while Katie and Lance are taking a short vacation this week, our preacher tomorrow will be none other than Malissa Endsley.

As with many of my other reasons for maintaining my church membership, this reason—the women—is intensely local and personal. Sixty years ago I sat in the third grade of a one-room school run by Freed-Hardeman College in Tennessee. I admired a bright fifth-grader, John Endsley, whose father was the college's entire science department. Almost twenty years later, when I was in graduate school at Abilene Christian College in Texas, my buddy, Don Haymes, introduced me to his friend, Albert Endsley. Albert was John's younger brother. Then, two years ago in Boston, I attended an informal gathering of Churches of Christ in New England, where I met a young woman who was one of the leaders of a church-planting mission in a challenging environment in the Bronx. When she introduced herself as Malissa Endsley, I asked whether she had an uncle named John; a grandfather, J. R.; and a father, named Albert. She was surprised, and I was delighted, to unpeel yet one more layer on the onion of fellowship.

I love the serendipity of discovering these kinds of relationships. (It's a small church!) I have discovered similar connections in a dozen different states and several foreign countries. An extended spiritual family in God is a blessing, an intimate way for me to connect with God our Father, Christ our Brother, and the Holy Spirit. Through having learned what Christian fellowship really means on the smaller scale within the Churches of Christ, I am learning likewise to cherish similar connections with Lutherans, Catholics, Anglicans, Presbyterians, and Jews.

Malissa and Katie—two women famous among the saints! Not long ago, when Donna and I spent a week studying Spanish in Antigua, Guatemala, I met again the indigenous minister of a large congregation in Guatemala City with whom I had worked in the surgical clinic for the Mayas of the highlands. Before walking to church, he introduced us to another guest in his home, and when that person heard that we were from West Islip, New York, he responded: "Then you probably know my cousin, Katie—she's a minister of the church there!" Indeed, we do know Katie, and Malissa, and the new generation of their sisters and daughters rising up to bless the churches everywhere with their ministry.

Change inevitably overwhelms tradition, sometimes for the good, sometimes not; but no little boy with his finger in the dike has ever been able to stop the process. God isn't finished with us yet, any of us, and not with the Church of Christ, either. I am hopeful, for I believe He loves us, despite the faults that we all can see, and the other faults that He alone can see. He will stay with us, if we do not leave Him, and maybe even if we do. I close with a prayer and an exhortation:

> *May the Churches of Christ come to emphasize grace rather than guilt; the faith of Galatians rather than the works in James; tolerance of variation instead of preoccupation with micro-judgment of other people's theology; and joy over good works performed in Christ's name by all believers, even those who are not of our party. Amen.*

> *Meanwhile, let peace and blessings accompany those who for conscience's sake need to depart! Whether leavers or stayers, we can pray together that the dear old Church of Christ of our background may grow to reflect more of God's love and less of our own harmful habits and frail traditions. And Amen.*

02/16/06 - of. Warren Lewis - $45.00 US $-66.86 Cdn
             Hans Rollman $12.00 US S/H   Duty $8.64